C000321232

Footprint

New Zealand

Handbook

The travel guide

Darroch Donald

Kia Hora Te Marino
Whakapapa-pounamu
Te Moana, Kia Tere
Te Karohirohi I mua I
Tou huarahi...

May the calm be widespread
May the sea glisten like greenstone
May the shimmer of light
dance before your path...

Maori blessing

New Zealand Handbook
First edition

Published by Footprint Handbooks
6 Riverside Court
Lower Bristol Road
Bath BA2 3DZ. England
T +44 (0)1225 469141
F +44 (0)1225 469461
Email discover@footprintbooks.com
Web www.footprintbooks.com

ISBN 1 900949 96 2
CIP DATA: A catalogue record for this book is available from the British Library

Distributed in the USA by Publishers Group West

Neither the black and white nor coloured maps are intended to have any political significance.

Credits

Series editors
Patrick Dawson and Rachel Fielding

Editorial
Editor: Alan Murphy
Maps: Sarah Sorensen

Production
Typesetting: Richard Ponsford, Emma Bryers, Leona Bailey and Davina Rungasamy
Maps: Robert Lunn, Claire Benison and Shane Feeney
Colour maps: Kevin Feeney and Robert Lunn
Proof reading: Catherine Charles
Cover: Camilla Ford

Design
Mytton Williams

Photography
Front cover: ImageBank
Back cover: Darroch Donald
Inside colour section: Darroch Donald, Patrick Syder and Robert Harding Picture Library

Print
Manufactured in Italy by LEGOPRINT

Every effort has been made to ensure that the facts in this Handbook are accurate. However, travellers should still obtain advice from consulates, airlines etc about current travel and visa requirements before travelling. The authors and publishers cannot accept responsibility for any loss, injury or inconvenience however caused.

New Zealand

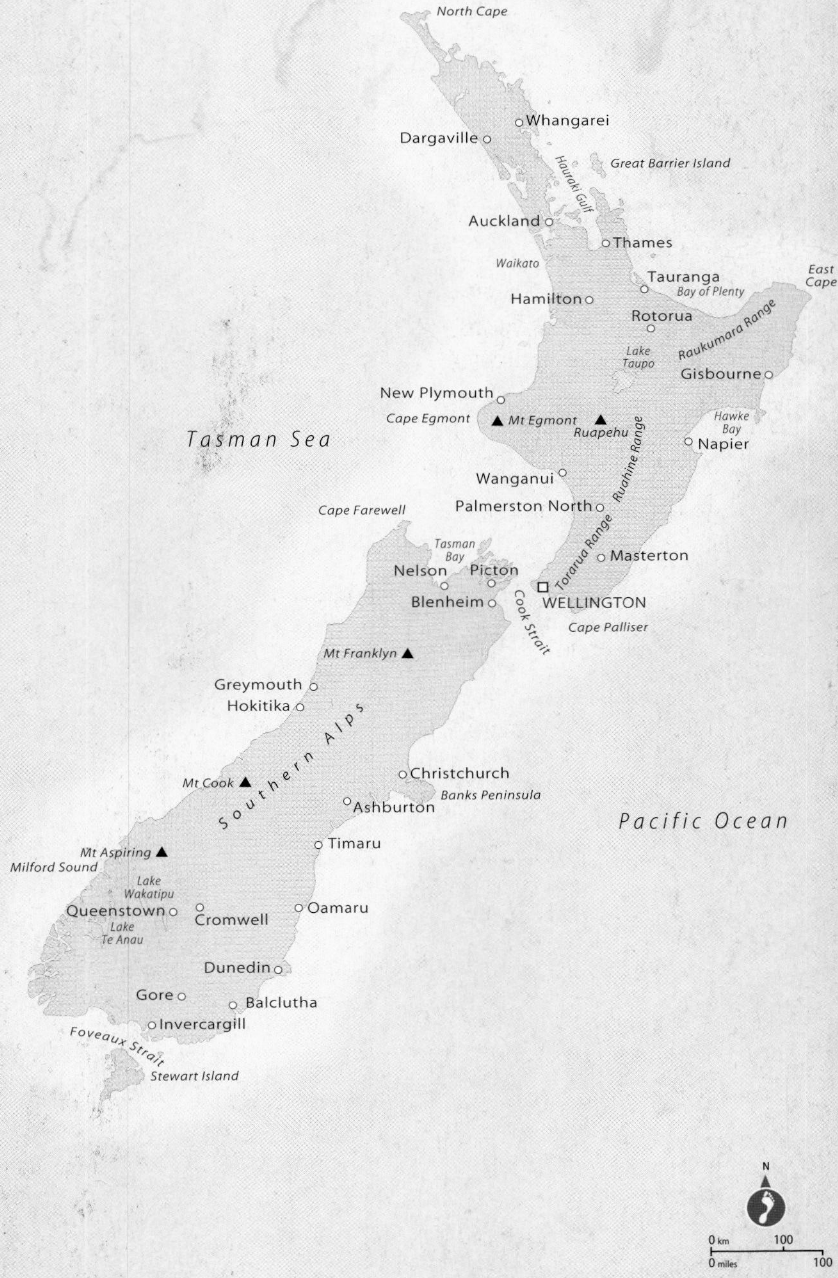

North Cape
Whangarei
Dargaville
Hauraki Gulf
Great Barrier Island
Auckland
Thames
Waikato
East Cape
Tauranga
Bay of Plenty
Hamilton
Rotorua
Raukumara Range
Lake Taupo
Gisbourne
New Plymouth
Cape Egmont
Mt Egmont
Ruapehu
Hawke Bay
Napier
Tasman Sea
Ruahine Range
Wanganui
Palmerston North
Cape Farewell
Tasman Bay
Tararua Range
Masterton
Nelson
Picton
Blenheim
WELLINGTON
Cook Strait
Cape Palliser
Mt Franklyn
Greymouth
Hokitika
Southern Alps
Christchurch
Mt Cook
Banks Peninsula
Ashburton
Pacific Ocean
Timaru
Mt Aspiring
Milford Sound
Lake Wakatipu
Queenstown
Cromwell
Oamaru
Lake Te Anau
Dunedin
Gore
Balclutha
Invercargill
Foveaux Strait
Stewart Island

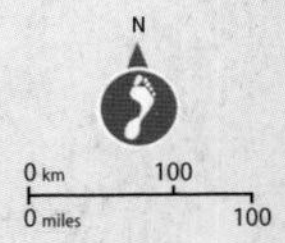

Contents

Left*: Maori carving in the Maori Arts and Crafts Institute, Rotorua.*

***Right**: Sunrise brings a golden hue to the landscape of the Catlins Coast.*

A foot in the door

Right: *Trams ply the streets around Cathedral Suqare in Christchurch, New Zealand's most Anglified of cities.*
Below: *Not for nothing is Auckland known as the 'City of Sails'. Here, the ubiquitous sight of yachts in Waitemata Harbour, with the omnipresent Sky Tower serving as a backdrop.*

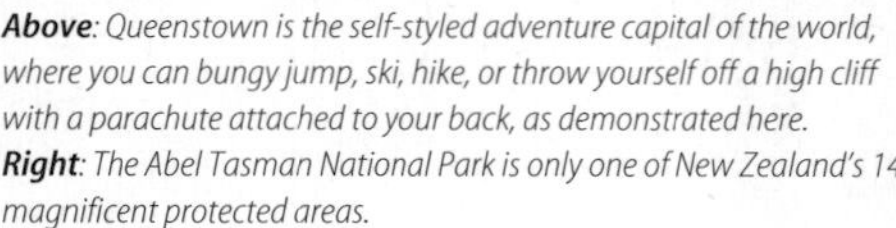

Above: *Queenstown is the self-styled adventure capital of the world, where you can bungy jump, ski, hike, or throw yourself off a high cliff with a parachute attached to your back, as demonstrated here.*
Right: *The Abel Tasman National Park is only one of New Zealand's 14 magnificent protected areas.*

Highlights

Put Steven Spielberg, Charles Darwin and Claude Monet in a room with six bottles of vodka and a party pack of recreational drugs and combined, they could not come close to the concept of New Zealand. If nature had a design studio full of her most surreal and stupendous ideas, it would be 'The Land of the Long White Cloud'. Nowhere else on earth can the tourist experience such a vast array of wild and wonderful activities. Or such diverse and spectacular scenery in such a compact country. To choose New Zealand as a travel destination is to make an appointment with Doctor Nature and her able assistant, nurse Adrenaline.

One country or three Islands?

On the map the physical geography of New Zealand looks simple, yet in content it is incredibly diverse and complex. The three islands – North Island, South Island and Stewart Island – are all very different in looks and personality. North Island is home to over two-thirds of New Zealanders – or kiwis – who live life to the beat of a faster rhythm than their countrified neighbours to the south. South Island, however, is said to provide the 'true essence' of New Zealand. To travel through it is like a fun-filled lesson in geography. Vast empty beaches where you feel almost guilty leaving footprints; endless mountain ranges blanketed in snow and rainforest; lakes, waterfalls and fiords; glaciers, volcanoes and hot pools; vast limestone caves and arches; massive crystal clear springs…the list and variety is endless. There are even parts that have not changed since Captain Cook first explored over 100 years ago. Stewart Island, the smallest of the three main islands, lies just off the coast of Southland and, having just been designated the country's 14th national park, offers peace, solitude and a wealth of unspoilt scenery.

Old habits die hard

Despite its relatively brief history, New Zealand provides a fascinating mix of cultures. Before the early Europeanexplorers paved the way for widespread colonial immigration, the native Maori had developed their own way of life. And though, like any other displaced people, they have struggled to maintain this identity and culture, thankfully 'Maoritanga' (Maoridom) is enjoying something of a renaissance in modern day New Zealand. Particularly in North Island, you will be exposed to their very different world and traditional lifestyle and, whether it is through a stay on a *marae*, a cultural performance, *hangi* (feast) or simple friendship, it will enhance your visit and a provide a sense of hope that biculturalism has indeed an optimistic future. You will also find that through the solid roots of Maoridom and colonialism a unique 'kiwi' culture and identity is growing both strong and steadfast.

***Next page**: The beautiful Otago Peninsula is home to a natural history encyclopedia's worth of wildlife, including sea-lions, penguins, fur seals and albatrosses*

Right: *If you're after a hooker, then look no further than Cannibals Bay Beach on the Catlins Coast. But don't get too close – they're not as out of condition as they look!*
Below: *Mount Taranaki stands proud and implacable in the heart of Egmont National Park. This dormant volcano offers some great walks as well as rewarding views from its snow-tipped summit.*

Above: *The steep-sided, windswept promontory of Nugget Point, with its 'nuggets', the jagged stacks of rock, lying just offshore.*
Right: *This bubbly is certainly not chilled. The hot, steaming Champagne Pool, in Wai-o-Tapu thermal Reserve, near Rotorua.*

The Clean and the Green

New Zealand is often advertised as the 'Clean Green Land' and nowhere is this more evident than in the glossy tourist brochures. There is no doubt that the environment and nature are the country's greatest asset, but don't be fooled. While the average New Zealander cares deeply about their country's awe-inspiring scenery and wildlife, the country's reputation is derived more from simple demographics rather than an extraordinary conservation ethic. New Zealand has a total head count equal only to that of many European capitals or US cities. If it had an average world population density it would certainly be a very different place. But though this basic reality may disappoint some of you, the environment and scenery will not. New Zealand really is as good as it gets when it comes to a pristine environment, and, thankfully, it is pretty well looked after.

Paradise lost?

Experiencing wildlife in New Zealand has been described as being as close to being on another planet as one can get. Millions of years of isolation have resulted in the evolution of a veritable Noah's Ark of unique species from the bizarre and whimsical kiwi to the prehistoric tuatara. Blanketed by native rainforest and with so few mammals, it was the birds that dominated, and with no ground predators many became flightless. Yet in reality it is now a biodiversity under siege and a paradise that has essentially been lost forever. From the day that man first arrived and planted an indelible footprint on the environment, it began an almost inevitable journey of destruction. Introduced animals and plants like the rat, the cat and the possum, together with unsustainable hunting and gathering methods, devastated both native flora and fauna with many species becoming extinct or replaced. Today, for example, for every native plant there is one introduced.

Fighting back

However, although nature will never be the same again, modern-day New Zealand is still home to an incredible range of wildlife, most of which you will see nowhere else on earth. Your encounters will be many and memorable: from enchanting penguins to graceful albatrosses; cheeky keas to manic fantails; rotund sea-lions to breaching whales. Given the fragility of its species, New Zealand is on the 'front-line' of the global conservation war and thankfully there has been some fine and victorious battles. Sterling efforts are being made in the war of conservation by governmental departments, for example the Department of Conservation, as well as independent organizations and individuals. Numerous captive breeding and predator eradication programmes have been initiated to stop, or at the very least slow down, the decline of so many species. As a visitor you will be given a stark reminder of the effect we are having on the world.

***Next pages**: Portrait of the author as a whale's dinner. Taking a well-earned break by a whale mural in Kaikoura, Canterbury.*

Outdoor Activities

Outdoor activities are not so much a tourist attraction in New Zealand as a way of life. The national psyche seems to crave adventure and the environment lends itself to being a natural Disneyland. There is a veritable smorgasbord of possibilities: from sea kayaking, cruising or jet boating, to swimming with dolphins, whale watching or tandem skydiving. Such is the average New Zealander's love of new and exciting activities, that they have become famous for creating their own bizarre, almost unimaginable pursuits. Where else in the world can you roll down a hill inside a clear plastic bubble, launch yourself from the nation's tallest building tied to a bungy cord of , or fly at 120 kph strapped to a stretcher with a small engine attached?

Adrenaline rush Without doubt New Zealand's most famous 'adrenaline high' is the bungy jump. Since the mid '80s, the country has led the world in the creation of safe, commercial, jumping sites and operations. Now, for young and old alike, it is almost considered rude to visit the country and not to take the plunge. Let's face it, if a 91-year-old can do it, why can't you? Some people even get married before they jump; others have jumped in a canoe, a kilt (thus confirming the rumour), on their bike and, before you ask, even naked! Though bungy jumping and countless other activities are on offer throughout the country, it is Queenstown in Otago, South Island, that is the place to be for all self-respecting adrenaline junkies. With over 150 activities and operations to choose from, surrounded by world-class scenery, it is little wonder it is dubbed the adventure capital of the world.

Wilderness tramping Many people come to New Zealand to experience some of the best walking and hiking (tramping) on earth, especially South Island which has been dubbed the walking capital of the world. The country's 14 national parks offer everything from hour-long coastal walks, to 10-day wilderness expeditions. Ever since the National Geographic Magazine dubbed the 54 km, four-day Milford Track the 'Greatest Walk on Earth', people have been drawn to sample the scenic delights and challenges of this famous track. And there are others with more evocative names: Kepler, Dusky, Rees-Dart and Greenstone, to name but a few. Each different and blessed with a range of features from volcanoes and glaciers to viaducts and waterfalls. But what also makes New Zealand so special is the unbeatable service, access, management and accommodation offered and administered nationwide by the Department of Conservation. They will be your guide,your interpreter and, if you have an accident, your saviour.

Left: *Whitewater rafting on the Shotover River, Queenstown.*
Below: *Too late to turn back now! Halfway across the swingbridge which is highly strung over the Waiohine Gorge, Wairapara.*
Next page: Getting back to your roots on The Domain, in Auckland.

Above: *This intrepid soul enjoys the remarkable view from the Remarkables Range, which tower over Queenstown.*
Left: *Taking the plunge at Nevis Highwire bungy, the highest jump in the countryworld, at a terrifying 134 m.*

ROBERT

Essentials

Essentials

Planning your trip

A word of advice about New Zealand: it **is** everything you have heard about it, and an awful lot more besides. If you can only go for two to three weeks, unless you stay put in one area, or visit just a few places, it is going to be an exercise in frustration. Just think about it: you are probably about to travel to the other end of the earth, so make the most of it. Three weeks is pushing it, six is better, and eight weeks about right, short of actual emigration.

If New Zealand presents an irresistible lure, you are are probably nature-friendly and also a very active and independent person. The main ingredients of the average 'New Zealand Happy Traveller Cake' is unspoilt nature, stunning scenery, with just a light icing of interesting history. Bake that in a pleasant climate and cover it in lashings of 'great things to do' and voila – the perfect trip. Start planning well in advance. You will find comprehensive sights and activities listings in each location section throughout this book. The web is also a major source of information. It's a good idea to secure your own transport on arrival, or even before. New Zealand is small and relatively easy to get about, but independence is a major advantage. If you are in a group consider the many campervan options (see page 48). New Zealand is very well geared up for this type of travel.

You might also consider buying a car (see page 47). Second-hand cars are cheap in New Zealand and, provided it's still in one piece, you can usually sell them again when you have completed your journey. If you cannot afford your own wheels, then New Zealand is pretty well set up for public transport. Listings for public transport can be found in the Ins and outs and Transport sections of the book and also on the web.

Essentials

Where to go

Should you decide to concentrate on one island, or alternatively spend a week in one and then two in the other, South Island has the upper hand

Three weeks tends to be the most common 'quick trip' people can afford. However, the 'two to three week' listing below has been divided into 'North Island' and 'South Island', with about 14 days outlined in each. This hopefully will give you further flexibility and a better idea of the best basic recommendations of each island. As already mentioned, covering the best of both islands in anything under a month is very hard and in reality you would be better focusing on one island (the South preferably) or a particular region. The top regions are Otago, Fiordland and Nelson/Marlborough in the South Island and The Bay of Plenty (Rotorua) and Taupo and Ruapehu in the North.

Two weeks: North Island

You will almost certainly arrive in **Auckland** – the main international airport. Although the Auckland Region has a lot to offer, only spend a day there, then move on quickly. Auckland is a great city – but a city nonetheless. It is modern and in many ways is not at all typical of New Zealand. In Auckland take a quick look from the top of the Sky Tower, at the Auckland Museum, followed by Devonport or one of the West Coast beaches. Then the following day head for Northland and the **Bay of Islands**, where you can go to see the islands or go dolphin-watching. Don't miss Russell (the first significant European settlement) and Waitangi (the site where the Maori/*pakeha* Treaty was signed). The following day take a one-day trip to **Cape Reinga**, the northern tip of New Zealand. Then return to Auckland and dine in Ponsonby. The following day head southwest for two days in the **Coromandel**. In the 'Coro' don't miss Coromandel township, Colville and Cape Colville and Cathedral Cove. From Coromandel head to **Rotorua** for two days. From Rotorua head southwest to **Taupo**. Make sure you see the Huka Falls and enjoy a hot pool. If the weather is fine the following day attempt 'The Tongariro Crossing', a full day walk, or take a cruise on the Lake Taupo, followed by a jump out of a plane at 12,000 ft. Alternatively from Taupo, get underground with a day trip to the **Waitomo Caves**. From Taupo take one of two recommended routes south. Either head south on SH1,

Eco-tourism operators in New Zealand

Auckland

***Kiwi Wildlife Tours**, PO Box 56389, Dominion Rd, Auckland, T09-3094367, F09-4242505, www.kiwi-wildlife.co.nz 11-18 day guided birdwatching trips.*

***Tiri Tiri Matangi Island**, Tiri Supporters, PO Box 24-229, Birkenhead, Auckland, peter@naturaledge.co.nz (see Auckland Region).* ***Miranda Shorebird Centre**, RD1, Pokeno, T/F09-2322781, shorebird@xtra.co.nz Specialist wader field centre on internationally significant site, accommodation available.*

Northland

***Aroha Island Ecological Centre**, PO Box 541, Kerkeri, T09-4075243, F09-4075246, www.aroha.net.nz*

Waikato

***Hamilton Zoo and The Free-Flight Sanctuary**, Brymer Rd, Hamilton, T07-8386720, F07-8490293, hamzoos@wave.co.nz*

Bay of Plenty

***Lakeland Queen Cruises Ltd**, PO Box 1976, Rotorua, T07-3486634, F07-3471766, www.lakelandqueen.co.nz Lake cruises and birdwatching trips on a paddle steamer to Mokoia Island nature reserve on Lake Rotorua.*

Taupo and Ruapehu

***Tongariro Eco-Tours**, PO Box 281, Turangi, T0800-101024, rafting@xtra.co.nz Two-hour trips by boat to unique wetlands on Lake Taupo.* ***Kiwi Encounters**, PO Box 146, Ohakune, T/F09-3859505, whakamanu@hotmail.com Three-hour guided trips to track and spot kiwi in the Waimarino Forest.*

East Coast

***Mount Bruce National Wildlife Centre**, RD1, Masterton, T06-3770723, F06-3772976, www.mtbruce.doc.govt.nz (see Masterton section, East Coast).*

***Gannet Beach Adventures**, PO Box 1463, Hastings, T06-8750898, F06-8750849, gannet.tractor.tours.napier@xtra.co.nz Four-hour guided trips to see New Zealand's largest gannet colony.* ***Gannet Safaris Overland**, RD2, Hastings, T06-8750888, F06-8750893, www.gannetsafaris.co.nz*

Wellington

***Nga Manu Nature Reserve**, Ngarara Rd, PO Box 126, Waikanae, T/F04-2934131, ngamanu@clear.net.nz (see Kapiti Coast section, Wellington Region)* ***Kapiti Island Alive and Kapiti Island Nature Reserve**, Kapiti Nature Lodge, PO Box 28, Otaki, T/F06-3648818, john.barrett@xtra.co.nz Day trips and overnight stays on a unique island nature reserve (see Kapiti Coast section, Wellington Region).*

Nelson and Marlborough

***Dolphin Watch Marlborough**, PO Box 197, Picton, T03-5737906, F03-5738040, www.dolphinwatchmarlborough.co.nz Bird/dolphin-watching trips in the wildlife-rich Queen Charlotte Sound.* ***French Pass Sea Safaris**, French Pass, Marlborough Sounds, T/F03-5765204, www.seasafaris.co.nz Flexible eco-trips to see dolphins and seabirds in the outer Marlborough Sounds.* ***Farewell Spit Tours**, Tasman St, Collingwood, T03-5248257, F03-5248939, www.FarewellSpit.co.nz Trips along the wildlife rich and internationally significant Farewell Spit to see seabirds including gannets and migrating wading birds.* ***Albatross Encounter with Ocean Wings**, 58 West End, Kaikoura, T03-3196777, F03-3196534, www.oceanwings.co.nz*

taking SH47 at Taurangi around the western side of the **Tongariro National Park**. If you can, take a scenic flight above the mountains from Whakapapa Village or drive up the Mountain Road from **Ohakune**. Stay in Ohakune. Next day get yourself to **Wellington** as soon as possible. Alternatively, head southeast to **Napier** and the **Hawkes Bay**. Enjoy Napier itself or visit a winery or Cape Kidnappers and take in the view from Te Mata Peak in **Havelock North**. From Havelock head south through the **Wairarapa** stopping at Mount Bruce wildlife centre and, if you can, take in the coast at Castle Point. The following morning try to visit the remote **Cape Palliser**, the southernmost tip of North Island. Once in **Wellington**, take a trip up the Cable Car, see the view from Mount Victoria and

Boat trips to see wide variety of rare seabirds. ***Dolphin Encounter,*** *T03-3196777, F03-3196534, info@dolphin.co.nz Dolphin-watching and swimming in Kaikoura Bay.* ***Whale Watch Kaikoura,*** *PO Box 89, Kaikoura, T03-3196767, F03-3196545, res@whalewatch.co.nz The world famous and original whale-watching operation in Kaikoura.*

Canterbury

Akaroa Harbour Cruises, *Akaroa, T03-3289078, F03-3288699, info@blackcat.co.nz Dolphin-watching cruises including the endangered hectors dolphin.* ***Kaki (Black Stilt) Visitor Hide Guided Tours,*** *Wairepo Rd, Twizel, T03-4350802, F03-4350852, kakivisitorhide@doc.govt.nz Guided trips to see one of the rarest waders in the world.* ***Heritage Expeditions,*** *PO Box 6282, Christchurch, T03-3389944, F03-3383311, www.newzealandalive.com Guided birdwatching trips and expeditions throughout New Zealand and the Sub Antarctic Islands.*

West Coast

White Heron Sanctuary Tours, *PO Box 19, Whataroa, T03-753420, F03-7534087, www.whiteherontours.co.nz Guided boat trips to see New Zealand's only white heron breeding site.* ***Okarito Nature Tours,*** *PB 777, Hokitika, T/F03-7534014, iljames@minidata.co.nz Specialized boat tours and kayak trips on the wildlife-rich Okarito Lagoon.* ***Moeraki Wilderness Lodge,*** *PB Bag 772, Hokitika, T03-7500881, F03-7500882, lakemoeraki@wildernesslodge.co.nz Accommodation, guided nature walks and kayak trips in World Heritage Park.*

Otago

Elm Wildlife Tours, *Elm Lodge Backpackers, Dunedin, T03-4741872, F03-4778808, www.elmwildlifetours.co.nz Superb guided nature tours of the Otago Peninsula. Hooker's sealions, fur seals, albatross and yellow-eyed penguin.* ***Nature Guides Otago,*** *PO Box 8050, Dunedin, T03-4545169, F03-4545369, www.nznatureguides.com Guided trips on the Otago Peninsula, Catlins Coast and Stewart Island, B&B accommodation available.* ***Royal Albatross Centre,*** *PO Box 492, Dunedin, T03-4780499, F03-4780575, www.albatrosses.com Observation of the only mainland breeding colony of royal albatross in the world.* ***Monarch Wildlife Cruises and Tours,*** *PO Box 102, Dunedin, T03-4774276, F03-4774216, www.wildlife.co.nz Nature cruises on Otago Harbour with the highlight of the albatross colony at Taiaroa Head.*

Southland

Catlins Wildlife Trackers, *Papatowai, Owaka, T/F03-4158613, catlinw@es.co.nz* ***Eco-tours and accommodation on the Catlins Coast***

Fiordland Ecology Holidays, *PO Box 40, Manapouri, T/F03-2496600, www.fiordland.gen.nz Research and holiday cruises of the Fiordland Sounds and Stewart Island.* ***Ruggedy Range Wilderness Experience,*** *Oban, Stewart Island, T21-91066, www.ruggedyrange.com* ***Kiwi Wilderness Walks,*** *based in Riverton, T08-00248886, www.riverton.co.nz Guided nature tours on Stewart Island, kiwi a highlight.*

check out the Museum of Wellington City and the Sea and Te Papa – New Zealand's multi million dollar national museum. The following day drive back to Auckland (nine hours) or head across early by ferry for a week in South Island.

Two weeks: South Island

By ferry from Wellington, try to arrive in **Picton** early in the day so you can join one of the trips out into the **Marlborough Sounds** – either dolphin-watching, kayaking or a half-day walk to Ship Cove. The following day drive to Blenheim and have a quick look at one or two of the vineyards before heading through Havelock and then make your way to **Nelson**. Enjoy the rest of the day in Nelson then make your way to Motueka via

Mapua. Next day take a day-walk or kayak-trip in the **Abel Tasman National Park**. Then make your way to the West Coast and **Franz Josef** taking a quick look at the Nelson Lakes National Park. In Franz Josef be sure to take a scenic flight around Mount Cook, or at the very least a glacier walk on the Franz. The following day, drive from Franz Josef, stopping at Ship Creek and Haast to make **Wanaka** by evening. Next day go canyoning, tandem skydiving, or for a walk up the Rob Roy Valley. Alternatively, take a scenic flight to Milford Sound. Head for **Queenstown** and spend the day deciding what to do. The bungy is a must as is the Shotover jet and the views from the gondola. Take another day visiting **Milford Sound** – it's best to bus in (to see Te Anau and the **Milford Road**) and fly out.

For the following three days there is an alternative to head for Christchurch first or go via Dunedin. For Christchurch drive from Queenstown to **Mount Cook** village. Spend the rest of the day taking in the scenery by foot, by bike or with a scenic flight. Next day drive to Christchurch taking a look at Tekapo and the McKenzie Country, arriving in **Christchurch** late evening. Alternatively spend the first two days in**Dunedin** and the Otago Peninsula with the following day in the **Catlins**.After a day in Christchurch, head for **Kaikoura** where you can go whale-watching or dolphin swimming, leaving yourself enough time to catch the late ferry from **Picton** that night.

Three weeks: North Island

Add to the above these alternatives: In Auckland try to get out on the **Hauraki Gulf**, visit **Tiri Tiri Matangi Island** ('must do'), **Rangitoto** or **Great Barrier Island**. Spend some time exploring the Waitakeres and the West Coast beaches. In the city visit Kelly Tarlton's Underwater and Antarctic Encounter and/or the Waterfront and the Maritime Museum.

In Northland on the way to the Bay of Islands, don't miss the **Whangarei Heads** (Ocean Beach) and/or the **Tutakaka Coast**. While there consider diving the **Poor Knights Islands**. In the Bay of Islands consider a two-day kayak trip on and around the Islands or walk to **Cape Brett**. Break your bum on the fast boat to the 'Hole in the Rock'. Heading north, take a peek at historic **Kerikeri** and the delights of the scenic coast road to Whangaroa. After visiting the Cape head southwest to the **Hokianga**. Just south of the Hokianga don't miss 'Tane Mahuta', the 1500-year-old kauri in the **Waipoua Forest**. Then learn more about the great trees at the Kauri Museum in Matakohe. Heading south from Auckland, spend a couple more days exploring the Coromandel. Go fishing from **Whitianga**. Don't miss the Driving Creek Railway in Coromandel Township.

From Coromandel head to the Bay of Plenty. Spend a day enjoying one of the many activities in **Tauranga**. There is plenty to detain you in the Tongariro National Park and you could also consider a kayaking trip down the Wanganui River, in the neighbouring **Wanganui National Park**, before heading south to Wellington. North from Rotorua you can negotiate the **East Cape** via **Whakatane**. While in Whakatane visit the active volcano **White Island** or swim with the dolphins. If you head west from Rotorua or Taupo, a day underground in the Waitomo Caves is a must. If at all possible and you can afford it, try the 'The Lost World' trip. From Waitomo you can follow the coast to **Taranaki** and spend some time around the mountain and the **Mount Egmont National Park** – arguably the most beautiful mountain in the country. From **New Plymouth**, which is a great town in itself, you could also take in **Wanganui** and a trip on the Wanganui River before heading south to Wellington.

If you head west from Rotorua or Taupo, spend more time in Napier and consider spending a night at **Lake Waikaremoana** in the **Urewera National Park**. Then from Napier head south via Havelock North, through the Wairarapa taking in Castle Point, the **Waiohine Gorge** and Cape Palliser. From all these directions you will then end up in Wellington and can spend more time in the city. For a superb day trip get yourself to the wildlife paradise of **Kapiti Island**. From Wellington again it is a nine-hour drive direct via SH1 back to Auckland, though the flight on a clear day between Mount Taranaki on one side and Ruapehu on the other is a delight.

Regional tourist boards

North Island

***Tourism Auckland**, PO Box 5561, Wellesley St, T09-3077999, www.aucklandnz.com*

***Tourism Bay of Plenty**, CPO Box 13325, Tauranga, T07-5776234, www.visitplenty.co.nz*

***Tourism Coromandel**, PO Box 592, Thames, T07-8685985, www.thecoromandel.com*

***First Light Tourism Eastland**, PO Box 2000, Gisborne, T06-8672000, www.gisborne.govt.nz*

***Hawkes Bay Tourism**, PO Box 123, Napier, www.hawkesbaynz.com*

***Destination Lake Taupo**, 72 Lake Terr, Taupo, T07-3779888, www.laketauponz.com*

***Destination Manawatu**, PO Box 474, Palmerston North, T06-3546593, manawatu.visitor-info@xtra.co.nz*

***Tourism Northland**, PO Box 365, Paihia, www.destination-nz.com*

***Tourism Rotorua**, 1160 Arawa St, Rotorua, T07-3484133, www.rotoruaNZ.com*

***Destination Ruapehu**, 15 Miro St, Ohakune, T06-3858364, www.ruapehu.tourism.co.nz*

***Tourism Taranaki**, PB 2058, New Plymouth, T06-7579909, www.tourismtaranaki.org.nz*

***Tourism Waikato**, PO Box 970 Hamilton, T07-8393360, www.waikatonz.co.nz*

***Tourism Wairarapa**, PO Box 814, Masterton, T06-3787373, www.nz.com/travel/wairarapa*

***Tourism Wanganui**-'River Region', T06-3453513, www.river-region.org.nz*

***Totally Wellington Tourism**, PO Box 10017, Wellington, T04-9161205, www.wellingtonNZ.com*

South Island

***Christchurch and Canterbury Marketing**, PO Box 2600, Christchurch, T03-3531184, www.christchurchnz.net*

***Tourism Dunedin**, PO Box 1446, Dunedin, T03-4718042, www.CityofDunedin.com*

***Destination Fiordland**, PO Box 155, Te Anau, T03-2497959, www.fiordland.org.nz*

***Destination Marlborough**, Level 1, 45 Queen St, Blenheim, T03-5775520, www.destinationmarlborough.com*

***Tourism Nelson**, corner of Trafalgar and Halifax Sts, T03-5466228, www.nelson.net.nz*

***Destination Queenstown** PO Box 353, Queenstown, T03-4427440, www.queenstown-nz.co.nz*

***Tourism Southland**, PO Box 903, Invercargill, T03-2149720, www.southland.org.nz*

***Central South Island Tourism**, PO Box 524 Timaru, T03-6840201, www.southisland.org.nz*

***Waimate District**, 75 Queen St, Waimate, T03-6897771, www.waimate.org.nz*

***Lake Wanaka Tourism**, PO Box 147, Wanaka, T03-4431574, www.lakewanaka.co.nz*

***Tourism West Coast**, Mackay St, Greymouth, T03-7686633, www.west-coast.co.nz*

Three weeks: South Island

Added to the above listings under South Island, there are many additional excursions and activities. In Nelson and Marlborough consider an extra day or two in the Marlborough Sounds. Do part of the Queen Charlotte Track, a full-day cruise, a multi-day kayak trip from Havelock or **Picton**, or better still, spend a day or two getting to **French Pass**. From Nelson consider doing the **Abel Tasman Coast Walk** or a multi-day kayak trip. From Motueka, venture over Takaka Hill to **Golden Bay**. Visit the Pupu Springs, Farewell Spit and do not miss **Wharariki Beach**. While in Golden Bay consider doing the **Heaphy Track** or exploring the northern sector of the Abel Tasman or **Kahurangi National Parks**.

Returning to Motueka, head for the West Coast via the Nelson Lakes National Park. Consider the **Angelus Hut Walk** in the Nelson Lakes then head to **Westport** via the Buller Gorge. From Westport venture north to **Karamea** and see the incredible karst scenery of the **Oparara Basin**. Walk part of the Heaphy Track coastal stretch. From Karamea head south down the West Coast to Franz Josef, taking in the arts and crafts of **Hokitika**, the **white heron colony** near Whataroa and the secluded delights of **Okarito**. Then, give yourself an extra two-three days around the Glacier Region. As well as the glaciers be sure to visit **Lake Matheson** and the coast.

Heading south to Haast, stop at **Munroe Beach** and/or Ship Creek. Spend at least two days around **Haast**, take a jetboat trip and/or explore further south to **Jackson's Bay** and the **Cascade Saddle**. Having negotiated the **Haast Pass** to Wanaka spend more time there, enjoying the scenery and wealth of activities, particularly the local walks. From Wanaka head for Queenstown via the **Cardrona** Road and lose yourself in the incredible range of activities.

For a break from the chaos head north and explore the **Glenorchy** area, **Arrowtown** or climb to the top of the **Remarkables**. From Queenstown drive to **Te Anau**, consider doing the Kepler, Routeburn or Milford Tracks or a multi-day kayak trip on Milford or **Doubtful Sound**. Be sure to make the scenic drive to Milford Sound and give yourself an extra day there. Just south of Te Anau, take in the stunning scenery and atmosphere of **Lake Manapouri** and Doubtful Sound. From Manapouri negotiate the **Southern Scenic Route** to Dunedin, and en route consider doing the **Humpridge Track**, visiting **Stewart Island** (to see kiwi) and certainly give yourself three days exploring the Catlins Coast. Spend two-three days in Dunedin allowing at least one on the **Otago Peninsula**. Take a tour to see the **Albatross colony** and the **yellow-eyed penguins**.

From Dunedin head north to Oamaru then inland to Mount Cook. Spend some time exploring the area and its activities. Via Tekapo and the McKenzie Country, head to Christchurch giving yourself more time in the city. While in Christchurch spend a day exploring the **Banks Peninsula**. North of Christchurch, as an adjunct to Kaikoura, head inland to enjoy a hot pool and perhaps a mountain bike ride in **Hanmer Springs**. From Hanmer Springs and Kaikoura enjoy the stunning coastal road that will deliver you back to **Picton** via the **vineyards** of Marlborough.

When to go

For travellers from the Northern Hemisphere spending Christmas day on the beach, sunbathing while digesting a hearty BBQ, or seeing a Santa Parade under cloudless skies in shorts, is really quite a bizarre experience. The summer or **high season** lasting from **November to March** is, of course, the busiest, and at these times you'll be joining battalions of Kiwis also on holiday throughout the country. At these times, especially over Christmas and for the whole of January, almost the entire country shuts up shop and heads for the beach or the mountains. Accommodation therefore is at a premium and the roads to the major tourist destinations can be busy. But again, 'busy' roads in New Zealand, especially in the more remote parts of South Island, equates perhaps to a car passing you every five or ten minutes. You get so used to being alone that the sight of other cars can be quite a shock.

The months of late spring (**September/October**) or early autumn (**March/April**) are often recommended. At these times you are almost guaranteed accommodation everywhere and the weather still favourable. It is also cheaper. The winter or **low season** sits between **April/May to August/September**. At these times prices are often reduced with special deals (especially at weekends) abounding in many, mainly mid-range, accommodation establishments. Bear in mind that some places are closed in winter but generally speaking, in New Zealand, tourism is a year-round affair. Also bear in mind some places like Queenstown (the principal tourist destination in South Island) are as busy in the winter months with skiing activities as they are with general activities in summer. Taking all the above in to account the best months to visit, unless you enjoy the busy tourist/holiday buzz, are **October/November or February/March**.

Climate

New Zealand has what is called an 'ocean temperate' climate, which to you and me basically means it is generally agreeable. As the country is fairly elongated and lying very much at a north to south angle, the weather varies greatly. The north is therefore consistently a few degrees warmer than the south. As you might expect, the warmest region of the country is generally Northland and the coldest Southland. In Auckland the winter (June-August) and summer (December-March) average temperatures are 8°C-15°C (48°F-59°F) and 14°C-23°C (57°F-74°F) and in Dunedin 4°C-12°C (39°F-53°F) and 9°C-19°C (48°F-66°F) respectively. When it comes to sunshine various regions vie for the title of 'sunniest place'. This year it was Nelson in South Island. But next year it could just as easily be Napier on the relatively dry and sunny East Coast of North Island or Whakatane in the Bay of Plenty. Wellington and Auckland, too, boast a lot of sunshine. Wellingtonians also suffer from wind – but thankfully not of the beans variety. The West Coast and Fiordland in Southland, too, have their extremes of wind and rain. But having said that, the beauty of a place like New Zealand is that even in winter, it doesn't rain for long periods. In summary, the weather is very favourable in New Zealand: you can swim in the sea, wear shorts in summer and not be forced indoors for days. One other word of advice. Thanks to ozone depletion, the sun in New Zealand is **dangerous**, so always wear a hat and the strongest possible sun block.

Organized tours

Although New Zealand is very much the domain of the independent traveller there are a number of specialist tour operators. As you might imagine most of these are either eco- or activity-based. The New Zealand Tourism Board (NZTB – see box on page 23) has detailed operator listings on its website, www.purenz.com For operators within New Zealand consult the 'Activities' sections throughout the book. See also box of Eco-tourism operators on page 20 For New Zealand operators in your own country see the 'Discount Travel Agents' boxes in the 'Getting there' section. Those listed below are just a few of the main players.

Nature safaris

Kiwi Wildlife Tours, (see box on page 20) 120 New North Road, Auckland, T09-3093467, Guided birdwatching tours of New Zealand and the Pacific from 11-18 days. Guides with over 35 years, NZ conservation experience. ***Manu Tours New Zealand***, 106 Ocean Beach Road, Tairua, T07-8647475, www.nzbirding.co.nz Another one for avid 'twitchers' with a national hunt to see as many endemics as possible. ***Nature Quest New Zealand***, T03-4898444, www.maturequest.co.nz Guided or organized independent birding trips with one of the country's best 'twitchers'. ***Adventure South***, PO Box 33, 153 Christchurch, T03-3321222, www.advsouth.co.nz Eco-based cycling and hiking trips and a specialist mid-life 13-day adventure tour for 41-55 year olds.

Coach tours

Great Sights, T0800-808226, www.new-zealand.com/GreatSights A wide range of tours throughout the country from day city tours to 2-11 day excursions. ***Greenworld Tours***, T0800-623827. Based in Auckland. Day trips to Auckland, Rotorua, Waitomo and Bay of Islands. ***Scenic Pacific Tours***, T0800-996699, www.scenictours.co.nz Deluxe coach trips with emphasis on activities as much as sightseeing. ***Thrifty and Freestyle Tours***, PO Box 31-257 Milford, Auckland, T09-4783550, www.tourmasters.co.nz Budget-conscious tours with flexibility. Range of options in both islands. Thrifty specials to Waitomo, Rotorua and the Bay of Islands.

Backpacker bus tours

Kiwi Experience, 170 Parnell Road, Auckland, T09-3669830, www.kiwiexperience.com ***Contiki***, 1st Floor, 15-17 Day Street, Newton, Auckland, T0800-CONTIKI, www.contiki.com

18-35 Travel specialists

Magic Travellers, 132-138 Quay Street, Auckland, T09-3585600, www.magicbus.co.nz ***Flying Kiwi Wilderness Expeditions,*** Koromiko, Blenheim, T03-5738126, webnz.com/flying_kiwi/ Specialize in activity and nature based trips. For trips especially designed for women try ***Bushwise Women,*** T03-3324952, www.bushwise.co.nz

Finding out more

English is of course the principal language spoken in New Zealand. Maori is the traditional

One of the best ways to source information from abroad is on the web. To get started see the useful websites listed on page 68. Again the NZTB website is a good place to start, but almost all the regions have excellent, informative websites and these are listed in the text. The national and regional tourist boards and local information centres are generally good at replying to specific enquiries, especially by email, and of course are usually willing to send heaps of useful information by snail mail. The area tourist boards are listed on page 23.

Disabled travellers

For travellers with disabilities, visiting New Zealand can, like most places, be a frustrating affair. While most public facilities are well geared up for wheelchairs, older accommodation establishments and some public transport systems (especially rural buses) are not so well organized. However, things are improving and it is now a requirement by law to have disabled facilities in new buildings. The larger airlines like ***Air New Zealand*** and ***Qantas*** are well-equipped and this applies both to international and domestic flights. Disabled travellers usually receive discounts on travel, and some admission charges. Parking concessions are also available for the disabled and temporary cards can be issued on receipt of a mobility card or medical certificate.

You are advised to research options thoroughly before you leave and this can often be done with the assistance of organizations in your own country. For more information within New Zealand contact the ***Disability Information Service***, 314 Worcester St, Christchurch, T03 3666189, dis@disinfo.co.nz ***Project Enable*** T0800-801981 and ***The Disability Resources Centres*** in Auckland, T09-6258069: Palmerston North, T06-3562311;

There are few specialist tour companies acting specifically for the disabled. One exception is ***Accessible Kiwi Tours Ltd***, owned and operated by Allan and Shona Armstrong, based in Opotiki in the Bay of Plenty, T07-3156988, F07-3155056, info@accessible-tours.co.nz

Gay and lesbian travellers

For more information on gay and lesbian New Zealand contact the New Zealand Gay and Lesbian Tourism Association, PB MBE P255 Auckland, T09-3742161, info@nzglta.org.nz

Homosexuality (except for in some rather bigoted rural outposts) is generally well accepted in New Zealand and indeed in some parts it is flourishing. Auckland has a thriving homosexual and transvestite community heavily focused around the Ponsonby and Karangahape Road (K'Road) areas, where there are many gay and gay-friendly clubs, cafés and pubs. Some specialist publications and independent groups are also in evidence. Each February Auckland hosts the popular 'Hero Parade', which is the national gay event of the year. This popular and growing festival involves a street parade and entertainment in the Ponsonby area. Although not quite on the scale of the world famous Sydney 'Gay Mardis Gras' it can still blow your wig off and is enjoyed by thousands, both gay and straight. Not to be outdone, Wellington also has a parade/festival, the 'Devotion Festival' usually held in November.

There are a few independent companies offering holiday packages and advice and these include: ***Wayne Leigh, Harvey World Travel***, 293 Ponsonby Road, Ponsonby, T09-3765011, www.gayholidays.co.nz and the ***Wilson Group Ltd***, 8/25 Mana Street, Vogeltown, Wellington, 6002, T/F04-9390562, twg@paradise.net.nz The website

Foreign consulates in New Zealand

Auckland

Australia, *7th Floor, 132-138 Quay St, City, T3032429;* ***Canada***, *T3098516;* ***Croatia***, *131 Lincoln Rd, Henderson, T8365581;* ***Denmark***, *T5373099;* ***Finland***, *10 Heather St, Parnell, T3092969;* ***France***, *T4883453;* ***Germany***, *6th Floor, 52 Symonds St, City, T9133674;* ***Italy***, *102 Kitchener Rd, Milford, T4861888;* ***Japan***, *Level 12, ASB Bank Centre, 135 Albert St, City, T3034106;* ***Korea***, *2nd Floor, 350 Queen St, City, T3790818;* ***Netherlands***, *L j Hooker House, Level 1, 57 Symonds St, City, T3795399;* ***Peru***, *199-209 Great North Rd, Grey Lynn, T3763047;* ***Russia***, *T5289237;* ***Samoa***, *283 Karangahape Rd, City, T3031012;* ***Sweden***, *13th Floor, 92-96 Albert St, City, T3735332;* ***United Kingdom***, *NZI House, 151 Queen St, City, T3032971;* ***USA***, *General Building, 4th Floor, corner Shortland and O'Connell St, City, T3032724.*

Wellington

Australia, *72 Hobson St, T4736411;* ***Canada***, *61 Molesworth St, T4739577;* ***France***, *42 Manners St, T3842555;* ***Germany***, *90 Hobson St, T4736063;* ***United Kingdom***, *44 Hill St, T044726049, www.brithighcomm.org.nz;* ***USA***, *29 Fitzherbert Terr, Thorndon, T4722068.*

www.gaynewzealand.co.nz is also useful. For specific information on the Auckland and Wellington gay scene see those relevant city sections of the handbook.

Working in the country

For work visas, see page 28

Backpackers can occasionally work for their keep at some farmstays (see page 39). One organization that will help you locate these is ***Farm Helpers***, T0800-327681. ***Farm Hosting in New Zealand*** (FhiNZ), Kumeroa Lodge Stud, RD1, Woodville, also have listings and a booklet ($15), T06-3764582. ***New Zealand Farm Holidays*** based in Orewa near Auckland also produce a helpful free catalogue listing almost 300 establishments, T09-4265430, farm@nzaccom.co.nz

There is also an option of working voluntarily on organic farms through an organization called ***Willing Workers on Organic Farms*** (WWOOF). Reports of this network are good and you can often get free comfortable accommodation in return for a few hours of daily work. For more information and a booklet listing over 300 venues ($20), T03-5449890.

Before you travel

Passports & visas

For detailed visa information consult the Visiting section of the New Zealand Immigration Service (NZIS) website, www.immigartion.govt.nz Or contact them at NZIS, Private Bag, Wellesley St, Auckland, T09-9144100

All visitors must be in possession of a passport that is valid for three months beyond the date you intend to leave the country. Australian citizens or holders of an Australian returning resident visa do not need a visa and can stay in New Zealand indefinitely. UK citizens do not need a visa and are automatically issued with a six-month visitor's permit on arrival. To find out the visa status of other countries check out the Visiting New Zealand section of the New Zealand Immigration Service website, or ask your travel agent. All visitors making an application for a visitor's permit require: (a) a passport that is valid for at least three months after your departure from New Zealand; (b) an onward or return ticket to a country you have permission to enter; (c) sufficient money to support yourself during your stay (approximately NZ$1000 per month). The sufficient funds factor can be waived if you have a friend or relative in New Zealand (citizen) who officially agrees to sponsor you i.e. guarantee to support you financially during your stay. If you must apply for a visitor's visa. You can do this at your nearest New Zealand Embassy or by downloading the relevant forms from the website.

New Zealand embassies abroad

Australia *High Commission: Commonwealth Av, Canberra, ACT 2600, T02-62704211 Consulate General: 14th Floor Goldfields building, 1 Alfred St, Circular Quay, Sydney, (PO Box 365), NSW 2000, T02-92471999.*
Canada *High Commission: Suite 727, Metropolitan House, 99 Bank St, Ottowa, Ont K1P 6G3, T613-2386097 Consulate General: Suite 1200-888 Dunsmuir St, Vancouver, BC V6C 3K4, T604-6847388.*
France *NZ Embassy: 7ter, Rue Leonard de Vinci, 75116, Paris, T014-5002411.*
Germany *NZ Embassy: Atrium Friedrichstrasse, Friedrichstrasse 60, 10117, Berlin, T30206210 Consulate General: Heimhuderstrasse 56, 20148, Hamburg, T404-425550.*
Ireland *Consulate General: 46 Upper Mount St, Dublin 2, T016-762464.*
Netherlands *NZ Embassy: Carnegielaan 10, 2517 KH, The Hague, T703-469324.*
UK *High Commission: New Zealand House, Haymarket, London SW1Y 4TQ, T020-79730366.*
USA *NZ Embassy: Observatory Circle NW, Washington DC, 20008, T202-3284848 Consulate General: Suite 1150, 12400 Wiltshire Blvd, Los Angeles. CA 90025, T310-2071605 Other Consulate: 6810 51st Av NE, Seattle, WA 98115, T206-5259881.*

Essentials

Longer stays & work visas

It is illegal to work on a visitor's permit. Citizens of Canada, Japan and the UK aged 18-30 can apply (from their own country) for a Holiday Work Visa which entitles you to work for 12 months. Australians do not require a work permit. To study in New Zealand student visas come under a separate category. You can also get extensions on your visitor's permit for up to nine months but you must meet certain criteria. For detailed information contact the NZIS direct. For a general Residence Visa an application must be made from your own country. It involves a points system relating to factors such as age, education, occupation and so on. The golden target number required goes up and down depending on the perceived demand for immigrants and 'to a degree' politics. For details consult the 'Migration' section on the website or contact the NZIS direct. Be warned – you will need endless supplies of patience and determination.

Customs regulations

Comprehensive advice for travellers is available on the New Zealand Customs Service website, www.customs.govt.nz

New Zealand's environment and highly unique bio-diversity has literally been decimated by unwelcome and non-native flora and faunaa. Not surprisingly, it has imposed strict bio-security laws. Be extra vigilant that you are not carrying or have packed any fruit, or animal and plant matter of any kind without prior permission. Heavy fines are imposed on those who flaunt the rules. You will find details of restricted items on the Customs website. The usual rules and regulations are also in force regarding pets or any live animals, drugs and firearms.

Duty free goods

New Zealand duty free liquor is some of the cheapest in the world

Apart from your personal effects and as long as you are over 17 years of age you are allowed the following importation concessions: 200 cigarettes or 250 g of tobacco or 50 cigars, or a mix of all three weighing no more than 250 g; 4½ litres of wine or beer and one 125 cl bottle of spirits, liqueur or other libation. Goods of value up to NZ$700 are duty and tax-free.

Insurance

Although New Zealand does not exactly suffer from crime-ridden society, accidents and delay can still occur. If you can afford it, full or part travel insurance is advised. For peace of mind, at the very least get medical insurance and coverage for personal effects. The New Zealand Accident Compensation Scheme covers visitors to New Zealand for personal injury by accident. Benefits include some medical expenses, but do not include loss of earnings. **Accident Info Services**, a private company can give 24-hour advice to visitors on how best to access the New Zealand health system, T0800-263345.

Points to note Always read the small print carefully. Check that the policy covers the activities you intend or may end up doing. Also check exactly what your medical cover includes, i.e. ambulance, helicopter rescue or emergency flights back home. Also check the payment protocol. You may have to cough up first (literally) before the insurance company reimburses you. It is always best to dig out all the receipts for expensive personal effects like jewellery or cameras. Take photos of these items and note down all serial numbers.

Insurance companies You are advised to shop around. ***STA Travel*** and other reputable student travel organisations offer good value policies. Young travellers from North America can try the International Student Insurance Service (ISIS), which is available through ***STA Travel***, T1-800-7770112, www.sta-travel.com

Other recommended travel insurance companies in North America include: ***Travel Guard***, T1-800-8261300, www.noelgroup.com ***Access America***, T1-800-2848300; ***Travel Insurance Services***, T1-800-9371387; ***Travel Assistance International***, T1-800-8212828; and ***Council Travel***, T1-888-COUNCIL, www.counciltravel.com Older travellers should note that some companies will not cover people over 65 years old, or may charge higher premiums. The best policies for older travellers (UK) are offered by ***Age Concern***, T01883-346964.

Vaccinations

There are no vaccinations required to enter NZ but as with any country, you are advised to get a tetanus injection or ensure that your boosters are up to date.

What to take

New Zealand is a well-developed nation and all you will need, from pharmaceuticals to camping gear, is readily available throughout the country. There is also a wealth of quality maps and travel books available. Given the favourable dollar rate if you are coming from Europe or North America you may be advised to travel light and buy as you go. Auckland can supply just about all your needs. Backpackers naturally are advised to bring a good sleeping bag and a bed sheet. These are not always provided in hostels and certainly not available in the backcountry tramping huts. A good pair of boots and a large rucksack is a good idea. A good camera is essential and you are advised to bring lots of film with you, it will be cheaper than buying it in New Zealand. Remember to bring a compatable electrical adapter plug (available in duty free shops). Binoculars are recommended as is a sun hat, sunscreen and sunglasses.

Money

The New Zealand currency is the dollar ($), divided into 100 cents (c). Coins come in denominations of 5c, 10c, 20c, 50c, $1 and $2. New Zealand notes come in denominations of $5, $10, $20, $50 and $100.

Travellers' cheques

The safest way to carry money is in travellers' cheques. These are available for a small commission from all major banks. ***American Express*** (Amex), ***Visa*** and ***Thomas Cook*** cheques are widely accepted. Most banks do not charge for changing travellers' cheques and usually offer the best exchange rates. Be sure to keep a record of your cheque numbers and keep the cheques you have cashed separate from the cheques themselves, so that you can get a full refund of all uncashed cheques should you lose them. It is best to bring NZ$ cheques to avoid extra exchange costs.

Credit cards, ATMs & EFTPOS

All the major credit cards (*Visa*, *MasterCard*, *Amex*, *JCB* and *Diners*) are widely accepted. New Zealand has a wonderful system called EFTPOS (Electronic Funds Transfer at Point of Sale) which is essentially like having thousands of mini-ATMs at points of sale throughout the country. Most hotels, shops, retail outlets and petrol stations have them and it has revolutionized the need to carry around wads of cash. Of course it is best suited to those who have a bank account in New Zealand and carry the various cash/cheque cards, but credit cards can be used with the relevant pin number. The real beauty of the system, other than its sheer convenience, is that you are not charged exorbitant fees for using it. If you intend to stay in New Zealand for a while you may be able to open an account with one of the major banks and secure an EFTPOS/ATM card and PIN. That way your money is in the bank and safe. The standard ATMs are readily available in almost all towns and though they accept non-host bank cards, it's best to stick to your own bank's ATMs so you do not incur hidden fees. Credit cards can of course be used and some banks are linked to foreign savings accounts and cards by such networks as Cirrus and Plus. Check with your own bank and card provider and ask what you can and cannot do before you leave.

Banks

Almost all towns and villages throughout the country have at least one of the major bank branches and an ATM. The main banks are the ***Bank of New Zealand***, the ***National Bank of New Zealand***, the ***ASB Bank***, ***Post Bank*** and ***Countrywide Bank***, with other trans-Tasman banks, like ***Westpac Trust*** and ***ANZ*** also in evidence. Major Internet banks like Bank Direct also do a healthy business in New Zealand. Bank opening hours are Monday-Friday 0900-1630 with some city branches also remaining open on Saturday mornings until 1230. Exchange offices like ***Thomas Cook*** and ***American Express*** tend to have longer opening hours, sometimes staying open until 2100 in the cities.

Money transfers

If you need money quickly or in an emergency the best way is to have it wired to you, via any major bank with the ***Western Union***, T0800-270000 or via ***Thomas Cook*** and ***Moneygram***, T0800-872893. This transfer can be done in less than an hour or up to a week depending how much is being transferred and how much you are willing to pay (about $30-80). Charges are on a sliding scale; it will cost proportionately less to wire out more money.

Cost of living/ travelling

If you are coming to New Zealand from the UK or the US you will be amazed at how far a pound or a US dollar will go. In late 2000 the NZ$ dropped to a record low with the US$ and after a slight rally with the UK£ in the mid-1990s the NZ$ is back hovering around £0.30. Those travelling from the UK and US will find things generally a lot cheaper, though some things such as beer are about the same price. Eating out is relatively cheap and should be enjoyed to the full. Accommodation can be expensive. Hostel accommodation will range from about $15-18 for a bunk, while a basic single or double room will cost up to double that. A non-powered site in a motor camp will cost from $8-12. A powered site is usually about the same or just a few dollars more. B&B accommodation varies, ranging from $70 for a basic double to over $200 for luxury. Motel prices vary but a double can be secured for as little as $60. A more luxurious motel will cost up to $175. Petrol is expensive at around $1 per litre ($4 per gallon). Many organized activities are also expensive. A highly mobile few weeks on the road alone, using non-powered sites, buying your own food and partaking in essentially free activities like tramping will still cost no less than about $80 per day. In New Zealand, money ultimately evaporates just as quickly as anywhere else, so it is wise to budget.

Youth & student discounts

There are various official youth/student ID cards available. The most useful is the **International Student ID Card** which will secure discounts in many accommodation establishments, some admissions and activities. In New Zealand you can also secure domestic air travel at up to half price and great reductions on rail and ferry services.

Getting there

Air

There are six airports in the country which handle international flights with Auckland being the principal international airport. Wellington, Palmerston North and Hamilton in North Island and Christchurch, Dunedin and Queenstown in South Island have services to eastern Australia.

Buying a ticket

There is a mind-boggling array of fares and deals available from the various airlines serving New Zealand (see following pages), but simply because of the distance involved in getting there from anywhere except Australia, it is going to be expensive. Fares are more expensive in the summer or high season (December-March) and cheaper in the winter or low season (May-August). However, fares do also tend to drop a little in the 'shoulder season' months of March/April and September/October. Through inter-airline competition and 'sudden offers', or if you book well in advance, you may also be able to secure a good deal.

Given the fact that your airfare will be your single biggest expense it is well worth shopping around and one of the best ways to do this is on the web. There are numerous sites where you can check out prices or even book tickets. You can search in the travel sections of your web browser or try the sites of the discount travel companies and agents listed in this section. If you have plenty of time it is well worth considering a Round the World (RTW) or Circle Pacific ticket, even if you do not intend to stay long in other countries.

Some useful websites for securing good deals, other than those already listed, include:
www.travelstore.com
www.lastminute.com

Flight prices

The following give you some idea of the airfare price range with the average airline: Australia to New Zealand standard return fare: A$370-A$550 (eastern seaboard) / RWT from A$1700.

Los Angeles to Auckland standard return fare: US$900-US$1400 / RWT from US$1350.

London to Auckland standard return fare: UK£500-UK£1000 / RWT from UK£1200.

Many travellers come to New Zealand on these tickets stopping for a week of sunbathing in Fiji or Papua New Guinea or en route from Australia. As well as surfing the web, a visit to your local travel agent for advice is often worthwhile. Also worth checking are: www.Teletex.co.uk; www.QXL.com; www.firedup.com (flight auction sites).

For some strange reason it is almost as expensive to fly from the US on a return ticket as it is from Europe, at almost twice the distance. As well as the RTW and Circle Pacific options you may also be able to secure an 'open-jaw' ticket, which would allow you to fly into Auckland and depart from Christchurch at no extra charge. When trying to find a good deal make sure you check the route, the duration of the journey, stop-overs allowed, travel restrictions, minimum and maximum periods away, cancellation policies and all the small print. It is also wise to book your ticket with a reputable travel agent. In the UK for instance most travel agents are registered with the Association of British Travel Agents (ABTA). Should your travel agent go bust prior to or during your trip ABTA will guarantee refunds or arrange alternatives. In New Zealand one recommended travel agent in Auckland is ***Destinations Unlimited***, T09-3734033, F09-3734032, destinations1@atlasmail.com Close to your time of departure check your reservation direct with the airline.

Cheap flight tickets fall into two categories – official and unofficial. Official tickets are called budget fares, Apex, super-Apex, advance purchase tickets, or whatever a particular airline chooses to call them. Unofficial tickets are discounted tickets which are released by airlines through selected travel agents. They are not sold directly by airlines. Discounted tickets are usually as low or lower than the official budget price tickets. You may also be able to secure a heavily discounted 'Courier fare' ticket whereby you personally take important courier company business documents to New Zealand. But bear in mind you may lose your full baggage allowance and only be allowed carry-on luggage.

One word of **warning**. If you have never experienced a 12-30 hour flight schedule before, even with stops, it is pretty gruelling. Think twice about the very cheap long haul multi-stop offers with the lesser-known airlines. You will also almost certainly arrive in New Zealand looking and feeling a lot older. Even with the top airlines 12-24 hours of flights and connections is an ordeal. The few extra pounds or dollars it costs to get you there quickly and reliably are worth their weight in gold.

From the UK & Europe

The routings are usually west via the USA (Los Angeles, San Francisco and Honolulu) or Canada (Vancouver and Toronto) or east via a number of stopovers in Asia, including Bangkok, Delhi, Kuala Lumpur, Tokyo, Brisbane, Sydney or Melbourne. But, especially with an RWT ticket, routes and stopovers vary and can change. Almost all flights depart from Heathrow or Frankfurt, so you may have to arrange connecting flights. Overall the choice of routes, types of ticket and, to an extent, airline and price, is huge so shop around. Use the listings in this book or the national newspapers to try to secure the best deal and one that is suitable to your requirements. Although New Zealand is well-geared to independent travel, you should also look at the numerous organized tours and package deals. If you have plenty of time look very seriously at buying a RWT.

Airlines to New Zealand from Australia

Air New Zealand, *T132476, www.airnz.com*
Freedom Air, *T1-800-122000, www.freedomair.co.nz*
Qantas, *1-800-062123, www.qantas.com.au*
Singapore Airlines, *T131011, www.singaporeair.com*
United Airlines, *T131777, www.ual.com*

Airlines to New Zealand from North America

Star Alliance Partners, *T800-2416522, www.star-alliance.com*
Air New Zealand, *US T1-800 2621234, Canada T18006635494, www.airnz.com*
Canadian Airlines, *T1-888 2472262*
Qantas *T1-800 2274500, www.qantas.com*
Singapore Airlines, *T1-800 7423333, www.singaporeair.com*
United Airlines, *T1-800 5382929, www.ual.com*

Airlines to New Zealand from the UK

All Star Alliance Partners, *www.star-alliance.com*
Aerolineas Argentinas, *T020-74941001*
Air New Zealand, *T020-87412299, www.airnz.com*
Britannia, *(occasional charters), T0800-000747*
British Airways, *T0845-7799977, www.british-airways.com*
Canadian Airlines, *T0870-5247226 (Ireland T1-800 626747)*
Cathay Pacific, *T0345-581581*
Garuda Indonesia, *T020-74863011*
Japan Airlines, *T020-74081000*
Korean Air, *T0800-413000*
Malaysian Airlines, *T020-73412020*
Qantas, *T0345-747767, www.qantas.com*
Singapore Airlines, *T020-87470007 (Ireland T016-710722; also fly out of Manchester), www.singaporeair.com*
Thai International, *T020-74919113, www.thaiair.com*
United Airlines, *T020-89909900, www.ual.com*

From North America

Almost all flights from within the USA are routed via Los Angeles (LAX). In Canada most go via Vancouver and Honolulu or again Los Angeles. From LAX several flights leave daily and you are looking at a direct flight of around 12 ½ hours, one of the longest direct flights in the world. Use the listings in this book or national newspapers to secure a good deal. Again, if you prefer to have your trip organized, or have special interests, look at the numerous package deals available. If you have plenty of time consider a RWT or a Circle Pacific ticket. Most people will have to arrange connecting inter-state flights. You should be able to secure these at a reduced cost or sometimes (especially for students) for free.

From Australia

A flight from Sydney to Auckland takes 3½ hrs

As you might expect there is a huge choice and much competition with trans-Tasman flights. Traditionally most flights used to go from Cairns, Brisbane, Sydney and Melbourne to Auckland but now many of the cheaper flights can actually be secured to Wellington, Christchurch and Queenstown. Other destinations include Palmerston North, Hamilton and Dunedin. The New Zealand based ***Freedom Air*** service to Dunedin is cheap (as low as NZ$420) but with only a few flights a week they must be booked well in advance. Flights and especially ski packages to Queenstown can also be cheaper and have been heavily promoted in recent years, but conditions usually apply, giving you limited flexibility. At any given time there are usually special deals on offer from the major players like ***Qantas***, ***United*** and ***Air New Zealand*** so shop around. Use the listings in this book, the web, your local travel agent and the national newspapers. From Australia you are likely to be interested in 'open-jaw' tickets that will allow you to fly in to one city and

Discount travel agents in Australia

Flight Centres, 82 Elizabeth St, Sydney, T131600, www.flightcentre.com.au Branches in other main cities.
STA Travel T1-300 360960, www.statravelaus.com.au 702 Harris St, Ultimo, Sydney and 256 Finders St, Melbourne.
Travel.com.au, 80 Clarence St, Sydney, T029-2901500, www.travel.com.au

Essentials

Discount travel agents in North America

Air Brokers International, 323 Geary St, Suite 411, San Francisco, CA 94102, T1-800-8833273, www.airbrokers.com Consolidator and specialists on RWT and Circle Pacific tickets.
Council Travel, 205 E 42nd St, New York, NY 10017, T1888-COUNCIL, www.counciltravel.com Student/budget agency with branches in many other US cities.
Discount Airfares Worldwide On-Line, www.etn.nl/discount.htm A hub of consolidator and discount agent links.
International Travel Network/Airlines of the Web, www.itn.net/airlines Online air travel information and reservations.
STA Travel, 5900 Wiltshire Blvd, suite 2110, Los Angeles, CA 90036, T1-800 7770112, www.sta-travel.com Discount student/ youth travel company with branches in most major US cities.
Travel CUTS, 187 College St, Toronto, ON M5T 1P7, T1-800 6672887, www.travelcuts.com Student discount fares, IDs and other travel services. Branches in other major Canadian cities.
Travelocity, www.travelocity.com Online consolidator.

Discount travel agents in the UK

Council Travel, 28a Poland St, London, W1V 3DB, T020-7437 7767, www.destinations-group.com
STA Travel, 86 Old Brompton Rd, London, SW7 3LH, T020-7361 6161, www.statravel.co.uk Branches throughout the country and specialists in low-cost student/youth flights and tours. Also good for student IDs and insurance.
Trailfinders, 194 Kengsington High St, London, W8 6FT, T020-7938 3939.
Usit Campus, 52 Grosvener Gardens, London, SW1 OAG, T020-7730 3402, www.campustravel.co.uk Student/youth travel specialists.

depart from another. This will almost certainly be more expensive and, given the many restrictions and conditions imposed, they are often hard to secure at a good price. Always be careful to check the conditions of the cheaper 'temporary' deals with regard to your minimum or maximum allowed length of stay, cancellations, refunds etc.

Touching down

Airport Information For detailed information on negotiating Auckland International Airport see Auckland Ins and Outs, page 74. Before you leave your own country check their excellent website www.auckland-airport.co.nz Other points of entry and their websites include: Wellington Airport, www.wellington-airport.co.nz and Christchurch, www.christchurch-airport.co.nz

Taxes There is a 12.5% GST (Goods and Services Tax) placed on almost every bought item in New Zealand. Prices quoted almost always include GST, but on bigger quotes or services it pays to check.

Getting to and from Auckland airport

Airport to city
Take the main exit road from airport (George Bolt Memorial Drive) to the intersection with SH20. Follow signs for Auckland City and take the motorway to Queenstown Road exit. Turn right into Queenstown Road and continue straight ahead, through the roundabout into Pah Road that becomes Manukau Road (SH12). Follow Manukau Road and turn right at the traffic lights (before Newmarket) into Alpers Avenue. At the end of Alpers Avenue turn right into Gillies Avenue then almost immediately left to join the SH1 motorway. The last exit to the central city is Nelson Street (right hand lane).

City to airport
On the Southern Motorway (SH1) take the Gillies Avenue exit. Turn right into Gillies Avenue then left at the traffic lights into Owens Road. At the end of Owens Road turn right on to Manukau Road (SH12). Go straight over the roundabout at Pah Road then turn left on to the motorway. Follow the motorway and join George Bolt Memorial Drive to the airport.

On leaving New Zealand there is a **Departure Tax** of $20-$25 depending on which airport you leave from. This is not included in your ticket price.

Essentials

Tourist information

Generally speaking the information centres provide a comprehensive and friendly service. There is also a huge amount of free material

The New Zealand Visitor Information Network (VIN) is made up of three categories of visitor information centres, with almost 100 centres throughout the country. **National Visitor Information Centres** (code red): These are based in Auckland and Christchurch as well as the main tourist centres, like Rotorua and Queenstown.Open seven days a week, they provide a comprehensive information service including accommodation bookings and domestic airline, bus and train ticketing. Souvenir shops and occasionally other retail outlets, currency exchange and cafés are often attached. **Regional Visitor Information Centres** (code green): These are found throughout the country and there may be more than one in each region. They provide a general information booking service usually seven days a week. **Local Visitor Information Centres** (code blue): These can be found almost anywhere providing local information as well as assistance in accommodation and transport bookings. They are open at least five days a week, but are subject to varying seasonal and weekend hours.

Maps

For major map stockists in Auckland *see page 77*

Detailed urban and rural maps are readily available throughout New Zealand. ***Wises*** are the major city and provincial town map company producing a range of handbooks and fold-out city maps. If you intend to do a lot of travelling, their provincial town maps for both North and South Islands are invaluable. Most large bookshops stock ***Wises***' maps and others. Almost all the information centres in the larger towns provide free leaflet maps and the coverage is generally excellent. **DOC** offices are also very well stocked with National Park and rural maps. For really detailed maps the **Land Information New Zealand** offices can provide all your needs. Major libraries have stocks which can be photocopied. ***Mapworld*** in Christchurch is an excellent outlet and also stocks complete CD-ROMs of all New Zealand national, regional and town maps, T0800mapworld, maps@mapworld.co.nz

Safety

For legal advice contact the local Citizens Advice Bureau, in Auckland, T09-5240298

Despite appearances, or what you may have heard, New Zealand has its fair share of crime. There are more guns in New Zealand than there are people and many in the hands of the poor, the drug gangs, the mad and the bad. Tourists are rarely targeted for anything other than petty crime but you still need to be vigilant. Theft, especially in Auckland, is rife and

Touching down

Business hours
Weekday business hours are usually 0900-1700. Most retail outlets close at 1730 and in the larger towns many are also open at the weekend. Also, in the main centres, the larger supermarket chains are open in the evenings. The modern city malls usually offer one or two late shopping nights: usually Thursday or Friday. Most Government offices are open from about 0830-1630.

Electricity
The New Zealand supply is 230/240 volts (50 hertz). Plugs are either two or three pronged with flat pins. North American appliances require both an adapter and a transformer. UK and adapter only and Australian appliances are the same. Adapters and transformers should be available at your local hardware store or at the airport.

Emergencies
For Police, Fire or Ambulance T111.

Laundry
Most towns, villages and accommodation establishments have laundries. They tend to operate with $1 or $2 coins. A full wash and dry will cost about $4.

Smoking
Smoking is not allowed on airlines, on most public transport, and in many public places. It is still possible to smoke in many restaurants, in segregated sections. Almost all pubs and clubs allow unrestricted smoking.

Time
At 1200 in NZ it is 0900 in Sydney, 1100 yesterday in the UK, 0800 in Japan, 1500 yesterday in Los Angeles or 1800 yesterday in New York. Allow for daylight saving ie from the first Sunday in October to the third Sunday in March the clock goes one hour forward.

Toilets
Public toilets are readily available and very rarely are you charged for the privilege.

Weights and measures
New Zealand uses the metric system. Distances are in kilometres, petrol is measured in litres.

Essentials

tourist accommodation establishments are not exempt. Cars and their contents are also regularly targeted. Do not relax your guard, keep money safe and out of sight. Keep your vehicle locked at all times and put valuables in the boot (trunk). It may sound ridiculous but you also need to be wary of other tourists. Having suitable insurance cover is also wise. Urban New Zealand has its fair share of rapes, some brutal, so women should be just as vigilant as they need be in the more populous and notorious nations.

Drink driving and speeding laws are very strict in New Zealand: do not even think about driving while under the influence, and keep your speed down. Thanks to the heavy road toll (though some say its principally a major source of government revenue) speed cameras and patrol cars are omnipresent. Drug laws are also strict so don't get caught in possession.

Rules, customs and etiquette

Tipping Tipping in New Zealand is at the customer's discretion and not really expected. However, In a good restaurant you should leave a tip of 10-15% if you are satisfied with the service, but the bill may included a service charge. Tipping is appreciated in pubs and bars and taxi drivers also expect some sort of tip. On a longer journey 10% is fine. As in most other counties, hotel porters, bellboys, waiters and waitresses should all be tipped to supplement their meagre wages.

How big is your footprint?

*Much of the **Environmental Code** advocated by DOC is common sense. Overall, the entire concept can be summed up with two words and an age-old cliché – **respect** and **awareness** and **'take nothing but pictures, leave nothing but footprints'.** Given the unbelievable damage we humans have already inflicted on New Zealand's unique and ancient biodiversity surely that attitude is not only particularly poignant, but also naturally demanded. For a listing of Eco-tourist operators throughout the country see page 20.*

*The independent organization **New Zealand Royal Forest and Bird Society,** 172 Taranaki St, Wellington, T04-3857374, www.forest-bird.org.nz are excellent and produce a quarterly magazine for its members. The monthly Wilderness Magazine, www.surfingnz.com is also good containing comprehensive outdoors and Eco-activity information and is available in most newsagents and bookshops.*

Responsible tourism

For the vast majority of tourists it is New Zealand's environment and nature that are its greatest attraction. Yet regardless of your interest or your intention, the moment you set foot in New Zealand you are by definition an **'Eco-tourist'**. In essence though your hosts may not demand it the environment does. There is no doubt whatsoever that the environment is the biggest and brightest jewel in the tourism crown and a resource that is not only precious, but requires considerable protection.

Yet one could argue that environmentalism and tourism is, in essence, a contradiction in terms. Surely what makes New Zealand so special, so attractive, is the very lack of humanity and its areas of almost inaccessible wilderness. There is no doubt this is true, but thankfully the New Zealand psyche is such that it seems to successfully marry tourism and environmentalism and bestow upon the union a blessing that has so far resulted in a congenial, if naturally imperfect relationship. So good in fact, that the country has earned the reputation as one of the best Eco-tourism destinations in the world. Part of this success is due to the vast area that is protected as forest parks, national parks, nature and marine reserves – almost a quarter of the entire country – all coming under the committed, yet under-resourced advocacy and administration of the **Department of Conservation**.

Before you arrive you can avail yourself of a wealth of information on its excellent website www.doc.govt.nz and throughout your travels you will find dedicated information centres and field stations in all cities, major provincial towns and national parks. If you intend to go walking or to embark on a longer tramp then you will find DOC invaluable and through its system of backcountry huts and campsites an essential aspect of the experience.

Given the country's natural resources New Zealand is, not surprisingly, on the cutting edge of Eco-tourism. The sheer choice and quality of activities, let alone the location in which they can be experienced are superb, from whale watching at Kaikoura, or tramping in Fiordland to exploring the island sanctuaries of Kapiti or Tiri Tiri Matangi. New Zealand is one of very few countries where you can see rare or endangered species (especially birds) at close hand and in solitude. For many this is a new and welcome experience and in deep contrast to the constraints of a being in a busy hide or being surrounded by an orgy of 'twitchers' all falling over each other to compare the size of their telescopes.

Essential telephone numbers

Emergency: T111
National directory assistance: T081
International directory assistance: T0172
International direct-dial access code: T00
International operator: T0170
Local and national operator: T010
New Zealand country code: T64
Toll help desk: T123

Where to stay

Bear in mind that given the vast range of choice, we can only list a number of reputable establishments in each location

Besides actually getting there, accommodation in New Zealand will be your biggest expense. There is generally a wealth of choice and though you will rarely end up without a bed for the night, you are advised to book ahead during the high season. At the present time the New Zealand Tourist Board are heavily plugging the homestay or farmstay options (see below). You are advised to try this at least for a few nights to encounter real Kiwi hospitality and general Kiwi life.

Visitor Information Centres are a great help when it comes to accommodation and generally stock all the highly illustrated leaflets. They can also offer plenty of good advice regarding the range of options and administer bookings. The web is also a major source of information with almost all reputable establishments now having at least an email address. There are also many books available including the ***AA Accommodation Guides, Jasons Motels and Motor Lodges Guide, The New Zealand Bed and Breakfast Guide*** and numerous motor camp, motel, campsite and backpacker guides (most of which are free). A visit to a national Visitor Information Centre will see you suitably stocked up.

Hotels

The numerous hotels in New Zealand can generally be listed under one of four categories:

Large Luxury Hotels There are a surprising number of large modern and luxury (four to five star) hotels in the major cities. Auckland in particular seems to benefit the most, with many new establishments like the *Grand Metropolis* or the *Hilton* being only months old. There are so many luxury rooms and apartment blocks in the city centre it is amazing they can all survive. These major hotels tend to be part of major international or trans-Tasman chains and the prices range from about $250-$500 per night. As you would expect, all rooms are equipped with the latest technology including laptop plug-in ports, Sky TV, etc. They also have restaurants and all the usual leisure facilities, including swimming pools, spa pools and gyms.

Standard Chain Hotels These range in age and quality and include such familiar names as *Quality Hotels*, *Novetel* and *Copthorne Hotels*. Available in all the major cities and most of the larger provincial towns, their standard prices vary from about $175-$300. Again most have in-house restaurants and additional facilities such as a heated pool.

Boutique Hotels These vary in size and price but tend to be modern and of a high and luxurious standard. The smaller, more intimate boutique hotels are, like elsewhere, beginning to overtake the major chains in popularity. On average double rooms here can cost anything from $175-400.

Traditional Pub and Budget Hotels Many of the rural towns have kept the traditional old wooden hotels. Don't be fooled, however. Some of these may look grand from the outside, but often the interior doesn't match up. However, a basic cheap and

Accommodation price codes

*Accommodation prices in this book are all coded with the letters below. These ratings are based on a double room (usually with en-suite) during the high season. Cheaper rooms are of course readily available with shared bathrooms or more basic facilities. Note that many places, especially the large hotel chains, offer low season and weekend specials. All the places listed are generally recommended as providing good service and value within their respective category. Note that price codes for hostels are grouped in the **C-D** sections. A bed in a shared dormitory will vary from $12-$18, depending on the establishment and the time of year:*

LL	*$220 plus*
L	*$175-$220*
AL	*$120-$175*
A	*$80-$120*
B	*$50-$80*
C	*$20-$50*
D	*$20 and under*

Essentials

comfortable room can still be found. Beware the bars in many of these places, unless you're quick on the draw. Also note that prices are often dropped at weekends and during the off season.

Lodges & B&Bs

There are a growing number of luxury lodges all over New Zealand and most sell themselves on their location or classic 'bush setting' as much as their architecture, sumptuous rooms, facilities and cuisine. Prices tend to be high, ranging anywhere from $200 to the mind-bending $2000 per night of the highly exclusives. Most of these lodges are listed in the text.

Although there are not as many B&Bs in New Zealand as there are in Europe, you can still find them in most places. They vary greatly in style, size and quality and can be anything from a basic double room with shared bathroom and a couple of boiled eggs for brekkie to a luxurious en-suite or self-contained with the Full Monty breakfast. Again prices vary, with the standard cost being as little as $70-90. Some of the more luxurious, however, are extortionate. When looking at prices bear in mind a full breakfast costs at least $10 in a café or restaurant. Many lodges and B&Bs also offer evening meals. Sadly the great Kiwi B&B has still got a long way to go before reaching the standard of its Scottish Highland counterpart, but you will find most hosts to be very congenial and helpful folk.

Homestays & Farmstays

The local Visitor information Centres can help you locate homestays or farmstays and the NZTB website also has a detailed listing of farmstays nationwide, www.purenz.com

The term 'homestay' in New Zealand is one that is often touted about, but its actual meaning is often vague. Generally speaking if an establishment advertises itself as a homestay it will deliberately lack the privacy of the standard B&B and you are encouraged to mix with your hosts. Depending on your preference and personality this is designed to give you an insight into Kiwi life. Other than that they are very similar to B&Bs, with breakfasts usually standard and an evening meal often being optional. Farmstays of course give you the added agricultural and rural edge and this form of accommodation is generally recommended. Accommodation can take many forms from being in-house with your hosts or fully self-contained, and breakfasts and evening meals are often optional and included. You will often find yourself helping to round up sheep or milking a cow and if you have kids (and farmstays usually welcome them) they will be wonderfully occupied for hours. Both homestays and farmstays tend to charge the same, or slightly lower, rates as the standard B&Bs. For farmstay options in Southland contact the very helpful ***Western Southland Farm Hosting Group***, T2258608, www.nzcountry.co.nz/farmhost

Motels

Motels are the preferred option of the average Kiwi holidaymaker. They are literally everywhere and reproducing even as you read this. They vary greatly, from the awful, stained love shacks to the new and luxurious condos. There is usually a range of rooms available and almost all have at least a shower, kitchen facilities (with coffee and tea) and a TV – though whether it actually works and has Sky TV, or doubles as a plant pot, depends on the price. Most are clean and comfortable and nicely appointed, while in others you may find yourself trying to sleep next to the main road. Prices vary from studio units at about $60-$80, one-bedroom units from $70-$100 and suites accommodating families and groups for an additional charge for each adult. Many of the bigger and better establishments have a restaurant and a swimming pool. Many also make the most of the country's thermal features and have spas, sometimes even in your room.

Hostels

In the high season and especially over Christmas through to March you are advised to pre-book everywhere

Being such a popular destination for the independent traveller/backpacker New Zealand is well served with hostels and budget accommodation establishments. Naturally, they vary greatly in age, design, location and quality. Some enjoy a busy atmosphere in the centre of town while others provide a quiet haven of sanctity in the country. They also range in the type of beds they offer, with many having separate double and single rooms as well as the traditional dormitory. Dorms are usually single sex but sometimes optionally mixed, which can make for an entertaining or frustrating night, depending on your pioint of view. Camping facilities within the grounds are also common. Generally, hostels are good places to meet other travellers, managers are usually very knowledgeable and helpful, and pick ups are often complimentary. Bikes, kayaks or other activity gear can often be hired at low cost or are free to use. Wherever you stay you will have access to equipped kitchens, a laundry, games or TV room, plenty of local budget orientated information ,and of course, phones and the internet. Prices vary little for a dorm bed, ranging from $12-$18 depending on season. Single rooms and doubles tend to be under $40 or about $20 per adult.

YHAs

The Youth Hostel Association NZ is part of a worldwide organisation with over 4500 hostels in 60 countries. There are 57 establishments throughout New Zealand. Being part of a large organization, most are on a par if not better than the private or independent backpacker hostels. They all offer very much the same in standard of accommodation and facilities. YHAs are only open to members but you can join in your home country (if YHA exists) or in New Zealand for an annual fee of $30. Non-members can also stay at hostels for an additional charge of $4 per night for the first six nights, by which time you become a member. YHA membership cards are very handy even if you do not intend consistently to stay at YHA hostels, entitling you to a number of discounts, including up to 30% off air and bus travel. There are also a number of Associate YHA hostels where no membership card is required but where members get a small discount.

Backpacker organizations

There are three major backpacking membership organizations and networks in New Zealand which provide detailed hostel information listings and certain discounts, including a dollar off each night's stay and other discounts on transport operators and activities. About 80 New Zealand establishments are members of the ***VIP*** group, PO Box 80021, Green Bay, Auckland, T09-8276016, www.vip.co.nz *VIP* have an annual membership fee of $30. ***Budget Backpacker*** (BBH), 99 Titiraupenga Street, Taupo, T/F07-3771568, www.backpack.co.nz have almost 300 member establishments and their 'Blue Book' is free (from VICs). The new kid on the block in New Zealand is ***Nomad***, www.nomadsworld.com They offer the same kind of deal for an annual membership of $30. Their principal agent in New Zealand is the ***Travellers Contact Point***, 87 Queen Street, T09-3007197. It is well worth joining one or more of the above.

Motor camps & cabins

New Zealand's fairly compact size and quality road network lends itself to road touring. Given that so many visitors and Kiwis take the campervan or camping option, New Zealand is very well served with quality motor camps and campsites. In fact it is hailed as one of the best in the world. Motor camps can be found almost everywhere and not necessarily just in towns. The hub of many a remote beach, headland or bay is often the great Kiwi motor camp. The quality and age does of course vary. Some are modern and well-equipped while others are much less so. Almost all motor camps are equipped with laundry facilities and most will charge a small fee ($0.20-0.50) for hot showers. Prices are generally very reasonable and range from $8-12 per person (child half-price) for non-powered sites. Powered sites are often the same price.

Most motor camps have a range of cabins which range from dog kennels to quite well-appointed alpine-type huts. They range in price but are rarely more than $50 per night (for two) with an additional charge of $12-15 per person after that.

The ***Top Ten*** chain of motor camps, which has almost 50 camps nationwide, though up to $3 more expensive per night, is generally recommended.

DOC Campsites & huts

The DOC website www.doc.govt.nz is also a good source of information

Naturally most motor camps cater for campers and the charges are generally the same as a non-powered site ($8-$12). This gives you access to all the facilities. **DOC** has over 100 basic campsites all over the country with many being in prime locations. They tend to provide clean running water, toilet facilities and BBQ areas. The National Parks are also excellently facilitated with comfortable well-equipped huts. The nightly camping fee is $3-6 while fees for huts are about $12-20 per night. If you plan to use DOC campsites and huts you are advised to research their locations, fee structures, rules and regulations and book ahead.

Holiday homes & cottages (baches)

This is one accommodation option very often overlooked by visitors. The country has a wealth of holiday homes and baches (seaside huts, cottages or mansions) which are made available for rent throughout the year. While in summer they will most probably be frequented by the owners, in the off-season in particular you can sometimes find a real bargain. The best place to look is in the national newspapers, travel or house rental sections. The regional VICs can also often be of assistance. Most operate on a minimum weekend or week stay basis and costs vary depending on quality and location. This type of accommodation is of course little use to the single traveller, but if you are a family or a group it is well worth looking into.

Getting around

Public transport in all its forms (except rail) is generally both good and efficient. All the main cities and provincial towns can be reached easily by air or by road. Although standard fares, especially by air, can be expensive there are a vast number of discount passes and special seasonal deals available, aimed particularly at the young independent traveller. Although it is entirely possible to negotiate the country by public transport, for sheer convenience, you are advised to get your own set of wheels. Many of the country's delights are only to be seen off the beaten track and certainly a long walk from the nearest bus stop. You will also free yourself of organized schedules. Long term vehicle hire or temporary purchase is generally viable (especially if the costs are shared) and whether you go the way of a standard vehicle or campervan, you will find the country is well geared up for this mode of travel. Having said that, petrol costs are expensive and need to be taken into account.

At the time of going to print domestic air and rail travel in New Zealand was in a state of relative chaos. Although ***Air New Zealand Link*** remain the principal domestic air carriers, with the dramatic and unexpected liquidation of its main competitor

Travelling times and distances to Auckland

Distance	(km)	Car	Bus/Coach	Train	Air
Wellington	647	8 hrs	9 hrs	10½ hrs	1 hr
Christchurch	1000	2 days	2 days	2 days	1¼ hrs
Dunedin	1358	2-4 days	2-4 days	3 days	2½ hrs
Queenstown	1484	2-4 days	2-4 days	–	2 hrs 35 mins
Bay of Islands	241	3 hrs	4 hrs	–	50 mins
Rotorua	235	2½ hrs	3½ hrs	4 hrs	45 mins

Qantas New Zealand in April 2001, the skies have been opened to a number of interested parties. Although none are yet properly established these include *Qantas* (Australia), *Origin Pacific*, *Freedom Air*, *Ansett Australia* and *Virgin Blue*. Since *Qantas* is the most likely of these to succeed and dominate and given the fact they may well retain the same contact details, all previous *Qantas New Zealand* details have been left in the text for this edition. Coming editions will see the companies and routes firmly established and their details listed accordingly.

Worse still is the state of rail travel. In July 2001 *TransRail* announced that every domestic route except the Auckland/Wellington (*Northerner*), Christchurch to Greymouth (*TransAlpine*) and Christchurch to Picton (*Coastal Pacific*) was to close or was at least threatened. Again only time and future editions of this book will tell.

Air

As well as the principal international airports of Auckland, Wellington and Christchurch New Zealand has many smaller provincial town airports that are well served on a daily basis. *Air New Zealand Link*, T0800-737000, www.airnz.co.nz and *Qantas New Zealand*, T0800-800146, www.qantas.co.nz (formerly Ansett New Zealand), are the principal domestic operators. *Origin Pacific*, T0800-302302, www.originpacific.co.nz also operate a number of domestic services but exist on a lesser footing. All are highly professional and efficient and you will rarely have problems with delays or poor service.

Apart from the major domestic operators there are numerous smaller companies offering scheduled services. These include: *Great Barrier Airlines* (Great Barrier, Coromandel and Northland), *Eagle Air* (offering a viable alternative to the ferry between North and South Islands) and *Southern Air* (between Invercargill and Stewart Island). All these companies are listed in the relevant sections. Note that flying anywhere in New Zealand is, on a clear day, a scenic delight and often worth the expense.

Domestic discount fares

If you can, book domestic flights well in advance and through your travel agent before you arrive in New Zealand. There are a number of deals available that will save you between 15% and 25% depending on season. You will also avoid paying GST of 12.5%. The best discounts obviously apply if you have adjunct domestic travel added to your international ticket. Both *Air New Zealand* and *Qantas* offer an Air Pass system which can offer attractive discounts. They work on a zone and coupon system and can be booked prior to arrival. For more information ask your travel agent or see the relevant website (www.airnz.co.nz or www.qantanz.co.nz). Student and backpacker discounts of up to 50% are readily available on domestic flights on presentation of an ISIC, YHA, VIP or BBH card. Conditions and rates vary, so research and book well in advance.

Airline offices in New Zealand

International

Aerolineas Argentinas*, Auckland: 15th Floor ASB Centre, 135 Albert St, T09-3793675; 29 Customs St West, T09-3777999; corner of Customs and Queen Sts, City, T09-3573363. Wellington: 41 Panama St, T04-4748950. Christchurch: 702 Colombo St, T03-3532800.* ***Air New Zealand Link****, T0800-737000, www.airnz.co.nz* ***Air Pacific****, Level 12/17 Albert St, City, Auckland, T09-3792404.* ***Air Vanuatu****, 2nd Floor West Plaza Building, corner of Customs and Albert Sts, City, Auckland, T09-3733435.* ***American Airlines****, 15th Floor Jetset Centre, 48 Emily Pl, City, Auckland, T09-3099159.* ***British Airways****, T09-3568690.* ***Canadian Airlines****, 6th Floor, 18 Shortland St, Auckland, T09-3793371.* ***Cathay Pacific****, 11th Floor, Arthur Andersen Tower, 205 Queen St, Auckland, T09-3790861.* ***Freedom Air****, T0800-600500, www.freedomair.com* ***Garuda Indonesia****, Westpac Trust Tower, 120 Albert St, City, Auckland, T09-3661862.* ***Japan Airlines****, Westpac Trust Tower, 120 Albert St, Auckland, T09-3799906.* ***Korean Airlines****, 92 Albert St, City, Auckland, T09-3073687.* ***Lufthansa Airlines****, T09-3031529.* ***Malaysia Airlines****, 12th Floor Affco House, 12-26 Swanson St, T09-3732741.* ***Polynesian Airlines****, Samoa House, 283 Karangahape Rd, City, Auckland, T09-3095396.* ***Qantas****, T0800-808767, www.qantas.com.au Auckland: 191 Queen St, T09-3578700. Wellington: ASB Bank, 2 Hunter St, T04-4721100. Christchurch: 119 Armagh St, T03-3796504.* ***Singapore Airlines****, West Plaza Building, corner of Albert and Fanshawe Sts, City, Auckland, T0800-808909, www.singaporeair.co.nz* ***Thai Airways****, 22 Fanshawe St, City, Auckland, T09-3773886.* ***United Airlines****, Lumley House, 7 City Rd, City, Auckland, T09-3081747, www.ual.com*

Domestic

Air New Zealand Link*, corner Customs and Queen Sts, Auckland, T0800-737000, www.airnz.co.nz* ***(Former) Qantas New Zealand****, 650 Great South Rd, Ellerslie, Auckland, T0800-800146, F0800267329, www.qantas.co.nz* ***Great Barrier Airlines****, Auckland International Airport (Domestic Terminal), T09-2566500.* ***Great Barrier Express****, Auckland International Airport (Domestic Terminal), T0800-222123.*
Mountain Air*, T0800-222123.*
Mount Cook Airlines*, T09-3095395.*
Origin Pacific*, T0800-302302.*

Essentials

Road

Bus
National bus travel in New Zealand is generally well organized and the networks and daily schedules are good

The two main bus companies are ***Newmans***, www.newmanscoach.co.nz and ***Intercity***, www.intercitycoach.co.nz For information and reservations call the following regional centres: Auckland, T09-9136100; Wellington, T04-4725111; Christchurch, T03-3799020; Dunedin, T03-4749600 and Queenstown, T03-4425628. ***Intercity*** are the only truly national company operating in both North and South Islands, while ***Newmans*** operate throughout North Island, except in Northland where ***Northliner Express***, T09-4383206, www.nzinfo.com/northliner co-operates with ***Intercity***. Other companies in North Island include ***White Star***, T06-3588777, who serve the route between New Plymouth and Wellington, taking in Wanganui and Palmerston North, and the ***Little Kiwi Bus Co***, T0800-759999, who operate between Auckland and Rotorua via Hamilton

The principal backpacker touring bus companies are: ***Kiwi Experience***, T09-3669830, www.kiwiexperience.com; ***Magic Travellers***, T93585600, www.magicbus.co.nz; and ***Flying Kiwi***, T0800-693296, flyingkiwi@xtra.co.nz They have a wide range of flexible routes and options available for reasonable prices. There are also many local operators and independent companies that provide shuttles to accommodation establishments, attractions and activities and these are listed in the Ins and Outs and Transport sections of the main travelling text.

Intercity and Newmans key agents

North Island

***Auckland**: Sky City Coach Terminal, 102 Hobson St, T09-9136100.*
***Gisborne**: Gisborne VIC, Grey St, T06-8687600.*
***Hamilton**: Hamilton Travel Centre, corner of Angelsea and Ward Sts, T07-8343457.*
***Hastings**: Hastings Travel Centre, Caroline St, T06-8780213.*
***Kaitia**: Kaitia Travel, 170 Commerce St, T09-4080540.*
***Napier**: Napier Travel Centre, Munroe St, T06-8342720.*
***New Plymouth**: The Travel Centre, 32 Queen St, T07-7599039.*
***Paihia**: Paihia Travel Centre, Maritime Building, T09-4027857.*
***Palmerston North**: PN Travel Centre, corner of Pitt and Main Sts, T06-3546155.*
***Rotorua**: Tourism Rotorua, 1167 Fenton St, T07-3480366.*
***Taupo**: Taupo Travel Centre, Gascoigne St, T07-3789032.*
***Tauranga**: Tauranga VIC, Willow St, T07-5713211.*
***Thames**: Thames VIC, 206 Pollen St, T07-8687284.*
***Wanganui**: Wanganui Travel Centre, 156 Ridgeway St, T06-3454433.*
***Wellington**: Tranz Rail Travel Centre, Railway Station, Bunny St, T04-4725111.*
***Whakatane**: Transbay Coach Lines, Pyne St, T07-3086169.*
***Whangarei**: Northland Coach and Travel, 11 Rose St, T09-4382653.*

South Island

***Ashburton**: Conway Travel, corner of East and Havelock Sts, T03-3088219.*
***Blenheim**: Blenheim Station Travel Centre, Sinclair St, T03-5772890.*
***Christchurch**: Christchurch Travel Centre, 123 Worcester St, T03-3770951.*
***Dunedin**: Dunedin Travel Centre, 205 St Andrews St, T03-4778860.*
***Fox Glacier**: Alpine Guides, Main Rd, T03-7510701.*
***Franz Josef**: The Glacier Shop, Main Rd, T03-7520131.*
***Greymouth**: Greymouth Travel Centre, Railway St, Mackay St, T03-7687080.*
***Hokitika**: Hokitika Travel Centre, Tancred St, T03-7558557.*
***Invercargill**: Invercargill Travel Centre, Railway Station, Leven St, T03-2140598.*
***Kaikoura**: Kaikoura VIC, West End, T03-3195641.*
***Nelson**: Nelson Travel Centre, 27 Bridge St, T03-5481538.*
***Oamaru**: La Gonda Milk Bar, 191 Thames St, T03-4348716.*
***Picton**: Picton Travel Centre, Ferry Terminal Building, T03-5737025.*
***Queenstown**: Queenstown VIC and Travel Centre, corner of Camp and Shotover Sts, T03-4428238.*
***Te Anau**: Air Fiordland, 70 Town Centre, T03-2497559.*
***Timaru**: AJ's Station Café, Railway Station, 22 Station St, T03-6847195.*
***Wanaka**: The Paper Place, 84 Ardmore St, T03-4437885.*
***Westport**: Craddocks Motors, 189 Palmerston St, T03-7897819.*

Concession fares

Note that Economy Fare cancellations must be made up to 2 hrs in advance to avoid a loss of 50% on the ticket price

All the bus companies offer a variety of concession fares. With ***Intercity*** and ***Newmans***, infants less than 5 years travel free and children 5-15 years travel at 60%. Travellers over the age of 60 travel at 30%, backpackers (YHA, VIP, BBH, Nomad cardholders) and students 20%. There are super fares of 30% and supersaver fares of 50% available but these should be pre-booked. ***Intercity*** also offer two special fare deals: a 'Y'all Come Back Now' fare offering a discount of 20% on a standard economy fare (if you book and pay for both the outward and return journeys at the same time) and the Frequent Travellers Card. This offers regular travellers the opportunity of obtaining greater discounts. Once 10 journeys have been completed the 11th is free. ***Newmans*** offer special discounts through their 'Pegasus Club'. It operates on a travel points system and costs nothing to join. There are also special family fares available.

Bus passes
There are lots of good value number of bus passes available, most with Intercity

Intercity North Island bus passes The 'Twin Coast Discovery' operates in a loop throughout Northland. It takes in the Bay of Islands, Kaitia, the Hokianga, Waipoua Forest and Dargaville; $85, child $57. The 'Coromandel Busplan' allows you to travel from Auckland to Thames, then loop around the Coromandel Peninsula back to Thames. From Thames you can then return to Auckland or go on to Rotorua; $89, child $60. The 'Forests Islands and Geysers' takes in a combination of Northland, Coromandel, Bay of Plenty (Rotorua) destinations before offering the choice of southwards travel to Taupo and Wellington or the Waikato (Waitomo Caves) and return to Auckland; $275, child $184. The 'Pacific Coast Highway Traveller' goes from Auckland to Thames (taking in the loop around the Coromandel Peninsula), through Tauranga and Rotorua and then rejoins the coast at Whakatane before travelling through the Waioweka Gorge to Gisborne and Napier (for an additional $40 you can then travel southwards to Wellington); $149, child $99. The 'North Island Value Pass' is a flexi-plan ticket between Auckland and Wellington taking in a number of chosen destinations; $99, child $66. 'Combo Passes' allow you to combine two of the above and range from $164 (child $110) to $23 (child $157).

Intercity South Island bus passes The 'West Coast Passport' operates between Nelson and Queenstown taking in Wesport, Greymouth and Hokitika; $125, child $84. A connection with Picton costs about $20 extra. The 'Milford Bound Adventurer' is available on services from Christchurch via Mount Cook to Queenstown and then into Milford Sound; $132, child $88. The 'East Coast Explorer' allows travel from Picton to Invercargill via Queenstown and Te Anau or Dunedin; $132, child $88. There is a combination option, the 'South Island Combo', which allows you to combine two of the three options above. These range in price from $252 (child $169) to $270 (child $182).

Newmans and Northliner Express passes *Newmans* offer a lesser range of similar options coming under the banner of their Stopover passes. There is an Auckland to Wellington Pass for $95 and Christchurch to Milford Sound pass for $129. *Northliner Express* offer discount backpacker passes throughout Northland from $49 to $109 and a 2-4 day travel and accommodation package from $149.

Car

Other than a campervan this is by far the best way to see New Zealand. Although petrol is expensive (about $1 a litre or $4 a gallon) it will give you the flexibility, range and freedom required to reach the more remote and beautiful places. Outside the cities and peak holiday periods traffic congestion and parking is rarely a problem. In many remote areas, especially in South Island, the roads are single track and unsealed, so a little more skill is required. Generally keep the speeds and gears low while on these roads. Also, in most rural areas, you will almost certainly encounter livestock of all shapes and sizes along the road verges, so be careful. At night you should of course take extra care and though there are very few mammals in New Zealand, one thing you will encounter is the cat-sized and brush-tailed possum. With 70 million of the little critters denuding the countryside of its native vegetation and wildlife, no one will mind the occasional roadkill.

Rules & regulations

In New Zealand you drive on the left (though some Aucklanders drive where they like). The give way to the right rule applies except when turning left; ie the oncoming car has right of way. This will seem mighty strange for the UK driver, who, if unaware of this rule, will end up on the receiving end of much abuse. If you do come a cropper and everyone is OK then just exchange insurance details. Make sure you avail yourself of the rules before setting out ('NZ Road Code' booklets are available from AA offices). The accident rate in New Zealand is high so extra vigilance is definitely required. Speed limits on the open road are 100 km/h and in built-up areas it is 50 km/h. Police patrol cars and speed cameras are omnipresent so flaunt it and you will almost certainly be caught. A valid driving licence from your own country or an international licence is required to get behind the wheel in New Zealand and certainly must be produced if you rent a vehicle. Finally, never leave (or hide) valuables in your car and lock it at all times.

Parking in the cities can be very expensive. Do not risk parking in restricted areas or going over your time allotment on meters. There are still many old meters in the cities (especially Wellington) which only take 20 or 50 cent coins so take a supply. Also, it is very important to note that (like the US) you must park with the flow of traffic, never against it.

For AA enquiries, T0800-500444, membership@nzaa.co.nz For breakdowns, T0800-500222

Motoring organizations The Automobile Association (AA) is the principal motoring organization in New Zealand. They have offices in most provincial towns. They also provide a great range of maps and travelling information as well as the usual member benefits. If you have bought a vehicle and intend extensive travel throughout New Zealand the basic annual membership fee of around $60 (which provides the basic breakdown assistance) is recommended. If you intend travelling down the West Coast and to Fiordland and to a lesser extent Southland in South Island, breakdown cover is highly recommended. Members of equivalent motoring organizations in other countries may qualify for reciprocal benefits.

Car hire

The general rule of thumb is that you get what you pay for and the cheaper the rate the more the risk

Almost all the major reliable companies (like ***Avis***, ***Budget*** and ***Hertz***) are represented in New Zealand and you will find offices at airports as well as the major airports, cities and provincial towns (listed in the directory sections throughout the text). There are also many local operators, but if you intend to travel extensively you are advised to stick with one of the major companies as they generally offer better cars, have more extensive networks as well as sound insurance and accident coverage. You must be over 21 and in possession of a valid driver's licence to hire a vehicle and insurance premiums for the under 25s can be high. Small, older and typically Japanese cars (1600 cc) start at about $75 per day but rates, naturally, vary depending on season, kilometres covered and the length of time you have the car (getting cheaper the longer you rent it). A medium sized 2000 cc car will cost around $100 per day with unlimited kilometres. Without unlimited kilometres you are looking at around $0.30 per kilometre.

There are of course cheaper deals out there (up to 50%) but not without risk. The best bet is to rent a vehicle in one of the major cities (Auckland being the cheapest) and drop it off at another. This will almost certainly involve a drop-off fee of around $100 but this is often worth it, just for the sheer convenience. In the summer high season, if you are returning to Auckland, it is worth shopping around and trying some bargaining since many operators have a glut of cars needing to be driven back north. Overall, the choice is vast so you are advised to shop around, but beware of cowboy operators and always read the small print before you sign. Some of the cheaper companies have an insurance excess of $700 even on minor repairs, so be careful. Always go over the car with a company representative and get them to acknowledge and list any dents or scratches that you see on the vehicle. This may avoid considerable frustration trying to prove you were not to blame. If you do not have a credit card you may also have to leave a substantial cash deposit of between $500 and $1000. Although it comes at extra cost, a 'Collision Waiver' can often be secured which means you do not automatically lose this deposit in the event of an accident. Note also you may not be covered on certain roads. You will certainly not be covered if you venture onto any of the 'sand highways' on the coast, like Ninety Mile Beach, and many companies do not provide cover in the Catlins (Southland).

There are a few motorcycle rental firms in Auckland (see page 114) and although not cheap, it can be a superb way to see the country, especially in South Island.

Buying a car

Although not essential, having a set of wheels in order to see New Zealand is highly recommended. Many people take the hired campervan option, but this can be expensive. Given the fact that second-hand cars are generally cheap, readily available and are not hard to find, it is well worth some serious consideration. Many people, even on low budgets and with limited capital, can buy a car, share running costs, then hopefully re-sell on leaving. If you arrive into Auckland you are in a good place to buy, but as with anything second-hand, choose carefully.

Buying procedure and legalities

Licence*: A current international or accepted driver's licence is essential.*

W.O.F (Warrant of Fitness)*: All cars need a safety certificate to be legally on the road and to obtain registration. Most garages and specialist 'drive in drive out' Vehicle Testing Stations (VTS) will do a WOF test which, if passed, lasts six months (see 'Warrant of Fitness' in the Yellow Pages). It costs about $30. If you buy a car with a WOF it should not be more than 28 days old.*

Registration*: Registration can be obtained with legal ownership and a valid WOF certificate for six ($83) or 12 ($160) months.*

Change of ownership*: The buyer and seller must fill in a MR13A that can be obtained and submitted at any NZ Post Office. Cost $9.20.*

Insurance*: Not compulsory but Third Party highly recommended.*

Highway code*: There are a few subtle differences in New Zealand road rules (the right of way while turning right being a prime example). You are advised to familiarize yourself with the 'Road Code' booklet available from AA Centres or major bookshops. $15.*

Automobile association*: AA membership costs $85 per annum. This covers you for emergency breakdown service for simple problems or towing to the nearest garage. Other benefits include free maps. Auckland AA, T3774660.*

Vehicle inspections*: The AA do a professional and comprehensive inspection as do a number of companies found under 'Vehicle Inspection Services' in the Yellow Pages. Cost $80-100. This is highly recommended.*

You are advised to have the car's legalities checked before purchase. T0900-909777. Quote chassis and licence plate numbers.

Where to buy a car

*There are a number of auto magazines available at newsagents (*Auto Trader *or* Trade and Exchange *on Monday and Thursday) but the major daily newspapers (*New Zealand Herald*, Wednesday and Saturday) and the auctions are also recommended.*

Car fairs

Oriental Markets*, Car Park, Beach Rd, City, Auckland. Sat 0900-1200.*

Ellerslie Racecourse*, off Greenlane Roundabout, Auckland. Sunday 0900-1200, T8109212.*

Manukau City*, (Park and Sell) Car Park, Sunday 0900-1300, T3585000.*

Sell It Yourself*, 1106 Great South Rd, Otahuhu. 7 days 0800-1830, T2703666 and 60 Wairau Rd, Glenfield. 7 days 0700-1900, T4433800.*

Car auctions

Turners*, corner of Leonard and Penrose Rd, Penrose, T5251920 (Wednesday, 1200) and 31 Hillside Rd, Glenfield, T4412690 (Saturday 1000, Wednesday 1800).*

Hammer Auctions*, 830 Great South Rd, Penrose, T5792344 (Monday–Friday 1800, Saturday 1030).*

Guaranteed buy back companies

(read the small print):

Budget Car Sales*, 12 Mt Eden Rd, Mt Eden, T3794120.*

Used Cars- Rex Swinburne*, 825 Dominion Rd, Mt Roskill, T6206587.*

Enduro*, 78 Henderson Valley Rd, Henderson, T8371117.*

Fastlane Autos*, 48 Henderson Valley Rd, Henderson, T8388338.*

Campervans New Zealand is well geared up for campervan hire and travel with a number of reputable international companies being in evidence. Being a fairly compact country it is certainly a viable way to see the entire country with complete independence. Although hire costs may seem excessive, once you subtract the inevitable costs of accommodation, and provided you are not alone and can share costs, it can all work out cheaper in the long run. You will find that motor camps are readily available even in the more remote places and the costs of a powered site will be around $10-15 dollars per night. Note that lay-by parking is illegal and best avoided, but if you are lost or stuck, you will rarely be confronted. Again, like car rental rates, campervan rates vary and are seasonal. Depending on which model you choose, the average costs for a basic two-berth/six-berth are around $130/ $250 in the high season and $90/ $150 in the low season.

The three most popular rental firms are ***Britz***, T0800-831900, ***Maui***, T09-2753013, www.maui-rentals.com, and ***Kea Campers***, T09-4444902, www.kea.co.nz There are some lesser known but equally reputable firms that can offer better deals, if not quite such plush vehicles, and these are listed in the relevant city or town Essentials sections. Although there are fewer risks involved with campervan hire, the same general rules apply as with car hire. You generally get what you pay for but shop around and check the small print. The average campervan works out at about 12 litres per 100 km in petrol costs. Diesel is obviously recommended.

Cycling Cycling touring in New Zealand is highly recommended and becoming increasingly popular, especially in South Island. Although it is not exactly flat, New Zealand is, let's just say, 'topographically manageable'.

Hitching Hitching is still quite heavily practised in New Zealand but not entirely safe. As ever, it is not advised for those travelling alone or single women. If you do decide to take the risk, try to keep to the main highways and restrict your hitching to the daylight hours. The usual common sense applies and if in doubt, don't. Another good tip is never take off a rucksack and put that or a bag in the car first. For the opportunist thief this can be like Christmas, and as they speed off you will be left standing there minus gear, feeling a bit of a Charlie.

Sea

Ferry

For details on the inter-island crossing, see page 402; for Stewart Island services, see page 658

Other than a few small, harbour-crossing vehicle ferries and the short trip to Stewart Island from Bluff in Southland, the main focus of ferry travel is of course the inter-island services across Cook Strait. The two ports are Wellington at the southern tip of North Island and Picton in the beautiful Marlborough Sounds, in the northern South Island. There are two services: the ***Interislander*** and the faster ***Lynz***. Both are owned and operated by ***Tranzrail***, T04-4983000, www.tranzrail.co.nz

Train

A trip from Auckland prior to the match and to the venue of an international rugby test (especially Rugby League), can be a bit like the Wild West – all that is missing are the Indians chasing alongside

The rail network throughout New Zealand is disappointing and in a seemingly incessant state of flux. New Zealand has struggled for years to maintain anything other than a core network between its main centres of population and provincial towns. Within North Island there are two daily services between Auckland and Wellington – the daytime 'Overlander' and overnight 'Northerner'. Within South Island, there are daily services between Picton and Christchurch (the 'Coastal Pacific') and Christchurch to Greymouth (the 'TransAlpine'). These services, though sparse, can be fun and quite an adventure.

Having slated the general network the trains are, in themselves, pretty comfortable, the service good and most have a great viewing carriage at the rear. However, unless you are desperate, avoid the overnight Auckland-Wellington service – it is strictly 'lights out' at 2200. But elsewhere any discomfort or boredom will be quickly forgotten with the stunning scenery. Fares range greatly from Standard to Super Saver so it is advised to check carefully what you are entitled to and what deals you can secure.

All fares are of a single class. The 'Trans Alpine' from Christchurch to Greymouth and the 'Coastal Pacific' from Picton to Christchurch are world class journeys offering South Island scenery at its best. Reservations and timetables from the Railway Station Information Centre, Visitor Information Centres or travel agents throughout New Zealand. Also contact ***TransScenic***, T0800-802802 (0700-2200), www.transrail.co.nz who also offer specialist packages, namely 'Great Train Escapes', a range of 2-8 day packages including accommodation. The 'Trains, Planes and Ferries' provides a combo travel choice of 12 destinations starting from $125 return. The 'Best of New Zealand Pass' combines savings on train, ferry and coach and 'The Train Day Escapes' offers day trips to selected tourist attractions around New Zealand. All are good value.

Combination travel passes

The New Zealand Travel Pass, T0800-339966, www.travelpass.co.nz allows you to combine unlimited bus and limited rail and air travel at discount prices. There are a range of 2-, 3- and 4-in-One passes allowing coach/ferry, coach/ferry/rail, coach/ferry/rail/short-flight and coach/ferry/rail/long-flight packages. These range from 5-22 days of travel over six months. Prices range from a 2-in-One 5-day package for $309, child $207, to a 4-in-One 22-day package for $1079, child $723. For details from overseas visit the website or ask your travel agent. In New Zealand phone direct or enquire at your local VIC.

Keeping in touch

Internet

New Zealand has the 'love it or hate it' computer disease as bad as any other developed nation. Internet cafés and terminals are now springing up everywhere and if you are amongst the many afflicted, who start walking funny or dribbling if you do not get your daily 'email-in-box-fix' you should be fine. The major cities are very well served with Internet outlets and most towns have cafés or terminals somewhere. Libraries and VICs are also a good bet, but unlike the free US system, they charge the same standard rates of $5-10 per hour. Thankfully, due to growing competition, rates are getting cheaper, but you are still advised to shop around. Internet venues are listed under Ins and outs or the Directory sections throughout the guide.

Post

Post offices (most often called 'Post Shops') are open from Monday-Friday, 0900-1700, Saturday 0900-1200. Mail can also be sent to 'Post Restante', CPO (Chief Post Office) in the main cities, where it will be held for up to 30 days. Within New Zealand standard (local) post costs $0.45 for medium letters and postcards; $0.80 for airmail (fast post) to domestic centres; $1 for all international postcards and $1.80 for standard overseas letters ($1.50 for North America, East Asia, Australia and South Pacific). Domestic mail takes one to two days, perhaps a little longer in rural areas. When sending any cards or letters overseas be sure to use the free blue 'Air economy' stickers. Books of stamps are readily available as are pre-paid envelopes and a range of purpose-built cardboard boxes. Average delivery times vary depending on the day of the week posted, but a standard letter to the UK can take as little as four days (scheduled 6-12 days). North America is scheduled 4-12 days and Australia and the South Pacific 3-8 days.

Telephone

The rather attractive Telecom payphones are readily available throughout the country and colour coded. Although there are both coin (blue) and credit card (yellow) booths available, the vast majority are 'phone-card only' so you are advised to stock up. They come in $5, $10, $20 and $50 and are available from many retail outlets, post and visitor information offices and hostels. Unless you want to see just how fast digital numbers can disappear on screen, do not use these Telecom cards for anything other than

Post Restante pick-up points

***Auckland**: Wellesley St Post Shop, Bledisloe St.*
***Wellington**: Wellington Railway Post Shop, Bunny St.*
***Christchurch**: Cathedral Square Post Shop, Cathedral Square.*
***Dunedin**: Metro Post Shop, 283 Princess St.*
***Queenstown**: Main Post Office, corner of Camp and Ballarat Sts.*

domestic calls within New Zealand. There is now a wealth of cheap international calling cards and call centres available. One of the best is **E Phone**, www.eph.co.nz, a calling card that accesses the net through an 0800 number. The cards, which again vary in price (usually from $10 to $50), can be bought from many retail outlets (look for the E Phone flag signs outside the shops). They come with simple instructions and can be used from any landline telephone. Voice instructions will tell you what to do and how much credit you have available before each call. Note that local non-business calls are free from standard telephones in New Zealand, so it is not too offensive to ask to use a host or friend's domestic (non-business) telephone for that purpose. 0800 or occasionally 0508 precede toll-free calls. Try to avoid 0900 numbers as they are usually very expensive. Mobile phones are prefixed by 025 (Telecom) or 021 (Vodaphone).

Media

Although not on the grand scale or blessed with the same choice as countries like the UK, the newspapers in New Zealand are pretty good, featuring fairly comprehensive and factual sections on local, national and international news as well as sport, business and travel.

The principal daily newspapers (except Sundays) are the *New Zealand Herald* (Auckland and upper North Island), the *Dominion* (Wellington and lower North Island) and the *Press* (Christchurch and central South Island). If you wish to sample any of these before you leave log on to www.nzherald.co.nz or the general website, www.nzstuff.co.nz a good site from which to access both national and regional news.

There are a few national magazines which may be of interest to the visitor, including: *North and South* – a magazine covering a wide range of traditional and contemporary issues; *New Zealand Geographic* – the quality New Zealand version of the great US national icon; *New Zealand Wilderness* – a glossy outdoor activity magazine and *New Zealand Outside* – a similar effort. These are readily available at bookshops or post shops while most mainstream International newspapers and magazines can be found at specialist magazine outlets like ***Maggazino*** in Auckland and Christchurch (see the Essentials sections of those cities).

Although New Zealand radio is quite good, television is a shocker. Whether due to a lack of population, revenue or simple imagination the four principal terrestrial channels have very little to offer. Bar good news and current-affairs programmes you are bombarded with the usual insidious UK or US soaps, or the wretched 'Who Wants to be a Millionaire'. Most New Zealanders (including tourist accommodation establishments) and the average Kiwi sports fanatic, has now subscribed to Sky TV. Perhaps the most aggravating thing about New Zealand television is the advertising. With such a low population, subsequent lack of variety and ineffective standards authorities, most of the advertising is offensively repetitive. It is not unusual to get the same ad every 10 minutes for days. A number of individuals have also made their fortunes in New Zealand with the use of the off-peak, special offer product advertising. Yes, those heinous 'Only $29.99'; 'Send no money, we'll bill you' and 'Wait, there's more' products. Sadly, this seems to work. Under many a bed in New Zealand you will almost certainly find one or two of the following: a broken, unused buttock firmer; a set of Jinsu kitchen knives (with free banana slicer); and the full set of extra absorbent, luminous incontinence pants for the obese (that double as a cat basket).

Food and drink

Don't forget to try some of New Zealand's excellent wines

Depending on your budget you are in for a treat. Both the quantity and the quality of food in New Zealand are superb. Although there are many types of traditional cuisine and restaurants in evidence, the principal style is 'Pacific Rim'. It dips into the culinary heritage of many of the cultures of the Oceania region, with inspiration and influences from Thailand, Malaysia, Indonesia, Polynesia, Japan and Vietnam as well as others further afield like Europe. For dishes that have a distinctly Kiwi edge look out for the lamb (arguably the best in the world), pork and venison and freshwater fish like salmon and eel. Despite its reputation as perhaps the best trout-fishing country in the world, you cannot buy trout commercially. Although this is a shame, it does provide the added incentive to catch your own, which many restaurants are delighted to cook for you.

As you might expect there is a heavy emphasis on fine seafood. Here, the choice is vast with many warm-water fish like snapper, kingfish, hoki, hapuka and orange roughie. Often you can catch these yourself and done in a BBQ style, fresh off the boat, it will provide a memorable culinary experience. Other seafood delights include crayfish (the South Pacific equivalent to the lobster), fine oysters (the best being from Bluff in South Island), paua (abalone), scallops and the famous green-lipped mussels. These mussels are very substantial, delicious and should not be missed. They are also relatively cheap and readily available. There are also some treats in store from below the ground. The kumara (sweet potato) will shed a whole new light on the humble 'spud', while many of the international vegetables like asparagus and broccoli come cheap (especially while in season) and always fresh. From the tree the fruit of choice is of course the succulent kiwi fruit or 'Chinese gooseberry' which although not exclusively grown in New Zealand is deservingly celebrated. Other fine fruits include feijoa and tamarillo. The celebrated dessert in New Zealand is the pavlova; a sort of mountainous cake made of meringue and whipped cream. For a real traditional feast try a Maori hangi (see page 52). Done properly and without ketchup you will be amazed just how good and different fish, meat and vegetables can taste when cooked underground.

Where to eat

Wellington boasts more cafés and restaurants per capita than New York

There are eateries to suit every taste and budget from the ubiquitous fast food joints to world-class seafood restaurants. Auckland and Wellington are particularly rich in choice with a vast selection of cafés, café-bars, brasseries and traditional and specialist restaurants flying the flag of many countries and styles and giving added puff to the celebrated 'Pacific Rim'. You will find that there is often a very fine line in the distinction between café and restaurant with the vast majority being essentially the same thing. Many cafés, although providing a more informal atmosphere and placing much emphasis on a broader range of cheaper light meals during the day, happily simmer on into the night with more substantial dishes. They also almost always serve coffee, breakfast or brunch, are licensed (or at the very least BYO – which means bring your own) and often provide outdoor seating. The restaurants are similar with few expecting formal attire. You can find up-market, snooty establishments if you wish, but they will not provide the celebrated, laid-back, food-centred focus of the vast majority. Also note that cost does not necessarily relate to quality.

Vegetarians are generally well-catered for in the main centres and provincial towns, while the more remote and rural corners of New Zealand still offer the 'half cow on the barbie'. Ask for a vegetarian dish on a South Island backcountry station and you'll most probably be shown the door. Also bear in mind that many of the top hotels, motels and lodges are open to non-residents and often provide fine dining at

The Hangi

Pronounced 'hungi', this is the traditional Maori and Pacific Island feast or method of cooking. To the uninitiated, the concept of cooking your dinner in the ground may seem a bit odd, but it is actually incredibly efficient and produces a certain taste and texture in the food that is extraordinarily good. Hangis were designed for the masses and were as much a social occasion as anything else. Traditionally the men would light a large fire and place river stones in the embers. While the stones are heating a pit is dug in the earth. Then the stones are placed in the pit and sacking placed upon them (before sacking it was suitably fashioned plant material). Then, presumably, the boys went off for a beer while the good ladies of the tribe prepared the meat. Nowadays this includes chicken, wild pig and lamb, but was formerly moa, pigeon and seafood. Vegetables are also added, particularly the kumera, a sweet potato. Once cleaned and plucked, the smaller items are wrapped in leaves (now foil) and the whole lot placed in a basket (now wire-mesh;in the past woven leaves from the flax plant) and then everything is covered with earth. The steam slowly cooks the food for a couple of hours, then it is dug up and eaten. The succulence and smoked flavours of the food are gorgeous.

Although, due to modern-day health and safety requirements, it is not really possible to sample a proper hangi, the commercial offerings by the Maori tourist concerns are worth the experience. Rotorua is the principal venue (see Rotorua section). If you ever have the opportunity to sample a real one, do not pass it up.

affordable prices. As well as the vast amount of cafés, café/restaurants and restaurants, you can generally find good 'pub-grub', with the cities and most major towns offering at least one Irish or old-English style pub with everything from the Full-Monty' breakfast, and Irish stew to good ol' fish and chips – all for under $18.

Generally speaking, eating out in New Zealand is pretty cheap. For those visitors revelling in the more than favourable dollar exchange rates you are probably going to end up a very happy little hoglett and certainly need to renew that annual gym sub on your return home. Backpackers on a strict budget will of course fare less well and experience a painful exercise in frustration. But no matter what the budget, you should treat yourself at least once. The vast majority of eateries fall into the 'mid-range' bracket. Price codes for eating out are given in the box above.

As far as opening hours are concerned, again it varies and they are often seasonal. Most cafés open for breakfast between 0700 and 0900 and remain open until at least 1700. Many also remain open until late into the evening or even the wee small hours. This usually applies seven days a week with special Sunday brunch hours provided. Most mid-range restaurants open their doors daily for lunch (often 1100-1400) and dinner (from 1800). The more exclusive establishments usually open for dinner from about 1800, with some (especially in winter) only opening some weekday evenings and at weekends.

There are a number of useful (mainly Auckland and Wellington) café and restaurant guides available from the major bookshops, while many VICs provide free promotional leaflets. Note however that many of these only list those restaurants that paid for the advertising. Some of the best are therefore not necessarily listed. In summary nothing beats a stroll around the main café or restaurant areas or streets (often listed) and a stomach-rumbling muse at the menus and interiors before making your decision.

If you intend to do your own cooking and buy in your own food then you will find food shopping is uncomplicated, convenient and offers a wide choice of fare. The main supermarket chains are Big Fresh and New World, with Pac-n-Save being marginally cheaper. When buying fresh vegetables and fruit always try to stick to the numerous roadside or wholesale fruit markets where the difference in price and quality can be astonishing.

Eating categories

In this book eateries are divided into three categories: ***expensive*** *(over $25 for a main/ US entrée);* ***mid-range*** *($15-$25 for a main/US entrée) and* ***cheap*** *(under $15 for a main/US entrée) All the places listed are recommended as offering relatively good value, quality and standards of service within their respective price category. Some are also noted for having particularly pleasant or unusual surrounds.*

Drinks

Other than L&P (a fairly unremarkable soft drink hailing from Paeroa. New Zealand lacks a national drink. If there is one, it is the highly sub-standard and over rated beer called Lion Red. This and a number of other equally watery relations are drunk not so much by the pint, as the jug, and are all backed by a very 'Kiwi-bloke' image, which is regularly promoted with omnipresent and less-than-PC advertising. Having abused the traditional Kiwi beer you can, however, rest assured that all the main internationally well-known bottled beers are available, as are some good foreign tap ales like Caffrey's and Kilkenny. Depending on which pub and how it is kept and poured, you can also get a good Guinness (see the Pubs & bars sections of cities).

Beer and lager is usually sold by 'the handle, or 'the glass' (pint) or 'the jug' (up to three pints). Half-pints come in a 12-fl oz (350ml) glass. Rarely is a pint a proper imperial pint, being just under. Drinks generally cost from $4-6 for a pint, about $4-5 for a jug of Lion Red and up to $6 for a double shot. Drinks are much cheaper in rural pubs and RSAs (Retired Servicemen's Clubs), where you can usually get yourself signed in. The minimum drinking age has just been reduced from 21 to 18. Liquor shops are everywhere and alcohol can generally (in most places) be bought seven days a week. There is a thriving coffee culture almost everywhere in the main towns and cities, so you will not go without your daily caffeine fix.

Generally speaking, the drinks do not match the food in New Zealand and although the vast majority of Kiwi blokes would argue against it, other than a few exceptions, New Zealand still has a long way to go in offering fine beers, ales and lager. Its wine however, is an entirely different story.

New Zealand wine

New Zealand's rich diversity of climates and soil types has borne an equally rich array of wines and after over a century of development the country now boasts many of internationally recognized standards. Wine is produced the length and breadth of the country but the Hawkes Bay and Nelson/Marlborough areas are the principal wine producing regions. New Zealand Sauvignon Blanc is rated throughout the world as one of the best, but there is growing recognition for its Chardonnay, Pinot Noir, Methode Traditionelle sparkling wines, Riesling, Cabernet Sauvignon and Merlots. Fruit wines, including the unusual 'kiwi fruit wine' are also in evidence. The choice is vast and whether a connoisseur or a novice you are advised to experiment. If you can, visit one of the many vineyards that offer tastings and cellar sales.

Entertainment and nightlife

Most cities are blessed with numerous venues hosting first-class concerts and shows. **Theatre, orchestral concerts, ballet, dance, comedy, rock and jazz** are all well represented. Many international rock stars now include at least one gig in Auckland in their itinerary. On a smaller scale you will find a vibrant nightlife in New Zealand cities and major provincial towns. Although not necessarily world class, the **nightclubs,**

cabarets, pubs and local rock concerts will certainly have you 'shaking your pants'. There's even Country and Western and line dancing (no comment). New Zealand also boasts two large, modern, 24-hour **casinos** in Christchurch and Wellington. *Ticketek* are the national administrators for information and ticketing and a comprehensive listing of up and coming shows and events can be sourced from their website, www.ticketek.co.nz or the website www.nz-events.co.nz

Essentials

Pubs & bars

Pubs and bars are generally open from 1100-2230 with many having an extended licence to 2400 and sometimes even 0300 at weekends

The pub scene has come on leaps and bounds over the last decade with new establishments opening up almost everywhere. Before the 1990s the vast majority of pubs in New Zealand were the archetypal male bastions–establishments where ashtrays were built into the tables, pictures of the local hairy rugby team donned the walls and the average Saturday night consisted of a good argument about sport, a band playing Deep Purple's 'Smoke on the Water', followed by a fight, copious wall-to-wall vomiting and a failed attempt to get home. Of course such places still exist, but generally speaking pubs and bars are now a much more refined and classy affair yet still retain that congenial and laid-back 'traditional pub' atmosphere. Now you can enjoy a good beer and conversation over an open fire in winter or the sun in summer and women (at least in groups) will not always be hassled by frustrated young farmers or dirty old men. New Zealand has also caught on to the 'Irish pub' fad and although some are the usual gimmicky affairs others are very good, offering fine surroundings and beer to match.

Many drinking establishments are also now attached to restaurants and cafés with outdoor seating. In summer these can be great places to while away an afternoon. If you really must sample the old-fashioned Kiwi pub you will find them often in the hotels or main streets of the rural towns. While not all bad, do not walk in with a pair of pink shorts, or without knowing what an 'All Black' is.

Shopping

Although on first acquaintance (especially in the cities) you might be forgiven for thinking it is all fluffy sheep or kiwis in rugby jerseys, shopping in New Zealand can be a rewarding and interesting experience. For a country so lacking in population there is a surprising wealth of quality goods on sale, from international designer label clothing to traditional Kiwi arts and crafts.

Arts & crafts

Beyond the international and the kitsch there are a number of things to look out for. New Zealand arts and crafts consist of a vast array of South Pacific, Maori and contemporary Kiwi styles and influences. Much of the art is very colourful, reflecting the beautiful bright blues and greens of the environment, while two-dimensional works are often beautifully carved panels, figures, bowls and furniture made of native woods like kauri and rimu.

Pottery and ceramics abound. There are Maori pendants (*tiki*) carved from bone (whale bone) and greenstone (*pounamu*). These have been made and worn by the Maori for centuries and often depict sacred animals or spirits. If you buy one it is customary to offer it as a gift. They are also often associated with *mana* (power or standing) and fertility. Note, however, that there are many cheap and nasty versions on sale, especially in the city souvenir shops and on the street. If you want quality look in specialist arts and craft or museum shops. Almost everywhere you will also see the stunning hues of the abalone shell (or *paua*). You can buy the half shells polished and varnished for about $20 or choose from the many jewellery pieces created or indented with colourful fragments.

Public holidays in New Zealand

If you are a tourist public holidays can be an inconvenience since shops and banks close. School holidays are particularly bad with the months of January and February being the worst. During these times you should book accommodation and activities well ahead. Bear in mind this also applies to the winter season at the major ski resorts like Tongariro, Wanaka and Queenstown.

January 1-2 *New Year*
February 6 *Waitangi Day*
April 13 *Good Friday*
April 15 *Easter*
April 16 *Easter Monday*
April 25 *Anzac Day*
June 12 *Queen's Birthday*
October 22 *Labour Day*
December 25 *Christmas Day*
December 26 *Boxing Day*

Essentials

Tapa cloth is a pacific brown or fawn-coloured material with unique and specific black-dyed designs. This is widely available but the best place to get the cloth, is at Auckland's United Tongan Church about one kilometre down Richmond Road, off Ponsonby Road, on Saturday mornings. They are very reasonably priced, original, light and easy to pack. As you might expect, woollen goods are everywhere. There is everything from jumpers and gloves to full sheepskins and cosy slippers. Although not cheap these goods are usually homespun and hand-knitted and of the highest quality.

Clothing

On the clothing front look out for the famous red or blue plaid Kiwi 'swandry'. It's a sort of thick woollen shirt/ jacket and offers the best protection from the cold. You will also see the world-famous All Black rugby jerseys all over the place. Although the real thing is now made by Adidas (in a much less appealing synthetic material) the 'Canterbury' rugby tops have to be the best cotton made tops in the world and last for years. Make sure the one you buy is made by the Canterbury Clothing Company (CCC). They have a factory shop in Christchurch (see page 485). For modern fashion wear look out for the award-winning Kiwi labels, Zambesi, NomD, Karen Walker and World.

Shopping hours

Most shops and businesses are open Monday-Friday, 0900-1700. Many shops are also open on Saturdays and Sundays. The large mall multi-complexes are also open daily and offer at least one late shopping night a week. The larger supermarket chains are open most evenings every day and the humble Kiwi 'dairies' (found in almost every high street) are often open until 2000-2300. Depending where you are petrol (gas) stations are open until about 2300 with some remaining open 24 hours. Many are following the trend of also selling a substantial (if not more expensive) range of supermarket type items.

Holidays and festivals

Local VICs have listings of up and coming events and the NZTB website, www.purenz.com has a detailed database. Regional and city events are listed in the relevant sections

There are a huge range of organized events and festivals held throughout New Zealand every year, ranging from the bizarre Gumboot Throwing Festival in Taihape (see page 370) to the huge, spectacular Opera in the Park in Auckland. One of the more obscure events is the **Wildfoods Festival** on the South Island's West Coast, an extravaganza of gourmet 'bushtucker' based on natural food resources from the land and sea. Some of the most popular national events include '**Opera**' and '**Christmas in the Park**'. Held annually in the Auckland Domain, the Operat can attract up to 400,000 people. The many regional and provincial town **Food, Arts and Wine Festivals** are usually held in summer and provide a fitting and lively celebration of the country's wealth of creations. There are also many traditional (if a little commercial) **Maori**

cultural performances in the main centres and particularly in Rotorua. Although not annual, and subject to winning in order to retain it, the internationally famous **America's Cup** will once again be defended by New Zealand in early 2003. This mammoth yachting event has in many ways put Auckland and New Zealand on the international tourist map and attracts millions of dollars of income, as well as thousands of visitors and of course, if the great 'Team New Zealand' win again, considerable prestige.

Sport and special interest travel

Bungy Jumping

The highest jump in New Zealand was done by A.J Hackett himself off Auckland's Sky Tower (192 m) in 1998. Believe it or not, this is set to become the latest big tourist attraction

The strange practice of attaching a rubber band to your ankles and diving off a very high bridge has now become synonymous with a visit to New Zealand and the best-known of all this country's weird, wonderful and downright suicidal tourist activities. The concept was professionally developed, though not invented, by A J Hackett, who jumped from the Eiffel Tower in 1986 (and more recently from the Sky Tower in Auckland). It is actually the Papua New Guineanians who invented bungy jumping, apparently as a test of manhood. There are now bungy sites throughout New Zealand, varying in type and height from the 'tasters' of about 40 m (from a crane) to the underwear-soiling 134 m (from a gondola above a canyon). Most are in Queenstown in South Island. There, you can do it from a bridge, suspended high above a canyon, at night, and even from a helicopter, the choice is yours. Other (low) sites include Taupo, the Agrodome in Rotorua and Hamner Springs in Canterbury.

Suffice to say it is indeed mad, but thankfully very safe, though care must be taken. Your life, after all, is literally in their hands. There are many rumours flying around that bungy jumping can detach retinas and send various bodily organs into disarray, but there is little evidence to support these, and although certain bodily parts can go into uncontrolled fits of clenching, pulsating or shrinking, the rush of adrenaline more than makes up for it. The bungy is not just the domain of the mad youth either. Many a wonderfully loony pensioner has done it, too. Respect due! There are also many variations on the theme. Folk have jumped together, in numerous costumes, in canoes, on bikes and, yes, of course butt naked. The top award however has to go to a Scot who jumped in his kilt, revealing to the world's press just exactly what is worn beneath ('freedom'). At around $100 a bungy jump is not cheap (so save your dollars) but as a once-in-a-lifetime experience, it has got to be worth it.

Caving

The underground world of the **Waitomo Caves** in the Waikato, North Island, is a magnificent natural wonder as well as a renowned playground. There are over 360 mapped caves – the longest of which is 14 km. Most have underground rivers which carve a wonderland of caverns, pools, waterfalls and rapids. These are negotiated with a headlamp in a wetsuit, attached to a rubber ring, which is an unforgettable experience. Added to that, there's a 300-m abseil into the awesome '**Lost World**' as well as the spectacle of **glow-worms**. Truly awesome. There are a huge range of activities on offer. Almost all involve getting wet – whether paddling, swimming, floating, abseiling and jumping, or just wetting yourself laughing. Although it may seem dangerous, all the companies take great care of you and are highly professional. ***Waitomo Adventures*** are particularly recommended. Prices range from a four-hour trip at $60 to a seven-hour trip at $300. If you can possibly afford it, try the seven-hour 'Lost World' experience. Like the bungy, it is a once-in-a-lifetime experience and worth every cent. There are many other caves throughout the Waitomo region and elsewhere in the country, all of which provide an insight into the delicate natural history that lives below. As in the rest of New Zealand, treat the environment with respect; screaming loonies in wetsuits should really not be down there.

Fishing

New Zealand is fishing heaven. Although noted as one of the best and most unspoilt trout fishing venues in the world, it also provides some superb sea and big game fishing. The lakes of the Taupo and Rotorua regions are the prime trout fishing spots, as is Gore in Southland, and there is ample opportunity to get out on the water. Both the experienced and the novice are well-catered for with numerous boat charters and guides from the relatively affordable $50 an hour to the all-mod-cons versions at $100.

The warm Pacific waters that grace North Island's shores also attract a huge range of salt-water species from snapper to massive marlin. Areas particularly well- geared up for game and sea fishing include the Bay of Islands, Tutakaka (Northland), Whitianga (Coromandel) and Tauranga/Whakatane (Bay of Plenty). However, there is excellent sea fishing from boat and shore from just about everywhere in New Zealand.

Costs vary from the three-hour novice trip to the highly organized but still affordable three-day 'Hemingway' trips to catch that prize marlin. This is something you might have though it was reserved for the idle rich, but in New Zealand you too can watch the seabirds, the odd dolphin (sometimes even a whale) and the amazing flying fish erupting from the water. Then suddenly the line from your rod and barrel-sized reel goes off like the wheel of a formula one car at the start of a race and your jaw drops in sheer awe as you see a huge marlin sail out of the water at incredible speed, and the fight is on. Though big-game fishing is hard work, you do not need to be Arnold Schwarzenegger to do it.

Flight-seeing

For those of you who have only ever flown in a commercial jetliner you must try the far more precarious experience of a small fixed-wing aircraft or a helicopter. Even without the stunning views, it is a wonderful experience and one that gives you a far better insight into what flight is all about. There are endless locations countrywide where you can get up in the air with almost every provincial airport, airstrip or local flying club offering flights. It is also surprisingly cheap. A 10-15 minute flight at $60 by helicopter or a 30 minute flight in a small fixed-wing for the same price may seem expensive, but you will not regret it. In North Island three places are recommended: over the volcanoes of the Tongariro National Park (from Whakapapa); Mount Tarawera (from Rotorua); and White Island (from Rotorua, Tauranga or Whakatane). In South Island, Kahurangi National Park (Nelson) and just about anywhere down 'The Great Divide' and Mount Cook and Fiordland are highly recommended. There are numerous operators in Wanaka, Queenstown, Te Anau and Milford and these are listed in the relevant sections in the main travelling text. If you can only afford one flight, then make it the helicopter flight around the **glaciers** and summit of **Mount Cook**. Most operate out of Franz Joseph or Fox Glaciers. This 30-minute $200 trip on a clear day is truly awesome. It really is what New Zealand is all about.

For a more sedate ride you may also like to consider a trip by **hot-air balloon** which, although not so common and more expensive, is available in a number of locations including Auckland, the Waikato and Canterbury. For the full Biggles experience you can also don the goggles and scarf and get strapped into a **bi-plane**. Locations include Auckland, Rotorua in North Island and Gore and Wanaka in South Island.

Fly-by-wire

Picture a metal hospital stretcher with a microlight engine on the back, suspended from a wire in a valley and flying like a pendulum, speeding through the air at up to 100 kph. Now imagine yourself strapped to this flimsy device, squealing like a schoolkid. This seemingly suicidal experience is available in Paekakariki, on the Kapiti Coast near Wellington, or in Queenstown. It costs $99 for 10 minutes – extra underwear optional.

Golf

New Zealand is blessed with hundreds of golf courses, from those that require a cute wedge shot to avoid sheep to others with well-manicured greens fit for an open championship. Have you ever played a steaming golf course? Didn't think so. Well, in Taupo and Rotorua you can. From little fumeroles on the fairways steam vents from the ground. Lose your ball down there and you won't find the solution in the R&A rulebook. There are many world-class courses in New Zealand like the new Gulf Harbour in Auckland, Wairakei in Taupo and the Millbrook in Otago – to name but a few.

Green fees vary, from newer courses costing over $100 to some that can be played for as little as $35. No wonder so many Asians come to New Zealand just to play golf. On a New Zealand course, if you go early and in the off-season, it can be rare to even see another player. No doubt you had to leave your clubs at home, but most courses have clubs for hire. A little word of warning – do not come to New Zealand expecting the same strict attitudes to golfing etiquette found in Europe and North America. This is not St Andrews and the courses are not the hallowed turf like the Old Course, or Pebble Beach. In New Zealand when a group of seven (maximum should be four) likely Kiwi lads drop their trousers on the 18th tee to play a 'provisional', just accept it – it's apparently traditional.

Horse trekking The New Zealand landscape is ideal for horse trekking and it can be experienced around almost every provincial town. Both the experienced and the novice are well-catered for, but the latter take note – horses just know when a complete 'buffoon' has climbed on their back. It will only cost around $30 for two hours, after which you'll be walking like John Wayne after a hearty plateful of beans. There are a wealth of operators and horse riding is available throughout the country. For a very informative leaflet and additional information countrywide contact the **International League for the Protection of Horses** (ILHNZ), PO Box 10-368 Te Rapa, Hamilton, T07-8490678, ilphnz@xtra.co.nz

Jet boating You have probably seen it. A red boat packed with tourists, all wearing the same 'well isn't this fun' expression, while thinking 'get me out of here now'. It is quite an unnerving experience whizzing down a river, heading straight at some rocks at insane speeds and closing your eyes in the face of inevitable death, only to open them again to find yourself still, remarkably, alive. Then, as a last hurrah, to be spun about in a 360° turn, just to make sure *all* your underwear is wet. That said, it is actually great fun and very safe – it just looks scary. There is jet-boating available on many North Island rivers, especially the Waikato (Taupo), Wanganui (Wanganui or Taumarunui) and the Motu (Opotiki), but it is the red boats on the Shotover River in Queenstown that are the best known. Not all are adrenaline-pumping trips with some (especially in North island) being more scenic affairs. Costs are reasonable, with a 30 minute trip being around $50.

Kayaking New Zealand is a renowned playground for this mode of water transport whether on river, lake or sea. You can just about do it from every major town, especially if there are lakes or ocean waves near by. For novices, kayaking just takes just a wee bit of time to get used to, but before you know it, you'll be off and paddling before you can say 'Deliverance'. One word of warning – kayaks and canoes are better designed for little people. Another word of warning – never share a canoe with a loved one. Within five minutes there will be a major argument, threats of violence and floods of tears. If you find it to your taste (the silence, the solitude and the scenery can be heartwarming) then consider a multi-day trip. The best of these are available in the Bay of Islands, Abel Tasman National Park and (most recommended) Fiordland. Inland you also have the Wanganui National Park in North Island. The coastal scenery is often best taken in by kayak and there are some great guides out there. You never know, you might even come across a friendly dolphin or fur seal. Costs again vary slightly but you can hire your own kayak for about $15 per hour while a three-hour trip will cost about $60 and a four-day affair $450.

Marine mammal watching & dolphin swimming

Both whale-watching and dolphin-watching/swimming is a memorable activity that is highly recommended

The New Zealand coastline is world famous for its rich variety of marine mammals. Almost everywhere around the coast pods of dolphin can regularly be seen, from the large, common bottlenose to the tiny and endangered hectors dolphin. Being on the main whale migration routes, the New Zealand coast is also a great place to see these great leviathans. For the tourist, the beauty is not only the whales and dolphins themselves, but also the relative ease to encountering them. The most popular venue is Kaikoura on South Island's northeast coast. Here a deep coastal trench that comes close to shore attracts whales within a short boat-ride from Kaikoura, making it one of the world's best and most convenient whale-watching locations. Closer to the shore, huge pods of dolphin frolic in the surf and seem to delight in the prospect of investigating any clumsy human who ventures into the water. Other than Kaikoura, the principal location for dolphin-watching and swimming are the Bay of Islands and Whakatane in North Island and the Marlborough Sounds, Punakaiki, the Catlins Coast and Akaroa (Banks Peninsula) in South Island. Note that encounter success rates (ie finding them) are generally very high in New Zealand. So much so that many operators offer a refund, or another trip, if the whales and dolphins are not located. A 2 ½-hour whale-watching trip in Kaikoura will cost $95, $30-60 for children . A 2-hour dolphin swimming experience (about 30 minutes in the water) anywhere around the coast will cost around $100.

Mountain biking

New Zealand is, as you might expect, a paradise for the avid mountain biker. With its wide range of magnificent landscapes, the country offers numerous tracks, both long and short and mainly through native bush or commercial forest. You can do it almost everywhere. Bike hire is readily available and quite cheap, so at some point you must try it. Whether you go down vertical rock faces and submerge yourself in mud pools, or stick to the straight and not-so-narrow, is up to you. Such is the quality of landscapes, there is perhaps no single place to be recommended for the sport in New Zealand – the exception being, perhaps, Hanmer Springs and Riverton, South Island, which are superb.

Mountaineering

It would take a lifetime to climb all the major peaks in New Zealand. Mount Cook at 3753 m is the country's highest. Although not especially high, the New Zealand peaks are no less spectacular. Neither are they any less of a challenge or indeed dangerous. The vast majority of peaks are in South Island with the Mount Cook Range, Mount Aspiring (Wanaka) and the peaks of the Nelson Lakes National Park being the most accessible and attractive.

Mount Taranaki in North Island is the country's most climbed mountain. There is just something about it. To look at on a clear day is to stand in awe. Its symmetry and isolation just beckons you up its precarious slopes. Other grand peaks in North Island include Mount Ruapehu and the little climbed (but superb) Mount Hikurangi in Eastland. If you have never done any mountaineering before this is the perfect country in which to catch the mountaineering bug. You are after all in Sir Edmund Hillary's back garden. Like the great man himself and limited numbers before you, once you scale that first peak and feel the sense of achievement, you will almost certainly be hooked. But if you are a novice seek advice and above all go well prepared, check the weather forecast and tell someone of your intentions. Many tourist lives have been lost through sheer stupidity and over-confidence. Although it is expensive there are numerous guided trips available especially around Taranaki and Mount Cook (Franz and Fox Glaciers). For specialist enquiries contact the **NZ Alpine Club**, based in Christchurch, T03-3777595. The **NZ Mountain Guides Association**, info@nzmga.co.nz/www.nzmga.co.nz are also a very good organization to consult for further information and contacts.

Paraflying & tandem parapenting

First question – what is the difference? Well, both involve a bit of hanging around. One is done around hills and coastal slopes, the other is done from the back of a speedboat over water. It's basically a bit like glorified kite flying with you attached to it. Paraflying is the easier and more commercial of the two and is practised at many coastal resorts including the Bay of Islands and Mount Maunganui in North Island, but also on inland lakes like Wakatipu (Queenstown). Basically you are strapped to a cradle below a special parachute and kept in the air by a speedboat. It's great fun and will have you screaming like a banshee and gesticulating wildly to your highly amused compadres. A 10-minute flight will cost about $50.

Parapenting (or paragliding) is great fun but takes a lot to master. Like skydiving the novice is taken in tandem with an expert. There are a limited number of tourist venues, but Te Mata Peak in Hawkes Bay is North Island's top venue while Wanaka and Queenstown are the capitals of the South. A 20-minute flight costs about $120.

Rafting

This is another 'must do' New Zealand activity. The principal locations in the country for white-water rafting are the rivers of central and east North Island and generally throughout South Island. In North Island the main places are Taurangi and Rotorua and the Tongariro, Rangitaiki, Wairoa, Kaituna, Mohaka and Motu Rivers. In South Island most of the regions have excellent opportunities and the river list is endless. The rivers and the rapids are graded from I to VI.

Although the quick 45-minute trips at about $60 are great fun and packed with adrenaline-pumping moments, the real rafting experience only comes with a multi-day trip ($500). There are many on offer, but if one stands out head and shoulders above the rest it is the four-day trip down the wild and remote Motu in Eastland, North Island. Provided water levels are favourable, this trip has to be one of the best New Zealand outdoor experiences on offer. It is the sheer isolation as well as the scenery and rapids that is so memorable. On a multi-day trip down a river you also experience the growth of the river itself, from the gently flowing headwaters to raging rapids and then, the gentle meander to the coast. The trips are generally well organized and safe. Most will even do the campfire cooking for you.

If the multi-day trip is beyond your budget and your timeline then the best experience is the 45-minute trip down the Kaituna Rapids near Rotorua. The highlight of this trip is the 7-m drop down the Okere Falls, the highest commercially rafted falls in the world. Here you, your 12-ft raft and all your shipmates literally submerge headfirst in the chaotic foam before bobbing up again like a cork. It is truly unforgettable. There is little time to learn the ropes, but the guides will keep you alive.

River sledding

This is the ludicrously simple but superb concept of rafting down a river on a body-board with little except a wet suit, flippers, a crash helmet and a PHD in lunacy. The prime location for this is again the Kaituna River in Rotorua. However, there is also the option of doing it down the man-made falls of a dam in Hawera, Taranaki. A 40-minute dunking will cost you about $50.

Rock climbing

This exciting activity is on the increase in New Zealand. The principal locations in North Island include the Mount Eden Quarry in Auckland and various locations near Taupo, Cambridge and Te Awamutu. In South Island the main bases are Christchurch and Dunedin for operators, while Fiordland and the Kahurangi National Park offer the most spectacular venues.

Sailing

New Zealand, and Auckland in particular, is famous for sailing. Indeed, the Kiwis are the proud holders of the world's biggest sailing trophy – the America's Cup – and are now considered not only the best sailors in the world but also the best designers and speed racers. Auckland is not called the city of sails for nothing. An estimated one in four of its inhabitants owns a recreational boat of some kind and this trend is echoed throughout the country. For the experienced sailor New Zealand and especially the Hauraki Gulf off Auckland and the Bay of Islands provides one of the best sailing playgrounds in the world, and for the novice, too, it is highly recommended. It's all great fun, but like any of the favoured sports, a bit of an 'art form'. At least a few hours out on the water are recommended but, if you can, try a multi-day trip. This will give you an insight into what sailing is all about. There are numerous opportunities to get out on the water in a proper yacht, though if you plan a longer trip there must obviously be someone present with the relevant experience and 'tickets' – and the Sir Peter Blakes of this world don't come cheap.

Scuba diving

Like sailing, New Zealand has some world-class diving venues including the celebrated Poor Knights Islands off Tutakaka in Northland. Although there are many locations and a number of superb marine reserves all around the country, the Poor Knights is where most budding Jacque Cousteaus gravitate. It is the combination of geology, marine life and perhaps, above all, water clarity that make them so special. With up to 80 m of visibility you can go head to head with a huge grouper or clench your rubbers at the sight of a shark. Of course the trained and the qualified fare better but in many locations local operators will take you for a full or half-day basic first dive experience for around $150 including gear hire. If the thought of all that is too much you can also go snorkelling, which gives you a great insight into the wonders of the deep for minimum effort. There is also some fine wreck-diving available with the old navy frigates *Tui* and *Waikato* deliberately sunk for diving off the east Northland coast. Another fine trip is the one to pay homage to the Greenpeace vessel *Rainbow Warrior* that was laid to rest off Matauri Bay. The great *Warrior* was bombed in Auckland by French terrorists in 1985. Other than Northland the main diving locations are the Hauraki Gulf (Auckland), Coromandel (Whitianga), New Plymouth (Taranaki) and the Marlborough Sounds and Fiordland in South Island.

Shark encounters

While the vast majority of the human race still have nightmares at the mere suggestion of a fin surfacing in the water, it appears there is a lunatic fringe who actually wish to have a picnic with them. If you are one of these people and wish to encounter these fascinating creatures in their own habitat from the relative safety of a cage, you can do so in New Zealand. The principal locations are Tutukaka and Napier in North Island and Kaikoura in the South. A four-hour trip will cost about $110, prosthetic limbs extra.

Skiing & snowboarding

Ski-field contact details are listed in the relevant sections

New Zealand is a principal southern hemisphere skiing and snowboarding venue and although it is of course seasonal (May-August), the slopes are highly accessible to the tourist and the beginner. Most of the major commercial ski-fields are in South Island. They include Coronet Peak and the Remarkables near Queenstown, Treble Cone, Cardrona and Waiorau near Wanaka, Mount Hutt, Mount Potts and Porter Heights west of Christchurch and the Arthur's Pass, Hanmer Springs and Nelson regions. The choice is vast. In North Island the main commercial venues are on the slopes of Ruapehu (Whakapapa and Turoa) in the Tongariro National Park.

Although they vary, the average cost of hire for skis, boots and poles is around $25, snowboard and boots $39. An all-day lift pass will cost around $54 ($29 for youths). There are inevitably a number of packages available at many fields which might include lift pass, equipment hire and one-hour lesson for $49 ($29 for youths). There may also be 'Lift and Ski Hire Packages' which cost $69 ($35 for youths). A group lesson will cost about $20 while a private lesson will cost about $80. A 'youth' is aged 16 and under.

Surfing

New Zealand is a world-class surfing venue but often overlooked by the surf set and because of this it is quite special. In New Zealand as yet, surfing is pretty uncommercial, but still practised in many locations, with an almost religious following. North Island's

West Coast locations of Taranaki, Raglan (Waikato) and Piha (Auckland) are perhaps the most famous venues, but other great surf spots include Whangamata (Coromandel), Eastland, Gisborne and Napier. You can get excellent and relatively cheap tuition in many locations (especially in Taranaki and Raglan). If you want a beginner's taste of what surfing is like, try boogie-boarding or bodysurfing. Boogie-boards are about half the size of a surfboard and made of compressed foam. They are readily available and are cheap to buy or hire. With this and a pair of flippers you can then go pseudo-surfing and take out the difficult bit – standing up.

Swimming Although swimming in the sea is kept mainly to the summer months, you can do your strokes year round in man-made pools and the numerous hot pools throughout the country. Rotorua and Taupo are the natural hot-pool capitals but there are also others in Waiwera north of Auckland, Te Aroha in the Waikato, Tauranga in the Bay of Plenty and numerous other venues throughout the country. There is something quite special about swimming around a large hot pool that is the temperature of a bath tub and for the uninitiated you will be reluctant to ever get out. One word of warning – coastal swimming can be very dangerous and at some popular locations there are notorious rips (currents that carry you off to Australia) so when you are swimming at the beach, take care and if directed swim only 'between the flags'. If in difficulties all you need to do is raise your arm and keep it aloft, and before you know it you'll be hauled into a rubber dinghy by hunky life-guards (sorry boys, this is not '*Baywatch*').

Tandem skydiving Adrenaline aside, the beauty of taking the jump in New Zealand is the scenic factor. Once you have recovered from that falling feeling the view of the land below hurtling towards you at about 120 kph is truly unforgettable. In New Zealand you can do a tandem in many locations throughout both islands. There is some scant instruction before the actual jump but you are essentially in very safe hands. A location recommended for value and height is Parakai (Auckland) and for scenery it is Taupo, Wanaka and Queenstown. Jumps range in height from 9000 ft to 15,000 ft. The latter will give you about 40 seconds free-fall. At no less than $200 it is undoubtedly expensive but worth it. The price, obviously, increases the higher you go, though commercial operators will generally not take first timers beyond 15,000 ft.

Tramping (Hiking) Even before the *National Geographic* proclaimed the Milford Track as 'the world's best walk', New Zealand could, without doubt, claim to be the tramping (or hiking) capital of the world. Not only is it one of the principal pastimes for many New Zealanders, it is also the reason many visitors come to the country. There is a vast network of routes and literally thousands of kilometres of track the length and breadth of the country, from the well-formed and trodden highway of the famed Milford Track, to the sporadic trail and markers of the lesser known Dusky Track. The range of habitats is immense, from remote coastlines, through rainforests, beside volcanic lakes, over mountain peaks to island traverses, with most penetrating vast and fully protected national parks.

Other than the sheer scenic beauty and scope of opportunities in New Zealand, what makes tramping so popular is the ease of access and maintenance of the tracks. Under the administration and advocacy of the **Department of Conservation** (DOC) all advertised tracks are clearly marked, well-maintained and have designated campsites and huts offering clean water, basic accommodation, cooking facilities and toilets. Add to that the wealth of detailed information available from route descriptions and access, to up-to-date weather forecasts, it is little wonder that tramping is perhaps New Zealand's biggest and most uniquely precious tourist asset. Even **safety** is well managed, with the tracks classified by type and fitness required. Guided trips are available for the more inexperienced and even an 'intentions sheet' system administered for major excursions. All this for a meagre $4 per tent site, or about $10 in nightly hut fees.

Tramping – it is no walk in the woods!

If you have never been tramping before and intend to embark on one that involves a number of days, you need to be warned that it will be a challenge. A challenge of not only your physical but also your mental self. Tramping is not walking the dog. You can, and will, get extremely tired, hot, wet, thirsty, hungry, smelly and bitten alive. But the rewards are immense. You will experience nature at its best (or worst) and your senses will be bombarded. There will be no lattes, no email, no warm duvets or clean, flush toilets. You are going to wake up tired because you were sharing a dorm with what sounded like a small family of warthogs. Everyday you are out there, you are going to eat a meagre breakfast, put those wet boots on again, what feels like a small house on your back, and not for the first time, set off thinking – what the hell am I doing here? Once the day's walking is done and you have reached your shelter it is the simple things that matter – a log fire for warmth, or a cup of tea. You are either going to love it or hate it, but you are going to have to accept the challenge and take the risk to find out which. Above all, like any challenge or any risk, it is the best way to learn a bit more about yourself and others. A word of advice, travel light – really light. In South Island take lots of insect repellent. One other thing: leave your bad moods at home – because, as you will soon find out, nature doesn't care.

Essentials

The most famous track is, deservedly, the magnificent **Milford Track**, a 54 km four-day trek that combines lake and mountain scenery. Also in the Te Waipounamu World Heritage Park is the **Routeburn**, **Kepler**, **Dusky**, **Greenstone**, **Hollyford** and the newest, the **HumpRidge Track**. But these are only a few of the many tasty options.

The most popular tramps come under the heading of New Zealand's (DOC) 'Great Walks'. In North Island these include the **Tongariro Northern Circuit** in the Tongariro National Park (including the volcanic delights of the **Tongariro Crossing**) and the beautiful circumnavigation of **Lake Waikaremoana** in the Te Urewera National Park. In South Island there are others including the highly popular bays and estuary crossings of the **Abel Tasman Coast Track** in the Abel Tasman National Park, the beautiful coastal stretches of **The Heaphy** in the Kahurangi and the muddy delights of the **Rakiura Track** on Stewart Island (the newest of the country's 14 national parks). Quieter and still spectacular tramps in South Island include the **Travers-Sabine** in the Nelson Lakes, **Rees-Dart-Cascade Saddle** between Glenorchy and Wanaka and the stunning but difficult **Dusky Track** in Fiordland.

It would be easy just to recommend the likes of the Milford, Kepler and Abel Tasman, but a word of warning: many of the tracks are becoming very **busy** and are now not so much tracks as public highways. The Milford, Kepler, Heaphy and Abel Tasman are considered the worst in this respect. Of course that does not mean that they should be avoided. They are still worth doing, and no less spectacular, but if you like a bit of solitude with your tramp, we recommend you consider other options or at the very least go towards the start or the end of the tramping season (October to April). To give you some idea of how busy they are, the Milford now hosts about 10,000 trampers annually and the Abel Tasman up to 300 a day in mid-summer. This not only means a lot of company, it also means you must book accommodation sometimes weeks in advance.

Tramping Information, booking & safety

For detailed information about all the major tramping tracks and 'Great Walks' contact the local **DOC** Field Centre (listed under the relevant location) or visit the website www.doc.govt.nz For **accommodation bookings** and **information** call in person or book via the website www.greatwalksbooking@doc.govt.nz

Tramping track classifications

All DoC managed and maintained walks from short five-minute boardwalks to mountain traverses have a classification, as follows:

Path *Easy, generally low-lying and well formed. Suitable for all ages and levels of fitness. No walking boots required.*

Walking track *Easy and well formed. Can involve short or steady climbs. Suitable for all ages and the reasonably fit. Shoes are OK, walking boots preferable.*

Tramping track *Requires relevant skill and experience. Generally continuous track but may be vague in parts. Expect full range of topographies up to scrambling. Suitable for people of average fitness. Walking boots required.*

Route *Requires high degree of skill and route finding experience. Track may only have markers as guidance. High level of fitness and equipment (including maps) required.*

There are two price systems for hut accommodation and four categories. The first are the **Great Walks Huts** ($10-35 per night) which have bunks with mattresses, basic cooking facilities, usually a log fire plus a clean water supply and long-drop toilets. Categories 2-4 are **Backcountry Huts** ($4-18) ranging from those offering similar facilities to the above to mere shelters with just water and toilets. An annual Hut Pass can be purchased for $65. All Great Walk Huts must be **pre-booked**, sometimes weeks in advance, and all huts (except those run by guided walk companies) operate on a first come first served basis. **Camping** is permitted at some huts or at designated campsites ($4). DOC produce excellent **leaflets** for each track ($1), stock **maps** and can provide up to date information as required.

You are advised to consult the local DOC office before embarking on any of the major tramps regardless of experience and weather conditions and if required fill in an intentions sheet. Always make sure you are well-prepared, equipped and of the required level of fitness Unless you are experienced, tramping on the more remote and quieter tracks alone is not advisable.

Walking

The opportunities are endless. New Zealand is a walker's paradise and most VICs or regional DOC offices compile lists of the most notable long and short walks in each region. There is everything from coastal or bush walks to historical trails. Two of the best one-day walks are the Tongariro Crossing in the Tongariro National Park (best accessed from Taupo) and the Tarawera Falls Walk near Rotorua in North Island. In South Island there are simply too many to list or recommend, but you should at least try the coastal walk at Wharariki Beach, Nelson Region.

Multi-day walks enter the realm of Tramping, the New Zealand term for hiking. The country is world famous for this, offering some of the best tramping trails in the world (see Tramping above). For more local short or long walks you can also consult the web. The best site is of course the DOC site, www.doc.govt.nz but another useful one is the independent site www.hillarysport.co.nz

Wildlife watching

Wildlife watching in New Zealand is usually of the 'bird' variety. However, you will also have the opportunity to see dolphins, fur seals and whales. The Bay of Islands and Whakatane are the dolphin-watching and swimming capitals of North Island, while Kaikoura is the world-famous venue for both dolphins and whales in South Island. The endangered Hectors dolphin can also be viewed from Curio Bay in the Catlins, Southland.

Given the fact that so much of the country and especially the mainland has been raped of its wildlife you are advised to visit at least one of the offshore island reserves. Tiri Tiri Matangi Island north of Auckland and Kapiti Island north of Wellington are easily accessible, world-renowned sanctuaries which are home to many unique and endangered species. On either of these islands you can really get a feel for the paradise that New Zealand once was. With little or no effort, you will also see many of those rare species close up since many are naturally very tame.

Perhaps the best and most comical is the **takahe**, an ancient species that looks like a large prehistoric purple chicken. Only about 200 remain. Then of course there is the **kiwi** – that remarkable nocturnal bird with no wings, an awfully long beak and an ability to lay an egg the size of a small melon. There are many commercial nocturnal houses where you will get a reasonably good view of one, even though it is very dark. The sight of a kiwi in the wild is of course a far more special and intimate experience, but for this you will have either to be exceptionally lucky or to go to Stewart Island or elsewhere on an organized or specialist trip (see Ohakune). At night they can sometimes be attracted by taped mating calls.

Sadly, like most of the country's native wildlife, the kiwi is becoming increasingly rare and is fast heading for complete extinction on the mainland. As usual we are to blame. There are very few places in the world where you can see, let alone have such free access to, such rare and beautiful birds, so make the most of it. Overall the scope, opportunities and locations to see and experience New Zealand's incredible wildlife first hand are endless. DOC's Mount Bruce Wildlife Centre near Masterton in the Wairarapa, North Island, or their Te Anau Wildlife Centre are recommended and of course the city zoos are also great places to see captive native wildlife at close range. While travelling keep your eyes open for organized eco-trips by foot, boat or kayak. For specialist wildlife operators see page 20 and more information see the Wildlife and Vegetation section in the Background chapter.

Essentials

Windsurfing

New Zealand is very well suited to the experienced windsurfer and offers endless locations. Windsurfing schools and board hire is available at most of the principal beach resorts.

Zorbing

Last and by no means least is zorbing. This is a most bizarre concept that could only be the creation of incredible Kiwi ingenuity. Described as a 'bi-spherical momentous experience', it involves climbing into a clear plastic bubble and rolling down a hill. Sadly, the organized venture involves a short hill that takes about 10 seconds and relieves you of about $50 – a bit of a rip-off. But what you could do with your own zorb blows the mind. Although a bit expensive you can have your own momentous experience in the Bay of Islands (Northland) and at the Agrodome in Rotorua. Incidentally, you can also do a wet run and be joined inside the bubble with a bucket of water.

Health

For free information on how best to access New Zealand's health system contact the 24-hr Accident Info Services, T0800-263345

No vaccinations are officially required for entry into New Zealand. You are however advised to get a tetanus shot or ensure your booster is up to date. The standards of public and private medical care are generally high, but unless you have a genuine accident it is important to note that these services are not free. Health insurance is recommended. A standard trip to the doctor will cost around $35 with prescription charges on top of that. Dentists and hospital services are expensive.

Safety precautions

Other than the occasional crazed driver, there are very few dangerous creatures in New Zealand. One exception is the **Katipo Spider**. It's a cute little black number, about 25 mm from leg tip to leg tip, which is found on beaches, under stones and in driftwood throughout North Island and parts of the South. It is not uncommon and can be fatal, with agonizing pain in the vicinity of the bite. Antivenin is readily available in hospitals. Although sharks are a common sight around New Zealand shores, shark attacks are rare. The last fatal attack occurred in Eastland in 1976.

There is one nasty little blighter, which, although not poisonous, will annoy you beyond belief – the dreaded **sandfly**. Particularly common in the wetter and coastal areas of Fiordland (but present almost everywhere), these black, pinhead sized 'flying fangs' have a successful hit rate that makes laser-guided missile systems look archaic. Open your car door and within seconds a vast cloud of the little devils will descend and your entire party will look like a crowd of deranged loonies at a 'rave' dance. There are numerous sprays available such as : *Off* and *Repel*.

There are a few other safety factors worth mentioning. **Giardia** is an equally offensive little nemesis of the bacterial variety. He's an ugly wee water-borne parasite on the increase in New Zealand, which, if allowed to enter your system, will cause wall-to-wall vomiting, diarrhoea and rapid weight loss. The best bet is not to drink water from lakes, ponds or rivers without boiling it first. The **sun** too is dangerous. Ozone depletion is heavy in the more southern latitudes and the incidence of melanomas and skin cancer is above average. Burn times, especially in summer, are greatly reduced so get yourself a silly hat and wear lots of sun block.

Other than that it is very much down to common sense. Bear in mind New Zealand's **weather**, especially at the higher elevations, is changeable and can sometimes be deadly. If you are climbing, tramping, or going anywhere 'bush' make sure you are properly clothed and shod, take maps, a first aid kit and a compass. Above all inform somebody of your intentions.

Volcanic eruptions and **earthquakes** are also an exciting factor. Although major events are rare they can (and have) of course happened and proved fatal. Such is their power and magnificence all you can say here is keep your fingers crossed and hope you are not in the wrong place at the wrong time. In the event of an earthquake, stand in a doorway, get under a table and if you are in the open, get indoors or keep away from loose rock formations and trees.

One other thing. Should you come across any **injured wildlife** call the nearest DOC office and try to ensure the animal is taken to one of the few local wildlife rehabilitators. DOC officers are very busy and the entire department is generally underfunded. Provided the animal is not on the 'Don't touch list' (ask DOC) and you use common sense, capture the animal and put it in a dark, fully enclosed box with some ventilation holes. Then find out the location of the nearest rehabilitator and take it there yourself. If in doubt don't. If you come across a **whale stranding** or an obviously sick seal on the beach from 10 kg to 300 kg (!) call DOC immediately or, in South Island, Marine Watch, T02-5358909 for advice.

Further reading and useful websites

Non-fiction pictorial, natural history & environment

As you might expect there is a vast array of pictorial books celebrating New Zealand's stunning scenery. The best known photographers are **Craig Potton, Andris Apse** and **Robin Morrison,** to name but a few. Their numerous books are of a very high production quality and contain some exquisite photographs. There are a few good wildlife guidebooks and field guides. **Geoff Moon's** *New Zealand Birds* is an old favourite while the new *Field Guide to New Zealand Wildlife* by **Rod Morris** and **Terence Linsey** (Collins) is recommended. From a far the pictorial websites of www.photonewzealand.com / www.andrisapse.co.nz / www.craigpotton.co.nz are all excellent.

History, politics & culture

The History of New Zealand by **Keith Sinclair** is a dated but celebrated historical work that is a complete history starting from before the arrival of Europeans. *Maori: A Photographic and Social Study* and *Being Pakeha*, both by **Michael King**; *The Old-Time Maori* by **Makereti**; *The Treaty of Waitangi* by **Claudia Orange**; and *The New Zealand Land Wars* by **James Belich** are all equally celebrated works covering the often contentious historical issues of the Maori and Pakeha. For an overall insight *The New Zealand Historical Atlas: Ko Papatuanuku e Takoto Nei* is highly visual, easy to read and generally recommended.

Biographies & travelogues

A good starting point is *The Dictionary of New Zealand Biography*, a three-volume anthology covering the period post 1769. **Barry Crump** is a recently deceased, iconic author famous for his humorous 'Kiwi bloke' hunting travelogues. Perhaps his most famous title is the aptly named *'Good Keen Man'* (1960). *An Angel at My Table* is a fine work by **Janet Frame**, a highly acclaimed contemporary writer receiving increasing recognition. The book tells of her childhood and life as a student, patient in a mental hospital and later as writer. The story has recently been made into a film of the same name directed by New Zealand's most famous film director **Jane Campion**, who directed *The Piano* (1993). New Zealand's own Hodder Moa Beckett is the principal sports biography publisher.

Outdoor activities

For tramping, the *Moirs Guides* (NZ Alpine Club) and *New Zealand's Great Walks* by **Pearl Hewson** (Hodders) are recommended. Also check out titles by **Craig Potton**, www.craigpotton.co.nz For cycling, the word is that **Bruce Ringer**'s *New Zealand by Bike* (Mountaineers) is excellent.

Guide books & reference

The Mobil New Zealand Travel Guide by **Diana and Jeremy Pope** offers a general place-oriented guide, with interesting background reading and historical insights into each place listed. If you can get your hands on an old copy of *Wises New Zealand Guide*, available in most second-hand bookshops, they are brilliant. For B&B guides the *New Zealand Bed and Breakfast Guide* by **J Thomas** (Moonshine) and the *Friars B&B Guide* are recommended.

Fiction

The **New Zealand Book Council**, PO Box 11-377, Wellington, T04-4991569, are an excellent source of information on New Zealand Literature and fiction books. They provide listings of books, places of literary interest to visit and literary events.

There are many celebrated fiction writers in New Zealand and when **Keri Hulme** won the Booker Prize in 1985 for the *Bone People* and children's writer **Margaret Mahy** the Carnegie Medal twice that same decade for *The Haunting* and *The Changeover*, New Zealand writing was put on the international map. Previous to that it was really only the celebrated short stories by the Wellingtonian writer **Katherine Mansfield** (1888-1923) that had received international recognition. *The Collected Stories of Katherine Mansfield* is her best known literary export. Other notable names and titles include **Maurice Shadbolt's** *Season of the Jew*, a story about dispossessed Maori identifying with the Jews of ancient Israel. **Maurice Gee's** is another well-known writer. His *Going West* is the story of unravelling relationships amidst the backdrop of Auckland and Wellington. The *Plumb* trilogy is recommended, as are his entertaining children's

Useful websites

www.purenz.com *Official website of the New Zealand Tourism Board packed with useful information, listings and contacts. Excellent first stop.*
www.searchnz.co.nz *One of the countries best national search engines. Great way to access main links through general search.*
The **www.nzcity.co.nz** *link has regional news and a superb weather satellite picture.*
www.nzstuff.co.nz /
www.nzoom.co.nz *Useful national web sites with regional news links.*
www.yellowpages.co.nz *Useful for any national telephone and address listing.*
www.maps@mapworld.co.nz *The best map supplier in New Zealand including CD-ROMS.*
www.discover.co.nz /
www.travelplanner.co.nz /
www.newzealandvacations.co.nz *Other useful tourist/visitor based sites with good links.*
www.govt.nz doc *The invaluable and fast developing website of the Conservation Department with detailed information on Regional Conservancies, national parks, tramping and short walks.*
www.travel-library.com *Detailed general travel site packed with good tips on buying flight tickets etc.*
www.nzherld.co.nz *Excellent website of the Upper North Island's main daily newspaper, with national, international news, sport, weather and travel.*
www.Intercitycoach.co.nz *Website for Intercity Buses with detailed bus information, fare concessions and package deals.*
www.tranzrail.co.nz *Provides all your rail and inter-island ferry information needs.*
www.auckland-airport.co.nz / **www.christchurch-airport.co.nz** *Perhaps worth a quick look before you enter the country.*
www.hillarysport.co.nz *Useful national walks guide.*
www.backpack.co.nz /
www.yha.org.nz /
www.kiwiexperience.co.nz *Principal backpacker and backpacker travel organizations.*
www.jasons.co.nz /
www.aaguides.co.nz *Useful general New Zealand travel and accommodation information.*
www.nz-travel.co.nz /
www.worldtouring.co.nz /
www.tourism.net.nz /
www.Expedia.com /
www.travelstore.com /
www.lastminute.com / **www.QXL.com** / **www.firedup.com** /
www.travelocity.com *Good general travel sites with general information and competitive airfares for NZ.*
www.photonewzealand.com /
www.andrisapse.co.nz /
www.craigpotton.co.nz *Some of the best photographers, photographs and pictorial references of New Zealand.*

works. **Witi Ihimaera's** *Bulibasha* is an affectionate look at Maori sheep shearing gangs in Eastland and **Alan Duff's** much acclaimed *Once Were Warriors* is a disturbing and powerful insight into Maori domestic life in Auckland's suburbs. The film of the same name is a 'must see' providing a reality check and the complete antithesis of New Zealand's clean green and peaceful image.

For excellent information on the full range of New Zealand titles, subjects and authors contact the **Book Publishers Association of New Zealand**, T09-4802711, www.bpanz.org.nz Also for general titles and worldwide availability consult www.Amazon.com

North Island

North Island

Auckland

Auckland

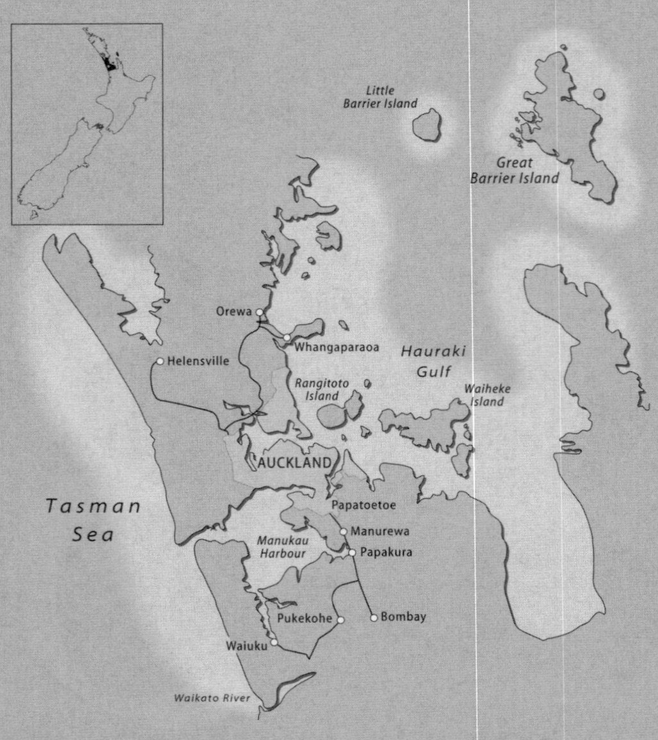

Little Barrier Island
Great Barrier Island
Orewa
Whangaparaoa
Hauraki Gulf
Helensville
Rangitoto Island
Waiheke Island
AUCKLAND
Tasman Sea
Papatoetoe
Manurewa
Manukau Harbour
Papakura
Pukekohe
Bombay
Waiuku
Waikato River

With a population of just over a million, Auckland is New Zealand's biggest city and home to almost a third of the population. For the vast majority of visitors to New Zealand, Auckland will be their arrival point and their first introduction to the country. Many will treat it only as a gateway to better things, but you'd be pleasantly surprised with what she has to offer.

Thanks to its spacious suburban sprawl, Auckland covers over 500 sq km – twice that of London and close to that of Los Angeles – but because the city is built on an isthmus and constantly fragmented by coastline, you are never far from water. The sea pervades almost every aspect of Auckland life, from recreation to cuisine. Aucklanders own more recreational boats per capita than any other city in the world, and it is subsequently and affectionately called the ***'City of Sails'****.*

No surprise then that it is currently the proud home to the world's most prestigious yachting trophy, the America's Cup. Most sailing is done in Auckland's backyard, the beautiful aquatic playground and island-studded waters of the ***Hauraki Gulf****, one of the most beautiful sailing venues in the world. As well as sailing, you can go fishing, swimming or surfing, all within minutes of the city centre and, in some places, have the beach to yourself. The city also boasts some impressive man-made attractions such as the stunning 360° views from the hypodermic* ***Sky Tower****, and its bustling city centre streets and trendy suburbs are home to a thousand world-class restaurants.*

Auckland

Phone code: 09
Population: 1,076,100

Auckland has been labelled the largest Polynesian city in the world, but in reality it enjoys a cosmopolitan make-up of Pacific, European, Asian and indigenous Maori. Modern Auckland is in fact the fusion of four cities: **North Shore**, an expanding, predominantly European and contemporary area of greater Auckland north of the bridge, with attractive beaches and quiet modern suburbs; **Auckland City** itself, the heart and hub, with its central business district around Queen St growing ever skywards, together with its waterfront and its happening inner-city suburbs; **Waitakere**, to the west, a mix of low and high income suburbs dominated by the bush-clad Waitakere Ranges; and **Manakau** to the south, with its lively low-income suburbs of predominantly Maori and Pacific Island citizens. All combine to create a huge cosmopolitan sprawl of modern humanity, in which, naturally, it is very easy to get lost.

Ins and outs

Getting there

Air

Qantas (ex Ansett), Air New Zealand and Mount Cook Airlines are the main carriers (see page 41)

The vast majority of visitors will arrive by air. Auckland airport, a relatively small, modern and friendly gateway to the nation, is 20 km from the city centre.

Facilities A small but adequate Airport Information Centre, T3076467, is located on the ground floor and open from 0500 till the last flight at night. They can help book accommodation and provide transport details. Also feel free to ask the Hospitality Ambassadors (the smiley folk in bright blue jackets) or Customer Service Officers (red jackets and splendid hats) for assistance. Shops, food outlets, mail boxes, free showers (towel hire from the Airways Florist on the ground floor $5, plus deposit), phones and practically everything else are all readily available at the airport.

There's also baggage storage (open 0600 – 2300) on the ground floor after emigration at 'The Collection Point', and dayrooms (containing a bed, desk, TV, coffee, tea and shower facilities) are available daily for $30 up to 4 hrs, or $40 for over 4 hrs.

The domestic terminal is only a short distance from the International and free transit shuttles operate between both terminals every 20 mins

Transport The *Airport Shuttle* costs about $18 and takes about 40 mins to the city centre, depending on traffic. The *Airbus*, T0800-247287, is another cheap option leaving every 20 mins between 0630-2030 and costs $10 one way and $16 return. Independent **taxis** are also readily available immediately outside the terminal and will cost you about $30. *Super Shuttle*, T3075210, also provides a door-to-door service. All the regular and well-known rental car operators are located at both international and domestic terminals on the ground floor.

Getting around

Bicycles, scooters & motorcycles

For bicycle, scooter and motorcycle hire (see page 114)

These are a brave option in Auckland, given the way people drive, unless you are a seasoned courier or experienced city cyclist. Within the city stick to walking, buses or a car. Outside the city keep bicycles to the mountain or touring variety. If you want a more unusual mode of transport try a *Tuk-Tuk*, a sort of metal rabbit hutch on wheels with fearless drivers; T3601988.

Things to do in Auckland

- *Climb the 'hypodermic' Sky Tower – take in the 360° views, dine in the revolving restaurant and climb the mast.*
- *Take a cruise across the Auckland Harbour to historic Devonport. Browse the galleries, enjoy a glass of wine or a latte in one of the cafés.*
- *Introduce yourself to Kiwi history, wildlife and culture in the Auckland Museum. Rediscover your childhood curiosity in the 'Discovery Centre'.*
- *Sample the café culture and nightlife of Ponsonby, K'Road and Parnell.*
- *Find solitude on the Waitakere West Coast beaches of Whatipu, Karekare or Bethell's.*
- *Mix with rare and endangered species on Tiri Tiri Matangi Island.*
- *Cruise the stunning Hauraki Gulf islands, by ferry, yacht or launch.*
- *Watch the sunrise from the volcanic cones of Mount Victoria or Mount Eden.*

Bus
For individual local operators within the city centre see page 113

The **Downtown Bus Terminal** (DBT) is located centrally on Commerce St near the waterfront. Although a little rundown and seedy, it is functional and the information kiosk staff will provide timetables and prices. Major tourist information centres can also provide detailed information. *Rideline*, T3666400, has a detailed telephone information service on all major local city routes, prices and connections with ferry services.

Car
For most visitors hiring a car or camper van is one of the first things on the 'to do' list after finding accommodation

Most of the major tourist sights and attractions are located centrally and can be easily accessed by foot, bus or ferry. For longer stays, due to the huge urban sprawl a car is highly recommended. Car ownership per capita in Auckland is one of the highest in the world and you will quickly see that Auckland is not only a 'city of sails' but also a 'city of wheels', many, unfortunately, with certifiable owners! The public transport system, although adequate for the average visitor, is generally poor and planned improvements are long overdue. Formal metered or multi-storey parking is readily available in the city. Parking costs up to $3 an hr, and traffic wardens are everywhere.

Dial-a-driver

If you own a car and have been drinking, there is a wonderful service available in Auckland called 'Dial-a-Driver' (similar services are available elsewhere in New Zealand). Some strange loophole in car insurance laws allows their employees to drive you and your car to your chosen destination – preferably home – while another driver follows behind in a company car. This service is understandably immensely popular. The drivers are generally friendly and immensely stoic. *Dial–A-Driver*, T2675799.

Ferry

Almost all, except for the few commuter ferries, depart from around the historic Ferry Buildings located on the waterfront, at Quay St. A limited commuter service to some waterside suburbs has been developed and is expanding, but the vast majority of ferry traffic is tourist based. There are numerous excellent island or harbour locations, trips and tours to choose from. Fares are generally very reasonable. The main ferry company is ***Fullers*** who have an Information Office on the ground floor of the Ferry Building; T3679111. Tourist Information Centres can provide all the details.

Taxi

All Auckland taxi drivers are required to belong to a registered taxi company, which sets standards, but that is no guarantee of good English or not being taken via 'the scenic route'. Meters are usually based on time, not distance, so it often pays to get an estimate first. Typical rates are $2 flag call and then $1.50 per km. Taxis are generally widely available and can be flagged down, ordered by phone or picked up at the numerous city-centre ranks. ***Discount Taxis*** T529100; ***Auckland Taxi Co-op*** T3003000; or for the up-market option, ***Corporate Cabs*** T6311111.

24 hours in Auckland

Once you have secured your accommodation, and provided the weather is fine, head straight away for the ***Sky Tower*** *and its all-encompassing view. From the main observation deck you can see the vast sprawl of the city and pinpoint various sights to visit. Once back down to earth head to the* ***America's Cup Village*** *on the waterfront and have lunch in one of the many, mainly up-market restaurants (Cin Cin in the Ferry Building, Euro on Princess Wharf, and Kermadec over-looking the America's Cup Village are recommended). From the Ferry Building then catch a ferry to* ***Devonport*** *and take a leisurely walk east to* ***North Head*** *from where you will get a memorable view back towards the city centre. Once back in the heart of Devonport, enjoy a coffee or glass of wine in one of its pavement cafés. If you still have some energy walk to the top of* ***Mount Victoria*** *for more good views. Back in Auckland sample the commercial delights of* ***Queen Street*** *and/or* ***Victoria Park Market*** *and enjoy some retail therapy, though you should ignore the souvenir shops as the regional centres and the major museums are often a better bet. In the evening relax with a stroll along* ***Ponsonby Road*** *and choose a dinner venue from the huge range of cafés and restaurants.*

Orientation and information

The best place to find your bearings is the observation decks of the amazing Sky Tower, especially on a clear day

The heart of the city centre is the **CBD** (Central Business District) and the main drag of **Queen Street**. On either side, the jungle of high-rises gives way occasionally to older buildings like the **Auckland Art Gallery** and the green inner city sanctuaries of **Albert Park** and **The Domain,** with its crowning glory, the **Auckland Museum**. Immediately to the north the **Waitamata Harbour** calls a halt to the concrete, and ferries and sails take over on the **waterfront** where the historic **Ferry Building** looks almost out of place compared to the ugly, modern tower blocks that back it.

Along the waterfront is the yachting focal point of the **Viaduct Basin**, the **America's Cup Village** and the **Maritime Museum**. Across the Harbour Bridge is the huge expanse of **North Shore City**, while closer, and immediately across the **Waitamata Harbour**, is the small and attractive suburb of **Devonport**, with its village feel. It boasts the two volcanic cones of **Mount Victoria** and **North Head**, both of which offer great views. Around the corner are the relatively calm and safe **beaches** of the North Shore, stretching its length to the **Whangaparaoa Peninsula** and the edge of the city 40 km away.

East of the Whangaparoa Peninsula is the **Hauraki Gulf**, with its glistening waters and magical islands playing host to swarms of yachties. To the north, just off the Whangaparoa Peninsula, is **Tiri Tiri Matangi Island**, an open bird sanctuary. Beyond Tiri is the small but mountainous **Little Barrier Island**. East again, in the far distance, is **Great Barrier Island**, Auckland's beautiful getaway. Closer, is the most obvious and famous island, **Rangitoto**, with its classic volcanic cone and green botanical blanket, guarding the entrance to the Harbour. Next to Rangitoto are Browns and Motuihe Islands and, behind them, **Waiheke** the Gulf's most visited and populous island.

Back on the mainland, the eastern suburbs of **Mission Bay** and **St Heliers** stretch towards the distant Asian enclave of **Howick**. These seaside suburbs attract many visitors and Aucklanders alike, most of whom follow the waterside **Tamaki Drive** to soak up the sun on the beaches or bathe in the shallow bays.

Dominating the southern horizon are two of the most well-known volcanic mounts in the city, **Mount Eden** and **One Tree Hill**. South from these impressive landmarks, the low-income suburbs of South Auckland spread unceasingly to the southern city limits of the **Bombay Hills**. Within these suburbs are the **Auckland Botanical Gardens**.

Thankfully, nature has called a halt to city expansion to the west in the impressive form of the bush-clad **Waitakere Ranges**. The lower income suburb streets of Henderson and Glendene give way to the expensive dwellings of Titirangi. The inner western suburbs host the **Auckland Zoo** and **Museum of Transport and Technology (MOTAT),** both of which border the pleasant lakeside park of Western Springs.

Maps

Perhaps your first purchase in Auckland should be a map. All your needs can be met in that department right in the centre of the city. The ***Auckland Map Centre***, 1A Wyndham St, has a fine selection of national and local maps of varying scale, as does ***Speciality Maps***, 46 Albert St, and ***Whitcoulls*** on the corner of Queen St and Victoria St. *Whitcoulls* also has a comprehensive national travel book section on the ground floor.

Various free tourist handouts have some colourful maps of the city, but if you are serious get the 'Wises Auckland Compact Handi Map Book' at $20, or at the very least the foldout version at $10. Other than that, you will probably quickly find yourself slipping in to the local habit of using the Sky Tower as seemingly omnipresent beacon, and the main volcanic cones and the harbour as guidance and orientation.

Tourist information

There are Information Centres at both airport terminals: International, T2756467; Domestic, T2568480. There are 2 main Auckland Information Centres in the central city: at 287 Queen St, open Mon-Fri, 0830-1730, Sat and Sun 0900-1730, Apr-Oct, Mon-Fri 0930-1700, and the quieter American Express New Zealand Cup Village next to the Maritime Museum, T9792333, www.aucklandnz.com

If you venture north across the bridge, the North Shore Visitor Information Centre is located at 49 Hurstmere Rd, Takapuna, T4868670, or Devonport, T4460677. All information centres provide piles of free leaflets and handouts, but don't miss the readily available *Auckland A to Z*, *Auckland What's On*, *TNT Magazine* and the *Backpackers News* all excellent, up-to-the-minute publications. The *New Zealand Herald* is the main Auckland and North Island daily. For all things environmental and ecological, including nature walks, get yourself to the Department of Conservation (DOC) Information Centre, Ferry Building, Quay St, T3796467, on the waterfront; open Mon-Fri 0830-1700, Nov-Feb Sat 0900-1630 and Dec-Jan Sun 0900-1630.

History

According to Maori legend, when Maui (founder of New Zealand/Aotearoa) fished up the North Island, his efforts to subdue his catch created the islands of the Hauraki (the scales) and the bays and the beaches of the Isthmus (the wounds). Maori Gods of the Ocean and Wind further shaped and modified the geography and created the warm moist climate. It was the Gods of the resident giant, Mataaho, who created the volcanoes (legend has it he was cold) with their most recent piece of central heating being Rangitoto Island which guards the mouth of the Waitamata Harbour.

The first Maoris to settle in the area were thought to be Moa hunters (Moa being the once numerous, but now extinct, flightless New Zealand bird) before AD 1000. But later, from the 12th to 14th centuries, further migrations and Waka (Maori canoes) brought first the Nga-Oho and later the Nga-Tai and Nga-Marama tribes. The latter, led by the ambitious Kiwi Tamaki, ruled the roost for sometime, taking up residence in *Pa* (which were Maori settlements, often fortified) on almost every volcano in the district, including a main *Pa* on what is now named One Tree Hill. But his reign did not last and, after an ugly dispute and subsequent brutal conflict with other *Hapu* (sub tribes), particularly the Ngati-Whatua from the Kaipara district to the north, he succumbed. This, together with an epidemic of smallpox, brought by the early Europeans, meant the area became relatively unpopulated.

This all changed when the first official visit by *Pakeha* (white Europeans) came in 1820 in the form of the Reverends Samuel Marsden and John Gare Butler, two missionaries who were keen to expand their teachings beyond the Bay of Islands. From that point more organized integration and low-key European settlement began. But it was not until 20 years later, in 1840, on the signing of the Treaty of Waitangi, that New Zealand's Lieutenant-Governor, Captain William Hobson, bought a 3000 acre 'pie shaped' part of the Isthmus from the Ngati-Whatua for £55 and a few blankets. He called this area Auckland, after George Eden second Baron Auckland, then Governor General of India, probably in return for giving him command of *HMS Rattlesnake* in which Hobson first visited New Zealand in 1837. Hobson's intention was to create a new capital of New Zealand, the original settlements of the Bay of Islands, particularly Russell, having a distinctly unsavoury and disobedient population.

And so, for a short time, Auckland became the capital and the focus for the invading pioneers. One such pioneer, a Scots medic called Logan Campbell, took full advantage of Hobson's acquisition for the Crown, and in the first

Greater Auckland

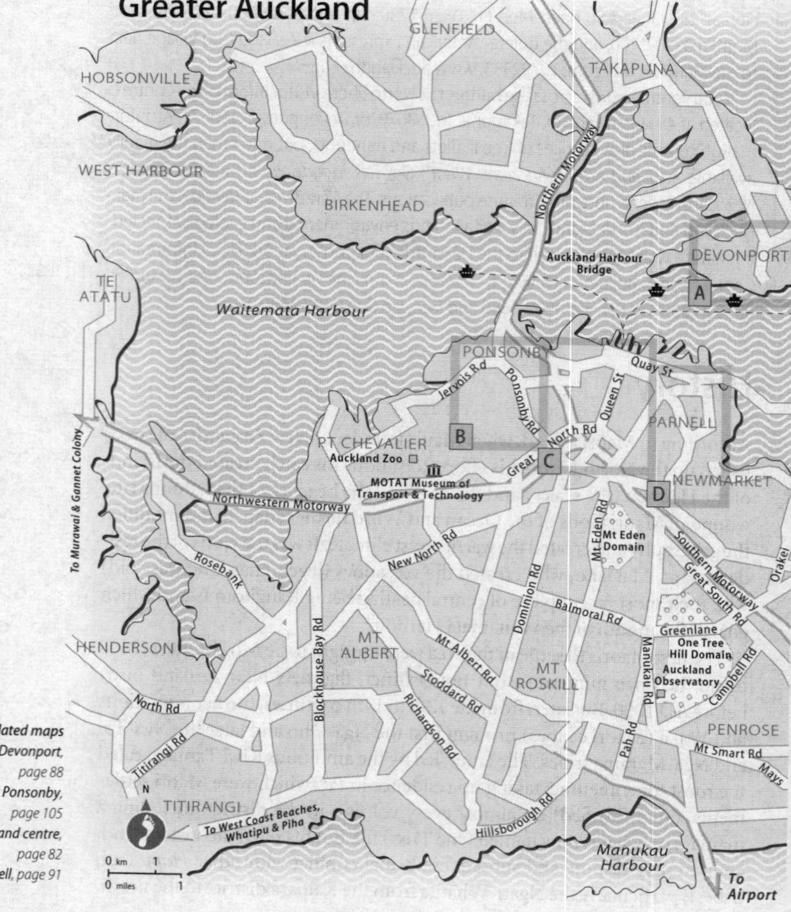

Related maps
A Devonport, *page 88*
B Ponsonby, *page 105*
C Auckland centre, *page 82*
D Parnell, *page 91*

years of its existence took almost total control of half the fast expanding 'pie'. He became Mayor of the settlement, and the so-called 'Father of Auckland'.

The rapidly growing demand for more land created great conflict with the Maori, contributing in part to the New Zealand Land Wars of the 1860's. Presumably, the Maori were beginning to realise that, in exchange for a few quid and some basic goods, they were fast losing '*Mana*' (presence, standing, integrity or honour) as well as their indigenous and rightful control.

Thanks to the Land Wars, and the discovery of gold elsewhere in Otago and in the nearby Coromandel, Auckland floundered a little. To add insult to injury in 1865 Auckland lost its status as capital to Wellington and with it the seat of Government.

However, towards the end of the 1800's, thanks to her fertile soils and climate and the brief but explosive 'Kauri' years – when there was widespread deforestation of the Kauri tree – Auckland's fortunes changed and the 'squashed pie' rapidly became the 'full bakery'. The rate at which Auckland continued to develop during the 20th century was astonishing. The irresistible combination of geography, climate, industry, agriculture and business opportunities has seen the population explode, creating the thriving cosmopolitan city we see today.

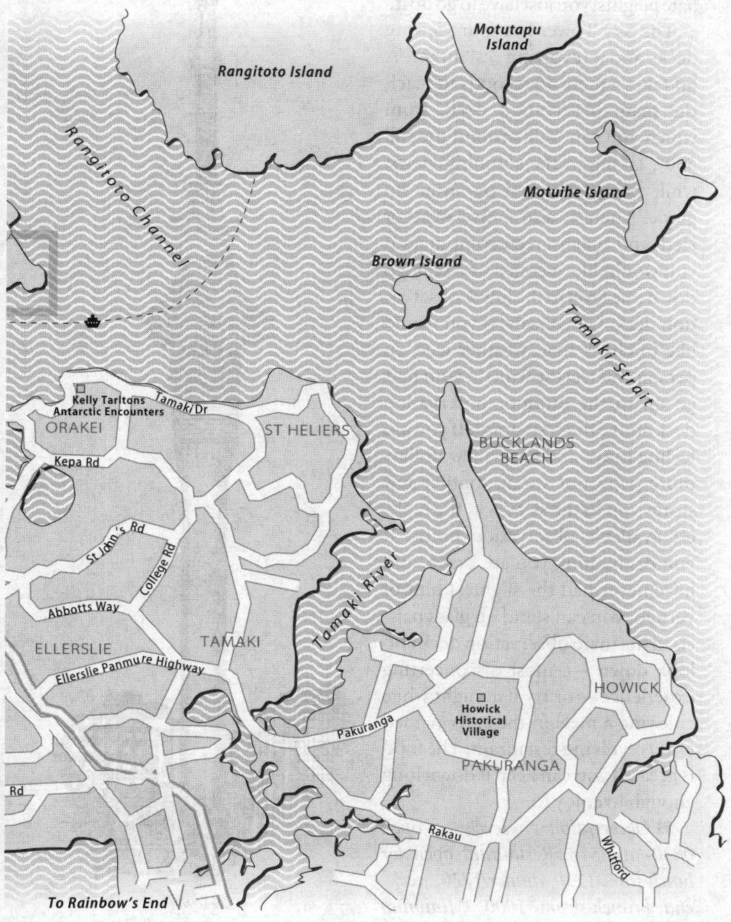

Sights

City centre

Sky Tower, Sky City & the Casino

For many Aucklanders in the early 90s the prospect of a casino and a futuristic 328-m **Sky Tower** smack bang in the city centre made them quake in their jangles (sandals). Construction began in 1994, on the corner of Victoria and Federal Streets, for the following 32 months and Aucklanders watched with disbelief and awe as Sky City sprouted its great hypodermic into the heavens. It was naturally the talk of the town, finally opening in 1997 in a hail of publicity. No one at the time denied the unbelievable imagination, construction, technology and logistics it took to create, but many still criticized the tower, saying it was too futuristic and a blot on the landscape. But Aucklanders have grown to love their tower – perhaps because it really is like a beacon. It's an awesome sight and, unless you hate heights, you just have to go up it.

The Sky Tower has four viewing decks and a revolving restaurant. A lift takes a mere 40 seconds to reach the main observation deck, from which you can walk around the full 360°, taking in the stunning views, while being educated by an audio guide. There is also a 'live weather feed' and touchscreen computers If you would like a coffee or a seat, go down one level to the lower observation deck. Conversely, if you would like to check that 'weather feed' in person and feel the wind in your hair go up to the outdoor observation deck above the restaurant. If you are feeling brave and have a few dollars more, why not shoot another few storeys up to the sky deck, the highest available observation point. If you really think you are brave, and have never had the slightest hint of vertigo, you can stand on glass panels in the main observation deck and look down – a most disconcerting experience – or try it at night while enjoying a meal in the aptly named *Orbit* revolving restaurant. The food is great, if you can keep it down long enough to enjoy it!

■ *Observation levels open 0830-late. $18. Restaurant open for lunch from 1130, dinner 1730, weekend brunch from 1000. Minimum*

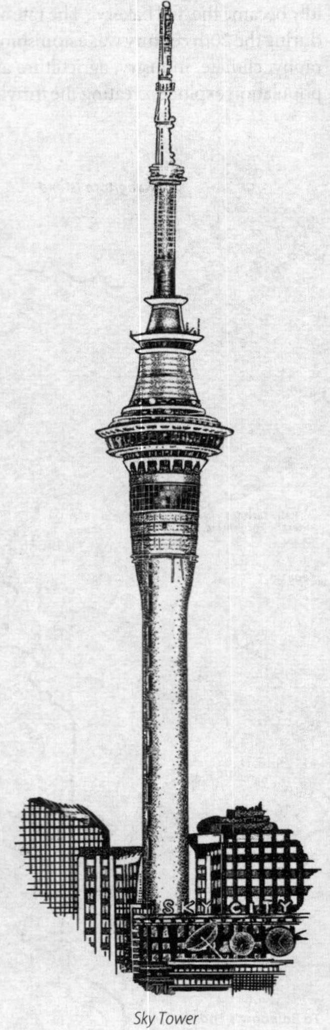

Sky Tower

Sky Tower – some statistics

The Sky Tower was opened in 1997 and took two years and eight months to build.

At 328 m tall it the tallest man-made structure in the Southern Hemisphere and 23 m taller than the AMP Tower in Sydney. The tower's shaft measures 12 m in diameter and its foundations go 15 m down into the earth. It houses the highest weather station, post box and restaurant in the Southern Hemisphere. The restaurant completes a 360° revolution every sixty seconds. The Sky Tower is designed to withstand a magnitude 8.0 Earthquake and 200 km/hour winds. Such winds would only create a 1 m sway of the entire structure. During construction the tower was kept absolutely vertical using complex telemetry including three global satellite-positioning systems. There are 1257 steps to the Sky Deck. The fastest recorded time of ascent during the annual 'Sky Tower Vertical Challenge' is five minutes 57 seconds. In 1998 bungy guru A.J.Hackett made a 192 m bungy jump from the main observation deck. This is the highest bungy jump ever attempted from a ground structure.

Auckland

charge $25. Enquiries and restaurant bookings; T9126400. *From mid-2002 you will be able to make a controlled bungy jump from the observation deck (190 m) for around $190, or climb the communications mast to 270 m. For more information, T0800-7592489, or visit www.skycity.co.nz*

Sky City Hotel is one of the largest in New Zealand (see Sleeping, page 96)

Sky City claims to be Auckland's largest multi-faceted entertainment and leisure destination. The main casino provides all kinds of gambling and gaming options, bars and live entertainment 24 hours a day, and has seen the ruin of many. The *Alto Casino and Bar*, T0800-7592489, is a more intimate and sophisticated experience with a higher standard of dress. One for the real wheelers and dealers. Sky City Theatre is a 700-seat, state of the art entertainment venue, staging national and international events and productions. Information and bookings; T9126000. As well as the Tower's *Orbit* restaurant there are five other eateries offering everything from Pacific Rim to Chinese, traditional buffet or café-style options. Information and bookings; T0800-7592489. Ample car parking is provided in a seemingly endless rabbit warren below the complex.

The waterfront & America's Cup Village

The once sandy beaches of the waterfront have now become cliffs of glass and concrete as the city has grown relentlessly outwards and upwards over the last 150 years. Radiating from the historic **Ferry Building**, built in 1912, the waterfront is the place where the city of concrete becomes the City of Sails and where the locals would say she takes on her proper and distinct character. The waterfront has always been a focus of major activity. In the early years it was the point where exhausted immigrants first disembarked to begin a new life in a new land. Later, the immigrant ships gave way to the fleets of log-laden scows bringing Kauri to the timber mills. Today, recreation has taken over, as modern ferries come and go and lines of expensive yachts rock gently together in the breeze at the **Westhaven Marina**, the largest in the southern hemisphere.

As a yachting nation and city, the waterfront has seen perhaps the most rapid development of all centred around the **Viaduct Basin**, home of the new America's Cup Village. Even before New Zealand took the cup from the USA's tight grasp in 1995, the Viaduct Basin was a stopover point for the Whitbread Round the World Race (also won by New Zealand in 1994) and the place has become an aquatic stadium of profound celebration. New Zealanders are proud of their yachting heritage and, even outwith the fierce

Auckland centre

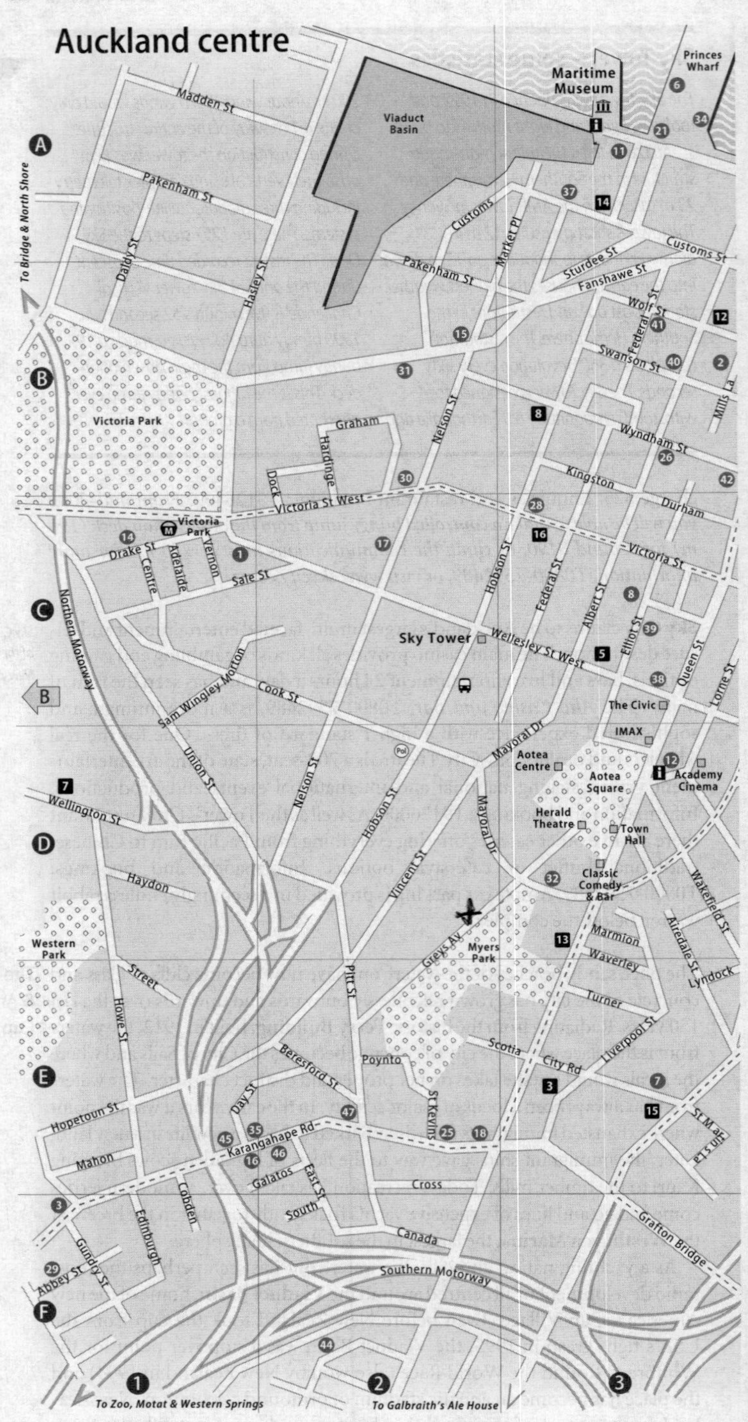

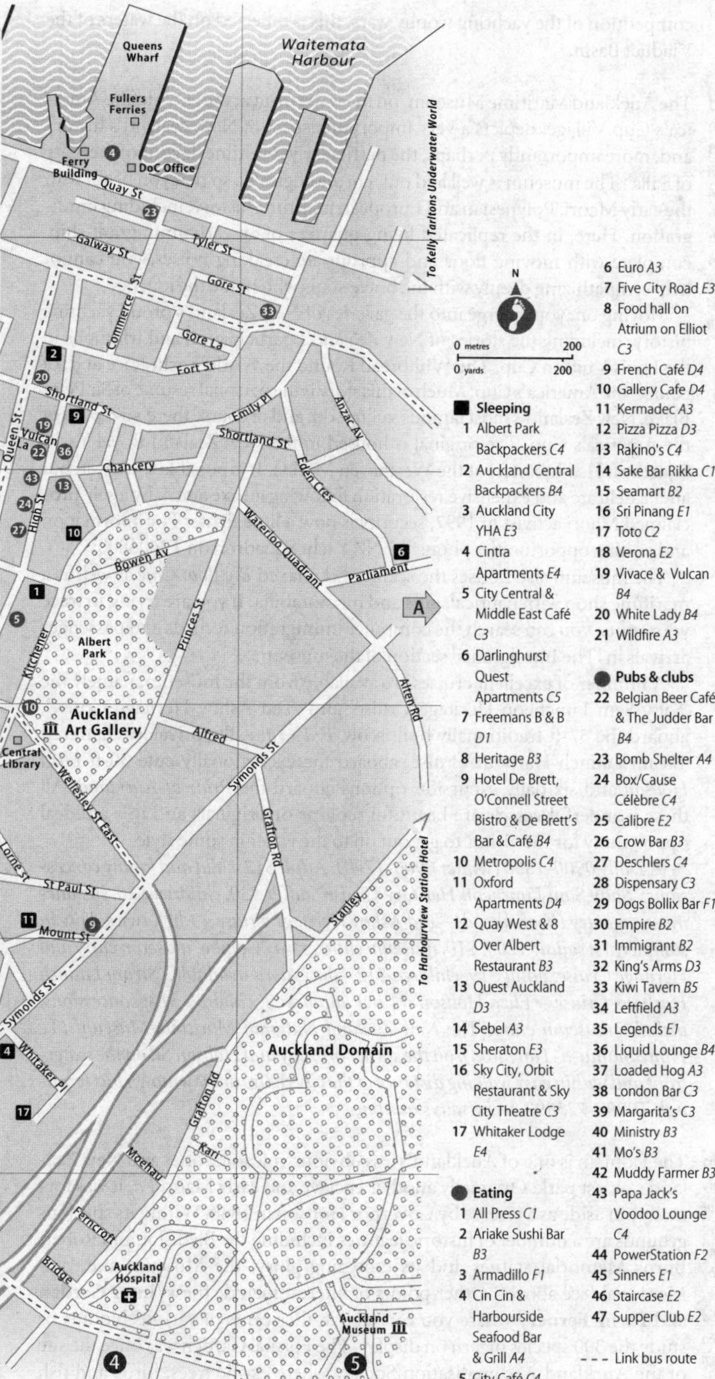
Waitemata Harbour
Queens Wharf
Fullers Ferries
Ferry Building
DoC Office
Quay St
Galway St
Tyler St
Gore St
Commerce St
Gore La
Fort St
Shortland St
Emily Pl
Anzac Av
Vulcan La
Queen St
Chancery
Eden Cres
High St
Waterloo Quadrant
Bowen Av
Parliament
Princes St
Albert Park
Kitchener
Alten Rd
Auckland Art Gallery
Central Library
Alfred
Symonds St
Wellesley St East
Grafton Rd
Lorne St
St Paul St
Mount St
Stanley
Whitaker Pl
Auckland Domain
Karl
Moehau
Ferncroft
Bridge
Auckland Hospital
Auckland Museum
To Kelly Tarltons Underwater World
To Harbourview Station Hotel
A
N
0 metres 200
0 yards 200
Sleeping
1 Albert Park Backpackers C4
2 Auckland Central Backpackers B4
3 Auckland City YHA E3
4 Cintra Apartments E4
5 City Central & Middle East Café C3
6 Darlinghurst Quest Apartments C5
7 Freemans B & B D1
8 Heritage B3
9 Hotel De Brett, O'Connell Street Bistro & De Brett's Bar & Café B4
10 Metropolis C4
11 Oxford Apartments D4
12 Quay West & 8 Over Albert Restaurant B3
13 Quest Auckland D3
14 Sebel A3
15 Sheraton E3
16 Sky City, Orbit Restaurant & Sky City Theatre C3
17 Whitaker Lodge E4
Eating
1 All Press C1
2 Ariake Sushi Bar B3
3 Armadillo F1
4 Cin Cin & Harbourside Seafood Bar & Grill A4
5 City Café C4
6 Euro A3
7 Five City Road E3
8 Food hall on Atrium on Elliot C3
9 French Café D4
10 Gallery Cafe D4
11 Kermadec A3
12 Pizza Pizza D3
13 Rakino's C4
14 Sake Bar Rikka C1
15 Seamart B2
16 Sri Pinang E1
17 Toto C2
18 Verona E2
19 Vivace & Vulcan B4
20 White Lady B4
21 Wildfire A3
Pubs & clubs
22 Belgian Beer Café & The Judder Bar B4
23 Bomb Shelter A4
24 Box/Cause Célèbre C4
25 Calibre E2
26 Crow Bar B3
27 Deschlers C4
28 Dispensary C3
29 Dogs Bollix Bar F1
30 Empire B2
31 Immigrant B2
32 King's Arms D3
33 Kiwi Tavern B5
34 Leftfield A3
35 Legends E1
36 Liquid Lounge B4
37 Loaded Hog A3
38 London Bar C3
39 Margarita's C3
40 Ministry B3
41 Mo's B3
42 Muddy Farmer B3
43 Papa Jack's Voodoo Lounge C4
44 PowerStation F2
45 Sinners E1
46 Staircase E2
47 Supper Club E2
Link bus route

Auckland

competition of the yachting trophy wars, this is reflected on the waters of the Viaduct Basin.

Auckland Maritime Museum

Even if you are an avid landlubber and have little interest in boats or sailing this is a wonderful museum and well worth a visit

The Auckland Maritime Museum, on the waterfront at the entry to the America's Cup Village, depicts a very important aspect of New Zealand's history and, more importantly perhaps, the particularly maritime flavour of the 'City of Sails'. The museum is well laid out, chronologically, so that you begin with the early Maori, Polynesian and European maritime history, including immigration. Here, in the replicated living quarters of an early immigrant ship, complete with moving floor and appropriate creaking noises, you cannot help sympathizing deeply with the brave souls who made the journey.

Moving on, you emerge into the galleries of New Zealand's proud yachting history, including the stories of New Zealand's participation and triumphs in the Louis Vuitton Cup, The Whitbread Round the World Yacht Race and, of course, the America's Cup. Much of this story is the personal resumé of Sir Peter Blake, New Zealand's most famous sailing son, and of course there's a replica of the America's Cup. The original is housed in the New Zealand Royal Yacht Squadron Headquarters at the Westhaven Marina. It is possible to view it, but after a delicate and expensive restoration following an axe attack by a self-proclaimed Maori activist in 1997, security is now a little tighter For information and visiting opportunities phone the NZ Yacht Squadron on T3606800.

The museum also houses the scenic and relaxed *Big Boat Café* as well as a maritime shop with nautical, gifts and memorabilia. If you are trying to trace your roots, you can search the computer immigration records and passenger arrivals in 'The Immigrants' section of the museum.

A number of excellent cruises are available from the museum, namely the 'Salty Sam Luncheon Heritage Cruise' and 'Ted Ashby Heritage Cruise', aboard the 57-ft traditionally built scow *Ted Ashby*, the privately chartered 'Steam Launch Harbour Cruise' aboard the exceptionally cute 30-ft *Eliza Hobson* and six daily excursion options aboard the *Pride of Auckland*. All these wonderful vessels are beautiful replicas or originals and it is an ideal opportunity for the visitor to get out on to the water in some style.

■ *Daily 0900-1800 (winter 0900-1700). Adult $12, child and family concessions. 'Salty Sam Luncheon Heritage Cruise': adult $30, children $20, includes museum entry (book ahead). 'Ted Ashby Heritage Cruise' (1 hr), twice daily in summer, 1st sailing 1200: $10, museum entry extra. 'Combo' museum entry and Heritage Cruise: adult $19, children $12, concessions available. 'Steam Launch Harbour Cruise – Eliza Hobson' (1 hr): adult $22, children $13, concessions, includes museum entry. The New Zealand National Maritime Museum (Te Huiteananui-a-Tangaroa), on the corner of Quay and Hobson St, on the waterfront and within easy walking distance of the city centre or Downtown bus terminal. T0800-725897, www.saltysam.com*

The Domain

If you get hungry during your wanderings or have forgotten a picnic then the Domain kiosk by the duck pond serves basic snacks and refreshments (open daily 1000-1500)

The Domain is one of Auckland's less obvious volcanic cones and New Zealand's oldest park. Originally another enclave and early Maori *Pa*, it was formally put aside as a reserve by Governor Hobson in 1840. Within its spacious grounds are a number of historic features including the Bledisloe and Robert Burns Memorial statues and its crowning glory, the Museum and War Memorial (see above). Other points of interest include the **Winter Garden** and **Fernz Fernery** where you can take in the scents of various blooms or study the 300 species of fern on display. The Formal Garden was once the site of the Auckland Acclimatisation Society where exotic trees, birds and fish were kept before being released to reap their havoc on indigenous species. The

The America's Cup

The America's Cup is to the world of yachting what the British Open (and the 'Claret Jug') is to golf, or the Ashes (the 'Urn') is to cricket. Although not exactly considered a mainstream spectator sport, it is a sporting prize worthy of considerable international prestige – especially in a small 'yachting-crazy' nation like New Zealand. The America's Cup, which is both the title and the prize, has been contested for over a century, usually every four years. For the first 132 years it remained in the possession of the New York Yacht Club, before an Australian challenge, led by magnate Alan Bond, took it from American leader Dennis Connor's grasp in 1983. In Australia there was of course considerable celebration, but the party was not to last. Four years later Connor first defeated the New Zealanders for the right to challenge Australia then swept Australia aside, returning the cup to the United States. The win against New Zealand was shrouded with controversy after Connor accused the New Zealanders and their team leader Sir Michael Fay of cheating. This was seen not only as an insult to Fay but to the nation as a whole. After three more unsuccessful attempts, most of which degenerated in to bitter accusations and court cases surrounding the legalities of boat specification and a personal battle between Connor and Fay, New Zealand finally took the cup and settled the score in San Diego, in 1995. It was an achievement that caught the imagination and stirred the passions of New Zealanders to a level normally only associated with the 'All Blacks' rugby team. On the day syndicate leader Peter Blake and his team returned home, over 350,000 people lined Queen Street in Auckland to welcome and applaud their heroes. Almost immediately the New Zealand syndicate started making plans for the Auckland defence of 2000, an event that would see the transformation of Auckland's Waterfront Basin to the America's Cup Village and further unprecedented spending in the city. By now the America's Cup was big business.

In February 2000 the New Zealand boat 'Black Magic' took the honours in five straight races. Auckland will stage New Zealand's defence of the cup again in 2003, but there is huge public concern that the attempt will fail, as the vast majority of the original crew have been persuaded, financially or otherwise, to race or design for foreign teams.

park also has a number of quiet inner-city bush walks, some with alluring names such as 'lovers walk', which can fool you in to the belief you are far from the city, were it not for occasional glimpse of the omnipresent Sky Tower through the branches.

■ *Domain Winter Gardens and Fernz Fernery 0900-1730, winter 0900-1630. Free. T3792020. To get there, see Auckland Museum above. The Domain is the venue for a number of major orchestral and operatic outdoor events in summer and over Christmas.*

Auckland Museum (Te Papa Whakahiku)

The museum has undergone major improvements in recent years and the result is a modern day masterpiece

The Auckland Museum, an impressive edifice that crowns the spacious surroundings of the Auckland Domain houses some wonderful treasures, displayed with flair and imagination. Its most important collection is that of Maori *Taonga* (treasures) and Pacific artefacts which, combined, is the largest such collection in the world. Other special attractions include an award-winning Children's Discovery Centre, Social and Settlement History Sections, Natural History Galleries, and 'Scars on the Heart', the story of New Zealanders at war, from the Maori Land Wars in the late 1800s, to the campaigns in Gallipoli and Crete in the two World Wars of the last century. The museum also houses a major national War Memorial and hosts the traditional dawn gathering of veterans on Remembrance (Anzac) Day on the forecourt.

If you are short of time make sure you see the **Maori Court**, a fascinating collection of pieces from woven baskets to lethal hand weapons carved from bone or greenstone, all centred round the huge 25 m Te Toki a Tipiri war canoe (*Waka*) and *Hotunui*, a beautifully carved meeting house. The authentic Maori concert held twice daily at 1100 and 1300 by the Pounamu Maori Performance Group is also worth seeing ($10 admission).

All in all, this is a must-see attraction

In the **Natural History Galleries** pay particular attention to the 'Human Impacts' section, which will give you a frightening reality check of how New Zealand has been systematically raped of the vast majority of its once huge indigenous biodiversity from the first day man set foot on the shores of this unspoilt paradise. The **Children's Discovery Centre** is a 'sensory learning feast' you, and the kids, might find it hard to drag yourself away from There are computers, games, things to jump on, look through, poke or prod;The museum café is on the ground floor, and there is a well-stocked, quality museum shop.

■ *Daily 1000-1700. $5 donation, Maori Concert $10 extra, children $5. Most city tour buses stop at the museum, as do buses 63 and 65 from the Downtown Bus Terminal. The Museum is also on the 'Coast to Coast' Walkway. T3067067, www.akmuseum.org.nz*

Auckland Art Gallery (Toi-O-Tamaki)

For other Auckland Art Galleries consult the Auckland Gallery Guide, Art Out West and Parnell Arts Trail leaflets available from main Tourist Information Offices

The Auckland Art Gallery is essentially two buildings situated in Kitchener Street and on the corner of Wellesley and Lorne Streets in the central city. They combine to form the largest and most comprehensive collection of national and international art in the country. The first building and old gallery (Kitchener Street) is over 100 years old and, although it has undergone major reconstruction and has added extensions over the years, it retains its French Renaissance revival character and charm.

The gallery spaces within its walls display exhibitions from the permanent collections. These include small collections of some of the better known international masters, particularly 17th-century pieces, but it is the New Zealand works by **Charles Goldie** and **Gottfried Lindauer** that are of particular interest. Goldie and Lindauer were two early European settlers who specialized in oil landscapes and portraits of Maori elders in the late 18th and early 19th century. The works of Goldie are impressive to say the least, with their almost Pre-Raphaelite detail bringing the portraits to life, particularly the delicate detail of the Moko, or facial Maori tattoos. However, one has to be a little wary of the romanticism of the depictions of Maori life as seen through early European eyes. Remember that they represent the warrior savages being civilized by those who think they know better.

The independent Gow Langsford Gallery just across the road from the Main Gallery is also worth a look

The New Gallery, which opened in 1995, is nearby on Wellesley Street. It houses mainly temporary exhibitions and artists' installations that explore new art, new ideas and media. The **Colin McCahon room**, which displays the works of this more contemporary and hugely respected New Zealand artist, demonstrates the often very conceptual nature of these more modern works. The installations can vary from the fascinating to the ridiculous depending on your artistic bent.

■ *Main Building: daily 1000-1700. Free guided tours at 1400 daily. Collection displays free; charge for temporary exhibitions. T3077700. New Gallery: daily 1000 –1700. Adult $4, concession $2, children free. T3074540. www.akcity.govt.nz/attractions/artgallery/ Both galleries are in close proximity and within easy walking distance from Queen St, Central City. The 'Link' bus stops right outside the gallery every 10 mins.*

Behind the Art gallery is **Albert Park**, the informal lunchtime an escape for the city suits and nearby university students. The Park was formerly another Maori *Pa* and later, during the Second World War, the site of concrete bunkers. These sites and the park as a whole have now thankfully been replaced by nicely manicured flowerbeds, statues, a floral clock and old spider-like fig trees. It is a great place to bring a sandwich, escape the noise and look up at the Sky Tower. On the park's western fringe, housed in a small cottage, is the **Bruce Wilkinson Collection** of ornate clocks and ornaments, which is worth a look if only to remind you that it is time to move on.

City North

North Shore City, or The North Shore, as it is better known, is most famous for the miles of coastline and pretty bays that fringe its quiet eastern suburbs. Many British immigrants reside north of the bridge and in summer you will find them on one of the many sheltered beaches enjoying the sun and aquatic delights they never could back home. The commercial centre of the North Shore is Takapuna, with its attractive range of modern shops, popular restaurants and bars.

North Shore Information Centre, 49 Hurstmere Rd, Takapuna, T4868670, www.nscc.govt.nz

Auckland

Ins & outs

Getting there **Car**: Devonport is 12 km from Mid City across the Harbour Bridge. Take the Takapuna off ramp, turn left on Lake Rd and just keep going.

Bus: Bus and ferry combo by *Link* buses from the DBT; T3666400.

Ferry: *Fullers Ferry* (Ferry buildings, Quay St, Auckland City, T3679111, www.fullers.co.nz), every 30 mins until 1900 weekdays, 2000 weekends and hourly after that until 2300; $7 return. The Devonport Explorer Tour is a combination of ferry, bus and walking which is personally guided and includes North Head and Mt Victoria (hourly 1000-1500,daily; $22). Tours with dinner options are also available. Information and bookings; T3576366. Devonport Ferry and Movie Package includes ferry and an evening movie at the Devonport Cinema; adult $10, children $8.

Devonport, Mount Victoria & North Head

The heart of North Shore City is in Devonport. This is the shore's oldest and most popular settlement, lying on the shores of its southernmost edge. Devonport's greatest asset is the fact it is so near yet so far from the city centre, creating a distinct village feel. It is a popular spot with both locals and visitors, and there is plenty to see and do. Only a 10-minute ferry ride from Mid City, or a 12 km drive across the Harbour Bridge takes you immediately to the heart of this historic and picturesque little suburb. Victorian villas, craft shops, sidewalk cafés and pleasant short walks all lie in wait, dominated by its two volcanoes, Mount Victoria and North Head, both of which offer great views. For a longer stay try in one of its many quaint bed and breakfast hideaways.

According to Maori tradition the great ancestral canoe, Tainui, rested here on its coastal explorations in or around the 14th century before both Mount Victoria and North Head were, not surprisingly, settled by the Maori and used as *Pa*. A village called Flagstaff on the western side of Mount Victoria was one of Auckland's earliest European settlements before land sales expanded in all directions to form eventually the suburb and naval base called Devonport, after its namesake in southwest Devon, England.

Your first stop in Devonport should be the **Visitor Information Centre** located in the shadow of the huge fig trees and pohutukawa in the **Windsor Reserve** on Victoria Road. The centre and its friendly staff will provide information on historic sights, the best short walks and places to stay. ■ *Daily 0900-1700. T4460677, visitorinfo@nthshore.govt.nz*

For Sleeping and eating in Devonport, see pages 97 and 102

If time is short your best bet is to take the short walk to **North Head** which guards the entrance to Waitamata harbour. Follow the shore east along the pohutukawa-lined King Edward Parade from which you can enjoy the view of the harbour, alive with all manner of craft, from jet-skis to huge supply ships. From there you can climb up and all around North Head and enjoy the commanding views back across the city, the North Shore suburbs and out across the Hauraki Gulf. The warren of underground tunnels and bunkers built amidst the hysteria of various potential invasions during both World Wars provide added interest.

From North Head climb down to **Cheltenham Beach**, a popular swimming and sunbathing spot in summer and one that gives the most spectacular and almost surreal view of the volcanic island of **Rangitoto**. It is a particular delight at sunrise. On your return to the village, if you have time and are feeling energetic, try to include a climb to the summit of **Mount Victoria**. Equally stunning views of the city can be had from here, and its slopes retain the remnants of the Maori *Pa*. From there you can descend to Victoria Road for a coffee, lunch or some shopping before catching a ferry back to the city.

There are three museums in Devonport. The largest, the **Naval Museum**, is really best left to those with a specific interest. ■ *Daily 1000-1630. Free. T4455186.* The more centrally located **Jackson's Museum** on Victoria Road is a better bet with its mish-mash of 'automobilia, sounds, Victoriana and collectibles'. ■ *Wed and Sun only, 1000-1600. Adult $10, children $6. T4451599.* The low-key **Devonport Museum**, at 31a Vauxhall Road in the Cambria Reserve, is relatively small but still worth a look. ■ *Weekends 1400-1600. Free. T4452661.*

The Devonport Food and Wine Festival is held every Feb and is a very light-hearted and inevitably alcoholic event with some fine New Zealand wines to be sampled

Devonport is famous for its resident artists and there are a number of quality galleries. *Art of this World*, T4460926, on the Queens Parade across the road from the Wharf, is the newest and the best but the *Flagstaff*, T4451142, and *Watercolour Galleries*, T4457545, on Victoria Road, and *Art by the Sea*, T4456665, on King Edward Parade, are all worth a look. The Devonport Arts Festival is held every March. Shopping in the village is a delight and there are a number of interesting craft shops, but you may be hard pressed to drag

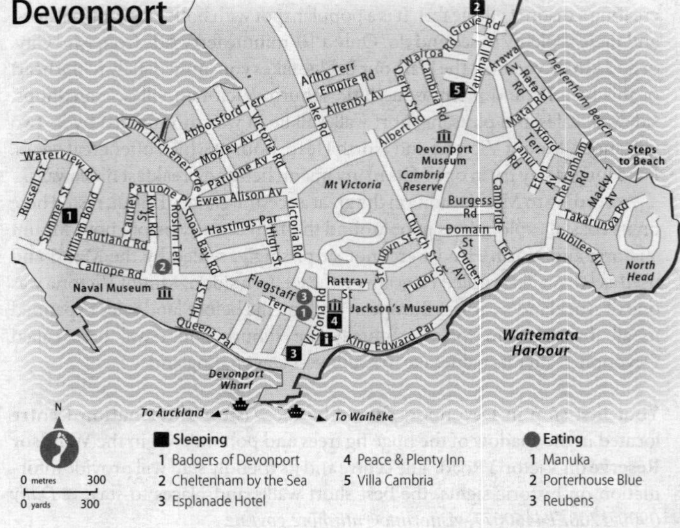

yourself away from the two excellent second-hand bookshops, *Evergreen Books* and *Baxter and Mansfield*, on Victoria Road.

City East

Kelly Tarlton's Antarctic Encounter & Underwater World

A 10-minute drive east of the city centre alongside the picturesque Tamaki Drive is Kelly Tarlton's Antarctic Encounter and Underwater World. The whole development is housed within the walls of Auckland City's old disused sewage-holding tanks beneath the car park and Tamaki Drive itself. It is a fascinating concept, and typical of the imagination, ingenuity and determination of New Zealand's most famous and best-loved diver, treasure hunter and undersea explorer, Kelly Tarlton, who was the founder and driving force behind the project. Sadly Kelly died only seven months after it opened.

The attraction is divided into two main parts. The first, **The Antarctic Encounter** (opened more recently in 1994) takes you through a range of informative displays relating the story of early Antarctic Exploration, including the triumphs and tragedies of Shackleton, Admundsen and 'Scott of the Antarctic'. Before you enter a replica of Captain Scott's 1911 hut in the Antarctic, you are primed by a weather update from the modern day base. The barely imaginable sub-zero temperatures, wind speeds and familiar words of 'snowing today' make the famous and tragic story of Scott's last expedition in 1910 all the more poignant. The replica hut itself is an impressive and faithful representation, complete with piano.

From there you board a snow cat which takes you through the equally impressive **Penguin Encounter**. A running commentary describes the huge king and smaller, more genteel geentoo penguins in their carefully maintained natural conditions. Such is the standard of the facility and the care of the birds that they breed happily and if you are lucky you will see, at close range, the huge and hilarious down-covered chicks. On the freezing snow they stand upright and dozing in their tatty attire, as if waiting in a queue for a much-needed new fur coat.

After more information about Antarctica and a 'Conservation Corridor', you enter the original **Underwater World**. This is a world-class live exhibit for which Kelly Tarlton pioneered the concept of viewing sea life through fibreglass tunnels. It is a strange mix of distance and intimacy as you walk beneath huge sting ray and sharks gliding gracefully and menacingly right above your head. Other smaller tanks contain a host of other species from beautiful seahorses to ugly moray eels and the highly poisonous scorpion fish. Open rock pools and a separate education facility provide a tremendous learning experience for kids. There is also a well-stocked shop in which to purchase a memento of your visit.

■ *Nov-Feb 0900-2200; Mar-Oct 0900-1800. Adults $22 (expensive but worth it), children free or up to $10 depending on age, family concessions available. T5280603, www.kellytarltons.co.nz There are a number of options to get to Kelly Tarlton's. The 'Explorer Bus' runs hourly from downtown Auckland, as does the Yellow Bus Company from the Downtown bus terminal every 15 mins. Fullers 'Harbour Explorer' ferry service departs from the downtown ferry terminal on Quay Street 6 times daily, package available with a return bus. Taxis cost about $10 one way. Or for the poor or energetic it is a scenic 6 km walk along the waterfront and Tamaki Drive.*

Tamaki Drive, Mission Bay & St Heliers

Bike and rollerblade hire is readily available along the route for $5 per hour

If you have not already visited Kelly Tarlton's Antartic and Underwater World then this is your chance; it's just around the corner

On a sunny afternoon, especially at the weekend, there is almost no better place to be in central Auckland than somewhere along Tamaki Drive. It is both a buzz of activity and a haven of relaxation, all along its 9 km length. Round every corner the view of Rangitoto and yachts plying the harbour predominate. You will see people who rollerblade, walk, jog and cycle in both directions, and leave the road to the vintage cars and city posers.

If you have time, take the short walk up the hill to the **M J Savage Memorial Park**, from where the view of the harbourmouth and Rangitoto is wonderful. This is a rather elegant memorial to the nation's first Labour Prime Minister. It was here, at Bastion Point, where one of the most serious recent altercations occurred between Maori and *Pakeha* in the late 1970s. The matter, as ever concerning land ownership and sale, was eventually settled after a 17-month stand-off between police and the local Nga-Whatua, whose fine *Marae* sits on the southern edge of the park. There are many fine cafés and restaurants along Tamaki, and in **Mission Bay** and **St Heliers** from which to sit back and watch the sun set before perhaps taking in a movie at the art deco Berkley Cinema in Mission Bay. **Achilles Point**, at the very end of Tamaki Drive, with its secluded beach, is a favourite spot for lovebirds and naturist bathers, and has wonderful views over the Gulf and back towards the city.

Parnell & Newmarket

Trendy Parnell, 2 km east of the city centre, was once a rather insignificant rundown suburb, but in recent years it has undergone a dramatic transformation which has seen it almost overtake Devonport and Ponsonby in the popularity and fashion stakes. It has the same village within a city feel as Devonport, with tiny brick-paved lanes and boutique style outlets, and boasts some of Auckland's finest galleries, speciality shops and restaurants.

At the top of Parnell Rise is the recently finished **Auckland Cathedral of the Holy Trinity**, whose angular structure is aesthetically interesting but nothing compared to the beautiful stained-glass windows and 29 ton organ within. Guided tours and audio-visual available, T3027203. The older **Cathedral of St Mary**, which now rests in its big sister's shadow, is one of the largest wooden churches in the world and its wonderfully peaceful interior is a delight. The stained-glass windows are beautiful, as is the entire wooden construction. There is usually a volunteer guide on hand who will proudly explain the 110 year history and show you pictures of how the grand old building was moved to its present site from across the road in 1984. *BB's Café* on the cathedral forecourt has some great food,and is an excellent place to sit and admire its unusual architecture (open daily from 0700). ■ *Both cathedrals open Mon-Fri 1000-1600 Sat, Sun 1300-1700. Free.*

Around the corner in Ayr Street you will find **Kinder House** and **Ewelme Cottage**. The former is a two-storey building built in 1856, erstwhile home of pioneer churchman and artist John Kinder. It displays the works of the artist. Ewelme Cottage was built in 1863 as the Auckland home of the family of Archdeacon Vicesimus Lush. It was altered in 1882 but has remained largely unchanged and contains a collection of colonial furniture and household effects. ■ *Kinder House open Mon-Sat 1100-1500. $1. Ewelme Cottage open Wed-Sun 1030-1200 and 1300-1630. $3.*

Back towards the harbour in Judges Bay, is the very cute **St Stephens Chapel**, one of a number of examples designed by Frederick Thatcher, the favourite architect of the former prominent missionary bishop, George Selwyn. It was one of Auckland's first churches. Although it is not generally open to the public you can have a peek in the window. Access to the park is off Gladstone and Judges Bay Roads. **Parnell Rose Gardens** nearby are a charming escape with rows of scented varieties.

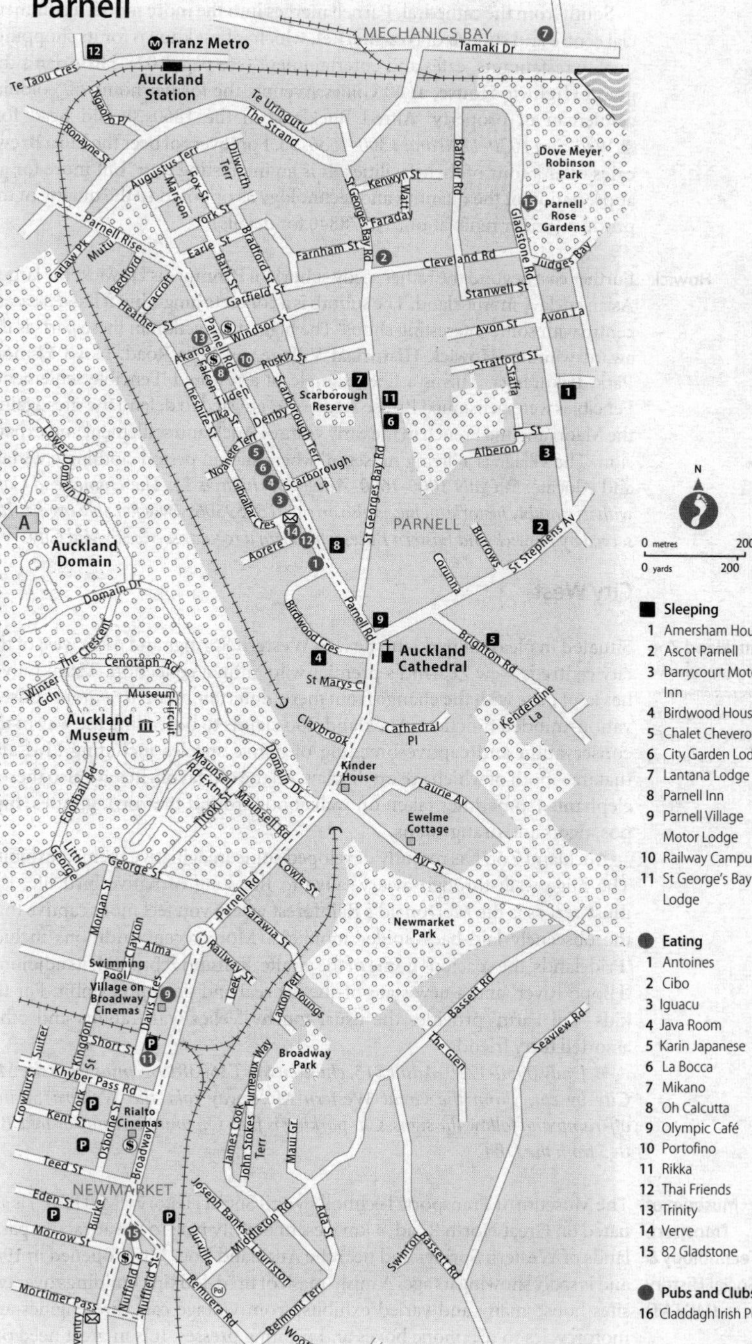
Parnell
Tranz Metro
Auckland Station
MECHANICS BAY
Tamaki Dr
Te Taou Cres
Ngaoho Pl
Ronayne St
Te Uringutu
The Strand
Augustus Terr
Dilworth Terr
Marston
Fox St
York St
Earle St
Bath St
Bradford St
Kenwyn St
Watt
Faraday
St Georges Bay Rd
Balfour Rd
Dove Meyer Robinson Park
Parnell Rose Gardens
Gladstone Rd
Judges Bay
Carlaw Pk
Parnell Rise
Mutu
Bedford
Cracroft
Heather St
Farnham St
Cleveland Rd
Garfield St
Stanwell St
Avon St
Avon La
Windsor St
Parnell Rd
Akaroa
Falcon
Ruskin St
Stratford St
Staffa
Tilden
Cheshire St
Tika St
Denby
Scarborough Reserve
Scarborough Terr
Alberon
Noahere Terr
Gibraltar Cres
Scarborough La
PARNELL
Burrows
Corunna
St Stephens Av
Aorere
Lower Domain Dr
A
Auckland Domain
Domain Dr
Birdwood Cres
Auckland Cathedral
Brighton Rd
The Crescent
Cenotaph Rd
Winter Gdn
Museum Circuit
Auckland Museum
St Marys Cl
Claybrook
Cathedral Pl
Kenderdine La
Maunsell Rd Extn
Maunsell Rd
Domain Dr
Titoki St
Kinder House
Laurie Av
Ewelme Cottage
Ayr St
Football Rd
Little George
George St
Cowie St
Morgan St
Parnell Rd
Sarawia St
Newmarket Park
Clayton
Alma
Swimming Pool/ Village on Broadway Cinemas
Davis Cres
Railway St
Leek
Laxton Terr
Youngs
Bassett Rd
Seaview Rd
Short St
Kingdon St
Suiter
Khyber Pass Rd
Broadway Park
Furneaux Way
The Glen
Crowhurst
York
Kent St
Osborne St
Rialto Cinemas
Broadway
Teed St
James Cook
John Stokes Terr
Maui Gr
NEWMARKET
Eden St
Burke
Morrow St
Joseph Banks
Middleton Rd
Ada St
Durville
Lauriston
Swinton
Bassett Rd
Nuffield La
Nuffield St
Mortimer Pass
Remuera Rd
Belmont Terr
Coventry
Wootton
Ely Av
N
0 metres 200
0 yards 200
Sleeping
1 Amersham House
2 Ascot Parnell
3 Barrycourt Motor Inn
4 Birdwood House
5 Chalet Cheveron
6 City Garden Lodge
7 Lantana Lodge
8 Parnell Inn
9 Parnell Village Motor Lodge
10 Railway Campus
11 St George's Bay Lodge
Eating
1 Antoines
2 Cibo
3 Iguacu
4 Java Room
5 Karin Japanese
6 La Bocca
7 Mikano
8 Oh Calcutta
9 Olympic Café
10 Portofino
11 Rikka
12 Thai Friends
13 Trinity
14 Verve
15 82 Gladstone
Pubs and Clubs
16 Claddagh Irish Pub
Link Bus Route

South from the cathedral, Parnell merges into the more modern commercial centre and suburb of **Newmarket**, which is best known for its shopping, quality restaurants, cafés and entertainment (see page 102). Historian's the grand **Highwic House**, at 40 Gillies Avenue, the former home of 'colonial gentleman of property' Alfred Buckland in the 1860s,should head for. ■ *Wed-Sun 1030-1200 and 1300-1630. $5.* For lovers of beer the **Lion Breweries** offer a tour of their facilities. It is an interesting tour, but more for an appreciation of the quantity and technology as opposed to the quality of the product (under renovation, T3778840 for details).

Howick Further east beyond the rather seedy suburb of Panmure is Howick, the largest Asian enclave in Auckland. The suburb is a concrete jungle but it has a pleasant centre with some interesting shops. The biggest attraction in these parts is the award-winning **Howick Historical Village**, on Bells Road, Lloyd Elsmore Park, Pakuranga. This is a fine example of a restored 'Fencible settlement'. Fencibles were pensioned British soldiers re-enlisted to defend the sites against the Maori and the French in the early years of Auckland settlement and expansion. The village is a 'living museum' where staff in period clothing entertain and educate. ■ *Daily 1000-1600. Adult $9, children $4. The Homestead Café, with its suitably historic theme, is also on site. T5769506, www.fencible.org.nz It is served by Howick and Eastern Buses which run a regular service to Mid City.*

City West

Auckland Zoo

Like most progressive, conservation-minded zoos, Auckland Zoo is worth a visit, even for the sceptics

Situated in pleasant parkland next to Western Springs and 6 km west of the city centre is New Zealand's premier wild animal collection. Thankfully it has kept pace with the change from mere 'entertainment' to a more conservation-minded function. Auckland Zoo claims to be leading the way in the conservation and captive breeding of native species including kiwi and tuatara – both of which are on display. All the old favourites are also there – elephants (sometimes taken on walkabout around the zoo), giraffes, hippos, tigers and orang-utans.

Auckland Zoo has recently developed some imaginative themed exhibits. The huge walk-through aviary, alive to the song of native bird life, is a must-see, as is the McDonald's Rainforest where you feel more captive than the obscenely laid-back spider monkeys. More recent additions include 'Pridelands' the spacious home of the giraffe, lion and zebra with its adjoining 'Hippo River' and a new state-of-the-art seal and penguin exhibit. For the kids 'Tui Farm' provides the usual touchy-feelies with rabbits and other assorted furry friends.

■ *Daily 0930-1730. Adult $13, children $7. T3603819. 5 mins from the Mid City by car. From the Great Western Motorway take the Western Springs off-ramp and follow the signs. Car parking is free. On tour bus route or take Bus 045 from the DBT.*

Museum of Transport, Technology & Social History (MOTAT) The Museum of Transport, Technology and Social History ('MOTAT') is situated on Great North Road, 4 km west of the city next to the attractive parklands of Western Springs and near the Auckland Zoo. It was opened in 1967 and is sadly showing its age. A mish-mash of tired-looking buildings over two sites house many and varied exhibits, from vintage cars, fire engines and motorcycles to telephone boxes and printing presses. It is in great need of a major revamp, but trainspotters, and those of you looking for somewhere else to take the kids on a rainy day, may find it worth a visit.

The second site, the **Sir Keith Park Memorial Site** (named after New Zealand's most famous war time aviator) concentrates on all things aviation, rail and military, including a restored flying boat and a Lancaster bomber. Both sites are connected by a working Tramline ($2 return) which passes Western Springs Park and stops at the Zoo on the way. ■ *Daily 0900 –1630. $10. T8467020, www.akcity.govt.nz/MOTAT The Colonial Arms Licensed Restaurant on site serves light lunches and cream teas. You can get to MOTAT by car via the Western Springs Motorway, taking the Western Springs turn off, or take a Yellow bus 045 from Customs St in the city; every 15 mins, 30-min journey.*

City South

Mount Eden

Mt Eden is a long walk from Mid City, and given the climb you might be better to take bus No 274 or 275 from the DBT in the CBD

At 196 m Mount Eden, the closest volcano to the city centre, provides a spectacular view and the vast, almost surreal crater gets your imagination running wild as you picture it 'going off'. Without doubt the best time to come here is at dawn, especially on misty winter mornings, when it can be a photographer's delight, and you can avoid the coach-loads of visitors. At the southern base of Mount Eden, **Eden Gardens** at 24 Omana Avenue, are a great place for lovers of all things green that grow. It is an all-seasons garden with a fine variety of flowering shrubs and New Zealand natives. ■ *Daily 0900-1630. Adult $5, children free, concessions available. T6388395. A Café (open 1000-1600) serves freshly baked delights with morning or afternoon tea.* Mount Eden village itself is worth a look, boasting a fine delicatessen, *Mount Eden Deli* (try a kumera pie), some interesting shops and a number of fine cafés and restaurants.

Cornwall Park & One Tree Hill

Just south of Mount Eden, and 5 km to the south of the Sky Tower, is Cornwall Park, a great escape from the hustle and bustle of city life, as the hordes of joggers and picnic-carrying locals will testify. It is famous not only for its crowning glory, the monument and the tree, but also the well-preserved remains of Maori *Pa* on and around the summit. Kiwi Tamaki the great chief of the Nga Marama lived here during the mid-18th century with his thousands of *whanau* (family) and followers, attracted by the rich pickings of the region's coast and its fertile soils. His claim to the region ended after being routed by sub-tribes from the north and his people being decimated by a smallpox epidemic introduced by the Europeans. Around the summit, if you look carefully, you will see the grass-covered terraces on which sat dwellings and the 'kumara pits' scattered beside them. With the land essentially vacant on the arrival of the first European settlers, it was the Scot, Logan Campell, the most powerful and well known of the new capital's residents, who eventually took ownership. Shortly before his arrival, a single Totara tree stood proudly on the summit. This had already given rise to the hill's Maori name, Te Totara-I-Ahua, meaning 'Hill of the single Totara'. This tree was rudely cut down in 1852 by early settlers and it was Campbell who planted several trees in its place, including the lonesome pine you could see until very recently. The prosperous Campbell, Mayor and 'Father of Auckland', donated his estate, now the park, to the people of New Zealand to commemorate the visit in 1901 of the heirs to the throne, the Duke and Duchess of Cornwall – hence the name.

At the base of the hill is a visitor centre housed in **Huia Lodge**, Campbell's original gatekeeper's house. Directly across the road is the simple and faithfully restored **Acacia Cottage** in which Campbell himself lived, though the building itself originally stood in the centre of the city and was relocated here in the 1920s.

One Tree Hill becomes None Tree Hill

In October 1999 Auckland lost its greatest landmark – the beautiful Monterey pine which gave its name to One Tree Hill. Both the tree and the hill have a long and controversial history. Long before the Europeans arrived One Tree Hill, or 'Maungakiekie' as the Maori then knew it, was a strategic Pa site. Much evidence still remains with clearly visible terraces and kumara (sweet potato) storage pits. Although the Ngati Whatua had all but abandoned the site by 1790, it is said that a totara tree grew upon the hill from a stick used to cut the umbilical cord of a boy named Koroki, born earlier that century. Once this tree grew, the site was known as 'Te-totara-a-ahua', or 'totara which stands alone'. Although early European documentation suggest the tree may have in fact been a pohutukawa, what is known from newspaper reports is that the remains of this lone tree were felled for firewood by a settler in 1852. The site and the tree were considered tapu (sacred) to Maori and its demise at the hands of the European was seen as an affront to their mana (integrity). In an attempt to make amends Sir John Logan Campbell, who first purchased the site from the Maori, attempted to replant native totara in 1875. In order to protect the tree from its exposed aspect he also planted Monterey pines around it. The first native tree died and another was planted to replace it in 1910. Sadly, it too died and only a few of the remaining pines took hold. In 1940 there were two pines and in 1960 only one after vandals felled the other. This remaining pine tree grew to form the famous and much loved icon. But, given the site's troubled history, it became the focus of much controversy and a target of Maori activism.

In 1994 the tree was almost completely felled by a Maori activist who cut through the main trunk with a chainsaw before being apprehended. Despite admirable attempts to save and support the tree with surgery techniques and supporting wires, its days were numbered. After yet another attack in early 1999 the damage proved terminal. In October of that same year the Auckland City Council took the controversial decision to fell the tree. The response was dramatic. Hundreds of people from all walks of life turned out on the day of its demise to say goodbye. A Maori karakia (farewell service) was held at dawn before the final felling took place. Although there is a plan to plant a native totara, further protected by a ring of pohutukawa, they will all take decades to grow. So for now the historic hill is treeless. For Aucklanders it seems the skyline may never look quite the same again. The old pine remains a much-lamented icon kept alive only in story, image and the famous U2 song. It even has its own website, www.onetreehill.co.nz

If you arrived in Auckland from the airport the chances are **One Tree Hill** (Maungakiekie) was the first New Zealand landmark that you saw. Crowning the 186-m cone of this dormant volcano was an old pine, planted by Campbell and shadowing his grave. The monument – a tribute to the relationship of Maori and *Pakeha* – has had a hard time over the years and was controversially cut down in 1999 (see previous page).

Also located within the park boundary at its southern end is the **Auckland Observatory.** This is the official home of Auckland's star gazers, and also contains the **Stardome Planetarium**, a cosmic multimedia experience played out on the ceiling for the general public. Outdoor telescope viewing sessions and special events are also held, depending on what the weather and the heavens are up to. You can even 'Adopt a Star', an interesting concept that will probably have you trying to find it again, for the rest of your life.

■ *Cornwall Park Visitors centre: 1000-1600. Free. Café and free 'points of interest' trail leaflet available. Acacia Cottage: open dawn till dusk. Free.*

Auckland Observatory: times and events vary, T6256945, www.stardome.org.nz *To get there by car: from state Highway 1 take the Greenlane off ramp, the main entrance to the park is off Green Lane West. By Bus: Nos 302,305 or 312 depart regularly from Mid City.*

Rainbow's End

Rainbow's End is situated near the main Manukau Shopping complex (the largest shopping mall in New Zealand), on the corner of Great South and Wiri Station Road, Manukau. Advertised as '23 acres of fun' it is New Zealand's largest theme park, boasting rides and attractions with such alluring and stomach-churning names as the 'Corkscrew Rollercoaster', 'Goldrush' and the mighty 'Motionmaster'. Along with these are old favourites like dodgems, go-karts, bumper boats and an interactive games arcade. Even small kids and cowardly parents are catered for in the more sedate 'Dream Castle'.

■ *Daily 1000-1700. All day unlimited rides: adult $30, children $20.* *www.rainbowsend.co.nz* *To get there by car, head south and take the Manukau off ramp from State Highway 1 and drive the ½ km to the park. By bus take either the 327,347,447,457,467,487 or 497 from the Downtown bus Terminal.*

Botanical Gardens

Keep your eyes open for some interesting native birds that reside in the gardens, including native pigeon and tui

In Manurewa, 20 minutes south of the city centre, is the Auckland Botanical Gardens. Since planting first began in 1974 an extensive 64-ha, 10,000-plant collection has sprouted, mostly of New Zealand natives. There is also an ornamental lake, a nature trail and a handsome and wonderfully fragrant display of New Zealand bred roses. The gardens also nurture an interpretative visitor centre, an outdoor café and a library. The annual Ellerslie Flower Show, which is the Southern Hemisphere's most illustrious gardening and horticultural event, was recently relocated here from the Ellerslie Showgrounds, and usually takes place during the last week of November.

■ *Gardens: daily 0800-dusk. Free. Visitors Centre: Mon-Fri 0900-1700, Sat and Sun 1000-1600. Café: 0830-1630. T3031530. To get there by car: head south, take the Manurewa off ramp from State Highway 1, turn left into Hill Rd. By bus: Stagecoach buses (Papakura, Pukekohe or Drury) leave from platform 4 at the Downtown Bus Terminal in the city centre, half-hourly weekdays, hourly at weekends. Alight in Great South Rd, Manurewa, just before Hill Rd.*

Otara Market

The southern suburbs are the poorest part part of the city. It can be dangerous, and is not a place to stray – especially at night. But it is definitely the place to experience the atmosphere of urban Maori or Pacific Island living. The Otara Market, held every Saturday morning in the Otara town centre car park, 18 km south of the city centre, is ideal for this and is thought to be the largest Maori and Polynesian market in the world. Like most street markets there is always a lot of nonsense for sale but some of the clothes, fabrics and certainly the fruit and vegetables are weird, wonderful and reasonably priced. Try some yams or taro, a type of vegetable and traditional staple diet for many native Polynesians.

■ *Every Sat 0530-1100. To get there by car, head south and take the Otara off ramp from State Highway 1. Buses 487 or 497 from the Downtown Bus Terminal (1 hr).*

Essentials

Sleeping

All the main Tourist Information Offices will help you find what you are looking for and provide a booking service (see page 77)

Auckland

As you might expect of the country's largest city and principal arrival point Auckland is not short of accommodation. Most of the major **hotels** are to be found in the city centre, particularly on the waterfront or on either side of Queen St. There are hundreds of **B&Bs** and **homestays** available, but these tend to be concentrated in the better-known suburbs like Parnell and Ponsonby. Homestays are, in effect B&Bs, but tend to involve a closer interaction with the hosts, often under the same roof, as opposed to the traditional B&Bs which tend to be self-contained premises and offer more privacy. Further afield, in the surrounding countryside, the **farmstay** is a growing sector of the accommodation market and one that is being heavily plugged by the Tourist Board. It is said to be the best way to experience real New Zealand life. If you like the sound of this option contact the New Zealand Farm Holidays Ltd, PO Box 558, Orewa, Auckland, T4265430, F4268474, farm@nzaccom.co.nz There are lots of **motels** throughout the city, mostly in the suburbs of Greenlane and in Manukau and Mangere, the latter two being near the airport. **Self-catering** can be readily found in all types of accommodation, but the city centre plays host to a number of plush apartment buildings, most at the higher range of the market. Auckland is huge when it comes to **'flatting'**, and if you are alone and intend to stay longer this is undoubtedly the best and cheapest way to go. Flats and flat shares are to be found every Sat in the *New Zealand Herald*, but start hunting early. With New Zealand being such a huge backpacker destination, there are many **hostels**, from the awful to the plush, rowdy to the sedate. They, too, are mostly to be found in the city centre or the more happening suburbs like Parnell. The popular and professional **YHA** has 2 hostels in Auckland and many more throughout the country. There aren't many **motor camps** in Auckland and most **campsites** are where they should be, amidst the beauty of the surrounding countryside parks and on the many islands of the Hauraki Gulf.

City Centre

L *Heritage Hotel*, 23 Hobson St, T3798553, F3798554, www.heritagehotels.co.nz The Heritage has more rooms than any other hotel in the country and is indeed more like a village complex than a hotel. It offers a wide range of luxury and standard en suite options, most of which have great views. The indoor and outdoor recreation areas are superb, as is Henry the Cockatoo who lives in the Foyer. Unlike the concierge, Henry welcomes visitors by biting them when they say 'who's a pretty boy then' and attempt to stroke his chin. **L** *Quay West*, 8 Albert St, T3096000, F3096150, www.mirachotels.com.au This unassuming hotel has been a big award winner since its recent opening and it is not hard to see why. The rooms are exquisite, the views even better and the Roman pool and spa is so cute you will probably spend most of your stay there. The *8 over Albert* bar and restaurant attached are also 1st class (see Eating). **L** *Metropolis*, 1 Courthouse La, T3008800, F3008899, www.somerset.com/auck.htm The new Metropolis is marketed as 'the definitive' luxury hotel in Auckland. It is an all-suite hotel, well positioned, and offers a range of rooms from the deluxe to the premiere. Rooms with a view are about $30 a night extra. All the trimmings are there and the recreation area is worth a look in itself. **L** *Sky City Hotel*, corner of Victoria St and Federal St, T9126000, F9126210, www.skycity.co.nz The obvious trump card here is the convenience, excitement and 24-hr action, with the casino next door and Sky Tower as an attic. It rates itself as a 4-5 star hotel. Special rates often apply. **L** *Sheraton Auckland*, 83 Symonds St, T3795132, F3779367, www.sheraton.com/auckland This old favourite has had to keep pace with the new hotels with a recent full refurbishment. Although the views are nothing spectacular, it is well appointed and often the venue for visiting stars. Tom Jones was here recently filling the foyer with cigar smoke and presumably his adoring fans' underwear. **L** *The Sebel*, corner of Hobson St and Customs St West, T9784000, F9784099, www.mirachotels.com.au After the Hilton, the newest hotel in Auckland's centre. It is ideally situated overlooking the Viaduct Basin so will no doubt be well booked up and pumping during the next America's Cup. It offers the same high standards of suite-style accommodation and service as its sister hotels overseas.

Accommodation price guide

LL	*Over $220*
L	*$175-$220*
AL	*$120-$175*
A	*$80-$120*
B	*$50-$80*
C	*$20-$50*
D	*Under $20*

A *Freemans B&B*, 65 Wellington St, T3765046, F3764052. Best known for its location than anything else. Within walking distance of the city centre.

B *Hotel De Brett*, 2 High St, T3772389, F3772391, www.acb.co.nz/debrett A cheaper hotel, well-sited right in the happening zone of the city centre. Art deco interior. A good range of clean and spacious rooms from single to family. Breakfast included. **B** *City Central Hotel*, corner of Wellesley St West and Albert St, T3236000, F3073388. Another cheaper option, well-placed, clean and comfortable. **B-C** *Harbourview Station Hotel*, 131 Beach Rd, T3032463, F3582489, aucklandcityhotel@extra.co.nz A grotty building but clean and comfortable accommodation at a good price.

C-D *Auckland Central Backpackers*, 9 Fort St, T3584877, www.acb.co.nz The best and busiest backpackers in the central city with simple clean accommodation, 24-hr reception, security, café, bar, internet and a travel shop attached. The travel shop staff are very knowledgeable and helpful. Always a buzz of activity. **C-D** *Albert Park Backpackers*, 27-31 Victoria St East, T3090336, F3099474. A smaller slightly quieter version of the above. **C** *Auckland City YHA*, corner of City Rd and Liverpool St, T3092802 F3735083, yhaauck@yha.org.nz One of 2 YHAs in Auckland, the other is just around the corner. Modern and clean. Good kitchen facilities, pleasant friendly atmosphere, in-house bistro.

Motels AL-A *Whitaker Lodge*, 21 Whitaker Pl, T3773623 F3773621. Despite the fact this old established motel is out of the sun and does not have very good views, it is ideally situated and offers large clean rooms, a friendly service and free car parking right in the heart of the city. Winter deals available.

City North

L-AL *Emerald Inn*, 16 The Promenade, Takapuna, T4883500, F4883555, www.emerald-inn.co.nz Wide range of options with suites, units, a cottage and villas, close to the beach and all amenities. **L** *Peace and Plenty Inn*, 6 Flagstaff Terr, Devonport, T4452925, F4452901, peaceandplenty@extra.co.nz A top B&B located on the waterfront and offering luxury accommodation and fine food.

AL *Badgers of Devonport*, 30 Summer St, Devonport, T4452099, F4450231. Fine villa accommodation with a liberal dash of antiques. Homely and friendly. **AL** *City of Sails Motel*, 219 Shakespeare Rd, Milford, T4869170, F4869179, city.of.sails@extra.co.nz New, with modern, clean rooms. Near Milford cafés and shops. **AL** *Parklane Motor Inn*, corner of Lake Rd and Rewiti Av, Takapuna, T4861069, F4862658, www.parklane.co.nz More a hotel than a motel with modern décor, spa baths available and close to the beach and Takapuna. **AL** *Villa Cambria*, 71 Vauxhall Rd, Devonport, T4457899, F4460508, www.villacambria.co.nz One of the better known and most popular B&Bs in Devonport. Victorian villa with all mod cons. Has a great self-contained 'loft'.

A *Amoritz B&B House*, 730 East Coast Rd, Browns Bay, T4796338. Budget rates, close to the beach, shops and transport. **A** *Cheltenham by the Sea*, 2 Grove Rd, Devonport, T4459437, F4459432. Contemporary and spacious, ideally situated next to Cheltenham beach. The best on the shore. **A-AL** *Esplanade Hotel*, 16 The Promenade, Devonport, T4451291, F4451999. One of Auckland's oldest hotels nicely renovated and situated right on the promenade with fine views of the bustling harbour. **A** *Poenamo Hotel*, 31 Northcote Rd, Takapuna, T4806109, F4180365. This is a traditional sports hotel and was until recent years the temporary home for the All Blacks for pre-match training in Auckland. Adequate facilities. Irish-style bar and restaurant attached. Golf course and range only a wedge away. **A** *Takapuna Homestay*, 9b Elderwood La, Takapuna, T4895420. 1 en suite and 1 family room, comfortable, quiet and friendly. **A** *Waiata Tui Lodge*, 177 Upper Harbour Dr, Greenhithe, T4139270. Situated on the outskirts of the city in 9 acres of pasture and bush. Swimming pool.

City East

LL *Amersham House*, corner of Gladstone Rd and Canterbury Pl, Parnell, T3030321, F3030621, www.amershamhouse.co.nz Luxurious and elegant with all you would expect for the price, each room wonderfully appointed with a PC to boot. Outdoor pool and spa.

L *Aachen House*, 39 Market Rd, Remuera, T5202329, F5242898, www.aachenhouse.co.nz Boutique hotel in an Edwardian mansion full of antiques. Not everyone's cup of tea, but the rooms are spacious with en suite bathroom, and the beds themselves are magnificent. **L** *St George's Bay Lodge*, 43 St George's Bay Rd, Parnell (close to Parnell Rd), T3031050, F3031055, enquiry@stgeorge.co.nz Elegant Victorian Villa situated down a quiet street and tastefully renovated and decorated.

AL *Ascot Parnell*, 36 St Stephens Av, Parnell, T3099012, F3093729, AscotParnell@compuserve.com An historic and characterful house with huge rooms. Terrific breakfast included. **AL** *Barrycourt Motor Inn*, 10-20 Gladstone Rd, Parnell, T3033789, F3773309, www.barrycourt.co.nz An ugly box of a building, but well situated in Parnell. Wide range of well-appointed rooms with fine views of the harbour. Restaurant within yards, and ample car parking. **AL** *Birdwood House*, 41 Birdwood Cres, Parnell, T3065900, F3065909, info@birdwood.co.nz Typical Parnell villa with typical Parnell interior and themed rooms. Tasteful, with Kauri staircase and open fire. Close to Parnell Rd. **AL** *Chalet Cheveron*, 14 Brighton Rd, Parnell, T3090290, F3735754, chaletchevron@extra.co.nz Charming, well-appointed rooms with nice views. Very friendly. **AL** *Seaview Heights*, 23a Glover Rd, St Heliers, T5758159, T5758155, seaview@bitz.co.nz 2 well-appointed suites with views towards the harbour and Rangitoto.

A *Parnell Inn*, 320 Parnell Rd, Parnell, T3580642, F3671032, parnelin@ihug.co.nz 16 clean and comfortable studio units, 3 with kitchenettes. Right on Parnell Rd but still quiet. Café attached. **A** *Parnell Village Motor Lodge*, 2 St Stephens Av, Parnell, T3771463, F3734192. Perfectly situated with large comfortable rooms and very friendly hosts. **A** *The Railway Campus*, 26-48 Te Taou Cres, Parnell, T3677100, F3677101, railcamp@auckland.ac.nz Primarily student accommodation, this place has been cleverly incorporated in to the old Railway Building. The entrance is very grand with its huge ceilings, marble floor, ticket office (now reception) and old clock. What used to be the platform corridors now house a café, extraordinary large and well-equipped cooking facilities and a laundry, while the old offices house the rooms, and the waiting room a study and library.

C-D *City Garden Lodge*, 25 St George's Bay Rd, Parnell, T3020880. A huge mansion of a place with wooden floors and Kauri staircase. Clean, comfortable and friendly with all the necessary facilities. Emphasis is on offering a quiet location in which to escape the city pace or recover from your arduous travels. **C-D** *Lantana Lodge*, 60 St George's Bay Rd, Parnell, T3734546. Another quiet option. Recently redecorated with various room types. Long-term storage available. Owner looks after his clients well.

City West

For accommodation further west see page 119

L ***Waitakere Park Lodge***, 573 Scenic Dr, Waitaura, T8149622, F8149921, reg@waitakereparklodge.co.nz Off the beaten track and situated in 80 acres of bush at the base of the Waitakere Ranges. Close to the vineyards and West Coast beaches. 17 accommodation suites with bush and city views. À la carte restaurant.

AL ***Great Ponsonby B&B***, 30 Ponsonby Terr, Ponsonby, T3765989, F3765527, www.dmd.co.nz/pons/, great.ponsonby@extra.co.nz One of the best B&Bs in the city, oozing quality and comfort. Close, but not too close, to Ponsonby Rd. Very friendly, helpful hosts.

A ***Abaco Spa Motel***, 59 Jervois Rd, Ponsonby, T3760119, F3787937, abacospa@extra.co.nz An old motor inn, but comfortable and conveniently situated for Ponsonby and the city centre. Within walking distance of 30 restaurants. Spa rooms available. **A** ***Colonial Cottage***, 35 Clarence St, Ponsonby, T3602820, F3603436. Olde worlde charm in an old Kauri villa. Alternative health specialists. **A** ***Unicorn Motel***, 31 Shelly Beach Rd, Herne Bay, T3762067, F3760685, unicorn.motel@pin.co.nz Fine location and recently refurbished.

C-D ***Brown Kiwi Backpackers***, 7 Prosford St, Ponsonby, T3780191, www.brownkiwi.co.nz The best and most recent Backpackers west of the city. Earning a good reputation and full of character. Close to the happening Ponsonby Rd and link bus service.

City South

L ***Central Auckland Airport***, corner of Kirkbride Rd and Ascot Rd, Mangere, T2751059, F2757884, www.centra.com.au Only 4 km to the airport, 14 km from the city. Country club style and atmosphere. Winter rates apply. **L** ***Langtons***, Haydn Av, One Tree Hill, T6257520, F6243122, thelangtons@extra.co.nz A lovely peaceful villa right next to Cornwall Park. Feels almost like the country. Swimming pool. Excellent food and wine.

A ***Bavaria Guest House***, 83 Valley Rd, Mt Eden, T6389641, F6389665, bavaria@extra.co.nz Spacious and comfortable, nice deck and garden. German spoken. **A** ***Hotel Grand Chancellor***, corner of Kirkbride Rd and Ascot Rd, Airport Oaks, T2757029, T2753322, www.grandchancellor.com A safe bet if you need to be, near the airport. All the trimmings, like pool and restaurant.

C-D ***Budget Travellers Inn***, 558 Great South Rd, Manukau, T2788947, F2784233. A highly affordable option close to the airport. Clean and friendly. **C-D** ***Oaklands Lodge***, 5a Oaklands Rd, Mt Eden, T/F6386545, info@oaklands.co.nz A budget option for those wishing to enjoy the more relaxed atmosphere of this congenial suburb.

There are a huge number of motels on **Great South Rd**. They are all very similar in style and price and include: **A** ***Ascot Motor Lodge***, T5204833, F5246680; **A** ***Greenlane Manor***, T5712167, F5712196; and **A** ***Oak Tree Lodge***, T5242211, F5249875; There are also lots of motels on **Kirkbride** and **McKenzie Rds,** in **Mangere**, near the international airport.

Self-catering

Bear in mind that many other types of accommodation (particularly B&Bs) offer self-catering. The following are at the high end of the market, come recommended, and are all located in the city centre: **L** ***Quest Auckland***, 363 Queen St, T9809200, F9809300, www.questauck@extra.co.nz; **AL** ***Oxford Apartments***, 15 Mount St, TT3674100, www.allfields.co.nz; **AL** ***Darlinghurst Quest Apartments***, 52 Eden Cres, T3663260, F3663269, www.questapartments.com.au **AL** ***Cintra Apartments***, Whitaker Pl, T3025670, T3796277.

Motor camps

All are B-D price range

North Shore Motels and Holiday Park, 52 Northcote Rd, Takapuna, T4182578, F4800435, www.nsmotels.co.nz Offers lodges, motel and cabin accommodation as well as the usual motor camp facilities. 5 mins to the beach. ***Remuera Motor Lodge and Inner City Camping Ground***, 16 Minto Rd, Remuera, T5245126, F5245639, remlodge@ihug.co.nz The only traditional-style motor camp near the city centre.

Quiet bush setting with all the usual facilities. ***Avondale Motor Park***, 46 Bollard, Av, Avondale,T8287228, F8283344, avondale@kiwicamps.co.nz 15 mins from the city centre, with all the usual facilities. ***Manukau Central Motor Camp***, 902 Great South Rd, Manukau City, T2668016, F2684209, camperak@ww.co.nz Handy for the airport and a good stopover for heading south.

Campsites *Auckland Regional Parks Campsites*, T3031530. There are 22 Regional Parks in and around Auckland and 39 basic facility vehicle and backpack campsites. From $4 per night. *DOC* also have many regional campsites and administer almost all the Hauraki Island campsites. For Information contact DOC Information Centre, T3796479.

Eating

Service is generally good and refreshingly friendly. Tipping is not essential but appreciated. BYO means bring your own bottle

When it comes to eating, Auckland is said to be on a par with New York and London. With almost 1,000 restaurants in the city it is not surprising to learn that 'dining out' is New Zealand's 3rd biggest retail spend.

When looking for a place to eat it is important, in most instances, not to try to differentiate between restaurant and café. Very often, in this part of the world, they are essentially the same thing with the latter perhaps just being a bit more casual. The cafés listed separately below are some of the traditional favourites; those particularly noted for their character, ambience and/or coffee. The central city offers waterside dining indoors and out, with spacious brasseries, intimate silver service, or romantic balconies overlooking the harbour. Elsewhere, in High St and Vulcan La, you can find a more casual setting in the many cafés that line these streets. To the west of the city centre, Ponsonby (Ponsonby Rd) has for years managed to hold on to its reputation as the culinary heart of the city, with Parnell coming a close 2nd.

City Centre

Most of the top restaurants in Auckland are now centred along the waterfront

Expensive *Euro*, Shed 22, Princes Wharf, Quay St, T3099866. Like many other waterfront restaurants, Euro is one of the new kids on the block designed to capture the America's Cup crowds, and boasts of being the best of the best. It has a very luxurious clean-feel interior with a large mesmerizing clock projected onto the wall, and offers new and imaginative cuisine in the revered Pacific Rim style. Open daily for lunch and dinner, and brunch Sat and Sun from 1030. Licensed, outdoor dining available. Almost next door is ***Wildfire***, also on Princes Wharf, Quay St, T3776869. This new addition offers amazing wood-fired pizzas and skewered meats amongst other dishes, all with a Mediterranean flavour. Open daily from 1130, licensed, outdoor dining available.

Perhaps the best restaurant in town, and arguably the best seafood venue, is ***Kermadec***, 1st Floor, Viaduct Quay Building, corner of Lower Hobson and Quay St, T3090412. Here you can tickle your tastebuds with the many delights of the Pacific Ocean as well as more traditional fare. There are 2 private rooms in a Japanese style decor that contain small ponds. Don't miss the seafood platter. Open for lunch Mon-Fri and dinner daily, licensed and BYO, private rooms available.

Staying on the waterfront there's ***Cin Cin***, Ferry Building, 99 Quay St, T3076966. It has been established as one of Auckland's top restaurants for years, but has changed hands recently. With its location right next to the ferry docks it is very much a happening place, serving Pacific cuisine to the highest standard. The service here is outstanding, as is the wine list. Licensed, outdoor dining available. Open Mon-Fri from 1100, Sat and Sun from 0930, Fri and Sat until 0300. Right above *Cin Cin* is the ***Harbourside Seafood Bar and Grill***, 1st Floor, Ferry Building, T3070556. It is advertised in all the tourist publications and seems to live up to all the praise. This is a good opportunity to try New Zealand snapper or green-lipped mussels. Open 7 days from 1130, licensed.

Five City Road, 5 City Rd, T3099273. An old favourite that has recently been given a new lease of life. It offers contemporary food, nicely cooked and presented and one of those diet-busting dessert menus. Open lunch Wed-Fri, dinner Mon-Sat, licensed, private rooms available. ***Orbit***, Sky Tower, corner Victoria St and Federal St, T9126000. Over two thirds of the way up the Sky Tower, so it has the best view of any restaurant in the city, if not the entire hemisphere. The restaurant also revolves, though sadly at a sedate speed. Although the food is not as good as the view, it is comprehensive in selection and has a good reputation. Open daily 1730-2200, Sat/Sun 1000-1200, licensed.

Mid-range *Ariake Sushi Bar*, Stamford Plaza Building, Swanson St, T3778881. Fine sushi in a well-respected establishment at affordable prices. Open lunch Mon-Fri, dinner Mon-Sun, licensed. ***The City Café***, 20 Lorne St, T3096960. A tiny restaurant that at times seems to burst at the seams due to its popularity. A fine place for a healthy substantial breakfast. Open Mon 0930-1530, Tue-Fri 0930-2300, licensed and BYO. ***8 Over Albert***, *Quay West Hotel*, 8 Albert St, T3096000. Shares the same popularity as the hotel and deservedly so, offering a fine menu of Pacific and Mediterranean dishes. The bar downstairs is also commendable. Open breakfast, lunch and dinner, Mon-Sat, breakfasts Sun, licensed.

O'Connell Street Bistro, corner of O'Connell St and Shortland St, T3771884. Another intimate, tiny venue serving fine examples of Pacific Rim. Express menu for theatregoers. Open lunch, Mon-Fri, dinner 7 nights, licensed. ***Sake Bar Rikka***, 19 Drake St, Victoria Park Market, T3778239. One of the best Japanese restaurants in town. Fine seasonal dishes in a wood-beamed warehouse, in character with the Victoria Park Market. Open lunch, Mon-Fri, dinner Mon-Sat, licensed. ***The French Café***, 210 Symonds St, T3771911. Recently revamped favourite, earning an even better reputation. Fine starters also available as main courses, and excellent fish dishes always available. Open lunch, Tue-Fri, dinner Mon-Sat, licensed. ***Toto***, 53 Nelson St, T3022665. Large, lavishly decorated Italian-style restaurant offering some of the finest Italian food in the city. Open lunch, Mon-Fri, dinner 7 nights, licensed, outdoor dining and private rooms available.

Vivace, 1st Floor, Norfolk House, corner High St and Vulcan La, T3022303. A well-known and lively favourite hidden away upstairs in Norfolk House. Fine traditional Mediterranean-style offerings. Open lunch, Mon-Fri 1200-1500, dinner Mon-Sat, licensed. ***Seamart Restaurant***, corner Fanshawe St and Market Pl, T3794928. Being attached to one of the main fresh seafood outlets in town you cannot really go wrong. Great chowder and smoked fish, but something simple and never tried before would be best for newcomers. Open lunch and dinner 7 days from 1100, licensed.

Armadillo, 531 Karangahape Rd, T3033515. Very slick interior with designer open fire. A top trendy spot for locals looking for generous servings of traditional favourites like crayfish and steak. Open 7 days from 1700, licensed. ***Vertigo***, Top Floor, Novotel Hotel, 8 Customs St, T3778920. A bit more down to earth than the *Orbit* restaurant in the Sky Tower, but still an impressive view and good modern dishes to go with it. Open daily breakfast, lunch and dinner, licensed.

Cheap *Middle East Café*, 23a Wellesley St, T3794843. This Dutch-owned and operated 'camel lovers' café offers the finest cheap meal in the city. The famous Middle East Café shwarma – a $6 lamb shwarma you drown in 2 delectable sauces – is so good it is practically impossible to eat just one. Open 1200-2100. ***Mexican Café***, 67 Victoria St West, T3732311. A favourite cheap and cheery café that has been around for years (no mean feat in Auckland), so it must be good. Open Mon-Fri 1200-1430, 1700-late, Sat/Sun 1700-late.

Pizza Pizza, 57 Lorne St, T3093333. If you're stuck with no notes, just coins, this is a good option. You can't beat that no-nonsense pizza. Open Mon-Fri 1030-2230, Sat/Sun 1630-2230. ***Food hall on Atrium on Elliot***, Elliot St. A convenient cheap multi-option venue during the day. ***White Lady***, corner Queen St and Shortland St. Open all night. Believe it or not this is a caravan that looks more like a train, which seems to appear from nowhere each night, towed by an old tractor. Within its battered walls are 2 battered-looking gentlemen, serving various battered items of food, most of which look like a serious road accident before you have even sunk your teeth in to them. But they taste amazing (as do most things at 0300). The *White Lady* is the best 'post-drink munchies' venue in the city that is open until the sun rises.

Cafés ***Vulcan***, Vulcan La, T3779899. Unpretentious old favourite. ***Verona***, 169 Karangahape Rd, T3070508. Perhaps The K'Rd's favourite café, colourful in character and clientele. ***All Press***, 192 Victoria St West, T3583121. Contemplate life and fitness over fine coffee amidst the posers from the local trendy gym. ***Gallery Café***, 1st Floor, Auckland Art Gallery, corner of Wellesley St East and Kitchener St, T3779603. A great wee café, even without all the in-house artworks. ***Rakino's***, 1st Floor, 35 High St, T3583535. Hard to find but worth it. Great coffee and traditional café fare.

Auckland

City North

Mid-range ***Manuka***, 49 Victoria Rd, Devonport, T4457732. The pick of the bunch in Devonport with its much-loved wood-fired pizzas and laid-back atmosphere. Open Mon-Fri 1100-late, Sat-Sun 0900-late, licensed. ***Reubens***, 59 Victoria Rd, Devonport, T4456911. A no-nonsense Indian takeaway, ideal if the ferry beckons. ***Porterhouse Blue***, 58 Calliope Rd, Devonport, T4450309. A well-kept secret worthy of the walk up the hill. Mainly European-style food in old-fashioned surroundings. Open dinner Mon-Sat 1800-late, licensed. ***Catalonia***, 129 Hurstmere Rd, Takapuna, T4893104. A top French restaurant that is one of the North Shore's favourites. Huge servings. Open lunch and dinner Tue-Sun, no lunch Sat, licensed. ***Killarney Street Brasserie***, 2 Killarney St, Takapuna, T4899409. Extensive menu selection with servings to match. Open Mon-Fri 1130-late, Sat-Sun 1030-late, licensed.

Cheap ***Shahi Café***, 1/1 Milford Rd, Milford, T4894798. The North Shore base for good Indian food at affordable prices. Open 7 days lunch 1200-1430, dinner, 1800-late, licensed.

City East

Expensive ***Antoines***, 333 Parnell Rd, Parnell, T3798756. Parnell's best and on a par with anything in the city. French cuisine with some firm favourites with the regulars – the duck is apparently exquisite. Very professional outfit. Open dinner Mon-Sat. Lunch Mon-Fri, licensed. ***Cibo***, 91 St George's Bay Rd, Parnell, T3092255. Fine outdoor dining, reliable in quality and service. Open for lunch Mon-Fri, dinner Mon-Sat. Licensed.

Mikano, 1 Solent St, Mechanics Bay, T3099514. A little out of the way, sited next to the helicopter base and container wharves but with a great view across the harbour and serving a very high standard of mainly Asian-inspired fare. Well worth the trip. Has maintained a good reputation for years. Open Mon-Fri 1100-late, Sat, 1700-late, Sun 0930-late, licensed. Further along Tamaki Drive is ***Hammerheads***, 19 Tamaki Dr, Orakei, T5214400. A tourist seafood favourite sited right next to Kelly Tarlton's Underwater World. A reputation for poor service, but the food makes up for it. Open 7 days 1130-2200, licensed.

Mid-range ***Iguacu***, 269 Parnell Rd, Parnell, T3584804. Parnell's most popular 'place to be seen', especially with the younger set. Not a place at night for the casually dressed or happily single female, but still immensely popular both night and day. Mainly traditional menu from snack size to feast. Top breakfast spot. Open Mon-Fri 1100-0100, Sat-Sun 1000-0100, licensed. ***Java Room***, 317 Parnell Rd, Parnell, T3661606. Fine selection of Asian and Pacific Rim cuisine at affordable prices. Open dinner Mon-Sat 1800-late, licensed and BYO. ***Karin Japanese***, 237 Parnell Rd, Parnell, T3567101.

Parnell's Japanese offering with a wide range of traditional favourites and prices. If you are a newcomer, take some advice about the options available. Open 7 days lunch 1200-1400, dinner 1800-2200. ***Oh Calcutta***, 151 Parnell Rd, Parnell, T3779090. A traditional favourite in Parnell. The Indian option and a fine and reliable one at that.

Rikka, 73 Davis Cres, Newmarket, T5225277. An offshoot of the city-centre Japanese establishment that is no less popular. Fantastic interior. The Tenshin section of the menu is more expensive but highly recommended if you are new to Japanese food. Open 7 days 1200-1500, 1800-2400, licensed. ***Bluefins***, corner of Tamaki Dr and Aitkin Av, Mission Bay, T5284551. The best choice in Mission Bay, with generous, mainly seafood dishes. Open lunch Mon-Fri. Dinner 7 nights, licensed. ***Saints***, 425 Tamaki Dr, St Heliers, T5759969. Situated at the end of the road along 'The Bays' but worth the journey. Great views and hearty traditional, Mediterranean and Asian dishes. Open lunch and dinner Mon-Fri. Dinner Sat/Sun, licensed.

Auckland

Cheap *La Bocca*, 251 Parnell Rd, Parnell, T3753260. A café with a recent and imaginative seafood adjunct. Both café and restaurant (which hopefully will soon open all year round) can boast great quality at very affordable prices. Open dinner Mon-Sat 1800-late (summer only), licensed. ***Portofino***, 156 Parnell Rd, Parnell, T3733740. Long-standing favourite, reliable and affordable, Italian style. Open lunch and dinner 7 days, licensed and BYO. ***Thai Friends***, 311 Parnell Rd, Parnell, T3735247. A friendly Thai restaurant whose menu will draw you back more than once. Open lunch Tue-Sat. Dinner 7 nights from 1800-2300, licensed and BYO. ***Verve***, 311 Parnell Rd, Parnell, T3792860. A great 'all rounder' in every way both day and night. Always busy and a top breakfast spot. Open 7 days from 0730. Dinner Tue-Sat licensed.

Olympic Café, 19 Davis Cres, Newmarket, T5248997. Well sited in busy Newmarket, the Olympic is a local favourite offering simple Mediterranean/Asian fare. Open lunch Wed-Fri (summer). Dinner 7 nights, licensed and BYO. ***White Lady***, corner of Broadway and Remuera Rd, Newmarket. The sister of the infamous *White Lady* in the city centre (see above). It has seen its fair share of loonies turning up in the wee hours trying to read the extensive menu, but the stalwart owners remain in control. Open all night. ***Venus***, 93 Upland Rd, Remuera, T5221672. A popular spot for locals and an intimate venue in the evening. Newmarket's best breakfast. Open Tue-Sat 0900-2130, Sun 0900-1500, licensed and BYO.

Cafés *82 Gladstone*, 82 Gladstone, Parnell, T3033032. A bit pricey, but well-situated next to the Rose Gardens and away from busy Parnell Rd. Very good coffee. ***Trinity***, 107 Parnell Rd, Parnell, T3003042. Prompt no nonsense service and a good hearty breakfast. Fine coffee. ***Café Jazz***, 563 Remuera Rd, Remuera, T5240356. A good place to go if you find yourself in Remuera and need a coffee or some lunch. ***Kenzie***, 17a Remuera Rd, T5222647. Good 'chill over a coffee and watch the world go by' establishment on the edge of busy Broadway.

City South

Kingsland looks set to become the 3rd 'fine dining' suburb in Auckland, after Ponsonby and Parnell

Mid-range *Sitar Indian Restaurant*, 397 Mount Eden Rd, Mt Eden, T6300321. The most popular Indian restaurant south of the city centre. Open dinner Tue-Sun 0600, licensed. ***Antiks***, 248a Dominion Rd, Mt Eden, T6386253. Offers a huge selection of mainly European dishes in a bustling, eclectic environment. Open lunch and dinner 7 days from 1100, Sun from 1030, licensed and BYO. ***Berlin Restaurant***, 423 Mount Eden Rd, Mt Eden, T6306602. Another favourite with the local residents, German food and décor. Great venison and, of course, sausages and strudel. Open dinner Mon-Sat, licensed. ***Dawsons***, 278 Dominion Rd, Mt Eden, T6389965. Good value, hearty international. Fine service. Open dinner Tue-Sat 0630-late, licensed and BYO. ***Roasted Addiqtion***, 487 New North Rd, Kingsland, T8150913. Becoming increasingly popular both for its fine coffee and highly imaginative evening menu.

Cheap *Crucial Traders*, 473 New North Rd, Kingsland, T8463288. Laid back café favourite that lures those tired of the Ponsonby scene. ***Frazers***, 434 Mount Eden Rd, Mt Eden, T6306825. A popular spot for locals, students and backpackers after a good selection of light meals and fine coffee at affordable prices.

City West **Mid-range** *Anglesea Grill*, corner of Ponsonby Rd and Anglesea St, Ponsonby, T3604551. Essentially a seafood establishment with an enthusiastic Scots chef who has applied his fine cooking skills to the fine local produce. Some argue that this is the best seafood restaurant in the city. Don't miss the yellow-finned tuna starter. Also serves good chicken and steak dishes. Open lunch Wed-Fri, dinner Mon-Sat, licensed. ***GPK***, 262 Ponsonby Rd, Ponsonby, T3601113. One of Auckland's most successful restaurants, with another branch in Mt Eden. Always busy with a lively happening atmosphere. The bar is as popular as the menu. Open Mon-Fri 1100-late, Sat/Sun 0900-late, licensed. ***Masala***, 169 Ponsonby Rd, Ponsonby, T3784500. Perhaps the best and certainly the busiest Indian restaurant on Ponsonby Rd. Good for a quick late-night supper. Good vegetarian selection. Open Mon-Fri 1200-late, Sat/Sun 1700-late, licensed and BYO.

Tuatara, 198 Ponsonby Rd, T3600098. A favourite with the trend-setters and 'Ponsobites'. Reliable eating venue and a favourite for lovers of the New Zealand sweet, pavlova. ***Kwans***, corner of St Mary's Rd and Jervois Rd, T3781776. A friendly, reliable Thai option. ***Prego***, 226 Ponsonby Rd, Ponsonby, T3763095. A big favourite with the locals who know they will get good food and good service. Italian-style menu. Great wood-fired pizza and fish. Open lunch and dinner 7 days, licensed. ***Bella***, 165 Ponsonby Rd, Ponsonby, T3602656. Good for the casual diner and outdoor eating. Great place to watch the 'Ponsobites' go by. Predominantly Mediterranean fare. Open lunch and dinner Mon-Fri. Dinner Sat/Sun, licensed. ***Musical Knives***, 272 Ponsonby Rd, Ponsonby, T3767354. So named because the chef and owner has been tour chef for a number of well known international music stars such as Madonna. Very popular for its health and figure-conscious fare, particularly organic vegetables, herbs and fruits. Open Tue-Sun from 1700-late, licensed.

Provence, 44 Ponsonby Rd, Ponsonby, T3768147. Formerly an Irish bar, this property has now taken on a French feel. The Provençale food, fine wines and pleasant decor would certainly seem to suggest it will do better than its predecessor. Open dinner Mon-Sat from 1800, licensed. ***Andiamo***, 194 Jervois Rd, Herne Bay, T3787811. Always busy, with a great all-day breakfast selection. Open Mon-Fri from 0700-late, Sat/Sun from 0800-late, licensed. ***Essence***, 70 Jervois Rd, Herne Bay, T3762049. Relatively small portions for those who love an imaginative menu with a highly artistic presentation. Good breakfast or brunch venue. Open 7 days, 1100-late, Sun brunch 0900-late, licensed.

Vinnies, 166 Jervois Rd, Herne Bay, T3765597. This is considered to be one of Auckland's finest, with such classics as Russian caviar. Professional in style, quality and presentation. Special menu is available allowing you to sample a wide variety of tastes. Very popular so book ahead. Open daily from 1830, licensed. ***The Hunting Lodge***, Waikoukou Valley Rd, Waimauku, T4118259. Plugged as Auckland's top countryside restaurant, serving traditional fare like beef and lamb and set in the heart of vineyard country. Hugely popular after a day's wine tasting. Open lunch and dinner Wed-Sun (daily in summer), licensed.

Cheap *Joy Bong*, 521 Great North Rd, Grey Lynn, T3602131. A bit out of the way but a quality, value for money Thai option. ***Lord Ponsonby's***, 267 Ponsonby Rd, Ponsonby, T3765260. A fine deli, ideal for picnic takeaways. ***Shahi Café***, 26 Jervois Rd, Ponsonby, T3788896. The 3rd *Shahi* venue and just as good as the others. Small and intimate, great for that romantic dinner. Open daily, lunch 1200-1400, dinner from 1800-late. Licensed and BYO. ***Ponsonby Fresh Fish and Chip Co***, 127 Ponsonby Rd, Ponsonby,

T3787885. Always popular and always busy. Try the local Pacific fish, you will probably be back again. Portions were large but are diminishing with time and popularity. Open daily 1100-2130.

Ponsonby Pies, 134 Ponsonby Rd, Ponsonby, T3613685. You must not leave Auckland without trying a 'Ponsonby Pie'. This is the base for an operation that

Ponsonby

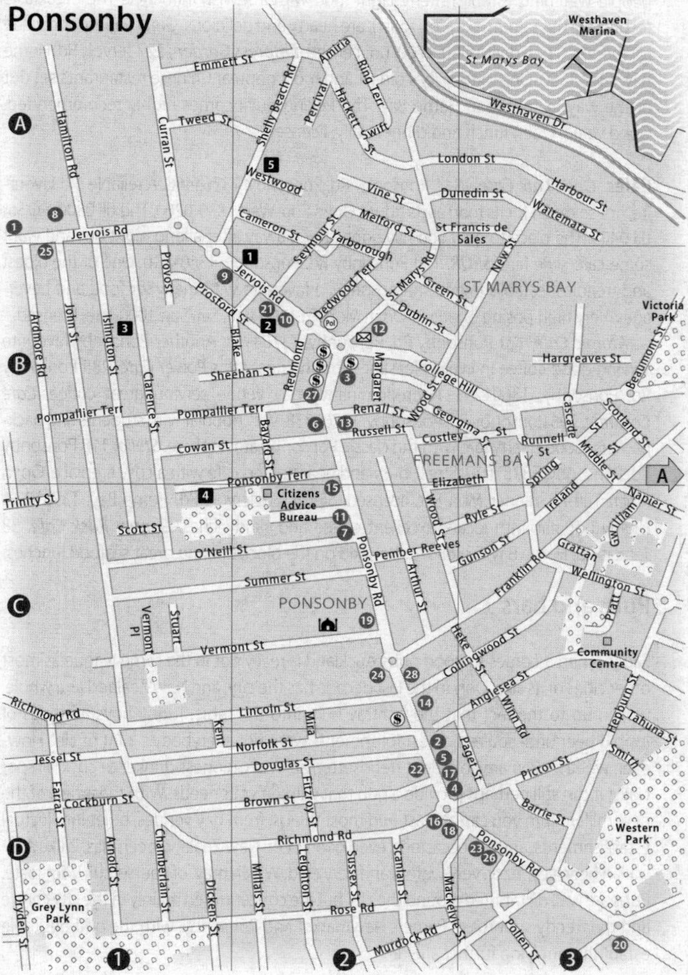

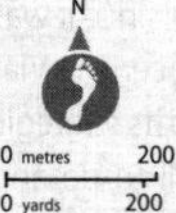

Sleeping
1 Abaco Spa Motel *B2*
2 Brown Kiwi Backpackers *B2*
3 Colonial Cottage *B1*
4 Great Ponsonby B & B *C1*
5 Unicorn Motel *A2*

Eating
1 Andiamo *A1*
2 Anglesea Grill *D2*
3 Atlas Power Café *B2*
4 Atomic Café *D2*
5 Bella *D2*
6 Café Cezanne *B2*
7 Dizengoff *C2*
8 Empress Garden *A1*
9 Essence *B1*
10 Gannet Rock Café *B2*
11 GPK *C2*
12 Kwans *B2*
13 Lord Ponsonby's *B2*
14 Masala *C2*
15 Musical Knives *C2*
16 Open Late Café *D2*
17 Ponsonby Fresh Fish & Chip Co *D2*
18 Ponsonby Pies *D2*
19 Prego *C2*
20 Provence *D3*
21 Sierra *B2*
22 SPQR *D2*
23 Stella *D3*
24 Tuatara *C2*
25 Vinnies *B1*

Pubs & clubs
26 Grand Central *D3*
27 Java Jive *B2*
28 Surrender Dorothy *C2*

Related map
***A Auckland centre**, page 82*

distributes the famous pies to food outlets city-wide. The fillings are imaginative, incredibly fresh and for about $3 you cannot go wrong. Everything from the standard steak and onion to silverbeet and cheese. Open daily 0900-1700. ***Dizengoff***, 256 Ponsonby Rd, Ponsonby, T3600108. A fine counter service operation offering takeaway or sit in items that attract a wide ranging clientele, making it another great people-watching establishment. Light food with a Jewish influence. The breakfasts (especially the salmon eggs on toast), are hearty and delicious. Great variety and value for money. Open daily 0700-1700, unlicensed. ***Empress Garden***, 227 Jervois Rd, Herne Bay, T3765550. One of the city's oldest and most popular Chinese restaurants set out of the way in suburban Herne Bay. The Peking duck comes highly recommended. Good value. Open lunch and dinner daily, licensed.

Cafés ***Open Late Café***, 134A Ponsonby Rd, Ponsonby, T3764466. A reliable old favourite, not so much for its food as its hours. Open Sun-Wed 1830-0200, Thu till 0300, Fri/Sat till 0400. The place to go if you have got carried away after a long night out and want some café-style fare. ***SPQR***, 150 Ponsonby Rd, Ponsonby, T3601710. One of the oldest and trendiest establishments in Ponsonby, a favourite with many for food and beverages. Very high posing quotient. Open Mon-Fri 1100-late, Sat/Sun 1000-late, licensed.

Atomic Café, 121 Ponsonby Rd, Ponsonby, T3764954. Another Ponsonby favourite serving good coffee in lively, pleasant surroundings. ***Atlas Power Café***, 285 Ponsonby Rd, Ponsonby, T3601295. A predominantly gay venue serving great coffee. ***Café Cezanne***, 296 Ponsonby Rd, Ponsonby, T3763338. Very popular with students and backpackers. Good hearty fare with the classic Ponsonby atmosphere. ***Stella***, 118 Ponsonby Rd, Ponsonby, T3787979. Small, busy and unassuming café with a cosy fireplace. Open lunch Tue-Fri, dinner Mon-Sat, licensed. ***Sierra***, 50 Jervois Rd, Herne Bay, T3781273. Highly popular with locals, excellent coffee and sandwiches. ***Gannet Rock Café***, 38 Jervois Rd, Herne Bay, T3768072. New kid on the block offering great seafood lunches.

Pubs and bars

Sadly, when it comes to good pubs Auckland is really not in the same league as most other cities of its size. Only in the last decade has the city, and New Zealand as a whole, woken up to the fact that the 'ashtray built into the table, rugby boys and jugs of insipid beer until you're sick' establishments were not everybody's 'pint of ale'. However, whether you are an ardent trendsetter, an avid Guinness drinker or cocktail specialist it can still perhaps provide a pub that will suit your needs. With the arrival of the new millennium you can at least find most things, from gay venues, quiet intellectual establishments, and, on occasions, even good beer. New Zealand beer, alas, is like Australian beer: very fizzy, very watery and very cold. Which may, of course, suit your taste. Pubs are well distributed around the city but are concentrated mainly in the city centre and the trendy suburbs of Parnell, Newmarket and Ponsonby, with the odd desirable establishment lying further afield.

City centre

Centred in High St and Vulcan La are a number of Auckland's top spots

The Loaded Hog, on the Viaduct Basin, T3664691, has been hugely popular since it was opened in 1993 shortly before the Whitbread Round the World Yacht Race. The Viaduct Basin, which acted as the yacht base, is right outside its doors. Due to its strategic location it has never looked back and is frequented, mainly by the well-to-do and trendy both day and night. Its huge interior and interesting agricultural and sailing theme décor is worth a look in itself. They also brew their own beer and serve good food. Nearby, ***The Muddy Farmer***, 14 Wyndham St, T3361265, is a more recent venue, similar in size and popularity and décor having that ever-popular Irish theme. The bar is great but the beer is expensive. Around the corner is ***The Empire***, corner of Nelson and Victoria Sts, T3734389. This is a fine-looking establishment that is a real party spot at weekends, offering live music at night and a fine espresso by day in its either frantic or peaceful courtyard. Check out its impressive website on www.empire.com

On the corner of Victoria St West and Hobson is the 24-hr ***Dispensary***, T3092118. Although the pub and its décor are nothing spectacular, this can be a very interesting establishment in the wee hours when all the others are shut. From about 0300 the place fills with real party animals and clocked-off bar persons, all with a story to tell. Heading back towards the waterfront and Queen St is ***Mo's***, corner of Wolfe and Federal St, T3666066. It is a tiny, very popular bar that is a fine place for conversation, as opposed to posing.

Back on the Quay, ***Leftfield*** is a new and highly trendy bar that is cold and clinically decked out. It is designed to host a weekly TV sports programme, and with the cleverly designed fold-away stands of seating can also house a big crowd while presenting live sporting events on a big screen. Definitely for the trendy or sports orientated. At the other end of the waterfront, and far more traditional, is the ***Kiwi Tavern***, 3 Britomart Pl, T3071717, an old favourite especially with backpackers. It is nicely relaxed and tries hard to push that Kiwi pub feel.

With Queen St clubs and a number of the major Backpackers nearby, the following bars all rage on well in to the night; they are also popular by day and most serve a fine lunch. The new ***Belgian Beer Café*** (ex-Occidental), 6-8 Vulcan La, T3006226, tries hard to push the Euro feel with favourable results. ***The Judder Bar***, 35 Vulcan La, T3097602, is one of a small chain with the same name that is very popular with locals and city types. Has that wine bar feel and seems to be the place to be seen. ***Deschlers***, 17 High St, is a cocktail lounge with lounge lizard music. A big favourite at the weekend with trendy young things with wandering eyes.

City East

There are a number of bars nestled in amongst the cafés and shops of the Parnell Rd, which are, along with those in Ponsonby, considered to be the trendiest drinking spots in the city. ***Iguacu***, 269 Parnell Rd, T3584804, is the old favourite and the kick-off venue for others. From there just follow the designer clothing and high heels.

In Newmarket, near Parnell, there are a number of pubs, including the old favourite, ***The Carlton***, on the corner of Khyber Pass Rd and Broadway, T5290050. Further along Broadway, at 372, is the ***Claddagh Irish Pub***, T5224410. The Claddagh is one of the best pubs in the city and is considered the new *Kitty O'Briens* (the infamous favourite near Victoria Park that shut in recent years). The much-loved Noel and Margaret, from Limerick, part-owners of *Kitty's*, went on to open the ***Claddagh*** in 1995 and the result is a wonderful homely Irish pub and a favourite haunt of Irish and Scottish visitors and immigrants. Throughout the day it is wonderfully quiet and welcoming, with its crackling open fire, but as the day progresses and the locals start to come in, it becomes busier and busier, till eventually (especially at weekends) it is jumping to the sound of Irish music late into the night. Along with the ***Northcote Tavern*** across the Harbour Bridge, the *Claddagh* pours the finest Guinness in New Zealand.

City North

The North Shore has its fair share of pubs, and there are a number of favourites that certainly deserve to lure locals and visitors across the Bridge

The Northcote Tavern at 37 Queen St, Northcote (almost immediately across the bridge), is very popular with both Kiwis and immigrants, who flood in after work before disappearing into the vast suburbs of the shore city. It has two very relaxed contrasting public and lounge bars, the latter of which supports a fine Scots theme. Great Guinness. ***R'Toto***, 134 Hurstmere Rd, Takapuna has a huge sports theme bar that fills like the pint glass at the weekends, so it must be popular. The main North Shore base for boy meets girl.

Heading North, Speakers Corner English ale House, at 7 Anzac Rd in Browns Bay, T4796060, is situated next to the beach and hugely popular for its range of fine, mainly British beers and good pub grub which is available daily from 1100. Just north of Orewa and 40 km north of the city, the ***Puhoi Hotel and Tavern***, T4220812, in the tiny settlement of Puhoi, may be well out of your range, but worth the trip. It is more an experience than a watering hole, very popular in summer and a favourite haunt of bikers on Sun afternoons. Basic, but richly decorated with an historic interior and interesting clientele.

City South *Galbraith's Ale House*, 2 Mount Eden Rd, Mt Eden, T3793557, used to be the old Grafton library and is perhaps the only notable pub south of the City Centre. Within its grand exterior a fine range of foreign and home-brewed ales are available (at slightly elevated prices) as is a fine menu. Further south of here beyond Mt Eden and into the depths of South Auckland the pubs are not generally recommended.

City West The main drinking venue west of the city centre is Ponsonby, which is very similar to Parnell. Here trendy young things parade up and down the sidewalks in and out of the many cafés and small bars which fringe them. The ***Chill Bar***, 116 Ponsonby Rd, is a local favourite and gets fairly riotous at weekends. Others escape for the more intimate surroundings of the ***Grand Central***, 126 Ponsonby Rd, and the ***Garage Bar***, 152 Ponsonby Rd, T3788237. If you are looking for another Irish pub and something different then the *Dogs Bollix*, corner of K'Rd and Newton Rd is a wonderful venue, famed not so much for its interior and its beer, but the band of the same name. A weekend night when the boys get going can be highly entertaining.

Entertainment

The after-sunset scene in Auckland is getting increasingly better and now boasts some fine venues for dancing, comedy or huge outdoor summer events in the Auckland Domain; infoline, T3671077

The Edge is a conglomerate of Auckland's main venues offering the top international performance events. It combines the ***Aotea Centre, The Civic, The Auckland Town Hall, and Aotea Square.*** For all enquires contact *The Edge*, T3075075, www.the-edge.co.nz, and ask for the regularly updated event schedule leaflets at all the main information centres. The free publication *'What's Happening'* is also a very useful guide, again available from information centres. For up to the minute information and comment tune in to *bFM's* gig guide on the radio.

Clubbing

Most venues have a cover charge of about $5, and drinks will be at least that again. Dress codes often apply

Most nightclubs in Auckland are centred in the city centre on **Queen St**, **Vulcan La**, **High St** and **Karangahape Rd** (or K' Rd – noted especially for its gay and transvestite scene). Some venues in **Ponsonby** and **Parnell**, although not considered clubs, also remain open well in to the wee hours with less emphasis on actual dancing.

Most of the clubs are open nightly, warming up towards the end of the week before going off at the weekend. Pubs vary greatly with their attempts at last orders, but generally speaking the solid drinking stops from midnight to 0300, and from then on it's clubbing till dawn.

On K' Rd although most of the clubs are essentially gay oriented they are very welcoming and popular with allcomers and can provide a very entertaining night out

The ***Staircase***, 340 K' Rd, ***Legends*** at 335 and ***Sinners*** at 373 (across the road) and ***Calibre***, basement 179, are the top spots and the dance music can be excellent. If you really want to hit the floor – on your own, or as a small group – then *Sinners* is good, especially if you go around midnight. Later on, as it gets busy, don't be surprised (or indeed offended) if a very large Pacific Island gentleman called Dina, with the most amazing scarlet number, high heels and a huge fruit filled hat, gives you a cheeky squirt with his large water pistol – it's all done in the best possible taste. Also near K' Rd, the ***Supper Club***, 2 Beresford Sq, open nightly, DJs Thu, Fri and Sat 2230-late.

If you are a true party animal head up to the Dispensary on the corner of Victoria and Hobson

For more traditional options, head down to the bottom of Queen St and join the queues outside venues in High St and Vulcan La. ***The Box/Cause Célèbre***, 35 High St, is a dual theme establishment and an old favourite. ***Cause Célèbre*** offers the quieter escape with local jazz and, at times, some talented live contemporary dance bands. Round the corner at 9 Vulcan La is ***Papa Jack's Voodoo Lounge***. It is another busy venue with a large bar playing mixed dance music and rock. ***The Liquid Lounge***, 5 O'Connell St, and the ***Red Zone*** are other popular options nearby, as is the ***Bomb Shelter***, 6-8 Commerce St, nearer the waterfront.

On the other side of Queen St, up at 26 Wyndham St, tucked downstairs, is the ***Crow Bar***. It can be excellent, but the dance floor is very small and at times it's like trying to dance in a phone box. Don't be surprised to see the odd 'All Black' wander in and out with an arrogant swagger, followed closely behind by a string of adoring and vacuous young ladies. ***The Ministry***, 17 Albert St is another trendy place, as is ***Fever***, 2/129 Hurstmere Rd, Takapuna, across the bridge, which is the North Shore City's top night spot. Back in the city centre and back towards K' Rd again is ***Margarita's*** at 18 Elliot St which has a larger dance floor and is especially popular as a venue in which to find that temporary 'mate'.

Comedy

There is a healthy comedy scene in Auckland, and stand-up New Zealand humour (on stage) can be very similar to that found in the US and Europe. Mike King, Brendon Lovegrove and the wonderfully bizarre 'Sugar and Spice' are some of the best performers. The main venues for regular comedy are the ***Classic Comedy and Bar***, 321 Queen St, T3734321, and the ***Silo Theatre***, Lower Grays Av, T3735151. See the *New Zealand Herald* for details. There is an Annual Comedy Festival held generally in late Apr at various venues throughout the city.

Cinemas

There are many cinema complexes throughout the city. New Zealand often receives films before Europe due to film distribution arrangements. For a daily guide to all venues and films consult the *New Zealand Herald* entertainment section. Admission is around $10, cheap nights are usually on a Tue. For specialist films the ***Academy***, 64 Lorne St, T3732761, is the best bet, and if you fancy a ferry journey for added entertainment there is always the ***Fullers*** *'Devonport Ferry and Movie Package'*, a dual ferry/cinema ticket for the Devonport 3 Cinema $10, T3679111. The newest movie attraction in the city is the big screen ***IMAX*** at the *Force Entertainment Centre*, 291-297 Queen St, T9792405. Films change on the hour every hour Fri and Sat 0900 –0300, Sun-Thu 0900-2400. There are also 12 cinemas in the *Force Centre*.

Theatres

The high profile theatre venues in the city are at the 700-seat ***Sky City Theatre*** in Sky City, corner of Victoria and Federal St, T9126000, www.skycity.co.nz; ***The Herald Theatre***, Aotea Square, Queen St, T3092677; and the ***Bruce Mason Theatre***, corner of Hurstmere Rd and the Promenade, Takapuna, on the North Shore, T4883133. The University's ***Maidment Theatre***, corner of Princess St and Alfred St, T3082383, and the ***Silo Theatre***, Lower Grays Av, T3735151, www.silo.co.nz, offer the more 'off the wall' performances. The Auckland Theatre Company can be contacted for further information T3090390, www.auckland-theatre.co.nz All listings again can be found in the entertainment section of the *New Zealand Herald*, particularly the weekend edition.

Gay & lesbian

The main club venues are listed above in the clubbing section. Other popular gay venues are the suggestively named ***Surrender Dorothy***, 175 Ponsonby Rd, Ponsonby, and ***The Kase***, 340 K' Rd. The Auckland gay scene is kept up to date with the *Express Magazine* ($2) which can be bought from the magazine outlets Magazzino (see Shopping, books). This publication and the local gossip can also be found in the predominantly gay cafés ***Atlas Power, Three Lamps, Ponsonby*** and ***Sublimate*** in Grey Lynn.

Music venues

The best bet for schedules is the New Zealand Herald

Auckland is well served with local, national and international gigs and venues. Most major concerts take place (usually as a one night in New Zealand affair) at the ***Aotea Centre*** and ***Western Springs*** or ***Ericsson Stadium***. Although New Zealand is isolated 'it's not unusual' to hear the Cranberries, Corrs, Moby, or to be seen throwing your knickers at Tom Jones. The main local music venues are described below.

Rock *King's Arms*, 59 France St, Newton, T3733240. ***Masonic Tavern*** (every Fri night), 27 King Edward Par, Devonport, T4450485. ***Temple Bar***, 486 Queen St, Live music nightly, T3774866. ***Devonport Bar and Brasserie*** (every Fri and Sat nights), 5 Victoria Rd, Devonport, T4453142. ***PowerStation***, 33 Mount Eden Rd, Mt Eden, T3773488.

Jazz, Rhythm and Blues *De Brett's Bar and Café* (Mon, Fri and Sat), 4 High St, T3770080. ***Iguacu*** (Sun brunch and most evenings), 269 Parnell Rd, Parnell, T3584804. ***Manifesto*** (Sun), 315 Queen St, T3034405. ***Cause Célèbre***, 33-35 High St, T3031336. ***London Bar*** (Fri and Sat), corner of Wellesley and Queen St, T3733684. ***Java Jive***, 12 Pompallier Pl, Ponsonby, T3765870. ***Grand Central***, 126 Ponsonby Rd, Ponsonby, T3601260.

General and Irish Folk/Rock *Devonport Folk Music Club* (Mon night), The Bunker, Mt Victoria, Devonport, T4452227. ***The Claddagh*** ('diddly dee' jam session Mon nights, regular bands most others), 362 Broadway, Newmarket, T5224410. ***Immigrant***, 104 Fanshawe St, T3732169. For a great night and a great band – the Dogs Bollix – do not miss Connor and the boys on a Sat and Sun – the ***Dogs Bollix Bar***, corner of K'Rd and Newton, T3764600.

Festivals

There are a number of annual events and festivals held in Auckland that are worth seeking out if your visit coincides

Jan: Last week; ***Sky City Starlight Symphony*** – a wonderful-free-open-air event held annually (sometimes with a different name) in the Auckland Domain, attracts over 300,000. Also the ***Auckland Anniversary Weekend Sailing Regatta*** held on the Waitemata Harbour.

Feb: 3rd week; ***Devonport Food and Wine Festival*** (see page 88). Also the ***Hero Parade***, a highly entertaining gay pageant held along Ponsonby Rd.

Mar: First week; ***Pacifica Festival***. New Zealand's largest Pacific culture festival with food, arts and crafts and music performances. Third week; ***National Dragon Boat Festival***, Viaduct Harbour. ***Round the Bays Fun Run***, a mainly charitable event that attracts over 7000 competitors.

Apr: ***Waiheke Jazz Festival*** (see Waiheke page 133). ***Sky Tower Vertical Challenge***. Competitors from 10 years old and up, race up and down the Sky Tower with mixed results.

Jun: ***New Zealand Boat Show***.

Jul: 1st week; ***Auckland International Film Festival***. 3rd week; ***Rally of New Zealand***. Part of the world series. 25 stages that start and finish from Auckland's mid city.

Nov: Last week; ***Ellerslie Flower Show***. The biggest horticultural event in the Southern Hemisphere, held at the Auckland Botanical Gardens.

Dec: 4th week; ***Christmas in the Park***. An equally popular and free precursor to the Symphony in the park, again held in the Auckland Domain and hugely popular. Last week; ***NZ Golf Open*** and the ***Great New Zealand Craft Show***.

Shopping

If you fancy some serious retail therapy then Auckland should not disappoint. And given the currency exchange rates, if you are coming from Europe or the US, you are in for a treat

Whether it is the bustling malls and open-air markets, high-fashion stores or historic boutiques and specialist or factory outlets, Auckland has them all. The most popular shopping spots are to be found in the central city and also Parnell and Newmarket to the east and Ponsonby to the west. But almost every major suburb has the ubiquitous mall that provides both quality and quantity. In recent years Auckland has led the way in the general expansion of opening hours throughout New Zealand. Generally you will find most major stores and malls throughout the city are open from 0900-1730 weekdays and 1000-1600 on weekends – if not longer, with some offering once weekly night shopping until 2100. The major shopping malls are the **Downtown Shopping Centre**, 11-19 Customs St, City, T3792180; **St Luke's Shopping Centre**, 80 St Luke's Rd, Mt Albert, T8462069; **Shore City Galleria**, corner of Lake Rd and Como St, Takapuna,T4864064; **West City Shopping Centre**, Catherine St, Henderson, T8362009; **The Plaza Pakuranga**, Main Highway, Pakuranga,T5720264; and the largest in New Zealand, the **Manukau Shopping Centre**, corner of Great South and Wiri Station Rd, Manukau City, T2621917.

If you are looking for products specific to New Zealand then it is a good idea to whet your appetite by visiting the **New Zealand Trade Centre**, 105 Queen St, City, T3666879. Although you cannot buy here, it will give you a great insight in to what is available. The '*Official Auckland Shopping Guide*' and individual leaflets are available from tourist information centres, and there are a few specialist shopping tours available, the best of which is '*Let's Go Shopping New Zealand*', a friendly personalized tour for $99 including coffee and lunch and a Factory Shop Tour at $40. Invaluable specialist advice is also available. T3601155, www.letsgoshopping.co.nz

Auckland

Art

There are plenty of quality art galleries in the city, and if you are serious about buying or viewing get the detailed 'Auckland Gallery Guide' from the main tourist information centres and allow a full day. Pacific and especially New Zealand art is unique, appealing and colourful – reflecting the very nature of New Zealand itself. Prices vary. The best gallery venues are Parnell (ask about the 'Parnell Arts Trail'), Devonport, Titirangi and the Central City. Some quality original artwork is also available on the 2nd floor of the Auckland International Airport at cheaper prices.

Although a good trek, the rugs of artist Kate Wells at the Breaksea Gallery,12 York Rd, Titirangi are beautiful– if quite expensive, T8179399. If you go to Titirangi check out the Lopdell House Gallery, Cnr Titirangi and South Titirangi Rds, at the same time.

Books

Auckland, like most major cities in the world, is seeing a revolution in book-selling with the smaller traditional stores being suffocated by the internationals with their huge product lines. ***Borders***, 291-297 Queen St, T3093377, arrived in 1999, and it dwarfs the largest of the more traditional stores like ***Whitcoulls***, 210 Queen St, T3565400, or ***Dymocks***, on the Atrium on Elliot, T5223343. These majors should meet all your traditional needs, with *Whitcoulls*, *Dymocks*, *Bennetts* and *London Bookshops* all having smaller outlets in most major suburbs and shopping malls. For the smaller, more personalized and sedate outlet try the ***Unity Bookshop***, 19 High St, Auckland City, T3070731.

For the specialist: ***Touchwood Books*** (horticulture) 35 High St, Auckland City, T3792733; ***The Woman's Bookshop***, 105 Ponsonby Rd, Ponsonby, T3764399; ***The Children's Bookshop***, Jervois Rd, Ponsonby, T367283; and, if you have completely blown your mind with all the shopping, head for ***Psychic Books***, 78 Felton Mathew Av, St Johns, T5283470 – apparently a haven for all your spiritual and psychic needs. The best second-hand bookshops are ***Evergreen***, T4452960, and ***Baxter and Mansfield***, T4460300 on Victoria Rd, Devonport, and the delightful rabbit warren-like interior of the *Hard to Find Bookshop* (harder to find your way out!), 171-173 The Mall, Onehunga, T6344340. For magazines the major bookstores should serve your needs or try the *Magazzino* outlets in the city, T3766933

Camping & tramping gear Although there is a good selection of camping and tramping clothes, boots and equipment to be found in Auckland and New Zealand, surprisingly there does not seem to be the range or the quality that is available in Europe or the United States. However, you will probably find all you need at ***Katmandu***, 305 Queen St, City, T3094615, and 200 Victoria St West, City, T3777560. Others include: ***Bivouac Outdoor***, 109 Queen St, City, T3661966, and 326 Broadway, Newmarket, T5292298; ***Canvas City***, Cnr Cook and Hobsons Sts, City, T3732675, and ***Living Simply***, 1st Floor, 241 Broadway, Newmarket, T5247957.

Clothing Most of the leading international brands and labels can be found in numerous outlets in the central city. Newmarket and Ponsonby are also other favourite spots. For menswear try ***George Harrison***, T3667788, ***Ermenegildo Zenga***, T3785545, and ***Saks***, T3734688, all on Queen St, and ***Barkers*** throughout the city, T5248846. For womenswear: ***Studio Works*** in Newmarket, T5290855; ***Zebrano***, T3772138; ***State of Grace*** (in the city) and numerous specialist boutiques on Ponsonby Rd. For both men's and womenswear: ***Atrium on Elliot***, ***Country Clothing*** (on Queen St), T3663940; ***Outdoor Heritage***, and ***Zambesi***, T3772220. O'Connell St in the city is also famous for its designer fashions – look out for Feline, Tanya Carlson, Karen Walker and Morrison Hotel. The best factory shops are to be found in the extensive ***Dressmart*** outlets in suburban Onehunga.

Gifts, jewellery & souvenirs

Remember, you will probably find better, cheaper souvenirs elsewhere in New Zealand

Auckland City Centre has souvenir shops everywhere packed with everything from cute furry kiwis in All Black shirts to the omnipresent bone or greenstone Maori pendants – which, traditionally you are not supposed to buy for someone else. So take your pick. Parnell and K' Rd are also recommended. But, the more discerning buyer should wait to see the smaller more provincial souvenir shops which tend to offer more specialist, unique stock. If you like the look of Kauri or other wood crafts and are heading for Northland wait and buy there, it may well be better quality and also cheaper.

Those in a rush or looking for the simple classic Kiwi Souvenirs try ***The Great New Zealand Shop***, T3773009, or ***Touch the Earth***, T3664474, both on the ground floor of the Downtown Shopping Centre, Queen St, City. Also try ***Aotea New Zealand Souvenirs***, Lower Albert St, City, T3795022, and ***NtoZ***, Victoria Park Market, Victoria Park, City, T3772447. One of the best craft shops in town is ***The Elephant House***, 237 Parnell Rd, Parnell, T3098740, and amongst the largest and the newest is ***Craftworld***, 15 mins from Mid City in West Auckland in the new Westgate Shopping Centre, Fernhill Dr, Massey.

For quality New Zealand jewellery try ***Marshals***, 93 Queen St, City, T3660807. For original knitwear – ***Great Kiwi Yarns***, 107 Queen St, T3089013, and the reasonably priced ***Breen's***, Tower Centre, 6 Customs St West, City, T3732788.

If you want a really original gift head for the United Tongan Church about 1 km down Richmond Rd, off Ponsonby Rd. On Sat mornings the original Tapa Cloths are displayed outside and are for sale. They are very reasonably priced, light and easy to pack.

Markets The most famous market in Auckland is the **Victoria Park Market** opposite Victoria Park, just a few minutes walk west of the city centre. It provides 7-days-a-week shopping with a variety of outlets from shops to stalls that expand in to the car park on Sat. There are a wide variety of products with a market theme, a number of good cafés, a food hall and a pub, all in pleasant surroundings. T3096911, www.victoria-park-market.co.nz While in the Victoria Park Market be sure to visit ***NtoZ*** for New Zealand-made crafts and souvenirs.

K'Rd (or Karangahape Rd), at the southernmost end of Queen St, is an excellent area for unusual shops, particularly Polynesian clothing and craft items. The Sat morning market on the bridge over the motorway can also produce the odd unusual bargain. If you would prefer a less commercial, raw Polynesian feel then an excursion to the Otara Market in the rather dodgy suburb of Otara in South Auckland is the best place to go (see page 95).

Photography

Film is readily available throughout the city, but for specialist film and equipment needs try ***Camera and Camera***, 162 Queen St, City,T3031879, and ***The Photo Warehouse***, 154 Queen St, City, T3090715. The best professional lab is ***PCL***, 86 Parnell Rd, Parnell, T3098090. Print film costs about $9 for 24 and slide $10-$13 for 36.

Sports

Quality sports stores can be found throughout the city and suburbs, but in this land of rugby and for that world-famous sporting souvenir – the All Blacks Jersey – head no further than ***Canterbury*** of New Zealand, corner of Queen and Customs St, City, T3794937. For all things nautical, and for the America's Cup souvenir and clothing range, try the 'in house' Maritime Museum Shop on the waterfront.

Tour operators

Auckland Central Travel, 16 Shortland St, City, open Mon-Fri 0800-1800, Sat-Sun 0800-1700, T3584874, F3584871, www.acb.co.nz New Zealand's largest domestic adventure travel shop, free information and discounted rates on rentals, rail, coaches, ferries, tours; ***STA Travel***, 10 High St, City, T3090458; ***Thomas Cook***, 159 Queen St, City, T3793924. ***Flight 2000 Cloudriders***, T2977299, F2982325, www.cloudriders.co.nz Based at Ardmore airport, 10 mins from *Manukau Cloudriders*, a company that offers tours and scenic flights of the Auckland Region on board a restored DC3.

Transport

Air

Auckland Airport Information: International, T2756467; Domestic, T2568480.

Bus (local)

Public transport generally is a major bone of contention in Auckland as traffic congestion and higher than average car ownership clogs the city's roads and pollutes the air

Most central and suburban buses stop at the Downtown Bus Terminal (DBT), centrally located opposite the wharves on Commerce St. Information can be obtained from staff at the kiosk or from all major tourist information offices and by phone, *Rideline*, T3666400.

The 'Auckland Busabout Guide', available from the Downtown Bus Terminal and all major tourist information offices, shows routes and departure points for the main city attractions. Daily unlimited passes are available on board buses for $7; 3-day passes $17.

The Double Decker 'Explorer' bus offers all day sightseeing with commentary; $20 day pass. 'City loop' provides a free service around the immediate city centre. The 'United Airlines Explorer Bus', T8366337 (24 hrs 7 days), offers a service to the 'big 14 attractions' for an all day pass of $20, or $30 for 2 days. It departs every 30 mins from the Ferry Building on Quay St. The excellent loop service 'Link' offers a flat fare of $1 to all stops and is an ideal way to get about the central city. It claims to provide a bus every 10 mins, 0600–1800 weekdays and every 20 mins evenings and weekends, but you will still feel like a sardine at rush hour. The Auckland City Loop 'Link' bus Route (goes both ways) is: Downtown-Railway-Parnell-Newmarket-Museum-Domain-hospital-University-AIT-Library-K'Rd-Ponsonby-Victoria Park-Casino-Mid Queen St-QEII Square-Downtown.

Bus (national)

Newman's (www.newmanscoach.co.nz) and ***Intercity Coach Lines*** (www.intercitycoach.co.nz) are the 2 main players providing standard coach travel from Auckland to destinations throughout New Zealand day and night. A wide range of standard and concession fares apply, all pretty reasonable. Various special passes are offered (see Essentials, page 45). For those travelling on their own, coach travel is a good option and well catered for throughout the country. All coaches arrive and depart from the Sky City Coach Terminal, 102 Hobson St, City (round the corner from the Sky Tower), T9136100, 0700-2200 Mon-Fri, 0700-2000 Sat-Sun.

Northliner Express offers a valued service to a number of North Island destinations, especially Northland. Concession fares apply. They arrive and depart from the Northliner Travel Centre, HSBC Building (opposite the Ferry Building) 172 Quay St, T3075873, www.nzinfo.com/northliner

Bicycle, scooter & motorbike
See also page 74

Outwith the central city and major suburbs cycling and motorcycle touring can be a joy. A number of cycle shops offer bikes for hire. ***Adventure Cycles***, 1 Fort La, Central Auckland, offer a great service and provide a free helmet, lock, tool kit and water bottle, plus maps and tips. Prices range from about $25 a day to $190 a month. They also offer a 50% buyback up to 6 months, which equates to the rental rate for 1 month when an inexpensive bike is purchased, and is a good deal. T0800335566, www.bikenet.co.nz ***Hedgehog Bikes*** also hire out bikes and have outlets in Takapuna and New Lynn (the latter being ideal for exploring the Waitakeres and West Coast Beaches), T4896559, inquiries@hedgehog.co.nz

For **scooters** contact *Zippy Scooter Hire*, Downtown Shopping Centre, corner of Tinley and Quay Sts, City, T08004AZIPPY. Cost from $18 a day.

There are a number of **motorcycle** rental companies in Auckland, so shop about; the most convenient is perhaps the award-winning and national ***NZ Motorcycle Rentals***, 31 Beach Rd, Downtown Auckland, T3772005. They hire out a range of bikes from the 50cc sensible sewing machines to the 1100cc scary monsters, all at reasonable rates. For the connoisseur, contact ***Shaft Motorcycles***, 234 Khyber Pass Rd, Newmarket, T3007500, shaft_motorcycles@extra.co.nz

Car
Driving in Auckland can be hazardous and rush hour is a nightmare

There are more car rental companies then you could shake a gearstick at in Auckland, ranging from fully insured, nearly new cars, to rather dodgy looking rent-a-dents. Most start at about $25 a day, are fully insured and have few hidden costs. Take time to find a good deal, depending on your requirements, through the main visitor information centres. For a cheap, no nonsense deal, try ***Dollar Save***, 200 Victoria St West, T0800486677, dollar-save@xtra.co.nz – ask about their 'City Limits Rate' at $19 per day all-inclusive. (For more car rental companies see page 115). If you are feeling extravagant, why not consider buzzing about Auckland in a limousine – after all there are over 40 operators.

Many people in for the long haul buy a good second-hand car. There is currently a glut of second-hand cars in New Zealand (since they can't really go anywhere!), especially in Auckland. Some amazing deals can be found with some careful effort. However, it always pays to have your wheels checked by the AA before purchase. They provide a mobile professional check and are usually present at most car fairs and Auctions – cost about $100 (see 'Buying a Car', on page 47).

Camper vans

With so many tourists taking to camper vans there are numerous companies offering a huge range of models and deals, especially in Auckland. Generally speaking they are not cheap and neither is petrol, but for many, travelling as couples or families, it remains the best and most economical option. The major companies are naturally the most reliable and convenient. Shop around for the best deals and, especially in the off season (Apr-Sep), try to negotiate. Prices range from backpacker models at $35 per day up to luxurious hotels on wheels that in peak season cost about $250 (see page 48).

Train
For all information: T0800-802802, www.tranzrail.co.nz

Local and intercity trains arrive and depart from behind the former and rather grandiose Railway Building on Beach St, 1 km east of the city centre, which has a small information centre, T2705143. Information can also be obtained from all local visitor information centres. Reservations and information from all mainstream travel agents. Two main lines west to Waitakere and to South Auckland serve only a few major suburbs of little interest to the tourist.

Directory

Airline offices

International *Aeorlineas Argentinas*, 15th Floor ASB Centre, 135 Albert St, T3793675. *Air New Zealand*, corner of Customs and Queen St, City, T3573363, www.airnz.co.nz *Air Pacific*, Level 12/17 Albert St, City, T3792404. *Air Vanuatu*, 2nd Floor West Plaza Building, corner of Customs and Albert St, City, T3733435. *American Airlines*, 15th Floor Jetset Centre, 48 Emily Pl, City, T3099159. *Ansett Australia*, T3796409. *British Airways*, T3568690. *Canadian Airlines*, T3090735. *Cathay Pacific*, 11th Floor, Arthur Andersen Tower, 205 Queen St, T3790861. *Garuda Indonesia*, Westpac Trust Tower, 120 Albert St, T3661862. *Japan Airlines*, Westpac Trust Tower, 120 Albert St, T3799906. *Korean Airlines*, 92 Albert St, City, T3073687. *Lufthansa Airlines*, T3031529. *Malaysia Airlines*, 12th Floor Affco House, 12-26 Swanson St, T3732741. *Polynesian Airlines*, Samoa House, 283 K' Rd, City, T3095396. *Qantas Airlines*, 191 Queen St, City, T3578900. *Singapore Airlines*, West Plaza Building, corner of Albert and Fanshawe St, City, T3032129, www.singaporeair.co.nz *Thai Airways*, 22 Fanshawe St, City, T3773886. *United Airlines*, Lumley House, 7 City Rd, City, T3081747, www.ual.com

Domestic *Air New Zealand*, corner of Customs and Queen St, City, T3573363, T0800-737000, www.airnz.co.nz *Qantas New Zealand*, 194 Broadway, Newmarket, T3022146. *Great Barrier Airlines*, Auckland International Airport (Domestic Terminal), T2566500. *Great Barrier Express*, Auckland International Airport (Domestic Terminal), T0800-222123. *Mountain Air*, T0800222123. *Helicopter Flights*, T0800206406. *Mount Cook*, T3095395.

Banks

American Express Currency Exchange: 105 Queen St, City; NZ Cup Village, Quay St, City; 67-69 Symonds St, City; 113 St Lukes Shopping Centre, Mt Albert, T0800-801122. *ANZ Banking Group*, corner of Queen and Victoria St, T3589200. *ASB Bank Ltd*, corner of Queen and Wellesley St, T3063000. *Bank of New Zealand*, 80 Queen St, T3799900. *Bank of Tokyo Ltd*, 151 Queen St, T3033554. *Hong Kong Bank*, 290 Queen St, T3670868. *National Bank of New Zealand*, 205 Queen St, T3599826. *Westpac Trust*, 79 Queen St, T3024200.

Car hire

Action Rent-a-Car, free pick up, 24-hr service, T2622279. *Affordable Rental Cars and Vans*, 12 Kenyon Av, Mt Eden, T6301567, F6303692, afford.rent@extra.co.nz *Alternative Rental Cars*, 115 Beach Rd, City, T3733822. *Apex Rental Cars*, 29 Beach Rd, City/ 30 Rennie Dr, Airport, T2570292, F3792647, free phone within NZ T0800-500660. *A2B Rentals*, 11 Stanley St, City, T0800-616888. *Avis*, 17/19 Nelson St, City, T3792650. *Big Save Car Rentals*, 39-43 The Strand, Parnell, T3033928 (free phone within NZ, T0800-422771). *Budget*, 83 Beach Rd, City, T0800652227, www.budget.co.nz *Hertz*, Airport, T2568692. *Rent a Dent*, City, T3090066. *Rent a Diesel*, 4083 Great North Rd, Kelston, T8182655. *Thrifty Car Rental*, 79 Fanshawe St, City/143 George Bolt Memorial Dr, Airport,T3660562, www.thrifty.co.nz

Campervan hire *Adventure Campervans*, 142 Robertson Rd, Mangere, T0800-844255, www.nzmotorhomes.co.nz *Backpacker/Kiwi Campa Motorhomes*, T0800-4222672, www.kiwicampa.co.nz *Britz Motorhomes*, 36 Richard Pearse Dr, Mangere, T0800-831900 *Kea Campers*. 100 Wairau Rd, Glenfield, T4444902, www.kea.co.nz *Maui Motorhomes*, Richard Pearse Dr, Mangere, T2753013, www.maui-rentals.com *Newmans Motorhomes*, T0800-808226.

Communications **Internet** *Auckland City Library*, 44-46 Lorne St, City, T3770209. ***Citinet Cyber Café***, 115 Queen St, City, T3773674. ***Click City***, 674 Dominion Rd, Balmoral, T6235001. ***Cyber City***, 29 Victoria St, City, T3033009. ***Cyber Gates***, 409 Queen St, City, T3776409. ***Cybercation Café***, 1st Floor, 241 Broadway, Newmarket, T5229790. ***Discount Dialing***, 7 Fort St, City, T3557300. ***Global Communications***, 137 K' Rd, City, T3094412. ***Login 1***, 1/12 Rialto Centre, 163 Broadway, Newmarket, T5229303. ***Net Central Internet Café***, 5 Lorne St, City, T3735186. ***Net Zone***, Shop 3/44 Queen St, City, T3093190. ***Stages Plugged In***, 62 Queen St, City, T3661917. Perhaps the best place to email is the ***Travellers Contact Point***, 87 Queen St, City, T3007197. Free coffee. **Post offices** Main post office and post restante, Wellesly St West, City. Open Mon–Thu 0900-1700, Fri 0900-1800, Sat 0900-1200, T3796714.

Disabled facilities *Auckland Disabilities Resource Centre*, 14 Erson Av, Royal Oak, T6258069, drc@disabilityresource.org.nz ***Flyability Paragliding Flights***, T4438405.

Embassies & consulates ***Australia***, 7th Floor, 132-138 Quay St, City, T3032429. ***Canada***, T3098516. ***Croatia***, 131 Lincoln Rd, Henderson, T8365581. ***Denmark***, T5373099. ***Finland***, 10 Heather St, Parnell, T3092969. ***France***, T4883453. ***Germany***, 6th Floor, 52 Symonds St, City, T9133674. ***Italy***, 102 Kitchener Rd, Milford, T4861888. ***Japan***, Level 12, ASB Bank Centre, 135 Albert St, City, T3034106. ***Korea***, 2nd Floor, 350 Queen St, City, T3790818. ***Netherlands***, LJ Hooker House, Level 1, 57 Symonds St, City, T3795399. ***Peru***, 199-209 Great North Rd, Grey Lynn, T3763047. ***Russia***, T5289237. ***Samoa***, 283 K' Rd, City, T3031012. ***Sweden***, 13th Flr, 92-96 Albert St, City, T3735332. ***UK,*** NZI House, 151 Queen St, City, T3032973. ***USA***, General Building, 4th Floor, corner of Shortland and O'Connell St, City, T3032724.

Gay & lesbian ***Gay Link travel***, 177 Parnell Rd, Parnell, T3020553, www.akltravel@gaylink.co.nz ***Pride Centre***, 33 Wyndham St, City, T3020590, F3032042. *Express Magazine* available from outlets of ***Maggazzino*** (see page 112).

Laundry *Clean Green Laundromat*, 18 Fort St. Open Mon-Sat 0900-2000, T3584370.

Left luggage *Sky City Bus Terminal*, Hobson St. Open daily 0700-2200. ***Downtown Bus Terminal***, corner of Quay and Albert St. Open Mon-Fri 0700-1900, Sat-Sun 0700-1800. ***Auckland International Airport***. Open daily 0600-2300, T2756467.

Libraries *Central City Library*, 44-46 Lorne St, City. Open Mon-Thu 0930-2000, Fri 0930-2100, Sat 1000-1600, Sun 1300-1700. T3770209.

Medical services Hospitals: ***Auckland Hospital***, Park Rd, Grafton, T3797440. ***Greenlane Hospital***, Greenlane Rd West, Greenlane, T6389909. ***Middlemore Hospital***, Hospital Rd, Otahuhu, T2760000. ***North Shore Hospital***, Shakespeare Rd, Takapuna, T4861491. ***Waitakere Hospital***, Lincoln Rd, Henderson, T8386199. **Accident and Medical Centres: *Shorecare,*** 209 Shakespeare Rd, Takapuna, T4867777. ***Westcare,*** 57-75 Lincoln Rd, Henderson, T8366000. ***White Cross Ponsonby,*** T3765555. ***White Cross St Lukes,*** 52 St Lukes Rd, St Lukes, T8153111.

Police Emergency: dial 111. Main Police Station is located at corner Cook and Vincent St, City, T3794240.

Sports **Leisure centres** *Village on Broadway Cinemas*, 77 Broadway, Newmarket, T5200806. Olympic pools and fitness centre right beside the cinema complex, T5224414.

Around Auckland

The Southern Kaipara, Helensville and Parakai

The **Kaipara Harbour** is one of the biggest natural harbours in the world, with a combined coastal length that exceeds 3200 km. It was of huge economic significance in the Kauri logging and export days of the mid to late 1800s with the ports of **Helensville** to the South and Dargaville to the North being of particular importance. Looking at Helensville today, it is hard to imagine it as a buzzing port. Sadly, these days it is a rather dull place, with little to attract the visitor except perhaps a reminder of yesteryear in the **Pioneer Museum**, on Commercial Street. ■ *Open daily, 1300-1500 or by arrangement. Free. T4207468.* Other than that most sights and activities are water-based, with a number of **fishing charters** available: *MV Joy*, T4208460, and tours that leave from Helensville to link up with others in Dargaville. **Kaipara Tours** have a great range of options, from three hours to two days; T4208466.

Nearby, **Parakai** is most famous for its hot pools at **Aquatic Park Parakai Springs**, 150 Parkhurst Road, which, after a horse trek on the beach or a 15,000-ft jump out of a plane, can be a delight. ■ *Daily 1000-2200. $9, private spa $5. T4208998.*

Sleeping & eating

A *Malolo House*, 110 Commercial Rd. Comfortable old villa-style accommodation T/F4207262, www.helensville.co.nz/malolo.htm **A** *Kaipara House B&B*, corner of SH16 and Parkhurst Rd. Offers 3 spacious rooms with thermal baths, T4207462, www.helensville.co.nz/kaipara.htm For food there is really only one place to go for a fine meal – ***Gallery 88***, 88 Commercial Rd, which is open most evenings and for lunch Wed-Sun only, T4207984.

Transport

The Yellow Bus Co run from Auckland DBT, Nos 064, 066-69, Mon-Sat only. By car go via State Highway 16 off the Great Western Motorway in the city.

Some 40 km north of the city centre (but a mere stone's throw from the northern edge of it) is the **Hibiscus Coast** – a coastline dominated by the 3 km beach adjacent to the main town, **Orewa.** Around Orewa there are the more sheltered bays of the **Whangaparaoa Peninsula** to the south and the **Wenderholm Regional Park** and **Puhoi** River to the North.

Whangaparaoa Peninsula

At the ever-expanding northern fringe of Auckland City is the Whangaparaoa Peninsula. Bar the scenery, it is essentially a rather dull enclave for the northern Auckland suburbanites. There is little on the visitor menu here except the **Whangaparaoa Steam Railway**, at 400 Whangaparaoa Road, Stanmore Bay. ■ *Open Sat-Sun, 1000-1700, T4245018. $4. www.rail.co.nz* There's also the **Gulf Harbour**, with its posh waterfront marina village and golf course (T4244735, www.gulf-harbour.co.nz). During the America's Cup it is pumping, but if you have ventured this far out and left your BMW and golf clubs at home, then you would be far better off heading for the **Shakespear Regional Park**. There, beyond Gulf Harbour, you will encounter fine views, a few walks and the occasional quiet beach. Alternatively, if your timing is right, take the Fullers ferry from the Gulf Harbour Marina to the beautiful open bird sanctuary of **Tiritiri Matangi Island** (see page 125).

Coast Dive Centre, 673 Whangaparaoa Road, offers a range of dive trips, T4248513. But if you don't want to get wet try the **Hibiscus Coast Leisure Centre**, 159 Brightside Road, Stanmore Bay, T4241914, or the **Serious Fishing Company**, 985 Whangaparaoa Road, T/F4240588.

Orewa

Although the coastal resort of Orewa is not essentially part of Auckland City it has, with the recent motorway connection and ever-encroaching housing developments, become a satellite town. But Orewa is still a staunchly independent community. It boasts a fine beach which lures the city slickers and visitors in increasingly healthy numbers in summer, but otherwise there is not a great deal on offer, except perhaps as a coffee and snack stop before heading north.

Hilary Square is the focus of the town and it boasts a statue of the great man himself. Sir Edmund Hilary is New Zealand's best-known explorer and climber, the first to conquer Mount Everest.

Sleeping If you intend to stay, the staff at the **Hibiscus Coast Information Centre** on the main drag, adjacent to the Orewa Beach Holiday Park and next door to *KFC* (open daily, T4260076, F4260086), will fill you in on what local activities are available and where best to stay. In summer you will struggle to find accommodation so book ahead.

The main luxury option in the area is within the Gulf Harbour development with the **LL** *The Gulf Harbour Lodge*, 164 Harbour Village Dr, Gulf Harbour, Whangaparaoa Peninsula, T4281118, F4281119. Cheaper weekend rates apply.

Motels dominate the northern end of Orewa and almost all of them can be found on either side of the main drag – The Hibiscus Coast Highway (HCH). **A** *Anchor Lodge Motel*, 436 HCH, T4263410. **A** *Beachcomber Motel*, 246 HCH, T4265973. **A** *Edgewater Motel*, 387 HCH, T4265260. **A** *Hibiscus Palms Motel*, 416 HCH, T4264904.

There are a number of B&Bs and Homestays in the area, including the affordable **B** *Orewa Homestay*, 54 Walton St, Red Beach, Orewa, T4266963, and the more expensive **AL** *Orewa Moontide Lodge*, 19 Ocean View Rd, Orewa, T4262374. There are 2 comfortable backpackers on offer, **C-D** *Marco Polo Tourist Lodge*, 2D Hammond Av, Hatfields Beach, Orewa, T4268455, with its palm tree painted bedroom walls, and **C-D** *Pillows Traveller's Lodge*, 412 Hibiscus Coast Highway, Orewa, T4266338.

The 2 main motor parks in Orewa are the *Orewa Beach Holiday Park*, 265 Hibiscus Coast Highway, T4265832, F4267883, and the *Puriri Park Holiday Camp*, Puriri Av, T4266396.

Eating There are numerous small cafés and takeaways in Orewa, but by far the best sit-down meal can be found at the *Walnut Cottage Restaurant* in the very congenial grounds of Orewa House, 498 Hibiscus Coast Highway. Closed Mon, BYO and licensed T4266523. The *Plantation Café*, right on the waterfront at the southern end of Orewa, T4265083, offers quality, convenience and a hearty all-day breakfast.

Transport Auckland's *Yellow Bus Company*,T3666400. Offer a regular daily service to and from Orewa and the Whangaparaoa Peninsula from Auckland; *Rideline*, T 3666400.

Orewa to Warkworth

Waiwera & Wenderholm At the northern end of Orewa you will pass the scenic **Red Beach** before winding your way to **Waiwera**, a small resort built around natural hot springs, where you can laze about in a purpose-built resort that has large pools, spas, and water slides for the kids, and even a separate covered pool where you can take in a movie – presumably to emerge afterwards looking like a walnut. **Waiwera Thermal Resort** ■ *Open Sun-Thu, 0900-2200, Fri-Sat, 0900-2230, Adult $14, Child $8, T4265369, www.waiwera.co.nz* Should you need to hang yourself out to dry overnight the **A** *Coach Trail Lodge*, T4264792, offers comfortable accommodation and is within walking distance of the hot pools.

Just 1 km north of Waiwera is **Wenderholm Regional Park**. This is one of the region's most handsome regional parks, sited on a sand spit deposited by the Puhoi River and now grassed over and dominated by beautiful large pohutukawa trees. The beach is often wild and windswept and offers a wonderful view of the small offshore islands and the mountainous Little Barrier Island to the north. The park has some excellent walking tracks ranging from 20 minutes to 2½ hours. There is a choice of coastal walks, or the more challenging headland walks, where you may see, or hear the fluid song of, the Tui and clattering wings of the Keruru or native pigeon. If history is your preference, the park's administration block is dominated by the old 1860s colonial homestead **Couldrey House.** ■ *Open Sat-Sun 1300-1600. The No 895 bus terminates here on summer Suns.*

Puhoi

Before leaving Puhoi you may ask yourself if it has the smallest library on the planet

The small and picturesque village of Puhoi is situated just off State Highway 1, 5 km north of Wenderholm. It has an intriguing history as a Catholic Bohemian settlement established in 1863. Although most of the memories are focused in the **Puhoi Historical Society Museum** in the former convent school (open December-April 1300-1600; April-December Saturday, Sunday and public holidays, 1300-1530; donation), much of the story is evident in the historic **Puhoi Tavern**. It is a fascinating little pub full of historic clutter and characters. Provided no one is playing pool you can read all about the early settlers and sympathize with their desperate cause. It is a depressing and unhappy story of a seemingly never-ending struggle with the land, of hunger and desperation. Despite the awful stories the pub is very appealing and on the second Friday of each month a local Bohemian band play their toe-tapping tunes. On a fine summer Sunday afternoon the river can be a fine place to be, as you gently wind your way downstream to Wenderholm Regional Park in a canoe. *Puhoi River Canoe Hire*, 84 Puhoi Valley Road, T4220891; $30 for the full river adventure or $15 per hour.

Waitakere City

From the centre of the city the Great Western Motorway straddles the inner inlets of the Waitemata Harbour before taking you to the western suburbs of Auckland. From these western fringes of the city the **Waitakere Ranges** rise to form a huge area of bush with an extensive network of walking tracks. These seemingly endless hills then eventually reach the sea and the **wild west coast beaches** that offer a huge contrast to the quiet Pacific beaches of the Hauraki Gulf.

West Auckland has a diverse type of suburb that makes up **Waitakere City**. Te Atatu, Swanson, Henderson, New Lynn and Glendene are relatively low-income areas of little note, except as being home to the 'Westie', a peculiar type of Aucklander who dresses predominantly in black, loves rock 'n' roll, does not believe in hair salons, and simply loves anything on wheels that goes fast, burns rubber and makes lots of noise. The Great Western Motorway pays homage to this almost nightly, with almost every dawn presenting a trail of abandoned vehicles that never made it home. Further west and south is

Titirangi where, on the slopes of the ranges around **Scenic Drive**, the more well-to-do citizens enjoy their secluded, often beautiful bush dwellings, with wonderful views across the city. Titirangi, 'the gateway to the Waitakeres', is a very pleasant little village that is worth a visit in itself, with a number of nice cafés, interesting shops and a good art gallery, *Lopdell House*, on the corner of Titirangi and South Titirangi Roads; open daily 1000-1630, free, T8178087. Over all, Waitakere City is most famous for its liberal attitudes, art, **vineyards** and orchards and its spectacularly wild unspoilt bush and beaches. It has, as a result, proclaimed itself Auckland's Eco–City with the Kumeu area being called the 'Gannet and Grape district' of the city.

The Waitakeres

The 'Waitaks', as they are affectionately known, are one of the region's biggest and most attractive regional parks, offering a 200 km network of walking tracks, many of which hide such scenic delights as large Kauri trees, waterfalls and large dams. Before embarking on any activities in the area, visit the **Arataki Information Centre** perched on the hill at the southern end of Scenic Drive, 6 km from Titirangi. It is a newly renovated centre that provides a vast amount of information, interesting interpretative displays, an audiovisual, nature trail, education centre and dominating the scene – an impressive Maori *pou* (carving), which lost its rather impressive 'manhood' a couple of years ago, though another was duly carved and the glint in his paua shell eye, restored.

Ins & outs

Getting there The Waitakeres, beyond Titirangi to the south and Swanson to the north and especially the West Coast beaches, are not at all well-served by public transport. The Tranz-Metro train does have a service from the city station to Henderson and Waitakere, and with a hire bike this could be a workable option. Other than that, organized tours and car hire are your only option.

Getting around One of the newest and most unique attractions in the area is the **Watercare Rain Forest Express**, a fascinating and fun trip on the small gauge railway train that still plies the numerous lines and tunnels to service and maintain the local dams. Regular scheduled trips Sun 1400 and 'glow-worm special' 1730 (summer only), Adult $12, Child $6, Bookings essential, T6344809. ***Bush and Beach*** is an excellent company that open's up the Waitakeres and west coast beaches to those visitors without their own transport. It offers a wide range of exciting activities and options, both half-day 1230-1700, $60, and full-day 0930-1700, $99. T0800423224, www.bushandbeach.co.nz ***Off the Beaten Track*** offers a smaller scale personalized set up, T0800356686.

Information The **Arataki Information Centre,** T3031530, is open daily 0900-1700. From here make sure you take detailed advice on all the walks in the Waitakeres that you wish to try, and buy the relevant maps. The Waitakeres have seen their fair share of lost trampers over the years. Don't forget to pick up the 'Welcome Out West', 'Art out West' 'Artists and Artisans Trail' and 'Accommodation Out West' leaflets, as well as numerous walking maps and options from the centre, all free.

Sights The 28-km **Scenic Drive** is the best way to get an immediate impression of the area as it winds along the eastern fringe of the Waitakeres, offering stunning views across the city both by day and by night. One of the best views can be seen from the garden of **Hellaby House**, just below the TV masts at its highest point, a short drive from the Arataki Information Centre. Its elderly owner, Rose, who loved the Waitakeres with a passion, donated Hellaby House to the city, and given the view from her backyard this is not surprising. The house is situated at 515 Scenic Drive. ■ *Gardens open daily 0900-1800. House open Sat, 1300-1600, Sun, 1100-1700. Free. T8149205.*

West Auckland is one of the best-known wine-producing areas of the country, containing nearly 20 wineries with such famous names as Corbans, Coopers Creek, Matua Valley, Nobilo and Babich. The northern areas of Waitakere City host most of these, especially in the Kumeu area. Most wineries offer tours and tastings. *Auckland Adventures*, offer one of the best wine tour packages available, T3794545, as do *Auckland Wine Trail Tours*, T6301540, costing $47. The wineries themselves almost all have websites, and copies of the official 'Wine Trail' and free 'Winemakers of Auckland' leaflets can be collected at the Kumeu and District Visitors Centre, Main Road, T4129886, and the main city Visitors Information Centres.

The Wild West Coast Beaches

Whatipu

If you are looking for solitude and a real sense of wilderness, without doubt one of the best places to go in the region is Whatipu. Situated 45 km from the city centre, at the southernmost tip of the Waitakere ranges, its huge expanse of sand in part forms the narrow mouth of the **Manukau Harbour**. At the terminus of the winding, unsealed road, past the picturesque little settlements of **Huia** and **Little Huia**, is a small cluster of buildings that make up *Whatipu Lodge*. The lodge is the last sign of habitation and chance of accommodation before you head north along the 6 km-long beach that stretches all the way to Karekare. If you can pull yourself away from the sound of the surf, head inland across the 700 acres of sand dune and wetland. Hidden in the undulations of dune grasses and cabbage trees are extensive wetlands that are home to noisy paradise shelduck, delicate pied stilt and elegant black swan. At the foot of the bush clad hills are the remains of the **Parahara Railway** that once hauled huge Kauri from Karekare in the 1870s. A boiler and a small tunnel still remain, even though the tracks have long been swallowed by the sand.

If you are on foot you can head north to Piha. Just before the road falls down the hill to Whatipu, take the Donald McLean Road up to the summit of **Mount Donald McLean**. The summit itself is a short 10-minute walk from the road end, and the view across the Waitakeres, the harbour and back across to the tiny Sky Tower is magnificent.

Sleeping and transport Book a cabin or a tent site at the **C-D** ***Whatipu Lodge***, T8118860, which will give you plenty of time to explore the area before heading back to the city the following day. There is no public transport out to Whatipu. Those without a car will have to hire their own, or a bike from ***Hedgehog Bikes*** in New Lynn, T4896559, inquiries@hedgehog.co.nz By bike you can take your time stopping in Titirangi village before heading out the 27 km to the point and Whatipu.

Karekare

If you want to swim at Kare Kare take great care and stay between the flags

Karekare beach is now most famous for the fact that the opening scenes of the 1993 film *The Piano* were filmed there. Like most of the West Coast beaches, the bush-clad hills of the Waitakeres fall dramatically into the sea and form a natural amphitheatre of vegetation and cliff, with the beach as its stage, the wind its song and the surf its applause.

Getting there **Bus**: There is no public transport to Kare Kare. **Car**: From the information centre at Arataki, head north along Scenic Drive before turning left down Piha Rd. 1 km before the road falls down the hill to Piha turn left down Kare Kare Rd.

For accommodation or shops you will have to head north over the hill to Piha

There are a number of short walks and tracks around Kare Kare, some of which head inland or south to join the extensive Waitakere network. For long inland excursions, make sure you carry a map and supplies. The short walk up the Taraire Track to **Karekare Falls** is worthwhile, especially if you intend to swim in the pool beneath it. Another is the **Colmans Track** from the end of Watchmans Road, where the path creeps up the hill at the northern point of Kare Kare beach and terminates with a magnificent view. Looking south you can see well past Kare Kare beach to the huge expanse of Whatipu beach beyond, as well as the tiny, inaccessible Mercer Bay, immediately below and north. If you are feeling energetic, keep going along the track which follows the coast to meet Te Ahahu Road eventually, at Piha.

Piha

Piha has been luring dreamers and surfers for years and is, along with Muriwai, one of the West Coast's most popular beaches

It is very hard to spend the day at Piha beach without contemplating packing it all in to live here. And as you climb down the windy road you will quickly realise that, for a few lucky souls, the dream has become reality. Although it can be very busy in summer – it still retains a distinctly isolated charm – perhaps due to the lack of public transport. After you are fed up sunbathing, swimming or trying to hold on to your surfboard in the fierce surf, there are two things you must do. The first and most obvious is to climb **Lion Rock** (a strenuous 30 minutes), the guardian of the beach that looks with menace out to the ocean. From the summit you can look down on the **surfers** bobbing about in search of the perfect wave. The other thing to do, especially in a wild winter storm or at sunset, is to take the **Tasman Lookout Track** at the south end of the beach to **The Gap**. Here you can sit and watch in awe at the power of the breakers as they pound and crash in to the narrow gap.

There is also an interesting, if less dramatic, walk at the northern end of Piha Beach, which leads to the isolated and beautiful **Whites Beach**. If you have time, also try to see the **Kitekite Falls** from the Kitekite Track down Glen Esk Road behind the main camping ground. If you swim at Piha you can do so in relative safety, but always stay between the flags and under the vigil of the lifesavers. Piha has been the watery grave for many shore fishermen and uninitiated swimmers. If you get into trouble, raise an arm and keep it aloft – you will be in an inflatable rescue boat before you know it.

Sleeping and eating **AL** *Piha Adventure Homestay*, 117 Piha Rd, T09-8128595, F09-8128583. Two self-contained units. Large pool and spa. **A** *Piha Cottage*, T/F09-8128514, www.bnb.co.nz A secluded self-contained cottage in quiet bush surroundings. *Piha Domain Motor Camp*, in the heart of the village, tent sites and on-site vans. Bookings advisable, T812 8815. For other local B&B options contact the Arataki Information Centre, T3031530, or consult the free 'Staying Out West' leaflet available from all TICs.

Eateries are equally scant. The *RSA*, T09-8128138, across the river from the motor camp, and the *Surf Club*, T8128896, at the southern end of the beach, offer great value meals, but you will have to ask a member to sign you in, and opening times vary. Other than that there are the usual sad-looking pies to be had at the general store near the motor camp, or burgers and the ubiquitous fish and chips at the burger bar, next to the Surf Club (summer only).

Transport There is no public transport to Piha. Piha Surf Shuttles can be of assistance, mainly for groups, T09-6267642. By car it is easily accessible from the Arataki Information Centre on Scenic Dr.

Muriwai

Muriwai, 15 km north of Piha and 45 km west of the city centre, is the West Coast's most visited beach. On summer weekends it plays host to locals and visitors alike, who nestle down in the black sands to soak up the sun, surf, fish, play, or look over the **gannet colony**. These angry looking birds have taken up residence on the flat rock outcrops at its southern end to breed, forming a small seabird city. It is a delight in spring, when you can witness at close range the stomachs of the fluffy white chicks being kept full by the comings and goings of their bad-tempered parents. Muriwai boasts the only major north island colony, after Cape Kidnappers on the East Coast, near Napier.

Muriwai itself is well serviced for locals and tourists and boasts a fine golf course (T4118454). If Muriwai beach is too busy for you then try **Maori Bay**, another favourite surf spot just south of Muriwai, reached via Waitea Road. If you find the huge stretch of beach heading north a bit daunting, a good way to venture up it and explore the surrounding bush is on horseback (*Muriwai Riding Centre*, 290 Oaia Road, T4118480; two hours will cost about $45).

Sleeping and eating There are a number of B&B's and Farmstays in Muriwai. One of the best is the **AL** *Skovholm Country Lodge*, Hinau Rd, Waimauku, T/F4118326, skovholm@yahoo.com Very comfortable and run by a very friendly Danish couple. Other more basic accommodation is available at the *Muriwai Beach Motel*, 280 Motutara Rd, T4118780, the *Muriwai Beach Motor Camp*, T4119262, or the **C-D** *Muriwai Backpackers Accommodation*, Muriwai Rd, T4118320. For B&B and Farmstay options contact the Arataki Information Centre, T3031530. The Waterfront general store serves light meals and refreshments. For a more up-market option nearby try the 'lovers loft' at the *Hunting Lodge*, Waikoukou Valley Rd, open for lunch and dinner Wed-Sun, T4118259.

Transport Helensville buses Nos 064 and 066-069 to Waimauku; from there flag down a car. By car via State Highway 16, heading north from the Great Western Motorway in the city.

South of the city

Once you leave the city southbound through the **Manukau City** and **Franklin Districts** there is little to lure the visitor off State Highway 1, which climbs over the Bombay Hills then falls to meet the Waikato River towards Hamilton. However, if you have ample time and are interested in exploring the **Franklin District**, let the folks at the **Franklin Information Centre**, Mill Road, Bombay, T2360670, tourism.franklin@extra.co.nz, persuade you to do so.

If you are heading to the Coromandel Peninsula then the best way is to follow the **Pacific Coast Highway** via **Howick** and **Whitford**. The route is generally well marked (with the Pacific Coast Highway logo) and offers a number of interesting stops on the way. Just before you hit the coast proper you pass the **Omana Regional Park**. This small park offers outstanding views of the Gulf across to Waiheke and has a pleasant beach with a rock platform that provides safe and shallow swimming at high tide and is ideal for kids. Camping available, T3031530.

Further south and inland again, is the farming town of **Clevedon**, home to Auckland's Polo Club, T2928556, who have games on Sundays in the summer. There are also a number of cafés in which to grab a cup of tea and contemplate a trip to **Montgomerie Farm**, Pioneer Road, T2928724. Here they offer a traditional farm show with a demonstration of sheep shearing, and in spring, lamb-feeding for the kids. Horse trekking is also available. South of Clevedon (but a diversion off the Pacific Coast Highway) is **Hunua,** on the edge of the **Hunua Ranges Regional Park**. These bush-clad ranges contain the watersheds for a number of dams that supply Auckland with most of its water. Although the park and the ranges are not in the same league as the Waitakeres west of Auckland, there are a number of interesting walks – the best of which is an all-day hike that takes in the Wairoa River, Cossey's Dam and the 30-m **Hunua Falls**. For information visit the **Hunua Ranges Park Visitor Centre** in Hunua, open daily 0800-1630, T3031530, or the **Clevedon Information Centre**, 9 North Road, Clevedon, T2928660.

From Miranda it is a short 35 km drive across the pancake flat Hauraki plains to Thames – the gateway to the Coromandel Peninsula

Back on the Pacific Coast Highway east of Clevedon you will hit the coast again. It is a very pleasant drive framed by pohutukawa trees and an area famous for its bird life. Christened the **Seabird Coast,** it is well worth stopping at the **Miranda Shorebird Centre**, home of the Miranda Naturalist's Trust. The Firth of Thames offers an internationally important habitat and stopover point for thousands of migrating wading birds. The 'target' birds at Miranda (for study not shooting) are the native wrybill – a strange little wader with a crooked beak designed for specialist feeding – and the rare New Zealand dotterel. Both join the near 60 other transitory species that stop over for a short time in spring and autumn to refuel for migration. The godwit, a medium-sized wader that breeds in Alaska, makes the journey to spend the Northern Hemisphere winter in New Zealand. Recent studies suggest that they do this journey non-stop, in a week! They are known to fly at a height of 4,000-6,000 m and to reach speeds of 60-70 km per hour. **The Miranda Shorebird Centre**, Pokeno, T/F2322781, open daily, 0900-1700. Just a few kilometres south of the Shorebird Centre are the **Miranda Hot Pools** and Holiday Park. The pools are open 0900-2200 all year. Adult $7, Child $4. Private spas are also available. Temperatures up to 40C. T0800-468777.

Sleeping **L** *The Inverness Estate*, Ness Valley Rd, Clevedon, T2928710, wwwinverness@extra.co.nz Luxury accommodation in a country setting with fine food and their own estate wine. **A** *Miranda B&B*, Findlay Rd, Miranda, T2327735. Country home in a garden setting. Dinner on request. **A** *The Miranda Holiday Park*, 595 Front Miranda Rd, T/F8673205, mirandaholidaypark@extra.co.nz A fine holiday park with wonderful facilities including their own hot pools. The **C-D** *Miranda Shorebird Centre* offers a fine roost if you are looking for accommodation in the area. Bunk, single/double room and self-contained accommodation is available from $10 to $35. Great value.

Eating The *Kaiaua Fishery fish and chip shop* in Kaiaua, north of Miranda, has a great reputation, T2322779, and the *Bay View Hotel*, Kaiaua, T2322717, offers takeaways and snacks as well as a restaurant serving mainly seafood. Open 7 days, Sun from 1700.

Hauraki islands

Rangitoto Island

Rangitoto seems to dominate your views of the Hauraki Gulf from almost every vantage point in the city, so it is only a matter of time before its classically shaped cone lures you across the water to take a closer look. Rangitoto first emerged from the sea in a series of eruptions about 600 years ago. When, Maori were known to be inhabiting the area.

One Maori myth suggests that the eruption occured after a casual dispute between the gods of fire and volcanoes, but many years later, science put it all down to being the latest of the many eruptions to take place in the area over the millennia. It is only a 30-minute journey by ferry to take a closer look, and to enjoy one of the island's many walks.

Most of these walks culminate at the summit from where there is a 360° view of the gulf and the city and you can peer down into its bush-clad crater. The vegetation of the island is of international importance with the recent botanical blanket boasting 200 species of native tree (the most prolific and famous being its pohutukawa) and flowering plants, 40 kinds of fern, some orchids and, of course, many lichens. All this is interspersed with the ankle-breaking mounds of loose laval scoria.

There are a number of walking options on the island, all neatly presented in an essential piece of kit – DOC's guide to the island – available from the DOC office in the Ferry Building. If you have plenty of time and want to get away from the crowds that immediately make for the summit (two hours), follow the tracks from the wharf to the summit via McKenzie Bay. It can take six hours but gives you a great feel for the island, its plant life and provides great sea-level views.

Motutapu Island – the contrasting island connected to Rangitoto by a short causeway – has a few interesting Maori archaeological sites but is best visited as part of the extensive winter replanting programmes that are taking place in conjunction with DOC. As you can see from Rangitoto, Motutapu needs it! Motutapu Tree Planting Day Trips, 0930-1730, adult $14, child $7, includes ferry. Contact *Fullers*, T3679111, or DOC, T3079279.

Getting there

A *Fullers* ferry from the Ferry Building on Quay St departs daily at 0930 and 1145 (1400 extra sailing in summer); adult $18, child $9. *Fullers* also offer a ferry/tour package with the 'Rangitoto Explorer' – a carriage pulled by a tractor that winds its way around the island, giving an interesting commentary and making regular photo stops: adult $35, child $17.50. Bookings essential for all trips. In the winter phone before departure; T3679111, www.fullersakl.co.nz Be sure to take plenty of water, sun block and a hat – the black scoria can emanate terrific heat. There is a small shop on the island that is open in summer, but you are advised to take your own picnic.

Tiritiri Matangi

Even if you are not particularly interested in wildlife 'Tiri' (as it is affectionately known) is well worth a visit. This jewel in the Hauraki is one of the few 'open bird sanctuaries' in New Zealand and has become an internationally famous conservation success story. Situated 4 km off the Whangaparaoa Peninsula, north of the city centre, the 220-ha island was originally leased for farming from 1855 to 1971, during which time the native forest was reduced

If you want to join the 'Supporters of Tiritiri Matangi' and be a part of the island's future and further development, ask on the island or T4794490

to 6% of its former glory. Thankfully, the island was recognized by The New Zealand Wildlife Service (now DOC) as having great potential as a wildlife sanctuary. A nursery was set up in 1983 and from 1984 volunteers from all walks of life became involved in planting over 250,000 trees and shrubs, and the island is now 60% revegetated. A vital poison drop rid the island of rats making it predator free and ready for the arrival of most of its current avian residents. Now Tiri has become the safe haven for numerous rare and endangered species including the famous takahe, little spotted kiwi, kokako, whitehead, saddleback, North Island robin, kakariki, stitchbird and brown teal. Being an open sanctuary, members of the public can visit and experience what New Zealand used to be like, with the bush alive with the sound of birdsong. The takahe – those big friendly purple chickens with red beaks – are perhaps the most famous of its current tenants. These amazing, almost prehistoric birds, were thought to be extinct until a small group were rediscovered in the wild Fiordlands of South Island. Since then a successful breeding programme has increased numbers and, given there are only about 200 of these birds left in the world, seeing them is an unforgettable experience.

The island has a numerous and varied network of walks on which you are almost certain to 'encounter' takahe and spot many of the other species. The coastal scenery and sea views are also magnificent. Do not miss the little blue penguin boxes near the wharf (ask) or the 'Wattle Track'. Kiwi are nocturnal birds, so don't expect to see one unless you stay at the bunkhouse overnight. Ray and Barbara are excellent hosts, as are the volunteer guides who formed the highly committed and professional outfit called the 'Supporters of Tiri Tiri Matangi'. For details on volunteer work, T4794490. Book well in advance.

Getting there Several ferry operators run a service to from Auckland to Tiri, principally – ***Fullers*** from Pier 3 (adjacent to the Ferry Building) on Thu at 0830, Sat and Sun at 0900; or the same ferry from Z Pier, Gulf Harbour on the Whangaparoa Peninsula, 45 mins later. Trips return by 1600. From Auckland; adult $30, child $18. From Gulf Harbour; adult $25, child $15. ***Fullers Ferries***, Ferry Building, Quay St, T4245561, www.gulfharbourferries.co.nz

If you want to arrive at the island (or sail the gulf) in style ***The Adventure Cruising Company*** also stop off at Tiritiri in their wonderful sailing ship the *Te Aroha*. They offer night walks and dawn chorus trips in association with DOC (your chance perhaps, to see a wild kiwi); T4449342. DOC guided tour is $5 extra. There is a souvenir shop on the island but it does not sell food so take a packed lunch. Coffee and snacks are available on the ferry, and free coffee and tea is available at the shop on the island.

Other islands in the Hauraki

Motuihe This small unusually shaped island of 179 ha lies between Motutapu and Waiheke. There is archaeological evidence that suggests the island was inhabited and used extensively by Maori before it was purchased and farmed by European pioneer W H Fairburn in 1839. Ownership changed hands again a few times before it was finally bought by the Crown in 1872 and used as a quarantine station. This station would be used as a prisoner of war camp in the First World War (prisoners included the infamous German Captain Felix von Lucker), an emergency hospital during the influenza epidemic in 1918, and a naval training base in the Second World War. In 1967, when the Hauraki Gulf Marine Park was established, the island came under the control of the Auckland City Council. Today, although the island is still farmed and is a DOC reserve, it is essentially a recreation venue, popular for swimming, fishing and escaping the city. A number of walks from 30 minutes to three hours are available, taking in a number of geological formations, archaeological sites, and the graves of those who died during the influenza epidemic.

Sleeping and eating There is a holiday home ($12 per person, $60 minimum), bunkhouse ($7) and camping ($4) available on the island. T5348095. In summer a small kiosk on the island sells basic snacks and refreshments.

Transport *Fullers* run a ferry to Motuihe on Fri at 1800 and Sun at 0930. Additional summer sailings are also available: adult $20, child $10. There is also a longer trip available on board the old ferry, *The Kestrel*, which departs Auckland at 1030 and is designed particularly for groups and families: adult $20, child $10. T3679111.

Little Barrier Island

The original Maori name, Hauturu, means 'resting place of the winds'

On a clear day it is just possible to see the mountainous bush-clad peaks that make up Little Barrier Island from the city. Little Barrier lies 90 km north of Auckland and 18 km west of her big sister, Great Barrier. This island is a plant and wildlife reserve of international value and significance. Being predator-free, it is sanctuary to a host of native birdlife, such as black petrel, cooks petrel and brown teal (all endangered). Other unusual inhabitants include the tuatara (a prehistoric native reptile), rare skinks and New Zealand's only bat (and native mammal) – the short-tailed bat. There are also 350 species of native plant on the island. But perhaps the most famous inhabitants are the kakapo. These flightless heavyweights (up to 3½ kg) are the rarest parrot, and one of the most endangered birds, in the world. At present only 62 known individuals remain in captivity or on protected off shore islands around New Zealand.

Little Barrier Island can only be visited with a permit and permission from DOC; T3662166. They run a volunteer programme and accommodation is provided, but the waiting list is huge. An alternative is to take a nature cruise aboard the sailing ship *Te Aroha* (November-April, four days for $400, T4449342).

Waiheke Island

At 93 sq km, Waiheke is the largest island in the gulf and, only 20 km (a 35 minute ferry ride), from the city it is also the most visited and heavily populated. It has plenty of beaches, activities, easy access, fine restaurants and accommodation, but if you are looking for a real 'island experience' then you are far better going to Great Barrier.

Ins and outs

Getting there

Air *Waiheke Air Services* fly twice daily for $65 return. Scenic flights by helicopter and fixed wing are also available from $25 (minimum 2),T3725000. The airport is 3 km east of Ostend and can be reached by local taxi (T3727756), or bus (T3728823). ***Heletranz*** offer a 'Heletranz Dining Adventure' by helicopter taking in one of the top restaurants on Waiheke, T4791991, www.heletranz.co.nz

Ferry *Fullers* offer a regular (passenger only) service every 2 hrs from 0815-1600 (additional sailings in summer): adult $23, child $10.50. T36791190. ***Pacific Ferries*** offer a cheaper deal from Pier 2 and 3 Quay St, but the fare does not include a bus pass (see below): adult $17, T3031714, www.pacificferries.co.nz ***Subritzky Shipping*** run a less salubrious passenger and vehicular service 5 times daily from Half Moon Bay to Kennedy's Point, at 0645, $110 family car and driver, extra passengers $20. Bookings essential; T5345663. www.subritzkyshipping.co.nz

Getting around **Bus** *Fullers* offer a 4-route service to and from the main Matiatia wharf and connect with all ferries. Route 1 runs a regular service to and from Onetangi taking in Oneroa, Blackpool, Surfdale and Ostend. Route 2 goes from the wharf to Oneroa, Little Oneroa, Hauraki Store, Palm Beach and Ostend to Rocky Bay and back. Route 3 from the wharf to Oneroa, Blackpool, Surfdale, Hauraki store, Palm Beach, Ostend, Onetangi to Rocky Bay and back; and Route 4 to Oneroa, Surfdale, Ostend to Onetangi and back. Tickets and $7 day pass available on the bus, T3728823. 'Bus and Boat' specials are often available (May-Oct); 'Bus and Boat Combo' (adult $20, child $10) include a free bus return as far as Onetangi. A $2 all-day bus pass is available with every *Fullers* or Link full fare ticket T3679111.

Waiheke Island

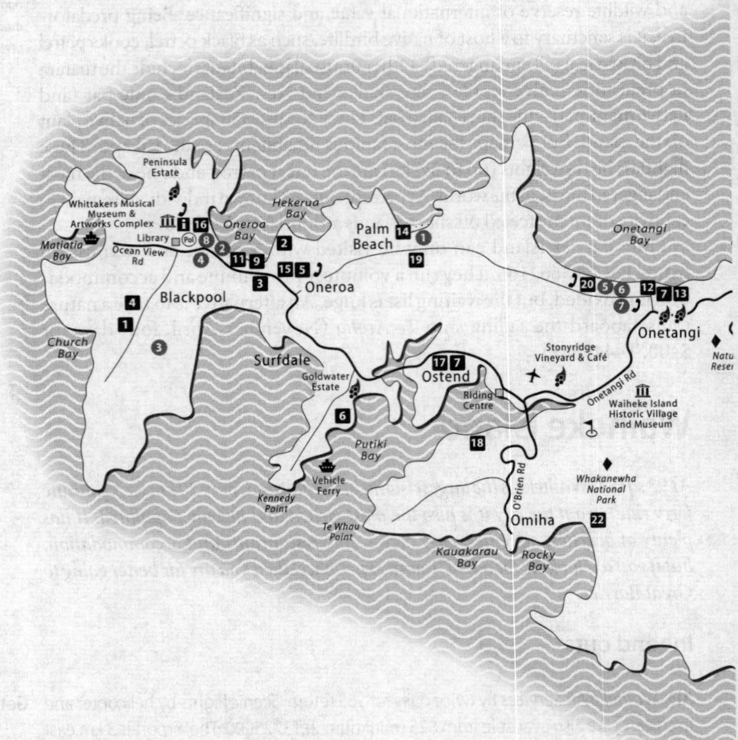

■ **Sleeping**
1 Ardens
2 Le Cedar House
3 Chalet Waiheke Apartments
4 Glenora Estate
5 Hekerua Lodge
6 Kennedy Point Vineyard Guesthouse
7 Midway Motel
8 Miro
9 Omaru Bay Lodge
10 Oneroa
11 Oneroa Lodge
12 Onetangi Beachfront Apartments
13 Onetangi Road Vineyard
14 Palm Beach Backpackers & Palm Beach Lodge
15 Punga Lodge

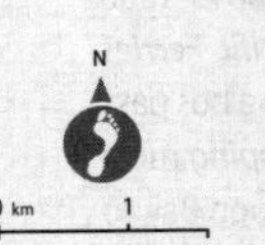

Vehicle hire *Waiheke Auto Rentals*, T3728998, www.ki-wi.co.nz/ auto.htm, operate a fleet of cars, station wagons, 4WDs, sports cars and a minibus. ***Waiheke Rental Cars***, T3728386, rent cars, minibuses, jeeps, motorbikes and scooters.

Taxis *Waiheke Island Shuttles*, T3727756, or ***Waiheke Taxi Co-op Ltd***, T3728038. Waiheke Island and Trika Shuttles provide a fun option with 3-wheeled open-sided vehicles, T3727756.

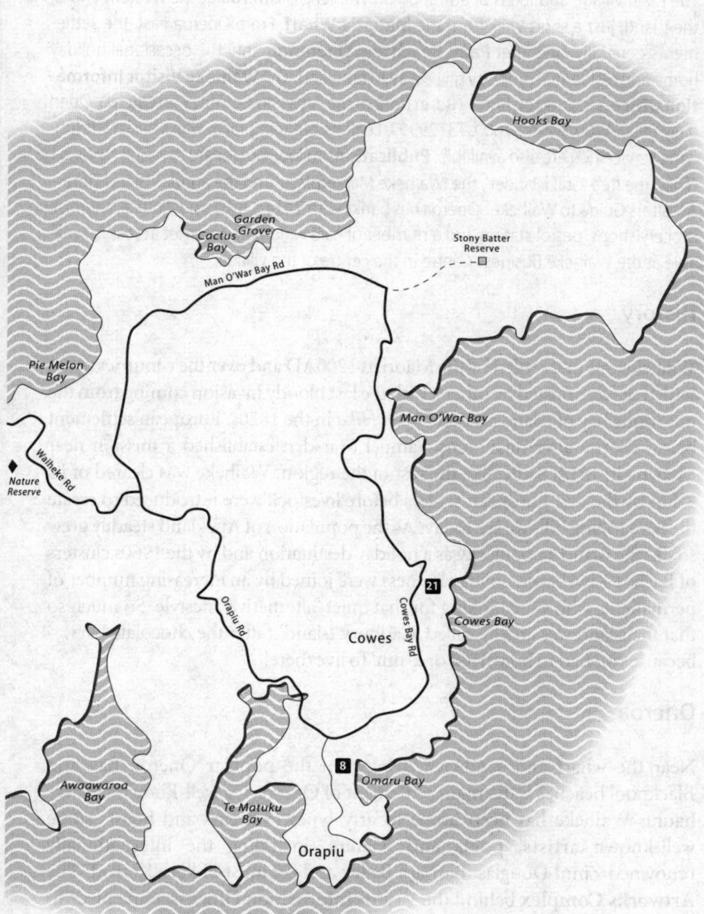

16 Seadream Holiday Apartments
17 Tawaipareira Farmhouse B & B
18 Te Whau Lodge
19 Waiheke Island Resort
20 Waiheke Island YHA
21 Waikopou
22 Whakanewa Regional Park

Eating

1 Cat's Eye Bar & Grill
2 Dolphin Café
3 Mudbrick
4 Nautico Bar
5 Onetangi Beach Hotel
6 Palaver
7 Strand Café
8 Vino Vino
9 Waiheke Resort

All Fullers tour enquiries, T3679111, www.fullers.co.nz

Tours *Fullers* offer the following: 'Island Explorer Tour and Ferry', a bus tour with commentary, departing Auckland 1000 with an optional return time, adult $34, child $18.50, bookings essential; the 'Waiheke Vineyard Explorer' tours, which are a 5½-hr tour taking in 3 world-class vineyards, summer Wed-Sun, winter Sat-Sun, departs Auckland 1200 with an optional return time, adult $56, bookings essential; 'Beyond and Back' Tour and Ferry is a 5½-hr tour that explores the whole island including remote areas, departs Auckland 1000 daily, return time optional, adult $40, child $20, bookings essential. For the kids Fullers also offer a farm visit on the 'Top of the Island' tour, Nov-Apr, departs Auckland 0815, adults $69, child $35.

Orientation & information

The major island event of the year is the Waiheke Jazz Festival held at Easter. It is hugely popular and attracts top national and sometimes international artists, www.waihekejazz.co.nz

The main village and focus of attention on Waiheke is **Oneroa** at the western end of the island, just a short walk from the **Matiatia Wharf**. From Oneroa east, the settlements generally fade after **Palm Beach** and **Onetangi,** until the occasional holiday home and residential property gives way to farmland. The **Waiheke Visitor Information Office** is located on Korora Rd, in front of the Artworks Complex , in Oneroa. Open daily 0900-1700, winter 1600. T3729999. Leaflets outlining local walks and a left luggage service ($2) are also available. **Publications** to look out for are the 'Gulf News' $1 (Thu), the free 'Gulf Islander', the 'Waiheke Marketplace' and the annual 'Island Time – A Visitors Guide to Waiheke'. Oneroa has banks with 24 hr ATMs, a post office, chemist, grocery shops, petrol station and a number of cafés and bars. Internet access is available at the Waiheke Business Centre in the centre of the village.

History

Waiheke was first settled by the Maori in 1200AD and over the centuries tribes settled or were ousted by others, with the last bloody invasion coming from the notorious Bay of Islands-based *Hongi Hika* in the 1820s. European settlement began shortly after missionary Samuel Marsden established a mission near Matiatia in 1818. Sadly, like the rest of the region, Waiheke was cleared of its Kauri by the first European settlers before livestock were introduced to create the bare rolling hills we see today. As the population of Auckland steadily grew so did the island's popularity as a holiday destination and by the 1960s clusters of Bachs (Kiwi beach holiday homes) were joined by an increasing number of permanents who were looking for that quiet 'alternative' lifestyle. So much so that the island was cruelly called 'Cadbury Island' (after the chocolate bars) – because you had to be a 'fruit' or a 'nut' to live there!

Oneroa

Near the wharf and sandwiched between the popular Oneroa Bay and Blackpool beaches is the main settlement of Oneroa – a well-known creative haunt. Waiheke has been home to arty types for years and boasts some well-known **artists, poets and writers**, including the internationally renowned Zinni Douglas, Barbara Bailey and ceramist Hillary Kerrod. The **Artworks Complex** behind the Visitor Information Office is a fine place to start your activities on Waiheke with a look at some of the local art and crafts available. It also has a theatre, a library, a café and the **Whittakers Musical Museum** which displays over 100 musical instruments dating back 500 years, and has live performances daily (except Tuesday) at 1300. ■ *Adults $7, child $5. Donation outside performance times. T3725573.*

Within a few kilometres of Oneroa are two fine examples of Waiheke's other claim to fame – vineyards. **The Peninsula Estate**, 52a Korora Road, offers free tastings and tour by arrangement, T3727866. **The Mudbrick**

Vineyard, 2 km west of Oneroa on Church Bay Road, is open daily in summer. It houses one of the island's best café/restaurants, The *Mudbrick Restaurant*; T3729050, bookings essential.

Beyond Oneroa

Within walking distance east of Oneroa along **Oneroa Bay** and up through the pleasant reserves and back roads is the next community, **Palm Beach** (two hours), with its small collection of houses and lovely sandy beach, with a secluded spot for naturists. There is also a General Store that offers bike, boogie board and snorkelling gear hire (from $10 a day). From Palm Beach it is about 3 km to **Onetangi**, site of Waiheke's longest and perhaps most popular beach. The Onetangi Beach Store hires out equipment for watersports from $5 a day. The **Waiheke Island Historic Village and Museum**, 165 Onetangi Road, is overlooked by a 700-year-old Maori *Pa* and has cottages and a small museum exhibiting collections of farm machines, engines and assorted bric-a-brac. ■ *Sat-Sun (daily on school holidays) 1200-1600, Free.* Also close by on Waiheke Road is the Forest and Bird Society's **Nature Reserve** which may, if you are lucky, produce the odd tui or native pigeon amidst its native tree plantations. East of Onetangi, the habitation diminishes and farmland, the odd vineyard and secluded bay takes over. If you have time the **Stony Batter Reserve**, on the islands north east headland, is worth a visit (1½-hour walk from the delightful **Cactus Bay**). It consists of an underground complex linked by a series of tunnels which, like others in Auckland, were built in the Second World War in fear of foreign invasion.

The two most famous **vineyards** on Waiheke are the **Goldwater Estate**, 18 Causeway Road (visits by appointment; T3727493) and **Stonyridge Vineyard**, 80 Onetangi Road, which produces New Zealands's most sought-after red. ■ *Tours and tastings, Sat-Sun, 1130. $10. There is also a fine café but times vary; T3728822.* You can see these and the other vineyards on the island on an organized tour (see getting around, page 130).

South of Oneroa are the scattered settlements of **Blackpool, Surfdale, Ostend** and **Omiha**, which provide little in the way of real in interest, though Ostend does have a market every Saturday from 0800-1300 while Omiha boasts the **Whakanewa Regional Park** – a pleasant scenic spot and one of the regions newest parks.

Essentials

Sleeping

Given its popularity and proximity to the city, Waiheke is very well-served with accommodation options, but in recent years the focus seems to be mainly on couples or honeymooners. There are a number of lodges, motels, hostels and over 100 B&B's to choose from, many with the ever-inviting 4-poster bed. The Information Office can assist where necessary and make all the appropriate bookings, T3729999. ***Fullers*** provide an accommodation service and packages from the mainland Fullers Information Centre at the Ferry Building on Quay St, T3679122, www.fullers.co.nz, with Club Waiheke, T3726565, also offering a similar service.

In Oneroa The Mediterranean-style **L** ***Oneroa Lodge***, 187 Ocean View Rd, T3728897, F3728244, is well-placed and appointed with 3 en-suites, all with fine views. Also well placed is the extraordinarily named, **AL** ***Oneroa –50 Yards to Beach, Bus and Bistros'***,159 Ocean View Rd, T3727433. Which seems to practise what it preaches. For more privacy try the self-contained flat or 3 bedroom cottage of **AL** ***Cedar House***, 69

Queens St, T3729434, F3729163, www.waiheke.co.nz/deco.htm Close to the beach are the **A** ***Seadream Holiday Apartments***, 35 Waikare Rd, T3728991, F3728091. They have 2 well-appointed units, 1 studio and 1 larger unit with lounge and separate bedroom. A little further out is **A** ***Le Chalet Waiheke Apartments***, 14 Tawa St, T/F37275. 10 apartments in a quiet bush settingwith fully self-contained rooms and private decks.

In **Little Oneroa** you have a number of options including the **AL** ***Punga Lodge***, 223 Ocean View Rd, T3726675, www.ki-wi.co.nz/punga.htm Set in garden and bush it has comfortable self-contained or bed and breakfast units. Also in Little Oneroa is the **C-D** ***Hekerua Lodge (Waiheke Backpackers)***, 11 Hekerua Rd T/F3728990, collrich@clear.net.nz, set in private bush and offering all the usual facilities including spa pool and internet access.

Church Bay just outside Oneroa has a number of luxurious options including the **L** ***Glenora Estate***, 160 Nick Johnstone Dr, T3725082, F3725087, nestled in its own 8 acres and offering wonderful accommodation in 17th-century style farmhouse and barn – ideal for couples. **AL** ***The Arderns***, 241 Church Bay Rd, T3725487, F3725489, also offers luxury in more expansive surrounds.

In Palm Beach **AL** ***Waiheke Island Resort*** on Bay Rd, Palm Beach T3727897, F3728241, www.waihekeresort.co.nz One of Waiheke's better-known luxury establishments with en-suite villa and chalet accommodation for up to 130 people. Attached is a fine restaurant and swimming pool. Also in the vicinity is **L** ***Palm Beach Lodge***, 23 Tiri View Rd, Palm Beach T/F3727763, www.ki-wi.co.nz/palmlodge.htm It has spacious Mediterranean-style suites with fine views. The fine **C-D** ***Palm Beach Backpackers***, 54 Palm Rd, T3728662, is only 50 m from the water's edge, provides a campsite, and hires kayaks and mountain bikes. The bus stops at the front door.

In Onetangi **AL** ***Onetangi Beachfront Apartments***, 27 The Strand T3727051, F3725056, www.onetangi.co.nz Has 8 new fully self-contained luxury apartments, 9 refurbished and 6 standard units. Barbecues, spas, sauna and free use of kayaks. There are 2 options among the vineyards: **AL** ***Miro***, Browns Rd T3727854, F3727056. Advertised as the ultimate in romance with a self- contained Tuscan-style villa. A homestay-style double is also available; **AL** ***Onetangi Road Vineyard***, 82 Onetangi Rd, T/F3726130. Also offers a similar set up for 2 in a private vineyard cottage. The interestingly decorated **C-D** ***Waiheke Island YHA***, Seaview Rd, T3728971, F3728971. Offers a cheaper, more wide-ranging option with en-suite doubles, doubles, family and twin bunk rooms with 'a $2 million view', TV lounge, BBQ and mountain bikes available.

In Ostend **A** ***Tawaipareira Farmhouse B&B***, 28 Seaview Rd, T/F3726676, www.waiheke.co.nz/tawa.htm A redecorated farmhouse with spacious and comfortable double and single rooms at affordable prices. **A** ***The Midway Motel***, T3728023, F3729669, www.waiheke.co.nz/midway.htm Has small and large units, an indoor heated pool, spa and spa room suites.

Elsewhere on the island **L** ***Omaru Bay Lodge***, T/F3728291, www.waiheke.co.nz/omarubay.htm Situated on the water's edge at the eastern end of the island, it offers a fine luxury option in 6 en suite guestrooms. Also at the top of the range is **L** ***Waikopou***, Cowes Bay Rd T3727883, F3729971, www.waikopou.co.nz A luxurious earth-brick lodge retreat in 22 acres of bush with fine views. **L** ***Te Whau Lodge***, 36 Vintage La, Te Whau Point, T3722288, F3722218. Overlooks Putiki Bay and provides 4 guest suites in a fine setting, fully licensed, breakfast and dinner included. **AL** ***Kennedy Point Vineyard Guesthouse***, 44 Donald Bruce Rd, T3725600, F3726205. Offers another vineyard retreat in affordable well-appointed guest suites.

If you have a tent, you can have your own 270 acre retreat with fine views at the ***Whakanewa Regional Park***, for $4, T3031530, 'Parksline'.

Eating

There are numerous mid-range eateries on the island, especially cafés that serve fine food and snacks

Oneroa is the centre of cuisine on Waiheke with the best and most expensive eating to be had at the ***Mudbrick Restaurant*** attached to the vineyard, T3729050, offering great seafood and, of course, a fine wine to wash it down, bookings essential. The ***Waiheke Resort Restaurant*** near Palm Beach is also at the top end and has outdoor decks with fine views across the Gulf, T3727897, bookings also essential. ***The Onetangi Beach Hotel***, on the Strand, offers cheaper barbecues, spit roasts and seafood in less luxurious surroundings, T3727583, and the ***Palaver***, T3728785, is great for chilling out with a pizza or a cup of tea. The ***Dolphin Café***, on Ocean View Rd, has enormous value burgers, and the licensed ***Vino Vino*** up the road offers good value and choice with fine views. The ***Strand Café*** in Onetangi is laid-back and offers a good breakfast. For lunch a popular weekend haunt is the ***Stonyridge Café***, at the Stonyridge Vineyard which is open from 1130-1700 weekends and Thu-Sun in summer.

Entertainment

In Oneroa the ***Nautico Bar*** and restaurant in the Pendragon Mall, T3728785, is usually where it all happens when bands visit from the mainland. Live performances can also be had, especially on summer weekends, at a number of low-key eating venues including ***Vino Vino***, T3729888 and the ***Cat's Eye Bar and Grill***, T3727884, in Palm Beach. When there's a big match on TV head for the big screen at the ***Onetangi Beach Hotel***, T3727583.

And then there's the mighty **Jazz Festival** every Easter, when Waiheke really pulls out all the stops.

Tours & excursions

Ananda Tours, 20 Seaview Rd, Ostend, offer excellent Art, Eco and Scenic tours, T3727530, www.waiheke.co.nz/anadatours.htm ***Tour De Waiheke Island*** is a luxury personally guided tour that takes in a scenic flight, vineyard visit and dinner at one of the top restaurants; T3725624. ***Ross Adventures Sea Kayaking***, Matiatia, offers half (4 hr), full, multi-day and night trips, T3570550. ***Waiheke Tours*** also offer kayak trips, vehicles and accommodation at Onetangi Beach Chalet (2 bedroom units near the beach), T3727262. ***Shepherds Point Riding Centre***, Ostend Rd, T3728104, and ***Sunset Coral Scenic Rides***, Dolphin Point, Church Bay, T3726565, offer trips of the 4-legged variety for around $60 for 2 hrs. ***Wharf Rats Trading Co*** hires bikes from the wharf, T3727937. ***Gulf Island Sailing Safaris***, T3267245, and ***Waiheke Island Yacht Charters***, T3729579, offer a variety of water-based day trips from about $85.

Great Barrier Island

Unlike Waiheke, Great Barrier (or the 'Barrier' as it is affectionately called) has not yet been spoilt by the influences of the city and still offers the visitor a true island adventure. The ferry to the Barrier is a joint island service that at first is packed with commuters and visitors before it empties dramatically at Waiheke and you are left amongst the Barrier locals,and the fishing rods and rucksacks of the odd intrepid backpacker. The bar on the boat suddenly takes a hammering and the conversation turns to local Barrier gossip, kingfish and snapper. The orange glow of the city gradually fades behind Rangitoto and you begin to feel a welcome isolation close in. Great Barrier is the second largest island in the gulf and lies almost 90 km northeast of Auckland. It used to be part of what is now the Coromandel Peninsula and in a way shares the same isolated, under-developed feel, with rugged hills, numerous bays and beautiful quiet beaches. The Barrier is 'possum free' so a precious habitat for some rare and endangered species – the brown teal and New Zealand's largest skink, the cheveron, being the most notable. For invading humans out to do some diving, fishing, tramping, surfing, sailing and relaxing it is unsurpassed in the region.

Ins and outs

Getting there Great Barrier is accessible by sea and air. The main airfield is at **Claris** in the centre east of the island about 17 km from Tryphena's **Shoal Bay Wharf**. Another airfield is at **Okiwi** north of Claris. Ferry services access the island mainly at Tryphena but also **Whangaparapara** and **Port Fitzroy**.The '**Great Barrier Island Combination Pass**' allows you to use a range of ferries and upgrade to air if you so wish. Contact *Fullers*, T0800-767786.

Air *Great Barrier Airlines* are the main carriers, and their aircraft are hard to miss with their tails beautifully painted with examples of New Zealand's native bird-life. They offer a highly professional and friendly service to the island from Auckland and North Shore airports, as well as connecting flights to the Coromandel (Whitianga) and Whangarei in Northland. Great Barrier Airlines have offices at the Auckland Domestic Terminal, T2566500, F2566509, gba@gbair.co.nz, and at the airfield on the Barrier at Claris. 3 flights go daily 0745,1015 and 1600 from Auckland, 0900,1300 and 1700 from Claris, with additional flights in summer on demand. A standard return will cost you $169 and a single $89, same day return $149. Concessions apply. These prices are cheap when you consider the scenic extravaganza on offer on a clear day. ***Mountain Air's Great Barrier Express***, T2567025, F2567026, www.mountainair.co.nz, offers a similar service and also proudly advertises that dogs, surfboards and bikes are welcome! Both Airlines offer pick-up and drop shuttle services throughout the island (see getting around below) and a 'fly and boat' package for about $100 which is highly recommended. ***Waiheke Air Services*** also fly to the Barrier but less frequently and on demand, T0800-3725000; as do ***Sunair Aviation*** to and from Tauranga in the Bay of Plenty, T0800685050.

Ferry *Fullers* offer a passenger-only service from the city (2 hrs), on Fri at 1830 and Sun at 1100, additional sailings in summer, $99 return, concessions available, bookings essential; T3679111, F4290004. ***Sealink (Subritzky Shipping)*** offers a vehicular and passenger service on board the 'MV Sealink'. Sailings daily except Tue and Sun (3½ hrs). Departs from Jellicoe Wharf, City, $65 return. T3734036, F3071505, www.subritzkyshipping.co.nz ***Gulf Trans***, T0800GULFTRANS, offer a 6-7 hr voyage on board the 'MV Tasman' every Tue at 0700, departing from Wynyard Wharf and costing $20 each way, though this is the really uncomfortable option.

The Central Backpackers in Auckland has a sister establishment on Great Barrier – The Stray Possum Lodge – which offers the excellent value '**Possum Pursuits Pass**' which includes daily transport, tours, use of mountain bikes, body boards, wet suits and snorkel gear. Contact The Auckland Central Backpackers Travel Centre, T3584874, or the Stray Possum Lodge, T4290109. The package costs $110, including travel to and from the island.

Getting around A network of mainly metalled roads connects the main settlements, but most of the island remains inaccessible by vehicle. However, transportation around the island is fairly well organized and readily available. A swarm of vehicles will meet you at the Tryphena Wharf (Shoal Bay). Many accommodation centres will also provide their own pick ups but, if you have not yet booked, the following taxis and shuttles will take you to the Information Centre in Tryphena or beyond: ***Bob's Island Taxis***, T4290988; ***Barrier Taxis***, T4290527; ***Aotea Tours*** (Okiwi), T4290055. ***Quality Cabs*** (Port Fitzroy), T4290046; ***Safari Tours***, T4290448.

Bus A regular bus service around the island was, in early 2000, not available but this is set to change. For information consult the Information Office in Tryphena, T4290033. ***Sanderson's Transport*** are worth a try, T4290640; typical fare Tryphena to Claris is $10. Both ***Great Barrier Airlines*** (GBA) and ***Mountain Air*** provide shuttles to and from the airport: Tryphena to Claris $7 each way; Claris to Medlands $5 each way.

Car hire *Bob's Island Tours* (Tryphena), T4290988; ***Wheels Down Under*** (Tryphena), T4290110; ***Safari Tours***, T4290448; ***Great Barrier Lodge*** (Whangaparapara), T4290488; ***Better Bargain Rentals*** (Tryphena), T4290092; ***Aotea Tours*** (Okiwi), T4290055, and ***Quality Cabs*** (Port Fitzroy), T4290046. All these companies offer rental options with a range of well-used vehicles from hatchbacks to 4WDs, but it is a captive market and prices are not cheap at about $90 per day, dropping slightly for long-term rental.

Cycle hire (see activities below).

Hitching Hitching is generally a safe method of transport – but don't be surprised if you find yourself on a steam roller or a quad bike, or, in fact, anything that goes.

Tours *Safari Tours*, T4290448; ***Aotea Tours***, T4290156, and ***Bob's Island Tours***, T4290100, offer highly informative daily tours around the main sights of the island for about $45. The Stray Possum Lodge has tour options attached to its excellent package deal.

Orientation & information

The main arrival point (by sea) and centre of population on Great Barrier is **Tryphena** which is essentially split into 3 areas or bays – Shoal Bay where the wharf is located, Pa Beach and Mulberry Grove. In Pa Beach and Mulberry Grove you will find most of what you need from bread to petrol, accommodation to car hire. Most shops are to be found in the **Stonewall Complex**, including the **Fullers office** next to the Stonewall Store, T4290004, open daily 0800-1700, where long-term resident Tamara is a terrific source of information and advice. The traditional **Information Centre** is located in the post shop in Claris and serves visitors arriving by air; T4290033, www.greatbarrier.co.nz, open daily 0800-1800.

It is advisable to take **detailed maps** to Great Barrier if you intend to explore its wild interior. Free handouts are available from the Fullers Information Centre, the main **DOC office** at Port Fitzroy, T4290044, Mon-Fri 0800-1630, and the Information Centre in Claris (The DOC leaflets are the most detailed and informative) but nothing beats the real thing.

Two **publications** are of particular value; 'The Essential Guide to Great Barrier' is essential (available from Fullers office and the Information Centre at Claris), $5.95, and the 'Barrier Bulletin' will fill you in on all the latest gossip and events.

The main and increasingly popular annual festival on the Barrier is the Port Fitzroy **Mussel Festival** held in Jan (for details contact the Port Fitzroy Boating Club, T4290072). The long-board **Surf Classic** is held in early Jan (depending on weather), T4290966. The Barrier Island Sports and Social Club in Claris hosts a monthly **market**, which can be a great way to mingle with the locals, T4290260.

History

The Maori name for Great Barrier is *Aotea* meaning 'White Cloud' or 'Clear Day'. Before the Europeans arrived over 12,000 Maori were settled on the island but that population has all but disappeared with only a few descendants of the first tribes still remaining. It was that man Captain Cook again, who on his 1769 voyage, renamed the island (along with its more mountainous sister,

Great Barrier Island

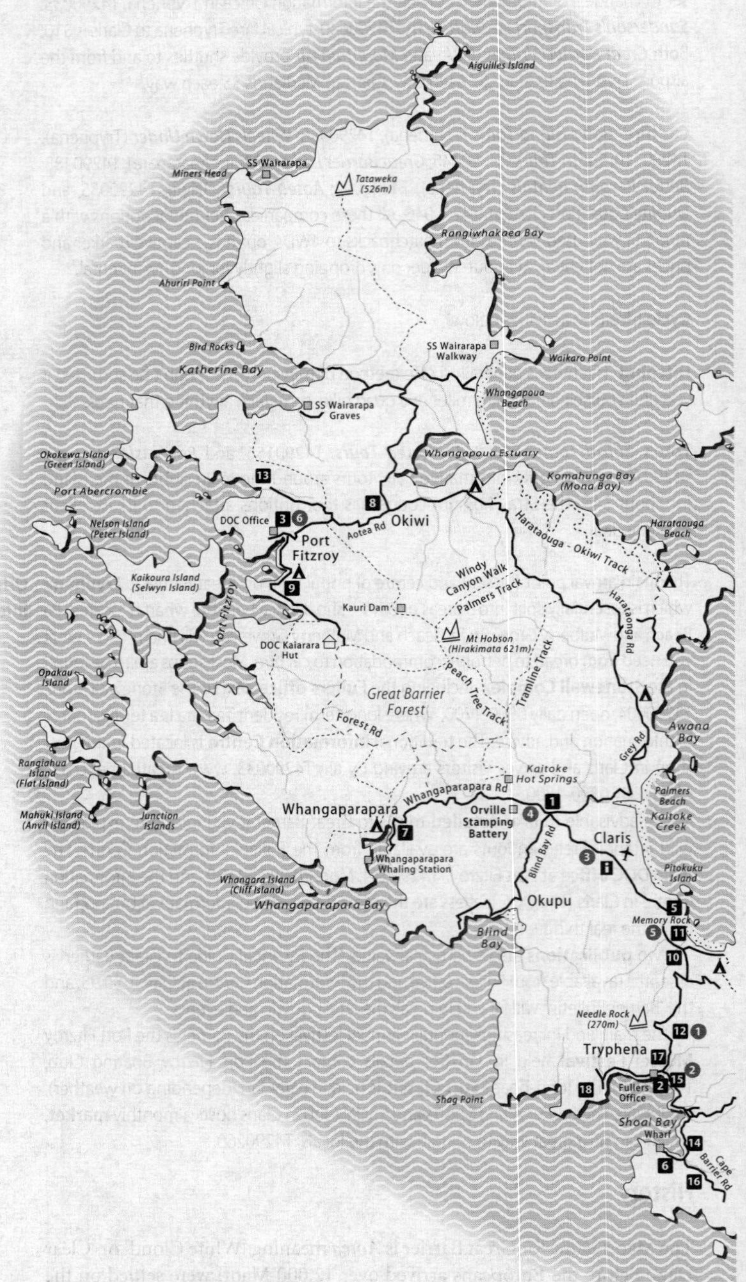

Little Barrier). 'Great Barrier' being an obvious name for the island's placement between open ocean and the inner gulf. The European history, like that of so much of the upper North Island, was initially centred on the Kauri industry and for a while it prospered through sweat and saw. Once cleared, attentions turned underground, to the mineral deposits of gold, silver and copper, which did not prove very productive. The plunder above and below ground complete, the sea became the focus, with a thriving whaling station being set up in Whangaparapara (the remnants of which still remain). Now, 100 years on with the Kauri, minerals, whales and human population depleted, the island has been left to the alternative, almost self-sufficient lifestylers – people who thankfully are much more conservation minded. The DOC now own and administer over half of the island, The current permanent population of the island juggles around 1000, but increases dramatically with visitors in the summer months.

Sights

Great Barrier is an activities destination, from sunbathing on its beaches, to multi-day tramps within the huge **Great Barrier Forest**, which is where you will find the most notable 'sights' both natural and historical. There are numerous **walks** or tramps from one hour to two days and the best source of information on these is the DOC office in Port Fitzroy. The 'Essential Guide to Great Barrier' (see previous page) also highlights the best walks and routes. Most tramps start or finish from various access points on the road between Port Fitzroy and Whangaparapara. The most popular starting point is Port Fitzroy, where both supplies and information can be gathered at the wonderfully stocked general store and main DOC office.

Auckland

Rakitu Island (Arid Island)

Whakatautuna Point

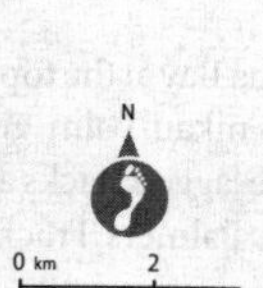

Medlands Beach

Windy Hill (361m)

Rosalie Bay Rd

4

Vol Ruahine (402m)

Cape Barrier

Sleeping

1 Crossroads Backpackers
2 Earthsong Lodge
3 Fitzroy House
4 Flowerhouse
5 Foromor Lodge
6 Gibb's Landing
7 Great Barrier Lodge
8 High Tide & Green Grass
9 Jetty Tourist Lodge
10 Medlands Beach Backpackers
11 Medlands Beach House & Cottage
12 Oasis Lodge
13 Orama Christian Community
14 Pigeon's Lodge
15 Pohutukawa Lodge
16 Stray Possum Lodge
17 Tipi & Bob's Holiday Lodge
18 Trilliam Lodge

Eating

1 Barrier Oasis
2 Currach Irish Pub
3 Claris Texas Café
4 Great Barrier Island Sports & Social Club
5 Medlands Lodge
6 Port Fitzroy Boating Club

Needle Rock (270 m) Located about 4 km north of Tryphena, this is a fine place to start. It is a rough 20-minute scramble to the summit which offers a great view back to Tryphena and the Coromandel to the south and all that awaits you to the north.

Medlands Beach This is perhaps the most popular beach on the island, especially with surfies, but it is also a fine place to swim, fish, sunbathe or take a walk around the headlands.

Kaitoke Hot Springs North of Claris, in the heart of the island, is a crossroads. Heading directly north about 3 km is the access point for the Kaitoke Hot Springs – a flat, easy one-hour walk past the Kaitoke Swamp to a series of pools in which you can relieve tired limbs.

Orville Stamping Battery Located 2 km along and south of the Whangaparapara Road on the Te Ahumata track. The concrete foundations are all that remain of this battery that once crushed quartz from the Te Ahumata gold field.

Palmers Beach and Awana Bay Heading east from the Claris crossroads you cross the river and up around the headland to Palmers beach with its shroud of pohutukawa trees falling chaotically to the beach. This is a fine beach to explore but access is not easy. The far more accessible Awana Bay is another fine spot, popular again for surfing and all other aquatic and beach-orientated activities.

Windy Canyon (20 mins) and the Kaitoke Springs (1 hr) are two of the best short walks on the island

Windy Canyon About 8 km north of Awana Bay at the top of Okiwi Hill is Palmer's Track. A 20-minute walk through nikau palm groves and up a well-built boardwalk will find you amongst the jagged stacks and spires of the canyon. The summit offers spectacular views. Palmers Track offers perhaps the best access point to Mount Hobson.

Mount Hobson (Hirakimata) At 621 m, Mount Hobson is the island's highest point. On a clear day it is unsurpassed in its 360° view of the island and beyond. The summit is the principal nesting site for the rare black petrel. Only about 4,500 remain and they are only found on Great and Little Barrier Island. They spend most of their life out at sea and are nocturnal on land, so don't expect to see any. They also nest in burrows so make sure you keep to the paths. From the summit the track splits – The Kaiarara track offering a route west to Port Fitzroy (with some fine remains of Kauri Dams on the way) or south via the Peach Tree Track that terminates at the Kaitoke hot springs.

Kauri Dam The well-preserved remains of a Kauri Dam can be seen along the Kaiarara Track. Kauri Dams were used by loggers to drive large numbers of Kauri downstream, allowing access to remote areas of bush. The lower one at Kaiarara was one of the largest driving dams to be built in New Zealand and is one of the best examples in the region.

'SS Wairarapa' Walkway The 'SS Wairarapa' was one of many ships wrecked on the island and certainly the most tragic, with the loss of 130 lives. It ran ashore near Miners Head in 1894. The 30-minute walk along the Whangapoua Beach to Tapuwai Point from the road end takes you to one of two graveyard sites on the island – the other being at Onepoto Beach at Katherine Bay on the west coast.

Whangapoua Estuary This estuary is a top spot for wildlife and is home to many interesting coastal and wetland species including spotless crake, banded rail and brown teal. If you spot a brown teal – a rather nondescript little brown duck – consider yourself very lucky as you will have seen one of only about 1200 left in the world. Great Barrier is home to 80% of these.

Whangaparaparapa Whaling Station The remains of the Barrier's old whaling station can be seen from the Whangaparapara Harbour. The oceans around the Barrier were the killing fields for thousands of whales from the 1950s before operations thankfully ceased in the 1960s .

Activities

Boating A wonderland awaits you. Boats can be hired from *Barrier Boat Hire*, T4290110; *Hot Pursuit*, T4290070; and *Fitzroy House Outdoor Centre*, T4290091.

Diving The waters around the Barrier are wonderfully clear. Great diving can be found all around the island, but preferred spots are Tryphena Harbour, around Port Fitzroy and off Harataonga Bay. There are three companies/individuals offering escorted trips to known locations: *Ron Gillard*, T4290110; *Fitzroy Dive Station*, T4290591; *Kevin Reynolds*, T4290468. **Dive Gear hire:** *Mobile Dive Centre*, T4290654 ($65 a day). Refills available; *Great Barrier Lodge* T4290488; and *Fitzroy Dive Station* (above).

Fishing Generally it is a good idea to bring your own gear for excellent land and sea fishing. Charters available include: *Fishing Charters*, T4290007; *Mokum*, T4290485; *Barrier Boat Hire*, T4290949; *Snappa-attack*, T4290007; *Vitamin C*, T4290949; and *Hot Pursuit*, T4290070. Some of the best land-based spots are Lighthouse Point (Shoal Bay, Tryphena), Cape Barrier, Shag Point, 'Shark Alley' (south headlands of Medlands Beach) and Haratoanga.

Golf Yes, the Barrier has a golf course, but mind the pukekos. Lessons (Saturday) and meals available; *Claris Golf Club*, T4290420

Horse trekking *GBI Adventure Horse Treks*, T4290274.

Kayaking The Barrier is a sea kayaking paradise. The following offer hire and trip options. The complete circumnavigation of the island takes about five days and is an awesome trip needing careful planning, local help and knowledge. *Aotea Kayaks*, T4290664; *Kayak Hire and Adventure Tours*, T4290520; *Safari Tours*, T4290448; and *Fitzroy House Outdoor Centre*, T4290091. All cost about $45 a day.

Mountain biking This is a great way to explore the island and both airlines and ferry operators are bicycle friendly. For environmental reasons most tracks are off limits, but a fine track that is accessible is the DOC Forest four-wheel drive track off Whangaparapara Road. You can hire bikes through *Bob's Island Tours*, Tryphena, T4290988; *Barrier Boat Hire*, Stonewall, Tryphena, T4290949; *Great Barrier Lodge*, Whangaparapara, T4290488; and *Barrier Hire*, Claris, T4290488. All about $25 a day.

Tramps **2 Days**: From the start of Palmers Track at the top of Okiwi Hill take a look at Windy Canyon before continuing to the summit of Mount Hobson. From there check out the Kauri Dam remains before continuing along the track and staying the night at the DOC Kaiarara Hut (24 bunks, a wood stove, toilet and cold water, $10, book with DOC, T4290044). Then the following day take the Forest Road and Tramline Tracks to finish your tramp in style at the Kaitoke Hot Springs. You will need to arrange pick up from the Whangaparapara Road access point.

1 Day Follow the route above but from Mount Hobson take the Peach Tree Track directly to the hot springs with pick up again from Whangaparapara Road.

Both the Harataonga – Okiwi Track (five hours) and Rosalie Bay Road end to Claris (five hours) are also fine walks.

Swimming Swimming (especially for kids) is best kept to sheltered West Coast bays, but the big eastern beaches are fine for adults if you are vigilant. Best bet is to take flippers and a boogie board.

Surfing The best spots are Medlands, Kaitoke, Palmers and Awana Bays.

Auckland

Essentials

Sleeping Great Barrier is both remote and basic, with no mains power, street lights, reticulated water supply or extensive road network, but when it comes to accommodation you can either enjoy that simplicity or be utterly spoilt. *Fullers* offer accommodation packages and advice from their office on the mainland (Ferry Building), T3679122. But perhaps your best bet is to contact the Fullers office or the general TIC on the island.

The Barri5er is very popular in summer so book well in advance

In Tryphena **LL** *Earthsong Lodge*, is a centrally located, luxury option that overlooks Tryphena Harbour and offers fine cuisine, T4290030. **LL** *Oasis Lodge*, Tryphena, is set amid a vineyard and is an old favourite. It has luxury en-suite and a cheaper cottage-style option available, meals included, T4290021. **LL** *Trilliam Lodge*, Puriri Bay, is a beautiful luxury Canadian log-style dwelling offering the full 5-star treatment, 6 double suites, T4290454.

AL *Flowerhouse*, operates an organic farm and offers a 1-bedroom option. Fine lunch venue, T4290464. The **A** *Pigeon's Lodge* is a fine B&B with en-suite rooms and set in quiet bush, T4290437. **A** *Tipi and Bob's Holiday Lodge* is and old favourite with 6 self-contained units, located close to all amenities, T4290550. **B** *Gibb's Landing*, Little Shoal Bay (near the wharf), offers beachfront, self-contained accommodation with a great view. Bike and car rental available, T4290654. In an ideal location next to the fine Irish Bar is the **A** *Pohutukawa Lodge* at Pa Beach. Close to shops, restaurants and that essential pint of Guinness. Also offers backpacker accommodation (**C-D**), T4290211, plodge@extra.co.nz **A-D** *Stray Possum Lodge* – the pick of the budget bunch on the island. An excellent backpackers located near the wharf and offering bunk-style, double room and chalet options in a lovely bush setting. Bar, Sky TV, Internet and pizza café available. Very friendly management and staff. Tours also available and bikes, boogie boards and wet suits for hire. See also 'Possum Pursuit Pass' (page 134).

Whangaparapara There is really only 1 place to stay in Whangaparapara and it is the **A** *Great Barrier Lodge*. Accommodation is in cottages in the grounds and, being out of the way, just about all you need is available. Car, bike and equipment hire, licensed bar and restaurant, T4290488.

Medlands Beach and north **LL** *Foromor Lodge* is another 'helicopter arrival' type venue on a fine beachfront location at Medlands, T4290335. Meals and activities included. **A** *Medlands Beach House and Cottage* is a mid-range self-contained accommodation option, right on the surf beach, T4821238. **C-D** *Medlands Beach Backpackers* is a basic cheap option with 1 bunkroom and 4 detached double rooms. Boogie boards, fishing and snorkelling gear available. Get well stocked up with food – it is remote. Surfies' favourite, T4290320. The **C-D** *Crossroads Backpackers*, just north of Claris, is well-situated in the heart of the island. It looks a bit clinical but offers fine accommodation has good facilities and Internet, T4290889.

Port Fitzroy and around **A** *Fitzroy House* offers 2 self-contained cottages in a wonderful setting and has heaps of activities available, T4290091, ftzhouse@voyager.co.nz **AL** *Jetty Tourist Lodge* is well placed and offers self-contained chalets and backpacker style dorms. Bar and restaurant, and within walking distance of the well-stocked general store, T4290050. **A** ***High Tide and Green Grass***, Okiwi, set in its own 12 acres of pasture and bush offering isolation and peace, T4290190. **A** ***Orama Christian Community*** offers self-contained flats and cottage, guestroom, cabin and bunkroom accommodation in a very scenic spot. It is located near Port Fitzroy and has its own library, shop and laundry facilities, T4290063.

Camping There are 6 DOC campsites and 1 DOC hut available (The Whangaparapara Hut having burnt to the ground recently). Bookings are advised and current charges (average $6) are available on enquiry at the main DOC office in Port Fitzroy, T4290044. Campsites are available at Akapoua Bay (Port Fitzroy), Whangaparapara, Whangapoua, Medlands, Harataonga and Awana. For convenience Akapoua Bay is advised, and perhaps the best of the more secluded campgrounds is Harataonga. The ***Akapoua Campsite*** also has a guest lodge which sleeps 8. The ***Kaiarara Hut*** has 24 bunks and costs $10 per night. Private campgrounds are also available at ***Great Barrier Island Campground***, Tryphena, $8.50, T4290184; ***Sugarloaf Campground***, Kaitoke Beach, $6, T4290229; and ***Mickey's***, $4.40, T4290140. Mickey's is run by a mad Irishman and is probably the most entertaining camping venue on the island.

Auckland

Eating

There are essentially very few restaurants on the Barrier with most eateries being attached to accommodation centres, many of which offer excellent cuisine

Tryphena *Barrier Oasis*, Stonewall, T4290021, offers top-quality cuisine for guests and visitors, lunch and dinner. Bookings essential. ***Currach Irish Pub***, Stonewall Complex, Tryphena, T4290421. Good pub food with a wicked seafood chowder. ***Earthsong Lodge***, T4290030. Excellent, specializing in French cuisine. Bookings essential. ***Flowerhouse***, Rosalie Bay, T4290464. Favourite local lunch spot, pick-ups available. ***Pigeon's Lodge***, T4290437. Set menu of mainly French and Italian specialities, bookings essential. ***Tipi and Bob's***, T4290550. Full menu including snacks and fish and chips, licensed (takeaways). ***Stray Possum Lodge***, T4290109. Pizza kitchen.

Whangaparapara *Great Barrier Lodge*, restaurant and bar, T4290488.

Medlands *Medlands Lodge*, à la carte French, Provincial and Italian, T4290352.

Claris *Great Barrier Island Sports and Social Club*, basic takeaways, Wed, Fri, Sat, T4290260. ***Claris Texas Café***, open daily 0900-1600. Fine food all day and from 1800 Thu-Sun evenings, best coffee on the island, T4290811.

Port Fitzroy *Port Fitzroy Boating Club*, Sat only menu (takeaways), T4290072. ***Jetty Tourist Lodge***, Kiwi food and seafood (summer only), T4290050.

Entertainment

In summer the bays are alive to the sound of clinking gin bottles and laughter from the parties taking place on yachts and expensive launches, but on the mainland there are 2 fine places to go to drink and have fun. ***The Currach Irish Pub*** at the Pohutukawa Lodge, T4290211, offers live entertainment with an unusual Kiwi/Irish flavour, while ***The Stray Possum Lodge***, T4290109, has a delightful little bar, where the manager and staff will entertain the beer-deprived visitors and occasional locals with a great collection of 80's hits. The odd wild party often ensues.

Directory

There is no mains electricity or streetlights on the island , so bring a torch. All electricity is self generated which gives the island much of its charm, but this may mean lights out at 2200. Water is sourced from streams or tank storage but considered safe

Banks There are no banks on the island but Eftpos is readily available in most shops, cafés, main accommodation places and restaurants. **Communications** **Post office**: Outpost, Tryphena (Stonewall Complex), T4290610. Port Fitzroy Store, T4290056. Okiwi, Fitzroy-Harataonga Rd, T4290156. You can even send a message by pigeon at the Pigeon Post, Claris, T4290219. **Telephones**: Generally available at main centres and sometimes in the most ridiculous places around the island. **Fax/photocopying**: ACC Service Centre, Claris, T4290258. **Fuel Petrol and Diesel** Available at Tryphena (Mulberry Grove), Claris, Whangaparapara and Port Fitzroy. **Gas**: refills at 143 Hector Sanderson Rd, Claris, and 428 Shoal Bay Rd, Tryphena. **Laundry** Claris Fuel and Laundromat, T4290075. **Medical services** **Doctor**: Health Centre, Claris, T4290356. **Pharmacy**: very amusing and based in Claris. **Public Toilets** Shoal Bay, Whangaparapara, Port Fitzroy Wharves, Mulberry Grove and Pa Beach Tryphena, Medlands, Claris and the Airfield.

Northland

Northland

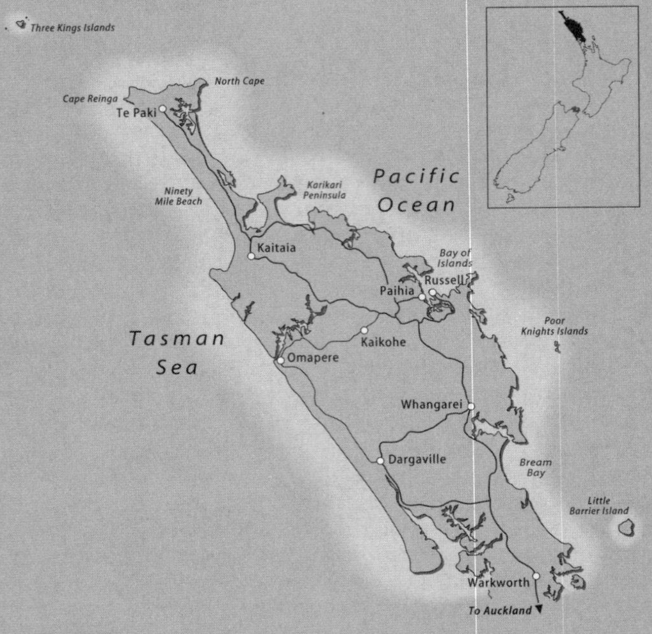
Three Kings Islands
North Cape
Cape Reinga
Te Paki
Ninety Mile Beach
Karikari Peninsula
Pacific Ocean
Kaitaia
Bay of Islands
Russell
Paihia
Poor Knights Islands
Kaikohe
Tasman Sea
Omapere
Whangarei
Dargaville
Bream Bay
Little Barrier Island
Warkworth
To Auckland

Northland is often called the 'cradle of the nation' and 'the 'winter-less north', a region rich in history, with a fine climate and boasting some of the most contrasting and stunning ***coastal scenery*** *in the country. It was here that the first Maori set foot in New Zealand, about 1000 AD, followed over 800 years later by the first European settlers. Here also, in the Bay of Islands in 1840, the Treaty of Waitangi was signed – the document that launched the relationship between two deeply contrasting peoples. A relationship reflected in the calms and the storms of unsettled ocean currents that unite uneasily at New Zealand's northernmost point,* ***North Cape****. Lost in time in the Waipoua Forest, making all that human history seem like yesterday, stands one of the few remaining 'ancient' kauri trees, the mighty '****Tane Mahuta****', nearly two millennia old. All in all, for the modern day visitor, Northland must feature as one of the most aesthetically and historically interesting regions to visit in New Zealand. Most of what it has to offer is signposted and detailed as the aptly-named and celebrated '****Twin Coast Discovery****'.*

Things to do in Northland

- *Watch the sunrise from Ocean Beach near Whangarei, and then synchronise watches at the Museum of Clocks in the Town Basin.*
- *Dive the Poor Knights Islands or go sea fishing from Tutukaka.*
- *Explore the Northland Coast from the Old Russell Road to the Bay of Islands.*
- *Go dolphin swimming, kayaking, sailing, big game fishing or for a fast jetboat ride in the beautiful Bay of Islands.*
- *Discover the 'Birth of the Nation' at the Waitangi National Reserve.*
- *Enjoy a day-trip to Cape Reinga, the northernmost tip of New Zealand. Go dune surfing, then drive back down Ninety-Mile Beach.*
- *Stand in awe below the massive 1500-year-old kauri tree 'Tane Mahuta' in the Waipoua Forest Park. Then learn more about the great trees at the award-winning Kauri Museum in Matakohe.*
- *See the bizarre garden decorations of Te Kopuru, near Dargaville.*

Ins and outs

Getting there **Air** ***New Zealand Link***, T0800-737000, and ***Great Barrier Airlines***, T0800-900600, service Whangarei, with the former also servicing the Bay of Island's (Karikari) and Kaitaia.

Road State Highway 1 up the East Coast is the main road to Northland via Orewa, Warkworth, Whangarei, Paihia and north to the Cape. The roads back down the West Coast from Kaiatia to Dargaville and back on to SH1 at Brynderwyn are more remote and less easily negotiable. The best bet is to follow the well-signposted '**Twin Coast Discovery Route**,' which encompasses both main coast roads, and take any small diversions from there. The free map and routeplanner 'Twin Coast Discovery' is available from all VICs and will keep you right. Most people travel anti-clockwise round the coast but you can go either way. The 2 main **coach** lines servicing Northland are ***Northliner***, T0930-75873, leaving from Auckland's Downtown Airline Terminal, and ***Intercity***, T0991-36100, which leaves from the Sky City Terminal. These services connect with the West Coaster service, which negotiates the West Coast from Dargaville and Paihia, T4383206. For backpackers, ***Kiwi Experience***, T3669830, offer a popular package to Northland attractions up the East Coast.

Information There are Visitor Information Centres (VICs) throughout Northland that provide free and comprehensive information on all that the region has to offer and places to stay. They will also book travel and sell local attraction tickets. Details of the VICs are given under the relevant town. You'll find them in Orewa, Warkworth, Whangarei, Paihia, Kaitaia, Omapere and Dargaville. All Auckland VICs are also well-endowed with information about the neighbouring region.

Warkworth

Phone code: 09
Population: 2000

Although of some historic significance as a former kauri-milling town, Warkworth is now essentially a farming service centre located on the banks of the Mahurangi River, 70 km north of Auckland. Although not geographically within Northland, it is for most a starting point and a gateway to the region. Most travellers, in their haste to reach Whangarei or the Bay of Islands (on State Highway 1), miss out sleepy Warkworth altogether, while others stop for lunch or a coffee by the river before taking the slower and more scenic route north, along the Kowahi coast, via Leigh, Mangawhai and Waipu. But whatever your intention, Warkworth and the pleasant coastal bays, peninsulas and islands to its east, are certainly worthy of a brief stop.

Ins & outs

Getting there *Intercity* and *Northliner* coaches stop daily outside the VIC, T9136100. *Gubb's Motors* also have weekday buses that connect with the Auckland *Yellow Bus Company* in Silverdale, T4258348.

The Warkworth Visitor Centre is located at 1 Baxter St, T4259081, F4257584, www.warkworth-information.co.nz It's open Christmas-Feb, Mon-Fri, 0830-1730, Sat-Sun, 0900-1500; Mar-Christmas, Mon-Fri, 0900-1700, Sat-Sun, 1000-1500.

Sights

Much of the local history is nicely presented in the **Warkworth and District Museum** located within the **Parry Kauri Park** on Tudor Collins Drive on the southern outskirts of the town, T4257093. The museum, which falls under the shadow of two impressive 6-800 year old kauri trees (the tallest on the east coast of Northland), explores, in a number of carefully recreated rooms, the life of the early pioneers and the influence of the great kauri industry upon them. There is also a small but pleasant nature trail next to the museum. ■ *Daily summer 0900-1600, winter 0900-1530. Adult $4, child $0.50.*

Staying south (4 km), and in stark contrast, is the **Warkworth Satellite Station** which is the Telecom NZ national base for international satellite communications. Under the shadow of two huge satellite dishes, is a small 'unmanned' visitor centre. It is all very impressive, for technophiles and technophobes alike. ■ *Daily 0900-1500. Free. T4258059, www.telecom.co.nz*

Back on SH1 again, and less than 1 km further south, you can get back to nature and all things sweet and communal at the **Honey Centre**, Perry Road, T4258003. It provides an interesting insight in to the industry and a close up look at a resident hive, and provides an ideal opportunity to buy a tub of the golden stuff for the kids to spread gratuitously all around the hire car. ■ *Daily 0900-1700. Free. T4258003.*

About 4 km north of Warkworth is **Sheepworld**. If the foot falls heavy on the accelerator at the very prospect of such a place, then just hold on. It is actually quite entertaining and worthy of the stop. Although chasing them is rightly frowned upon, you are allowed to feed the lambs and get involved in some shearing. The souvenir shop more than caters for the reminder of your visit. Café on site. ■ *Daily 0900-1700. Show 1100 and 1300 or T0800-227433. Adult $9, child $4.50. Www.sheepworld.co.nz* A further 3 km north is the **Dome State Forest,** which provides a number of walks ranging from 40 minutes to three hours. The best walk takes 1½ hours climbing to the Dome Summit from where you can spot the Auckland Sky Tower on a clear day. All the walks start at the *Top of the Dome Café*, which is open daily.

To the east of Warkworth, on the scenic Mahurangi Peninsula, are the popular coastal holiday venues of **Snells Beach** (with the *Salty Dog Tavern*, an old English style pub with good beer and pub grub, T4255588), **Algies Bay** and **Martins Bay**, the latter having the best beach, and **Sandspit**, from where the ferry departs to **Kawau Island** (see below).

Sleeping

The Warkworth area seems to have a glut of luxurious B&B accommodation

L ***Kauri Grove Lodge Homestay***, Thompson Rd, Kaipara Flats, T4225775, F4225785, www.kaurigrove.co.nz Fine country living, food and wine with 4 luxury guest rooms. **L** ***Sandpiper Lodge***, Takatu Rd Peninsula, Matakana, T4227256. Located near the beautiful Tawharanui Regional Park. Pool and restaurant attached. **L** ***Uhuru Farmstay***, 390 Pukapuka Rd, Mahurangi West, T4220585, T4220545. A spectacular, new and spacious house in farm and bush setting overlooking a private bay. **A** ***Bellgrove B&B***, 346 Woodcocks Rd, T/F4259770. A modern house located 3 mins from the town in a quiet setting with pool and friendly hosts.

Within the town itself a small number of affordable options are available including **A** ***Central Motel***, Neville St, Warkworth, T/F 4258645, and **B-D** ***Warkworth Inn***, 9 Queen St, Warkworth, T4258569, F4259696. The latter is the town's original hotel built in 1860 with comfortable, good value B&B and backpacker-style accommodation. Campervans are also welcome to use the facilities for a small fee.

There is a wide range of accommodation options in the satellite coastal villages from B&Bs to motels and motor parks. The VIC in Warkworth has extensive listings and will arrange bookings, T4259081, F4257584.

Eating For daytime eating try the ***Arts Café***, Baxter St (with its interesting local art gallery attached), open Mon-Fri 0700-1700, Sat-Sun 0900-1500, T4258971, or the ***Duck's Crossing Café***, Riverview Plaza. Open daily 0730-1630. T4259940. For something more substantial the ***Warkworth Pizza Company***, Neville St, open daily 1100-1500, is a local favourite and also opens in the evening from 1700-late. ***Pizza Construction***, Mahurangi East Rd, Snells Beach, also has a good local reputation. Open daily 1700-2200, T4255555. Also the ***Riverbank Café***, Wharf St. Open Thu-Sun, T4257383. For fine dining the ***Kauri Grove Lodge***, T4225775, and ***Sandpiper Lodge***, T4227256 (see accommodation above) are the best options. Bookings essential.

Kawau Island

Kawau island is a popular holiday resort situated 8 km off the coast on the Mahurangi Peninsula. In summer its sheltered bays are almost more popular than terra firma, as yachties from far and wide drop anchor to enjoy the surroundings, fish, swim, dive or party long in to the wee hours. In pre-European times the island was the headquarters of Maori raiders who made numerous pirate attacks on surrounding tribes from their villages and *pa*.

Ins & outs **Getting there** From Auckland ***Fullers Ferries*** run selected summer trips from the Ferry Building, Quay St. Ferry departs 1000 and returns 1630, adult $40, child $20. For schedule information, T3679111, enquiries@fullersakl.co.nz Also from Auckland the ***Kawau Kat*** runs a seasonal ' Paradise Cruise' departing from the Auckland Waterfront daily at 1000 and leaves Kawau at 1500, arriving back at Auckland at 1630. For schedules, T4258006. All other organized trips depart from Sandspit about 6 km east of Warkworth. To get to Sandspit from Warkworth contact ***Gubb's Buses***, T4258348. ***Matata Cruises*** offer a daily 'Coffee Cruise' departing at 1000 (and 1400 Christmas and Easter); adult $25.There is also a lunchtime champagne cruise that departs at 1000 for $35, bookings essential. Both trips allow some time on the island, T0800225292, matata.cruises@extra.co.nz

Kawau Kat Cruises have 2 trips: 'The Royal Mail Run' departs at 1000, adult $45, child $15. The 1½-hr trip takes in the scenic bays before landing for a while at the main Wharf; the 'Paradise Cruise' – see above, T4257650, www.kawaukat.co.nz For thrillseekers there is the seasonal 'Kawau Jet', a fast boat which offers a short blast around the island and the regulatory stop at the Mansion House, T4257650. There are other irregular ferry sailings from Sandspit mainly at 0800,1000 and 1400. For information, T0800-8880006.

Around the island European ownership dates back to 1837 when the island became the focus for mining activites – first manganese, then copper – with operations ceasing in 1869. There are still remnants of copper mines a short walk from the wharf. In

1862 Sir George Grey in his second term as Governor of New Zealand purchased the island for a mere £3500 commencing a 26 year stay in Bon Accord Harbour, where he created perhaps the biggest modern day tourist draw, **The Mansion House**. Grey was very interested in botany and zoology, developing a small collection of exotic animals and plants and also using the island as an acclimatization centre. He even had a pair of zebra brought from Africa to pull his carriage, which resulted in their death a short time after arriving. Sadly, our George was also blissfully unaware of the monumental environmental damage he was unleashing on the increasingly threatened New Zealand native flora and fauna. To this day the odd wallaby hops through the bush, accompanied by the laughing of the Australian kookaburra. In 1967, 79 years after Sir George Grey went home to England, the island became part of the Hauraki Maritime Park. Some 176 ha were put aside as public domain, the Mansion House turned from guesthouse to museum and the rest of the island went to farmers and the wallabies. ■ *Open daily 1000-1530. $4.*

Northland

Sleeping & eating

There are a number of accommodation options on the island, mainly B&Bs and camp grounds

L ***St Clair Lodge***, Vivian Bay, T4228850. Luxury hostel. **A** ***Cedar Lodge***, Smelting House Bay, T4228700. **A-D** ***Pah Farm Lodge and Camp***, Moores Bay, T4228765. Fishing Lodge, bar and restaurant. **B** ***Mansion House*** (DOC Cottages), Bon Accord Harbour, T4228882. If you would like to stay in the DOC bunkhouse for free in return for some voluntary work contact DOC, T3079279. There is a restaurant attached to the Pah Farm Lodge and a kiosk on the island, but it is not very well stocked and you would be advised to take your own picnic.

Kowhai Coast and Bream Bay

The Kowhai Coast extends from Wenderholm Regional Park just north of Waiwera to Pakiri Beach and contains three Regional Parks, Kawau Bay, including Kawau Island, the Marine Reserve at Goat Island and over 26 accessible beaches popular for boating, fishing, diving and walking.

Matakana

Located 8 km north of Warkworth on the main Warkworth to Leigh Road is Matakana. Blink and you may miss it, but the surrounding countryside, if not the village itself is worth a mention.

The **Morris and James Country Pottery and Café**, Tongue Farm Road, T4227116, uses clay sourced from the Matakana River to produce a wonderful array of terracotta pots and tiles that have become famous throughout the country. There are free weekday pottery tours and the café serves up delicious food and fine local wines in a relaxed garden setting. ■ *1000-1700, pottery tours weekdays at 1130. Café open daily 0830-1630, summer until late, winter Thu-Fri until late.*

The **Heron's Flight Vineyard**, 49 Sharp's Road, is one of a number in the vicinity producing a fine nationally recognized product. Tours and tastings are available and again a fine café is on site. ■ *Daily 1000-1800. T/F4227915, heronfly@planet.wk.gen.nz*

Tawharanui

For Information 'Parksline' T3031530. Permit camping is available

If you have time do not miss the biggest countryside and northernmost coastal park in the region, Tawharanui. It takes some getting to via Takatu Road just north of Matakana, but is well worth the effort. Even before you reach the park you are afforded spectacular views of Kawau Island and beyond. Being so isolated it is quieter than most other parks and offers beaches, walks and scenery unrivalled in many other eastern coastal parks. A heaven for native birds, you are almost sure to see noisy paradise shelduck, together with pied stilts and variable oystercatchers. Plans are afoot to turn Tawharanui into a 'mainland island' protected with predator-free fences, which would be an exciting prospect. The two main beaches are ideal for relaxing or swimming and look out across Omaha Bay to Leigh. Extended walks out to the headland offer even better views.

Sleeping and eating L *Sandpiper Lodge*, Takatu Rd (see Warkworth sleeping). **L** *Hurstmere Lodge*, Tongue Farm Rd, Matakana, T4229220. **L** *The Castle*, 378 Whitmore Rd, Matakana, T4229288, mail@the-castle.co.nz, are all fine top range options. In the budget bracket there is the **C-D** ***Matakana Backpackers***, 19 Matakana Valley Rd, Matakana, T4229264. Pick-ups available from Warkworth; dormitory and twin share.

Both the cafés at the ***Morris and James Pottery*** and ***Heron's Flight Vineyard*** are excellent for daytime eating while the unusually named ***Rusty Pelican*** in the heart of Matakana offers an affordable evening meal and value roasts on Sun; open Mon-Wed 1600-2300, Thu-Fri 1100-0100, Sat-Sun 1100-2300, T4229122. For fine dining the *Sandpiper Lodge* (see above) is recommended. Bookings essential.

Leigh and the Goat Island Marine Reserve

The original name for Leigh was Little Omaha, which was common sense given its position on the west of Omaha Cove, 13 km from Matakana. However, to avoid confusion with its sister settlement of Big Omaha, located slightly inland, the name was changed, to Leigh. Why 'Leigh' remains a mystery. Whatever, Leigh is a small fishing community the nature of which is best summed up with its rather mundane street names like 'Wonderview', 'Barrierview', 'Grandview' and, yes, even 'Seaview'!

Matheson's Beach is situated 1 km to the west of the village and is a popular spot in summer for all beach and aquatic pursuits, but by far the main focus of attention lies 4 km north of Leigh, around Goat Island and the Marine Reserve. Although the island itself, 300 m offshore, is fairly nondescript, the waters that surround it are very special. These waters were established in 1975 as New Zealand's first marine reserve. Treated essentially like any reserve on land, the entire aquatic flora and fauna is fully protected, and no angling or shell fishing is allowed. Essentially, nothing can be taken except photographs and scientific samples. The result is an astonishing abundance of marine life that brings hordes of divers to the area year round. The added allure is that you do not need to be Jacques Cousteau to enjoy it. From the shore swimmers and snorkelers can (particularly in summer) find themselves surrounded by shoals of inquisitive fish looking for an easy meal. In the early days it was possible to feed the fish, but it quickly became obvious a diet of cheese slices and crisps was not conducive to their good health. Indeed a sign just before the beach now states: 'Do not feed the fish, it can make them sick'.

Wet suits and belts ($25), tank refills and snorkelling gear ($11) can be hired from *Seafriends*, 7 Goat Island Road, 1 km before the beach. Full dives cost $60 and can be done daily 0900-dusk. There is also a restaurant on site and a small series of aquariums containing local sea creatures for children to see and for educational purposes. T4226212, www.seafriends.org.nz The glass-bottom boat *Habitat Explorer* offers a number of trips around the island for up to 45 minutes, giving good views of the fish and abundant marine life, weather dependent; October-June, adult $18, T4226334, F4226901.

Sleeping & eating

C-D ***Goat Island Backpackers***, Goat Island Rd, T4226183. Well-situated close to the beach and also has powered sites for campervans, but may be closed in winter. The **C-D** ***Leigh Sawmill Café***, 142 Pakiri Rd, Leigh, T4226019, has accommodation, while there is always the beachfront and friendly **C-D** ***Whangateau Holiday Park***, 559 Leigh Rd, Whangateau, T4226305.

For daytime eating try the ***Sawmill Café***, 142 Pakiri Rd, T4226019. Open summer daily 7 days 1000-late, winter Thu-Sun 1000-late. ***Seafriends***, 7 Goat Island Rd, T4226212, also has a restaurant. Given the fishy nature of the village and the area as a whole it would perhaps be rude not to sample the delights of ***Leigh Fish and Chips***, Cumberland St. Open daily 1100-2230 (later on weekends)

The main road north of Leigh splits in to a series of metalled roads that begins to give the first raw impressions of rural Northland life. Just 10 km north of Leigh is the very pleasant and fairly isolated beach at **Pakiri**. If you wish to stay, the *Pakiri Holiday Park* has some nice cabins that face right on to the beach, T4226199. There is also a rather intriguing homestay option at '*Miller's Ark*' just north of Pakiri, T4315266. Horse trekking is available nearby with the popular *Pakiri Beach Horse Treks* ($25 per hour, $85 per day, two-day safaris also available), who also provide their own basic or more comfortable homestay accommodation, T4226275.

Mangawhai Heads

From Pakiri the metalled roads wind their way up to **Mangawhai**, a short distance from the sweeping coast and beaches of the Jellicoe Channel. Slightly inland the rather exposed **Spectacle** and **Tomorata Lakes** play host to local water-skiers and jet-skiers. If you have the gear very pleasant accommodation can be found at **AL** *Lake View Chalets*, 662 Ocean View Road, T4314086, www.chalets.co.nz The best spot at which to access the beach and coastal views is at **Te Arai Point**, just north of Spectacle Lake. There is little in the way of habitation here, which adds to the peace and isolation. North along the beach from Te Arai there is a **wildlife refuge** that takes in the impressive sand spit of the **Mangawahi Harbour**, but this is best accessed just south of Mangawhai village on Bull Road (off Black Swamp Road).

Some 10 km north of Te Arai is Mangawhai, a small farming village which offers a limited range of motel and motor camp accommodation. The Mangawahi Harbour was once famous for its stingrays – 'Whai' in Maori – hence the name of the village – 'Manga' meaning stream. Mangawhai Heads, a short distance to the north of the village, is basically a scattering of holiday houses frequented by the wealthy in summer. The beaches around both villages are popular with surfies and beach-goers, and 'The Heads', as it is better known, is also a popular base for deep-sea and game fishing.

There is no information centre in Mangawhai but a fairly comprehensive information booth is located next to the main drag, Molesworth Drive, near the Golf Club. Here you can see the various accommodation options (beyond those mentioned below) and local activities available. The leaflet '*Magical Mangawhai*' is also comprehensive and available from Regional Tourist Offices and most local shops and motor parks.

Sleeping and eating **L** ***Kainganui Lodge***, Mangawhai Heads, T4191342. The best luxury option in the area. **A** ***Milestone Cottages***, Moir Point Rd, Mangawhai, T4314018, milestone.cottages@clear.net.nz Self-contained, near the beach with pool and kayaks. **A** ***Hidden Valley Chalets***, corner of Te Arai Pt Rd, Mangawhai, T4315332. Quiet surrounds with outdoor spa. Two of the best Motor Camps are the ***Mangawhai Heads Motor Camp***, Mangawhai Heads Rd, T4314675, and the ***Riverside Holiday Park***, Black

Swamp Rd, Mangawhai, T/F4314825, the latter being close to the beach and the sand spit wildlife refuge.

The ***Naja Garden Café***, Molesworth Dr. Fully licensed and offers contemporary food and an all-day breakfast. Open daily 7 days 0830-1700, and for dinner 7 days, Thu-Sat winter. T4315226. ***Sail Rock Café***, Wood St. Offers an à la carte menu, plus pizzas and café lunches, bar and BYO. Open 7 nights in summer, T4314051. For a quick coffee and to check your email head for the ***Cyber Café***, 7 Wood St, T4315430.

Waipu and around

North of Mangawhai the road negotiates the headland and falls to the beautiful shoreline settlements of **Lang's Beach** and **Waipu Cove** at the southern end of **Bream Bay**, before turning inland to the proudly Scottish enclave of **Waipu**.

Waipu was founded in 1853 by a party of 120 Scottish settlers who were part of a group of 400 that originally left their homelands under the resolute leadership of the Reverend Norman McLeod. They did so in desperation during the terrible Highland Clearances, which resulted in mass migrations in the early 1800s. Their first stop was Novia Scotia but after a series of bad winters and crop failures they left for the new colonies in Australia and then New Zealand on board sailing ships they skilfully built themselves. With their resettlement a relative success, word was sent to Nova Scotia and a further 850 followed to settle the area. Hints of the ethnic origins are all around the village with street names like Braemar Lane, Argyll Street and Caledonian Park.

Also, in the village square is the grand war memorial monument which is made of Aberdeen Granite and was shipped especially from Scotland in 1914 to commemorate the 60th anniversary of the town's founding.

Sights

The small community is very proud of their Scottish heritage and no visit to Waipu would be complete without a look inside the **Waipu Museum** with its large Nova Scotian flag outside – a flag that combines the ancient Scottish Saltire and Lion Rampant designs. Inside the museum, walls decked with the photographs and faces of early immigrants, proud and brave, look down on cases full of personal effects, from spectacles to spinning wheels. Log books listing the immigrant arrivals and the ships on which they arrived have been carefully created and are being continuously updated. It is little wonder that many Nova Scotians come especially to Waipu to trace their ancestors and at times find family heirlooms amongst the treasured pieces. The staff in the museum are very knowledgeable and will, if you linger, tell you many a fine story of both past and present. ■ *0930-1600, $4. T4320746.*

Every New Year's Day since 1871 the **Waipu Highland Games** (the largest and longest running in the Southern Hemisphere) gets into full swing with highland dancers, pipe bands and the statutory kilted, caber-tossing men, all of whom descend on the village from far and wide. For details contact the Waipu Caledonian Society, T4320746. The **Old Waipu Firehouse Art Gallery** in the old Waipu fire station on West End Street is worth a look with some fine examples of local art at affordable prices. ■ *7 days. T4320797.* On the eastern edge of Waipu adjacent to Johnston Port Road is the **Waipu Wildlife Refuge,** where you can see a variety of native shorebirds in an easily accessible area situated around the mouth of the Ruakaka River.

The **Waipu Caves** 13 km to the west of Waipu (via Shoemaker Road), offer a great opportunity to see glowworms through a 200-m passage, part of an extensive limestone cave system. The cave has free access, so caution is advised. Going alone is not recommended and obviously do not enter without a torch and appropriate footwear. A map giving directions is available in the museum and the cave is signposted from Waipu Caves Road. If you would prefer to see the sights above ground using the four-legged option, or take a guided tour of the cave, *North River Horse Treks* can oblige, T4320565. Again, take appropriate clothing, your swimsuit and a torch.

North of Waipu and back on SH 1 you follow the edge of Bream Bay (beach best accessed at Uretiti 6 km north of Waipu) before turning inland towards Whangarei. At the northern end of Bream Bay and the entrance to Whangarei Harbour is the unsightly **Marsden Oil Refinery.** This is where all of New Zealand's crude oil is imported. Sadly, even with all the best technology in the world, the refinery and its tanker traffic poses a significant threat to Northland's pristine coastline and remains a potential environmental disaster. However, see if the **visitors centre** at the refinery can persuade you otherwise. ■ *Daily 1000-1700. T4327620.*

Sleeping

There are a number of good B&Bs and Lodges in the area including the **L** ***Wychwood Lodge***, Lang's Beach, T4320757, which has 4 luxury suites with breakfast included. Also, **L** ***Vane House***, Lang's Beach, T4320356, which is self-contained. More affordable options include the **A** ***Lochalsh B&B***, Cove Rd, Lang's Beach, T4320053; the **A** ***Stone House B&B***, Cove Rd, Waipu, T4320432; and the **A** ***Flower Haven B&B***, 53 St Ann Rd, Waipu Cove, T4320421. There are only a few motels, including the **A** ***Waipu Clansman Motel***, 30 Cove Rd, Waipu, T4320424, and the **A** ***Waipu Cove Motel***, Waipu Cove, T4320348. For budget accommodation there is the **C-D** ***Ebb and Flow Backpackers Hostel***, Johnston Point Rd, T4320217, and the ***Waipu Cove Reserve Caravan and Camping Ground***, Waipu Cove, T4320410.

Eating

There is not a great deal to tickle the tastebuds in Waipu and sadly not a haggis or a 'clooty dumpling' to be had anywhere (in public that is!). However, ***Waipu Cove Takeaways***, Cove Rd, T4320636; ***Granz Café***, The Centre, open daily in summer, T4320254; ***Pizza Barn and Bar***, 3 Cove Rd, Waipu, T4321011; and the ***Clansman Motel and Restaurant***, 30 Cove Rd, Waipu, T4320424, will no doubt all do their best for you with conventional Kiwi fare.

Whangarei and around

Phone code: 09
Population: 47,000

First impressions of Whangarei are not good. Perhaps it is the lure of the Bay of Islands to the north, but there is an almost inevitable sense of disappointment on arriving here. But, despite its rather dull appearance, if you do choose to linger and use it as a base, you will find that it is surrounded by gems. One such gem is, very simply, to sit on Ocean Beach, Whangarei Heads, just after a storm, and watch the sunrise.

Ins and outs

Getting there

Although there is a rail link with Auckland there is no passenger service

Air The district is serviced by ***Air New Zealand***, T0800737000, www.airnz.co.nz ***Great Barrier Airlines*** also run a Sun service, T2566500. Onerahi Airport is located 9 km west of the city and is linked to the city centre by shuttle bus, $7, T4370666.

Car If you are arriving by car, take extra care on the stretch of road from Waipu to Whangarei. This stretch of road is a notorious black spot and is known locally (rather morbidly) as 'the killing fields'.

Bus Both ***Intercity***, T4382653, and ***Northliner Coaches***, T4383206, have a daily service to and from Auckland and further north. The depot for both is in Rose St, downtown Whangarei.

Whangarei

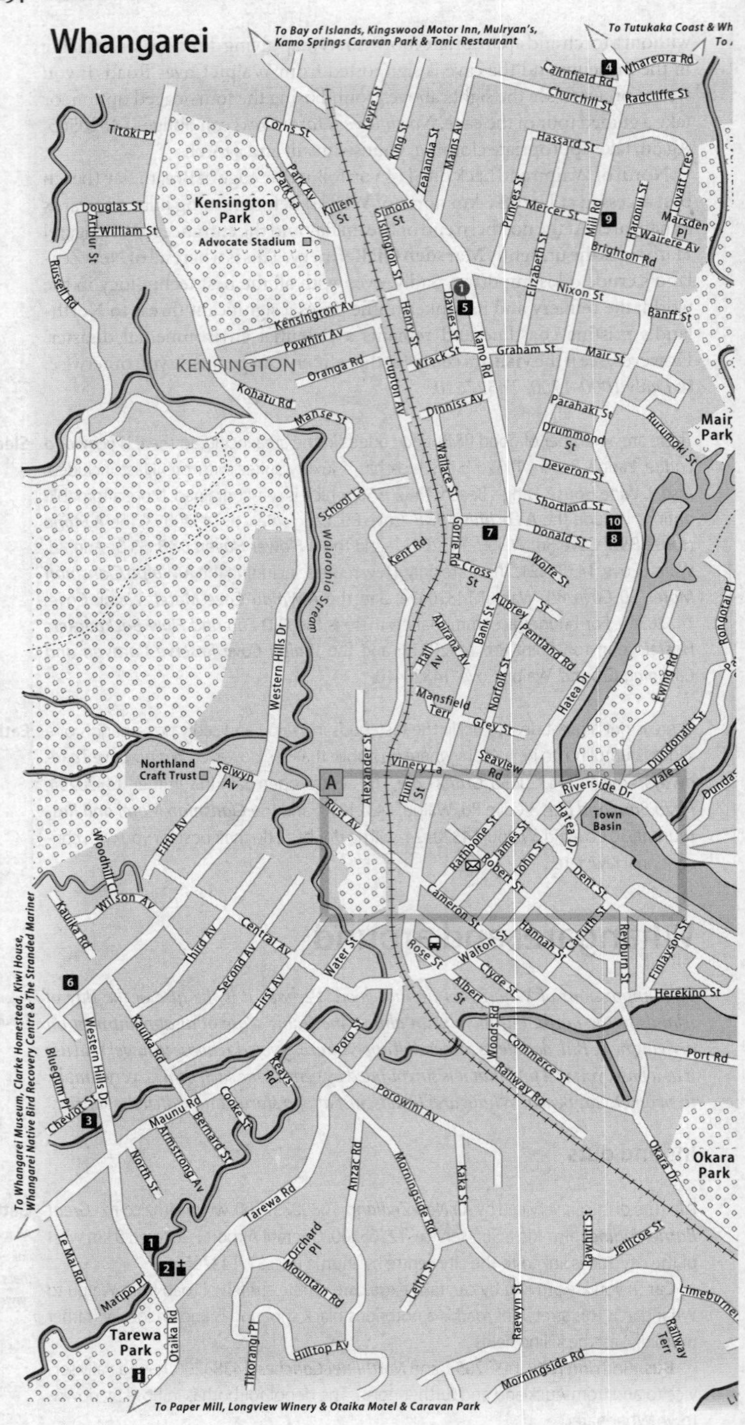
To Bay of Islands, Kingswood Motor Inn, Mulryan's, Kamo Springs Caravan Park & Tonic Restaurant
To Tutukaka Coast & Wh
Kensington Park
Advocate Stadium
KENSINGTON
Northland Craft Trust
Town Basin
Mair Park
Okara Park
Tarewa Park
To Whangarei Museum, Clarke Homestead, Kiwi House, Whangarei Native Bird Recovery Centre & The Stranded Mariner
To Paper Mill, Longview Winery & Otaika Motel & Caravan Park
Wairoahia Stream
Whareora Rd
Cairnfield Rd
Churchill St
Radcliffe St
Hassard St
Mercer St
Brighton Rd
Nixon St
Banff St
Mair St
Graham St
Parahaki St
Rurumoki St
Drummond St
Deveron St
Shortland St
Donald St
Wolfe St
Aubrey St
Pentland Rd
Hatea Dr
Riverside Dr
Vale Rd
Dundonald St
Ewing Rd
Rongotai Pl
Dent St
Reyburn St
Finlayson St
Herekino St
Port Rd
Okara Dr
Rawhiti St
Jellicoe St
Limeburner
Railway Terr
Morningside Rd
Raewyn St
Titoki Pl
Douglas St
William St
Arthur St
Russell Rd
Corns St
Park Av
Park La
Killen St
Keyte St
King St
Zealandia St
Mains Av
Simons St
Islington St
Princes St
Elizabeth St
Mill Rd
Haronui St
Lovatt Cres
Marsden Pl
Wairere Av
Kensington Av
Powhiri Av
Oranga Rd
Kohatu Rd
Manse St
Henry St
Davies St
Kamo Rd
Wrack St
Lupton Av
Dinniss Av
Wallace St
School La
Kent Rd
Gorrie Rd
Cross St
Bank St
Apirana Av
Hall Av
Norfolk St
Mansfield Terr
Grey St
Seaview Rd
Vinery La
Hunt St
Alexander St
Western Hills Dr
Selwyn Av
Rust Av
Rathbone St
James St
Robert St
John St
Hatea Dr
Cameron St
Walton St
Hannah St
Caruth St
Rose St
Clyde St
Albert St
Woods Rd
Commerce St
Railway Rd
Fifth Av
Woodhill Cl
Wilson Av
Kauika Rd
Third Av
Central Av
Second Av
First Av
Water St
Poto St
Reays Rd
Porowini Av
Bluegum Pl
Cheviot St
Maunu Rd
Armstrong Av
Bernard St
Cooke St
North St
Te Mai Rd
Tarewa Rd
Anzac Rd
Morningside Rd
Kaka St
Orchard Pl
Mountain Rd
Leith St
Matipo Pl
Otaika Rd
Tikorangi Pl
Hilltop Av
A
1
2
3
4
5
6
7
8
9
10

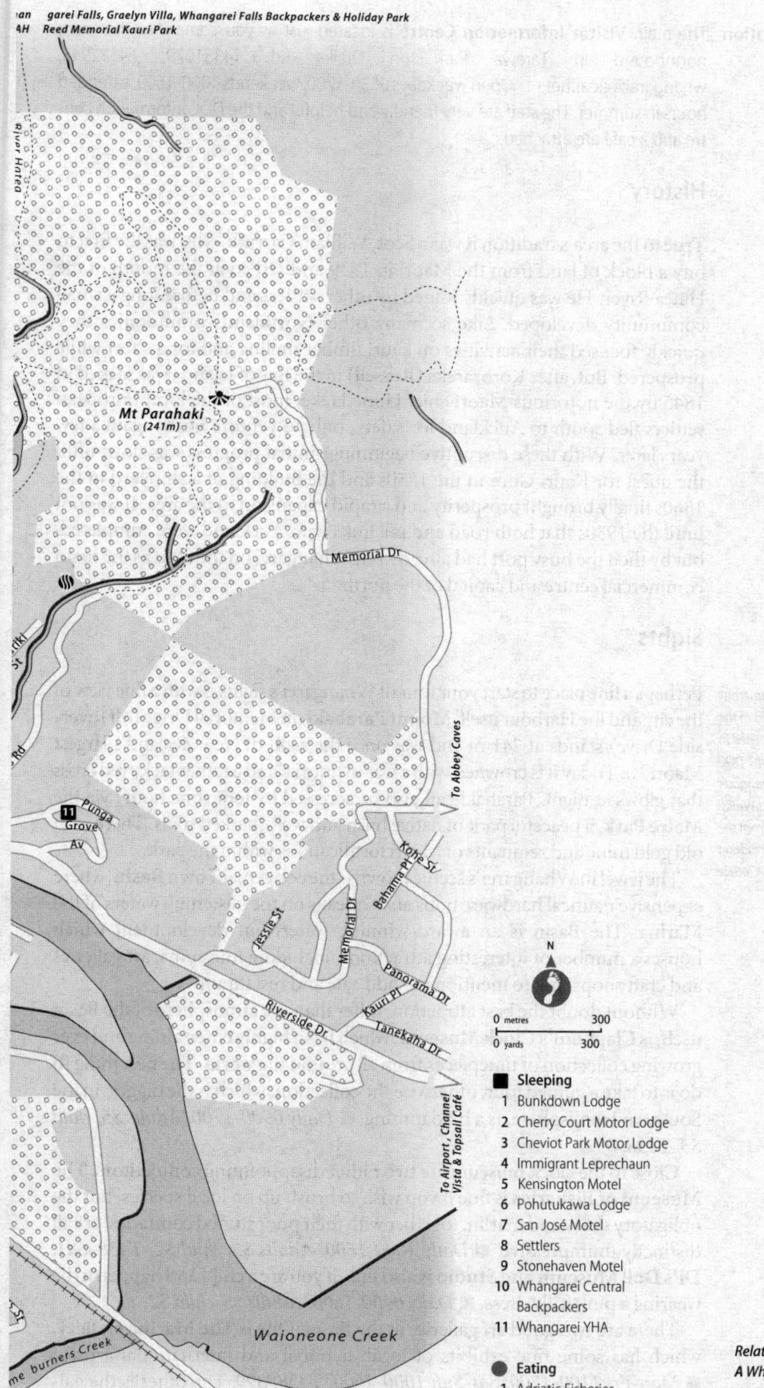

Related map
A Whangarei centre, page 157

Information The main **Visitor Information Centre** is located just as you come into the town northbound in Tarewa Park on Otaika Rd, T4381079, F4382943, whangarei@clear.net.nz Open weekdays 0830-1700, weekends 1000-1600, extended hours in summer. The staff are very friendly and helpful and the DOC information centre and a café are attached.

History

True to the area's tradition it was a Scot, William Carruth, who was the first to buy a block of land from the Maori in 1839 and settled at the mouth of the Hatea River. He was quickly joined by other settlers and before long a small community developed. Like so many other Northland communities they quickly focused their activities on kauri timber milling and for a short while prospered. But, after Kororareka (Russell) in the Bay of Islands was sacked in 1845 by the notorious Maori chief Hone Heke, most of the local European settlers fled south to Auckland for safety, only to venture north again a few years later. With these disruptive beginnings initial progress was slow, until the quest for Kauri Gum in the 1850s and the building of a shipyard in the 1860s finally brought prosperity and a rapid expansion to the area. It was not until the 1930s that both road and rail links with Auckland were completed, but by then the busy port had already put Whangarei on the map as the main commercial centre and capital of the north.

Sights

There are numerous fine walks in the district outlined in detail in the DOC pamphlet 'Whangarei District Walks' available from the Visitor Information Centre or DOC office

Perhaps a fine place to start your tour of Whangarei's sights is with a fine view of the city and the Harbour itself. **Mount Parahaki** on Memorial Drive (off Riverside Drive) stands at 241 m and was once the sight of New Zealand's largest Maori *Pa*. Today it is crowned with a war memorial and a rather tacky red cross that glows at night. Parahaki can also be accessed by foot (one hour) via the **Maire Park**, a peaceful park of native bush and well-marked trails. There is an old gold mine and remnants of Maori fortifications within the park.

The jewel in Whangarei's scenic crown is the congenial **Town Basin**, where expensive nautical hardware bobs and squeaks on the glistening waters of the Marina. The Basin is an award-winning waterfront development which houses a number of interesting attractions, including museums, art galleries and craft shops, not to mention the odd café and restaurant.

Without doubt the best attraction, other than the atmosphere of the Basin itself, is **Clapham's Clock Museum**, which has a highly entertaining and ever growing collection of timepieces from all around the world. The best thing to do is to take a guided tour, otherwise the collection, which is the biggest in the Southern Hemisphere, is a bit daunting. ■ *Daily 0900-1700. Adults $5, child $3. T4383993.*

Close to the clock museum are two rather disappointing competitors. **The Museum of Fisheries** is fine if you wish to brush up on local species, but the obligatory shark and marlin, together with their poor stuffed comrades, are all distinctly unimpressive. ■ *Daily 1000-1600. Adults $5, child $2. T4385681.* **Di's Doll Museum and Studio** is also fine, if you are a child and happen to be wearing a pink frilly dress. ■ *Daily 0900-1600. Adults $5, child $2.*

There are two good art galleries at the Basin. One is **The Marina Gallery**, which has some fine exhibits of local, national and international artists. ■ *Mon-Fri 1100-1700, Sat-Sun 1000-1600. T4388899.* The other is the gallery in the historic colonial **Reyburn House** (oldest in Whangarei), which features displays of local art. ■ *Tue-Fri 1000-1600, Sat-Sun 1300-1600.* For lovers of beer, Northland Breweries, 104 Lower Dent Street, T4384664, near the Basin offers free beer tasting – but there is a limit! ■ *Mon-Sat 0900-1800.*

West of the town Basin, located in the peaceful and pleasant **Cafler Park and Rose Gardens**, is the **Whangarei Art Museum**, a small, modern museum that shows the best of local art past and present and also hosts touring national exhibitions. ■ *Tue-Fri 1000-1630, Sat-Sun 1200-1630, donations. T4307240.* A short walk will take you to the **Margie Maddren Fernery and Snow Conservatory**. The fernery houses New Zealand's largest collection of ferns, while the conservatory is filled with ever-changing displays of flowers. ■ *Daily 1000-1600. Free. T4384879.* Near the park on Rust Avenue is the **Forum North Cultural Complex** (see Entertainment, page 160).

On the outskirts of town at the end of Selwyn Avenue is the celebrated creative heaven of the **Northland Craft Trust (Craft Quarry)**. It's an impressive collective of working artists and crafts people producing an array of works from pottery and lithographs to traditional Maori carvings – worth a visit. ■ *Daily 1000-1600. Free.*

Further west and 6 km out of town, in the suburb of Maunu, is the **Whangarei Museum, Clarke Homestead** and **Kiwi House**. It is an indoor/outdoor complex with a colonial farming block and homestead and a modern building housing a number of significant Taonga or Maori treasures, including Kiwi feather capes and a musket that belonged to the great northern warrior Hone Heke. The display is deliberately indigenous in content and perspective. 'Live Days' are held regularly during the summer with special events like bullock riding, vintage car displays and horse drawn carriages. The Kiwi House is one of the better examples in the country with museum-style exhibits of native flora and live kiwi on show. Note that there is usually only one. This is deliberate since kiwi are solitary birds and fiercely territorial. ■ *Daily 1000-1600, Adult $3, $7 all sites. T4389630, www.whangareimuseum.org.nz*

Next to the museum is the **Whangarei Native Bird Recovery Centre**, T4381457. Although not freely open to visitors you may be allowed to visit by prior arrangement and for a donation. This charity has the main centre in the north for wild bird rehabilitation and has an excellent and successful kiwi egg incubation facility. To the south of the city on State Highway 1 is **The Paper**

Northland

Whangarei centre

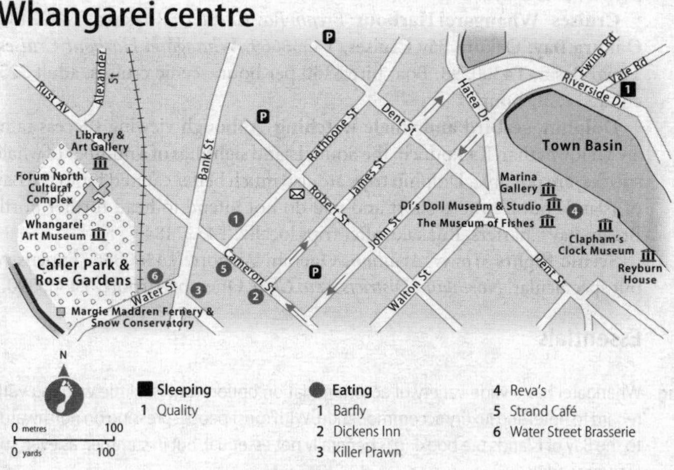

Mill. This tourist attraction is growing in popularity and deservedly so. It gives the visitor an insight into traditional craft papermaking using recycled materials in an historical setting, and you can even try to make some yourself. ■ *Mon-Fri 1000-1200, 1300-1400. $4, $6 to make paper. T4382652.* Just 1 km further south is the **Longview Winery**, a 30-year-old estate producing popular and award-winning wines. ■ *Mon-Sat 0830-1800 in summer, 0830-1730 in winter, Sun 0900-1700.*

To the north of the city on Ngunguru Road, Tikipunga, is the slightly over-rated 23 m **Whangarei Falls** which are worth a peek if you are passing. Perhaps a better way to experience them is to abseil down them with *Northland Outdoors*, T4303474. The **AH Reed Memorial Kauri Park** on Whareora Road is the pick of the local parks with some fine examples of native Kauri trees up to 3 m in diametre and 500 years old. They are impressive, but nothing compared to the 1500 year old Tane Mahuta on the west coast which in turn is nothing compared to some monsters that once were. The park has a number of short walks and tracks and a very pleasant waterfall thrown in for good measure.

Although they are hard to find and a bit out of town, the **Abbey Caves** are worth a visit. If you take a right off Memorial Drive (up Mount Parahaki) on to Old Parua Bay Road and on to Abbey Caves Road you will, with a little difficulty, find a DOC sign next to the road. Provided you have adequate footwear, a torch and are not alone (or have kids in tow), then follow the footpath and signs past the weird and wonderful limestone foundations that lead to the caves. Do not venture too far in to the caves without a guide. If you are brave switch off your torch and amidst the sound of trickling water, enjoy the small galaxy of glow-worms above. It is easy to get lost in and around the caves so the best option if you have time is to join a guided tour, Bill McLaren: Hatea House Hostel, Hatea Drive, T4376174, $12.

Tours & activities

Bush Safaris *The Bushwacka Experience*, Highway 14, Maungatapere, T4347839, F4347539. Thrilling trips in a four-wheel drive vehicle with frequent stops, barbecue and abseiling. Daily four-hour trip $85, two-hour $55. Recommended. *Farm Safaris*, Maungakaramea, T4323794, fmsafari@ihug.co.nz Morning, afternoon and twilight tours on four-wheel bikes. One hour (minimum four people) $50, two hours (minimum three people) $90. 20 minutes south of the city on SH1.

Cruises **Whangarei Harbour**: *Bream Bay Charters*, Ruakaka, T4327484. **Oakura Bay**: Oakura Bay Cruises, T4336669. *Whangarei Harbour Cruises*, Town Basin, T4300598. Boat hire $150 per hour, scenic cruises, adult $25, child $12, 2½ hours.

Dolphin, seabird and whale watching Although viewing success rates are far lower than Kaikoura in the South Island sightings of a number of whale species, are possible. Dolphin trips are also much better catered for in the Bay of Islands but if time is short and you do not intend to head further north Bream Bay Charters, Ruakaka offer trips locally, T4327484.

Scenic flights *Tower Aviation*, Onerahi Airport, T4360886. Expensive but spectacular. *Northland Districts Aero Club*, Onerahi Airport, T4360890.

Essentials

Sleeping

Whangarei has a wide variety of accommodation options but is a little wanting with regard to hotel and luxury accommodation. With most people pressing on northwards to the Bay of Islands pre booking is generally not essential, but in summer, as ever, still recommended.

AL *Quality Hotel*, 9 Riverside Dr, T4380284, F4384320, quality.whangarei@extra.co.nz Guest rooms and suites, laundry, licensed restaurant and bar. Overlooks the marina and Town Basin.

A *Channel Vista*, 254 Beach Rd, Onerahi, T/F4365529, tancred@igrin.co.nz Fully self-contained and traditional bedrooms, great harbour views. **A** *Cherry Court Motor Lodge*, 35 Otaika Rd, T4383128, F4387972, www.cherrycourt.co.nz Swimming pool, laundry, licensed restaurant nearby. **A** *Cheviot Park Motor Lodge*, corner of Cheviot St and Western Hills Dr, T4382341, F4380442. Units with kitchen facilities and – for the non-sea sick or downright kinky – waterbed suites. **A** *Kingswood Motor Inn*, 260 Kamo Rd, T4375779, F4375780. 5 mins north of the city centre, paraplegic units, laundry, spa. **A** *Mulryan's*, Crane Rd, Kamo, T4350945, F4355146, info@mulryans.co.nz Comfortable B&B style accommodation in a restored kauri villa. Quiet country setting and a great breakfast. **A** *Pohutukawa Lodge*, 362 Western Hills Dr, T4308634, F4308635. New studio units, some with spas, laundry. **A** *Settlers Hotel*, Hatea Dr, T4382699, F4380794, settlers@ihug.co.nz Located in a nice setting over looking the river and within walking distance of the Town Basin. En-suite bedrooms, laundry, pool and private spas, licensed à la carte restaurant. **A** *Stonehaven Motel*, 30 Mill Rd, T4376898, F4595940. Clean, comfortable and within walking distance to city centre. **A** *The Stranded Mariner*, State Highway 14, T4389967, F4387967. Separate self-contained unit and traditional B&B accommodation. Unusual house with a veritable den of unusual teddy bears and a craft shop.

B *Graelyn Villa*, 166 Kiripaka Rd, T4377532, F4377533, graelyn@extra.co.nz Nicely restored villa, comfortable and homely. **B** *The Immigrant Leprechaun*, 2 Cairnfield Rd, Kensington, T4377991, F4373986. Comfortable, clean and friendly with an Irish flavour. **B** *Kensington Motel*, 85-87 Kamo Rd, T/F4370555. Another budget option. **B** *San Jose Motel*, 10 Cross St, T4387459, F4385669. Adequate budget motel option.

C-D *Bunkdown Lodge*, 23 Otaika Rd, T4388886, F4388826, bunkdown@ihug.co.nz Without doubt, one of the best Backpackers in the country, Large, modern, more like a B&B and even has a bath. Very helpful friendly hosts who have nothing short of another tourist information centre attached. Popular, so book ahead. **C-D** *Whangarei Falls Backpackers and Holiday Park*, Ngunguru Rd, Tikipunga, T4370609. A great wee backpackers which doubles as a small motor camp. All the usual amenities plus a small pool, spa and TV room. **C-D** *Whangarei YHA*, 52 Punga Grove Av, T4388954. **C-D** *Whangarei Central Backpackers*, 67 Hatea Drive, T4376174, F4376141, centralback@extra.co.nz Popular with divers heading for Tutakaka.

Motor camps and campsites *Otaika Motel and Caravan Park*, 136 Otaika Rd, T/F4381459. *Kamo Springs Caravan Park*, 55 Great North Rd, T4351208. *Whangarei Holiday Park*, 24 Mair St, T4376856, F4375897, whangareiholiday@actrix.co.nz

Eating

Expensive *Killer Prawn*, 28 Bank St, T4303333. A swish and busy restaurant/bar considered the best eatery in town, offering a wide selection of traditional and specialist seafood options. Try the namesake 'Killer Prawn' – a small pond of seafood in which to bathe your tastebuds. *Water Street Brasserie*, 24 Water St, T4387464. Open Tue-Sat, BYO. Fine traditional cuisine in modern surroundings. *Tonic*, 239A Kamo Rd, T4375558. Licensed, contemporary French cuisine and a fine Sun brunch from 0900. *Topsail Café*, 1st Floor, Onerahi Yacht Club, Beach Rd, Onerahi, T4360529. Open Mon-Sat from 1800, Sun brunch 1000-1500. Continental style cuisine and a local seafood favourite. *Reva's on the Waterfront*, Quayside Town Basin, licensed, T4388969. International cuisine in very pleasant surroundings. Live music most nights.

Mid-range *Barfly*, 13 Rathbone St, T4388761. Café-style fare including wood-fired pizza and good coffee. *Dickens Inn*, corner of Cameron and Quality St, T4300406. One of Whangarei's most popular pubs. Pub-style cuisine, breakfast, lunch, dinner and snacks, children's menu.

Cheap *Adriatic Fisheries*, Kensington, 91 Kamo Rd, T4373874. The best fish and chippy in town. The *Strand Café* in the Strand Arcade is also a value snack stop with a great cheap breakfast.

Entertainment

Whangarei touts itself as the cultural centre of the north

The main **cinema** in the city is on James St. *Cinema City Five*, T4388550. The well-equipped *Forum Theatre* is one of the best in the country for cultural and performing arts; T4383815. There are a number of nightclubs in the city. Try the *Powderhound*, Vine St, and the *Metro Bar* or *Planet Earth* on Bank St. All 3 are pretty lively but, as you would expect, have that small town atmosphere. For something a little quieter head for the *Dickens Inn* in Cameron St, *Barfly* in Rathbone or *The Killer Prawn* in Bank St. The latter is the local 'place to be seen'.

Sports

Kensington Park and the Advocate Stadium, Western Hills Dr, T4373021. A modern venue for hockey, cricket, soccer and athletics, while the stadium caters for basketball, volleyball, bowls, shows and concerts, and also has an 8-m high rock wall. **Diving** Whangarei is used as a base for the Tutukaka coast, which offers world class diving around the Poor Knights Islands (see below). **Fishing** The harbour and more especially the Tutukaka coast offers excellent sea fishing. Big game fishing charters are available at Tutukaka with record catches in summertime. **Golf** Whangarei has some fine courses. *Whangarei Golf Club*, Denby Cres, T4370740, is the best. Also, *Northland Golf Club*, Pipiwai Rd, Kamo, T4350042. *The Pines*, Parua Bay, T4362246. *Sherwood Park*, Millington Rd, Maunu, T4346900. **Hang-gliding** Weekends with local club *Northland Hang Gliding*, Guntram Gross, T4360268. **Horse riding** *Manaia Horse Treks*, McLeod's Bay, T4340165. Bush and beach treks around the beautiful Whangarei Heads. *Whananaki Trail Rides*, Whananaki, T4338299. **Rugby** Okara Park in the city is the venue for local and provincial games as well as international test matches. **Sea Kayaking** *Escape Sea Kayaking Tours*, 1 Riverside Dr, Town Basin, T4388280. 2-hr to 4-day adventures in the Whangarei Harbour, offshore islands and Tutakaka Coast with experienced guides. Summer only. *Northland Coastal Adventures*, Parua Bay, T4360139. Fishing, kayaking, snorkelling, boogie boarding. Bill McLaren, Hatea House Hostel, Hatea Dr, T4376174. Provides local tours especially suited for beginners. **Skateboarding** *The Skateboard Park*, William Fraser Memorial Park, Riverside Drive, has a modern 1500 sq m facility. **Swimming** *Whangarei Aquatics*, Riverside Drive, T4387957. Olympic sized outdoor pool and a large indoor heated pool. Spas and sauna also available; open daily, $2.50.

Transport

Whangarei has a fairly comprehensive bus service operated and administered by the Regional and District Councils. Timetables are available from the VIC or infoline, T4384639. Standard fare within the city is adult $2, child $1. The main taxi company is *Kiwi Carlton*, 24-hr service, T4382299.

Directory

Banks Most are situated in Bank St (funnily enough). **Car rentals** *Avis*, Okara Dr, T4382929. *Budget*, 22 Maunu Rd, T4387292. *Rent-a-Cheepy*, 69 Otaika Rd, T4387373. **Communications** **Internet** is available at the Library and at the Town Basin Post Shop. **Main Post Office** is located at 16-20 Rathbone St. **Library** Rust Av, T4307260. **Medical services** *Primecare*, 12 Kensington Av, T4371988. 0830-2200.

Whangarei Heads

If you do only one thing in the Whangarei district, then make sure it's a trip to watch the sunrise at **Ocean Beach,** 35 km west of the city. Ocean beach is one of Northland's best: it's quiet, beautiful and, in a raging easterly wind, a place where the senses are bombarded with nature at its best. On the way you will begin to note the prevalence of evocative Scots place names like McLeod's and Urquart's Bay and street names like McDonald Road – all family names of the 'overspill' Scots settlers from the Bream Bay and Waipu enclaves. Above these quiet communities and scenic bays are the towering peaks of **Mount Manaia,** the base of which can be accessed from the car park next to the Manaia Club. It is an excellent, but steep walk through native bush that takes about three hours return. You cannot climb to the peak summits themselves – they are *tapu* (sacred and off limits) – being steeped in Maori legend. Other fine coastal walks are to **Peach Cove** (three hours) and **Smugglers Cove** (one hour) both of which are accessed from **Urquart's Bay**.

Sleeping

There is little in the way of accommodation at the heads beyond McLeod's Bay but the small communities of Parua Bay just before it, and Pataua and Taiharuru a few kilometres north, have a number of options. **A** *Parua House*, Parua Bay, T4365855, F4365702. A farmstay with en-suite and private facilities, fine views. **A** *The Old Lady*, 13 Norfolk Av, Reotahi, T4340575, is an historic homstead that offers 2 rooms with their own sitting room and balcony. **A** *Tide Song*, Taiharuru Estuary, Beasley Rd, T4361959, is self-contained in a bush and seaside setting. **D** *Treasure Island Trailer Park*, Pataua South, T4362390, has a beachfront campsite.

Eating

If venturing back into Whangarei is too much effort then try the *Parua Bay Tavern*, Parua Bay, T4365856. It offers bistro style lunches and evening meals. Beyond that it is groceries or snacks at the general store at McLeod's Bay.

Transport

There is no public transport available to the Heads, but cycling is an option. For hire contact *Hedgehog Bikes*, 29 Vine St, Whangarei, T/F4382521.

The Tutukaka Coast

Even if fishing and scuba diving did not exist, the Tutukaka coastline would still deserve to be one of the finest coastal venues in Northland. But its rugged scenic bays are best known throughout New Zealand and beyond as the gateway and safe harbour to some of the best deep-sea fishing and diving in the world. **The Poor Knights Islands** which lie 25 km offshore are an internationally significant nature reserve both above and below the waterline, with a wide range of flora and fauna. Here the nutrient-rich currents meet in water of unusually high clarity to create a showcase of marine life much of which is seen nowhere else in the country. Although landing is forbidden without a permit the islands themselves are home to rare terrestrial species, like the prehistoric tuatara, a reptile that has changed little in 60 million years. Most activity in the area takes place from **Tutukaka** with its large sheltered marina while the village of **Ngunguru**, 5 km before it, has most of the visitor and resident amenities.

Ins & outs

Getting there If you are not going on a tour with one of the Whangarei diving, fishing or tour companies you will need your own wheels to get to Tutukaka. The village is on the loop road that also takes in Ngunguru and **Matapouri** before turning inland again back to SH1 and Whangarei. From the city suburb of Tikipunga take the Ngunguru Rd past Whangarei Falls. On the outskirts of the city in Glenbervie the roads become lined by 'drystone' walls giving the area a distinctly British countryside feel (no doubt a legacy of the early settlers) before New Zealand bush takes over once again and you hit the coast at Ngunguru.

The Poor Knights Islands

The Poor Knights Islands, lying 24km off Tutukaka, are the remnants of a large volcano, which erupted over 10 million years ago. The islands themselves provide a predator-free refuge for land animals like tuatara, native lizards, giant weta, flax snails, giant centipedes and a wide variety of rare seabirds. They are also home to several species of distinctive plants, including the Poor Knights lily, found only on 'The Knights' and the Hen and Chicken islands off Whangarei Heads. But it is the marine reserve, and the wonderful spectacle below the water, for which the islands are most famous. A rich habitat of caves, arches, tunnels and sheer cliffs attract a wide variety of marine life from sharks to black coral. Sponge gardens, kelp forests and gorgonian fields are inhabited by a myriad of fish, shellfish, urchins and anemones and there even tame grouper, which welcome divers with their distinctively vacuous look. All this combined with the exceptional water clarity make 'The Knights' one of the top dive sites in the world.

Activities

Diving Tutukaka is the main dive base with companies offering personalized tours and equipment hire. Most boats leave for the Poor Knights about 0830 and return at 1600. As well as the Poor Knights, wreck dives are also available to the sunken navy frigate *Tui* located just offshore from Tutakaka, and the *Waikato*, another warship sunk in 2000. A two-dive trip costs about $150 with full gear hire. Tuition, snorkelling and kayaks are also available for the novice.

The main dive company is *Tutukaka Dive* who run a very professional outfit from their base right on the marina. They offer a range of over 10 site dives with such evocative names as 'The Labyrinth' and 'Maomao Arch' as well as tuition, snorkelling, kayak and whale and dolphin watching activities, T4343867, F4343884, www.diving.co.nz Another reputable company offering a similar package is the *Tutukaka Charter Boat Association*, Tutakaka Marina, T4343818, F4343755. Based in Whangarei are: *Pacific Highway Charters*, T4373632, F4372469; *Knight Diver Tours*, 30 Heads Road, Whangarei, T4362584, www.poorknights.co.nz *Dive HQ*, 41 Clyde Street, Whangarei, T4381075, F4300854; *Dive Connection*, 140 Lower Cameron Street, Whangarei, T4300818, F4300562. The latter two offer full dive courses. If you would like to try **Shark Cage Diving** contact *Sports Fishing Charters*, T4343233, hookem@igrin.co.nz If they can locate a shark or six they will happily scare the life out of you for about $120. Post-dive prosthetic limb hire extra!

Fishing There is no fishing allowed within the marine reserve of the Poor Knights but the surrounding ocean has some of the best deep-sea fishing in the world, with numerous species like shark and marlin. The 'big game' season runs from December to April. A day trip as a group will cost at least $200 a head. Most of the main charter companies are based in Tutukaka including; *Delray Sportsfishing Charters*, T/F4343028, delray@igrin.co.nz; *Lady Jess Charters*, Tutakaka, T4343758; *Whangarei Deep Sea Anglers Club*, Tutukaka, T4343818.

Horse treks *Sandy Bay Horse Park*, Sandy Bay (near Matapouri), T4343327.

Jet-skiing, mountain biking, kayaking, surfing, boogie boarding Equipment hire is available at *Water Sport Hire*, 14 Kopipi Crescent, Ngunguru, T4343475, and the *Ngunguru Holiday Park*, T/F 4343851.

Walking One of the best walks in the area is at Tutukaka Head. To reach the car park take the 'right of way' sign right off Matapouri Rd, 400 m past the *Tutukaka Hotel* and marina. From there the track goes over the headland before falling to a small beach and a series of small rock stacks. After negotiating the stacks (beware at high tide), climb the hill to the light beacon (2 km; one hour return), from where there are magnificent views along the coast. A few kilometres north of Tutukaka, just before the road turns inland again, are a number of small settlements and attractive bays and beaches. Matapouri and Whale Bay 1 km to the north are both well worth a stop.

Sleeping

AL *Waipouri Lodge*, Tutukaka, T4343696, mckillop@extra.co.nz Self-contained 3 bedroom home. **A** *Dreamstay*, Sandy Bay, T4343059, dreamstay@homenet.net.nz B&B, homestay or self-contained options. **A** *Pukepoto Orchards*, 521 Ngunguru Rd, Glenbervie, T4375433, F4373533. Self-contained unit in garden setting. **A** *Malibu Malls Divestay*, Tutukaka Block Rd, Kowharewa Bay, T4343450, malibumal@extra.co.nz Self-contained units or B&B. **A** *Pacific Rendezvous Motel*, Tutukaka, T4343847, F4343919, www.oceanresort.co.nz The most celebrated motel in the area offering spectacular views across the Tutukaka Harbour. **A** *Seabreeze Motel*, Ngunguru, T/F4343844. **A** *The Sands Motel*, Whangaumu Bay, Tutukaka, T4343747, F4343192. 6 spacious self-contained units. **A-D** *Ngunguru Holiday Park and Backpackers*, Ngunguru, T4343851.

Eating

One place not to miss is the *Snappa Rock Café* by the marina in Tutukaka, T4343774. Open 7 days and nights. People come here from miles around to enjoy the seafood, the atmosphere and talk about the one that got away.

Whangarei to the Bay of Islands

Most people take State Highway 1 to the Bay of Islands, though a far more interesting route is via the **Old Russell Road** which leaves SH1 for the coast at Whakapara, about 26 km north of Whangarei. Here you are entering a mobile-phone-free-zone, on roads with more animals than cars, and with communities whose houses have and streets on which the children (predominantly Maori) do not mind walking in the rain. Welcome to rural Northland and the simple spirit of the north. After simply enjoying the countryside and its atmosphere you reach the coast at **Helena Bay** which, along with **Whananiki** and **Mimiwhangata** to the south and the **Whangaruru Peninsula** to the north, offer remote and beautiful coastal scenery.

From Whangaruru the road passes the neck of the beautiful **Cape Brett Peninsula** which offers great **walking** in equally stunning coastal scenery before turning inland and slowly negotiating its way to Russell. If you intend to reach Paihia you can get the vehicular ferry at Okiato (last ferry Saturday-Thursday 2050, Friday 2150).

Accommodation here is somewhat basic and sparce

Sleeping There are basic motor camps with backpacking facilities mainly at Oakura (just north of Helena bay). The **C-D** *Oakura Beach Camp*, Oakura Bay, T7527861, and **C-D** *Whangaruru Beachfront Camp*, Whangaruru, T4336806, are both near the beach. DOC have relatively cheap facilities with a self-contained lodge, cottage, beach house (book well in advance) and a campsite at *Mimiwhangata Bay* and *Coastal Park*. Bookings can be made through the Tarewa Park Visitor Centre, T4302007. Basic DOC camping facilities are also available at Whananiki and Whangaruru; contact DOC, T4302007.

The Bay of Islands

If you arrive in **Paihia** by road, the Bay of Islands will be a huge disappointment, because you can't see them. You can see plenty of 'no vacancy' signs, plenty of people and boats – including a ferry that crosses the bay to the small village of **Russell** – and plenty of sales people in ticket offices, but no islands. Well, don't worry, they are out there. All 150 of them.

The Bay of Islands is one of the major tourist draws in the country offering the visitor a combination of numerous water-based activities and superb coastal scenery. The area is also of huge historic significance being the site of the first European settlement and the signing of the **Treaty of Waitangi** – the document that began the uneasy 'voyage' of New Zealand's bi-cultural society. You can explore the islands by kayak, by yacht, or by sailing ship, go big game fishing for marlin or shark, dive amidst shoals of blue maomao, swim with the dolphins, bask in the sun or jump out of a plane.

Ins and outs

Getting there The Bay of Islands **airport** is located between Paihia and Kerikeri. ***Air New Zealand Link***, T0800-737000. A shuttle bus meets planes. Most people, though, arrive at Paihia via SH1 from Whangarei. A more scenic route via the Old Russell Rd will bring you in 'the back door' via Russell. A vehicle **ferry** connects Russell and Paihia via Opua (see below). ***Northliner*** and ***Intercity*** run regular daily **coach** services to the Bay of Islands from Auckland and all major points north and south on SH1. The journey from Auckland will take about 4 hrs. In Paihia all buses arrive outside the Maritime Building on the Wharf.

Getting around Paihia is not big and everything is in walking distance including Waitangi. Russell can be reached by passenger ferry from the wharf every half hour or so from 0720 to 2230 (reduced in winter). Adult $4, child $2.

A vehicle ferry leaves about every 15 mins from Opua 9 km south of Paihia (Sat-Thu 0650-2100, Fri 2200) car and driver $7, camper van $12, passenger $1 one way). For trips further afield and a guided tour ($45) contact ***Bay Mini Tours***, T4075373.

Orientation & information Paihia is the main **resort town** in the Bay with the focus being on the waterfront, where the vast majority of your activities on or around the islands and **Bay of Islands Maritime and Historic Park** can be booked and boarded. Paihia was the site of New Zealand's first church and missionary centre. Waitangi, which is a short walk north, is a pleasant contrast as a site of celebrated national heritage. The Treaty of Waitangi was signed here in 1840 at the historic **Treaty House**, which is now a national museum and visitor's centre on the **Waitangi National Reserve**. Paihia is also the base for a number of tours and excursions further north.

Tourist office Located on the waterfront by the wharf, Marsden Rd. T4027345, F4027314, visitorinfo@fndc.govt.nz Open daily, Oct-Mar 0700-1900, Apr-Sep 0800-1700.

Paihia and Waitangi

Unless you have a fetish for motels there is little in the way of sights in Paihia itself, with the town acting primarily as a base, accommodation and amenity centre for tourists. There is a small aquarium on the wharf with the highly imaginative name of **Aquatic World**, but its café hosts more delights than its tanks of incarcerated sea creatures. For the best of land-based attractions you are far better to head the short distance north to Waitangi with the possible diversions of the collection of fierce looking Maori *pou* (carvings) and the sailing ship the 'Tui' on the way. This 1917 'Tui' houses **Kelly Tarlton's Shipwreck Museum**. Kelly was by all accounts a wonderful fellow and New Zealand's best-loved diver, underwater explorer, treasure hunter and the founder of the impressive Undersea World in Auckland. However, here in Waitangi, the offering is far less impressive, focussing on Kelly's collection of underwater lost and found, with a bistro and café attached. Sadly the bottle of 100-year-old whisky is not on the drinks list. ■ *Daily 0900-1730. Adult $7, child $2.50. T4027018.*

Waitangi Visitor Centre & Treaty House

For an excellent personally guided tour of the reserve contact, Culture North, T4019301, CultureNth@extra.co.nz, $13 (includes entry)

A little further along, across the bridge, is Waitangi and the very impressive Waitangi Visitor Centre and Treaty House set in the **Waitangi National Reserve**. This is the heart of New Zealand's historical beginnings. The haunting sound of piped Maori song leads you in to the visitor centre where your first stop should be the audio-visual display before taking the pleasant walk around the reserve. This is quite nicely done but does give you a rather 'politically correct' outline of events that led to the signing of the Treaty of Waitangi in 1840 and the significance of the document right up to the present day (see page 688). The main focus of the reserve is the beautifully restored **Treaty House.** It was built in 1833-34 and was once the home of British Resident James Busby who played a crucial role in the lead up to the treaty signing. The house is full of detailed and informative displays that help clarify the quite confusing series of events surrounding the creation of the treaty. Near the Treaty House the reserve boasts perhaps the most visited **Whare Runanga** (Maori meeting house) in the country. To merely call this, or any *Whare* merely a house would be a minimalist view. They are essentially artworks, with all the meaning, soul and effort therein and the Whare Runanga at Waitangi is a fine example.

In front of the Treaty House and Whare Runanga is a spacious lawn overlooking the bay to Russell. From the lawn it is a short walk down to the shore where the **war canoe** (*waka*) 'The Ngatokimatawhaorua' is housed. This impressive 35-m long craft is named after the canoe in which Kupe, the great Maori ancestor and navigator, discovered Aotearoa (New Zealand), and was commissioned along with the Whare Runanga as a centennial project commemorating the signing of the treaty. The Ngatokimatawhaorua continued to be launched every year as part of the high profile Waitangi Day commemoration ceremonies hosted on and around the National Reserve. However, in recent years, after attracting protesters, Waitangi Day was scrapped and there was a call for a more progressive and low key 'New Zealand Day'. ■ *Daily 0900-1700. $8.* T4027437.

The Huia Creek Walkway, which begins near the Treaty House, is an easy walk through the reserve to the unremarkable **Haruru Falls**, taking in a fine example of mangrove habitat on the way (two hours). Running adjacent to the reserve is the **Waitangi Golf Course**, which along with **Mount Bledisloe** 3 km away, commands fine views across the bay.

Around Paihia

You might think it ridiculous to recommend a public convenience as a major attraction but if you have time, a visit to the **Kawakawa 'Hunterwasser' Public Toilets** in the centre of Kawakawa, 17 km south of Paihia, is a must. You can get to Kawakawa in style on the Opua to Kawakawa **Bay of Islands Vintage Railway**. The train leaves the small port and marina base of **Opua** 2-3 times daily and the journey takes 45 minutes each way; $16 return, $10 one way. T4040684.

Paihia & Waitangi

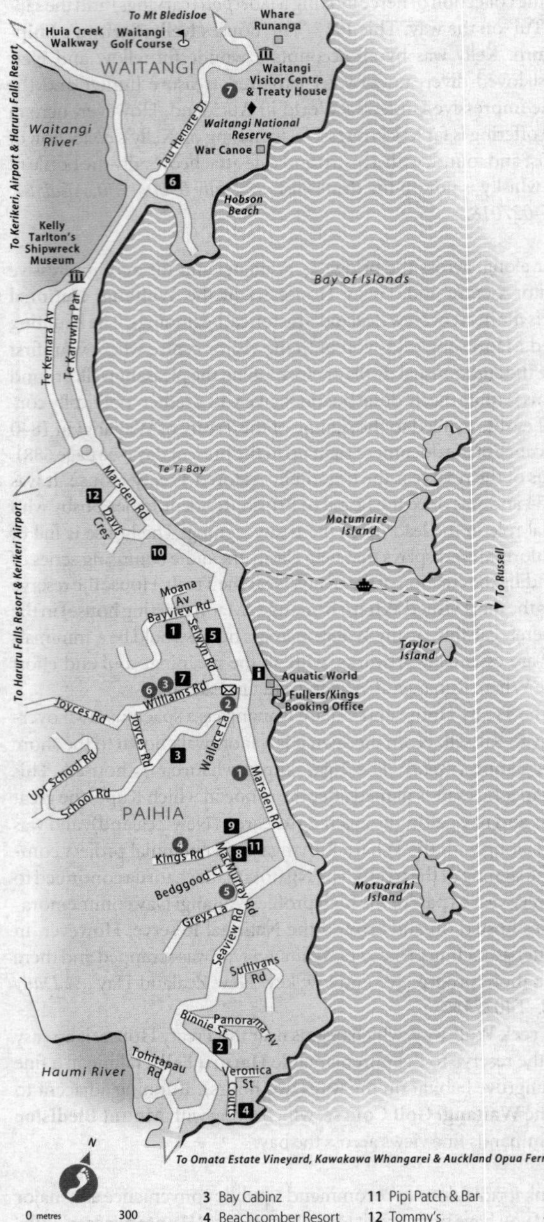

Sleeping
1 Abri Apartments
2 Aloha Garden Resort Motel
3 Bay Cabinz
4 Beachcomber Resort
5 Centabay
6 Copthorne Resort
7 Dolphin Motel
8 Lodge Eleven
9 Mousetrap
10 Paihia Beach Resort
11 Pipi Patch & Bar
12 Tommy's

Eating
1 Bistro 40 & Only Seafood
2 Caffé Over the Bay & Lighthouse Tavern
3 Esmae's
4 Paihia Pacific 'Oasis'
5 Park Lodge
6 Ruffino's
7 Waikokopu Café

Activities & tours

It is better not to book ahead, unless you have researched the options thoroughly, or you will lose much freedom of choice

The minute you arrive in Paihia you are under pressure to book, book, book and buy, buy, buy. Sadly it has become the nature of the place, as the huge range of tour and activity operators vie for your attention and dollar. The best thing to do is to take your time and to take advice from the unbiased VIC before venturing in to the 'booking mall' on the waterfront to be mauled by the sales sharks. The two main players are *Fullers*, T4027422, www.fullers-bay-of-islands.co.nz (not the same company as the ferry operators in Auckland), and *Kings*, T4028288, www.kings-tours.co.nz Both offer very similar tours ranging from relaxed day trips around the islands and swimming with dolphins, to the bum-breaking speedboats that head out to Cape Brett and 'The Hole in the Rock'. Bear in mind there is fierce competition. The booking offices are open daily from 0700-2130, 1830 in winter. For detailed information you are best to get your hands on both agencies' *Awesome Adventures and Dolphin Encounters, Bay of Islands Leaflets* (available from the waterfront VIC or booking offices or from Auckland VICs and the Bay of Islands Travel Centre, Customs Street, Auckland).

Northland

Boomnetting This is the rather novel idea of clinging on for dear life to a large net slung alongside a cruise boat. The boat stops if dolphins are spotted in the hope they venture near. Boomnetting is done as part of a six-hour cruise trip including the 'Hole in the Rock'. *Kings*, T4028288. Complete trip: adult $79, child $45.

Cruising Huge choice, again in combination with sightseeing, dolphin encounters and the 'Hole in the Rock' – a huge natural arch in a rock outcrop at the very tip of Cape Brett through which the cruise boats navigate the ocean swell. Trips range from about three hours (adult $50, child $25), or six hours (adult $80, child $45). Some cruise options take in a stop on **Urupukapuka Island**, a favourite haunt of Zane Grey, the famous American author and big game fisherman. The bay at Otehei is beautiful, spoilt only perhaps by the rather gimmicky yellow submarine *Nautilus* in which you can venture under the water, $12 (no Beatles songs allowed). If you wish to stay on the island to take in the atmosphere, sights, archaeological walks (see DOC leaflet) and would prefer to pick up a later ferry later, there is the basic *Zane Grey Lodge*, T4037009, or DOC campsites. The Zane Grey restaurant in front of the lodge will see you right for a decent meal.

Very popular (especially in high swell) is the bone-crunching, high speed 'Hole in the Rock' trips in *Kings*' 'Mac Attack', T4028180, or *Fast Boat Company*'s 'Excitor', T4027020. Multiple trips daily, 1½ hrs, $50-$60. There is an informative commentary and stops on the way. You can take a camera but you will probably return with blurred pictures of the posterior of the person in front, and forget wearing specs unless fitted with automatic wipers. Persons prone to seasickness – don't even think about it. For the more traditional approach the rather grand Gaff Rigged Square Tops Schooner, the 'R Tucker Thompson', is a delightful way to see the islands. A six-hour trip will cost you $85. Tea and a barbecue lunch are provided. There is the opportunity to hoist sails and, if you wish, enjoy a swim after walking the plank. *Fullers*, T4027421.

Kayaking *Coastal Kayakers* do half or full day guided trips (some up river to Haruru Falls) and also the excellent three-day experience. Three days on a remote bay with a kayak to explore the islands can be a wonderful adventure, and is a fine chance to encounter dolphins alone or watch the skate and assorted shoals of fish come right up to the water's edge at camp. All equipment and food provided. Half day trip $43, full day $65, multi day $110-$500; independent hire available $10 per hour, $40 per day. T4028105, F4038550, www.nzinfo.com/seakayak/coastalkayakers.htm *Sea Kayak Adventures* offer an equally excellent service and trips at $125 per day, with a special for backpackers at $175/$250 for 2-3 days . All equipment and food provided. T025-2081319, T/F4028596, nzakayak@clear.net.nz

Diving The bay is a fine dive venue and trips are also available for the Greenpeace 'Rainbow Warrior Wreck Dive'. *Paihia Dive*, T4027551, F4027110, www.divenz.com Two dives all gear $145. *Dive North*, T4027079, divenorth@xtra.co.nz Similar set up specialising in the Rainbow Warrior Trip. Also *Captain Buckos* (see below).

Dolphin watching The Bay of Islands is a top spot for dolphins, orca and the occasional migratory whale. There is much debate about the impact of tourist activities on the creatures, though the jury is still very much out. Only three companies are allowed actively to approach the dolphins, and all offer a similar experience of observation and encounter, including a scenic trip (with commentary) around the islands and out to the 'Hole in the Rock'. Limited numbers are allowed in the water at a time, so it can be slow and frustrating, but the animals obviously must come first. All three companies have high success rates and will take you out again the following day for free if your trip proves to be a 'water encounter'. *Dolphin Encounters* (Fullers), T4027421, reservations@fullers-northland.co.nz October-April, depart daily at 0800, returning at 1200 and 1230-1630. May-September, 0800-1200. Adult $85, child $45. Trip with Island stop (Urupukapuka), October-April, daily at 0800-1730, no extra charge. *Dolphin Discoveries*, T4028234, F4026058, dolphin@igrin.co.nz Offer two trips daily at 0900-1300, a 'Discover the Bay' sightseeing and watching trip for $58 and a dolphin swimming trip for $85. *Awesome Adventures*, T4026985, F3021444. September-May, daily at 0800-1200 and 1230-1630; June-August at 0800-1200. Island stop available (Urupukapuka). Adults $85, child $45.

Fishing The Bay and the upper Northland Coast is the best sea angling and big-game fishing venue in the country and one of the best in the world. You may imagine this activity is the preserve of rich, cigar-chomping business men, but think again – a trip can be just about affordable for the average Joe at about $200-$250 a day. It is a very exciting experience, especially if you are 'in the chair' when you hook a big one. There are numerous reputable charter boats operating from Paihia and Russell. Contact the Paihia VIC for details. For beginners and standard sea-fishing options (including diving) try *Captain Bucko's*, T4027788, cptnbucko@acb.co.nz Snorkel trip $55, dive $130, fishing $65 (four hours).

Parasailing A far more sedate option to the tandem skydive which operates along the foreshore in Paihia. *Flying Kiwi Parasail*, T4026078.

Sailing Again, there are numerous independent sailing charters and options in the Bay, contact the Paihia VIC for details. One of the cheaper is *Great Escape Yacht Charters*, Opua, T4027143, www.greatescape.co.nz

Scenic flights *Salt Air* do a range of spectacular scenic flights including a trip to Cape Reinga and back, with a stop and four-wheel drive trip. Expensive at $269, but worth it. T4028338, F4028302, info@saltair.co.nz

Tandem Skydive The customary 'must do' in the region is based at the Airport. *Sky-Hi Tandem Skydive Ltd*, T02-5756758. From $185.

Tours Paihia acts as base for a number of full-day coach trips to the far north and **Cape Reinga**. The trip entails a number of stops to view kauri in the **Puketi Forest**, the lighthouse at the cape and a dune surfing experience, whereby you throw yourself down huge sand dunes on a boogie board. *Fullers*, *Kings*, *Northern Exposure*, T4028644, and *Awesome Adventures*, T4027421 (recommended), offer the trip for around about $75. There is also a four-wheel drive 'Dune Rider', also for $75. T4028681.

Zorbing Described as a 'Bi-Spherical Momentous Disturbance' (once had one of those after 15 pints of beer and a dodgy takeaway in Glasgow). This is the wonderfully silly pursuit of climbing inside a large clear plastic ball and being pushed down a hill. The experience costs $35 and is located 5 km west of Haruru Falls on Puketona Road, T025-2081319.

Northland

Sleeping

If you are looking for peace and quiet you would be better staying across the water in Russell where you will find the best lodges and B&Bs

Paihia is well served with most types of accommodation to suit all budgets, with luxury hotels, a plague of motels and a number of backpackers. Despite a wealth of beds, in summer – especially over Christmas and through Jan and Feb – it is essential to book ahead. Bear in mind the Bay of Islands is also the favoured holiday spot for hundreds of New Zealanders.

AL-L *Beachcomber Resort*, T4027434, F4028202, www.beachcomber-resort.co.nz A popular hotel resort with New Zealanders, located at the other end of town to the Copthorne. Studios and family suites. Right next to the beach. Fine buffet breakfast. **AL** *Copthorne Resort Hotel*, Tau Henare Dr, T4027411, F4028200. l45 guest rooms. Nice location near the Waitangi Reserve. Large and unusual outdoor pools and spas. In the centre of town the **AL-L** *Paihia Beach Resort*, 116 Marsden Rd, T4026140, F4026026, www.paihiabeach.co.nz, and the **AL-L** *Quality Hotel*, T4027416, F4028348 (also on Marsden Rd), are reliable and offer views directly across the bay. There are many self-contained accommodation options in town including the new and delightful **AL-L** *Abri Apartments*, 10 Bayview Rd, T4028003, F4028035, www.abri-accom.co.nz, and the cedar cabins of **AL** *Bay Cabinz*, 32-34 School Rd, T4028534, F4028536, sleeping 1-4.

There are motels all over town, mostly centrally located, ranging in both standard and price. At the top of the range the **A** *Aloha Garden Resort Motel*, 32-36 Seaview Rd, T4027540, F4027820, has a good reputation. In the medium range is the **A** *Dolphin Motel*, 69 Williams Rd, T4028170, F4028666, dolphin@extra.co.nz

There are 8 backpackers in Paihia most of which vary only slightly. The most popular and busy is **B-D** *The Pipi Patch*, 18 Kings Rd, T4027111, F4028300, www.acb.co.nz/pipi.html, which has a great selection of value options from bunks to doubles. It also has a great bar attached, which for travellers is the main focus and meeting venue in town, as well as the haunt of a few good-value locals. Other reputable establishments include the quieter and very arty **C-D** *Mousetrap*, T4028182; **C-D** *Tommy's*, 44 Davis Cres, T/F4028668, tommy's@xtra.co.nz; **C-D** *Centabay*, Selwyn Rd, T4027466, F4028145, centabay@xtra.co.nz; and **C-D** *Lodge Eleven*, corner of MacMurray and King's Rd, T/F4027487. With so much competition in these parts all of them have to maintain good standards so you can't go far wrong.

Motor camps and campsites The *Haruru Falls Resort*, T0800-757525, 6 km north west of Paihia on the Old Wharf Rd has powered sites and camping facilities as well as motel units and a pool. The Haruru Falls are directly in view. ***The Twin Pines*** pub and restaurant is a short walk up the hill, T4027195.

Eating For daytime eating undoubtedly one of the best places to eat is the ***Waikokopu Café*** in the pleasant surrounds of the Waitangi National Reserve, T4026275. It has a highly imaginative menu including the sumptuous 'Whalers Breakfast'. Open daily 0900-1700, BYO and licensed. For fine dining it is worth the trip to the ***Omata Estate Vineyard***, Aucks Rd, Russell, which on a fine summer's day or for an evening treat is expensive but superb, T4038007, info@omata.co.nz

As you would expect, there are plenty of choices in Paihia, most serving local fish and seafood. The ***Paihia Pacific 'Oasis' Restaurant***, 27 King's Rd, T4028221, and the ***Park Lodge***, corner of Seaview and McMurray Rd, T4027826. Open 0700-late. Both offer reliably good à la carte cuisine. For traditional New Zealand fare try ***Esmae's*** at 41 Williams Rd, T4028400. Licensed. For the best seafood in town the upstairs, downstairs ***Bistro 40***, T4027444 (lunch from 1200, dinner from 1800, licensed), and ***Only Seafood***, T4026066 (open daily from 1700, licensed) sit together at 40 Marsden Rd. If it is just a snack you are looking for in a central location the pizzas at ***Ruffino's***, 39 William's Rd, T4027964 (open daily from 1730, licensed), are good and the ***Caffé over the Bay*** right on the waterfront has a nice healthy variety of snacks and good coffee. Breakfast from 0800. For an evening cruise including evening meal, $45, contact ***Darryl Honey Cruises***, T4027848.

Entertainment The best pub in town is attached to the ***Pipi Patch Backpackers***, 18 Kings Rd, T4027111, while clubbing (almost literally) takes place at the ***Lighthouse Tavern***, upstairs in the Paihia Mall.

Directory **Communications** Internet and cheap overseas calls available at ***Internet Access***, Selwyn Rd, T4026632. **Medical services** Doctor, T4028407.

Russell

About 2 km across the water from Paihia is the contrasting settlement of Russell which enjoys a village feel and a rich history that eludes its frenetic, tourism-based neighbour. The original name for Russell was Kororareka, which derived (so legend has it) from the utterings of a wounded Maori chief who, after being given some penguin soup, said 'Ka-reka-te-korora' (how sweet is the penguin). With the advent of the first European settlement Kororareka quickly grew to be the base for whalers, sealers and escaped convicts and soon earned the sordid and notorious reputation as 'the hellhole of the Pacific'. The earliest missionaries tried their best to quell the unholy mob with mixed results. When the Treaty of Waitangi was signed in 1840, although it was the largest European settlement in New Zealand, William Hobson, the then Governor, decided it was not a very good marketing ploy to give it capital status and instead bought land in what is now Auckland. To make matters worse the Treaty was beginning to be seen by local Maori as a fraud and not as beneficial as promised, with financial benefits in particular failing to materialize. The focus of their scorn (led by the infamous chief Hone Heke) was placed on the Flagstaff near Russell, which proudly flew the Union Jack. Heke and his band of not so merry men, duly cut it down, not once but four times, the last felling causing a major battle in which Kororareka was sacked and the first Maori Wars began. Once relative peace returned the authorities decided to make a new beginning and lose the notorious label by calling it Russell.

Today Russell, along with Kerikeri (also in the Bay of Islands), is flaunted as the most historic village in New Zealand and, although it bustles with transitory tourists in the summer and is inundated at New Year, it manages admirably to maintain a sedate and close community feel, which if you stay, can warm the heart.

Ins & outs

Getting there By car via the Opua Ferry (see page 164). By ferry every 20-30 mins from Paihia Wharf, $3.

Tourist office There is no official tourist centre in Russell but the DOC **Bay of Island's Maritime and Historic Park Visitor Centre** on The Strand, T4037685, open daily, summer 0830-1700, winter 0900-1600, will meet most of your needs. Bradley's Office at the end of the wharf, T4038020 (0830-1700), and the Fullers Office on Cass St, T4037866 (open daily 0730-1700), can also help with excursion information. **Activities** Most of the Paihia-based tours stop off to pick up in Russell on their way out to the islands. For information and times contact tour operators or the VICs.

Sights

For a detailed historic indulgence head for the **Russell Museum**, on the corner of Pitt and York Streets. It has an interesting collection of early settler relics and, having being built to commemorate the bi-centenary of Captain Cook's visit in 1769, features a host of information on the explorer, including a very impressive 1:5 scale model of Cook's ship 'The Endeavour'. ■ *Daily, Jan 1000-1700, Feb-Dec 100-1600, $3. T4037701.*

A short distance south along the shore from the museum is **Pompallier House**. This historic 1842 dwelling was originally set up by the early missionaries as a printing works. It later served as a tannery and a private home before becoming a small museum in 1990. ■ *Daily 1000-1700. $5. T4039015.* On the corner of Church and Robertson Streets is the 1836 **Anglican Church** which was one of the few buildings to survive the 1840s sacking and Maori war (bar a few visible musket ball holes) and remains the oldest church in New Zealand. For a grand view it is worth the steep climb to **Flagstaff Hill** (Maiki). Parts of the current pole were erected in the late 1850s over a decade after Hone Heke's attempts at clear felling. Looking a further 1 km north, the earth terraces of the ancient *Pa* on the **Tapeka Point Reserve** are tempting for a pleasant walk.

Long Beach, 1 km behind the village, is also a nice spot and a fine venue on a hot summer's day. If the history of Russell is of particular interest the Heritage Trails leaflet from the DOC Visitor Centre is excellent or there is **Russell Mini Tours**, T4037866, that departs three times daily (1000/1300/1500) from outside the Fullers Office on Cass Street; $15, one hour.

Cape Brett Walk

The track is on Maori Trust land so stick to the rules

This is one of the finest walks in Northland following the ridge of Cape Brett to the lighthouse and DOC Cape Brett Hut. With a clear view across the Bay of Islands it provides some spectacular coastal scenery. The track starts near Rawhiti 29 km from Russell in Oke Bay (secure parking is available at Hartwells, Kaimaramara Bay, end of Rawhiti Road, small fee). It will take an entire day to walk the 20 km to the Hut but if you cannot face the return journey you can book a water taxi to pick you up just below the hut for $30, *Kaimaramara Bay Tours*, T4038114. To attempt the walk and stay in the hut you must first pay a hut fee of $8 and a track fee of $15 at the DOC visitor Centre in Russell. You can post the fee to the centre (PO Box 134, The Strand, Russell) but you will probably still need a key. Keys, essential maps and all the relevant information are available from there.

Sleeping

Russell boasts the widest selection of B&Bs north of Whangarei

L-AL *The Duke of Marlborough*, T4037829, F4037828, the.duke@extra.co.nz Well located right on the waterfront, oozing all the gracious charm its 150 years deserve. 28 guest rooms, bar and à la carte restaurant. **L** *Pukematu Lodge*, Flagstaff Hill, T/F4038500, pukematu.lodge@clear.net.nz Perched high on the hill with spectacular views this superb B&B is run by a very friendly couple, one of whom is the local Maori policeman. En-suite rooms. Breakfast almost surpasses the company and the view. **AL** *Orongo Bay*, Aucks Rd, T4037527, F4037675, orongo.bay@clear.net.nz En-suite rooms in what used to be New Zealand's first American Consulate (1860). Organic gourmet dinners by arrangement. **A** *Inn-The-Pink*, 1 Oneroa Rd, T/F4037347, www.bay-of-islands.co.nz/inthepnk Self-contained, double and single options with fine views. **A** *Arcadia Lodge*, 10 Florence Av, Matauwhi Bay, T4037756, F4037657, arcadialodge@xtra.co.nz Historic Tudor House with 8 comfy rooms, great breakfast. **A-D** *Orongo Bay Holiday Park*, Aucks Rd, T/F4037704, orongabayholidaypark@xtra.co.nz The budget-friendly option. **A-D** *Russell Lodge*, corner of Beresford and Chapel St, T4037640, F4037641. Studio and self-contained units and 13 backpacker cabins. Internet. **A-D** *Russell Top Ten Holiday Park*, Long Beach Rd, T4037826, F4037221, russelltop10@xtra.co.nz Motels, flats, cabins and backpackers. Reliable and fairly modern.

Northland

Eating

Expensive Some of the best eating in the region can be had at the very congenial *Omata Estate Vineyard*, Aucks Rd (halfway between Opua and Russell), T4038007, F4038005, info@omata.co.nz Overlooking the vines and the bay this is a great place to be on a summer's day or evening. Expensive lunch and dinner but worth it. Booking essential. Recommended. The Somerset restaurant in the *Duke of Marlborough Hotel* (see above), is an old favourite, with a great atmosphere right on the waterfront. Open for lunches and dinner.

Mid-range For cheaper meals the *York St Café*, York St, T4037360, is recommended. Great pizzas, seafood and breakfasts. Licensed. Then there is always the *Some Thing's Fishy* fish and chippie on Cass St, T4037754.

Events

Jan: *Tall Ships Race*. Apr: *Bay of Islands Arts Festival*. Aug: *Jazz and Blues Festival*. Sep: *Russell Oyster Festival* (recommended), *Food and Wine Festival*.

Russell

Kerikeri

Phone code: 09
Population: 2000

You have never tasted a mandarin until you have been to Kerikeri. Travelling north from Paihia the rolling hills give way to corridors of windbreaks that hide the laden trees of citrus, grape and kiwifruit for which the area is famous. The word Keri means 'dig', and it was here, in pleasant little 'Dig Dig', that the first plough cut into New Zealand soil in 1820. Along with Russell, Kerikeri is rich in Maori and early European history with the Kerikeri Basin, 2 km northeast of the present town, being the nucleus of New Zealand's first European colonization.

Ins & outs

Getting there Kerikeri **Airport** is about halfway between Paihia and Kerikeri. Arrivals and Departures, T4078419. Kerikeri is 22 km north of Paihia just off SH1. Both ***Intercity*** and ***Northliner*** coaches stop in the centre of town on Cobham Rd.

Getting around For guided tours contact *Tour Kerikeri*, T4079904, leaves Paihia 1315, $45.

There is a small **Visitor information Centre** at the town library on Cobham Rd, T4079297. The VIC in Paihia has detailed information about Kerikeri (see Paihia page 164). The **DOC** information office, 34 Landing Rd, T4078474, can provide advice on local short, or longer walks in the Puketi Forest. Rewa's Village Visitors Centre, 1 Landing Rd, T4076454, can also provide general local information.

Sights

For a sense of history and atmosphere head straight for the **Kerikeri Basin** past the main commercial centre. There the road falls to meet the babbling Kerikeri River and the dominant and attractive **Stone Store**. This was New Zealand's first stone building and was completed in 1835. It was used by the first Anglican bishop George Selwyn as a library in the early 1840s and later as an ammunition store during conflicts between Ngapuhi chief Hone Heke, before assuming its intended purpose as a general mission store. Today it is neatly laid out as testimony to that function with a museum on its top floor. ■ *1000-1700. $2.50.*

Almost immediately next door is the two-storeyed **Mission House** or Kemp House. This is the oldest surviving building in New Zealand (at the very young age of 179). It was established by pioneer missionary Samuel Marsden on land offered to him by the great local Maori warlord Hongi Hika, who accepted 48 felling axes for the land and also offered Marsden and his staff protection from invading tribes. In 1832 it became the home of catechist-blacksmith, James Kemp and his family, generations of which lived in the house until 1974, when it was passed over to the nation as an historic site. The house is now packed with Kemp family relics. ■ *Daily 1000-1700. Combined entry with Stone Store $6, children free.* Overlooking both buildings is the more ancient **Kororipo Pa** which was chief Hongi Hika's more basic domain (until, not surprisingly, he had a European-style house built nearby in the 1820s).

Located a short stroll across the river is **Rewa's Village**. This is an authentic recreation of a pre-European Maori fishing settlement, or *Kainga*, named after Hongi Hika's successor. With its very basic ponga tree fern trunk huts and shelters you can only wonder what the early Maori must have thought of the Euro-architecture of the time. ■ *Daily, $2.50.*

The **Kerikeri Basin** offers a number of pleasant short walks along the river, the most notable of which takes in the 20-m **Rainbow Falls** (also accessible 3 km north from Waipapa Road; leaflet available from DOC). Another fine short walk is to **Ake Ake Point and Pa**, accessible from the pretty Opito Bay, 20 km east of the city.

As well as its fruit, Kerikeri is also famous for its **arts and crafts**. The free leaflet 'Kerikeri Art and Craft Trail' lists a number of venues, the best of which is **Origin Art and Craft Co-op** on SH10, T4071133 (open daily 1000-1700). It has a wide range of works on display and for sale from pottery to stained glass. The **Kauri Workshop**, just as you come in to town on Kerikeri Road,

T4079196, has a quality range of kauri and other native wood products. From there you can take a stroll next door to the **Makana Chocolate Factory**, T4076800, where you can watch the stuff being made while wondering why all the employees are not the size of small houses.

On an ecological theme is the excellent **Aroha Island Ecological Centre** on Kurapari Rd, 12 km east of the town. Aroha Island and the neighbouring Rangitane Scenic Reserve are important remnant habitats of the brown kiwi. The island is kept predator-free and therefore offers a small but valuable sanctuary for a few birds. Alas, with the kiwi being nocturnal, daytime visitors will only be able to see interpretative material in the visitors centre. However, if you stay overnight you may get the opportunity to see, and certainly hear, the birds after dark on a guided tour. ■ *Daily (may be closed 1 month in winter), T4075243, kiwi@aroha.net.nz (see also Sleeping below).*

Activities **Diving**: *Octopus Divers*, T4078381, hoyle@igrin.co.nz Offer a range of dive trips including the Rainbow Warrior wreck. From $90 per day. **Fishing**: *Black Rocks Charters*, T4078505. *Learae Charters*, T4708689. *Earl Grey Charters*, T4077165 ($80 per hour). **Horse Trekking**: *Lakeside Horse Treks*, T407422. $20 per hour. **Scenic Tours**: (see Ins and outs above). **Fruit Picking**: If you intend to find work in the orchards of Kerikeri, the hostels will provide advice and occasionally transportation. **Walking**: The Puketi and Omahuta forests west of Kerikeri can be accessed between Waipapa and Kapiro on SH1. These forests contain a number of impressive Kauri that are also included on the agenda for most of the Cape Reinga coach tours from Paihia. For details on camping and walks contact DOC in Kerikeri, T4078474.

Sleeping Accommodation in Kerikeri is plentiful and generally less expensive than Paihia. Although not as busy it is still advised to book ahead, especially at Christmas and in Jan. Hostels also tend to fill up between the fruit harvesting of Apr-Aug.

LL *Sommerfields*, Inlet Rd, T/F4079889, www.sommerfields.co.nz Luxury, modern B&B accommodation set in 5 acres outside Kerikeri. **AL** *Kerikeri Village Inn*, 165 Kerikeri Rd, T4074666, F4074408, www.kerikeri.village.inn@xtra.co.nz New B&B in a contemporary Santa Fe style house. Fine views and sumptuous breakfast. **AL** *Puketotara Luxury Accommodation*, T4077780, F4075480, moods.holdings@xtra.co.nz Another countryside retreat with fine organic cooking. **A** *Colonial Cottage*, Inlet Rd, T/F4079240. Comfortable B&B in an attractive 1890s cottage. **A** *Kauri Park Motel*, Kerkeri Rd, T/F4077629, kauriprk@igrin.co.nz Relatively new and set in sub-tropical garden setting. Large nicely appointed units, some with private spa.

B-D *Aranga Holiday Park*, Kerikeri Rd, T4079326, F4079897. Modern motor camp, centrally located next to the river. **B** *Aroha Island Ecological Centre*, Kurapari Rd, T4075243, F4075246. Cottage-style accommodation (sleeps 5), B&B, camper vans and campsites. Kayaks and kiwi-watching at night. **B** *Glenfalloch Homestay*, Landing Rd, T/F4075471. Variety of rooms, swimming pool. **B** *Wairawa B&B*, Landing Rd, T/F4079888. Private bed-sitting room with own entrance and en-suite bathroom.

C-D *Hone Heke Lodge Backpackers*, 65 Hone Heke Rd, T/F4078170, honehekelodge@hotmail.com Dorm, single and double, some en-suite, tent sites. **C-D** *Kerikeri YHA*, 44 Kerikeri Rd, T4079391, www.yha.org.nz Located in large forested grounds. Double, twin and family rooms, self-contained cottage, campsites. **C-D** *Kerikeri Farm Hostel*, SH10, T4076989. Self-contained unit on a 15-acre citrus orchard. Try some fruit picking.

Eating **Expensive** *Marx Garden Restaurant*, Kerikeri Rd, T4076606. Try the 'Orgasmic Seafood Platter' for $30 – speaks for itself.

Mid-range *The Black Olive*, Main Rd, T4079693. Equally orgasmic food of the pizza variety. Sit in or take away. BYO. Open daily 1700 till late. ***Café Gecko***, Kerikeri Rd, T4077958. Wood-fired pizza and cuisine. Licensed. ***Stone Store Tearooms and Restaurant***, Kerikeri Basin. Located across the road from the stone store in a great setting. Beautiful on a sunny day. Open daily 0900-2100.

Cheap *Café Jerusalem*, Cobblestone Mall, T4071001. Cheap Middle Eastern food, sit-in or take away. Vegetarian snacks. Open Mon-Fri 1100-2300, Sat 1500-2300. *Kerikeri Club*, Cobham Rd, T4078585. Cheap food and lots of it in the local RSA, bridge and tennis club. Open Mon-Sat 1300-2200, Sun 1500-2200.

Keri Pies are widely available – try one of Northland's finest

Kerikeri to Kaitaia

Provided you have your own transport, the roads that branch off SH1 to the coast north of Kerikeri offer stunning coastal scenery and some secluded beaches that are well worth the visit. About 15 km north of Kerikeri the road loops to the coast taking in the small settlements and peaceful hideaways of **Matauri Bay**, **Te Ngaire**, **Wainui**, **Mahinepua** and **Tauranga Bay** before rejoining SH1 again near **Whangaroa**. From there you meet the sweeping shores of **Doubtless Bay** with its mainly retirement communities of **Mangonui**, **Coopers Beach** and **Cable Bay**, before cutting across the picturesque **Karikari Peninsula** on your way to the last significant northern outpost and predominantly Maori enclave of **Kaitaia**.

Matauri Bay

The views above Matauri Bay are stunning, with the numerous **Cavalli Islands** offering a sight that almost surpasses that of the Bay of Islands. Captain Cook named the islands after travalli (a species of fish) bought by Cook from local Maori. The Samuel Marsden **memorial church** in Matauri Bay commemorates New Zealand's pioneer missionary who first preached the gospel in the Bay of Islands on Christmas Day 1814.

The area remains a top venue for **deep sea fishing** and **diving**. Matauri Bay has always been a popular holiday spot, but assumed additional national fame when the wreck of the Greenpeace Vessel *Rainbow Warrior* was laid to rest off the Cavallis in 1987. The famous flagship was bombed by French secret service through a ludicrous act of terrorism in Auckland in 1985. The intellectually bankrupt idea was to prevent her leading a protest flotilla to the French nuclear test grounds on the Pacific atoll of Mururoa. Her sunken hull, 3 km offshore, provides the poignant home to a myriad of sea creatures while an impressive **memorial** on the hill overlooking the islands near the beach pays tribute to the ship, her crew (one of which was killed) and the continuing cause for a nuclear-free region. The incident, rightly, caused an international outcry and New Zealanders are in no hurry to forget, or forgive. There is an echo of Maori history, spirit and support in the Bay with the *Waka* (war canoe) Mataatua II located near the campground. The history of this legendary canoe led to the local tribe the Ngati Kura offering the remains and the *mana* of the modern day *Rainbow Warrior* a final resting-place.

Activities

Diving: The *Rainbow Warrior* is a well-known and popular wreck dive. A number of companies offer trips from Whangarei, Tutukaka and Paihia (see page 168). *Matauri Bay Charters* based at the Matauri Bay Holiday Park, T/F4050525, are the local company. **Golf**: the Kauri Cliffs Golf Course, Kauri Cliffs, Matauri Bay Road, T4051900, www.kauricliffs.com, is one of the most scenic golf courses in the country, but expensive at $200 a round.

Sleeping & eating

The area, like the Bay of Islands, is very popular so book in advance

LL *Huntaway Lodge*, Te Ngaere Bay (4 km north of Mataure Bay), T09-4051611, greg@huntawaylodge.com New exclusive lodge in superb setting overlooking the ocean. 2 en suites with decks. Activities arranged and gourmet breakfast included. **L** *Cavalli Beach House*, T4051049, www.cavallibeachhouse.com Luxurious accommodation in a fine setting and a most unusually designed beachfront house. Fine cuisine. **A** *Oceans Holiday Village*, T4050417, www.matauribay.co.nz/oceans/ Perfect waterfront location a stone's throw from the beach. A range of self-contained units and family lodges. Boat hire and charter, dive gear and tank refills, kayaks, internet. **C-D** *Matauri Bay Holiday Park*, T4050525. Set right on the beach in the shadow of the Rainbow Warrior memorial hill (which sadly affects the view). All the usual facilities for camping and camper vans but no units. The *Oceans Holiday Village* has a fully licensed restaurant/café attached. Winter hours vary, T4050417.

North to Whangaroa

From Matauri Bay the road follows the coast to the picturesque bays and settlements of **Te Ngaire** and **Wainui**. A branch road, just past Wainui, will take you to **Mahinepua Bay**, which provides a classic touch of seclusion, scenery and the only campsite (DOC). From there the road climbs the hill again, offering fine views inland at Radar Heights (an old radar station), before temporarily leaving the coast towards **Tauranga Bay** and **Whangaroa**. Tauranga Bay hosts a basic **A-B** *Tauranga Bay Motel*, T4050222, and the *Tauranga Bay Holiday Park*, T/F4050436, and is home to *Northland Sea Kayaking*, T4050381. This company offers great value $60 day trips with an extra $10 for accommodation in cabins with cooking facilities. They provide a $15 shuttle pick-up from the main bus route at Kaeo.

Northland

Whangaroa

Whangaroa is located along the eastern shoreline of the Whangaroa Harbour which, due to the hills and the subsequent unsighted narrow entrance, has more of a feel of an inland lake than a coastal settlement. It is modern day base for a number of deep-sea fishing charter companies and boasts the historic claim as the site where the sailing ship *Boyd* was sunk after a *Pakeha*/Maori disagreement in 1809. A small gallery based in the well-stocked general store will enlighten you. Whangaroa was also home to the first Wesleyan Mission, which was established in 1823, and is where the infamous Maori chief Hone Heke died in 1828.

The settlement is dominated by the almost globular volcanic plug, St Paul, that provides a great view. It is a short but stiff climb best accessed from the top of Old Hospital Road.

Activities

There are a number of fishing charters available from the marina beside the Whangaroa Big Game Fish Club, T4050347, and quality, good-value trips can be had aboard the yacht *Snow Cloud* from $60 a day, T4050523.

Sleeping & eating

LL *Butterfly Bay*, T4050681, F4050686, bbay@voyager.co.nz Luxurious self-contained hideaway with its own beach. Fine local seafood. **L** *Kingfish Lodge*, T4050164, F4050163, www.kingfishlodge.co.nz This is a famous, 50-year-old establishment that is a favourite isolated haven for sea anglers and only accessible by boat. 14 fully serviced rooms, silver service cuisine, gym, sauna and a well-stocked bar (also open to day visitors). Under recent new ownership. **A** *Whangaroa Motel*, Church St, T/F4050222. Self-contained units with views across the water. **C-D** *Sunseeker Lodge*, Old Hospital Rd, T/F4050496, sunseekerlodge@xtra.co.nz Backpacker accommodation with 2 motel units and 2 doubles. Friendly and comfortable. Internet. *Whangaroa Harbour*

Retreat (Motorcamp), Whangaroa Rd, T/F4050306, DYLEEWhangaroa@xtra.co.nz All the usual facilities. Can arrange dive and fishing trips and charters.

The ***Whangaroa Big Game Fish Club***, has a restaurant and pleasant veranda bar, but winter hours are limited, T4050399. The ***Marlin Hotel*** across the road provides some rather unremarkable fare, T4050347.

Mangonui and around

Although historically noted as a port for whaling ships and kauri exports, today the congenial waterfront community of Mangonui is today most famous for its fish and chip shop. Once you've tasted them you'll no doubt agree that this is a change for the better.

Ins & outs

Getting there All the main Doubtless Bay settlements are serviced by ***Northliner*** or ***Intercity*** coaches, which stop in Mangonui. There is a visitor centre on the waterfront at Mangonui, T4061190, F4061197, www.doubtlessbay.co.nz Open daily 0900-2100 Dec-May and 0900-1700 Jun-Nov. The free *'Doubtless Bay Visitors Directory'* contains a host of local information.

Northland

Just beyond Mangonui are the small beachfront settlements of **Coopers Beach** and **Cable Bay** (a former terminus for ocean cable). This is very much the habitat of the rich retiree, but the beaches themselves and the view across **Doubtless Bay** make up for their lack of depth and character. Thankfully, history comes to the rescue a little further along the coast at **Taipa**, the spot where Maori legend proclaims Kupe, the discoverer of Aotearoa, first landed. His honourable footprints are now followed by the bucket and spade brigade, who descend in their hundreds in summer. The 1840s **Butler House, Gardens and Whaling Museum**, based at Butler Point, towards HiHi, is worth a visit if you are interested in the local history. ■ *$5, T/F4060006.*

Activities & tours

Dolphin Bay Dolphin Rendezvous, T4061190, and *Paradise Connection*, T/F4060460, offer the local Cape Reinga day excursion, and its sister operation *4x4 Exclusive Tours* takes the personalized approach with day or multiday tours to the Cape and other local attractions, T4060406. The information centre has details of local fish or dive charter companies, T4061190.

Sleeping

L ***Coopers Beachfront Suites,*** 18 Bayside Dr, Coopers Beach, T4061018, coopers@voyager.co.nz 2 self-contained suites in a quiet location. **L** ***Breaker House***, Cable Bay, T4060412, breaker@xtra.co.nz Fine all mod cons accommodation particularly suited to couples. **AL-A** ***Acacia Lodge***, Mill Bay Rd, Mangonui, T/F4060417, www.acacia.co.nz Popular lodge located right on the waterside in the heart of Mangonui. Luxury to standard units available. Tours and excursions arranged. **A** ***Mangonui Motel,*** 1 Colonel Mould Dr, T/F4060346, mangonui.motel@xtra.co.nz HiHi Beach Holiday Camp, HiHi Beach Rd, HiHi, T/F4060307. Situated in a peaceful beachfront location. **A** ***Old Oak Inn,*** Waterfront Rd, Mangonui, T4060665. Characterful historic kauri hotel with good-value, clean doubles. Café bar and licensed restaurant attached.

Eating

There are a number of cafés scattered along the waterfront offering fine local seafood. The ***Waterfront Café***, Beachfront Rd, T4060850 is one. The ***Old Oak Inn*** (above) is a good choice for breakfast, lunch or dinner. However, when it comes to eating in Mangonui, everything revolves around the delights of the licensed ***Mangonui Fish and Chip Shop***, just north of the village on Beach Rd. Open 0800-2100, T4060478. Enjoy!

Karikari Peninsula

The temptation is to miss the Karikari peninsula and head straight for Kaitaia or the Cape but, if you have time, its isolated and remote beaches have considerable appeal. This T-shaped peninsula separates Doubtless Bay and the mangrove swamps of **Rangaunu Harbour**, with the broad empty sweep of **Karikari Bay** to the north. This bay is a natural danger zone for whale strandings with the last involving over 100 beached pilot whales in 1995. Sadly, despite an initial successful refloatation of many, the resilient efforts of locals and DOC were in vain, when almost all rebeached the following day and died. **Whatuwhiwhi** is the main settlement on the peninsula and is serviced by a shop, service station, takeaway and the *Whatuwhiwhi Holiday Park*, Whatuwhiwhi Road, T4087202, which offers a peaceful holiday location next to the beach. The **Cape** itself is worthy of investigation and there is a popular campsite located at **Maitai Bay** (DOC). Rock fishing here is said to be excellent. Karikari Beach can be accessed from a number of marked points along the way. The western side of the peninsula, which forms part of the Rangaunu Harbour, is more sheltered offering quiet, but slightly less picturesque beaches. You can book accommodation at **A** *Reef Lodge*, Rangiputa Beach, T4087100, or the **A** *White Sands Motor Lodge*, T4087080.

Kaitaia

Population: 2700
Phone code: 09

Almost every night on the national television weather forecast, Kaitaia takes the honours of being the hottest place in the country and, although the place itself is nothing to write home about, the weather and its general friendliness is notable. The town is primarily the main rural service centre for the Far North. It is predominantly Maori with an interesting smattering of Dalmation blood – mainly Croats who came during the kauri gum boom years of the late 1800s. For the tourist it provides a gateway to the **Aupouri Peninsula**, with its famous, uninterrupted sweep of **Ninety Mile Beach** (actually just over 100 km) to **Cape Reinga** and **North Cape**, the northernmost tip of New Zealand.

Ins & outs

Getting there Kaitaia **Airport** is located 6 km north of the town and is serviced by Air New Zealand Link services. Kaitaia is serviced by ***Northliner*** and ***Intercity*** coaches which drop off and pick up outside Kaitaia Travel Bureau, 170 Commerce St, who also handle ticketing.

Information Far North is located in the Lighthouse, Jaycee Park, South Rd, T4080879, F4082546, visitorinfo@fndc.govt.nz Open daily 0830-1700 (closed weekends in winter).

Sights

The **Far North Regional Museum** next door to the Information Centre is worth a peek. Although hardly outstanding it is well laid out and proudly boasts a number of important exhibits and Maori *Taonga* including the Kaitaia Carving (one of the earliest Maori carvings in existence) and a very impressive 1500 kg anchor left by de Surville in 1769. Other collections include some interesting Moa remains and the far more modern remnants from the wreck of the *Rainbow Warrior*. There is also the regulation collection of kauri gum and digging items that feature heavily in every museum in Northland. ■ *Mon-Fri 1000-1700. T4081403.* The **Okahu Estate** on the corner of Okahu Road and the Ahipara/Kaitaia highway, 3½ km from Kaitaia, is New Zealand's northernmost winery. It is in pleasant surrounds and offers free tastings. ■ *1000-1800 (closed winter weekends). T4080888, okahuestate@xtra.co.nz.*

Further afield on Beckham Road west of Kaitaia is the **Nocturnal Park** featuring its glow-worm cave and Kiwi exhibits. Although fine in itself, with an added token restaurant and micro-waterfall, this is perhaps only worth the drive if you will not have a chance to see better venues or exhibits elsewhere. ■ *Daily from 1000 until after the night tour at dusk, adult $10, child $3. T4084100, www.kiwi-glowworms.park.co.nz* The **Ancient Kauri Kingdom** in Awanui, 8 km north of Kaitaia, has a range of beautiful kauri furniture and crafts, but is fairly unremarkable, except for the impressive 50 tonne log centrepiece, the old kauri logs drying in the car park, and the date scones in the café. ■ *7 days. Free. T/F4067172, www.ancientkauri.co.nz*

Activities & tours

For other activities near Kaitaia see Ahipara, page 180

A number of quality day trips leave Kaitaia for the **Cape Reinga/Ninety Mile Beach** circuit. These tours generally offer more time at the Cape and various other stops than their distant counterparts operating out of Paihia. Most stop at the Ancient Kauri Kingdom, Wagener Museum at Houhoura (see page 181), the Cape and the Te Paki Stream sand dunes (for dune surfing) before running almost the entire length of Ninety Mile Beach.

Harrison's Cape Runner, 123 North Road, Kaitaia, T4081033, F4083003, capetours@xtra.co.nz Leaves daily at 0900, returning about 1700. Adult $40, child $20, lunch included. *Harrison's* also operate a more personalized *4x4 Reef Runner* tour which takes in a half-day of four-wheel driving, spectacular views and sand tobogganing. Twin tour discounts apply.

Sand Safaris, 221 Commerce Street, T4081778, F4083339, www.sandsafaris.co.nz Another full-day tour that goes in the reverse direction taking in Ninety Mile Beach first. Usual stops and activities apply. Departs daily 0900, returning about 1700. Adult $55, child $29.

Tall Tale Tours, 237A Commerce Street, T4080870, F4081100, www.Tall-Tale.co.nz Offer a unique Maori cultural package including a visit to a Marae interspersed with learning about protocol, language, arts and crafts, herbal remedies (make your own), stories, myths and legends. Far less commercial than other such experiences around the country.

If it happens to rain during your visit you might try your hand with a .22 rifle at the *Far North Indoor Shooting Gallery*, Hillcrest Road, T4080097.

For details about local walking and mountain biking routes consult the '*Kaitaia Area Walks*' leaflet, available from the VIC, $1.

Sleeping

LL *Taharangi Marie Lodge*, Sandhills Rd, Ninety Mile Beach, T4086282, ronnybear@xtra.co.nz A spacious house situated in perfect isolation among the sand dunes of Ninety Mile Beach. Knowledgeable hosts and a fine base for explorations further north. **A** *Lake Ngatu Countryside B&B*, Sweetwater Rd, Lake Ngatu, Waipapakauri, T/F4067300. Situated some distance from town but worth the effort. **A** *Sierra Court Motor Lodge*, 65 North Rd, T4081461, sierracourt.kaitaia@xtra.co.nz Basic but comfortable 1 and 2 bedroom units centrally located. **A** *Wayfarer Motel*, 231 Commerce St, T4082600, F4082601. Centrally located. **C-D** *Main Street Backpackers*, 235 Commerce St, T4081275, F4081100, mainstreet@xtra.co.nz Maori-operated offering the opportunity of a great cultural experience.

Eating

Kaitaia is not exactly a culinary capital, but those listed are recommended

Mid-range *Beachcomber Restaurant*, The Plaza, 222 Commerce St, T4082010. Open Mon-Fri 1100-1430, Mon-Sat 1700-late. *Blue House Café*, 14 Commerce St, T4084935. Open 7 days from 0700. Seasonal closing from 1530-2200. **Cheap** *Michaelangelo's Pizza*, 26 Commerce St, T4082001. Open 7 days from 1000, closed from 1700 Tue-Thu. *Bushman's Hut Steak House*, corner of Bank St and Puckey Av, T4084320. Open 7 days Sun-Wed 1700-2100, Thu-Sat 1700-2200. Live music weekends. Good value, stuff your chops venue.

Events The annual *Te Houtaewa Challenge* in Mar is a gruelling 60 km run up Ninety Mile Beach with added 5 person relay, 42 km marathon, 21 km half marathon and a leisurely 6 km walk for the lazy! The event runs in parallel with a 4-day Festival of Maori arts and crafts. For details, *Pop Runner Promotions*, T5702222, poprun@xtra.co.nz

Directory **Jeep rental**: *Beach Rentals*, T4067217. **Internet**: *Hackers internet Café*, 84 Commerce St, T408499. Open Mon-Wed 0900-2100, Thu-Sat 0900-late, Sun 1000-2100.

Ahipara Ahipara forms the southern extremity of Ninety Mile Beach and is located 14 km west of Kaitaia. Formerly a 2000-strong gum-digging community it is now a shadow of its former self but nonetheless a pleasant, scenic spot offering the tourist a number of beach-based activities. The VIC in Kaitaia will provide all the relevant information or you may wish to visit the local website, www.ahipara.co.nz The hill at the far end of town offers fine views up Ninety Mile Beach.

Horse trekking: *Jayar Horse Treks*, Foreshore Road, T4094888. **Quad Biking**: *Aidriaan Lodge*, Reefview Road, T4094888. *Tua Tua Tours*, Ahipara Road, T/F4094875, tuatuatours@yahoo.com Guided quad bike tours – lots of fun – three hours $115, 1½ hours $70. **Fishing**: *Wildcat*, T4094729.

Sleeping & eating **AL** *Beach Abode*, 11 Korora St, T/F4094070. Wide range of self-contained accommodation on the beachfront. **A** *Pinetree Lodge Motor Camp*, Takahe Rd, T4094864, F4092118. **A-D** *Adriaan Lodge Motel*, Reefview Rd, T/F4094888. Suitable for backpackers. Does its own quad bike hire. For an evening meal try the licensed *Bayview Restaurant* at the Adriaan Lodge Motel (above). Open 7 days from 0600, Fri-Sat 1900, Sun 1600.

North to the Cape

Human nature being what it is, one is naturally drawn up the Aupouri Peninsula to reach the northernmost tip of New Zealand. The peninsula itself, which is bounded by **Ninety Mile Beach** to the west and **Great Exhibition Bay** and the **Rangaunu Bay and Harbour** to the east, used to be covered in kauri forest, but today mainly consists of extensive dune systems and swamps, interspersed with commercial forestry. Although the orange dunes that back Ninety Mile Beach cannot fail to impress, it is the white silica sands of **Kotoka** – the huge sand spit on the Parengarenga Harbour – that stands out the most. This remote peninsula offers one of the best coastal walks in the country and in spring and autumn is alive with flocks of migratory wading birds. The highest point south of the Cape is the 236 m **Mount Camel** near Houhoura, which stands out like a sore thumb. Sadly access is some distance from the north and to enjoy its view is a major hike. **Houhoura** is home to the **Wagener Museum** which holds an amazing collection and is a 'must-see'. From Houhoura you pass the village of **Pukenui** before winding your way towards the remote and highly spiritual lands and landscapes of the Cape itself with **Cape Reinga** to the west and **North Cape** – the true northernmost point, to the east.

Ins & outs

If you are short of time the best way to see the peninsula is to join the many coach tours from Paihia, Mangonui or Kaitaia *(see page 179)*

Getting there With your own wheels it will take about 1½ hrs to reach the Cape from Kaitaia. The road is sealed to Te Paki Station, which is about 21 km from the Cape. Beyond this point the road is metalled so watch your speed - many a budding rally driver in their Maui camper van has come to grief along this stretch. Although Ninety Mile Beach is classified as a highway, it is not advised to take anything other than a 4WD vehicle on to the sand. Again, for those in rental cars (that are not insured on the sand) who cannot resist the temptation to do so, it will probably all end in tears. But, if you must and cannot resist the urge, contact ***4x4 Beach Rentals*** in Kaitaia, T4067271, who will hire you a suitable vehicle – at a cost (from $99).

The Homestead, which was the original family residence is particularly authentic and also worth a look

Houhoura is a small fishing village on the shores of Houhoura Harbour. It is home to the **Wagener Museum and the Subritzky/Wagener Homestead**. The only way to describe this museum is that it is essentially a collection of collections and one of the best in the country. It houses the largest private collection in New Zealand that was initiated in 1969 by the Wagener family. Since then the collections have grown to incorporate everything from a stuffed 440-kg (locally caught) marlin, to butterflies, chamber pots, miniature letters, guns and gramophones. It is a delight to wander through or better still take a guided tour (preferably by Owen Wagener himself). Whatever you do, do not leave without asking to see the old washing machine working. It's like putting Mike Tyson in a locked metal cage and then calling him names. There is a café attached to the museum. ■ *0830-1630. $6. T4098850.*

Pukenui is the last major settlement on the way to the Cape, so it may pay to grab some petrol or a coffee at the café and general store, or on your return quench your thirst at New Zealand's northernmost pub the *Houhoura Tavern*. This is a fine place to mix with the locals. Sharkophobes should not enter – there are very gruesome pictures on the wall. Twenty-five kilometres north of Pukenui you reach the small Maori enclave of **Te Kao**. This is the best place to park up and access the **Kotoka Sand Spit**. The forestry gate is about 1 km up the road but vehicular access is forbidden. Ensure you have maps and a compass since the myriad of forestry roads to reach the sand spit are difficult to negotiate. Eventually you will emerge, preferably on the beach to the west. From there walk north to the sand dunes which are wild, remote and stunning. Allow eight hours.

Northland

Cape Reinga

From Te Kao the road passes through the basic motor camp at Waitiki Landing before entering the huge **Te Paki Station and Recreation Reserve** towards North Cape, Cape Reinga and the lighthouse. This reserve has a total area of 23,000 ha and contains some of the most extraordinary landforms in New Zealand. The Maori call this area Te Hiku o te Ika (the tail of the fish) from the legend that tells how the giant fish (North Island) was pulled from the sea by Maui from his canoe (South Island). Geology posits a less prosaic theory . The rocks that form the Cape were formed about 60 million years ago which later separated from the mainland. Then around two million years ago sand moved northwards from Kaitaia forming a huge tombolo and the peninsula we see today. The area supports a wide variety of coastal scenery from cliffs to wide sweeping beaches. There is a great network of short and long walks in the area (information from DOC) but access may be denied, or permission required, T4097831. Local Maori own almost a quarter of the land, and areas around North Cape are particularly sacred. The tip of North Cape, the northernmost point of New Zealand, is a scientific reserve with limited access. For most visitors, sadly, the visit to this amazing area will be all too brief and revolve around Cape Reinga and the lighthouse. The views from the hill above the lighthouse are stunning and in stormy weather you can see the Tasman Sea and Pacific join in an uneasy union, and to the Three Kings Islands, 57 km offshore. The northland coastline has claimed over 140 vessels and many lives since 1808, with the majority falling foul around the Cape. The lighthouse, which is a rather dumpy rotund little unit, was built in 1941 and contains the lens from the original lighthouse built on Motuopao Island to the south. Beside the lighthouse is the obligatory multi-destination signpost for that vital memento for Mum.

Sleeping & eating

The accommodation north of Kaitaia is fairly basic, with Houhoura, Pukenui and Waitiki Landing offering the best base (the latter being the last available beds before the Cape)

A *Houhoura Chalets Motor Lodge*, corner of Far North and Houhoura Heads Rd, T4098860, F4098864. Comfortable A-frame unit accommodation near the Wagener Museum. **A-D** *Pukenui Lodge Motel and Youth Hostel*, SH1, Pukenui, T4098704, pukenui@igrin.co.nz **B-D** *Waitiki Landing*, SH1, T4097508, F4097523. Tent sites, bunk and cabin. Restaurant. *Pukenui Holiday Camp*, Lamb Rd, T4098803, F4098802, john.horsnell@xtra.co.nz This motorcamp provides better facilities than the very basic, but more scenic Houhoura equivalent. There are **DOC campsites** (**D**) at **Rarawa** on the east coast just south of Te Kao, at **Kapowairua** next to the beautiful Spirits Bay and **Tapotupotu Bay**, near the Cape. T4086014. The café at the *Wagener Museum* (seasonal hours), the *Houhoura Pub*, the café and takeaway in the centre of *Pukenui*, and the basic restaurant at *Waitiki Landing* are your only hope.

South to the Hokianga

From Ahipara the road turns south to **Herekino**, through Broadwood and **Kohukohu** to **Narrows Landing** on the **Hokianga Harbour**. There you meet the Ferry to **Rawene** and the heart of Hokianga. This road is fairly torturous and once again the familiar Northland Mobile-Phone-No-Service-Zone country sights apply. There is little of interest on the road itself but two venues in the area are of particular note. First is the **Golden Stairs Walkway** on the southern shore of the mouth of the **Whangape Harbour**. If you can muster the courage and tackle the route to the little settlement of Pawarenga, this walk is well worth it. The mouth of the Whangape Harbour is like a small fjord and out of character with the other larger harbours along the west Northland Coast. The walk is fairly short but steep and culminates at the northern tip of the vast and wild beach. From here you could continue down the beach to Mitimiti, where there is a fine and remote backpackers (see below). The following day could be spent exploring the coast before being dropped of at the end of the Golden Stairs Walkway again, from where you negotiate the return to retrieve your car. Be sure to secure all belongings out of sight and lock the car.

The second venue is actually **Mitimiti** and the wild **Warawara Forest,** which is the second largest kauri forest in New Zealand, still containing some whoppers. The 41 km it takes by road to get to Mitimiti from Narrows Landing is quite arduous but worth the drive simply for the views and nature of the remote Northland countryside, not to mention the broad stretch of coast and wild beach at its terminus. Once again, if you stay at the *Manaia Hostel* at Mitimiti you can just about have 50 km of beach to yourself for fishing, walking or (careful) swimming. The Maori owner of the hostel will happily take you for a 'blat' in the 'sand banger', or eight-wheel quad bikes, up and down the beach, and while doing so give you a fascinating insight in to the Maori history of the area. The *Tree House* is another fine Youth Hostel located near the Narrows Landing Ferry.

Sleeping & eating

B-D *Manaia Hostel*, T4095347, F4095345, mitimiti@xtra.co.nz Great budget accommodation, 2 twins and a double, in a truly remote Northland location. Internet. **B-D** *Tree House*, West Coast Rd, Kohukohu, T4055855, F4055857, tree.house@xtra.co.nz A positive sanctuary of a place set in 17 acres of bush and orchards. 2 doubles, 2 twins, 2 bunkrooms and a house bus! Camping. Friendly hosts. When it comes to eating it's the general store or the sandwich bar - or if you're at Manaia, you'll be catching your own.

Rawene

Rawene is essentially the gateway to the heart of Hokianga from the north, but has a heart of its own that seems strangely broken. Even in the earliest years of

The Souls Departing

The Northern tip of New Zealand is steeped in Maori legend and tradition. The name Reinga means 'Place of Leaping' and it is here, according to Maori lore, that the souls of the dead depart Aotearoa to the after-life. After travelling up the West Coast to Spirits Bay, the dead are believed to descend the slopes of the headland to the roots of an old, lone pohutukawa tree, before falling in to the sea. From there they are said to re-emerge on Ohaua, the highest point of the Three Kings Islands, where, still within view of Aotearoa, they bid their last farewell, before returning to the lands of their ancestors – Hawaiki.

Maori and European settlement, when a large sawmill and shipyard was established in the area, Rawene saw its fair share of conflicts, both internally and externally, that has left it wanting. Today, although it is a pretty place with lots of potential, it struggles with unemployment, drugs and poverty and many think that only tourism and the building of a bridge across the harbour, can come to the rescue. One hopes that it can, but meantime, there is little to hold the visitor back, except the laid-back **Boatshed Café and Gallery,** T4057728, and the historic 1868 **Clendon House**, both on the waterfront. Clendon House is the former residence of James Clendon, a local dignitary who was, amongst other things, the former Hokianga district magistrate. ■ *1000-1230, 1300-1600. $2.*

Getting there The Rawene Ferry operates daily from 0730-1930, light vehicle $13, foot/car passenger $1.50 T4052602.

Sleeping and eating A *Hokingamai B&B*, 12 Gundry St, T4057782, david.gill@xtra.co.nz **B** *Masonic Hotel*, Parnell St, T4057822. One of the best bets for simple and affordable accommodation and food. *Rawene Motor Camp*, 1 Marmot St, T4057720. Small but adequate with backpacker accommodation. Swimming pool. Another option for a decent evening meal is the *Harp of Erin*, on Russell Esplanade (weekends).

Kaikohe

Just south of Rawene you join the SH12 to Opononi and Omapere and all points south to Dargaville. East of here is the small service town of Kaikohe just before SH1. There is a **Visitor Information Centre** here at Broadway, T4011693 (open daily 0900-1700, closed winter weekends), but really there is little to stop for. One possibility is **Kaikohe Hill**, which offers a good view, perhaps followed by a soak in the wooden hot tubs of the **Ngawha Springs and Waiariki Pools**, south east of the town. The springs are said to cure some rheumatic, lumbago, arthritic and skin conditions. The old Maori warrior Hone Heke recognized the remedial power of the springs, bringing his wounded here for treatment after the British assault on his fortified Ohaeawai Pa. ■ *Open daily 0700-1930. $2.50. Camping and campervan sites available.*

Opononi and Omapere

These two converging waterfront villages are the main resorts in the Hokianga. The villages and the harbour entrance are dominated by the impressive bare sand dunes that grace its northern shore. They rise to a height of 100 m and at sunset glow with an orange radiance. It was here in the Hokianga Harbour, in the 10th century, that the great Polynesian explorer

Kupe first set foot in Aotearoa (New Zealand) from his homeland of Hawaiiki. After a short stay he went home again leaving a small group behind. Although Kupe himself never returned his ancestors did and it was christened Hokianganui-a-Kupe meaning 'the place of Kupe's great return'. The area is also known as Te Kohanga o Te Tai Tokerau or 'the nest of the northern tribes'. Indeed it remains the centre point from which most Northland Maori trace their ancestry. Both Opononi and Omapere were somewhat insignificant until the appearance of a solitary wild dolphin in 1955. 'Opo', as she was christened, won the hearts of the nation and subsequently put little Opononi on the map.

Ins & outs Getting there ***Intercity*** run a service through Omapere from the south (Tue, Thu and Sun) to Paihia and returning south from Paihia (Mon, Wed and Fri). A ***Northliner*** 'Loop Pass' is also accepted by *Intercity*. ***West Coaster*** also offers a service from Paihia to Auckland, T4397069. All buses stop at the VIC where bookings can be arranged.

The **Visitor Information Centre** is situated on the main road roughly between the 2 communities, T4058869, F4058317, hokianga@hotmail.com Open daily 0900-1700.

Sights The small **Omapere Museum** housed above the Information Centre has some interesting historical stories, pictures and items, of which the original and highly entertaining 'Tally Ho' video about Opo the dolphin stands out. ■ *0900-1700. Free.*

You can forget the **statue of 'Opo'** on the waterfront at Opononi. It is showing its age and should be outside a supermarket on springs, with a coin slot. Far better to head for the southern edge of Omapere and the **Arai-Te-Uru** headlands. The tip of the headland supported a signal station that for many years used to help ships negotiate the tricky harbour entrance. The headland offers a great view across to the sand spit (North Head) or *Niua* to give it its Maori name. The **Ocean Beach track** takes you down to the rocky coast below, where a blow hole and cave can be explored (turn left and watch the tide). The **Coastal Walkway** also starts here and winds its way round to the remote and beautiful beaches to the south. **Pakia Hill** at the southern end of Omapere also offers spectacular views of the Harbour and the dunes. **The Labyrinth Woodworks and The Amazing Maize Maze** is worth a look, is located along Waiotemarama Gorge Road next to the Kauri Forest Walk. The Labyrinth offers a range of quality crafts while the maze is an imaginative alternative use of the crop. There is complimentary tea or coffee and the **Kauri Forest Walk** is a nice 10-minute amble that takes in a waterfall, but you can go the full hog with a six-hour hike up to Mount Haturu; 4054581. Back in the centre of Omapere the *Mamaku*, SH12, is the rather cute looking outlet for a local craft co-operative set up in 1979. Fine wood, fibre, glass works and bone carvings, T4058662.

Activities & tours *Quad Bike '8 wheel' Adventures*, T4095347. It is possible to hook up with the Manaia Hostel tour from Omapere. $60 includes a water taxi across to the dunes. *Northland Coast to Coast Tours*, T4059460, offers, local tours throughout the Hokianga and beyond. *Hokianga Express Charters*, T4058872, F4058863, offer trips across to the dunes to explore or go sandboarding ($12). Also fishing and dive trips. *Alma 80 Scow*, T4057704, g.darroch@xtra.co.nz Cruising the Hokianga aboard a 78-ft kauri ship. Regular cruise from Rawene on Thursday at 1000 and fishing from Opononi on Friday at 1800 December-April. *Okopako Horse Treks*, Mountain Road, T4058815. Three hours, about $40.

Sleeping

A *Omapere Tourist Hotel and Motel*, SH12, T4058737, F4058801. A fine spot right next to the beach and the wharf. A range of 26 well-equipped units are available, as are powered sites and campsites. Heated pool, spacious lawns, restaurant and bar. **A** *B&B in Omapere*, Signal Station Rd, T4058641, F4058643, whaley_bnb@paradise.net.nz Peaceful spot with great views. **A** *Dawn Homestay*, Omapere T/F4058773. Again nice spot on the hill – quiet, friendly and secluded. Yacht trips available. **B-D** *Globe Trekkers*, SH12, Omapere, T/F4058183, shirley@xtra.co.nz Bigger establishment offering private chalet plus dbl/twin/share/tents, campervan sites. Bike and scooter hire. **C-D** *House of Harmony*, SH12, Opononi, T/F4058778. Small and friendly backpackers offering scooter hire.

Eating

Expensive/mid-range *Omapere Tourist Hotel* (above) has a fine restaurant offering the traditional Kiwi fare, as does the ***Opononi Resort Hotel***, T4058858. Both licensed.

Cheap *Calypso Café*, SH12, Omapere, T4058708. Mediterranean offerings and fine coffee. Open Mon-Sun 0900-2300, BYO.

The Kauri Coast

Just south of Omapere you bid farewell to the coast and the Hokianga and enter 'kauri country'. Waipoua, Mataraua and Waima Forests make up the largest remaining tract of native forest in Northland, and the **Waipoua and Trounson Kauri Forests** contain 300 species of tree including the great kauri and the two finest examples and living monuments to these magnificent and awe inspiring trees. The mighty kauri forests used to blanket much of the upper North Island but, thanks to the activities of man, those forests have been plundered and raped and remain as a mere suggestion of their former selves. The Waipoua forest is home to the largest remaining individuals, including the much-loved and ancient **Tane Mahuta** or 'Lord of the Forest'. For lovers of life and for those who have a healthy respect for nature, to visit this great tree is something of a pilgrimage. For those who have never really thought about it, it is a fine place to start.

Waipoua Kauri Forest

The 15,000-ha Waipoua Forest includes the 9105 ha Waipoua sanctuary of which 2639 ha contain mature kauri trees. The original block of forest was bought from the local Maori chiefs for $4,400 in 1876 and, although the original intention was to use the land for 'settlement purposes', most of the forest was reserved for government forestry purposes in 1906. Thankfully, due thanks to much local and national pressure, which came to a head in 1952 with a 70,000-strong petition, the forest is now safely under the administration of DOC. The 20 km drive through the forest is appealing in itself, with roadside kauri and umbrella-like ponga ferns giving you just a hint of what Northland and much of the entire country used to be like.

Walking tracks at the northern end of the forest, immediately next to the highway, give access to the two largest known kauri specimens, **Tane Mahuta**, or 'Lord of the Forest' and **Te Matua Ngahere**, the 'Father of the Forest'. Tane Mahuta can be reached within five minutes and is an awesome sight, with a trunk height of 17.7 m, girth of 13.8 m and total height of 51½ m. It is estimated to be over 1500 years old. Two kilometres south of Tane Mahuta is a car park where you pay a $2 security fee (such was the level of car theft from the most destructive of New Zealand's introduced mammals – the human). From here, there are a number of short or long walks. Te Matua Ngahere, the second largest tree, can be reached in about 20 minutes, while the 'Four Sisters', a stand of four trees growing together like a huge botanical oil rig, are only 100 m from the car park. The Yakas Track is 6 km in length and takes in another monster, the Yakas Kauri, before emerging at the visitor centre. A lookout point 1½ km from the park's southern boundary is worth a look on the one hour trek from the visitors centre.

The **Waipoua Forest Visitor Centre** (DOC) is located just off SH12 towards the southern end of the park. It contains a small, interesting museum and can provide all walking or sundry information. ■ *Mon-Fri 0800-1630, Sat-Sun 1000-1600. T4390605.*

Sleeping & eating

A *Waipoua Lodge*, SH12, T/F4390422, www.waipaualodge.co.nz Fine comfortable self-contained accommodation in former wool shed and stables. Restaurant attached. **B-D** *Kaihu Farm Backpackers*, Kaihu, T4394004.Backpackers and twin/double. 20 km South of Waipoua. **C-D** *Waipoua DOC*, T4390605. 2 and 4 bed cabins are available at Waipoua. Hot and cold showers and some with cooking facilities. Campsites and non-powered campervan sites. The ***Kauri Coast Holiday Park***, Trounson Park Rd, Kaihu, T4390621. Cabins, powered sites and cabins set in a very pleasant site next to the river. Clean, relatively modern and almost homely. Guided night tours to Trounson Kauri Reserve in summer to hear kiwi. $15. For eating out the ***Waipoua Lodge*** is really the best and only bet for miles. T4390422.

Northland

Trounson Kauri Park & Kaihu

There is also a smaller but impressive kauri forest in the 450-ha Trounson Kauri Reserve, which is located 17 km south of Waipoua. The road is signposted about 40 km north of Dargaville and goes through Donelly's Crossing, which has everything bar the saloon and stagecoach. At the reserve there is a 40-minute **loop walk** that starts near the DOC campsite, taking in some of the finest kauri specimens in the country. A 'teepee' site is available, and facilities include hot showers and a communal cookhouse ($7). Powered sites also available. Guided night tours in summer to hear kiwi, $15, T4390621. The forest has a healthy population of North Island browns due to its isolation from other predator-rich forests by a sea of farmland. The camp is closed in winter; T4390605. For other accommodation see above.

Just south of Trounson is the small settlement of **Kaihu**. The *Nelson's Kaihu Kauri* is a noted retail outlet for quality kauri crafts (open 0900-1700 Monday-Saturday).

Kai Iwi Lakes

About 30 km south of Waipoua and 10 km towards the coast is the aquatic summer playground of the Kai Iwi Lakes. This is a favourite Northland holiday spot for those wanting to enjoy the combination of endless beach and surf, together with the more sedate inland waters of the three main lakes – **Kaiiwi, Taharoa** and **Waikere**. Here, mainly in summer, you can enjoy sailing, windsurfing, water-skiing, jet skiing and fishing. Lacking much cover and being so close to the beach bear in mind the lakes can be a little exposed at times.

Sleeping A *Country Cottage*, Kai Iwi Lakes Rd, T4390303, F4390302. 2 self-contained cottages located nearer the lakes than above. Jet-skis for hire, $90 per hr. **A** *Hilltop Studio*, SH12, T4396351, F4396353, rwatt@igrin.co.nz Single self-contained unit in bush setting, about 10 km from the lakes but handy to Dargaville. **A** *Waterlea*, Kai Iwi Lakes, T/F4390727. 2 self-contained units right next to the lakes. Host of aquatic activities and relevant equipment. Fishing trips and boat hire, $65 per hr. **Camping** with very basic facilities is available at Pine Beach on the shores of Taharoa, and Promenade Point, $6, T4398360.

Dargaville and around

Dargaville is a rather dull township located on the bank of the **Wairoa River**, the Kaipara Harbour's largest and longest tributary. Like many Northland settlements it has, in modern times, with the exhaustion of the kauri forests, become a shadow of its former self. It was founded in 1872 by Irish timber merchant Joseph Dargaville, when the district was already the enclave of a large group of Dalmatian settlers. Kauri timber was again the name of the game , and for many years Dargaville was an important export centre. The rivers north of the bustling port were choked with kauri being worked downstream, and it was from here that much of Northland's kauri was shipped to Australia and elsewhere. With the myriad tributaries and branches of the Northern **Kaipara Harbour** inundating the region, access in those days was only possible by boat from the sister port and timber-milling town of Helensville, located on the south of Kaipara Harbour, north of Auckland.

Today Dargaville is a main service centre for the farms with their barren fields on which the great kauri once stood, and the river meanders quietly by, transporting little except ducks. The region as a whole is also known as the 'Kumara Capital' of the country producing the best of this mouth-watering sweet potato introduced by the early Polynesian navigators.

Ins & outs

Getting there *Intercity* and *Mainline* have connecting services to Auckland. *West Coaster* run an Auckland to Paihia service and back. Buses stop on Kaipa St. Information and ticketing at the VIC.

The Kauri Coast **Visitor Information Centre** is located on Normanby St, T/F4398360, www.kauricoast.co.nz Open summer Mon-Fri 0830-1730; Sat-Sun 0900-1600. Winter, Mon-Fri 0830-1700; Sat 0830-1700, closed Sun.

Sights

The low point on the tour has to be the statue of the Dalmation pioneer in Hokianga Road, who looks like a cat has just peed in his pocket

Although generally considered principally the gateway to the Kauri Coast, and an important supply or overnight stop on the developing and popular Twin Coast Highway, there is the odd significant thing to see in Dargaville. A number of tour operators and local activities are also based here. If you are intrigued by the region's rich history the information centre has put together an **Historic River Walk**, with an interesting free leaflet. It is 5 km and takes about an hour. One of the highlights is the **Dargaville Maritime Museum**, which bears the remnants and relates the sorry tales of the many ships that were wrecked trying to negotiate the notorious Kaipara Bar. It also boasts its fair collection of Maori taonga and pioneer exhibits and, at 84 kg, the largest piece of kauri gum in the world (carrying just a few grammes more than a similar piece in the Kauri Museum at Matakohe). ■ *Daily 0900-1600. $5. T4397555.*

Another useful leaflet from the VIC outlines the **Kauri Coast Craft Trail** which details the various galleries and outlets at which to see kauri and other native woods being crafted, on display or for sale. There is no doubt that this is your best opportunity to buy quality kauri products at competitive prices. One 'working' studio, the *Woodturners Kauri Gallery* at 4 Murdoch St, is run by Rick Taylor, who has been turning and chipping away at kauri for over 23 years. ■ *Open daily. T4394975, www.stop.at/rickys*

It is worthwhile taking a look at the coast near Dargaville and the ridiculously long **Ripiro Beach** – if only to have an inkling of what 104 km of almost uninterrupted sand looks like. It is accessible at a number of places, the most well-serviced being **Baylys Beach**, 14 km west of Dargaville. But if you fancy a look at the local countryside (and the locals) followed by a truly remote walk to the disused 1884 **Kaipara Lighthouse** and the seemingly endless sand dunes of the **Kaipara Heads**, then take the road to the tiny outpost village of **Poutu**. It is a strangely disconcerting 69 km south from Dargaville and gives one an inkling of the staggering length of the Kaipara Harbour's shoreline, at 3,000 km thought to be one of the longest natural harbour coastlines in the world.

Before you leave Dargaville or supposing you have only an hour or so then head to the rather seedy village of **Te Kopuru** (12 km southwest) and take a look at what must be one of the most interesting and bizarrely decorated gardens on the planet. Located at 51 Norton Street and next door and round the corner in Wilson St, it puts a whole new meaning to the words buoy and ballcocks, and makes Barbara Cartland's collection of earrings look tedious. One can only shudder at what exactly goes on in such a disturbed mind.

If you are not on a tour or cannot be bothered with the 69 km to the Kaipara Heads and the remote walk to the **Kaipara Lighthouse** then there are three interesting peaks to conquer in the vicinity, all of which offer interesting views of the vast Kaipara Harbour. **Mount Tutamoe** is a 4-5 hour walk; the 221 m **Mangaraho Rock** (11 km south of Dargaville) is 45-minutes around base and 30 minutes to summit; and the very knobbly **Toka Toka Peak** (17 km south) is a 20-minute walk. For directions and more information call at the VIC.

Northland

Activities & tours

Most of these tours link to Helensville on the Southern Kaipara Harbour just north of Auckland

Taylor Made Tours, T4391576. Scenic beach excursions by coach or the four-wheel drive 'Big Foot' along Ripiro Beach. Shipwreck sites, Kaipara Heads Lighthouse, sand tobogganing, fishing from $45. *Pouto Quad Bike Tours*, T4398360. Can work in conjunction with Taylor Made Tours. *Kaipara Kapers*, T4398360. Jet Boat trip up the river Wairoa, $35, or longer trips in conjunction with above, up to $155. *Curel Cruises*, 3A Lorne Street, Dargaville, T/F4391805, www.only.at/kaipara A variety of cruises and activities aboard the historical schooner 'Te Aroha', from $10 2 hrs, lunch cruise $30, dinner $35, fully licensed. *Baylys Beach Horse Treks*, T4398360. Ripiro Beach rides, $33. Transport from Dargaville.

Sleeping

L *Lighthouse Lodge*, Pouto Point. A remote and luxurious hideaway at the very end of the northern Kaipara peninsula at Kaipara Heads, a long drive and most probably not a 1 night stay, but worth the journey. Fishing trips and quad bikes. **AL** *Kauri House Lodge*, Bowen St, Dargaville, T4398082. Spacious kauri-built house with comfortable en-suites.

A *Awakino Point Lodge*, Awakino Point, Dargaville, T/F4397870, apl.j.hyde@xtra.co.nz Quiet and comfortable, 2 mins from town. **A** *Parkview Motel*, 36 Carrington St, Dargaville, T4398339, F4398338, www.onward.to/parkview Pool spa and children's play area. **C-D** *Greenhouse Backpackers*, 13 Portland St, Dargaville, T4396342. Camping $10.

Selwyn Park Motor Camp and Backpackers, Onslow St, Dargaville, T/F4398296, selwynpark@xtra.co.nz Central location, usual facilities plus 10-bed backpacker lodge. *Baylys Beach Motor Camp*, 22 Seaview Rd, Baylys Beach, T/F4396349. Small and functional near the beach.

Eating

Not a huge selection beyond the usual takeaways. *Uno Restaurant and Bar*, 17 Hokianga Rd, T4395777. Lunch and dinner, à la carte. Good coffee. Open 7 days 1100-late. Closed Mon in winter. This is prime kumara country (sweet Polynesian potato), so try a kumara dish. *Steakhouse and Bar*, corner of Victoria and Gladstone St, T4398460. Good family venue. Open 7 days. *New Asian Restaurant*, 14 Victoria St,

T4398388. Palatable local Chinese. Open 7 days 1100-2200. ***Blah, Blah, Blah Café and Bar***, 101 Victoria St, T4396300. Good for breakfast, blah blah, blah.

Directory

Communications Internet at *Kauri Computers*, 85 Victoria St, open Mon-Fri 0900-1730, Sat 0900-1230.

Matakohe and the Kauri Museum

The village of Matakohe, 45 km south of Dargaville, is home to the **Kauri Museum**. The museum, at Church Road, is one of the finest in the country and provides a fitting finale to the Twin Coast Discovery Highway before the SH12 meets the main SH1 at Brynderwyn and heads back south to Auckland.

Ins & outs

Getting there The museum is located on SH12, 26 km from SH1 at Brynderwyn, which is 114 km north of Auckland. All major coach companies that take the Twin Coast Discovery Highway stop at the museum.

Tours *Kauri Country* offers a unique experience with a wonderful 3-hr Eco-tour, where you join in with a real bullock team on a 'hands-on' kauri tree and gum discovery adventure. On the way you will learn about the trees, the tools and the methods once used and stop for real 'billy' tea. Pick up from the museum, T4316007, F4316289, www.kauricountry.co.nz Adult $65, child $40.

A well-stocked souvenir shop offers a great opportunity to purchase some finely crafted pieces of kauri including some 'Swamp Kauri' pieces, which are tens of thousands of years old

The museum houses a number of highly imaginative displays which offer a detailed insight in to the natural history of the kauri and man's exploitation and love affair with the great tree. Starting in the Volunteer Hall one cannot fail to be impressed with the 22½ m cross section of the Balderston Kauri, a local specimen which was killed by lightening. It is a massive example but a relative youngster. On the wall at its base this is dramatically highlighted with life-size circumference outlines of larger recorded trees. The largest outline, depicting a tree that once grew in the Coromandel, has a diameter of 8½ m, which makes the Balderston slice seem like a piece of cress and even dwarfs Tane Mahuta. Around the edges of the hall there are some exquisite examples of kauri furniture and finely crafted models of some of the many kauri scows that used to ply the Kaipara Harbour.

Next to the Volunteer Hall is a recent edition to the museum, the **Steam Sawmill**. This is an impressive working mock-up which takes you through the complex and ingenious methods used to cut the huge logs. Additional detailed displays in the **Smith Wing** outline examples of wood types and ages, the extraction of kauri gum and include some monstrous moving equipment and saws that show what a mammoth task it was get the tree from bush to mill. That unenviable effort and detail is cleverly and subtly highlighted right down to a bead of sweat from a mannequin's nose!

Other wings of the museum display mock-up pioneer family rooms, fine kauri furniture, timber panels and carvings. Downstairs is the world's best kauri gum display with some fine (and some not so fine) carvings, busts and ornaments, all carefully fashioned from the tree's resin or sap. This 'amber' (its other name) is of varying ages, some of it hundreds of thousands of years old. Within the museum grounds there are some nicely restored examples of kauri buildings, including the 1867 Pioneer Church and 1909 Post Office.

All in all the museum is well worth a visit and stands as a wonderful tribute to man's imagination, skill and sheer hard work in the extraction and use of the kauri. However, if there is to some criticism it is that there is not enough to echo the fact that mans love affair with this, New Zealand's greatest native tree, has been, for the species as a whole, an incredibly damaging and unsustainable affair. ■ *Daily 0830-1730 Nov-Apr, 0900-1700 May-Oct. Adults $7, child $2.50 . T4317417, F4316969, thekauri@xtra.co.nz*

Sleeping **A** *Matakohe House*, Church Rd, T4317091, F4316002, mathouse@xtra.co.nz Situated only 50 m from the museum. Comfortable modern double and twin rooms. Communal lounge. Evening meals available. Café and art gallery next door. **A** ***Maramarie Farmstay***, Tinopai Rd, Matakohe, T4316911. A pleasant kauri homestead located 4 km from the museum. **C-D** *Matakohe Motor Camp*, T/F4316431. Fairly modern and located 350 m from the museum. Tent sites. **C-D** *Old Post Office Guest House*, Cnr SH12 and Oakleigh, Paparoa. T/F4316444. Old World character and charm homestead with 1 room an ex-prison cell! Located 6 km east of the museum.

Eating *Matakohe House*, next to the museum, doubles as a café offering quiches, pasta, teas and fine coffee. Open 7 days from 0900-1730. T4317091.

5 The Coromandel Peninsula

The Coromandel Peninsula

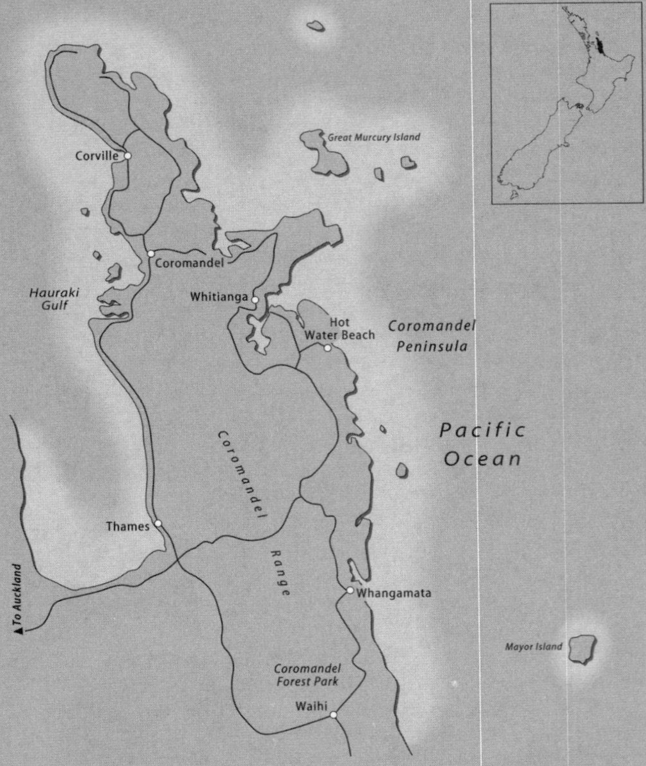

In many ways the Coromandel Peninsula is like a compact and easily accessible mix of Northland and Great Barrier Island. It offers varied and spectacular coastal scenery, rugged mountain bush and a relaxed lifestyle, which together make it the main attraction on the Pacific Coast Highway. The West Coast, bounded by the Firth of Thames, is the most undeveloped side of the peninsula. It has a ragged coastline of islands and pebble beaches, lined with some of the best examples of pohutukawa in the country. For three weeks in December the olive evergreen leaves that crown the gnarled trunks, flower in a radiant mantle of crimson, earning them the label of New Zealand's Christmas tree. In contrast, the East Coast is a plenitude of beautiful bays and sandy beaches, with ***Cathedral Cove*** *and* ***Hot Water Beach*** *being two of the most celebrated in New Zealand. Here you will find most of the development, activity and population, from the transitory tourist in the holiday townships of* ***Whitianga*** *and* ***Whangamata*** *to rich retiree in the rather sterile resorts of Matarangi and Pauanui. Between the two coasts a dominating backbone of bush-clad mountains make up the* ***Coromandel Forest Park****, with its wealth of walks and historic logging and mining remains. One word stands out as the key to this almost timeless and beautiful region – relaxation. Enjoy it and respect it – like so much of New Zealand there are few places, so spoilt, yet so unspoilt, on earth.*

Things to do in Coromandel

- *Chill-out in laid-back Coromandel township and take a ride on the unique Driving Creek Railway.*
- *Climb Castle Rock and see the views across the peninsula.*
- *Explore the old kauri dams, then spend a night in the DoC Pinnacles Hut in the heart of the Coromandel Forest Park.*
- *Explore the pohutukawa coast and northern tip of Cape Colville, stopping for supplies in the Colville General Store, north of Coromandel Township.*
- *Go swimming, or take a stroll along the beautiful New Chum's Beach near Whangapoua.*
- *Go sea fishing or kayaking from Whitianga, or try bone carving in the town centre.*
- *Be the first to see the sunrise, and lay the day's first footprints in the sand at Cathedral Cove.*
- *Dig your own hot pool on Hot Water Beach, find total peace and quiet at Opoutere Beach or go surfing at Whangamata.*

Ins and outs

Getting there ***Air Coromandel*** and associate airline ***Great Barrier Airlines*** operate a twice daily service to and from Auckland (around $80), servicing Whitianga, Pauanui, Matarangi, Thames and Coromandel Town airfields. There are also scheduled flights to and from Great Barrier Island and Whangarei in Northland. There are some excellent fly/boat/bus packages with ***Fullers***, ***Sealink*** and ***Intercity***. ***Great Barrier Airlines***, T09-2566500, F092566509, gba@gbair.co.nz If you wish to arrive in luxury by helicopter contact ***Miller Helicopter Services***, T07-8686100.

Getting around *The Coromandel can be reached in around 90 mins from Auckland*

The Coromandel Peninsula is the premier destination on the North Island's '**Pacific Coast Highway**' tourist route that links Auckland to the north, with Napier and Hawkes Bay to the east. Like the 'Twin Coast Discovery' in Northland, the route is well signposted, with free leaflets and maps readily available at all VIC's. Throughout the Peninsula there is a mix of sealed roads (linking the main towns) and unsealed roads (linking west to east and the further up the north of the Peninsula you venture), making for difficult and time-consuming driving. The main highway that loops the peninsula is SH25. All the roads are very scenic but very windy, so the advice is to relax and take your time.

There are regular ***Intercity*** coach services to and from the Coromandel, and three special passes. The 'Peninsula Loop Pass' goes from Thames to Coromandel Township and Whitianga, then back to Thames ($47). With the Coromandel 'Busplan' you can travel the Coromandel SH25 loop then, from Thames, have the option of carrying on to Rotorua or returning to Auckland. The third pass is the popular 'Forests, Islands and Geysers' whereby you fly to Whitianga (via Great Barrier Island) from the Bay of Islands in Northland, then bus on to Rotorua and beyond ($275). There are a number of Peninsula, and Auckland based bus tour companies offering shuttle, personalized or specialist tour options. These include: ***Aotearoa Tours***, T8662807, F8664583, aotearoa@tournz.co.nz (to and from Auckland plus two and three day tours); ***Go Kiwi Shuttles***, T8660336, F8660337, nzwild@xtra.co.nz (Auckland, Thames, Whitianga shuttle plus tours and charter); ***Coromandel Heritage Tours***, T6369339, F6369309, www.corotours.com (small, personalized eco-adventure safaris).

There are Tourist Information Centres throughout the Coromandel that provide free and comprehensive information on all that 'the Coro' has to offer as well as places to stay. They will also book travel and sell local attraction tickets. Details of the TIC's are given under the relevant town. You'll find them in Thames, Coromandel Town, Whitianga, Tairua, Whangamata and Waihi.

Information
Useful websites: www.worldtouring.co.nz/www.PacificCoast.co.nz

Thames

Phone code: 07
Population: 7000

Thames is located at the western base of the Coromandel Peninsula at the mouth of the Waihou River and fringe of the Hauraki Plains. Behind the town rise the bush-clad hills of the **Coromandel Forest Park.** Thames serves as the gateway to the peninsula, either north to Coromandel town and the west coast, or across the heart of the Forest Park to Tairua and the east coast. Thames is the largest town in the Coromandel and was one of the largest towns in New Zealand during the peak of the kauri logging and gold mining eras of the late 1800's, though you would not guess it now. Other than essential services there is little in the town to hold the tourist back, except perhaps a few historic buildings and the old **Gold Mine and Stamper Battery**. On its back door, the **Kauaeranga Valley**, the main access point to the **Coromandel Forest Park**, is well worth a visit.

Ins & outs

Getting there For transport to and from Thames see Ins and outs on previous page. Coaches stop outside the VIC on Pollen St.

Getting around For car rental try *Michael Saunders Motors*, 201 Pollen St, T0800-111110, or *Rent-A-Dent*, 503 Queen St, T8688838. For bike-hire: *Price and Richards* on Pollen St. Taxis: *Thames Gold Cabs*, T8686037.

Visitor Information Centre 206 Pollen St, Thames, T8687284, thames@ihug.co.nz/www.thames-info.co.nz Mon-Fri 0830-1700, Sat-Sun 0900-1600. Internet access. **DOC** is located at the Kauaeranga Valley Visitor Centre, T8679080. Daily 0800-1600. Most of Thames' amenities are on Pollen St, which runs the length of the town from south to north. The VIC has free street maps.

Sights

Perhaps the best place to start and to get your bearings is the **War Memorial Monument Lookout** on Waiotahi Creek Road, at the northern end of the town. From there you can get a fine view of the town and across the Hauraki Plains and Firth of Thames. Also, at the northern end of town, on Pollen Street, is the **Thames Gold Mine and Stamper Battery**. It offers regular tours which take in the impressive ore-crushing stamper and various horizontal tunnels, with an informative commentary about the process and history of goldmining along the way. ■ *Daily 1000-1600. $6, child $3. T/F8688514, rskeet@xtra.co.nz*

Along the same mining and mineral theme, the **Thames School of Mines and Mineralogical Museum**, on the corner of Brown and Cochrane Streets, has a varied and interesting collection of rocks and minerals from around the world. ■ *1100-1500. Adult $3.50, child free*. T8686227. Given the significance of the area for both kauri logging and gold mining the **Thames Historical Museum** on the corner of Pollen and Cochrane Streets is worth a peek, although it is quite small. ■ *Daily 1300-1600. Adult $2.50, child $1. T8688509.*

There are a number of notable **gardens** and **art and craft galleries** in the area including *Lyndell and Stony Creek Gardens*, *Libby's Pottery*, *In Vogue Gallery* and the Maori craft gallery, *Te Whare Whakairo*. Details of these plus the historical **Thames Heritage Trail** leaflet can be obtained from the VIC.

The Bach

The word bach (or crib in South Island) is one that almost every visitor to New Zealand will encounter. A bach is essentially a second home, or holiday house, built traditionally at the coast. For many years they were very basic wooden huts with a corrugated iron roof, with furniture created from second hand-materials, or even driftwood. An electricity supply was not usually connected and fresh water was collected from the roof and stored in a tank. But in the modern-day the world of traditional bach building has changed dramatically and they can now be anything from the decrepit hut of a reclusive artist, to the million dollar 'pride and joy' of the stockbroker. Some of the first bachs were built on freehold land on Rangitoto Island in the Hauraki Gulf, but the Coromandel, the favoured summer playground for Aucklanders, is a favourite location. If you have time, especially out of season, a rental stay in a traditional bach can provide a traditional and highly relaxing kiwi experience. Local newspapers provide listings.

Market Day in the town is on Saturday and is held in Grahamstown at the north end of Pollen Street.

Sleeping There are a number of B&Bs in and around Thames ranging in price from the **AL** *Grafton Cottage*, 304 Grafton Rd, Thames, T8689971, with its five very smart en-suite chalets with fine views, to the more affordable **A** *Cotswold Cottage*, Maramarahi Rd, T/F8686306. This is a restored villa set in spacious grounds and offering a range of 3 en-suite rooms. The best hotel option is the **A** *Brian Boru Hotel*, 200 Richmond St, T8686523, F8689760, brianboru@xtra.co.nz Established in 1868, it provides affordable, traditional NZ hotel and standard motel-style accommodation. The hotel is most famous for its Agatha Christie-style 'Mystery, Intrigue and Murder Weekends', which provide a bit of role-playing and added fun to your explorations of the Coromandel. Although it is designed for corporate and block bookings you may be able to join in the fun and surround yourself with bad actors in weird and wonderful outfits for a night.

There are also some pleasant B&Bs located out of town in the Kauaeranga Valley, including the wonderfully spacious **A** *Kauaeranga Country B&B*, Kauaeranga Valley Rd, T8686895, and the two-bedroom **B** *Huia Lodge*, T8686557. The pleasant streamside **B-D** *Dickson Holiday Park* is located 3 km north of Thames, T8687308. The 3 hr return, 'Rocky's Goldmine Trail' begins from here. There are cheaper hostels, including the **C-D** *Sunkist Lodge*, 506 Brown St, T8688808, sunkist@xtra.co.nz which is well located and comfortable. The owner is also a mine of information on the Coromandel. There is also the recently renovated and lively **C-D** *Adventure Coromandel Backpackers*, at 476 Pollen St, T8686200, which was formerly the Imperial Hotel.

Motels include the **A** *Coastal Motor Lodge*, 608 Tararu Rd, T8686843, F8686520, which is nicely situated looking over the Firth of Thames, just north of the town. In town itself the **B** *Rolleston Motel*, 105 Rolleston St, T8688091, F8688783, is fine; and the **B** *Brookby Motel*, 102 Redwood La, T/F8686663, is one of the cheaper motel options.

Eating The *Brian Boru Hotel* (see above) offers breakfast, lunch and dinner is open from 0730 and is licensed. The ***Buffet House*** 648 Pollen St, T8688634, offers a great 'all you can eat' smorgasbord, while the ***Gold Bar and Restaurant***, 404 Pollen St, T8685548, offers good-value all day and evening meal menus. Both are licensed. ***The Sealey Café***, 109 Sealey St, T8688641, open 1000-late (0800 Sat /Sun), is perhaps the most popular café with occasional live jazz. ***Food For Thought***, 574 Pollen St, T8686065, is also good value. Open 0730-1700. Just south of Thames, the ***Kopu Station Hotel*** has standard pub grub and is a good place to mix with travellers coming and going from the Peninsula, as is the

Udder Bar below the Adventure Coromandel Backpackers. If it is just a good ol' fish and chippie you are looking for, try the *Majestic Fish Shop*, at 640 Pollen St.

Tour operators

Coromandel Adventure Treks offer good value Eco-based tours in the area including kayak trips, T8682436, www.coromandel-ecotours.co.nz *Triple Challenge Tours*, T8684891, offer multiple 4x4 bike, boat and abseil adventures from about $60. *Adventure Abseiling*, T/F8687181 and *Kauaeranga Horse Treks*, T8688742, are also based in Thames.

Around Thames

Coromandel Forest Park (Kauaeranga Valley)

The Coromandel Forest was, in the late 1800's, one of the most extensive kauri logging areas in the North Island. At the head of the Kauaeranga Valley, 13 km east of Thames, there is a fine DOC visitor centre, set in a very pleasant recreation area. From there a number of fine **walks** spread through the Forest Park. These vary from a few hours to a few days, taking in some of the best scenery the park has to offer and a few remnants of the old logging days, including the impressive **Dancing Creek Dam.** The **Kauaeranga Kauri Trail** (leaflet from the Visitor Centre) is the most popular walk taking trampers to the interesting **Pinnacles** rock formation.

A fascinating audio-visual gives you an insight into the life and times of the early pioneer loggers

Getting there The **Kauaeranga Visitor Centre** is located at the end of Kauaeranga Valley Rd that is accessed via Parawai Rd at the southern end of town. If you do not have your own wheels the *Sunkist Lodge* (see above) in Thames offers a shuttle service; $20 return, T8688808.

Sleeping The 80 bunk **C-D** *Pinnacles Hut*, located on the track, is run by DOC and is a fine place to stay, but beds must be booked in advance, T8679080. There is also a DOC campsite near the visitor centre.

Thames Coast & North to Coromandel Town

The coast road to Coromandel township is scenic, but very windy and quite dangerous, so take your time. On the way, the **Rapaura Watergardens**, about 6 km up the Tapu-Coroglen Road, are worth a look, with numerous paths and lots of 'Monet-like' lily ponds. After your explorations you can enjoy a 'cuppa' and a snack in the Trellis Tearooms. ■ *1000-1700. $5. T8684821.*

Just east of the gardens, a little further up the road and along a fairly steep track, is the impressive '**Square Kauri**' estimated to be over 1,000 years old. Ask at the gardens for detailed directions. While on the Tapu-Coroglen Road (on the right about 2 km before the gardens) it is worth a stop to see the quirky work of sculptor Heather Stevens at the *Mahara Garden Pottery*, T8684817. Another pleasant garden with the added attraction of butterflies is the **Butterfly and Orchid Garden** just 3 km north of Thames. If you have not seen a Monarch yet, this is your chance. ■ *Daily summer 1000-1600, winter 1100-1500. Café and shop. T8688080.*

Just north of Kereta SH25 climbs, turns inland and at the crest of the hill, offers a magnificent **view** of the northern part of the Coromandel Peninsula.

Sleeping If you are beginning to feel dizzy trying to negotiate all the bends in the road, this stretch of coast has some fine accommodation in which to recover, or indeed base yourself to explore the Peninsula. The **AL** *Te Puru Coast View Lodge*, 468 Thames Coast Rd, Te Puru, T8682326, F8682376, tepuru-lodge@xtra.co.nz A boutique Mediterranean-style getaway with excellent views and fine cuisine. At the lower end of the market is the **B-D** *Te Mata Lodge* cabins and campsite off Te Mata Creek Rd, 20 km north of Thames, T8684834, temata@wave.co.nz For camper vans there are a number of options including the popular but basic beach/riverside **C-D** ***Tapu Motor Camp***, 18 km north of Thames, T8684837. Nearby the **A** ***Santa Monica Motel***, Ruamahanga Bay, has seven self-contained units and a restaurant. T8682429.

Coromandel Town

Phone code:07
Population: 3500

Coromandel Town has a wonderful bohemian village feel and a warm atmosphere. The locals, many of whom are artists, are friendly and contented souls who walk about with a knowing smile, as if they are well aware they have come to the 'right' place. It is refreshingly free from the drearily ubiquitous High Street chains or rows of unsightly advertising hoardings, and only a lamppost opposite the road junction as you arrive in the heart of the town bears any signs or place names. The village, and indeed the whole Peninsula, derives its name from the visit, in 1820, by the *HMS Coromandel*, which called in to load kauri spars. Again, gold and kauri in the late 1800s were the attraction, and some old buildings remain, though sadly not the beautiful native bush that once cloaked the hills. Just north of the town one of New Zealand's most famous potters, Barry Brickell, has created – along with many fine works from his kiln – a unique and quirky **Driving Creek Railway** (see below).

Ins & outs

The **Visitor Information Centre** is at 355 Kapanga Rd, T8668598, F8667285, coroinfo@ihug.co.nz Open Mon-Fri 0900-1700, Sat/Sun 1000-1300 (extended summer hours). In keeping with the village the staff are very friendly and helpful. The same office also provides DOC information and internet facilities.

Sights

There are a number of fine garden visits in the immediate area; the VIC has details

The **Coromandel Mining and Historic Museum**, at 841 Rings Road, is a fairly small affair but provides a worthy insight into the rapacious days of gold mining, when the town had three times the population it does now. ■ *Daily in summer, 1000-1600; winter Sat/Sun, 1330-1600. Adult $2, child $0.50.* The 100 year-old operational **Coromandel Gold Stamper Battery** on Buffalo Road is set in very pleasant surrounds with a waterwheel and stream in which you can (for a fee) try your hand at gold panning. ■ *T8667186. Daily, summer 1000-1700. Closed in winter. Tours $5, child $3.*

The **Driving Creek Railway** created by Kiwi sculptor Barry Bricknell is well worth the visit. Barry has lived in Coromandel for years and his artistic creations, open-air studio and railway line all ooze character and charm. Building began on the narrow-gauge railway in 1975 as a means of transporting clay to the kilns at the base of the hill. Now 25 years on the line winds its way almost 2 km up the hill through regenerating bush. It is a delight and a construction of budget engineering genius, together with artistic creativity and environmental respect and sensitivity. Tunnels and embankments built of empty wine bottles (the fuel of the railway builders), together with some of Barry's evocative, and at times quite erotic sculptures, decorate the route. There is an entertaining and informative commentary along the way with the occasional stop (one of which is to see some impressive creepy-crawlies). There are plans to build a spectacular terminus complete with viewing deck at the top and, near the base terminus, a predator-free bush area and museum. The present base terminus, with its brickworks – where all the bricks used along the railway were made –, kilns and shop are all fascinating. ■ *Trains run daily at 1000, 1400, also 1200 and 1600 in summer. Adult $12, child $6, family $30. T/F8668703, www.drivingcreekrailway.co.nz*

The one hour **short walk** at Long Bay Scenic Reserve west of Coromandel is very pleasant, taking in bush and beach (for the beach turn right to Tucks

Bay on reaching the road). It begins at the end of Long Bay Road and is accessed at the Long Bay Motor Camp. The view from the short walk to the **Tokatea Lookout**, at the crest of the hill, up Kennedy Bay Road (via Driving Creek Road) is well worth it.

Don't miss the **craft shops** along Coromandel's main street. The *Weta Design Store* at 46 Kapanga Road is particularly good. The VIC and the free '*Coromandel Craft Trail*' leaflet will point the way to others.

Sleeping

There is a good range of accommodation in and around Coromandel town, mainly in the form of B&Bs, motels, motor camps and backpackers. The VIC has comprehensive information about B&Bs. In summer you are advised to book ahead everywhere

LL-L *Buffalo Lodge*, 860 Buffalo Rd, T/F8668960, www.buffalolodge.co.nz Tasteful, 5-star luxury in a bush setting with sweeping views. Fine cuisine. **AL-A** *Coromandel Colonial Cottages*, 1737 Rings Rd, Coromandel, T/F8668857, coromandel_colonial_cottages@xtra.co.nz Self-contained cottage-style motel units with large grounds and a swimming pool. **AL** *Karamana Homestead*, 84 Whangapoua Rd, Coromandel, T8667138, F8667477, karamana@xtra.co.nz A delightful 1872 kauri villa with three large rooms, all antiques, fine food and luxury. **A** *Celadon B&B*, corner of Alfred St and Oxford Terr, T/F8668058, wilsonmc@wave.co.nz Offers very fine, private and romantic B&B and self-contained options within walking distance of the town centre. **A** *Jacaranda Lodge*, SH25, T/F8668002. Spacious and friendly B&B located just south of the village. **A** *Pottery Lane Cottage*, 15 Pottery La, T/F8667171, r&bmartin@xtra.co.nz A well-situated, cute self-contained cottage. **A** *Coromandel Court Motel*, 365 Kapanga Rd, T8668403, F8668403, corocourt@xtra.co.nz New, well equipped and in a very central location behind the VIC. **B** *Country Touch B&B*, 39 Whangapoua Rd, Coromandel, T/F8668310. Good value en-suite units in country setting.

There are three **backpackers** in and around Coromandel, all of which are clean and comfortable. The centrally located **C-D** *Coromandel Town Backpackers*, 732 Rings Rd, T8668327, is small and handy for all amenities. The **C-D** *Whitehouse*, corner of Frederick and Rings Rd, T8668468, is a larger conglomerate of houses, while the **C-D** *Tui Lodge*, 60 Whangapoua Rd, T8668237, has a good range of accommodation, a campsite and free bikes. The **A-D** *Tidewater Tourist Park*, 207 Tiki Rd, also offers backpacker accommodation.

Similarly the **Motor Camps** are located in and around town. Centrally you have the **A-D** *Coromandel Holiday Park*, at 636 Rings Rd, T8668830, F8668707. North of town on the beach is the **C-D** *Shelly Beach Holiday Park*, Colville Rd, T8668988, and west is the **B-D** *Long Bay Motor Camp*, 3200 Long Bay Rd, T/F8668720.

Eating

The main eateries are all centrally located on Kapanga Rd

The award-winning *Peppertree Restaurant and Bar,* T8668211, has fine dining with a lunch and mainly seafood dinner menu. It has a pleasant interior, bar and outdoor eating area. Open daily from 0900. On summer evenings bookings are advised. The *Coromandel Café* and *Success Café*, T8667100, are opposite each other and both offer good snacks during the day with the Success being open late for evening dining year round. Again seafood is the speciality.

Tour operators

If the museum and stamper battery have whet your appetite to learn more about the history of gold mining, *Dave's Gold Country Treks* offers guided bush-walks and panning trips. Who knows it might be your lucky day. T8668987. $15, two hours, child $7. For fishing two local charter companies are *Coho Boat Charters*, T8668007, coho@xtra.co.nz ($40, three hours), and *Papa Aroha*, T/F8668818, papa.aroha@xtra.co.nz who also hire out kayaks. For a 'blat' around the coast in a small 'fast-cat', contact *Coro Tornado*, T/F8667271. $35, one hour. Horse treks can be arranged with *White Star*, T/F8666820.

Transport

Intercity runs a twice-daily service to and from Thames and a daily service to Whitianga stopping in the town centre. For information and tickets contact the VIC. *Carter's Tours* also offer trips to Thames and elsewhere around the Peninsula on demand (with enough people) and also operate the town's taxi service, T8668045. **Car rental** is at *Rent-A-Dent*, T8668626, and **bikes** can be hired from *Pack-n-Pedal*, T8667753, Tidewater and Tui Backpackers (see above).

South on the 309 Road

The old 309 road, which starts just south of Coromandel Town, then winds its tricky 22 km to Whitianga, has a number of fine attractions. It is one way to get to Whitianga – the other being the SH25.

First stop on the 309, 4½ km from Coromandel, is the charming **Waiau Waterworks**, which is a garden full of fascinating whimsical water sculptures and gadgets. Like the Driving Creek Railway it is Kiwi ingenuity and imagination at its wonderfully eccentric best. ■ *Daily 0900-1700.Closed in winter. Adult $6, child $3. T8668161.*

A short distance further up the road from the waterworks there is a track on the left that takes you a further 2 km to the start of the Castle Rock Walk (standard cars will be fine). The aptly named **Castle Rock** is a very knobbly looking volcanic plug that commands a wonderful view of the northern end of the Peninsula. It is a stiff climb and one to two hours return depending how fit you are. Wear suitable footwear as the track is more like a stream in winter, but the view is well worth the effort.

Just over 7 km up the 309 are the **Waiau Falls**. It is a 15-minute walk to a very pleasant glade where the falls crash over a rock face. Less than a kilometre further up the road is the **Kauri Grove**, a stand of ancient kauri, some of the very few left alone and protected, and all the more impressive for it. The walk takes about 20 minutes. From here you can return to Coromandel Town or carry on to Whitianga.

North to Colville & the Cape

North of Coromandel Town, the Colville Road rejoins the coast at **Papa Aroha** (Land of Love) and **Amodeo Bay**. From these charming bays you will be able to feast your eyes once again on Mount Moehau and what is called the **Pohutukawa Cape**. These wonderfully old and gnarled 'pohutas' that grace the shoreline are some of the best examples in the country, and in December flower in a gorgeous crimson mantle. From this point you are entering perhaps the most remote and scenic area of the Coromandel Peninsula with an atmosphere all of its own. The beach at **Waitete Bay**, about 5 km north of Amodeo Bay, is a cracker and a favourite haunt in summer. From here the road climbs over the hill and falls again to the historic settlement of **Colville**, with its amazingly well stocked general store (open Monday-Thursday 0830-1700, Friday 0830-1800, Saturday 0900-1700, Sunday 0930-1700). Next door, the *Colville Café* is a great place to stop for a coffee or a snack.

Just north of Colville you can cross the Peninsula northeast on the Port Charles Road to **Port Charles** or back down southeast to **Kennedy Bay**, then back to Coromandel. Port Charles is the northernmost settlement on the East Side of the Peninsula and has a great bay and beach. Kennedy Bay is less well-endowed than Port Charles in both scenery and amenities, but gives the passer-by an insight into real Coromandel Peninsula life. Note the St Paul's Anglican Church which must have a very small congregation.

The **Port Jackson Road** which heads north of Colville is an absolute delight with the Moehau Range looming on your right and pebble beaches to the left. The road itself becomes almost completely shrouded by huge gnarled pohutukawa trees. About 13 km north of Colville you will reach the small Te Hope Stream and the beginning of the Mount Moehau Track. **Mount Moehau** is 893 m and the highest peak anywhere near Auckland. Indeed, on a clear day the Moehau range is visible from the city. Mount Moehau is a superb climb, but somewhat frustrating, because the last few hundred metres to the summit (and what must be incredible views) is sacred to the Maori and out of bounds. So if you do make the climb, show suitable respect and settle for nearly reaching the top. The first 2 km of the walk, which follows the river, are still superb with numerous clear pools (sadly swimming is prohibited) and small waterfalls to enjoy. The track, before it starts to make a serious ascent, is a delight and you are almost certain to see native wood pigeon and hear tui.

Information about the walkway is available at the VIC

After negotiating numerous idyllic pebble bays, the road eventually climbs round the northern tip of the cape and falls steeply to **Port Jackson** and **Fletcher Bay**, where the road ends. From here you can enjoy great views of Great Barrier Island, seemingly only a stone's throw away across the Colville Channel. Fletcher Bay marks the beginning of the popular **Coromandel Walkway** which connects Fletcher Bay with Stony Bay and effectively the east coast road and all points south. There are two tracks about 7 km in length and they take about three hours one way. The steeper of the two tracks offers better views and also doubles as a fine mountain biking route. If you do not have your own wheels *Carter's* in Coromandel will drop off and pick up for about $60, T8668045.

There are a number of accommodation options at Papa Aroha and Amodeo Bay

Sleeping The **B** *Pohutukawa Coast Chalets*, near Papaaroha, just north of Coromandel, T8668379, are comfortable, good-value, self-contained 'A Frame' cabins, some of which have fine views. Discounts for 5 days or more. The **A** *Papa Aroha Motel*, T/F8668440, is a Spanish-style standard motel with a restaurant, while the basic **C-D** *Papa Aroha Holiday Park* is a place to camp or park up with the campervan. It also offers fishing charters, boat and kayak hire. At Amodeo Bay is the excellent **A-D** *Anglers Lodge*, T8668584, F8667352, anglers@clear.net.nz, which offers motel units and a campsite, with swimming pool, spa, shop, kayak hire and charter boat, all on site. There is also the **A-B** *Amodeo Bay Motel, B&B and Homestay* at Waitete Bay, T/F8668322, which has a good range of accommodation close to the beach.

Near Colville the **A-D** *Colville Lodge* is the Peninsula's northernmost motel and motor camp. It has a spa and backpacker beds, and campsites are also available. The popular **B-D** *Colville Farm*, T/F8666820 has self-contained, lodge, backpackers and camping facilities. The northernmost backpackers is **C-D** *Fletcher Bay Backpackers*, T8666172, js.lourie@xtra.co.nz which offers a remote but welcome overnight stop if you have done the Coromandel Walkway. **DOC** operates 5 **campsites** with basic facilities at Fantail Bay, Port Jackson, Fletcher, Stony and Waikawau Bays. For site information and availability, T0800-455466. Bookings are essential at Waikawau Bay in summer, T8666852.

Eating When it comes to eating, the well-stocked *Colville Store and Café* will more than suffice, considering the location. Open 7 days from 0800. Café from 0800 and evenings on Sat, every evening in summer.

SH25 to Whitianga

From Coromandel Town the SH25 winds its way east, over the ranges, offering fine views, before descending steeply to Te Rerenga and Whangapoua Harbour. **Whangapoua** village, 4 km north of the junction at Te Rerenga, is essentially a conglomeration of holiday homes and beaches that come alive in the summer months. A short 30 minute-walk north from the road end in Whangapoua is **New Chums Beach**, which is one of the best beaches in the Coromandel. The fact that you cannot drive there and have to negotiate the headland by foot seems to protect its beauty, enhance its character and make it a truly magical place. Even in bad weather it is worth the walk.

Back on SH25 and east is the sterile real estate settlement of **Matarangi**, which is saved only by its sweeping beach and great golf course. About 6 km further on at the end of the beach is **Kuaotunu** a nice spot in itself, especially for swimming. Kuaotunu also acts as the gateway to **Opito Bay** via the scenic and intriguingly named Black Jack Road. Opito has a lovely beach with magnificent views across to the Mercury's and numerous other small Islands. In summer this is a great spot to escape the crowds.

Sleeping and Eating There is a campsite is at Whangapoua (Hamiora), T8667183, and a general store that can also assist in bach rentals, T8668274. The **A** *Castle Rock Winery* in Te Rerenga has a comfortable flat, and an amazing range of fruit wines (you may never leave!),T8664542. Open 0900-1800.

There is a well-stocked store at Kuaotuna and two holiday parks: the **B-D** *Kuaotuna Beach Holiday Park*, T8665172 and the **B-D** *Kuaotuna Motor Camp*, T8665628. There's also the **C-D** *Black Jack Backpackers*, T8662988, carl@black-jack.co.nz, and two B&B's on Gray's Av: **B** *Drift In B&B*, 16 Gray's Av, is good value and has great views, T/F8664321; and **A** *Kaeppeli's, T8662445, which is similar, and run by a Swiss/ Kiwi family and chef, so is also renowned for its fine cuisine.*

Whitianga

Phone code: 07
Population: 4000

Whitianga is a very popular holiday town on the shores of beautiful Mercury Bay, which was given its planetary name by Captain Cook during a spot of astronomy on his brief visit in 1769. 'Whiti' (pronounced 'fitty') – as it is affectionately known – has much to offer, including a number of fine beaches within walking distance of the town. But it also acts as a convenient short-cut access point, across the narrow Whitianga Harbour entrance and Ferry Landing, to two fine smaller resorts – Cooks Beach and Hahei. Although there is an abundance of leisure activities to choose from, Whiti is perhaps most famous as a sea and big game fishing base and, like the Bay of Islands, a trip on the water is highly recommended. In summer and especially at Christmas and New Year, Whiti's growing resident population increases dramatically, resulting in excellent of tourist services and amenities year round.

Ins and outs

Getting there & around The **airport** is 3 km south of the town and is serviced by *Air Coromandel* (see page 194). *Intercity* and *Newmans* **buses** drop off and pick up outside the VIC in the centre of town. Other smaller shuttle companies operate to and from Auckland and around the peninsula (see also page194). *Hot Water Beach Conxtions* are a local company offering a full day hop-on, hop-off service from Ferry Landing to Cooks Beach, Cathedral Cove, Hahei and Hot Water Beach. There are about 5 departures a day and a day pass costs $20. Some buses connect with Auckland services at Dalmeny Corner. T/F8662478. The 5-min **ferry** crossing to Ferry Landing operates continuously in summer from 0730-2300. In winter the hours are 0730-1200, 1300-1830 and for 30 mins at 1930 and 2130; $1, child $0.50. **Car rental** is available at the *Rental Car Centre*, 19 Coghill St, T8665901. **Bikes** can be hired at *Whitianga Mowers and Cycles*, 15 Coghill St, T/F8665435. The local taxi service is *Mercury Bay Taxis*, T8662047.

Information The often overstretched **Visitor Information Centre** is located at 66 Albert St in the centre of town, T8665555, F8662205, whitvin@ihug.co.nz/www.whitianga.co.nz/ www.mercurybay.co.nz Mon-Fri 0900-1700, Sat 0900-1300, 7days in peak season.

Sights

The rather tired **Mercury Bay Museum** on the Esplanade is fairly small, but nicely showcases the area's rich human history which goes back over 1000 years, when Maori explorer Kupe made landfall here. Cook's visit is also documented. ■ *Daily summer, 1100-1400 Tue-Thu-Sun winter. Adult $3, child $1.50.* The main waterfront beach is called **Buffalo Beach**, named after *HMS Buffalo* which was wrecked here in 1840. It is a fine beach but gets a little hectic in summer. **Flaxmill Bay** across the water just beyond Ferry Landing, and better still **Lonely Bay**, at the eastern base of the Shakespeare Cliff Scenic Reserve, are often a better bet.

There are a number of fine craft shops and galleries in and around Whitianga; for information see the VIC

Whitianga

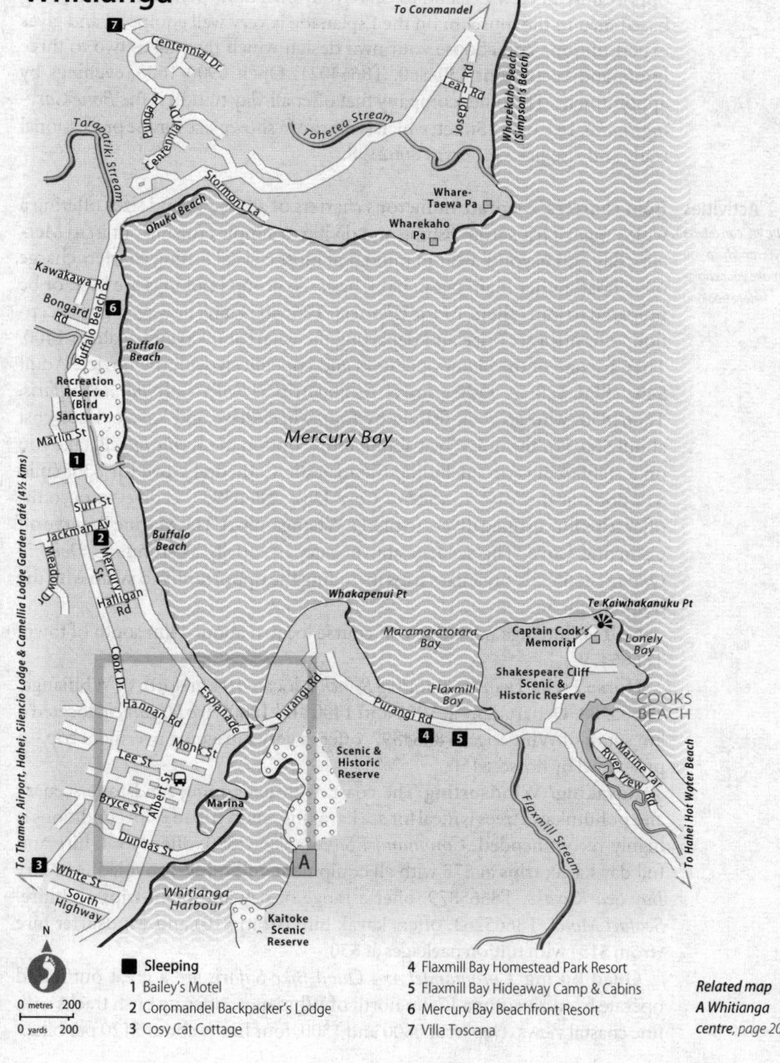

Related map
A Whitianga centre, *page 205*

Even if you do not intend to go as far as Cooks Beach and Hahei, the short ferry ride across to **Ferry Landing** is worthwhile. The **wharf** itself was built in 1837 and, though it is one of the oldest in New Zealand, is less than attractive with its concrete coating. However there is a nice café and a number of fine **coastal walks** nearby. Immediately to the right of the wharf is the Whitianga Rock Walk (20 minutes) which takes in a Maori *Pa* and offers a great view back over Whiti. The Maramaratotara Bay Walk (40 minutes) joins the Rock Walk and also has good views. A little further down the road opposite the Flaxmill Bay Resort is the access point to the Shakespeare Cliff Scenic Reserve. Climb the path to the right then cross the hill to the viewpoint where you are rewarded with a wonderful view across the Bay.

Whiti has two **Bone Carving Studios** which between them offer the best opportunity in New Zealand to carve your own bone pendant. *Bay Carving* based next to the museum on the Esplanade is very well equipped and gives expert tuition. You choose your own design which then takes two to three hours and costs from $30-$60. T8664021. Open 0900-1600, evenings by appointment. The other company that offer all-day tuition is the *Bone Carving Studio*, 16 Coghill Street, which is more of a showpiece for the professional trade and also has a gallery, T8662158.

Activities

The VIC can advise you and help you make your choice before booking

Boat charters There are numerous charters of all shapes and sizes offering a wide range of trips from fishing and diving to simple cruising out in to Mercury Bay and beyond. Bear in mind that most coastal fishing charters charge on a 'boat' rather than 'per person' basis, so group bookings are best, or be prepared to join others. *Marie Charters*, T8664054, are, however, one exception, offering a set price and departing the wharf at 0900 and again at 1400. They are one of the better operators and cope nicely with the novice. Adult $45, child $20. A rather novel fishing trip is with *Coromandel Safaris*, T8662850, who go rock fishing by four-wheel drive and kayak. Trips cost about $60. For the noisy 'blat about' cruise option the *Scenic Jet* will take you on a sightseeing trip, including the majestic Cathedral Cove for $30, child $15.Book at the VIC. *Cathedral Cove Dive*, T8663955, ccdive@xtra.co.nz, offer trips for certified divers to the Te Whanganui-A-Hei Marine Reserve off Cathedral Cove. The scenery above water is equally as stunning. *Dolphin Quest*, T8665555, organizes trips including the opportunity to swim with the dolphins for $85.

Golf Whitianga has a fine golf course located about 4 km south of town, T8665479.

Horse Treks *Twin Oaks Riding Ranch* is located 9 km north of Whitianga. T8665388. Depart daily at 1000 and 1400 and 1800. *Ace Hi Ranch*, located 8 km south of Whitianga, T8664897, offers a very intriguing overnight trip – a pub-crawl by horse. $150.

Kayaking/ Windsurfing The coast, with its eroding sandstone scenery and pohutukawa trees is ideal for sea kayaking, and a trip in calm conditions is highly recommended. *Coromandel Safaris*,T8662850, offer kayak hire and full day kayak trips at $75 with all equipment and meals provided. *Mercury Bay Sea Kayaks*, T8665879, offer a range of day and night trips and hire. *Seafari Motel*, T8665263, offers kayak hire (from $10) and windsurfer hire (from $15) with tuition packages at $30.

Quad biking *Coromandel 4x4 Quad Bike Safaris* are a great outfit and operate from Kuaotuna 17 km north of Whitianga, offering bush tracks with fine coastal views. Depart at 0800 and 1300, four hours about $120 per bike.

If you want to make a complete Charlie of yourself you should have a go on the **Whiti Banana Boat**. This is a large inflatable yellow 'phallus' that blats around the bay at high speed, with you desperately trying to hold on – actually a great laugh. There are a number of trip options including the Hell Bender, the Thrill and Kiddies Ride. Call at the VIC, $10.

Essentials

Sleeping

There is a huge range of accommodation in Whitianga to suit all tastes and budgets. The TIC has all the information and can pre-book, which is highly recommended in summer

LL *Villa Toscana*, Ohuka Park, is a superb Italian-style villa set on 2 ha of native bush near Whitianga, with a self-contained designer suite that seems of equal size. Total luxury, T8662293, F8662269, www.villatoscana.co.nz A bit more affordable but still at the luxury end is the **L** *Silenco Lodge*, again out of town, set in 14 acres of bush. Spa log fire, the works, T8660304, F8660304, Gavin@enternet.co.nz

Amongst the best in town is the **AL-A** *Mercury Bay Beachfront Resort*, 111-113 Buffalo Beach Rd, T8665637, F8664524. It has a prime beachfront location and all mod cons. **A** *Whitehouse B&B*, 129 Albert St, T/F8665116, is well-situated and very comfortable; as is the human-friendly and very cat-friendly **B** *Cosy Cat Cottage*, 41 South Highway, T/F8664488. There's also a wide range of motels. At the lower end of the market is the older but comfortable **B** *Bailey's Motel*, 66 Buffalo Beach Rd, T/F8665500, which is still beachfront and close to town.

Whitianga centre

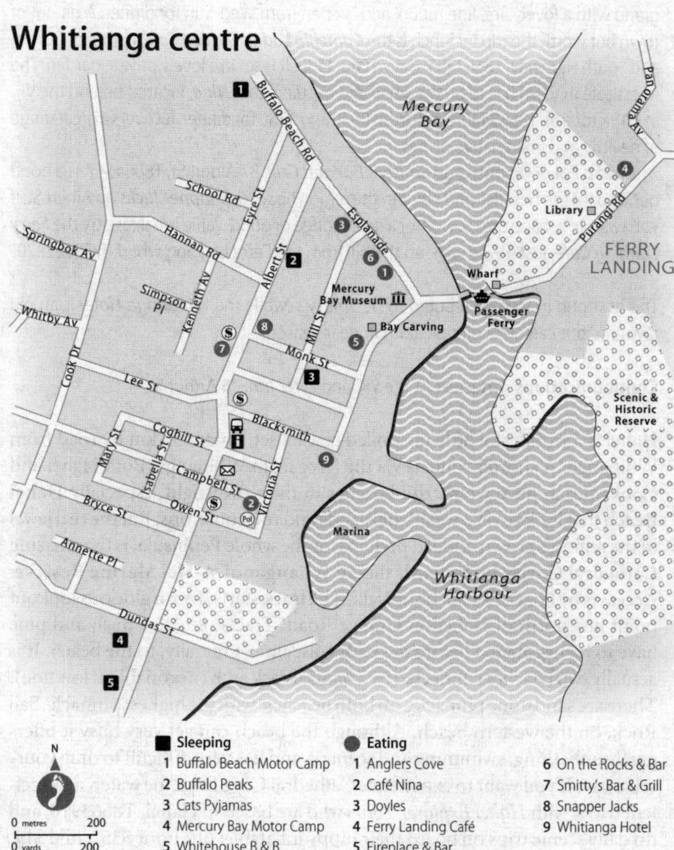

The **C-D** *Cat's Pyjamas*, 4 Monk St, T8664663, is the smaller of three backpackers in Whiti and a fine one to boot. Buster the owner is building a plane in the garage, in which he hopes, one day, to fly to Australia. The hostel is well located, clean and comfortable. The alternatives are the **C-D** *Buffalo Peaks*, 12 Albert St, T8662933, buffalopeakslodge@xtra.co.nz and the **C-D** *Coromandel Backpacker's Lodge*, 46 Buffalo Beach Rd T8665380, corobkpk@wave.co.nz The latter has bikes and kayaks for hire.

There are a few motor camps including: **B-D** *The Mercury Bay* at 121 Albert St, T/F8665579, and the **B-D** *Buffalo Beach*, Eyre St, T/F8665854. Two great alternatives in a quiet and wonderful location near Ferry Landing is the **B-D** *Flaxmill Bay, Hideaway Camp and Cabins*, T/F8662386, and the **B-D** *Flaxmill Bay Homestead Park Resort*, T/F8665595. Both provide a range of accommodation from log cabins to self-contained units and backpacker bunks, but it is only accessible by road via Cooks Beach, a ferry ride and walk from Whitianga.

Eating

Whiti is well served with fine eating establishments, most of which offer a variety of fresh seafood; the best are located along the Esplanade

Mid-range *The Anglers Cove*, 17 The Esplanade, T8665623. Daily from 0900 summer and 1100 in winter; and *Doyles*, 21 The Esplanade, T866 5209. Open for lunch and from 1700 for dinner, are both fine places for seafood, and fully licensed. Perhaps the best is the award-winning *On the Rocks Bar and Restaurant*, 20 The Esplanade, T8664833. Open from 1100. The new *Fireplace Restaurant and Bar*, also on the Esplanade, is very grand with a lovely fire, fine menu, and is open from Wed-Sun for dinner. A bit out of town but worth the trip for lunch is the *Camellia Lodge Garden Café*, corner of Golf Rd and South Highway, T8662253. Daily 1000-1530. It is set in a lovely private garden. The finest café in town has to be the small and bustling *Café Nina*, located behind the VIC at 20 Victoria St, T8665440. Open from 0930 and 1730 for dinner. It covers a great range of healthy and imaginative dishes.

Cheap For good pub grub *Smitty's Bar and Grill*, 37 Albert St, T8664647, is a good bet, and for the best fish and chips in the region head for *Snapper Jacks* on Albert St. If you want to escape the crowds for a quiet coffee or good-value breakfast, try the *Ferry Landing Café*, just a wee walk up the hill from the Ferry Landing wharf, T/F8662820.

Entertainment

The best pub in town is reputed to be *Smitty's* ,while the *Whitianga Hotel* is an old favourite but can get a bit ridiculous in peak season.

Directory

Communications Internet At the VIC and *LyNZ Inn*, 25 Arthur St.

Hahei, Cooks Beach & Hot Water Beach

Seeing the sunrise at Cathedral Cove is an unforgettable experience

Hahei is a wonderful little unspoiled coastal settlement 35 km by road from Whitianga. A shorter route is via the ferry from Whitianga. Both Hahei and Cooks Beach have wonderful beaches in their own right, especially **Hahei Beach** that looks over a wealth of islands and rock outcrops. But the real jewel in the region's crown, indeed perhaps for the whole Peninsula, is the amazing **Cathedral Cove** which guards the **Te Whanganui-A-Hei Marine Reserve**. Access is by boat or a half-hour walk. The track starts from a glorious lookout point just north of Hahei on Grange Road. Tracts of native bush and pine have to be negotiated before the path falls, almost literally, to the beach. It is actually two beaches connected by a natural rock arch (negotiable at low tide). There are sandstone pinnacles on both beaches, with the highest pinnacle, Sail Rock, on the western beach. Although the beach can get very busy it offers great sunbathing, swimming and scenery, and it is very difficult to drag yourself away. If you want to experience Cathedral Cove from the water, an excellent trip is with *Hahei Explorer Tours* who are based in Hahei, T8663910, and do daily scenic trips on board their nippy inflatable; one hour $35, child $17. The tour also takes in some caves and a blowhole not accessible by foot.

About 15 km south of Hahei is **Hot Water Beach** which offers the fairly unique experience of digging a hole in the sand to access natural hot water. You should do this about two hours each side of low tide. Once filled, you can settle in to read a book or watch the surfers doing what you can't. The beach in itself is very pleasant, but be warned: it is also very dangerous with notorious rips. The *Hot Water Beach Store* hires out spades for $2, or, if you are lucky, you can borrow someone else's.

Sleeping and eating At the top end of the market is the **L-B** *Hanlyn Park Lodge*, 11 Christine Rd, Hahei, T/F8663888. Perched on the hill the range of self-contained units and rooms are immaculate and offer unforgettable views. There is a swimming pool and spa. The **A** *Spellbound B&B*, 77 Grange Rd, T8663543, is at the opposite end of the village, but is almost as good with equally good views which will leave you spellbound. The **A** *Church*, 87 Beach Rd, T8663533, F8663055, is full of character and offers en-suite cottage-style B&B accommodation. It also has a fine à la carte restaurant. The **A-D** *Hahei Holiday Resort* right on the beach is a fine facility and offers backpacker accommodation. The **A-D** *Tatahi Lodge* is also an excellent motel and backpackers located on Grange Rd, T8663992. At Hot Water Beach is the **B-D** *Hot Water Beach Holiday Park*, complete with thermal pools, T8663735, and the friendly **B** *Auntie Dawn's Place*, Radar Rd, T8663707, F8663701, which has a couple of units and in-house B&B.

For fine dining the ***Church*** is popular (see above). Otherwise, try ***Breakers Restaurant and Café***, 7 Grange Rd, T8663502. Open 7 days in summer from 0900, weekend dinners in winter. Alternatively, ***Café Luna***, nearby at 1 Grange Rd, T8663016. Open 7 days in summer from 0800 until late and winter Thu to Sun daytime from 0800 and Fri-Sat for dinner. The *Luna* does a great breakfast.

Tairua and Pauanui

Tairua is also the main gateway to Alderman, Shoe, Slipper & Mayor Islands

Only the Tairua Harbour and a resulting 20 km-road trip separate these deeply contrasting communities. Tairua, which was settled as a milling and farming town, is the older, smaller and more accessible of the two, situated on SH25. Pauanui, in contrast, is full of expensive holiday and retirement homes with fussy gardens, four-wheel drives and luxury watercraft. A place where men wear polyester shorts and knee-length nylon socks with fawn coloured dress shoes, and the women support the latest clinical blue-rinse hairdo. Not exactly the haunt of the happy-go-lucky traveller. Perhaps the best thing about the two towns is the setting and the memorable view from **Paku Hill** which dominates the harbour entrance. It can be accessed from the end of Tirinui Crescent off Paku Drive.

Other than that there are a number of attractive water-based activities operating mainly out of Tairua, a fine surf beach at Pauanui and the popular **Broken Hills** Recreation Area walks (leaflet from the VIC).

Ins and outs The ferry to Pauanui leaves from Tairua Wharf on Wharf Rd. In summer she sails at 0900, 1100,1300,1500 and 1700, winter weekends only. $4 return. T025970316. The Tairua **Visitor Information Centre** is in the heart of Tairua on SH25, T/F8647575, info.tairua@xtra.co.nz Open summer daily 0930-1600, winter, 1000-1400. They can assist with the plentiful accommodation options or book water-based activity or island trips.

Sleeping and eating **LL** *Puka Park Lodge*, Pauanui Beach, is reputed to provide perhaps the most luxurious accommodation on the Peninsula. Fine private bush chalets with a restaurant and bar in the main lodge house. **A** *Kotuku Lodge*, 179 Main Rd, T/F8647040, kotuku@wave.co.nz A very popular hillside lodge with fine view and sumptuous breakfast. **B** *Walnut Tree*, 167 Main Rd, T8647428. Cosy, good value B&B.

A-AL *Pacific Harbour Lodge*, Main Rd, T8648581, F8648858, Pacific.Harbour@xtra.co.nz One of the best motels with a good restaurant. The **A-AL** *Pauanui Pines Motor Lodge*, 168 Vista Paku, Pauanui Beach, T8648086, pauanuipines@clear.co.nz, is a fine award-winning motel in Pauanui. There are two good hostels the **C-D** *Flying Dutchman*, 305 Main Rd, T8648446, and the very activity-based **C-D** *Tairua Backpackers Lodge*, at 200 Main Rd, T8648345. There are plenty of motor parks in the area including the **B-D***Tairua Holiday Park*, 4 Manaia Rd, T8648871.

For eating, the fine dining option has to be at the *Puka Park Lodge* (see above), bookings advised. In Tairua, for lunch, the *Out of the Blue Café* on Main Rd can serve good coffee, imaginative lunches and snacks and a fine breakfast, T8648987, 0900-1700. About 12 mins north of Tairua the *Colenso Country Café* on SH25 is a top spot with fine food, T8663725. 1000-1700. Back in town, *Shells Restaurant*, also on Main St, is a convenient place for a good-value, standard dinner. T8648811.

Opoutere

Opoutere is one of the Coromandel's best-kept secrets. It has a quiet and magical atmosphere with a gorgeous sweeping white-sand **Ocean Beach**, guarded by the Wharekawa Harbour and a narrow tract of forest. At the tip of the sand spit is the **Wharekawa Wildlife Refuge**, where oystercatcher and rare New Zealand dotterel breed in summer. Special care should be taken not to enter this area and disturb the birds (dogs are strictly forbidden). The beach can be accessed from the car park around the corner from the **B-D** *Opoutere Youth Hostel*, T8659072, which is a fine, peaceful place to stay and has great facilities, short walks nearby, and a lovely view across the harbour. Opoutere can be reached by bus from Whangamata, T8658613.

Whangamata

Whangamata is well serviced with luxury and budget accommodation, eateries and mainly water-based activities

Whangamata is a very popular holiday spot and the main **surfing** venue on the Coromandel. As such, it acts as a magnet to youngsters, especially at New Year. There are a number of good short coastal **walks**, while south of the town the **Wentworth and Parakiwai Valleys** offer longer walks taking in remnants of the gold mining years and waterfalls. The often busy **beach** at Whangamata is over 4 km long, while the quieter **Whiritoa Beach** and lagoon, 12 km south of Whangamata, also offers a lovely bush walk, heading north. There is a quality **art and crafts** trail in the area (see VIC) and, like Tairua, Whangamata, is also a base for trips to the outer islands, including **Mayor Island**.

The Whangamata **Information Centre** is located at 616 Port Road, T/F8658340, info-whangamata@xtra.co.nz Open Monday-Saturday 0900-1700, Sunday 1000-1600. It can assist in finding accommodation and book the numerous water-based trips and activities. *Kiwi Dundee Adventures*, T/F8658809, www.kiwidundee.co.nz Offers an extensive and imaginative range of Eco-tours. Half and full-day trips, taking in natural sights and gold mining remnants. The *Whangamata Surf Shop*, Port Road, is the focus for the latest surfer's gossip and board hire. **Internet** access at *Internet and Graphics*, 712 Port Road, T8658832.

There are many options for accommodation in Whangamata and you are advised to consult the VIC and book in advance in summer, well in advance for New Year

Sleeping **LL** *Brenton Lodge*, 1 Brenton Pl, T/F8658400, brentonlodge@xtra.co.nz A gorgeous boutique country retreat with romantic, cottage-style suites and lots of pampering. **L-AL** *Bushland Park Lodge*, 444 Wentworth Valley Rd, T8657468, F8657486, bushparklodge@xtra.co.nz Another fine establishment in a lovely location, 'Euro' in style, emphasis on health and a quality restaurant attached. **A** *Fairway Homestay*, 130 Kiwi Rd, T8657018, F8657685. Set next to the golf course and 5 mins from the beach. Two guestrooms with shared bathroom. **A** *Breakers Motel*, 324 Hetherington Rd, T8658464, F8658991, breakersmotel@whangamata.co.nz A new motel with great facilities including swimming and private spa pools. **B** *Estuary*

Retreat Motel, 105 Marie Cres, T8659563. Quality budget motel with good cheap breakfasts and close to the beach. **B-D** ***Garden Motor and Tourist Lodge***, Cnr Port and Mayfair, T/F8659580, gardenlodge@xtra.co.nz Well maintained, farm style accommodation with backpacker facilities. **C-D** ***Whangamata Backpackers***, 227 Beverley Tce, T/F8658323. Small but well situated close to all amenities. The two main motor camps are the **B-D** ***Pinefield Holiday Park***, 207-227 Port Rd, T/F8658791, and the **B-D** ***Whangamata Motor Camp***, Barbara Av, T8659128. There is a basic DOC **campsite** at Wentworth Valley on Wentworth Valley Rd, T/F8657032.

Eating For fine dining head for the cosy ***Nickel Strausse*** at Bushland Park (see above). In town, ***Café 101***, 101 Casement Rd, T8656301, does acceptable breakfasts, lunch and dinner, while ***Ginger's*** at 601 Port Rd, is the place to head for health food and ***Vibes Café***, also on Port Rd, for the best coffee.

Waihi

The VIC is on Seddon St, T8636715; open daily, 0900-1700 in summer, and 0900-1630 in winter

Although gold mining once flourished all around the Coromandel, Waihi was in many ways the capital of operations, with 1,200 mines producing half of the country's gold. The scale of operations earned Waihi the reputation as the most famous mining town in New Zealand. The town itself, although well serviced, is nothing remarkable, but it boasts a heart of gold and seems to retain a sort of Wild West feel.

The most impressive evidence of the town's mining history is the huge **Martha Mine**, which sits like a huge, but strangely discrete bomb crater, right in the centre of town . The Martha Mine was one of the originals that reopened after a brief redundancy in the mid-1900s. Today, from a lookout behind the Information Centre, you can watch huge earthmoving trucks relentlessly winding their way in and out of the massive terraced hole. The Waihi Gold Mining Company, Barry Road, offers free guided tours most weekdays, T8639880, info@waihigold.nzl.com The **Waihi Arts Centre and Museum**, Kenny Street, is worth a look. It displays an array of mining memorabilia and interesting working models, including a miniature stamping battery. ■ *Open Mon-Fri 1000-1600, Sat-Sun 1330-1600. Adult $3, child $1.50. T8638386.*

Nearby the Ohinemuri River winds its dramatic way west, through the **Karangahake Gorge**, where there are a number of interesting walks and mining relics (DOC leaflet available from the VIC). The **Goldfields Railway**, a vintage steam train, runs 8 km into the gorge from Waihi to **Waikino**. It leaves from Wrigley Street, daily at 1100,1230,1400. Adult $10, child $7 return. T8638251.

There are also two wineries in the area, two fine golf courses and a generous collection of gardens, including the pretty **Waihi Waterlily Gardens** at Pukekauri Rd. ■ *Daily in summer 100-1600. Adult $4.50, children free*. For other venues ask at the VIC. If you want to go to the beach, head for the popular surfer's hangout at **Waihi Beach**, 11 km to the east. A pleasant 45-minute coastal walk at the northern end of the beach will take you to the very pretty **Orokawa Bay**.

Waihi and Waihi Beach, 11 km to the east are well serviced with the full range of accommodation options

Sleeping The **A** ***French Provincial Country Homestay***, 5 km from Waihi on Golden Valley Trig Rd North, T8637339, is at the top end of the market and popular with honeymooners, as is the popular self-contained **A** ***Goose Farm Cottage***, Owahara Falls, Karangahake Gorge, T8637944. In town **B** ***Chez Nous B&B***, 41 Seddon St, T8637538, is central and good value. For motels you are best to head for Waihi Beach and the relatively new **A** ***Sea Air Motel***, Emerton Rd, Waihi Beach, T8635655. There are a number of motor camps: in Waihi the **B-D** ***Waihi Motor Camp***, 6 Waitete Rd, T8637654, has chalets, cabins and tent sites. At Waihi Beach the **A-D** ***Waihi Beach Holiday Park***, 15 Main

Beach Rd, Waihi Beach, T8635504, has some fine cabins, while the **B-D** ***Athenree Holiday Park***, on Athenree Rd, T/F8635600, offers all the usual with the added attraction of hot springs.

For something different if your timing is right you could try the evening dinner train run by Goldfields, which runs the first Sat of each month, $35, T8638251

Eating The ***Chambers Wine Bar and Restaurant***, 22 Haszard St, , T8637474, is in the old 1904 Council Chambers building, offering a mix of Mediterranean and Antipodean dishes. Open 1100-late. The smaller log cabin-style ***Grandpa Thorns***, 4 Waitete Rd, T8638708, is in a nice setting and does good seafood. Open summer, Tue-Sun from 1730. The ***Waitete Orchard Café***, Waitete Rd, off SH2, T8638980, is a great lunch venue with organic flare and fruit wines. Daily from 0830-1730. In the imaginatively named ***Jellyfish and Custard***, 31 Wilson Rd, T/F8635840, serves just about everything but. Daily lunch and dinner.

The Waikato

The Waikato

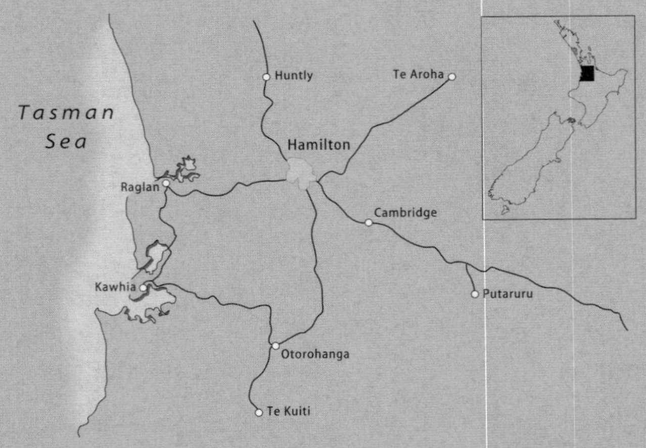

Tasman Sea
Huntly
Te Aroha
Hamilton
Raglan
Cambridge
Kawhia
Putaruru
Otorohanga
Te Kuiti

The Waikato is one of the country's richest agricultural areas where the eponymous river, the longest in the country, snakes its way through a landscape of green rolling hills and fields. The Waikato is rich in Maori history and is home to the Tainui people, one of the largest tribes in the land, as well as being home to the current Maori queen and head of state. The first Maori king was elected here in 1858 and the subsequent formation of the Maori King Movement, in direct opposition to rule under the British monarchy, led to much bloodshed. After almost a year of fierce battles and confrontation the British finally quashed the Kingites, who fled to southern Waikato, which is now also known as ***King Country****. Today, peace reigns, but the memory lives on. Waikato also boasts New Zealand's fourth largest city,* ***Hamilton****, which, despite being an unremarkable commercial centre, is increasingly seen as an alternative base to Auckland. Although not a major tourist destination, the Waikato is a region with considerable diversity, from the famous* ***surf beaches*** *on its coast, to the jewel in the crown of the King Country, the* ***Waitomo*** *District, a wonderland of limestone caves and subterranean activities that deservedly make it one of the North Island's premier tourist attractions.*

Things to do in Waikato

- *Encounter a kiwi, a kea or a kokako in Otorohanga's famous Kiwi House.*
- *Go underground with style in the 'Haggas Honking Holes' or descend 100 m in to the awe-inspiring 'Lost World'.*
- *Hug an Angora rabbit, see the highly entertaining Woodlyn Park agricultural show, or marvel at glow worms in Waitomo Caves Village.*
- *Take the back roads from Waitomo to the intriguing coastal village of Kawhia, stopping at the misty Marokopa Falls on the way.*
- *Dream about VW Beetles and 'left-hand breaks' with the surfies in laid-back Raglan.*
- *Climb Mount Te Aroha then relax in a hot pool in the Te Aroha Domain.*

Hamilton

Phone code: 07
Population: 120,000

Perched on the serpentine banks of the famous Waikato River, 129 km south of Auckland, Hamilton is New Zealand's fourth largest city and main service centre for the rich fertile agricultural region of the Waikato. Being located so close to the major tourist destinations of Auckland and Rotorua, Hamilton struggles to attract visitors for any length of time. It has few major attractions but can be an attractive alternative 'arrival base' to Auckland and is ideally located for explorations around the Waikato Region. Hamilton is also a university town and plays host to some major national events, including the annual ***National Agricultural Fieldays*** *in June and the colourful* ***Hot Air Balloon Fiesta*** *in April. Visitors stopping briefly in the city can enjoy a ride down the Waikato on the MV Waipa Delta paddleboat and visit the celebrated, museum, gardens and 'Free-flight Aviary' of* ***Hamilton Zoo****.*

The Waikato

Ins and outs

Getting there

Air Hamilton has a busy International **Airport** located 15 mins south of the city, T8433623. ***Freedom Air*** (T0800-600500) fly regularly to Eastern Australia while ***Air New Zealand*** (T0800-737000) and Quantas New Zealand service major domestic destinations.

Bus Hamilton is well serviced by ***Intercity*** (T8343457), ***Mount Cook*** (T0800-800287) and ***Newmans*** (T0800-777707) which arrive and depart from the Transport Centre on Anglesea St, T8393580.

Car Both SH1 and the main Auckland to Wellington trunk line run through the heart of the Waikato. An alternative route south is SH27, which branches off SH1 just south of Auckland at the Bombay Hills and also accesses Waikato east. SH27 passes through Matamata before rejoining SH1 again at Tirau. The principal signposted touring route is called the **'Thermal Explorer Highway'** which goes from Auckland via Hamilton, Rotorua and Taupo to Napier. A free touring map is available from all major VIC's.

Rail Hamilton is on the main trunk **rail** line with services daily to Auckland, Wellington, Rotorua and Tauranga, T0800-802802. The rail station is on Fraser St, in Franktown.

Information & orientation

The Hamilton **Visitor Information Centre** is located at the Hamilton Transport Centre, Anglesea St, T8393580, F8393127, hamiltoninfo@wave.co.nz/www.hamiltoncity.co.nz Open Mon-Fri 0900-1700, Sat-Sun 1000-1700. **DOC** is located on London St, T8391393.

History

The earliest recorded settlers in the Hamilton area were Maori from the Tainui canoe that settled on the banks of the river. At that time, the Waikato River was the major means of communication, transportation and trade with other settled areas. In the 1860s the first Europeans began to settle, during the Land Wars and the notorious 'raupatu' or land confiscations. A military outpost was established in Hamilton East and existed for a number of years before communications and relations improved and agriculture developed. In 1867 the road was opened to Auckland, followed ten years later by the railway. From that point on settlement began in earnest and the city developed as a major agricultural service centre. The town was named in honour of Captain John Charles Fane Hamilton, the commander of *HMS Esk*, who was killed while leading the naval brigade at the Battle of Gate *Pa* near Tauranga in 1864.

Sights

Waikato Museum of Art & History

There is also a fine café/restaurant attached to the museum, selling interesting fare such as ostrich antipasti and kangaroo loin, amongst other things

The modern Waikato Museum of Art and History overlooks the river on the corner of Victoria and Grantham Street. It presents a wide-ranging programme of both permanent and temporary exhibitions, including a balance of contemporary and historical art of regional significance and national importance. The history of Hamilton and the region is naturally explored with a particularly impressive collection of Tainui Maori *taonga* (treasures). The highlight of the collection has to be the beautiful carved and decorated *Waka*, 'Te Wainika' , gifted to the museum in 1973 by Te Arikinui Dame Te Atairangikaahu, the Maori queen. '**Excite**' is an adjunct science and technology centre located on the ground floor. It offers all the usual whizz-bang earthquake simulation stuff, which is great for little kids and big kids alike. ■ *Daily 1000-1630. Donations. Special exhibitions: adult $10, child $4. T8386533.*

The VIC has a free and comprehensive 'Architrek' Heritage Trail leaflet, another outlining 'Hamilton's Walkways' and the 'Waikato Vintage Wine Trail'

While near the river it is worth taking a stroll to soak up the almost English atmosphere, with its row boats and pleasant gardens. On the eastern bank, just across from the museum, the historic paddleboat the **MV Waipa Delta** (the original of which first plied the Waikato in 1876) runs various cruises, including a lunch (1200, $30), afternoon tea (1445, $20) and dinner cruise (1800, $45, child $22.50), T0800-472335. The food is less than remarkable. Just south of the city centre and east of Cobham Bridge are the celebrated **Hamilton Gardens**. These are a conglomerate of Japanese, Chinese and English flower gardens, mixed with numerous smaller and more traditional themed displays. The gardens also host a popular café and restaurant. ■ *Open from 0730-sunset, café from 1030. Free. T8563200.*

Hamilton Zoo

Don't miss the very grumpy Kune pig in the heart of the park

Located 8 km from the city is **Hamilton Zoo.** It is both modern and progressive in its outlook, not only acting as a major attraction, but also attempting to mix a considerable collection of native New Zealand species with others important to international conservation breeding programmes. The highlight is the 3,800 sq m, walk-through, 'Free-Flight Aviary', which houses ten species of indigenous, rare and endangered New Zealand birds within a native bush setting. It is often difficult to spot the birds, the best method being simply to take your time and wait. Other attractions include the 'Waikato Wetlands' and 'Out of Africa' exhibits. ■ *Daily from 0900-1700, with extended hours in Jan. Adult $7.50, child $4. T8386720, www.hamiltoncity.co.nz/ hamiltonzoo To get to the zoo from the city centre take the SH23 Raglan Rd, turn right on to Newcastle Rd, then go straight ahead down Brymer, following the signs.*

Essentials

Sleeping

Hamilton has plenty of mid-range accommodation and you should not have much difficulty finding somewhere to stay without pre-booking

LL-L *Novotel Tainui Hotel*, 7 Alma Rd, T8381366, F8381367, book_hamilton@novotel.co.nz This is a new hotel with all the usual Novotel mod cons, centrally located and overlooking the river. The *Café Alma* (attached) offers both indoor and outdoor à la carte dining. Located halfway between the city and the airport is the **AL-A** *Glenview International Hotel*, corner of Ohaupo Rd and Resthills Cres, T8436049, F8433324, glenview.int@xtra.co.nz It is relatively new and has excellent facilities including a restaurant, three bars, spas and a pool. **AL-A** *Narrows Landing*, 431 Airport Rd, Tamahere, T8584001, is also near the airport and offers self-contained accommodation, with country views and a fine restaurant attached. Back in town the **A** *Commercial Hotel*, corner of Victoria and Collingwood St, T8394993, F8342389, healey@xtra.co.nz is a cheap, traditional hotel located right in the centre of town.

Ulster St, just north of the city centre is the main motel drag. They include: **A** *Sails Motel*, 272 Ulster St, T8382733, bookings@sails-motorinn.co.nz Fairly new with fine spas; the **A** *Ambassador Motor Inn*, 86 Ulster St, T8395111, F8395104, with a restaurant attached; and **A** *Chloe's*, 181 Ulster St, T8393410, F8393427, which also has a restaurant adjacent. The **B** *Cedar Lodge*, 174 Ulster St, T8395569, is one of the cheapest. On Abbotsford St is the quality **A** *Abbotsford Court*, T8390661, F8389335.

There are not many B&Bs in Hamilton. The VIC has full listings

B&Bs include the **A** *Sefton Park B&B*, 213b River Rd, T8559046, jshort@xtra.co.nz, located by the river in the city. 10 mins from the city is the rural and rather grand looking **A** *Anlaby Manor*, 91 Newell Rd, RD3, T8567264. It has pleasant gardens and a pool. The **C-D** *Flying Hedgehog Backpackers* has recently moved to 1157 Victoria St, T/F8392800, and is subsequently and suitably fresh. The **C-D** *J's Backpackers*, 8 Grey St, T8568934, bookme@jsbackpackers.co.nz, has comfortable dorms, twins and doubles. They also organise trips and have internet. The **C-D** *Hamilton YHA* is located near the river at 1190 Victoria St, T8380009. The **B-D** *Parklands City Motel*, 24 Bridge St, T8382461, also has basic backpacker facilities and is centrally located.

There are two fairly basic motor camps with camping facilities in East Hamilton about 3 km from town: The **C-D** *Hamilton East Motor Camp*, 61 Cameron Rd, T8566220; and the **C-D** *Municipal*, 14 Ruakura Rd, T8558255.

Eating

Hamilton boasts an amazing number of café/restaurants (mainly located along the southern end of Vicoria St), all trying to outdo each other in interior design, theme and cuisine

Expensive *Tables on the River*, 12 Alma St, T8396555, is an award winner – overlooking the river. International and traditional Kiwi fare. Open Mon-Sat from 1200. *The Bank Bar and Brasserie*, corner of Hood and Victoria, is a spacious local favourite, especially with the suits at lunchtime and trendsetters at night. Big servings. Open Sun-Thu 1100-2300, Fri-Sat 1100-0300.

Mid-range *Museum Café/Restaurant*, Grantham St, T8397209. You cannot go far wrong here, with an eclectic menu for lunch and dinner. It is open daily from 1130 and has jazz on Thu nights. *The Sahara Tent Café and Bar,* 254 Victoria St, T8340409, is a Middle Eastern style establishment which is worth seeing, never mind eating in. *Scotts Epicurean,* 181 Victoria St, T8396680, is a funky little café with a highly imaginative lunch and brunch menu, including, to its eternal credit, a fine bowl of porridge.

Cheap *Planet Burger*, 206 Victoria St, T8391444, offers fresh burgers the size of flying saucers and is open daily, 1200-late.

Bars

The traditional Irish pub, *Biddy Mulligan's*, 724 Victoria St, or the Fox and Hounds on Ward St, are amongst the favourites, with *Biddy's* hosting bands at the weekend. For the trend-setters, *The Bank* on the corner of Hood St, or the *Loaded Hog*, at No 27, are the places to be, particularly at weekends when you can rip your tights and shake your

Te Kooti

Te Kooti – or Rikirangi Te Turuki – (1830-93) could arguably be considered the William Wallace (Braveheart) of Maoridom. And although the battles were less bloody, his death far less gruesome, his resolve and integrity (or mana – to use the proper Maori term) was certainly on a par with the great Scot. Born near Gisborne, of a good family and of no particular chiefly rank, he was given a sound education at the Waerenga-a-hika Mission School before becoming a horse-breaker and later, a seaman on a small schooner trading the East Coast of the North Island. During the Maori uprising and siege of Waerenga-a-hika in 1865, Te Kooti actually supported the pakeha, but was accused of supplying the hauhau Maori rebels with ammunition and intelligence regarding the positions of Colonial Government troops.

Without trial and after being essentially 'set-up' by a local pakeha-allied Maori chief, he was exiled to the Chatham Islands with a group of hauhau rebels in 1866. Te Kooti had constantly protested his innocence, but his claims were ignored. During his two years on the Chathams Te Kooti studied the New Testament and, after claiming he had experienced a divine revelation, he established the tenets of his own 'Ringatu' faith. Convinced that the Government had no intention of releasing him, Te Kooti and a small group of other exiles captured a ship and forced the crew to take them back to the east coast of the North Island. Now a fugitive and considered dangerous, he was immediately pursued by government forces. Again, after writing to the Government and claiming his innocence, his protestations were ignored. Given little choice, Te Kooti had to fight and, gathering considerable support, he did so with a vengeance.

In a fierce battle at Matawhero against a large force commanded by one Colonel Whitmore, he and his men killed 33 Europeans and 37 allied Maori. Still outnumbered and closely pursued he retreated to the Urewera Forest. Ropata Wahawaha, who was a Maori chief allied to Whitmore, executed 120 of Te Kooti's men. For the following three years Te Kooti was relentlessly pursued and harried not only by government forces, but also European colonials and allied Maori tribes. When battles ensued Te Kooti fought with courage or always managed to cleverly elude his enemies. In 1872 he sought refuge in The Waikato where the Maori 'King Movement' had been established by fellow Maori rebels. There he spent much time peacefully, still proclaiming his original innocence as well as consolidating and spreading the word of his Ringatu religion. Te Kooti was finally pardoned in 1883 and died back on the East Coast, ten years later- a free man. To this day and in to the future his Ringatu religion lives on in the Bay of Plenty and his memory in the hearts of all Maori.

pants to modern dance music. For more traditional Kiwi pub atmosphere and for younger crowds, try the ***Outback***, ***Judder*** or ***Diggers Bars***,also on Hood St, which must get pretty messy in the small hours!

Entertainment

For information and bookings contact the VIC or Theatre Services, T8386603

The main ***Village 7 Cinema*** is located in the Centreplace Mall on Ward St. There are three **theatres** in Hamilton: ***The Founders***, 221 Tristram St, offers opera, ballet/dance and musicals; the ***Westpac Community Theatre***, 59 Clarence St, offers drama, ballet/dance, concerts, musicals and comedy; and the ***Meteor***, 1 Victoria St, is the smallest offering drama, dance, bands and comedy.

Shopping

Hamilton has two large shopping centres: the ***Hamilton Central Shopping Centre***, T8342020; and the ***Chartwell Square Shopping Centre***, corner of Hukanui and Comries Rd, Chartwell, T8548934. ***R&R Sports***, 934 Victoria St, have a wide range of outdoor equipment for sale and hire, including skis and accessories, tramping gear and boots ($10), wetsuits ($15), surfboards ($15) and kayaks ($25), T8393755. For New Zealand souvenirs try ***New Zealand World***, 24 Garden Pl. ***Crow's Nest Books***, Worley Pl, is a good second-hand bookshop.

Hamilton

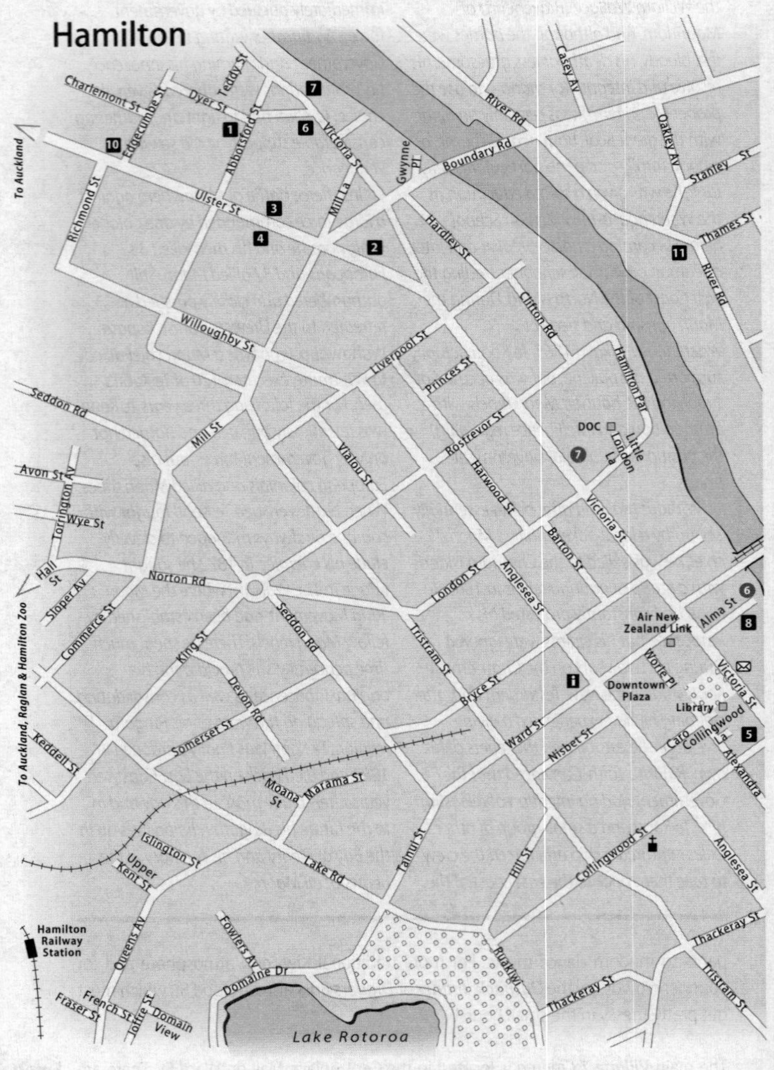

Sleeping
1 Abbotsford Court
2 Ambassador Motor Inn
3 Cedar Lodge
4 Chloe's
5 Commercial
6 Flying Hedgehog Backpackers
7 Hamilton YHA
8 Novotel Tainui
9 Parklands City Motel
10 Sails Motel
11 Sefton B & B

Eating
1 Bank Bar & Brasserie
2 Museum Café & Restaurant
3 Planet Burger
4 Sahara Tent Café & Bar
5 Scotts Epicurean
6 Tables on the River

N

0 metres 200
0 yards 200

Transport

Air Hamilton Airport is 12 km from the city centre. The Airport Shuttle is about $7, T8475618.

Bus For all regular daily *Intercity*, *Newmans* and *Mount Cook* services information contact the Hamilton Travel Centre, corner of Ward and Anglesea St, T8343457. **Local buses** operate from the Travel Centre. For information on services within Hamilton, contact *Hamilton City Buses*, T8564579.

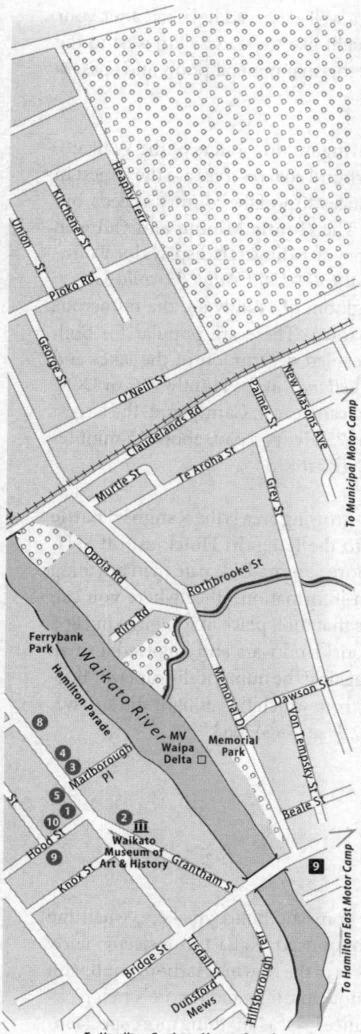

Car Rental *Rent-A-Dent* and *First Choice*, 383 Anglesea St, T0800736823, T8391049. *Waikato Car Rentals*, Brooklyn Rd, T8550094. **Bike Rental** *R&R Sports* (see shopping).

Rail Regular services run north and south to Wellington and Auckland with special commuter services to and from Auckland with *Tranzmetro*, T8564579. Auckland, single, $21. The No 8 bus runs from the city centre to the station.

Taxis *Hamilton Taxi Society*, T0800-477477.

Directory

The **AA** Centre is at 295 Barton St, T8391397. **Banks** All the main banks have branches on or around Victoria St. *Thomas Cook*, Garden Pl, T8380149. For foreign exchange. **Communications Internet** At VIC, library, Garden Pl, and *MBE Business Service Centre*, corner of Collingwood and Anglesea. **Post Office** Victoria St, opposite Garden Pl. **Medical services** *Waikato Health Ltd*, Pembroke St, T8398899.

To Hamilton Gardens, Airport, Otorohonga & Waitomo, J's Backpackers, Anlaby Manor, Glenview International & Narrows Landing

Pubs & clubs
7 Biddy Mulligan's
8 Fox & Hounds
9 Loaded Hog
10 Outback, Judder & Diggers

Waikato North

Ngaruawahia

For information regarding the Waikato North region, contact The Huntly Visitor Information Centre which is located next to the river on 160 Great South Rd, SH1, Huntly. T8288623, F8286409, wdea@xtra.co.nz

Ngaruawahia, 19 km north of Hamilton, is the Maori capital of New Zealand, housing the Maori Queen, Te Atairangikaahu (first queen and sixth person to hold office), and one of the best and most significant Maraes in the country – the **Turangawaewae marae**. This marae, which is beside the river on River Road, is only open once a year in March, during the annual regatta, when a number of *waka* (canoes) are displayed on the river. The town is located where the Waipa meets the mighty Waikato. Another point of interest in Ngaruawahia is the **Mahinarangi House**, built in 1929. It is beautifully carved both inside and out, with the royal coat of arms on the giant doors, entitled 'Te Paki o Matariki' announcing the hope of peace and calm between Maori and *Pakeha*. Next door is the Queen's official residence. As well as the rich historical interest, Ngaruawahia has a number of good walks including the **Hakarimata Walkways** and **Taupiri Mountain**, the site of the Waikato's most sacred burial ground. If you fancy a well-deserved hot soak after your walk or explorations of the town you might like to head 23 km west to the **Waingaro Hot Springs**, featuring large thermal mineral pools and spas. ■ *Open 0900-2200. $5. T8254761.*

Huntly

The SH1, both north and south of Huntly, is a notorious accident blackspot, so drive with care

With its power station and the slow-moving muddy waters of the Waikato, Huntly is not a pretty place. The underground coal reserves are the largest in New Zealand and the power station produces 20% of the country's needs, but that boast does not help the aesthetics! The **Huntly Mining and Cultural Museum**, at 26 Harlock Street, may tempt you to linger. It displays local mining history. ■ *Mon-Fri 1000-1500 and Sat 1300-1500. Adult $3, child $1.*

In direct contrast to the man-made gloom of Huntly are the numerous lakes and **wetlands** that surround the town. These are popular for both watersports and birdwatching. For a detailed description of the lakes and walks ask for the DOC leaflet '*Waikato Wetlands*' at the Huntly VIC or DOC offices in Hamilton. If you have kids and can bear it, **Candyland**, the largest candy shop in New Zealand is located at 75 Henry Road, about 15 minutes southeast of Huntly. ■ *Daily 1000-1700. T8246818.*

Te Kauwhata

The Rangiriri Hotel across the road from the centre is a congenial, old-fashioned country pub that offers a fine pub lunch

The main attraction in this mainly grape-growing area is the **Rangiriri Battle Site Heritage Centre**, which sits next to the Rangiriri Hotel just off SH1. Although the place seems to function more as a roadside café than anything else, there is some memorabilia and an information office where you can arrange to see an audiovisual. The battle that took place in Rangiriri in 1863 was one of the bloodiest during the Maori land wars and involved a small group of Maori who made a brave stand against the numerically superior British Forces. The remains of the redoubts from which they fought still survive, as does the cemetery. ■ *Open 0900-1700. Free. T8263663.*

Waikato coast

Kawhia

Population: 600

Outside the summer influx of mainly domestic holidaymakers, when the population almost triples, Kawhia (pronounced 'Kafia'), is a sleepy, fairly unremarkable, coastal village on the shores of the Kawhia Harbour southwest of Hamilton. But perhaps due to its remote location and nature's rich pickings, Kawhia seems in no hurry to announce itself as anything more spectacular, and has the contented atmosphere of a place entirely happy with its lot. And it would seem that this has always been the case. Kawhia (which actually translates to 'place of abundance') was home to the Tainui people who first arrived here some 750 years ago. So happy were they with the place and its natural provision, that it took them over 300 years before heading inland to settle other parts of the Waikato. Even then, it was only through inter-tribal disputes, which ironically were over the abundant fishing grounds.

Sights

Most of Kawhia's points of interest are on the shoreline in the town and extending around to the harbour entrance and **Ocean Beach**. This is the most popular beach with summer visitors and it is best accessed through the Tainui Kawhia Forest Track southwest of the town centre. Ocean Beach boasts the **Puia Hot Springs** (a far less commercial echo of Hot Water Beach in Coromandel). Here, too, you can dig your own 'spa bath' in the sand, but it's difficult to know where exactly you do this, especially in the off season. It is perhaps best to join a local tour to access the best spots (see below). Back in town if you want to immerse yourself in Kawhia's interesting history and learn more about the Tainui landing, the small **Kawhia Museum**, which sits next to the Wharf, will proudly oblige. The '*Best of the West*' Heritage leaflet will pinpoint and explain specific sites. The museum also acts as the **visitor information centre** and has seasonal opening times with the regular hours of 1100-1600 on weekends.

When the Tainui people first made landfall they tied their canoe to a pohutukawa tree and named it **Tangi-te-Korowhiti**. Although the specific tree is not marked, it is one of a small grove at the northern end of Kaora Street. What is marked is the site of its burial with two stones **Hani and Puna** which can be seen behind the **Maketu Marae** about 500 m south of the landing site (ask for permission at the *marae* to see them)

Activities & tours

The friendly and enthusiastic four-wheel drive 'Sand Rover' tour, which operates out of the *Kawhia Camping Ground*, will take you fishing and for a picnic at the Te Puia Hot Spings, T/F8710863, dinic@xtra.co.nz $8. *Kawhia Harbour Cruises*, T8710149, offer a number of trips around the harbour, 1000-1300; adult $15, child $8.

Sleeping & eating

The newest motor/camping ground is the **B-D** ***Kawhia Camp Ground***, at 73 Moke St, T/F8710863, dinic@xtra.co.nz Internet access. The **B-D** Kawhia Beachside S-Cape, T8710727, located as you come into town, offers the usual range of motor camp accommodation with a backpacker caravan. The historic **B** ***Rosamond House B&B*** is one of the few B&Bs. Built in 1901 it was a former residence, boarding house and doctor's surgery, now tastefully renovated. There is one basic motel, the **B** ***Kawhia Motel***, located centrally on the corner of Jervois and Tainui Sts, T8710865.

Around the corner on Jervois St is the ***Wee Knot Inn***, a congenial little pub which also does backpacker accommodation. Next door is ***Annie's Café*** which offers traditional fare and is open from 1000-1600, 1800-late. The ***Kawhia Hotel*** also serves basic meals, but perhaps the best bet is the fish and chips from Kawhia Fisheries on the wharf.

Transport

The drive to Kawhia from anywhere is quite arduous but scenic. If you are peckish be sure to stop for a home-made pie at the Oparau petrol station. If you do not have your own wheels try ***Kawhia Bus and Freight*** who run a service to and from Te Awamutu, T8710701.

Raglan

Phone code: 07
Population: 3100

Raglan is the Waikato's main seaside resort, and internationally renowned for its fine surfing. So, when you arrive in the heart of the village, with its palm trees and laid-back cafes, don't be surprised if you end up being sandwiched in a queue or sharing your lunch table with a colourful length of fibreglass with 'Ride' em Baby', 'The Big Phallus' or 'No Fear' written on it. In Raglan these strange, almost religious objects seem to make up half the population. The village itself is located on the quiet Raglan Harbour with all the 'surf action' on beaches a short drive away heading west. One of those beaches – Manu Bay – has apparently one of the best 'left hand breaks' in the world.

Ins & outs

Getting there *Pavlovich Coachlines* run regular weekday services to Hamilton, departing from the VIC, T8564579.

The small but highly efficient **Visitor Information Centre** is on Bow St, T8250556, F8250557. Open daily from 1000-1600.

Sights

The main attractions around Raglan are its beaches

The most convenient and safest swimming beach is **Te Kopua**, which borders the Raglan campground. Access is via the camp access road west, or across the footbridge at the end of Bow Street in the centre of the village. All the main surf beaches are located west of town. **Ocean Beach** is the first and as well as surfing, it is also popular for swimming and the view across the 'Raglan Bar' (harbour entrance). Access is off Wainui Reserve Road via a walking track. Surf lifesavers operate in summer, and as always, you must swim between the flags. The infamous 'left-hand break' **Manu Bay** is next and the best spot to surf or spectate. Further still is **Whale Bay** which is a great spot for both surfers and the uninitiated alike, but it can only be accessed over rocks.

For wild coastal scenery **Ruapuke Beach** is popular, but remote. Follow the old coast road (taking in the scenery and impressive **Te Toto Gorge** on the way), then follow Ruapuke Beach Road and walk from there. Other beaches near town that are safe and child-friendly are **Cox's Bay** (accessible from Bayview Road and Daisy Street or the walkway along Government Road) and **Puriri Park** (Aro Aro Bay) at the end of Wallis Street.

If you are interested in local history the small **Raglan and District Museum** has mainly European material and is located on Wainui Road. It has a voluntary staff so hours vary (see the VIC). Further afield on SH23 are the aptly named 55 m **Bridal Veil Falls**, which are a bit of a trek but worth it, particularly after heavy rain. If the 756 m summit of **Mt Karioi** beckons it is best accessed from Te Toto Gorge, 12 km southwest (see above). There are fine views from the top; allow six hours. It is known by the Maori as 'the sleeping lady', the reason for which is obvious if you study its outline.

Activities & tours

There are several of the obligatory **fishing and harbour cruise** charters including *Cloud Nine*, T8258303, *Crystal Blue Ocean Safaris*, T8298870, and *Raglan Harbour Cruises*, T8250300, $15. The latter will take you on a trip to see the unusual Pancake Rock formations (no description necessary there). *Jet Safari Tours* offer the fast-adrenaline option to see Okete Falls and Sugar Loaf Island (one hour), T025-6267585.

The local **horse trekking** company, *Horse Trekking Te Mata*, is located a 30-minute drive south of Raglan. They offer treks that take in great scenery, including the Bridal Veil Falls, so make a day of it. They also offer Farmstay accommodation, T8256892. You can also go **Paragliding** near Raglan on summer weekends, T025-730799 or jump out of a plane with a chap attached to your back (plus parachute) with *Skydive Raglan*, T025-2804288. If you want to try your hand at **surfing** contact the *Raglan Surfing School*, T8256555.

Sleeping

The **A** *Luxury Retreat*, 6 Upper Wainui Rd, T/F8258684, is one of the better B&Bs in the area, as is **B** *Raglan by the Sea B&B*, 191 Hills Rd, and the **B** *Rangimaarie Seaside Retreat*, 78G Moonlight Bay, Greenslade Rd, T8257567, Rangimaarieretreat@xtra.co.nz The latter has a self-contained option and also specialises in natural therapies and scrumptious organic cooking. The **B** *Harbour View Hotel*, 14 Bow St, T8258010, is a traditional Kiwi hotel, worth mentioning because it is nicely renovated, cheap, clean, centrally located and has a good restaurant attached. The **B** ***Raglan Palm Beach Motel***, 50 Wainui Rd, T8258153, is popular and is located towards the main beaches. The **B-D** ***Raglan Kopua Holiday Park***, T8258283, is almost on an island of it's own, with a beach and linked to the village by a short bridge.

If you are looking for something completely different there really is only one place to stay in Raglan and that is the amazing **B** ***Railway Wagon Cabins***, 7 km west of the village centre at 611 Wainui Rd, T8258268. Here the owners have gone to great pains to relocate and renovate an array of railway wagons as colourful accommodation units from dorm to self-contained. There is also a veritable menagerie of animals on-site including a couple of ex-wild kaimanawa horses, saved from the government bullet in central North Island a few years ago. It's good value and highly recommended. The main backpacker accommodation is at **C-D** ***Raglan Backpackers***, 6 Nero St, T8250515. This is quite a small hostel but purpose-built and well situated. Popular of course with the surfing set. Kayak and bike hire.

Eating

The two most popular eateries are the ***Tongue and Grove Café***, 9 Bow St, T8250027, (open Mon-Sun 0900-late), and ***Vinnies***, 7 Wainui Rd, T8257273, (Open Tue-Sun 1100-2000, weekends from 0800). Both serve traditional cuisine at affordable prices with the latter having the seafood edge. The Harbour View Hotel's ***Verandabah*** restaurant, T8258010, and the ***Molasses Café***, T8257229, both on Bow St, are also popular light meal and lunch spots. The ***Raglan Fresh Fish and Takeaways***, 33 Bow St, has good fish and chips, but it would seem the service is rotten unless you are a local or are attached to a surfboard.

Directory

Communications Internet: at the ***Tongue and Groove Café***, the library and the video shop, which are all on Bow St.

Waikato South

Te Awamutu

Phone code: 07
Population: 9500

Te Awamutu is in the heart of Waikato dairy farming country and the Waipa District, which also takes in Cambridge to the east. It is most famous for its **Rose Gardens**, which are on Gorst Avenue (across the road from the VIC). The gardens contain hundreds of varieties which are nurtured to be at their smelly best for the *Rose and Cultural Festival* held during the first week in November.

Ins & outs

Getting there *Hodgson Motors*, Ohaupo Rd, offer a regular service to and from Hamilton for $4.50 one way, T8716373. Te Awamutu is also on the main North/South trunk line.

The rose-covered **Visitor Information Centre** is at 1 Gorst Av, T8713259, F8712888. Open Mon-Fri 0900-1630, Sat-Sun 1000-1500.

Sights

Te Awamutu has an interesting history, and you can pick up a detailed Heritage Trail handout at the VIC

The **Te Awamutu District Museum**, on Roche Street, takes a bizarre leap of time, culture and theme, with some fine examples of local Maori *taonga* (treasures) mixed with a celebration of the towns two best-loved sons – Neil and Tim Finn, of the rock bands Split Enz and Crowded House. Somehow, it seems a bit like running a video of Freddie Mercury, strutting his stuff next to the original Crown Jewels in the Tower of London, but such is the dilemma faced by the New Zealand small town museum. ■ *Mon-Fri 1000-1600, Sat-Sun 1000-1300. Free. T8714326.*

The Waikato

You can hang around – literally – at the **Wharepapa Rockfields**, about 20 km south east of the town. The crags include the 'Froggatt Edge', which is considered the best sport-climbing crag in the North Island, with over 115 climbs. The VIC will give you information and directions to the fields, as will the *Wharepapa Outdoor Centre* and the aptly named *Boulderfield Café*.

There are numerous walks around Te Awamutu, and the town also acts as the gateway to the **Pirongia Forest Park**. Dominated by the 959 m Mount Pirongia, the park offers some fine long and short walks, including the seven-hour summit track, which rewards you with great views. Again the VIC will provide directions and information (which is best described in the DOPC leaflet 'Pirongia Forest Park'). On four legs you could try *Pirongia Horse Treks*, one hour, $25, T8719960, or pay a visit to the home of the **DB Clydesdale Team**, a team of Clydesdale horses sponsored by New Zealand's largest brewing company. The well-groomed horse and carriage appear regularly on TV along with their fictional owners, who are an annoyingly good-looking couple who call everybody 'mate' and seem to do nothing but mend fences and drink beer. ■ *Open daily. T8719711.*

Sleeping There are over 500 B&B and **Farmstay** beds in the area, and The Te Awamutu Farmstay is a great place to experience New Zealand rural life. The VIC has listings of these and local motels. The **B-D** ***Road Runner Motel and Holiday Park*** is at 141 Bond Rd, Te Awamutu, T8717420, F8716664. For eating, the ***Ngaroto Nurseries Café***, 208 Ngaroto Rd (5 km north of the town), T8715695, is recommended. Open 7 days 0930-1630.

Directory **Communications Internet**: at the library on Roche St.

The Waikato

Otorohanga The small agricultural service town of 'Oto', as it is better known, is so close to Waitomo with its famous caves that it struggles to attract anything other than the passing tourist. However, it does fancy itself as the gateway to the caves and boasts one of the best kiwi house and displays of native New Zealand birds in the country.

Getting there *Intercity* buses run a regular service North and South from outside the TIC. Otorohanga is on the main Auckland to Wellington trunk line and the train station is located a short distance behind the VIC. To get to the Waitomo Caves see page 226.

The **Visitor Information Centre** is on the main SH3 drag at 87 Maniapoto St, T8738951, F8738398. Open Mon-Thu 0830-1730, Fri-Sun 1000-1600. Internet here and at the Library.

Established in 1971, The **Otorohanga Kiwi House and Native Bird Park**, on Alex Telfer Drive, is one of the oldest native bird and reptile parks in the country, housing over 50 species, including three of the four known species of kiwi. It provides the familiar delicate and uneasy balance of visitor attraction with vital conservation activity, attracting thousands of visitors a year and yet, behind the scenes, successfully breeding a number of inmates, including over 65 kiwi since 1975. The park's main attraction is the unique double nocturnal house where you are almost certain to see a kiwi going about its fascinating and comical hunt for food. They do this with their long sensitive beaks, locating grubs with the nostrils which are located at the tip. Once you have reaccustomed your eyes to daylight you can go on to see a number of raptors, waterfowl and reptiles, including the prehistoric tuatara and cheeky native parrot, the kea. The walk culminates with a large walk-in aviary where other rare birds can be spotted. Throughout the park there are also some fine examples of native trees. ■ *Daily 0900-1700. Adult $8, child $3.*

If you happen to be in Oto in February you may catch the *Otorohanga Country Fair*, when the streets are decked with flower baskets and the gumboot- clad locals have fun parading down the street on floats. If you want to see some action at the livestock sale-yards then Wednesday is the day to go. Beware – as you sip your coffee or stroll about town, you may be befriended, and highly embarrassed, by the town's summer mascot 'Wiki' – an underpaid and sweaty person in a kiwi suit.

Sleeping The accommodation in Otorohanga is limited and the VIC can assist, but the **B** ***Otorohanga and Waitomo Colonial Motels*** (T/F8738289) on the main road, towards the north of town, are fairly modern, clean and comfortable. The **C-D** ***Oto-Kiwi Backpackers,*** 1 Sangro Cres, T8736022, oto-kiwi@xtra.co.nz, has a good reputation with adequate facilities. They also organise trips, including to the caves and back. The **D** ***Otorohanga Holiday Park*** is basic and tiny, but located right next to the Kiwi Park. At night you can hear the kiwi screeching away, which is not (strangely) that unpleasant. The park's owner is very helpful and friendly and also runs the shuttle to the caves.

Eating The options are limited. The most modern and popular venue is the ***Regent Café and Bar***, on Maniapoto St, next to the library. Open 7 days, Mon-Sun 0630-1700, Fri/Sat-2100.

Te Kuiti
Phone Code: 07
Population 4500

Te Kuiti is fairly unremarkable but is often used as a base for the Waitomo Caves, 19 km to the north. It is a small provincial town known as the sheep-shearing capital of New Zealand (witness the rather grotesque statue at the southern end of town). For a number of years it was home and refuge to the rebellious East Coast Maori chief Te Kooti who built the highly aesthetic **Te Tokanganui-o-noho Marae** at the south end of Rora Street. Also worth a stop is the new and magnificent Te **Kuititanga-o-nga-Whakaaro Millennium Pavilion** which is located next to the railway, near the VIC on Rora Street. Its carvings, stained and sandblasted window designs are a great work of art. The big event of the year is the annual *Te Kuiti Muster* in April when the town celebrates its reputation with sheep-shearing championships, the 'bloated sheep race' and street celebrations and entertainment. There are some fine gardens in the area, outlined in the free '*King Country Gardens*' leaflet available from the **Visitor Information Office**, on Rora Street in the centre of town, T8788077, F8785280. It can assist with bus information, tickets and other accommodation options in the area. **DOC** is located at 78 Taupiri Street, T8787297.

Sleeping, eating and transport The basic **C-D** ***Te Kuiti Camp Ground*** is located on Hinerangi St, T8788966, while the comfortable **C-D** ***Casara Mesa Backpackers,*** T8786697, is on Mangarino Rd. Breakfasts, transport and bike hire available. There are numerous rather forgettable cafés and eateries on Rora Rd, with ***Tiffany's*** standing out from the rest. ***Tiffany's*** is also where the Intercity buses arrive and depart. ***Perry's*** is the local bus company serving Waitomo to the coast, T8767596. The train station in Te Kuiti is on the main Auckland to Wellington trunk line.

Waitomo and the Caves

The district of Waitomo ('wai' meaning 'water' and 'tomo' hole), with its underground wonderworld of limestone caves, is the region's (and one of North Island's) biggest tourist attractions. Above ground, the typical farmland and the tourist village itself almost completely belie what lies below.

The Formation of Limestone Caves (Karst)

Limestone is a fossil rock made from the layered remains of countless marine animals. The limestone around Waitomo was therefore formerly the seabed, formed about 30 million years ago. Over the millennia these layers have been raised by the action of the earth's plates. In some places the limestone is over 200 m thick. Through its gradual uprising the limestone bends and buckles creating a network of cracks and joints. As rainwater drains in to these cracks it mixes with small amounts of carbon dioxide in the air and soil forming a weak acid. This acid slowly dissolves the limestone and the cracks and joints widen. Over time small streams flow through converging cracks and eventually forming underground caves.

Once these caves are created the same acidic water seeps from the cave walls or drips from the roof, leaving a minute deposit of limestone crystal. Slowly these deposits form stalactites, stalagmites and various other cave features. The size and rate of their formation depends on the rate of flow. Stalactites form from the drips falling from the ceiling of the cave and stalagmites grow up as the drips fall to the floor. When the two join, pillars are formed and when they spiral around they are called helictites.

Various minerals in the soil like iron oxide can add colouration to the formations. The growth rates of caves and limestone features in general vary considerably depending on topography, vegetation, and of course the weather. It is also important to realise that like everything else the caves have a 'lifespan' eventually collapsing to form gorges, holes or arches. The 'Lost World' near Waitomo is a fine example of part of a cave system that collapsed in on itself. These caves are also home to a unique range of plants and animals of which the New Zealand glow-worm is the most spectacular example.

The Waikato

Although only the geologically trained eye would suspect it, there is an astonishing network of over 360 recorded caves in the area, the longest being over 14 km. If you come here and have time, and a towel, you should pack a promise to yourself that you will try at least one of the amazing underground activities below and beyond the highly commercialised tour of the **Glow-worm Caves**. Wherever you go down there (somewhere), it is pretty unforgettable.

Ins & outs **Getting there** By car, note there is no fuel available in Waitomo Village. By bus, locally, the ***Waitomo Shuttle*** operates a regular service from 0900-1730, between Otorohanga's bus depot, railway station, motels, backpackers, caravan parks and Waitomo. T8738279, $7 one way. The ***Waitomo Wanderer*** runs a daily service from Rotorua and Taupo. It departs Rotorua at 0730 and arrives in Waitomo at 0930, departing Waitomo again at 1600. T8737559, F8737509, From $25. ***Intercity, Newmans*** and ***Great Sights*** offer highly commercial day-trips to the Glow-worm Caves from Auckland and Rotorua, but unless you are really stretched for time (or intend to stay overnight and return the following day) these are best avoided, $136.

The best idea is to get to Otorohanga on a standard ***Intercity*** bus and get to Waitomo independently from there. ***Magic Traveller Buses*** and ***Kiwi Experience*** also allow more flexibility than the day trip option. There is also the train, but the trip from Auckland to Otorohanga alone is pretty dull.

Information and orientation The Waitomo Museum of Caves **Visitor Information Centre** is located at the heart of operations in the small tourist village of Waitomo, T8787640, F8786184, waitomuseum@xtra.co.nz Open daily 0830-1730, 2000 Jan/Feb. Almost all the above-ground attractions, below,-ground activity operators, booking offices and tourist amenities are within walking distance. Although compact it can be confusing, so the best bet (if you have not already researched from other VIC's, leaflets and the web) is to absorb the information here first and take your time. There are numerous and often, very similar activities on offer. Then, let the staff book on your behalf, or go to the relevant tour operator for more information. There is a shop attached to the ***Waitomo Adventure*** booking office, and *Cavelands Café* next door to the VIC, which also sells limited supplies, stamps and has internet access.

Sights below ground

The **Glow-worm Cave** is Waitomo's biggest attraction, but it is also the most commercial. From 0900-1700, lines of buses park outside and group after group are herded underground. The caves were first extensively explored in 1887 by a local Maori, Tane Tinorau, and English surveyor, Fred Mace. Further explorations eventually led to the opening of the caves to tourists in 1889. They now attract almost 250,000 visitors annually. Although the caves remain impressive, you cannot help feeling that you're on some Steven Spielberg film set, about to sit on Santa's knee and ask him for an extension to your MasterCard. Having said that, the highlight of the 45-minute tour – the silent, almost religious homage to see the glow-worm galaxy by boat – is incredible and well worth it, especially if you have never seen these amazing insect larvae before. The cave also has the obligatory shop and café attached. ■ *Tours begin every half-hour from 0900. Arrive early. Adult $20, child $10. Cave combo ticket (Glow-worm and Aranui) adult $30, child $15. Glow-worm Cave and Museum Combo, adult $22, child $10. T8788227, F8788858, www.waitomocaves.co.nz*

The **Aranui Cave** by contrast is a far more realistic and sedate experience, located a short 3 km drive west of the Glow-worm Cave near the Ruakuri Scenic Reserve. Their discovery, by Maori hunter Ruruku Aranui, occurred by accident in 1910.While out pig hunting, Rukuru's quarry disappeared into the small entrance, followed enthusiastically by his dog. After a year of further explorations and amidst much excitement, the caves were opened to tourists in 1911. Whilst underground, with effective lighting, the colour and variety of the stalactites and stalagmites, and the sound of a thousand drips of water, you can let your imagination run wild and emerge from the cave satisfied that you have experienced a real limestone cave. ■ *Tours are hourly from 1000-1500 and limited to groups of 20. Book at the Glow-worm Caves. Adult $20, child $10. Cave Combo Ticket (Aranui and Glow-worm) adult $30, child $15.*

Activities below ground

There is a wide range of choice and competition between operators is fierce; research the options carefully and take your time

As usual it all comes down to bucks, but generally speaking with whatever activity or operator you choose, it will be money well spent. A combination of trips that offers value for money, a high level of safety and professionalism, as well as the best mix of activity is the 'Lost World Epic' (if you can afford it) followed by the 'Hagas Honking Holes' run by *Waitomo Adventures*. Both are highly recommended. The activities last from 2-7 hours, are all great fun and usually involve a combination of abseiling, crawling, swimming and floating (note that the water is cold). A brief description of the main tours is listed here followed by a list of the relevant operators. Note that there are also price reductions for trip combinations with some also offering free museum entry.

Tumu Tumu Toobing (*Waitomo Adventures*) This trip, along with the Hagas Honking Holes, is ideal if you are limited for time. The least strenuous of *Waitomo Adventures*' tours, it involves a highly entertaining walk, swim and float down an underwater stream with glow-worms and interesting rock formations. ■ *Daily 1100 and 1530. $65. 4 hrs, about 2 hrs underground.*

Hagas Honking Holes (*Waitomo Adventures*) Slightly more full on, this trip involves an abseil, rock climbing and an intimate encounter with a waterfall, as well as all the usual crawling and scenery. Great fun. ■ *Daily 1115 and 1615. $125. 4 hrs, about 2 hrs underground.*

Lost World (*Waitomo Adventures*) This is a unique and famous trip in a unique setting. It involves an incredible and mind-bending 100 m (300 ft) abseil in to a huge and forbidding hole in the earth. Once negotiated you follow the river for a short distance into a huge cave system and the aptly named, 'Lost World'. The atmosphere of the place is unforgettable. No abseiling experience necessary, and perfectly safe. ■ *Daily 0700 and 1130, $195. 4 hrs.*

Lost World Epic (*Waitomo Adventures*) If you can afford it and are fit enough this has to be one of the best and most unusual full-day activity trips in the country, if not the world. It involves the same exciting descent into the gaping hole but is followed by the exhilarating and highly entertaining three-hour negotiation of the cave system and underground river. It involves walking, climbing, swimming, wading, jumping and even racing, with the final stage a quiet reflection of the trip under a galaxy of glow-worms, before emerging, like some intrepid latter-day explorer, at the river entrance. If you can splash out, it is a once-in-a-lifetime experience and worth every cent. ■ *Daily 1130 (min. 2 people), dinner included. $300. 7 hrs, 5 hrs underground.*

Black Water Rafting I (*Black Water Rafting*) This trip involves floating down a subterranean river negotiating a waterfall on the way and taking in the cave formations and glow-worms. ■ *Departs every 45 minutes from 0900-1630. 3 hours, 1 hr underground. $65; includes museum entry, showers, soup and bagels.*

Black Water Rafting II (*Black Water Rafting*) This trip is more adventurous and strenuous than the above, also involving a 30 m abseil. ■ *Departs 0930, 1100, 1430. 5 hrs, 3 hrs underground. $125 (also includes museum, showers, soup and bagels).*

Waitomo Down Under This Maori-run operator offers three cave-tubing adventures similar to the above, with one trip involving a 50 m (150 ft) abseil in to the impressive 'Baby Grand' cave. ■ *Several trips daily, 2-3 hrs, 1 hr underground. $50-$65 (includes free museum entry). Showers available.*

Long Tomo Rafting (*Waitomo Wilderness Tours*) This fairly new adventure involves a 27 m (80 ft) abseil into a cave, then a float through a river system with a great display of glow-worms. ■ *Daily. 5 hrs, about 2 hrs underground. $65 (includes free museum entry).*

Black Water Dry (*Black Water Rafting*) This mainly eco-based adventure is the trip for those who want to remain dry, and involves an informative guided trip into a cave system. ■ *Daily on demand. 2-3 hrs, about 2 hrs underground. Adult $30, child $15 (includes free museum entry).*

Pink Gumboot Cave This is a family-based adventure out at Woodlyn Park with Barry Woods. It takes in an informative bush and cave-walk incorporating a treasure hunt. ■ *1¾ hrs. Adult $13, child $10. T8786666.*

Shady Acres Cave Reserve This is an excellent eco-based trip that's uncommercial, relaxed and friendly. The tour takes place in a part of the longest cave in the area. The local animal-mad couple that run it rightly concentrate on the delicate fragility of the caves, our impact on them and their conservation. See amazing cave *wetas* (huge insects) and plant a native tree. ■ *2-5 hrs. From $60. Contact Paul or Karan, T8785255.*

Tour operators *Waitomo Adventures Ltd* (office located next to the VIC), T0800-924866, T8787788, F8786266, www.waitomo.co.nz *Black Water Rafting* (office

2 km east of Waitomo Information Centre), T0800228464, T8786219, F8785190, www.blackwaterrafting.co.nz *Waitomo Down Under* (office next to the Information Centre), T8786577, F8786565. *Waitomo Wilderness Tours*, T0800-228372 Simon_Hall@xtra.co.nz

Sights & activities above ground

This museum is now considered the best limestone cave museum in the world

A fine initiation and insight into the area can be found at the **Museum of Caves** which is located in the visitor centre. It offers interesting and highly informative displays about cave formation, the history surrounding the local caves and the natural history, including the spectacular and intriguing glow-worms. If you are claustrophobic and shudder at the very thought of going underground then there is also a fake cave to crawl through. ■ *Daily 0830-1700, 1730 in summer. Adult $4, child free (free entry with some activities). T8787640.*

The **Waitomo Walkway** (three hours return), begins opposite the Glow-worm caves and follows the Waitomo Stream, taking in a number of limestone features before arriving at the **Ruakuri Scenic Reserve**. This reserve encompasses a short walk that is hailed as one of New Zealand's best. Although it does not deserve quite that billing, it is well worth it, with a circular track taking in interesting caves and natural limestone bridges, hidden amongst lush, native bush. At night, just before the path crosses the stream, you can see a small 'scintilla' of glow-worms. These are the only glow-worms you'll see around here for free! Take a torch.

Another popular walk is the **Opapaka Pa Walk** which takes about 45 minutes return and is located 1 km east of Waitomo. The view is memorable and there are also some interesting interpretation points explaining about the *pa* and the medicinal uses Maori made of surrounding flora.

Woodlyn Park is the above-ground entertainment 'must see' in Waitomo, if not the region. Like the Driving Creek railway in the Coromandel it is a typical example of Kiwi imagination, ingenuity and that simple 'can-do' mentality. The 'show', hosted by ex-shearer Barry Woods, is an informative, interactive (and at times comical) interpretation of old and modern day Kiwi country life, and is very hard to describe. It involves a clever pig, a not so clever pig, an axe, a homemade ingenious computer, dogs, sheep, a 'kiwi bear' and a pair of underpants. Enough said – you'll just have to go and see it! As the visitor book says – 'look out Bill Gates'. ■ *Shows are staged on demand, book first. Adult $12, child $6. T/F 8786666, woodlyn_park@xtra.co.nz. Also on the grounds Barry has built a large tyre-lined pond on which you can blat about in a jet boat for $35.*

About ½ km north down Waitomo Valley Road from Woodlyn Park, in Waitomo Village, is the **Shearing Shed**, where cute Angora bunnies are cuddled to within an inch of their little lives and then given a short back and sides so that their highly-prized fur can be used for knitting. ■ *Show held daily at 1245. Free. Shop open daily 0900-1630. T/F8788371.*

Still on the animal theme the **Altura Garden and Wildlife Park**, located 4 km south of Waitomo village, provides a diversion if you have kids or wish to stay above ground. A range of animals are on display, with all the regulars, including emus and horses. ■ *Open daily summer 1000-1600. Adult $6, child $3.*

Waitomo Horse Treks is based at Juno Hall Backpackers, about 1 km east of Waitomo Village. Local character 'Juno' (and staff) will take you on half-day, full-day or overnight trips through the surrounding countryside. These trips are fun and come recommended due to the views and varied limestone scenery. From $30. (Overnight $200), T8787649. The **Waitomo Big**

Red 4x4 is the local quad bike adventure company offering trips to suit all ages and experience; $65 for two hours, T8787640.

Sleeping

There is a wide range of accommodation in Waitomo Village, but in summer pre-booking is essential

AL-D *Waitomo Caves Hotel and Hostel*, T8788240, F8788205. Situated on the hill overlooking the village this historic hotel offers a wide range of comfortable rooms and has a restaurant attached. There is also a recently renovated YHA and Backpackers on site. **A** *Abseil Inn B&B*, T8787815, aseilinn@xtra.co.nz The new and aptly named Abseil Inn is located up an 'exciting' driveway within walking (or climbing) distance of all amenities. The very friendly hosts are both cave guides, so full of good tips. Recommended. **A** *Waitomo Guest Lodge*, T878641. A slightly older, but well situated and comfortable B&B for more mature clients. **B** *Waitomo Express*, T8786666. If it is the unusual you are looking for, look no further than Barry Woods at Woodlyn Park (1 km down Waitomo Valley Rd) and his converted train carriage accommodation. The **A-B** *Glow-worm Motel* (T8738882) and *Caves Motel* (T8738109) are located 8 km east of Waitomo Village at the junction with SH3. Both are fine, and the latter has a good restaurant. **A-D** *Waitomo Caves Holiday Park*, T/F8787639, stay@waitomopark.co.nz A modern, convenient and very friendly motor camp located right in the heart of the village. **B-D** *Juno Hall Backpackers*, T8787649. This is a great log-cabin style hostel with a pool and log fire. Courtesy van. Home of *Waitomo Horse Treks*.

Eating

For à la carte the *Waitomo Caves Hotel* offers fairly good traditional cuisine, but the best-value evening meal is currently reputed to be available at the *Caves Motel*, 8 km east of Waitomo Village (see above). For lunch the best venue is *Roselands Restaurant* which is located 3 km from Waitomo Village up Fullerton Rd, T8787611. They specialise in hearty BBQ lunches and salads in a lovely garden setting. Open for lunch only, daily summer 1100-1430. There are three cafés in Waitomo run by the operators: the *Waitomo Adventures' Cavelands*; *Black Water Rafting's Black Water* and the *Glow-worm Caves Café*. All are open daily from 0800-1730 (later in summer). The *Black Water Café* does a fine breakfast for $12. For cheap and basic pub grub and a pint with the locals head for the *Waitomo Tavern*, near the Information Centre, T8788448.

Waitomo to Kawhia

The **Marokopa Road** that winds its way to Te Anga and the small coastal town of Marokopa, before heading north to Kawhia, is a long but pleasant trip with a number of worthwhile stops on the way. If you have your own wheels the first stop should be the slight diversion to see the impressive view looking back towards Waitomo from 3 km down Waipuna Road. The road is on the left, 11 km from Waitomo. Once back on the main road sit back and enjoy the scenery until you reach the **Mangapohue Natural Bridge Scenic Reserve**. Here a short streamside walk (10 minutes) will take you to an impressive natural limestone arch, complete with unusual stalagmites. This arch was once part of a large cave and it is hard to imagine that the rather inconspicuous little stream essentially created it all. About 5 km further on are the **Piripiri Caves**, accessed by a short but stiff climb up a boardwalk. These caves are in stark contrast to the well-lit, tourist-friendly offerings in Waitomo. They are dark and forbidding, and the path in to them is steep and quite dangerous. If you are alone do not venture far and be sure to take a torch.

A little further on and about 35 km from Waitomo are the beautiful 32 m **Marokopa Falls** which have to rate as amongst the best in North Island, though due to their remote location they are not celebrated as such. A 15-minute walks descends to a lookout. If you go beyond the lookout to take photographs prepare to get very muddy. From the falls it is a short distance to the small settlement of **Te Anga** where there is a tavern selling lunches and the basic *Bike'n Hike Backpackers*, T8767362.

From Te Anga you have a choice of a very scenic road heading north to **Kawhia** or carrying on to the coast and **Marakopa**, a small, remote fishing village with black-sand beaches. From Marakopa it is possible to drive all the way to **Awakino**, another small coastal settlement, on the main SH3 New Plymouth road, but it is long, unsealed and fairly arduous. If you do not have your own wheels, *Perry's Buses* of Te Kuiti do a weekday coastal run from Taharoa to Te Kuiti and back, T8767595, $12. There is a basic **camping ground** with powered sites in Marokopa, T8767400.

Waikato East

Paeroa

Poor Paeroa. It's neither here nor there – and that seems to be its problem. People are always rushing through on their way to the Coromandel or the Bay of Plenty and rarely stop. And if they do, it is only very briefly, to get their photograph taken beside a huge plastic bottle of 'Lemon and Paeroa' (L&P), which is New Zealand's only national soft drink. Although not made in Paeroa, the additive spring water was discovered here in 1900 and made the place famous. This old, once thriving port, has little to offer, but don't write the place off entirely. The **Paeroa Museum**, on Belmont Road (Open Monday-Friday 1030-1500), does its best with displays about local history, bone china collections and some Maori artefacts. For view junkies, **Primrose Hill**, near the town centre, offers great views back across the Hauraki Plains – which, alas, for poor Paeroa, are flat and boring!

If you are in Paeroa on the third Sunday in February you will find the place pumping with the motorcycle extravaganza 'Battle of the Streets'. This increasingly popular annual event attracts bikers from far and wide, but if the notorious gangs turn up, the event could end up being very aptly named. Lucky this does not coincide with the other major event in the same month – the Pipe Band Tattoo – otherwise it would be like Mad Max meets Braveheart. The very friendly VIC is on Belmont Road, T/F8628636. Open Monday-Friday 0900-1700, Saturday-Sunday 1000-1500.

Te Aroha

Phone code 07
Population 4000

In 1875 Te Aroha was little more than a single house in the shadow of the mountain occupied by Irish pioneer Charlie Lipsey, and subsequently known as 'Lipseytown'. With the discovery of gold nearby in 1880 the settlement expanded, but only temporarily, as the mining returns proved relatively poor. Later, with the discovery of the hot soda water geyser, the Hot Springs Domain were born and today this remains the jewel in the crown of this mainly agricultural service town. The name of the town and the mountain means 'The Love' and comes from the story of a Bay of Plenty Maori chief who once made those utterings in relief after getting lost and seeing the glorious views south, homewards to his *pa*.

Ins & outs

Getting there *Turley-Murphy Connections* are the main local bus operator with services to and from Hamilton and Thames most days, T8848208, or T8848052 (VIC).

The Te Aroha **Information Centre** is located in the original Te Aroha Hot Springs Domain ticket office at 102 Whitaker St, T8848052, infotearoha@xtra.co.nz Mon-Fri 0900-1700, Sat/Sun 1000-1400.

Sights There are two major attractions in Te Aroha, **Mount Te Aroha** and the **Hot Springs Domain**. As far as activity goes the two could hardly be more opposite, but the 5-6 hour return climb up the 950 m summit can be duly rewarded afterwards with a dip in the pools, providing the perfect marriage of the two. The mountain path is accessed at the rear of the Domain. The Whakapipi or Bald Spur Lookout about halfway up is easily reached after about 45 minutes and offers a fine view west. But, if you can, carry on to the summit and take in the spectacular 360° view, north across the Coromandel and south to the Bay of Plenty. For track information see 'The Te Aroha Mountain Tracks' leaflet available from the VIC.

On your return you can fall straight in to the **Te Aroha Mineral Pools** near the track entrance. The pools, which were originally created in the late 1800's, are the world's only naturally flowing hot soda spa pools. ■ *Open daily 1000-2100/2200. $7 for private pool, ½ hr. T8848717.*

The **Wynborn Leisure Pools** are located just a short distance further on. They offer both hot and cold outdoor pools and more modern renovated bathhouses. ■ *Open daily 1100-1900. Adult $4, child $2. T8844498.* Next door you can complete your pampering with an hour-long massage and aromatherapy ($35). Behind the pools is the **Mokena Geyser**, which is one of very few soda water geysers in the world. Named after the Maori chief and benefactor of the land on which the Domain now stands, the geyser does its 3-m high thing about every half-hour.

Also on the Domain is the **Te Aroha Museum**. Housed in the original bathhouse (which was once said to be possibly the most attractive building in the country and 'the sanatorium of New Zealand'), it now contains some interesting displays on the mining and agricultural development of the town. Oh, and two rather pretty toilets! ■ *Open weekends 1300-1600, additional hours mid-summer. Donation. T8844427.* Also of considerable historical interest, but not housed in the museum, is the 1712 Queen Anne Pipe Organ in **St Mark's Church** (T8848052). The town has a fairly unremarkable arts and crafts trail, and a gardens and heritage trail; ask for leaflets at the VIC. For a pleasant easy grade short walk there is the wildlife rich Howarth Memorial Wetlands Walk, located on the banks of the Waihou River. Ask at the VIC for directions and leaflet.

Sleeping B&Bs include the **AL** *Little Brook Cottage*, 63 Gilchrist St, T8849798, the **A-B** *Lavender Hills*, 19 Hamilton St, T8847726, and the intriguing **B** *Historic Jailhouse*, 2 Kotuku St, T8847572. The lone motel is the **B** *Te Aroha Motel*, 108 Whitaker St, T/F8849417. There's also the **B-D** *Te Aroha Holiday Park*, 217 Stanley Rd, T/F8848739, and **C-D** *Te Aroha YHA Hostel*, Miro St, T8848739.

Accommodation is fairly limited in Te Aroha

Eating Two places stand out: The *Domain House*, in the Domain, which serves a traditional style à la carte menu. Open Tue-Sun. And the stylish *Café Banco*, 174 Whitaker St, which offers good value breakfast, lunch and dinner, Wed-Sun 1000-2300. Interesting antiques and art.

Directory **Communications** **Internet**: at Te Aroha Library and VIC.

Matamata Matamata lies in the heart of Waikato's rich and fertile agricultural landscape and is the epitome of affluent rural Kiwi life. Large ranches and spacious farmsteads would seem to suggest that the domestic and export agricultural worth of New Zealand is alive and well. Although it is pleasant enough, there is not a great deal here to attract the tourist. The **Visitor Information Centre** is at 45

Population: 8000

Broadway, T8887260, F8885653. Open Monday-Friday 0830-1700, Saturday/Sunday 1000-1500. They can assist with all accommodation enquiries.

The historic and well-armoured landmark **Firth Tower**, on Tower Road, was built in 1882 by Yorkshireman Josiah Firth, and is the town's main attraction. Why exactly it was so well fortified and therefore cost so much to build, is a matter of debate. The tower is the centrepiece of the historical **museum** which explains the intriguing history. ■ *Daily 1000-1600. Adult $3, child $0.60.*

About 6 km from Matamata, the **Opal Hot Springs** are a popular spot, and compete with Te Aroha's Domain, with a pool complex of mineral and private spa pools, T8888198. **Longlands Farm and Restaurant**, Burwood Road, is an award-winning dairy farm that offers a working farm experience with commentary and fine dining. Bookings essential, T8886588. Back in town if you have an interest in pigeons **Keola Lofts**, 428 Hinuera Road, is a unique and lively presentation about these intriguing masters of navigation. ■ *Open 1000-1600, T8881728.*

Cambridge

Cambridge is a popular spot to stop while heading south to Taupo or beyond

Also located on the Waikato River, 20 km south east of Hamilton on SH1, is the pleasant country town of Cambridge. Recognised nationally as a centre for thoroughbred horse studs, antiques, arts and crafts, and known locally as 'the town of trees', Cambridge has a distinctly English feel.

Ins & outs

Most of the main bus operators heading north or south on SH1 stop in Cambridge. For local bus information and Hamilton services contact *Cambridge Travelines*, T8277363. The Cambridge **Information Centre** is located on the corner of Queen and Victoria St, T8233456, cvc@wave.co.nz Open daily 0900-1600, 1000 weekends. Don't leave without the free *'Cambridge Welcomes You'* booklet.

Sights

The VIC has some excellent leaflets outlining the numerous antique, art and craft outlets in the town. The most famous is the Cambridge **Country Store**, 92 Victoria St, T8278715, which is housed in an old church. It has a wide range of crafts including native New Zealand wood pieces, ceramics, knitwear, Maori carvings, wines and foods. The *All Saint's Café* attached does a fine job of serving fresh snacks and home baking. Open daily 0830-1700. For horse and pony fanatics the **Cambridge Thoroughbred Lodge**, SH1, Karapiro, 6 km south of the town, puts on an entertaining hour-long 'New Zealand Horse Magic Show' where a range of horse breeds are shown and perform to order with much horsy humour and audience participation. ■ *Daily 1000-1600, shows at 1030 Tue-Sun, afternoon by arrangement. Adult $12, child $5. T8278118, www.racing.net.nz/cambridge*

For museum buffs the small **Cambridge Museum** is housed in the old courthouse on Victoria Street and is open from 1000-1600 Tue-Sat. There are a number of good **walks** in and around Cambridge. For a short walk the **Te Koutu Lake** on Albert St is very picturesque, while the tramp up **Maungatautari Mountain** (at the terminus of Maungatautari and Hicks Road, off SH1, a few kilometres south of town) is a more strenuous affair, rewarded with fine views of the river and beyond. For a spin (quite literally) down the river, contact '*Camjet*', T8436114, $45.

Sleeping & eating

VIC has information regarding the full range of accommodation

A *Birches B&B*, Maungatautari Rd, T8276556. Farmhouse located in a quiet country setting just south of town. In-house or separate cottage options, open fire and spa-bath. **A** *Riverside Motor Lodge*, 27 Williamson St, T8276069, is perhaps the best motel in town. **B-D** *Cambridge Country Lodge*, 20 Peake Rd (north off SH1), T8278373. Self-contained and backpacker bedrooms in rural setting, friendly, good facilities and bike hire available. **B-D** *Cambridge Motor Camp*, 32 Scott St, T/F8275649. Basic but well located. For dinner *Souter House*, 19 Victoria St, T8273610, and *Alphaz*, 72 Alpha St, T8276699; for lunch *The Gallery*, 64c Victoria St, T8230999; and for a fine breakfast, *Sazarac Caffe*, 35 Duke St, T8276618.

Tirau

Tirau is located at the junction of SH1 and SH27 which are the two main routes south – making Tirau a popular coffee stop. The highlight of the town is not hard to miss and comes in the form of a giant corrugated iron sheep on the Main Road. This edifice houses the **Big Sheep Wool Gallery** which sells an array of New Zealand – made woolly products and kitsch sheep souvenirs. The **Tirau Country Store**, Main Road, T8831539, is the 'younger sister' of the popular Cambridge Country Store, selling a wide range of New Zealand art and crafts with a specialisation in ceramics. Gourmet food is also available. The *Loose Goose* is a new café/restaurant at 7 Main Road, T/F8831515, which, along with *Alley Cats* and the *Oxford Landing* (also on Main Road), are the most popular eateries and coffee stops. The Tirau **Visitor Information Centre** is – you guessed it – on Main Road, T8831202, F8831202. They can assist with all accommodation enquiries and bookings.

Putaruru & Tokoroa

Tokoroa is a major forestry base and takes its name from a Maori chief who was killed during the Maori Land Wars of the mid 1800s. The main attraction here (other than the toilet or a coffee) are the various walks and mountain biking tracks in the surrounding forest. **Hatupatu Rock** is an interesting place steeped in Maori legend. In Putaruru the **Timber Museum** is the main draw. It has a steam engine and some ancient native logs and is located just south of the village on SH1. ■ *Open 0900-1600. T8837621*. Both Putaruru (T8837284) and Tokoroa (T8868872) have **Visitor Information Centres**, both located on SH1. They can assist with accommodation enquiries, bookings and details about local walks and attractions. If you are looking to park up for the night the **B-D** *Tokoroa Motor Camp and Backpackers*, 22 Sloss Road, Tokoroa, T/F8866642, is your best bet.

The Bay of Plenty

The Bay of Plenty

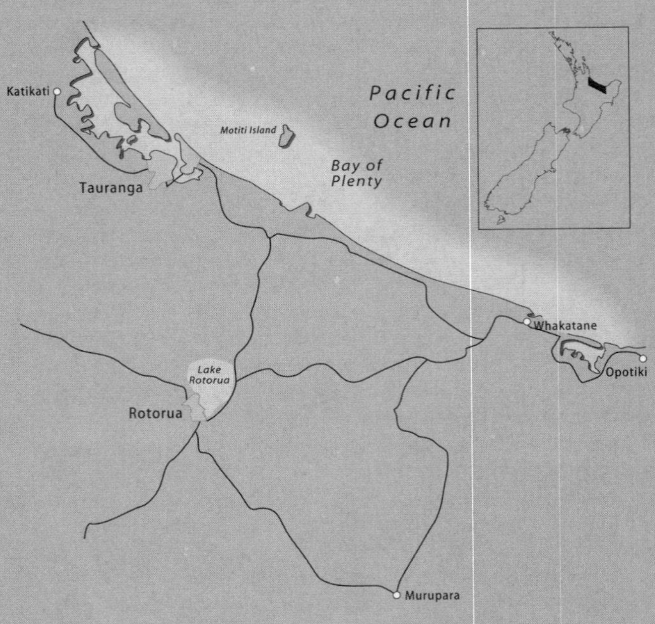

The Bay of Plenty. The obvious question – is it? Well, if statistics are anything to go by the answer is categorically, yes. By population, the Bay of Plenty is the North Island's fastest growing region, with the real estate figures of Tauranga now generally accepted as being a barometer to the health of the national economy. The region is also the most-visited tourist destination in the North Island and is where the very idea of New Zealand tourism began. ***Rotorua****, or 'Roto-Vegas' as it is known, is the thermal and* ***volcanic capital*** *of New Zealand, with geysers, hot pool and vents of bubbling mud. Rotorua also has a rich and fascinating human history.* ***Tauranga*** *is another tourist hot spot. Its sunny climate and beaches, as well as its proximity to Coromandel and Auckland, attract visitors by the bus load. Even the cruise ships have started visiting this busy port. The outlying towns, too, get their turn on the tourist merry-go-round. Proud* ***Whakatane*** *offers not only a lovely coast and congenial atmosphere but its own distinct attractions. One minute you can be swimming with* ***dolphins****, the next reeling in a marlin, or staring down the steaming barrel of* ***White Island's*** *volcanic crater.*

Things to do in the Bay of Plenty

- *Tour the incredible thermal reserves around Rotorua, not missing Wai-o-Tapu or Hell's Gate.*
- *Cruise or fish Lake Rotorua or Rotoiti; raft the Okere Falls; try white-water sledging; mountain biking in the Whakarewarewa Forest Park; or the infamous 'luge'.*
- *See the trout 'sub-aqua' or the huge, octogenarian native eels at Rainbow Springs.*
- *See the Tarawera Falls and walk up the Tarawera River to Lake Tarawera – the best walk in the region (if not the North Island).*
- *Do the tourist thing and compare cameras at the Agrodome 'Sheep-Shearing and Sheep Dog Show'.*
- *Experience Maori culture, song, dance and food on the Tamaki Twilight Cultural Tour and hangi.*
- *Go dolphin watching or visit the active White Island volcano from the congenial seaside town of Whakatane.*

Ins and outs

Getting there From the north the Bay of Plenty is accessed by **road** via SH2 from Auckland to Tauranga (route known and signposted as **The Pacific Coast Highway**) or SH1 and SH5 via Hamilton and Tirau (route known and signposted as **The Thermal Explorer Highway**). From the east coast and Napier, Rotorua is accessed via SH5, while Tauranga is accessed from Gisborne via SH2 or round East Cape via SH35. By **air** the Bay of Plenty is served by ***Air New Zealand Link*** from the two provincial airports at Tauranga and Rotorua. With New Zealand's fast-failing **train** network there is no longer any service to Rotorua.

Information The principal **Visitor Information Centres** are located in Rotorua and Tauranga with smaller centres available in Mt Maunganui, Whakatane and Opotiki. **DOC** offices are available in Tauranga, Rotorua and Murupara. All these centres and offfices are listed in the relevant sections. The main regional **websites** are www.rotoruanz.com/ www.tauranga.govt.nz and www.whakatane.govt.nz

Rotorua

Phone code: 07
Population: 52,000

Rotorua – alias 'Sulphur City' – is the 'thermal and volcanic capital' of New Zealand. A place that can sometimes be smelled before it's seen, though they say you get used to it. Of all the places in 'The Bay of Plenty' nature has indeed given Rotorua 'plenty'. The natural thermal wonders first attracted the Maori in the 14th century and later the Europeans, though nature has not always been so kind. The violent eruption of Tarawera in 1886 led to the loss of 150 lives.

Rotorua is deserving of its 'most visited' tourist status. The city and the region probably offer more unique sights and activities than anywhere else in New Zealand. And although, like Taupo, it is particularly famous for its thermal and volcanic features, lakes and fishing, the region offers a multitude of other things to do and see. Here you can join in a Maori concert or gorge yourself at a Maori hangi (feast), throw yourself down a 7 m waterfall in a raft, jump out of planes, bike, walk or shop till you drop and then 'take the cure' in one of the city's many hot thermal pools.

24 hours in Rotorua

Most people allow more than one day in Rotorua. There is so much on offer both in sights and activities that three to four are recommended. If one day is all you have, begin your first with a visit to the ***Rotorua Art and History Museum*** *and* ***Government Gardens****. This will give you a valuable insight into the history that shaped the region and the town. Be sure to take a wander around the gardens and around the lake edge. Then make your way to the town centre and lunch at* ***Fat Dog Café*** *or* ***Freos Café****. In the afternoon enjoy one of two activities: either an exhilarating rafting trip with* ***Kaituna Cascades****, or head for the* ***Skyline Gondola*** *to enjoy the views and the infamous luge. If you go to the Skyline Gondola you will then have time to skirt the northern edge of Lake Rotorua and head east on SH30 to* ***Hell's Gate*** *Thermal Reserve. That evening, experience a hangi and Maori cultural performance with* ***Tamaki Tours****.*

Ins and outs

Getting there
Rotorua is 234 km from Auckland, 658 km from Wellington and 80 km from Taupo

By air Rotorua is serviced by ***Air New Zealand Link*** with daily flights to Auckland, Wellington and other principal domestic centres. The airport is located on the eastern shores of Lake Rotorua, about 10 km from the town centre, T3486299. **By car** Rotorua is reached via SH4, which branches off SH1 at Tirua from the North and Taupo from the South. It is a major destination on the signposted '**Thermal Explorer Highway**' tourist route. ***Intercity*** and ***Newmans*** **buses** service Rotorua daily and stop outside the VIC on Fenton St. Specialist travel centre within the VIC handles all enquiries and bookings, T3485179.

Getting around

Super Shuttle, T3493444, and the main taxi companies provide transfers to and from the airport (shuttle $10 one way, taxis about $15). The 'Thermal' and 'Cultural Shuttle' provides daily transportation to the Tamaki Maori Village, Waimangu Volcanic Valley, Waiotapu Thermal Wonderland and Waikite Valley Thermal Pools, with scheduled and flexible non-scheduled pick ups and drop-offs available, $20. T0800-2872968. ***Santa Fe Shuttles*** offer a daily return service to Wai-O-Tapu, with flexible pick-ups from 0915. $15 return. T3457997. For **Car Rental** and **Cycle Hire** see page 115. For specific **Tour buses** see under Activities and tours, below.

Information & orientation

The rather grand Tourism Rotorua **Travel and Information Offices** are located at 1167 Fenton St. They are one of the oldest and busiest tourist offices in the country. It is the principal base for all local information, as well as the bus arrival and departure point. The in-house travel centre administers local and national bus, coach, air and rail ticketing. There is a **currency exchange** office (open 0800-1730), toilets, showers, a shop, a café and even a hot thermal footbath outside. T0800-768678, F3486044, info@tourism.rdc.govt.nz/www.rotoruanz.com Open daily 0800-1800. **DOC** are located at 1144 Pukaki St, T3497400, F3497401. Open Mon-Fri, 0800-1600. The **Map and Track Shop**, just a short distance south of the VIC at 1225 Fenton St, offers a comprehensive range of local and national maps and guides. Open Mon-Sat 0900-1800 T/F3491845.

History

Ohinemutu on the shores of Lake Rotorua and Whakarewarewa to the south of the present city, were first settled by Maori from the Arawa Canoe around the 14th century. These early Maori were quick to utilise the many benefits offered by the local thermal activity and for almost four centuries they thrived happily

Hinemoa and Tutanekai

Once there lived a beautiful and high-ranking young maiden by the name of Hinemoa, daughter of a very influential Maori chief. They lived at Owhata on the eastern shores of Lake Rotorua. Because of her rank, Hinemoa was declared puhi *(tapu or sacred). A husband would be chosen for her when she reached maturity by the elders of her* hapu *(sub-tribe) and her family. Many people came from far and wide to seek the hand of Hinemoa, but none of the potential suitors won approval.*

On Mokoia Island lived a family of several brothers, each of whom had set out in vain to win the hand of Hinemoa. Tutanekai was the youngest among them, born of an illicit affair between his mother and Tuwharetoa, who hailed from another tribe. Tutanekai was also smitten by Hinemoa's beauty and grace but he knew that, because of his lowly birth, he would never win the approval of her tribe and family. Tutanekai, however, was a very handsome fellow who excelled at the games which Maori used to develop co-ordination and battle skills. His physical prowess caught the eye of Hinemoa and she fell in love with him. This love grew in strength but, despite their mutual longing, it was almost impossible for them to communicate.

Tutanekai would sit on the shores of Mokoia with his friend Tiki and play soulful music on his flute. This music would waft across the waters to where Hinemoa also sat aching with passion, knowing she could never marry anyone but Tutanekai. Her people began to suspect this was the case and in order to prevent her from eloping they pulled all their waka *(large canoes) on to the shore. Night after night she listened for Tutanekai's flute until her heart could take no more. She decided she would attempt to swim the lake.*

The next night, after making suitable excuses to her family, she went down to the waterfront where she collected six calabashes from the cooking house. At Iri Iri Rock (which can still be seen at Owhata) she made the calabashes into primitive water-wings and slipped into the lake to swim for Mokoia. Guided only by the music played by Tutanekai, she finally made it to the island, where she hid behind a rock in a

and peace reigned. Then, in 1823, the Te Arawa were invaded by the Ngapuhi chief Hongi Hika from Northland. Despite the fact that Hika's warriors were armed with European muskets, the Te Arawa, determined to defend their little piece of paradise, put up a valiant fight, inflicting heavy losses on the intruders.

By the 1840's the first missions had been established on the shores of Lake Rotorua and Lake Tarawera. However, their sanctity was soon disrupted by more inter-tribal warfare, this time from the Waikato Maori to the west. During the Waikato campaigns and Maori King Movements of the New Zealand Wars, the Te Arawa elected to side with the New Zealand Government and, in 1864, a force of East Coast Ngati Porou attempted to cross Arawa lands to assist the Waikato tribes, only to be repelled by the Te Arawa and sent packing. This led to further reprisals from the Waikato tribes, which were subsequently repelled with Government assistance. It was not until the end of the New Zealand Wars that any substantial European settlement began. With the obvious attraction of both the aesthetics and therapeutic qualities of the thermal sights and waters of the region, the population rapidly expanded and tourism flourished. With the eruption of Mount Tarawera in 1886, settlement was temporarily halted, but as confidence returned so did the tourists and, now over a century on, that attraction and popularity continues.

thermal pool, as she was naked and too shy to approach his whare *(house). At that moment Tutanekai suddenly became thirsty and sent his slave to fetch a calabash of water. The slave had to pass quite close to Hinemoa, and as he passed she called out in a deep voice 'Mo wai te wai'? (for whom is the water?). The slave answered; Mo Tutanekai (For Tutanekai); 'Give it to me' she demanded. As soon as the slave did so she smashed the calabash on the rock. When the slave returned to Tuntanekai and related his tale, Tutanekai grew angry and sent the slave a second time. The same thing happened and this time a furious Tutanekai went down to the pool to investigate, armed with his* mere *(greenstone weapon). Once there he challenged the stranger to show themselves. No one moved, so Tutanekai reached behind the rock and, feeling a body, grabbed Hinemoa by her hair dragging her clear. 'Who are you' he cried, 'who dares annoy me'? She answered 'It is I Hinemoa, I have come to you Tutanekai'. Tutanekai could not believe his luck and when she stepped from the water Tutanekai took off his cloak and wrapped it around the naked Hinemoa, and then they went into the* whare *to sleep (if you believe that).*

The next morning the people of the pa *rose and after preparing breakfast remarked that Tutanekai must be sleeping late, which was unusual as he was well known for being the first to rise. After a while his father began to think ill of him and sent a slave to investigate. Such was his surprise on recognizing Hinemoa. he began to call out 'It's Hinemoa, it's Hinemoa', but no one would believe him. Only when Tutanekai emerged from his* whare *with Hinemoa on his arm did reality sink in. Then they noticed the* waka *approaching the island and, knowing it to be Hinemoa's tribe, they feared a great battle would ensue. However, this did not occur and, proud of her determination and bravery, both tribes celebrated the union and the couple lived happily ever after. The story of Hinemoa and Tutanekai is apparently not legend but truth, and her bones are buried on Motutawa Island on the Green Lake (Rotokakahi).*

Sights

Lake Rotorua

Lake Rotorua is the largest of the 17 lakes in the Rotorua thermal region, covering an area of 89 sq km and sitting at a height of 279 m above sea level. It is, as you might expect, a flooded volcanic crater. A feature of many of the launch trips based on the city's lake front is the bush-clad nature reserve of **Mokoia Island**, scene of the classic love story of the Arawa princess Hinemoa and her suitor Tutanekai (see short). But Mokoia was also the site for far less romantic encounters. During the invasion of Hongi Hika's warriors in 1823, the Arawa *pa* on Mokoia was sacked, but having sustained such heavy losses, the invaders could not hold what they had temporarily conquered. Today the lake is a top venue for recreational activities including boating, water skiing, and above all, trout fishing. For cruising on Lake Rotorua see 'activities and tours' below.

On the northern shores of the lake, at 733 Hamurana Road, are the **Hamurana Gardens** where the largest spring in the North Island erupts with a beautiful clarity and a volume of over one million gallons an hour. The gardens also feature a tract of giant Redwoods. ■ *Adult $5, child $2. T3323866.*

Ohinemutu

Situated on the lakefront within the city, and reached via narrow streets lined with steaming drains, is the former Maori settlement and thermal area of Ohinemutu. The focal point of the village is the **Tamatekapua Marae**, a beautifully carved *whare-runanga* (meeting house), erected in 1939. It is often used as the focus for Maori events and performances, and despite its fairly modern renovation, still contains carvings from the 1800s. It was named after the head of the original Arawa canoe which first made landfall in the Bay of Plenty in the 14th century. Just opposite the marae is the Tudor-styled **St Faith's Church** built in 1910. Its interior pillars, beams, rafters and pews are beautifully carved with Maori designs and on a sandblasted window overlooking the lake a 'Maori Christ' is portrayed, dressed in a *korowai* (chief's

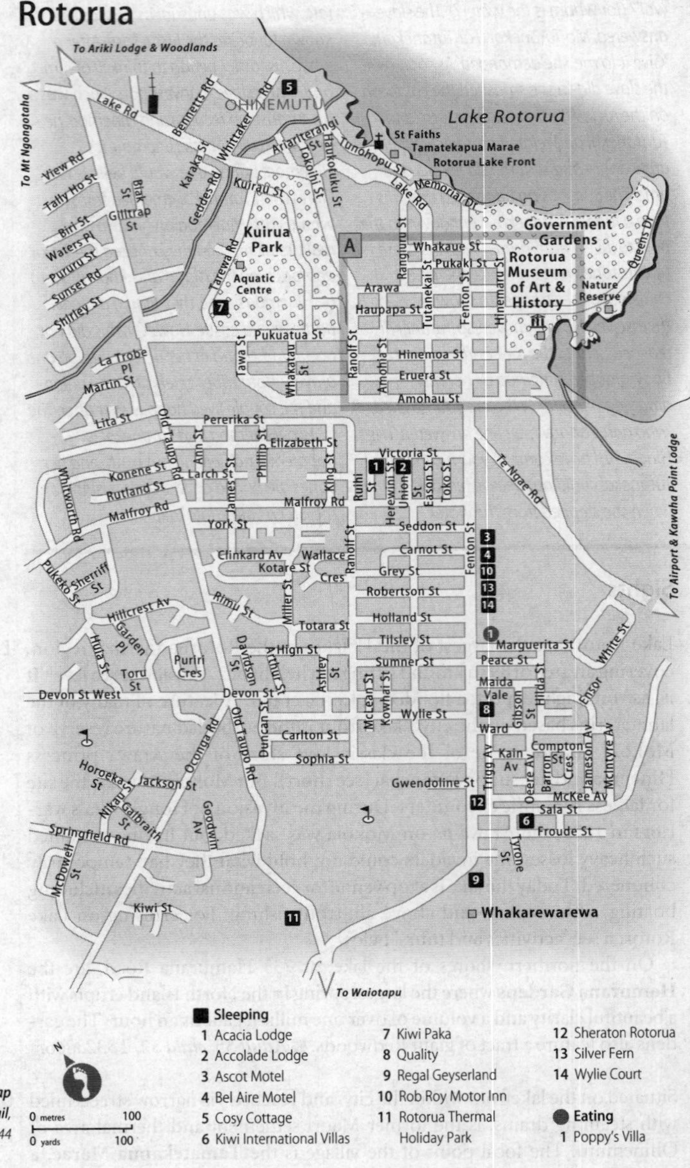

Related map
A Rotorua detail, page 244

cloak). ■ *Open daily 0800-1700. Free.* Buried in the **graveyard** are many notable members of the Arawa tribe, among them the only European to be admitted to full chieftainship, the colonial force officer Captain Gilbert Mair (1843-1923). He twice saved the Arawa from inter-tribal attacks. It is interesting to note that the graves are built above ground to protect them from the thermal activity and intense heat. Had they been buried in the conventional style they would have been cooked before the last sod of earth had been replaced. At the entrance of the churchyard is a four-gabled canopy under which a bust of Queen Victoria used to sit. It was presented to the Arawa in 1870 by Prince Albert, the first member of the British royal family to visit New Zealand. The bust recently disappeared in mysterious circumstances. All around the village you can see quite intense thermal activity that was enjoyed and utilised by the first Maori settlers. There is still a boiling pool near the church that is frequently used for boiling eggs and cooking meat – and perhaps the occasional member of the British monarchy.

Government Gardens & the Rotorua Museum of Art and History

Just West of Ohinemutu are the elegant and beautifully maintained Government Gardens. There, as a backdrop of the grand former bathhouse and current museum, are the well-manicured bowling greens and croquet lawns, ponds and scented roses, which create a distinctly Edwardian, colonial atmosphere.

The **Rotorua Museum of Art and History** is housed in the once-famous **Bath House**. Built in 1908, it was designed along the lines of the European Spas and attracted hundreds of clients the world over that hoped to take advantage of the thermal water's therapeutic and curative powers. At the time the soothing waters were thought to be a cure for any ailments, as diverse as anxiety and even obesity. Its popularity in 'taking the cure', together with the added volcanic features and attractions surrounding the city, made the Bath House the focus of the New Zealand Government's first major investment in the new concept of tourism. In one wing of the museum you can see some of the original baths, changing rooms and equipment, together with photographs. Given the rich local Maori history it is not surprising to find a superb collection of Te Arawa *taonga* (treasures) which contrasts nicely with collections of modern artworks by local Maori artists. There are also displays that feature the great Tarawera Eruption of 1886 as well as temporary, national touring exhibitions and more modern dynamic offerings. One display not to miss is the excellent audiovisual display entitled 'Rotorua Stories'. It screens every 20 minutes and is a 15-minute introduction to the great historical legends and stories of the area. It comes complete with shuddering pews during the fascinating account and depiction of the Tarawera eruption. ■ *Daily 0930-1700 in winter, 0930-1800 in summer. Adult $7.50, child $3. T3494350. The museum has a shop and a café.*

A short distance from the museum are the **Blue Baths** (Blueys). Built in the Spanish Mission style during the Great Depression of 1933, the pools soon flourished as one of the major social and recreational venues in the city, and were one of the first public baths to offer 'mixed' bathing. Sadly, due to competition elsewhere and social change, the Blueys' popularity declined and they were finally closed in 1982. Still much loved, they were restored and re-opened in 1999 as functional hot pools, museum and tearooms. There is an entertaining video presentation relating the story of the pools, and the museum displays are imaginatively set in the former male and female changing room cubicles. You can combine a visit to the museum with a dip in the hot pool or a cuppa in the faithfully restored tearooms. ■ *Daily 1000-1600 in winter, 1800 in summer. Pools open till 2100 in summer. From $5, child $2. T3502119.*

Behind the Blue Baths is the highly popular **Polynesian Spa** complex. Rain or shine this is a Rotorua 'must do' and, although often very busy, it is a delight. There is a luxury spa complex and hot springs and pools, private spa pools, a family spa, shop and café. A range of massage treatments are also available. If you cannot afford the luxury spa then the therapeutic adult hot springs will not be a disappointment. Set outside in timber-style tubs, the springs overlook the lake and range in temperature from 33°C to 43°C. It is a great place to ease the aches and pains of your far more active tourist pursuits and a fine place to mix with the locals, though the omnipresent tour groups can make it all very chaotic. The best times to go are at lunch and dinnertime when the tour buses are elsewhere. ■ *Daily 0630-2300. From $10, child $4. T3481328.*

Alongside Hinemaru Street and close to the Garden's entrance, are the slightly overrated **Orchid Gardens**. As well as a range of hot house orchids, New Zealand ferns and other tropical blooms, there is a water organ, which is an hourly, 15-minute choreographed light and water display with over 800 jets of water. Microworld, which is a 'techno-observatory' on the life and times of insects, and the reputable *Garden Café* are also housed within the gardens. ■ *Daily 0830-1730. Adult $10, child $4. T3476699.*

Rotorua detail

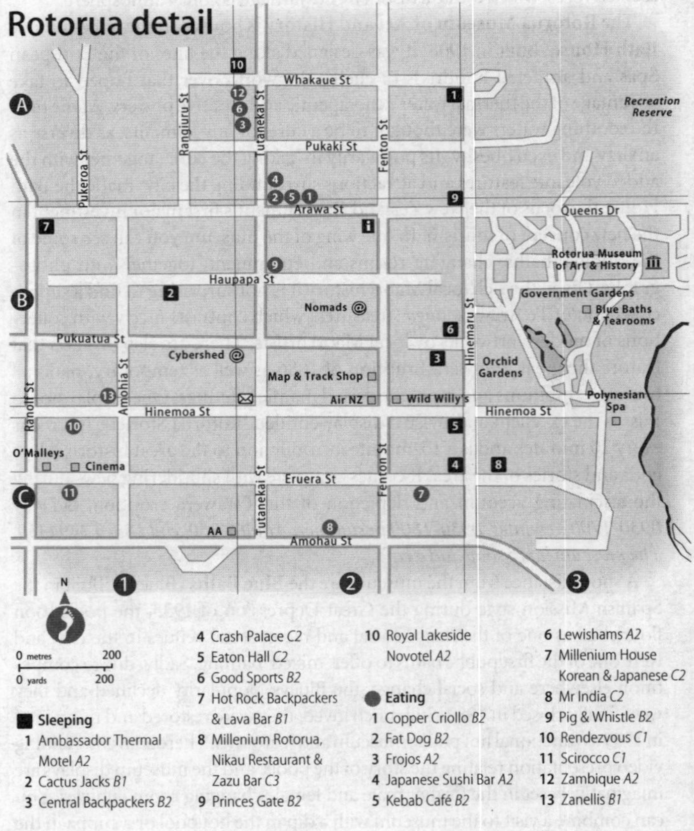

Other than the obvious attractions, the Government Gardens are well worth a thorough investigation and a further muse. If you follow the road around the lakeshore you will encounter a thriving **nature reserve** complete with hungry swans and a colony of prehistoric looking pied shags.

Whakarewarewa

'Whaka' (pronounced 'Fuckka') is the most famous and historic of the region's thermal reserves, with New Zealand's largest geyser, the much celebrated **Pohutu**, being its star attraction. As well as the great spout there are also boiling pools, silica terraces and the obligatory bubbling mud. Also attached to the complex are the **Rotowhio Marae**, the **Mai Ora Village** (a replica of the former Te Arawa Maori settlement) and the modern **Maori Arts and Crafts Institute**.

Although worth the visit to see ol'Pohutu doing its thing and the many interesting Maori aspects, Whaka suffers a little from tourist overkill and is by far the most commercial of the thermal reserves. On entering you have the option of self-guided or a (recommended) Maori guided tour around the reserve. A series of paths branch out from the main visitors block and take in a strictly 'showpiece' nocturnal kiwi house before passing the large and at times, fairly inert Ngamokaiakoko ('Leaping Frog') mud pool, before the path delivers you at the geyser formations. There used to be many geysers in Whaka (about 60), but now there are essentially two. The famed Pohutu or 'Big Splash' goes off like a broken water hydrant, 10-25 times a day (more recently for days on end), to a height of over 30 m, while the more impotent Prince of Wales (sorry Charles) geyser nearby, is less spectacular. The tracks then negotiate the other small mud pools and volcanic features of the valley before arriving back near the entrance and the Rotowhio Marae. There are many features in this functional marae, including a banquet and weaving house and a *waka* (canoe).

The marae also hosts daily **cultural performances** which feature a traditional *powhiri* (welcome), demonstration of the *taiaha* (warrior's weapon), *haka* (posture dance), *poi* (women's dance) and a range of traditional Maori songs. A longer performance in the evenings includes a *hangi* (feast). The Maori Arts and Crafts Institute was established in 1963 to ensure that the traditional artist aspects of Maori culture are not lost. A viewing platform allows visitors to see students at work in the woodcarving studio before taking them through other galleries and display areas where pieces of completed work can be seen and are for sale. There is also a shop and a café on site. The Whakarewarewa Valley is located about 3 km south of the city centre along Fenton Street (just head for the steam) ■ *Open from 0800-1800. Guided tours are optional and depart hourly. Adult $18, child $9. There are daily cultural performances at 1115 and 1400 and in the evening ('Mai Ora' – 'Essence of Maori' performance, which costs $65, child $35). T3489047, www.nzmaori.co.nz*

Whakarewarewa Forest Park

On the southern outskirts of Rotorua is the recreational playground of the Whakarewarewa Forest Park, well known for its excellent **walking** and **mountain biking** opportunities. The best way to choose from those opportunities is to visit the Fletcher Challenge Information Centre located along Long Mile Road, off Tarawera Road, which in turn is just off SH30 heading east. ■ *Mon-Fri 0830-1800, Sat/Sun 1000-1700. T3462082.* It has a number of interesting interpretative displays as well as all track information and colour-coded track maps. The walks range from 20 minutes to eight hours, with the shortest taking in a tract of giant Californian **Redwoods** (along Long Mile Road) and the longest taking in the shores of the Blue and Green Lakes. For mountain bike hire see 'Activities and tours' section below.

Kuirua Park If you arrive in the city from the SH4 north, the steam that issues from the thermal features in Kuirua Park will be your first sight and smell (if not taste) of the city's volcanic activity. This park is 25 ha with gardens linked by tracks to a number of low-key thermal pools and features, as well as the cutely named 'Toot and Whistle' miniature steam railway, which is perfect for kids. There is also a miniature golf course and the city's Aquatic Centre. ■ *Open 0600-2100.* While in the vicinity of Kuirua take a short drive down **Tarawera Road**. On the left heading south, you will see two fenced-off sections that are billowing steam. These were – believe it or not – former properties until 1998, when new boiling springs literally erupted in the driveway. Under a system of Government volcanic damage compensation the families were forced to move and the land given back to nature!

If you want a great view of the city and the region as a whole, then **Mount Ngongotaha** to the west of the city is easily accessible by car. From SH5 heading north, take Clayton Road at the crossroads with the Old Taupo Road. After about 3 km Mountain Road is signposted off Clayton to the right. The Aorangi Peak Restaurant is near the summit.

Activities and tours

Agrodome **The Agrodome Complex**, just north of Rotorua on SH5, offers a wealth of activities including **bungy-jumping, jet boating, 'The Swoop', Zorbing** and **'Dirtthingz'** (see page 258). T3574350, www.agrodome.co.nz

Climbing There is a climbing wall in Rotorua at 1140 Hinemoa Street. Open daily. Outdoor trips can also be arranged for $20; T3501400.

Cruising The two main cruises around Lake Rotorua (including Mokoia Island) and beyond, to Lake Rotoiti are provided by the paddle steamer *Lakeland Queen* and the unfortunately named *Scatcat*. The *Lakeland Queen* offers breakfast, from $26, child $13 (0800-0900); lunch from $28, child $14 (1230-1330); a dinner cruise from $40, child $20 (1900-late); and a 3½ hour cruise from $45, child $22.50; T0800862784. The *Scatcat* offers one-hour cruises to Mokoia leaving at 1000,1100,1300 and 1400, $25; two-hour trips to Hamurana Gardens and springs, $30; and a lake cruise, $48. T3479852. There are also self-drive speedboats available for hire from the waterfront.

Eco-Tours *Nature Connection* based in the city offer a range of excellent fully guided, fully equipped half to full-day trips to local sights and the Whirinaki Forest Park, from $70. T3471705.

Fishing As you might expect there are numerous guided and self-guided charters that mainly operate on Lake Rotorua or Lake Tarawera. Ernie Scudder is a very congenial local fisherman who offers a great trip aboard the '*Silver Hilton*', from $65 an hour. T3323488, www.troutfly.co.nz Other reputable charters include: *Clearwater* (Lake Tarawera), T3628590; *The Trout Connection*, T3472363; *Hamill Charters* (sea and freshwater), T3628199. Prices start at about $70 per hour.

Four-Wheel Drive & Quad Bikes *Off Road NZ*, Amoore Road (off SH5 north), are a fine outfit and offer a range of thrills and spills in a range of four-wheel drive vehicles and buggies. From their base near the city you can go uphill and down dale (including a monstrous 15 m 'luge' drop) and through some very large mud pools. There is also clay-bird shooting and archery available. Tours daily 0900-1700, from $60. T3325748, www.offroadnz.co.nz

Mount Tarawera 4WD Tours are the principal four-wheel drive operators for the mountain. They offer a fully guided, fully equipped, half-day trip to the summit. You spend about two hours at the edge of the crater, with the option of a guided walk. It costs $110, child $55.T3482814.

Hill Hoppers offer the complete range of off-road four-wheel drive experiences in a range of vehicles. Trips include the 'Bogs Bunny', the 'Wet Wabbit' and 'Run Rabbit Run' – all from $55. The only slight drawback is that they are located at Longridge Park, near Te Puke, well to the north of the city.T5331818.

Mountain Action is the local quad bike operator and is located near Rainbow Springs on SH5 north. Horse trekking also available. From $80. Pick-ups provided. T3488400.

Golf

There are six courses in and around Rotorua. The best is the **Arikikapakapa Course** at the southern end of Fenton Street, Rotorua Golf Club, T3484051. There is also a range and a short nine-hole course in the **Government Gardens**, T3489126.

Horse Trekking

Foxwood Park Horse Treks are located at the edge of the Whakarewarewa Forest Park and offer trips from 30 minutes to full-day, from $30, T3332977. *Paradise Valley* are based near the Paradise Valley Springs, 11 km west of the city on Claydon Road, one hour for $25, T3488195. *Peka Horse Treks*, SH30, T3461755, are ideally situated close to Whakarewarewa Forest Park; one hour from $25.

Kayaking

Adventure Kayaking, offer half or full-day tours to a number of lakes and rivers in the region, as well as fishing trips and twilight paddles, from $35. Independent hire is also available. T3489451, www.adventurekayaking.co.nz *Go Kayaking* offer similar trips with more emphasis on teaching the beginner; from $50. Independent hire also available. T3624222.

Maori concerts & hangis

A trip to Rotorua is not complete without the Maori cultural experience of a concert and/or *hangi* (feast). There are numerous options, some good some not so good. The least commercial and recommended are the well-established *Tamaki Tours Marae Experience* and the daily *Magic of the Maori* performance at the Tamatekapua Marae at Ohinemutu. The former involves a daily, twilight *marae* tour, performance and *hangi* with some audience participation; from $60. They provide pick-ups from your accommodation. T3462823, www.maoriculture.co.nz The latter is a one-hour concert that kicks off at 2000; $20. Pick-ups available. Bookings are preferred, but you can also just turn up. T3493949. During the day and again in the evening there are also the cultural performances at the **Whakarewarewa Village**, at 1115 and 1400. T3493463 (see page 245).

The major hotels almost all offer *hangis* and concerts, but these tend to be less grand affairs than the above. The *Matariki Hangi and Concert* at the *Royal Lakeside Novotel* takes place daily at 1830 and is one of the best on offer, T3463888. A hotel *hangi* and concert will cost you about $50.

Mountain Biking

The **Whakarewarewa Forest Park** is just one of many popular and challenging venues for mountain biking around Rotorua, with over 30 km of trails (see page 245). For organised trips try *Planet Bike*, T3489971, www.planetbike.co.nz Combo kayak trips and independent bike hire also available. From $49. For more track and operator information, T3484581.

Rafting & White Water Sledging *Kaituna Cascades* are a very professional, safe and experienced company that offer a range of white-water rafting and tandem kayaking trips, on the Kaituna, Rangitaiki Wairoa Rivers and nearby lakes. The most popular trip is the recommended 45-minute blast down a stretch of the Kaituna, which negotiates 14 falls. The largest of these is the famous and highly entertaining 7 m drop down the Okere Falls – the highest commercial rafted falls in the world. Trips range from $65 (45 minutes) to $385. You get a photo of the drop down the falls. *River Rats* are a similar company offering a wider scope of multi-activity adventure packages that include jet boating, bungy jumping, four-wheel drive, bikes and more, T3476049, www.riverrats.co.nz *Wet-n-Wild* are another reputable company offering all the local trips but also specialising in multi-day trips on the Motu and Mohaka Rivers, From $65. T3483191. White-water sledging is the new and exciting concept of doing all you do in a raft, except alone on a type of 'head-first' water toboggan. To try it and learn something about Maori culture on the way, contact *Kaitiaki Adventures*, T2785555.

Sightseeing Tours

The VIC offers reductions and package deals which are well worth looking at

There are a wealth of independent operators. *Carey's Tours* are a Maori-owned and operated company and one of the largest local tour operators in Rotorua. They offer a wide range of tour options from half to full-day and from $25 to $145. They are based at 1108 Haupapa Street, near the VIC, T3471197, www.careys.co.nz *Volcanic Sightseeing and Adventure Tours* are similar to the above with half to full-day trips with a little more emphasis on action as opposed to just sightseeing, T0800-697444. From $49-$254. *Te Kiri Treks* are a new, Maori-operated company that provide an excellent day out in a four-wheel drive, taking in Ohinemutu, Whakarewarewa, Waiotapu, Tarawera and a few secret spots on the way. Lunch is provided in a beautiful self-built bush camp. All for $120. T3455016. Good value, entertaining and recommended. *Sonny's World* are another new Maori-operated tour company, also offering the genuine and fun Maori perspective. Half-day $48. T3490290. *Harmony Tours* offer a range of trips locally and farther afield and are flexible with their itinerary, T2677768. Day trips from $125. *Taylor's Tours* are similar, from $35-$320. T3323387.

Scenic Flights *Volcanic Air Safaris* have a fleet of fixed-wing aircraft and helicopters that take in all the local sights and go as far as White Island in the Bay of Plenty. From $50 to $625. T0800-800848. *Heli-Kiwi* operate out of Wai-O-Tapu and offer helicopter trips from five minutes above Wai-O-Tapu ($45) to 30 minutes over Mount Tarawera ($205). *New Zealand Helicopters*, based at the Whakarewarewa Thermal Reserve, offer local flights from 10 minutes to four-hour White Island flights, from $55-$650. They are one of the principal operators allowed to land on the summit of Tarawera. *Red Cat* offers the old bi-plane option above the city and the lake, and operates from Rotorua airport, from $95. T3459369.

Skyline Skyrides Accessed by a scenic gondola there are a number of activities available on the slopes of Mount Ngongotaha. These include the infamous Luge, a flying fox, flight simulator and helicopter trips, T3470027.

Tandem Skydiving *Tandem Skydiving Rotorua* operate from the airport daily, weather permitting. From 9,500 ft for $195 (13,000 ft, $225), T3457520.

Walking

There are a wealth of walking opportunities in the Rotorua region, ranging from a short walk around **Government Gardens** and the waterfront, to the **Tarawera summit** climb (see page 253), the 20-minute to eight-hour walks through the **Whakarewarewa Forest Park** (see page 245), and the superb **Tarawera Falls** walk (see page 256). Other excellent walking tracks are to be found around Lake Okataina in the **Lake Okataina Scenic Reserve**. These are best accessed from SH30 at Ruato (Lake Rotoiti) or Lake Okareka (Tarawera Falls Road). The **Okere Falls** walk (30 minutes) is accessed from SH30 east and then SH33 (16 km) and worth the trip, while a great view can be had from the summit of **Rainbow Mountain** (two hours) which is accessed off SH5, 26 km south of Rotorua. For more details contact the VIC or DOC. Maps can be bought at *The Map and Track Shop*, just a short distance south of the VIC at 1225 Fenton Street, T/F3491845.

Essentials

Sleeping

There are over 12,000 tourist beds in Rotorua, so the choice is huge

Many of the main hotel chains are here and there are lots of motels situated on either side of Fenton St, between the centre of town and Whakarewarewa. Pre-booking is advised throughout the year. Whatever you do and where ever you end up, make sure there is an accessible hot pool in-house or nearby.

LL-AL *Royal Lakeside Novotel*, lake-end of Tutanekai St, T3463888, F3471888. Located right in the heart of town and Lake Rotorua, and also near Government gardens. Good reputation with in-house spas, and a popular restaurant and bar. It also offers one of the best hotel Maori concerts and *hangis*. **LL-AL** *Sheraton Rotorua*, Fenton St, T3495200, F3495201. One of Rotorua's best and most expensive. Located close to Whakarewarewa Village and thermal reserve. Pool, spas, gym, café, restaurant and even an Irish pub attached. Maori concert and feasts nightly. **L-AL** *Okawa Bay Lake Resort*, SH33, Lake Rotoiti, T3624599, F3624594, www.okawabay.co.nz A good hotel option out of town, in an idyllic lakeside setting. Full amenities including restaurant and private beach.

There are a number of luxury lodges around town, most lakeside and offering peace and quiet with all mod cons. These include: **LL** *Solitaire Lodge*, Lake Tarawera, T3628208. Highly celebrated hideaway with ten luxurious suites over looking the lake; **LL** *Woodlands*, Hamurana Rd, Ngongotaha, T3322242, www.woodlands.co.nz Luxurious mansion overlooking Lake Rotorua. Beautifully appointed; **L** *Kawaha Point Lodge*, 171 Kawaha Point Rd, T3463602, www.kawahalodge.co.nz Lakeside, 5 mins from the airport. En suite double or twins, two with spa baths, garden with pool; **L** *Namaste Point*, Lake Rotoiti, T3624804. On its own peninsula on Lake Rotoiti, luxury self-contained accommodation, spa, pool, beach and free canoe hire.

AL-A *Ariki Lodge*, 2 Manuariki Av, Ngongotaha, T3575532, F3575562. Spacious, well-appointed lakeside B&B north of the city. **AL** *Lake Tarawera Lodge*, Te Mu Rd, Lake Tarawera, T3628754, www.laketarawera.co.nz Beautiful location. Country-style cottages, 6-roomed Mission House and campsite. Very popular with the fishing fraternity with trips by arrangement. **AL** *Millennium Rotorua*, corner of Eruera and Hinemaru Sts, T/F3471234. Popular and very tastefully appointed. Only metres from the Polynesian Spa (discounts to guests), reputable in-house bar. **AL-A** *The Princes Gate*, 1 Arawa St, T3481179, F3486215, www.princesgate.co.nz An award-winning establishment that hails itself as being 'historically boutique' and keeps its promise. Also in a great location between the city centre and Government Gardens. **AL-A** *Quality Hotel*, Fenton St, T3480199, F3461973. Comfortable mid-range option with good facilities including pool, spa and gym. **AL** *Regal Geyserland*, 424 Fenton St, T3482039, F3482033. Famed for its location overlooking the Whakarewarewa Thermal Reserve. You can literally hear the geyser Pohutu going off and look down on a pool of bubbling mud. All the usual facilities including in-house hot pools.

With so much motel competition there are few B&Bs in town but the **A-B** *Eaton Hall*, 1255 Hinemaru St, T/F3470366, is good value, comfortable and well situated close to the Polynesian Spa. Also well situated is the **A** *Accolade Lodge B&B*, 30 Victoria St, T3482223, F3482238, though it is more a cross between a motel and a B&B, but seemingly popular all the same.

B *Good Sports Hotel*, 1209 Hinemaru St, T3481550. Kiwi pub-style, low budget option. Comfortable and well situated.

Rotorua is not lacking **Backpacker Hostels** The award winning **B-D** *Kiwi Paka*, 60 Tarewa Rd, T3470931, www.kiwipaka-yha.co.nz is the pick of the bunch, with a fine range of dormitory, unit, motel, camper van and campsite options. The staff are great and the amenities are excellent, including a large kitchen and sitting room, a bar and café and a thermal pool. Activities arranged. It is a bit out of town but most operators provide pick-ups. Also popular but ageing is the **C-D** *Hot Rock Backpackers*, 1286 Arawa St, T3479469, www.hotrock@acb.co.nz It has in-house spa pools and a lively, popular bar on-site. The **C-D** *Central Backpackers*, 1076 Pukuatua St, T/F3493285, is a congenial, friendly and more historic establishment that is deservedly growing in popularity. Beds not bunks, single rooms and an in-house spa. **C-D** *Cactus Jacks*, 54 Haupapa St, T3483121, well-established, its artistic delights seem a little out of place but well-located and friendly with an in-house spa, . For the quieter more homely treatment head for the newly renovated **C-D** *Crash Palace*, 1271 Hinemaru St, T3488842, www.crashpalace.co.nz

Bay of Plenty

There are almost 100 **motels** in Rotorua, most on Fenton St, so the choice is vast. Most are modern and very much the same and, given the fierce competition, you will rarely be let down. The following are just a few examples, and some that are particularly recommended or well situated: **AL-A** *Ambassador Thermal Motel*, Cnr Whakaue and Hinemaru Sts, T3479581. Ideal location close to Polynesian Spa and city centre. **AL** *Silver Fern*, 326 Fenton St, T3463849. Hailed as one of the city's best. Wide range of suites with spa pools; **AL-A** *Wylie Court*, 345 Fenton St, T3477879. 36 suites with pool and restaurant; **A** *Acacia Lodge*, 40 Victoria St, T3487089. Well situated close to the city centre, outdoor heated pool and spas; **A** *Ascot Motel*, 247 Fenton St, T3487712. Spas in all units; **A** *Bel Aire Motel*, 257 Fenton St, T/F3486076. Good value; **B** *Rob Roy Motor Inn*, 291 Fenton St, T3480584; **B** *Kiwi International Villas*, 11 Tryon St, T3473333; **B** *Kiwi Paka*, 60 Tarawera Rd, T3470931, Recommended.

Motor camps and campsites The **B-D** *Cosy Cottage*, 67 Whittaker Road, T3483793, is an excellent motor camp located just north of the city centre, almost lakeside. It is one of the only motor camps in the world that can boast 'naturally heated' campsites. It has a wide range of cabins, good amenities and spa pools. At the other end of town the **B-D** *Rotorua Thermal Holiday Park*, Old Taupo Rd, T3463140, is also excellent with some fine log cabins and within walking distance of the Whakarewarewa Thermal Reserve. If you are looking for a quiet country spot then look no further than the Top Ten **B-D** *Blue Lake Holiday Park* on the banks of Blue Lake on Tarawera Rd. There is a beach across the road for swimming, kayak hire and a lovely walk around the lake, T3628120.

Eating

There are more than 50 restaurants in Rotorua offering a wide range of cuisine to suit all budgets

Most of the restaurants are located on or around Tutanekai St towards the lake. Visitors to Rotorua should of course consider sampling one of the many Maori *hangis* available. Although few of them are truly authentic, having neither the time nor the stringent health and safety requirements to dig earth pits and cook the food underground, they will still give you just a taste of how good a Maori *hangi* can be (for options see page 247). For dinner afloat don't forget the *Lakeland Queen* paddle steamer that leaves for a cruise/dinner from the lakefront at 1900, from $40, T3486634.

Expensive ***Lewisham's Café and Restaurant***, 1099 Tutanekai St, T/F3481786 has a good reputation, offering traditional European dishes with a definite Austrian edge. The venison and wiener schnitzel are recommended. Open daily 0900-2200. ***The Rendezvous***, 1282 Hinemoa St, T3489273, is a popular award-winning restaurant offering fine pacific rim dishes in very congenial surroundings. There is venison, quail and even emu on the menu. Open Tue-Sat from 1800. For Kiwi cuisine ***Poppy's Villa,*** 4 Marguerita St, T3471700, is recommended. Open daily from 1800. ***Zanelli's,*** 1243 Amohia St, T3484908, is touted as the best Italian restaurant. ***The Nikau Restaurant*** in the *Millennium Hotel* (see Sleeping above) has a good reputation and offers traditional European and Kiwi-style fine dining without being too formal. The bar is also popular, T3471234.

Mid-range ***The Pig and Whistle*** ,corner of Haupapa and Tutanekai Sts, T3473025, offers great pub food at affordable prices and you can wash it all down with their own brews. Open daily from 1130-2130. ***The Copper Criollo Restaurant***, 1151 Arawa St, T3481333, offers an intriguing mix of contemporary Maori (*hangi*-style), Cajun and Creole dishes, cheap breakfasts. Open daily 0730-2400. ***Frojos***, lake end of Tutanekai St, T/F3460976, is a busy little café/restaurant that offers traditional Kiwi fare and obviously does it well: it has a loyal following. Open daily from 0830. ***Zambique***, also on Tutanekai is well known for its creative modern dishes and good coffee. Open daily from 0800-late. ***Mr India***, 1161 Amohau St, T3494940, is perhaps the best Indian in the city keeping up the traditions and reputation of other national outlets. Open daily from 1130. All-you-can-eat specials on Tue/Wed. For traditional Asian fare try the ***Japanese Sushi Bar***, 1148 Tutanekai St, T3460792. Open daily 1100-1400 and 1700-2200; or the ***Millennium House Korean and Japanese***, 1074 Eruera St, T3493309. Open daily 1100-1400, 1800-2300. For Middle Eastern dishes look no further than the ***Kebab Café***, 67 Arawa St, T3488411. Open daily 1100-1500, 1700-2200. Out of town a fine affordable lunch and dinner spot with a distinctive Scots flavour is the very friendly ***Landings Café***, Spencer Rd, Lake Tarawera, T3628502. Open daily from 0900. Book for dinner.

Cheap The best café in town is the ***Fat Dog***, 1161 Arawa St, T3477586. It is certainly always busy and friendly, and offers an imaginative blackboard menu. Open Mon-Fri 0900-late, Sat/Sun 0800-late. Other good cafés include the ***Scirocco***, 1280 Eruera St, T3473388, and, for traditional afternoon teas, the historic tea-rooms at the ***Blue Baths***, Government Gdns, T3502119, are a good option, open 1000-1600. The ***Robert Harris Coffee House***, on 227 Tutanekai St, is also an old faithful, with the usual reliable snacks and breakfast. Open daily from 0730.

Pubs & entertainment

The ***Pig and Whistle***, corner Haupapa and Tutanekai Sts, is nicely decorated, brews its own ales and has a congenial atmosphere. It also has bands at the weekends, T3473025. The Irish pub ***O'Malley's***, 1287 Eruera St, is also popular with good beer, bands on Fri night and the obligatory round pool table, T3476410. Locals are apparently secretly hanging out in the classy ***Zazu Bar*** in the *Millennium Hotel* (see Sleeping section), T3471234. The happy hour on Fri at 1930 and Sat at 1730 are especially popular. For the younger set the ***Lava Bar*** at the Hot Rock Backpackers, 118 Arawa St, is especially popular with travellers, while ***Wild Willy's***, 1240 Fenton St, is the place to shake your pants of a Wed, Fri and Sat from 2100, T3487774.

The **Cinema** complex is next to the Irish pub on Eruera St, T3492994.

Events

Jan: ***Opera in the Pa***; World-class opera performed amidst the geothermal splendour of the Rotowhio Marae. **Feb**: ***Lakeside 2002***; Annual concert and entertainment in the soundshell on the lakeside. **Mar (3rd week)**: ***International Two-Day Walk***; 10, 20 and 30 km walks through Rotorua forests and city.

Apr (last week): ***Rotorua Marathon***; 42 km run around Lake Rotorua. **May (3rd week)**: ***Rotorua Tagged Trout Fishing Contest***; Catch the tagged trout in Lake Rotorua and become a rich fishing-person. **Jul (1st week)**: ***Sheraton Concerto***; a showcase of national classical musicians; **3rd week**; ***Catseye Moonride***; a night-time mountain biking event held in the Whakarewarewa Forest Park (unfortunately lights are allowed).

Sep: ***Rally of Rotorua***. **Oct**: ***Lockwood Aria***; New Zealand's largest classical singing competition with both classical and contemporary disciplines and Maori cultural music. ***New Zealand Trout Festival***; marks the opening of the Rotorua lakes season. **Nov**: ***International Trout Tournament***; 3-day tournament with major prizes attracting anglers worldwide. **Dec**: ***New Year's Eve Mardi Gras***, wild shenanigans down at the waterfront to welcome in the New Year.

Shopping As you might expect, there are plenty of souvenir shops in Rotorua. Most are located on Fenton St. ***The Souvenir Centre***, at 1231, is one of the better ones. The mainly authentic Maori souvenirs attached to ***Carey's Tours,*** 1108 Haupapa St, are also worth a peek. For Maori Art don't miss the ***Maori Arts and Crafts Institute,*** at the Whakarewarewa Thermal Reserve, SH5, or the ***Maori Art Gallery*** at Tamaki Maori Village, also on SH5. For outdoor and camping equipment the ***Outdoorsman Headquarters***, 6 Tarawera Rd, T3459333, is the best in the city.

Directory **Airlines**: *Air NZ*, corner of Fenton and Hinemoa Sts, T3461001. **Banks**: All the major branches are in the town centre, on Hinemoa St. **Car Rental**: *Rent-A-Dent*, 14 Ti St, T3493993; ***Budget***, Fenton St, T3488127; ***NZ Link Rentals***, 108 Fenton St, T3491629. **Communications: Internet** is available at ***Nomads Cyber Café***, 1195 Fenton St, and ***Cybershed***, 1176 Pukuatua St. **Post Office**: Hinemoa St. Open Mon-Fri 0830-1700. **Cycle hire**: *Rotorua Cycle Centre*, 1120 Hinemoa St, T3486588; ***Lady Janes***, corner of Tutanekai and Whakaue Sts, T3479340; ***Cactus Jacks Backpackers***, Haupapa St, T3483121; ***Planet Bike***, T3489971; ***Pins Cycles***, 1275 Fenton St. **Medical Services**: **Doctor** 0800-2300, T3481000. **Money Exchange**: *Travelex*, VIC. Open daily 0830-1800, T3480373; ***Thomas Cook***, corner of Fenton and Hinemoa Sts. Open Mon-Fri 0900-1700, Sat 0930-1230, T3480640 **Police**: Fenton St, T3480099. **Taxis**: T3481111. **Useful addresses**: Amohau St, T3483069.

Around Rotorua

Blue & Green Lakes Southwest of the city, off SH30, Mount Tarawera Road takes you to some of the most celebrated lakes of the Rotorua region. The road runs adjacent to the Whakarewarewa Forest Park, before arriving at the **Blue** and **Green Lakes**. Blue Lake (Tikitapu) has a very cheery atmosphere and is used for boating and swimming and walking, with a very pleasant track that circumnavigates its shores, while Green Lake (Rotokakahi) is *tapu* (sacred) and off limits to all recreational activities, due to the fact that Motutawa Island was used as a former Maori burial ground.

Buried Village Past these two contrasting lakes the road enters the Te Wairoa Valley, home of the Buried Village. Prior to the 1886 eruption, the Te Wairoa Valley was the focus for Maori guided tourist trips to see the pink and white terraces at the foot of Mount Tarawera. The sudden and violent eruption of Tarawera on the evening of 10th June 1886 was witnessed by the tourists staying at the village hotel. Sadly for them and many of the settlers, this sight of the mountain was their last. Much of the area, the village and its hotel were laid waste with a blanket of rock and ash falls. Interestingly it was the Maori *whare* (houses) that fared better due to their stronger construction and steeply sloping roofs. There is a small and fascinating **museum** which relates the sorry tale, complete with everyday items excavated from the ash almost a century later. Of particular interest is the treatment of the poor Maori elder who, hours before the eruption, made the prediction it was about to blow. After the interior displays of the museum a pleasant walk takes you around the remains of some of the original buildings. To complete the walk you have the option of a 10-minute extension to see the 80 m Te Wairoa Falls. You can take a guided or a self-guided tour of the village. There's also the obligatory shop and café on-site. ■*Daily 0900-1700. Adult $12, child $4. The Santa Fe Shuttle leaves for the Buried Village from Rotorua daily at 0930, 1330 and 1530, $12 return, T3457997.*

Lake Tarawera

Lake Tarawera is almost the same size as Lake Rotorua and lies at the slightly higher elevation of 315 m. With a shoreline sparsely populated and almost entirely rimmed with bush, the lake has a pleasant atmosphere, dominated by the slopes of the jagged volcanic ridge of Mount Tarawera on its western shore. The lake has been altered in both shape and depth by Tarawera's eruptions over the centuries.

It was on Lake Tarawera on 31 May 1886 that two separate boat loads of tourists, on their way to see the then world-famous Pink and White Terraces (since obliterated), caught sight of a fully manned *waka* (war canoe) in the mists. Both the Maori and the *Pakeha* knew there was no such *waka* in the region and, due to the fact it was seen by so many independent eye witnesses, it was taken as a bad omen. Just eleven days later Tarawera erupted and the whole area was laid waste with the loss of 150 lives. Today the lake is an almost deceptive picture of serenity and is the venue for fishing and other water-based recreational activities. **Hot Water Beach** on its northern edge is a poplar spot where thermal activity creates an area of warm water.

Lake tours The best way to visit the beach and to take in the atmosphere and learn more of the area's diverse and, at times, violent history, is on board the *MV Reremoana*, a charming little launch which operates from the jetty just off Lake Tarawera Rd. A 2-hr cruise leaves daily at 1100 with a 30-min stop over (allowing about 45 mins to visit the shores of Lake Rotomahana – the former site of the 'pink' and 'white terraces'). From $27, child $13.50. Another 45-min scenic cruise leaves on demand until dusk (seasonal). T3628595. The smaller *SS James Torrey* operates out of Boat Shed Bay just a bit further along Mount Tarawera Rd and offers 3-hr and 45 minute cruises for $28, child $14 and $16, child $8. T3628698. The ***Landing Café***, opposite the jetty, is part of the launch business and is a fine venue for breakfast, lunch and dinner, T3628502.

There are 3 DOC campsites and numerous walking opportunities around Lake Tarawera, including the excellent Tarawera Falls Track *(see below)*

Mount Tarawera

For mountain activity operators *see page 248*

Standing at 1,111 m, with a 6 km converging gash of craters, is the dormant volcano Mount Tarawera. In looks it is very different to the higher, classic snow-capped cones of Ngauruhoe and Ruapehu in central North Island. Mount Tarawera is essentially a conglomerate of three mountains: Wahanga to the north, Ruawahia in the centre and Tarawera to the south. All three were obviously very different in appearance prior to their eruption in 1886.

A number of scenic helicopter flights and four-wheel drive tours give the tourist the opportunity to see its colourful interior, but generally speaking it is hard to access independently and is on Maori Reserve Land. Indeed, there is no public transport for miles around and, due perhaps more to greed than upkeep, conservation or tradition, independent access is almost actively discouraged, with the cost of climbing the summit now an insulting $24. If you

Around Rotorua

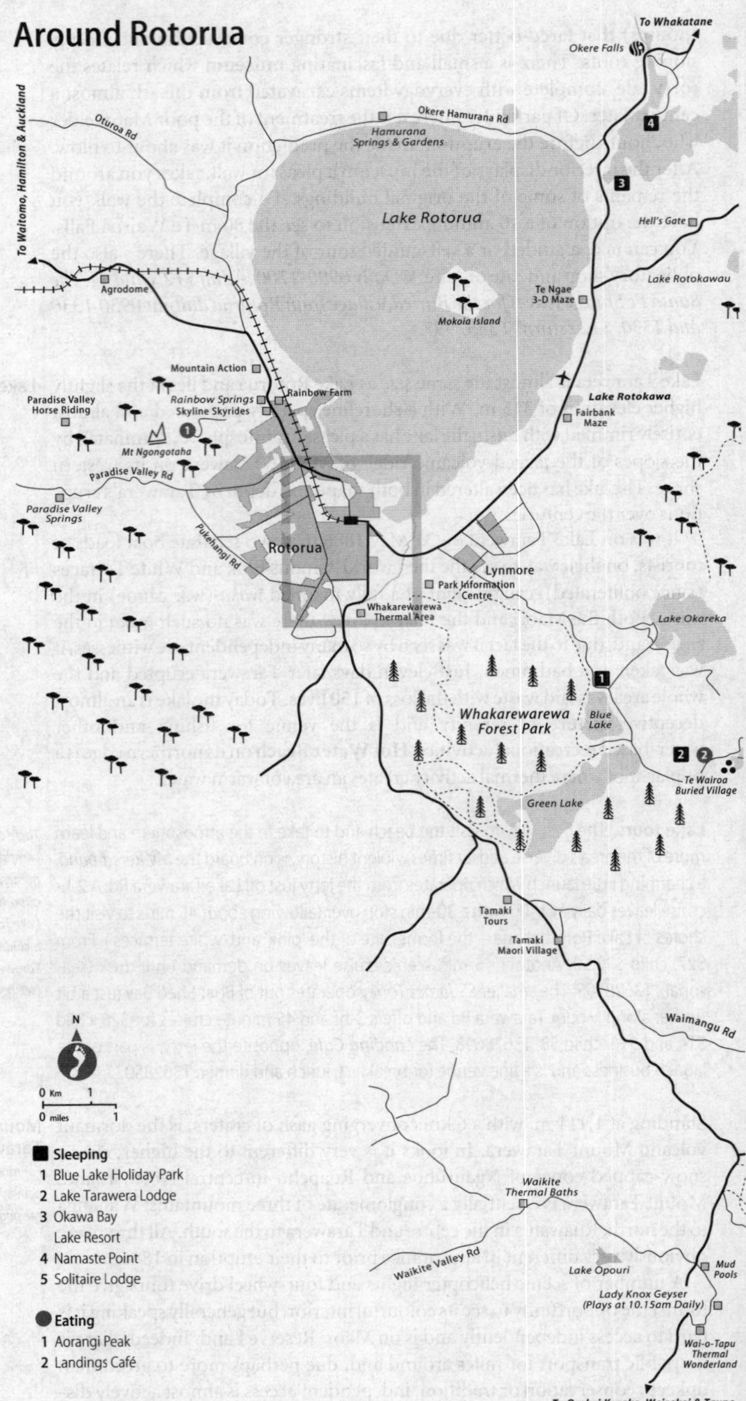

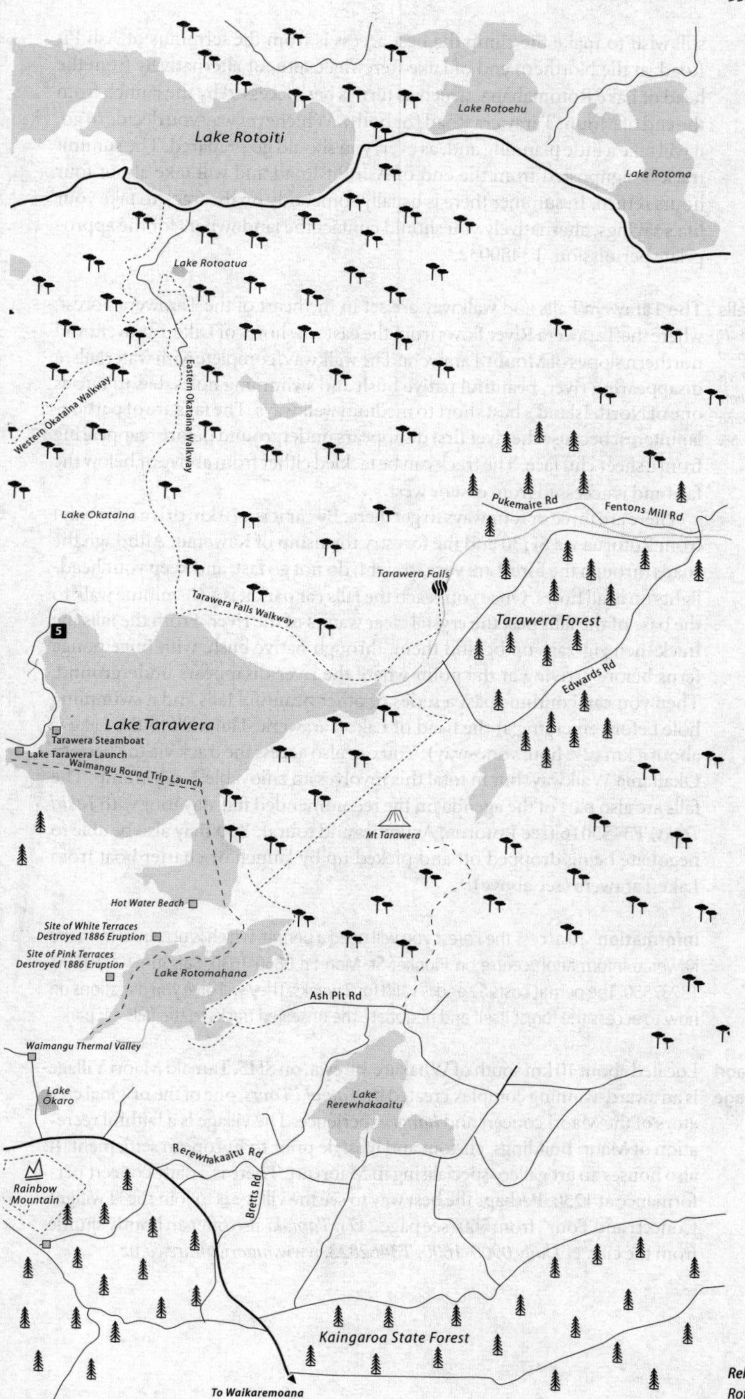

Related map
Roturua, page 242

still wish to make the climb the best access is from the terminus of Ash Pit Road, at the Northern end of Lake Rerewhakaaitu, or alternatively from the head of Lake Rotomahana, which in turn is best accessed by the launch from the end of Mount Tarawera Road (or both). Whichever way you decide to go, it will take a little planning and, as ever, you should go prepared. The summit track is signposted from the end of Ash Pit Road and will take about four hours return. In summer there is usually somebody on the track to take your life's savings, alternatively you should contact the landowners for the appropriate permission, T3480032.

Tarawera Falls

The falls are remote and hard to access, but this is part of their charm, and the effort is definitely worthwhile

The Tarawera Falls and walkway are set in the heart of the Tarawera Forest, where the Tarawera River flows from the eastern shores of Lake Tarawera and northern slopes of Mount Tarawera. The walkway, complete with waterfalls, a disappearing river, beautiful native bush and swimming holes, has to rate as one of North Island's best short to medium walkways. The falls are of particular interest because the river first disappears underground before reappearing from a sheer cliff face. The track can be tackled either from above or below the falls and is accessed from east or west.

There are three or four ways to get there. By car it is a 70 km drive (one way) from Rotorua via SH30 and the forestry township of Kawerau. Although the roads through the forest are very straight, do not go fast, and keep your headlights on at all times. Once you reach the falls car park it is a 10-minute walk to the base of the falls past the crystal clear waters of the river. From the falls the track then zig-zags up behind them, through native bush, with huge ponga ferns before arriving at the point where the river disappears underground. Then you can continue past a series of other beautiful falls and a swimming hole before emerging at the head of Lake Tarawera. The walk to the Lake is about 4 km (2½ hours one-way). You can also access the track via the Eastern Okaitania Walkway, but in total this involves an enjoyable 2-day tramp. The falls are also part of the agenda on the recommended full-day tour with ***Tekiri Treks***, T3455016 (see Rotorua, Activities and tours). You may also be able to negotiate being dropped off and picked up by launch or charter boat from Lake Tarawera (see above).

Information To access the Forest you will need a permit, which is obtained from the Kawerau Information centre on Plunket St. Mon-Fri 0830-1630, Sat/Sun 1000-1500. T3237550. The permit costs $2 and is valid for 2 weeks. They will give you directions on how to access the forest itself and negotiate the unsealed tracks to the falls car park.

Tamaki Maori Village

Located about 10 km south of Whakarewarewa, on SH5, Tamaki Maori Village is an award-winning complex created by *Tamaki Tours*, one of the original creators of the Maori concert and *hangi* experience. The village is a faithful recreation of Maori buildings, custom and lifestyle prior to European settlement. It also houses an art gallery specialising in Maori art. There is a daily concert performance at 1230. Perhaps the best way to see the village is to join the 'Twilight Concert and Tour', from $60 (see page 247). *Tamaki* also offer an hourly shuttle from the city. ■ *Daily 0900-1600. T3462823, www.maoriculture.co.nz*

Wai-O-Tapu
The park is 29 km south of Rotorua off SH5 and is not to be confused with the Waimangu Thermal Valley, which is about 4 km before it

Wai-O-Tapu is, without doubt, the best thermal park in the region, with an almost surreal and colourful range of volcanic features, from mud pools and silica terraces to the famous and beautiful 'Champagne Pool'. If you can, time your arrival with the daily 1015 eruption of the **Lady Knox Geyser**, which is signposted on the Wai-O-Tapu Loop Road (off SH5).

Just before the Geyser, again on the Loop Road, are a number or globulous mud pools that are separate from the park itself. These, too, are worth a peek. The thermal park proper is at the southern end of the Loop Road. The full self-guided walk around the park will take about two hours. Along the first section of track there are a number of features including steaming caverns, mud pools and cavernous holes, with evocative names like **Devil's Home** (good one for that photo), the **Devil's Ink Pots** and **Thunder Crater.** The track then arrives at a lookout across the aptly named **Artist's Palette,** a multi-coloured silica field. It really is a wonderful sight to behold with pastel shades of yellow, green and blue, fading in and out of swathes of billowing white steam. A boardwalk takes you across the silica fields, where you can either go on to investigate a silica waterfall, some 'alum cliffs', 'frying pan flat' and some colourful lakes, or (more likely) get entirely engrossed with the **Champagne Pool**. This is hard to describe, but essentially is a bright orange edged, steaming, fizzing pool of about 60 m in diameter. Without doubt it is the highlight of the park and certainly rates as a ten out of ten on the 'awesometer'. What you are looking at is in fact a 62 m-deep flooded volcanic vent, the base of which boils the water to a surface temperature of around 74°C. Hot stuff. From the Champagne Pool it is a short meander past more steaming, gurgling crevasses and a pastel green lake, before returning to the visitors centre. The visitors centre also has a shop and café. ■ *Daily 0830-1700. Adult $13, child $4. T3485179, www.geyserland.co.nz*

Although it is expensive, another excellent way to see Wai-O-Tapu is with a five-minute flight by helicopter: a good way to see all the colours of the park combined. Contact *Heli-Kiwi*, T3666611. Flights are about $45 for five minutes. The base is just next to the car park.

Waimangu Volcanic Valley
The Waimangu Volcanic Valley is 26 km south of Rotorua, off SH5

The volcanic features here are all very recent and were created as a result of the 1886 eruption of Tarawera. Lake Rotomahana is essentially a water-filled crater which, before the eruption, was once the site of the famed pink and white silica terraces. Sadly, both of the terraces were completely obliterated by the eruption, but what were created in their place are the lake and a number of new volcanic features around it. These include the **Waimangu Cauldron** – the world's largest boiling lake – the **Inferno Crater Lake** that rises and falls up to 10 m a month, steaming cliffs, and numerous boiling springs and steaming fumeroles. At the turn of the last century the now inactive **Waimangu Geyser** used to be the largest in the world, spouting water to a staggering 500 m. The park is self-guided and is seen partly by foot and partly by boat. ■ *Daily 0830-1700. There is a walk only or walk and boat option from $20, child $5. T3666137.*

The **Waikite Thermal Pools** are located off SH5, between the Waimangu and Wai-O-Tapu thermal reserves. They consist of large family and adult hot pools in a country setting. Ideal for family picnics. Private pools are also available. From SH5 turn west on to Waikite Valley Road at the Waiotapu Tavern. The pools are about 4 km on the right. ■ *Daily 1000-2200. T3331861, from $4, child $2.*

Hell's Gate The aptly named Hell's Gate thermal reserve is located 15 km from Rotorua on SH30 towards Whakatane. It is not the most colourful of the reserves, but certainly one of the most active, and a thoroughly steamy affair. The 10-ha reserve is set on two levels separated by a tract of bush, yet subtly connected by a warm thermal stream, complete with steaming waterfall. The pools of bubbly mud and water on the lower levels, with such evocative names as 'Sodom and Gomorrah' and 'The Inferno', hiss with menace and are quite scary, reaching temperatures well over 100°C.

The upper level of the reserve is not much better, with steaming lakes and a myriad of tiny steaming vents, scattered with features including mini mud volcanoes, and cauldrons of boiling water. Best of all is the **Devil's Cauldron**, a small pit that is home to a lively globular mud pool which makes the most wonderfully disgusting noises. Thankfully the entire reserve is connected with a boardwalk, from which, for obvious reasons, you are encouraged not to stray. There is a small shop and café on site selling postcards. ■ *Daily 0900-1700. No guided tours, but informative leaflet provided. T3453151. Adult $10, child $5. The Santa Fe Shuttle leaves for Hell's Gate from Rotorua daily at 0930,1330 and 1530, $15 return, T3457997.*

On the way to Hell's Gate you may like to stop at one of the two maze gardens. The **Fairbank Maze** is 9 km from the city on SH30 East, opposite the airport. It is the country's largest hedge maze with a pathway of over 1 ½ km, set amongst pleasant gardens with ponds and birdlife. The **Te Ngae Park 3D Maze** is 3 km further east on SH30. This is a timber maze, slightly longer than the hedge maze and once again set in bush and pleasant surroundings. ■ *0900-1700. Adult $5, child $2.50. T3455275.*

Agrodome
Try to attend the busiest show: mid-morning or mid-afternoon

The Agrodome Complex, 10 km north of Rotorua on SH5, is a principal tourist attraction on the Rotorua circuit, and deservingly so. It has a wide array of attractions from the full-on bungy jump to some more sedate farm activities. The focus of the complex and its principal feature attraction is the **Sheep Show**. If the very thought of such an event leaves you cold, then think again: it is highly entertaining. This ovine spectacular features over 19 breeds of sheep – all of which are highly domesticated, wonderfully tame and co-operative. Before the show starts the 'stars' are available for copious stroking, and perhaps an autograph if you're lucky. The actual animal show is very informative, entertaining and professional. There is much audience participation and the opportunity to see a sheep fully shorn and bottle-feed lambs. As for the audience, well, they are almost as entertaining, as they attempt to video the entire show.

Surrounding the Agrodome there are a wealth of activities including a **farm tour** (optional extension to the sheep show, combo $20, child $10), **bungy jumping** (43 m, $99), **helicopter rides** (from $69) and **jet boats** ($35, child $25), as well as the '**Swoop**', '**Zorbing**', and '**Dirthingz**'. The 'Swoop' is a glorified swing, whereby you are strapped into a body harness then dropped from a height of 40 m. Apparently somewhere on the way down you reach over 130 kph, with a G-force of three, which roughly translated means your kidneys seek an unexpected and rapid exit out of your back passage. However, it all seems to go down very well ($45, child $30). 'Zorbing' is the unique New Zealand invention of rolling down a hill in a large clear plastic bubble, filled, if you so wish (though God knows why), with a bucket or six of water. It is highly entertaining, but a bit of a rip-off as the entire episode lasts about ten seconds and costs $40. 'Dirthingz' are essentially motorized skateboards on which you hurtle around a paddock dodging cowpats ($35). There is a shop and café on site. ■ *Agrodome is open daily. Shows at 0930, 1100 and 1430. Show only $13, child $6.50.* T3574350, www.agrodome.co.nz

Trout Springs

The Rotorua region is rich in freshwater springs, the streams from which are home to thousands of both brown and rainbow trout. Trout are not native to New Zealand and were introduced to the region in the 1800s. Some of these springs have been developed into tourist resorts where you can observe both wild and captive trout above and below the water or feed the swirling masses. Some streams are also home to the unbelievably huge native New Zealand eels.

The largest and most popular springs resort is **Rainbow Valley Springs**, which are 5 km from the city centre on SH5 north. Here the attraction of the trout is mixed with additional wildlife attractions, including kiwi and other native birds in a free-flight aviary. The underwater viewing area is particularly popular. There are also fluffy farm animals for the kids to stroke. There are regular guided tours of the park, farm animal shows and a café on site. ■ *0800-1700 (1930 in summer). $18, child $7. T3460641.*

The smaller but quite charming **Paradise Valley Springs** are 11 km from the city along Claydon Road which is straight on at the Koutu Corner intersection, as you head north out of the city on the Old Taupo Road. The attraction is very much the same, with the same features (with added lions), but it enjoys a quieter, more congenial atmosphere. There is also a small bottling plant which utilises the pure spring water. ■ *Daily 0800-dusk. $14, child $7. T3489667.*

Skyline Skyrides

There is a night luge which is only for the insane

If you are physically able, everyone who visits Rotorua should call in to the Skyline Skyrides to take a ride up the mountain in the gondolas and have a go on the infamous **Luge**, which is basically throwing yourself down a concrete course on a plastic tray with wheels and primitive brakes. Once down, and if still alive, you can then hitch a ride on a secondary chairlift to repeat the operation. You are given brief instructions, a plastic helmet and a chance to try the 'family' course first, just to get the hang of it. This is very slow – so much so that you can have a conversation with complete strangers, if not tea and cakes on the way down – and once completed you can attempt the main course with its savage turns and precipitous jumps. As well as the Luge and scenic gondola there is a far less exciting 'sidewinder' metal track and a flight simulator, as well as helicopter trips and a scenic restaurant, with a memorable view across the city and lake. ■ *Daily from 0900 until late. Gondola and 5 rides $24, child $18, T3470027.*

Whirinaki Forest Park

Whirinaki Forest Park is one of New Zealand's finest remaining podocarp forests, aptly described by one famous botanist as a 'dinosaur forest'. The park is off the beaten track but that is part of its charm. There are a number of excellent walking tracks taking in the diverse remote forest landscape with giant trees, waterfalls, river valleys and lagoons. There are DOC campsites and huts within the park to allow longer multi-day tramps. For detailed information of how to access this excellent forest park contact DOC in Rotorua, or better still call in at the DOC Field Centre on the main road in Murupara, which is the nearest township lying at the northern edge of the park, T3661080. Murupara is about 60 km southwest of Rotorua on SH38 (Waikaremoana road off SH5). For organized walking tours within Whirinaki, contact Nature Connections, Rotorua, T3471705, half-day from $70 (see page 281).

Tauranga

Phone code: 07
Population: 88,000
Being a principal destination on the celebrated Pacific Coast Highway, as well as a fine place in which to base yourself, an extended stay in Tauranga, can only be recommended

Tauranga has enjoyed tremendous growth in recent years. So much so that it is used as a barometer to the general state of the economy and national real estate prices. As well as its thriving commercial and business centre, busy port (the name means 'sheltered anchorage') and rich horticultural farmland, it seems Tauranga is also proving the ideal place in which to enjoy the archetypal Kiwi lifestyle. With the combination of location, climate, attractive beaches and the many associated activities, as well as its proximity to the delights of Rotorua, it has much to offer both the native and the visitor. Dominating the scene is the harbour and of course the volcanic dome of Mount Maunganui to the north, which guards its precarious entrance. Nowadays there are almost as many cruise liners negotiating that narrow entrance as there are merchant ships, and the town's tourist allure seems almost set to overtake its popularity with the natives.

Ins and outs

Getting there
Tauranga is located on SH2, 210 km, southeast of Auckland and 83 km north of Rotorua

Tauranga is a major destination on the signposted **Pacific Coast Highway**, which connects Auckland with Napier in the Hawkes Bay. Tauranga **airport** is located 4 km east of the city centre and is served daily by ***Air New Zealand Link***, T0800-737000, and ***Origin Pacific***, T0800-302302. A taxi to the airport costs about $10. ***Intercity***, T5777285, and ***Newmans* buses** operate daily services to most North Island destinations arriving and departing from the VICs in the city and Mount Maunganui. Both VICs handle bookings and ticketing. ***Supa-Travel*** are a local company that offer a daily service (except Sat) to Hamilton, Rotorua and Auckland (connecting with ***Northliner*** services to Northland). They also operate from both Tauranga and Mount Manganui VICs, T5710583. ***Call-A-Bus*** offer a similar daily mini-bus service to Auckland, T0800-100550, www.callabus.co.nz

Bay of Plenty

Getting around Tauranga city centre is fairly compact and easily negotiable by foot. ***Newloves*** are the local suburban bus company operating regular daily services to Mount Maunganui. They depart from the corner of Wharf and Willow St beside the VIC, T5786453; $3 one way. ***Te Puke*** Bus Services serve Te Puke via Papamoa, and depart from Wharf St, T5736949; $4.50 one way. For Car Rental and Taxi Companies see Directory, below.

Information The Tauranga **Visitors Information Centre** is at 95 Willow St, T5788103, F5787020, www.tauranga.govt.nz Open Mon-Fri 0700-1730, Sat/Sun 0800-1600. For quick reference be sure to avail yourself of the free 'What's to See and Do' leaflet. DOC is located at 253 Chadwick Rd, Greertown, T/F5787677. Open Mon-Fri 0800-1630.

History

The shores were already quite heavily settled by the Maori by the time Captain James Cook passed the area on his circumnavigation of New Zealand in 1769. The earliest European settlement took the form of several flax traders and the missionaries of 'The Elms' mission that was established on the Te Papa Peninsula in 1834. Due to inter-tribal warfare this mission was temporarily abandoned before enjoying resurgence from 1838. With the gathering momentum of the Maori King Movement in the Waikato region in the early 1860's the government set about blocking supply routes from outlying areas of the East Coast. Troops were dispatched and redoubts built on the Te Papa Peninsula. With such a build up of forces it was perhaps inevitable that conflict would ensue, and the first major battle with the Ngaiterangi Maori occurred at Gate *Pa* in April 1864. As a result of the conflict and government victory, over 20,000 ha of land were confiscated and a military presence remained to secure the peace. From this point, as road access improved, settlement grew steadily. It is only in recent years, with the development of the port and the obvious attractions of the 'lifestyle' element, that the population has boomed.

Tauranga orientation

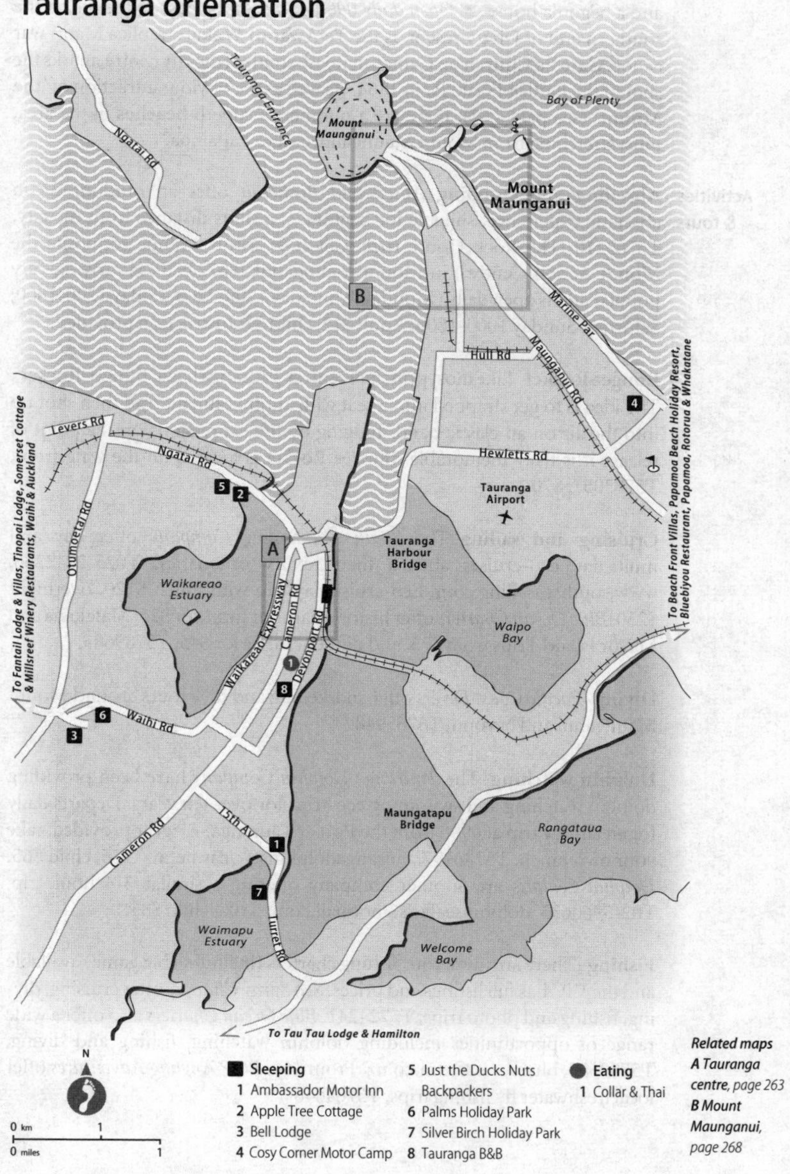

Related maps
***A Tauranga centre**, page 263*
***B Mount Maunganui**, page 268*

Sights

The main historical attraction in Tauranga is the **Elms Mission House** set amidst pleasant grounds on Mission Street, on the Te Papa Peninsula, which was the site of the original mission, established in 1834. *Open Sun 1400-1600. $5.* Nearby in **Robbins Park** on Cliff Road on the eastern side of the peninsula are the remnants of the **Monmouth Redoubt**, built by government forces during the New Zealand Wars. The gardens have rose gardens and a begonia house. ■ *Open daily 0900-1800.* At the base of the hill, at the southern end of Dive Cresent, is the **Te Awanui Waka**, a replica Maori war canoe. **Gate Pa Church** on Cameron Road, south of the city centre, marks the spot of the Battle of Gate *Pa* in 1864. As well as the obvious attraction of '**the Mount**' (see page 267), there are a number of superb **beaches** in the area, most stretching from Mount Maunganui east to Papamoa.

Activities & tours

Abseiling and climbing *Abseil and Bushcraft* offer an outdoor 25 m abseiling experience, suitable for beginners, a short distance from the city, T5765410. The Rock House rock wall at 9 Triton Avenue (opposite the Mount Action Centre), in Mount Maunganui, T5724920, is proving very popular and is open daily (Monday-Thursday 1200-2200, Friday 1200-1800, Saturday/Sunday 1000-1800. Adult $12, child $7. Instruction provided.

Bungee Rocket Like most principal centres Tauranga has a 'Bungee Rocket'. The idea is to get strapped into a seat with another lunatic and then shot up into the air on an elastic band. Judging by the expressions on the point of release it is truly memorable. Bungee Rocket is located on the waterfront, T5783057; $70.

Cruising and sailing The *South Sea Sailing Company* offer day and multi-day eco-cruises aboard their luxury catamaran, T025-2242266, www.southseasailing.com Eco-cruise day trip with lunch $120, overnight $250. *Blue Ocean Charters* offer historic harbour tours for $25, Matakana and Mayor Island Trips from $75, and dinner cruises for $45, T5789685.

Diving *Pacific Coast Divers* offer snorkelling and dive tours around Mount Maunganui and beyond, T5765948.

Dolphin watching The *Tauranga Dolphin Company* have been providing dolphin watching and swimming eco-trips for over ten years. Departs daily for an all-day trip at 0900 from the Port at Tauranga. All gear provided, take your own lunch, T5783197, taurangadolphins@clear.net.nz $85, child $65. *Dolphin Seafaris* are another company offering a similar 3-4 hour trip, T02-5960633, dolphinseafaris@hotmail.com $100, child $85

Fishing There are numerous fishing charters (including big game) available and the VIC has full listings and prices. *Sea Spray Charters* offer cruising, diving, fishing and photo trips, T5724241. *Blue Ocean Charters* also offer a wide range of opportunities including dolphin watching, fishing and diving, T5789685, blueocean@xtra.co.nz From $60. *BOP Angling Adventures* offer local freshwater fly fishing trips, T5764646

Four-wheel drive and quad biking *Hill Hoppers* are one of the region's best four-wheel drive activity operators and are based in Te Puke. They have over 3 km of track and a wide range of vehicles. Suitable for the novice and owner, T5331818, www.adventure4wd.co.nz From $55, child $25. *Argo Adventures*, based at the Athenree Pancake House and restaurant, SH2, offer bush rides on eight-wheel drive vehicles, T5492520. From $10.

Golf There are a number of good courses in the area, including the *Tauranga Golf Club*, Cameron Road, T5788465, and the *Mount Maunganui Club*, Fairway Avenue, T5754487.

Horse trekking *Papamoa Adventure Park*, 1162 Welcome Bay Road, T5420972; *Faraway Farm*, No 3 Road, Te Puke, T5735400 (accommodation available); *World of Horses*, SH2 between Tauranga and Katikati, offer trekking, display corral, show stable and café, T5480404; *Windsong*, 161 Peers Road, Owanawa (off SH29 west), is a miniature horse stud and training centre offering tours and displays, T5433132.

Hot air ballooning *Max's balloon Adventures*, 41 Strathmore Drive, Katikati, T5491614.

Tauranga centre

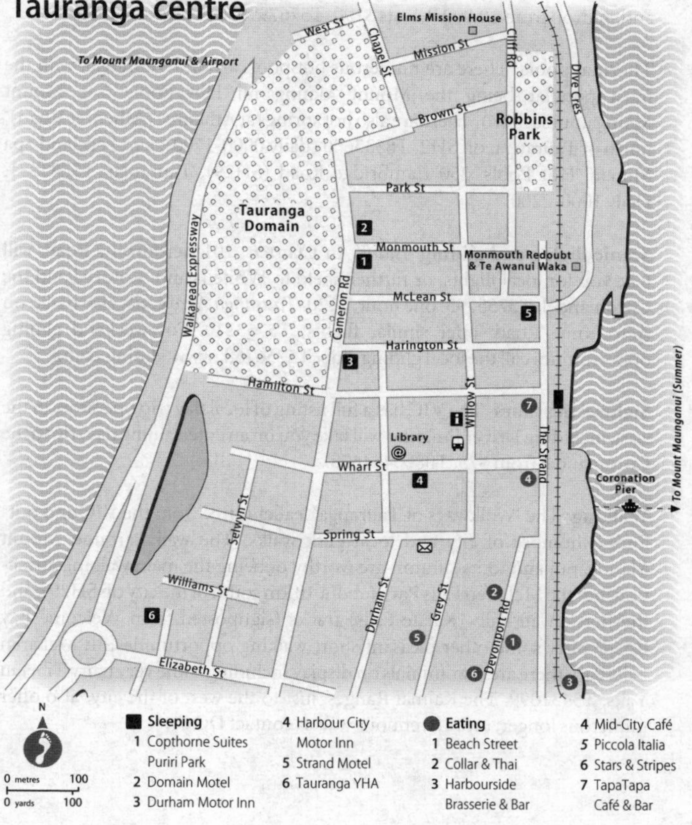

Jetboating and jet skiing Longridge Park, in Te Pukes offer a thrilling jet boat ride amongst its many activities and attractions, T5331515. $59, child $35. Jet skis can be hired from *Bay Marine*, T5776005; *Bay Jet Ski*, T02-5844062; and *Tauranga Jet Skis*, T02-5520865.

Kayaking *Waimarino Adventure Park*, Bethlehem, T5764233, www.kayaks.co.nz, offers a range of guided and self-guided day trips. *Sea Kayak Tranquility*, based in Tauranga, do harbour, lake and moonlight trips, T02-5542866.

Mountain biking Oropi Grove, 3 km up Oropi Road from SH28 – accessed off Joyce Road (off Pyes Pa Road) – is considered the best track in the area, T5773055.

Para-sailing and water-skiing *Parasail BOP* offer 'the lift of a lifetime' and the 'dry' or 'the dunk', T5747333. 15-minute flight.

Rafting The Wairoa and Rangitaiki Rivers near Tauranga are major venues for white-water rafting. For operators see page 248.

Tandem skydiving *Tauranga Tandem Skydiving* is located at the airport and. A drop from 10,000 ft costs $190. T5767990, freefall@xtra.co.nz

Thermal pools There are numerous hot pools around Tauranga, with the most popular being the Mount Maunganui Hot Pools (see Mount Maunganui section). There are also hot springs at Athenree (Athenree Road), north of Tauranga, on SH2, T8635600 (daily 0900-1700); and Fernland Spa Mineral Hot Pools, 250 Cambridge Road (SH29), Tauranga, T5783081. Daily 1000-2200.

Scenic flights and gliding *Island Air Charters*, 101 Aerodrome Road, will take you for local flights, or further afield to White Island, Rotorua and the Coromandel, T5755795; one hour, $120. *Tauranga Aero Club*, also based on Aerodrome Road, offer similar flights, T5753210. For weekend gliding opportunities call the local gliding club, T5756768, www.gliding.co.nz

Sightseeing tours The VIC has a full listing of local day trip operators in the area, including Driver Jim, who will take you on an entertaining day trip to the Coromandel from $75, T0800454678.

Walking The 'Walkways of Tauranga' leaflet is free from the VIC and outlines a number of city and local park walks. The walks around Mount Maunganui and to its summit are worthy of being the main walking attraction, but the McLaren Falls Park (about 10 km south of the city on SH29), and the Rerekawau Falls (Kaiate Falls) tracks (signposted from Welcome Bay Road) offer some other pleasant short walking opportunities. In McLaren Falls Park there are also animals on display including some very hairy Tibetan Yaks, T5431099. The Kaimai Ranges, just to the west of the city, also offer numerous longer, more strenuous walks (contact DOC).

Essentials

Sleeping

There is plenty of choice in Tauranga City and Mount Maunganui, but it's best to book ahead in mid-summer when the area is hugely popular with Kiwi holidaymakers

LL *Fantail Lodge and Villas*, 117 Rea Rd, T5491581, F5491417, www.fantaillodge.co.nz Located 25 mins north of the city, this country lodge estate, which consistently rates in the country's top ten, offers all-suite luxury accommodation in beautiful surroundings. Fine cuisine. **LL** *Tinopai Lodge*, 20 Tinopai Dr, Omokoroa, T5481515, F5481525, www.tinopai.com A 14-acre waterfront property with views across the harbour. Beautifully appointed suites and fine facilities including hot pools, gym and golf. Fine cuisine. **L-AL** *Taiparoro House B&B*, 11 Fifth Av, T5779607, F5779264, kl.kelly@clear.net.nz Historic 1882 restored villa close to the city centre. Range of rooms and suites, all en suite. Organic food a speciality. **L-AL** *Copthorne Suites Puriri Park*, 32 Cameron Rd, T5771480, F5771490. Tauranga's principal centrally located hotel. Wide range of modern rooms and facilities.

AL-A *Tau Tau Lodge*, 1133 Pyes Pa Rd, T5431600, F5431601, jevkerry@wave.co.nz New, good-value boutique lodge located between Rotorua and Tauranga in elevated bush setting. Private en suites and spa. **A** *Tauranga B&B*, 4 Ninth Ave, T5770927, F5770954. Comfortable and friendly, affordable and centrally located. **A** *Beach Front Villas*, 535 Papamoa Beach Rd, T/F5720816, www.papamoabeach.co.nz Although a few miles from Tauranga in Papamoa, this complex and villas are on the beachfront and recommended.

C-D *Bell Lodge*, 39 Bell St, SH2 North (Waihi Rd), T5786344. Very smart purpose-built complex located north of the city in park surroundings. Large kitchen and comfortable en suite rooms or dorms, open fire, tent sites. Free trips and bikes. **C-D** *Tauranga YHA*, 171 Elizabeth St, T5785064, F5785040, yhataur@yha.org.nz Well-established hostel, comfortable, friendly and centrally located. Twin, doubles, dorm and camping options. Internet. **D** *Just the Ducks Nuts Backpackers*, 6 Vale St, T5761366. Small, but with a name like that an inevitably popular, laid-back hostel with usual facilities including an open fire and bike hire. **D** *Apple Tree Cottage*, 47 Maxwells Rd, T5767404. Small private house located on the edge of the harbour about 1 km from the city centre. Quiet, relaxed and friendly.

Motels **AL** *Durham Motor Inn*, corner of Cameron Rd and Harrington St, T5779691, F5779635. One of the best motels in the city centre. 20 clean modern units, pool and spas. **AL-A** *Harbour City Motor Inn*, 50 Wharf St, T5711435, F5711438, taurangaharbourcity@xtra.co.nz One of the city's newest upper-range motels, ideally located with well appointed rooms and fine facilities. **A** *Ambassador Motor Inn*, 9 Fifteenth Av, T5785665, F5785226, ambassador.tga@xtra.co.nz New motel at the estuary end of the Av. Wide range of units, spa and heated pool. **A-B** *Domain Motel*, corner of Monmouth St and Cameron Rd, T5789479, F5781912. Mid-range option close to city centre. **B** *Strand Motel*, 27 The Strand, T/F5785807, strandmotel@xtra.co.nz Comfortable, basic, budget motel located close to all amenities.

Motor camps and campsites There are a number of motor camps in the city, with the *Silver Birch Holiday Park*, 101 Turret Rd, SH2, T/F5784603, and the *Palms Holiday Park*, 162 Waihi Rd, T/F5789337, being adequate options. **A-D** *Top Ten Papamoa Beach Holiday Resort*, 535 Papamoa Beach Rd, T/F5720816. A fine absolute beachfront camp with fine facilities.

Eating

Tauranga has a fine selection of restaurants and cafes to suit all tastes and budgets. Most are located on or around The Strand over looking the harbour

Expensive The ***Harbourside Brasserie and Bar*** enjoys a loyal following and the reputation as Tauranga's best restaurant. Located as much on the water as beside it at the southern end of The Strand, it offers an excellent and imaginative all-day blackboard and à la carte menu, with an emphasis on local seafood. Open 1130-late, T0800-721714. Away from the city centre, at 30 Bethlehem Road, is the ***Somerset Cottage Restaurant***, a small, congenial place serving a classic range of international cuisine to suit a wide range of tastes. Bookings essential, T5766889. For lunch and dinner, another out-of-town option are the culinary delights of the ***Millsreef Winery and Restaurant*** which is renowned for its good food, especially of the sea and with gills variety. Open daily from 1000, T5768844. ***The Bluebiyou***, 559 Papamoa Beach Rd, T572209, which is right next to the beach in Papamoa, is also great if you want to get away from the city. Open daily from 1100.

Mid-range *Piccola Italia*, 107 Grey St, T5788363, is a fine Italian restaurant that combines excellent cuisine, congenial authentic atmosphere, fine service and a great Italian wine list. It has a popular local following. Open Wed-Fri 1130-1430, Mon-Sat from 1800. Back on the waterfront ***Beach Street***, 82 Devonport Rd, is another fine choice overlooking the harbour. It offers imaginative traditional dishes and great pizzas. Open daily from 1000-late, T5780745. For Thai food you can't go wrong at the ***Collar and Thai***, Goddards Centre, 21 Devonport Rd, T5776655. Open Mon-Fri 1130-1400, Mon-Sun 1730-late. For good Indian food the ***Talk of India***, corner of Cameron Rd and Third Av, T5787360, is the oldest and reputedly the most popular. Open daily.

Cheap *TapaTapa Café and Bar*, 67 The Strand, offers a fine combination of Pacific Rim and European dishes in a café atmosphere. Open daily, T5788741. ***The Stars and Stripes***, Shop 1 and 2 West Plaza, Devonport Rd, has a good selection of traditional steak and burgers at affordable prices, T5771319. For a range of great lunchtime snacks, a fine cheap breakfast and fairly good coffee try the popular ***Shiraz Café***, Wharf St, T5770059. Open Mon-Sat from 1100.

Entertainment & pubs

The Crown and Badger, on the corner of Wharf and The Strand, is a popular spot especially on sunny evenings when the clientele spills out on to the street. ***Flannagan's Irish Pub***, 14 Hamilton St, T5789222, is another good pub with regular gigs, especially at weekends. The ***Harrington Nightclub*** is on Harrington St. The ***Grumpy Mole***, 41 The Strand, T5711222, is another very wooden pub and entertainment venue that has a 'hump-day' every week, whatever that is supposed to mean.

Events

Jan: Brightstone Blues Brews and Barbecues; outdoor performances with both national and international celebrities, mixed with boutique brewery product and barbecue food; **Port of Tauranga Half-Iron Man**; hailed as the country's premier Half-Iron Man event attracting over one thousand national and mainly Australian competitors.

Feb: **Tauranga Food and Wine Festival**; a celebration of fine local and national food and wine.

Mar: **Zespri Lifestyles Festival of Tauranga**; held over the entire month, local, national and international events cover beach and surf, harbour and sailing, art exhibitions and shows, food, wine, shopping, sports and leisure activities.

Apr: **Montana National Jazz Festival**; considered (after Waiheke Auckland perhaps) to be the country's premier national jazz event, performed in the Baycourt Theatre, bars and cafés.

Oct/Nov: **Arts Festival Tauranga**; biennial event from 2001 with street performers, dance, theatre, exhibitions and literary events.

Nov: **Décor Greenworld Garden and Arts Festival**; another biennial event held early in the month and alternates with the Arts Festival and held over one weekend.

Whakaari (White Island)

White Island, 50 km offshore in the Bay of Plenty, is currently New Zealand's only constantly erupting volcano, and part of the Taupo Volcanic Zone. Thought to be between 100,000 and 200,000 years old, what is seen above sea level is only one third of the island's actual size. Although the highest point is only 321 m above sea level, in actuality it is higher than Mount Ruapehu in the central North Island. The vent is actually below sea level but shielded from flooding by high crater walls. The crater is continually active with almost constant steam (which can be seen from the mainland) and occasional ash and rock eruptions. Around the crater there are boiling pools, steam fumeroles, lakes of acid, sulphur holes and geysers. Between 1899 and 1934, when major activity was not forcing occasional closure, the White Island Products Company extracted sulphur and gypsum in commercial quantities. In 1914 the first factory was destroyed and a group of 11 men were obliterated when another major eruption, occurred. These days the island is uninhabited but home to numerous seabirds and hardy species of plants that cling to its unstable slopes. The island is privately owned but open to tourist operators in Rotorua, Tauranga and Whakatane (see the relevant Activities sections). The volcano is closely monitored and activity fluctuates. Many believe White Island is due for another major eruption but don't let that deter you from a visit; there would probably be plenty of warning. The Island was named White Island (for obvious reasons) by (guess who) Captain Cook in 1769. The Maori name Whakaari means 'uplifted to view'.

Regional gardens are opened to the public and visual art exhibitions are staged throughout the city.

Directory

Banks: All the major branches have offices and ATMs in the city centre. **Car Rental**: ***Avis*** 69 2nd Av, T5783911; ***Budget***, Intercity Building, Dive Cres, T5785156; ***Johnny's Rentals***, 115 Hewletts Rd, T5759204; ***Rite Price Rentals***, 25 Totara St, Mt Maunganui, T0800-250251. **Communications**: **Internet**: Tauranga Library, Willow St, Maunganui Library, Maunganui Rd; ***Cybersurf***, Piccadilly Arcade, Grey St; ***Tapa Tapa***, The Strand, T5788741. **Post Office**: 17 Grey St. Open Mon-Fri 0830-1700, Sat 0900-1200. **Cycle Hire**: ***Bike and Pack Warehouse***, Dee St, Mt Maunganui, T5752189; ***Gravities Edge Cycles***, Maunganui Rd, Mt Maunganui, T5758997. **Medical Services**: Baycare, 10th St, T5788000. Open 1700-0800. Hospital, Cameron Rd, T5798000 **Taxis**: ***Tauranga Taxis***, T5786086.

Mount Maunganui

Dominated by its namesake **'Mount'** and graced by golden **beaches**, Mount Maunganui, 6 km north of Tauranga, has held an irresistible appeal to both locals and visitors for years. In winter the town is quiet, its streets and beach almost empty, but in summer and particularly over the New Year, the place is a tourist battleground with the Mount crowned with an army of view junkies and the beach with battalions of soporific sunbathers. The Mount itself (also known as 'Mauao') is 232m in height and guards the entrance to the Tauranga Harbour.

Ins & outs

Getting there **By bus** ***Intercity***, ***Newmans*** and the local operator ***Supa-Travel*** serve Mount Maunganui. For information and ticketing contact the VIC. ***Newloves*** is the local suburban bus company in Tauranga operating regular daily services to Mount Maunganui. They depart from the corner of Wharf and Willow St in Tauranga,

T5786453; $3 one way. There is a bridge toll of $1 to get across to Mount Maunganui. Seasonal ferries run between Tauranga's waterfront and Mount Maunganui and cost around $6.

The Mount Maunganui **Visitor Information Centre** is on Salisbury Av, T5755099. Open Mon-Fri 0900-1700, Sat/Sun 0900-1600. **Internet** is available at the *Mount Backpackers*, 87 Maunganui Rd.

Sights Once an island and an almost impregnable Maori *Pa*, the Mount now serves as an obvious tourist attraction and a landmark for ships negotiating the harbour's treacherous entrance. There is a network of pathways which criss-cross the Mount, offering a range of pleasant walks to suit all levels of fitness. The summit climb, which is best accessed to the south of the motor camp, takes about 45 minutes one-way and, as you might expect, is rewarded with a memorable view.

From the narrow neck of the Mount, **Ocean Beach** begins a stretch of sand that sweeps almost uninterrupted, east to the Cape. Just offshore from Ocean beach are the two small islands Moturiki and Motuotau. Moturiki can be

Mount Maunganui

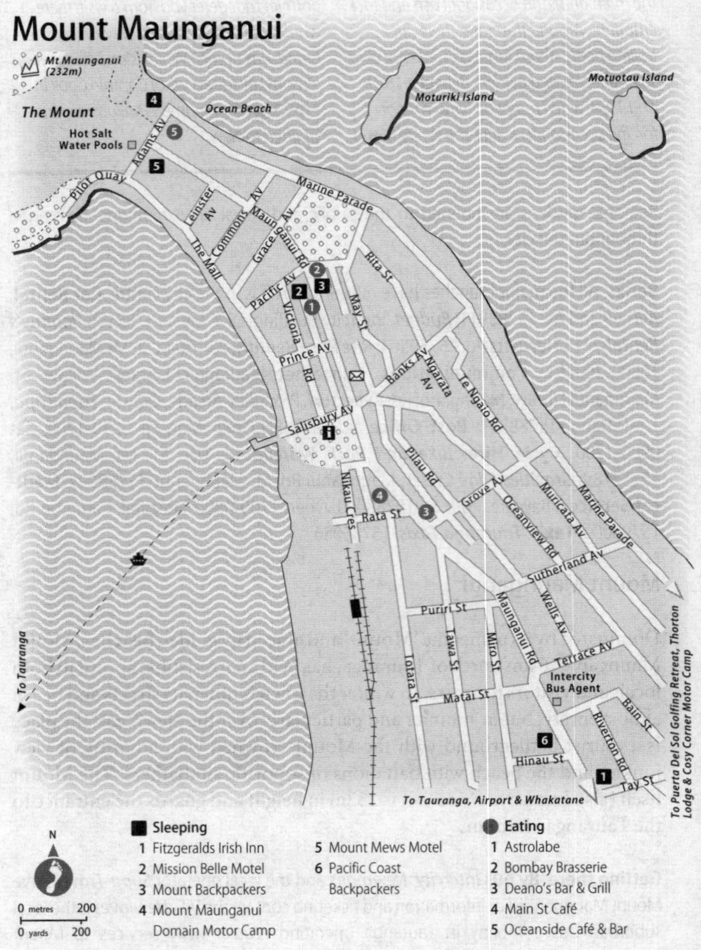

Sleeping
1 Fitzgeralds Irish Inn
2 Mission Belle Motel
3 Mount Backpackers
4 Mount Maunganui Domain Motor Camp
5 Mount Mews Motel
6 Pacific Coast Backpackers

Eating
1 Astrolabe
2 Bombay Brasserie
3 Deano's Bar & Grill
4 Main St Café
5 Oceanside Café & Bar

reached from the shore and is a popular spot for fishing, while Motuotau is important for its wildlife.Other than the Mount and the beaches the major attraction in the town is the Mount Maunganui **Hot Salt Water Pools**, at the base of the Mount on Adams Avenue. Here, therapeutic salt water is heated to 39°C in a number of large communal and private pools. ■ *Mon-Sat 0600-2200, Sun 0800-2200. From $2.50, child $1.50. T5750868.*

Sleeping

LL *Thorton Lodge*, 171 Oceanbeach Rd, T5755555, F5755554. Luxury beachfront lodge with 8 well-appointed apartments, suites and a penthouse with spa. **LL** *Puerta Del Sol Golfing Retreat*, 214 Oceanbeach Rd, T5758665, F5758695, www.puertadelsol.co.nz Situated right next to the Mount Maunganui golf course and close to the beach, 3 large luxury en suite rooms, open fire, pool and spa.

AL *Mission Belle Motel*, 1 Victoria Rd, T5752578. Modern, luxury Spanish-style motel located in the heart of town. **A** *Mount Mews Motel*, 8 Maunganui Rd, T5757006, F5753999, Well-established, close to all amenities. Spas. **B** *Fitzgerald's Irish Inn*, 463 Maunganui Rd, T5754013. Hasn't quite got the round pool table, but just about everything else. Comfortable and characterful.

C-D *Pacific Coast Backpackers*, 432 Maunganui Rd, T5749601. Large and lively with excellent range of comfortable doubles, singles and bunks. Wide range of activities organized, often with price reductions. **C-D** *Mount Backpackers*, 87 Maunganui Rd, T/F5750860. Smaller more centrally located backpackers. Internet. **C-D** *Mount Maunganui Domain Motor Camp*, Adams Av, T5754471. Ideally located at the base of the Mount and next to both the beach and the hot pools. **C-D** *Cosy Corner Motor Camp*, 40 Oceanbeach Rd, T5755899. Quieter camp located further along the beach.

Eating

The combination restaurant, bar and café facilities of the *Astrolabe* (not named after a space ship, but a shipwreck), 82 Maunganui Rd, is to be recommended. It offers breakfast, lunch and dinner with a range of fine and imaginative traditional dishes. Live bands often play at weekends. Almost directly across the road is the *Bombay Brasserie,* at 77 Maunganui Rd, an excellent, affordable, Indian restaurant. Open daily from 1800, T5752539. The modern and trendy *Oceanside Café and Bar,* below the Twin Towers on Adams Av, is a safe bet, with a wide range of choice from seafood to vegetarian, T5758030. Open Mon-Thurs 1700-2100, Fri 1700-late, Sat/Sun 1200-late. For a good-value steak, *Deano's Bar and Grill,* 305 Maunganui Rd, is recommended and there is often entertainment at weekends. Open daily 1200-1400 and 1800-2200, T5756675. For a good cheap breakfast with the locals head to the *Main St Café,* just south of the roundabout on Maunganui Rd. Open from 0700.

Whakatane

Phone code: 07
Population: 17,000

Whakatane is the principal town in the Eastern Bay of Plenty, situated at the mouth of the Whakatane River. It has a vibrant atmosphere that is often lacking in many New Zealand towns of the same size. There is just something about it – something that can warm the heart.

Ins and outs

Getting there

Whakatane **Airport** is located just northwest of the town off SH2 and is served by *Air New Zealand Link*, T0800-737000. The airport **shuttle** will get you into town for about $12, T3080222. For **taxis** use the same number. *Intercity* **buses** serve Whakatane and the VIC acts as the agent.You can connect with the East Cape and Opotiki shuttle from Whakatane (see page 273).

Information The Whakatane **Visitor Information Centre** is located in the heart of the town on Boon St, behind the main street, The Strand. T3086058, F3086020, www.whakatane.govt.nz Open Mon-Fri 0900-1700, Sat 0900-1300.

History

Whakatane has a rich Maori history going back to AD1150 when the Polynesian explorer Toi-te-Hauatahi landed and was reputed to have settled. Later, in the mid 14th century, the ancestral canoe, Mataatua, captained by one Chief Toroa, is believed to have also landed. Due to the New Zealand Wars in the 1860s there was not any major European settlement initiated until later in the century, and more especially in the early 1900s, when land drainage opened up the land for farming.

The name Whakatane means 'to act like a man', and it came about after the heroic acts of Wairaka, the high-spirited daughter of Toroa. When the *waka* landed at the river mouth, the men came ashore to investigate. As was the case in those days, the women were instructed to stay in the canoe, but they were so busy nattering away they didn't notice the canoe drifting. This left them in a bit of a predicament as the oars were *tapu* to the womenfolk (out of bounds). However, young Wairaka, the spirited daughter of the chief, took up the oars and, rowing furiously for the safety of the shore, proclaimed; 'Ka Whakatane au I ahau' which roughly translated means 'we must now play the part of men'. A very beautiful and evocative statue of Wairaka now stands on a rock at the harbour entrance – a reminder to us all of her heroinism!

Sights

The town also enjoys some of the highest annual sunshine hours in the country

The major attraction of Whakatane is as a gateway to visit the active volcano **White Island**, which can, on a clear day, be seen 50 km offshore, steaming away merrily. The other major activities are dolphin swimming, fishing and, to a lesser extent, walking locally and beyond, in the Urewera National Park, Whirinaki Forest Park and Tarawera Falls areas.

If you have your own transport, perhaps the best thing to do first is to get your bearings. To do this take Hillcrest Road south from the centre of town and the road over the hill west towards Ohope Beach. At the crest of the hill turn left and follow the signs to the **Kohi Point Scenic Reserve**. At the headland (which was the *pa* site of the first Maori settlers) you will get a grand view of the town, the coast and White Island. From here you can also embark on a number of short or long, scenic coastal walks.

The island close to shore is Whale or **Moutohora Island** (which does indeed look like a whale from the side). Moutohora is another less active volcano which has some hot springs and a number of historic *pa* sites. It is privately owned and a wildlife refuge administered by DOC. Although generally off limits, DOC do offer occasional guided tours in the summer months (contact the VIC).

Back in the town centre another natural feature is the **Pohaturoa**, a large rock outcrop located at the corner of The Strand and Commerce Street. For some six centuries this was used by the Maori as a meeting place and was also where the local Ngati Awa tribe signed the Treaty of Waitangi in the 1840s. While the summit was used as sacred place for the bones of early chiefs, the newborns were given a form of baptism and dedicated to the Gods in a stream at its foot. More local historical information can be gleaned at the **Whakatane District Museum and Gallery** on Boon Street. As well as a wealth of historical displays and a fine dynamic gallery space, it houses a large collection of over 20,000 photographs. ■ *Tue-Fri 1000-1630, Sat 1100-1330. Entry by donation. T3079805.*

No trip to Whakatane would be complete without a short drive west along to the harbour entrance to see the gorgeous, svelte sculpture of **Wairaka** – a fine tribute to the town's roots and womanhood. There is also an interesting **mural** on the wall at the corner of The Strand and The Quay. It depicts a bi-cultural scene of Maori and *Pakeha* (whites). If you look closely you will see the head of Captain Cook has been defaced a number of times. This is a reflection of some strong feelings which still exist in the area regarding bi-culural and land issues. The Tuhoe Iwi, whose lands lie to the south of Whakatane, are well known for their particulary staunch stand.

Just 8 km over the hill from Whakatane, heading east, is the 11 km long sandpit called **Ohope Beach**, guarding the entrance to the Ohiwa Harbour. Principally a beach resort, it is a fine place to while away a few hours in the sun, swimming, sunbathing or just watching White Island billow with steam off in the distance. There are several places to stay here, listed below under Sleeping.

Activities and tours

Diving and snorkelling *Dolphin Down Under* (see below) offer dive trips and snorkel trips off the various offshore islands, three hours. Over a dozen other **charters** offer dive trips from Whakatane. For details contact the VIC.

Dolphin watching and eco-tours The Bay of Plenty is rich with schools of playful dolphin, and encounters with schools of over one thousand are not uncommon. *Dolphin Down Under*, T3087837, are the principal operators, offering a weather-dependent, four-hour trip for around $100, child $75. If a school of dolphins is encountered (highly likely) you can either observe of get in the water. Trips several times daily in summer, by demand in winter. Booking essential. Ohiwa Harbour Tours is a new local eco-tour which encompasses a trip by road to take in natural and human historical facts, followed by a 2½ hour cruise on the wildlife rich Ohiwa Harbour. Light refreshments are provided, but take your own food. Three hours in total. $40. Recommended. *Pohutukawa Tours*, T3086495, do an interesting volcanic feature based tour ($75) as well as trips to the beautiful Whirinaki Forest Park ($95) and Mount Tarawera ($90).

Fishing guided line *Beach and Rock Fishing Adventures*, T3086227, offer fishing and sightseeing trips by four-wheel drive with all equipment and food included, from $50. There are 18 other charters available ranging from $40-$1350. Contact the VIC for listings.

Horse trekking *Tui Glen Farm* (2 km from Kawerau, south), T3236457. $20 for one hour, $30 for three hours. *Toketehua Horse Treks*, two hours for $40, T3129176.

Hot pools The nearest hot pools to Whakatane are the basic but relaxing Awakeri Hot Springs, which are located just off SH30 to Rotorua southwest of the town, T3049117.

Jet boating *Kiwi Jet Tours*, T3070663, offer a 1½-hour trip down the Rangitaiki for $60, child $40.

Kayaking See *Dolphin Down Under* (above).

Rafting *Whakatane Raft Tours*, T3087760, offer half to multi-day trips on the Motu, from $65. Another excellent company operating out of Opotiki is *Wet'n Wild*, T3496567. Their 5-day trip down the Motu when the river is normal to high is great value and highly recommended.

Walking The VIC has details and leaflets outlining local short and long walks, craft and historic town trails. *Tramplite Walks*, T3049893, are a local company offering a varied and interesting three-day hike for a very reasonable $220, which includes accommodation, food and transport .

White Island tours and scenic flights There is the choice of boat trips or scenic flights: *Te Kahurangi* operating as *Blue Sky Tours*, T3237829, is a Catamaran. It leaves at 0830 for a five to six-hour trip to the island. Lunch provided. $85. Bookings essential.The other highly commercial operator is *Pee Jays*, 15 Strand East, T3089588, www.whiteisland.co.nz, which offers a five to six-hour trip leaving at 0900. Lunch and refreshments provided. They will often deviate off schedule if dolphins are spotted. $95. Bookings essential. *Vulcan Helicopters*, T/F0800-804354, www.vulcanheli.co.nz, operate out of Whakatane Airport. Three-hour tour, one hour on the island. From $315. *East Bay Flight Centre*, T3088446, offer a 50-minute trip in a comfortable fixed wing for $150.

Essentials

Sleeping **AL-A** *White Island Rendezvous*, 15 Strand East, T3089500, F3080303, www.whiteisland.co.nz Part of the *Pee Jay* White Island Tour operation. New, well-appointed waterfront motel. Café and spa. **AL-A** *Pacific Coast Motel*, 41 Landing Rd, T3080100, F3084100. Another modern option. Luxury one-bedroom or studio units. Spa. **AL-A** *Barringtons Motor Lodge*, 34 Landing Rd, T0800-830130. Modern units, some with spa and disabled facilities.

B *Nau Mai Motel*, 61 Landing Rd, T3086422. Budget motel option close to town centre. **AL** *Motuhora Rise B&B*, off Waiewe St, T3070224, jtspell@xtra.co.nz Fine B&B located on outskirts of town with well-appointed rooms, open fire and spa. **A** *Clifton Manor Motel and B&B*, 5 Clifton Rd, T/F3072145. Spacious home within walking distance of town centre. Pool. **A** *Te Ruru Log Cabin*, 659 White Pine Bush Rd, T/F3129069. Self-contained double with en-suite in log cabin-style in country location. Horse treks available. **A** *Briar Rose*, 54 Waiewe St, T3080314. Charming cottage in bush setting close to town. Double, single and studio en suite.

B-D *Whakatane Hotel*, The Strand, T3071670. Basic but sound backpacker-style accommodation. Singles and share. Great Irish pub downstairs and a noisy nightclub next to that, so be sure to get a room in the west wing. **C-D** *Whakatane Motor camp*, McGarvey Rd, T3088694. Basic but next to the river.

In Ohope There are numerous **motels** along the waterfront, including: **A** *The Ocean View*, 18 West End, T3125665; **A** *Surfs Reach*, 52 West End, T3124159; **A-B** *Jody's on the Beach*, 31 West End, T3124616; **A-B** *Alfresco Court*, 5 Moana St, T3125061. Good **B&Bs** include: **A** *Turney's B&B*, 28 Pohutukawa Av, T3087748; **B** *The Rafters*, 261A Pohutukawa Av, T3124856. The **C-D** *Ohope Beach Top Ten*, 367 Harbour Rd, is a good motor camp in a quiet spot at the west end, right on the beach.

Eating There is quite a good chioce in Whakatane and all are pretty affordable. ***The Wharf Shed,*** Strand East, is a fine and relatively new restaurant. Imaginative mainly seafood menu. Open daily from 1100, T3085698. Closer to town, also on Strand East, ***The Chambers,*** T3070107, which has a nice ambience and serves a superb lamb dish. Open daily from 1000. Also doubles as a café and has Internet. ***The Harbourside,*** 62 The Strand, T3086721, is one of the more established restaurants in town, with reliably good and affordable traditional Kiwi and seafood dishes. Two other reputable eateries are ***Go Global*** on Commerce St, T3089000, and the ***Why Not Café ,*** T3071006, below the Whakatane Hotel. For a cheap snack, street-side coffee and a grand date scone, head for the ***Main St Café***, 3/15 The Strand.

In Ohope For eating try the popular ***Pohutukawa Café*** on the Main Rd, or the ***Ohope Beach Resort*** on West End Road, T3124692.

Entertainment

The *Whakatane Hotel* plays host to a superb small, cosy Irish pub, *The Craic*. Next door is a new nightclub which hopefully won't ruin the place.

Directory

Communications Internet is available at ***Artex***, Boon St, opposite the VIC and at the ***Chambers Café Restaurant***, Strand East. The **post office** is on Commerce St. Open Mon-Fri 0830-1700, Sat 0900-1200.

Opotiki

Phone code: 07
Population: 10,000

The small fairly unremarkable town of Opotiki is 60 km southeast of Whakatane near the mouths of the Waioeka and Otara Rivers. Although some are attracted to its fine beaches, most visitors use Opotiki as the gateway to the East Cape. Like Whakatane, the town is rich in Maori history, with settlement taking place before the great migrations of the 14th century. Opotiki was the base of the Hauhau – an almost religious sect of Maori rebels who were fierce enemies of the early *Pakeha*.

Ins & outs

Internet is available at 38 King St, T3157683

Getting there Opotiki is served daily by ***Intercity* buses** which stop on Elliot St. For bookings and information contact the VIC. For shuttle buses going around the East Cape (SH35) see East Cape section.

The very friendly Opotiki **Visitor Information Centre** is located on the corner of St John and Elliot Sts, T3158484, opovin@nzhost.co.nz Open Mon-Fri 0830-1630, Sat/Sun 1000-1500. **DOC** is an adjunct to this office, T3156103. The comprehensive and free booklet 'Opotiki and East Cape Free Holiday Guide' is a must for anyone touring the area.

Sights

The **Hukutaia Domain** is about 6 km from the town and signposted to the left after the Waioeka Bridge. It is a hectare of bush with many New Zealand native trees, including a historic 2000 year-old puriri tree called 'Taketakerau', with a girth of about 22 m and a height over 23 m. The hollow in this tree was used by the local Iwi to store the preserved bones of their dead, in an elaborate ritual and as protection from enemy desecration. Also of historical interest is **The Church Of Hinoa** (St Stephen's Anglican Church) at the north end of Church Street. It was originally built for the Church Missionary Society and the Reverend Karl Volkner, who first arrived in 1859. Sadly, given local bad feeling towards the *Pakeha*, he was considered a government spy and killed by Hauhau emissaries in 1865. There naturally followed much unrest in the region.

There are several operators in Opotiki who offer kayaking, horse riding and jet boating. For details contact the VIC. Opotiki is home to the *Wet n' Wild* rafting company, T3496567. They offer one of the North Island's best wilderness expeditions, the multi-day trip down the remote Motu River. Provided the river levels are good, this is an unforgettable experience that will cost around $590. Recommended. The main Jetboat operator for the river is *Motu River Jet Boat Tours*, T3158107. Two hours $85, child $50.

Sleeping & eating

There are several motels, farmstays, B&Bs and Backpackers in Opotiki, and the VIC have full listings. **A** ***Riverview Cottage***, SH2, T/F73155553, riverview.cottage@xtra.co.nz Well-appointed self-contained cottage, 10 min from Opotiki, next to the Waioeka River. The **C-D** ***Central Oasis Backpackers***, 30 King St, is a small traditional cottage that is in the heart of town, T3155165. The **C-D** ***Opotiki Holiday Park***, Potts Av, is the only motor camp located within the town – basic but adequate, T3156050. For eating, the ***Flying Pig Café***, Church St, is fine and fully licensed, T3157618.

Taupo and Ruapehu

Taupo and Ruapehu

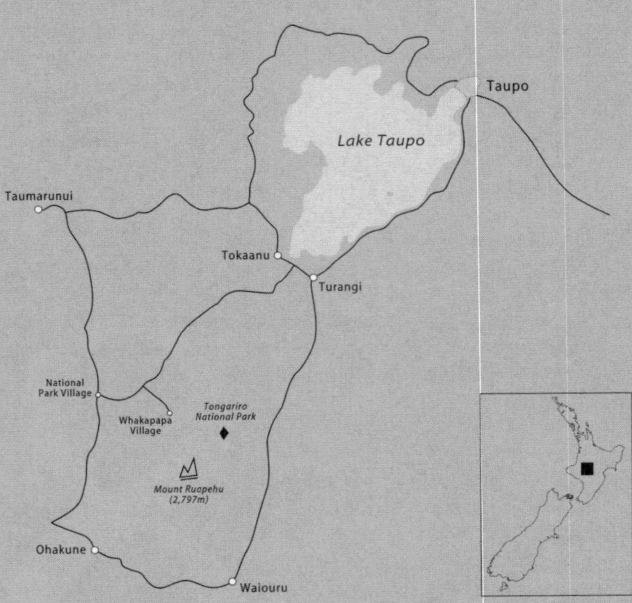

*From space **Lake Taupo**, the largest lake in New Zealand, looks like a large bullet-hole shot through the heart of the North Island. This is perhaps fitting given that its placid waters, now world famous for **trout fishing**, mask a frightening heritage of **volcanoes** and **thermal activity** – one that is the trade mark of the Taupo and Ruapehu Region. Here are the remains of the largest volcanic eruption in the last 5,000 years. Now, during its dormancy, Lake Taupo is home to a bustling tourist town, **Taupo**, renowned not only for its **fishing**, but a host of other **activities**, from rafting and mountain biking to tandem skydiving. After exerting yourself, aches and pains can be soothed away in the town's popular **hot pools**.*

*All around the region is the evidence of ancient and ongoing volcanic activity. Nowhere else is this more apparent than the **Tongariro National Park**. A place that is steeped in Maori legend and spirituality, and New Zealand's oldest national park, boasting the still active volcanoes of **Ngauruhoe** and **Ruapehu** – the North Island's highest peak, which erupted in spectacular fashion as recently as 1996. When both mountains are in less aggressive mood the park provides excellent skiing, tramping and walking opportunites, including the great **Tongariro Crossing**, a walk full of volcanic wonder, considered one of the best day-walks in the country.*

Things to do in Taupo and Ruapehu

- *Go cruising, sailing or trout fishing on the huge flooded 'caldera' that is now Lake Taupo.*
- *Explore the 'Craters of the Moon', the Volcanic Activity Centre and the thunderous Huka Falls in the Wairakei Park.*
- *Play golf on one of Taupo's first-class 'steaming' golf courses.*
- *See the spectacular view from the summit of Mount Tauhara near Taupo.*
- *Try the memorable 'Tongariro Crossing' in the Tongariro National Park – one of the best day-walks in the country – followed by a relaxing soak in the Taupo Hot Springs.*
- *Find peace at the Orakei Korako Thermal Reserve.*
- *Climb to Mount Ruapehu's Crater Lake from the Whakapapa ski-field and ski back down.*
- *Join an evening trip to hear wild kiwi from Ohakune.*

Ins and outs

Getting there

Situated in the heart of North Island, with SH1 running through its heart, the Taupo and Ruapehu region is easily accessible

By **road** Auckland is 278 km north of Taupo via Hamilton and SH1, while Rotorua is 80 km northwest via SH5. Taupo is also on the signposted '**Thermal Explorer Highway**' tourist route that runs from Auckland via Rotorua, through Taupo to Hawkes Bay. ***Intercity*** and ***Newmans*** run regular daily services to Taupo, from where public transport to Turangi and the Tongariro National Park can be easily arranged. Taupo **airport** is serviced by ***Air New Zealand Link***, with daily domestic flights to Auckland and Wellington, and connecting services to provincial towns and the South Island.

Information

The principal **Visitor Information Centre** is located in Taupo, with smaller centres available in Turangi and Ohakune. The main **DOC** visitor centre servicing the Tongariro National Park is located in the Whakapapa Village in the heart of the park. These centres are all listed in the text. The websites www.thinkfresh.co.nz, and www.laketauponz.com, are both a wonderful source of information for the entire region, while www.whakapapa.co.nz, and www.doc.govt.nz, will tell you all you need to know about the National Park.

Taupo and around

Population: 20,000
Phone code: 07

For the tourist heading south, Taupo is really the first place that begins to satisfy the imagination for what New Zealand is 'supposed' to look like: wide open spaces with snow-capped mountains and clear blue lakes. As you come over the hill into town on a clear day, the scene hits you like the first sip of a fine wine, with the huge expanse of Lake Taupo dwarfing the distant snow-tipped volcanoes of the Tongariro National Park. Take a while to enjoy it from the roadside lookout above the town before merging into the picture in the sure knowledge that it gets even better from here.

Because of its position in the centre of the North Island, Taupo is the commercial headquarters for the central districts of Taupo and Ruapehu, as well as a major tourist resort. The town is very pleasant, busy, friendly and well set out, it is also nestled close to the source of the Waikato River (the longest in the country) and lies on the northernmost bank of the huge lake, once a mighty volcanic crater. The region has a multitude of activities to enjoy. Fishing is, of course, the principal attraction but you can also try the more adrenaline-pumping pursuits of bungy jumping and tandem skydiving, as well as mountain biking, golf, sailing and walking. Beyond the town and its lake, the glorious mountain peaks of the Tongariro National Park will lure you into further investigation, with that omnipresent edge of fear that maybe, just maybe, another volcanic eruption will strike.

Ins and outs

Getting there

Taupo is located on SH1 280 km South of Auckland and 82 km from Rotorua and is a major stop on the tourist 'Thermal Explorer Highway'. The town is well serviced by both road and by air. The **airport** is located just off SH1, 10 km south of the town, T3785428. ***Air New Zealand Link*** operates direct daily flights to Auckland and Wellington with connections to the South Island, T0800-800737. By **bus** Taupo is serviced daily by ***Newmans*** and ***Intercity*** which arrive and depart from the Travel Centre on Gascoigne St, T3789032.

Getting around

Shuttles and taxis usually meet incoming flights at the airport. Shuttles can also be booked with ***Taupo Passenger Services***, T3782172. ***Alpine Scenic Tours*** operates between Turangi and Taupo, with additional services to the Tongariro National Park on Mon, Wed and Fri, T3786305. ***Taupo Fun*** operates a similar daily service, T3770435. ***Kiwi Value Tours*** operate more local services but go as far as the Orakei Korako Reserve, T3789662. The prominent London Double Decker Bus does 20-min town tours which depart from the lakefront gardens, corner of Tongariro and Redoubt Sts. T3770774, $5, child $2.50. For taxis, cycle hire and car rentals see Directory.

Information

The Taupo **Visitor Information Centre** is located on Tongariro St (SH1), T3789000, F3789003, www.thinkfresh.co.nz It has all the usual information, a good range of maps and also handles DOC enquiries. Specialist information available on the Tongariro Crossing (see Tongariro National Park) with up-to-date weather forecasts. Open daily 0830-1700. Another useful regional website is www.laketauponz.com

History

Prior to European settlement Taupo was called Tapuaeharuru, meaning 'resounding footsteps', and was allegedly christened by a Maori chief, who thought the ground felt hollow. The main *pa* site and fortified village was located near the lake outlet (the Waikato River). In 1868 an Armed Constabulary force established a garrison on the site of the present township to assist in the national campaign to rout the Maori rebel leader Te Kooti. By the late 1800s the area's thermal activity was already beginning to attract visitors and the land was bought from the Maori and trout introduced into the lake. From that point it seems Taupo's destiny was sealed and the tourism trade flourished.

Sights

Taupo's natural sights are mostly located outside the town itself. You are advised to consult both the 'Taupo' and 'Around Taupo' sections before deciding what you might like to see or do

The most immediate and dominant sight in town is of course the huge expanse of **Lake Taupo** itself – 619 sq km. On a calm day it can be almost mirror-like, disturbed only by the wakes of boats and ducks. But it wasn't always like this and the origin of the lake itself will make you quake in your walking boots, for Lake Taupo is in fact the tranquil remains of the biggest volcanic eruptions the planet has created in the last 5,000 years. The latest occurred in AD186 spewing out over 30 cu km of debris at up to 900 kph. For the statisticians amongst you that is about 30 times more than Mount St Helens spewed out. There was so much ash that the effects were seen in China and Rome.

The now placid waters are famous for their copious trout and very much the domain of the serious angler. But the lake is of course utilised for numerous other activities including, sailing, cruising, water-skiing and wind-surfing. Most of the longer cruises take in the remarkable **Maori rock carvings** (a huge face complete with moko or tattoos), which can only be seen from the water and adorn an entire rock face in Mine Bay, 8 km southwest across the lake. Although remarkable, they were only created in recent years, which does somewhat dampen the excitement. For cruising and other lake activities see 'Activities' section.

Near the very tacky oriental-style trout statue is the **Taupo District Museum of Art and History** on Story Place. Here there are some interesting photos and artworks that focus on the early days of the region, and a gallery that features regular exhibitions. ■ *Daily 1030-1630. Donation only. T3784167.* Just a little further west the **Waikato River** begins its 425-km journey to the Tasman Sea and winds its merry way north behind the town towards **Wairakei Park**. Before the park proper, off Spa Road, **Cherry Island**, which is set in the middle of the river, has been developed into a small wildlife attraction. There are a few aviaries, fluffy farm animals and some trout pools. Perhaps if you are not going to Rotorua where such attractions are on a far grander scale, you might like to pay a visit. ■ *Daily 0900-1700. $9.50, child, $4.50. Licensed café, gallery and shop. T3789028.*

Nearby, at 202 Spa Road, almost looking over Cherry Island, is the HQ for **Taupo Bungy**, which might be your first opportunity to get an elastic band tied to your ankles before throwing yourself over a 45 m cliff. Masochistic adrenaline junkies will be delighted to hear that the ones in South Island are at least twice this height. A jump in Taupo will cost from $89, which includes a video and some photos with which to terrify the folks back home.

Also on Spa Road, and not quite so harsh on the pacemaker, is **Spa Dinosaur Valley**, Taupo's answer to Jurassic Park, where the little monsters can run wild amongst some big concrete monsters. *Daily (except Tue) 1000-1600. $5, child $3. T3784120.*

The **AC Baths** at the top of Spa Road are one of two large thermal pool complexes in Taupo. Here you can soak away all your troubles in a range of outdoor and private spa pools while the kids do their thing on the hydro-slide. ■ *Daily 0830-2130. $4, child $2. T3773600.*

The other thermal complex is the excellent and recently refurbished **Taupo Hot Springs**, next to De Brett's just off SH5 (which heads west from SH1, along the lakefront at the southern edge of town). This is the better of the two complexes with all the usual facilities and a very congenial atmosphere. It's a fine place to mix with the locals, as well as celebrities (Xena Warrior Princess 'aka' Lucy Lawless). ■ *Daily 0700-2130. $7, child $2.50. T3776502.*

To the west of town looms the dormant volcano **Tauhara** (1088 m). Not only is it a grand site, but also a great walk with superb views which make the three-hour return trip well worth it. The track, which is about one-third grazing paddock to two-thirds native bush, begins from the bottom of Mountain Road, 5 km from Taupo on the Napier SH5 Road. Do not be fooled by the immediate summit in view, which is a false summit. The track enters the bush-filled crater to the true summit beyond it. Adequate footwear and patience are required.

Activities and tours

Bungy jumping *Taupo Bungy* (45 m) is located just off Spa Road, T3771135. From $89.

Charter boats As you might expect there are numerous boat charters plying the lake. The Marina office in Taupo at the Boat Harbour, along Storey Place, has all the information. The three main operators are: *Chris Jolly Outdoors*, T3780623, www.chrisjolly.co.nz; *Taupo Launchmen's Association*, T3783444; and the *Sailing Centre*, 2 Mile Bay, T/F3783299.

Climbing *Rock and Ropes*, between Rotorua and Taupo on the SH5, T3748111, have a low and high ropes course with a giant 15 m swing that is a lot of fun and has a good reputation; from $15-$85. There is also an excellent climbing wall at the AC Baths on Spa Road, T3773600, $6. For the real thing see Walking below or try *Wilderness Escapes*, T3783413, for abseiling, climbing and caving from $30.

Cruising There are numerous opportunities to cruise the lake in a number of varying craft offering daily trips, most of which leave regularly from the Boat Harbour on Storey Place. *Cruise Cat Scenic Cruises*, T3780623, offer 1½-hour trips (Monday-Saturday 1130-1300; Sunday 1030-1230), to see the Maori Rock Carvings in Mine Bay and the picturesque Whakaipo Bay. $38, child $26. One of the yacht options is 'The Barbary', a fine 50-ft ocean-going vessel which also takes in the Maori carvings and leaves daily at 1000 and 1400; $25, child $10. The 'Ernest Kemp' is a small replica steamboat that leaves from the Boat Harbour daily at 1000 and 1400 (1400 in winter). Again it takes in the Maori Rock carvings. T3783444; $22, child $11. *Taupo Fun*, T3770435, has had the novel idea of going the other way down the river taking in (and dropping off) at Cherry Island. You can also watch the mad fools at *Taupo Bungy* launch themselves into the abyss. Departs hourly 1000-1700, 1100-1500 winter. $19, child $15 (return). For a far faster trip you might want to try the 'Greatlake Super Jet', which is a one to two-hour trip on board a jet hydrofoil vessel. T0800-787222. From $39.

Eco-tours *Tongariro Eco Tours* provide a very interesting two-hour cruise of the lake wetlands and are based in Turangi, T0800-101024. $40. Recommended for the nature lover. *Eco safaris (NZ)* are a national operation with day or multi-day trips out of Kinloch near Taupo, T3770127, from $650. *Chris Jolly* also offers some good nature-based trips of the surrounding area, T3780623. From $45. *Kayaking Kiwi* offer excellent half, full-day and overnight eco-based kayak adventures from $55. T3785901.

Fishing As you might expect there are a wealth of operators out there willing to take you out and try to catch a 'monster trout'. Guides charge about $45 per hour for up to two persons. The obligatory license is $12 per day, $25 per week. A minimum three-hour trip is recommended to give you at least a chance, especially for beginners. For full listings see the VIC. Mike Aspinall, T3784453; Chris Jolly, T3780623; Paddy Clark, T3781364; Poronui Ranch, T3789680; and Ron Burgin, T3728112, are all recommended.

Gliding The *Taupo Gliding Club*, Centennial Drive, Taupo, offer tandem flights mainly at weekends, with more regular schedules in summer, weather permitting, T3785463. From $70.

Golf Taupo is one of the best golfing venues in the country, both the Wairakei (SH1 North), T3748152, and Taupo Clubs (Spa Road, then Centennial Drive), T3786933, are excellent. This is your chance to play one of the very few 'steaming' courses in the world. Green fees from $35.

Taupo

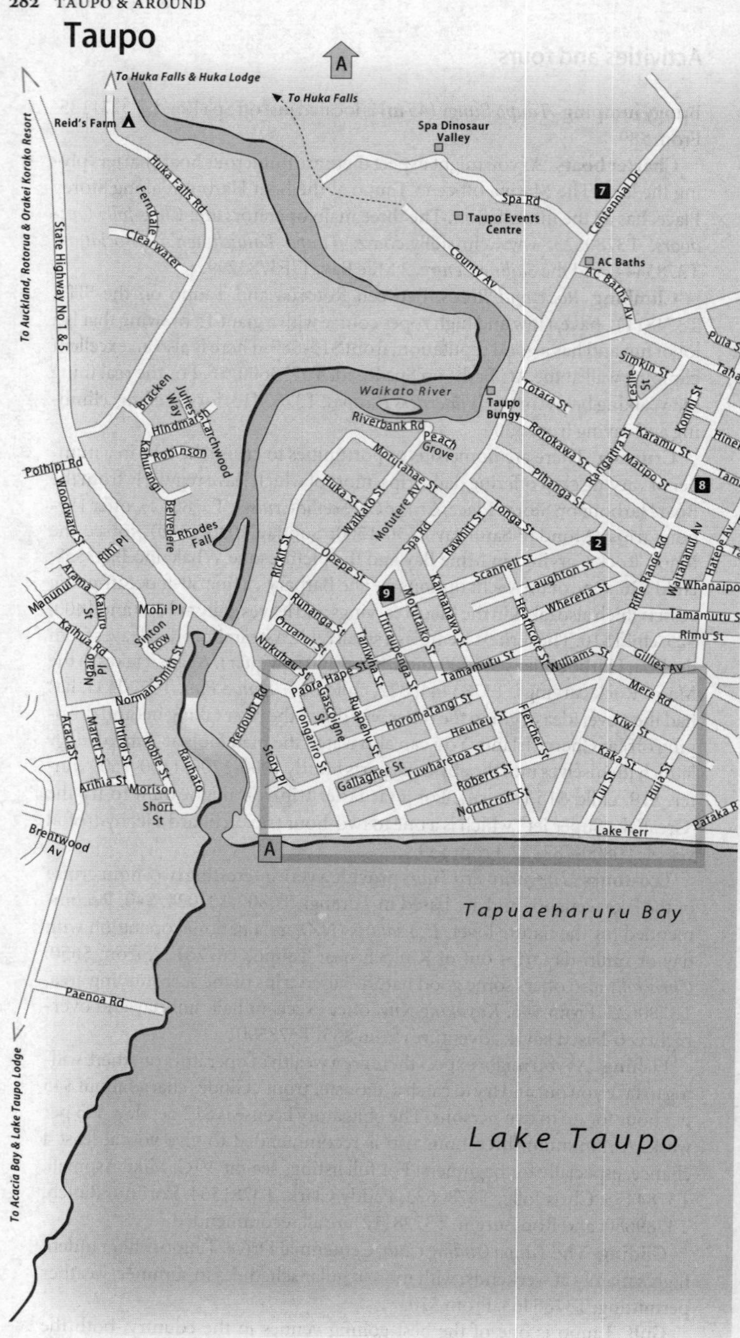

Related map
A Taupo centre,
page 285

Taupo and Ruapehu

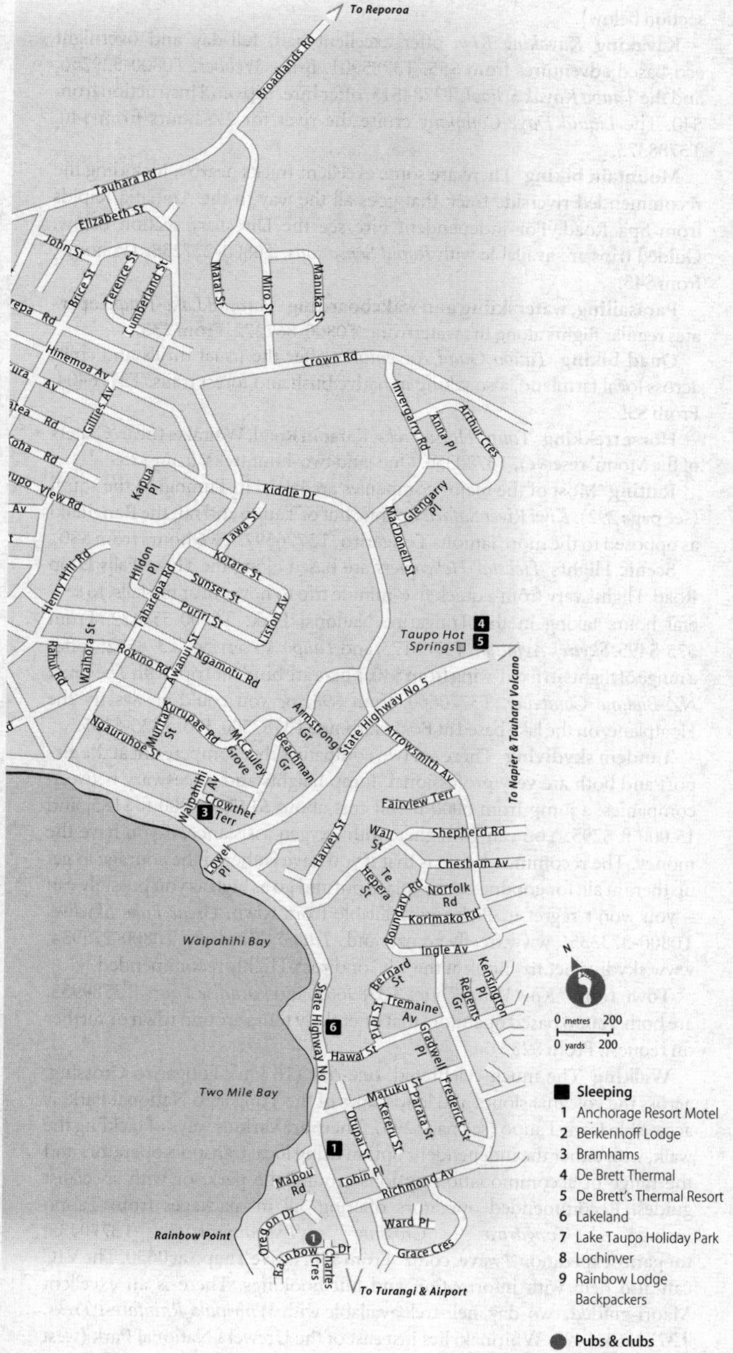

To Reporoa

Broadlands Rd

Tauhara Rd

Elizabeth St

John St

Brice St

Terence St

Cumberland St

Matai St

Miro St

Manuka St

Hinemoa Av

Gillies Av

Crown Rd

Invergarry Rd

Anna Pl

Arthur Cres

Kapua Pl

Kiddie Dr

Glengarry Pl

MacDonell St

Tawa St

Kotare St

Hildon Pl

Henry Hill Rd

Taharepa Rd

Sunset St

Puriri St

Liston Av

Taupo Hot Springs

Waihora St

Rahui Rd

Rokino Rd

Awanui St

Ngamotu Rd

State Highway No 5

To Napier & Tauhara Volcano

Armstrong Gr

Beachman Gr

Arrowsmith Av

Ngauruhoe St

Kurupae Rd

Muritai St

McCauley Grove

Waipahihi Av

Crowther Terr

Lower Pl

Fairview Terr

Wall St

Shepherd Rd

Harvey St

Chesham Av

Te Hepera St

Boundary Rd

Norfolk Rd

Korimako Rd

Waipahihi Bay

Ingle Av

Kensington Pl

Regents Gr

Bernard St

Tremaine Av

Piripi St

State Highway No 1

Gradwell Pl

Hawai St

Two Mile Bay

Matuku St

Kereru St

Parata St

Frederick St

Otupai St

Mapou Rd

Tobin Pl

Richmond Av

Ward Pl

Rainbow Point

Oregon Dr

Rainbow Dr

Rainbow Cres

Charles Cres

Grace Cres

To Turangi & Airport

0 metres 200

0 yards 200

Sleeping

1 Anchorage Resort Motel
2 Berkenhoff Lodge
3 Bramhams
4 De Brett Thermal
5 De Brett's Thermal Resort
6 Lakeland
7 Lake Taupo Holiday Park
8 Lochinver
9 Rainbow Lodge Backpackers

Pubs & clubs

1 Ploughmans Pub

Jet boats (See Wairakei Park and Aratiatia Rapids in the Around Taupo section below).

Kayaking *Kayaking Kiwi* offer excellent half, full-day and overnight eco-based adventures from $55. T3785901. *Bruce Webber*, T0800-529256, and the *Taupo Kayak School*, T3784515, offer hire, trips and instruction from $40. The *Liquid Dayz Company* cruise the river for 2½ hours from $40. T3788373.

Mountain biking There are some excellent tracks nearby, including the recommended riverside track that goes all the way to the Aratiatia Rapids from Spa Road. For independent hire see the Directory section below. Guided trips are available with *Rapid Sensations*, T0800-227238. 1½ hours, from $45.

Parasailing, waterskiing and wakeboarding *Parasail Lake Taupo* operates regular flights along the waterfront, T0800-867272. From £35.

Quad biking *Taupo Quad Adventures* offer the usual thrills and spills across local farmland, also taking in native bush and forest trails. T3776404. From $55.

Horse trekking *Taupo Horse Treks*, Karapiti Road, Wairakei (near 'Craters of the Moon' reserve), T3780356. One- and two-hour treks, from $25.

Rafting Most of the major companies are based in Turangi to the south (see page 292). *Kiwi River Safaris* operate out of Taupo and raft the Rangitaiki as opposed to the more famous Tongariro. T3776597. Two hours from $80.

Scenic Flights *Helistar Helicopters* are based along the Huka Falls Loop Road. Flights vary from a quick five-minute trip to hover near the falls, to several hours taking in the Tongariro National Park. T0800-554422. From $75-$495. *Skytrek Aviation*, T3788173, and *Taupo Air services*, T3785325, offer a range of flights in fixed-wing from $40. There are bi-plane trips with *The Great NZ Biplane Company*, T3770660, from $98, or you could always try the Floatplane, on the lake based at Boat Harbour, T3787500. From $35-$135.

Tandem skydiving There are two companies that compete out at the airport and both are very professional. Jump heights and prices vary between companies: a jump from 6000 ft will cost about $145; 10,000 ft $185; and 15,000 ft $295. You can go higher, with oxygen assistance, if you have the money. The recommendation is that if you have gathered the courage to get up there at all, for goodness sake splash out and go as high as you possibly can – you won't regret it. Pick-ups available from town. *Great Lake Skydive*, T0800-373335, www.freefly.co.nz, and *Taupo Tandem*, T0800-275934, www.skydive.net.nz Book at the VIC or direct. Highly recommended.

Town tours *Kiwi Value Tours*, T3789662, and *Paradise Tours*, T3789955, are both Taupo based operators that offer daily tours around town or further on request. From $25.

Walking The much-celebrated, one-day (16 km) Tongariro Crossing, across the volcanic slopes and landscapes of the Tongariro National Park, is accessible from Taupo (see page 293). There are various ways of tackling the walk, with either the independent option using local transport operators and the range of accommodation options around the park, or with specialist guides. Recommended operators offering 'all in' packages from Taupo include *Tongariro Crossing Expeditions*, T3770435, tongariroexpedition@wave. co.nz From $30. Leave Taupo at 0630. The VIC can also help with information and hut bookings. There is an excellent Maori-guided, two-day, heli-trek available with *Whirinaki Rainforest Treks*, T3772363. $495. Whirinaki lies just east of the Urewera National Park (west of Taupo) and has some of the most unspoilt rainforest in the North Island.

There are numerous other short and long walks in the area including the excellent climb to the summit of Tauhara (1088 m), west of the town (see Sights above). The VIC can provide detailed walking information and maps.

Essentials

Sleeping

There are many B&Bs, homestays and farmstays available, mainly around town and in Acacia Bay to the east of Taupo. For details contact the VIC

LL *Huka Lodge*, Huka Falls Rd, T3785791, www.hukalodge.com Luxury at its most luxurious in quiet seclusion beside the river. Mingle with heads of state and visiting stars. Watch your money evaporate. **LL** *Lake Taupo Lodge*, 41 Mapara Rd, Acacia Bay, T3787386. Another top establishment offering total luxury in 4 luxury suites with dining room, reading gallery, open fire. Includes exquisite cuisine.

AL-A *Caboose Taupo*, 100-102 Lake Terr, T3760116, www.taupo.caboose.co.nz A new and unusual luxury establishment with a 'colonial African' theme. Log cabin-style architecture and accommodation with an unusual range of suites and bunkrooms. Spas, pool, restaurant and bar. Recommended. **AL** *Lakeland*, SH1, Two Mile Bay, T3783893, www.lakeland.co.nz Mid to upper-range comfort next to the lake. Restaurant and bar, spas and pool.

In town **A** *Bramhams*, 7 Waipahihi Av, T3780064, bramham@reap.org.nz and **A** *Lochinver*, 33 Tamatea Rd, T3770241, are both friendly, comfortable and centrally located. **B** *De Brett Thermal Hotel*, Napier/ Taupo Highway (SH5), T3787080. Budget hotel within walking distance of hot pools complex.

C-D *Rainbow Lodge Backpackers*, 99 Titiraupenga St, T3785754, rainbowlodge@clear.net.nz Long-established, popular and congenial backpackers run by one of the longest serving managers in the game. Good dorms and excellent doubles. Recommended. The **C-D** *Taupo Central Backpackers*, corner of Tongariro and Tuwharetoa Sts, T3783206, and the **C-D** *Go Global* in the former Cob and Co Hotel across the road, T3770044, are the two most central and 'happening' hostels, but do not necessarily have the best, most modern accommodation, but with the top pubs in town within crawling distance, they are the best for nightlife and action. The *Central* has its own terrace balcony with fine view over lake and town. The **C-D** *Action Downunder Hostel*, corner of Kaimanawa and Tamamutu Sts, T3783311, is a recently expanded YHA

Taupo centre

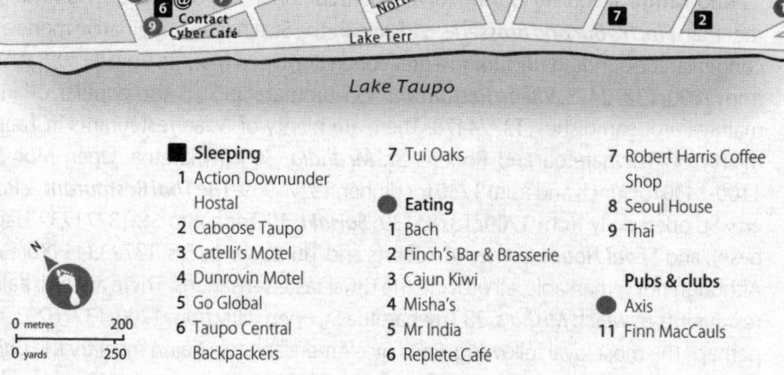

associate with great new rooms and facilities. Spa and bike hire. **C-D** ***Berkenhoff Lodge***, 75 Scannell St, T3784909, is a bit out of the centre but has a fine 'rambling house' atmosphere and is friendly and well kept. Bar, café, spa and free bikes.

There is a wealth of **motels** with the best being 'lakeview', located on or around Lake Terr and the waterfront. The cheaper options tend to be in the town's western suburbs. **AL-A** ***Tui Oaks***, corner of Lake Terr and Tui St, T3788305. One of the best in the upper range with great views across the lake, pool, restaurant and bar. **A** ***Anchorage Resort Motel***, Lake Front, Two Mile Bay, T3785542, F3787287. Situated a bit further along Lake Terr. Good facilities including pool, spas and gym. **A** ***Catelli's Motel***, 23-27 Rifle Range Rd, T3784477, F3784239. Comfortable mid to upper-range within walking distance of town. **B** ***Dunrovin Motel***, 140 Heu Heu St, T/F3787384. Budget option in western suburbs.

There are 6 **motor camps** in town. The **A-D** ***De Brett's Thermal Resort***, Napier/Taupo Highway (SH5), T3788559, F3772181, is an excellent establishment with great range of cabins as well as powered sites. Modern facilities. Right opposite hot pools complex. Recommended. The **B-D** ***Lake Taupo Holiday Park***, 28 Centennial Dr, T3786860, is an adequate alternative, closer to town and opposite the AC Thermal Baths.

If you want to linger a while at the Orakei Korako Thermal Reserve (see page 290) the **B** ***Orakei Korako Resort***, 494 Orakei Korako Rd, T3783131, ok@reap.org.nz, provides log cabin-style accommodation across the lake from the thermal reserve. Quiet, comfortable with modern facilities. Spa pool on the deck overlooking the lake. Recommended for superb peace and quiet.

There is controversial **free camping** just outside Taupo at ***Reid's Farm***, next to the river on the Huka Falls Rd. But it does get busy and can attract less than desirable neighbours.

Eating There is a wide selection of restaurants, brasseries and cafés in Taupo, with most being located in the many motels and in the heart of town, around the waterfront. If you have been looking forward to sampling a big fat juicy trout, the fine fish for which the town and the region are famous, you will be disappointed. Under the conservation act it is illegal to buy or sell trout. However, if you have had a successful fishing trip most restaurants are delighted to cook your catch for you.

Expensive Although you may not be able to afford to stay at the exclusive ***Huka Lodge***, Huka Falls Rd, you can sample its equally amazing culinary delights. The Lodge welcomes casual diners for breakfast, lunch and dinner, but book first, T3785791. Most of the upper-range motels and hotels have in-house restaurants that welcome non-guests. The ***Tui Oaks'*** 'Reflections in the Lake' can offer a pleasant candlelit affair overlooking said lake, T3788305, while the Serengeti Restaurant in the new ***Caboose Lodge*** has everything short of the full water buffalo, T3760116.

Mid-range If you are looking for a good traditional beef or lamb dish look no further than ***Finch's Bar and Brasserie***, 64 Tuwharetoa St. It has an imaginative menu and congenial surroundings including a great open fire. Open Mon-Fri from 1130, Sat/Sun from 1800. T3772425. ***Villino Restaurant***, 45 Horomatangi St, is also popular, offering mainly European dishes, T3774478. There are plenty of Asian restaurants in Taupo, mainly on Tuwharetoa and Roberts St: ***Mr India***, 30 Tuwharetoa. Open Mon-Sat 1100-1430 for lunch and from 1730 for dinner, T3771969; ***The Thai Restaurant***, 2 Roberts St, open daily from 1700, T3781139; ***Saisaki***, 19 Tongariro St, T3771232 (Japanese); and ***Seoul House***, corner of Roberts and Titiraupenga Sts, T3773344 (Korean). Although not remarkable, all provide the usual taste sensations. There are two Italian restaurants of which ***Misha's***, 28 Tuwharetoa St, open daily from 1700, T3776293, has perhaps the most loyal following. For a nice American-style Cajun meal try the ***Cajun Kiwi***, 92 Roberts St. Open Tue-Sun from 1730, T3785276.

Cheap *The Ploughmans Pub*, 43 Charles Cres, is a pleasant English-style pub just off SH1 heading south out of town. It offers good pub grub in quiet surroundings, T3773422. Back in town, the *Replete Café*, 45 Heu Heu St, is considered one of the best cafés and daytime eating establishments. Open Mon-Fri 0845-1700, Sat 0900-1430, Sun 1000-1430, T3780606. The *Robert Harris Coffee Shop*, 42 Roberts St, is an old favourite, nicely located on the waterfront. It is always busy and offers a fine selection of quick snacks, breakfasts and bottomless cups of coffee. Although away from the centre of town the *Bach Restaurant*, 116 Lake Terr, has the best pizza in town. Open daily from 1800, T3787856.

Pubs & entertainment

Most of the action eminates from Tongariro and Roberts St (waterfront) and their connecting blocks in the heart of town. The best pubs are the new Irish *Finn MacCauls*, T3786165, and the trendier *Axis Bar*, T3787624, both on the corner of Tongariro and Tuwharetoa Sts. Both have bands at the weekends. Along the waterfront there are fine lake views and a congenial atmosphere at the *Mad Dogs and Englishmen*, 80 Lake Terr, T3780457, while for a quiet (good) pint and traditional pub food in the old English pub-style head for the *Ploughmans* (heading out of town south) on Charles Cres, T3773422.

The **Cinema** in Taupo is located on Horomatangi St, T3787515.

Events

In the 1st and 2nd weeks of **Feb** the biennial *Lake Taupo Arts Festival* swings into action, attracting local and national artists and exhibitions. The street performances are excellent, T3771200. In the 1st week of **Mar** *Ironman New Zealand* attracts the obscenely fit from all over New Zealand, who compete in a 1-day triathlon event, www.ironman.co.nz **April Fools Day** sees the *Diamondback Flyer Cycle Race* from Rotorua to Taupo, and in the second week, the 3-day *Lake Taupo International Trout Fishing Tournament*. In the 1st week in **Aug** the *Taupo Half-marathon* sees all ages, shapes and sizes running (or crawling) around the lake, while late **Nov** sees them doing the same by bike, in the *Great Lake Cycle Challenge,* T3786655. Last but not least, **Dec** brings the 2-day *ETA Ripples Power Boats and Water Festival* on the lake, usually in the first week.

Shopping

For interesting New Zealand art and crafts take a look in the *Kura*, 47A Heu Heu St, T3774068.

Directory

Banks: All the major banks have branches and ATMs in central Taupo. **Car rental**: *A1*, corner of Tamamutu and Gascoigne, T3783670; *Avis*, 61 Spa Rd, T3786305; *Budget*, corner of Titiraupenga and Tuwharetoa Sts, T3789764; *First Choice*, 7 Nukuhau St, T3780985; *Rent-A-Dent*, 7 Nukuhau St, T3782740. **Cycle hire**: *Rent-A-Bike*, T025322729. **Communications Internet**: *Cyber Shed*, 115 Tongariro St, T3774168; *Contact Cyber Café*, 10 Roberts St, T3783697. **Post office**: Horomatangi St. Open Mon-Fri 0900-1700, Sat 0900-1200, T3789090. **Library**: Story Pl, T3787554. **Medical services**: **Hospital**, Kotare St, T3788100; **Taupo Medical Centre**, corner of Heuheu and Kaimanawa Sts, T3784080; **Late pharmacy**, Mainstreet, 67 Tongariro St. Open 0900-2030, T3782636. **Police**: Story Pl, Hotline, T3784935. **Taxis**: *Taupo's Top Cabs*, T3789250; *Taupo Taxis*, T3785100. **Travel agents**: *House of Travel*, 93 Tongariro St, T3772700; *Budget Travel*, 37 Horomatangi St, T3789799. **Useful addresses:** *AA*, 93 Tongariro St, T3786000.

Wairakei Park

Huka Falls

The Huka Falls are signposted from SH1 and are accessed via the Huka Falls Rd. There is a new information kiosk in the falls car park

No visit to Taupo would be complete without a muse of utter fear and trepidation at the mighty Huka Falls. Located in the heart of the Wairakei Park north of the town, these falls are arguably the most spectacular in the country. From a sedate steady flow the waters of the Waikato River are forced through a 15 m wide cleft of solid rock for 100 m, before falling 7 m into a cauldron of aquatic chaos and foam. From the car park a bridge crosses the rapids before joining a walkway down to the waterfall, where, depending on the flow (regulated at Lake Taupo for electricity generation), the falls vary from 9 m to 10 m in height, to a staggering 220 cu m per second of volume. Believe it or not some utter lunatics have attempted the ultimate adrenaline buzz of 'riding' the Huka by canoe. Last time it was attempted in 1994, two canoeists went down. One made it in about 60 seconds. The other disappeared in the torrent and reappeared minus canoe, and life, 40 minutes later.

The **walking tracks** that lead both north and south along the river from here are worthy of investigation on foot or mountain bike. Just up river is the exclusive retreat of *Huka Lodge* – an exorbitant luxury pad that hosts the filthy rich and occasional visiting dignitaries.

Honey Hive

Carrying along the Huka Falls Loop Road (north) you can take a small diversion to admire the view looking back at the falls, before passing *Helistar's Helicopters* (see page 284) and arriving at the Honey Hive. For honey monsters this is the 'place to bee' with some interesting interpretative displays, a working glass fronted hive and the hilariously titled *Beez Kneez Café*. There is also a shop where you can purchase a tub of Manuka Honey, the most delectable toast spread on earth. ■ *Daily 0900-1700. Free. T3748553.*

Volcanic Activity Centre

The next attraction along the road are the geological delights of the Volcanic Activity Centre. It is well worth a peek, if only to get an inkling of the scale and magnitude of the natural powers that lie beneath your feet. The Taupo district is in the heart of one of the most active volcanic zones in the world, the details of which are well presented in the centre. There are models and displays, all with the appropriate shaking and rumbling noises. ■ *Daily 1000-1700. $5, child $2.50. T3748375. There are also volcanic tours that are available in the area, T3785901. $80-$190. Their website www.volcanoes.co.nz is just fascinating and will give you all the latest status reports on national earthquakes and eruptions.*

Prawn Park

Carrying along Huka Falls Road you pass **NZ Woodcraft** (a glorified native wood souvenir workshop) before reaching the road end and the riverbank. Here you will find Prawn Park. Hailed as the world's only geothermal Prawn Farm, you can join an informative tour (to meet'em), see the prawns crassly anthromorphisised (and greet'em), before you are encouraged to tuck into a few (and eat'em), in the *Riverside Restaurant*. Thankfully, prawnless meals are also available. ■ *Daily 0900-1700. $6, child $1.50. T3748474.*

River trips

Alongside Prawn Park are the headquarters of the highly contrasting *African Queen* and *Huka Jet* river trips. You can take your pick between a sedate and historic trip on the 1907 'Otunui' or the raunchier Huka Jet boats. Both boats go up the river to view the Huka Falls. The 'African Queen' departs hourly 1100-1600 with an additional glow-worm trip at 2100 in summer and 1930 in winter, $25, child $15. T3785828. The Huka Jet is open daily and leaves every half-hour, $55, child $25. T0800-485253.

Craters of the Moon volcanic reserve

Back on SH1 and almost directly across it, you can access the Craters of the Moon volcanic reserve. This is a very steamy affair that is somewhat akin to taking a stroll through a smouldering bush fire. From almost every conceivable crack and crater along the 40-minute to one-hour walk, steam quietly billows into the air, with only the faintest hiss giving you an indication of the forces that lie below. The track is easy going, with most of it understandably made up of boardwalk. The reserve and the car park are staffed by friendly thermo-volunteers that will keep an eye on your car. ■ *Open daily. Free but offer a donation.*

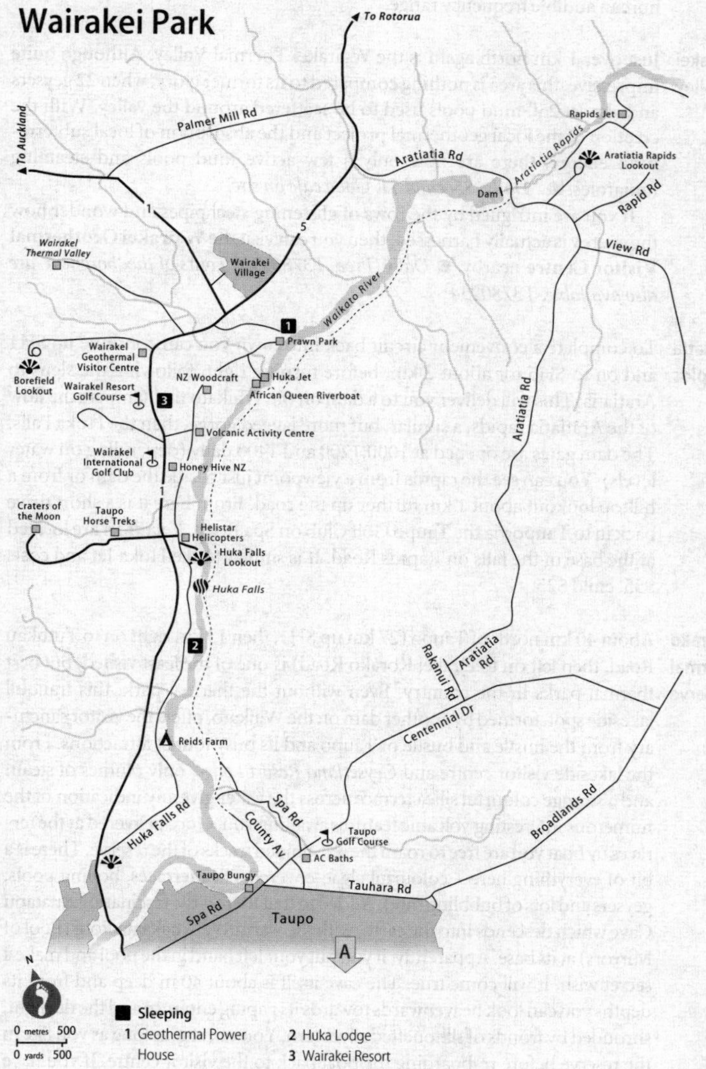

Heading north again up SH1 you pass the **Wairakei Golf Course** to the left. This is a superb course of international quality and, as far as golf courses go, very cheap and easy to access (if not easy to play). If you just happen to be there in August/September it is also one of the best places in New Zealand to see **tui**, the native bird which features in the course logo. If you go to the trees behind the clubhouse you can often see large flocks of them feeding amongst the flowering branches in an almost hyper feeding frenzy. Their call is one of the most unusual and entertaining in the avian world, with an inconceivable range of whistles, clicks and knocking noises, most of which are beyond the human audible frequency range.

Wairakei Thermal Valley

Just over 1 km north again is the Wairakei Thermal Valley. Although quite impressive, this area is nothing compared to its former glory, when 22 geysers and almost 250 mud pools used to be scattered around the valley. With the creation of the local geothermal project and the absorption of local subterranean energy, there are now only a few active mud pools and steaming fumaroles. ■ *Daily. $5, child $1. Good café on site.*

If you are intrigued by the rows of glistening steel pipes and wonder how the energy is actually harnessed, then you can visit the **Wairakei Geothermal Visitor Centre** nearby. ■ *Daily. Free. T3780913. Tours of the 'borefield' are also available, T3780254.*

Aratiatia Rapids

To complete a convenient circuit back into town you can continue up SH1 and on to SH5 for about 2 km, before turning right, following the signs to Aratiatia. This will deliver you to a dam on the Waikato that tempers the flow of the Aratiatia rapids, a similar, but more jagged gorge, than the Huka Falls. The dam gates are opened at 1000,1200 and 1400 daily (depending on water levels). You can see the rapids from a viewpoint just beside the dam or from a hilltop lookout about 1 km further up the road. From here it is a short drive back in to Taupo via the Taupo Golf Club on Spa Road. *Rapids Jet* are located at the base of the falls on Rapids Road. It is similar to the Huka Jet and costs $55, child $25.

Orakei Korako Thermal Reserve

About 40 km north of Taupo (27 km up SH1, then 13 km right on to Tutukau Road, then left on to Orakei Korako Road) is one of the least visited, but best thermal parks in the country. Even without the thermal park, this tranquil lakeside spot, formed by another dam on the Waikato, offers the visitor sanctuary from the hustle and bustle of Taupo and its busy tourist attractions. From the lakeside visitor centre and *Geyserland Resort Lodge* only plumes of steam and a strange colourful silica terrace across the water give any indication of the numerous interesting volcanic features awaiting you. Once delivered at the terraces by boat you are free to roam the self-guided tracks of the reserve. There is a bit of everything here – colourful algae-covered silica terraces, boiling pools, geysers and lots of bubbling mud. Added to that there is the fascinating Ruatapu Cave which descends into the earth, with the warm Waiwhakaata Pool (Pool of Mirrors) at its base. Apparently, if you put your left hand in the pool and make a secret wish, it will come true. The cave itself is about 40 m deep and from its depths you can look heavenwards towards its gaping entrance and the daylight, shrouded by fronds of silhouetted silver fern. You can stay as long as you like in the reserve before re-boarding the boat back to the visitor centre. If you have any questions about the reserve ask local guide Chris who is an entertaining 'geyser' of considerable knowledge. ■ *0830-1630 (hours vary according to demand). $17, child $6. There is a café and shop at the visitors centre which also acts*

A steamy relationship

In times of early Maori settlement the Orakei Korako thermal reserve was the sole domain of the Wahine (Maori women folk) who used to cross the lake and use the waters to beautify themselves. Legend has it that a Maori warrior from a neighbouring tribe (let's call him Wayne) found one of the girls in the cave (let's call her Waynetta). Though Waynetta was already spoken for, Wayne made advances on her. Her initial reaction was – of course – the expected 'bugger off big boy, my boyfriend is just around the corner', but Wayne was a very audacious fellow with a fine, muscular body, and further wooing apparently did the trick. When they heard the cuckolded boyfriend (let's call him Shane) calling for Waynetta, the pair quickly bolted, but they were spotted and followed by the now very angry Shane. The fleeing couple took a safe route across the silica terraces that only the women knew about, knowing that Shane would try to follow. This he duly did, only to run across a thin part of the terrace where he fell into a boiling pool and was cooked alive. So, gentlemen, take heed. The moral of the story is obviously get down to the gym and work on that six pack if you don't want to lose your girlfriend.

as the base for NZ Riverjet jet boat trips, T3337111, from $55, an interesting trip taking in some lovely lake and river scenery. You can also hire kayaks at the visitor centre, T3783131. Walter's Tours, based in Taupo, offer specialist tours to the reserve, T3785924.

Pureora Forest Park

This little-known forest park to the west of Taupo offers a number of easy short walks as well as the more demanding climb to the summit of Mount Pureora (1165 m). The park is also the focus for the successful reintroduction of the kokako (a native bird with a beautiful haunting song). Most of the main park sights can be taken in on a scenic drive that starts from Kakaho Road, south of the intersection of SH32 and Poihipi Road, to emerge again at Mangakino. For maps and more information see the Taupo VIC. There is also a DOC Field Centre in Mangakino, T8784773.

Turangi and Tokaanu

Population: 4000
Phone code: 07

Turangi, is located on SH1, 50 km south of Taupo and 4 km inland from the southeastern edge of Lake Taupo. It is a small, pleasant village, world famous for trout fishing on the scenic Tongariro River that flows past the eastern edge of the village before quietly spilling into the huge expanses of the lake. The village is well served with accommodation and amenities and is often used as a convenient base for exploring the Tongariro National Park. The neighbouring village of Tokaanu, 5 km to the west along SH41, also provides accommodation, amenities, thermal pools (Mangaroa St, $3, T3868575) and access to Lake Taupo.

Ins & outs

Getting there Turangi is well-served by both ***Newmans*** and ***Intercity*** which stop at the Avis Travel Centre on the corber of Ngawaka and Ohuanga Rd, T3868918. The VIC in Turangi acts as bus ticketing and AA agents. Local operators which provide shuttle transport to Tongariro National Park, Taupo and surrounding townships include: ***Alpine Scenic Tours*** (scheduled daily services to Whakapapa and National Park and Taupo Mon-Wed-Fri, from $15), T3868918; ***Bellbird Connections***, Bellbird Lodge Backpackers, T3868281; and ***Club Habitat***, T3867492.

The Turangi **Visitor Information Centre** is on Ngawaka Pl, just off SH1, T3868999, F3860074, www.turangivc@laketaupo.com Open daily 0830-1730. They have the obligatory fishing licenses and information about where to catch the 'big ones'. Internet is available here. There is also a wealth of information surrounding the other activities in the Kaimanawa Forest Park and Tongariro National Park. Hut bookings and ski passes can also be arranged. **DOC** is located on Turanga Pl, T3868607, F3867086.

Sights Turangi would not be content without proudly displaying some live trout somewhere and the **Tongariro National Trout Centre**, 3 km south of Turangi on SH1, does it admirably. Here you can see a trout hatchery in operation, adult fish in an underwater viewing area and learn about their interesting life cycle and the history of the sport in the region, ■ *Daily 1000-1500. Free. T3868607.*

Activities & tours **Eco-tours** *Tongariro Eco Tours*, Atirau Rd (SH1), T0800-101024. This is an excellent two-hour trip aboard the 'Delta Queen' which glides serenely through the extensive and wildlife-rich wetlands of Lake Taupo. There is an entertaining commentary on the way and binoculars are provided. Trips leave from Atirau Road daily from 0800, $40.

Fishing Taupo and the Tongariro River is New Zealand's premier trout fishing region. Provided you have a licence ($12 a day available from the VIC or DOC) you can fish all year round, though summer is considered the best time for brown trout, and winter for the rainbow variety. There are numerous boat charters and guided trips (from about $50 per hour, gear included) based in and around Turangi (consult VIC) and tackle can be hired from tackle shops on Taupehi Road, and *Sporting Life* (T3868996) and *Greig Sports* (T3867713) in the town centre.

Horse trekking There are two companies in and around Turangi: *Kiwi Outback*, T3866607, two hours for $70; and *Hinenamu Trail Rides*, T3867851 (also multi day trips) from $25 per hour.

Kayaking Ever tried an inflatable kayak? Well here's your chance with *Eddyline Adventures*, T/F3865081. Extra stable trips down the Tongariro from $58.

Maori culture Cultural performances and *hangis* (feasts) held on local *marae*. At 1730 every Thursday, Friday and Saturday; $35. T3866279.

Mountain biking The Rafting Centre, Atirau Road, T3866409, has bikes for hire (two hours from $20); while *Tongariro Hike'n'Bike* offer hire and trips, T3867588.

Quad biking *Kiwi Outback Tours*, T/F3866607. Two hours to full day/overnight. Three hours, $110.

Rafting The Tongariro River is a grade III and has over 50 rapids, while the Rangitaiki further afield, is a grade IV, providing a bit more action. *Tongariro River Rafting* is based at the Rafting Centre, Atirau Road (SH1), Turangi, T0800-101024. They offer a range of trips from conventional rafting to raft fishing and mountain biking. Rafting will cost from $75 for four hours. *Rapid Sensations*, Parklands Motor Lodge, Arahori Street, T0800-227238, also raft the Tongariro, from $80. *Rock'n'River*, Puanga Street, Tokaanu, T/F3860352. This company offer a range of trips on the Tongariro from one hour to overnight. From $75.

Walking One of the best short walks around Turangi is around **Lake Rotopounamu**, which is just off the SH47, 9 km south of the intersection of SH47 and SH41 towards National Park. It is a pleasant two-hour stroll through native bush around the lake. Sadly there are no views from here south to the volcanoes. For a nice view north you can climb **Mount Maunganamu** in about 20-30 minutes. This walk starts at the Scenic Reserve along a track turning right after the Tokaanu Tailrace Bridge on SH41. The DOC field centre in Turangi has details of other walks in the area.

Sleeping

LL *Tongariro Lodge*, Grace Rd, T3867946, www.tongarirolodge.co.nz Fine fishy establishment on the banks of the river. Range of very luxurious chalets, some with kitchen facilities. Resident fishing guides. Restaurant and bar.

AL-A *Anglers Paradise Resort*, corner of SH41 and Ohuanga Rd, T3868980. Convenient and well-appointed motel with swimming pool and spas. **A-B** *Parklands Motorlodge*, corner of SH1 and Arahori St, T3867515, info@prklands.co.nz Modern and comfortable, close to Rafting Centre. Restaurant and bar, activities organized.

B-D *Extreme Backpackers*, 26 Ngawaka Pl, T3868949, F3868946. Very tidy lodge-style accommodation. Open fire, Internet. **C-D** *Club Habitat*, Ohuanga Rd, T3867492, F3860106. Large motel, motor camp, backpackers (YHA) and camping park with good facilities. Restaurant, bar, sauna and spa. **C-D** *Turangi Cabins and Holiday Park*, Ohuanga Rd, T/F3868754. 96 cabins with basic facilities. **C-D** *Oasis Motel and Tourist Park*, SH41, Tokaanu, T3868569. Tokaanu's budget option. Good cabins.

Eating

Though you can't buy trout commercially in New Zealand, most establishments in the Taupo region will cook your catch for you

For the expensive à la carte option book at the *Tongariro Lodge*, Grace Rd, T3867946. Good food at affordable prices is available at the *Anglers Café* in the Anglers Paradise Resort (daily from 1800), The *Parklands Motorlodge* and *Tongariro Lodge* (see above). Other than that there is also the *Brew House Bar and Restaurant* in the Club Habitat Complex, 25 Ohuanga Rd, which offers good pub grub to wash down with its microbrewery ales. Breakfasts are also good. Open daily, 0700-2100, T3867496. *Valentino's* is a popular Italian in the town centre, T3868821. Open from 1830.

Tongariro National Park

In winter, skiing is the principal activity

Tongariro National Park is New Zealand's oldest national park, and the fourth oldest in the world. In 1887 Horonuku Te Heuheu Tukino, the then paramount chief of Ngati Tuwharetoa, gifted the central portion – essentially the volcanoes of Ruapehu, Ngauruhoe and Tongariro – to the nation. In more recent years the park has been substantially increased in size to cover an area of 75,250 ha, taking in the forest, tussock country and 'volcanic desert'. As well as its stunning scenery, Tongariro National Park offers the visitor some excellent walking opportunities, including the **Tongariro Northern Circuit**, considered one of New Zealand's great walks, with the **Tongariro Crossing** (part of the circuit) being haled as one of the best one-day walks in the country.

Ins & outs

Getting there and around The Park is bounded along its north, and western sides by SH47, with the principal settlements of Turangi, National Park and Ohakune, and to the east by SH1 (the famous Desert Road). The small township of Waiouru is located to the southeast. Whakapapa Village, at the northern base of Ruapehu, serves as the Park's main headquarters. All the surrounding townships are serviced by ***Intercity***, with Turangi also being served by ***Newmans***. The main Auckland/Wellington rail line runs through Ohakune and National Park. A number of local shuttle bus operators provide access to Whakapapa Village and major tramping drop-off/pick-up points around the park (see the relevant Ins and outs sections). You can also fly direct to Tongariro National Park from Auckland ($238 return) with ***Mountain Air***, T8922812. The airfield is located at the junction of SH47 and SH48.

Information The **DOC** Whakapapa Information Centre is located in the heart of Whakapapa Village on SH48, T8923729, F8923814, www.whakapapa.co.nz/ www.ruapehu.tourism.co.nz Open daily 0800-1700. It has a wealth of information on the park, interesting displays, maps and weather reports. Park hut bookings/fees are administered here. If you are intending a longer tramp or summit climb you are advised to fill in an intentions sheet at the centre.

For sleeping and eating within and surrounding the park see Whakapapa Village, National Park, Turangi and Ohakune listings. DOC hut bookings can be made at all major DOC field centres and the Whakapapa Visitor Centre. Campsites have been established near each of the huts. Hut fees are $14, youth $7 Nov-May; $10, youth $5 Jun-Oct. Camping fees are around $4-5 cheaper.

History According to local Maori legend, the volcanoes were formed back around the 14th century, when Ngatoroirangi, a navigator and priest of the Arawa canoe, came to New Zealand. Journeying inland from the Bay of Plenty Ngatoroirangi saw the majestic peaks and decided to climb them, thus laying claim to all that he saw. As he climbed, Ngatoroirangi was hit by a violent blizzard. Close to death he cried out to the gods in his homeland of Hawaiki to send fire to warm his body and revive him. In response to his plea a great fire was issued forth, forming White Island, Rotorua and Taupo, before erupting from Tongariro and saving his life. Apparently in gratitude, Ngatoroirangi then slew his slave, Auruhoe, who had accompanied him on the climb, throwing the poor soul in to the newly formed crater, which later formed Ngauruhoe. The name Tongariro means 'south wind' and 'borne away' and refers to Ngatoroirangi's pleas for help. Science, of course, offers a more boring theory. It suggests that they are in fact andesitic, single and multi-vented volcanoes of recent geological origin, dating back about two million years, reaching their greatest heights during the last ice age, when glaciers extended down the slopes of Ruapehu. Have you ever heard such nonsense?

Tongariro All of the National Parks sights are of course natural and dominated by the three majestic volcanic peaks of Tongariro, Ngauruhoe and Ruapehu. Although all three mountains are active volanoes they are quite different in size and appearance. Tongariro, the namesake of the park, at the northern fringe, is a fairly complex, flat-topped affair and the lowest at 1968 m. Of the three mountains it is the most benign with only a few mildly active craters, some hot springs, lakes, fumaroles and pools of boiling mud. From a purely aesthetic point of view its most attractive features are the aptly named **red crater** (which is still active) and the small **emerald lakes** at its base. Nearby are the contrasting **blue lakes** of the **central crater** and the **ketetahi springs**, which emerge on its northern slopes. All of these interesting features are included on the **Tongariro Crossing**, which can be completed in a day and is considered one of New Zealand's best one-day walks (see description below).

Ngauruhoe Just 3 km to the south of Tongariro is the classic symmetrical cone of **Ngauruhoe** (2291 m), the youngest of the three volcanoes. Its classic cone shape is due to its relative youth, but more especially because it has a single vent, as opposed to Ruapehu and Tongariro which have multiple vents. Although, Ruapehu and White Island (Bay of Plenty) have been far more active in recent years, Ngauruhoe has over the years been considered the most continuously active, frequently venting steam and gas and, occasionally, ash and lava, in more spectacular displays of pyroclastics. Its last significant eruption occurred in 1954.

There is plenty of evidence of these eruptions to be seen, most obvious being the old lava flows on its slopes. The Tongariro Crossing Track skirts the eastern flank of Ngauruhoe, while another popular three to four-day tramp is the **Northern Circuit Track**, which is one of New Zealand's great walks and encompasses both Ngauruhoe and Tongariro.

Ruapehu

About 16 km south of Ngauruhoe is the majestic shape of **Ruapehu**, with its truncated cone, perpetually snow-covered **summit peaks** and **crater lake**. It is the North Island's highest mountain, at 2797 m, and over the course of the last century has seen the the most violent activity of all the three volcanoes. Between 1945 and 1947, due to a number of eruptions blocking the overflow, the waters of the crater lake rose dramatically. On the stormy Christmas Eve of 1953, without warning, the walls of the crater collapsed and a mighty lahar rushed down the Whangaehu River, wiping out the rail bridge near Karioi. The night train to Auckland arrived moments later and 153 lives were lost. It erupted more recently, in September 1995, thankfully and miraculously without loss of life, and the same thing happened a year later, wiping out the entire ski season for both Whakapapa and Turoa and for almost another year. Ruapehu attracts thousands of visitors each year who come to ski or climb on its slopes, or enjoy its numerous long and short tramping tracks. The longest track is the **Round-the Mountain Track** which takes 5-6 days with overnight stays at a number of DOC huts on the way. Ruapehu is home to three ski fields: **Whakapapa** on its northern flank (serviced by Whakapapa and Iwikau Villages), **Turoa**, on the southern flank (serviced by Ohakune); and **Tukino,** the smallest and least popular of the three on the eastern slopes.

Skiing

For details, see Ohakune and Whakapapa Village sections

Tongariro National Park offers numerous walking tracks from a few minutes to six days. There are numerous DOC huts located throughout the park. The major tramps are the famed **Tongariro Crossing** (see previous page), the **Northern Circuit** and the **Round the Mountain Track**. Most of the shorter walks are located and accessed from Whakapapa Village and the Ohakune Mountain Road, which connects Ohakune with the Turoa Ski Field. Note that a number of local activity operators also offer guided walks and DOC run an excellent summer programme of organized and guided walks, which usually start from the Whakapapa Village Visitor Centre; $10-80. T8923729.

Walking

The Northern Circuit The Tongariro Northern Circuit winds its way over Mount Tongariro and around Mount Ngauruhoe passing through unusual landforms and volcanic features, including lakes, craters and glacial valleys. Taking 3-4 days to complete (with overnight accommodation provided in DOC huts), it is listed as one of New Zealand's great walks. The track officially starts from Whakapapa Village and finishes at the Mangatepopo Road just off SH47, but the track can also be accessed from Ketetahi Road (north) or Desert Road (east). Detailed information about the walk can be obtained from the Whakapapa Visitors Centre, where you can also arrange hut bookings and are also advised to fill in an intentions form. The DOC website www.doc.govt.nz also provides excellent details on the walk. If you do not have your own transport, the local shuttle operators will provide transportation (see relevant town/village listings). If you have your own vehicle do not leave valuables in parked cars.

Round-the-Mountain Track The Northern Circuit can be combined with the full Ruapehu Round-the-Mountain Track to create a mighty six-day tramp around all three mountains. Again comfortable accommodation is

The Tongariro Crossing

This excellent walk is hailed as one of the best one day walks in the country and provided the weather is kind, there is no doubt that the combination of views and the varied and unique volcanic features certainly make it a memorable experience. But to call it a walk is really an understatement. At about 16 km in length with some steep climbs and the odd bit of scrambling, it is really a mountain hike that can take up to ten hours to complete. In winter it can be impassable and even in summer dangerous, so despite what you may have heard, don't underestimate the walk or overestimate your abilities. But if you are fit and well-prepared and the weather is looking good, you should not pass up the opportunity.

The walk can either be tackled from north to south, or south to north, with a number of diversions along the way. The general recommendation is to start from the Mangatepopo Car Park (accessed off SH47 on the park's western edge), walk the 10 km north to Ketetahi Hut, stay the night, then either, descend from the Ketetahi Hut to SH47A (walk terminus), or return the 10 km back to Mangatepopo. The overnight stay is all part of the 'package' and is recommended if you have the time. There is a hut at the Mangatepopo end but it has neither the character nor the view that the Ketetahi enjoys.

From Mangatepopo the track makes a gradual ascent towards the southern slopes of Tongariro, while the steep slopes and lava flows of Ngauruhoe loom to the northwest. Sandwiched between the two mountains the track is then forced to make a steep ascent up the Mangatepopo Saddle. Before this ascent there is the choice of a short diversion to the 'Soda Springs' – a series of cold springs which emerge beneath an old lava flow, surrounded by an oasis of greenery. Once you have negotiated the Saddle you enter Tongariro's South Crater. The views of Ngauruhoe from here are excellent (and the especially fit can take in the summit diversion from here). A short climb then leads to the aptly named Red Crater and the highest point on the crossing (1,886 m). Following the rim of this crater you are then treated to the full artist's palette of colours on with the partial descent to the Emerald Lakes. It is the minerals from Red Crater that create the colours in the water. Just beyond Emerald Lakes, the track branches right to Oturere Hut, or continues to Ketetahi Hut across the Central Crater and alongside Blue Lake, which is another water filled vent. The track then straddles the North Crater taking in the stunning view north across Lake Taupo, before making a gradual zigzag descent to the Ketetahi Hut (1,000 m), without doubt the busiest and most popular in the park. If you have booked your stay in the hut bear in mind it operates on a first come first served basis, so get there early to claim your bunk. The huts all have mattresses, gas cookers (summer only), water supplies and toilet facilities. In the busy seasons there will be hut wardens present to provide information and latest weather reports. The hot Ketetahi Springs are on private Maori land only a few hundred metres away from the hut. Until recent years a highlight of the walk used to be a welcome soak in the pools of the stream, but sadly, due to unresolved disagreements between DoC and the local Iwi, the springs and stream are now out of bounds. From Ketetahi it is a two hour descent through native bush to the SH47A access point. For more information about 'The Crossing' and hut bookings contact the Whakapapa Visitor Centre. The DoC website www.doc.govt.nz, is also an excellent source of information. For transportation to either Mangatepopo Car Park or SH47A access see under National Park and Whakapapa Village.

available in DOC huts along the way. The Round-the-Mountain Track can be accessed from Whakapapa Village or the Ohakune Mountain Road. For information and hut bookings contact the Whakapapa Visitors Centre or DOC field centre on Ohakune Mountain Road, Ohakune (see page 301).

Ruapehu Crater Lake Both the summit and Crater Lake of Ruapehu are popular climbs in both summer and winter and are, in part, easily accessible via the Whakapapa Ski Field Chairlift. The climb to the crater and back takes about seven hours (four hours if you use the chairlifts). Once you reach the snow line it is tough going and can be dangerous. Ice axes and crampons are essential kit in winter and recommended even in summer. Whatever your intentions, always obtain all the necessary information before attempting this climb and let DOC know of those intentions. Ruapehu has claimed many lives. A few local operators offer guided walks to the Crater, T8923738 (see VIC).

A very close eye is kept on the mountain's seismic activity, and at the slightest sign of any action, an exclusion zone is placed around the crater

Whakapapa Village

Whakapapa Village is essentially the headquarters and information base for The Tongariro National Park and the gateway to the **Whakapapa Ski Field**. It is also home to the magnificent *Grand Chateau Hotel*, built in 1929. As well as the Chateau itself there are a number of accommodation and eating options available in the Whakapapa Village. There is also a store, the DOC field centre and, believe it or not, a golf course. Don't miss the excellent displays in the Whakapapa DOC Visitor Centre and especially the seismograph, monitoring the fickle moods of the mighty Ruapehu, which, lest you forget, is an active volcano that last let rip in the mid 1990s.

Look out for the bright yellow kiwi road sign. There are very few of these signs in the country. Due to their considerable 'souvenir' appeal the DOC got so fed up replacing them that the signs were almost withdrawn altogether

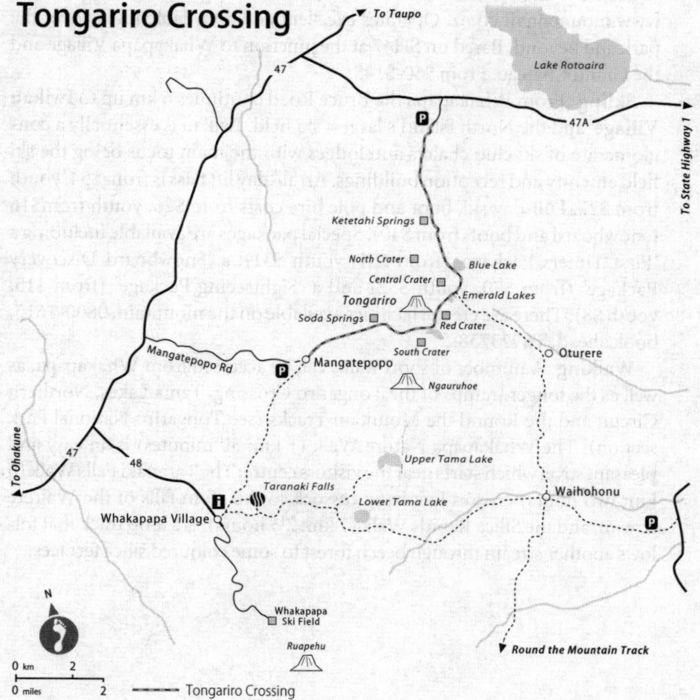

Ins & outs **Getting there** There is only shuttle bus transportation available to Whakapapa Village. Alpine Scenic Tours are a principal operator with daily schedules, T3868918. See also National Park Village and Turangi sections.

Information The DOC Whakapapa **Visitor Information Centre** is located in the heart of Whakapapa Village on SH48, T8923729, F8923814, www.whakapapa.co.nz Open daily 0800-1700. The centre offers a broad range of information on the park, with many displays and an audio-visual theatre to keep you interested on a rainy day ($3). The staff are expert in advising on walk options in the park. Note the seismograph quietly sitting in the corner, just waiting for the next major volcanic event.

Sights & activities Whakapapa can be used as a base for the numerous activities throughout the park (see Activities sections in National Park Village, Ohakune and Turangi). One local operator is *Plateau Adventure Guides*, a quality outfit offering a range of activities from mountaineering to kayaking, T8922740. For the luxury treatment you might like to try the Tongariro Trek Trip offered by the Grand Chateau. It includes the Tongariro Crossing and Crater Lake of Ruapehu as well as four nights in the hotel itself, all for $1000. T8923809.

Mountaineering Whakapapa provides the most accessible routes to the Ruapehu Summit(s) and the Crater Lake. In both summer and winter you can take the chairlift (T8923738), then reach either the Crater Lake and/or the summits from there; 6 km, four hours (9 km, seven hours minus chairlift). The highest summit is **Tahurangi** (2797 m) on the southwest fringe of the crater. The dome hut, which took a pummelling during the 1990s eruptions, is easily accessible at the crater's northern fringe. As always, make sure you are well-equipped.aprèst and leave details of your intentions with DOC at the visitor centre (see also Ruapehu Crater Lake Walk on page 297).

Scenic flights *Mountain Air Scenic Flights*, T0800-922812, www.mountainair.co.nz Operates excellent and affordable flights over the park and beyond. Based on SH47 at the junction to Whakapapa Village and the Grand Chateau. From $60-$145.

For ski Information, T8923738, www.whakapapa.co.nz Snowphone T0900-99333

Skiing From Whakapapa the Bruce Road continues 6 km up to **Iwikau Village** and the North Island's largest ski field. Iwikau is essentially a conglomerate of ski club chalets and lodges with the main focus being the ski field amenity and reception buildings. An all-day lift pass is from $54, youth from $27. Full-day ski, boot and pole hire costs from $26, youth from$16 (snowboard and boots from $40). Special packages are available including a 'First Timers Package' (from $51, youth $31); a 'Snowboard Discovery Package' (from $70, youth $52) and a 'Sightseeing Package' (from $15, youth $8). There are crèche facilities available on the mountain, 0800-1615, book ahead, T8923738.

Walking A number of short walks can be accessed from Whakapapa, as well as the longer tramps of the Tongariro Crossing, Tama Lakes, Northern Circuit and the Round the Mountain Tracks (see Tongariro National Park section). The Whakapapa Nature Walk (1 km; 30 minutes) is an easy and pleasant stroll which starts near the visitors centre; The Taranaki Falls Walk (6 km; two hours) crosses low-lying tussock to the 20 m falls of the Wairere stream; and the Silica Rapids Walk (7 km; 2½ hours), is a loop track that follows another stream through beech forest to some coloured silica terraces.

Sleeping

All prices rise in winter, and opening and closing times vary. For all winter accommodation, and even in summer, booking is advised

LL-AL *The Grand Chateau*, T8923809, F8923704, www.chateau.co.nz Traditional luxury in a grand location. 63 rooms, 1 executive suite and 9 villas. Excellent restaurant, bar and café. Pool and golf course. **AL-A** ***Skotel Alpine Resort***, T8923719, F8923777. Modern facilities with luxury and standard hotel rooms or self-contained chalets. Restaurant and bar. Pool, spa and gym, ski hire. **C-D** ***Whakapapa Holiday Park***, T/F8923897. Basic facilities but set in the heart of the village close to all amenities. Backpacker accommodation. **D** ***DOC Huts*** There are 9 DOC huts in the park with foot access only. Fees ($8-$15) bookings and information from DOC, T8923729.

Eating

The ***Grand Chateau*** has a restaurant with fine, traditional à la carte dining, the ***Pihanga Café*** that offers lunch and dinner from 1130 daily and the ***Whakapapa Tavern Pizzeria***, T8923809. The ***Skotel Resort*** also has a restaurant and bar that is open to non-guests for breakfast, lunch and dinner, T8923719. ***Fergusson's Café***, opposite the Chateau, is the best place for a light, cheap snack, and is open from 0800-1700. If you fancy a coffee (with a view), you can go up the Bruce Rd and take the chairlift to the (weather-dependent) ***Knoll Ridge Café***, T8923738. Chairlift $15, child $8. The ***Whakapapa Camp Store*** in the village also has light snacks and sells groceries at elevated prices, so stock up before you go.

National Park Village

Population: 500
Phone code: 07

The small, unremarkable and almost barren village of National Park is set overlooking Mount Ruapehu and Ngauruhoe, at the junction of SH4 (which links Taumaranui and Wanganui) and SH47. It is also on the main Auckland/Wellington railway line. National Park is a place graced only by its convenient location to both Tongariro and Wanganui National Parks and as such has a number of accommodation options, amenities and activity operators. It is naturally popular in the winter ski season. Its only notable 'sight' is its own impressive view across to the mountain.

Ins & outs

Getting there Some Auckland/Wellington trains stop at the station on Station Rd, while buses stop in Carroll St, the villages's main street. Bus tickets can be bought from Ski Haus, Pukenui and Howard's Lodges.

Getting around *Alpine Scenic Tours* operate a daily shuttle to and from National Park to Whakapapa Village (and the ski field), Tongariro Crossing access points and Turangi. They also connect with ***Intercity*** and ***Newmans*** buses at Turangi. Summer services may vary but they will run pretty much on demand, T3868918. Most of the major accommodation establishments offer shuttle services throughout the park. ***Tongariro Crossing Transport*** are based at Howard's Lodge and will get you to Whakapapa Village for $10 (return), the start of the Tongariro Crossing for $15 and the 42 Traverse (popular mountain bike trail) for $20, T/F8922827. ***Tongariro Track Transport*** offers a similar service, T8923716.

Activities & tours

There are a number of activity operators based in the village, again most being connected to the various lodges and backpackers. Walking equipment (including boots) can be hired from *Howard's Lodge*, *Pukenui Lodge* and the *Ski Haus* (see Sleeping below). *Pete Outdoors* offers a wide range of guided activities, T8922773.

Climbing wall The *National Park Backpackers* on Findlay Street has an 8 m wall that is open to non-guests. Open daily 0900-2100, $10.T8922870.

Fishing *Pete Outdoors*, T8922773. *Pukenui Lodge*, T8922882.

Horse trekking *Blazing Saddles*, T8922611.

Kayaking, canoeing and rafting National Park is often used as a base for Wanganui River Trips; the main lodges and backpackers will assist in arranging trips. For operators see Wanganui National Park section, page 376.

Mountain biking The 42 Traverse is a 46 km 3-7 hour track and the major biking attraction in the area, and the following provide information, guided trips or independent bike hire: *Pete Outdoors*, T8922773, *Pukenui Lodge*, T8922882, and *Go For It Tours*, T8922705.

Quad biking *Go For It Tours* based at the train station, T8922705.

Scenic flights *Mountain Air Scenic Flights*, T0800-922812, www.mountainair.co.nz Excellent and affordable flights over the park and beyond. Based on SH47 at the junction to Whakapapa Village and the Grand Chateau. From $60-$145.

Skiing Equipment hire is available from *Pukenui Lodge*, T8922882. *Howard's Lodge*, T8922827. *Ski Biz*, Carroll Street, T8922717. *Roy Turners*, Buddo Street, T8922757. *Eivin's*, SH4, T8922844.

Walking *Pete Outdoors*, T8922773. Full guided trips and instruction available.

Sleeping

All accommodation in National Park is in high demand in the winter ski season, when prices also rise. Booking is advised

AL-D *Howard's Lodge*, Carroll St, T/F8922827. Fine establishment with a wide range of comfortable rooms. B&B available. Spa. **A-D** *National Park Lodge and Motel*, Carroll St, T8922993, natparklodge@xtra.co.nz Self-contained units, comfortable backpacker accommodation and campsites available. Activities and transport pick-ups. **A-B** *Mountain Heights Lodge*, SH4, T/F8922833. B&B, self-contained, motorcamp and camping located just south of National Park Village. Friendly 'Eee by gum' Yorkshire owners with 'reet grand' home cooking. Activities and transport pick-ups arranged. **B-D** *Pukenui Lodge*, corner of SH4 and Miller St, T8922882, F8922900, www.Tongariro.cc Modern single-storey lodge. Various rooms, quad, double or single, some en-suite. Motel units and camping also available. Spa.

B-D *The Ski Haus*, Carroll St, T/F8922854, SkiHaus@xtra.co.nz Family and multi-share rooms, activities and transport arranged. **B-D** *National Park Hotel*, Carroll St, T8922805, F8922746. Basic but comfortable hotel and backpacker options. Restaurant and bar attached. Transport arranged. **C-D** *National Park Backpackers*, Findlay St, T8922870, nat.park.backpackers@xtra.co.nz Modern establishment with dorms and doubles with en-suites. Climbing wall. Activities arranged.

Eating

The ***Ski Haus*** and ***National Park*** have in-house restaurants offering breakfast, lunch and dinner to non-guests (see above). Other than that there is ***Schnapps Hotel***, Findlay St. Open 7 days from about 1100, T8922788; or ***Eivin's Café*** on the corner of Carroll St and SH4. Open daily from 0830, T8922844. Both are pleasant enough and serve traditional pub-style fare, including pizza. For fine dining in grand surroundings head for ***The Grand Chateau*** in Whakapapa Village, T8923809.

Ohakune

Population: 1320
Phone code: 06

The pleasant little ski-resort of Ohakune (meaning 'place to be careful'), near the southern edge of Tongariro National Park, changes its mood according to the season. In winter when (and if) the snows arrive, it attracts skiers in droves. But when winter brings little snow, or when spring arrives and the snow fades, it falls silent. So pretty little Ohakune is unpredictable, but whatever the season or the weather, it is worth lingering a while.

Ins & outs

Getting there Ohakune is serviced by *Intercity* buses (everyday except Sat) which stop in the centre of town at the VIC. About 2 km west of the centre, towards the mountain, is the principal 'après-ski' and mountain access point. The train station is also located here, and the daily Wellington/Auckland trains all stop on the way. For all booking and ticketing contact the VIC.

Getting around Although it has essentially 2 centres, and shuttling between them is awkward, everything in Ohakune is within walking distance. Shuttles operate up and down the Ohakune Mountain Rd (to the Turoa ski field) or elsewhere within the Tongariro National Park, pretty much on demand.

For shuttle bus companies see page 304

Information and orientation Ohakune has essentially 2 centres. The main centre is on Clyde St (SH49, where you arrive into the town) and this is the base for the VIC, the main cafés, restaurants and amenities. The other ' centre' is of the après-ski variety and is located about 2 km northwest, towards the mountain, up Goldfinch St and Mangawhero Terr. Here the focus is the *Powderhorn Chateau* (principal 'après-ski' base) with the railway station, the mountain access point (Ohakune Mountain Rd) and the DOC Field Centre also located here. The Turoa ski field is 17 km up the Ohakune Mountain Rd. The Ruapehu **Visitor Information Centre** is located in the main centre of town, at 54 Clyde St, T3858427 F3858527, www.ruapehu.tourism.co.nz Open Mon-Fri 0900-1700, Sat/Sun 0900-1530 (summer). The **DOC** Ohakune Field Centre is at the base of the Ohakune Mountain Rd, T3858578. Open daily 0800-1500. It has some excellent displays, (including video footage of the 1995 Ruapehu eruption), up-to-date weather forecasts and maps, and can advise on any aspect of park activities, including local short walks.

For Information on the Turoa Ski field, T3858456, F3858992, information@turoa.co.nz For local weather and regular snow updates in winter listen to Peak FM 95.8 FM, T3854919, or Ski FM 96.6 FM, T3859502

Sights

If the weather is foul you can always warm yourself up briefly with the video of the 1995 Ruapehu eruption in the DOC field centre

All of Ohakune's 'sights' are essentially 'natural' and revolve around **Mount Ruapehu** and its associate activities, with skiing and walking being the principal pursuits. There are a number of local short walks (mainly around the DOC field centre) as well as longer options, which come under the Tongariro National Park activities. If the weather is good, no trip to Ohakune would be complete without a drive to see the magnificent views from the top of the 17 km **Ohakune Mountain Road** and the **Turoa Ski field**. The road begins at the northwestern edge of town. **Lake Rotokura** is also worthy of a visit, and is located about 12 km south of Ohakune, on SH49. Take the track signposted to the left. There are actually two lakes, one above the other and both reached on foot through native bush (30 minutes). Both have a lovely, tranquil atmosphere, especially the upper lake, which reflects the top of Ruapehu on a clear, still day.

Activities & tours

Eco-tours *Kiwi Encounters*, T3859505. This is a local company offering touristy noctambulations into the Waimarino Forest to learn more about kiwi. If you are lucky you may actually see one, but if not, the screeching calls will certainly be forever ingrained in your memory. 2045-2300, $35, child $20. If you do see one, count your lucky stars: they reckon in 15 years the entire mainland population may be wiped out.

Fishing Lake Taupo and other local rivers and lakes offer the best freshwater fishing in the North Island. Two Ohakune-based operators are *Pete's Guiding*, T0800-754224, and *Tairoa Lodge Guided Fishing*, T3854882.

Horse trekking Contact *Ruapehu Homestead*, SH49, Ohakune,T3858799. One-hour beginner's trek $25, child $20; two hours $38; full day $70.

Kayaking, canoeing and rafting Ohakune is a popular base for river activities on the Wanganui River. For operators see page 380.

Mountain biking The area is an excellent venue for mountain biking of all grades of difficulty. For information on what tracks are available call into the DOC field centre or VIC. Bike hire is available through the *Powderhorn Ski*

Shop (Powderhorn Chateau), T3858888, and the *Ski Shed*, Clyde Street, T3858927. Full day $35. An organized trip is available with *Ohakune Mountain Ride*, T3858257. They will provide bikes and transport up to the ski field for a thrilling ride back down the mountain.

Quad bikes and four-wheel drive *Lahar Totally Off Road*, Lahar Farm, T/F3854136. Provide self-guided, guided or training trips for four-wheel drives, but only if you bring your own. Accommodation available. For Quad bikes you can hire, contact *4x4 Fun*, T0800-494386.

Skiing This is the tourist raison d'être for Ohakune, with the Turoa ski field being preferred by many to the larger Whakapapa field on the western slopes of the mountain. As well as offering some great runs and spectacular views, Ohakune sits head and shoulders above the rest for après-ski atmosphere and amenities. Although popular destinations for skiing, both Turoa and Whakapapa have suffered in recent years due to the Ruapehu eruptions in the mid 1990s and a lack of fresh winter snow. As a result, many have gravitated to the South Island ski resorts, with disastrous economic consequences for the town. However, when conditions are right there is no doubt Turoa can offer some of the best skiing in the North Island. There are numerous ski equipment hire shops in Ohakune as well as at the base of the ski field itself. The average cost of hire for skis, boots and poles is around $25, and snowboard and boots from $39. An all-day lift pass will cost from $54. There are a number of packages available on the mountain, including the 'Discover Skiing' package, which includes lift pass, equipment hire and one-hour lesson for around $49. The 'Lift and Ski Hire Package' is self-explanatory and costs from $69. A group lesson on the mountain will cost about $20 while a private lesson will cost $80. For further information on skiing see previous page. Also try to source the Turoa 2002 booklet. For transport services up the mountain see below.

Walking The Ohakune Mountain Road provides short and long walks, some of which join the Tongariro National Park's major walking circuits. There are two very pleasant short walks which depart from the DOC field centre at the edge of town. The 15-minute **Rimu Track** with its interpretative information posts is wonderful, even in the rain, while the one-hour **Mangawhero Forest Walk** follows the river valley up towards the mountain. Further up the road (11 km) the one hour **Waitonga Falls Track** is popular, as is the longer (five-hour) **Lake Surprise** tramp, which starts about 15 km up the road. The less active can try the 10-minute **Mangawhero Falls Walk** which is also accessed off the Mountain Road. For details, maps and the latest on weather call in at the DOC field centre, T3858578. The Tongariro Crossing is also accessible from Ohakune. For information see page 293. For shuttle transport see below.

Sleeping

As a main ski resort Ohakune offers a wide range of accommodation, though it operates on a seasonal basis. In winter, especially at weekends, you are advised to book well in advance. If you are stuck or want to avoid the high winter prices the far less salubrious village of Raetihi, 11 km to the east, has a number of cheaper options. For information, options and bookings contact the Raetihi Information centre, T3854805.

AL *Powderhorn Chateau*, corner of Mangawhero and Thames Sts, T3858888, F3858925. Alpine-style accommodation in the après-ski base of Ohakune. Spacious, well-appointed rooms. Excellent restaurant and bar attached. Ski/bike hire, indoor pool. In Rangataua, 5 km from Ohakune, are: **AL** *Whare Ora*, 1 Kaha St, T/F3859385, whareora@xtra.co.nz Beautiful, renovated, 5-level wooden house originally built in 1910. One en-suite with spa and sitting room, 1 attic en-suite room. Luxuriously appointed with great cuisine; **AL** *Ruapehu Homestead*, SH49, T3858799. Well-appointed rooms. In-house restaurant. Base for horse treks.

A *Tairoa Lodge*, 144 Magawhero Rd, T/F3854882, tairoalodge@xtra.co.nz Modern, spacious single-storey lodge in the centre of town. Range of en-suite rooms. Activities arranged. **B** *Waireka B&B*, 11 Tainui St, T/F3858692, richardmilne@xtra.co.nz Friendly, affordable B&B with local photographer and qualified naturopath. There are numerous self-contained chalet-style options in town including: **A** *Ossies Chalets and Apartments*, corner of Tainui and Shannon St, T3858088; **B** *Ruapehu Cabins*, 107 Clyde St, T3858608, ruapehu.cabins@xtra.co.nz **B-D** *Rimu Park Lodge and Chalets*, 27 Rimu St, T/F3859023 (also offers backpackers accommodation); and a range available through **AL-A** *Ruapehu Chalet Rentals*, 23 Clyde St, T3858149, accommodation@ruapehu.co.nz

There are also numerous **motels** including the recommended **A** *Hobbit Motor Lodge*, corner of Goldfinch and Wye Sts, T3858248, which has an in-house restaurant; **B** *Sunbeam Motel and Lodge*, 4 Foyle St, T3858470, bar and restaurant attached, spas and tour services. For a cheaper motel option try the centrally located **B-D** *Alpine Lodge Motel*, 7 Miro St, T/F3858758. Backpacker accommodation. Bistro attached. Spa pool.

There is plenty of budget accommodation in Ohakune. **C-D** *Ohakune YHA*, Clyde St, T/F3858724. Central location, range of rooms and dorms. **D** *Matai Lodge*, corner of Clyde and Rata St, T3859169, maitai.lodge@xtra.co.nz Fairly new establishment, comfortable. Bike hire. **C-D** *The White House*, 22 Rimu St, T/F3858413. Range of comfortable double and dorm rooms in modern building. Licensed lounge bar and spa. Wheelchair facilities. **D** *Station Lodge*, 60 Thames St, T3858797. Basic, laid back and close to all the nightlife. Spa. The **C-D** *Ohakune Holiday Park*, 5 Moore St, T/F3858561. Excellent facility with spotless amenities near the town centre and next to the Mangateitei Stream. Shuttle service available. Spa. For purist campers there is also the basic **D** *DOC Mangawhero Campsite*, on the Ohakune Mountain Rd, T3858578.

Eating

Expensive The *Matterhorn* and *Powderkeg* restaurants in the *Powderhorn Chateau*, corner of Mangawhero and Thames St, T3858888, are very popular for a range of fine traditional dishes. The Matterhorn is open daily year round, while the Powderkeg is closed in summer.

Mid-range The *Ohakune Hotel's* ***O Bar***, 72 Clyde St, T3858268, offers good traditional pub food both day and evenings throughout the year. Across the road the *Alpine Wine Bar and Restaurant* offers more formal dining, again every evening throughout the year from 1800. Round the corner in Miro St, the *Sassi's Bistro* has an intimate, congenial atmosphere and is also open for breakfast from 0700 and dinner from 1800 every night, year round. A number of motels have reputable in-house restaurants including the *Hobbit*, corner of Goldfinch and Wye St, T3858248. $10 specials on Fri nights.

Cheap *Le Pizzeria* and *Margaritas* on Thames St, at the northwestern end of town, are open late in the winter evenings and can alleviate the post-party munchies. In the centre of town, the slightly dodgy *Stutz Café* can fill a desperate gap, while for a good coffee and an altogether better snack (year round) head for the *Utopia Café* further north up Clyde St. Open 0900-1600 (extended hrs in winter). *The Fat Pigeon Garden Café* on the way back up towards the mountain on Mangawhero Terr is also a good café with in/outdoor seating, but has seasonal opening hours.

Entertainment

Without doubt the place to go is the *Powderkeg Bar* in the *Powderhorn Chateau*. It is spacious, nicely decked out in an alpine-style, is very popular, and above all has a great open fire. The most popular dance/late-night pub is *Hot Lava* along the road on Thames St (seasonal opening).

Transport *Tongariro National Park Shuttle Transport*, 5 Moore St, Ohakune, T0800-825825, offer an on-demand shuttle service throughout the park including, the Ohakune Mountain Rd ($15), Whakapapa Village and the Tongariro Crossing ($25). Two other local shuttle operators are ***Snowliner Shuttles***, T3858573, and ***Snow Express***, T3859280.The return fare up to the Turoa ski field is $15, child $6.

Directory **Communications Internet**: is available at the ***Snowbird Copy Centre***, 92 Clyde St, (open daily 0930-1700). ***The Video Shop***, also on Clyde St has access late into the evening. **Post Office**: Goldfinch St.

Waiouru & the Desert Road
Population: 2,500

Waiouru is at the junction of SH1 (Desert Road) and SH49 from Ohakune (27 km) on the southern fringe of the Tongariro National Park. It is essentially an army base and, for the traveller, a last resort for accommodation when the Desert Road is closed with snow. During the winter this can happen quite frequently and when it does (if conditions allow) all traffic is diverted to the west of the mountain via Ohakune and National Park. If this happens you can expect to add another 1-2 hours to your journey. The Desert Road is essentially the stretch of SH1 from Waiouru to Turangi (63 km), featuring Ruapehu and Ngauruhoe to the west and the Kaimanawa Mountains to the east. The broad flat valley is so called due to its barren landscape, given over only to grass and ancient volcanic ash fields. It has a strange kind of beauty only spoiled by the tracks of off-road army vehicles and rows of electricity pylons disappearing into the horizon. During eruptions, potential ash falls on these wires substantially threaten upper North Island electricity supplies.

There are few sights in Waiouru but, if you have time or the snow has fallen, the **QEII Army Memorial Museum** is worth a look. It has a generous collection of army hardware as well as a range of displays covering New Zealand's military history since the mid 1800s. There is also a dynamic Roll of Honour to remember those who have died for this great country. ■ *Daily 0900-1630. $8, child $5. Café. T3876911.*

Taumarunui
Population: 5000
Phone code: 07

Taumarunui is a small agricultural service town lying at the confluence of the Ongarue and Wanganui Rivers, on the western fringes of the Ruapehu District. Although nothing to write home about it, is often used as an overnight base for skiing in the Tongariro National Park, and as a base for kayak, canoe and jet boat tours of the Wanganui River and the Wanganui National Park.

For Wanganui River activity operators based in Taumarunui see Wanganui National Park section, page 376

Ins and outs Taumarunui is serviced by Intercity and Newmans and is also on the main Auckland/Wellington rail line. The TIC administers bookings and tickets. The Taumarunui **Visitor Information Centre** is located at the train station on Hakiaha St, the main drag through town, T8957494, F8956117, www.middle-of-everywhere.co.nz Open Mon-Fri 0900-1630, Sat/Sun 1000-1600. It has an interesting working scale model of the 'Raurimu Spiral' (see below). DOC is located on Cherry Grove, beside the river, T8958201.

The major attraction around Taumarunui is the **Raurimu Spiral**, an impressive feat of railway engineering on the main north/south trunk line, devised by the late RWHolmes in 1908. The track falls (or rises) 213 m at an incline of 1 in 50, by means of a complete circle, three horseshoe curves and two tunnels, which double the distance travelled. Check it out from the lookout, 37 km south of the town on SH4, or the working model in the VIC.

There are a number of walks around the town for which the VIC has details. For the very energetic there is the climb to the summit of the flat-topped **Mount Hikurangi** (770 m) behind the town. For detailed directions, and to confirm permission with the local landowner, ask at the VIC. The 155 km **Taumarunui to Stratford Heritage Trail** (scenic drive) begins or ends here, taking you through the Wanganui and Taranaki Regions to Stratford. The highlight of this trip is the tiny settlement of **Whangamomona**, which, after a run in with regional bureaucracies in 1995, declared itself a republic. It is an unremarkable little place with a population of less than 100. The village opens its borders on the anniversary of the great uprising in October each year, when there is a weekend of celebrations. No passport control or baggage checks necessary, just a pint glass. There is also an alternative scenic route from Taumarunui, across the hills via Ohura and SH40 to SH3 and New Plymouth. This is a rugged trip over remote country so make sure you are stocked up.

Sleeping and eating There is not a huge range of choice when it comes to accommodation but the VIC can advise. The best motor camp in town is the **B-D** ***Taumarunui Holiday Park***, near SH4 and next to the river, 3 km east of town, T/F8959345. For eating you can't go past the ***Main Trunk Café,*** set in an old rail carriage on Hakiaha St. Open Wed-Sun 1000-2200.

Taranaki

Taranaki

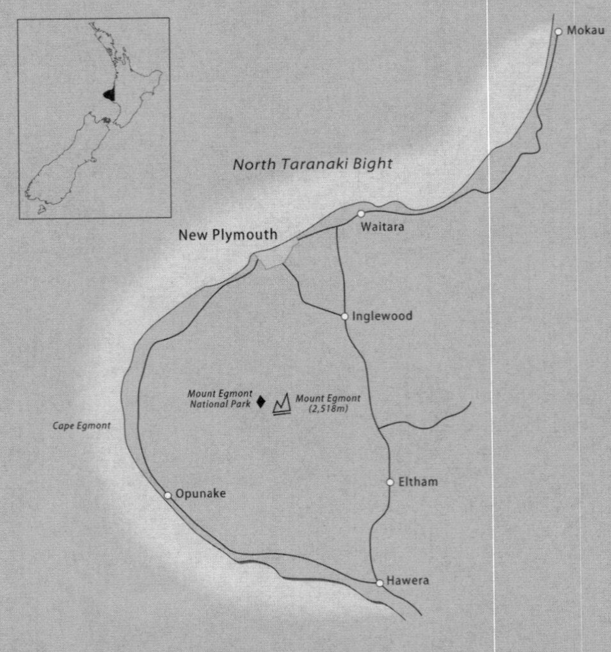

Mokau
North Taranaki Bight
New Plymouth
Waitara
Inglewood
Mount Egmont National Park
Mount Egmont (2,518m)
Cape Egmont
Eltham
Opunake
Hawera

In many ways Taranaki is more mountain than region. The awesome 2518 m snow-capped volcanic cone of the same name seems to dominate everything and, even shrouded in mist, it is still strangely omnipresent. Although it has been enjoyed by many, it has also been the death of a few, and they say it is due another eruption. But whether you look at it with reverence or fear, it will always be the region's one defining feature. The mountain has two names, Taranaki and Egmont, both official, but in a way controversial. Taranaki is the original Maori name, while Egmont is the result of Captain Cook's habit of to renaming anything in sight during his explorations in 1770. The largest town is New Plymouth, a proud, prosperous and modern centre that lies in the shadow of the great mountain on the northwest coast. Although a little bit out of the way, those who make the effort to visit the region will not be disappointed. As well as the superb scenery and range of activities on or around the mountain itself, the region boasts a fascinating history, fine parks, gardens, arts and crafts and, not least, a scenic coast which is internationally recognized for its excellent surfing.

Things to do in Taranaki

- *Enjoy the great Mount Taranaki, perhaps the most beautiful mountain in the country: climb it, ski down it, drive around it, or stroll through its Goblin Forest.*
- *Take a stroll through The Pukeiti Rhododendron Gardens or New Plymouth's Pukekura and Brooklands Parks .*
- *Try 'dam-dropping' in Hawera and go windsurfing in Oakura.*
- *Gaze at the bizarre contemporary artworks at the Govett-Brewster Gallery in New Plymouth.*
- *Climb up Paritutu Rock above the New Plymouth Power Station and see if you can see Mount Ruapehu.*

New Plymouth

Population: 50,000
Phone code: 06

New Plymouth is the main service town and population base of the New Plymouth district and Taranaki Region. Based on resources of rich agriculture land and natural gas and oil supplies, the town enjoys considerable prosperity, and this is reflected in its character and lively atmosphere. Like the entire region, the town is dominated by the mountain, which seems to dictate the general mood, like some huge meteorological barometer. On a clear day, when the mountain radiates, its sheer size and stature are mirrored proudly in the town and all around the region. But, when shrouded in mist and rain, both are equally dull and sombre. As well as being a fine base from which to explore the recreational delights on and around the mountain and the region as a whole, New Plymouth itself has an excellent art gallery, some interesting historic buildings and a fine marine and public park.

Ins and outs

Getting there **By air** The airport at New Plymouth is located about 10 km north of the town and is serviced by ***Air New Zealand Link***, T0800-737000, and ***Origin Pacific***, T0800-302302. **By road** New Plymouth is a little out of the way: 254 km from Hamilton and 172 km from Wanganui, and roughly halfway between Auckland and Wellington. SH3 that links New Plymouth to Hamilton is notorious for slips and is in a constant state of upgrading, while its continuation to Wanganui is a little better, but still quite slow. ***Intercity*** and ***Newmans*** run regular bus services to New Plymouth from Auckland and Hamilton to the north and Wanganui and Palmerston North to the south. They stop at the travel centre on the corner of Queen and King St, T7599039. ***White Star***, who are based at 25 Liardet St, also have daily freight and passenger services south, T7583338. Bookings and information at the VIC.

Getting around New Plymouth's central grid of streets has a very confusing one-way system, so patience is required. Shuttles to and from the airport are available from ***Withers***, T7511777, or ***Carter Travel***, T7599039, and cost about $12 one-way. The local bus company is ***New Plymouth City Services***, T7582799. ***Carter*** and ***Whithers*** also offer runs to hostels and the mountain, as do ***Cruise NZ Tours***, T7583222. A minibus operates between Inglewood and New Plymouth Mon-Fri, T7566193.

Information The New Plymouth **Visitor Information Centre** is located on the corner of Leach and Liardet streets, T7596080, F7596073, www.newplymouthnz.com, www.tourismtaranaki.org.nz Open Mon-Fri 0830-1700, Sat/Sun 0900-1700. **DOC** is located at 220 Devon St West, T7580433. Open Mon-Fri 0800-1600.

History

Like the mountain, New Plymouth and Taranaki as a whole has an unsettled and at times explosive human history. Prior to the arrival of Europeans there were several Maori *pa* in the vicinity of New Plymouth, particularly around the port area and the natural fortification of Paritutu Rock. The first *pakeha* to arrive in 1828 were whalers who soon found themselves joining forces with the local Te Ati-awa to defend against marauding tribes from the Waikato. In 1841, in an area now almost deserted as a result of these skirmishes, the New Zealand Company bought up large tracks of land, and European settlement began in earnest. With the return of exiled Maori, disputes quickly arose surrounding the sale of their land and, after unsuccessful arbitration by the crown and fuelled by the white settlers' greed, war broke out. The Maori in the Taranaki had not signed the Treaty of Waitangi so were treated as rebels and many land claims and transactions were highly dubious. The war was to last for 10 years, and battles between the Europeans and the Maori were amongst the fiercest ever fought in the country. As a result, most settlers deserted the area leaving New Plymouth little more than a military settlement. It was not until 1881 that formal peace was made and New Plymouth and the region as a whole settled down and began to prosper through its rich agricultural lands. New Plymouth was named after its namesake on the coast of Devon in England, from where many of the first settlers came. Today, as well as agriculture, economic booms have been enjoyed through the discovery of natural gas and oil.

Sights

One of the town's most celebrated institutions is the **Govett-Brewster Gallery**, on the corner of Queen and King Streets. Although it opened 30 years ago you would be forgiven for thinking the paint was still wet. The interior is on three levels and looks very modern, which befits its reputation as the premier contemporary art gallery in the country. Although perhaps not to everyone's taste, the mainly three-dimensional and highly conceptual pieces are well worth a look. The gallery doyen is Len Lye, a poet, writer and multi-media artist who specialized in pioneering animation work in the 1930s. His mainly abstract film works are regularly shown. ■ *Daily 1030-1700. Free. T7585149, www.govettbrewster.org.nz*

If you are interested in historical sites the VIC can give you details of a number of Heritage Trails in the area including an interesting 2-hr walk in town starting at Pukeariki Landing, a park with sculptures located by the shoreline

The **Taranaki Museum**, above the library on Ariki Street, is fairly small with the usual collection of Maori artefacts, mixed with pioneer exhibits and some rather tired-looking wildlife specimens. ■ *Mon-Fri 0900-1630, Sat/Sun 1300-1700. Free. T7589583.* There are some notable **historic buildings** and sites in the city, including the oldest stone church in the country, **St Mary's**, on Vivian Street. The original church was built in 1846. The interior contains some lovely Maori carvings and stained-glass windows. The cemetery echoes the military theme, with several soldiers' graves being a testament to the town's and area's colourful and, at times, bloody past. The quaint little **Richmond Cottage** on Ariki Street, near the museum, is a furnished colonial cottage built in 1853. ■ *Open in summer, Mon, Wed & Fri 1400-1600 and all year round on Sat/Sun, 1300-1600. $1.*

The **Fitzroy Pole** (Pou Tutaki) which stands proudly at the northern end of town on the corner of Devon Street East and Smart Road was erected by the Maori in 1844. It was done so to commemorate Governor Fitzroy's decision to question the legalities of white settlers and forbid their acquisition of huge tracts of land. Although not the original, the carving speaks for itself.

New Plymouth is famous for its parks, the oldest and finest of which are **Pukekura** and **Brooklands**, which merge. They are best accessed at Fillis Street, just east of the town centre. Pukekura, opened in 1876, is a well-maintained 20 ha of lakes and assorted gardens, with a cricket ground, fernery and tea-room serving refreshments and light meals daily except Tuesday. From here, on a clear and calm day, you will see the reflection of Mount Taranaki across the main lake, which is crossed by a Japanese-style bridge. Brooklands has an outdoor amphitheatre, ponds studded by lily pads, English-style and rhododendron gardens, an historic colonial hospital museum/gallery and a 2000-year-old puriri tree. There is also a small children's zoo with all the usual inmates including, kune-kune pigs, goats and miniature horses, as well as monkeys and a fine collection of parrots and parakeets. ■ *Daily from 0900-1800.*

Near the ugly towers of the power station and the busy port is the **Sugar Loaf Island's Marine Park**, with its eroded, volcanic rock islands. Designated in 1986, the park is home to New Zealand fur seals and a variety of nesting seabirds. Boat trips to visit the park and view the wildlife are available (see below). The shoreline of the park is part of an interesting 7-km Coastal Walkway, the highlight of which is the climb up **Paritutu Rock** – if you can. The climb requires considerable effort and involves pulling yourself up by a steel

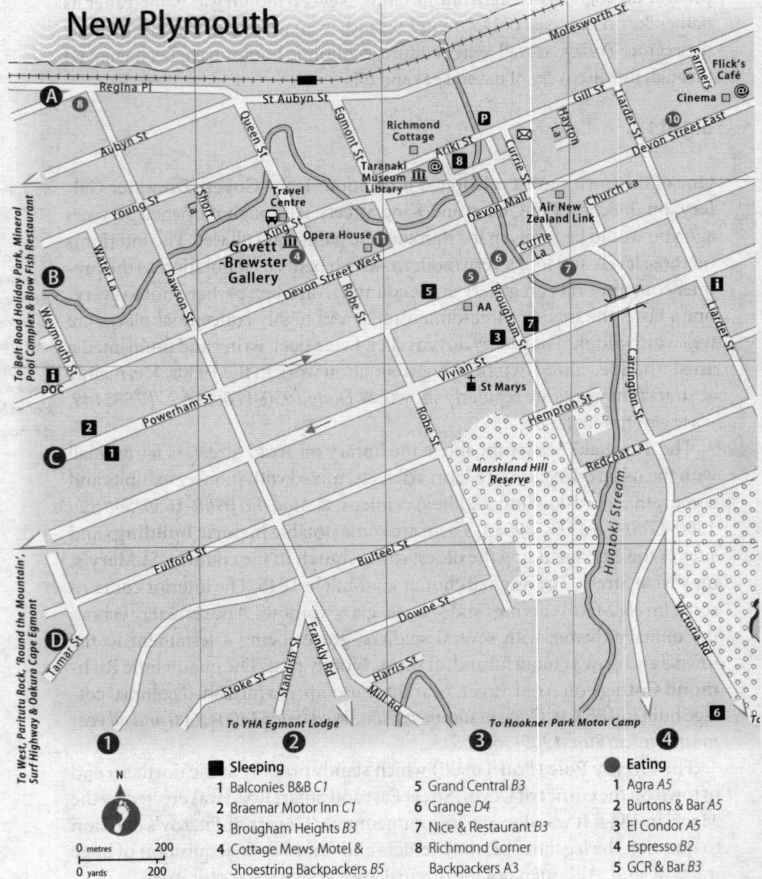

cable, but the view (though spoilt slightly by the power station and oil storage tanks) is worth the effort , with the ever-present Taranaki cone to the east and the town to the north, with Ruapehu and Ngauruhoe just visible on a clear day. Then you're faced with the descent, which is not so much a scramble, as an abseil. If the climb is too daunting, a fine view can also be had from Marshland Hill, off Robe Street, which was formerly the Pukaka *Pa*. It is also home to the New Plymouth Observatory. ■ *Open to the public on Tue 1930-2100. Donation only.*

Activities and tours

New Plymouth offers many of the usual activities with **Dam-dropping** and **Tandem-surfing** being the more unique options.

For mountain activities see page 318

Dam-dropping This is another of those 'Kiwi unique' adrenaline offerings. This time you throw yourself down a dam outlet with only a boogie-board and some other lunatics for company. The experience lasts three hours, costs from $80 and also takes in some Maori culture. *Kaitiaki Adventures*, based in South Taranaki, T2785555, www.kaitiaki.co.nz

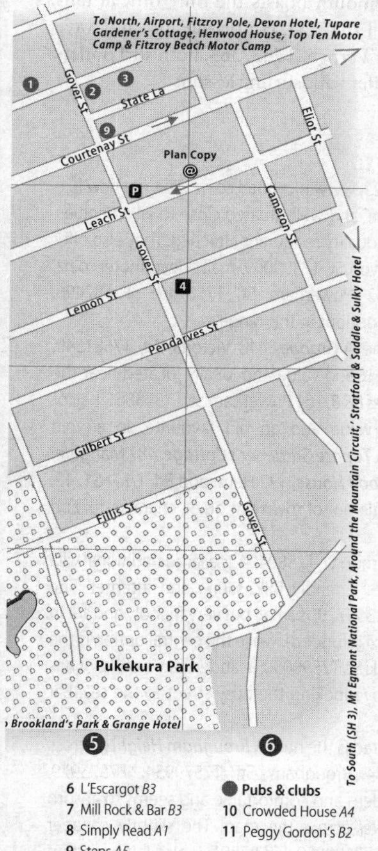

6 L'Escargot *B3*
7 Mill Rock & Bar *B3*
8 Simply Read *A1*
9 Steps *A5*

Pubs & clubs
10 Crowded House *A4*
11 Peggy Gordon's *B2*

Fishing, diving and cruising There are a number of boat charters and organized trips. For fishing or diving try *Compass Rose*, T7511573, *Taranaki Fishing Charters*, T7520731, *Fishy Business*, T7588095, or *Wild West Tours*, T02-5474532; also offer dolphin and shark-watching trips. *Chaddy's Charters* offer regular fishing and cruise trips to the marine reserve and are located at the Lee Breakwater Marina, Ocean View Parade, near the port, T7589133. It costs $20, child $10, fishing $10 per hour. For diving try *New Plymouth Underwater*, T7583348.

Horse and four-wheel drive treks *Windyglen Farm*, Bertrand Road, Waitara, T/F7520603. Treks depart daily 1030, 1330 (and 1830 in summer). *Off the Beaten Track Adventures*, T7627885, also offer canoe and four-wheel drive trips.

Kayaking For hire and local shoreline and marine park explorations, *Chaddy's Charters*, T7589133. For expeditions down the Mokau River in North Taranaki, *Wiseway Canoe Adventures*, T7529118, $65-$150.

Mineral pools Increasing in popularity in the town is the new Mineral Pool complex at 8 Bonithon Road. The complex is the result of a very tasteful renovation of the former mineral pool that has an artesian mineral well spouting 29,000-year-old water. It offers both communal and private pools (four people) with a range of professional massages and health treatments. The pools cost $15 for 30 minutes, but this is on a 'per pool' basis and they are freshly filled for each client. Very therapeutic. ■ *Daily 0730-2000. Bookings essential. T7591666.*

Scenic flights and tandem skydiving *Air Taranaki*, T7544375; *Taranaki Scenic Flights*, T7550500; *Taranaki Skydiving Club*, T7552426.

Sightseeing tours *Cruise NZ Tours* offer a popular city tour for about $40 and an all-day tour for $90, T7583222. *Newmans* also offer regular trips around the city, the mountain and farther afield for about the same price, T7584622.

Surfing, tandem-surfing and windsurfing The Taranaki or Egmont Coast is one of the best surfing venues in the country. The so called 'Surf Highway 45' which hugs the coastline between New Plymouth and Wanganui boasts some fine surf beaches, particularly at Oakura and Opunake. Particular gems also include Ahu Ahu Road, the Kumara Patch and Stent Road. In town, Footsore Beach is one of the favourites. Companies offering trips include: *Taranaki Surf Tours*, T2781285, tangaroa.adventures@xtra.co.nz Half–day $95. Also, if you have never tried surfing, have no fear: New Plymouth boasts the only official tandem-surfing operator in the country, T7527734. For private hire and wave information try *Sirocco*, T7527363, or *Vertigo*, T7527363, both surf outlets based out of Oakura. The latter also offer windsurfing lessons.

Essentials

Sleeping

For mountain accommodation see page 319

L *The Nice Hotel*, 71 Brougham St, T7586423, www.nicehotel.co.nz This is a new luxury boutique hotel that is indeed 'very nice' and well situated close to all amenities. There are a range of 'themed' rooms and a quality restaurant attached. They also offer nice tours! The **AL-A** *Devon Hotel*, 390 Devon St, T7599009, mail@devonhotel.co.nz, and the **AL-A** *Grand Central Hotel*, 42 Powerham St, T7587495, F7587496, grandhotel@hotmail.com, are the 2 nicest options in this range.

There are numerous **B&B** options. The **A** *Grange*, 44B Victoria Rd, T7581540, F7581539, cathyt@clear.net.nz, is modern, good value and ideally located near the Pukekura Park. The aptly named **B** *Balconies B&B*, 161 Powerham St, T7578866, balconies@paradise.net.nz, is cheaper, good value and an old favourite, in an old characterful home, centrally located. The **A** *Tupare Gardener's Cottage*, 487 Mangorei Rd, T7586480, F7586353, and the **A** *Henwood House*, 122 Henwood Rd, T/F7551212, henwood.house@xtra.co.nz, are both a little out of town but quiet, characterful and very pleasant.

The **B-D** *Shoestring Backpackers*, 48 Lemon St, T7580404, is a large traditional villa with a range of rooms and fine facilities. Friendly folk, sauna and internet. The **B-D** *YHA Egmont Lodge*, 12 Clawton St, T7355720, is small but very friendly and set in a quiet location a 15-min walk to town (taxi refunded); while the central option is the **C-D** *Richmond Corner Backpackers*, 25 Ariki St, T7590050, jrsanders@xtra.co.nz It has all the usual facilities with a great patio overlooking the busy street to the sea. Bar downstairs.

There are numerous **motels**. Well-located is the new **A** *Brougham Heights*, across the road from the *Nice Hotel* at 54 Brougham St, T7579954, F7575979, brougham_heights@clear.co.nz It is modern and comfortable and seems to absorb some of the niceties from the *Nice Hotel* across the road! The slightly cheaper **A** *Braemar Motor Inn*, 152 Powerham St, T7580859, F7585251, is also fairly modern and has a distinct Scottish theme with a restaurant attached.

For good value and fine folk head for the immaculate **B *Cottage Mews Motel*** suites attached to the Backpackers, 48 Lemon St, T/F7580403. There are numerous other motel options around town particularly along Coronation Av, heading southeast on SH3. These include the interestingly named **B *Saddle and Sulky*** at 188, T7575763. There is a **B-D *'Top Ten'*** motor camp in Taranaki, located centrally at 29 Princess St, Fitzroy, T/F7582566, New.Plymouth.TopTen@xtra.co.nz Nearer the water but overlooking the port is the **B-D *Belt Road Holiday Park***, 2 Belt Rd, T/F7580228, with the **B-D *Fitzroy Beach Motor Camp***, T/F7582870, located further north on Beach St, being less well endowed but more scenic. The quiet country option is the **B-D *Hookner Park Motor Camp***, T7536945, which is located on a working dairy farm along Carrington Rd about 10 km from town. Here you can join in with farm activities.

Eating

Expensive ***L'Escargot*** (André's) 37-43 Brougham St, T/F7584812. Open Mon-Fri from 1100, Sat from 1700. This is an old favourite offering award-winning, fine French-style cuisine in a congenial setting. ***The Nice Hotel***, 71 Brougham St. Well, it couldn't possibly be horrible could it? Fine à la carte with superb desserts and a good wine selection. Open Mon-Sat from 1600. ***Steps Restaurant***, 37 Glover St, T7583393. Another award-winning establishment with Mediterranean cuisine.

Mid-range The ***GCR Restaurant and Bar***, Brougham St, T7587499. A new modern restaurant and bar specializing in gourmet pizzas. Open daily. ***Agra, the Indian Restaurant***, 151 Devon St, T7580030, is deserving of a loyal following in the town and is good value. Open Sun-Thur 1730-2230, Fri/Sat 1730-late. Both ***Burtons***, corner of Devon and Gover Sts, T7585373 (Open daily from 0700), and ***The Mill Rock***, 2 Courtney St, T7581935 (Open Mon-Sat from 1100) are good pubs with pub grub to match. The latter has joined the growing trend of serving a variety of dishes on hot slabs of stone – the 'stone-grill'. For an Argentinian pizza head for the value ***El Condor***, 170 Devon St East, T7575436.

Cafés

The ***Simply Read***, 2 Dawson St, T/F7578667. In a sunny spot overlooking the sea, with a small bookshop attached. ***The Espresso***, attached to the Govett-Brewster Gallery, Queen St, T7599399, is a firm favourite, while ***The Blow Fish***, 406 St Aubyn St, T7591314, has no airs and graces and is good value.

Taranaki

Pubs & bars

Burtons (see above) seems to be a firm favourite, with fine ales and a fair weather Fri evening clientele that spills out on to the street. ***The Mill Rock*** (above) is another favourite, with a cosmopolitan clientele and live bands. ***Crowded House*** on Devon St is about the size of a football field and claims to be the official bar of the famed Taranaki Rugby Team supporters. ***Peggy Gordon's***, corner of Devon and Egmont Sts, is the town's Irish-style offering.

Entertainment

The TSB Showplace, Devon St, T7584947, stages regular national and occasional international acts. The ***New Plymouth Operatic Society*** puts on about 3 shows annually, and they are of an excellent standard. The **Cinema** is located at 125 Devon St East, T7599077.

Festivals & events

Feb/Mar: The ***Taranaki Festival of the Arts*** (every 'odd' year). High-profile and quality arts festival, involving dance, music, theatre, literary events, workshops and exhibitions. **Oct**: ***The Taranaki Rhododendron Festival*** involves a number of events and tours that take place at various major gardens, www.rhodo.co.nz **Dec-Feb**: The ***New Plymouth Festival of Lights***. Held in Pukekura Park, it involves the illumination of trees, waterfalls and fountains with additional staged events.

Shopping There are numerous excellent arts and crafts galleries and outlets in the region, for details see the VIC. The ***Rangimarie Maori Art and Craft Centre*** is located near Paritutu Rock on Centennial Dr, T7512880. See also ***Kina NZ Design and Art Space***, 101 Devon St West, T7591201.

Directory **Airlines** *Air New Zealand*, 12-14 Devon St East. **Banks** Most main branches can be found on Devon St. Currency exchange at *TSB Centre*, 120 Devon St East, T7595375. **Car hire** *Avis*, 25 Liardet St, T7575736. *Budget*, 72 Leach St, T7588039. *NZ Rental Car Centre*, 281 Devon St West, T7575362. **Cycle hire** *Raceway Cycles*, 207 Coronation Av, T7590391. **Communications Internet**: New Plymouth Library, Brougham St; *Flick's Café*, 125 Devon St East; *Plan Copy*, 53 Leach St. **Post Office**: Currie St, open Mon-Fri 0730-1800, Sat 0900-1300. **Medical services Hospital**: Taranaki Base, David St. Accident and Medical Clinic, Richmond Centre, Egmont St, open daily 0800-2200, T7598915. **Useful addresses** *AA*, 49-55 Powerham St, T7575646. **Police:** Powerham St, T7575449. **Maps**: TIC/DOC. **Taxi:** *New Plymouth Taxis*, T7575665.

Around New Plymouth

North on SH3 The 'Scenic 3 Highway', as it is called, has a number of attractions best described in the free 'Scenic 3 Highway' leaflet available from the VIC. However, there are a few attractions, walks and viewpoints that are definitely worth a visit. Heading north past Waitara and Urenui, which have some popular beaches in themselves, is the **White Cliffs Brewing Company**, a boutique beer brewery offering tastings and sales of some fairly heady brews. ■ *Mon-Fri 1000-1700, Wed 1500-1700.*

For detailed information get hold of the 'Walks in north Taranaki' from DOC or the VIC, $1

The **Whitecliffs Walkway** is the most celebrated in North Taranaki. The Whitecliffs, named after the famous Dover cliffs in England, although not on the same scale or grandeur, are quite impressive and dominate the shore for some 7 km. The track can be accessed from the south at the Pukearuhe Historic Reserve which is located at the end of Pukearuhe Road, north of Urenui. The total length of the track is 9 ½ km, terminating at the northern access point, on Clifton Road at the mouth of the Tongaporutu River. Much of the track is along the shoreline, so make sure you check the tides.

The immediate coastline either side of the Tongaporutu River is scattered with rock towers, caves and arches, though they are not easily accessed (low tide only). For a superb view of them head just north of the Clifton Road, across the bridge and up the hill on the other side. Turn left on to Cemetery Road. From the end a short walk across an accessible field will take you to the headland. There is also a fine view of the Whitecliffs from there.

Just north of Tongaporutu are **Mokau** and **Awakino**. Both are popular but remote holiday spots especially good for coastal walks and fishing. For canoe trips on the Mokau (see page 313) and cruises, T7529775, $30.

A lengthy diversion off SH3 along SH40 will take you to the 74-m **Mount Damper Falls**, the highest waterfall in the North Island. From SH40 take the Okau Road to the Mount Damper Falls car park, which is well marked. The 15-minute walk will take you to a lookout platform. The falls are best viewed after heavy rain.

Sleeping The **C-D** ***Seaview Motor Camp***, T7529708, located in Awakino, just before SH3 turns inland heading north, is excellent and has a café attached. In Mokau there is the basic **B** ***Mokau Motel***, SH3, T7529725, and a good backpackers, Palm House, T7529081 (affiliated with the YHA in New Plymouth).

Carrington Road

Carrington Road (off Victoria Road) heads southwest out of New Plymouth towards the mountain. It has a number of sights worth visiting. **Hurworth Homestead**, at 827 Carrington Road, was built originally in 1856 by young lawyer Harry Atkinson, who was also New Zealand's Prime Minister, not once, but four times. Young Harry and his family had to flee the house and the area during the Taranaki wars in 1860. The house today is a well-renovated tribute to the family. Viewing by appointment, T7533593. Further along at 1296 Carrington is the **Pouakai Zoo Park**, which is a small, private, enthusiastically run zoo, exhibiting a number of native and non-native species including meerkats and gibbons. ■ *Open 'every day, all day', T/F7533788. $5, child $2.*

The highlight on the Carrington Road, however, is the **Pukeiti Rhododendron Trust** gardens. These are 4-sq km gardens surrounded by bush that is world renowned for its beautiful displays of 'rhodies' and azaleas, which are best viewed in the spring/summer and especially during the Rhododendron Festival in late October. There is a restaurant, and a shop selling plants and souvenirs. ■ *Daily summer 0900-1700, winter 1000-1500. $8 ($5 in winter), child free. T7524141.*

If you continue on Carrington Road you will join the network of roads that surround the mountain. There is a fine walk and views of the mountain on the **Stony River** and **Blue Rata Reserves**. From Carrington take a left on to the Saunders Road dirt track and follow it to the end. From there, by foot, negotiate your way through the bush following the sound of the river. You will emerge on to the Stony River boulder-field. From here you can walk carefully east or west, under the shadow of the mighty mountain. The large Blue Rata, from which the reserve takes its name, is hard to find, about 100 m into the bush, on the river-side of the track, about halfway up its length.

Before re-joining SH45 and heading north or south, take a discreet peek at the memorial to the great man, prophet and Maori chief, Te Whiti, which is at **Parihaka Pa**, on Mid-Parihaka Road (signposted).

Sleeping The **A** ***Patuha Farm Lodge***, Upper Pitone Rd, T/F7524469. This 10-bedroom lodge is well placed in a quiet bush setting on the edge of the Pukeiti Rhododendron Trust gardens. Over all a fine relaxing retreat.

Lake Mangamahoe

There is something you simply must do on your visit to New Plymouth (weather permitting) and that is to soak up the beauty and serenity of Lake Mangamahoe. Located just 10 km southeast on SH3, this scenic reserve is one of the very view places you can see a reflection of the mighty mountain on water. After enjoying the lake itself, with its numerous swans, ducks and geese, head to the road end and take the right hand track up the steps to the lookout point. From here at sunset, or anytime when the mountain is clear, the view is magnificent. Take your camera.

Mount Egmont (Taranaki) National Park

Mount Egmont is one of the oldest national parks in the country, designated in 1900

Weather permitting, no trip to Taranaki would be complete without getting close to the mountain. At 2518 m, Mount Taranaki is not only in the heart of Egmont National Park, but essentially is the heart. This classically shaped, dormant volcano was formed by the numerous eruptions of the last 12,000 years. The most recent happened 350 years ago and they say she is presently 'overdue' , with the potential to 'go off' literally at anytime. Fatham's Peak, on the southern slopes, is a parasitic outcrop from the main vent, while the Pouakai and Kaitake Ranges to the west are much older andesite volcanoes which have eroded for much longer than Taranaki.

Ins and outs

Getting there The main access points to the park and the mountain are at North Egmont (Egmont Visitors Centre), Stratford (East Egmont) and Manaia (Dawson Falls).The Egmont Visitors Centre is located 16 km from North Egmont Village, at the end of Egmont Rd, which heads towards the mountain. East Egmont is accessed via Pembroke Rd, which heads 18 km towards the mountain from Stratford. Dawson Falls is located at the end of Upper Manaia Rd, via Kaponga on the southern slopes of the mountain. Dawson Falls is 24 km from Stratford. ***Whither's***, T7511777, ***Carter's***, T7599039, and ***Cruise NZ Tours***, T7583222, all offer shuttle services to the mountain from New Plymouth (particularly the Egmont Visitors Centre); $30 return.

Information Before attempting any walks on the mountain you should read all the relevant information. In New Plymouth the VIC (see page 310) can provide basic information particularly about getting there, while DOC (both in town and on the mountain) can fill in the detail with walking information, maps and weather forecasts. The **Egmont Visitor Centre** is open daily from 0800-1630, T7560990. The **Dawson Falls Visitor Information Centre** is open from Wed–Sun 0800-1630, Jan/Feb daily, T025430248. The **DOC** Stratford Field Centre is located on Pembroke Rd, T7655144.

Activities

Walks

The mountain has numerous walking tracks, two main summit routes, a round-the-mountain track and a ski-field.

The 140-km of short or long walks, which range in difficulty and from 30 minutes to four days, are well maintained by DOC. All are easily accessible from the main access points and information centres above. The forest and vegetation is called 'goblin forest' (due to its miniature 'hobbit-style' appearance the higher in altitude you go) and the entire mountain is drained by a myriad of babbling streams. Beware that the higher you go, obviously, the more dangerous it gets. In winter the slopes are covered in snow and ice, so climbing boots, crampons and an ice axe are essential. Even in summer crampons are advised on the summit, though the main enemy underfoot is the loose scree.

To the uninitiated Mount Taranaki looks deceptively easy and the weather is highly unpredictable. Many people have lost their lives on its slopes, so you must be well prepared. DOC has produced a number of leaflets that detail the walks. The 'Around the Mountain Circuit' and 'Short Walks in Egmont National Park' are both excellent. The visitors centres around the mountain can also advise on routes, hut accommodation options, prices and bookings.

The **Mountain Circuit** takes 3-5 days and is about 55 km in length. There are a number of huts to stay in en route, but these must be pre-booked. At Dawson Falls two of the best short-walk options include the track to the eponymous falls which can be accessed via the **Kapuni Loop Track** (one hour). This walk offers some good photo opportunities along the way, as does the **Wilkies Pools Track** (one hour), which takes in some very pretty 'goblin forest' and a series of plunge pools, formed by sand and gravel running over the lava. At North Egmont the 45-minute walk from the park entrance to the **Waiwhakaiho River** has some beautiful base native bush, while the **Ngatoro Loop Track** (one hour) takes in some beautiful 'goblin forest', and the **Veronica Loop Track** (two hours) some excellent views. Both of these tracks start from the top of the road. If you want to go the full nine yards and climb the summit, good luck: it's quite a hard climb, but boy, is it worth it.

Mountain guides If you want some experienced company and some great information en route then 2 main operators offer guided summit treks and other walks; Mountain Guides Mount Egmont, T7588261, mguide@voyager.co.nz, and MacAlpine Guides, T7513542. It is costly, at about $300 for the day.

Skiing

The only ski-field on Taranaki is on the Stratford Plateau 3 km past the Mountain Lodge, Pembroke Road, East Egmont which is accessed via Stratford. Ski hire is available at the Mountain Lodge, T/F7656100. For information call the Stratford Mountain Club, T7655493.

Essentials

Sleeping

For all mountain hut bookings contact and pre-book with DOC

North Egmont **C-D** *The Camphouse*, North Egmont Visitor Centre, T7560990. Basic bunk-style accommodation, with cooking facilities and hot showers near the centre. **C-D** *Missing Leg Backpackers*, 1082 Junction Rd, Egmont Village, T7522570. Very friendly and relaxed backpackers with log fire, bike hire and shuttle up the mountain.

East Egmont **AL-A** *Stratford Mountain House*, Pembroke Rd, Stratford, T0800668682, mountainhouse@xtra.co.nz Very popular hotel close to the slopes with an award-winning restaurant attached, Swiss-style cuisine. **A** *Anderson's Alpine Residence*, 922 Pembroke Rd, T7656620. 3-storeyed Swiss-style chalet with 3 guestrooms. Affiliated to the Mountain House.

Dawson Falls **A** *Dawson Falls Tourist Lodge*, Manaia Rd, Dawson Falls, T7655457. Another alpine-style lodge, comfortable rooms, log fire and all mod cons, in-house restaurant. **C-D** *Konini Lodge*, Dawson Falls, T025430248. A poor relation to the above, but comfortable nonetheless.

'Surf Highway 45'

If you fancy doing the 175 km trip around the mountain, it involves at least a full day via the 'Surf Highway 45' and SH3. But on a clear day the mountain will be good company throughout, and there are a number of interesting places to see and visit on the way.

Heading south from New Plymouth the view of the mountain is shielded by the Kaitake and Pouakai Ranges for a short while, then you arrive in **Oakura** which is famous for its surf, windsurfing and swimming beach. There is also an interesting craft shop called the *Crafty Fox* in the heart of town next to the

Main Road. Various local art and craft pieces are for sale and there is a railway wagon café next door.

Sleeping in Oakura **B** *Oakura Motel*, 53 Wairau Rd, Oakura, T/F7527680. Basic but only 3 mins to the beach. **C-D** *Oakura Beach Camp*, 2 Jans Terr, T7527861. Again basic but has a store and is across the road from the beach.

Lucy's Gully, 3 km south of Oakura, is a pleasant picnic spot with exotic trees and ferns including redwoods. There are also walking tracks in to the Kaitake Range. Around the small settlement of **Okato** the mountain comes back into view and the road edges its way closer to the coast. You can satisfy your desire to see it again at the **Cape Egmont Lighthouse**, about 3 km down Cape Road. Although the lighthouse is closed to visitors it is still worth seeing. It seems strangely out of place, standing in a field with a huge mountain in the background! Just south of Cape Road back on SH45 is Mid Parihaka Road. Two kilometres up is **Parihaka Pa** (see page 317).

Back on SH45, you can enjoy the scenery or explore the many side roads until you reach **Opunake**, which has a fine surf and swimming beach and a 7 km walkway, starting at Opunake Lake, which takes in lake, beach and river scenery. See the **Visitor Information Office** in the Library on Tasman Street for accommodation options, T7618663. Open Monday-Thursday 0930-1700, Fri 0930-1830. The next settlement south of Opunake is **Manaia** which is the place to leave SH45 if you want to get a bit more intimate with the mountain at **Dawson Falls**. There is not a lot in Manaia itself, a small settlement of about 1,000, named after a Maori Chief. Country and Western fans might like to pop into the **Taranaki Country Music Hall of Fame**, 11 Surf Highway. Yee-ha! ■ *1000-1600. T2748442*.

Hawera

Phone code: 06
Population: 8000

Hawera is the largest of the southern Taranaki townships and is located on the coast at the confluence of SH45 and SH3. From here it is about 70 km to complete the circuit around the mountain, north to New Plymouth. It is a good place to stop for a break and offers a number of interesting sights and attractions.

Ins & outs The **Visitors Information Centre** in Hawera is at 55 High St, T2788599, F2786599, visitorinfo@stdc.govt.nz Open Mon-Fri 0830-1700, Sat/Sun summer 1000-1500.

Sights Hawera is an interesting wee town with many architecturally significant buildings, the most obvious of which is the **water tower**, built in 1914. Apparently, it was built at the request of insurance underwriters who were getting somewhat dismayed at the town's amazing propensity to burn down, which it did to varying degrees in 1884,1895 and 1912. The VIC has an 'Historic Hawera' heritage trail leaflet that details the major buildings. Strangely enough there is not an old fire station.

The **Tawhiti Museum**, 401 Ohangai Road, is an amazing little museum that uses realistic life-size exhibits and scale models to capture Taranaki's past. It is a private museum with an interesting history of its own. Its founders Nigel and Teresa Ogle make the models and figures on site. There is also a small gauge railway. ■ *Fri-Mon 1000-1600 summer. $3, child $1. Only Sun in winter. $5, child $1.50.*

Equally unusual is the **Elvis Presley Memorial Room**, 51 Argyle Street, where avid collector and fan Kevin Wasley has amassed memorabilia and 2000 of The King's records. ■ *Phone for appointment, T2787624. Donation only*. If you have not seen enough of dairy fields and cows, the 'udderly amazing' **Dairyland**, on the corner of SH3 and Whareroa Road, is the region's equivalent to Sheepworld in Northland or The Agrodome in Rotorua. Here you can take a simulated milk tanker ride and learn how the mechanical mega-suckers have taken over from the old hand-and-bucket method, plus so much moo-re. There are interactive audio-visuals and also a revolving café, which is supposed to simulate a revolving rotary milking shed. ■ *Daily 0900-1700. $5, child $3. T2784537.*

Hawera is the base for the imaginative **Dam-Dropping** experience.

Sleeping & eating

A-B ***Kerry Lane Villas Motel***, 2 Kerry La, T/F2781918. The newest motel in Hawera in quiet rural setting 5 mins from town. **C-D** ***Ohangai Backpackers***, Urupa Rd, T2722878. Well-equipped farmstay backpackers 5 km from town (turn right in front of the museum). **B-D** ***King Edward Park Motorcamp***, Waihi Rd, T2788544.

For eating try ***Morrison's Café and Bar*** on Victoria St, open Mon-Sat 1100-0100, Sun 1100-2230. Dairyland and the Tawhiti Museum also have cafés attached.

SH3 from Hawera to New Plymouth

Eltham

Eltham is well known for its dairy products, especially its production of cheese, but for the tourist the attractions are mainly its surrounding lakes. **Lake Rotokare** (Rippling Lake), 11 km southeast on Sangster Road, is in a pretty setting with a one-hour walk and picnic sites. Further afield, **Lake Rotorangi** on Glen Nui Road (via Rawhitiroa Road) is 40 km in length and was formed by the damming of the Patea River. It is popular for water sports and fishing. For information regarding other local attractions and accommodation, contact the Eltham **Information Centre** in Eltham Library, High Street, T7648838. Open Monday-Friday 0930-1730.

Stratford

A glance at the street names in Stratford will soon confirm your suspicion that this rural service centre and eastern gateway to the Egmont National Park was named after its namesake and Shakespeare's birthplace in England. But there the similarity really ends. Stratford New Zealand is a pleasant little town but there is little to detain the visitor beyond a meal, a coffee and a quick wander round, before perhaps moving on up towards the mountain, or back to New Plymouth. The main attraction in town is the **Taranaki Pioneer Village**, on SH3, which consists of 50 re-sited buildings on 10 acres, all faithfully equipped to depict the Taranaki of the early 1900s. ■ *Daily from 1000-1600. $7, child $3.T7655399. The café is deservingly popular and open same hours.*

For more information on accommodation and local attractions, contact the Stratford **Information Centre**, Broadway South, T/F7656708, stratford@info.stratford.govt.nz Open Monday-Friday 0830-1700, Saturday/Sunday 1000-1500.

Sleeping and eating Stratford has a **B-D** ***'Top Ten' Holiday Park*** on Page St, T/F7656440, stratfordholpark@hotmail.com For eating the ***Backstage Café*** on Main St is considered one of the best bets. For other Sleeping and eating options, see under Egmont (Taranaki) National Park.

If you have kids, Inglewood, 13 km south of New Plymouth, has the **Fun Ho National Toy Museum**, on the corner of Rata and Maitai Streets. It is small but may keep them occupied for a few milli-seconds. ■ *Mon-Fri 0900-1700, Sat/Sun 1000-1600. T7567030. $5, child $2.* To recover, head for the popular *McFarlanes Café* on Kelly Street, T7566665.

10

East Coast

East Coast

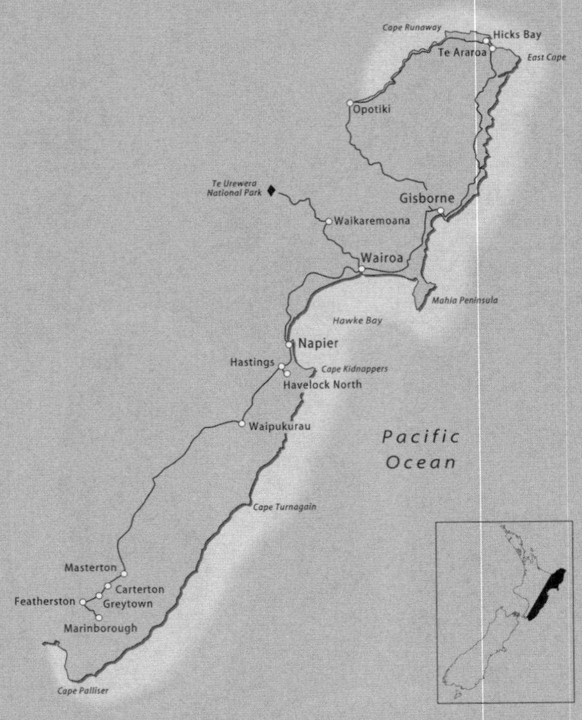

Cape Runaway
Hicks Bay
Te Araroa
East Cape
Opotiki
Te Urewera National Park
Gisborne
Waikaremoana
Wairoa
Mahia Peninsula
Hawke Bay
Napier
Hastings
Cape Kidnappers
Havelock North
Waipukurau
Pacific Ocean
Cape Turnagain
Masterton
Carterton
Featherston
Greytown
Marinborough
Cape Palliser

The East Coast of the North Island is all about ***sun, wine*** *and remote* ***coastal scenery****. The East Cape (the 'heel' of the 'upside-down boot') is where you can witness the day's first warming rays and a little further south, the coastal town of* ***Gisborne*** *prides itself on being the first place* ***Captain Cook*** *set foot in New Zealand in 1769. Inland from Wairoa (south of Gisborne) and the enchanting* ***Mahia Peninsula****, are the dense forests of the* ***Te Urewera National Park****, a place of almost spiritual beauty and particularly famous for its 'Great Walk' that circumnavigates its most scenic jewel, Lake Waikaremoana. Back on the coast you enter the wine country of Northern* ***Hawkes Bay*** *and the pretty coastal town of Napier, almost completely flattened by an earthquake in 1931 and now reborn as an international showpiece for its art deco buildings*

South again on the bleached cliffs that caress Hawkes Bay is the largest gannet colony in the country, at ***Cape Kidnappers****. Further south is one of the most stunningly beautiful and remote parts of North Island, the* ***Wairarapa****, where, from* ***Castle Point*** *to the lighthouse at* ***Cape Palliser*** *– the southernmost tip of the North Island – the peace and isolation is unsurpassed anywhere in North Island.*

Things to do in East Coast

- *Raft the wilderness Motu River and lose contact with civilization for days.*
- *Be one of the first in the world to see the day's sunrise at the East Cape Lighthouse.*
- *Climb spiritual Mount Hikurangi and see the Maori 'millennium sculptures' en route.*
- *See the best of Napier's Art Deco architecture and revisit the day of New Zealand's worst earthquake in the Hawkes Bay Museum.*
- *Tour the premier Hawkes Bay vineyards or the gannet colony at Cape Kidnappers.*
- *Visit the wild scenery of Castlepoint on the Wairarapa's remote coastline.*
- *Cross the swingbridge at Waiohine Gorge near Carterton.*
- *Explore the coast road to the Cape Palliser Lighthouse – the southernmost tip of the North Island.*
- *Walk into the 'chancel' of the Putangirua Pinnacles.*

Ins and outs

Getting around Although the more remote parts of the East Coast, particularly the East Cape, Wairarapa and the Urewera National Park are difficult to reach by public transport, much of the region is easily accessible. The East Cape road, SH35, is part of the well-publicised Pacific Coast Highway which can be completed comfortably in about 2 days from Opotiki in the Bay of Plenty, to Gisborne in Hawkes Bay, or in reverse. It is well signposted and shuttle buses operate in both directions. If you are limited for time, SH2 cuts out the East Cape through the Waioeka Gorge. If you wish to visit the Urewera National Park from Rotorua or Wairoa, south of Gisborne, SH38 will get you there and it is worth the trip. But bear in mind the road is both long, mostly unsealed and there is no public transport from one end to the other. The principal destination on the East Coast is Napier, which is easily reached from Taupo via SH5, or from Gisborne to the north and all points south via SH2. Gisborne is also the principal destination on the Pacific Coast Highway Route. SH2 is really the only main route through the Wairarapa with small minor roads (some unsealed) connecting the small towns with its more remote, scenic, coastal locations.

Information The East Coast section covers the East Cape, Hawkes Bay and Wairarapa Regions and includes the Te Urewera National Park, the fourth largest in the country. The main VICs are in Napier and Gisborne, with smaller local VICs in Opotiki, Wairoa and Masterton. The best websites are: www.gisbornenz.com; www.eastland.tourism.co.nz; www.hawkesbaytourism.co.nz; www.hastingsalive.co.nz

East Cape

Phone codes: Bay of Plenty District (Opotiki to Waihau Bay) 07 Gisborne District (Lottin Point to Gisborne) 06 Population: 6500

Those with a healthy imagination and good sense of geography will recognise East Cape as the 'heel' of the 'upside-down boot' that is New Zealand. Along with the Wairarapa, East Cape is the least-visited area in the North Island. This is due not so much to its isolated location but its geography. Almost the entire peninsula is sparsely populated, remote and mountainous. Indeed, much of the Raukumara Range which makes up most of its interior, remains impenetrable by road, with only wild rivers like the Motu and Mata carving their way through the wilderness.

Ins and outs

Getting there

Both Opotiki and Gisborne are serviced by ***Intercity*** buses. Beyond those places getting around the East Cape by public transport is possible, but unpredictible. Your best bet is with ***Polly's Passenger and Courier Services***, T8644728. They operate a return service from Hick's Bay (at the top of the Cape) to Whakatane, Mon-Sat and a similar service from Hick's Bay to Gisborne Mon-Sat. The service around the Cape is excellent because it provides a flexible timetable on a single fare of about $50. The bus departs Whakatane VIC at 1230, Opotiki VIC for the Cape at 1400, and from Gisborne VIC at 1300, but check for changes. ***Matakaoa Coastline***, T0800-628252, also offer a Mon-Fri service between Whakatane and Hick's Bay. Also check with Opotiki and Gisborne VICs for any changes to schedule and price.

Getting around

There really is, logistically, only one way to explore the Cape and that is to drive the 334 km of SH35 from either Opotiki to Gisborne or do it in reverse. Although the trip can be done comfortably in 2 days, you may like to absorb the very laid-back atmosphere and take longer, perhaps exploring the numerous bays and beaches as you go, or attempting the climb Hikurangi, North Island's 4th highest peak. On a clear day, from this legendary summit, the entire East Cape laid out before you.

East Cape

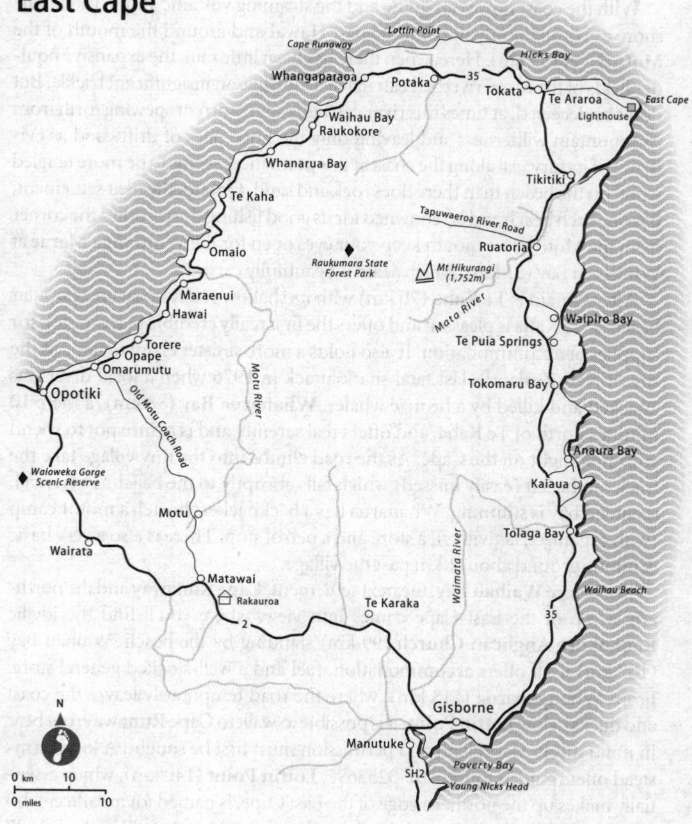

East Coast

Rise and shine

East Cape has earned the label of North Island's 'last wilderness'. People come here to get away from it all and go down a few gears. But it is not only the remoteness which attracts visitors. They also come for the sun. Not in the sense of soaking up the rays but to experience the joy and strange sense of pride at being the first souls on Earth to witness the day's sunrise.

Information The Opotiki **Visitors Information Centre** (see page 273) has 2 excellent free handbooks, the *'Opotiki and East Cape Holiday Guide'* and the *'Eastland Visitor Guide'*, both essential pieces of kit for the trip.

Opotiki to East Cape Lighthouse

The Cape road, SH35, begins at Opotiki (see page 273) and very soon you will be aware that you are entering the another world. Change your watches to 'Cape Time' which really means taking the batteries out. Maori influences are also almost immediately apparent in the first small settlement of **Torore** (24 km) and the beautiful carvings which adorn the gates to its school.

With the coast now your guide and the steaming volcanic White Island offshore as companion you continue past **Hawai** and around the mouth of the **Motu River** (49 km). Here, when there has been little rain, the expansive boulder fields of the Motu riverbed can make it look like an insignificant trickle. But don't be deceived, at times this river can be a raging torrent spewing forth from its mountain wilderness and leaving only the huge piles of driftwood as evidence of its fury. All along the coast at this point there seems to be more tangled wood on the beach than there does rock and sand. **Omaio,** the next settlement, has one such beach and is renowned for its good fishing. Just around the corner from the Motu River mouth keep your eyes open for the **Whitianga Marae** at Whitianga Bay (51 km), which again is beautifully carved.

After Omaio is **Te Kaha** (70 km) with its shallow rocky coast and popular beaches. Te Kaha is pleasant and offers the first really credible place to stop for supplies or accommodation. It also holds a more sinister claim to fame as the site of New Zealand's last fatal shark attack in 1976 when a local diver was attacked and killed by a bronze whaler. **Whanarua Bay** (88 km), a mere 10 minutes north of Te Kaha, and offers real serenity and is a fine spot to spend your first night on the Cape. As the road climbs into the tiny village take the track on the left (easily missed) which falls abruptly to the beach. This small, secluded bay is stunning. Whanarua has a backpackers hostel, a motor camp (with organized activities), a store and a petrol stop. There is also a very basic camping ground about 1 km past the village.

Just before **Waihau Bay**, the next settlement, **Cape Runaway** and the northern sweep of the East Cape comes into view, where you'll find the idyllic **Raukokore Anglican Church** (99 km) standing by the beach. Waihau Bay (107 km) itself offers accommodation, fuel and a well-stocked general store. From **Whangaparoa** (118 km), where the road temporarily leaves the coast and ducks below **Lottin Point**, it is possible to walk to **Cape Runaway**, but bear in mind this is Maori land and permission must first be sought. A local farmstead offers guided tours, T07-3253697. **Lottin Point** (140 km), which essentially makes up the northern edge of the East Cape, is named for an officer who sailed with French explorer Jules Sebastian Cesar Dumont d'Urville in1827 (presumably the latter's name was too long for people to remember). Lottin

Point has one of the most remote motels in the country, at the very end of Lottin Point Road, offering sanctuary and also, apparently, fine rock fishing.

From Lottin Point the road meets the coast again at **Hick's Bay** (151 km), this time named for one of Captain Cook's sidekicks. Hick's Bay has a wild surf beach and an old wharf at its northern end. There is also a small store and a petrol stop. Around the corner from Hick's Bay is **Horseshoe Bay,** which is also impressive.

Before reaching East Cape and the lighthouse you pass through the tiny settlement of **Te Araroa** (160 km) before negotiating about 21 km of unsealed road. There are two particular points of interest in and around Te Araroa. The first is the pohutukawa tree which dwarfs the school grounds (it is believed to be one of the largest in the country and over 600 years old). The second is the new **Manuka Oil Distillery** between Te Araroa and Hick's Bay (about 4 km from the Gisborne junction). There is a factory shop at the distillery selling the delicious Maneka honey. ■ *Mon-Fri, 0900-1600.*

If you want to see the sunrise at **East Cape**, Hick's Bay and Te Araroa are your best (and only) options for accommodation. The coast road to the lighthouse and the most easterly point of New Zealand is beautiful, with numerous rock platforms, small rivers, pohutukawa trees and a long and empty stretch of beach worthy of investigation. The *Coastal Arts Gallery*, which is open seven days, is also worth a peek, T8644890.

The **Lighthouse,** which only comes into view at the last minute, sits proudly on a hilltop all of its own. It can be easily accessed through a gate and via a set of seemingly never ending steps, beyond a small group of derelict buildings.

Sleeping & eating

Torore, Te Kaha and Whanarua Bay **A-B** *Te Kaha Hotel and Motel*, T/F3252830. Rooms and 2 modern beachfront units overlooking a sheltered beach and bay. Bar and restaurant serving lunch/dinner in-house, recoomended only for the local seafood. **A** *Tui Lodge B&B*, Copenhagen Rd, T/F3252922. Spacious modern home, dinner on request. **A** *Waiwaka B&B*, T/F3252070. In a beautiful spot 2 km north of Te Kaha and 12 km from Whanarua Bay.

If you want to sample real East Cape life and see a bit of pig-dog training try the **B** *Torore Homestay*, T3158228. **B-D** *Te Kaha Holiday Park*, T/F3252894. Basic amenities with backpacker beds. **B-D** *Rendezvous Holiday Park*, T/F3252899. Usual amenities but also offers fish and dive trips and bike hire. **C-D** *Robyn's Place*, T3252904. Almost next door to the Holiday Camp and within walking distance to the bay. **D** *Maraehako Camp Ground*, T3252047. Beachfront, 1 km past the holiday park.

Waihau Bay and Lottin Point **A** *Waihau Bay Homestay*, T3253674, n.topia@clear.net.nz 2 self-contained units and double overlooking the beach. **A** *Oceanside Apartments*, T3253699, F3253689. Located at the far end of Oruaiti Beach, 3 km Northeast of Waihau. Excellent apartments or B&B rooms, fishing charters. **A** *Lottin Point Motel*, T/F8644455. Amazing location. New and expanding number of units. Licensed restaurant in summer. **B** *Waihau Bay Lodge (Hotel)*, T3253804, F3253875. Comfortable rooms with shared facilities, licensed bar and restaurant. Campsite available. **B-D** *Waihau Bay Holiday Park*, T3253844. Located opposite the beach, store and café with dubious coffee!

Hicks Bay and Te Araroa **B-D** *Hicks Bay Motel Lodge*, T8644880. Located up the hill just past the village. Licensed restaurant. **C-D** *Hicks Bay Backpackers* , T/F8644731, hicksbaybackpackers@xtra.co.nz Small cosy and friendly place set next to the bay. Popular with surfies. Spa and Internet. Also arrange trips/transport. **B-D** *Te Araroa Holiday Park*, T8644873, F8644473. Located at the other end of the bay, west of the village. Modern facilities including a store and off licence.

East Cape to Gisborne

The eastern side of the Cape is more populous than the west and for much of the time the road winds its way through countryside between coastal settlements. If you wish to access the coast this is best done at these settlements, or with short diversions using a detailed map. From Te Araroa you head south and gain the first sight of Mount Hikurangi before arriving in **TikiTiki**. Here the Anglican Church is worth a visit boasting some fine Maori designs. It was built in 1924 as a memorial to local Iwi tribesman (Ngati Porou) who died in the First World War.

Just before the Mata River crossing is the turn-off to **Mount Hikurangi**. Even if you do not intend to climb the mountain it is worth the short diversion to enjoy the river and mountain views. The road which flirts with the Tapuwaeroa River is a bit of an obstacle course as you dodge stray pigs, chickens, horses, sheep and cattle. Back on SH35 it is only a short distance to **Ruatoria** (206 km), the main administrative base of the predominant East Cape Iwi, the *Te Runanga O Ngati Porou*. It has a food store and petrol station where you can have a light-hearted chat with the locals.

Turning your back on the mighty Hikurangi, next stop is **Te Puia Springs** (232 km) whose eponymous hot thermal pools can be located behind the hotel (see below). Access to the pools is available to non-residents but hours are seasonal, T8646755.The village also has a small Information centre in the District Council Building, T8646853, a store and a petrol station. A short diversion from Te Puia is scenic **Waipiro Bay** with its three *marae*. The beachside holiday resort of **Tokomaru Bay** (243 km) is next, where you can find accommodation and food (see below). Between Tokomaru and Tolaga Bay is **Anaura Bay**, a 7 km diversion from SH35, where there's a very pleasant, relatively easy grade coastal walk (two hours). **Tolaga Bay** (279 km) is the largest coastal town and resort on the East Coast. Worth a visit is the at 660 m-long wharf (reputed to be the longest in the Southern Hemisphere) which can be accessed down Wharf Road to the south of the town. Also here is Cook's Cove. Our intrepid explorer stopped here to make repairs and gather supplies, though ship's naturalists Banks and Solander were particularly interested in the coastal scenery and unusual rock formations which can be seen on the (three-hour) walkway.

From Tolaga Bay the road leaves the coast for a while before reuniting at Tatapouri and Makorori, both well known as fine surfing spots. **Wainui** is essentially a beachside suburb of Gisborne with all the attendant amenities (. On its fine surf beach there is an interesting 'Sperm Whale Grave' which was the inevitable result of a mass stranding of 59 sperm whales in 1970. From Wainui you have just about reached your East Cape journeys end (or beginning) and Gisborne.

Sleeping & eating

Te Puia and Waipiro Bay B-D *Te Puia Hotel*, T8646755. Basic but saved by the hot thermal pools. The ***Mountain View Café***, just south on SH3, has good food and coffee. **C-D** *Waikawa Lodge*, Waikawa Rd, Waipiro Bay, T8646719. A remote and charming backpackers which although quite small offers a perfect getaway. Also home to Waikawa Horse Adventures.

Tokomaru Bay AL *Rahiri Homestay*, 263 Mata Rd, Tokomaru Bay, T8645615, www.rahiri.com Farmstay homestead on sheep and cattle station. Well appointed, very comfortable and with great amenities. **B** *Te Puka Tavern*, Tokomaru Bay, T8645466. 2 comfortable motel units close to beer and food. **B** *Tokomaru Bay Homestay*, 641 Mata Rd, Tokomaru Bay, T8645619, F8645620. Comfortable with

Climbing Mount Hikurangi

Hikurangi is an attractive mountain though it does not look 1,752 m high (the highest non-volcanic mountain in the North Island).The name means 'Sky Peak' and refers to well-loved peak in Hawaiki, the ancient ancestral home of the Maori. It is relatively accessible, but the summit return will take at least nine hours so give yourself plenty of time. If you follow the Tapuwaeroa River Road almost to the end you will see an iron bridge which crosses the boulder-fields of the Tapuwaeroa River to several farm buildings on the hill. At the far side of the bridge a sign will remind you that you are on Maori (private land), but once you park your car down the side road towards the river, you can still use the track which heads up and past the houses, over the hill and beyond, towards the summit. Once you reach the top of this first hill you will clearly see the climb that lies before you. Follow your nose and the stiles up a clear sheep track which goes almost two thirds of the way to the summit. It terminates at Hikurangi's 'well kept secret' – the Millennium Maori Pou *(carvings). These are beautifully crafted pieces full of spiritual meaning, standing in a circle. From here head upwards and find the white bunkhouse. From behind the bunkhouse things start to get difficult. Climb up the scree slope to the rock outcrops and the path which leads through a tract of mountain bush. Beyond the bush it is a hard slog to the main summit, which is reached after several almost equally high false summits'.On a clear day the view is spectacular.*

For more information on the mountain and guided tours contact the local Iwi (tribe), Ngati Porou, T/F8678436, porou.ariki@xtra.co.nz It is both polite and respectful to let the Ngati Porou know that you intend to climb the mountain and seek official permission, and, if the weather turns nasty, it is added security.

swimming pool and tennis courts. **C-D** ***Tokomaru Bay Backpackers***, Potae St, Tokomaru Bay, T8645858. Intimate wee backpackers with friendly hosts.

Tolaga Bay B-D ***Tolaga Bay Motor Camp***, 167 Wharf Rd, T8626716. A bit tired and basic but the only one for miles. **B** ***Tolaga Bay Motel***, corner of Cook and Monkhouse, T8626888. Basic but adequate.

Activities & tours

Fishing ***Kiwi Boyz Charters***, Waihau Bay, T3253850. **Horse treks** ***Waikawa Horse Adventures***, Waikawa Rd, Waipiro Bay, T8646719. ***Marae stay Ngati Porou Outdoor Pursuits*** (see also Climbing Mount Hikurangi above) offer summit climbs with a stay in the mountain hut, fascinating cultural information and marae stays. T8678436, porou.ariki@xtra.co.nz

East Coast

Gisborne

Phone code: 06
Population: 30,000

The busy agricultural service town, port and coastal resort of Gisborne attracts many visitors in search of the sun, eager to jump on a surfboard or explore the East Cape. Being the most easterly city in New Zealand, Gisborne prides itself on being the first city in the world to see the sunrise. It is also the first place that Captain Cook set foot in New Zealand. On top of that, it boasts an almost subtropical climate with long hours of sunshine and rich fertile plains. You'd be forgiven for expecting the place to be brimming with with pride and vitality, yet somehow Gisborne seems a little tired.

Ins & outs

Getting there By air There are 5 ***Air New Zealand Link*** flights a day to both Wellington and Auckland, T8671608. The airport is about 2 km west of the town centre. ***Link Taxis*** operate an airport shuttle, T8674765, $10.

By car Gisborne is linked with all major points south, to Wellington 550 km and north (via the Waioeka Gorge) to Auckland (504 km) by SH2. Is a major stop on the well-signposted 'Pacific Coast Highway' which includes SH35. This 330 km trip terminates at Opotiki, where SH35 re joins SH2.

By bus Gisborne is regularly serviced, daily by ***Intercity*** buses which arrive and depart from the VIC.

Getting around Most of the city is easily negotiable by foot but ***Gisborne Taxi Buses***, T8672222, operate a bus service on weekdays. Car Taxi companies includes ***Sun City Taxis***, T8676767.

The Gisborne **Visitor Information Centre** is located at 209 Grey St, T8686139, F8686138, www.gisbornenz.com Open Mon-Fri 0830-1715, Sat/Sun 1000-1700. **DOC** is located at 63 Carnarvon St, T8678531.

History The first Maori to settle were thought to be from the Horouta and Te Ikaroa-a-Rauru *waka* (canoes) which landed at the base of the Kaiti Hill in 1350. When Captain Cook made the first European landing at the same site in 1769, in search of supplies, he was met by a threatening and hostile group of Maori. Cook promptly scarpered, leaving only the name 'Poverty Bay' behind. Although the area was home to a whaling station, European settlement would not occur in earnest until the 1840s with the establishment of several Christian missions. Captain G E Read, who settled in 1852, was a pivotal figure in the town's development. After a period blighted by numerous threats and attacks by Maori, eventually things settled down in the 1860s when steady growth and development continued.

Sights After the VIC your first stop should be **Cook's Landing Site and National Historic Reserve** next to the main port and the base of Titirangi (Kaiti Hill).To get there, cross to the northern bank of the **Taruheru River** which flows through the centre of the town. The reserve marks the spot where Cook first set foot, on 9 October 1769, to a hostile response from local Maori. Above the reserve the **Titirangi Domain or Kaiti Hill** provides great views across the city and the second of three Cook memorial edifices. At the summit of the hill is the **Cook Observatory**, which frankly has seen better nights. ■ *Open to the public on Tue at 1930, T8688653.*

There are a number of interesting gardens, walks (including heritage, antique and art and craft trails) and wineries. Details and leaflets from the VIC

Set in trees at the foot of the hill to the west is the **Te Poho-O-Rawiri Marae** which was built in 1930 and is one of the largest carved meeting

Captain James Cook

houses in the country. Nearby the **Toko Toru Tapu Church** is also worth a peek. For visits to both, T8685364.

Before re-crossing the river it is worth taking a look at the Inner Harbour Area. *The Works* on the Esplanade is home to the well-known *Longbush Wines* who have been producing a fine range for 35 years. There are tastings, an outlet and also a good restaurant within the renovated warehouse. ■ *1000-1800, T8631285.* Opposite the nearby *Wharf Café* is a wall which has been colourfully adorned with children's self portraits, created for the millennium.

Head to the beachside reserve on the southern bank of the river to see another Cook memorial. A little further along is a statue of Cook's cabin boy, **Young Nick**, who is credited as being the first to sight land. He was rewarded by having the promitory Young Nicks Head (which forms the southern edge of Poverty Bay) named in his honour. He also apparently won himself a bottle of rum, the customary reward for the first able seaman to see land. These statues are of particular interest simply due to their location with the backdrop of the port and huge steel hulled cargo ships.

To learn more about young Nick and the region's history head for the small but effective **Gisborne Museum** on Stout Street. It houses all the usual stuff with a particular bent towards the fascinating Maori history and, of course, that man Cook. There are also ever-changing exhibitions of national and international contemporary art. Attached to the museum (quite literally) is the wheelhouse of *HMS Canada*, which floundered at the base of Kaiti Beach in 1912. It forms part of the Maritime section of the museum. ■ *Mon-Fri 1000-1600 Sat/Sun 1330-1600. Entry by donation*. T8673832.

There is one other, less remarkable museum in the city, of particular interest to transport and technology buffs, the **East Coast Museum of Technology**, Main Road, Makaraka. ■ *Daily 0930-1630. $2, child $0.50.*

The **Ngatapa Valley** is of particular interest and lies to the west of the town. At the time of writing the good people of Gisborne were trying hard to secure funding to create the largest standing sundial in the world. Exactly where it will go remains to be seen. Only time will tell.

Activities & tours

Cruising *Bay Discovery Cruises*, T8672039. Day and evening cruises aboard the 15 m 'MV Tokerau'. Leaves from the Inner Harbour, licensed.

Fishing and shark cage experience *Surfit Charters*, T8672970. Another chance to encounter those persecuted denizens of the deep. From $120.

Horse trekking *Waimoana Horse Treks*, T/F8688218. Based a short distance north of Gisborne, combine bush and beach on two trips departing at 1000 and 1400; two hours, $30.

Surfing *Pines Alley Surf Tours*, 24B Moana Road, Okitu, T8672882. Based in Wainui, just north of Gisborne, this company can provide a taste of the region's fine surf beaches. Huge range of options available.

Cultural *Ao-Marma First Light Tours*, T8685444, firstlighttoursltd@amcom.co.nz Local and extended tours up the East Cape with informative visits and traditional cultural experiences. *Te Runganga-o-Turanganui-a-Kiwa*, Nga Wai E Rua, Grey Street, T8678109, www.trotak.iwi.nz An introduction to the historical and cultural sites in and around the city by the local mandated tribal authority. Recommended. *Te Wainui Tours*, T8621511, p.wainui@paradise.net.nz Maori village trip and experience including *hangi* (feast), $65.

Sightseeing and 'Station Experience' *Trev's Tours*, 1641 Wharekopae Road, Ngatapa, T8639815, www.gizbiz.co.nz/ngatapa Local knowledgeable tour operator offering a range of trips to a variety of old and modern attractions locally and farther afield. From $45. *Tangihau Station Enterprise* , Rere,

Gisborne

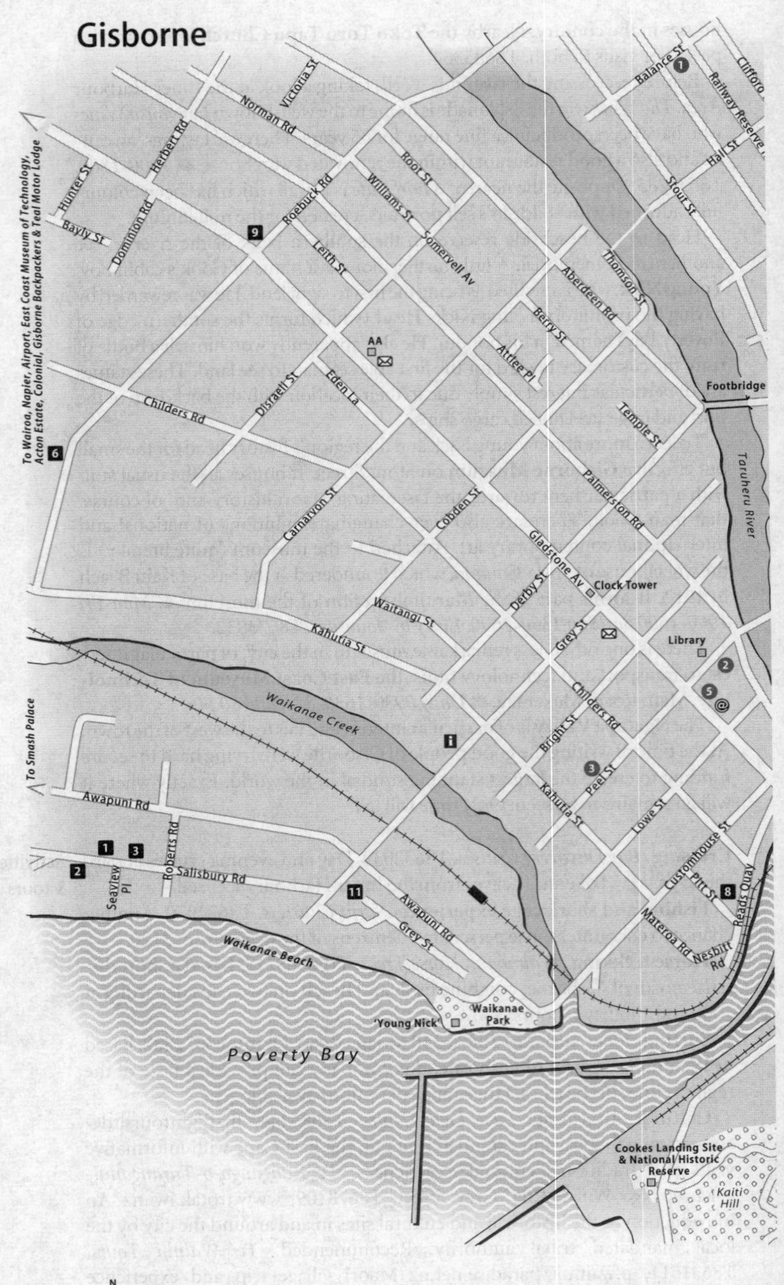

Sleeping

1 Beachcomber
2 Blue Pacific
3 Casa Blanca
4 Cedar House B & B
5 Fawnbridge B & B
6 Flying Nun Backpackers
7 Gisbourne YHA
8 Pacific Harbour
9 Teal Motor Lodge
10 Thompson Homestay
11 Waikanae Beach Holiday Park

East Coast

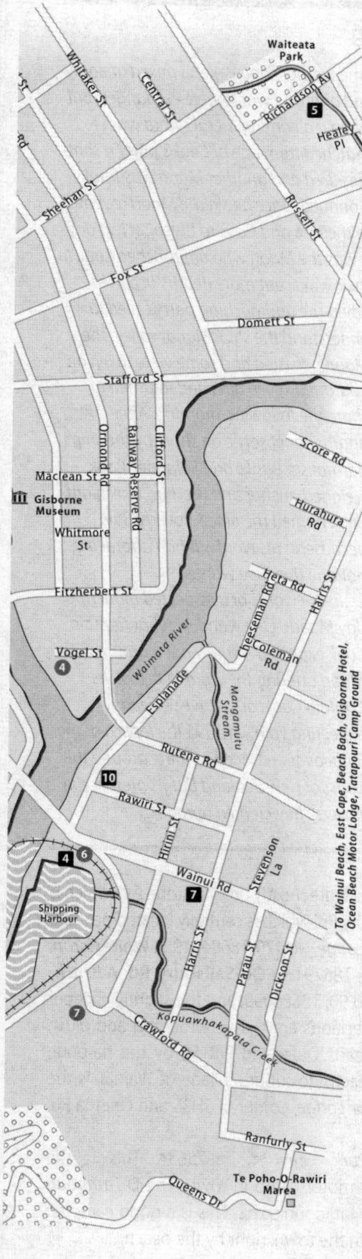

Gisborne, T8670837, F8675043. This is a new and interesting venture offering a range of New Zealand Station life experiences from a shepherd's muster, to tours and hunting. From $75-800. *Air Gisborne*, T8674684. The local fixed-wing scenic flight operator. From $55.

Sleeping

Gisborne is a popular summer resort so you are advised to book ahead in the high season

LL *Acton Estate*, 577 Back Ormond St, T8679999, F8671116. The top range hotel in town, this is a restored Edwardian-style mansion in spacious grounds, offering all mod cons and fine cuisine. **AL** *Cedar House B&B*, 4 Clifford St, T8681902, F8671932, www.cedarhouse.co.nz Similar Edwardian-style to *Acton Estate* but cheaper and centrally located. **AL** *Beach Bach*, 52 Wairere Rd, Wainui Beach, T8686605. You're own little bach on Wainui Beach, just north of town. **A** *Gisborne Hotel*, corner of Tyndall and Huxley Rd, T8684109, F8678344, info@gisbornehotel.com One of Gisborne's few hotels. Comfortable with very friendly hosts but not particularly well located. Tour arrangements a speciality. **A** *Fawnbridge B&B*, 29 Richardson Av, T8688823. Semi-rural option. Cosy and quiet with fine views, a spa and good cooking. **B** *Thompson Homestay*, 16 Rawiri St, T/F8689675. Well established cheaper B&B within walking distance of town.

There are currently 3 backpackers in Gisborne: **C-D** *Gisborne YHA* is located near the inner harbour at the corner of Wainui Rd and Harris St, T8673269, yha.gis@clear.net.nz is well-run, friendly and has had a recent renovation. The **C-D** *Gisborne Backpackers*, 690 Gladstone Rd, T8681000, gisbornebp@xtra.co.nz A vast establishment offering a wide range of accommodation options in an old orphanage. It has beds as opposed to bunks, a bath and Sky TV and all the usual facilities. The **C-D** *Flying Nun Backpackers* on 147 Roebuck Rd, T8680461, yager@xtra.co.nz Looks very unusual and comically ecclesiastical from the outside, but although perhaps not the best backpackers in town, the interior is modern enough and the place certainly has character.

☛ Culture clash – Cook's first landing

On 8 October 1769 a group of Maori living on a pa just to the east of the Turanganui River looked out to sea and saw what they thought was an enormous bird on the horizon. It was, in fact, Cook's ship, the 'Endeavour'. The Maori dispatched a party of warriors to investigate, while Captain Cook and his men were rowing ashore in search of supplies and eager to make contact with any 'savages'. Cook disembarked and the first ever footprint of a shoe was made on New Zealand sand. He and his men took some gifts to the local whare *while others guarded the longboats. As they waited on the shore the warriors emerged and performed a* haka. *Utterly terrified and taking this to be a sign of imminent attack, the* Pakeha *fired warning shots, one of which felled a Maori warrior. Both the Maori and Cook 's men hastily retreated. That night the Maori kept a close watch on the great 'bird' in both fear and amazement. Next morning Cook tried a second landing. A party of warriors once again met the landing party and performed a* haka. *This time, accepting the fearful dance as a bizarre welcoming ritual, Cook kept his muskets silent. For a time warriors and* Pakeha *mixed uneasily and gifts and words were exchanged. But when a gleaming metal sword was snatched from one of Cook's party a shot was fired and another Maori was fatally wounded. Once again the Maori retreated to their* pa *and Cook to his ship. Next day it was the Maori who approached Cook in their* waka, *but more deaths occurred when the approaching party failed to understand the ship's signal volley. The Maori persisted and some were taken on board, fed, given gifts and returned to shore the following morning. After another brief sortie on shore by the ship's naturalists, Banks and Solander, Cook weighed anchor and the 'bird' took flight. Cook named the place 'Poverty Bay' because, in his words: 'It had afforded us not one thing we wanted'.*

In the words of a respected modern day Maori: "One wanders what Captain Cook expected – surely not a group of Maori uttering the words 'Oh look its Captain Cook, at last, we've been expecting you!'" In 1995 the replica of the 'Endeavour' retraced its route around the coast of New Zealand but its presence in Poverty Bay created uproar.

East Coast

There's the usual selection of **motels**, which are mostly on Gladstone Av, which is essentially the main drag (SH35), and Salisbury Rd, which is centrally located near the beach. **On Gladstone Av**: **A-AL** *Teal Motor Lodge*, No 479, T8684019; **A** *White Heron*, No 474, T8671108; and **A** *Colonial*, No 715, T8679165. **On Salisbury Rd**: **A** *Beachcomber*, No 73, T8689349; **A** *Blue Pacific*, No 90, T8686099; and the slightly cheaper **A** *Casa Blanca*, No 61, T8677107. Two exceptions are the very modern and plush **AL-A** *Pacific Harbour*, on the corner of Reads Quay and Pitt St, by the harbour, T8678847. A little further afield, in the beachside suburb/village of Wainui, is the newest motel, the **AL-A** *Ocean Beach Motor Lodge*, corner of SH35 and Oneroa Rd, Wainui Beach, T8686186.

The **B-D** *Waikanae Beach Holiday Park*, Grey St, T8675634. This is the best-equipped and most centrally located motor camp in town. The **D** *Tatapouri Camp Ground*, 5 Innes St, T8683269, www.tatapouri.co.nz This is a good camping option located 15 mins north and away from the town, right by the beach.

Eating **Expensive** *The Acton Estate* (see Sleeping) is open to non guests and offers a 4-course, à la carte culinary experience prepared by their in house award-winning chef. Bookings essential, T8679999. *The Wharf Café*, 60 The Esplanade, The Wharf, T8684876. This is not very expensive but still at the high end, very popular with wide-ranging menu. Open daily 0900-late. *The Marina Restaurant*, Vogel St, T/F8685919.

Well-established eatery next to the marina. Fine International cuisine (especially steaks) and good wine list.

Mid-range ***The Fettucine Brothers Restaurant***, 12/14 Peel St, T8685700. Mediterranean in décor and food. Popular with the locals. Open 7 days 1800-late. ***The Works***, The Esplanade, Inner Harbour, T8631285. Home of *Longbush Wines* so no need to recommend the wine list. Good venue for lunch. Open from1130-late. Wine tasting 1000-1500.

Cheap ***The Irish Rover***, Peel St, T/F8671112. Not only the best pub in town but the best pub grub. ***Verve Café***, 121 Gladstone Rd, and ***Café Villagio*** in Balance St village are 2 of the best cafés in town.

Pubs & bars

There are 2 great pubs in Gisborne the ***Irish Rover*** on Peel St which is the town's offering to the mighty leprechaun and the highly unique ***Smash Palace***, Bank St. The Rover is especially good during happy hours (around 1700-1900) and on Fri evening. The *Smash* is a local legend and deservedly so, supporting the most amazing décor which is best seen from over the rim of a glass, not described. It also has a local wine outlet next door.

Entertainment

The ***Odeon*** **cinema** is located at 79 Gladstone Rd, T8673339, while ***The Irish Rover*** hosts regular bands.

Shopping

The ***Ukaipo Art Gallery***, 133 Ormond Rd, T8671177. Promotes local Maori artists and often hosts some lovely work. There is a **flea market** which starts at an ungodly hour every Sat morning in Alfred Cox Park across from the VIC.

Directory

Banks: All the major banks have branch offices on Gladstone Rd. **Internet**: *Cyberzone*, 83 Gladstone Rd. ***Verve Café***, 121 Gladstone Rd. ***VIC***, Grey St.

South to Wairoa

From Gisborne, SH2 climbs the **Wharereta Hills** offering great views back across Poverty Bay. On the southern slopes, 60 km south of Gisborne, are the **Morere Hot Springs**. Here, public and private thermal pools are set among a pleasant bush setting with a number of good short walks. ■ *The pools are open Dec-Apr 1000-1800, $6. T8378856. There is accommodation and a café across the road.*

At the tiny junction settlement of **Nuhaka**, 8 km south of the springs, a scenic coastal road leaves SH2 towards the **Mahia Peninsula**. The Mahia is a barren, windswept peninsula 21 km long and about 12 km wide that marks the coastal boundary between the Pacific and Hawkes Bay. The Mahia used to be an island and is now joined to the mainland by a sandspit or tombolo. Almost totally devoid of trees, infested by sheep and deeply rutted by eroded green valleys, the peninsula has a strange appeal. One of the great Maori migration *waka* (canoes), the Takitimu, made landfall here in the 14th century, after circumnavigating the northern and east coasts from its first landfall at Awanui near Ninety-Mile Beach. Some of its crew never left and the peninsula was also home to one of North Island's biggest whale stations. Today, at the neck of the peninsula is the small holiday village of **Mahia Beach** which forms a link between two beaches: **Mahanga Beach**, lying to the east, is exposed to the elements of the open ocean and a popular surf spot; **Opoutama Beach**, on the Hawkes Bay side (west), is much more sheltered and therefore better for swimming. On the eastern edge of the peninsula are the settlements of **Oraka** and **Mahia**, connected by a rows of holiday bachs which hug the shore like a string of pearls. In summer the peninsula is a very popular spot for surfing, windsurfing, swimming and fishing, but year round it enjoys the erstwhile island atmosphere, which makes it an idyllic spot in which to get away from it all. You will need your own transport.

From Mahia it is a 44 km drive to Wairoa past farmland and coastal lagoons renowned for their birdlife.

Booking ahead in summer is advised

Sleeping and eating **A** *Cappamore Lodge*, 435 Mahia East Coast Rd, T8375523, oconellcappamore@clear.net.nz This is like Scandinavia by the sea. The log cabin has full self-catering facilities and a view across the ocean. **A** ***The Quarters Te Au Farmstay***, Te Au Farm, Nuhaka (Mahanga) T8375751, m.rough@xtra.co.nz Modern isolated farmstay with deck overlooking the ocean. **B-D** ***Mahia Beach Motel and Holiday Park***, 43 Moana Dr, Mahia Beach, T/F8375830. The centre of activity on the peninsula, with café and camp store. For eating there is little except the ***Beachfront Café***, Moana St, Mahia Beach or ***Sunset Point Sports Bar and Bistro***, Newcastle St, Mahia Beach, T8375071.

Wairoa
Population: 5200

Wairoa is the eastern gateway to the Te Urewera National Park and sits on the coast at the junction of SH2 and SH36. Also strategically placed on the banks of the Wairoa River, it was once a thriving port. These days however, it has little to hold the visitor except perhaps a brief peek at the relocated and reconstructed 1877 **lighthouse** which once shone away on the Mahia Peninsula. Sadly these days, looking somewhat incongruous in the centre of town next to the river, it only seems to attract local graffiti artists. The town has a number of shops in which to stock up and small takeaways to grab a snack before heading north, south or inland to **Waikeremoana** via SH36. There are a limited number of accommodation options available in town and the VIC has details. The Wairoa Visitor **Information Centre** is located on the corner of SH2 and Queen Street, T/F8387440, wirvin@nzhost.co.nz Open November-March 0900-1700 daily, April-October 0900-1700 Monday-Friday. Internet facilities.

Te Urewera National Park

Phone code: 06

Te Urewera is daunting and mysterious; a place of almost threatening beauty. The National Park encompasses the largest block of native bush in the North Island and is the fourth largest national park in the country. The main focus of the park is ***Lake Waikaremoana****, the 'Sea of Rippling Waters', while the track which circumnavigates it, the* ***Lake Waikaremoana Circuit****, is one of the most popular walks in the country. The vast park is home to a wealth of wildlife: some native and welcome, including kiwi, kaka and kokako (one of New Zealand's rarest and most endangered birds); others introduced and very unwelcome, such as the omnipresent possum, stoats, goats, rats and feral cats. The park is also a favourite haunt for pig hunters, though, thankfully, few known banjo players.*

Ins and outs

Getting there & around
Frasertown to Waikaremona is about 50 km; Waikaremoana to Murupara is another 75 km

Although various companies have tried (and will no doubt continue to do so) there is essentially no public transport to the heart of the park via the hardy SH38. This almost completely unsealed highway links Murupara on the western boundary of the park with Frasertown, near Wairoa to the east. It is pretty heavy going, very windy, often subject to fallen trees and, if you break down, you're on your own. The park and all the amenities of Lake Waikaremoana are best accessed from the east via Wairoa and Frasertown. This will allow you to get intimate with the park on foot from Waikaremoana before building up the strength to explore the the western part.

There is a privately owned shuttle bus (Waikaremoana Shuttle Service) which runs around the lake, from $10 one way, T8373729. A water taxi travels on the lake taking trampers to and from trailheads. It is based at the Waikaremoana Motor Camp and costs from $10 one way, T8373729. Two private companies offer chartered services from Wairoa to the park in conjunction with accommodation/walk packages ***Out and About***, T8386712, and ***Big Bush Holiday Park***, T8373777. *Big Bush* also have a café and provide a complete 3-day package on the Waikaremoana Track for around $300.

Information

The **DOC** Aniwaniwa **Visitor Centre** is located on SH38 at Lake Waikaremoana, T8373900, T8373722, www.urewerainfo@doc.govt.nz Open daily 1000-1700. It has modern displays, an audio visual show ($1) and a gallery which is entrusted to care and display the controversial **Urewera Mural** by Colin McCahon. The staff can assist with the limited but surprisingly good accommodation options and also handles all the walk information, fees and hut bookings. There is also a DOC Office in Murupara, SH38, T07-3661080.

History

The Te Urewera area is home to the Tuhoe people, known as 'the children of the mist'. They have always been amongst the most determined of Maori tribes. Before the European arrived the Tuhoe effectively ruled over the forest. Even other Maori were fearful of their *mana* (standing, integrity) and legendary bush skills. So when the Europeans arrived to lay claim to the forest it was obvious trouble would ensue.

During the New Zealand Wars of the 1860s and 70s the great Maori leader and rebel, Te Kooti (see page 217) took refuge in Te Urewera with the Tuhoe. From here he fought his enemies until the Tuhoe made peace and Te Kooti was forced to seek exile in the King Country of the Waikato. With the end of the Wars in 1872, and after being pardoned 11 years later, Te Kooti died a free man. But although the official wars ended in the Te Urewera, the troubles and hard feeling did not. Tuhoe religious prophet and leader Rua Kenana, who headed a thriving religious community in Maungapohatu, remained a thorn in the *Pakeha*'s side until his arrest in 1916. Thereafter, leadership crumbled and so did the Tuhoe's hold on the region. Along with the rest of the country, the kauri fell, the land was 'acquired' and the *Pakeha* took control. Many Tuhoe still live in Te Urewera and although most would argue that the forest is no longer 'officially' theirs, in spirit it remains so.

Sights

Lake Waikaremoana

The lake covers 5500 ha; it stands at a height of 600 m; its deepest point is 256 m

This beautiful lake was created only 2000 years ago when the Waikaretaheke River was dammed by a huge landslide between the Ngamoko and Panekiri Ranges. One section of that landslide is claimed to have been 3 km long by 1 km wide. This relatively new addition to the landscape sits beautifully with the equally impressive bush which cloaks its indented shores. The main activities on the lake are trout fishing and boating, but it is most famous for the network of excellent walks around its shores.

Most of the short walks radiate from the main settlement of Waikaremoana, which is little more than a scattering of DOC buildings and the motor camp at the northeastern end of the lake. There are two waterfalls within 15 minutes of the DOC vistors centre. The first, the **Aniwaniwa Falls**, is less than 1 km from the centre and is accessed from a track right beside it. The slightly higher and more impressive **Papakorito Falls** are up a short track

The Waikaremoana Circuit Track

The Circuit track, a 46-km walk of moderate difficulty, completely circumnavigates the lake. It can usually be done in 3-4 days taking in a variety of bush types, full of birdlife and rocky and sandy bays ideal for fishing and swimming. Most of the route is fairly easy going with the exception of a 900 m ascent of the Panekiri Range, which offers a spectacular view of the lake. There are five modern and comfortable DOC huts and five designated campsites along the route, which provide basic amenities. The walk can be done in either direction from the southern access point at Onepoto (which climbs Panekiri first) or from the most popular starting point, Hopuruahine, on the lake's northern shores. Although there is parking at both access points at Onepoto and Hopuruahine, most people leave their vehicles at the Waikaremoana Motor Camp ($3) and take the water taxi to either starting point. The ferry will also pick up or drop off from various designated points along the way, which is ideal for those who only wish to walk part of the circuit. Weather can be changeable throughout the year and positively ugly in winter, so, as always, go well equipped. The walk is very popular in summer, so either late spring or early autumn is advised. Bookings are essential and conditions apply. The huts cost $14 per night, child $7. Campsites are $10, child $5. For all information, leaflets and bookings contact the DOC Aniwaniwa Visitor Centre (see above). For web booking and information log on to greatwalksbooking@doc.govt.nz

opposite the centre (or by car to within a five-minute walk). There is a short and pleasant 2 km track connecting the visitor centre with the motor camp called the **Black Beech Track** (30 minutes). If you fancy something more demanding and scenic, the **Ngamoko Track** (2½ hours) just south of the motor camp climbs the mountain through a delightful tangle of native bush before emerging at a 1099 m trig and viewpoint.

Better still is the four-hour tramp to see the idyllic **Lake Waikareiti**, which is a smaller body of water formed in the same way as Lake Waikaremoana. Set 300 m above Lake Waikaremoana, it is almost like a lost world with a magical atmosphere and shores entirely cloaked by bush. The DOC Sandy Bay Hut is available for an overnight stay (book at the visitor centre, $14) and there is also boat hire. Most serious trampers, however, come to Lake Waikaremona to experience the scenic **Waikaremoana Circuit Track,** a national tramping top ten (see next page).

East Coast

There are numerous other walks and huts in the park including the 3-5 day **Whakatane River Round Trip**, the three-day **Manuoha-Waikareiti Track** and the two-hour **Onepoto Caves Track**. For more information and bookings contact DOC or call at the Aniwaniwa Visitors Centre.

There is boat and kayak hire ($45 per day) available at the motor camp. Fishing (from $54 per hour), fishing licenses, hunting trips, horse treks and lake cruises (from $20, 1½ hours) can also be arranged from there. T8373826, www.lake.co.nz

Sleeping & eating Accommodation is available at Waikaremoana or the settlements of Kaitawa and Tuai at the southeast entrance to the park. Booking is advised in summer. **B-D** *Whakamarino Lodge*, Tuai, T8373876, F8373872, whakamar@ihug.co.nz Comfortable self-contained units, rooms and backpacker accommodation 5 km from Waikaremoana. **B** *Homestay*, 9 Rotten Row, Tuai, T8373701. Thankfully Judy's hospitality and the accommodation does not reflect the street name. **B-D** *Waikaremoana*

Motor Camp, T8373826, F8373825, misty@lake.co.nz Well-situated right next to the lake near most major short walks and the visitor centre. Modern range of cabins and units as well as petrol and a well-stocked store. Kayak hire and base for water taxi.

Napier and around

Napier is a bright, dynamic place with the pleasant vibe of a Mediterranean coastal town. On the surface it seems to enjoy the perfect relationship with nature and the rich fertile land and the warming sun have made it the wine-producing capital of North Island. But even though it paid a heavy price in 1931 when an earthquake almost raized the town, the fiercely proud and determined people used this to their advantage and set about its rebuilding with a collection of Art Deco buildings thought to be amongst the finest in the world. Now, as it enters the new millennium, Napier seems in the best of health.

Population: 54,900
Phone code: 06

Ins and outs

Getting there

By air Napier is serviced by ***Air New Zealand Link***, T0800-737000 and ***Origin Pacific*** T0800-302302. There are regular daily flights to both Wellington and Auckland and other principal national destinations. The airport is located just north of the town on SH2. There is an Airport Shuttle service costing around $10 one-way, T8447333.

By bus Napier is serviced by ***Intercity*** and ***Newmans***. Buses arrive and depart from the Napier Travel Centre at the train station on Munroe St. Open 0830-1700,T8352720.

By car Napier is on SH2, 321 km north of Wellington. The junction with SH5 and SH2 is about 6 km north of the town and from there it is 117 km to Taupo and 397 km to Auckland. Napier is the premier east coast destination on both the 'Thermal Explorer' (SH5) and 'Pacific Coast Highway' (SH2) touring routes. These routes are well signposted and advertised.

Getting around

Much of the city is negotiable on foot and, given the architectural appeal, is best appreciated from the street. The local suburban bus company is ***Nimbus***, T8778133. They operate weekdays only and a service to Hastings. For car rental companies, cycle hire and taxis, see page 115.

Information

The Napier **Visitor Information Centre** is on the seafront at 100 Marine Parade, T8341911, F8357219, www.hawkesbaytourism.co.nz Open Mon-Fri 830-1700, Sat/Sun 0900-1700. They have information and leaflets on local and regional Heritage Walks, Gardens and Art and Craft Trails. **DOC** is at 59 Marine Parade. Open Mon-Fri 0900-1615, T8343111. It has information about Cape Kidnappers Gannet Colony (plus tide times), as well as the Te Urewera and Ruahine National and Forest Parks.

History

Before the earthquake of 1931 Napier looked very different. Bluff Hill, which now forms part of the town, was practically an island, surrounded by swamps which formed the estuary of the Tutaekuri River. When Captain Cook first mapped the Bay in 1769 Maori were already happily ensconced on local *pa* and harvesting the local marine resources. This harvest was expanded in the 1830s when seasonal whalers arrived from Australia to be joined a decade later by missionaries and another decade after that by the first significant group of European settlers. In 1854 the town was named after British general Charles Napier.

The Big Shake

February 2nd 1931 at around 1030 there was a ferocious quake measuring 7.9 on the Richter Scale. The effect was devastating. Survivors recall that the land became 'almost fluid' and to a deafening roar, buildings were toppled, trees were uprooted and over 3,600 hectares of coastline had been thrust upwards by several feet. The few buildings the earthquake did not destroy, fires would and with the loss of any water supply, let alone the organized means with which to fight them, all the shocked survivors could do was watch. By the time it was all over, Napier was essentially flattened and 161 lives had been lost. In Hastings to the south the damage was less, but older buildings still collapsed and 93 people were killed. In rural areas as far away as the Wairarapa, roads and bridges were destroyed, rivers became lakes and communications were cut off. But although many lives were lost and the town was destroyed, the spirit and determination of those survivors was not. Despite the enormity of the task, within two years, the town was rebuilt and as a whole, actually benefited through the availability of new land that had previously been seabed. Undoubtedly another benefit was the manifestation of its Art-deco architecture, which is ideal in its resistance to further earthquake damage. The quake remains, for now, the worst in New Zealand's human history.

During the New Zealand Land Wars of the 1860s the residents, with the help of local Maori, managed to defend against aggressive tribes from the north and, with the development of agriculture, the settlement flourished. But though everything was destroyed by the devastating earthquake of 1931, the subsequent rebuilding led to great improvements. The land surrounding Bluff Hill had been raised several feet and huge tracts of land, previously underwater or covered in swamp, were now available for use. The redesign of the city encompassed the widespread creation of earthquake resistant concrete boxes of Art Deco design and within a decade the town had a new face and a new future. Although the earthquake remains a painful memory, it has, in many ways, shaped the coastal town that Napier is today.

Sights

Art Deco architecture

The main attraction of Napier is its famous Art Deco architecture

On foot, the two central streets **Emerson** and **Tennyson** have many examples. On Emerson Street is the **ASB Bank** with its Maori incorporated designs and fine doorway, while on Tennyson Street the highlights are (from east to west) the **Daily Telegraph Building**, restored **Municipal Theatre** and the **Desco Centre** (*Art Deco Shop*).

Further afield is perhaps the most attractive building of all, the façade and entrance of the 1932 **Rothmans Pall Mall Building** at the corner of Bridge and Osian Streets. Although somewhat distant from the town centre (in the port area of Westshore), it is worth the diversion. The building is even more impressive at night, when it is beautifully and imaginatively lit. During the day it is possible to have a look at the interior which is equally impressive. For a more modern example of Art Deco take a wander inside the pharmacy at the southern end of Emerson Street.

The best way to see the pick of the buildings and get some insight into their significance and history is to join the enjoyable **Art Deco walks**. There are three principal walks/tours on offer, the morning walk, afternoon walk and the Promenade Walk, all of which operate daily in summer. The morning walk (one hour, $8) leaves from the VIC at 1000, while the afternoon walk (two hours, $10) leaves at 1400 from the *Art Deco Shop*, 163 Tennyson Street. The Promenade Walk (two hours, $15) leaves at 0930 from the VIC. In winter, only the afternoon walk is available, on Saturday, Sunday and Wednesday. The tours are hosted by the Art Deco Trust, an organisation set up in 1985 to help preserve and promote Art Deco in the region. Included in the morning and afternoon walks is an audio-visual and free refreshments at the *Art Deco Shop*. The shop stocks a wide range of Art Deco products and is open daily 0900-1700, T8350022, www.artdeconapier.com If you wish to see the best of the buildings on your own, or are pushed for time, pick up a copy of the excellent 'Art Deco Walk' leaflet ($2.50) from the VIC. There are also 'Art Deco Scenic Drive' maps available.

Marine Parade
For a guided walk *see above*

Marine Parade creates an impressive perspective with its long promenade lined with **Norfolk Pines** and old wooden houses (the few that survived the earthquake). There are a number of waterfront attractions to add to its Mediterranean/English ambience. At the northern end are some elegant gardens including the **Centennial Gardens** at the base of Bluff Hill (free). Almost opposite are other gardens containing a **floral clock**, the **Tom Parker Fountain** (no Elvis connections here) and **'Pania of the Reef'** statue. The fountain is just your average garden fountain by day but by night comes alive with a multi-coloured aquatic light show. 'Pania' is a small, attractive statue of a Maori maiden, with her legend of love described accordingly in a shower of the fountain's mist.

Heading south is the Art Deco **Colonnade** and **Soundshell**. The Colonnade was once used for dancing and skating and is home to the **Veronica Bell** and memorial. The *Veronica* was a naval vessel which was in port at the time of the quake and her crew was pivotal in the first attempts to save lives in the rubble. The bell is rung to commemorate their efforts every New Year. Opposite the Soundshell, which is occasionally used for open-air concerts, is the **Art Deco Tower** (A&B building), which is also nicely lit at night and the Art Deco **Masonic Hotel**.

Past the modern VIC and Mini Golf Park are the **Sunken Gardens**, complete with ponds of waterlily and a lazy waterwheel. Further south is **Marineland**. Here seal and dolphin displays are mixed, perhaps with a twinge of guilt, with an ongoing programme of wild penguin and gannet rehabilitation. You can also touch, feed and swim with the dolphins. Thankfully, all the animals seem to be in both caring as opposed to strictly commercial hands. ■ *Daily 1000-1630. Shows at 1030 and 1400. $9, child $4. Touch the Dolphins Tour at 0900 ($15, child $7.50). Swim with the Dolphins, daily sessions ($50). Penguin Recovery Workshop at 1300 ($15). T8344027, www.marineland.co.nz*

The Hawkes Bay Museum, 9 Herschell Street, offers a wide range of exhibits relating to the history and art of the region in modern surroundings. *Nga Tukemata* (The Awakening) presents the art and *taonga* of the local Maori and a rare presentation of evidence that dinosaurs once existed in New Zealand. Special attention is of course afforded to the earthquake of 1931. Relics plucked from the rubble go with the audio-visual descriptions and touching memories of survivors. ■ *Daily 1000-1630. $5, child free. T8357781.*

Although somewhat spoiled by the port and hard to reach, the view from **Bluff Hill** at the northern tip of the town is worth the effort. A good view down Marine Parade and across the city can be had from Lighthouse Road above the Centennial Gardens (accessed up Lucy Road, off Coote).

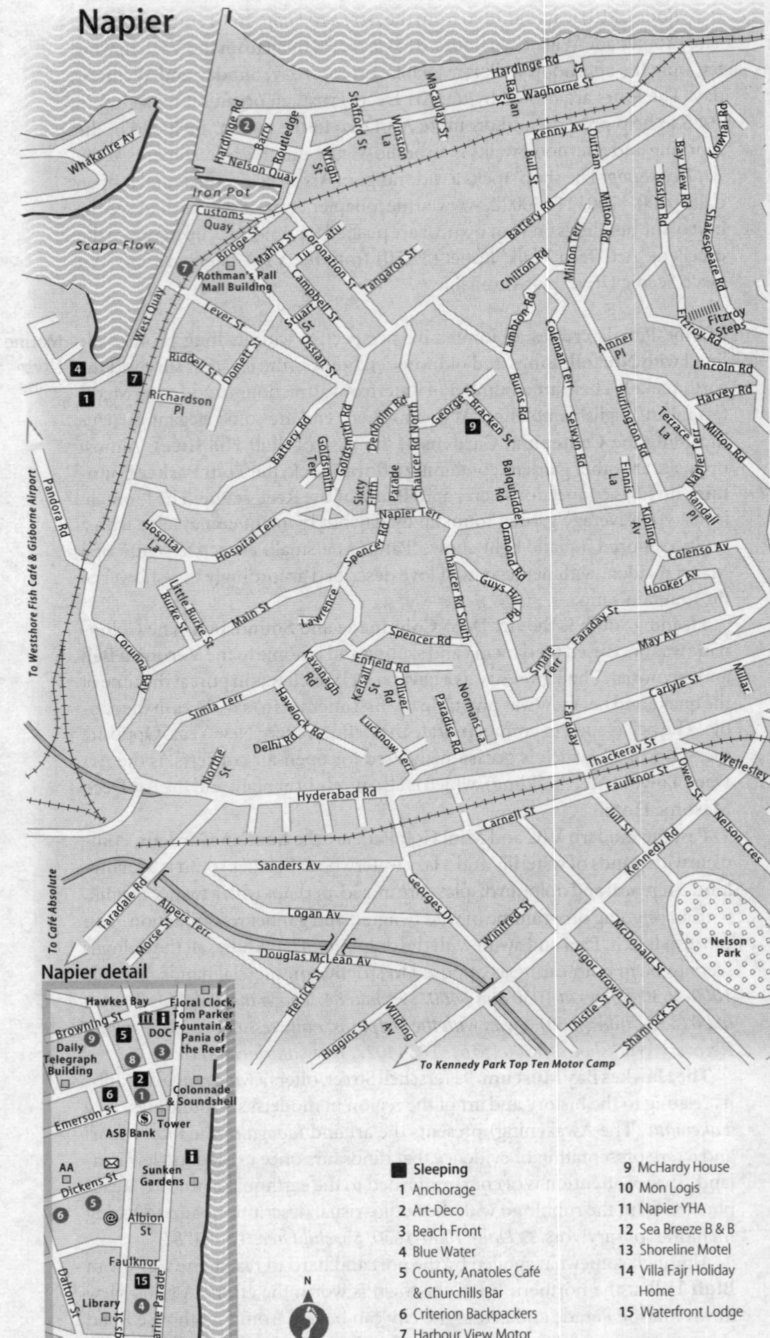

Napier
Hardinge Rd
Waghorne St
Raglan St
Macaulay St
Winston La
Stafford St
Hardinge Rd
Barry
Routledge
Nelson Quay
Wright St
Whakarire Av
Iron Pot
Customs Quay
Scapa Flow
Bridge St
Mahia St
Tu atu
Coronation St
Tangaroa St
Campbell St
Stuart St
Ossian St
Rothman's Pall Mall Building
West Quay
Lever St
Riddell St
Domett St
Richardson Pl
Kenny Av
Bull St
Outram
Milton Rd
Milton Terr
Battery Rd
Chilton Rd
Lambton Rd
Coleman Terr
Burns Rd
Selwyn Rd
Amner Pl
Burlington Rd
Roslyn Rd
Bay View Rd
Kowhai Rd
Shakespeare Rd
Fitzroy Steps
Fitzroy Rd
Lincoln Rd
Harvey Rd
Milton Rd
Terrace La
Napier Terr
Randall Pl
Finnis La
Kipling Av
Colenso Av
Hooker Av
George St
Bracken St
Balquhidder Rd
Ormond Rd
Denholm Rd
Chaucer Rd North
Sixty Fifth Parade
Goldsmith Rd
Goldsmith Terr
Battery Rd
Napier Terr
Spencer Rd
Chaucer Rd South
Guys Hill Rd
Hospital La
Hospital Terr
Little Burke St
Burke St
Main St
Lawrence
Corunna Bay
Pandora Rd
To Westshore Fish Café & Gisborne Airport
Spencer Rd
Enfield Rd
Kavanagh Rd
Kelsall St
Oliver Rd
Paradise Rd
Normans La
Smale Terr
Faraday St
May Av
Carlyle St
Millar
Faraday
Simla Terr
Havelock Rd
Delhi Rd
Lucknow Terr
Northe St
Thackeray St
Wellesley
Faulknor St
Owen St
Hyderabad Rd
Carnell St
Jull St
Kennedy Rd
Nelson Cres
Nelson Park
Sanders Av
Georges Dr
Logan Av
Winifred St
McDonald St
Taradale Rd
Alpers Terr
Morse St
To Café Absolute
Douglas McLean Av
Herrick St
Vigor Brown St
Thistle St
Shamrock St
Higgins St
Wilding Av
To Kennedy Park Top Ten Motor Camp
Napier detail
Hawkes Bay
Browning St
Daily Telegraph Building
DOC
Floral Clock, Tom Parker Fountain & Pania of the Reef
Colonnade & Soundshell
Emerson St
ASB Bank
Tower
AA
Dickens St
Sunken Gardens
Albion St
Faulknor
Dalton St
Library
Hastings St
Marine Parade
N
0 metres 200
0 yards 200
Sleeping
1 Anchorage
2 Art-Deco
3 Beach Front
4 Blue Water
5 County, Anatoles Café & Churchills Bar
6 Criterion Backpackers
7 Harbour View Motor Lodge
8 Masters Lodge
9 McHardy House
10 Mon Logis
11 Napier YHA
12 Sea Breeze B & B
13 Shoreline Motel
14 Villa Fajr Holiday Home
15 Waterfront Lodge
Eating
1 Acqua Brasserie

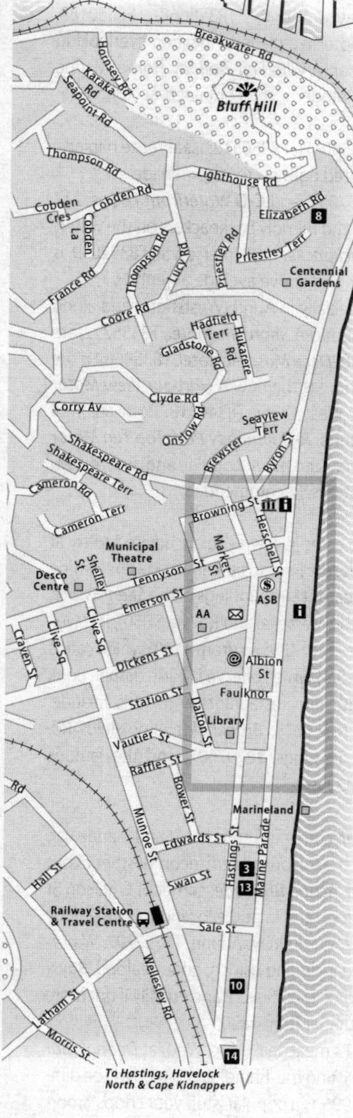

2 Bayswater Bistro
3 Breakers Café
4 Deano's Bar & Grill
5 Golden Crown
6 Mossy's
7 Shed 2

Pubs & clubs
8 Flaherty's
9 Rosie O'Gradys

Activities & tours
For details contact the VICs

Ballooning: T/F8588480, $230, child, from $150. **Canoeing**: Trips and hire, T8747721. **Climbing wall**: *Salty Rock Adventure Company*, T8343500. **Fishing**: *Ross Mossman*, T8351397. *Jack Trout*, T8777642. **Horse treks**: *Te Awanga*, T8750541, Riverlands (Mohaka River), T8349756. **Jet boat tours**: T8444568. **Quad biking**: *Karamea Adventures*, T8746661, from $90. **Rafting/kayaking**: *Riverlands (Mohaka River)*, T8349756. *Salty Rock Adventure Company*, West Quay, T8343500. **Scenic flights**: *Napier Airport*, T8356192, from $39. **Sightseeing tours**: *Bay Tours and Charters*, T8436953. *Liberty Tours*, T8359888. **Swimming**: Note that the beach in Napier is pebble, deeply shelved and too dangerous for swimming. **Vineyard tours**: see page 349. **Walking**: The Whana Valley Walk is an organized 3-day event taking in very pleasant countryside and accommodation lodges (meals optional and extra), $135, T8742860, www.whana-valley-walk.co. nz **Windsurfing/sailing**: *Sail'n Surf*, T/F8350684, from $40.

Essentials

Sleeping
Napier is a popular holiday spot so, in summer, you are advised to book ahead

LL *McHardy House*, 11 Bracken St, Hospital Hill, T8350605, F8340902, www.mchardyhouse.com One of Napier's oldest estates, centrally located with 4 suites and 2 rooms. Luxuriously appointed with fine dining (in-house chef) and panoramic views. **LL** *Masters Lodge*, 10 Elizabeth Pl, Bluff Hill, T8341946, F8341947, www.masterslodge.co.nz 2 luxury private suites, solarium, in-house museum and veranda with commanding views. Dinner on request.

AL-A *County Hotel*, Browning St, T8357800, F8357797, countyhotel@xtra.co.nz Restored Art Deco Edwardian Hotel in the centre of town. Popular award-winning restaurant *Anatole's* and *Churchill Bar* attached. **AL** *Mon Logis*, 415 Marine Par, T/F8352125, monlogis@xtra.co.nz French-style waterfront accommodation with fine French cuisine.

East Coast

A *Blue Water Hotel*, 10 West Quay, Ahuriri, T8358668, F8350188, bluewaterhotel@xtra.co.nz Napier's newest hotel in a pleasant location overlooking the Westshore Marina. Spas, restaurant and bar. **A** ***Villa Fajr Holiday Home***, Marine Par, T8350584, www.villafajr.co.nz Excellent, modern, self-contained accommodation in traditional wood beachfront house.

B *Sea Breeze B&B*, 281 Marine Par, T8358067, F8350512, seabreeze.napier@xtra.co.nz Tidy, comfortable, guesthouse located right on the promenade.

The **C-D** ***Napier YHA***, 277 Marine Par, T8357039, and **C-D** ***Waterfront Lodge***, 217 Marine Par, T/F8353429 are both comfortable and friendly backpackers on the waterfront with internet, while the **C-D** ***Criterion Backpackers***, 48 Emerson St, T8352059, is an Art Deco former hotel with spacious rooms and above average amenities.

There are numerous **motels** in Napier, especially in Auriri (Westshore) and along the promenade. **A** ***The Beach Front***, T8355220, and **A** ***Shoreline Motel***, T8355222, are new and the best on Marine Par, while the **A** ***Art-Deco Masonic Hotel***, T8358689 is the slightly cheaper, older style option. At Westshore is the new **A** ***Harbour View Motor Lodge***, T8358077, and the **A** ***Anchorage***, 26 West Quay, T8344318. Both are well appointed and look over the harbour and marina. **A-D** ***Kennedy Park Top Ten Motor Camp***, Storkey St, T8439126, www.kennedypark.co.nz A popular and well established motor park offering a wide range of options. Recommended.

Eating

Although there are some fine restaurants and cafés in town you are advised to try at least one lunch or dinner at one of the **vineyards**. Perhaps the finest cuisine can be found amidst the amazing architecture and pleasant surroundings of the ***Sileni Estate***. Although some way from Napier (34 Km) on the Maraekakaho Rd (via SH50), it is well worth the journey. There are 2 restaurants: the *Mesa Alfresco* (from 1130) which caters for day-time cuisine and *RD1* (from 1800 Wed-Sat) which offers à la carte dinner. Book ahead, T8794831. Some other vineyards with fine restaurants and cafés include: ***Crab Farm***, 551 Main Rd North, Bay View, T8366678; ***Brookfields***, Brookfields Rd, Meeanee, T8344615; ***Te Awa***, Roys Hill Rd, Hastings, T8797602; and the famous ***Mission Estate***, 198 Church Rd, Taradale, T8442259.

In Napier Mid-range: ***Breakers Café and Bar***, corner of Tennyson St and Marine Par, T8358689. Central location, perhaps a bit over the top on modern 'neon' aesthetics but fine food, again with an emphasis on seafood. ***Acqua Brasserie***, corner of Emerson St and Marine Par, T8358689. Modern, good seafood and in prime location. Get a seat by the aquariums. Open from 1130 daily. ***Shed 2***, West Quay, Ahuriri, T8352202. Waterfront location, imaginative international menu including ostrich, good seafood. ***Bayswater Bistro***, 5 Hardinge Rd (East Pier), T8358517. Near Shed 2 and equally if not more popular. Stylish international cuisine. Open Tue-Sat from 1830.

Cheap: You can't go far wrong with the $13 meal deal (Mon/Wed) at ***Deano's Bar and Grill***, at 255 Marine Par, T8354944, but resisting the 'Rhino' sized steak will be difficult. ***The Golden Crown***, 38 Dickens St, T8355996, is a popular 'stuff your chops' smorgasbord Chinese.

Cafés

Mossy's, 88a Dickens St, T8356696. Open daily 0800-late. An intimate, cosy café with candles and tasteful décor. Good value and live music on Sat nights. ***Café Absolute***, 120 Taradale Rd, T8434322. Modern-style award winner. ***Anatole's Café***, 12 Browning St, T8357800.Open seven days 0730-late. Another award winner with good coffee and a wicked raspberry tandoori chicken and fine breakfasts. ***Westshore Fish Café***, 112a Charles St, Westshore, T8340227. One of the better seafood options.

Pubs & entertainment

There are 2 Irish pubs in Gisborne, ***Rosie O'Gradys*** and ***O'Flaherty's*** , both on Hastings St. Although not notable for their interior aesthetics, they do occasionally 'go off' with live bands at the weekends. The place to be seen at the moment is the ***Gintrap*** on West Quay. It is like a cross between a wool shed and a Nasa's mission control centre with music that may well result in 'lift off'. If you want to have a bit of fun over a fat cigar and G&T, head for ***Churchills Bar*** below the County Hotel in Browning St. There staff are well used to merry clients doing awful Churchill impersonations but quite rightly draw the line when it gets to... 'Never, in the field of human drinking....'

Festivals

Napier and the Hawkes Bay has a nationally famous itinerary of annual events that which attract people both from home and abroad.

Feb *Harvest Hawkes Bay*: a weekend of fun and games celebrating the region's wine production. Grown men race around a park in wine barrels, tremendous stuff. ***International Mission Estate Concert***: an outdoor concert at the renowned Mission Estate Winery drawing large crowds and famous names like, Dame Kiri Te Kanawa, Dionne Warwick and the Beach Boys, to name but a few.

Art Deco Weekend: Napier's biggest and most popular event celebrating the Art Deco Style. Vintage cars, period costume, parades and Devonshire teas on the promenade.

Mar *Horse of the Year Show*: The largest horse show in the Southern Hemisphere attracting over 1000 riders and 8000 spectators.

Jun *Winter Arts Festival/ Winter Solstice Fire Festival*: A celebration of the arts with theatre, restaurant theatre and vocal arts all enhanced by a spectacular fire show at the Soundshell.

Nov *Month of Wine and Roses*: A month of private garden tours, music and wine releases.

Directory

Car Rentals: *Hertz* T8356169. *Xpress*, T8358818. **Communications Internet:** Available at *Cybers*, 98 Dickens St (open Mon-Fri 0800-1700, Sat 0900-1200) **Cycle hire**: *Marineland*, 209 Marine Parade, T8344027. *Napier Cycle Centre*, Tennyson St, T8359528. **Library**: Station St, T8344180 **Medical servies**: 30/32 Monroe St, T8354696. **Useful addresses Police**: T8354688. **AA**: Dickens St, T8353725.

Around Napier

Cape Kidnappers Gannet Colony

Cape Kidnappers is the jagged white peninsula which marks the southern boundary of Hawkes Bay. It gets its name from another rather unfortunate incident involving Captain Cook and the local Maori. Believing Cook's Tahitian interpreter was being held against his will, the Maori sent a *waka* to bring him back to shore. Doubtless a little confused, the Tahitian captive escaped back to the Cook's ship, which promptly weighed anchor and left, leaving only a name behind – Cape Kidnappers.

The Cape is famous for its colony of gannets. These large, elegant seabirds have lots of attitude, and weighing in at about 2 kg with deadly 6-in beaks designed to spear fish, they have every right to be so. They hunt by gliding high over the surface of the water and diving with wings folded back at tremendous speed to catch the unsuspecting fish beneath. In the summer months up to 15,000 gannets gather at Cape Kidnappers to breed, forming the biggest mainland colony in New Zealand, and one of the biggest in the world. Perhaps given their attitude and armoury, gannets are not particularly fearful of anything or anybody, which makes them very approachable, particularly when grouped together and guarding their own little breeding patch. Being so approachable makes them the perfect tourist attraction, as they simply stare at you with an expression of complete contempt. The tourist-visiting season runs from October to late April, with the best time to view being early

November and late February. The first fluffy white chicks hatch in early November with the last chicks fledging and leaving the colony on their migration to Australia during May.

There are a variety of tours available to see the gannets. Most negotiate the beach and the tides below the peninsula, while others go overland. Provided the tides are right you can walk the 8 km to the colony yourself. The walk starts from the Clifton Motor Camp but it is generally hard going. Given the time restictions due to the tides, you are advised to join a tour operator. If you are determined to go it alone, you can get the latest tide times at T8343111.

All trips are subject to season and tide times. There is a Cape Shuttle between Napier and Clifton or Te Awanga, $20.Contact the VIC

Tour operators There are 5 operators. The oldest is ***Gannet Beach Adventures***, T8750898, gannetbeach@xtra.co.nz This 4-hr tour leaves from Clifton Beach by tractor and allows about 90 mins with the gannets, from $22, child $15. ***Gannet and Coastline Tours Ltd***, T864664, www.gannet.co.nz offer a similar 4½-hr tour in a 4-wheel drive truck but leave from Napier giving less time with the gannets, from $25, child $17. ***Gannet Safaris***, T8750888, m.neilson@xtra.co.nz based at the Summerlee Station on the Cape (near Te Awanga), go overland by shuttle bus, which involves very little walking. The 3-hr tours depart daily at 0930 and 1330, from $38. Still on wheels is the quad-bike 3-4 hr option with ***Quadventures***, T8366652, from $95. Again they go via the beach. If walking is your thing you can join a half or 3-day Cape walking experience with Cape Kidnappers Walks, T8750837, p.julian@xtra.co.nz From $50.

Contact the VIC for details of B&Bs in the area

Sleeping and eating Both the **C-D** ***Clifton Motor Camp***, Clifton Beach (road terminus) T8750263, and the **B-D** ***Te Awanga Motor Camp***, 52 Kuku St, Te Awanga, T/F8750334, offer adequate beachside accommodation near the Cape and the 2 main operators *Gannet Beach Adventures* and *Gannet Safaris*. For eating the excellent new ***Clifton Bay Café and Bar***, T8750096 (open daily in summer, Mon-Fri winter, 0900-1700) is near the entrance to the motor camp and overlooks the beach.

Other sights

Old (or young) rock'n rollers should not miss the unique **Jukebox Museum**, at 158 Main Highway, in Clive, at the mouth of the Ngaruroro River, 10 km south of Napier. Numerous old models are on show playing all the old favourites. ■ *Daily 0930-1700. $3, child free. T8700775.* Staunch British 'petrol-heads' should pay homage to the **British Car Museum**, 63 East Road, Haumoana, which is near Cape Kidnappers. It's quite small but its eccentric owner is very proud of his many old favourites, including the legendary Mini. ■ *Open daily but call first. $5.T8750561.*

For keen photographers there is the **Millennium Museum** in Te Awanga, which is also near the Cape. It boasts a moderate range of classic cameras and microscopes. ■ *Open by appointment. T8750987.*

Even if you have seen enough sheep the **Classic Sheepskins Tannery**, 22 Thames Street, Pandora (near Napier airport) is worth a visit. It offers a tour of the premises to see just how those hearthrugs and car seat covers are made. Drying lines with row after row of stretched sheepskins does prove a bizarre sight and conjures up an image of a flock of naked, embarrassed sheep hiding somewhere in the fields beyond. ■ *Mon-Fri 0730-1700, Sat/Sun 0900-1600. From $8, child $4.50. T8359662, www.classicsheepskins.co.nz*

Hawkes Bay Wineries

Given the climate and the soils in the Hawkes Bay it was inevitable that it would not take long for the first grape vine to be planted by the first Europeans settlers. Back then wine was produced primarily for religious use and it was the Catholic Society who founded a Mission Vineyard, in Taradale in 1851. Since that first harvest, the vines and the industry have boomed, making Hawkes Bay second only to Marlborough as the country's top wine producing region. The two regions combined produce a range of wines which can compare with the world's best. Hawkes Bay offers a particularly wide range of wines due to the composition of the land and diverse 'sub regions'. Two such established 'sub-regions' are Bay View and the Esk Valley. There are over 25 vineyards in the region so, unless you are a connoisseur, knowing which to visit can be a dilemma. Thankfully the 'Hawkes Bay Wine Trail', as outlined in the free leaflet of the same name, gives details of what each vineyard offers. Some have stunning architecture, some are particularly famous or more established, others have fine restaurants or cafés. Most offer sales and tastings. You can either embark on a tour according to your own choice and itinerary, or join a number of organized tours (see below). If you know little about wines, and New Zealand wine in particular, an organized tour is advised.

Recommended vineyards

Sileni, Maraekakaho Rd, Hastings, T8798768. Stunning modern architecture, top restaurant and a fine range of wines. Open 1000-1700, top class (and top range) restaurant open until late. ***Mission Estate***, corner Avenue and Church Rds, Taradale, T8442259. The oldest vineyard in New Zealand. Famous labels, restaurant and established tours. Open Mon-Sat 0830-1730, Sun 1100-1600. ***Church Road***, 150 Church Rd, Taradale, T8442053. Formerly the McDonald's Vineyard. Owned by the internationally famous Montana Estates. Wine-making museum and restaurant. Open daily 0900-1700. ***Te Mata***, Te Mata Rd, T8774399. Another architectural stunner. Reputable label. Mon-Fri 0900-1700, 1000 Sat, 1100 Sun. ***Te Awa***, Roy's Hill Rd, SH50, T8797602. Interesting building, fine labels and good café. Open 0900-1700, Sat/Sun 1000-1800. ***Clearview***, 194 Clifton Rd, Te Awanga, Hastings, T8750150. One not to miss if you are visiting Cape Kidnappers. Quality not quantity with a classy Mediterranean style café. Open daily 1000-1700.

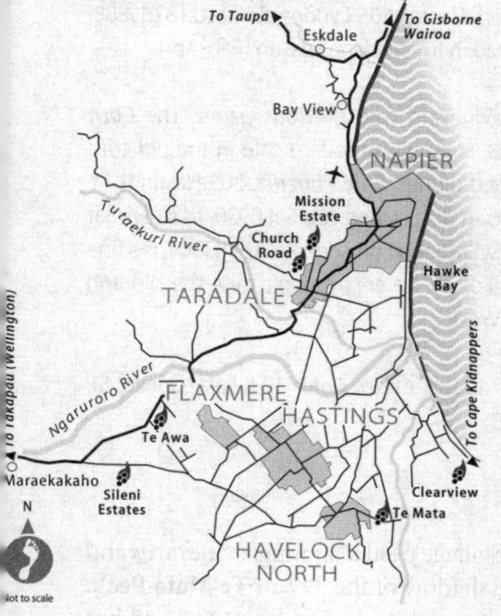

Wine Tours

Most of the tours available are flexible to your needs

Hawkes Bay in a Glass, T8432478, F8432474, www.qualityhb.co.nz High quality customized tours arranged to your own time schedule and tastes. Price varies. **Wine Tours**, Napier, T8436953. Established in 1982. Range of tours from $40. ***Vince's Vineyard Tours***, T8366705. Personalized tour with friendly, local, knowledgeable guide. In operation for 10 years. Flexible itineraries from $35. ***Vicky's Vineyard Tours***, T8439991. Good range of imaginative tours from added sightseeing to committed connoisseurs. From $35. ***On Yer Bike Winery Tours***, Hastings, T8798735. The energetic option, by bike (requires supreme coordination and orientation skills towards the end of the day).

Hastings

Population: 50,000
Phone code: 06

Hastings is a lively, sprawling, mainly agricultural service centre 20 km south of Napier and, like Napier, it was reduced mostly to rubble by the 1931 earthquake, with the loss of 88 lives. In rebuilding the town the architects echoed Napier's Art Deco and Spanish Mission styles, much of which can clearly be seen in the town centre. The two best examples are the **Westerman's Building** on Russell Street and **Municipal Theatre** on Hastings Street. The prominent Art Deco **clock tower**, situated right in the centre of town, was erected in 1935 to house the bells from the old 1909 Post Office Tower which collapsed in the quake. Architect Sydney Chaplin won 25 Guineas ($52) for its design.

Ins & outs The Hastings **Visitors Information Centre** is on Russell St North, T8735526, F8735529, www.hastingsalive.co.nz Open Mon-Fri 0830-1700, Sat/Sun 1000-1500.

Sights Modern day attractions in Hastings include the **Hawkes Bay Exhibition Centre**, 201 Eastbourne Street. It is the region's premier arts venue offering a varied programme of national and international touring exhibitions. Science and history also feature and there is an in-house café. ■ *Mon-Fri 1000-1630, Sat/Sun 1100-1600. Usually free depending on exhibitions. T/F8762077.*

Given the dangerous nature of the beaches in the region, **Splash Planet**, a new themed water-park on Grove Road, is proving very popular. There is an ice rink, hot pools and the inevitable slides and rides to keep the kids happy for hours. ■ *Daily 0900-late. $15, child $10. T8769856.* If wine tasting doesn't whet your appetite, the **Pernel Fruitworld**, 1412 Pakowhai Road (north towards Napier), offers an interesting orchard tour and experience. Café on site. *Daily 0900-1700, $8, child $4. T8783383.*

Sleeping **L-AL** *Hawthorn Country House*, 420 SH2, T/F8780035, www.hawthorne.co.nz Award-winning luxury B&B in country setting. Range of spacious rooms. Sumptuous breakfasts. **A** *Angus Inn*, Railway Rd, T8788177, F8787496. Large complex with on-site restaurant and pool. **A-B** *Aladdin Motel*, 120 Maddison St, T8766322, F8766736. Slightly cheaper motel option, centrally located. **B-D** *Hastings Holiday Park*, Winsor Av, T8786692, vin_norma@clear.net.nz Located within walking distance of 'Splash Planet'. **C-D** *Hastings Backpackers Hostel*, 505 Lyndon Rd East, T8765888. The pick of the 4 hostels in town. Book ahead in fruit picking season (Feb-Apr).

Eating For fine dining near Hastings see *Selini* Vineyard (see previous page). The *Corn Exchange*, 118 Maraekakaho Rd, T8708333, is a stylish modern café in the old corn exchange building. Open daily for lunch and dinner. *Café Phoenix*, 205 Hastings St, T8734530, is an award winner amidst classic art deco. Open Tue-Sat 0930-1430, Fri/Sat 1700-late. *Saporito*, corner of Heretaunga St East and Lumsden Rd, T8783364, is a fine budget Italian. Open Tue-Sat 1600-2000. For an ice cream don't miss the old and famous *Rush Munro's*, 704 Heretaunga St West.

Directory **Communications Internet** is available at the *Cyber Café*, 102 East Queen St, T8764876.

Havelock North

Population: 9000

Havelock North is a very pleasant little village nestled amongst vineyards and orchards towards the coast and in the shadow of the 399-m **Te Mata Peak**. The view from the summit of Te Mata on a clear day is a 'must see' and it is easily reached by car via the village and Te Mata Peak Road. Weather permitting it is also a top spot for **Paragliding**. Tandem flights are available with Peak Paragliding, T8778804, from $120.

As well as the numerous wineries surrounding Havelock North it is also home to another one of nature's great delights, honey. **Arataki Honey Ltd**, 66 Arataki Road, was established in 1944 and is one of the largest beekeeping enterprises in the Southern Hemisphere, with a staggering 17,000 hives. There is a guided tour available, a shop and the spectacular 'wall', with its army of 40,000 live and very busy bees. ■ *Mon-Sat 0830-1700, Sun 0900-1600. $10, child free. T8777300.*

Sleeping

There are a number of magnificent traditional and modern 'country house style' B&Bs and lodges in the area. For full listings contact the VIC

LL *Mangapapa Lodge*, 466 Napier Rd, Havelock North, T8783234, F8781214, Mangapapa.lodge@xtra.co.nz A world famous small luxury hotel in 100 year-old refurbished country house. Magnificent range of accommodation and fine in-house restaurant. **LL** *Lombardi Wines*, Havelock North, T8777985, F8777816, lombardi@xtra.co.nz Lombardi have 2 self-contained options, a barn and a cottage, both situated in the heart of the vineyard. Expensive, but superb. **L-AL** *Te Mata Lodge*, 21 Porter Dr, Havelock North, T8774880, F8774881, temata.lodge@xtra.co.nz Comfortable, self-contained and centrally located in the village, spas. For the more traditional accommodation options try the **A** *Havelock North Motor Lodge*, 7 Havelock Rd, Havelock North, and T8778627. Quality, modern motel, well-located. **B-D** *Arataki Motel and Holiday Park*, 139 Arataki Rd, Havelock North, T/F8777479. Heated indoor pool. **C-D** *Peak Backpackers*, 33 Havelock Rd, T8771170. This is a new, modern establishment, clean, comfortable and well-situated right in the heart of the village.

Eating

See also page 130

The *Bradshaw Estate Winery*, Te Mata Rd, T8775795,has a classy restaurant offering lunches from 1200 and dinner Fri/Sat. Coffee all day. In the village the *Olive Tree*, 17 Joll Rd, T8770222, does snacks and has good coffee. For a magnificent view head for the *Peak House Restaurant* on Te Mata Peak Rd. T8778663. Open Wed-Sun from 1800 for dinner, Wed-Mon 1200-1400 for lunch. Licensed.

Pubs & entertainment

Lovers of good pubs and fine ale should not miss the *Rose and Shamrock* a spacious and delightful Anglo/Irish style pub in the centre of the village. For the complete opposite pop your head in to the infamous *Happy Tavern* nearby.

Transport

The major national coachlines stop in the centre of Hastings. *Nimbus* is the local operator, T8778133.

Southern Hawkes Bay & south to the Wairarapa

From Hastings SH2 winds its lonely way towards the little-visited, but stunning region of the Wairarapa, before arriving in Wellington. On SH2 there are a number of small towns including **Waipawa, Waipukurau, Dannevirke** and **Norsewood** (the latter two having obvious Scandanavian links). Although these settlements have little to offer the visitor there are plenty of activities avilable in the area, including ballooing and tramping. The wild **Kaweka** and **Ruahine Ranges** offer some fine tramping but you are advised to plan carefully and go well prepared.

Getting there From Waipukurau take the coast road towards Porangahau. After about 40 km take a right. Follow the AA 'Historic Place Sign'. From Porangahau it is possible to take the back road to Wimbledon and undertake the alternative route to the Wairarapa, re-emerging on SH2 at either Eketahuna or Masterton. This will allow you to take in the stunning Castle Point on the way.

Information DOC (Napier) or the field station in the historic village of **Ongaonga**, 15 km west of Waipukurau, will provide all the necessary information and leaflets, T8566808. The **Visitor Information Centre** in Waipukurau, Railway Esplanade, T8586488, F8586489, chbinfo@xtra.co.nz, can assist with activity and accommodation bookings.

Before leaving Hawkes Bay region proper, there is one other place worth visiting. But, bear in mind it is on the 'alternative' route into the back country of the Wairarapa and involves a bit of a hike. For the sheer sake of it, it is worth the trip to see a sign that points at a distinctly unremarkable hill called '**Taumatawhakatangihangakoauauotamateaturipukakapikimaungahoronukupokaiwhenuaktanatahu**' and declares it as having the longest place name in the world. Roughly translated it means 'The place where Tamatea, the man with the big knees, who slid, climbed and swallowed mountains (known as land eater) played his flute to his loved one'. As you carefully contemplate both sign, place and meaning, as well as your annoyingly inquisitive nature, you can be sure of one thing – old Tamatea may have been a big eater but he was also a lousy lover if this was his idea of a romantic spot.

The Wairarapa

*The Wairarapa is one of the least-visited regions in the North Island. Most visitors miss it out in their rush to reach Wellington via SH1, which lies to the west beyond the natural barrier of the **Ruahine** and **Tararua Ranges**. If that simple fact is not appealing enough, the remote and stunning coastal scenery and relaxed atmosphere will, if you make the effort to visit, confirm that this is a place worth getting to know. The highlights, other than the delights of rural towns like **Martinborough**, which lie like a string of pearls along SH2, is the coastal splendour of **Castle Point** and **Cape Palliser**, the North Island's most southerly point.*

Masterton

Population: 18,000
Phone code: 06

Given its relative geographical isolation (thanks to the Tararua Ranges), Masterton was not settled to any great degree until the late 1850s, but with rich fertile soils and a favourable climate, growth was rapid. Today, the town is the chief commercial centre for the Wairarapa Region. Masterton also gives Te Kuiti in the Wiakato (the 'sheep-shearing capital of New Zealand') a run for its money in the big woolly event stakes. The 'Golden Shears' is the major date event in the local young farmer's calendar and offers moderate fame and fortune to the fasted clipper around. It is held at the beginning of March, lasts about three days and ends with a big 'dinner' and 'cabaret'.

Ins & outs

Getting there **By bus** *Tranzit Coachlines* run regular weekday services between Wellington and Palmerston North (including Mount Bruce), T3771227, wai@tranzit.co.nz **By train** The rail link with Wellington provides regular services and has the added attraction of the long Rimutaka tunnel across the ranges. There is a special day excursion fare of $15, child $8. Contact *TranzMetro*, T04-4983000. The train station is located on Perry St, about a 15-min walk from the town centre.

Getting around Car rental is available with *Greame Jones Car Rental*, 81 Dixon St, T3786667. *Wairarapa Coachlines* offer a regular weekday and limited weekend services between Masterton, Martinborough and Featherston, T0800-666355.

Information The Masterton **Visitor Information Centre** is at 5 Dixon St, 3787373, F3787042, tourwai@xtra.co.nz The staff are very friendly and it acts as the main VIC in the region. They hold a comprehensive information base on the wealth of B&B beds all over the Wairarapa Region. Mon-Fri 0900-1700, Sat/Sun 1000-1600. The **DOC** Masterton Field Centre is on South Rd (continuation Queen St),T3770700.

Sights

Within walking distance of the VIC and town centre is the much loved and celebrated **Queen Elizabeth Park**. First planted in 1878, today it boasts a lake (with boats for hire), sportsgrounds, a miniature railway, swing bridge, aviaries, a deer park and the usual tracts of tree and manicured herbaceous borders. A little further out of town, on Colombo Road, is **Henley Park**, with lakes, offering fishing and lakeside walks. **The Wairarapa Arts and History Centre**, Bruce Street, has just been given a major, new lease of life and is worth a look. It has an in-house café. ■ *1000-1600.* On lesser scale is the **Museum of Childhood**, 40 Makora Road, with displays of toys and games dating from 1800 to the late 1900s. ■ *Visits are by appointment, T3774737. Donation.*

Masterton has a number of interesting gardens and **Heritage Trail Walks** (1-2 hours) which are part of an eight-walk Regional Heritage Trail. Information and leaflets for all can be obtained from the VIC. If you are a budget traveller, or just simply a little tired from your endless travels, be sure to check out the bronze statue and charmings story of **Russian Jack**, the erstwhile Wairarapa 'Swag' man, on Queen Street.

For recreational walks the **Mount Holdsworth** area offers access to the Tararua Range with short and long walk options. Details are outlined at the car park. To get there take Norfolk Road just south of the town (17 km). Another short scenic walk with added Glow-worms and Flying Fox is at **Cavelands Glow-worm Caves** ($5) Cavelands Road, which also offers great Homestay accommodation (**A**), T3727733.

Activities & tours

Canoeing: *Seven Oaks*, T3723801. Canoe trips to the Whareama River, 1030 and 1330, from $25, child $10. **Climbing wall**: *Oasis*, 2 Akura Road, T/F3788789. **Jet boat**: *Wairarapa Jet Adventures*, T/F3772114. Thrills and spills on the Ruamahanga and Manawatu Rivers. **Sightseeing**: *Laura's Wairarapa Tours*, T3773534. Tailor-made trips with long term resident. **Skydiving**: *Wairarapa Parachute Centre*, T02-5428805. **Swimming**: *Recreation Complex*, Dixon Street. Heated indoor and outdoor pools. **Walking**: *The Kaiwhata Walk*, Ngahape Road, T3722772. Well-organized coastal walk with accommodation and transport arranged, from $125.

Sleeping

The Wairarapa is renowned for its ever-increasing number of B&Bs which comfortably cater for the huge numbers of Wellingtonians, whocross the hills into the Wairarapa in droves on summer weekends and during the holiday periods . Given the sheer number of beds, standards are generally high and competition is fierce. The choices therefore (if not necessarily the prices), are excellent.

L *The Fresh Egg*, Bute Rd, T3723506, F3723505, hosts@freshegg.co.nz Silly name but top of the range country B&B with pool, sauna, spacious rooms and fine cuisine. **AL** *Acorn Cottage*, Bowlands, Bideford, T3724842, www.bowlands.co.nz Charming, well appointed,130 year old cottage in country location. Fully self-contained with log fire. **AL** *Camellia Estate Homestay*, 39 Renall St, T3709088, camellia@wise.net.nz Spacious 1903 villa set in quiet location within walking distance of the town centre. Pool and tennis court. **AL-A** *Copthorne Resort*, High St South, T3775129, F3782913. Very popular due to its extensive range of amenities including pools, spas, squash courts and solarium and high quality accommodation.

AL-A *Masterton Motor Lodge*, 250 High St, T3782585, www.masterton-motorlodge.co.nz Wide range of top quality, modern units, pool, spa, in-house restaurant and bar.

A *Koeke Lodge*, Upper Plain Rd, T3772414, koekelodge@bigboulders.com Huge house close to town and complete with library and snooker room. **B** *Amaru Cottage*, Amaru, T/F3786256. Small, cute and affordable cottage located 6 km from town. Fully self-contained. **B** *Empire Lodge,* 94 Queen St, T3771902. Main budget hotel in town, with ensuites and in house restaurant. **B-D** *Mawley Park Motor Camp*, 15 Oxford St, T3786454. All the usual basic amenities situated close to town and beside the river. **C-D** *Masterton Backpackers*, 22 Victoria St, T3782877. A comfortable suburban house which also serves as the regions main YHA.

Eating There is not a huge amount of choice in Masterton but *Burridges Café* on Queen St, T3771102, offers a good range of traditional fare. It has a bar attached and Mediterranean style décor, open daily for breakfast, lunch and dinner, while in the centre of town, the *Slug and Lettuce*, 1st Floor, 94 Queen St, has good value pub grub. The *Regent Bistro*, also on Queen St, is fine for a quick snack and coffee.

Directory **Communications Internet** is available at the library, Queen St, T3789666.

Mount Bruce The main focus of Mount Bruce, 30 km north of Masterton on SH2, is the **Mount Bruce National Wildlife Centre**. This centre is the flagship of DOC's conservation and endangered species breeding programme. Although much of what happens at Mount Bruce takes place behind the scenes, (and involves dedicated staff acting as surrogate mothers) the public can see many species rarely seen by the average visitor. There is something very special about sitting on the veranda, sipping a coffee and overlooking an enclosure with a takahe (a charming prehistoric-looking purple bird, not dissimilar to a large chicken) going happily about its business, in the knowledge that there are only 200 or so left in the world. Likewise, taking a stroll through the native bush, to see other enclosures hiding stitchbirds and kokako, all of which you will probably never see again in a lifetime.

There is a nocturnal kiwi house which rates as amongst the best in the country and leaves you in no doubt as to the numerous threats which this national icon faces in the modern world. Other highlights include the eel feed at 1330 and the kaka feed at 1500. The wild eels live in the stream running through the reserve and gather beneath the bridge at feeding time in a swirling mass. This particular species are native to New Zealand, are far larger than the average eel and live up to at least 80 years. The kaka is a cheeky and at times raucous, native bush parrot. There is a small colony at Mount Bruce that have been bred and now live wild in the area. They all have names and will quite happily nibble your hair (if you have any) or your ear before cracking open a peanut with their powerful beak. If you go to the feeding area just before 1500 they will usually be hanging about in the trees, available for interviews and photographs. Within the main building there are some fine displays, a shop and a café. ■ *The centre is open daily from 0900-1630. $8, child free. T4725821, www.mtbruce.doc.govt.nz*

Mount Bruce Pioneer Museum, 10 km south of Mount Bruce (SH2) houses a fairly unremarkable collection of pioneer and early settler relics from tractors to vacuum cleaners. ■ *Daily. $3, child $0.50.*

Shelling out for paua

The inner shell casing of the paua (a sea-mollusc) has to be one of the most beautiful and colourful things in nature. The paua is very closely related to the abalone, of which there are about 130 species worldwide, and both are related to snails and limpets. The Maori has long valued paua as a source of both food and decoration and the same is true today. To protect paua as a sustainable resource, strict quotas are in place in New Zealand and no paua harvesting is allowed with compressed air. This makes their collection, with only a snorkel, often in cold southern waters over 12 m in depth, quite an art. Dives of up to two minutes are not uncommon. What comes up from those depths is not the radiant casing that you see in the souvenir shops, but a drab coralline coated shell which, once removed of its flesh, must be ground down to reveal the beautiful patterning beneath. The paua industry is well established in New Zealand, not only for seafood, but more especially for the shell from which the polished jewellery is made. You will encounter the huge range of designs in almost every souvenir shop throughout the land. In some parts of the country the humble paua has even reached iconic status. In Bluff, near Invercargill, an elderly couple (in that typically eccentric New Zealand style) decided to decorate almost their entire house (in and out) with paua. The result is the famous 'paua house', which must feature in many a photo album all over the planet.

Castlepoint

It is a major diversion to get to this remote coastal settlement (65 km from Masterton) but the trip is well worth it

Castlepoint is considered to be the highlight on the Wairarapa's wild and remote coastline and it certainly deserves the honour. At the eastern end of the main beach a stark rocky headland, from which sprouts the weather-beaten Castlepoint Lighthouse, sweeps south to enclose a large lagoon. The picturesque bay, a popular spot with surfers and swimmers, is dominated at its southern entrance by the aptly named 162-m Castle Rock. If you're temped to climb the rock it can be accessed from the southern end of the bay. The lighthouse can be accessed across the sand tombolo which connects it to the mainland via a boardwalk. Parked up on the beach you will see huge tractors and metal rigs which launch the local fishing boats. Just below the lighthouse there is a cave which can be explored at low tide, but beware – Maori legend has it that it is the hiding place of a huge menacing octopus. One word of warning, a small memorial stone testifies to those who have drowned while exploring the offshore reef, so take care. On its eastern side, huge ocean waves can catch you unawares. While contemplating the memorial stone look closely at the rocks that surround it and you will see hundreds of fossil shells embedded therein.

There are **fishing charters** operating out of Castlepoint including *Castlepoint Charters*, T3726619, and *Legionnaires Charters*, T3726613. There are fishing competitions in summer. The *Okau Station* (see below) offers a range of activities in their vast 'Wilderness Park'. The main beach is the venue for a famous horse race in March.

Sleeping and eating There is a well-equipped motor camp, a tidy motel, a beach store at Castlepoint and a number of B&Bs nearby. **B** *Okau Station*, 7 km north of Castlepoint, T/F3726892. Tidy self-contained cottage near the beach with log fire. **B** *Castlepoint Motel*, T3726637. Old and new units right in the heart of the village. **B** *Whakataki Hotel*, 4 km before Castlepoint, T3726852. Kiwi country pub with budget rooms and cabins available. **B-D** *Castlepoint Holiday Park*, T3726705. Good value, basic, but adequate amenities and sits next to the beach overlooking the headland. There are no restaurants, so the village store and the Whakataki Hotel 4 km north are your best bet.

Transport There is no public transport to Castlepoint. You may however be able to hook up with the holiday park or hotel staff on supply trips to Masterton.

Riversdale Beach & Flat Point The small coastal resort of Riversdale is 35 km northeast of Te Wharau which is itself east of Masterton, (130 km round trip). The beach is long and sandy and, as it's patrolled in summer, offers safe swimming as well as surfing, fishing and diving. The Flat Point to Honeycomb Rock section of coast is wilder than Riversdale with interesting rock formations and an old shipwreck. *Trekkers Horse Treks*, T3723523, offer great coastal treks from $25.

Sleeping and eating At Riversdale Beach there is a store, a motor camp and a number of B&B's nearby. **A** ***Blairlogie***, (between Riversdale and Whareama), T/F3723777. Beautiful old homestead and self-contained cottage in spacious grounds. **A** ***Caledonia Coastal Farmstay***, (Flat Point Rd), T/F3727553, wendakerr@xtra.co.nz A well-appointed self-contained cottage in prime position overlooking the beach. **C-D** ***Riversdale Beach Camping Ground***, T3783482.

Carterton

Carterton acts as a secondary service town to Masterton and is famous in spring for its daffodils (first planted in 1920). Although not aesthetically as nice as its neighbouring settlements, it is perhaps worth a stop to see the **Paua Shell Factory** and use the town as an access point to the **Mount Dick** Viewpoint and the Tararua Forest park at **Waiohine Gorge**.

Sights The **Paua Shell Factory** on Kent Street is one of the few places in the country that converts the stunningly beautiful Paua (abalone) shells into jewellery and souvenir products. It is possible to see how the shell is crafted and to watch a video about the paua itself, with complimentary coffee or tea. This is all cleverly designed to get you in to the shop, where there is a vast range of paua shell items on sale, some of which is painfully kitsch. ■ *Daily 0800-1700. Free. T3796777, www.pauashell.co.nz*

Sporting your new paua shell earrings and keyrings, and provided the weather is fair, you can then go and see one of the best views in the Wairarapa, from **Mount Dick**. At the southern end of town turn into Dalefield Road which heads straight towards the hills like a never-ending runway. At the very end of the road keep going and just before its terminus look for a farm track on the left. This track, which is negotiable without four-wheel drive (just), goes about 3 km up to a viewpoint; 14 km total.

The trip to **Waiohine Gorge** (22 km) at the entrance to the **Tararua Forest Park** is well worth it for the scenery itself, let alone the walks on offer and the heart-stopping **swingbridge**, one of the longest in New Zealand. The road is signposted just south of the town on SH2. Eventually an unsealed road connects you with the riverbank which gradually rises high above the river gorge. At the road terminus you can embark on a number of walks from one hour to several days, almost all of which involve the initial negotiation of the swingbridge which traverses the gorge at a height of about 40 m. Even if you do nothing else at Waiohine, a few trips back and forth on the bridge is great fun. Although it is perfectly safe, bear in mind that jelly has less wobble.

Sleeping & eating

There are numerous friendly B&Bs available. For the full range contact the VICs

A ***Courthouse Cottage***, 16 Hilton Rd, South Carterton, T3798030. Very pleasant self-contained option right in the heart of town. As the name suggests the cottage was the former 1860s Courthouse. **A** ***The Bothie***, Admiral Rd, Gladstone, T3727724, F3727770. This is a fine wee cottage, which although in the nearby settlement of Gladstone (as opposed to Carterton) is well worth the journey. It is in perfect isolation amongst bush and has a wonderful ambience, with a nice interior, decks and a log fire.

Towards the Waiohine Gorge is the good value **A** ***Waiohine Farmstay***, Fire 21, T0800-387437, www.waiohine.co.nz Close to all gorge and forest activities, if you can ever drag yourself away from the farm itself. **B** ***Matador Motel***, 187 High St, T/F3798058. Not as dodgy as the name suggests and the town's only motel. Carterton's basic **D** ***Campground*** is located on Belvedere Rd, T/F3798267.

In Carterton itself the ***Buckthorn Bar and Grill***, 20 Memorial Sq, T3797972, open Tue-Sat 1130-late, Tue-Sun 1200-1430, from 1800, offers pub grub in congenial surroundings while the new ***Square***, corner of Memorial Sq and High St, offers café style day and à la carte evening meals. Near Carterton the ***Gladstone Inn***, Gladstone Rd, T3727866 (open daily from 1000), and the ***Gladstone Vineyard Café***, T3798563 (open Summer Fri/Sat/Sun 1100-1500) also on Gladstone Rd, are both recommended.

Greytown

Greytown is a great spot to stop and wander around the old buildings and quaint shops before enjoying a coffee and moving on

Greytown, along with Martinborough, is the prettiest of the Wairarapa settlements and is best known for its antique, art and craft shops and roadside cafés. Given its historic village feel it is not surprising to learn that Greytown was one of the first places settled in the area. Settlement began in earnest in the 1850s, on land purchased by Sir George Grey, one of New Zealand's first governors and after whom the town is, of course, named. There is a small **Visitor Information Centre** in the Council building, 110 Main Street, T3049008. ■ *Fri/Sat/Sun 1000-1600. The free 'Taste of Greytown' leaflet is especially useful.* The **Cobblestones Museum**, 169 Main Street, is a collection of buildings and memorabilia from the early settler days. ■ *Daily from 0900-1630. $2.50, child $1. T3049687.*

Greytown is the base for **The Adventure Centre**, 76 Main Street. They offer a wide range of activities including rafting (from $55), kayaking (from $65), abseiling (from $55) and caving (from $95), mainly centred around the Waiohine Gorge. The full-day 'extreme trip', which is a combination of these activities, costs a very reasonable $95. T3048565, www.ecoadventure.co.nz If the weather is settled *Ballooning NZ*, will take you up, up and away for an early morning 2-3 hour flight for about $200, breakfast included; T/F3798223.

Sleeping & eating

Greytown and the immediate area also has its fair share of lovely B&Bs details of which are available at the VICs. There is a basic **D** campground on Kuratawhiti St, T3049837. In the heart of town, the ***Main St Deli*** has a large outdoor eating area and offers breakfast, lunch and dinner along with some great snacks and coffee, good value. Open daily from 0700-1800, Fri/Sat for dinner, T3049022. For both lunch and dinner ***Fredricks***, 83 Main St, is also recommended. Open daily, live jazz, T3049825. Just north of the village, and next to the golf driving range, ***Swingers Café*** is also popular for daytime eating and evening dining (must book). Open daily from 0830, T3049952.

Marinborough

Marinborough is located towards the coast from SH2, 16 km southeast of Greytown. It is not dissimilar to Greytown but enjoys its country location and a quiet town square as opposed to the bustling SH2. First settled by a nationalistic Briton, John Martin in the late 1880s, the Village Square and the streets running off it form the shape of the Union Jack. With names like Kansas, Texas and Ohio, it is clear that Martin had as much a love of the US as he did his homeland. Described as a unique **wine village**, with a staggering 20 vineyards within walking distance of the square, and blessed with as many charming B&Bs, it is a favourite romantic haunt for Wellingtonians in search of a quiet weekend followed by a savage headache on the following Monday morning. The Martinborough **Visitor Information Centre** is at 18 Kitchener Street, T3069043, F3068033, mboroinfo@xtra.co.nz Open daily 1000-1600.

Sights Of local historical interest is the **Colonial Museum** on the Square, which was itself the former village library built in 1894. It is furnished with all the usual early settler artefacts. ■ *Sat/Sun 1400-1600. Donation. T3069736.* The 'Vintage Village Heritage Walk' available from the VIC will pinpoint other sites of historical interest like the rather grand and recently restored *Martinborough Hotel*. Again there are a number of 'open gardens' for which the VIC will point the way.

The **Patuna Chasm**, Patuna Farm, Ruakokopatuna Road, is an interesting limestone gorge featuring stalactites, fossils and waterfalls and a host of native wildlife. The chasm is on private land but guided walks are available from $15. Book through the VIC. Along a similar theme the **Ruakokopatuna Glow-worm caves** nearby are also on private land but can be accessed with permission from Blue Creek Farm, T3069393. Take a torch and your gumboots. About 20 km southeast of the village are the busy white propellers of the **Hau Nui Wind Farm**, White Rock Road. Although you are not free to wander amongst them there is a viewing platform provided. From there you might consider going all the way to the remote coast at **Tora** or **White Rock** which offers some great walks and coastal scenery.

If you are around in Nov your visit may coincide with the immensely popular 'Toast Martinborough' celebrations, a festival of fine wine and food toast@toastmartinborough.co.nz

The main attraction is of course the **vineyards** and a most offer tastings and some tours, but bear in mind not all of them are open all year round to visitors. The web site www.nzwine.com is useful. There is also a wine museum planned for Martinborough and the VIC produces 'The Martinborough Wairarapa Wine Trail' which will get your grand tour started. The **Ata Rangi Vineyard** is one of the better known, producing a fine Pinot Noir, for which the village is now famous. ■ *Sep-Mar, Mon-Fri 1300-1500, Sat/Sun 1100-1700. T3069570.*There are a number of local tour operators who can arrange specialist **wine tours**, including *Burgiss's South Wairarapa Tours*, T3089352, *Mercury Buses*, T3069603 and *U Name It*, T3089878.

Activities & tours In an effort to lure the well-heeled Wellingtonians there are a wide range of activity operators around Martinborough. You have the choice of canoeing, quad and mountain biking, skydiving, horse trekking, clay-bird shooting, diving and jet boating. The VIC will fill you in with all the detail and book on your behalf. *Tora Walks* offer an interesting and varied three-day **coastal tramp** with an equal variety of accommodation types. Recommended. T3078862, toracoastalwalk@wise.net.nz $120 (meals optional extra)

Sleeping

Martinborough has an huge selection of B&Bs and self-contained cottages. You are advised to to the VIC to choose and book

LL *Wharekaukau Country Estate*, Western Lake Rd, Palliser Bay, T3077581, www.wharekaukau.co.nz This is one of the region's (and one of the country's) top luxury lodges. It is quite simply incredible. **L** *Aylstone*, Huangarua Rd, T3069505. Top range lodge offering total pampering and fine wine and cuisine. **L-AL** *Marinborough Hotel*, The Square, T3069350, www.martinboroughhotel.co.nz Recently refurbished, luxury rooms in elegant surroundings, restaurant and bar. **A** *Margaret and Bruce Craig*, Dublin St, T3069930, have three cottage style B&Bs on offer including the charming *Craigievar*, set in its own gardens and orchard. For real romantics (and fans of pop group, the B52's) there is always the **A** ***'Love Shack'***, 23 Ferry Rd, a private (very private) self-contained country cottage, T02-52951666. One hopes that anyone staying there, who can last the entire weekend without singing the hit song, gets a free bottle of wine. **A** ***Claremont Motels***, 38 Regent St, T/F3069162. One of the few places in New Zealand where the tables are turned and a motel is hard to find! This one seems to live up to its near singular standing. For determined campers there is a very basic **D** campground on the corner of Princess and Dublin St, T3069336.

Eating

As you might expect Martinborough is not short for choice. The ***Marlborough Hotel*** is suitably popular for breakfast, lunch and dinner. Open daily 0800-late, T3069350. There are a number of good cafes, some within vineyards. The ***Post and Vine Café***, Puruatanga Rd is one of the newest and is earning a good reputation. Open Fri-Sun from 1100, book for evenings, T3068552.

Shopping

While you are in Martinborough don't miss ***Moazark Wind Toys and Whirligigs***, 3 Kitchener St,T3069375. Open Wed-Sun 1000-1600. Here a wonderful range of wooden wildlife runs for its life at the slightest sign of a breeze.

Also at ***Thrive***, 8 Kitchener St, you will find the famous 'Thunderpants' – apparently an entirely new concept in modern technology knickers. They are very popular because (by all accounts) they 'do not go up your bum'!

Cape Palliser, Ngawi and Lake Ferry

The day long drive to see the Cape Palliser Lighthouse epitomizes the region and is highly recommended. On the way you can take in the bizarre rock formations of the **Putangirua Pinnacles**, the charming coastal fishing village of **Ngawi** and a colony of enchanting, languid fur **seals**, before the road terminates at the steps of the **lighthouse**.

Getting there

From Featherstone or Martinborough make your way down Lake Ferry Rd, towards Lake Ferry. Just before the village turn left for Ngawi. From here the lighthouse is about 40 km. Once the road joins the coast and if it is a clear day, you may be able to see the snow-capped Kaikoura Ranges of the South Island.

Sights

After about 15 km keep your eye open for the **Putangirua Pinnacles** car park. The pinnacle formations are a bizarre series of eroded gravel spires and turrets. They are about an hour's walk down a streambed, so proper footwear is advised. Once you reach the entrance to the pinnacles (on the left, after about 30 minutes) you have the choice of climbing a steep path through bush to a viewpoint (30 minutes), or entering the pinnacles stream bed and going into heart of the formation. You should not miss the viewpoint but both trips are worth it.

From the car park the road continues, hugging the cliffs before opening out across a wide coastal plain, with a beautiful shore of rock and sand, well-known for its excellent surfing. The coastal village of **Ngawi** soon comes into view and you will be immediately struck by the amazing collection of old tractors and bulldozers on the beachfront with rigs supporting a raft of fishing boats of all shapes and sizes. It is well worth a stop here to take a closer look and watch as one of the dearly loved machines is used to launch a boat.

From Ngawi the red and white tower of the lighthouse can be seen. On the rocks just before it is a colony of New Zealand **Fur Seals**, though you have to look carefully so as not to miss them. Like fat, brown barrels they doze the day away amongst the boulders. All they're missing is a TV, a can of beer and a remote. By all means take a closer look, but do not go too near (no more than 10 m). If you do, be warned: their soporific attitiude will evaporate in an explosion of rippling blubber as they charge towards the surf.

From the seal colony it is only a short distance to the **Lighthouse**, with its steep climb of steps and rewarding views. Here you are at the southernmost tip of the North Island. Once you return to Lake Ferry Road it is worth the short diversion to see **Lake Ferry** itself. The *Lake Ferry Hotel* is a fine place to enjoy a meal or a drink while watching the sunset and whitebaiters sifting the shallows on the banks of **Lake Onoke**

Sleeping & eating **A** *Hamenga Lodge*, Cape Palliser Rd, T3078010, F3078051. Licensed lodge with a range of comfortable rooms, open fire. **B** *Ann's Abodes-Mangatoetoe*, T/F3077728. A modern, self-contained house in a perfect spot, near the lighthouse and seal colony. **B** *Lake Ferry Hotel*, Lake Ferry Rd, T3077831, F3077868. Basic, affordable, hotel accommodation, restaurant and bar attached. **B-D** *Lake Ferry Motor Camp*, Lake Ferry Rd, T3077873. Busy, waterside and wi thin walking distance to the hotel. If hunger strikes before Lake Ferry there are snacks and refreshments available at the ***Top House Tea Garden***, in Ngawi (follow the signs), T3078229.

Featherston

Featherston is the southern gateway to the Wairarapa (or the last settlement depending on which way you came) and sits in the shadow of the Rimutaka range that was, and continues to be, the 'great divider' between the Wairarapa and Wellington. Although not particularly remarkable in history or aesthetics, Featherstone is best known as 1870s base of operations, in the mammoth task of connecting the Wairarapa and Wellington by rail.

The Featherston Visitor **Information Centre** is housed in the Old Courthouse (SH2) in the village, T3088051, F3088051. Open daily 1000-1500.

Sights The main attraction in Featherston is the **Fell Engine Museum**, on Fitzherbert Street. It houses the beautifully restored Fell Engine (the only one of its type in the world) that used to climb the steep 265 m slopes of the Rimutaka Incline. ■ *Sat/Sun1000-1600, or on request. Donation. T3089777.*

The railway line now goes through a tunnel and the **Rimutaka Incline** has been opened up as a walkway, which starts at the end of Cross Creek Road, 10 km south of Featherston. It takes a whole day to reach the summit or traverse the ranges to Kaitoke (17 km). There is a comfortable *YHA* in Kaitoke should you need a bed at the other end, T5264626.

As you leave the Wairarapa by road (or indeed arrive) a fine departing (or introductory) view can be seen from the **Rimutaka Trig** (725 m) at the crest of the ranges road. The track (one hour return) starts beside the road, just below the summit café, on the Wellington side. From the top you will get a great view of **Lake Wairarapa** and the coast.

Sleeping & eating Featherstone has a surprising number of luxury and mid range lodges, B&Bs and self-contained cottages. The basic **C-D** *Leeway Caravan Park and Backpackers* is located at 8 Fitzherbert St, T/F3089811. For details and bookings contact the VIC. For eating you will be well rewarded with a stop at the Loft, 38 Donald St. It is set in an old historic barn and offers a delightful breakfast, lunch and dinner menu. Open Wed-Sun from 1000, evening meals Thu-Sun, T3088173.

11

Wanganui and Manawatu

Wanganui and Manawatu

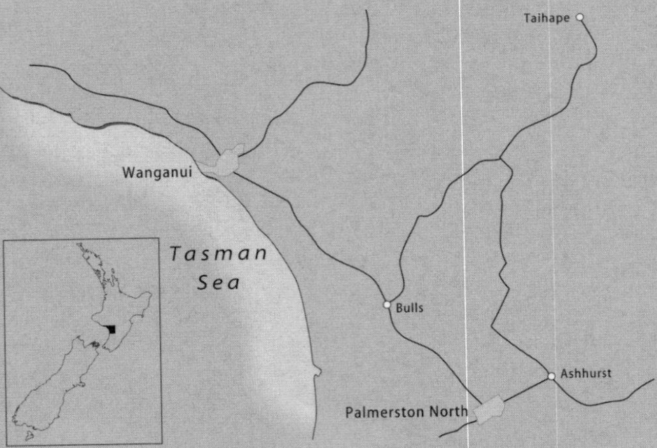

Stretching from South of Levin to just north of Taumarunui, and from Wanganui on the West Coast across to Cape Turnagain in the east is the Wanganui/Manawatu Region, scythed almost in half by the ***Wanganui River****, the longest navigable river in the North Island. Steeped in history, and supporting a rich watershed of remote hills adorned with native bush, much of the region is protected within the boundaries of the* ***Wanganui National Park****. Settlement began with groups of Maori moa hunters between 1400 and 1650, who were in turn followed by the first Europeans; whalers from Kapiti Island. The rich agricultural lands have now made the region the sixth most populace in New Zealand with almost half of that within the urban boundaries of* ***Palmerston North*** *and* ***Wanganui****. Palmerston North is also a major seat of learning, home to New Zealand's largest university. Although not blessed with the tourist bounty of other parts, the region still has much to offer. The National Park is especially worth exploring, being a magnet to kayakers and trampers, who can leave civilization behind for days on end.*

Things to do in Wanganui and Manawatu

- *Take a few days to explore the historic Wanganui River by kayak or jet boat, and take a side trip to the 'Bridge to Nowhere'.*
- *Take the mail-run up the Wanganui River Road through the historic mission settlements of Atene, Koriniti, Hiruharama (Jerusalem) and Pipiriki.*
- *Pay homage to the 'All Blacks' at the New Zealand Rugby Museum in Palmerston North.*
- *Be sure to pass through the 'incredi-bull' township of Bulls.*
- *If you are around in November don't miss the World Annual Gumboot Throwing Festival in Taihape, the 'Gumboot Capital of the World'.*

Ins and outs

Getting there
Both Wanganui and Palmerston North have airports with provincial links

The principal towns are Palmerston North and Wanganui. Although SH1 cuts straight through the heart of the region making it readily accessible, both towns will require a diversion. Wanganui is best accessed from the south via Bulls and SH3 while Palmerston North is a short distance east of SH1 also from Bulls or Levin. The Wanganui National Park is fairly remote and best accessed from the north via National Park or Ohakune or from the south via Wanganui itself.

Information There are TIC's in Palmerston North and Wanganui, both of which provide comprehensive information on the region. The principal websites for the region are www.manawatunz.co.nz/www.wanganui.co.nz The DOC office in Wanganui and the DOC website can provide information on the Wanganui National Park. All of these are listed in the text.

Palmerston North

Population: 75,000
Phone code: 06

Located on the banks of the Manawatu River and in the heart of flat, rural Manawatu, is the pleasant university and agricultural service town of Palmerston North. Although set away from SH1 and not exactly blessed with a wealth of touristical product, 'Palmy' (as it is known) is an important gateway west, through the impressive Manawatu Gorge, to the Wairarapa and Hawkes Bay. Other than Massey University, which is the second largest in the country, the town is perhaps most famous for its Rugby Museum, a place of almost spriritual significance, where many New Zealand rugby fanatics come on a pilgrimage to pay homage to their All Black Heroes.

Ins and outs

Getting there
Palmerston North is 140 km from Wellington and 546 km

By air *New Zealand Link*, *Quantas New Zealand*, and *Origin Pacific* fly regularly to most domestic centres, while *Freedom Air* T0800-600500 fly to the eastern seaboard of Australia. The airport is located about 4 km northwest of the city, T3514415. A taxi from the centre costs around $8. **By car** Palmerston North is about 30 km west of SH1. It is the main gateway to the Wairarapa and Hawkes Bay via SH3 to SH2 at Woodville. **By bus** *Intercity*, *Newmans*, *Tranzit* (T3574136) and *White Star* (T3588777) operate from Palmerston North. *White Star* run a regular service to Wanganui and New Plymouth and stop at the Courthouse, Main St, while the others run through to Wellington, Auckland and Napier and stop at the Palmerston Travel Centre at the corner of Main and Pitt Sts, T3554955. **By rail** Palmerston North is on the main north south rail line.

Palmerston North

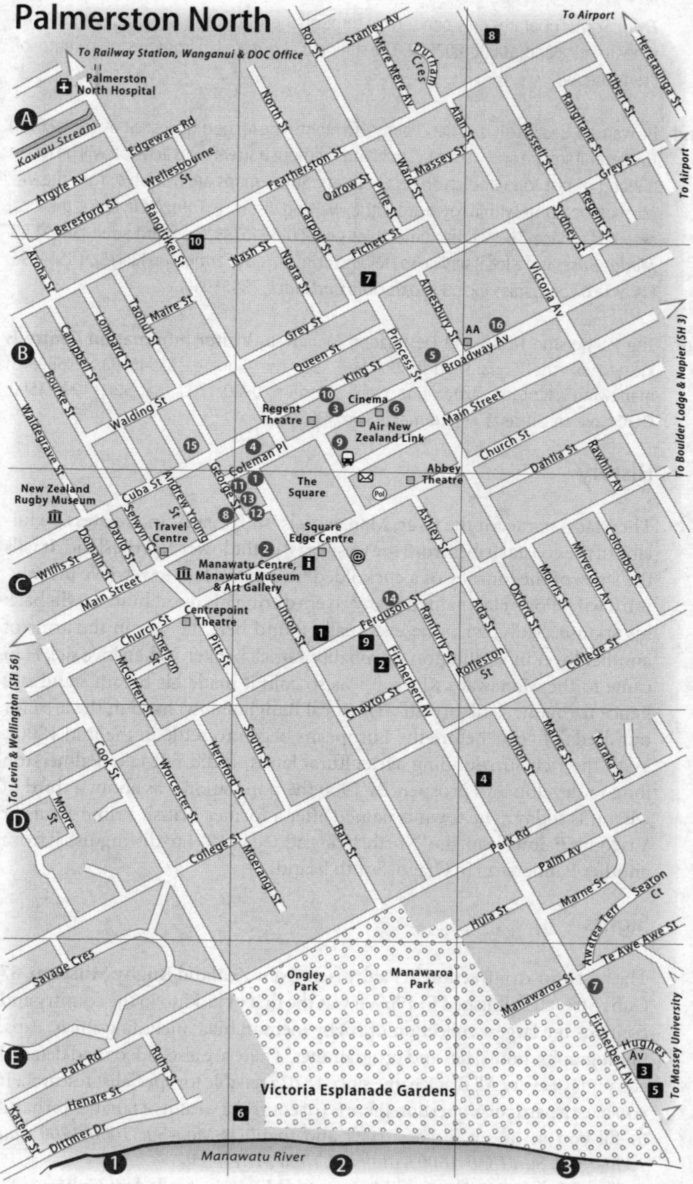

Sleeping
1 Camelot *C2*
2 Coachman *C2*
3 Colonial Court *E3*
4 Gables B & B *D3*
5 Harringtons *E3*
6 Palmerson North Holiday Park *E2*
7 Peppertree Backpackers *B2*
8 Plum Tree B & B *A3*
9 Quality *C2*
10 Sherwood *B1*

Eating
1 Bella's Café *C2*
2 Burger Extreme *C2*
3 Celtic Inn *B2*
4 Costa's *B2*
5 Déjeuner *B2*
6 Downtown on Broadway & Robert Harris Coffee Shop *B2*
7 Elm Café & Brasserie *E3*
8 George St Deli & Café *C1*
9 Highflyers *B2*
10 Link on King *B2*
11 Loaded Hog *C1*
12 Moxies *C2*
13 Mr India *C2*
14 Pompeii *C2*
15 Spostato *B1*
16 Vavasseur *B3*

Tranz Scenic operates only one service through the region, the Overlander and Northerner to Auckland, T0800-802802. The station is about 2½ km from the town centre off Tremaine Av.

Getting around Be warned. Because it is so flat, 'Palmy' is a nightmare for getting lost. Stray too far from the central square and visible tall buildings without a street map and you will be lost in a world of fast food and chain retail outlets. Street maps are available from the VIC. Most of the sights within town are within walking distance. ***Tranzit Citylink*** is the local area bus service. The VIC has timetables or T050-8446749. Standard adult fare $1.50. ***Madge Buses*** run a local service to Fielding from outside Farmers on King St, T3564896. Local Taxi companies include ***Taxis Gold and Black***, T3555059.

Information The Palmerston North and Destination Manawatu **Visitor Information Centre** is located in the Square edge Building, 52 The Square, T3546593, F3569841, manawatu.visitor-info@xtra.co.nz Open Mon-Fri 0900-1700, Sat/Sun 1000-1500. **DOC** have an Office at 717 Tremaine Ave, T3589004.

History

The Maori name for the river, Manawtu, is 'still breath' and relates to a lullaby of the coastal tribes from the west coast of the lower North Island. It tells the story of the journey of a cuckolded husband, Hau, to retrieve his wayward wife. Poor Hau named many rivers during his quest hunt to win back his spouse. Sadly, when he eventually found her, she was in the arms of another lover in Wellington – probably a stock broker. When love sick Hau came to the Manawatu River, it was so cold it made his breath stand still hence the name, 'still breath'. The local Rangitane Iwi lived in the area for hundreds of years before the Europeans began to settle in the mid 1800s. With the rich surrounding agricultural lands, it did not take Palmerston long to develop and prosper. By 1930 the population was about a third of what it is today. The town is named after a former British Prime Minister Viscount Palmerston, the 'North' being added in 1871 to distinguish it from another Palmerston in Otago, South Island.

Sights

The best known attraction in Palmy is the **New Zealand Rugby Museum**, 87 Cuba Street. Established in 1969, it was the first of its kind in the country and contains the largest collection of rugby memorabilia, including shirts, caps, photographs, boots, ties and programmes. There are also videos and detailed accounts of every All Black game since 1870 available for specialist research. If you have a particular question there is (of course) a wealth of fanatics on hand to fill you in on every pass, ruck and maul. ■ *Mon-Sat 1000-1200 and 1330-1600, Sun 1330-1600. Adults $3, child $1. T/F3586947.*

The **Manawatu Centre, Manawatu Museum and Art Gallery**, Te Aweawe Complex, 396 Main Street, is a progressive and modern centre that integrates the usual social, cultural and artistic heritage with hands-on science displays. It is split in to three main parts, the museum, gallery and science centre, all of which are worth visiting. There are the some interesting Maori *taonga* and a fascinating and rather sad depiction of the rise and fall of one of New Zealand's most celebrated, but now extinct birds, the huia. Like so many others birds around the world (and New Zealand in particular), it's demise came about through the decimation of habitat, the introduction of non-native predators and man's ridiculous desire to feel important by sticking colourful feathers in his hat. The gallery upstairs often hosts important national touring exhibitions. ■ *Daily 1000-1700, $6, child $4.*

If you head west towards the university and the river (Fitzherbert Avenue, then Park Road) you can access the **Victoria Esplanade Gardens**, a very pleasant mix of bush, lawn and gardens that grace the banks of the river. There are numerous walking tracks and a playpark complete with miniature railway for the kids. Open dawn to dusk. As usual there are leaflets available from the VIC outlining other city walks and open gardens in the area. On a rainy day, Mr and Mrs Fit and the wee fitettes can head for the city's climbing wall at *City Rock*, 38A Grey St. It is a 10-m high top rope and boulder wall. ■ *Daily 1000-2200, $8, T3574552.*

While you are wandering around Palmerston North you may occasionally glimpse the graceful white blades of the **Tararua Wind Farm** towers, on the hills to the west of town. If you fancy a closer look there is a private access route from Centre and Back Roads (off Fitzherbert East Road from Massey University) and via Jackson's Farm to Hall Block Road on the east side of the Manawatu Gorge (SH3). Bear in mind, however, that access is restricted and you may be best going with a tour operator (see below).

Activities & tours

Gliding Weekend flights are available with the local gliding club at the Fielding Airfield, Taonui, T3238389. **Golf** There are a number of good courses in the area including Brookfields, Te Matai Road, T3580749 and Fielding Golf Course, Fielding, T3238636. **Horse trekking** *Timeless Horse Treks*, Manawatu Gorge, T3766157. Half to multi day trips. **Jet boats** *Manawatu Jet Tours*, Pohangina Valley, T3294060, man-jet-tours@inspire.net.nz Rafting, Clay bird shooting and four-wheel drive also available. **Quad bikes** Yes, the darn things are here too; *Go 4 Wheels*, George Road, Balance, T3767136. **Scenic flights** *Helipro*, T3571348, www.helipro.co.nz Offer a range of flights including the City Panorama, $60, 10 minutes and the Windfarm Wizzer, $95, 20 minutes. **Sightseeing and specialist tours** Both *Bush Pigeon Tours*, T3766288 and *Tui Tours*, T3574136 do trips around the town and beyond. **Swimming** *Lido Aquatic Centre*, Park Road. Open Mon-Fri 0600-2000, Sat/Sun 0800-2000, T3572684.

Essentials

Sleeping

AL-A *Coachman Hotel/Motel*, 134 Fitzherbert Ave, T3565065, www.coachman.co.nz Pleasant, well appointed with café, gardens and an open fire. **A-B** *Quality Hotel/Motel*, 110 Fitzherbert Ave, T3568059, F3568604. Along with the Coachman, the Quality is one of Palmy's few hotels but doesn't let the side down, restaurant, bar, spa and sauna. **A** *Gables B&B*, 179 Fitzherbert Ave, T/F3583209. Refreshing historic homestead on the main motel drag. **A** *Plum Tree B&B*, 97 Russell St, T3575200, F3575214. Well appointed self-contained lodge close to town centre. **A** *Boulder Lodge*, Pohangina Valley West Rd, Ashurst, T3294746, F3294046, www.boulder-lodge.co.nz Located some distance from Palmerston North this is a popular and isolated, self-contained wooden cabin. You arrive by 4-wheel drive and can have a bath outside in an open fire heated tub under the stars. It has no electricity but that is part of the charm.

There are over 40 **motels** in Palmerston North, with most being located either side of Fitzherbert St. These include, the modern and comfortable **A** *Colonial Court*, (305), T3593888 and the very friendly **A** *Harringtons* (301), T3547259, harringtons@clear.net.nz, which is almost next door. Closer to the centre of town is the rather plush **A** *Camelot*, 295 Ferguson St, T3554141, camelotmotorlodge@xtra.co.nz, while to the north is the slightly cheaper **A** ***Sherwood***, 250 Featherston St, T3570909, townsley@iconz.co.nz

C-D *Peppertree Backpackers*, 121 Grey St, T3554054. This is by far the best backpackers in town. A YHA associate set in an old rambling, single storey house, close to the centre of town. Excellent facilities open fire and garden where you can watch the owner constructing a racing car. **C-D** *Palmerston North Holiday Park*, 133 Dittmer Drive, T/F3580349. Modern facility located next to the river and adjacent to the Esplanade Park.

Eating

The town is well blessed with good restaurants and cafés. Most are on Broadway Av, George St and Cuba St, just off the main square

Expensive *Dejeuner*, 159 Broadway. A small restaurant that is well established in the town and offers an imaginative blackboard menu. Open Mon-Sat 1800-late, T3561449. ***Vavasseur***, 201 Broadway is similar in style and an award winner, particularly well known for its New Zealand lamb dishes. Open Tue-Sat 1830-late, T3593167. In the centre of town on Cuba St is the Italian style ***Spostato*** at 213, considered at the top end of the Cuba St offerings. Open daily from 1800-late, T3555505.

Mid-range Most of the **pubs** (mentioned below) offer good affordable lunches and dinners. ***Bella's Café***, 2 The Square. Popular and offers a mix of Italian, Thai and traditional Pacific Rim dishes. Open for lunch Tue-Sat from 1100 and for dinner Mon-Sat 1800-late, T3578616. ***Costa's*** at 282 is a popular Tex/Mex style. Open daily from 1800, T3566383, while round the corner ***Mr India***, 79E George St, has a loyal following and is open daily from 1730. Also on George is the new café ***Moxies*** at 81. It has already established itself as a popular spot for breakfast, lunch and dinner offering an interesting blackboard menu. It is open daily from 0730. Although a bit away from the centre of town, the ***Elm Café and Brasserie***, Fitzherbert St, T3554418, is worth the distance with great traditional cuisine in rather grand Tuscan-style surroundings. Open daily 0900-1700 and Wed-Sat 1830-late.

Cheap The ***George St Deli and Café***, corner of George and Main St, has one of the finest breakfasts and perhaps the best coffee in town. It is open Mon-Sat 0600-1800, T3576663. For a pizza you can't go far wrong with ***Pompeii***, 353 Ferguson St, T3590059. Open daily from 1630 (deliveries available). For huge burgers head for ***Burger Extreme*** at the Old Grand Hotel, 339 Church St, T3577224. Open daily 1200-1400 and 1700-2100, (deliveries available). There ***Celtic Inn*** (see below) has about the best cheap pub lunch. For a quick snack and reliable cuppa, there are 2 ***Robert Harris*** coffee shops in 2 malls in town, the ***Downtown on Broadway*** shopping mall and the other in the ***Link on King***.

Pubs

For traditionalists the ***Celtic Inn*** tucked down the Regent Arcade off Broadway is the best bet, T3575571. For the trend-setters and modernists the aptly named ***Highflyers*** on the corner of The Square and Main St (T3575155) or the ***Loaded Hog*** on corner of George and Coleman St, (T3565417) are the places to go.

Entertainment

The ***Centrepoint Theatre***, corner Pitt and Church St, was established in 1974 and is one of the few North Island best theatres that can boast its own full time professional theatre company. There are regular shows, many of national importance, covering comedy to classic dramas, with an emphasis on New Zealand plays, T3545740, www.centrepoint.co.nz Another major venue is the ***Regent Theatre*** on Broadway. Opened in 1998 and with a seating capacity of almost 1500 it hosts larger events including ballet, musicals, orchestral performances and comedy, T3502100. Other mainly musical (rock and pop) events are held in the ***Abbey Theatre***, 369 Church St. For other mainly local performances and art displays head for the ***Square Edge Centre***, 52 The Square, above the VIC, T3585314.

For most performances in the town you can get more information and book with *Ticketek*, T3581186.

Shopping

For New Zealand art and crafts try *Ivy and Moss*, 481 Main St and *Something Different*, 117 Victoria Ave, while for fine art is the excellent *Taylor Jensen Gallery*, 39 George St, T/F3554278, www.finearts.co.nz Also on George St is the *Bruce McKenzie Bookshop*, which makes a refreshing change from the large bookshop chains, T3569922. There is an excellent open-air **market** held in the square on Sat mornings.

Directory

Airline offices *Air NZ*, 30 Broadway Av, T3518800. **Car rental** *Ward Hire*, 445 Tremaine Av, T3553043. *Rental Car Centre*, 320 Rangitikei St, T3574316. *Rent-A-Dent*, T3555227. **Communications** Internet: *Online Computers*, 366 College St, T3571213 (Open Mon-Thu 0900-1800, Fri 0900-1900, Sat 1000-1400, Sun 1000-1700). **Post office**: 338 Church St, T3536900. **Medical services** Palmerston North Hospital, Southern Cross, 21 Carroll St, T3569169. City Health, 22 Victoria Av, T3553300. **Useful addresses** AA, 185 Broadway Av, T3577039. **Police** Church St, T3579999.

Around Palmerston North

Levin and **Foxton**, both southwest of Palmerston North lie in the heart of the Horowhenua region. This narrow strip of land bordered by the Tararua Ranges to the west and the Tasman Sea to the east is known for its rich alluvial soils and subsequent fruit and vegetable growing industries. Earlier industries included flax milling and timber exports. The Horowhenua **Visitors Information Centre** is located at 93 Oxford St, Levin, T3678440, F3670558, horowhenua.visitor@clear.net.nz Open Monday-Friday 0900-1730, Saturday/Sunday 1000-1500. They can assist with all accommodation and transportation bookings.

The **Tokomaru Steam Engine Museum** is the highlight (if not the sum total) of **Tokomaru** village, 32 km north of Levin. The museum offers the enthusiast or the layperson the chance to see the country's largest collection of working steam engines. There are a number of static displays and the occasional 'Steam Up' (by all accounts). ■ *The museum is on SH57 and is open Mon-Sat 0900-1500, Sun 1030-1500. $5, child $2. T3298867.*

The **Lake Papaitonga Scenic Reserve**, 4 km southwest of Levin, offers a delightful short walk (30 minutes) through some superb native bush, before reaching two viewpoints across the lakes. The atmosphere here, particularly at sunset, is magical. The area is rich in both Maori history and birdlife, details of which are outlined at the park's entrance.

Taihape

Population: 2000 (4000 gumboots)
Phone code: 06

North of 'Palmy' in SH1, in the odd little region of **Rangitikei**, is Taihape, a fairly nondescript town quietly serving the local dairy farming industry. At first sight, there appears to be little of interest, other than a few unremarkable cafés, motels and shops, but there are some notable activities in the area and some of the major river adventure companies are based in the town. The VIC can provide information about a number of garden visits and heritage tours in the area, and then, of course, there's Taihape's famous and very silly festival, which brings some life and 'sole' to the town.

Information The Rangitikei **Visitor Information Centre** is in the Town Hall, Hautapu St, T3880350, F3881090, rangitikiei.tourism@xtra.co.nz

Activities

Bungy jumping *High Time Bungy*, Torere Junction, T3889109. Operate North Island's highest (80 m) bungy off a rail bridge spanning the Rangitikei,

World Gumboot Festival

Its October and an air of serious anticipation has fallen on the town of Taihape. In a town usually full of chatter and gossip, words are few and the looks distrustful. The town's men-folk gather in the pub and huddle around tables, whispering. When a stranger walks in they don't look up, but down at his feet. It's time. They disperse and from behind closed doors the 'Skellerup Perth' is coming out of the closet. Muscles are flexed. In to the night and down in the gardens, covert practice sessions take place. Cats scatter and the moonlit sky fills with the silhouettes of hurling Gumboots. The great festival is nigh.

The World Gumboot Throwing Festival is a unique and inevitably highly entertaining festival that takes place in November of each year in Taihape – the self proclaimed 'Gumboot capital of the world'. Apparently, it involves both 'serious' and 'novelty' throwing for teams and individuals of all ages. How quite one becomes a 'serious' thrower of a gumboot, or throws one 'seriously' (without wetting oneself with laughter) is a mystery, but seriously, it can be with a prize of $5000 for a new New Zealand record (currently; men 38.66 m/women 24.92 m) Note that the actual world record is held by the Fins – perhaps Sven and Anna Bolic – at an astonishing, men 63.98 m/and women 40.78 m (strong folk those Fins).

from $120. **Fly fishing** *Rangitikei Anglers*, Kawhatau Valley, Mangaweka, T3825507, raineys@xtra.co.nz Both rafting and flyfishing trips on the Rangitikei. Accommodation available. **River adventures** *River Valley*, T3881444, www.rivervalley.co.nz A range of activities including white water rafting ($80), horse trekking ($35) and kayaking ($40). Accommodation available. Rangitikei River Adventures, Main Road, Mangaweka, T0800-655747, nzrivers@hotmail.com A variety of river trips including rafting, kayaking, overnight campouts and wilderness safaris, $25 to $120. Four days $500. **Scenic flights** *Wanganui Aero Works*, Valley Rd, T/F3881696. Helicopter fishing, hunting and sightseeing trips.

Festivals

If you want to take part and fancy your chances with the size 8, there is a participation fee of $4 for individuals, $20 for groups, T3881126, gumbootcountry@xtra.co.nz

The World Gumboot Throwing Festival (see above) is a serious event. Not just any old 'wellie' can be used. It must be: "A Skellerup Perth size 8 Men's, of ordinary standard stock, and be available from a regular vendor of footwear, and have no structural or design changes. It cannot be weighted or lightened. The height of the gumboot must be a minimum of 36 cm/14 in and weigh not less than 964 grams/34 oz. The boot may not be folded, twisted or distorted. The boot must be approved for throwing by the organizers". As well as the official throwing there are numerous other secondary gumboot events including a 'Gumboot Art Competition', 'Shoot-the-boot', 'Carve-a-boot' and 'Flycast-a-boot'. There are also food, art and craft stalls and some of the other, far more traditional activities of shearing, milking and shoeing to boot. All in all the festival is great fun and highly recommended.

Sleeping & eating

A *Taihape Motels*, Kuku and Robin St, T/F3880456. Range of comfortable units with good amenities in the centre of town. **C-D** *River Valley Lodge* (see River Valley, 'Activities' section). **C-D** *Abba Motor Camp*, Old Abattoir Rd, T/F3880718. Basic motor camp located 3 km north of town.

For eating the best bet is ***The Brown Sugar Café***, Huia St, T3881880. It is the best café in town with good coffee, breakfasts and an open fire. Open daily 0900-1700, Fri/Sun until 2030. There are a number of restaurants on Hautapu St: ***The Venison Kitchen***, 65B Hautapu St, T3881011, is a fairly unique venison café; ***Al Centro*** is an

Italian at No 105 (Open Tue-Sun from 1700), T3880593; ***New Win Wah*** at No 94 (open daily 1100-2300), T3881744, is a traditional Chinese.

Mangaweka

Mangaweka is best known for its **DC-3**, which sits next to SH1 and houses a café. It is also the base for the *Rangitikei River Adventure Company*, which operates a variety of adventure packages on the river (see previous page). There is a basic camping ground in the village and a number of local walks established by DOC.

Bulls

Population: 3898

The small agricultural service town of Bulls stands of the junction of SH3 and SH1, midway between Wanganui and Palmerston North. Blink and you'll miss it, but take a closer look and you may be surprised to learn that the township was not named after our four-legged friends, but one James Bull, who was one of the first settlers in 1858. By all accounts he was quite the entrepreneur and created so much of the town's infrastructure that in 1872 the government approved the replacement of the original name for the settlement – Rangitikei, with Bulls. But our James has a lot to answer for. In the desperate effort to put Bulls on the map, the community has gone to ridiculous lengths to incorporate its name into every one of its amenities. Take a look around and you'll find the Information Centre which is 'Inform-a-Bull', the chemist which is 'Dispense-a Bull, the fire station 'Extinguish-a-Bull', the police station' Const-a-Bull' and the church, which is 'Forgive-a-Bull', and so it goes on. It is interesting to note a few major omissions in town, like the public toilets and pub however, and as you head out on SH3 there seems to be the most glaring omission of them all-a sign saying – 'Antique and Collectibles' – clearly owned by the black sheep of the town. Annoyingly, this is all very infectious, and for days you will find yourself suffering from this chronic 'Voca-Bull-ary' affliction. Some may find Bulls entertaining, but others may find such behaviour 'Question-a-Bull'. The 'Access-a-Bull' **Visitor Information Centre** is at 113 Bridge Street, T3220055, F3220033, rangitikiei.information.centres@xtra.co.nz They can help with finding 'Afford-a Bull' accommodation requirements and that's no bull.

Ohakea

At the RNZAF base at Ohakea which is on SH1 between Sanson and Bulls is the **Ohakea Wing RNZF Museum**. Here there are historical and hands-on displays, as well as a flight simulator, videos and a café. Great for kids. ■ *Daily 0930-1630. $8, child $3. T/F3515020.*

Wanganui

Population: 41,000
Phone code: 06

Wanganui lies at the mouth of the Wanganui River roughly half way between Wellington and New Plymouth. Proud of its river and once a bustling port, Wanganui is now principally an agricultural service town and the southern gateway to the Wanganui River National Park. The town boasts a rich heritage and retains some fine buildings as well as a reputable museum and a number of parks and gardens. In summer the main street is ablaze with a thousand hanging baskets of flowers and throughout the year the restored steamboat 'Waimarie' plies the great river, reminding both locals and visitors of days gone by.

Ins & outs

Getting there **Wanganui airport** is located near the coast about 5 km to the southwest of town and is serviced by ***Air New Zealand Link***, T0800-737000. Wanganui is on the main SH3 coastal route 172 km southwest of New Plymouth and 196 km north of Wellington (via SH1 which joins SH3 at Bulls). SH4 from Te Kuiti (250 km North) terminates in Wanganui. ***Newmans*** and ***Intercity*** **buses** stop at 156 Ridgeway St. ***White Star*** operate a service between New Plymouth and Wellington stopping at 161 Ingestre St, T3476677. The VIC facilitates all national bus bookings.

Getting around Wanganui has 4 looped bus routes which run Mon-Fri (weekends vary) by ***Tranzit Citylink***, linking the main suburbs, including Castlecliff on the coast. All start from Maria Pl in the centre of town, off Victoria Av. Standard fare is $2. For information T050-8446749 or pick up a timetable from the VIC. There is an airport shuttle operated by ***Ash's Transport***, T3438319 (Palmerston North included). Note that there is a **Mail Run** service operating to Pipiriki and the Wanganui National Park via the Wanganui River Rd (see River Road Tours, page 379).

Cycle hire is available at ***Wanganui Pro Cycle Centre***, 199 Victoria Av, T/F3453715. From $35 per day. **Car rental** *Avis*, 161 Ingestre St, T3457612. *Rent-a-Dent*, T3451505. **Taxis** *Wanganui Taxis*, T3435555.

Information The Wanganui **Visitor Information Centre** is at 101 Guyton St, T3490508, F3490509, www.wanganui.co.nz Open Mon-Fri 0830-1700, Sat/Sun 1000-1400. The **DOC** Wanganui Conservancy Office is located in the Ingestre Chambers, 74 Ingestre St, T3452402.

History The Wanganui River was an important focus for the Maori and provided a vital supply route both north and south. Even great Polynesian explorer Kupe was believed to have travelled up the river in AD800 and the first Maori settlement dates back to about 1000. Intertribal conflicts were common and came

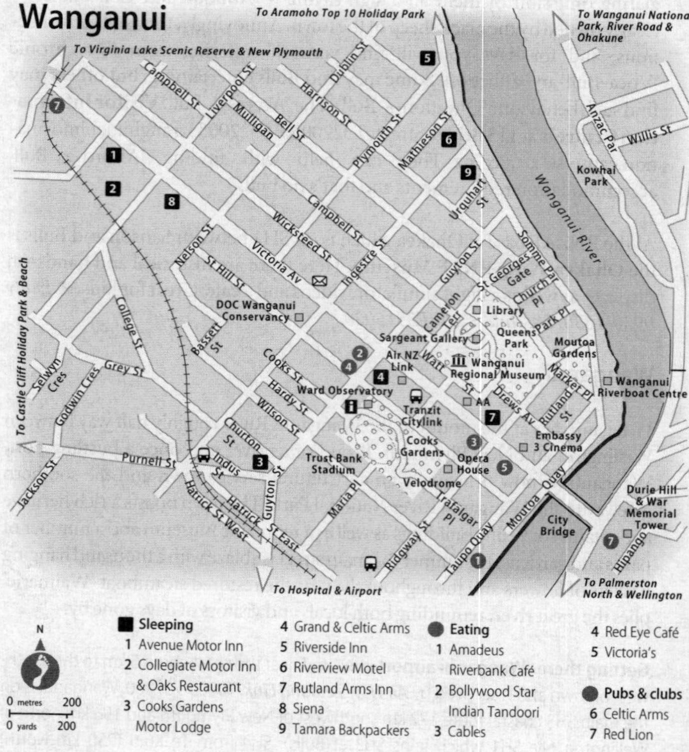

to a head (literally) in the 1830 when Ngati Toa, chief Te Rauparaha from Kapiti Island, sacked the local tribe and celebrated with a cannibal feast. Heads continued to roll with the arrival of the first Europeans in 1831 in the form of trader Joe Rowe, reputed to be a dealer in preserved Maori heads. Sadly for ol' Joe it was a case of what comes around goes around and in a dispute with the Maori his head was also lopped off and preserved, with the rest of him providing dinner. Thankfully, in 1840 the missionaries arrived and for a while, everyone began to keep the head as opposed to loosing it. About the same time the New Zealand Company, keen to extend land purchases beyond Wellington, made a rather dubious deal with the local Maori and 'bought' 40,000 acres. Once the Maori realized that this spurious transaction meant the permanent loss of their land, almost a decade of bitter wrangling followed. British troops were brought in, but eventually, after arbitration an agreed cash payment was made in 1848. The Maori went on to assist the *Pakeha* during the Taranaki Land Wars of the 1860's. With the establishment of a railway linking New Plymouth, via Wanganui to Wellington, together with the importance of the river as a communication link north, the town prospered.

Sights

The VIC has details about local gardens visits and the Wanganui Heritage Walk

Queens Park was a former British stockade site during the New Zealand Wars of the 1860's and is located east of Victoria Ave. It is essentially the cultural heart of the city and home to the Wanganui Regional Museum, the War Memorial, the Alexander and District Libraries and the Sargeant Gallery.

The **Wanganui Regional Museum** is of particular note due to rich local history and the influence of the river down the years. There is a fine collection of Maori *taonga* (treasures) in the *Te Atihaunui-a-Paparangi* (the Maori Court) including an inevitable collection of *waka* (canoes), the finest of which is the beautifully carved Te Mata-o-Houra. Of particular interest is also the range of displays showing the ingenious methods and traps the early Maori used to catch fish on the river and birds in the bush. Upstairs there is a large and rather tired looking collection of wildlife exhibits, including numerous native birds and moa bones. Elsewhere temporary galleries feature a programme of changing exhibitions. ■ *Mon-Sat 1000-1630, Sun 1300-1630. $2, child 60c. T3457443.*

A short distance away from the museum, proudly crowning Queens Park hill, is the **Sargeant Gallery**, set in a grand building and reputed to be one of the best in the country. Home to over 4,000 permanent artworks, there is an ever changing programme of local and national touring exhibitions and occasionally an international show. ■ *Mon-Fri 1030-1630, Sat/Sun 1300-1630, Donations. T3490506.*

The **Wanganui Riverboat Centre** on the riverbank on Taupo Quay, has been a hive of activity in recent years as committed enthusiasts have been hard at work fully restoring the old paddlesteamer *The Waimarie*. This steamer worked the river for 50 years carrying a wide variety of cargoes and tourists, before she came to grief and sank at her moorings in 1952. In 1993 she was removed from the mud and over the next seven years faithfully restored to be relaunched on the first day of the 21st century. Now, she is sailed proudly up the river daily with a loving crew and cargo of admiring tourists. Although the riverboat centre no longer houses *The Waimarie* there are displays of photographs and memorabilia from the river era. The Waimarie sails daily at 1400 (two hours), T/F3471863; $25, child $10. If you do go for a trip be sure to ask if you can take a look at the restored steam engine that pumps the pistons below decks. It is quite a sight and testimony to the loving care and attention that is now bestowed upon the old girl since she was pulled from the mud.

Immediately across the road from the Riverboat centre are the **Moutoa Gardens** which, though unremarkable, are famous as the spot where the deed was believed to be signed between the New Zealand Company and the Maori for the dubious land deals of 1840. This notoriety and the continued displeasure felt by Maori regarding land deals lead to an occupation of these gardens in 1995. High profile court battles followed and an ugly confrontation with police was only avoided with face to face meetings and thankfully a peaceful end to the 83-day occupation.

Cooks Gardens which grace the western heart of the town on St Hill Street are home to the 1899 colonial style **Opera House** the modern **Trust Bank Stadium** (with its wooden cycling velodrome) and the **Ward Observatory**. This observatory was originally built in 1901 and houses the largest telescope of its kind still in use in the country. ■ *Open for public viewing on most Mon nights from 2000-2130.*

Just across the bridge from Taupo Quay is the unusual access to the **Durie Hill** and the **War Memorial Tower**. A tunnel, almost immediately across the bridge takes you 200 m in to the hillside where you can get the '**Earthbound Durie Hill Elevator**' to the top. This highly considerate service is available Monday-Friday 0730-1800, Saturday 1000-1800, Sunday 1100-1700 and costs $1. From the top you can then climb the Durie Hill War Memorial Tower, built of fossilized rock. The view from the top is engaging and on a clear day can include Mount Taranaki and Ruapehu, but don't expect to get any photographs of Ruapehu, unless you want a water tower in the way.

There are a number of good **parks and gardens** in the town and surrounding area. At the top end of Victoria Avenue up the hill is the **Virginia Lake Scenic Reserve** with the usual lake, themed gardens and aviary. There is a nice walk that goes around the lake and once completed you might like to celebrate by setting off the coin-operated lake fountain.

If you have kids the star attraction in Wanganui has to be the excellent **Kowhai Park** located on the eastern bank of the river just across the bridge to Anzac Parade. Here you can find a wonderful array of interactive attractions including a dinosaur slide, a pirate ship, a flying fox, roller beetles and sea serpent swings, as well as the traditional bike and skateboard tracks all of which will keep them happy for hours. The **beach** at Castlecliff 7 km west of the city is renowned for good surf and safe swimming. Bus No1 and No2 will get you there.

Activities and tours As well as being the main gateway to the National Park, Wanganui is well known for its excellent mountain biking. Favoured tracks and routes include Lismore Forest, Hylton Park, Bushy Park Loop, the Wanganui River Road and Pauri Village Forest. The VIC has details about all these venues and the *Wanganui Pro Cycle Centre*; 199 Victoria Avenue, hires bikes and will also provide advice, T/F3453715. For all river activities based in or around Wanganui see page 379. Note that there is a Mail Run Tour service operating to Pipiriki and the Wanganui National Park via the Wanganui River Road.

Sleeping

Other than motels there is not a large amount of choice in Wanganui and B&Bs are particularly thin on the ground

AL *Rutland Arms Inn*, corner Victoria Av and Ridgeway St, T3477677, F3477345. Centrally located. 8 well appointed suites in the old English style. Bar, restaurant and courtyard café attached. **A-B** *Grand Hotel*, corner St Hill and Guyton Sts, T3450955, F3450953. A 1920's hotel in the heart of town. Nothing spectacular but good value with, spa, bar and good restaurant attached. Internet.

There are over 20 **motels** in Wanganui with the top end of Victoria Av being home to some of the newest and the best including: The **AL-A** *Siena*, 355 Victoria Av, T3459009, sienaml@ihug.co.nz **A** ***Avenue Motor Inn***, 379 Victoria Av, T3450907, dot@xtra.co.nz Elsewhere the **A** ***Collegiate Motor Inn***, 122 Liverpool St, T3458309, collegiate.motorinn@xtra.co.nz, is recommended as is the **A** ***Cooks Gardens Motor Lodge***, corner of Guyton and Purnell Sts, T3456003. For a cheaper motel try the **B** ***Riverview Motel***, 14 Somme Pde, T3452888. **C-D** ***Tamara Backpackers Lodge***, 24 Somme Pde, T3476300, F3458488, tamarabakpak@xtra.co.nz An excellent establishment with a locally streetwise manager set in a large 2-story villa overlooking the river. A range of older rooms or new en suite units. Large garden, free bike hire, internet. River trips organized. **C-D** ***Riverside Inn***, 2 Plymouth St, T/F3472529. YHA affiliate, located round the corner from the Tamara. Also comfortable but quieter and more sedate. **C-D** ***Aramoho Top 10 Holiday Park***, 460 Somme Pde, T/F3438042, aramoho.holidaypark@xtra.co.nz A bit out of the centre but worth the drive. Quiet, modern facilities next to the river. Friendly owners. **C-D** ***Castlecliff Holiday Park***, 1A Rangiora St, T3442227, F3443078. The more basic coastal option close to the beach, bus and stores.

Eating

For à la carte dining ***Victoria's***, 13 Victoria Av, has a good reputation offering traditional New Zealand fare. Licensed. Open Tue-Fri from 1200, Tue-Sun from 1800, T3477007. ***Cables***, 51 Victoria Av, T3487191, is modern and offers affordable evening dining. Open Thu/Fri/Sat 1800-2200. Licensed. The ***Oaks Restaurant*** at the Collegiate Motor Inn, 122 Liverpool St, has a good reputation and offers à la carte and café style cuisine as well as a seafood smorgasbord on Sat. Open Wed-Fri from 1200 for lunch daily for dinner. Licensed. T3458039. For the best Indian meal in town head for ***Bollywood Star Indian Tandoori Restaurant***, 88 Guyton St. Open for lunch Tue-Sun 1100-1500 and dinner daily from 1800. Licensed. T3459996.

Cafés

The ***Amadeus Riverbank Café***, 69 Taupo Quay. It does a fine value breakfast, has good coffee and outdoor seating overlooking the river. Open Mon/Tue 0700-1600, Wed-Fri 0700-late, Sat/Sun 1000-late. Licensed. T3451538. ***Red Eye Café***, 96 Guyton St. Has a loyal following and also serves a good coffee. Open Mon-Fri 0800-late, Sat 1000-late, Sun 1000-1800.T3455646.

Pubs

The main pubs in town are the ***Red Lion*** on Anzac Pde, which also offers à la carte dining and the ***Rutland Arms Inn*** (see above) which seems to attract a good clientele. The fairly dull Irish style offerings are the ***Ceilidh Bar***, attached to the Grand Hotel, Guyton St and the ***Celtic Arms***, 432 Victoria Av.

Entertainment

The small but very grand ***Royal Wanganui Opera House*** on the edge of Cooks Gardens, St Hill St, is a regular venue for touring shows from opera to rock 'n' roll. For details about up and coming performances contact the VIC or T3490511. The Art-deco ***Embassy 3 Cinema*** is at 34 Victoria Av, T3457958.

Festivals

Wanganui in Bloom runs from Dec to Mar when the streets are adorned with 1,000 hanging baskets of flowers. The highlight is the festival weekend in Jan, when there are various events including a raft race, vintage car procession and street bands.

Directory

Airline offices *Air NZ*, 133 Victoria Av, T3454089. **Communications Internet** is available at the VIC and the library (Queens Park). **Post Office**: Victoria Av (between Ingestre and Plymouth Sts). **Library**: Queens Park, T3458195 (Open Mon-Fri 0900-2000, Sat 0900-1630). **Medical services** *Wanganui Hospital*, Heads Rd, T3481234. *After Hours*, 163 Wicksteed St, T3488333. **Useful addresses** **Police**: Bell St, T3454488. **AA**: 78 Victoria Ave, T3489160.

Wanganui to Hawera

About 5 km northwest of Wanganui, down Rapanui Road (towards the sea) is **Westmere Lake**. Set aside as a wildlife refuge with native bush, the lakeside provides a pleasant spot for a picnic. For the more energetic there is a 40-minute walk that circumnavigates the lake. A little further down Rapanui Road is the **Bason Botanical Gardens**, which were bequeathed to the Wanganui Regional Council in 1966 by local farmer Stanley Bason. They consist of 25 ha of gardens, with native and introduced plants, a conservatory, begonia house, camellia garden and lake with a lookout. ■ *Daily from 0930-dusk.* If you have time you may like to follow the road to the sea (14 km) and the small village of Mowhanau, blessed with the black-sand **Kai Iwi Beach** which is surrounded by cliffs but still provides a safe spot for swimming.

Back on SH3 and a further 20 km northwest is the **Bushy Park Forest**, a picturesque 90-ha reserve with a rich variety of native flora and fauna. Some of the trees are magnificent and they include the great girth and twisted trunk of 'Ratanui', a Northern Rata that is thought to be the largest living Rata in the Southern Hemisphere. To get to the Bushy Park Reserve turn right at the village of Kai Iwi and follow the signage (8 km). ■ *Daily, $3, child $1.* Also in the park is the **A-D** *Bushy Park Homestead*, built in 1906 which provides grand B&B and budget accommodation, T/F3429879.

Ashley Park, 29 km northwest of Wanganui near the village of Waitotara is a similar to Bushy Park, but more commercial, with farm animals, pony rides, a swimming pool and a café. There is also motel, B&B, Farmstay and campsite accommodation available, T3465917, F3465861.

Wanganui National Park

Springing from high on the volcanic slopes of Tongariro in National Park, the Wanganui River begins its 290 km journey to the sea, carving its way through some of the most remote and inaccessible country in the North Island. At its most remote mid to lower reaches, it cuts deep in to the soft, sand and mudstone and is joined by tracts of intact lowland forest, which form the heart of the Wanganui National Park. Although the river is not the longest in the North Island (that honour going to the Waikato) it is the longest navigable river for generations. As a result the river is rich in both Maori and European history, from the first days of early exploration and settlement through to the river's renaissance as a tourist and recreational attraction. Although the entire area is hard to access (which is undoubtedly part of its charm), there is the opportunity to explore the historical sites of the river and enjoy its atmosphere. You can do this, in part, on its banks by road and walking tracks, or on the river itself, by jet boat or kayak.

Ins and outs

Getting there & around

The 3 principal gateway settlements to the river are Taumarunui to the north, Raetihi to the northwest and Wanganui to the south. Physical access to the river and the park is from 6 main **access** points: from the north, Ohinepane, 21 km down river from Taumarunui; from the East Whakahoro (linked to SH4 by roads from Owhango and Raurimu), Pipiriki (accessible from Raetihi), Ohura Rd (from SH4 north of Raetihi); from the south via the River Rd off SH4 (just North of Wanganui) to Pipiriki, and from the West via way of Stratford/Ohura Rd (SH43) where Brewer Rd and Mangaehu Rd lead on to Kohi Saddle and the Matemateaonga Track. As well as the daily **Mail Run** service from Wanganui to Pipiriki, T3442554, most tour operators will provide transportation in and out of the park for about $50 return. Other than that you are on your own.

Note that both the back roads, tracks and the river itself is subject to slips and flooding so always consult with DOC before attempting a major excursion. Summer is undoubtedly the busiest and safest time to visit the park. During this time you are advised to pre book all accommodation.

Information

DOC deals with all **information** enquiries and hut/campsite bookings and fees. There are a number of good books available about the river and the park (available from main DOC offices) while DOC produce detailed leaflets, including the helpful (though rather outdated) 'In and Around Wanganui National Park' and the 'Wanganui Journey'. There

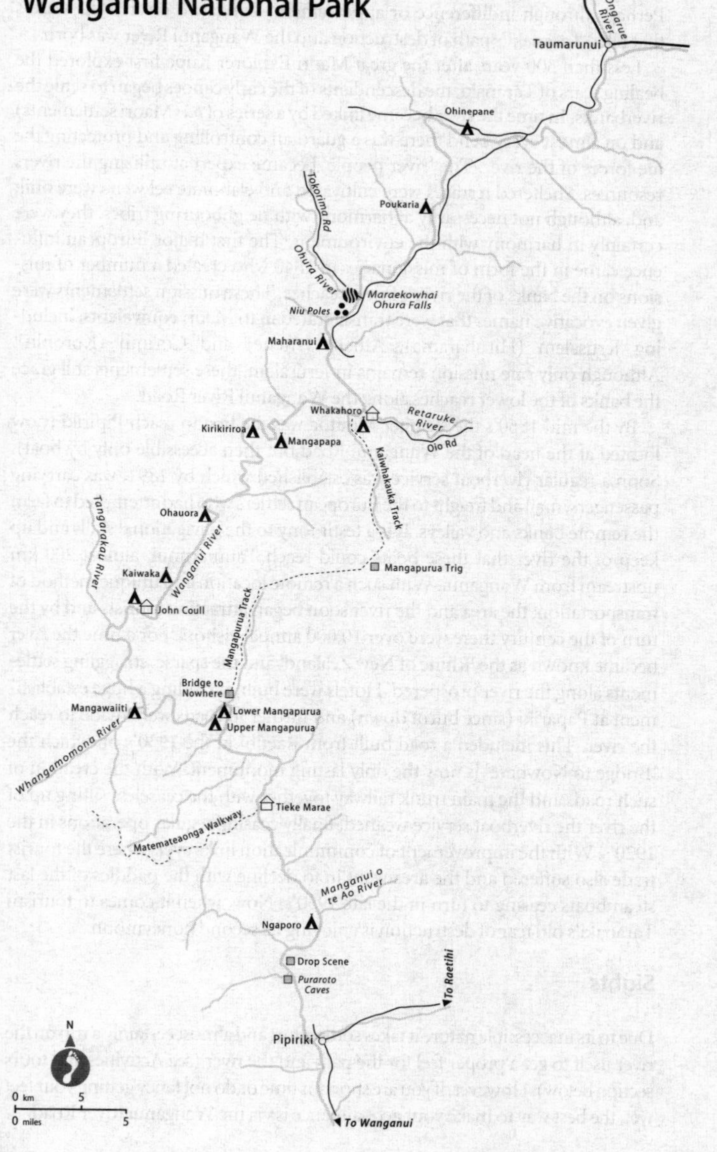

are DOC offices in Wanganui, T3452402, Taumarunui, T07-8957494 and Pipiriki, T3854631. For DOC bookings also refer to their website greatwalksbooking@doc.govt.nz

History

Legend has it that the Wanganui was created as a result of a mighty love feud between the mountains of Tongariro and Taranaki in the central North Island. When both fell in love with the beautiful Mount Pihanga, a battle ensued. Taranaki lost the fight and, wild with grief and anger, ripped himself from his roots and tore a path towards the coast, where he now stands alone – in a mighty huff. Perhaps through indifference or appeasement, Tongariro created the waters that filled Taranaki's path of destruction and the Wanganui River was born.

Less than 300 years after the great Maori Explorer Kupe first explored the healing scars of Taranaki, the descendants of the early canoes began to settle the riverbanks. In time the river became linked by a series of *pa* (Maori settlements) and on almost every bend there was a guardian controlling and protecting the life forces of the river. The 'river people' became expert at utilizing the rivers resources. Sheltered terraces were cultivated and elaborate eel weirs were built and, although not necessarily at harmony with neighbouring tribes, they were certainly in harmony with the environment. The first major European influence came in the form of missionaries in 1840 who created a number of missions on the banks of the river's lower reaches. These mission settlements were given evocative names that were transliterated in to Maori equivalents, including Jerusalem (Hiruharama), Athens (Atene) and Corinth (Koroniti). Although only one mission remains in Jerusalem, these settlements still grace the banks of the lower reaches along the Wanganui River Road.

By the mid 1860's the steamer Moutoa was the first to reach Pipiriki (now located at the head of the Wanganui Road but then accessible only by boat). Soon a regular riverboat service was established which by 1891, was carrying passengers, mail and freight to the European settlers who had attempted to farm the remote banks and valleys. It is a testimony to the navigational skills and up keep of the river that these boats could reach Taumarunui, almost 200 km upstream from Wanganui. With such a remote location and unique method of transportation, the area and the river soon began attracting tourists and by the turn of the century there were over 10,000 annual visitors. For a time the river became known as the 'Rhine of New Zealand' and the sparse, struggling settlements along the river prospered. Hotels were built, including a huge establishment at Papariki (since burnt down) and further in roads were made to reach the river. This included a road built from Raetihi in the 1930's on which the 'Bridge to Nowhere' is now the only lasting monument. With the creation of such roads and the main trunk railway together with the ceaseless silting up of the river the riverboat service weaned, finally ceasing regular operations in the 1920's. With the improvement of communication links everywhere the tourist trade also suffered and the area went in to decline with the paddles of the last steamboats ceasing to turn in the late 1950's. Now, when it comes to tourism Taranaki's old tear of destruction is enjoying its second honeymoon.

Sights

Due to its inaccessible nature it takes some effort and almost certainly a trip on the river itself to get a proper feel for the park and the river (see Activities and tours section below). However, if you are short for time or do not fancy getting your feet wet, the best way to make your acquaintance is via the Wanganui River Road.

Wanganui River Road

The road originally opened in 1934 and took 30 years to construct

This windy scenic road branches off SH4 15 km North of Wanganui and follows the river to Pipiriki, before turning inland to Raetihi where it rejoins SH4. The entire trip is 106 km and although the road is slow and for the most part unsealed, it can be done comfortably in about four hours. As well as the scenery itself, there are a number of small historically significant settlements, specific historic sites, *marae* and some fine short- to medium-length walks along the way.

From South to North after the Aramoana Walkway and Lookout (now closed) the road joins the river proper. The first specific point of interest is the Pungarehu Wharenui (meeting house) just before the settlement of **Parikino**, which used to be located on the other side of the river and now occupies a former Maori village. Just after Parikino the road cuts in to a series of **Oyster Shell Bluffs** (once seabed) before reaching **Athene** (Athens), the first of a number of mission settlements created in the 1840's by the Reverend Richard Taylor. Just before the village is the access point to the **Atene Skyline Track**. This recently upgraded DOC track crosses farmland before climbing to take in rewarding views of the entire region before continuing to rejoin the River Road further north (viewpoint 1½ hours return; full walk 6-8 hours).

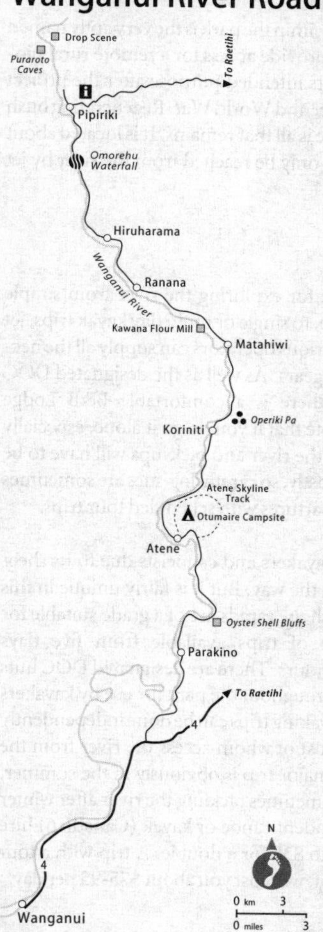

The next settlement and former mission settlement is **Koriniti** (Corinth). Formerly the Maori settlement of Otukopiri, it still retains a fine *marae* that welcomes visitors. The Anglican Church dates back to 1920. Keep your eyes open here too for flood markers, one of which is half way up a barn, giving you a shocking reminder of the potential dangers of the river. The **Operiki Pa**, just north of Koriniti, was the original home of the Koriniti Maori and the site of the first Anglican Church built in 1840. About 6 km further north is the **Kawana Flour Mill**, a fully restored example from 1854, complete with millers cottage. Both the mill and the cottage are a short walk from the main road and well worth a quick look. **Ranana** (London) is the next small settlement. Ranana was one of the largest former mission settlements first established in the 1890's and its church is still in use today.

After Ranana is **Hiruharama** (Jerusalem) the most picturesque of all the former missions. Originally a larger Maori village known as Patiarero, it was once home to famous New Zealand poet James Baxter and French Sister Mary

Aubert whose catholic mission still remains to this day. You can visit the church which was built in the late 1800's. From here the road climbs to a fine viewpoint and the Omorehu Waterfall Lookout before delivering you at **Pipiriki**. Pipiriki used to be the major tourist destination at the turn of the century, complete with a large hotel. These days, although not so well blessed with luxurious accommodation, it is still an important settlement, serving as the main southern gateway to the heart of the National Park via the river itself. Although the large hotel *Pipiriki House* that once stood here has long since burnt down, a former **Colonial House**, remains and serves as a small museum and information centre, as well as a reminder of the former glory days. ■ *Summer from 1000-1600, $1, child 50c.*

The small DOC office in Pipiriki can assist with information and also provides overnight parking. On the way you will pass the rather sorry remains of the former 1903 steamer *MV Ongarue*, which plied the river until the late 1950's. Although restored in 1983 and placed high and dry on the hill for all to see, she is clearly much in need of some attention and a new lick of paint. From Pipiriki the road then turns inland and winds its way for 27 km to the small township of Raetihi, where it rejoins SH4.

One of the major man-made 'sights' within the park is the very aptly named **'Bridge to Nowhere'**. Built in 1936 to provide access for a remote rural pioneer settlement, it never really served its intended purpose after the project was abandoned with the advent of the Second World War. Regenerating bush quickly covered the track and the bridge is all that remains. It is located about 30 km upstream from Pipiriki and can only be reached from the river by jet boat, canoe or by a three-day walk.

Activities and tours

There are numerous options available for exploring the river from simple independent and self guided canoe hire, to single or multi day kayak trips, jet boat trips and multi day tramps. The various operators can supply all the necessary equipment (including camping gear). As well as the designated DOC huts and campsites along the way there is a comfortable B&B Lodge (Ramanui) in the heart of the park. Note that if you do go it alone, especially tramping, the tracks essentially end at the river and pick-ups will have to be arranged. If you are alone this may be costly, so careful logistics are sometimes necessary to time your arrivals and departures with scheduled tour trips.

Kayaking The Wanganui is very popular with kayakers and canoeists due to its sheer length, and the 239 listed rapids along the way. But it is fairly unique in this sense, in that for almost its entire length the rapids are of a grade suitable for beginners. There are a wide range of trips available from five days (Taumarunui to Pipiriki) to just a few hours. There are designated DOC huts and campsites with basic amenities, throughout the park for use by kayakers and trampers (see Sleeping below). Kayaking trips can be done independently or with the various tour operators, most of whom access the river from the north. The best time to embark on a major trip is obviously in the summer, though more experienced canoeists sometimes tackling the river after winter rains. Costs vary but standard independent canoe or kayak (Canadian) hire starts at about $25 a day for a single, to $35 for a double. A trip with a tour operator, which includes all equipment, will cost you about $75-95 per day.

The principal operators according to base:

Wanganui *Rivercity Tours*, T3442554, F3447642. 1-4 day guided trips (equipment, food and transport with pick-ups included). From $75 per day. Independent canoe, kayak and camping equipment hire available.

Wairua *Hikoi Tours* (Jerusalem/Wanganui River Rd), T3453485, T/F3428160. Maori operator with emphasis on cultural aspects. 1-3 day trips self guided $45 or guided $95 per day. Transport from Wanganui $25 extra. Recommended.

Omaka Farmstay, (Wanganui River Rd, near Athene), T3425595. 1-3 hr canoe trips available, from $15.

Ohakune *Yeti Tours*, T3858197, F3858492, www.canoe.co.nz Range from luxury to economy 4-6 day trips. From $125. Recommended for the longer excursion. *Canoe Safaris*, T3859237, www.canoesafaris.co.nz Canoe and rafting trips throughout the area. Wanganui 4-5 day guided trips from $560 (all-inclusive).

Raurimu *Plateau Adventures*, T/F8922740, T.parker@xtra.co.nz 2-5 day guided trips (2 day $260). Independent rentals and transport ($50).

Whakahoro (Wades landing) *Wades Landing Outdoors*, T8955995. Canoe, Kayak and jetboat trips.

Taumarunui *Blazing Paddles*, T/F078958074. 1-5 day trips. Self-guided from $33 per day. Guides can be arranged.

Jet boating

Since the 1980s jet boats have been the principal fast transport link up and down the river. There are various operators providing sightseeing trips from 15 minutes to two days (including the drop off for the 40-minute 'Bridge to Nowhere' walk) and picks ups from the river ends of the Matemateaonga Walkway and Mangapurua Track. Again costs vary but a five-hour trip to the bridge will cost about $85.

Current operators are listed below according to base:

Wanganui *River Spirit Jetboat Tours*, T3421718, F3421007. From 2½ hrs, $50.

Whakahoro (Wades Landing) *Wades Landing Outdoors*, T8955995. Canoe, Kayak and jetboat trips.

Pipiriki *Bridge to Nowhere Tours*, T/F3854128. 20-min to 4-hr bridge trip (4 hr, $70).

Tramping

As well as the 'Bridge to Nowhere' track which is accessible only by jet boat canoe or by foot there are 2 main tramps in the park: the Matemateaonga Walkway and the Mangapurua Track.

Matemateaonga Walkway This track which penetrates deep into the heart of the park, traversing an expanse of thick bush-clad hill country between Taranaki and the Wanganui River, is considered one of the North Island 'great walks'. It uses an old Maori trail and former settlers' dray road and for the most part follows the ridges of the Matemateaonga Range before arriving at the river and the Ramanui Lodge. The highlight is a short 1½ hour diversion up the 730 m Mt Humphries for a fine view. The track is 42 km in length, considered 'moderate' in difficulty and takes about 4 days to complete. There are 3 DOC huts along the way for which a fee must be paid (see Sleeping below). Bear in mind that transport must be arranged with one of the jet boat operators either to pick you up or drop you off at the river end of the track. From the west the track is accessed from SH43 at Strathmore, near Stratford. Look for the signpost that indicates the road to Upper Mangaehu Rd and the track which begins at Kohi Saddle.

The track is easily accessed at the end of the Whakahoro Rd

Mangapurua Track The Mangapurua Track is about the same length as the Matemateaonga Walkway and takes 3-4 days to complete. It starts from Whakahoro up the Kaiwhakauka Valley past the Mangapurua Trig (663 m) and then descends through the Mangapurua Valley, via the 'Bridge to Nowhere' to meet the river at the Mangapurua Landing, 30 km upstream from Pipiriki. There is only 1 hut at Whakahoro but a number of good campsites along the way. Again you will need to arrange jet boat transportation back to base.

Essentials

Sleeping

Wanganui National Park Both the walking tracks and the river itself within the park are well endowed with DOC huts and campsites. During the period 1 Oct-30 Apr you must buy a hut and campsite pass from DOC (or VIC and some operators) before staring your journey. This pass costs $35 ($25 if bought before your journey), child $12.50 and is valid for 6 days. Concessions are available for some canoe and jet boat trips. Campsites provide a water supply, toilets and shelters with benches for cooking. Huts have bunks with mattresses, stoves, benches, tables and cooking facilities. In winter campsites are free of charge while hut users must have hut tickets or an annual hut pass. The Teieke Hut on the eastern riverbank near the Matemateaonga Landing is fairly unique in that it is also a *marae*, where you can experience the traditional *marae* stay (traditional protocol must be observed).

Besides the DOC facilities and the marae there is the immensely popular **AL-D** *Ramanui Lodge*, which is located in a very remote spot on the riverbank in the heart of the park. Access is either by boat, canoe or by foot which makes the place very special. There is B&B, cabin and campsite accommodation available, along with a bar and positively exquisite home cooking, T025480308, F3421007.

In Whakahoro, *Whakahoro Wilderness*, Oio Rd, Lower Retaruke, offer **D** backpacker and campsite accommodation, T078966232.

Wanganui River Road **B** *Omaka Homestay*, (Parikino), T3425597. A 1,000-ha hill farm. Homestay, backpacker (in a comfortable working woolshed) and camping options available. Campervans also welcome. Very friendly with lots to see and do. **B** *Flying Fox*, Koriniti, T/F3428160. The Flying Fox is on the western bank of the river and is only accessible by an exciting aerial cableway or by jetboat. The accommodation consists of B&B, 2 self-contained cottages and campsites. There is a very cute outdoor wood-fired bath, some fine 'home brew' to sample and the home cooking is superb. **B** *Operiki Farmstay*, Operiki, T3428159. Traditional single storey house close to the river. Good value. **C** *Backcountry Lifestyles*, Matahiwi, T/F3428116. Basic, cheap and comfortable. **D** *Jerusalem Catholic Church Backpackers*, Jerusalem, T3428190. Basic but angelic. There is additional camping available at **D** *Kauika Campsite* (near Ranana), T3428061 and with DOC in Pipiriki, T3854631.

12

Wellington

Wellington

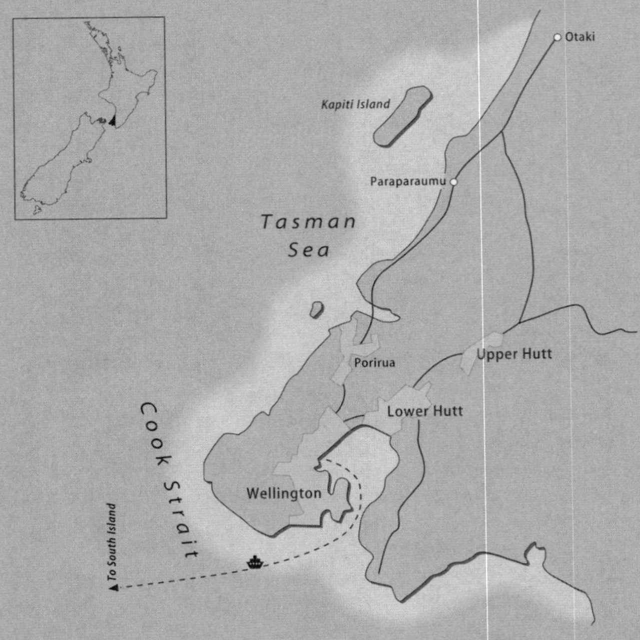

Otaki
Kapiti Island
Paraparaumu
Tasman Sea
Porirua
Upper Hutt
Lower Hutt
Cook Strait
Wellington
To South Island

Though Wellington is the nation's capital, it enjoys a small-town atmosphere. With its surrounding hills, generally compact layout and well-preserved historical buildings, it has far more character than sprawling Auckland or monotonously flat Christchurch. In saying all that, Wellington is a vibrant, cosmopolitan city, noted for its arts and café culture, with almost as many restaurants and cafés per capita as New York. Its most famous visitor attraction, the multi-million-dollar ***Te Papa Museum****, is situated on the city's recently revamped and buzzing waterfront. Some of the best shopping in the country can also be found in the compact city centre. If you are heading for the South Island by ferry, you will inevitably encounter Wellington and you are advised to give it more than a cursory glance, while waiting for your ferry.*

To the east of the city are the rather unremarkable commuter towns of Upper and Lower Hutt, from where you can reach the beautiful, off-the-beaten-track region of the Wairarapa, with its remote coastline. First, though, you must negotiate the ***Rimutakas*** *– 'the hill' – a natural barrier that has always prevented the spread and pace of settlement and development. To the north, both major rail and road links hug the scenic* ***Kapiti Coastline****, with its pleasant coastal towns and their associated beaches and attractions, the most noteworthy being the nature reserve of* ***Kapiti Island*** *looming a short distance offshore.*

Things to do in Wellington

- *Try to avoid information overload and find enough time to explore the impressive Te Papa – The National Museum of New Zealand.*
- *Give the Museum of Wellington, City and Sea a chance to impress further.*
- *Take the city centre Cable Car to the Botanical Gardens. Enjoy the views, stop and smell the roses, then walk back down to the city centre via the Parliamentary District.*
- *Try rollerblading on the Wellington Waterfront then follow it up with an al fresco lager.*
- *Enjoy the city views from Mount Victoria. On a windy day, watch the planes make the tricky landing into Wellington Airport below you.*
- *Sample Wellington's world-class cafés and restaurants in or around Cuba Street or Courtenay Place.*
- *Experience a wildlife paradise on a day trip to Kapiti Island off the scenic Kapiti Coast.*
- *Get strapped to the fast and funky stretcher-cum-microlight and 'Fly By Wire' at Paekakariki.*

Ins and outs

Getting there

Air Wellington Airport, T3855100, www.wellington-airport.co.nz is in the suburb of Miramar, about 6 km to the south of the city centre. It has been recently given a major revamp and is now highly modern and efficient, handling both international and domestic flights. It is perhaps the most infamous airport in the country due to its short runway, nestled precariously between populated hillsides. During southerly storms the nightly news often shows the latest 'interesting' landing from Wellington, whereby the aircraft 'come dancing' into land. That, and the fact you can practically make eye contact with the residents in the houses that nestle on the hillsides, makes a departure or arrival by air rather memorable.

Although there are dozens of ***Trans-Tasman*** and ***Pacific Island*** flights per week, Wellington primarily operates a busy domestic schedule, with regular daily flights to most principal centres. ***Air New Zealand***, T0800-737000, and ***Origin Pacific***, T0800-302302, are the principal carriers. Additionally, a number of smaller operators fly to upper South Island destinations. These include ***Soundsair***, T48010111, and ***Taka Valley Air***, T03-5258613, who offer regular and very reasonable fares from $50 one-way to Picton, Nelson and Blenheim. The new terminal has all the usual facilities including food outlets, shops, left luggage and an information centre, T3885100. All the major car rental companies are represented at the airport. There are plenty of taxis to meet you and the standard fare in to town is about $20. Shuttle buses, T5699017, can be shared for about $8. They also run regular scheduled services, with frequent city centre stops, to and from Wellington Railway Station ($5).The ***Stagecoach Flyer*** is the regular bus service to and from the airport to the city, $3.50, 0720-2020 call ***Ridewell*** T8017000.

Bus ***Intercity***, T09-9136100, ***Newmans***, T09-9136120 are the principal operators and arrive and depart from the Railway Station. ***White Star***, T4784734, operates services to Palmerston North, Wanganui and New Plymouth. Tickets available from ***Freeman's Lotto and Café***, Rutherford House, 23 Lampton Quay.

Car Auckland is 658 km from Wellington. The principal route is via SH1. SH2 is the principal route to the Wairarapa and the East Coast. Wellington is the terminus for all vehicular traffic by ferry to **South Island** (see box on page 403).

Windy Wellington

Wellington is often called 'Windy Wellington', especially by rival Aucklanders (Wellingtonians simply fight back by replacing the Au with Dor). 'Wind' is something of a swear word in Wellington, since most of its proud residents would baulk at the very idea that Wellington receives nothing but its fair share of settled weather. However, it does have to be said that when a southerly sweeps in from the south, and essentially Antarctica, with no obstacles except the odd iceberg, it has quite an interesting effect. Most amusing are the city suits, with their bright silk ties, out and about at lunchtime, who take on the appearance of Biggles in the cockpit of his First World War fighter plane, replete with scarf, goggles and an expression befitting a man in whose pocket a seagull has just copiously pooped. If you do arrive and the place seems deserted, you can be fairly certain, most have attempted to put up an umbrella and are now in Fiji.

Train The Railway Station is located next to the Quay on Bunny St and has an information centre, T4983000. ***Tranz Rail*** operate a regular service north to Auckland (Overlander/Northerner) and also own and operate the Interislander Ferry, T4983108, F4983090, www.tranzrail.co.nz

Getting around

For taxi, car rental and bike hire see page 403

Bus *Stagecoach Buses* operate daily from 0700-2300. City and suburban coverage is good and there is a 'ten-trip' ticket system available. The City Circular Bus runs every 10 mins (Mon-Fri 0730-1800, Thu 2100, Sat 0900-1800, Sun 0950-1800) from the Railway Station taking in major sites including Te Papa, Cuba Mall, the Cable Car on Lampton, and Parliament Buildings. It costs $1 (child $0.50) with a $7 'Star Pass' ticket ($10 group of 4) available in conjunction with ***Stagecoach Wellington*** services. For information call ***Ridewell***, T8017000, and get your hands on the free 'Wellington bus and train guide' from the VIC.

Car Parking can be a nightmare in the city centre. It is heavily metered and fiercely patrolled. If you struggle to find a spot in the centre, try the 'park and display' areas around the Railway Station, north and south of the centre, and Te Papa Museum. You can walk from there.

Train *Tranz Metro* operates regular daily suburban services between Wellington City and Upper Hutt, Melling and Paraparaumu. There is a day rover ticket available for $10. For information call ***Ridewell***, T8017000.

Walking Wellington city centre is quite compact and you should not have much trouble getting around on foot. Indeed, given the road system, with its numerous one way networks and omnipresent traffic wardens, this would seem to be the best thing to do.

Orientation & information

Wellington is generally easy to negotiate and, unless you are in a car and swept away on its one way systems, you should not get too lost. All roads lead into the centre since there is nowhere else for them to go.The central city is essentially sandwiched between the hills and the waterfront and those arriving by road will be delivered right in the heart, within a stone's throw of Lampton Quay, the main business and shopping street. Lampton then doubles back north to meet Molesworth St, Thorndon and the Parliament District. The Harbour, with its merging main roads of Quay, Customhouse, Jervois, Cable St and Oriental Parade, sweeps back south and east, encompassing the modern and highly developed waterfront, including the dominant Te Papa Museum. From the heart of the waterfront south, Willis and Jervois connect with Victoria, Cuba and Courtenay Pl, where you'll find many of the restaurants and cafés. Behind the Central Business District (CBD) are the spacious Botanical Gardens and hillside suburbs of Kelburn. Dominating the view south east is Mount Victoria, a 'must see' lookout and an ideal place to get your bearings.

There is a specialist **Map Shop**, on the corner of Vivian and Victoria Sts (near Cuba St), as well as the stocks available at major bookshops *Whitcoulls* and *Dymocks* (see page 401). The Wellington **Visitor Information Centre**, 101 Wakefield St (Civic Sq), T8024860, F8024863, www.wellingtonNZ.com Mon-Fri 0830-1730, Sat/Sun 0930-1630. The VIC also has a shop, a café and internet access. There is also an information centre at the airport, T3855123. **DOC** Information Centre, Government Buildings, Lampton Quay, T4727356, www.doc.govt.nz Open Mon-Fri 0900-1630, Sat/Sun 1000-1500.

Useful free guides include '*Wellington Visitors Guide*', '*What's On Wellington*', the '*Wellington Arts Map*' and the '*Wellington Fashion Map*'. Also the weekly newspapers '*City Voice*' and '*Capital Times*' are designed for visitors. The main daily in the lower North Island is the *Dominion*, but the *New Zealand Herald* (Auckland and upper North Island) is also available.

History

According to Maori legend it was Kupe, the great Polynesian explorer who first made landfall in the region in about AD 950, and his descendants, the Ngai Tara and Rangitane tribes, became the first permanent settlers. The first European ships to enter the harbour were the *Rosanna* and the *Lampton* on a preliminary exploration for the first New Zealand Company in 1826. But it was not until 1839/40, when other ships, the *Tory* and then the *Aurora* brought the first settlers, that the inevitable dubious land deals with the local Maori were made. Initially the first blocks of land purchased were at the northern end of the harbour towards what are now Petone and the Hutt Valley. But the land was found to be unsuitable for building, so the settlers moved south, to what is now Thorndon, in the heart of modern day Wellington. Along with the rest of the country, Wellington suffered three decades of Maori/*Pakeha* friction surrounding the various land deals. But despite this, and a major earthquake in 1855 (which actually had the positive effect of creating new and ideal flat land for building), Wellington prospered. By the 1860s, with the various inroads being made in to the South Island and the then capital Auckland suffering due to its geographical position, it was decided to move the seat of government and make Wellington the capital in 1865. The name Wellington was bestowed in honour of yet another British general, Arthur Wellesley (1769-1852), the first Duke of Wellington. Although modern day Wellington is a proud buzz of human life and celebrated development, deep down there is the ever present fear of further earthquakes and the hope that history will not repeat itself and that nature will not spoil the party.

Sights

Mount Victoria Lookout
Take a No 20 bus

Most of Wellington's major attractions are all within walking distance, or a short bus ride from each other. Perhaps the best place to start, and an ideal spot to get a sense of place, is the (196 m) Mount Victoria Lookout. Looking south-east from the city centre it is not hard to miss, but to the uninitiated, reaching the lookout can be somewhat akin to an expedition up K2. The best ascent is by car. Head straight for the hill up Majoribanks Road (at the bottom of Courtenay

Place). From Majoribanks turn left on to Hawker, carry on up Moeller , Pallister, and then Thane. The entrance to the lookout is on the right, off Thane. If you get lost in the web of residential hillside streets, just make sure you keep going up and eventually you will reach the summit. You might like to investigate the **Byrd Memorial**, a rather modernist edifice pointing south towards the Antarctic, in honour of the American Admiral Richard Byrd. The view is also spectacular at sunrise and after dark. If you are on foot the summit is part of the 'Southern Walkway' (details and leaflets from the VIC).

The Parliamentary District

The Parliamentary District is on Bowen Street, at the northern end of Lampton Quay and just west of the rather grand looking **Railway Station** building, on Bunny Street. You will be immediately struck by the rather odd and aptly named **Beehive**, which houses the various governement offices. Designed by British architect, Sir Basil Spence, and built in 1980, it is either loved or hated. Far more pleasing is the 1922 **Old Parliament House** next door and next door to that, the **Parliamentary Library**, which is older still. There is an excellent **visitors centre** in the ground floor foyer of Parliament House. Regular tours are available and you can also see parliament in session. ■ *Mon-Fri 0900-1700, Sat 0930-1600, Sun 1130-1600. Tours Mon-Fri 1000-1600, Sat 1000-1500, Sun 1200-1500. 1 hr. Free. T4719999.*

While in the vicinity of Parliament House take a peek or stop for lunch in the **Backbencher Pub**, across the road, on Molesworth Street facing the High Court. Adorning the walls are some superb cartoons and 'Spitting Image' style dummies of past and present Prime Ministers. The best has to be the less than flattering one of Rob Muldoon (perhaps New Zealand's most famous Prime Minister). It is particularly grotesque, looking for all the world like the alien slug-like character 'Jabba the Hut' from the film 'Star Wars'.

Just a short stroll from the Backbencher Pub on Lampton Quay are the historic **Old Government Buildings** built in 1876 to house the Crown Ministers and public servants of the day. It has an interesting interior with a rather grand staircase and cabinet room, but it is worthy of above average scrutiny externally as well. The building was designed to look like stone but actually constructed of wood. An expensive restoration was completed in 1996 and it now houses the Victoria Universities Law Faculty and the DOC information centre. It is partially open to visitors, T4727356. Also in the Parliamentary District is the **National Library** building with its impressive collection of research books, colonial photographs and in-house gallery. It also has a shop and a café. ■ *Mon-Fri 0900-1700, Sat 0900-1630, Sun 1300-1630. T4743000.*

From the library, heading towards the water are the **National Archives of New Zealand**, 10 Mulgrave Street. Within its hallowed walls are housed a number of important historical documents including the original and controversial Treaty of Waitangi. ■ *Mon-Fri 0900-1700, Sat 0900-1300. Free. T4995595.*

Also on Mulgrave Street is the **Old St Paul's Cathedral**, an 1866 Gothic style church adapted from traditional stone to native timbers. It is worth a look, not only to see the superb timberwork of the interior, but also the impressive stained glass windows. ■ *Mon-Sat. Free. T4736722.*

On the corner of Jervois Quay and Cable Street is the **New Zealand Film Archive**, which houses a collection of New Zealand and overseas film and TV materials of artistic, social and historical value, dating back to 1897. It runs frequent specialist exhibitions. ■ *Mon-Fri 0900-1700. Free. T3847647.*

Wellington

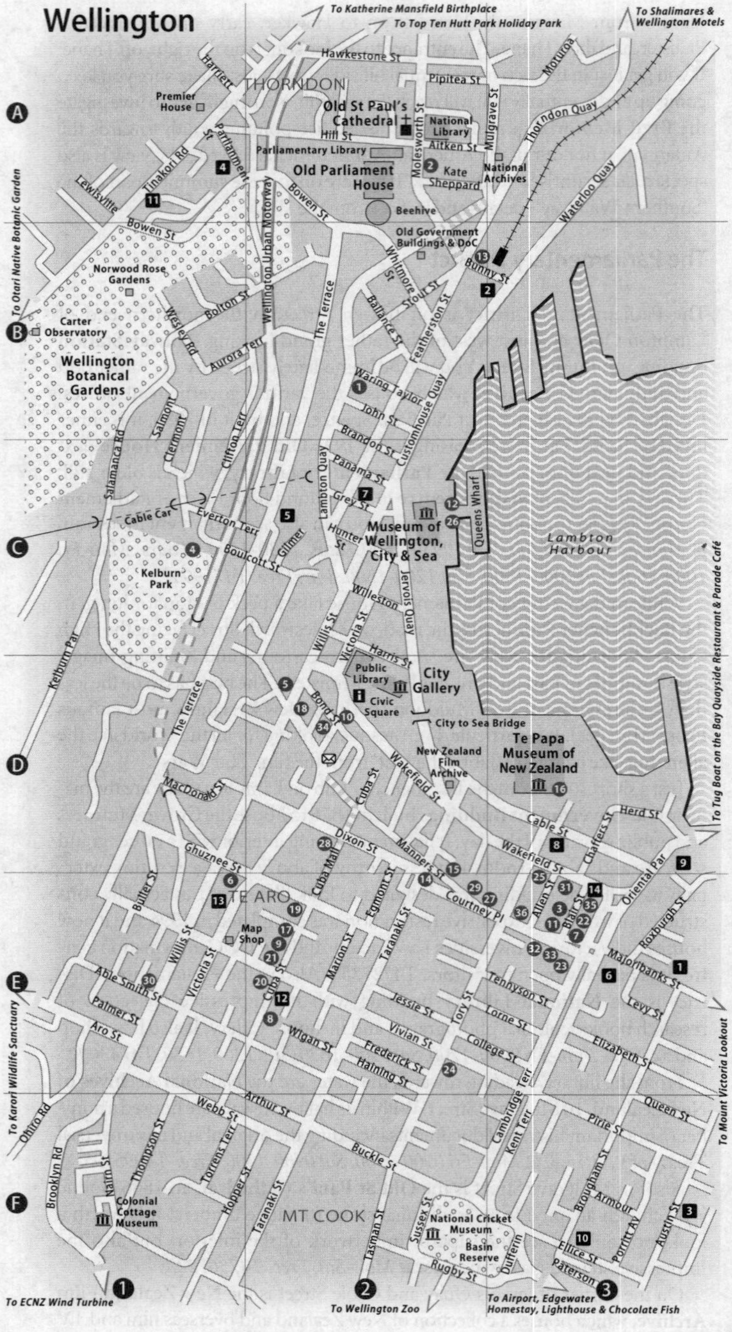

To Katherine Mansfield Birthplace
To Top Ten Hutt Park Holiday Park
To Shalimares & Wellington Motels
Hawkestone St
Pipitea St
Harriett
THORNDON
Premier House
Old St Paul's Cathedral
National Library
Hill St
Parliament St
Tinakori Rd
Parliamentary Library
Aitken St
Molesworth St
Mulgrave St
Thorndon Quay
Moturoa
Old Parliament House
Kate Sheppard
National Archives
Lewisville
Bowen St
Wellington Urban Motorway
Beehive
Waterloo Quay
Old Government Buildings & DoC
Bunny St
Norwood Rose Gardens
Whitmore St
Stout St
To Otari Native Botanic Garden
Bolton St
Wesley Rd
The Terrace
Ballance St
Featherston St
Carter Observatory
Aurora Terr
Wellington Botanical Gardens
Waring Taylor
John St
Customhouse Quay
Salmont
Clermont
Clifton Terr
Brandon St
Salamanca Rd
Lambton Quay
Panama St
Queens Wharf
Cable Car
Grey St
Everton Terr
Museum of Wellington, City & Sea
Lambton Harbour
Hunter St
Gilmer
Boulcott St
Kelburn Park
Jervois Quay
Willeston
Willis St
Victoria St
Harris St
Kelburn Par
Public Library
City Gallery
Civic Square
Bond St
City to Sea Bridge
The Terrace
Te Papa Museum of New Zealand
New Zealand Film Archive
Wakefield St
Cuba St
MacDonald St
To Tug Boat on the Bay Quayside Restaurant & Parade Café
Herd St
Cable St
Dixon St
Chaffers St
Wakefield St
Ghuznee St
Cuba Mall
Manners St
Oriental Par
Egmont St
TE ARO
Courtney Pl
Allen St
Blair St
Roxburgh St
Bulter St
Taranaki St
Willis St
Map Shop
Marion St
Victoria St
Majoribanks St
Able Smith St
Tennyson St
Palmer St
Jessie St
Tory St
Lorne St
Levy St
Aro St
Vivian St
College St
Wigan St
Frederick St
Elizabeth St
Haining St
To Karori Wildlife Sanctuary
Ohiro Rd
Arthur St
Queen St
Webb St
Cambridge Terr
Pirie St
Kent Terr
Thompson St
Torrens Terr
Buckle St
Brooklyn Rd
Nairn St
Hopper St
Taranaki St
Brougham St
Armour
Colonial Cottage Museum
MT COOK
Tasman St
Sussex St
National Cricket Museum
Basin Reserve
Dufferin
Porritt Av
Austin St
Ellice St
Rugby St
Paterson
To ECNZ Wind Turbine
To Wellington Zoo
To Airport, Edgewater Homestay, Lighthouse & Chocolate Fish
To Mount Victoria Lookout

Wellington

Not to scale

Sleeping
1 Apollo Lodge Motel *E3*
2 Downtown Backpackers *B3*
3 Dunrobin House B & B *F3*
4 Eight Parliament St *A1*
5 Grand Chancellor *C2*
6 Haswell Lodge *E3*
7 Inter-Continental Wellington *C2*
8 Museum *D3*
9 Quality Oriental Bay *D3*
10 Rowena's City Lodge *F3*
11 Shepherds Arms *A1*
12 Trekkers *E2*
13 Victoria Court *E1*
14 Wellington YHA *E3*

Eating
1 Astoria *B2*
2 Backbencher *A2*
3 Beacon Wood Fire Grill & Bar & Little India *E3*
4 Boulcott Street Bistro *C1*
5 Bouquet Garni *D2*
6 Brasserie Flipp *E1*
7 Brava & Opera *E3*
8 Café Globe *E2*
9 Café Istanbul *E2*
10 Café Lido *D2*
11 Café Paradiso *E3*
12 Dockside *C2*
13 Donald's Pie Cart *B2*
14 Dubliner & Molly Malones Pub *E2*
15 Expressoholic *D2*
16 Icon *D3*
17 Khmer Satay Noodle House *E2*
18 Kopi *D2*
19 Krazy Lounge *E2*
20 Logan Brown *E2*
21 Midnight Expresso Olive *E2*
22 Mondo Cucina *E3*
23 Oriental Thai *E3*
24 Petit Lyons *E2*
25 Satay Kampong *E3*
26 Shed 5 *C2*
27 Uncle Changs *E3*

Pubs & Clubs
28 Barney's Place *D2*
29 Big Easy *E2*
30 Bodega *E1*
31 CO2 *E3*
32 Coyote Bar *E3*
33 Grand *E3*
34 Loaded Hog *D2*
35 One Red Dog *E3*
36 Wellington Sports Café *E3*

The suburb of **Thorndon**, to which the Parliamentary District essentially belongs, is the oldest and most historic in Wellington. The '*Thorndon Heritage Trail*' Leaflet (from the VIC, $1) will outline other historical sites in the area. Two notable examples are the 1843 **Premier House** (still the official Prime Minister's residence) on Tinakori Road and, further north at 25 Tinakori Road, the **Katherine Mansfield Birthplace**. Mansfield is generally hailed as New Zealand's most famous writer having penned many internationally well-known short stories. Some of those stories ('*Prelude*' and '*A Birthday*') feature this house, where she lived until she was five. The house and gardens have been faithfully restored and there is an interesting video portrait of the writer. ■ *Daily 1000-1600. $5, child $2. T/F4737268.*

Civic Square and the waterfront

The **Civic Square**, just behind the VIC, was given a major revamp in the early 1990s and is blessed with some interesting architectural features. These include the instantly striking Nikau Palm columns adorning the modernistic **Public Library** and the imaginative and beautiful silver fern orb, cleverly suspended above the centre of the square. The Civic Square is often used for outdoor events and also houses the **City Gallery**. With Wellington being considered the artistic heart of the nation, the gallery strives (successfully it would seem) to present a regular programme of the very best of contemporary visual arts. There is an impressive array of media on show and the gallery also hosts special events, film screenings and performances. ■ *The gallery is open daily 1000-1700 and there is a good café on the ground floor. Free. T8013952.*

Also in the square is the kids paradise of **Capital E**, described as 'an inner city children's events centre' it offers an

Wellington

ever changing agenda of experiences, events and exhibitions. You won't be surprised to learn that there is a large and expensive toyshop attached. ■ *Daily 1000-1700. T3848502.*

From Civic Square it is a short walk across a very arty **City to Sea Bridge** that connects the square with the waterfront. The bridge sprouts a number of interesting sculptures that celebrate the arrival of the Maori in New Zealand.

The **Waterfront** has become a major focus in the city for its museums, aesthetics and recreational activities. On a sunny weekend it is a buzz of tourists and visitors alike, simply chilling out, sightseeing, roller-blading, kayaking or fishing.

To the north of Civic Square is **Frank Kitts Park** with its impressive children's play area complete with model lighthouse and slide. Further north is the classy revamped **wharf**, with its al fresco waterfront cafés and restaurants where you can relax over a beer and watch the sightseeing helicopter come and go and various water based activities taking place.

Museum of Wellington, City & Sea

Housed in the former Bond Store on Queens Wharf is the recently revitalized Museum of Wellington, City and Sea. Being in such close proximity to Te Papa, you might think its attempts to compete and woo visitors was an exercise in futility, but this museum is actually superb and, in its own way competes favourably with Te Papa. The interior multi-levelled design is modern yet rustic, maintaining the feel of its former function and the modern dose of sensual bombardment it now houses is very powerful. As the name suggests, the emphasis is on local history, with a particular maritime bent. Of particular note is the **Waihine Disaster Gallery** and the state of the art, holographic Maori legends display. The Waihine was a passenger ferry that came to grief at the harbour entrance in 1968 with the loss of 51 lives. Original film footage set to a suitably dramatic score, documents the chilling series of events. The 3D and holographic mix of the Maori legend display is simply stunning and leaves you in no doubt how much technology has transformed and injected new life in to museums as a whole. Recommended. ■ *Daily 0930-1730, 1800 summer. $5, child $2.50. T4728904, www.bondstore.co.nz*

Te Papa Museum of New Zealand

You will need a half a day at the museum, much more and you'll suffer from sensory overload

To the south of Civic Square and gracing the Harbour's eastern bank is the unmistakable Te Papa – Wellington's biggest tourist attraction. As if the exterior was not enough, the interior is also mind-bending. Heavily publicized and perhaps a little over celebrated, Te Papa has tried to faithfully represent the nation's heritage since 1998, at a cost of $317 million. They say there is something for everybody and this does seem to hold true. There is a heavy emphasis on Maori heritage and *taonga* (treasures) and biculturalism, mixed with the inevitable over kill of early settler material. This reflects the country's relative youth on the scale of world history and events. However, it does provide the usual high-tech sensual bombardment and you will find the hours passing happily by as you become inevitably engrossed. Given the fact it costs nothing, it is a good idea to have an initial quick recce and return later for a more in-depth investigation. One word of advice, go early and be sure to avoid the processions of noisy children.

There is an excellent shop on the ground floor but the café is less than impressive. Modern ideas may be great, but do we have to sit at our tables and watch a decorative tube of green slime doing what our lunch is about to? ■ *Daily 1000-1800, Thu 2100. Free. T3817000, www.tepapa.govt.nz*

The Botanical Gardens and cable car

Before going anywhere near the gardens you should pick up the free gardens map and leaflet, available from VICs

Wellington Botanical Gardens are really quite magnificent, but excruciatingly 'hilly', and although well worth the visit and a stroll, almost require oxygen and a base camp support team to do so. Gracing its precarious slopes are 26 ha of specialist gardens, radiant flowerbeds, foreign trees and native bush. Its crowning glories are the **Carter Observatory** and the **Norwood Rose Garden**.By far the most sensible and conventional way to visit the gardens is via the **Cable Car**, at 280 Lampton Quay, first built in 1902 and now a tourist attraction in itself. The almost completely subterranean single line has cables that haul the two lovely red carriages up and down, with four stops on the way. When your carriage glides in quietly to the summit (Kelburn) station you step out into the gardens and are immediately rewarded with a fine view across the city. ■ *The Cable Car runs every 10 mins, Mon-Fri 0700-2200, Sat/Sun 0900-2200. $1.50, child $0.70. T4722199.*

Having arrived in such style you are now in the perfect position to explore the gardens. At the crest of the hill and a short walk from the summit station is the **Carter Observatory** which has a static displays, planetarium shows and audio-visuals. ■ *Shows and telescope viewing are available from 1830-2230 on Tues/Thu and Sat. $7-$10, child $3-$5. T4728167.* Be sure to see another fine view over the city on the lawn, just in front of the observatory. The **Norwood Rose Gardens**, with its circular display of over 300 varieties, are at the northern end of the gardens, at the base of the hill and along with the café (open Mon-Fri 1100-1500, Sat/Sun 1000-1600) should perhaps be your last port of call. ■ *The gardens are free and open from dawn till dusk, T8013071, treehouse@wcc.govt.nz . The main entrance is on Glenmore St in Thorndon, which is on the No 12 bus route.*

The **Otari Native Botanical Garden**, 160 Wilton Road, in the suburb of Wilton (northwest of the Botanical Gardens) is another famous garden that concentrates in nurturing a fine collection of native flora. ■ *Open dawn to dusk. Free. T4753245. Take a No 4 bus.*

South of the city centre

On Manchester Street, in the suburb of Newtown, directly south of the city centre, is **Wellington Zoo**. Like Auckland and Hamilton, Wellington has embraced the need for the modern day zoo to be involved in conservation projects as well as be commerically-viable. Wellington has some fine exhibits of natives, including kiwi and tuatara and a wide variety of non-natives, including Sumatran tigers, Malayan sun bears and troupe of chimps, the second largest in the Southern Hemisphere. ■ *Daily 0930-1700 (last entry 1630). T3894577. $10, child $5. Take a No 10 bus.*

The **National Cricket Museum** is a small but worthy attraction, particularly to the enthusiast. It is housed in the Old Grandstand of the Basin Reserve (a ground that has hosted some famous encounters) and displays a range of national and international memorabilia dating back to 1743. Particular emphasis seems to inevitably be placed on encounters with the arch-enemy Australia. ■ *Daily 1030-1530, weekends only in winter. $3, child $1. T3856602.*

The **Colonial Cottage Museum**, 68 Nairn Street, Brooklyn, is housed in one of the city's oldest buildings dating back to 1858. Georgian in style, the faithfully restored and furnished interior takes you back to the early settler days. ■ *Wed-Fri 1200-1400, Sat/Sun 1300-1630. $3, child $1. T3849122.*

While visiting the Colonial Museum you might like to supplement the trip with a fine **city view** and the starkly contrasting **ECNZ Wind Turbine**, which slices the air above Brooklyn. From Brooklyn Road turn right in to Todman Street and follow the signs.

Around Wellington

There are a number of attractions around Wellington that are worth a visit. The **Karori Wildlife Sanctuary** is located in a valley of regenerating bush in the suburb and hills of Karori. In 1994, an area of 250 ha was set aside and protected with a predator-proof fence. Now, with the eradication of non-native pest species within the boundary of the fence, the benefits are already being seen. Reintroduced species are beginning a comeback and bird song is returning to bush that once lay silent. The Sanctuary has an information centre located on Waiapu Road in Karori. The area around the perimeter fence is already popular for walking and mountain biking. ■ *Sun 1000-1700. Guided tours are available. T9209200.*

Set in the middle of Wellington harbour is the **Somes or Matiu Island Reserve**. Once a quarantine station the island is now administered by DOC and is home to a number of protected native birds. The island can be reached by ferry which leaves from Queens Wharf and stops off at the island three times a day on its way to Days Bay near the coastal resort of Eastbourne (timetable, T4991273). ■ *Open daily to the public from 0830-1700. $14, child $3.50. T4991282.*

There are two New Zealand **fur seal colonies** near Wellington. The first and the most accessible is the Red Rocks colony accessed from the end of Owhiro Bay to the south of the city (see below). The second requires permission (DOC) and is located at Turakiae Head to the south east of Pencarrow Lighthouse. To get there take the Coast Road to Baring Head via Petone (Upper Hutt) and Wainuiomata. Then walk east to the headland (it's a half- to full-day trip).

There are a number of great **walks** in and around the city and details and free leaflets that cover these are available from the VIC or DOC. The **Heritage Trail** leaflet takes in many of the sights within the city above. There are **Northern, Southern, Eastern** and **Waterfront Walkways**. These range from an hour or two covering just a few kilometres to a full day's jaunt. They take in a range of city, suburb, waterfront, coastal and country scenery with both historic, contemporary or natural sights outlined. **Mount Kaukau** (430 m) to the northwest of the city is a good climb and offers a rewarding view of the region. It can be accessed from Simla Crescent in Khandallah (two hours). One of the most popular walks near the city is the walk to **Red Rocks** and the fur seal colony (see above) which is accessed via the quarry track at the western end of Owhiro Bay (4 km). Owhiro Bay is reached via Brooklyn and Happy Valley Road (take Nos 1, 4 then 9 buses).

Other good **beaches** in the area suitable for sunbathing and swimming can be found to the east of the city. From the airport follow the road round the headland to Palmer Head and **Scorching Bay** on the edge of Seatoun.

Activities and tours

Cruising/Sailing For day trips around the Harbour, to Somes Island and the eastern harbour seaside resorts of Days Bay and Eastbourne take the Eastbourne Ferry. It operates a regular sailing schedule from Queens Wharf and a day return to Days Bay is $14, child $7. T4991282 (timetable T4991273). There are also a number of **charter boats** available at Queens Wharf. *Shed 5* is a custom built 17 m luxury launch offering fishing trips and cruises with catering supplied by the *Shed 5* restaurant. T4999069, shed5@shed5.co.nz *Phantom of the Straits-NZL3900* is a 24 m maxi cruiser originally built for New Zealand's yachting legend Sir Peter Blake and offers harbour trips and occasional racing, T4773503. *Sweet Georgia Cruising* offer tailored cruises around the harbour or further afield across Cook Strait to the beautiful Marlborough Sounds. On board catering and accommodation is available, T02-5452641, F3863770. Charter boats for fishing leave just north of Queens Wharf.

Diving There is surprisingly good diving around Wellington. One company that offers gear hire, tuition and the opportunity to join trips are *Wellington Dive Adventures*, 58 Ohiro Bay Parade, Owhiro Bay, T3835473, www.dive.net.nz

Golf Note that *Paraparaumu Golf Course* just north of Wellington is an international standard golf links ranked 73rd in the world and graced by Tiger Woods at the NZ Open in 2001. T2984561. Closer to town is the so-so *Miramar Course* next to the airport, T3882099 and on the outskirts the more challenging *Karori Course*, T4767337.

Four-wheel drive Organized four-wheel drive tours of the colony and Red rocks are available and also take in the ECNZ Wind Turbine on the way; $40, 2½ hours. Book at the VIC, T8024860.

Horse trekking The *Country Club Riding Academy* in Johnsonville (Ohariu Valley) is New Zealand's largest equestrian centre specializing in horse trekking and tuition, T4788472.

Jet bikes For jet bike trips on the harbour contact *Wet & Wild*, T2359796, from $75 for 1 hour.

Kayaking *Ferg's Rock 'n' Kayak* based in Shed 6 on the Queens Wharf is hugely popular at weekends hiring out a range of single or double kayaks for self-guided or organized trips (night included) on the harbour. There is also a climbing wall on the premises ($12). ■ *Open from Mon-Fri 1000-2200, Sat/Sun 0900-2200. From $14 for 1 hr, trips from $35. T4998898, fergs.rock.n.kayak@clear.net.nz*

Mountain biking There are a number of good tracks around Wellington including the Karori Wildlife Sanctuary perimeter fence (from Brooklyn Hill), Karori Reservoir, parts of the Southern Walkway, Tinakori Hill and Mount Kaukau. For cycle hire see page 403. Information at the VIC.

Quad biking *All Track Adventures*, 20 minutes from the city, operate the area's quad bike tours. Trips zoom about rugged farmland, cliff tracks and beaches. ■ *From $90. T0800-494335, www.alltrack.co.nz*

Roller-blading Hugely popular along the waterfront. Blades can be hired at *Ferg's Rock 'n' Kayak* (see above) where tuition is also available for $30. Skates are also available for hire from *Cheapskates*, Chaffers Street Park (opposite

Cable Street) or from the southern end of Frank Kitts Park (on the waterfront). ■ *From $10, 1 hr.*

Scenic flights *Helipro* helicopter flights over the city, harbour or beyond are ideally placed on Queens Wharf and cost about $50(five minutes), $95(15 minutes).T4721550.

Sightseeing There are a number of specialist sightseeing operators offering a range of city tours or others that go further afield. These include the scheduled daily trips with the well established and entertaining *Wally Hammond's Tours*, T4720869, 2½ hours, $25 and the award winning *Wellington Explorer Tours*, operated by *Newlands Coaches*, T0800-287287. Depart twice daily 0900 and 1330, pick-ups available. For informative and entertaining **guided walks** around the city contact *Walk Wellington*, T3849590, walkwellington@xtra.co.nz $20, child $10.

Swimming The best beaches are to be found to the east of the city around the coast at Seatoun. The invitingly named Scortching Bay, 3 km north of Seatoun is a favourite. If the beach holds no appeal head for the *Freyberg Pool*, ■ *139 Oriental Parade. daily 0630-2100, Fri 1730. T3843107.*

Windsurfing/surfing Windsurfers can be hired from *Wild Winds Sail and Surf* at the Overseas Terminal near Te Papa, T3841010. Tuition available. There is also good windsurfing and hire available at Days Bay. *Wild Winds* can also advise on the best local surf spots.

Essentials

Sleeping
The range and standard of backpackers is poor

Although not as well-blessed as Auckland in quantity, Wellington does have the advantage that all types of accommodation are centrally located and within walking distance of most attractions. During festivals and in summer Wellington can get busy so you are advised to book ahead. Upper range hotels seem to dominate but, given the emphasis on weekday business, prices are usually halved at weekends.

LL-AL *Hotel Inter-continental Wellington*, corner of Grey and Featherston St, T4722722, F4724724, reservations@wellington.parkroyal.com.nz Located right in the heart of the city and a stone's throw from the waterfront, the best of the best on the hotel chain links. It has all the usual amenities including 3 restaurants and bars including the western theme *Arizona Bar*. **LL-AL** *Grand Chancellor Hotel*, 147 The Terrace, T4999500, F4999800. Another at the top range, with all mod cons, a fine piano bar and in an ideal spot to climb the steps down to Lampton Quay. **LL** *Shalimares*, 9 Shalimares Cres, T4791776, F4791786, www.shalimares.co.nz Modern house with luxury, tasteful and spacious accommodation overlooking the harbour on the northern outskirts of the city.

L *The Lighthouse*, 326 The Esplanade, Island Bay, T/F4724177, bruce@sportwork.co.nz Ever stayed in a lighthouse? Well, if not this is your chance. Built in 1993, the lighthouse offers suitable views across the harbour entrance and oozes character. Small kitchen and bathroom on one floor, living and sleeping areas above. Recommended. **L-AL** *Museum Hotel*, 90 Cable St, T3852809, F8028909, www.museum-hotel.co.nz A modern establishment Ideally located across the road from Te Papa and in the heart of the café, bar and restaurant areas.

AL *Dunrobin House B&B*, 89 Austin St, T3850335, F3850336. Elegant early 1900s villa with 2 romantic, classy rooms and quiet pretty gardens (where breakfast is often served). Centrally located. **AL-A** ***Eight Parliament Street***, 8 Parliament St, T4990808, F4796705, www.boutique/bb.co.nz A traditional, well-appointed villa with 3 en-suite rooms. Excellent breakfast. **AL** ***Quality Hotel Oriental Bay***, 73 Roxburgh St, T3850279, F3845324. Situated on the waterfront with wonderful views across the harbour and CBD, its is worth staying here for that reason alone. However it also boasts an indoor pool, licensed restaurant and is close to Te Papa. **AL** ***Shepherds Arms Hotel***, 285 Tinakori Rd, T4721320, F4720523. If you are fed up with the flash modern high-rise hotels, the 1870s *Shepherds Arms* will embrace you with the historic, tastefully restored option, in the quieter suburb of Thorndon.

A ***Apollo Lodge Motel***, 49 Majoribanks St, T3851849, F3851846, www.apollo-lodge.co.nz Standard modern unit interiors, most with kitchen facilities. Walking distance to Te Papa and Courtenay Pl. **A** ***Edgewater Homestay***, 495 Karaka Bay, Karaka Bay, Seatoun, T3884446, F3884649, www.edgewaterwellington.co.nz Modern and classy, situated near the airport and best city beaches. **A** ***Haswell Lodge***, 21 Kent Terr, T3850196, F3850503. Comfortable units sited well off the main street. Walking distance from Te Papa and Courtenay Place restaurants and cafés. **A** ***The Victoria Court***, 201 Victoria St, T4724297, F3857949, victoriacourt.nz@xtra.co.nz This is a new and nicely appointed motel in a perfect location for the mid-city and café, restaurant districts of Cuba and Courtenay. **A** ***Wellington Motel***, 14 Hobson St, T4720334. Closest motel to the South Island ferry terminals.

B-D ***Trekkers Hotel, Motel and Backpackers***, 213 Cuba St, T3852153, F3827872, info@trekkers.co.nz An award-winning establishment, with fine facilities but a bit of a rabbit warren. Some rooms are miles from the kitchen.

C-D ***Downtown Backpackers***, 1 Bunny St, T4738482, F4711073, www.downtownbackpackers.co.nz Not the most characterful place to be, but it's certainly 'happening', has adequate (ex-hotel) facilities, including an in-house bar and is well located next to the railway station. Internet. **C-D** ***Rowena's City Lodge***, 115 Brougham St, Mt Victoria, T/F3857872, rowenas@iconz.co.nz Pleasant, friendly hostel in large rambling house, far more intimate than the other backpackers. Value single rooms available. Camping available on the lawn. Internet. **C-D** ***Wellington YHA***, corner of Wakefield St and Cambridge Terr, T8017280, yhawgtn@yha.org.nz Very popular with comfortable rooms (with en-suite bathrooms), fine views and all in the heart of the café and restaurant areas and a stone throw from Te Papa.

Motor camps It is hard to believe that there is, as yet, no Motor camp within Wellington itself. The nearest is the excellent **B-D** ***'Top-Ten' Hutt Park Holiday Park***, 95 Hutt Park Rd, Lower Hutt, T0800-488872, www.huttpark.co.nz Although about 15 km from Wellington city centre it is worth the trek. Besides, there really is little choice.

Eating

Wellington prides itself on its thriving café and restaurant scene is often dubbed 'the café crazy capital'. More than 80 new establishments have opened up in the last 3 years and the choice is now vast, which means you are almost guaranteed good quality. The Courtenay quarter is where most are located, though Queens Wharf on the waterfront and Cuba St are also favourite haunts.

Expensive
For the more expensive restaurants booking is advised

On the waterfront's newly developed Queens Wharf the ***Dockside*** (T4999900) and ***Shed 5*** (T4999069) are proving 2 very popular eateries. Although both are fine evening venues they are particularly popular during the day and weekends, when the al fresco atmosphere and mainly seafood or Mediterranean lunches (or simply a cold beer while watching the world go by) never fails to attract. Both are open daily from 1100. Further round the waterfront the ***Quayside***, 245 Oriental Par, T8017900, is another popular harbour-side venue with a view that beats the other 2 and cuisine to match. It is open daily from 1200.

Between these waterfront locations is the ***Icon Restaurant*** in Te Papa, T8015300. As you might expect, although not enjoying the same al fresco atmosphere as the above, it is very classy and boasts another fine view – one that can be enjoyed in all weathers. *Icon* offers international cuisine with a Pacific Rim influence and is open daily from 1100. If you really wish to get intimate with the harbour the ***Tugboat on the Bay*** is a restaurant in an old tugboat in Oriental Bay. It offers the usual classy seafood dishes with traditional kiwi backups. Open daily for lunch and dinner, T3848884.

The top-end option on Cuba St is ***Logan Brown*** on the corner with Vivian St, T8015114. This is a well-established, multi award-winning establishment, offering international cuisine in the old historic and spacious banking Chambers. The interior is spectacular and comes complete with a huge chandelier.Open for lunch Mon-Fri and dinner Mon-Sun. Nearby, the ***Brasserie Flipp***, 103 Ghuznee St, T3859493, is another well-established award winner with character. Its menu consists of mainly traditional Pacific Rim and traditional Kiwi dishes. Open Mon-Fri from 1100, Sat/Sun from 1030. In the heart of the city the ***Boulcott Street Bistro***, 99 Boulcott St, T4994199, is another top restaurant in historic surroundings, this time a period wooden villa. The cuisine is mainly French mixed with some international dishes. Open from 1200 Mon-Fri and Mon-Sat from 1800.

Mid-range Blair St, off Courtenay Pl is practically wall-to-wall restaurants. A few stand out including the ***Beacon Wood fire Grill and Bar***, 8 Blair St, T8017275. It has plenty of atmosphere and walls decked with impressive artworks. The food as the name suggests is mainly wood-fired Mediterranean. It is open Mon-Sat 1730-late and for brunch on Sat/Sun. A few doors down, at 18, is ***Little India*** , T3849989. This is one of the city's best Indian restaurants and is open for lunch Mon-Fri and dinner daily from 1730. Across the road is the popular and modern ***Mondo Cucina***, T8016615, with a rich traditional menu and a fine bar. Again it has some interesting artworks on the walls. Open daily from 1730.

Most of the more classy pubs in the Courtenay Quarter offer fine, reliable and mainly international or Pacific Rim cuisine. On the corner of Blair and Courtney is an old favourite, the ***Café Paradiso***. For over a decade it has attracted a loyal following who enjoy its light, classical, traditional dishes, good service and busy atmosphere. It is open Mon-Wed from 1100, Sat 1100-0100, Sun 0900-1800, T3842675. At 2 Courtenay Pl is ***Brava***, which offers reliable fine dining but is most popular for its breakfasts and brunches at the weekend. It is open Mon-Fri 0800-late, Sat/Sun 0900-late, T3841159. At the other end of Courtenay is one of the better Chinese restaurants, ***Uncle Changs*** at 72 Courtenay Pl. It specializes in Taiwanese and Sezchuan. Open daily for lunch and dinner, T8019568. Still on the Asian theme and around the corner from Courtenay, at 58 Cambridge Terr, is ***The Oriental Thai***, which is considered the pick of Thai restaurants in the city. Open for lunch Mon-Fri 1200-1430, dinner daily from 1730, T8018080.

There are numerous small restaurants and cafés in the 'Cuba Quarter'. Restaurants that stand out include ***Petit Lyons***, 33 Vivian St, which offers moderate to expensive casual and fine dining in a characterful 3-storey building. It is open daily for lunch and dinner, T3849402. ***The Café Istanbul***, 156 Cuba St, is a fine Turkish style restaurant with a congenial interior. Open daily for lunch and dinner, T3854998. On Willis St back towards town the ***Bouquet Garni*** is both a bistro and wine bar set in an old wooden villa on the corner of Willis and Boulcott Sts. It offers fine or casual dining and is very proud of its beef and lamb dishes for which it has just won a national award. It is open daily from 1000, T4991095. Across the road at 103 Willis is the cute ***Kopi***, perhaps the best Malaysian restaurant/café in the city offering 'rotis' to die for. Open daily from 1000, T4995570. In the heart of the city is one of the best traditional Japanese restaurants ***Sakura*** on the corner of Whitmore and Featherstone Sts. Open for lunch Mon-Fri 1200-1400 and dinner Mon-Sat from 1800, T4996912.

Cheap

At the northern end of town a good pub lunch can be assured in the characterful ***Backbencher***, 34 Molesworth St, T4723065. In Cuba St there are numerous inexpensive cafés and takeaways of which, ***Midnight Expresso*** (178) and ***Khmer Satay Noodle House*** (148) are recommended. On Courtney Pl you can't go far wrong with a traditional pub lunch at *Molly Malone's* ***Dubliner*** restaurant upstairs (corner of Courtenay and Taranaki), T3842896. Around the corner at 262 Wakefield St is the basic and immensely popular Malaysian restaurant, ***Satay Kampong***, which is open for both lunch and dinner. If it is late at night, you are desperate and anywhere near the railway station, there is always the 24-hr ***Donald's Pie Cart***.

Cafés

Right in the heart of town, just opposite the VIC (which itself has a reputable café), is the ***Café Lido***, one of the most popular in the city and always busy. It is a fine place to mix with Wellingtonians and watch the world go by over good coffee. On the corner of Waring Taylor St and Lampton Quay is the ***Astoria Café***, a modern, popular café that fills with suits at lunchtime. It is also famous for the weird water sculpture outside that looks for all the world like a stand off between a group of rival sperm!

Cuba is the focus of the café scene and here ***Café Globe*** (213), ***Olive*** (170) and ***Midnight Expresso*** (178) and ***Krazy Lounge*** (132) stand out. On Courtenay the ***Expressoholic*** (128) is very laid back, open late and serves up great coffee, while further east on Oriental Parade the ***Parade Café*** (148) is an award winner. Further still the ***Chocolate Fish*** near the beach at Scortching Bay, is an award winner and hugely popular on sunny summer afternoons.

Pubs & bars

The main hot spots in the city are ***Courtenay Place*** and its off-shoot ***Blair St***, with the odd reputable drinking hole in Cuba St, Willis St and the Central Business District (CBD). With the vast range of cafés and restaurants, many of which are licensed, the main pubs tend to remain quiet until late, when, particularly at weekends, they fill with young and old and generally go off well into the wee small hours.

For sheer interest the ***Backbencher***, 34 Molesworth St, T4723065, is worth a look with the 'Spitting Image' type dummies and cartoons decking the walls keeping the country's politicians in check. It also is a good venue to watch sports, has live bands at the weekend and is a hugely popular venue on Fri nights. Another popular mid-city venue is the ***Loaded Hog***, 18 Bond St, T4729160 which has a wide ranging clientele and bands at the weekend. Still around the CBD, Queens Wharf is a great daytime drinking venue with a number of fine waterfront cafes providing the ideal spot for that relaxing afternoon libation. These include ***Dockside*** and ***Shed 5*** (see Eating above). ***The Bodega***, 286 Willis, T3848212, is a top, laid back, live music venue. ***Barney's Place*** is a similar venue at 80 Cuba St, T3848441, especially good for 80's music.

The selection on Courtenay and its off-shoot street of Blair is vast but the following are a few of the most popular: ***Molly Malones***, corner Taranaki St and Courtney Pl, T3842896 is the city's most popular Irish offering and hosts bands both folk and rock most nights. The beer too is reliably good. For huge contrast ***The Big Easy***, 74 Courtenay Pl is best known for the range of lingerie on show rather than the range of musical instruments. The other big names on Courtenay are: ***The Grand***, 69-71, T8017800; ***The Coyote Bar***, 63, T3856665, ***The Wellington Sports Café***, corner of Tory St, T8018015 (big screen for sports fanatics); and the rather grand ***Opera***, corner Blair St and Courtenay Pl, T3828654. All of these practically rub shoulders with each other, are hugely popular and interesting in themselves. On Blair St check out ***One Red Dog*** which is also good for pre-prandials and ***CO2***, the up-market 'bolly til' you're jolly' venue.

Entertainment

For up to date listings contact the VIC or check the daily newspaper The Dominion, as well as the tourist papers City Life and Capital Times

Although Aucklanders would disagree, Wellington probably has the edge when it comes to a good night out. There are numerous venues: from large concert halls like the ***Michael Fowler Centre*** offering both rock and classical; noted theatres like the ***St James*** and ***Circa***, offering contemporary drama, dance and comedy; and a plethora of pubs and clubs, particularly down Courtenay Pl and along Cuba St. For major events tickets can be booked or bought directly from *Ticketek*, located in the Michael Fowler Centre, 111 Wakefield St, T3843840, www.ticketek.co.nz Also note that the VIC offers discounts on theatre tickets subject to availability. Another useful website is browse is www.events.org.nz

Art galleries Wellington is a major national venue for the visual arts and there are some fine galleries. The VIC produces an excellent free guide – *'The Wellington Arts'* booklet. Main dealers in contemporary New Zealand art include: ***The Bowen Galleries***, T4997805 (open Mon-Fri 1000-1730, Sat 1000-1400) and the ***Christopher Moore Gallery***, T4734528 (open Mon-Fri 1000-1730, Sat 1000-1400) both on The Terrace; ***The Ferner Gallery***, 128 Featherstone St, T4999446 (open Mon-Fri 0930-1730, Sat 1000-1600); ***The Tinakori Gallery***, 330 Tinakori Rd, Thorndon, T4712636 (open Mon-Fri 0900-1700, Sat 1000-1500).

Cinemas Tue night is cheap ticket night and listings can be found in the daily papers. The ***Paramount***, 25 Courtenay Pl, is considered the best and most characterful cinema in town. In-house bar, T3844080, www.delux.co.nz Others include: ***The Embassy Theatre***, 10 Kent Terr, which has a giant screen, T3847657; ***Rialto Theatres***, corner of Cable St and Jervois Quay, T3851864; and ***Hoyts***, Manners St, T3843567.

Comedy Venues As well as the larger theatres (see above) the ***Indigo Bar*** and ***Venue***, 171 Cuba St, is well known for its laid-back comedy nights, T8016797.

Concert Halls ***The Michael Fowler Centre***, 5 Hania St, is Wellington's largest concert venue hosting a mix of rock and classical performances, T8014242. Tickets sold on site with *Ticketek*. The ***Wellington Town Hall***, T4711573, and the ***Queens Wharf Events Centre*** are 2 other popular concert venues.

Theatres There are 4 principal theatres in Wellington all with good reputations: ***Bats Theatre***, 1 Kent Terr, is a small characterful venue offering live professional theatre focusing on alternative works and New Zealand drama. T8024175, www.circa.co.nz

The ***Circa Theatre***, 1 Taranaki St, next to Te Papa is a well-established theatre that offers lively international drama, comedy and music. Performance times Tue/Wed 1830, Thu-Sat 2000, Sun 1600, In-house café, T8017992, www.circa.co.nz

The ***Downstage Theatre*** on Courtenay Pl is one of New Zealand's leading professional theatres presenting touring shows of classic contemporary drama, dance and comedy, T8016946, F8016948. The ***Opera House***, 111 Manners St, is also one of Wellingtons favourite venues for touring shows and has recently undergone major renovation,T8024060.

Last but not least is the ***Westpac St James Theatre***, also on Courtenay Pl, which was originally built in 1912. After a multi-million dollar refurbishment in 1998 it is now considered a premiere venue and a central focus to the performing arts. The James is also home to the Royal New Zealand Ballet, T8024060, stjames@stjames.co.nz

Gay & lesbian The ***Flipp Brasserie***, 103 Ghuznee St, T3859493 and the ***Evergreen Coffee House***, 144 Vivian St, are 2 main daytime venues while the ***Valve*** (also on Vivian St) and ***Ruby Ruby***, 19 Edward St, T3845211 go off into the night. For more information on gay and lesbian issues contact the Gay switchboard, T3850674, or Lesbian Line, T3851162.

Live music venues

Jazz ***Tatou***, 22 Cambridge, T3843112. Not exactly intimate but still fun with live jazz on most weekends. ***Petit Lyon***, 33 Vivian St, T3849402. Excellent intimate venue on Fri especially in the 'Oyster Bar'. ***Beacon Bar***, 8 Blair St, T8017275. Thu and Sat nights.

Classical Occasional classical concerts are staged at the ***University School of Music***, The ***Conservatorium of Music*** (Polytechnic) and ***St Andrews*** on the Terrace.

Rock There are numerous pub venues that host mainly weekend rock gigs including: The ***Opera***, corner of Blair St and Courtenay Pl, T3828654; ***Bodega***, 286 Willis St, T3848212; ***Wellington Sports Café***, corner of Tory St and Courtenay Pl, T8018015; ***Loaded Hog***, 14 Bond St, T4729160 (Sat); The ***Grand***, 69-71 Courtenay Pl, T8017800 (Thu); ***Backbencher***, 34 Molesworth St, T4723065; ***Matterhorn***, 106 Cuba St, T3843359.

Folk ***Molly Malones***, corner of Taranaki and Courtenay Sts, T3842896, can usually get the toes tapping most nights with the less traditional ***Kitty O'Sheas***, (a few doors down) coming in a close second.

Nightclubs ***Tatou,*** 22 Cambridge Terr, T3843112, has 2 levels the upper with comfy sofas and more laid back jazz while downstairs is where all hell lets loose. This is where will end probably end up, emerging in a sorry state at dawn. The rather trendy ***Opera***, and less uptight ***Coyote St Bar***, both on Courtenay Pl, are 2 popular weekend venues with modern dance music, T3856665. ***Café Paradiso (Blue Room)*** , 32 Blair St, has weekend DJs and occasional bands, T3842675. ***Chicago*** on Queens Wharf has weekend bands and traditional dance music, T4734900. ***Barneys***, 60 Dixon St, is a laid-back non-trendy place that plays lots of 80's and has a loyal local clientele, T3848441. Other popular dance spots include The ***Judder Bar***, 1-21 Allen St, T3852438 and the trendy ***Planet***, corner of Courtenay Pl and Tory St, T3829747.

Shopping

Wellington is reputed to be a fine city for shopaholics who generally find no difficulty in getting the right fix in the main shopping areas of **Lampton Quay, Willis, Cuba** and **Courtenay Streets**. The VIC has a number of free shopping leaflets and the '*Wellington Shopping Guide*' is the bible of choice.

Lampton Quay is nicknamed 'The Golden Mile' which probably relates more to the quality and sheer variety as opposed to the type of credit card or subsequent state of the savings account, afterwards. The highlights on Lampton are the elegant boutique shops of the ***Old Bank*** and Wellington's answer to Harrods – ***Kirkaldie and Stains***. Here you can indulge, browse or simply try the expensive scents before re-emerging on the street like a mobile flowerbed. ***Sommerfields*** at 199 Lampton is a grand shop for New Zealand souvenir hunters while the major bookshops ***Dymocks*** (366) and ***Whitcoulls*** (312) are also based here. **Willis St** is well known for its sheer variety with a number of popular clothing stores including ***Starfish***, at 128 and ***River***, at 89 Victoria St. ***Unity Books*** at the far end of Willis St is also an excellent bookshop specializing in New Zealand titles.

As you might expect **Cuba St's** wide variety of cafés and restaurants are echoed in the nature of its shops. Whether it be 70's clothing, second-hand books, utter kitsch, a pair of skin-tight pink plastic pants or even an erotic device with batteries, this is where to go. It is always good fun to muse at the other shoppers even if you do not indulge yourself. **Courtenay Pl** is a little more upmarket than Cuba but still retains a wide variety. Shops to take a peek in here, include ***Bloomsbury***, 16 Majoribanks St for arts and crafts and the fine souvenir shop in the Te Papa museum. The ***Wellington Market*** nearby on the corner of Wakefield and Taranaki Sts, is open Fri/Sat/Sun from 1000-1730 is the city's main market and is worth a look.

Ferries to South Island

Interislander Timetable
Wellington to Picton
Depart: 0110 0500 0930 1300 1730*
Arrive: 0430 0800 1230 1600 2030
Picton to Wellington
Depart: 0510 0900 1330 1700 2130*
Arrive: 0830 1200 1630 2000 1230
*Prices (One-way) Adult $49, child $29 (4-14 years); Car $175**; Bikes $10*
** Tue-Sat only. Schedules and fares subject to change*
*** Excludes drivers and passengers*

Lynx Timetable
Wellington to Picton
Depart: 0800 1300
Arrive: 1015 1715
Picton to Wellington
Depart: 1130 1830
Arrive: 1345 2045
*Prices: Adult $63, child $37 (4-14 yrs); Car $199***
*** Excludes drivers and passengers*

Festivals It seems that Wellington is happy and proud to host more 'events' than any other town or city in New Zealand and there is always something going on. The Jazz festival and Festival of the Arts are particularly, and deservingly well celebrated.

Jan: ***Foster's Wellington Cup Week***. This is a major sporting and social event for the city and the region's high point on the annual racing calendar. Usually held in the last week of the month.

Feb/Mar: ***Wellington Fringe Festival***. An exciting month-long event that begins in the last week of February and celebrates and showcases contemporary and modern theatre, music and dance, T3845143. ***Wellington Dragon Boat Festival.*** Usually held towards the end of the month this paddle-fest attracts over 2000 competitors. ***New Zealand International Festival of the Arts***. This is a biennial event and Wellingtons most celebrated. It lasts for 3 weeks and is currently the country's largest cultural event with a rich and varied pageant of music performers, drama, street theatre, traditional Maori dance, modern dance and visual arts. T4730149. ***Tareitanga Sculpture Festival***. A 2-week event where up to fifty artists create an exciting range of works at Frank Kitts Park on the waterfront, T3886390.

Apr: ***The Laugh Festival***. A national comedy event open to local, national and international talent, T3099241.

Jul: ***Wellington Film Festival***. A showcase of nationally and internationally celebrated films, T3850162.

Oct: ***(Biennial) Wellington International Jazz Festival***. An increasingly popular and growing celebration of national and international jazz talent, www.jazzfestival.co.nz

Nov: ***'Devotion'***. Wellingtons answer to Auckland's famous 'Hero Parade'. A gay and lesbian event with dance, music and a street parade, T4725006

Transport

Getting to the South Island The scenic 85 km journey across Cook Strait takes about 3 hrs. In adverse weather conditions the crossing can be bit of an ordeal. Sailings will be cancelled if conditions are considered too dangerous. If you can, schedule your trip so it is daylight during the 1 hr scenic and memorable approach through the 'Sounds' to Picton. Also note that access outside on the *Lynx* is very limited, so photographers should go on the older vessels. Both the year-round *Interisland* and faster, summer-only *Lynz* services are operated by *Tranz Rail*. Pre-booking is advised at all times, but especially in Dec/Jan. Most major VICs and Travel Agents administer bookings and tickets. **Reservations**: *Tranz Rail*, Railway Station, Wellington, T44983000, F44983090, www.tranzrail.co.nz

The Interislander ferry schedule

There are 2 passenger ferries in the *Interislander* fleet. On board facilities include a range of bars, foodcourts, cafés, a movie theatre and a Visitor Information Centre. There is also a children's play area and nursery and private work desks, although negotiating a lap top on stormy seas, can in itself provide, much entertainment for fellow passengers. The slightly higher Club Class ticket will give you access to a private lounge, complimentary tea and coffee, magazines, newspapers and a slightly better class of sick bag. A free shuttle bus to the terminal is available from the Wellington Railway Station, 35 mins before each scheduled ferry departure. At the Picton end a free shuttle is available to the Railway station connecting Picton with Christchurch.

Various day/limited-excursion, family and group fares and standard discounted fares are available but must be booked in advance and are subject to availability. At peak periods (particularly Dec/Jan) discounts are rarely available and whatever the discount, they are offered mainly in winter and for night sailings. Best of New Zealand Pass and Travelpass New Zealand are accepted, and kids under the age of four travel free.

The Lynx Ferry

The *Lynx* is a fast ferry that operates daily Dec-Apr taking 2¼ hr to do the crossing. There is one vessel in the fleet. On board facilities include a café and bar. Various discounted fares are available subject to availability. Best of New Zealand Pass and Travelpass New Zealand applicable with small additional charge.

Directory

Banks Foreign Exchange: *Thomas Cook*, 358 Lampton Quay, T4722848; *American Express*, Cable Car Complex, 280-292 Lampton Quay, T4737766. **Car hire** At the airport, also: *Ace*, 150 Hutt Rd, T4711176; *Darn Cheap Rentals*, T5682777; *Pegasus*, 51 Martin Sq, T3844883; *Kiwi Car Rentals*, T0800-5494227. **Communications Internet**: is available at the VIC. Also: *Net Arena*, 115 Cuba St; *Cyber Nomad*, 43 Courtenay Pl; *Full Stop*, 117 Custom house Quay, 20 Victoria St; *Cyber Internet*, Shop 17, Oaks Complex, Dixon St. **Post office**: 101 and 284 Lampton Quay, 43 Manners St. **Cycle hire** *Pins Cycles*, 126 Willis St, T4724591; *Penny Farthing*, 89 Courtenay Pl, T3852279. **Embassies and consulates Australia**, 72 Hobson St,T4736411; **Canada**, 61 Molesworth St, T4739577; **France**, 42 Manners St, T3842555; **Germany**, 90 Hobson St, T4736063; **UK**, 44 Hill St, T4726049; **USA**, 29 Fitzherbert Terr, Thorndon, T4722068. **Library** Victoria St (Civic Sq). Mon-Fri 0930-2030, Sat/Sun 1300-1700. **Medical services** Wellington Hospital, Riddiford St, T3855999; A&E Centre(and After Hours Pharmacy), 17 Adelaide Rd, T3844944. **Taxis**: *Wellington Combined*, T0800-384444; *Capital City Cabs*, T3884884, *Black and Gold*, T3888888. **Useful addresses AA**: 352 Lampton Quay. **Police**: corner of Victoria and Harris St, T3824000.

The Hutt Valley

Population: 130,000

To the east of Wellington, sitting obstinately right on a major fault-line and already split by the Hutt River, are the fairly unremarkable Wellington dormitory towns of Lower and Upper Hutt, or 'Hutt City'. There isn't much on offer for the visitor, but if you can drag yourself away from Wellington or just happen to be passing, there are a few sights and activities that may appeal.

Ins & outs

The Upper Hutt **Visitors Information Centre** is at 6 Main Rd, Upper Hutt, T5272141, F5279818, www.upperhuttcity.com Daily 0900-1700. The Lower Hutt City **Visitor Information Centre** is in the Council Buildings, 30 Laing Rd. Open Mon-Fri 0800-1700.

Sights The main attractions in Lower Hutt are the Petone Settlers Museum and The Dowse Art Museum. The **Petone Settlers Museum**, which is located right on the waterfront, is quite a small affair but no less effective in adequately highlighting the early historical significance of the area. ■ *Tue–Fri 1200-1600, Sat/Sun 1300-1700. Free. T5688373*. The **Dowse Art Museum** in the Civic Centre, Laings Road is a nationally respected showcase of contemporary art and crafts. It also has a good café on-site (not an easy thing to find in Lower Hutt). ■ *Mon-Fri 1000-1600, Sat/Sun 1100-1700. Free. T5706500*. Another gallery of note is the **Konae Aronui Gallery**, 58 Gutherie Street, Waiwhetu, T5604630.

In Upper Hutt the principal attractions are the **Silverstream Railway Museum**, Reynold Bach Drive, Silverstream, which houses a large collection of steam locos, some of which operate on a short track. ■ *$5, child $3. T5637348.*While a bit of a trek but still worth it is the **Staglands Wildlife Reserve**, Akatarawa Road, which is another capable steward and advocate of native New Zealand wildlife conservation. ■ *Daily 1000-1700. $8, child $4. T5267529, www.staglands.co.nz* The **Kaitoke Regional Park** is a popular recreational spot and the Upper Hutt area also gives access to the **Akatarawa Forest** and **Rimutaka Forest Park** (camping available)

Activities & tours Activity operators based in Lower Hutt include *Top Adventures* and *Wet and Wild* (see Wellington) Excellent Maori Insight Tours can also be arranged with *Indigenous Aotearoa New Zealand*, T5604630, gra.owen@xtra.co.nz Upper Hutt is the home to *Mt Devine Horse Treks*, Russell's Road, T5289191 and the *H20Xtream aquatic adventure centre*, corner of Blenheim and Brown Streets, which has water slides, a wave machine and a wide range of water activities. Open daily, T5272113.

Kapiti Coast

Just north of Wellington SH1 slices its way through the hills of a major fault-line and passes the rather dull dormitory town of ***Porirua*** *before joining the picturesque Kapiti Coastline. For the next 30 km the small coast and inland settlements of* ***Paekakariki, Waikanae*** *and* ***Otaki****, are shadowed by* ***Kapiti Island****, on one side and the* ***Tararua Forest Park*** *on the other. Kapiti Island itself is well worth a visit while Paekakariki, Paraparaumu and Waikanae offer a number of interesting local sights and activities. Otaki is the principal access point to the Tararua Forest Park.*

Ins & outs Paekakariki, Paraparaumu, Waikanae and Otaki are all on SH1 and the main rail line. Both the main bus companies and trains stop at these centres. Note the regional trains to and from Paraparaumu run frequently day and evening services and are relatively cheap. For Information and times contact ***Ridewell***, T0800-8017000 or the VICs. ***Day-trippers Tours*** and ***Charters*** also run regular trips to and from Wellington and around, T2970161. ***Blue Penguin Coaches*** and ***Shuttles*** also run Wellington and airport services and may also be able to assist, T3646899.

Paekakariki

Population: 1600 Paekakariki is a tiny seaside village, popular with visiting **train** enthusiasts, as well as adrenaline junkies eager to experience the infamous **'Fly by Wire'**.

Sights

The first thing to do in Paekakariki is to take a quick diversion up to the **viewpoint** on Paekakariki Hill Road (3 km) and take in the view. From here on a clear day you can get a great view of Kapiti Island and see the coast stretching all the way up to Wanganui. At the village Railway Station is the **Steam Inc Engine Shed**, where enthusiasts have faithfully and painstakingly restored a number of vintage trains, some of which still huff and puff along the tracks, T3648986, $5. A few kilometres further north, almost literally along the same tracks is the **Wellington Tramway Museum** in Queen Elizabeth Park. Here, historical displays and working trams take a nostalgic look at one of Wellington's former modes of transport. ■ *Weekends 1100-1700, T2928361.*

Activities

'Fly by Wire' is very hard to describe and is indeed, the stuff of dreams, literally. It all came about after founder Neil Harrap had dreamt (one can only presume after way too many lagers) that he was attached to a flying machine with a microlight engine on the back. It went around and around and around, like a dangling weight on a plumbline. On waking, so intrigued was Mr Harrap that he wrote it all down. But it didn't stop there. To cut a long story short – after a phone call to a friend who is a pilot, hours of design, even more hours of building and more finding a suitable location the dream began to take shape. Last but not least, after convincing those highly sceptical characters in the government's health and safety department that you won't kill tourists, the dream became reality and 'Fly by Wire' was born. If you want to live Mr Harrap's dream you can do so in perfect safety at speeds of up to 120 km an hour for a budget-denting (but still worth it) $99, 15 minutes, plus video. 'Fly by Wire' is located behind the BP station on SH1 where a video of the action is running and where bookings can be made. For more information T4991212, www.flybywire.co.nz

Paraparaumu and Waikanae

Population: 29,000

Paraparaumu is the principal township on the Kapiti coast and has close ties with Wellington both as commuter town and as a seaside resort, popular during the summer months. There are two main beaches, Raumati to the south and Paraparaumu Beach to the north. All the usual facilities are here and the town also serves as the gateway to Kapiti Island. A little further north on SH1 is the small satellite town of Waikanae, which also prides itself on its fine beach. Paraparaumu's main claim to fame came in 2001 when the legendary golfer Tiger Woods was lured with a rather attractive NZ$4 million appearance fee to play (or simply to turn up) at the NZ Open golf challenge on Paraparaumu's world class golf course.

Ins & outs

The Paraparaumu **Visitor Information Centre** is just off SH1 in the Coastlands shopping centre, T2988195. Open Mon-Sat 0900-1600. The main **DOC** office for the Kapiti Coast is at 10 Parata St, Waikanae, T2932191.

Sights

Other than the beach, the main attractions are scattered along SH1 just to the north of Paraparaumu and around **Waikanae**. The **Lindale Centre** 2 km north of town is essentially a kitsch and coffee stop for coach tours, but there is a Farm Park for kids with daily shows ($7.50, child $4) and a number of retail outlets, including the shop attached to *Kapiti Cheeses*. Here a delicious and imaginative array of gourmet products are available to tickle the taste buds. There is also a café nearby that will attempt to do the same.

Just a little further north still on SH1 is the **Southward Car Museum** boasting a huge collection of 250 vehicles dating from 1895. In addition to cars there are traction engines, motorcycles, bicycles and a model railway. ■ *Daily 0900-1630. $5, child $2. T2971221.*

On the outskirts of the pleasant village of Waikanae 5 km north of Paraparaumu is the **Nga Manu Nature Reserve.** Although principally an educational establishment, this reserve, which is set in delightful bush, with man-made lakes, bush walks and collections of native and non-native wildlife, is definitely worth the detour. Everything is well presented and this is one of the few establishments in the country that are not ashamed to display (as highly effective educational tools), the 'enemy' – the heinous non-native pests. There is a wonderful (well-enclosed) display of rats, some possums and the less well advertised, but obligatory mallard ducks on the lawn, eyeing up your picnic. Added to the refreshing 'pest' displays are the usual collections of native birds, geckos, tuatara and a nocturnal kiwi house. Eel feeds take place at 1400. *Daily 1000-1700. $7.50, child $3.50. T2934131.*

The reserve is quite hard to find but signposted from SH1. Back in town the **Kapiti Coast Museum**, 9 Elizabeth Street, (just over the railway lines at the traffic lights on SH1) houses a collection of early radio, telephone, local and general historic collections. ■ *Open weekends 1400-1600 or phone for an appointment, T2932359.* At some point along the coast it is well worth taking at least a look at the beach. This can be done at a number of access points, one of which is **Te Horo Beach** just north of Waikanae. The coast is piled high with amazingly sculpted pieces of driftwood.

Activities **Four-wheel quad bikes** *Kapiti 4x4 Adventures*,T0800-368794, fourX4@man.quik.co.nz More trailblazing bike trips based near Paraparaumu. One-hour, all day and overnight trips. **Horse trekking** *Ferndale Equestrian Centre*, Waikanae, T2936209, bramber@xtra.co.nz Horse treks over farmland and along the beach. **Scenic flights** *Kapiti Aero Club*, Kapiti Road, T9026536.

Kapiti Island

Kapiti Island is a very special place, a place that is not only a delight to visit but is like going back in time. A time when New Zealand was an unspoiled paradise. Kapiti Island lies 5 km offshore from Paraparaumu and is 10 km long, 2 km wide, with a total land coverage of 1,965 ha. Its highest point is Tuteremoana at 520 m.The island is now one of the most important reserves in the country and has an adjunct marine reserve, all of which is administered, protected and nurtured by DOC. It took a huge budget and six years of hunting and poisoning in the 1980s to rid the island of 22,500 possums, while further exhaustive helicopter poison drops in the 90s have been successful in keeping rats at bay. After numerous plant and animal reintroductions the results are the first signs of regeneration and hints of what once was. Here you are in wildlife territory – not human. You can walk on a number of well-kept tracks through proper New Zealand bush. Inquisitive birds like robin, saddleback and stitchbird flit about your head, while weka and takahe poke about for insects disturbed by your feet. At night you can hear kiwi, or share the coastal path with little blue penguins that do not run in fear, but merely stick their heads in the grass and croak at you with their wee white bottoms sticking in the air. And at dawn, if you are very lucky, you can hear one of the most beautiful bird songs ever to grace human ears – that of the endangered kokako.

Ins & outs

All access and landing permits are administered and must be pre-booked with DOC. Only 50 people can land per day and bookings need to be made well in advance. Landing permits cost $9, child $4.50. Although there is a well-equipped hut, it is mainly used for research purposes and no overnight stays are allowed, unless through prior arrangement with DOC. For detailed information call DOC or consult the booklet/ leaflets 'Kapiti Island Nature Reserve', available from the main Wellington DOC Office, Old Government Buildings, Lampton Quay, Wellington. T4727356.

Private boats are not allowed to land on the island but 2 principal private operators can get you there for a day trip: ***Kapiti Marine Charter***, T2972585, $30, child $20 and ***Kapiti Tours Ltd***, T0800527484, T3645042, F3648820, kapiti_tours@clear.net.nz / www.kapititours.co.nz from $30, child $20. Boats depart from Paraparaumu Beach in front of the Kapiti Boating Club at 0900-0930 and return 1500-1600. Sea Kayaking trips are also available with ***Tamarillo***,T02-52441616, www.tamarillo.co.nz $125. For sleeping and eating in Paraparaumu see below.

Otaki

Population: 5600
Phone code: 06

Otaki is the last (or first) settlement within the Wellington Regional Boundary. Steeped in Maori history there are a number of *marae* including the 1910, finely carved **Te Pou O Tainui Marae** on Te Rauparaha Street. The **Rangaitea Church** in the town was one of the finest restored Maori churches in the country. Sadly fire destroyed the church in 1995 and another restoration is planned. Otaki is the main eastern gateway to the **Tararua Forest Park**. Otaki Gorge Road, which is 2 km to the south of the town, takes you 19 km to **Otaki Forks** where a number of tracks lead in to the mountains. Information about the Tararua Forest Park, local sights and accommodation options can be obtained from the Kapiti Coast **Visitors Information Centre** which is located in Centennial Park, SH1, In the heart of the village, T3647620. Open Mon-Fri 0830-1700, Sat/Sun 0900-1500.

Activities The *Tararua Outdoor Recreation Centre* on Otaki Gorge Road, hosts a range of activities including kayaking, mountain biking and rafting. They were also the originators of 'night rafting' the novel idea of removing the 'see the rapids actually coming' factor. T3643110, TORC@xtra.co.nz From $30.

Sleeping

AL ***Te Horo Luxury Lodge***, 109 Arcus Rd, Te Horo, T3643393, tehoro.lodge@xtra.co.nz Luxuriously appointed homestay in the country and near the driftwood beach. Open fire and no shortage of wood. **AL** ***Te Nikau***, Kakariki Grove, Waikanae, T3568460, F3568460. Contemporary house with wooden interior set in coastal forest, 2 spacious doubles, spa and pool.

A ***Killara Homestay***, Ames St, Paekakariki, T2928242, www.killarahomestay.co.nz 2 rooms in a large comfortable beachfront villa. **A** ***Byron's Resort***, 20 Tasman St, Otaki, T3648121, F3648123. Quality motel units with all resort amenities including, pool, spa and sports facilities. **A** ***Copperfield Seaside Motel***, 13 Seaview Rd, Paraparaumu Beach, T2986414, F2988044. New motel with licensed restaurant 2 mins walk from the beach. **A** ***Sand Castle***, Paetawa Rd (off Peka Rd) Peka Peka, Waikanae, T2936072, F2933926. A delightful and aptly named motel right next to the beach.

C-D ***Paekakariki Backpackers***, 11 Wellington Rd, Paekakariki, T2928749. Very pleasant, comfortable wee place set on the hillside above the village. **C-D** ***Lindale Motor Park***, Main Rd North (SH1), Paraparaumu, T2988046. Ideally located next to all Lindale Tourist centre amenities. **C-D** ***Paekakariki Holiday Park***, Wellington Rd, Paekakariki, T2928292. This offers above average accommodation and amenities close to the beach. **C-D** ***Toad Hall***, Addington Rd, Otaki, T3646906. Amazing renovated homestead complete with cuddly cats and crafty canines.

D ***Ngatiawa Campsite***, Terrace Rd, Waikanae, T2935036. A lovely quiet campsite with cabins set in bush next to the Ngatiawa stream.

Eating From south to north the ***Fisherman's Table Restaurant and Bar***, SH1 in Paekakariki is a relaxed family seafood restaurant, T2928125. At the Lindale Tourist Centre just north of Paraparaumu the ***Aqua Vitae Wine Bar and Restaurant***, serves New Zealand and international style cuisine in congenial surroundings, T2989889. Further north in Waikanae the ***Country Life Restaurant*** on SH1 provides à la carte dining as well as daytime snacks and weekend brunches, T2936353, as does the quaint and award-winning ***Rumours Café***, SH1, T2934564. Near the beach in Waikanae the Breakers Restaurant, 1 Waimea Rd is another pleasant seafood venue, T2935711. In Otaki the best bet is the ***Brown Sugar Café***, corner of SH1 and Riverbank Rd., with lots of delicious home cooking in a garden setting, T3646359.

South Island

South Island

13 Nelson and Marlborough

Nelson and Marlborough

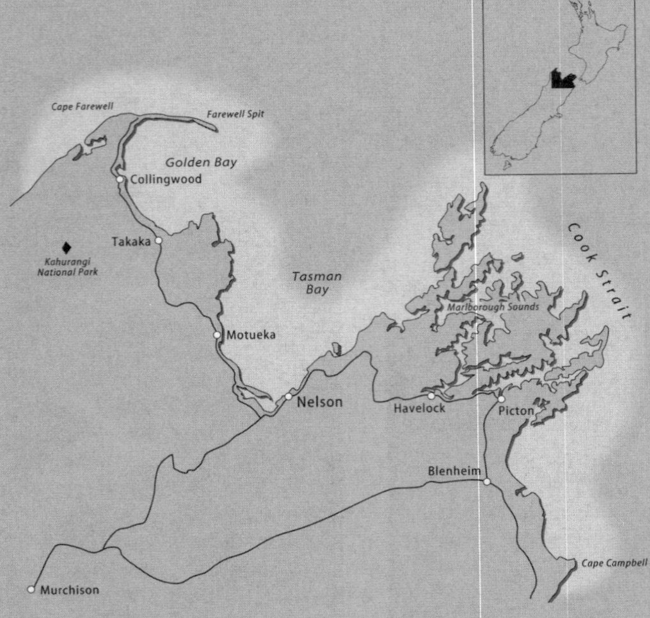

The regions of Nelson and Marlborough have all the classic New Zealand ingredients – mountains, lakes, golden beaches and great tramping tracks – all safe within the boundaries of its national parks and warmed by the sunniest climate in the country. If that weren't enough, it also has a relatively low population.

Those who do live here are a diverse bunch: from the farmers, fruit-growers and wine-makers in the valleys, to the artists and writers in the quiet creative havens of the Marlborough Sounds and smaller rural towns, like Motueka orTakaka. Despite the appealing lifestyle and obvious attractions, few have heard of this 'secret region'. Most travellers simply pass through on their way to the tourist honey pots further south, stopping only briefly in Picton, the main ferry port on South Island.

Things to do in Nelson and Marlborough

- *Explore the Marlborough Sounds by boat, kayak, or on foot.*
- *Take the back roads to the remote French Pass.*
- *Sample the world class wines of the Marlborough vineyards, and join the locals in a rain dance!*
- *Enjoy the buzz of seaside Nelson, the most popular coastal town in New Zealand.*
- *Walk the Coastal Track of The Abel Tasman National Park.*
- *See all three National Parks and the Marlborough Sounds in one day on a scenic flight from Nelson.*
- *Relax in arty Takaka, Golden Bay, and visit the crystal clear waters of its local Pupu Springs.*
- *Spend a day walking the spectacular coast from Cape Farewell to Wharariki Beach.*
- *Experience the strange and lonely sandscapes of Farewell Spit.*

Ins and Outs

Getting there For many, the Nelson and Marlborough Region, and the port of Picton in particular, is their first introduction South Island. It is arrival and departure point for the main car and passenger **ferries** from North Island (see page 402). SH1 resumes its route south from Picton via Blenheim, to Kiakoura, Christchurch and beyond. SH6 from Blenheim is the main route to Nelson, the Nelson Lakes National Park and ultimately, the West Coast. From Nelson SH60 heads northwest to Motueka, the Abel Tasman and Kahurangi National Parks, Takaka and Golden Bay. The main north/south railway hugs the East Coast of the region, with the 'TranzCoastal' running a daily service between Picton and Christchurch, stopping in Blenheim and Kaikoura on the way. Nelson and Blenheim are the principal **airports** in the region, but you can also fly from Wellington direct to Picton.

Getting around Generally the region is well serviced with public transport, with numerous bus and shuttle companies operating from the main centres. If you plan to venture out to the Marlborough Sounds this can be done relatively easily on the water with numerous water shuttles and taxis operating from Picton and Havelock. If you plan to do so by road, bear in mind that the roads are long, windy and mostly unsealed, so allow plenty of time.

Information The principal VICs in the region are in Picton, Blenheim, Nelson and Kaikoura. There are also major DOC offices in Nelson and Blenheim and DOC Field Centres in each National Park. For Ferry and train information contact the VICs or Tranzrail direct (T04-4983000 F4983090), www.tranzrail.co.nz

The Marlborough Sounds

The Marlborough Sounds is like South Island's giant foyer. This vast, convoluted system of drowned river valleys, peninsulas and islets, often dubbed New Zealand's 'little slice of Norway', is the island's scenic introduction, where you can enjoy stunning scenery, cruising, tramping, kayaking, wildlife watching or merely a few days of peaceful relaxation. The port of Picton is the gateway to The Sounds. From here it is then only a short journey to ***Blenheim*** *the region's capital. Although the town itself is fairly unremarkable, the area produces some of the best wines in New Zealand. A day visiting a few of the top* ***vineyards*** *is recommended. South of Blenheim is the pretty coastal settlement of Kaikoura, famous for its* *whale watching. Given its relative isolation on the coast and closer proximity to Christchurch, Kaikoura has been placed in the Canterbury chapter.*

On the map, it may look like the Marlborough Sounds take up a relatively small area of the South Island, but its myriad sounds (drowned river valleys as opposed to fjords, which are drowned glacial valleys) create an astonishing 1500 km of coastline. Although the endless inlets and bays are not bounded by the snow-capped peaks of Norway, the topography is just as intriguing and picturesque. Wildlife abounds and the area is particularly well known for its seabirds and dolphins. The two main inlets are the **Queen Charlotte** *and* **Pelorus Sounds***, the former being plied several times daily by the inter-island ferry between North and South Islands. The two principal towns are the port of Picton, at the head of the Queen Charlotte Sound, and Havelock at the head of the Pelorus.*

History

The Sounds exhibit evidence of Maori settlement from as early as the 14th century, but the most famous early historic association was with Captain James Cook, who visited the Sounds on each of his three voyages in 1770, 1773-4 and again in 1777. He was particularly fond of Ship Cove near the mouth of Queen Charlotte Sound, which he visited five times. A monument in Ship Cove commemorates his visits. As you might expect, Cook is responsible for many place names in the area.

Other, more brief and less celebrated visitations by other early explorers included that of Abel Tasman (before Cook) and French navigator Jules Dumont d'Urville in 1827. It was D'Urville who discovered the chaotic and incredibly narrow passage of water between the mainland and the D'Urville Island (no prize for guessing where the name came from), which guards the northwestern corner of the Sounds. He called this strait French Pass, or Passe des Français, and it remains as much of a threat to shipping today as it did to the early navigators. In the same year as D'Urville's visit, London whaler, John Guard, established Marlborough's first European settlement, and the countries first land-based whaling station, at Te Awaiti Bay, on Arapawa Island in the Tory Channel. Guard went on to explore and name Pelorus Sound in search of other sites that were suitable for settlement. Apart from the whaling stations and some early attempts at farming, the area, due to its topography, remained sparsely populated keeping much of its native bush intact. Sadly, much of that bush has now gone, giving way to the ubiquitous sheep.

Activities

Most activities are obviously based around cruising, tramping (see page 418) or kayaking, with the odd bit of dolphin and bird spotting thrown in. The VIC in Picton has a comprehensive list of activities which are cleverly listed by time of day, not operator, and well worth a look. They can also advise on horse trekking, winery tours, diving, tandem paragliding, scenic flights (from Picton airfield), fishing and independent boat charters.

Cruises

There are endless bays, coves and islands to explore in the Sounds, with a rich variety of wildlife including dolphins and rare seabirds. As you might expect, there is a mind-boggling range of cruise options available with fiercely competitive operators. Most are based on The Waterfront in Picton. It's a good idea to check at the VIC before parting with your cash.

Beachcomber Cruises, The Waterfront, Picton, T0800-624526, offer two popular half-day 'Mail Boat' cruises: the Pelorus Mailboat departs Tuesday/Thursday/Friday from Havelock at 0930 and Picton at 1015, returning mid-late afternoon, it takes in many mail stops and a mussel farm or two on the way, from $90; the Magic Mail Run explores the Queen Charlotte Sound, including a stop at Ship Cove and a salmon farm. It departs Picton Monday-Saturday at 1330, and returns at 1730; $58. Also on offer is a two-hour 'Round the Bays' cruise that takes in a number of Queen Charlotte Sound bays, including Double Cove where you stop briefly to feed tame fish. It departs daily at 1015 and 1415; from $35. Another is a six-hour luncheon cruise to the Portage Resort Hotel and Torea Bay, departing daily at 1015. A one-day 'Freedom Walk' (8 km) taking in part of the Queen Charlotte Track from Torea Bay, departs at 1015 daily (from $30), or 'Anakiwa Walk' (12 km), departing at 1015 (from $30).

The Cougar Line, also based on the Waterfront, T0800-504090, offer a similar series of cruises. The most popular is the day trip to Ship Cove where you have the option of a five-hour bush walk to Furneaux Lodge where you are picked up later in the afternoon. It departs at 0800 (from $43). Various short cruises are also on offer taking in up to 80 km of coastline in three hours with an informative commentary on the way. These depart at 1000 and 1330 (from $20). Cougar also offer a luncheon cruise to the Punga Cove Resort that leaves at 1000 (from $43 plus lunch) and a three hour-twilight tour that departs at 1800 (from $43).

The Marlborough Sounds

Both *Endeavour Express*, T5798465, based at the Waterfront, and *West Bay Water Transport*, T/F5735597, offer a similar range of options with a trip to the Motuara Island Bird Sanctuary being a speciality; it departs at 1030 (from $45). *Beachcomber Cruises* offer a similar package. *The Sounds Connection*, T0800-742866, also offer a flexible water taxi service.

Day walks

Most of the water-based operators offer a range of half/full-day walking trips. Two of the most trips are the **Ship Cove to Furneaux Lodge** (with *Endeavour Express* and *Cougar*, from $43) which takes in the Captain Cook monument and some lovely native bush and views. The other is the Eco-based trip to the **Motuara Island Bird Sanctuary** (with *Beachcomber Cruises* and *Endeavour Express*, from $48). The VIC or individual operators can advise. Cougar have the best boats and tend to offer the most modern, comfortable service, but competition is fierce.

Eco-Tours

Dolphin Watch Marlborough are based next to the VIC, T5738040, www.dolphinwatchmarlborough.co.nz They offer a range of trips from four hours including an excellent jaunt to the Motuara Island bird sanctuary (departing 0845/1345, from $60) or a Birdwatchers Special (departing 0845, from $60). The Sounds are not only home to seals and dolphins but also some rare birdlife such as the king shag (found only in the Sounds), New Zealand robins, little blue penguins and saddlebacks. Many of the land-based birds on the island are typically fearless and will constantly check your route for disturbed insects. Note that *Sea Safaris*, based in French Pass, also offer some superb, flexible wildlife trips, T/F5765204, www.info.SeaSafaris.co.nz (see page 432).

Sea Kayaking

Most travellers save their NZ kayaking experience for the Abel Tasman National Park, the most famous sea-kayaking venue in the country. However, Abel Tasman is now getting very crowded in summer and the idea of having a beautiful golden bay to yourself is a near impossibility. What the Sounds can offer that the Abel Tasman often cannot is almost guaranteed shelter and relative peace and quiet. Also note that Abel Tasman has about 50 km of coastline, whereas the Sounds have 1500!

The principal operator in Picton is the *Marlborough Sounds Adventure Company* on the Waterfront, T0800-283283. msac@msadventure.co.nz They offer a wide range of excellent trips from a few hours, (including a twilight trip), a four-day paddle/walk, to six days specialist itineraries. Prices range from one-day independent rental $50 (one day guided $85) to four-day guided paddle/walk $845. They are a highly professional company and very safe. Mountain bike hire also available. Other companies in the area include: *Sea Kayaking Adventure Tours*, based in Anakiwa, one-day trips and independent hire from $40, T/F5742765; and *The Sea Kayaking Wilderness Company*, Havelock Youth Hostel, T5742610, www.soundswild.com Trips from $75.

Self-drive

If you are pushed for time or want an alternative method of exploring the Sounds you can do so in part by road. Note however that the roads throughout the Sounds are tortuous, mostly unsealed and not entirely suitable for campervans, or indeed sightseeing. The popular Queen Charlotte Drive is a scenic 35 km drive from Picton to Havelock taking in a number of sheltered bays, campsites and viewpoints on the way. From Linkwater it is possible to then traverse the ridge between Queen Charlotte and Kenepuru Sounds by road (close to the route of the Queen Charlotte Track) before the road joins the main landmass of the Sounds. The intrepid explorer can reach the outermost bays from this road and combine some walking on parts of the Queen Charlotte Track, including the most popular day walk – the Endeavour Inlet to Ship Cove Track. On a clear day the half-day walk to the summit of Mount Stokes (the highest point in the Sounds) is recommended for the view. Campsites are available at Mistletoe Bay, Cowshed Bay, Punga Cove (Endeavour Inlet) and at Titirangi Bay. Note that some accommodation establishments are also accessible by road, including Punga Cove, The Portage, Te Mahia, St Omer House and Raetihi Lodge (see page 419).

For another fine and remote exploratory drive in to the Sounds see the French Pass section, page 432.

Tramping in the Sounds

Although most of what the Sounds has to offer can be accessed by boat it is possible to explore much of it on foot. There are two popular **tramping** tracks, the **Queen Charlotte Track** and the **Nydia Track** (see Havelock section).

The Queen Charlotte Track

The track itself is well maintained and is also open in part to mountain bikes (see leaflet from VIC, $1)

The Queen Charlotte Track is a 67 km, three- to- five-day tramp that winds its way along the peninsula from Anakiwa at the head of the Queen Charlotte Sound, to **Ship Cove** (the historic site of Cook's landings) near its mouth. The track passes through coastal forest, negotiates a number of historic and picturesque bays and traverses ridges with memorable coastal views. Note that in recent years, in summer and autumn, the track has been subject to total fire bans and even closed, such is the risk. The track is also becoming increasingly popular, so you are advised to plan and book well in advance. There are numerous DOC campsites and independent accommodation establishments to suit a range of budgets all along the route.

Boat access is also well organized and readily available. Given the ease of water access it is considered best to tackle the route from east to west, from Ship Cove to Anakiwa. Water taxis and cruise operators regularly stop, not only at Ship Cove, but many of the accommodation establishments or campsites en route so it is possible to do part of the track, or to stay in one place and simply chill out. Details of the Queen Charlotte Track are outlined in the relevant DOC leaflets and both the VIC and DOC in Picton can provide more comprehensive information and maps.

The *Marlborough Sounds Adventure Company* based in Picton (see previous page) offer guided walks (three-day, $600/ four-day $845) and self-guided walks (four-day, including food, transport and accommodation, $410). They also offer kayaking trips and an increasingly popular three-day walk/paddle/mountain bike adventure which is recommended. *Action in Marlborough*, based in Blenheim, also offer a range of guided one- to four-day walks throughout the region including the Queen Charlotte and Nydia tracks. From $799 (four day, all-inclusive), T/F5784531. Note that you can also do part of the track by kayak (see previous page) or as an organized walk (see below).

You are advised to book your movements around the Sounds

Getting there There are plenty of water-based operators who will drop off or pick up from a number of points along the track, with most offering day-walk options. Sea access is possible at Ship Cove, Resolution Bay, Endeavour Inlet, Camp Bay (Punga Cove), Bay of Many Coves, Torea Bay (the Portage), Lochmara Bay, Mistletoe Bay (Te Mahia) and Anakiwa. ***The Cougar Line***, based on the Waterfront in Picton is the most modern and comfortable, T5737925. They will drop you off at Ship Cove (departs Picton 0800/1330, $48) and pick up at Anakiwa (Tirimoana, 1430/1645). They can also deliver your pack to your accommodation and offer day-walk options (see below). ***Endeavour Express***, based in both Endeavour inlet and at the Waterfront in Picton, T5798465, offer the same service, departing Picton 0900/1030/1345, $45 and picking up Anakiwa (Tirimoana) 1600/1715. ***Beachcomber Cruises***, based in Picton have both scheduled trips to Torea and Anakiwa ($45) but will run drop off or pick up at any of the accessible points, T0800-624526. They depart Picton 0930 and pick up Anakiwa 1600, $45. Free tea and coffee. ***West Bay Water Transport***, based near the Ferry Terminal in Picton, serve the southern end of the Queen Charlotte Track, from Torea Bay to Anakiwa (single $15). They also offer half-day, track-walk options ($30), T5735597. ***Arrow Water Taxis***, also based in Picton, offer flexibility and will go on demand anywhere in Queen Charlotte Sound or Tory Channel for about the same price, T5738226 A typical single fare to Anakiwa is $15.

There are also options by road from Picton to Anakiwa. ***Sounds Connection***, T0800-742866 (minimum 4, $50), and ***The Rural Mail Run***, from $10, are 2 such options. Both must be booked and pre-paid via the VIC. If you have your own wheels road access is also possible at Camp Bay (Punga Cove), Torea Bay (The Portage) and Mistletoe Bay (Te Mahia).

Nydia Track

Details of the track are outlined in the relevant DOC leaflets and both the VIC and DoC office in Picton or Havelock can provide more comprehensive information and maps

The Nydia Track is the lesser-known and shorter of the two tramping tracks. It is 27 km in length and takes two days. The track, which is essentially a network of old bridal paths, begins at Kaiuma Bay (near Havelock) and traverses the Kaiuma and Nydia saddles, taking in the sheltered, historic timber-milling site at Nydia Bay, before ending at Duncan Bay. The track is particularly noted for its magnificent forest, much of which is untouched and a fine example of the native bush that once covered the region. Although the Nydia Track is more difficult than the Queen Charlotte and requires detailed planning and logistics, it offers a shorter, less busy alternative, though it is not so well-served by accommodation and public transport. From Havelock it is 12 km drive via SH6 to the turn-off at Dalton's Rd, then another 21 km to Kaiuma car park and the start of the track. Alternatively you can catch a water-taxi to Shag Point, from Havelock, T5729108.

Sleeping There are **DOC campsites** ($5) available in the northwestern corner of Nydia Bay: two in Tennyson Inlet and one in Duncan Bay. The DOC's **D *Nydia Lodge*** on the south coast of Nydia Bay sleeps 50, T5203002 while **C-D** Driftwood Cottage, a small backpackers, which is also in Nydia Bay is another option, T5798454.

Essentials

Sleeping & eating

The Queen Charlotte Track is well serviced with accommodation options with a broad range from DOC campsites ($5), to privately owned backpackers, self-contained units and luxury lodges. The VIC has full listings and will help you plan your itinerary and book your accommodation, but in summer you are advised to do this well in advance. There are also ample accommodation options elsewhere throughout The Sounds with most offering meals and some having in-house restaurants or at the very least adequate cooking facilities. Some can be reached by water taxi, others by road, or even by air. Again the VIC will advise. Some of the more noteworthy establishments are listed below.

L-AL *Raetihi Lodge*, Kenepuru Sound, T5734300, F5734323, www.raetihi.co.nz An excellent establishment and the most modern in the luxury bracket, offering some of the best accommodation in the sounds. 14 themed en-suite rooms, stunning views, licensed restaurant (à la carte from $50). **L-C *Punga Cove Resort***, Punga Cove, Endeavour Inlet, T0800-809697, www.pungacove.co.nz Wide range of options from private chalets, self-contained studios to rooms in the lodge. Facilities and services includes a licensed restaurant, shop, laundry, spa and canoe hire. **L-D** ***Pohuenui Island Sheep Station***, Pohuenui Island, T5978161. A place that comes recommended and The Sounds at its best. Remote seclusion on a working farm. Full board or bunkroom. Join in the work and feel a million miles from civilization.

AL-D ***Portage Hotel***, Kenepuru Sound, T/F5734309. A wide range of accommodation from spa rooms to bunkrooms. Shop and DOC campsite nearby and kayak and bike hire.

A-D ***Furneaux Lodge***, Endeavour Inlet, T/F5798259. Historic lodge set in idyllic gardens near a waterfall. Self-contained chalets and backpacker accommodation in a lovely stone 'croft'. Campsite available. Restaurant and bar. Ideal for a night stopover from Ship Cove. **A** ***Kamahi Lodge***, Resolution Bay, T/F5799415. Popular friendly homestay. Dinner available on request. Activities arranged. **A-D** ***Lochmara Lodge (Backpackers)***, Lochmara Bay, T/F5734554. Another popular backpackers with a great, laid-back atmosphere. Dorm and private studio chalets – if you can remove yourself from a hammock. Spa (in the bush!), open fire, free kayak, windsurfer hire, tea and coffee. **A-D** ***Resolution Bay Cabins***, Resolution Bay, T5799411. Accommodation ranges from cabins to self-contained cottages. Nice atmosphere and fine cuisine. **A-D** ***St Omer House***, Kenepuru Sound, T5734086. Historic villa with rooms (some shared), units, self-contained cottages, powered sites. Lovely setting with a private beach only yards away. Meals available. **A-D** ***Te Mahia Bay Resort***, Kenepuru Sound, T/F5734089, www.temahia.co.nz Popular new and old self-contained accommodation and backpackers. Store but no bar or restaurant.

C-D ***Smiths Farm Holiday Park***, Queen Charlotte Drive, Linkwater, T/F5742806. Tent and powered sites and cabins close to the track start at Anakiwa. **C-D** ***The Lazy Fish Guesthouse***, Queen Charlotte Sound, T/F5799049, www.lazyfish.co.nz A superb budget option only accessible by boat (or plane) about 12 km from Picton. Its motto is *'Ubi Dies Omnis Festus'* ('where every day is Sunday') and it is an apt description. It is a renovated, beautifully appointed homestead only a few metres from the water, with a range of rooms or cabins set in bush. There is spa, excellent kitchen facilities and windsurfer/canoe/fishing tackle hire. Recommended. **D** ***DOC campsites*** are available at Ship Cove, Camp Bay, Bay of Many Coves, Black Rock, Cowshed, Mistletoe Bay and Davies Bay.

Picton

Phone Code: 03
Population: 4000

Once you cross the Cook Strait and enter the 'The Sounds', you arrive in the pretty township of Picton, gateway to the The Marlborough Sounds and South Island. In summer Picton is a buzz of activity with visitors coming and going by ferry, car or train, but in winter it reverts to its more familiar role as a sleepy port.

Despite its size, Picton has had an interesting history. It was once an important Maori pa-site called Waitohi before the first Europeans settled and renamed it named Newton. For a while Newton was the proud capital of Marlborough (before Blenheim stole the honours) and later, after being renamed Picton, became a candidate for the country's capital. In more recent times there has been controversy. For almost a decade there has been the hotly debated issue of relocating the ferry port south, closer to Blenheim. Thankfully for 'the Picts' that option has just been dismissed by the government, who claim it is not financially viable. So, thankfully, as the gateway to both the South Island and the Sounds, pretty Picton looks set to remain.

Ins and Outs

Getting there

Picton is 27 km from Blenheim and 336 km from Christchurch south via SH1

By air Picton airfield is about 10 km south of the town and is serviced by ***Soundsair***, T0800-505005 from Wellington; $50 one-way and includes a free shuttle to town. Scenic flights are also available with Picton Air, T5738018.

By bus There are numerous bus companies that network their way south, or west, from Picton. The principal operators are ***Intercity***, T3195641 (Nelson, Blenheim, Kaikoura and Christchurch); ***Atomic Shuttles***, T3228883 (throughout South Island); ***Delux Travel Line***, T5785467 (Blenheim and beyond). Other smaller companies offering a range of options include: ***Southern Link Shuttles***, T3588355 (Christchurch and beyond); ***Knightline***, T5474733; ***East Coast Express***, T0508830900; ***Kiwilink***, T0800-802300; ***Kahurangi Bus***, T5259434 (via Blenheim to Nelson, Abel Tasman); ***Abel Tasman Coachlines***, T5480285; ***Sounds to Coast***, T0800-802225 (Greymouth via Blenheim and the Nelson Lakes National Park); and ***Alpine Coaches***, T0800-274888 (also to the West Coast, via Blenheim). A typical fare to Blenheim is $15, Nelson $30 and Christchurch $40. Buses all drop-off or pick-up at the Railway Station, Ferry Terminal or outside the VIC. For further details contact the VIC.

By ferry The *Interislander* ferries and *Lynx* dock in the rather plush terminal, about 500 m from the town centre. There are at least four sailings daily. For information on these sailings and prices see page 402, or contact T0800-802802.

By train The daily 'TranzCoastal' is the only daily train service to and from Christchurch and Picton, T0800-802802. It arrives daily at 0050 and departs at 1340, from $54. This trip is famous for its stunning coastal scenery.

Getting around

There are lots of **car hire** companies based just outside the ferry terminal, with a few others on High Street in the centre of town. These include: ***Rent-A-Dent***, T5737787; ***Ace***, T0800-422373; ***Apex***, T0800-422744; ***Pegasus***, T0800-803580 and ***Budget***, T5736081. The local taxi company is ***Blenheim taxis***, T0800-802225. ***The Sounds Connection***, T0800-742866 (located on the Waterfront) also rent out nifty scooters from $20 per hr.

Information

The Picton **Visitor Information Centre** is on the Foreshore, T5737477, F5735021, www.marlborough.co.nz Open daily 0830-2000 (1700 winter). Only a short walk from the ferry terminal. Very busy but staffed accordingly. Internet is available .There are many useful leaflets on offer including the invaluable '*What to Do In Picton*' and very useful '*The Queen Charlotte Track*'. **DOC** has an office in the same building an sell a range of books and maps on the region. The railway station (and ferry terminal) provides comprehensive information about train and ferry departures and prices. Open 0900-1700, T5738857.

Sights

The Edwin Fox

If you have arrived on the almost futuristic *Lynx* Ferry, with its comfy seats and state of the art radar screens, you will be immediately thanking your lucky stars for progress, when you encounter the old teak wooden hulk of the Edwin Fox. Located between the ferry terminal and the town centre, the remains of the 1853, once fully-rigged, East India trading ship is being lovingly restored to something of her former glory by the Edwin Fox Society. The vessel, which is the only remaining example of her type in the world, was formerly a troop carrier in the Crimean War before being commissioned to bring immigrants to both Australia and New Zealand. The interesting displays in the museum extend in to the impressive hulk of the ship. One thing is for sure – they don't make nails like they used to! ■ *Open 0845-1700 daily. $5*

Just a little further on London Quay, commanding prime position overlooking the Waterfront, is the **Picton Community Museum** lovingly maintained by the Picton Historical Society. It contains a cluttered but interesting range of items focussing mainly on the 1800s whaling operations in the Sounds (including an evil-looking harpoon gun), as well as the inevitable Maori *taonga* (treasures) and early pioneer settler pieces. ■ *Open 1000-1600 daily. $3, child $0.50.*

A short walk across the footbridge and the inlet to the eastern side of the Waterfront to Shakespeare Bay will deliver you to the **Echo Gallery and Museum**. The Echo is a former 'scow' built in 1905 that has now been lovingly and gradually restored after her retiral in 1965. She was formerly a trading vessel, apparently, the last commercial trader under sail in New Zealand before seeing further service in Second World War. There is no doubt that she has led an interesting, if not rather unfortunate existence. Indeed she is perhaps the most unfortunate vessel to sail the high seas. By all accounts she was stranded 15 times, damaged 16 times, had two engines, new propellers and shafts, had fires in 1911 and 1920, seven collisions involving 75 different vessels and was sunk twice. Be careful not to trip going up the gangplank. ■ *Open daily in summer. Adult $3, child $1.*

Walks around Picton

For the numerous activities based in Picton see page 415

For a comprehensive guide to the walks around Picton get hold of the excellent '*Picton by Foot*' broadsheet, available free from the VIC. There are a number of options, with most traversing the narrow peninsula to the northeast of the town separating Waikawa Bay and Picton Harbour. Most are around two hours return, with the longest being the **Snout Track**, taking in the **Queen Charlotte Lookout**. Other walks taking in fine views are the **Karaka Point Lookout** (20 minutes, located on the main road east of Waiwaka) and the **Tirohanga Walk Lookout**, above and south of the town (start point off Newgate St just east of the town centre, two hours return).

Essentials

Sleeping

There are few modern hotels but plenty of motels to choose from

AL *Waikawa Bay Seafront Apartments*, 45 Beach Rd, T5735220. A new establishment located beside the Waikawa Bay marina complex, east of Picton. Since its creation it has been receiving good reviews and offers luxury self-contained apartments, pool, spa, and café/restaurant/bar nearby. **A** *The Jasmine Court*, 78 Wellington St, T5737110, www.jasminecourt.co.nz Is one of the best, most luxurious motels offering a fine range of well appointed, modern units. Well located. **A** *Americano Motor Inn*, 32 High St, T0800104104, www.americano.co.nz Located in the heart of town this is a large, modern motel with a licensed restaurant attached. **A** *St Catherine's B&B*, 123 Wellington St, T/F5738580. A very relaxing historic former convent, great views from the balcony and a crazy dog called 'Wappo'. **A-B** *The Gables*, 20 Waikawa Rd, T5736772. Enjoys a good reputation, being spacious, well-appointed and ideally located. **A-B** *Picton Homestay*, 2 Canterbury St, T0800-274286. A modern, friendly and good value homestay, in a quiet location. Courtesy car.

B-C *Cottage International*, 25 Gravesend Pl, T/F5737935. A good value no-nonsense B&B-cum-backpackers 5 mins walk from the town centre. **B** *The Harbour View*, 30 Waikawa Rd, T5736259, has 12 fully self-contained studio units with fine views across the harbour. **B** *Tourist Court Motel*, 45 High St, T/F5736331. One of the better, well established budget motels, located near the town centre.

C-D *Sequoia Lodge Backpackers*, 3A Nelson Sq, T/F5738399, stay@sequoialodge.co.nz Although located about 500 m from the town centre and 1 km from the ferry terminal, this is an excellent hostel run by an enthusiastic manager.

Modern, recently renovated facilities with secure parking. Range of dorm and private single, twin and double rooms, some en-suite. Log fire, free tea and coffee and great home-made bread. Free pick-up/drop-off to ferry. Internet **C-D** ***The Villa***, 34 Auckland St, T/F5736598, www.thevilla.co.nz A deservingly popular, well-established and lively backpackers in a century old villa. Dorms, twins and doubles. Fine facilities and a great outdoor area with spa. The managers are a hive of information on local activities and can assist with plans and bookings. Free 'all you can eat' breakfast, tea, coffee, duvets, bike hire and shuttle service. Internet. Pre-booking advisable. **C-D** ***Picton Lodge***, 9 Auckland St, T5737788, picton.lodge@xtra.co.nz The closest hostel to the ferry terminal and close to the VIC and town centre, pub next-door. Singles, doubles/twins and small dorms. Large open plan living area. Free breakfast, blankets and bike hire. **C-D** ***Bayview Backpackers***, 318 Waikawa Rd, T/F5737668, bayview.backpackers@xtra.co.nz This is modern, friendly and rapidly expanding place in Waikawa Bay just east of Picton. Good value dorm beds, single/twin and double rooms. It offers the peace and quiet the bustling hostels in the town centre do not. Free pick-up/drop-off to the ferry. Free bikes, kayaks and sailing trips arranged. Internet.

Motorcamps **C-D** ***Blue Anchor Top Ten Holiday Park***, 78 Waikawa Rd, T0800-277444. This is an excellent award-winning holiday park and subsequently very popular. It is well located within walking distance from town, has tidy cabins and tourist flats and great facilities. Another large, but older less salubrious holiday park, the **C-D** ***Parklands Marina Holiday Park***, T/F5736343 which is located on Beach Rd, Waikawa, close to the marina.

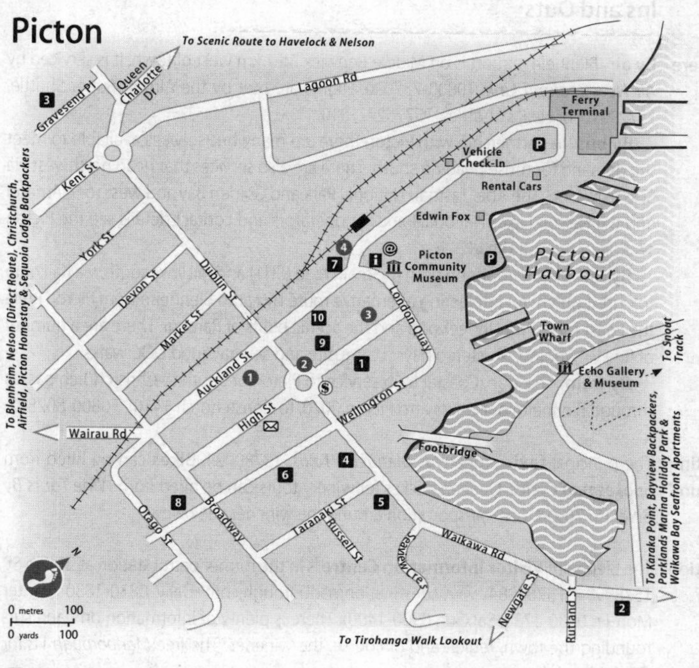

Sleeping
1 Americano Motor Inn
2 Blue Anchor Top Ten Holiday Park
3 Cottage International
4 Gables
5 Harbour View
6 Jasmine Court
7 Picton Lodge
8 St Catherines B & B
9 Tourist Court Motel
10 Villa

Eating
1 Expresso House
2 Holty's
3 Marlborough Terranean
4 Toot & Whistle

Eating The *Marlborough Terranean*, 31 High St, T5737122, is a popular little place and considered one of the best restaurants in the region. It has a nice atmosphere and offers both a European and Mediterranean-style menu. Good wine list with Marlborough wines a speciality. Open daily from 1800. ***Holty's***, 58 High St, T5738823, is another reliable venue with a café style menu specialising in gourmet pizza. Open daily 0900-2200. The best pub grub and beer can be found in the ***Toot and Whistle***, T5736086 located on Auckland St, near the ferry terminal. It's open from 0900 till late daily and can be a lively place, that has seen no doubt seen its fair share of clients miss the ferry! One of the best cafes in town is the ***Expresso House***, 58 Auckland St, T5737112. Fine coffee and great value, imaginative lunch and dinner menu. Open daily (except Wed) in season from 1100-late (Thu-Tue in winter).

Blenheim

Phone Code: 03
Population: 25,000

*Although it is depressingly flat and unremarkable looking, Blenheim – Marlborough's largest town – is a popular tourist base, primarily for those intent on sampling the region's fine wines. Most of the **wineries** lie just to the west of town, on the fertile soils of the **Wairau Plains**. In Blenheim you can be sure a local winemaker will never be far away. Wine making in Marlborough is big business and fiercely competitive and brings new meaning to the phrase 'designer label'.*

Ins and Outs

Getting there **By air** Blenheim airport is on Middle Renwick Rd 7 km west of town. It is serviced by *Air New Zealand Link*, T0800-737000. Flights are met by the Airport Super Shuttle, T5729910, or Neal's Shuttles, T5775277; $10.

By bus In partnership with Picton there are many bus services available to meet the demand for those heading south. There are also services that head northwest via SH6 to Nelson, The Abel Tasman National Park and Golden Bay and west to St Arnaud and the Nelson Lakes National Park. For operators and contact details see the Picton section or consult the VIC.

By car Blenheim sits on both the main road (SH1) and rail links south, via Kaikoura to Christchurch. An interesting alternative route by car to Blenheim from Picton is via the coast road, Port Underwood and the scenic bluffs of Rarangi. There are a number of fine viewpoints, sheltered bays a campsite and several good DOC walks.

By train The TranzCoastal train service to Picton or South to Christchurch passes through Blenheim once a day (to Picton 0020, to Christchurch 1410), T0800-802802.

Getting around The principal **taxi** company is *Blenheim Taxis*, T5780224. **Bikes** can be hired from *Spokesman Cycles*, Queen St. Bikes for winery tours can be hired from *Wine Tours By Bike*, T5776954. For Transportation around the wineries see below.

Information The Blenheim **Visitor Information Centre** is in the former petrol station at 2 High St, T5789904, F5786084, www.destinationmarlborough.com Daily 0830-1830 (winter Mon-Fri 0830-1730; Sat/Sun 0900-1400). There is plenty of information on hand surrounding the town, region and of course, the wineries. The free *Marlborough Visitor Guide* is useful.

Climate One of the rarest sights you will see in Blenheim is an umbrella. The Marlborough Region and the Blenheim area especially, have suffered in recent years from a severe lack of rain. Whether this pattern continues and how much it will affect wine growing in the area remains to be seen, but in the meantime slap on the sunscreen buy a hat and enjoy.

Sights and activities

Being primarily a service town, Blenheim has little in itself to offer the tourist in the way of sights, with most visitors simply joining the various winery tours based in town, or picking up the information to tour the vineyards themselves. However, of some historical interest is the provincial museum and archives complex at The **Brayshaw Museum Park**, New Renwick Road, 3 km south of the town. The museum is a mainly open-air affair, featuring an interesting reconstruction of an early settler's village along with the inevitable farm machinery and ancient vehicles. ■ *Open Sat 1000-1600, Sun 1000-1300. $2.* Also of some note back in town is **Pollard Park**, Parker Street – a pretty conglomerate of flowerbeds, ponds and rose gardens. Right in the centre of town is **Seymour Square** with its landmark clock tower. If you are interested in **arts and crafts** the free '*Art and Craft Trail*' leaflet from the VIC is an excellent guide.

Activities

Though rain appears to be in short supply recently, **rafting** on the Buller and Clarence River (recommended) can be exciting and *Action in Marlborough*, T/F5784531 will accommodate with half to multi-day trips from $70. The wilderness of the Marlborough backcountry and the remote Molesworth Station (New Zealand's largest cattle station) can be explored with *BackCountry Safaris*, T/F5757525. One to two-day excursions from $170. There are some fine **walking** venues in the region particularly around the Richmond Ranges, the Withers Farm Park and on the coast road, via Rarangi, to Picton. The ascent of **Mount Richmond** (1760 m) with its memorable views is recommended. For self-guided trips consult DOC or the VIC for their free leaflets. Several reputable operators offer specialist guided walking trips, including *Ramshead*, T5724016, www.ramshead.co.nz, offering good value one- to four-day options from $20. For **horse trekking** contact *High Country Horse Treks*, Ardnadam, Taylor's Pass Road, Redwood Village, T/F5779424, 2 ½ hours from $50. Finally, if you fancy a trip along the Opawa River on a small floating BBQ and bar, contact the very entertaining *Marlborough Riverboat Company*, T5757209, 1 ½ hours for $25 (BBQ only $10 extra).

The Wineries

The best time to visit the vineyards is in Apr when the heavily laden vines are ripe for the picking

The biggest attractions around Blenheim – and arguably the entire region – are the world-class wineries. Sun-baked Marlborough is New Zealand's largest wine-growing region, with over 50 wineries producing highly acclaimed Chardonnay, Riesling, Cabernet Sauvignon, Merlot, Pinot Noir, sparkling Methode Champenoise and some of best Sauvignon Blanc in the world. Montana sowed the first seeds of success in the early 1970s and is now the largest winery in the country. Three decades on, Montana has been joined by many other world famous names and is a major national export industry.

Like the Hawkes Bay in the North Island the wineries have been quick to take advantage of the tourist dollar, with most offering tours, **tastings** (free or small charge) and good **restaurants**. Although the competition in Marlborough is fierce the region's vineyards lack the architectural splendour or variety of Hawkes Bay. Perhaps they just leave the wine to do the talking.

If you are a complete novice you are advised to join one of the many excellent **tours** on offer. They tend to last a full, or half-day, taking in the pick of the crop and the widest variety of wine types. There is always an informative commentary on offer, very often a lunch stop, too and, of course, numerous tastings included in the package. If you know a bit about wines and have particular tastes, many tour operators will create a personal itinerary. If you wish to simply explore by yourself, there are plenty of maps and leaflets available at the VIC.

Most of the wineries are located off SH6 around the small village of **Renwick**, 10 km west of Blenheim. Should you get sick of all the wine, or pompous 'wine-speak', there are other distilleries, breweries, vineyards and orchards in the area, producing everything from liqueurs and fruit wines to olive oil. There is even a brewery producing its own beer at *The Cork and Keg*, an English style pub and brewery on Inkerman Street in Renwick. Add to this the many fine eating establishments and there is no doubt your visit to the area can get very expensive.

Information

Most wineries and some tour operators will organize shipping

Some excellent and detailed information about the region and New Zealand wines generally can be found in the magazine *'Campbell's Wine Annual'* which can be bought in most leading bookshops and magazine outlets. The VIC also produce *'The Wines and Wineries of Marlborough – Wine Trail Map'* and *'The Marlborough Wine Region'* broadsheet. With all of these you cannot go wrong so much as sozzled.

A comprehensive list of the wineries is beyond the scope of this guide, but some wineries of particular note are listed below.

Brancott Winery, Main South Rd, T5782099, www.montanawines.com On the main road (SH1) just to the south of Blenheim, it is almost rude not to visit this, the largest wine-producer in the country. The new visitor centre is very impressive and there are half-hourly tours, tastings, a restaurant with outdoor seating and a classy shop. This is also the venue for the now world-famous ***Marlborough Food and Wine Festival*** held in Feb. Open 0900-1700.

Hunters Wines, Rapaura Rd, T5728489. Another of the larger, most popular labels producing a wide variety of wines. Also home to a fine restaurant open for lunch (1100-1430) and dinner (from 1800). ***Allan Scott Estate***, Jacksons Road, T5729054, www.allanscott.com Established in 1973, producing fine Sauvignon, Chardonnay and Riesling wines. Popular '***Twelve Trees Restaurant***'. Open all day. ***Cloudy Bay***, Jackson's Road, T5728914. An internationally famous label. Tastings and tours daily 1000-1630.

Cellier Le Brun, Terrace Rd, Renwick, T5728859, www.lebrun.co.nz Offer a little contrast as the producer of fine Methode Champenoise. Café on site. Open daily 0900-1700. ***Johanneshof Cellars***, SH1 Koromiko, T5737035. 20 km north of Blenheim. Famous for underground 'rockcellars', lined with both barrel and bottle. Summer Tue-Sun 1000-1600. ***Seresin***, Bedford Rd, Renwick, T5729408, www.seresin.co.nz Noted not only for its wine, but also is artwork. Summer daily 1000-1630, winter Mon-Fri 1000-1630

Highfield Estate, Brookby Rd, T5728592, www.highfield.co.nz Fine wine, architecture and the best view of the lot, from its rampart tower. Reputable indoor/outdoor restaurant. Open daily 0900-1700. ***Prenzel Distillery***, Sheffield St, Riverlands Estate, T5782800. New Zealand's first commercial fruit distillery producing a range of products including fruit liqueurs, schnapps, and brandies. One of contrast to visit at the beginning of your days tasting!

Tours

There are a broad range of tours and many operators available all of whom will look after you every whim. Some offer more formal scheduled trips, while others can design a trip around your personal tastes. Others take in arts and crafts and garden visits. You can even go by bicycle.

Delux Travel Line, T0800-500511, www.deluxtravel.co.nz Marlborough's original Wine Trail Tour taking in Montana, Forrest, Hunters and Preznel. Tastings included, meal extra. Available from Picton and Marlborough. Departs daily, Picton 0945,

Blenheim 1025. From $40. ***Highlight Tours***, T5779046. Both full or half-day, morning and afternoon tours. Flexibility with venues (including craft and garden venues) and lunch (additional cost) included. From $40. ***Marlborough Wine Tours***, T/F5757525. Personalized tour of up to eight wineries. Flexible itinerary depending on taste. UK wine delivery service. ***Sounds Connection***, T5738843, www.soundsconnection.co.nz Scheduled and private half to full-day tours. Based in Picton. From $45. ***Marlborough Travel Centre Winery Tours***, T5779997, www.marlboroughtravel.co.nz Daily half or full-day tour packages including lunch. ***Wine-Tours-By-Bike***, T5776954, www.winetoursbybike.co.nz This is the new and delightfully common sense method of visiting the wineries – by bike. The great attraction here is the slow pace and the greater bombardment of the senses only felt on a bike. The drawback

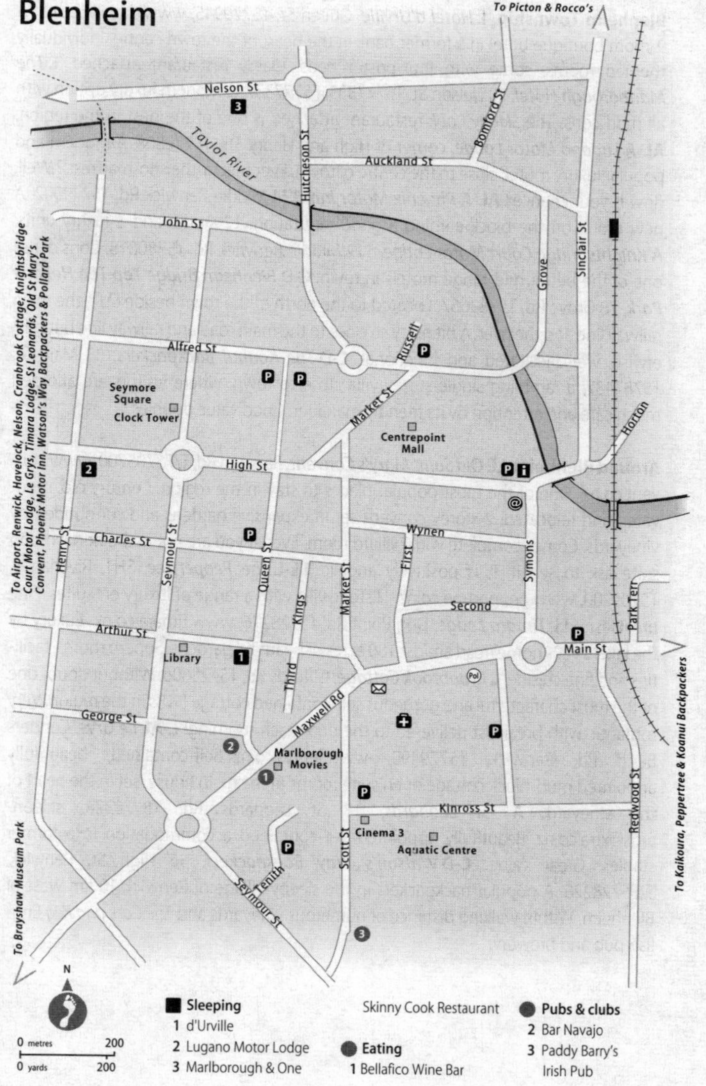

obviously is the steady deterioration of those senses as the day wears on and the ability to pedal in any direction after ten glasses of wine. You can join a guided tour or hire your own bikes.

Essentials

Sleeping There are no shortage of beds in Blenheim with hotels, motels and backpackers. The emphasis however is on the many excellent boutique style lodges, B&Bs and homestays outwith the town and often in the vineyards. The VIC has comprehensive listings and can book on your behalf. During the picking season (Apr/May) you are advised to pre-book backpackers in the region.

Blenheim Township **L** ***Hotel d'Urville***, Queen St, T5779945, www.durville.co.nz A 9-room boutique hotel in a former bank in the heart of the town centre. Individually themed rooms, some with four-poster beds. Classy restaurant attached. **L** ***The Marlborough Hotel***, 20 Nelson St, T5777333, F5777337. A modern luxury option with all mod cons. The *Skinny Cook* restaurant attached is one of the best in the region. **AL-A** ***Lugano Motor Lodge***, corner of High and Henry Sts, T5778808. A modern and popular luxury motel, close to the centre of town. Ever tried a 'thermo-mattress'? Well, now is your chance? **AL-A** ***Phoenix Motor Inn***, 174 Middle Renwick Rd, T5779002. A new motel on the block earning a good reputation. 12 studio and 3 luxury units. **A** ***Knightsbridge Court Motor Lodge***, 112 Middle Renwick Rd, T5780818. Considered one of the better mid-range motels in town. **C-D** ***Blenheim Bridge Top Ten Holiday Park***, 78 Grove Rd, T5783667. Located to the north of the town beside SH1, the main railway line and the river. A bit noisy so close to the main road and railway line but otherwise, well facilitated and functional. **C-D** ***The Koanui Backpackers***, 33 Main St, T5787487, a rambling single-storey villa close to town, where visitors are afforded much care and attention by its friendly manager. Good value doubles.

Around Blenheim **LL** ***Old Saint Mary's Convent***, Rapaura Rd, T/F5705700, www.convent.co.nz One of the most popular places to stay in the region. Century old, renovated and relocated, 2-storey convent set in expansive gardens and surrounded by vineyards. Comes complete with billiard room. Even if you are not in the honeymoon suite ask to see it, it is positively angelic. **LL-L** ***The Peppertree***, SH1, Riverlands, T5209200, www.peppertree.co.nz Historic villa with a range of luxury en-suites. Fine breakfast. **LL** ***Timara Lodge***, Dog Point Rd, T5728276, www.timara.co.nz Luxury by the lake! 1920s homestead amidst 180 acres of beautiful gardens. Superb rooms, facilities and fine cuisine. **L** ***Cranbrook Cottage***, Giffords Rd, T5728606. Without doubt one of the most characterful and gorgeous self-contained cottage B&Bs in the region. Very romantic with breakfast delivered to the door each morning! **L-AL** ***Le Grys***, Conders Bend Rd, Renwick, T5729490, www.legrys.co.nz Self-contained, beautifully appointed mud-block cottage or en suite rooms in the main house, set in the heart of the vineyard. **A** ***St Leonards***, 18 St Leonards Rd, T5778328, st.leonards@xtra.co.nz Beautifully appointed self-contained accommodation in a former stables. Great value. **C-D** ***Watson's Way Backpackers***, 56 High St, Renwick, T/F5728228. A popular backpackers in the sleepy village of Renwick 10 km west of Blenheim. Within walking distance of numerous vineyards and *The Cork and Keg* English pub and brewery.

Eating

With the influence of the wineries and the many gourmet travellers, the choice and quality are excellent

For fine dining in Blenheim, the ***Hotel d'Urville***, 52 Queen St, T5779945 (0600-midnight) and the ***One Skinny Cook*** at the Marlborough Hotel, 20 Nelson St, T5779821, are recommended. For mid-range try ***Rocco's***, 5 Dodson St, T5786940 (evenings only), a fine Italian restaurant, or the European offerings of the ***Bellafico Wine Bar***, 17 Maxwell Rd, T5776072 (open Mon 0930-1630/ Tue-Sat 0930 until late). For good pub grub ***Paddy Barry's Irish Pub***, 51 Scott St, or ***Bar Navajo*** on Queen St. Some of the larger wineries have fine restaurants or cafés offering indoor/outdoor seating and lunch and/or dinner. Some of the best can be found at ***Hunters*** (T5728489), ***Allan Scott*** (T5729054), ***Montana*** (T5782099), ***Cairnbrae*** (T5727018), ***Highfield*** (T5728592), ***Cellier le Brun*** (T5728859) and ***Wairau River Wines*** (T5729800).

For fine café-style cuisine heading south, ***The Store***, at Kekerengu (halfway between Blenheim and Kaikoura), is recommended, with crayfish a speciality! Open 0700-late, T5758600.

Entertainment and Events

The Marlborough Centre, Arthur St, is the region's principal entertainment venue with a variety of shows, exhibitions and performances on offer throughout the year. T5782009

Most of the Blenheim and Marlborough events obviously revolve around fine wines and food. The principal event of the year is the now, world-famous ***Marlborough Wine Festival***. Held on the second Sat in **Feb** it is a lively (and very alcoholic) celebration of the region's gourmet food and wines. Live music provided. For more information T5778977. Also of note, in the first week **Feb**, is the ***Blues, Brews and Barbecues*** annual festival. This is the breweries answer to their wine-making neighbours, whereby tents are raised and all kinds of ales dismantled, to accompanying live entertainment. There is even alcoholic lemonade. T5789457. The ***Bubbles and Balloons*** is a hot air ballooning festival held over Marlborough in **Jun**, T5778935. Where the bubbles come in to it we can only imagine! For further information on other annual events and specific dates contact the VIC or look up the regional website www.destinationmarlborough@xtra.co.nz

Directory

Communications **Internet** is available at *Internet Direct*, 15 High St, near the VIC. Open Mon-Fri 0830-1700, Sat 0930-1230.

Havelock

Phone Code: 03
Population: 500

From Blenheim SH6 passes through the small village of Renwick, before winding its way through the rolling hills of the Inner Marlborough Sounds to Nelson. About a third of the way (40 km), at the head of the expansive Pelorus Sound, is the enchanting little village of Havelock. Blink and you will miss it, but if you have time, a stop here is well worth it.

Ins & outs

Getting there Havelock is 41 km from Blenheim and 75 km from Nelson on SH6.***Intercity, Newmans, Kiwilink*** (T0800-802300) and ***Knightline*** (T5474733) all service Havelock (Main Rd) on their way back and forth to Nelson.

Information There are two independent visitor centres in the main street vying for tourist's attention. The first is ***Pelorus Enterprises***, 60 Main Rd, where Mandy and Sandy will take good care of you. Daily 0830-1800, T5742633, pelorusinfo@xtra.co.nz The other is the **Outdoor Centre**, 65A Main Rd, open daily 0830-2000 (1700 in winter) T5742114. They are also a booking agent for many activities in the area and hold most of the DoC information. Bike hire is also available. Internet is available in the Outdoor Centre and the YHA.

The village itself has little to offer except a friendly welcome, a fine café, restaurant, art and craft galleries, some rugby playing mussel shells (honest), a small museum and a fine Scottish pub, but it is an ideal base from which to explore the glorious Pelorus and other 'outer sounds'. As the quiet neighbour to the much-hyped Queen Charlotte Sound, the Pelorus does not receive as much attention, but it is no less impressive and, in summer, provides a much quieter alternative. Although you may find it hard to believe, Havelock was once, a thriving gold-mining town and also the boyhood home of one of New Zealand's most famous sons, Ernest Rutherford – the man 'who split the atom'. His former home is now the busy Youth Hostel. Havelock was also the latter-day home of another famous New Zealander, the writer Barry Crump. 'Crumpy', as he was affectionately known, was the archetypal 'kiwi bloke' whose humorous accounts of hunting and life in the bush has kept many a proud kiwi smiling in recognition. These days Havelock's gold is the green-lipped mussel, without doubt the finest-tasting thing in a shell and a major export industry within the Sounds.

Sights & Activities

Most of what Havelock has to offer and almost all of its services will be found on Main Road or down at the harbour, which is a short walk from centre of the village. The small but interesting Havelock **Museum** is on Main Road. ■ *Daily (seasonal) 0900-1700. Donation. T5742176.*

Pelorus Sound can be explored by boat or by road. There are numerous opportunities to get on the water from scheduled **cruises** to charter boats and kayak trips. The Mail Boat Run operated by *Beachcomber Cruises* is popular and leaves Havelock at 0930 on Tuesdays, Thursdays and Fridays, costing from $90, child free. It delivers supplies and mail to a number of the isolated settlements and visits one of the many **mussel farms** before returning at about 1730. If you fancy something more sedate '*Classic Cruises*' and '*The Mussel Farm Cruise*' on board the 40-ft kauri launch 'MV Mavis', are two other popular trips based in Havelock. Both take in the beautiful scenery of the Sounds will give you an insight in to how the famous mussels are bred and harvested. It leaves from the harbour at 1030 and again at 1330, costing from $45, T5742114. Note that **water-taxis** are available from Havelock and you can be flexible with your intentions and itinerary. The Outdoors Centre can help you plan and book. There are also **fishing** and **diving** charters available. If **sea kayaking** is your thing or you would like to try it, the Sounds provide excellent opportunities. Several companies can oblige including the *Havelock Kayaking Company*, T/F 5742114, sightsounds@hotmail.com (Havelock); *Marlborough Sounds Wilderness Company*, T5742610 (Havelock YHA); *Sea Kayaking Adventure Tours*, T/F5742765 (Anakiwa); and *Explore Pelorus Sea Kayaks*, T5480726 (Nelson). Trips are half to multi-day from $70 and independent hire is also available.

If you intend to explore the Sounds **by road** you can do this along the Kenepuru Road, which starts just past Linkwater (east of Havelock on Queen Charlotte Drive), or the Tennyson Inlet and French Pass roads, just north of Rai valley, west of Havelock (see below). Maps are available at the Picton or Havelock VICs. If neither water nor road appeal you can of course explore from the saddle with *Marlborough Sounds Horse Treks*, T5742534. And if you want to find your fortune, you can try your luck at **gold panning** for $35. Contact the Outdoors Centre, T5742114.

Walks

Havelock is the principal base from which to embark on the increasingly popular **Nydia Track** (see page 419). Both the Outdoors Centre and the YHA can advise. *Havelock Water-taxis*, T5729108 and *Wilderness Express*, T0800-990800 can help with transportation. About 18 km west of Havelock is the **Pelorus Bridge Scenic Reserve**. This is a pretty little spot where the azure waters of the Rai and Pelorus Rivers carve their way through the surrounding bush-clad hills. There are a number of walks from 30 minutes to 3 hours. A

Let's split

New Zealand's most eminent scientist, Ernest Rutherford, is best known for being the first person to split the atom. He was born at Spring Grove near Nelson in 1876 and after being awarded several scholarships, graduated with a Bachelor of Arts at the age of 17, and a Bachelor of Science two years later. By the age of 22 he was a professor at McGill University in Montreal and was already deeply involved in research surrounding radioactivity. Within a decade he had discovered the natural transmutation of elements, the development of techniques that allowed the radioactive dating of geological samples and also made the first deduction of the nuclear model of the atom. All this brought him to world prominence and was to earn him several prestigious awards, including the Nobel Prize for chemistry in 1908 and a knighthood in 1914. But despite all this his best work was yet to come, and at the end of the first World war he conducted an experiment which split the atom – something that would have far reaching consequences for mankind. Rutherford died in Cambridge, England at the age of 61.

number of DOC information boards or the tearooms near the car park will keep you right. At the very least stop and have a look at the river from the bridge.

Closer to Havelock itself is the climb to **Takorika Hill**. Located behind the town its ascent will be rewarded by fine views. The lazy, or pushed-for-time can reach the transmission tower by car via forest tracks (6 km). The entrance via Wilsons Rd is about 5 km west of Havelock on SH6.

Sleeping

There is little in the way of accommodation in Havelock itself with most being out in the Sounds

B ***Havelock Garden Motel***, 71 Main St, T5742387, www.gardenmotels.com Pleasant motel set in large gardens close to all amenities. **C-D** ***Rutherford YHA***, 46 Main Road, T5742104. Spacious YHA, the former home of world famous scientist Ernest Rutherford, run by a caring relative. Double, twin and bunks. Camping available. Internet. **C-D** ***Chill Inn***, Queen Charlotte Dr, T5741299, thechillinn@hotmail.com A new backpackers deserving of growing popularity. Dorms, twins and doubles. Relaxed atmosphere and nice setting. **C-D** ***Havelock Motor Camp***, 24 Inglis St, T5742339. Powered/tent sites and cabins close to the harbour.There is also a **C-D** *DOC campsite* with cabins and powered sites, T5716019

Eating

A stay in Havelock would not be complete without sampling the green-lipped mussels at the award-winning ***Mussel Boys Restaurant***, 73 Main Rd, T5742824 (open daily all day). Likewise a coffee or breakfast at the ***Darling Dill Café***, corner of Main Rd and Neil St, T5742824, or a pint and some fine pub grub in the ***Clansman Scots Pub***, Main Rd is recommended. There is also a fine Deli across the road from the Clansman, the ***Greenmarket***, T5742311, with a range of hard to find items including prime smoked salmon.

Tennyson Inlet, French Pass and D'Urville Island

The Ronga and Opouri Roads which connect the remote corners of the Outer Sounds are well worthy of investigation, offering some stunning coastal scenery of a type that is unsurpassed elsewhere in the country. Both roads can be accessed just beyond the small settlement of Rai Valley 48 km east of Nelson and 27 km west of Havelock. To explore both roads properly you should stock up with food and petrol and give yourself at least two days: one to take in Opouri Road and **Tennyson Inlet** (40 km), then back to Ronga Road to **French Pass** (70 km); and the second (or more) to spend some time in French

Pass before returning to SH6. From French Pass it is also possible to explore the most remote and largest of the Sounds islands – **D'Urville Island** – named after the intrepid French Explorer who first discovered and named it in 1827.

Getting there If you do not have your own transport you can join *Back Roads Transport* on their mail run to French Pass from Rai (Tue and Thu), T5765251.

Tennyson Inlet About 1 km from SH6 Opouri Road shadows the Opouri River and cuts through paddock upon paddock full of sleepy stock lying in the shade of sheds that have seen better days. Then it suddenly and dramatically straddles **Lookout Hill** (900 m) before falling like a stone to Tennyson Inlet. The view at the crest of the hill is almost as impressive as the hairpin bends which must be negotiated to reach the Inlet. But once there, the peace and tranquillity seems reward enough. If you are feeling energetic you might like to walk part of the **Nydia Track** to **Nydia Bay** where there is camping and accommodation available (see page 419).

French Pass Back on Ronga Road, the route cuts through the paddocks of a river valley before climbing through attractive native bush to reach the first stunning views of Croisilles Harbour and out to the west coast of D'Urville Island. The first settlement of any consequence is **Okiwi Bay**, a secret little haunt of many a 'boatie Nelsonite'. Okiwi provides a great base from which to go sailing or fishing in the quiet, undisturbed bays of the Sounds westernmost coastline. The *Okiwi Bay Holiday Park*, T5765006 has a small lodge, powered and tent sites and a small store.

Just past Okiwi Bay the road passes through some beautiful tracts of beech forest before becoming unsealed. It is another 40 km to French Pass but after just a few kilometres the views of the Sounds really open up and the damage to your hire car will be the last thing on your mind. From **Elaine Bay** the road clings precariously to bush-clad ridges giving you an occasional glimpse of the scenic splendour, before the trees peter out and D'Urville Island hoves into view. You then head steadily along the western side of the now bare ridge to French Pass. On the way take the short detour to the top of the hill with the transmitters. From there you can soak up another stunning vista of Tennyson Inlet.

French Pass is really nothing more than a row of houses and a DOC campsite in a small sheltered bay at the very tip of the mainland. French Pass takes its name from the nautical nightmare that is just around the corner. The best view of this alarmingly slim channel of water can be seen from a path that leads down to a viewing point from the road (about 1 km before the settlement). At anytime, but particularly mid-tide, the chaotic currents can be seen forcing their way between the mainland and D'Urville Island. First discovered by D'Urville in 1827, this passage is a very important point on the nautical map because it offers an enticing short cut between Wellington and Nelson. If you are lucky you can time your visit to coincide with the passage of a ship. Some are so large you swear they will never make it and you can almost shout hello to the captain on the bridge, wave, and then tell him to watch where he is going.

French Pass is not only famous for its scenery, pass or shipping. Without doubt the most famous sight and resident was Pelorus Jack (see previous page).

Pelorus Jack

The name of Pelorus Jack has been synonymous with the Marlborough Sounds, and particularly French Pass, for over a century. The tale relates not to some old pirate or explorer, but to a famous dolphin that paved the way to the concept of legal protection for all sea mammals.

The Marlborough Sounds, and the route from Wellington to Nelson, via the treacherous waters of French Pass, were regularly negotiated by trading and passenger vessels. By the turn of the 19th century, the antics of a particular dolphin – Jack as he was christened by the local fishermen – were becoming legendary. Almost every vessel that appeared over the horizon, east of French Pass, would be escorted to the entrance by Jack, who then disappeared, only to reappear in readiness to escort the next. Jack was a large Risso's Dolphin, a rare species which are not the classic 'dolphin' size, shape or colour, having a bumpy forehead and very pale skin. Before long, people from all over New Zealand were making the trip just to see the 'mysterious creature'. News quickly spread and through word of mouth, letters, postcards and newspaper articles 'Jack' began to gain notoriety around the world. Not all the stories of the day got the details right, however. One article even said he was protected by an Act of Parliament. This particular piece of misinformation inspired a junior clerk in the Government Weather Office to lobby for Jack's official protection. After much lobbying and personal determination by the junior clerk, an official act of parliament – the first of its kind protecting any sea mammal – was passed in September 1904 and as a result it became illegal to hunt or harm Jack or any of his kind in New Zealand waters. This made him even more famous and his sightings were listed in the social columns of the national papers. Visiting celebrities like Mark Twain took the Nelson voyage especially to see him and seafarers the world over gave a special toast at gatherings in respect and honour of his protection and guidance. 25 years after his first 'official' documented sighting, in the spring of 1912, Jack mysteriously disappeared. Although at the time, there was national outrage and a subsequent and unsuccessful witchhunt to find his 'killer', it is now known that he died of old age. Theories abound to explain his strange behaviour, but it is the Maori who have perhaps the best explanation. To them the dolphin (or 'Tahu-rangi') is said to be a 'taniwha' – or a spirit sent by the gods to be our guide and helper. Because he is a spirit he can never die and has, for the last century been resting in his ocean cave between spells of duty. And there are stories of the appearance of a dolphin when boats have been in peril or have been lost in the Sounds. So keep an eye out. Pelorus Jack may still be out there.

Sleeping

There are a number of places to stay and a surprising amount of activities based in or around French Pass

A-B *French Pass Motels and Sea Safaris*, T/F5765204, www.seasafaris.co.nz Here residents Danny and Lynn Bolton have created the main focus for activity operations in the area and have combined that with some delightful motel come backpacker accommodation. The trips they offer are flexible, half to multi-day ventures that can include diving, fishing, walking, or wildlife watching, with dolphins a regular sight. Many rare seabirds can also be seen on the trips. Audio-visual presentations and commentary provided. *Sea Safaris* also offer a water-taxi service to the remote D'Urville Island and the *D'Urville Island Wilderness Resort* (see below). Overall this operation is very friendly and professional and has the refreshing edge of placing conservation and promotion of the unique environment with utilisation and access. Bookings are essential. Recommended **A-B** *D'Urville Wilderness Resort*, T/F5765268, enquiries@Durvilleisland.co.nz It doesn't get much more remote than this! Comfortable accommodation and a waterfront café accessible only by boat. Ideal for that total getaway experience or for exploring D'Urville Island. **A-B** *Nagio Bay Homestead*, T/F5765287. Idyllic B&B with its own private beach, located on the western side of the peninsula. Homegrown, organic produce a speciality. **B-C** ***Anaru Homestead***, T5765260. Large homestead offering budget singles and four doubles. Fishing charters available. **D** ***DoC Campsite French Pass***. Small and basic but not surprisingly, popular. The *D'Urville Wilderness Resort* is the only place to eat. Other than that, there's a small store and a petrol station.

Nelson and around

Phone Code: 03
Population: 50,000

Nelson is known as the sunniest place in the country, though this label could apply to its atmosphere, its people and its surroundings, for as well as its Mediterranean climate, Nelson has a great deal going for it. It is lively and modern, yet steeped in history. Surrounding it, all within 100 km, are some of the most beautiful coastal scenery and beaches in New Zealand, not to mention three diverse and stunning National Parks, where you can experience some of the most exciting tramping tracks in South Island, plus a host of other activities. Little wonder that Nelson is one of the top holiday destinations in the country as well being considered the best place to live in New Zealand.

Ins and Outs

Getting there

By air Nelson is serviced by the small but efficient airport about 6 km southwest of the town centre on SH6, in the suburb of Nayland. ***Air New Zealand Link***, T0800-737000, www.airnz.co.nz and ***Origin Pacific***, T0800-302302, fly regular scheduled flights to Auckland, Wellington and Christchurch. Also of note are ***Tasman Bay Aviation*** who run a quality service with small fixed wing aircraft throughout the region, T5472378.

By bus The following companies provide regular services to/from Nelson and the region as a whole: ***Intercity***, 27 Bridge St, T5481539 (Christchurch via Blenheim/Picton/West Coast); ***Kiwilink***, T5778332 (Christchurch/Blenheim/Picton/Golden Bay/Heaphy Track/Abel Tasman/Kaikoura/West Coast); ***Knightline***, T5287798 (Blenheim/Picton/Motueka); ***Lazerline***, T0800-220001 (Christchurch via Lewis Pass); White Star, T5468687 (Christchurch) and ***Atomic Shuttles***, T3228883 (Blenheim/Picton/West Coast).

Operators servicing Motueka and the Abel Tasman National Park include Abel Tasman Coaches, 27 Bridge St, T5480285, and ***Knightline***, T5287798 and ***Kahurangi Bus***, T5259434. Buses going further nortwest to Takaka and Golden Bay are ***Abel Tasman Coaches*** and ***Kahurangi***, T5259434. Buses heading south to St Arnaud and the Nelson Lakes National Park and the Rainbow ski area include ***Nelson Lakes Transport***, T5475912 and ***Nelson Lake Shuttles***, T5211887.

The West Coast Express is a backpacker special that runs every Wed from Nelson to Queenstown via the West Coast, from $100, T5465007, www.westcoastexpress.co.nz

Average fares to Christchurch are from $40, Greymouth from $50, Takaka from $22, Heaphy Track $44 and Blenheim from $20. Most of the bus services stop right outside the VIC on the corner of Trafalgar and Halifax Sts. The VIC can assist with bookings and information.

By car Nelson is 144 km from Picton via SH6, 424 km to Christchurch via SH6, SH65 (Lewis Pass) and then SH1 and 226 km to Westport via SH6.

Getting Around

Super Shuttle operates to and from the **airport**, T5475782 (about $8). **Taxi** companies include ***Sun City Taxis***, T5482666 and ***Nelson City Taxis***, T5488223. The local **suburban bus** company are ***Nelson SBL***, T5481539 and are based at the terminal on Lower Bridge St. **Bikes** can be hired from ***Natural High***, 52 Rutherford St, T5466936

Information

The Nelson **Visitor Information Centre** is on the corner of Trafalgar and Halifax Sts, T5482304, F5469088, www.nelson.net.nz Open Mon-Fri 0830-1730 /Sat 0830-1700 Sun 9000-1700. The booklet *'Nelson-Live the Day'* is very useful. **DOC** has an adjunct office in the same building. The centre is well laid out and busy, but very efficient.

History

The Nelson Region has a rather bloody Maori history, with many of the early tribes who started arriving from the North Island in the 16th century being successively conquered by others migrating south. The Ngati Tumatakokiri (who gave Abel Tasman his hostile reception in 1642) were for a while the largest tribe, but they were effectively wiped out by the Ngati Apa (from Wanganui) and Ngati Tahu (also from South Island). This transition was short-lived however when, in the 1820s, the Ngati Toa from Kapiti arrived and conquered the lot. So, when the NZ Company's agent, Captain Wakefield arrived about two decades later, it was with Te Rauparaha (chief of the Ngati Toa) whom he negotiated land purchase. From the early 1840s Wakefield went on to effectively establish the company's largest New Zealand settlement – Nelson. However, very quickly problems arose when too many migrants arrived to too little work and not enough agriculturally viable land. To counter this Wakefield and a survey party went in search for more land in the Wairau Valley to the southeast. Wakefield though this land to be already his, but Te Rauparaha disputed that claim. The misunderstanding and subsequent disagreement lead to what was called the 'Wairau Affray' and the death of Wakefield, twenty one of his party and four Maori. This incident understandably retarded the development of early Nelson and to make matters worse the New Zealand Company went bankrupt in 1844 leaving many destitute and unemployed. Redemption arrived in 1857 when gold was discovered near Collingwood (Golden Bay) and a new impetus was brought to the region. By the end of the century, long after the gold had run out, the rich agricultural potential and sustainability of the region was finally being realised – a natural resource that remains the most important in the region to this day.

Sights

Sadly the appearance of central Nelson is spoiled by one thing you cannot miss. The **Civic Tower** across the road from the VIC, which dominates the central city skyline, is without doubt, the most hideous looking building in the country. An utter mess of concrete and steel, covered with aerials and radar, it looks like something that is about to take off. Whether to the moon or Mars, it would matter not, as long as the architect responsible was strapped to it. That aside, there are many more attractive sights to see in and around Nelson.

A fine place to start is a short climb (one hour return) to the **viewpoint** above the **Botanical Gardens**, which can be accessed off Milton or Maitai Roads. This site is claimed as the geographical centre of New Zealand, but other than offering a fine view of the town and giving you a sense of location, it is also the regular target for some delightful expressions of 'daring-do' and protest. Here, in the geographical centre of the country it is not at all unusual to see some wonderfully colourful and frilly lingerie fluttering from the flagpole! More recently it was a flag proclaiming disgust at the use of GM (genetically modified) foodstuffs. Sadly, after that, the attractive botanical gardens are admirable, but far less remarkable. The other heavens of green in Nelson include the very attractive **Queens Gardens** off Bridge Street, complete with the city's fair share of ducks and the vibrant flowerbeds of **Anzac Park** at the end of Rutherford Street. The **Miyazu Japanese Park** on Atawhai Drive has a traditional 'stroll' garden built to celebrate Nelson's links with sister city Miyazu in Japan. ■ *Open dawn to dusk. Free.* There are numerous other fine gardens to visit in the region and the VIC can provide further information. The leaflet *'Gardens of the Nelson Region'* free from the VIC is a handy guide.

The newest tourist attraction in the Nelson area is the **World of Wearable Art and Classic Cars Museum**, set in a 1 ha site in Quarantine Road, Annesbrook, just north of Nelson Airport, the complex has two galleries. The first is the Wearable Art Gallery showcasing the historic Wearable Art Garment collection (now an iconic aspect of the region). There is a fully scripted show that uses mannequins rather than live models but with all the usual elements of sound and lighting. The second gallery showpieces an impressive collection of classic cars formerly on view in the town centre. ■ *The complex is open daily 1000-1800 (1700 in winter), from $15, child $7. T5489299, www.worldofwearableart.com*

Although Nelson was at one of New Zealand's earliest and largest settlements, there is little architectural evidence. Of obvious notoriety, but hardly historical (having being finally completed in 1965), is the **Nelson Cathedral** which dominates the southern end of town. Although its exterior barely matches the view of Trafalgar Street from the steps that lead up to it, the interior contains some fine stained glass windows. ■ *Daily in summer 0800-1900 (winter 0800-1700) tour guides are on duty most days. Donations.*

Also worth a quick look is **Broadgreen Historic House**, 276 Nayland Road, in Stoke, which is 6 km southwest of the town centre via the coast road. It is an 11-room 1855 Victorian 'cob' house furnished accordingly and set amongst pleasant gardens. ■ *Summer Tue-Fri 1030-1630, Sat-Sun 1330-1630 (winter Tue, Wed, Thu, Sat and Sun 1400-1630). Adult $3, child $0.50. T5460283.*

While in Stoke a far better sense of history can be found at the **Nelson Provincial Museum** set in the lovely **Isel Park**. Accessed via Hilliard Street, it serves as the region's principal museum and contains all the usual suspects covering life from Maori settlement to the present day. It boasts a particularly large photographic collection dating from the 1870s. ■ *Exhibitions are open Mon-Fri 1000-1600 and Sat/Sun 1200-1600, T5479740. Adult $2, child $1. The free leaflet 'Nelson City of History' is available from the VIC.*

With over 300 artists resident in the town **art and crafts** feature heavily in list of attractions. A copy of the *'Nelson Regional Guide Book – Art in its Own Place'*, is a great guide and available from most bookshops. The **Suter Gallery** (Te Aratoi-o-Whakatu), 208 Bridge Street, heads the list of major art galleries. Located next to Queens Gardens, it boasts four exhibition spaces that showpiece both permanent and temporary historical and contemporary collections. There is also a café and cinema theatre on site that runs a programme of musical and theatrical performances. ■ *Open daily 1030-1630. $2. T5484699.*

There are many other galleries in the area displaying a vast array of creative talent. Of particular note is The **Hoglund Art Glass** at Korurangi Farm, Landsdowne Road, T5446500, which is home to the Hoglund Glass Blowing Studio. Here the internationally renowned pieces are created for sale and show in the gallery. There is also a café and the entire set-up is set in a park like environment. Also worth a visit is the **South Street Gallery**, 10 Nile Street West, T5488117. This is the historical home of the Nelson Pottery where 25 selected potters of national and international renown create their various wares. The street itself is also noted for its 16 working-class **historical**

Thou Art gorgeous, darling!

In 1987, Nelson Sculptor Suzie Moncrieff created and directed a unique stage show called ***Wearable Art****. The concept is very simple – to create a piece of themed artwork in any media and in a form that can be worn in motion. The names of previous entries sum up the potential creativity, imagination and fun: The 'Over the Shoulder Boulder Holder' (Bizarre Bra Section); 'Queen of the Night' (Man Unleashed Section); 'Flaming Avenger' (Illumination Illusion section) and 'Superminx' (Dynasty Section).*

Almost overnight the first show became a huge success and every year since it has grown in stature attracting more entries, more media coverage, more money and now major sponsorship. The Montana Wearable Arts Festival held every ***September*** *attracts entries representing disciplines as diverse as sculpture, architecture, fabric design, weaving and engineering, from artists and designers based in New Zealand, Australia, Europe, The Pacific and Asia. The prize too has increased with the Supreme Award winner now winning $7000. Award-winning entries can be seen at the new* ***World of Wearable Art and Classic Cars Museum****.*

cottages built between 1863 and 1867. *Art Encounter Tours*, Abel Tasman Drive, T5259008, offer a specialist tour from $65. On a rainy day, you can also try your hand at **bone carving** at 87 Green Street, T5464275. At only $45 for the full day course this is good value.

Beaches

No visit to Nelson would be complete without a trip to the beach and the most popular stretch of golden sand is to be found at the **Tahunanui Beach Reserve**, just a few kilometres southwest of the town centre. Although you will not find the same scenic beauty and certainly not the solitude of the other, more remote beaches in the region, it is a convenient place to lay back and soak up the rays, swim or fly a kite. It is a great spot for kids with a small **zoo** (open 0900-1600; adult $3, child $1) and a large play park nearby. Slightly further afield (20 km) towards Motueka (SH60) are the beaches and forest swathe of **Rabbit Island**. This seemingly never-ending beach offers a far quieter and expansive alternative. It is worth checking with DOC however to confirm that it is not closed due to fire risk. With recent droughts this is becoming a more regular occurrence.

Wineries

Wineries around Nelson are also a big attraction. Although the region and its fine winemakers perhaps suffer from the reputation and sheer scale of their much-hyped neighbours in Marlborough, the wine they produce can be of a very fine quality. For more information on Nelson Region wineries consult the website www.nelsonwines.co.nz A fine winery tour is available with *JJ's Wine Tours*, T5447081. From $50

Some of the better known wineries which all offer (at the very least) tastings include the **Seifried Estate Vineyard**, Redwood Road, Appleby, T5441555. This is the largest and oldest in the region and offers tours, tastings and has a fine restaurant. Also of interest are the combined operations of the Holmes Brothers, T5444230 and Te Mania Estate, T5444541, which come under the banner of the **Grape Escape**. Both located on McShane Road, Richmond they produce a wide range of wines including certified organic varieties. There is also an art and crafts outlet, a café and a nursery.

Others are the **Waimea Estate**, 22 Appleby Highway, Hope, T5444963, which also has a café and is open daily from 1000-2200, and nearby the **Greenhough Vineyard**, T5423868. In the pretty locale known as Upper Moutere there are a number of fine wineries including: **Moutere Hills**, Sunrise Valley, Upper Moutere, T5432288, noted not only for its wine but its café, open daily 1100-1800; **Neudorf**, Neudorf Road, which offer tastings; the very scenic **Ruby Bay Wines**, Korepo Road, T5402825; the popular and well-established **Spencer Hill Estate**, Best Road, T5432031. Last, but by no means least, is the **Glovers Vineyard**, Gardner Valley Road, T5432698, owned by the very congenial David Glover himself, who is considered something of institution when it comes to producing fine wines and sampling others. The great 'sorcerer' will be delighted to give you a taste, but best pre-book, since there may be a great tasting party raging. If you get lost, just head for the sound of classical music.

Lovers of beer will be relieved to learn that some local brewing talent is hot on the heels of the winemakers. **McCashin's Brewery** 660 Main Road, Stoke, T5475357, is home to the popular Mac's Ales. Open daily and tours are available at 1115 and 1400 daily. The **Founders Brewery** in the Founders Historic Park, 87 Atawhai Drive, T5484638, is a certified organic brewery offering a range of heady organic brews. It has a good café.

Activities

Nelson and the Nelson Region offers a wide range of activities from the crazy to the traditional. The VIC has listings of everything is on offer.

Nelson

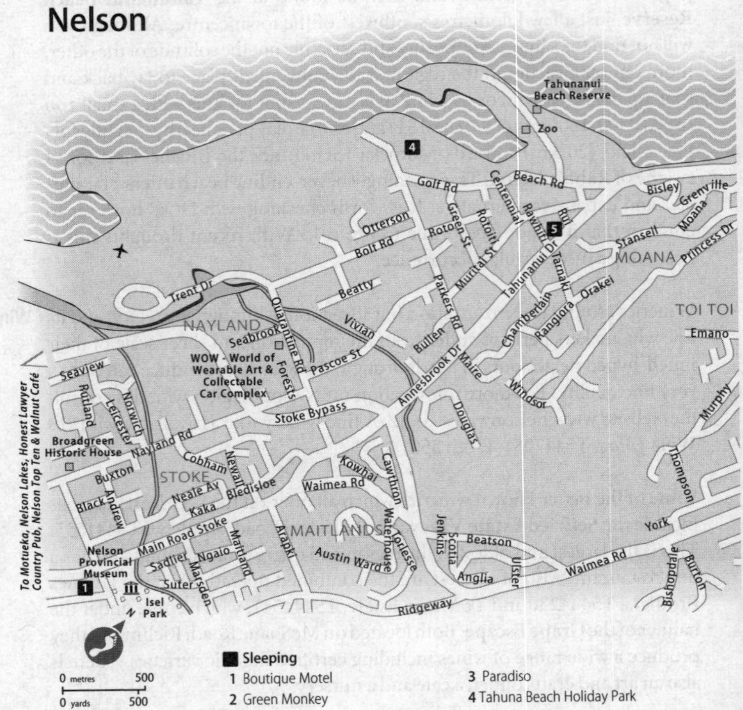

Horse Trekking

Western Ranges Horse Treks, Wakefield, T5433864, are a good outfit well suited to both beginners and the experienced, from $55 half-day. *Stonehurst Farm Horse Treks*, Stonehurst Farm, Clover Road, T5423823, from $30. *Thorndale Horse Treks*, T5451191, based north of Nelson (near Happy Valley Adventures), on Cable Valley Road are also recommended.

Mountain Biking

The Nelson area is very popular for mountain biking. *Natural High* based at 52 Rutherford Street, T5466936, www.natural-high.co.nz offer guided tours and independent hire from $15 per hour. A broadsheet outlining the best rides is available from DOC in the VIC.

Fishing

There are a number of private charters and guided trips available for both sea and fly-fishing. For details contact the VIC. *Cat-O-Nine Charters*, 262 Wakefield Quay, T5480202, are one of the most convenient. From $60 all gear provided.

Flightseeing

Tasman Bay Aviation, Nelson Airport, T5472378, are an excellent and friendly outfit offering both transportation and flightseeing options in the region. A flight around Abel Tasman and Kahurangi National Parks is recommended. From $35. Scenic Helicopter Flights are available with *Nelson Helicopters*, T5418178.

4WD Quad Biking

This is a speciality in the region with one of the oldest and best operators in the country based nearby. *Happy Valley Adventures*, 194 Cable Bay Road, Hira T5450304, offer back-country guided rides, taking in a mighty maitai tree and

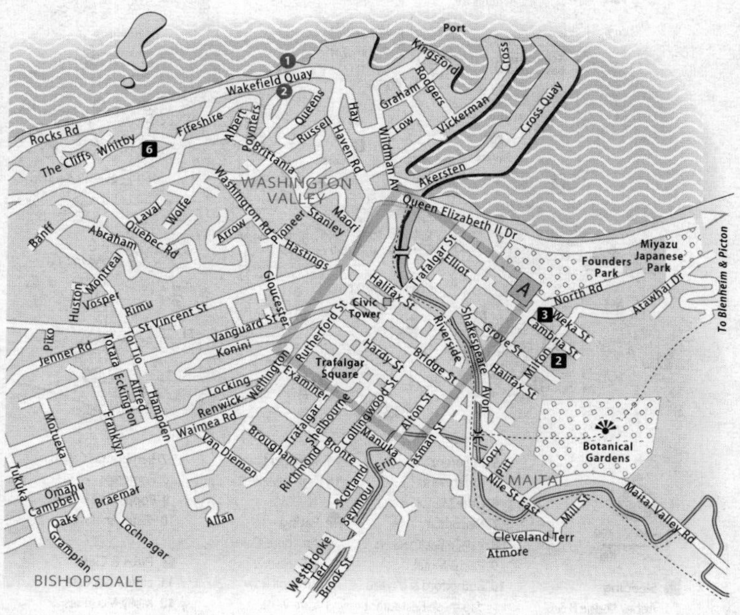

5 Tuscany Gardens Motor Lodge
6 Wheelhouse Inn

Eating
1 Boat Shed Café
2 Quayside Brasserie

Related map
A Nelson centre, page 440

some superb views. Interesting eco-based commentary. Kids fun rides in an eight-wheel drive also available and there is a café on site. Note this is an excellent wet weather option. Transportation available. From $75 for 2 ½ hours.

Golf Nelson is not short of quality courses including *Greenacres* in Richmond, T5448420 and the *Nelson Golf Club*, Bolt Road, T5485028. There is a driving range on Nayland Road, Stoke, T5472227.

Rock Climbing *Vertical Limits*, 28 Halifax Street, T5487842, www.verticallimits.com offer some excellent rock climbing trips to some notable venues in Golden Bay, From $120.

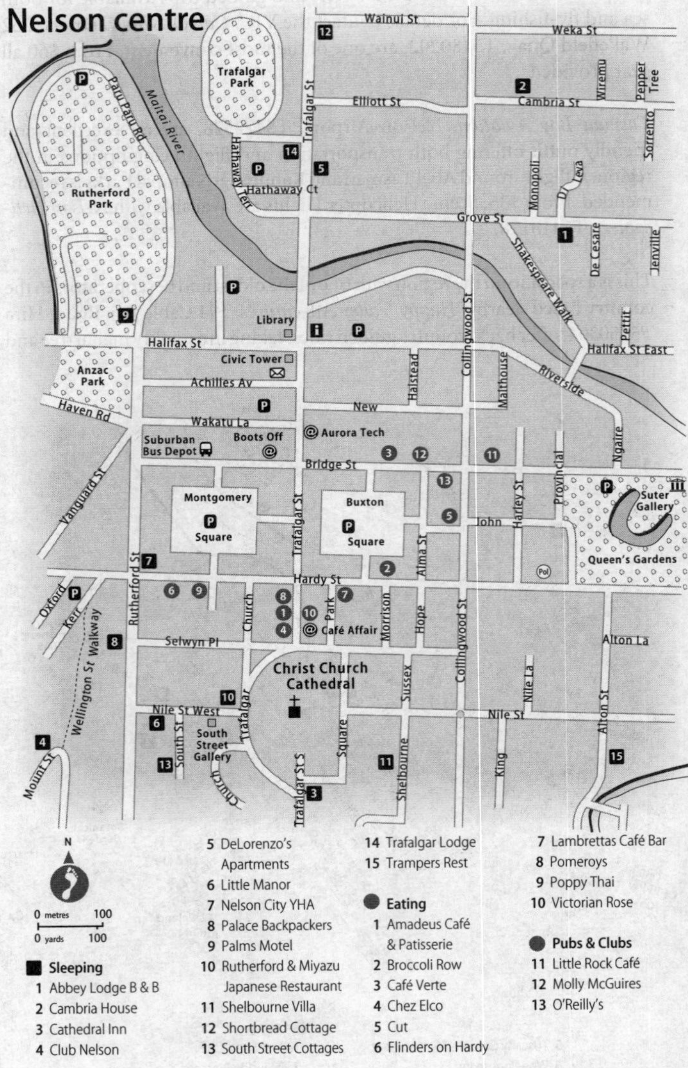

Sea Kayaking

If you intend to go sea kayaking in the Abel Tasman National Park you can organise the trip from the Nelson VIC or direct with operators (see page 447). There are many of operators and plenty of transport. You can also organize trips locally or to the much quieter, sheltered and expansive Marlborough Sounds. Independent hire is available from *Natural High*, 52 Rutherford Street, T5466936.

Sightseeing, Cruising, Sailing & Wine Tours

For sailing and cruising charters consult the VIC. The *Cat-O-Nine*, T5480202 based at 262 Wakefield Quay, are a well-established operator offering a range of trips and activities locally or to the Abel Tasman National Park. Half to multi-day trips on offer. There are numerous sightseeing tours available. Recommended operators include *JJ's Scenic and Wine Tours*, 279 Hill Street, T5447081; *Bay Tours*, 48 Brougham Street, T5457114; and *Nelson Day Tours*, T5484224, from $35.

Skydiving, Paragliding & Hang-gliding

If the weather is in your favour you can do your obligatory Tandem Skydive in the region with *Tandem Skydiving Nelson*, 19 Tamaki Street, T5452121, from $195. Tandem Paragliding and hang-gliding is offered by *Nelson Paragliding*, T5441182, *Tasman Tandems*, T5289283, and *Nelson Hang-gliding Adventures*, T5489151. From $130. Solo introductory courses are also available.

Diving & Shark Encounters

Dive trips are available with the *Nelson Dive Centre*, 21 Halifax Street, T5459385; *Big Blue Dive and Fish*, corner of Akersten and Wildman Avenue, Port Nelson, T5467411. From $80. Shark diving is on offer with *Orca Adventures*, T0800JAWSLIVE. Leaves at 0700 and 1230, from $95.

Walking

For a short walk the viewpoint above the Botanical Gardens is recommended while for longer excursions and more expansive views try the **Dun Mountain Walkway**, which is accessible via the Broom Valley. From Brook Street take a left on to Tantragee Road.

Water-skiing

Natural High, 52 Rutherford Street, T5466936. From $45. The broadsheet *'Water Ski Tasman'* is available from the VIC.

Whitewater Rafting

The *Rapid River Rafting Company*, T5457076, www.rapid-river.co.nz are based in Nelson offering half to five-day trips on the Buller, Gowan and Clarence Rivers. From $110.

Essentials

Sleeping

Being such a popular holiday destination there are no shortage of beds in Nelson with a few good hotels, numerous B&Bs and homestays, the usual rash of motels and more backpackers than almost anywhere else in New Zealand. Despite this mid-summer is very busy and you are advised to book ahead.

LL-AL *Cambria House*, 7 Cambria House, T5484681, F5466649, www.cambria.co.nz A well-established, beautifully appointed and well located B&B in a 130 year-old homestead. **LL-AL** *Cathedral Inn*, 369 Trafalgar St South, T5487369, F5480369, www.cathedralinn.co.nz Another well-located, historic option with a fine reputation. **LL-AL** *Shelbourne Villa*, 21 Shelbourne St, T5459059, F5467248, www.shelbournevilla.co.nz Located right next to the Cathedral, offering 3 king master en suites and 1 loft with 2 twins. Beautiful garden. **L-AL** *The Rutherford Hotel*, Trafalgar Square, T548229, F5463003, www.rutherfordhotel.co.nz is the principal hotel in the city and is centrally located. It has all the usual mod cons and a very good Japanese restaurant attached.

AL *DeLorenzo's Apartments*, 51 Trafalgar St, T5489774, F5489775, www.delorenzos.co.nz New, well-appointed and fully self-contained block of apartments close to town. **AL** *The Honest Lawyer Country Pub*, 1 Point Rd, Monaco, T5478850, F5478868, thl@ts.co.nz Although out of town (near the airport) this is well worth the effort. Lovely rustic en suite rooms and a quiet characterful pub with restaurant downstairs. **AL** *Little Manor*, 12 Nile St, T5451411, F5451417, a.little.manor@xtra.co.nz A charming, 2-storey, historic, self-contained cottage in the heart of town. **AL-A** *Palms Motel*, 5 Paru Paru RD, T5467770, F5467672, www.palmsnelson.co.nz One of the best upper-range motels in the centre of town. **AL** *South Street Cottages*, 1 & 12 South St, T/F5402769. Self-contained historic cottages in Nelson's most historic street. **AL-A** *Tuscany Gardens Motor Lodge*, 80 Tahunanui Dr, Tahunanui, T5485522, F5485401, tuscany@xtra.co.nz A relatively new luxury motel with a good reputation.

A *Boutique Motel*, 7 Bail St, Stoke, T5471439, F5471436, boutique@ts.co.nz A new and well-appointed establishment located in the quiet suburb of Stoke and near the airport. **A** *Wheelhouse Inn*, 41 Whitby Rd, T/F5468391. A new, spacious, timber-style establishment, with self-contained accommodation. Quiet bush setting with a superb view.

B *Abbey Lodge B&B*, 84 Grove St, T5488816, F5484220. Simple, no nonsense budget option 10 min walk from the town centre. **B** *Trafalgar Lodge*, 46 Trafalgar St, T5483980. A fine and well-located budget option with very friendly owners.

The choice of budget accommodation is vast with over 15 to choose from. The following are recommended

C-D *Club Nelson*, 18 Mount St, T5483466, clubnelson@xtra.co.nz A huge rambling villa with 45 rooms, a pool and tennis courts. **C-D** *The Green Monkey*, 129 Milton St, T/F5457421 thegreenmonkey@xtra.co.nz A small, new and quiet option with great doubles and fine facilities. **C-D** *Nelson City YHA*, 59 Rutherford St, T5459988, www.yha.org.nz A large, modern, purpose built YHA that is deservingly popular. Mainly twin and doubles. Well located in the town centre. **C-D** *Paradiso,* 42 Weka St, T5466703, www.backpackernelson.webnz.co.nz Club-Med in Nelson! A bit of a walk from the centre of town but a very popular with a pool, spa and sauna. Wide range of rooms, conservatory kitchen and internet. Busy so book ahead. Internet **C-D** *Palace Backpackers*, 114 Rutherford St, T5484691, thepalace@xtra.co.nz Another popular place set in a spacious historic villa over-looking the town. Wide variety of rooms. Great view, free breakfast/coffee, spa and a nice friendly atmosphere. Internet. Camping available. **C-D** *Shortbread Cottage*, 33 Trafalgar St, T5466681. Another small, homely and friendly backpackers with good facilities. Shortbread is excellent! **C-D** *Tramper's Rest*, 31 Alton St, T5457477. An excellent home-style backpackers with an owner who is a guru when it comes to tramping information. Small, but very friendly and cosy.

Motorcamps and holiday parks The pick of the bunch is the *Nelson Top Ten*, 29 Gladstone Rd, Richmond, T5447323. Although located 14 km away in Richmond it is worth it. Another possibility is the vast *Tahuna Beach holiday Park*, 70 Beach Rd, Tahunanui, T5485159. Set in a small continent close to the most popular beach in town. Shop on site.

Eating

There are over 50 cafés and restaurants in Nelson

Expensive *Miyazu Japanese Restaurant*, Rutherford Hotel, Trafalgar Sq T5482299. An excellent but expensive Japanese restaurant with a loyal regional following. Open daily. *The Cut* (formerly Ciao), 94 Collingwood St, T5489874. Undergoing a few alterations but will hopefully remain one of the city's top restaurants. Fresh, local seafood a speciality. Open daily from 1830. *Flinders on Hardy*, 90 Hardy St, T5488589. A classy minimalist décor establishment clearly under the influence of Auckland waterfront restaurants and of the same ilk. Best wear a tie! Open daily 1100-late.

Mid-range *Chez Elco*, at 296 Trafalgar St, T5487595, is one of the oldest cafés in the country with a loyal local following. Fine atmosphere, food, great coffee and breakfasts. Internet out back. ***The Quayside Brasserie***, T5483319 and particularly the Boat Shed Café, T5469783 on the waterfront (Wakefield Quay) are popular for the view and their seafood offerings. Open daily form 1100 for lunch and dinner ***Amadeus Café and Patisserie***, 284 Trafalgar St, T5457191. Great for either breakfast, lunch or dinner. Wide-ranging Euro-style menu and a plump range of great pastries and cakes. Open all day 0800-late. ***Pomeroy's***, 276 Trafalgar St, T5487524. Restaurant/wine bar with an imaginative menu and blackboard selection. Good coffee and breakfasts. ***Poppy Thai***, 142 Hardy St, T5488997. The pick of the affordable Asian restaurants Open daily 1730-2200. ***Walnut Café***, 251 Queen St, Richmond, T5446187. An award-winning establishment with a Euro-style menu. The pick of the eateries in Richmond should you be staying out that direction! Open daily for lunch and dinner.

Cheap *Lambrettas Café Bar*, 204 Hardy St, T5458555. This is another popular, good value café specialising in all things Italian, including scooters. Open 0900-late. ***Café Verte***, 123 Bridge St, T5457174. A good café to laze about over a latte and take your pick from an interesting blackboard menu. ***Broccoli Row***, 5 Buxton Sq, T5489621. Known for its seafood and vegetarian offerings. Pleasant outdoor area. Open 0930-2200. ***The Victorian Rose***, 281 Trafalgar St, T/F5487631. An olde English-style pub with very expensive beer but good value food. Cheap all-you-can-eat Sun roasts a speciality. ***The Honest Lawyer***, 1 Point Rd, Monaco (near the airport) is another fine pub worthy of the ale and steak lover's attention. There are a number of winery restaurants located out of town but worth the trip for a leisurely lunch. These include the café at ***Waimea Estates***, 22 Appleby Highway, Hope, T5444963, and the popular restaurant at the biggest winery the ***Seifrieds***, corner of SH60 and Redwood Rd, Appleby, Richmond, T5441555.

Bars & entertainment

When it comes to nightlife most of the action in Nelson (and it can be considerable) takes place on or around ***Bridge St***. Here you will find the very 'Mad-Max' ***Little Rock Café***, 165 Bridge St. It can go off with dancing at the weekend with the young set shaking their pants into the wee small hours. Nearby ***Molly McGuire's*** is Nelson's popular Irish pub featuring regular music sessions. ***O'Reilly's*** is an even better Irish option across the road. If you are fed up with the noise, like jazz or blues, or just want to watch some sport on the big screen, then head for the ***Victoria Rose***, Trafalgar St, but the good stuff (Irish and English beer) is expensive. The ***Honest Lawyer*** in Monaco is again a good venue for traditional Irish music at the weekends.

The **cinema** in Nelson is at the ***State Cinema Centre***, across the road from the VIC. It has a café upstairs. The ***Suter Gallery***, 208 Bridge St is the focus for more cultural events, including theatre, dance and non-mainstream films, T5484699.

Events

The most famous event in Nelson is the now world famous ***Wearable Arts Festival*** held annually in late Sep (see 437). Also of note are the ***Nelson Jazz Festival*** between Christmas and New Year and the ***Festival of Possibilities*** – a event that explores and contemplates the mind, the body, the spirit – and probably even your navel – held in late Feb.

Shopping

The ***Nelson Market*** on Sat (0800-1300) and ***Monty's Market*** held on Sun (0900-1300) in Montgomery Sq is popular and has a crafts edge. There are many specialist arts and crafts outlets including the renowned ***Hoglund Glass Gallery***, Korurangi Farm, Landsdowne Rd, Richmond, T5446500, ***The Wood Gallery*** 69 Point Rd, Monaco, T5477299, and ***Craft Habitat,*** a conglomerate of working studios on SH6, Richmond, T5447481. The ***Bead Gallery***, 18 Parere St, is excellent, T5467807. For detailed information on art and craft outlets get a copy of the *'Nelson Regional Guide Book – Art in its Own Place'*, available from most bookshops.

Directory **Banks** You will find all the main branches in or around Trafalgar St. **Car hire** ***Budget***, Nelson Airport, T5479586; ***Pegasus***, 83 Haven Rd, T5480884; ***Hardy Cars***, 8 Bridge St, T5481618; ***Rent-A-Dent***, 51 Collingwood St, T5469890. **Communications Internet** Available at the ***Boots Off Email Centre***, 53 Bridge St; ***Aurora Tech***, 161 Trafalgar St; ***Chez Elco***, at 296 Trafalgar St, and ***Café Affair***, 295 Trafalgar St. **Post Office** Corner of Trafalgar and Halifax, opposite the VIC. **Medical services** Nelson Hospital, T5461800, Emergency Pharmacy, T5483897. **Police**, T5488309

Nelson to Motueka

From Richmond, 14 km southwest of Nelson, SH60 follows the fringe of Nelson Bay, west, to Motueka. This route – often labelled as '*Nelson's Coastal Way*' – is the realm of vineyards, orchards, art and craft outlets and some pleasant seaside spots. One such spot worth a look, particularly around lunch or dinnertime is **Mapua**. A congenial little settlement at the mouth of the **Waimea Inlet** (and just a short diversion off SH60), it boasts one of the best restaurants in the region, *The Smokehouse Restaurant* which it is well known for its fine smoked fish and other seafood delicacies. The restaurant is set overlooking the river with a very pleasant outdoor eating area, where you can tickle your taste buds and sample a glass or two of local wine, while taking in the view, al fresco. Attached is a very popular fish and chip shop. Open daily for lunch and dinner, from 1100,T5402280.

Across the road is the rather unremarkable **Touch the Sea Aquarium and Gift Shop**, T5403557, which is maybe worth a look if you love seahorses or have kids. Activities in the village include *Shoreline Park Horse Treks*, 128 Aranui Road, T5402707.

Sleeping The **B-D** (clothing optional) ***Mapua Leisure Park***, 33 Toru St, T5402666 is an excellent camp, set amidst pine trees and sheltered surroundings, at the river mouth. It has numerous pretty areas to camp in, powered sites, cabins, chalets, sauna, pool and spa. There is also a small café and bar on the beach. If the holiday park is not to your tastes, there are a number of good B&Bs in the area, including the **A** ***Kinda Colada Health Retreat***, Kina Peninsula, T5266700. Here you can enjoy the congenial surroundings, a massage, sauna, or an oxygen, hydro and moor-mud therapy (what ever that might be). **LL-L** ***Bronte Lodge***, Bronte Rd East, T5402422, margaret@BronteLodge.co.nz is another luxury option set in beautiful gardens. 2 luxury suites and self-contained villas with all mod cons.

Motueka

Phone Code: 03
Population: 12,000

Motueka itself is a rather drab little place, of little note, but set amidst all the sun-bathed vineyards and orchards and within a short distance from some of the most beautiful beaches in the country, it seems to radiate a sense of smug satisfaction. Once a thriving Maori settlement, the first residents were quickly displaced by the early Europeans, who were also intent on utiliszing the area's rich natural resources. Today Motueka is principally a service centre for the numerous vineyards, orchards and market gardens that surround it, or for the many transitory tourists on route to the Abel Tasman National Park and Golden Bay. With such a seasonal influx of visitors Motueka is also a place of contrast, bustling in summer and sleepy in winter. One thing you will immediately notice on arrival is its almost ludicrously long main street – so long you could land a 747 on it and still have room for error.

Ins & outs

Getting there By air Motueka is serviced by ***Tasman Bay Aviation***, T5472378 (Nelson) and ***Takaka Valley Air Services***, T5258613, which fly a regular service to Wellington. The airport is located on College St (SH61) 2 km west of the town centre. **By road** Motueka is 51 km from Nelson on SH60. **By bus**, Motueka is serviced by ***Abel Tasman Coachlines***, T5480285; ***Kahurangi Bus***, T5259434; ***Knightline***, T5287798. **Bike rental** is available at ***Avanti Pro Cycle Shop***, 277 High St, T5289379.

Information The Motueka **Visitor Information Centre** is located on Wallace St in the town centre, T5286543, F5286563, www.motueka.net.nz It is a busy centre that prides itself on providing the best and most up to date information on the Abel Tasman National Park. Open daily 0800-1800. **DOC** have a field centre at the corner of King Edward and High Sts, T5281810, motuekaao@doc.govt.nz, with maps and leaflets available for the entire region plus hut bookings for the Abel Tasman Coastal Walkway, Kahurangi National Park and Heaphy Tracks. Open Mon-Fri 0800-1630.

Sights & Activities

For activities in the Abel Tasman and Kahurangi National Parks see the relevant sections. *Abel Tasman National Park Enterprises*, 265 High Street, T5287801, www.abeltasman.co.nz, offer a wide range of sea kayaking, and walking trips to the Abel Tasman National Park. The best **beaches** near Motueka (and before the national park) are in **Kaiteriteri**. For a local short **walk** try the Motueka Quay accessed via the waterfront west of the town centre. For other walks in the area contact DOC. The small **Mouteka Museum** is located in the centre of the town, on High Street, T5287660. ■ *Mon-Fri 1000-1500 (also weekends in summer). Donations.*

Sleeping

Given the proximity to the Abel Tasman National Park you are advised to book well ahead in summer

The area has many fine **Lodges**, **B&Bs** and **homestays**, most of which are located out of town. The VIC has full listings. The **LL-L** *Lodge at Paratiho Farm*, 545 Waiwhero Rd, T5282100, www.Paratiho.co.nz is touted as the most luxurious place to stay in the region. Set on a 900-acre farm in the country, it is rather stunning. It offers just about all a body could need, but at $1600 a night for a single occupancy, it would have to! The **LL** ***Motueka River Cottage***, Motueka Valley Highway, Ngatimoti, T5289533, www.rivercottage.co.nz is another popular establishment of sumptuous luxury near the town. If you would like to stay on a vineyard nearby then the **LL** ***Kahurangi Estate***, Sunrise Rd, T5432980, www.kahurangiwine.com, and the **AL** *Old Schoolhouse* at the Kina Beach Estate, T5266252, kinabeach@xtra.co.nz both offer beautiful self-contained cottages amid the vines.

In Motueka itself 2 far more affordable options are the **A** ***Rowan Cottage***, 27 Fearon St, T5286492 and **A** ***The Estuary B&B***, 543 High St, T5286391. Both are good value, modern and have good facilities with character.

There are a few fairly unremarkable motels in Motueka with the modern **A-B** ***Avalon Manor***, 314 High St, T5288320, being a possible exception. You would be far better to head for one of the main hostels in town, the award-winning **C-D** ***Bakers Lodge***, 4 Poole St, T5280102, bakers@motueka.co.nz It is an excellent establishment with a wide variety of rooms, modern facilities and a nice atmosphere. Its very popular so book well in advance. Of the other hostels in town the popular and spacious old villa, the **C-D** ***White Elephant***, 55 Whakarewa St, T5286208, gets the vote. The main motorcamp is the small but functional **B-D** ***Fernwood Holiday Park***, 519 High St (SH60), T5287488, beside the roundabout at the start of the never-ending main road through the town.

Eating & entertainment

The ***Jacaranda Park***, College St West, T5287797, has a good reputation and is a pleasant garden café set beside a nursery at the edge of town. In town itself the licensed ***Grain and Grape***, 218 High St, T5286103 and the funky ***Hot Mamma's Café***, 105 High

St, T5287039 (both open daily – 'ate' till late) have a loyal local following, good coffee and inviting blackboard menus. For dinner the ***Gothic Gourmet Restaurant***, 208 High St, T5286699, is also popular and there is a bar and nightclub attached.

Directory **Communications** Internet is available at the VIC and across the road at the *Cyberworld*, 15 Wallace St, T5280072.

Kaiteriteri and Marahau

Kaiteriteri and Marahau are both on the dead-end road to the southern boundary of the Abel Tasman National Park, which is accessed from SH60 just north of Motueka. **Kaiteriteri** (13 km) is a very pretty village with two exquisite **beaches** of its own and is a popular holiday spot. The main beach is the main departure point for scenic launch trips, water taxis and kayak adventures in to the Abel Tasman National Park. If you do nothing else in Kaiteriteri allow yourself time to take in the view from the **Kaka Pa Point Lookout** at the eastern end of the beach. There is a signpost appended with destinations and distances that will remind you how far you are from home – and how close to paradise. **Breakers Beach** below, looking east towards the park is truly idyllic.

Marahau a further 6 km east of Kaiteriteri is principally an accommodation and activity base at the main access point to the national park. There is a good range of accommodation options, a number of water-taxi and activity operators and a café to satisfy the needs of exhausted, hungry trampers. There is much controversy surrounding a $15 million resort development on environmentally sensitive wetlands, right at the entrance to the national park, which is expected to get building consent. If it does it sadly sums up the fears of many conservationists, that it may be the beginning (or confirmation of the beginning) of the end, for the unspoilt beauty of the Abel Tasman.

Other than the park oriented activity operators based in Marahau (see the Abel Tasman National Park below), there is *Marble Hills 4WD Adventures*, 92 Little Sydney Valley Road, T5278400, who provide some excellent scenic trips and 4WD fun from $70. On the main road near Kaiteriteri, you will doubtless be intrigued with the **Flying Fox**. This is more of a novel idea than a major adrenaline rush, but involves being hoisted 700 m up a hillside in a six-man carriage to descend at a reputed 100 km per hour into a small pond!-what will they think of next! ■ *Daily 0900-1900 in summer. $25, child $15.*

Sleeping **Kaiteriteri** **A** *Sea View B&B*, 259 Riwaka-Kaiteriteri Rd, T/F5289341 is a good value B&B in Kaiteriteri with one queen and one double/single. **A** ***Torlesse Coastal Motels***, Kotare Place, Little Kaiteriteri Beach, T/F5278063, is the best motel option with a choice of studio or 2-bedroom units. **A-B** ***Kimi Ora Holiday and Health Resort***, Martin Farm Rd, T5278134, www.kimiora.co.nz has 20 modern chalets, pool, spa and a health centre offering a range of treatments. In-house restaurant (open to non-guests) and courtesy pick-ups also available. Nearby, and across the road from the beach, is the popular **C-D** *Kaiteriteri Motor Camp*, T5278010, which has tent and powered sites and cabins.

Marahau **A** *Ocean View Chalets*, T5278232 are neat, self-contained cottages set on the hillside over-looking the bay, about 500 m from the main village. Nearby, the *Marahau Lodge*, T5278250, www.abeltasmanmarahaulodge.co.nz is slightly more up market with well appointed en suite units, pool, sauna and spa. Clients are well looked after. Further along the road and essentially at the entrance to the park is **C-D** *Old McDonald's Farm*, Harvey Rd, T5278288, which is a large but sheltered holiday camp complete with various animals, including a friendly and extremely dozey kune pig. There are plenty of sheltered tent and powered sites and a range of well appointed self-contained units, cabins, and a backpacker's dormitory. Small café on site and internet. Also on Harvey Rd is the **C-D *Barn Backpackers***, T5278043, which is a smaller but otherwise similar set up. Both of the latter can assist in park accommodation and activity bookings.

Eating

For eating there is the very popular ***Park Café*** just at the entrance to the park on Harvey Rd, T5278270. It has fine blackboard fare, a bar, good coffee and Internet. Great atmosphere. Open daily from 0800 (closed May-Aug).

Abel Tasman National Park

The Abel Tasman is the smallest and the busiest National Park in New Zealand, and one of the most beautiful, protecting 23,000 ha of some of the finest coastal scenery and beaches in the country. Rolling hills of native bush fall to azure coloured clear waters and a 91 km coastline, indented with over 50 beaches of golden sand. It is a paradise for trampers and sea kayakers and boasts the famous and increasingly popular 51 km ***Coastal Walkway****. The park is also home to the* ***Tonga Island Marine Reserve****.*

The park was opened in 1942 , after the tireless efforts of conservationist and resident, Perrine Moncrieff, and named after the Dutch navigator, Abel Tasman, who first sighted New Zealand in 1642. Many of the place names are accredited to the explorations and subsequent mappings in 1827, by the French explorer, Jules Sebastien Cesar Dumont d'Urville.

With over 170,000 visitors a year and up to 4000 on an average summer's day many feel the great 'Abel Taz' is loosing its appeal. More importantly, is in danger of being placed on an environmental precipice. Part of the problem lies not only in its sheer and understandable popularity, but also that DOC is somewhat powerless to prevent further damaging development. Although they administer the vast majority of the park the sections between the low and high water mark are essentially council owned. That does not necessarily mean the Tasman District Council is intent on ruining the place, but it does mean that development, money and greed can grow to rule the roost, while pure conservation looses its beautiful feathers and gets placed further down the pecking order. What will happen remains to be seen, but as it is, the Abel Tazman is everything it is cracked up to be and, if you can stand the company, respect and treat the place as such, it is well worthy of investigation. They say winter is now the best time to visit the park. In summer you must book well in advance for all accommodation and most activities.

Ins and outs

Getting there

Marahau, at the park's southern entrance, is the principal gateway to the park. Access from this point is by foot, water-taxi, kayak or launch. The northern (walk) gateway to the park is via Takaka (Golden Bay) at the road terminus on the eastern edge of Wainui Bay. There is road access (unsealed) in to the northern sector of the park terminating at Totaranui and Awaroa Bay. Note that you can also fly in to Awaroa Bay from Nelson or Motueka, contact ***Abel Tasman Aviation***, Nelson Airport, T5472378.

By bus Kaiteriteri and Marahau are serviced via Motueka by ***Intercity*** (connections), T5481538; ***Abel Tasman Coachlines*** (Nelson), T5480285; ***Kiwilink*** (Blenheim),

T5778332 and ***Kahurangi Buses***, T5259434. Abel Tasman Coachlines and Kahurangi Bus also service the northern sector of the park to Totaranui.

By boat There are numerous water-taxi operators that offer casual walkers or day trippers the option of being dropped off at one beach, to be pick up later at the same, or at another. For trampers this can also provide numerous options to walk some of the Coastal Walkway or to retire early in the attempt to walk its whole length. Note also that some operators will tow kayaks, giving you the option to kayak and walk or again retire early. Bags and backpacks can also be carried independently, but this tends to be in conjunction with organized trips. Alas, in the Abel Tazman these days it is actually possible to 'hail' a water-taxi, or at least gesticulate wildly to catch one, even though you are not pre-booked! Also note that most water-taxi companies can pick up or help arrange bus transport from Nelson and Motueka to coincide with departures and of course they also offer a huge range of 'suggested' itineraries for a set price.

In Motueka itself the principal operator (departing from Port Motueka Marina) is ***Abel Tasman Sea Shuttles***, T0800-732748. A one-way fare to Totaranui will cost from $30. In Kaiteriteri the principal beachfront operators are, again Sea Shuttles, above; ***Abel Tasman Water Taxis***, T5287497 and ***Abel Tasman Enterprises***, T0800223582.

In Marahau ***Abel Tasman Seafaris Aqua Taxi***, T5278083, have an office and café (where you also board your boat-first leg by tractor-trailer!). ***Abel Tasman Seal Swim and Water Taxi***, Marahau Valley Rd, T5278136, are located near the road terminus providing a similar service. Prices are reasonable and with so much competition kept very much the same. An average fare to Totaranui at the top end of the park will cost from $28 one-way. Most water-taxis depart between 0830 and 1000 from Motueka, Kaiteriteri and Marahau with additional sailings in the early afternoon, depending on the tides.

Information The **VIC** and **DOC** offices in Motueka (see Motueka section) are the best and principal sources of information on the park. They can assist with accommodation bookings and passes, transportation and activities. They can also provide tide times. DOC can also assist with general information, hut bookings, maps, and leaflets. Unmanned DOC information stations and intentions sheets are available at Marahau and Totaranui.

Activities

The choice is so vast that on initial acquaintance it is all very confusing. You can tramp, walk, kayak, walk/kayak, cruise or even swim with seals, but exactly how you do it and how much you pay is a headache. The advice therefore is to give yourself plenty of time to pre-plan and not to jump at the first option with which you are presented.

Organized trips & cruises

For other water taxi operators see above

There is a bewildering number of organized trips on offer designed to help make the decisions for you, but they can, if you are indecisive, make it very difficult to choose. All the water taxi operators offer a range of cruises and half- to full-day trips, with combinations of cruising and walking. *Abel Tasman Enterprises* based at 265 High Street, Motueka, T5287801, www.AbelTasman.co.nz, are a professional and reliable outfit. They offer a wide range of options from half- to full- to multi-day guided or non-guided trips, including transport only, transport/walk, kayak and kayak/walk. A transport-only fare can be as little as $20 and a day-cruise from $50, while a five-day guided walking trip weighs in at around $1,200, all in.

If you want to swim with the seals at the Tonga Island Marine Reserve, that lie within the park boundary, contact the *Abel Tasman Seal Swim and Water*

Taxi Company, Marahau, T08005278136, sealswim@xtra.co.nz They are the only operators that have a DoC concession to do so. From $65.

Most water-taxis depart between 0830 and 1000 from Motueka, Kaiteriteri and Marahau, with additional sailings in the early afternoon, depending on the tides. In summer wherever you are in the park it is basically a 0900-1700 operation with water-taxis plying the coast and various stops constantly between those times.

Sea kayaking

The Abel Tasman offers a world class sea-kayaking experience and it is, without doubt, the top venue in New Zealand. But it is very busy. On a mid-summer's morning the colourful flotilla of kayaks departing from Kaiteriteri and Marahau are a sight to behold and something that would probably even have had the early Maori paddling their *waka* for cover. There is an army of operators offering a wide range of options from simple independent day hire and self-guided day-trips, to multi-day, guided kayak/walking combinations. The choice is yours and the decision difficult.

If walking is not your thing, then a kayak only trip is obviously recommended. But to get the overall essence of the Abel Tazman a guided combination of both kayaking and walking is recommended. The beauty of the Abel Tazman, other than the scenery, the crystal clear waters and the wildlife, is the layout of its myriad bays and beaches, which makes a staged trip and the logistics eminently surmountable. Even if you have never been sea kayaking before, it is relatively safe and easy. The modern day sea kayak is very stable and all the major operators provide adequate training, guidance and have adequate safety standards. Serious sea kayakers tend to leave the Abel Tazman to the novice flotillas and are to be found hiding in the serenity of the Marlborough Sounds or Fiordland.

The principal and reputable kayaking companies include: *Abel Tasman Enterprises*, 265 High Street, Motueka, T0800223582, www.abeltasman.co.nz; *Southern Exposure*, Moss Rd, Marahau, T5278424, www.southern-exposure.co.nz; *Kaiteriteri Sea Kayak*, Kaiteriteri Beachfront, Kaiteriteri, T0800-252925, www.seakayak.co.nz; *Abel Tasman Kayaks*, Marahau Beach, T0800-5278022, www.kayaktours.co.nz; *Abel Tasman Sea Kayak Company*, 506 High St, Motueka, T8252925, www.seakayaknz.co.nz; *Ocean River Adventure Company*, Motueka, T0800-732529, www.seakayaking.co.nz *Planet Earth Adventures*, Pohara, Golden Bay, T5259095, www.seakayakingnz.com Popular and slightly differentant. *Sea Kayak Nelson*, Nelson, T0800-695494. *Abel Tasman Kayaks* and *Ocean River* are two of the older operators, but as you might expect competition is fierce and trips and standards are generally very similar. The best advice is to shop about and research thoroughly before deciding. Prices range from about $35 independent hire per day, $60 -$100 for a guided day trip, to $385 for a three-day trip (camping) with food provided. An all in three-day guided kayak/walk combo with *Ocean River*, including full catering and accommodation in B&B /Lodges costs $565.

Walking and tramping

The most popular walk, and one that is now world famous is the 51 km **Coastal Walkway**, while the **Inland Track** offers a quieter and more energetic tramp away from both the coast and the hordes of people.

The Abel Tasman Coastal Walkway

Given the popularity of the Coastal Walk you must book well in advance. In peak season it is not uncommon to have 200 people in the main campsites alone

This two- to five-day, 51 km walk requires medium fitness and the track itself is well maintained (and certainly well trod). The only obstacle encountered and sections that can cause difficulty are the two estuary crossings at Awaroa Inlet and Torrent Bay. Given this fact these two stretches must be negotiated at low tide, otherwise your swimming skills will be tested way beyond your walking.

There are a number of ways to tackle the track in whole or in part. The most popular route is from the south (Marahau) to the north (Wainui), or commonly from Totaranui in the north (by water-taxi from Marahau) back to Marahau in the south. There are plenty of DOC campsites and huts along the way and a few other, more salubrious independent lodges should you choose the luxury option. Detailed information about the track can be obtained from DOC in Motueka and the website www.doc.govt.nz. Their leaflet *'The Abel Tasman Coast Track'* ($1) is invaluable and they can provide the essential tide tables. Although the walk does take in many attractive bays, inlets and beaches, it does involve a lot of bush walking, where a view of the sea, never mind beaches, are obscured for long periods of time. So if you are not a seasoned tramper a water-taxi/ walk plan over part of the route is perhaps recommended. Although the whole trip is a delight the most scenic beaches are Torrent Bay and the Awaroa Inlet. Both of these should not be missed and have the added novelty of the tidal crossing-which will give you a mild taste of what tramping in New Zealand is all about.

A rough outline of the recommended route, distances and times (from south to north) is as follows:Marahau to Anchorage: four hours, 11 ½ km; Anchorage to Bark Bay: three hours, 9 ½ km; Bark Bay to Awaroa: four hours, 11 ½ km; Awaroa to Totaranui: 1 ½ hours, 5 ½ km; Totaranui to Wharwharangi: three hour, 7 ½ km; Wharwharangi to Wainui: 1 ½ hours, 5 ½ km. There are DOC huts at Anchorage, Bark Bay, Awaroa and Wharwharangi and numerous campsites along the way (see below).

Inland Track

The Inland Track is for obvious reasons less popular and links Marahau to Wainui via the Pigeon Saddle on the Takaka-Totaranui Road. It is a 37 km, 3-5day effort. The main attraction here, other than the fact it is far less trodden than the coastal track, is the beautiful undisturbed and regenerating bush and occasional fine views. You may also hear kiwi at night. The track can be tackled in whole or part and one recommendation is to start at the car park at Harwoods Hole. This way you can take in the impressive Harwoods Hole before tackling the remaining 20 km track north over the Pigeon Saddle to Wainui. Note that the track can also be tackled in part with the access point at Pigeon Saddle (Totaranui Road via Takaka). DOC can provide information and an essential broadsheet about the track. There are four huts but no separate campsites but they are not of the same standard (obviously) as those on the Coastal Track.

Two recommended day-walks in the Abel Tasman National Park

If you are short for time or cannot stand the sight of a paddle the following are two day-walks that will provide a pleasant taste to what the Abel Tasman is all about. They are also not too strenuous, having the added fun of getting your feet wet and take in a lovely cup of tea to boot. The first is accessed from the southern end of the park, the other from the north.

Torrent Bay to Marahau

(14 km 3-6hours)

From Marahau take an early morning water-taxi to Torrent Bay ($15). Make sure your arrival at Torrent Bay coincides with low tide. Take in the immediate delights of Torrent Bay, then take the Coastal Track heading south, for which you need to take off your boots and follow the markers across the estuary.

Return boots to feet and find the track again that climbs the small headland before falling to the exquisite Anchorage Bay Beach. Then, from half way up the beach, climb the hill, not forgetting to look back at the stunning view. Take the sidetrack (15 mins) from the top of the hill down to the incredibly cute (and hopefully quiet) Watering Cove. Climb back up to the coastal track and continue south. If you have time check out Stillwell Bay and certainly walk along Appletree Bay (re-access to main track at far end of the beach). From there complete the walk past Tinline Bay to the Marahau entrance point. If the tide is

Abel Tasman National Park

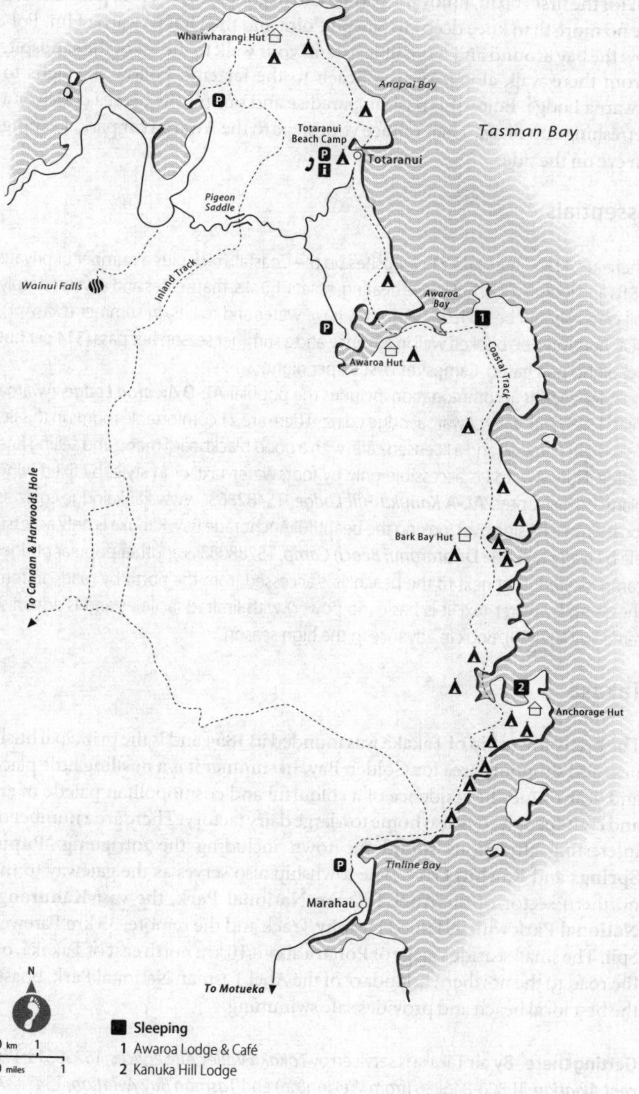

Nelson and Marlborough

in your favour, you can cross the bay directly just beyond Tinline Bay (where the path descends to beach level). Fall exhausted and happy in to the Park Café, reward yourself with a pint of beer, a glass of wine or the full seafood fettuccine. While there use the email facility to make friends back home.

Awaroa Bay *(6 km, 3-6hours)* From Takaka take the Totaranui Road via Pohara, Wainui Inlet and the Pigeon Saddle, enjoying the views on the way. From the Totaranui Road take a right on the Awaroa Road to the Awaroa car park. Make sure once again that your arrival coincides with an outgoing tide. Digest the view across the inlet and the walk you are about to do. Descend to beach and remove footwear. Cross the inlet in a direct line towards the sea, ignoring the especially muddy bit for the first 100 m. Enjoy the paddle and negotiate the deepest part (should be no more than knee deep) to Sawpit Point and the DOC Awaroa Hut. Follow the bay around and if possible extend your walk to the tip of the sandspit. From there walk along Awaroa beach to the far end. Follow the signs to Awaroa Lodge. Enjoy this oasis in paradise and sample the beer, a coffee or a refreshing cup of tea. Then retrace your steps to the Awaroa car park, keeping an eye on the tide.

Essentials

Sleeping There are 4 DOC huts and 21 campsites on the Coastal Track plus a number of private B&Bs and lodges. DOC huts have heating, toilets, bunks, mattresses and a water supply (all water should be boiled). Campsites have water and toilets. In summer (Oct-Apr), DOC huts must be booked well in advance and a summer season hut pass ($14 per hut per night) purchased. Campsites cost $7 per night.

Independent accommodation includes the popular **AL-D** *Awaroa Lodge*, Awaroa Inlet, T5288758, www.AwaroaLodge.co.nz There are 21 comfortable rooms in this little oasis in paradise and a licensed café, with a good blackboard menu and selling fine coffee. Note Awaroa is accessible only by foot, water-taxi, or in style, by fixed wing plane or helicopter. **AL-A** *Kanuka Hill Lodge*, T5482863, www.kaukalodge.co.nz is located on a hillside over looking the beautiful Anchorage Bay. Kanuka is only accessible by water taxi. The **D** *Totaranui Beach Camp*, T5288083 is another popular budget camp located right next to the beach. It is accessed from the north by road, or from the south by water-taxi. It is basic (no power) with limited facilities and is administered by DOC ($9). Book in advance in the high season.

Takaka

Phone Code: 03
Population: 1,100

The pretty township of Takaka was founded in 1854 and is the principal business and shopping area for Golden Bay. In summer it is a bustling little place and year round the residence of a colourful and cosmopolitan palette of art and crafts people. It is also home to a large dairy factory. There are a number of interesting attractions round the town including the intriguing **'Pupu' Springs** and **Rawhiti Cave**. The township also serves as the gateway to the northern sector of the **Abel Tasman National Park**, the vast **Kahurangi National Park** with its famed Heaphy Track and the remote, 35 km Farewell Spit. The small seaside village of **Pohara** about 10 km north east of Takaka, on the road to the northern boundary of the Abel Tasman National Park, boasts the best local beach and provides safe swimming.

Ins & outs **Getting there** **By air** Takaka is serviced by *Takaka Valley Air Services*, T5258613; *Vincent Aviation*, T0800-846236 (from Wellington) and *Tasman Bay Aviation*, T5472378 (from Nelson). These services also provide excellent scenic flights and also transportation from the southern end of the Heaphy Track. The airfield is located about 6 km west of the town on SH60. **By road** (SH60) Takaka is 109 km from Nelson and 50 km to Farewell Spit. **Bus** companies servicing the town include ***Abel Tasman Coachlines***, T5480285; ***Kahurangi Bus***, T5259434, and ***Kiwilink***, T5778332. Buses stop outside the VIC. **Bike** hire is available with ***The Quiet Revolution***, 7 Commercial St, T5259555. From $35 per day. They also offer local tours from $30.

Information and orientation Almost all the services the visitor requires can be found along the main street through town – Commercial St. The Golden Bay **Visitor Information Centre** is located on Willow St, at the southern entrance to Takaka, T5259136, F5259288, gb.vin@tourism-nelson.co.nz They stock the full range of information for the entire Golden Bay area, including Collingwood and Farewell Spit. The free 'Golden Bay Heart of the Parks Guide' is useful. Open daily 0900-1700. **DOC** is located at 62 Commercial St, T5258026. They have detailed information on both the Abel Tasman and Kahurangi National Parks (including the Heaphy and Abel Tasman Coastal Tracks). Open Mon-Fri 0800-1600.

Sights

In the town itself the local history and cream of local art and crafts are showpieced in the **Golden Bay Museum and Gallery** on Commercial Street, The museum has some fine collections of minerals and shells, along with the usual local treasures and special features on early explorer Abel Tasman's unfortunate first encounter with the local Maori. The gallery next door is well worth a look. ■ *Open daily 1000-1600. Closed Sun in winter. $1. T5259910.* There are many other independent studios and galleries in the area for which the VICs free *'Arts of Golden Bay'* leaflet is ideal.

The biggest attraction in the immediate area are the beautiful and crystal clear **Te Waikoropupu or Pupu Springs** (see short above). The springs are administered by DOC and are open daily. To get there follow SH60 north of Takaka, turning left just after the bridge over the Takaka River. Follow Pupu Valley and Pupu Springs Road to the car park. There are well-maintained paths and the reserve can be explored thoroughly in about 45 minutes. Nearby the **Pupu Walkway**, which starts at the end of Pupu Valley Road, retraces an old goldmining water race, taking in some interesting features and lovely bush. It is considered one of the best short walks in the region and takes about half a day.

Of the two limestone cave systems in the area, Te Anaroa (see page 455) and Rawhiti, it is the **Rawhiti Cave** that is the most impressive. It is however the least accessible. This ancient cave with its enormous entrance laden with thousands of coloured stalactites can be accessed independently, but a guided tour is recommended. ■ *3 hrs, from $25, child $15. T/F5257177.*

Also on the limestone theme and closer to Takaka are the odd and shapely 'karst' features of the **Labyrinth Rocks**, which are located just outside the town on Labyrinth Lane, Three Oaks. ■ *The rocks are open daily from 1300-1700 and will keep the kids occupied for hours, $5. T5258434.*

Also of note in this area, and accessed where Motupipi meets the Clifton Crossroads is the **Grove Scenic Reserve**. Here a short 10 minute walk will bring you to an intriguing spot where massive Rata trees grow out of curiously shaped karst rock outcrops. Nearby those with green fingers and the love of a fine view will enjoy the **Begonia House** and succulent gardens, Rocklands Rd, Clifton. ■ *Open 1000-1700. Free. T5259058.*

Again while in the immediate area it would be rude not to have a quick look at the **Abel Tasman Memorial** on the headland just beyond Tarakohe

Te Waikoropupu Springs

Borne of the Takaka Marble Aquifer, the turquoise waters of the 'Pupu Springs' bubbles out at an average rate of 13.2 cu m a second, creating a lake that is the clearest of any freshwater body outside Antarctica. To the scientific community they are of interest not only as an unusual landform, but also for the resident aquatic plants and animals. For divers, it provides a habitat of unsurpassed clarity and for the Maori; they are considered taonga, *a treasure, and* wahi tapu *– a scared place to be revered. It is a peaceful, beautiful place that has a palpable and rare sense of purity. If you are in the area, a visit is highly recommended.*

(Totaranui Road) and look then listen with eyes shut to the pretty **Wainui Falls** (Wainui Bay); an easy 40 minute walk. Note this road can also take you to the northern beaches and tramping access points of the **Abel Tasman National Park**.

Of some novelty are the famous Anatoki **tame eels** at **Bencarri Farm**, 6 km south of Takaka (signposted off SH60). The eels are reputed to be the oldest tame eels in the country with some individuals still enjoying a daily snack after 80 years of residence. Bencarri Farm also has a host of touchy-feely animals including llamas and some homesick Scottish 'Heelaan coos'. There is a good café (open 1000-late) and there are also numerous activities on offer including gold panning, four-wheel drive quad biking (from $49) and, yes, the obligatory 'milk the cow'. ■ *Bencarri is open daily 1000-1730. $8, child $4. T5258261.* If you just happen to fall in love with the llamas why not try one of the new and rather unique activities available in the region with **Llama Safaris**, Rangihaeata Road, T5258406, llamasafari@ihug.co.nz They offer treks by llama from two hours ($38, child $20) to three days ($420).

Sleeping The VIC has a full listing of B&Bs and homestays most of which are located near the beaches at Pohara. **AL** *Bay Vista*, Pohara, T/F5259772 is a single-storey, spacious and modern B&B with two doubles and a deluxe en suite with private lounge. Just 5 km south of Takaka itself the **A** *Rose Cottage Motel and B&B*, Hamama Rd, T5259048 offers a 3 unit motel and a cute two-bedroom B&B in a garden/country setting. In town the popular **A** *Anatoki Lodge Motel*, 87 Commercial St, T5258047, anatoki@xtra.co.nz is the pick of the motels providing modern facilities close to all amenities. Nearby and slightly more affordable, is the great value **B** *Sans Souci Inn*, Richmond Rd, Pohara, T/F5258663, reto@sanssouciinn.co.nz It is a mud-brick Mediterranean-style establishment with lovely detached bedrooms and a great, licensed in-house restaurant.

There are 4 backpacker hostels in the area. In town is the well-established and cosy **C-D** *Annie's*, 25 Motupipi St, T5258758, and the new **C-D** *Golden Bay Backpackers*, 114 Commercial St, T5257005. The latter offers free trips to the Pupu Springs. Near Pohara is the unusual **C-D** *Nook*, T5258501, offering comfortable in dorms, double accommodation in a straw-bale cottage or a four-berth house truck. At the other end of town and closest to the Pupu Springs is the century old pub-style **C-D** *River Inn*, Waitapu Rd, T5259425. It has a wide range of rooms with especially cheap singles. Free bike hire and Internet. The best motorcamp is the **B-D** *Pohara Beach Holiday Park*, Abel Tasman Dr, Pohara, T5259500, which has tent, powered sites and motel units, next to the beach.

Eating The *Wholemeal Café*, Commercial St, T5259426 is a bit of an institution in Takaka and the haunt of many a local artists. It has good coffee, breakfasts, blackboard menu and excellent service. Open daily 0730-1930. The *Dangerous Kitchen*, also on Commercial

St, T5258686, does fine pizza. Open daily 0830-late. For evening meals ***Milliways***, 90 Commercial St, T5259636, is a good choice with an imaginative menu and pleasant outdoor eating area. The ***Sans Souci***, Richmond Rd, Pohara, T/F5258663 is similar and open for lunch and dinner (seasonal). For a cafe experience surrounded by a veritable menagerie head for ***Bencarri Farm*** (south off SH60). Open daily 1000-late.

Directory

Internet is available at the ***Golden Bay Net Café***, 48 Commercial St, T5258355 (behind the Dangerous Kitchen Café) and ***Baylink Communications***, 6 Commercial St.

Golden Bay

From Takaka SH60 continues northwest, eventually reaching the coast and the tiny village of Collingwood, the gateway to ***Kahurangi National Park****, the* ***Heaphy Track*** *and Wharariki Beach, one of the most beautiful beaches in the country. From the end of terra-firma, 22 km north of Collingwood, the huge 35 km* ***Farewell Spit*** *extends like a golden rainbow out into ocean to envelope the vast mud flats of Golden Bay.*

Collingwood

Collingwood was formerly known as Gibbstown and was (believe it or not) once a booming gold mining town that was promoted as an eminently suitable capital for the nation. But that dream turned to dust when the gold reserves were laid waste and a fire almost destroyed the entire village. Rebuilt and renamed Collingwood in honour of Nelson's second-in-command, fire struck again in 1904 and yet again as recently as 1967 when the town hall, hotel and two shops were reduced to ashes. Despite its fiery history and now void of its once lofty social standing, Collingwood still retains a few historical buildings, including the characterful courthouse, which is now a café where you can sentence yourself to a lengthy tea-break. Collingwood itself also has a small and fairly unremarkable **museum** on Tasman Street. ■ *Open daily 0900-1800. Adult $2, child $1. T5248447.*

The area has a few other notable attractions worth visiting. South of Collingwood, in the attractive **Aorere River Valley** and back on the limestone theme, are the privately owned **Te Anaroa Caves**, Caves Road, near Rockville. These caves are 350 m in length and include the usual stalactite and stalagmite formations, plus fossilised shells and glow worms. Guided tours are available in summer at 1030,1230,1430 and 1630 (winter by arrangement), T5248131, from $15, child $6. At the end of Cave Road are two fairly unremarkable 'karst' (limestone) rock monoliths known as the **Devil's Boots** (presumably because they are upside-down). The walks and mountain bike tracks of the **Aorere Goldfields**, which were New Zealand's first, are accessed from the road end and are of far more interest. (See free DOC leaflet).

If you have time an exploration of the pretty **Aorere River Valley** (Heaphy Track Road) is recommended. Beyond the pleasures of the drive itself a stop at the river **gorge** at Salisbury Bridge (Quartz Range Road) and the old **Bainham Store** will both have the camera clicking. Access down to the river is possible, to the right just beyond Salisbury Bridge, while the Bainham Store is an original, still operative store that has changed little in decades.

Farewell Spit

Access on the spit is restricted so an organized tour is the only way to truly experience the place

The spit is formed entirely from countless tons of sand ejected in to the northerly ocean currents from numerous river mouths scattered all the way up the West Coast. It is a dynamic, almost desert like landscape, with sparse vegetation struggling to take root in the dry and constantly shifting sand. The vast majority of the Spit is a DOC nature reserve and the vast mud flats that it creates along its landward edge are one of New Zealand's most important wading-bird habitats. Over 100 species have been recorded around the spit, but it is the sheer numbers of each species that is most notable. Migrating flocks of godwit and knot can run well in to the thousands providing a memorable sight. Black swans also use the food rich mud flats of Golden Bay, and when the tide is in they gracefully tread the water in vast flocks. There is also a small colony of rapacious gannets at the very end of the spit.

Both Cape Farewell and Farewell Spit were noted by Tasman in 1642 (no doubt a little shorter than it is now) and named by Cook when he left the shores of New Zealand in 1770. The Lighthouse at the very tip of the spit was first erected in 1870. It has an interesting history, having been almost washed away once and relocated.

The Spit is a remarkable and memorable landscape if only for its powerful sense of isolation, but to see it from afar and from sea level is a strangely unremarkable experience. With its vast dune system, no more than 20 m in height, its sheer length and the omnipresent coastal haze, its very presence is, to say the least, muted. At best only a small grove of pine trees near its tip can be seen like some tiny far off island. If you cannot afford to go out on the spit or simply want to get a better impression of its scale from afar, the best place to view it is from the elevated hills around the Pillar Point Light Beacon, accessed from Wharariki Road and Puponga.

At the base of the Spit and just beyond the last small settlement of Puponga is the **Farewell Spit Café and Visitor Centre**. It stocks a range of informative leaflets and has a number of interesting displays surrounding the spit, its wildlife and the rather sad and repetitive whale strandings in Golden Bay. The café sells a range of refreshments and snacks and has a fine deck overlooking the bay and the spit itself. ■ *Open daily 0900-1700 (seasonal). T5248454.* Most of the established **walking tracks** leave directly from the centre. Note you can also book and join the Farewell Spit tours en route to the spit at the visitor centre ($45).

Tours to Farewell Spit

All the organized tours to Farewell Spit are based in Collingwood

The Original Farewell Spit Safari (Farewell Spit Tours), Tasman Street, Collingwood, T5248257, enquiries@farewellSpit.co.nz are, as the name suggests, the original tour operator and have been taking people out on to the spit for over 50 years. They are a very professional outfit and now offer a range of three tours. The most popular of these is the *Lighthouse Safari* which is a 5 ½ hour excursion to the end of the spit and the lighthouse. Transportation takes the form of robust but comfortable RL Bedford Trucks that can go where conventional wheels cannot. Along the length of the seaward side of the spit you will be introduced to the Spit's wildlife (which can include the odd, bleary-eyed basking fur seal) and allowed stops to take in the special atmosphere of the spit, before arriving at the lighthouse. There, you can climb to see the rather unremarkable view from the top, before descending again to learning a little of its interesting history over a welcome cup of tea. There is an interesting commentary throughout the tour. This tour costs a very reasonable $58, child $30.

Whale Strandings

Although science has yet to confirm the exact reasons for whale stranding, it is an undeniable and sad fact that the coastline of New Zealand is highly prone to this bizarre phenomenon. Almost every year, especially in summer, strandings occur around the country's coastline, with some bays like Keri Keri Bay in Northland, The Mahia Peninsula in the Hawkes Bay – and worst of all – Golden Bay in the Nelson Region, being the most notorious. New Zealand has led the world in the delicate art of refloating these mammoth, intelligent leviathans. At any given stranding, large numbers of volunteers, from all walks of life turn up to help in accordance with strict protocols and a national programme led by DOC and the charitable organization Marine Watch based in Christchurch. Through 'peacetime' training, many Kiwis are now well-versed in how to deal effectively with the emergency. Sadly, despite the huge effort, most whales die, but there have been some major successes, sometimes with almost every whale being returned to sea successfully. The biggest whale stranding in recent years occurred when a staggering 385 pilot whales stranded in Golden Bay in 1991. Only 15 died with the rest successfully refloated. To attend a whale stranding is an incredible experience both to witness its effect on people (bringing out both the best and the worst) and to sense the almost haunting presence of these intelligent creatures. For more information contact DOC or Marine Watch in Christchurch, T02-5358909. If you encounter a stranded whale or dolphin or even a freshly dead carcass, contact DOC immediately.

The Gannet Colony Safari (6 ½ hours, $65, child $35) is an extended trip that takes in the above and, as the name suggests, the gannet colony at the very end of the spit (this company are the only operators with the DOC concession to get up close). The *Wader Watch Safari* (3-4 hours, $50) is a specialist and fascinating trip to see the wading birds on the spit often numbering in the thousands. Although most suited to birdwatchers and somewhat seasonal (summer only) it would be of considerable interest to any nature lover, especially given the limited access to the spit. *Farewell Spit Nature Tours*, also based in Collingwood on Tasman Street, T5248188, www.farewell-spit.co.nz, are a newer operation offering a similar lighthouse tour with the exception of a diversion to visit the cliffs and seal colony at Cape Farewell and the elevated view of the spit from Pillar Point. $65, child $35. Book ahead for all of the tours above.

Wharariki Beach

Wharariki Beach has to be one of the most beautiful beaches in the country. Perhaps it is its very remoteness that makes it so special, but add to that its classic features, including caves, arches and dunes, and you have near perfection. It is so beautiful you almost find yourself feeling a corrupting sense of guilt at leaving your lone footsteps on its swathes of golden sand – let alone stripping off entirely and splashing about in the waves. You can access the beach by road from Puponga via Wharariki Road (20 minute walk) or make it the highlight on a longer and stunning coastal walk from Pillar Point Lighthouse. If you do not fancy using your own legs you can join a posse with *Cape Farewell Horse Treks*, Puponga, T5248031, who are blessed with some of the most scenic routes in the region. From $35.

Pillar Point to Wharariki Beach coastal walk *(13 km, 6-8 hrs)* From Puponga follow Wharariki Beach Road to the turn-off (right) up to Pillar Point Light Beacon ('Blinking Billy'). Note this is a rough, non-signposted road. Park your vehicle at the base of the hill below the light beacon. Climb the hill to Pillar Point and enjoy your first proper view of Farewell Spit before heading further north towards The Old Man Rock (155 m) along the crest of the hill. Take in the views of The Spit and Golden Bay before retracing your steps to Pillar Point. From Pillar Point follow the sporadic orange markers south, through a small tract of manuka trees. From there follow the markers and the cliffs taking in all the cliff-top views to Cape Farewell. Keep your eyes peeled for fur seals, whose plaintive cries will be probably be first to reach the senses. Continue south, along the cliffs before descending to Wharariki Beach. If the tide is in your favour walk its entire length and investigate the many caves and rock corridors along its length. Once at the base of Pilch Point (at the very end of all the beaches) retrace your steps to Pillar Point. Now *that* is a coastal walk!

Essentials

Sleeping Just before Collingwood township on SH60 is the luxurious and spacious **LL** ***Kahurangi Luxury Retreat***, T5248312, retreat@kahurangiNZ.co.nz It is well-appointed, and the friendly owners have a genuine desire to make your stay worthwhile, fine cuisine. Nearby, is the more affordable **A** ***Golden Bay Lodge and Garden***, Tukurua Beach, T5259275, www.GoldenBayLodge.webnz.co.nz It's a beautiful spot on the cliff-top with self-contained units and B&B rooms. In Collingwood itself is the superb **AL** ***Collingwood Homestead B&B***, Elizabeth St, T5248079, www.CollingwoodHomestead.co.nz It gets the vote as the best B&B in the entire region. Cheaper options in Collingwood include the comfortable **B** ***Skara Brae B&B and Motels***, Elizabeth St, T5248464, skarabrae@xtra.co.nz and the very basic **C-D** ***Collingwood Motor Camp***, 16 William St, T5248149. On the road to Farewell Spit you will find the hugely popular **C-D** ***Innlet and Cottage***, Main Rd, Pakawau, T5248040, jhearn@xtra.co.nz It oozes character and is in a lovely bush setting offering dorms, twins and doubles and two charming self-contained cottages that sleep 3-6. The owners are friendly, dedicated long-term residents. There is bike hire available and excellent harbour/ rainforest kayak trips from $65. Internet. **C-D** ***Pakawau Beach Park***, Pakawau, T5248327, is also an excellent motorcamp with modern facilities and some very colourful, value, self-contained huts overlooking the beach. There is a fairly unremarkable licensed café across the road.

Eating There are few options but the ***Mussel Inn***, Onekaka (roughly half way between Takaka and Collingwood on SH60), T5259241, offers good pub grub, great value mussels and the best beer around – and a toilet to remember. Open daily from 1100 in summer and 1700 in winter. In Collingwood the ***Courthouse Café***, corner of Gibbs and Elizabeth St, T5248572 is the best bet. Open daily 0830-late (seasonal). Then, at the very end of the road at Farewell Spit, the **visitor centre** also hosts a good café with a basic blackboard menu, T5248454. Open daily 0900-1730 (seasonal).

Transport ***Kahurangi Bus***, T5259434, and ***Abel Tasman Coachlines***, T5480285, offer daily services to Collingwood from Takaka and Nelson.

Kahurangi National Park

Opened in 1996, Kahurangi is New Zealand's second newest national park (the newest now being Stewart Island, opened in 2001). After Fiordland, it is also the largest. It is a vast and remote landscape of rugged alpine ranges and river valleys, the most notable of which is the Heaphy that meets, in part, the park's most famous tramping route, the ***Heaphy Track****. One of the most interesting features of the park is its ancient geology. It contains some of the country's oldest rock landforms, with spectacular limestone caves, plateaux, arches and outcrops. Kahurangi is home to over half of New Zealand's native plant species (over 80% of all alpine species) and over 18 native bird species, including the stealthy New Zealand falcon and the huge New Zealand land snail.*

Ins and outs

Getting there

Transport to the various trailheads is available from Motueka, Takaka, Collingwood and Karamea (West Coast). ***Kahurangi Bus***, T0800-173371; ***Abel Tasman Coachlines***, T5288805; ***Trek Express***, T5402042 and ***Karamea Express***, T7826617(West Coast) are the principal operators. ***Tasman Bay Aviation,*** Nelson, T5472378 offer flights to Karamea and Takaka.

Getting around

They say it takes a long time and many walks to acquaint yourself properly with Kahurangi and for many this is its very appeal. One of the best ways to see the park is from above. A scenic flight across the bare mountaintops and remote valleys is a truly memorable experience (***Tasman Bay Aviation***, Nelson, T5472378). The Heaphy Track is usually the visitor's first and only acquaintance with the park but the **Cobb Valley**, **Mount Arthur** and the **Tablelands** (accessed from the Cobb River Valley, 50 km south of Takaka and from the Flora car park 30 km south of Motueka) offer some shorter walk options. The view from Mount Arthur (four hours, 8 km), which is accessed from Motueka, is particularly recommended. Kahurangi Guided Walks, Takaka, T5257177, www.kahurangiwalks.co.nz ***Bush and Beyond,*** Motueka, T5289054, www.naturetreks.co.nz and ***Hideaway Hiking and Outdoors,*** also in Motueka, T5268234, www.hideaway-tours.co.nz all provide a range of guided walks in the park from $60 per day. ***Vertical Limits,*** Nelson, T8837842, www.verticallimits.com offer some excellent rock climbing trips to Kahurangi, From $120.

Information

The **DOC** field centres in the Nelson VIC, Motueka and Takaka stock detailed information on the park, including access, walking and tramping. On longer walks or tramps you are advised to go well prepared and, in summer, book the huts and passes ahead – especially on the popular Heaphy Track.

The Heaphy Track

The Heaphy Track is one of New Zealand's most popular 'Great Walks' and the most popular tramp in the Kahurangi National Park. It is a relatively low-level tramp of 82 km taking 4-6 days. The Heaphy is named after Major Charles Heaphy a noted soldier who was the first to traverse the coastal portion of the modern track in 1846. Although not famed for its mountainous vistas, the track does provide a wide range of interesting habitats and a superb coastal section. It is also noted for being 'open' for much of its length providing a fine sense of space and wilderness. Flannigan's Corner (915 m) near Mount Perry (880 m) is the highest point on the track and provides memorable views. The Heaphy is usually negotiated from west to east. The western trailhead starts about 15 km north of Karamea, while the eastern, starts 28 km south of Collingwood.

The approximate walking times are as follows-west to east: Kohaihai River Mouth to Heaphy Hut, five hours, 16 ½ km; Heaphy Hut to Lewis Hut, 2 ½ hours, 8 km; Lewis Hut to Mackay Hut, 3 ½ hours, 13 ½ km; Mackay Hut to Saxon Hut, three hours, 14 km; Saxon Hut to Gouland Downs Hut, 1 ½ hours, 5 km; Gouland Downs Hut to Perry Saddle Hut, two hours, 8 km; Perry Saddle Hut to Brown Hut, five hours, 17 km.

Ins & outs

Take plenty of insect repellent

Getting there The eastern Heaphy Track trailhead is accessed via Collingwood (28 km) and Bainham (Aorere River Valley) at the end of the Heaphy Track Road. The route is signposted from Collingwood. The eastern trailhead is served daily in summer and on demand in winter by ***Kahurangi Bus***, T0800-173371; ***Abel Tasman Coachlines***, T5288805; ***Trek Express***, T5402042. The western by ***Karamea Express***, T7826617. The average fare from Takaka is $15 and from Karamea $5.

Information The Golden Bay **Visitor Information Centre** in Takaka, T5259136, F5259288, gb.vin@tourism-nelson.co.nz and **DOC**, also in Takaka, T5258026, have detailed information on the Heaphy Track. Both administer hut tickets and bookings.

Sleeping

The 7 huts along the track are supplied with bunks, heating, water (must be boiled) and toilets. Hut passes are $12 (advance bookings) or $15 if purchased at the time of walking. Note a pass does not guarantee a bunk. Camping is $8, child $6. For more information and bookings contact DOC, or the major VICs. You can also book direct with DOC website www.greatwalksbooking@doc.govt.nz

Nelson Lakes National Park

The slightly underrated Nelson Lakes National Park protects 102,000 ha of the northernmost Southern Alps range. The park is dominated by its two long, scenic and trout-infested ***Lakes Rotoroa*** *and* ***Rotoiti****, cradled in beech-clad alpine ranges, hiding beautiful tussock valleys and alpine meadows. Although a quick look at the lakes are all that most people see of this park, the ranges and river valleys offer some superb walking. The two most noted tramps are the 80 km, 4-7 day* ***Traverse-Sabine Circuit*** *and the excellent 2-3 day* ***Robert Ridge/Lake Angelus Track****. There are a number of very pleasant* ***short walks*** *from 20 minutes to two hours that extend into the park from St Arnaud or Lake Rotoroa.*

The principal base for the park is pretty village of ***St Arnaud,*** *which nestles at the northern end of Lake Rotoiti. Almost all accommodation, services, major park access and activities are located here The park is also accessible from the more remote and sparsely populated* ***Lake Rotoroa****.*

Ins and Outs

Getting there

St Arnaud is 90 km from Nelson (via SH6), 100 km from Blenheim (SH63) and 163 km from Westport (SH6/63). To visit Lake Rotoroa, turn off SH6 at Gowan Bridge west of St Arnaud. An 11 km side road takes you up the Gowan Valley to the lake.

By bus St Arnaud is served by ***Coast Shuttles***, T7896837 (Nelson to Westport); ***Nelson Lakes Shuttles***, T5211887 (Nelson); ***Wadsworth Motors***, T5224248 (Nelson): ***Atomic Shuttles***, T3228883 and ***Nelson Lakes Transport***, T5475912 (ski season). **Water-taxis** operate on both Lakes Rotoroa and Rotoiti and offer scenic and/or fishing trips and tramping pick-ups/drop-offs: ***Rotoiti Water Taxis***, T5211894; ***Lake Rotoroa Water Taxi***, T5239199. From $25, lake's end one-way.

Information

The DOC Nelson Lakes National Park **Visitors Centre** in St Arnaud, T5211806, F5211896, StArnaudao@doc.govt.nz is an excellent centre which provides comprehensive displays and information on the park and local accommodation and transport. Open daily 0800-1900 (seasonal). The free *'St Arnaud & Nelson Lakes'* booklet is useful. The Nelson Lakes Village Centre on the main road serves as the main grocery store, petrol station, postal agency and has EFTPOS, T5211854. Open 0800-1830 (seasonal hours). Lake Rotoroa does not have a shop. Nelson Lakes also plays host to the popular Rainbow Valley and Mt Robert ski-fields (only accessible in winter).For skiing information contact T5211861, www.skirainbow.co.nz or freephone T0800-754724.

Mount Robert to Lake Angelus Basin walk

(2-3 days, 30 km)

If you are short for time this walk is touted as one of the best in the park. The destination (and highlight) is the beautiful Lake Angelus Basin and an overnight stay at the Mount Angelus Hut ($10) from which to take it all in. It is a walk that should only be considered by those of average fitness, in good weather conditions. Go prepared and pre-book your hut accommodation (and fill in an intentions sheet) at the DOC Visitors Centre.

From the Upper Mount Robert car park (accessed from West Bay, 5 km from St Arnaud) climbs the steep zig-zag track up the face of Mount Robert to the bushline shelter, near the summit (two hours). From there follow the marked route along the ridge and around the Mount Robert Ski-field to Flagtop summit (1690 m). Then descend briefly and continue on the saddle beneath Julius Summit (1794 m). The route now leaves the ridge briefly crossing rocky ground before retaining the ridge. At a small saddle marked by a metal pole, the route drops again to the west side and crosses a steep, rocky slope to another broad saddle at the head of Speargrass Creek. From here a short climb to the ridge reveals the beautiful Angelus Basin (five hours).

Stay the night at the Angelus Hut and get up for sunrise! To return you can either retrace your steps, or descend in to the Hukere Valley to join the Cascade Track to Coldwater Hut located at the southern end of the lake. From there the Lakeside Track will deliver you back to the lower Mount Robert car park. If you have no vehicle and have been dropped off, you may consider booking a water taxi from the southern end of the lake and reward yourself with a scenic cruise back to St Arnaud.

Sleeping

At St Arnaud and Lake Rotoiti, the range of accommodation includes hostels, motels, B&Bs and three camping areas. Lake Rotoroa has far fewer options. St Arnaud **AL-D** *Alpine Lodge*, T5211869, enquiries@alpinelodge.co.nz This is the mainstay of quality accommodation and eating in the village and comprises of a wide range of options from self-contained studio units to dorms. Licensed à la carte restaurant, café, bar and spa. Bike hire from $7 per hr. **A** *St Arnaud Log Chalets*, T5211882, www.nelsonlakes.co.nz Offer very pleasant modern self-contained units. Next door is the YHA associate **C-D** *Yellow House*, T5211887, which is modern and friendly with good facilities, including a spa. They can also provide good tramping information and gear hire. **A** *Tophouse*, Tophouse Rd, T0800-867468, is a very animal- (and people-) friendly, historic farm guesthouse located 9 km north of St Arnaud. It has 4 self-contained units and 5 comfortable B&B rooms. At one time it also boasted New Zealand's smallest bar. Café on site, Open daily to non-guests 0930-1700. Other reputable B&Bs in the area include the pretty and self-contained **B** ***Woodrow Cottage***, Tophouse Junction (5 km), T5211212; the luxurious **LL** ***Kikiwa Lodge***, Korere, Tophouse Rd, T5211020; and the quiet 2-storey **A** ***St Arnaud B&B***, intersection of Bridge/Holland and Lake Rd,

T5211028. There are DOC **campsites** with power at the edge of the lake in West and Kerr Bays, T5211806. (Deposit fees at DOC Visitor Centre)

The very limited options at Lake Rotoroa range from the exclusive and luxury fishing retreat **LL** *Lake Rotoroa Lodge*, T5239121, www.rotoroa.co.nz, to the excellent and friendly *Gowan River Holiday Camp*, Gowan River Valley Rd, beside the river, T5239921. Avoid the campsite by the lake, where the sandflys will eat you alive.

Murchison

Phone Code: 03
Population: 750

Murchison, 65 km further along SH6 from St Arnaud, at the head of the **Buller Gorge** and junction of the Matakitaki and Buller Rivers, is a service centre for the local farming community and for many, the gateway to the West Coast from the north. Although once an important gold mining town (and famous for being nearly wiped out by a violent earthquake in 1929), it is today a quiet place, primarily of interest to the tourist as the base for a number of interesting activities. It is also the haunt of the odd serious tramper intent on exploring the remote southern wilderness of the **Kahurangi National Park**.

Ins & outs

Getting there The West Coast bound buses all stop in Murchison outside Collins Tearooms, Beechwoods Restaurant or the VIC. The principal companies are *Coast Shuttles*, T7896837; *White Star*, T5468687 and *Intercity*, T5481538.

Information The Murchison VIC is on the main road through town, at 47 Wallar St (SH6), T5239350.Open 1000-1600 (seasonal).

Sights & Activities

The small Murchison **Museum** on Fairfax Street has interesting exhibits on gold mining and the town's somewhat shaky past. ■ *Open daily 1000-1600, donations.*

The principal activities in the area include fishing, white-water rafting, kayaking, caving, mountaineering and walking. The VIC has all the details

The **Murchison Adventure Centre,** 51 Fairfax St, T5239899, www.rivers.co.nz is the base for *'Ultimate Descents'*, that offer an attractive range of **rafting** and **kayaking** trips in the region from three hours to five days. One of their most popular activities is the '**river-bugs**' trip. This is three to seven hour blast down the Buller River sitting headfirst, in what can only be described as an inflatable deformed carrot. Its great fun and costs from $60 for two hours.The adventure centre also has a shop and a café on-site.

White Water Action Rafting Tours, Gowan Valley Road (behind the VIC), T5239581, action-tours@actix.co.nz offer a similar range of whitewater trips and their competitive colourful inflatable offering are the 'funyaks', which are basically indestructible blow up kayaks. Prices are from $75. Still on the water, Jetboat trips down the Buller are available with *Buller Jetboat Tours*, T5239880, www.murchison.co.nz from $50.

To catch the monsters that lurk beneath the water try one of the many good **fishing** guides in the region, including *Russell Frost's Ticklish Trout Tours*, T5239371. Independent fishing licences ($20 per week) are available from the VIC. The *Majik Places* (linked with *White Water Action* above) T5239581, also offer an exciting range of guided adventure activities including, canoeing, fishing, walking and gold-panning.

More sedate scenic tours are available with *Mt Murchison Scenic Tours*, 53 Fairfax Street (motel), T5239026, three hours from $45, or *Tiraumea Horse Treks*, T5239341. **Mountain bikes** can hired from Auto Engineering, 27 Grey Street, T5239425.

If you feel lucky and want to try **gold-panning**, the VIC hires pans and shovels for $5 ($20 bond) and will point you in the right direction. The VIC can also provide details and directions of the numerous short and long **walking** options in the area. The view from the **Skyline Walk** (1 ½ hours, 6 km) is recommended. If a walk seems to much one spot worth visiting are the **Ariki Falls** which are located 3 km from O'Sullivan's Bridge heading west down SH6, (turn left down the track 1 km after the statue of three people hugging). The pink rocks are even more attractive than the falls. But beware, take insect repellent.

Sleeping

The **LL** ***Moonlight Lodge***, Paenga Maruia Valley, T5239323, F5239515, www.moonlightlodge.com, is the most luxurious option in the immediate area offering all mod cons, in a pleasant bush setting next to the river. In Murchison itself is the pretty **A-B** ***Coch-y-Bondhu Lodge B&B***, 15 Grey St, T/F5239196, which is a cheaper option with five comfortable, well-appointed rooms. Fishing trips are a speciality. The **A-B** ***Kiwi Park***, 170 Fairfax St, T/F5239248, has tidy, modern motel units and powered sites. The **C-D** ***Riverview Holiday Park***, T5239591, 2 km north of town, by the river, is another popular spot for campers.

Eating

For eating you are limited to the ***Do-Duck Inn Café*** (formerly Collins) 67 Fairfax St, T5239078 or the slightly larger and more plentiful, licensed ***Beechwoods***, SH6 (southern end of town), T5239571. Open 0630-2130. Collins was something of a local institution for quick cheap snacks, but has recently changed hands. Another option for a quick lunch is The ***River Café*** at The Adventure Centre, 51 Fairfax St, T5239889. But, beware, you will be hard pushed to walk out without being lured for a trip down the river on the great inflatable carrots. And why not indeed!

Directory

Internet is available at the ***River Café***, Fairfax St or ***Beechwoods Café***, SH6.

[illegible] the VIC [illegible] gold-panning [illegible] palm and [illegible] (☎ 4[illegible]) [illegible] in the right direction. The VIC can also provide details and directions [illegible] and long walking options in the area. The view from the Skyline Walk (1 1/2 hours [illegible]) is recommended [illegible] walk seems to [illegible] spot worth visiting are the [illegible] Falls [illegible] located [illegible] (turn left down the track [illegible] after the [illegible]). The [illegible] even more [illegible] than the [illegible] Falls [illegible] repelling.

Sleeping

The [illegible] Lodge [illegible] (☎ 4[illegible]; www.[illegible]) [illegible] a [illegible] offering [illegible] a pleasant [illegible] setting next to the [illegible] The pretty [illegible] Lodge [illegible] is a [illegible] with [illegible] well appointed rooms [illegible] speciality. The A-B [illegible] Park [illegible] (☎ 4[illegible]) [illegible] and powered sites. The [illegible] Park [illegible] 1 km north of town by the river is another popular spot for campers.

Eating

For eating you are limited to the [illegible] (formerly [illegible]) [illegible] pub [illegible] and [illegible] meals [illegible] fine [illegible] down [illegible] ☎ 4[illegible] [illegible] is a [illegible] quick [illegible] Another option for a quick lunch is the River Café of the [illegible] Centre [illegible] [illegible] down the [illegible] not [illegible]

Directory

Internet [illegible] at the River Café [illegible]

14

Canterbury

Canterbury

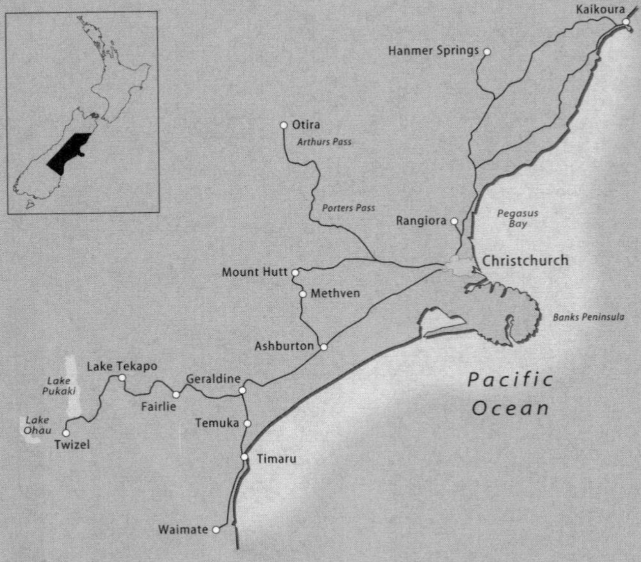

Kaikoura
Hanmer Springs
Otira
Arthurs Pass
Porters Pass
Rangiora
Pegasus Bay
Christchurch
Mount Hutt
Methven
Banks Peninsula
Ashburton
Lake Tekapo
Lake Pukaki
Geraldine
Fairlie
Pacific Ocean
Lake Ohau
Temuka
Twizel
Timaru
Waimate

Whichever way you arrive in Canterbury, by air or by road, the ***Canterbury Plains*** *dominate, giving an impression of flatness And yet, despite appearances, much of Canterbury is mountainous, home to New Zealand's highest peak, Aoraki or* ***Mount Cook*** *(3754 m). Canterbury is the largest region in the South Island, extending from the Pacific Ocean and the Canterbury Plains in the east to the Great Divide and Southern Alps to the west and from the south Marlborough Mountains and Kaikoura Ranges in the north, to the braided,* ***Waitaki River*** *in the south.*

Central Canterbury *is the hub of South Island with its capital* ***Christchurch****, the country's second largest city. Dubbed 'The Garden City', it also claims the title of New Zealand's favourite city, although it lacks the architecture and the remarkable friendliness of Dunedin.* ***North Canterbury*** *is home to South Island's 'little piece of Rotorua' in the form of the* ***Hanmer Springs*** *thermal resort, providing just one good reason to stop en route to the West Coast via the beautiful* ***Lewis Pass****. Along with* ***Arthur's Pass*** *to the south, these form the region's two main portals from the east coast to the west and are also the focus for skiers.*

In ***South Canterbury*** *the pleasant coastal port of* ***Timaru*** *provides a starting point from which to head west, via Fairlie and* ***Burkes Pass*** *to the* ***McKenzie Country****. Here, you will find the region's most stunning and diverse scenery, culminating in* ***Pukaki Lake*** *and* ***Mount Cook Village****.*

Things to do in Canterbury

- *Meet the ocean's 'Who's Who' in Kaikoura.*
- *Take a punt on Christchurch's Avon River.*
- *Visit the Antarctic and Arts Centres in 'The Garden City'.*
- *Take a gondola to the crater rim of the Banks Peninsula, then mountain bike back down.*
- *Explore the 'Banks' and find the 'French connection' in Akaroa.*
- *Enjoy a graceful balloon trip over the Canterbury Plains at dawn.*
- *Take one of the world's most scenic train trips to the West Coast.*
- *Say goodbye to your ancient training shoes at the unofficial shoe memorial in Burkes Pass.*
- *Go star gazing at Lake Tekapo.*
- *Let the mountains envelop you along SH80 to Mount Cook Village. Then take an unforgettable scenic flight around Aoraki (Mt Cook) and the glaciers.*
- *See one of the rarest birds in the world (the black stilt) in Twizel.*

Ins and outs

Getting there Canterbury is reached either by air, or by road from the north east coast via Kaikoura and SH1. Christchurch is the principal city (the country's second largest) and the region's capital. By **bus** the region is generally very well served. By **air** Christchurch is served by*Air New Zealand Link* from all major provincial airports including Auckland, Wellington and Queenstown. A the time of going to print the 'Southerner' **train** service from Christchurch to Dunedin and Invercargill was under threat, but this situation may change. The ***TranzCoastal*** service from Picton to Christchurch and the world-famous***TranzAlpine*** service to Greymouth and the West Coast remain.

Getting around Christchurch is 336 km south of Picton and 362 km north of Dunedin on SH1. Queenstown is 486 km southwest via SH1 and SH8 via the McKenzie Country and Mount Cook. There are many and regular **bus** services throughout the region that focus primarily on the SH1/SH8 routes. The principal operators are ***Intercity***, T4425628; ***Atomic Shuttles***, T4428178, and ***Southern Link***, T3588355. These plus the numerous other service providers are listed under each destination.

Information There are major **VIC**s in Christchurch (city, international and domestic airport terminals) and Timaru, with smaller local centres located in Hanmer Springs, Lyttleton, Akaroa (Banks Peninsula), Geraldine, Ashburton, Methven, Tekapo and Twizel. DOC has offices in Christchurch, Geraldine, Mount Cook and Arthur's Pass. These are all listed in the relevant sections.

The principal websites for the area are www.christchurchnz.net/www.kaikoura.co.nz/www.hurunui.com (Hanmer Springs)/www.adt.co.nz/tourism(Ashburton)/www.mtcook.org.nz/www.Akaroa.com/www.southisland.org.nz (South Canterbury)

Christchurch

Phone code: 03
Population: 320,000

What Auckland is to volcanic plugs, stark concrete and Polynesia, or Dunedin is to wildlife, fine architecture and Scotland, Christchurch is to the deciduous tree, gardens and England. Dubbed 'The Garden City', Christchurch is known as the most English of New Zealand's cities. Reminders of its Anglican roots are everywhere, from the formal blazers and straw hats of the city's schoolchildren, to the punts on the river and the distant chorus of 'Howzatt' from its myriad cricket pitches on lazy summer Sunday afternoons. Without doubt the key to its charm is the immense, tree-lined Hagley Park that borders its centre and has over the decades remained remarkably intact. With the park, its trees and the pretty Avon River that threads it all together, the aesthetics of Christchurch verge on the adorable. But natural aesthetics and its obvious English colonial feel aside, Christchurch has developed its own atmosphere that is also very Kiwi. It has the buzz and vitality of Auckland, the cosmopolitan 'town' feel of Wellington, and it shares a pride that only Dunedin can beat in heritage and architecture.

Ins and outs

Getting there

Air Christchurch Airport, (Domestic Terminal VIC, T3537774), T3537714, www.christchurch-airport.co.nz is located 12 km northwest of the city via Fendalton Rd and Memorial Av. It is a modern airport with both international and domestic terminals in a single easily negotiated building. The International terminal has direct links with Australia, Singapore and Japan, while the domestic serves all national provincial airports. There are travel and information centres in both terminals, and city transport is to be found directly outside the terminal building. At the time of going to print the domestic carriers at Christchurch were limited to ***Air New Zealand***, T3532800, or T0800-737767, and ***Origin Pacific***, T0800-302302, www.originpacific.co.nz , but this situation is set to change. With the demise of Qantas New Zealand in May 2001 (not Qantas Australia/International) the chances are several carriers will be available offering cheaper than ever fares – at least that is the hope. For the latest information contact the VIC. As it stands there are still regular daily flights to all major provincial airports in both Islands with flights to Wellington and Auckland almost every hour. For

Christchurch

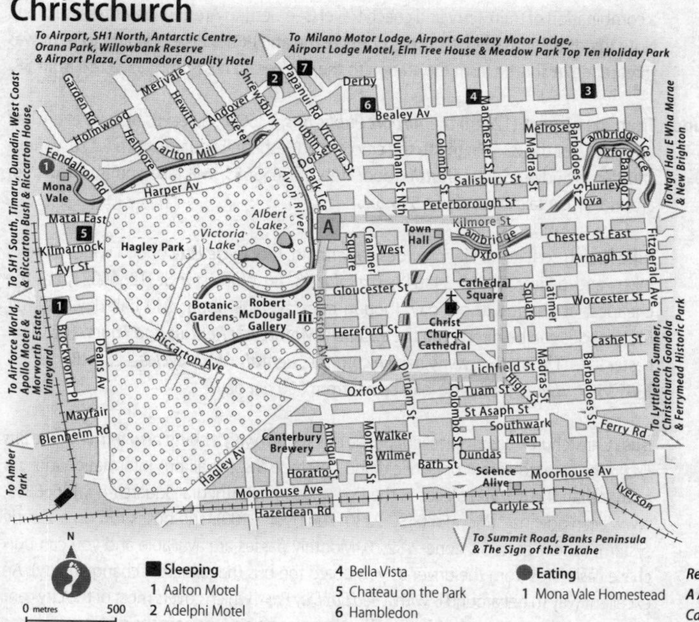

Sleeping
1 Aalton Motel
2 Adelphi Motel
3 Avalon Motel
4 Bella Vista
5 Chateau on the Park
6 Hambledon
7 Strathern Motor Lodge

Eating
1 Mona Vale Homestead

Related map A Around Cathedral Square, page 474

Canterbury

Bus *Intercity* is the main player, with daily services to most major towns in the South Island including Picton (5 ½ hrs), Dunedin (6 hrs), Mt Cook (5 ½ hrs), Wanaka (9 hrs), Queenstown (10 hrs). In Christchurch their agent is the ***Christchurch Travel Centre***, 123 Worcester St, T3770951; reservations T3799020, **www.intercitycoach.co.nz** *Great Sights*, T0800-808226, also offer more tour-based options. There are many shuttle services which are listed in 'Getting There' sections of the intended destinations. ***Atomic Shuttles***, T3228883, are the main Christchurch-based company offering excellent South Island-wide services. ***Southern Link***, T3588355, also offer services to Picton, Dunedin, Queenstown and Wanaka. ***Supa Kut – Price Shuttles***, T3777782, offer an 'unbeatable' price to Dunedin at $20 one-way, $30 return. ***White Star***, T3588355; *Coast to Coast*, T0800-800847; and ***Alpine Coaches***, T0800-274888, offer daily services to Greymouth and Westport on the West Coast while The ***Hanmer Connection***, T0800377378, offer a daily service to Hanmer Springs. For special deals, including ***The Best of New Zealand Pass*** which offers a combination of train, ferry and coach travel see 'Getting around', 'Essentials' section, page 41. The VIC has full details on national bus travel and can make bookings on your behalf.

Road By road Christchurch is 336 km south of Picton (Kaikoura 183 km) via SH1; 579 km north of Invercargill (Dunedin 362 km/ Timaru 163 km) on SH1. Queenstown is 486 km southwest via SH1/SH8, and Greymouth 258 km via Arthur's Pass and SH73.

Train The train station is 3 km from the city centre at the southwestern tip of Hagley Park on Addington St. TranzScenic, T0800-802802, www.tranzscenic.co.nz operate the daily southbound Southerner (departs 0815;Timaru/Dunedin/Invercargill); northbound TranzCoastal (departs 0730; Kaikoura/Blenheim/Picton); and the deservingly popular TranzAlpine (departs 0900; Greymouth). For details and fares get the *'Times and fares'* booklet from the train station or the VIC. The Best of New Zealand Pass offers a combination of train, ferry and coach travel (see Getting Around, 'Essentials' section). Note that the Southerner service is under revue and at the time of going to print was threatened. A shuttle from the station to the city centre costs from $5, a taxi from $8.

Getting around

From the **airport** (12 km) the ***Airport Public Bus***, T3668855, leaves at least every half hour daily for the 25-min trip to the city centre (Cathedral Square), from $2.70. Various shuttles including ***Super Shuttle*** (door-door), T3655655, will take you into town for around $10. A taxi costs about $18-$25.

Bike Being so flat the city provides easy riding. ***City Cycle Hire*** offer a wide range of bikes, and deliver, T0800-343848; ***Trailblazers***, 86 Worcester St, T3666033, are the cheapest at about $20 per day, though rates average about $30 half-day, $40 full. Motorcycles can be hired from the excellent ***Motorcycle Rentals and Tours***, 166 Gloucester St, T3770663, www.nzbike.com or ***Rental Motorcycles***, 28B Byron St, T3723537, www.motorcycle-hire.co.nz from $90 per day.

Bus Christchurch has an excellent public bus system with a brand new terminal, the *Bus Exchange*, located corner of Lichfield and Colombo Sts. For all bus information look no further than the *Bus Info* offices in the Exchange or in Cathedral Square (47), T3668855, www.ecan.govt.nz (Mon-Fri 0630-2230, Sun 0900-2100). The buses run on a 2-zone system; zone-1 costs $2, zone-2 $2.70. Monthly passes are available and you can purchase cash fares from the driver as you board the bus (have correct change ready). An excellent way to get around is with a *Red Bus Day Pass*, which covers most of the city centre and major attractions for $5 a day. They can also be bought from the driver or from the Bus Info offices. The electrified *Free Yellow Shuttle* takes in a north-south route from the Casino, through Cathedral Sq and down Colombo St and back, and operates every 10-15 min Mon-Thu 0800-2230; Fri 0800-2400; Sat 0900-2400 and Sun 1000-2000. It's worth jumping on at least once to get your bearings. For shuttle services to **Lyttleton** and **Akaroa** see relevant texts under 'Around Christchurch' section, below. There is a free shuttle to and from the Mt Cavendish *Gondola*, departing from outside the Bus Info Centre on Worcester St at 1000/1200/1400 and 1600.

Car You are far better on foot or going by public transport within the city. The one-way system is a little confusing, and although there are plenty of parking lots and meters they are almost as tightly patrolled as Auckland and Wellington. An hour in the city centre will cost about $2. A good idea is to park your car for free south of Moorhouse Av (the Old Train Station and Hoyts 8 Cinema) and catch the free shuttle from there.

Tram Between 1905 and 1954 Christchurch had a thriving tram system. Since 1995 the beautifully restored trams now follow a 2 ½ km loop around central Christchurch, passing various sights of interest on the way (commentary provided). The trams operate Apr-Oct 0900-1800 and Nov-Mar 0900-2100, from $6 for 1 hr (all-day $7, child $4) There is also a restaurant car that offers a daily dining tour, T3667511, www.tram.co.nz The trams can be boarded at many stops including Cathedral Square.

Taxi You have a choice of ***Blue Star***, T3799799 (24 hrs); ***Gold Band***, T3795795; or ***First Direct***, T3775555.

Orientation

The heart of Christchurch lies just to the west of Hagley Park with **Cathedral Square** being the most recognized focus. The borders of the city centre are known as the **'Four Avenues'**: **Deans Av** that borders the western fringe of Hagley Park, **Moorhouse Av** to the south, **Fitzgerald Av** to the east and **Bealey Av** to the north. One of the most attractive features of the city is the **River Avon** that winds its way through Hagley Park and the city centre from west to east. The city is essentially flat and has a basic grid system of streets extending in all directions from Cathedral Square, with the north/south **Colombo St** being the main shopping street. The city centre is easily negotiable by foot using the Cathedral and high-rises around Cathedral Square as a reference point. The **VIC** has a plentiful supply of free city maps. The major bookshops (see 'Shopping' below) also stock Christchurch city map books, and ***Mapworld***, Cnr Manchester and Gloucester Sts, T3745399, www.maps@mapworld.co.nz is an excellent source of city, town, provincial and national maps.

Information

The ***Christchurch Visitor*** Information Centre is located in the Old Post Office Building in Cathedral Square (West), T3799629, F3772424, www.christchurchnz.net Open daily Mon-Fri 0830-1700; Sat/Sun 0830-1600. There are also VICs in the International (T3537783/4) and domestic (T3537774/5) **airport** terminals.

There is a wealth of **free brochure** material, including the useful *Today and Tonight/Christchurch and Canterbury'*, which is a must. There are also numerous city attractions and 'drive' maps including *the 'Top Attractions'; 'A Guide to Christchurch's City Centre'; 'The Avon River Drive'; 'The Garden Drive'; 'The Antarctic Heritage Trail'; 'Wine Trail'* and *'Arts Trail'* maps. The **daily paper** in the Central South Island is the *Christchurch Press*. If you are computer literate and need contact addresses and numbers don't forget the www.yellowpages.co.nz website.

DOC are located at 133 Victoria St, T3799758. They can provide local, regional and South Island walks and tramping information. Open Mon-Fri 0830-1630.

History

Given Christchurch's strong and outwardly obvious English links, it is perhaps ironic that the first European settlers on the Canterbury Plains were in fact Scottish. Although having originally emigrated separately to Nelson and Wellington in 1840 and 1842, in search of better living conditions, brothers William and John Deans arrived on the plains and established themselves on land the local Maori called Putaringamotu in 1843, calling it Riccarton after their home town in Central Scotland. Five years later the New Zealand Government made a contentious land deal with the local Maori purchasing about 8 million ha of land for – we presume – little more than 'two sticks and a balloon', which paved the way for more concerted settlement.

In 1849 a prestigious 53-member organisation called the **Canterbury Association** was founded by Irishman Robert Godley. Comprising two Archbishops (of Canterbury and Armagh), seven bishops, 14 peers, and other notables, mainly from Godley's old university college of Christ Church, in Oxford, its aim was to establish a new utopian Anglican settlement in the new colony of New Zealand. The site of this new settlement was chosen by the association's surveyor, Captain Joseph Banks, who, presumably after seeing the Deans brothers' prize 'neeps' and 'tatties' (swedes and potatoes), saw the obvious potential of the rich alluvial plains for agriculture.

In 1850 the 'first four ships' – The 'Charlotte Jane', 'Randolph', 'Sir George Seymour', and 'Cressy', brought 782 colonial souls to the then whaling base of Lyttleton, which had already been established on the Banks Peninsula. Even before their arrival the Canterbury Association had already christened the great settlement-to-be, Christchurch. But perhaps, human nature being what it is, it seems little of either Christ or the church prevailed and bitter wrangling between members quickly led to the association's disintegration in 1855 and the effective end to the great Anglican settlement plan.

Despite these hiccups the new colony flourished and today its roots are obvious. One only needs to look at the trees and cricket pitches in Hagley Park, the gardens, the street names and the punting on the river, the public school boys skipping out of Christ's College in blazers and straw hats, to realise how much of its founding English influence prevails. Indeed, in Christchurch, to be in the slightest way related to anyone on 'the first four ships' is – 'darling' – to belong to the city's elite. As for the Deans boys, William drowned in 1851 on a journey to Australia to buy sheep, and John died in the cottage three years later after contracting tuberculosis.

Sights

City centre

Within the **'Four Avenues'**, and easily negotiated on foot, are a number of sights and attractions that easily take up one day. Ask at the VIC about the **Super Pass**, which can combine entry to a number of attractions at a reduced price.

Cathedral Square

Dominated by the Gothic revival Anglican **Christ Church Cathedral**, Cathedral Square has recently undergone a major revamp that has become the talk of Christchurch. The issue is highly contentious (even nationally), with most feeling the development is an aesthetic disaster and a crass waste of money. Certainly, it does seem hopelessly out of character with the rest of the city, with its sharp angles and dull façades of steel and concrete. And once again it seems to suffer from the scourge of the average New Zealand architect – a severe

Christchurch's most unusual visitor

He is a rebellious, moody, teenage star that weighs almost two tonnes. He does what he likes, when he likes and has very bad breath. He would not win any beauty contests but doesn't care. Anything blue he will attack, anything yellow he wants to play with and anything red makes him horny. He loves to throw his weight around and in doing so has destroyed boats, trees, cars, sheds and kayaks. But, he has injured nobody and has no desire to. He has had to be forcibly evicted from a garage several times, a woodshed twice and on one occasion even somebody's bedroom. He has tried to mount and make love with several boats and even a Toyota Corolla car (red, of course).

Yet, despite his behaviour (and perhaps because of it), he is an international star and while in Christchurch has over 6000 visitors a day. Some fear him; some hate him and some have even attacked him – but most love him dearly. He even has an entourage of carers who look after him, play with him when bored and keep those that want to hurt him away. His name is Dumbo.

He is a Southern Elephant Seal. Dumbo first turned up on the beaches of Christchurch in 1993 and for six consecutive years spent each summer there 'in moult' (a natural process of shedding and re-growing pelage that occurs annually in seals). Dumbo was a sub-adult and therefore in a state of 'solitary limbo', before becoming sexually mature and securing his own territory amongst others. Why exactly Dumbo chose the public beaches of Christchurch to moult, where he went in winter, or indeed, where he is now, is not known. But he was certainly a handful and provided an interesting insight into these magnificent creatures and at times, sadly, the darker side of human nature. The summer of 2000 was the first since 1993 that Dumbo failed to return. However, it is now felt that this is entirely natural and that he is now of an age to be elsewhere making love with seals as opposed to cars. But wherever he is now, one thing is for sure – he remains in the hearts of many and will always be the city's most unusual visitor.

For more information about Dumbo, contact his personal NZ agents, minders, secretaries and public relation executives at his 'Christchurch Office' c/o Marine Watch.

disregard for trees. Surely it does not take a PhD to realise that it is Christchurch's wealth of flora that essentially is its very appeal, so why create something of a complete antithesis at its very heart? With so much negative debate, one of New Zealand's most noted architects, Ian Athfield, has been brought in to assist in revamping the revamp, and at the time of going to print researchers are out on the streets asking 'the people' what they would like to see – perhaps something that should have been done in the first place. However, current aesthetics aside, the main feature worth looking at in the Square is of course the Cathedral itself. It houses a number of interesting memorials and boasts an interior design that is an interesting and eclectic mix of Maori and European. The spire can be climbed in part, offering a panoramic and memorable **view** of the city. There is also an audio-visual and a good café attached. ■ *Tours are available Mon-Fri 1100/1400, Sat 1100, Sun 1130, admission from $4, child $1.50 (tour $3), T3660046*. The Square is also home to two notable characters, one made of bronze, a memorial and pleasantly quiet; the other wearing a cloak, a pointy hat and that never stops talking. The former is the statue of **John Robert Godley**, the founder of the Canterbury Association and essentially Christchurch itself; the latter the iconic **Wizard**, a local eccentric who has been 'entertaining' the masses with his views on life the universe and just about everything contentious for decades. As a wizard he apparently travels without a passport and has been known to get through

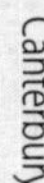

customs without one, presumably for the sake of some peace and quiet. ■ *The Wizard is in evidence Mon-Fri between 1300-1400 Nov-Mar. For an argument or more information visit his website, www.wizard.gen.nz* Also in the square is the **'Four Ships Court'**, a memorial to the 'first four ships' which stands outside the 1879 **Old Post Office** (which now houses the Christchurch VIC). Accessed through the VIC is the **Southern Encounter Aquarium**, T3779196, which seems remarkably out of place but is still worth a look, housing an interesting collection of local sea creatures, from \$10, child \$5. Open daily 0900-1630. Trout and salmon feeding 1300, marine tank dive and feeding 1500. **Guided City Walks**, offer informative 2-hour guided walks of the inner city for \$8. ■ *They depart Oct-Apr 1000 and 1300; May-Sep 1300, from the southeast corner of the Square, T3799629 (or book at the VIC).*

The Avon River

Heading west from Cathedral Square you immediately encounter (and not for the first time) the pretty **Avon River**. This is one of the city's greatest assets.

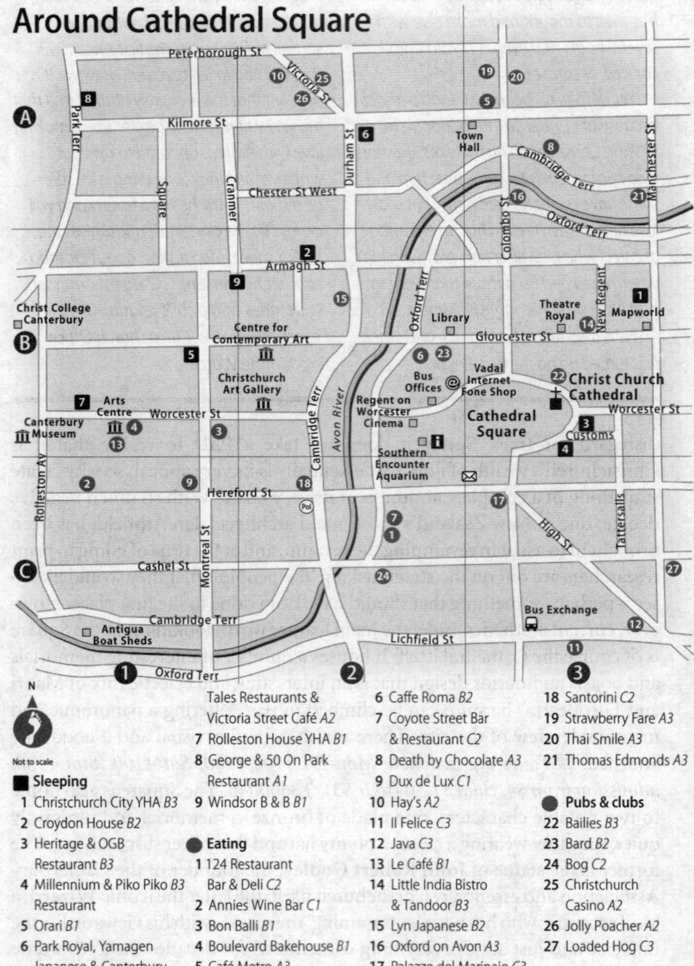

The river meanders like a snake from the northwest tip of the 'four avenues' through Hagley Park and the Botanical Gardens, through the city centre, before finally continuing its journey through the city's eastern suburbs to the sea. The river is particularly attractive in autumn when poplar and weeping willows are radiant in golden hues. It offers some lovely inner city walks that are outlined in the free *'River Walks of Christchurch'* available from the VIC. The *'Avon River Drive'* is another alternative. On the eastern bank of the river, just beyond Cathedral Square and beside the Worcester Street Bridge, is one base from where you can go **punting** on the river, T3799629. The punts operate daily usually from 0900-2100 (winter 1000-1600) and a 30 minute trip will cost from $15, child $7.50. Note also the 1917 statue of **Scott of the Antarctic** beside the river – not the first nor last reminder that Christchurch is a principal gateway to the Antarctic.

Across the bridge and on the right, further up Worcester Street, is the new **Christchurch Art Gallery**. Due to open in late 2002 this new building houses the collection formerly housed behind the Canterbury Museum in the **Robert McDougall Gallery**, T3650915. The impressive new gallery is poised to set the standard for galleries in South Island. As well as specialising in a formidable collection of New Zealand art, it will show contemporary works from the Canterbury Region and display travelling national and international exhibitions. Prices and times pending. The **Centre for Contemporary Art**, 66 Gloucester St, T3667261, is also worth visiting, five galleries and over 50 exhibitions per annum. Much of the art is for sale.

The Arts Centre

On the opposite side of the road is the **Arts Centre** of Christchurch, 2 Worcester Boulevard, T3660989, info@artscentre.org.nz Once the site of the original University of Canterbury, the old Gothic Revival buildings now house an excellent and dynamic array of **arts and crafts**, workshops, galleries and sales outlets, as well as **theatres, cinemas, cafés, restaurants** and **bars**. It is well worth a visit, particularly at the weekend when it hosts a lively arts and crafts **market**. It becomes very much the focus of attention for tourists with an International Food Fair and top local **entertainment**, from a local town crier to city buskers. There are also some notable historical features including the 'Den' of scientist **Ernest Rutherford** (see page 431), the **Great Hall** with its stained glass windows and the **Townsend Observatory** with its working telescope. Guided **tours** are available with the Town Crier and depart from the Centre's Information Centre in the Clocktower foyer, ■ *Mon-Fri at 1100, from $5, child, free. The free 'What's on at The Arts Centre' and 'Christchurch City Arts Trail' booklets are very useful. T3632836.*

Hagley Park & its attractions

At the western edge of the Arts Centre, Worcester Street meets Rolleston Avenue and the eastern fringe of **Hagley Park**. Amazingly intact after all the years of development, Hagley Park (over 200 ha) is divided in two portions by Riccarton Avenue, and comprises of pleasant tree-lined walkways, sports fields and in its central reaches the **Botanical Gardens**, enclosed by a loop of the Avon River. Well maintained and with a huge variety of gardens from 'herb' to 'rose', these provides a great escape from the buzz of the city year round. Autumn sees the gardens at their colourful best. The grounds open at 0700 and close at dusk. The Conservatory Complex is open daily from 1015-1600. The Information Centre and **Gardens Café** is located on Rolleston Ave, beside the Peacock Fountain, T3661701. ■ *Open daily Sep-Apr 1015-1600; May-Aug 1100-1500. Guided tours are available daily Sep-May, from 1000-1630 departing from the Information Centre ($6, child $4).*

At the entrance to the Botanical Gardens on Rolleston Avenue is the **Canterbury Museum**, T3665000. Housed in a grand 1870 neo-Gothic building and founded in 1867, it is well worth a visit, with the undoubted highlights being its impressive Maori collection and the Hall of Antarctic Discovery. In keeping with other museums in the country, it also hosts a dynamic Discovery Centre for kids and big kids alike. The Exhibition court displays a changing program of travelling national and international exhibitions. There is also a fine in-house shop and a café overlooking the Botanical Gardens. ■ *Daily 0900-1730 (winter 1700). General entry is free but there are charges for the Exhibition Court and Discovery Centre ($2). Guided tours are also available.*

Just north of the museum is **Christ College Canterbury**, which is without doubt New Zealand's most famous historic school. Built in 1850 it is an aesthetic and architectural delight, and in the late afternoon spills forth suitably clad and 'proper' scholars. ■ *Guided tours are available daily 4 Oct – 20 Mar (Mon-Fri 1030,1430,1900; Sat/Sun 1430), from $10, T3795570.*

At the southern end of Rolleston Avenue are the **Antigua Boat Sheds**, which were built in 1882, making them one of the oldest buildings in Christchurch. The former boatbuilders' premises now host a café and are the base for **Punting in the Park**, T3660337, who provide 30-minute punting trips daily from 1000-dusk, from $20. You can also **hire** canoes (one hour, $6); paddleboats (one hour $12); rowing boats (one hour, $20), T3665885.■ *0930-1700 (winter 1600).*

Canterbury Brewery

Near the junction of Riccarton and Hagley Avenues (Hagley Park), at 36 St Asphalt St, is the Canterbury Draught Brewery. Founded in 1854, its long established 'CD' is something of a libatious institution in the Canterbury Region. ■ *The brewery has a good* ***museum*** *and guided* ***tours with tastings*** *are available Mon-Thu, T3794940, from $8. Bookings are essential.*

Beyond the Four Avenues

City North and West

Mona Vale

Heading out towards the airport is **Mona Vale**, a beautiful Elizabethan-style homestead and gardens, built in 1905 on the land first settled by the Scots Dean brothers in 1843. While the Homestead itself now serves as a fine restaurant and café, the 5 ½ ha grounds are a spectacular array of features including a lily pond, rhododendrons, azaleas and exotic trees, all set in reverence to the lovely River Avon. Mona Vale is located just beyond the northwest corner of the 'Four Avenues' at 63 Fendalton Road, T3489660. The gardens can be reached by punt, and guided tours are available. Phone for details.

International Antarctic Centre

Also located out at the airport (signposted) is one of the city's 'must sees' – **The International Antarctic Centre and Hagglund Ride**, Orchard Road, T3589896, www.iceberg.co.nz Since the turn of the last century and the days of Scott and Shackleton, Christchurch has been a principal 'gateway to the Antarctic'. Today the Antarctic Centre, which opened in 1990, is a working campus and formidable array of buildings. In entirety it is home to Antarctica New Zealand (managers of New Zealand's activities in the Antarctic), the Antarctic Heritages Trust, The US and Italian Antarctic programmes, the International Centre for Antarctic Information and Research, and the Antarctic Passenger terminal and aircraft hangers, where you can often see the

Hercules that head off into the wild blue and very cold yonder. The Visitors Centre, which was opened in 1992, is an excellent introduction to the great white continent and a place from which would-be world travellers will emerge dreaming. Over all it is both informative and fun, with an excellent array of displays from the historical to the modern-day. One of the first displays encountered are the current Antarctic weather statistics (3832 km away and that day – minus 70° F) that send a shiver down your spine and your hands plunging into your pockets. Then, to get an even better idea of the real thing, you can don jackets and overshoes and enter the **Snow and Ice Experience**, a room kept at minus 5° F, replete with manufactured snow and ice. In contrast is a superb **audio-visual**, which beautifully marries images from the ice with inspiring music. From the displays you then emerge into the well and unusually stocked **Antarctic shop** and the 60° F **South Café and Bar**. ■ *The centre is open daily Oct-Mar 0900-2000; Apr-Sep 0900-1730, from $16, child $8. Guided* **tours** *are available from officers who have lived and worked on the ice or you can self-guide with the help of 'snow-phones' ($5)*. A recent addition to the Centre activities is the Antarctic Hagglund Ride. The Hagglund is a tracked vehicle that was originally used by the US and NZ Antarctic programmes in Scott and McMurdo bases. During the 45-minute ride you are taken to see some of the major facilities of the centre before experiencing the all-terrain abilities of the vehicle on a man-made adventure course, from $15, child $8. A combo Visitor Centre/ride costs $28, child $15. By public transport the City-Airport **bus** (from Cathedral Square) runs to the Centre every half-hour. The Centre also forms part of the interesting **'Antarctic Heritage Trail'** (free leaflet from the VIC). Note that the free Canterbury museum also hosts an excellent Antarctic display.

Orana Wildlife Park & The Willowbank Reserve

While out in the vicinity of the airport it is worth visiting one (or preferably both) of Christchurch's main wildlife attractions. **Orana Park** is New Zealand's largest captive wildlife reserve, set in 80 ha of parkland. It has a good mix of native and international wildlife with an emphasis on **African** animals. All the usual suspects are there from the lofty giraffes and horny rhinos to the ever-popular, inquisitive meerkats. And of course amongst the many New Zealand natives you will find a nocturnal kiwi house. Orana is located at 743 McLeans Island Rd (10 minutes from the airport) T3597109, www.oranawildlifepark.co.nz ■ *Daily 1000-1700, from $12, child $6.* Also near the airport (five minutes), 60 Hussey Road (off Gardiners Road), is the **Willowbank Wildlife Reserve**, T3596226. It focuses more on native wildlife and farm animals and provides daily guided tours ($2) and both night and day **kiwi** viewing. The reserve has a very successful kiwi breeding programme and you can also see the cheeky kea (mountain parrots) being fed. There is a great **restaurant** on-site offering buffet dinner from 1830-2030, from $37.50. ■ *Daily 1000-2200. Entry to the reserve costs $14, child $6. For transport book at the city VIC or T0800484485.*

Riccarton Bush & Riccarton House (Putaringamotu)

Located 3½ km west of the city centre on the banks of the Avon River, and set in 30 acres of parkland, is the historic Riccarton Estate. Once the home of the Scots pioneers and brothers William and John Deans (the first European settlers on the Canterbury Plains), it features the faithfully restored and furnished original 1843 **Deans cottage** in which they first lived, and the grand Victorian/Edwardian **homestead** that was built by the next generation from 1856-74. Within the house, which has recently been restored and redecorated in period style, you will find the detailed brochure *'The Story of Riccarton House'* which gives more details about the family and the lives they led. The main entrance to the reserve is at 16 Kahu Road. ■ *The cottage is open daily, while the homestead is open Mon-Fri 1300-1600, T3484277. Prices and times are under review.*

The Nga Hau E Wha Marae The Nga Hau E Wha National Marae or 'Marae of the Four Winds' is the country's largest marae. The meetinghouse (Whare Nui) is beautifully constructed and comes complete with greenstone (pounamu) inlaid steps (which should be rubbed for good luck). Guided **tours** are available, on which you will be given an introduction to Maori culture, protocol, history and tradition. You can also extend you visit and stay to experience the evening **performance** and **hangi** (feast). ■ *Daily, free. For evening performance and hangi, book ahead on T0800456898. Concert starts 1900, from $60, child $33. Includes performance, hangi and transport from the city. To get there independently from the city, take Hereford St (northeast) – turn right into Linwood Ave then left into Buckleys Rd, continue through to Pages Rd (250).*

City East East of the city centre the River Avon negotiates suburbia before emptying its contents into the Pacific. There is a **wildlife reserve** on the estuary that offers good birdwatching and short walk opportunities and a number of fine **beaches**. **New Brighton** is the main focus of activity, with a **bungy rocket** (from $35), **cafes** and a **pier** decked with hopeful anglers. New Brighton can be reached from the centre of the city, via Cashel St, then Buckleys Pages Road (8 km). South of the estuary via Ferry Rd (SH74) is the coastal resort of **Sumner** (12 km) which also has some fine beaches with safe swimming and plenty of cafés. The **scenic drive** to Lyttleton and the Lyttleton Harbour from Sumner (Evans Pass Road) is recommended.

City South

Airforce World If vintage aircraft are your thing then Airforce World on the old RNZAF Base at Wingram, Main South Road (15 minutes southwest) will appeal, T3439532. It has an impressive collection of 28 classic aircraft including a Spitfire and a Skyhawk. All of the aircraft have been faithfully restored and are theatrically displayed alongside special sections on World War II and the role of the modern-day RNZAF. It is worthy of a visit even if you are not a plane buff, and there is the added attraction of the Bi-plane joyrides (see activities below) and free flight simulators. Guided tours are available (1100, 1300 and 1500) and there is a café on site. ■ *Open daily from 1000-1700, from $10, child $5* .

Science Alive Although the Discovery Centre in the museum, the Antarctic Centre and wildlife parks are all obvious drawcards for kids, the Science Alive Centre on Moorhouse Avenue (Old Train Station), T3655199 is a great wet weather attraction. It is very much a hands-on place that could even see your kids waiting outside for you! ■ *Mon-Fri 0900-1700, Sat/Sun 0900-1800, from $6 (all day pass).*

The Christchurch (Port Hills) Gondola If only for the stunning **views**, the Christchurch Gondola is well worth the trip. The base terminal is located in the Heathcote Valley 10 km southeast of the city via Ferry Road. From there gondolas whisk you 945 m to the top of the Port Hills (1500 m) and the Summit Complex. The complex has all the expected shops and a café but also supports viewpoints from which you can gaze down to Lyttleton and across the Banks Peninsula. North, the view across the city is equally stunning, and on a clear day beyond the Canterbury Plains is the distant line of the Southern Alps. You can embark on a number of **walks** from the complex that explore the crater rim, including the Bridle Path which was once used by the early pioneers as the main route to Lyttleton. An attractive way of descending is by **mountain bike** (see activities below). ■ *The Gondola is open daily from 1000-2130, T3840700, from $14, child $7. A free* ***shuttle bus*** *leaves from the Visitor Centre at 1000,1400 and 1600.*

On the way or coming back from the gondola you might like to stop off at the **Ferrymead Historic Park** in the suburb of Ferrymead (Ferrymead Park Drive), T3841970. It's an entertaining mock up of a 1920 Edwardian township and a working museum with a wide array of period memorabilia including transport displays, Clydesdale horse-drawn carts, and a bakery selling freshly baked food. Trams and trains operate at weekends. ■ *Daily 1000-1630, from $8, child $4.*

Activities

One of the main activity operators in Christchurch is **Adventure Canterbury**, T3852508, www.adventurecanterbury.com They offer a wide array of trips and activities including, **Rafting** (September-May full-day $165); **Helicopter flightseeing** (from 15 minutes $140/ Heli-ski $945); **Jet boating** on the Waimakariri (two hours $49); **Horse trekking** (2½ hours $45); **Fishing** (5-6 hours $600); **Farm visits** (three hours $55); **Combos** from $89. Other activities and operators include:

Aerobatics Christchurch is well known for its Barnstormer and Pitt Stop Bi-planes. They operate out of the Wingram Airfield and Airforce World, 15 minutes southwest of the city (see 'Sights' above), T3439544 from $195.

Ballooning Ballooning over the Canterbury Plains is perhaps Christchurch's iconic activity. Two companies, *Up Up and Away*, T3814600, www.ballooning.co.nz and *Aoraki Balloon Safaris*, T3028172, calm@voyager.co.nz offer early morning flights of about one hour, with champagne breakfast from $200. Recommended.

Bone Carving There is a self-carving studio at 103 Worcester St, T3778942, www.bonecarving.co.nz where you can carve your own Maori-style pendants (tiki) from $35. Excellent value and a good wet weather activity.

Cruising For **wildlife** and **historic/scenic cruises** on the Lyttleton Harbour see page 488.

Fishing There are a number of operators offering half to full-day trips or tailormade options from $250. The VIC has listings.

Jet boating *Jet Thrills River Tours*, T025-387485; *Jet Stream Tours*, T3851478; and *Waimak Alpine Jet*, T3184881, offer a range of jetboating trips to the eastern Southern Alps rivers from $49-$90 with transport inclusive. Jetstream also offer a **heli-jetboat** option from $130.

Horse trekking *Waimak River Horse Treks*, T0800-873577, offer interesting 30 minutes or 1 ½ hours horse trek/jetboat combos or trekking only trips from $35; *Longspur Treks*, T3290005, are based near Lake Ellesmere and offer one to two-hour trips from $30.

Kayaking *Canterbury Sea Tours*, T344770, www.seafari.co.nz offer an interesting array of kayaking trips around the Banks Peninsula (from Lyttleton) from two-hour to full day, from $49.

Mountain biking There are some attractive options around Christchurch, with the Port Hills and Banks Peninsula being the main venues. *Mountain Biking Scenic Cycling*, T0800-424534, offer a good trip that goes up the Port Hills via the Gondola to then descend by bike, from $40; Other operators offering more far flung options are *Mainland Mountainbike*, T3298747, and *Adventure South* (see above), from $70. For independent hire see 'Directory' below.

Paragliding Paragliding is big in Christchurch, with a number of companies vying for the tourist dollar. All are safe and pretty similar in price; *Cloud Nine*, T3854739, offer tandem flights on a two-hour trip to the Port Hills area from $125; *Eagle Paragliding*, T3777834, offer 15-20 minutes flights from a number of local sites from $110; *Nimbus*, T3267922, similarly, offer a two-hour trip and flight daily at 1000 and 1300 for $110; *Pheonix*, T3267634, offer flights at $120 or full day courses for $150.

Punting For details see 'Sights-River Avon and Hagley Park' above

Rafting *Adventure Canterbury*, T0800-847455, offer full-day rafting trips (see above).

Tours The *TranzAlpine High Country Explorer Tour*, T0800-863975, www.high-country.co.nz is an interesting full-day trip that combines one hour transportation by coach across the Canterbury Plains; morning tea; a 15 km jetboat trip; a 65 km four-wheel drive safari; lunch; and then a 2¼-hour trip back to Christchurch from Arthur's Pass on the famous TransAlpine from $259. There is a huge range of tours operating out of Christchurch, encompassing everything from sightseeing, activity combos, wineries, gardens, walking and motorcycling. The VIC has brochures and full listings.

Skydiving *The Christchurch Parachute School*, T025321135, operate out of the Wingram Airfield 15 minutes south of the city, two-hour trip 10,000 ft, from $245.

Walking In town the **River Avon** and self-guided or guided **City Walks** (brochures from the VIC) are recommended, while further afield the **Port Hills Bridle Path** and **Crater Rim Walks** provide great views and can be tackled in part with the Gondola. Again the VIC has details, or see Christchurch Gondola in 'Sights' above. The beaches of New Brighton and Sumner offer good and easygoing **beach walks**. DOC has details and leaflets covering walks throughout the Banks Peninsula (see 'Information' above).

Essentials

Sleeping

As you would expect, Christchurch has plenty of accommodation covering all types and all budgets. Almost all the national chain **hotels** are in evidence in the city centre, with the majority being located in or around **Victoria** and **Cathedral Sq**. A few independent **boutique**-style options surround Hagley Park and overlook the River Avon. Likewise there are many **B&Bs** both in the city centre and a little further out, with some set in historic and spacious villas. Most of the **motels** are located northwest of the city centre along **Papanui Rd** and **Bealey Av** west (to SH1), or on **Riccarton Rd** heading south. **Hostels** abound in the city centre, from the small purpose-built, or old hotel/pub-style to the large and modern. All the **motor parks** are located on the city fringes in all directions, but mainly close to SH1 north and south. Over all you will find prices above average for South Island, but winter can see a drop in rates and some very reasonable deals, especially with the many competing hotels. Since Christchurch is the starting point for so many South Island travellers you are advised to pre-book in mid summer.

All the usual suspects are in evidence. At the top end is the popular **L** ***Park Royal***, corner Kilmore and Durham Sts, T3657799, F3650082, reservations@christchurch.parkroyal.co.nz Aesthetically, from the outside you will either love it or hate it, but there is no denying its prime position at the corner of Victoria Square. The Square acts like a garden and comes complete with river, fountains and a path leading right into the heart of the city. It has all the usual luxuries, a Japanese restaurant, a café and a very spacious, comfy atrium area on the ground floor. Overlooking all the action on Cathedral Square are the **L-AL** ***Millennium Hotel***, T3651111, F3657676, central.res@cdlhms.co.nz and the **A-AL** ***Heritage Hotel***, T3779722, F3779881, res.heritagechc@dynasty.co.nz both of which are modern, well-appointed and have all the usual facilities. The restaurants and bars are also popular with non-clients due to their ideal location. Located right next to the Avon River is the smaller and more discrete **A** ***Holiday Inn***, 356 Oxford Terr, T3791180, F3667590, reservations@holidayinnchristchurch.co.nz which is good value. Also over looking the river is the more expensive **A** ***The George Hotel***, 50 Park Terr, T3794560, F3666747, info@thegeorge.com It has a solid reputation with excellent, well-appointed suites, facilities and award-winning cuisine. Still near the river and retaining that 'Garden City' feel is the **AL** ***Chateau on the Park***, 189 Deans Av, T3488999, F3488990, www.chateau-park.co.nz Located at the northwestern edge of Hagley Park it is a little further from the action but that is part of its appeal. Its gardens are excellent and the restaurant and bar have a nice cosy atmosphere.

Out at the airport you will find the **AL** ***Airport Plaza***, T3583139, F3583029, www.airportplazahotel.co.nz and the cheaper **A** ***Commodore Quality Hotel***, T3588129, F3582231. Both are at the end of Memorial Avenue 5 min from the airport and the Antarctic Centre.

Motels There are literally dozens, offering affordable prices and located within walking distance of the city. On **Papanui Rd** in order of price you have **AL-A** ***Milano Motor Lodge*** (87), T/F3552800, milano@xtra.co.nz **A** ***Adelphi Motel*** (49), T3556037, adelphi@xtra.co.nz and the **A** ***Strathern Motor Lodge*** (54), T/F3554411, spa@xtra.co.nz On **Bealey Av**, again in order of price, you have the **AL-A** ***Tuscana Motor Lodge***, (74), T/F3774485, www.tuscana.co.nz **AL-A** ***Bella Vista*** (193), T3773363, www.bellavistamotel.co.nz The **AL-A** ***Avenue Motel***, (136), T3660582, avenuemotorlodge@xtra.co.nz The **A** ***Avalon Motel***, (301), T3799681, infoavalonmotel@xtra.co.nz On **Riccarton Rd**, The **AL-A** ***Apollo Motel*** (288), T3488786, www.apollomotel.co.nz **A** ***Aalton Motel*** (19), T3486700, welcome@aalton.co.nz Out at the **airport**, the **AL-A** ***Airport Gateway Motor Lodge***, 45 Roydvale Ave, T3587093, www.airportgateway.co.nz and the cheaper **A** ***Airport Lodge Motel***, 105 Roydvale Av, T3585119, airport_lodge@clear.net.nz, are recommended. Elsewhere, convenient to the town centre and good value, are the **B** ***City Worcester Motels***, 336 Worcester St T3664491, city.worcester@inet.net.nz, and the new units at the **B** ***Stonehurst Apartments***, 241 Gloucester St, T3794620, accom@stonehurst.co.nz

Again there is a huge choice of B&Bs & homestays . In order of price, in or near the **centre of the city**, are **LL** ***Weston House***, 62 Park Terr, T3660234, www.westonhouse.co.nz Neo-Georgian mansion offering luxurious suites and elegant surroundings opposite Hagley Park and the Avon River; **AL** ***Hambledon***, 103 Bealey Av, T3790723, F3790758, hambeldon@clear.net.nz A large and well-appointed historic 1856 mansion with lovely luxury en suites, a large collection of antiques and peaceful garden. Nearby **A** ***Eliza's Manor House*** at 82 Bealey Av, T3668584, elizas@ihug.co.nz is another vast, historic, well-appointed mansion with 12 rooms, 10 of which are en suites. The wooden façades and staircase of the ground floor are superb and the open fire gives a lovely cosy atmosphere. **AL** ***Orari***, 42 Gloucester St, T3656569, www.orari.net.nz is smaller, slightly cheaper with more modern décor and again is ideally located close to town, and the Arts Centre in particular. It has en suites and rooms with a private bathroom. The **AL** ***Croydon House***, 63 Armagh St, T366511, www.croydon.co.nz is another fine choice and is friendly and well located. Again, en suites or rooms with private bathroom. Nice to sit and watch the trams rattle past on the street outside. Good breakfast. Cheaper B&B options in the city centre include the **B** ***Ambassador***, 19 Manchester St, T3667808, the3ds@ihug.co.nz and the **A** ***Windsor B&B Hotel***, 52 Armagh St, T3661503, www.windsorhotel.co.nz

Further out in quieter locations, the 1857 **L-AL** ***Glenmore House***, 6 Pear Tree La, Hillsborough, T/F3328518, glenmorehouse@clear.net.nz, and the equally characterful **L-AL** ***Elm Tree House***, 236 Papanui Rd, T3559731, www.elmtreehouse.co.nz are both excellent and recommended.

There are plenty of hostels to choose from. The best mainstream, large establishment has to be the **B-D** ***Stonehurst Backpackers***, 241 Gloucester St, Latimer Sq, T3794620, www.stonehurst.co.nz It has just about everything – a wide range of good double, twin, single and dorm rooms (some with en-suites and self-contained), clean facilities, a pool, pizza bar, internet and a travel shop. It is deservingly popular so book in advance. The **C** ***Foley Towers***, 208 Kilmore St, T3669720, comes a close second and also has a great range of rooms and facilities, internet. It is a very friendly place and is more peaceful than the Stonehurst. Right in the centre of town are two YHA options. The **C** ***Christchurch City YHA***, 273 Manchester St, T3799535, yhachch@yha.org.nz, is the more modern. It is purpose-built so a little sterile but still has all the right facilities and comfortable rooms. The other YHA is the **C-D** ***Rolleston House YHA***, 5 Worcester St, T3666564, yhachrl@yha.org.nz Although a little tired it is still popular, with a good atmosphere and well positioned across the road from the 'happening' Arts Centre. There are several pub/hotel-style establishments and the **C-D** ***Occidental Backpackers***, 208 Manchester St, T/F3799284, freebreakfast@occidental.co.nz, is again a little tired but has clean comfortable double, twin, single and dorm rooms and a lively and popular bar downstairs, with great value meals. It's definitely a social establishment. Other good places include the very tidy, peaceful and friendly **C-D** ***Vagabond Backpackers***, 232 Worcester St, T3799677. The **C-D** ***Dorset House***, 1 Dorset St, T/F3668268, is an historic, upmarket place pitched somewhere between a backpackers and a B&B, with good doubles, twins and singles. It also has Sky TV and provides pick-ups; For women only there is the bohemian, health-promoting **D** ***Frauenreisehaus***, 272 Barbadoes St, T3662585. It prides itself in offering beds not bunks and has internet.

Motor parks At the northwestern end of the city is the **A-D** ***Meadow Park Top Ten Holiday Park***, 39 Meadow St (off Papanui Rd), T3529176, meadowpark@xtra.co.nz It has a great range of options from self-contained motels, lodges and flats to chalets, cottages and standard cabins, powered/tent sites. All are modern and the facilities are equally so including a spa pool, sauna and weight training room. South of the city centre is the older but tidy **B-D** ***Amber Park***, 308 Blenheim Rd, T/F3483327. It offers flats, cabins, powered/tent sites in a quiet garden setting.

Eating While Christchurch can't quite match Auckland, Wellington or Queenstown in its range of fine eateries, it is by no means 'wanting' and over all you will not be dissatisfied. Generally you will find a wide range of options to suit all budgets. Most of the modern eateries are to be found along the trendy **'Strip'** over looking the river from **Oxford Terrace**. This is a fine place for lunch and is very convenient for the city centre. **Colombo St** and **Manchester St** also offer a wide choice. Note Christchurch has 3 pretty unique dining options. For the romantic couple you can arrive at your restaurant by **punt** (see page 476). Another unusual option is the ***Tramway Restaurant*** car, T3667511 (see 'Sights' above), while the ***Willowbank Wildlife Reserve*** offers dining in view of the deer, before joining a complementary guided night tour to see kiwi, T3596226 (see 'Sights' above).

Expensive Hotel restaurants are popular, with the à la carte ***Yamagen Japanese*** and ***Canterbury Tales Restaurants*** in the *Park Royal* and ***The Piko Piko*** in *The Millennium* or the ***O.G.B*** in the *Heritage* all growing in popularity (see 'Sleeping ' above). The ***50 On the Park*** in the *George*, is another award-winning hotel option in a very pleasant setting, T3710250. ***Victoria Street Café***, which is in the Park Royal, is a good choice for lunch and fits nicely in the affordable bracket (open from 0630). The cuisine at the characterful and historic ***Dorothy's Boutique Hotel***, corner of Latimer Sq and Hereford St, T3656034, www.dorothys.co.nz has a fine reputation (open Mon-Sat from 1800, lunches Mon-Fri from 1200). A great romantic option is the ***Thomas Edmonds Restaurant***, in the rotunda, corner of Cambridge Terr and Manchester St. It is very different aesthetically, offering a fine imaginative, mainly NZ menu and, most importantly perhaps, can be reached by punt from the city centre. To book a punt see Avon River or Hagley Park 'Sights' above. A great lunch option that can also be reached by punt is the beautiful ***Mona Vale Homestead*** and gardens, 63 Fendalton Rd. They have an all-day menu (which is best to appreciate the surrounds), from 0930-1530 but are also open for dinner, T3489660. A good French option is the ***Bon Bolli***, corner of Worcester and Montreal St, T3749444, which is too modern in aesthetics but more than makes up for it with the cuisine.

Mid-range Two of the best options on the Strip (Oxford Terr) are the ***124 Restaurant, Bar and Deli*** (124), T3650547 (open breakfast, lunch and dinner), and the ***Coyote Street Bar and Restaurant*** (126), T3666055. Both offer imaginative dishes from seafood to pasta. ***Tiffany's Restaurant***, 95 Oxford Terr, T3791350, is another great choice for NZ cuisine.

Elsewhere, good affordable Asian choices include the excellent ***Thai Smile***, 818 Colombo St, T3662246; ***The Lyn Japanese Restaurant***, between Gloucester and Armagh Sts, T3654654 (open Mon-Sat for dinner from 1800 and Tue-Fri for lunch from 1200); ***The Little India Bistro and Tandoori***, corner of Gloucester and New Regent Sts, T3777997 (open Mon-Fri for lunch from 1200 and daily for dinner from 1700).

For Italian the ***Il Felice***, 56 Lichfield St, T3667535 (open Mon-Sat from 1800), is recommended; while ***Santorini***, corner of Gloucester St and Cambridge Terr, T3796975, is a good and very colourful Greek option. For seafood it would be rude not to mention the Italian-style ***Palazzo del Marinaio***, 108 Hereford St, T3654640 (open daily for lunch and dinner). For great NZ Lamb don't miss ***Hay's***, 63 Victoria St, T3797501 (open Tue-Sat from 1700 and Mon evenings in summer).

The Arts Centre is a great place to hang out during the day, especially at weekends. The ***Dux de Lux***, 41 Hereford St, T3666919, has a great vegetarian and seafood selection and a good atmosphere, while ***Annie's Wine Bar and Restaurant***, T3650566, is great for light lunches and has a good wine list. Open daily from 1100.

Lovers of weight gain and creative deserts should throw caution to the wind and try the ***Strawberry Fare Restaurant***, 114 Peterborough St, T3654897 (open Mon-Fri 0700-late, Sat/Sun 0900-late). It's great, and makes ***Death by Chocolate*** (209 Cambridge Terr, T3657323) look like the easy way out.

Cheap For huge, great-value lunches and dinners look no further than ***The Oxford on Avon***, 794 Colombo St, T3797148. It is a bit of a Christchurch institution offering set-price, no-nonsense buffet lunches and dinners, from 1130.

Out of the city Away from the town centre in the Port Hills (south via Colombo St then straight up Dyers Pass Rd) is the historic country house and restaurant at ***The Sign of the Takahe***, 200 Hackthorne Rd, T3324052, www.signofthetakahe.co.nz It offers award-winning cuisine and the views are better than anything in the city. Bookings are essential. The ***Morworth Estate Vineyard*** has a great restaurant/café providing a pleasant escape from the city. It is open for lunches from Wed-Sun 1000-1600 and is located in Broadfield (7 km southwest via Main South Rd, left on Hampton's Rd, then right on Block Rd), T3495014.

Cafés Again the ***Arts Centre*** is a fine café hang-out. ***Le Café***, T3667722 (open 0700-2400) in the heart of the complex has extended hours, making it one of the most popular social cafés in town. It also has great coffee, value breakfasts and internet. The ***Boulevard Bakehouse*** below is also popular, especially at lunchtime. Closer to town on Oxford Terr (176) is the ***Caffe Roma***, T3793879, which is also very popular, being a big breakfast/brunch hang-out at the weekend. ***Café Metro***, corner of Colombo and Kilmore Sts, T3744242, is another place with a loyal following and a good atmosphere, while the ***Java***, corner of High and Lichfield Sts, T3660195, is funky and a popular hang-out with the younger and more alternative crowd.

Pubs Christchurch's main drinking venue is a conglomerate of modern, well-appointed and lively restaurant/bars on ***Oxford Terrace*** called ***'The Strip'***. It is a good spot to be both in the evening and more especially during the day, when you can sup a bottle or glass of your favourite libation while watching the world (and the river) go by. Irish pub fans will be satisfied with the ***Bog*** near '*The Strip*' at the top of Cashel Mall, T3797141, and the older and more spacious ***Bailies*** in Cathedral Sq, T3665159. Other popular pubs include yet another ***Loaded Hog***, corner of Manchester St and Cashel St, T3666674; The ***Dux de Lux*** in the Arts Centre, corner of Hereford and Montreal Sts (especially daytime at weekends), T3666919; The ***Jolly Poacher***, Victoria St (opposite the Casino), T3795635; and ***The Bard*** an old English favourite on corner of Oxford and Gloucester Sts, T3771493. You will find most stay open to at least 2300 with some on 'The Strip' remaining open at weekends until 0230.

Music & dancing For listings of local gigs and visiting acts consult *The Press* newspaper. The web site www.bethere.org.nz can also be useful. There are plenty of pubs hosting live music, especially at weekends, and over all there is a lively and modern dance/club scene in the city centre. The best bet, if you can stand all the mobile phones, is to gather with the city slickers in the pre-club pubs along '***The Strip***' on **Oxford Terr**, then just tag along. In **Lichfield St** you will find a few of the main late-night clubs, with the popular and large establishment, the ***ministry*** (88-90), and nearby the smaller, cellar and gay-friendly ***Platinum*** (76), both good dance venues. Elsewhere the ***Base***, 674 Colombo St; The ***Edge*** (85) and the ***Occidental*** Pub on Hereford St are both pubs that go off into the wee hours. The 'Trendyphobic's best bet is ***Illusions***, corner of Chancery Lane and Gloucester St, which still puts on the 60s and 80s disco classics. For a good jig, joke and pint, head for the unfortunately christened Irish pub ***The Bog*** on 82 Cashel Mall, which has live music in the evenings from Wed-Sat.

Entertainment **Cinema and theatre** If you missed out on the Maori performances and hangis (feasts) in the North Island Christchurch provides one of the few opportunities in the South island (see Nga Hau E National Marae, 'Sights' above). **The Arts Centre**, Worcester Boulevard, is home to the Court Theatre, T3667256; the University Theatre; The Southern Ballet and Dance Theatre, T3797219; and the Academy Cinema, T3660167. There is a dynamic programme of events year-round listed at the Information Centre, T3660989. The Friday Lunchtime Concert Series featuring local, national and international musicians is held in the Great Hall of the Arts Centre, 1310, $8. The web site www.artists.co.nz/concerts.html is a good source of performance dates and venues. The Theatre Royal, 145 Gloucester St, T0800474697, is the other major events venue featuring everything from rock to jazz, while Kilmore St is home to the Town Hall, (86), T3778899, and the in-house James Hay Theatre. Mainstream cinemas include ***Hoyts 6*** in the Northlands Mall, T3666367; ***Cinema 3 Hornby***, Hornby Mall, T3492365; ***Regent on Worcester Cinemas***, T3663594; and ***Hoyts***, 392 Moorhouse Ave (Old Train Station), T3663791. For performance and cinema listings consult ***The Press*** newspaper.

Casinos The *Christchurch Casino*, 30 Victoria St, T365999, is a well-established institution and naturally a popular entertainment venue. Even if you do not get lured to the 'pokies', roulette and card tables, it can be a fascinating place to watch the desperate, cool or ecstatic go by. There are also various bars and good-value food outlets. Dress code is smart casual, the age limit is 20 years and it is open 24 hrs, T3659999.

Festivals

For details on events have a look at the useful web sites www.bethere.org.nz and www.showtimecanterbury.org.nz Noted annual events include:

Jan/Feb/Mar sees the ongoing events of the '*Summertimes*' programme, www.summertime.org.nz that includes summer theatre and retro events, twilight concerts and even a teddy bears picnic. The culminating outdoor Rick Armstrong Motors Classical Sparks on 3 Mar is the highlight, with a classical concert and fireworks in Hagley Park. In Jan (last week) the *World Busker's Festival* is a lively event attracting artists of all shapes, sizes and acts. Feb sees The Speight's *Coast to Coast*, a South Island icon event that is a gruelling combination of running, kayaking and cycling to the West Coast. Valentines night heralds a *Festival of Romance* with dancing and jazz in Victoria Square. The *International Garden City Festival of Flowers* between the 16-25 Feb offers over 30 events from garden tours to floral carpet displays. This event coincides with the *Jade Wine and Food Festival* on the 18th, which is a celebration of local produce held in Hagley Park. Mar sees the *Festival of Asia*, a day of Asian celebration at the Arts Centre (date pending); and *Le Race*, the South Island's largest cycling event is on the 31 Jul 2003 will include the biennial *Christchurch Arts Festival*, www.artsfestival.co.nz that includes theatre, dance, classical and jazz concerts, cabaret and exhibitions of the visual arts throughout the city. **Aug** sees the *Montana Christchurch Winter Carnival*, www.wintercarnival.org.nz a 10-day celebration of winter-themed events, while the *Showtime Canterbury* from 14-18 **Nov** is an annual carnival full of activities including the *A&P Agricultural Show*. From **Mar-Oct** look out for national and international **Rugby** 'Super Twelve' and Tri-Nations and Test matches at Christchurch's new Jade Stadium in the south of the city.

Shopping

There is a rash of **souvenir** shops in and around Cathedral Square selling everything from furry kiwis in rugby shirts to sheepskin slippers. One great souvenir would be your own self-carved, bone Maori pendant – or **tiki** – (see 'Activities' above), from $35. The **Arts Centre**, Worcester Boulevard is an excellent place to pick up **arts and crafts**, as is the weekend market on both Sat and Sun. **Rugby shirts** are always a great buy in New Zealand and Christchurch is home to *Canterbury of New Zealand* (CCC), which is the best label to buy. You can find a wide selection of apparel at their outlet at 5 Durham St, T3794220, or the *Champions of the World* outlets at 767 Colombo St, T3774100, and 88 Worcester Boulevard, T3798703. The main **bookshops** in the city are *Whitcoulls* and *Dymocks* on the Cashel Street Mall, just south of Cathedral Sq. A good second-hand bookshop is multi-storeyed *Smiths Bookshop*, 133 Manchester St, T3797976.

For **outdoor**, camping and tramping equipment try *Great Outdoors*, 54 Lichfield St, T3652178; *Mountain Designs*, 654 Colombo St, T3778522; and *Snowgum*, 637 Colombo St, T3654336. For the almost-famous Christchurch **alcoholic lemonade** visit the *Harringtons Brewery*, 945 Ferry Rd, T3846758.

Directory

Airlines *Air New Zealand*, 702 Colombo St, T3534899 (after hours T0800-737767); *Qantas*, T3747100 (after hours T0800-808767); *Mount Cook*, T3581210. **Banks** The *ANZ, ASB, BNZ, National and Westpac* are all to be found around Cathedral Sq. ATMs abound. Banking hours Mon-Fri 0900-1630. **Currency Exchange** Most of the major bank branches offer exchange services. *American Express*, 773 Colombo St, T3657366; *Asia Pacific World*, corner of Hereford and Manchester Sts, T3777703; *Interforex*, 65 Cathedral Square, T3771233; *Thomas Cook*, corner of Armagh and Colombo Sts,

T3796600; *Travelex*, 730A Colombo St, T3654194, www.travelex.co.nz (open til 2000). **Car hire** You will find all the major national companies at the airport and in town. Prices average about $35 per day with unlimited mileage; $750-$1000 credit bond; *Apex*, T0800-105055; *Hertz, T0800-654321; KiwiCar, T0800-5494227; Omega, T0800-112121; Pegasus, T0800-803580.* For cheaper deals try *Rent-A-Dent, T0800-736823; Cut Price, T3663800; Mac's T0800154155; Trusty, T3666329 and Shoestring Rentals, T3853647.* For motorhomes; *Maui T0800-651080, or Tomlinson Campers, T3745254.* **Disabled services** *Kiwiable, T3711774; Disability Information Service, 314 Worcester St, T3666189, dis@disinfo.co.nzang1033.* **Communications Internet** There are numerous places especially around Cathedral Sq. *Vadal Internet Fone Shop* is a vast place at 51-59 Cathedral Square (Bus Info corner), *T3772381, F3773281 (open daily 0800-2230). For a bit of peace and quiet and great rates try the E-Café,* 28 Worcester St, T3729436, in The Arts Centre (open 0800-2400); Others include the *Cyber Café, 127 Gloucester St, T3655183* (open Mon-Fri 0900-2100, Sat/Sun 0900-2000). **Post Office** Cathedral Sq, T0800-501501 (open Mon-Thu 0800-1800, Fri 0800-2000, Sat/Sun 1000-1600). **Library** Gloucester St (open Mon-Fri 1000-2100, Sat 1000-1600, Sun 1300-1600). **Luggage Storage** *Vadal Internet Force* 51-59 Cathedral Sq, T3772381. **Maps** Look no further than the excellent *Mapworld*, corner of Manchester and Gloucester St, T3745399. **Medical services** *Christchurch Hospital*, Riccarton Av, T3640640; 24 hr surgery corner of Bealey Av and Colombo St, T3657777; *Dentist* T3666644 (ext 3002); *Urgent Pharmacy*, 931 Colombo St, T3664439 (open til 2300). **Useful addresses Police** Central Station Cnr Hereford and Cambridge Terr, T37939999; Emergencies T111. **AA** 210 Hereford St, T3791280.

The Banks Peninsula

Jutting out into the Pacific Ocean from Christchurch, like the bulb on a jigsaw piece, is the Banks Peninsula. Distinctly out of character with the (now) connected and monotonously flat alluvial Canterbury Plains, it is a refreshing and rugged landscape of hills and flooded harbours formed by two violent volcanic eruptions. The two largest harbours, which now fill the craters and shelter their namesake settlements, are ***Lyttleton*** *to the north and* ***Akaroa*** *to the south. The first inhabitants of the peninsula were members of the Waitaha tribe who came south from the Bay of Plenty, but their claim was not to last. Around 1577 they were violently ousted by the Ngati Mamoe from Poverty Bay, who in turn fell to the onslaught of the Ngati Tahu, another East Coast tribe, in around 1700. For over 100 years peace reigned before yet another violent battle ensued between the Tahu and the invading Toa from Kapiti Island.*

Captain Cook was the first European to discover the peninsula, but actually thought it was an island and charted it as such, bestowing it the name Banks Island after his ship's naturalist Sir Joseph Banks. This confusion remained until 1809 when further surveys by Captain Stewart of the 'Pegasus' proved otherwise. Ironically, the Banks Peninsula was in fact once an island. After the violent eruption that created it, it was eventually connected to the mainland by the advancing alluvial plains that spread east from the Southern Alps.

By 1830 the seas around the South Island were plundered for their whales and seals and the sheltered harbours and bays of the Banks were an ideal base for a number of whaling stations. Permanent settlement began with the arrival of the French at Akaroa in 1840 and the British in Lyttleton three years later. In effect it was this pre-emptive settlement strike by the French that spurred the British to initiate the Treaty of Waitangi and effectively place New Zealand under British sovereignty and subsequent rule. Had they not, today, the Sky Tower in Auckland would perhaps be of the Eiffel variety and it would be Bonjour, not G'day – Oui?

The peninsula's two main settlements provide an interesting excursion from Christchurch, with Lyttleton, located only 12 km away via the Lyttleton Tunnel, being by far the more accessible. Akaroa is an 84 km drive from the city, south-east via SH75. Other than the obvious and refreshing hill and harbour scenery, both places offer some interesting historic sites and activities, including cruising and **dolphin watching**. The bays and waters that surround the peninsula are home to the world's smallest and rarest dolphin, the Hector's dolphin. The 3-4 day **Banks Peninsula Track** from Akaroa is also a popular attraction.

Lyttelton

Whichever way you arrive in Lyttelton, by the **Port Hills** scenic route, via **Sumner**, or through the **road tunnel**, it is quite an exciting delivery and will, along with the deeply contrasting scenery, provide a pleasant sense of escape from the city buzz and the flat vistas of Christchurch. Lying on the northern shores of the volcanic crater that now forms the **Lyttelton Harbour**, this busy, characterful port still has an air of history, befitting its stature as the place where the 'first four immigrant ships' arrived in 1850. It was also the port that Captain Scott and Lieutenant Shackleton used as their base to explore the Antarctic.

Ins & outs
Phone code: 03
Population: 3,000

Getting there By **road** Lyttelton is 11 km from the centre of Christchurch via the **tunnel** or about 20 km via the windy roads above Sumner. Both Sumner and Lyttelton are well signposted from Ferry Road at the southeastern corner of the city. The scenic **Port Hills** road is accessed via Colombo St via the Cashmere Hills. By **bus** Lyttelton is served by the No28 that leaves regularly from Cathedral Sq or the Casino in Christchurch.

Banks Peninsula

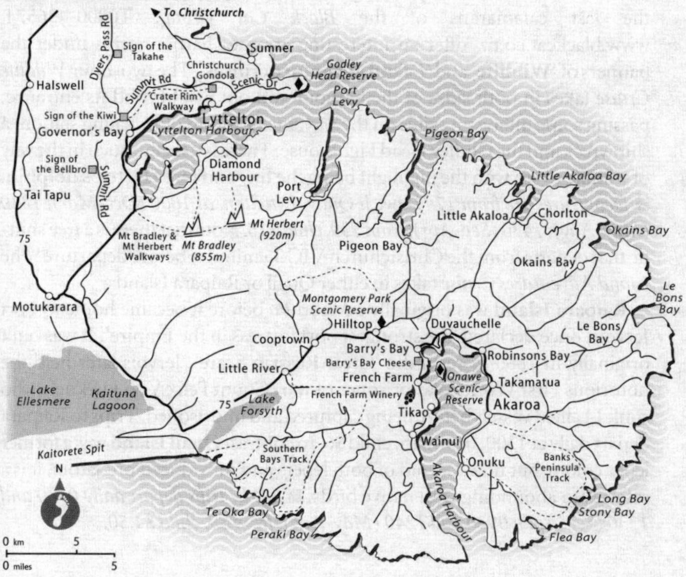

Information Most of the amenities in Lyttelton are to be found on or around London St, which runs parallel (and just north) of the waterfront and Norwich Quay. The Lyttelton **Visitor Information Centre** is located at 20 Oxford St, T3289093, F3289094, www.lytteltonharbour.co.nz Open daily 0900-1700. The staff are full of enthusiasm, and can provide all the relevant walks and activity leaflets. Of particular interest is the self-guided **historical walks** leaflet. They also have full accommodation listings and **Internet**.

Sights & activities

Relics from these times and its fascinating past can be found in the **Lyttelton Museum**, Gladstone Quay, T3288972. ■ *Tue/Thu/Sat/Sun 1400-1600, entry by donation.*

Also of historical interest is the **Lyttelton Timeball Station**, which sits high on the hillside off Sumner Road, T3287311. Built in 1876, it is the only survivor of three such contraptions ever built in New Zealand, and was used as an essential visual timing device to keep mariners accurate in their calculations of longitude. From 1876 to 1934 the large ball that is clearly visible at the top of a mast on the building's turret would drop at precisely 1300 in accordance with Greenwich Mean Time. ■ *After years of disuse the Station building, which is very grand both inside and out, was fully restored and is now open daily 1000-1700 (winter Sun-Thu), $2.50, child, free.*

As well as the historical walks around town and those up to the Christchurch (Port Hills) **Gondola**, the **Crater Rim Walkway** (19 km, four hours) provides a longer and spectacular walk with memorable views across the Banks Peninsula and the Canterbury Plains to the Southern Alps. Again the VIC can provide directions and all the relevant leaflets. Several **cruises** leave from the port from vessels both old and new. For the historical option try the 1907 **Steam Tug Lyttelton** which has been lovingly restored and taking passengers for historical cruises for 28 years. From September-June *The Tug Lyttelton Preservation Society*, T3228911, operate a 1 ½-hour Sunday afternoon cruise from No 2 Wharf, departing at 1430, from $12. In contrast the fast catamarans of the *Black Cat Group*, T0800-436574, www.blackcat.co.nz offer an interesting array of harbour trips under the banners of '**Wildlife**' and '**Island adventure cruises**'. The two-hour *Wildlife Cruise* takes in both sides of the harbour and out just beyond its entrance, passing some interesting sites on the way, including an old whaling station, a shipwreck and the Godley Head Lighthouse. There is usually much in the way of wildlife to see with the highlight being the tiny and rare **Hector's dolphin**. ■ *Departures are from 17 Norwich Quay, Lyttelton, at 1000 (Dec-Mar); 1330 (May-Aug); 1430 (Sep-Apr), from $39, child $15.* Note that there is a free shuttle that departs from the Christchurch VIC 35 minutes before departure. The *Island Adventures Cruise* takes in either Quail or Raipara Islands.

Raipara Island was originally a Maori *Pa* before it became home to Fort Jervois, once declared 'the strongest port fortress in the Empire'. It was built originally in 1886 to repel the 'Great Russian Scare'. Jervois later held the notorious First World War prisoner of war, Count Felix Von Luckner, who sunk 14 allied vessels before being captured and imprisoned. Trips to Raipara depart daily at 1300, from $15, child $6. In contrast **Quail Island** was a former leper colony but now, devoid of both lepers and introduced predators, it is a safe haven abounding with native birds. ■ *3-4 hr trips depart daily 0930 and 1330 (Sep-Apr); 0930 and 1240 (May-Aug), from $9, child $4.50.*

Sleeping & eating

There are a few good **B&Bs** within walking distance of the town centre. These include the **AL** ***Cavendish House***, 10 Ross Terr, T3289505, gsorell@xtra.co.nz which is a well-appointed Edwardian villa with doubles, an en suite with a spa and nice views; On Godley Quay is **A** ***Shonagh O'Hagan's B&B*** (16), T3288577, shonaghohagan@xtra.co.nz and the historic 1892 **A** ***Lochranza*** (14), T3328518, which both have comfortable queens, doubles and singles with good harbour views. On Sumner Road you will find **A** ***Randolph House*** (49), T3288877, randolph@netaccess.co.nz which has pleasant attic rooms and an en suite; and the modern **B** ***Dockside*** (22), T3287344. Again both have good views of the port and harbour. The tidy and friendly **C-D** ***Tunnel Vision Backpackers***, 44 London Rd, T3287576, has doubles, twins and dorms, and is right in the heart of town.

There are plenty of places to eat in Lyttelton, with most establishments on Norwich Quay or London Road. The brightly coloured ***Volcano Café and Lava Bar***, corner of London and Canterbury, T3287077, has a good traditional blackboard menu and good coffee. As a port there are no shortage of drinking establishments. The ***Lava Bar*** (see above) is very popular. Across the road is the new ***Rat and Roach***, T3287517, which also offers cheap pub food (Open lunch 1200-1400, dinner 1700-2030). The ***Irish Pub*** (also on London Road) is good with a deck overlooking the port. The ***Old Post Restaurant*** on Norwich Quay, T3287574, offers a traditional/Kiwi menu and is recommended. (Open Wed-Thu for dinner and all day Fri/Sat/Sun from 1100).

Akaroa

Phone code: 03
Population: 642

The name Akaroa, which is a variant on the Maori word 'hakaroa' – meaning 'Long Harbour' – gives no impression of Akaroa's distinctly French roots. In 1835 French whaler Jean Langlois established a whaling station in the harbour at French Bay and seeing its potential for settlement and as an ideal shipping port made a down payment on the land with the local Maori. Once he had secured the deal he returned to France to organise the colonisation of the newly acquired territory. Knowing nothing of the Treaty of Waitangi, which had effectively placed New Zealand under British sovereignty only 13 days before, a group of French settlers set sail on board *L'Aube* on Feb 19th 1840. When the French arrived there was a fractious period of political 'growling, lamppost sniffing and marking' before the French eventually agreed to accept the situation, sell their claims and integrate. Perhaps through their long association and history of dealing with such situations, this integration was thankfully successful and before long Akaroa had become a pleasant and cosmopolitan European community. They brought with them both their rich character and culture which gives Akaroa its modern-day legacy of fine architecture, place names and, still, a wonderful sense of community and friendship.

Ins & outs

Getting there and around By road Akaroa is 84 km southeast of Christchurch via SH75 which skirts past Lake Ellesmere, before turning inland into the heart of the peninsula. Just past the small settlement of Little River the road climbs, offering great views from the Hilltop Hotel, before falling to the head of Akaroa Harbour and into Akaroa itself. An alternative route is via Lyttelton but, due to the road network, this is no shorter. By bus Akaroa is served by the ***Akaroa Shuttle***, T0800500929, which departs from the Christchurch VIC daily Nov-Apr at 0900 and 1030 (also 1600 on Fri), returning from Akaroa at 1535 and 1630 (also 0930 on Fri); in winter daily from Christchurch at 1000 (also 1600 on Fri) returning at 1600 (also 0930 on Fri), from $30 return, $17 one-way. The ***Akaroa French Connection***, T3664556, offer a scenic day-tour to Akaroa and other places of interest on the peninsula, departing daily from the ***Intercity Travel Centre***, 123 Worcester St at 0910 or the VIC at 0930 in Christchurch, returning by 1730, from $38, $19 one-way. If you have time and can afford it, a hire car is the best way to explore the peninsula properly. Bikes can be hired from the ***Akaroa Village Inn***, 81 Beach Rd (opposite the Main Wharf), T3047421, *Chez La Mer Backpackers* and *Le Bons Bay Motor Camp* (see below).

Information & orientation Akaroa sits neatly on the shores of Akaroa Harbour, with the main street of Rue Lavaud being home to the VIC and most of the town's amenities. Further south, Lavaud Rd merges to form Beach Rd, which skirts around French Bay to the Main Wharf and beyond. The Akaroa **Visitor Information Centre** (Akaroa District Promotions) is at 80 Rue Lavaud, T/F3048600, www.Akaroa.com Open daily Oct-Apr 0900-1700; May-Sep 1000-1600. The staff are very helpful and will avail you of all the local knowledge regarding the village and the peninsula's more out-of-the-way places.

Sights Akaroa is a very pretty little place with a lovely atmosphere, made even more intriguing by its French street and place names. But perhaps before getting properly acquainted with the place you should take in the superb **view** of the locality from the hill to the south, via Rue Jolie and then Onuku Road (lighthouse road). Given the village's rich history the **Akaroa Museum** is worth a visit, located on Cnr Rue Lavaud and Rue Balguerie, T3047614. A 20-minute film provides a fine introduction backed up with collections focusing on early Maori, whaling, the French connection and the British succession.The **Custom House** at Daly's Wharf that dates from 1852, the old **Court House** and the **Langlois-Eteveneaux House** nearby, are three fine remnants that are an adjunct to the main museum. ■ *The museum is open daily; Nov to Apr 1030-1630; May–Oct 1030-1600, from $3.50, child $1.*

The VIC has Heritage Trail details and also offers an excellent Artisan's Trail leaflet that covers the wide diversity of artists to be found around the peninsula. Of more convivial and contemporary interest is Barry's Bay Cheese, Main Road, Barry's Bay (at the head of Akaroa Harbour), T3045809. This small family-owned operation makes a fine array of cheeses between October and May, and visitors are welcome to watch the process (alternate days between October-April) and sample the varieties, before purchasing their favourites in the shop. To visit other places of interest around the peninsula you can join Bayline Services, 108 Rue Jolie, T3047207, on their scenic mail run which departs from the VIC at 0820 Mon-Sat returning at lunchtime, from $20.

Activities There are a number of **harbour cruises** on offer, all of which depart from the Main Wharf. *Akaroa Harbour Cruises*, T3047641, www.canterburycat.co.nz offer a two-hour scenic/wildlife cruise at 1100 and 1330. Although the undoubted highlight is the probable sighting of hector's dolphin, you can also see little blue penguin, spotted shags and fur seals. The cruise costs from $33, child $15. *Dolphin Experience*, 61 Beach Road, T3047726, dolphins.akaroa@xtra.co.nz offer three-hour dolphin swimming and watching trips from $75, child $50 (viewing only $30). Trips depart November-April 0600, 0900 and 1200; May-Oct 0900 and 1200. Also on offer is a two-hour, purely scenic/historic cruise to the harbour entrance, departing November-April 0830, 1130 and 1430; May-October 1100 and 1400. *Dolphins Up Close*, also based on the Main Wharf, T3047641, offer similar trips; and *Bluefin Charters*, T/F3047866, offer independent boat charter. *Akaroa Seal Colony Safari*, T/F3047255, Double.L@xtra.co.nz offer an interesting 2 ½ hour road trip via the rim of the crater to a fur seal colony on the eastern bays, from $50, child $30. Trips depart from the VIC at 0930 and 1300. *Shireen Helps*, T3048552, akaroapenguins@paradise.net.nz offers two tours, one a full day-tour of various historical and scenic sites with a sea kayaking and snorkelling option, from $50, child $25, or a three-hour specialist tour of the DOC Little Blue **Penguin Reserve**, from $35, child $20.

You can also further investigate the surrounding countryside on four legs, **horse trekking** with Mount Vernon Stables, T3047180 (3-4 hours, $85), or on four wheels and quad bikes with *Akaroa 4 Wheel Bike Safaris*, T3047866, two hours from $79. Kayaks can be hired from *Akaroa Boat Hire*, Foreshore, Beach Road, T3048758 (half-day $25).

The 3-4 day, 35 km **Banks Peninsula Track** is a popular tramp across private farmland, the hills and outer bays, and is recommended. It is very much an off the beaten track experience, with great huts provided for accommodation. For more information T3047612, www.bankstrack.co.nz The track is open from October-May and costs from $150, which includes an introductory talk, booklet, transport to the first hut and four nights accommodation. You must take your own food. There is also a two-day option for $100. For other **day-walk** options on the Banks contact DOC or the VIC in Christchurch.

Sleeping

Note that there are some attractive and more remote accommodations throughout the peninsula. The VIC has full listings.

In Akaroa the French-influenced **L-A** ***Akaroa Village Inn***, opposite the main Wharf on Beach Rd, T3047421, F3047423, www.akaroa.co.nz, is the best of the hotel offerings with 40 units, several self-catering luxury apartments and courtyard cottages, most with views over the harbour. Swimming pool and spa and bike hire. They also administer the charming 1856, fully self-contained ***Rebecca's Cottage*** which is a dream for the romantic couple. There are a few good motels including the new **AL-A** *Criterion Motel*, 75 Rue Jolie, T3047775, AkaroaCriterion@xtra.co.nz which has spacious luxury studios and en suites close to the village centre. At the wharf end of Beach Road the **A** *L'Hotel Motel* (75), T3047559, d-tork@xtra.co.nz has good units overlooking the harbour and a licensed Italian-style restaurant downstairs.

There are plenty of characterful, well-appointed **B&B's and homestays** in and around Akaroa, with most boasting an historic and/or French flair, and you are advised to see the full listings at the VIC. Of particular note are the **AL** *Blythcliffe*, 37 Rue Balguerie, T/F3047003, www.blythcliffe.co.nz **AL-A** *Lavaud House*, 83 Rue Lavaud, T/F3047121, lavaudhouse@xtra.co.nz and the distinctly cute, purpose-built and self-contained **L** *Maison des Fleurs*, 6 Church St, T/F3047804, maison.des.fleurs@xtra.co.nz **L-AL** *Oinako Lodge*, 99 Beach Rd, T3048787, www.oinako.co.nz and the charming **AL** *Mill Cottage*, Rue Grehan, T/F3048007, are also recommended upper-range options.

There are 2 main **hostels**: The **C-D** *Bon Accord Backpackers*, 57 Rue Lavaud, T3047782, bon-accord@xtra.co.nz is under new ownership and has tidy dorms, cosy, good-value doubles and offers a warm and friendly Scots welcome. Be sure to ask about the progress on unearthing the intriguing Scots/French heritage of the house. Across the road the equally well placed **C-D** *Chez-la-Mer Backpackers*, T/F3047024, chez_la_mer@clear.net.nz, is in a nice historic house with a secluded garden. It also offers dorms, doubles, twins and singles. The **B-D** *Akaroa Top Ten Holiday Park* is located off Morgan Rd at the entrance to the village, T/F3047471. It is the best-facilitated **motor camp** and offers flats, tourist/standard cabins, powered/tent sites and nice views across the harbour.

Eating

Again, given the French influence, Akaroa offers some fine restaurants and cafés, but bear in mind that many are subject to seasonal hours. Arguably the top restaurant in

Akaroa is the French-style ***C'est La Vie***, 33 Rue Lavaud, T3047314, which offers great meals (especially seafood) by candlelight (open daily for lunch and dinner; dinner only in winter). Other more traditional options are the nautical surroundings and seafood of ***The Dolphin Café and Bar***, 6 Rue Balguerie, T3047658, and the modern beachfront ***Harbour 71***, 71 Beach Rd, T3047656. Both are licensed and open daily for lunch and dinner. A more affordable no-nonsense dinner can be found at the à la carte ***Jolly Rodger Restaurant*** in the ***Grand Hotel***, 6 Rue Lavaud, T3047011, which is also open daily for breakfast and dinner. The ***Turenne Coffee Shop***, corner of Rue Balguerie and Rue Lavaud, T3047005, seems to be the most popular daytime café and has good coffee, light snacks and internet (open daily 0700-1800). For great fresh bread and a good breakfast, head for the ***Akaroa Bakery***, 51 Beach Rd (open daily 0730-1600). The most happening **bar** in town is at the *Grand Hotel*.

Directory **Internet** is available at the ***Akaroa Library***, 141 Rue Jolie, T3048782 (open Mon-Fri 1000-1600, Sat 1000-1300), and the ***Turenne Coffee Shop***, Cnr Rue Balguerie and Rue Lavaud (see below). The **post office** is next door to the Visitor Centre, and the very attractive BNZ **bank** is across the road. There is no ATM. (Open Mon-Fri 0900-1630.) For **police** call T3041030; **doctor** T3047004.

North of Christchurch

From Christchurch SH1 heads north through the unremarkable settlement of Amberley before reaching the junction with SH7 and the **Waipara Valley**. From here SH7 heads northeast, through the **Hurunui District** to **Hanmer Springs** and the West Coast via the **Lewis Pass**, while SH1 heads north to **Kaikoura** and eventually Blenheim. Another road, SH70 leaves SH7 just north of Culverden, offering a scenic short cut from Hanmer Springs to Kaikoura. These routes are known collectively as the (signposted) **Alpine Pacific Triangle**, which is designed to combine the lesser attraction of The Waipara Valley **vineyards** with its two star destinations, Hanmer Springs and Kaikoura. Although many people visit Kaikoura (which actually lies in Marlborough, not Canterbury) on their way to Christchurch from the north, this 'triangle' offers an attractive multi-day trip from Christchurch. There is much to see and do in both Hanmer Springs and Kaikoura, but they are very different. In landlocked Hanmer the wealth of activities includes **skiing**, rafting, horse trekking and perhaps its year-round speciality – **mountain biking**. All these activities of course are added to the more obvious and soporific attraction of its hot pools in the **thermal resort**. Kaikoura, in contrast, set on the spectacular northeast coastline and almost miniaturised in the shadow of the Kaikoura mountain ranges, is equally a-buzz with activity. But here the emphasis is most definitely in the colder waters of the ocean and its inhabitants. At Kaikoura you can see and even swim with an impressive list of the oceans 'Who's Who', including albatrosses, seals, sharks (yes sharks!), **dolphins** and of course Kaikoura's very own **whales**.

Hanmer Springs

Phone code: 03
Population: 576

Hanmer has long been popular with Kiwi holiday-seekers, and has only recently come in to its own as a top national tourist venue. Its biggest attraction is of course its **Thermal Reserve**, but it is also very popular as a base for mountain biking and walking in the **Hanmer Forest Park** nearby and, in winter, as a base for the **Hanmer and Lyford Ski fields**. After these two activities, and when winter snows lie on the ground or spring rain plays on the puddles, the hot pools provide the perfect place to be. Hanmer offers a wide range of modern accommodation options, some good restaurants and numerous other activities from bungy jumping to horse trekking. The town is particularly beautiful in autumn when the forest and tree-lined streets are flush with golden hues and falling leaves. The name Hanmer derives from the name of Canterbury pioneer Thomas Hanmer. We can only wonder how Thomas managed, but the word Hanmer is far more often pronounced Hamner by mistake, even on official maps.

Ins & outs

Hanmer Springs is 136 km north of Christchurch and 219 km east of Greymouth

Getting there By bus Hanmer is served by ***White Star***, T3236156 (Westport/Nelson/Christchurch daily); ***Lazerline***, T3157128 (Christchurch/Nelson daily); ***East West***, T0800142622 (Christchurch/Wesport and return daily), and ***Hanmer Connection***, T3157575 (Christchurch/Kaikoura, Thu/Tue/Sat).

Getting around There are scheduled or on-demand shuttles to both the Hanmer and Lyford Ski fields, from $20. For details contact the VIC.

Information

The Hanmer Springs **Visitor Information Centre** is located just in front of the Thermal Reserve, corner of Amuri Av and Jack's Pass Rd, T/F3157128, www.hurunui.com Open daily 1000-1700. The VIC holds DOC walks information.

Sights

The Hanmer Springs Thermal Reserve Although it may be the last thing on your agenda after activities, the Hanmer Springs Thermal Reserve, on Amuri Avenue, T3157511, is undoubtedly the top attraction. The springs were first discovered by the Europeans in 1859 and later became a commercial venture and public attraction in 1807 when the first facilities and a hotel formed the beginnings of the resort and subsequently the town as a whole. The resort is an oasis of various pools ranging from the open and landscaped to the freshwater, swimming and a children's playpool variety, all connected by steaming boulder streams. The mineral-rich waters range in temperature from a luke warm 32°C to a balmy 42°C. Other facilities include a massage clinic, private hot pools, saunas, a steam room, a licensed café and a picnic area. ■ *Daily 1000-2100, from $8, child $4 (day pass $11, child $5.50).*

Activities

There are plenty to choose from, with mountain biking and skiing being the most prominent. The *Thrillseekers Adventure Centre (TAC)* is the hub of most activities and is based 9 km south of the town at the Waiau River Bridge, T3157046, www.thrillseeker.co.nz Bookings can also be made in their shop in the Mall, T/F3157346. Also located in the town centre is the *Hanmer Springs Adventure Centre (HSAC)*, 20 Conical Hill Road, T/F3157233. Open daily. They offer a wide range of activities and specialise in mountain biking trips, but also offer the independent **hire** of mountain bikes (one hour $14, full day $28), scooters, motorbikes, ATV's, fishing tackle, rollerblades and ski equipment. *Rainbow Adventures (RA)*, T3157401, are the third major, multiple activity operator. Note the latter offer 'combination' activity packages.

Bungy jumping is available through the *TAC*. It is a fairly tame 37 m jump from the bridge over the Waiau River 9 km south of the town, perhaps most suitable for the faint-hearted or as a practice run, from $95. **Canyoning** trips are offered by *RA*, three-hour trips, three times daily, from $52.

There is excellent local **fishing**, and the VIC sells licences ($13 per day) and lists local venues and guides. *Amuri Helicopters*, T0800-888308 offer eight-minute to one-hour **flightseeing** trips over the forest park and surrounding mountain ranges, from $75-$410. **Four-wheel drive Adventures** are offered by *Backtrax*, T3157684. A 2 ½-hour trip across farmland and the hills bordering the Waiau River will cost $98 while a longer four-hour trip cost from $169. *Molesworth and Rainbow Station Tours*, T3157658, offer half or full-day four-wheel drive trips to the largest cattle station in New Zealand from $65. *Argo Adventures*, T3157387, offer 45 minutes to 1½ hours **8WD** adventures from $50.

Hanmer Forest Park and the surrounding countryside is superb **horse riding** country. *Rainbow Horse Trekking*, T3157444, offer one-hour to full-day rides from $35. *Alpine Horse Treks*, Hawarden, T/F3144293, offer some excellent multi-day trips in the region from $330 (two-day) to $2480 (11 day). You can also go on an exciting five-day **wagon trekking** adventure with *Hurunui Horse Treks*, T/F3144204, from $1600. **Jet boating** trips (30 minutes) down the Waiau are offered by *Amuri Jet* and *TAC*, from $65. Amuri are based beside the bungy jumping site and bridge 9 km south of the town. Kayaking of the inflatable (carrot) '**Fun Yak**' variety is offered by *RA*, T3157401, half-day from $68.

If you are exhausted even reading this list, or fancy some pampering after your activities, then a **massage** can be secured at the Thermal Resort (see above). Kids might like to lose themselves, or adults might like to lose their kids, in the new and fairly unremarkable **Hurunui Maze**, located roadside as you come into town. It's fun but you cannot help wondering if it was only ever a rock garden project gone horribly wrong. ■ *From $5.50, child $4.50 (open 1000-1730)*. **Mountain biking** is a major reason why many come to Hanmer Springs, and the Forest Park offers some superb tracks from easy and moderate to the wonderfully muddy. The *HSAC* offer bike hire from $14 (one hour) to $28 (full day). *RA* also offers tandem **paragliding** from Wallace Peak (924 m) near the town from $140. The Waiau, Hurunui and Clarence Rivers are good venues for rafting, and trips from half a day to multi-day are offered by both *RA* and *TAC* from $65 to $580.

Skiing is another major reason many flock to Hanmer in winter. The two fields are the **Hanmer Springs Ski Area**, T3157233 (45 minutes) and **Mount Lyford**, T3156178, which is off SH70 (75 minutes). The Hanmer field has two rope tows, poma and lodge and accommodation facilities while the Lyford field has four pomas, ski hire, lodge and a restaurant. Lift Passes start at about $35. For more information contact the VIC or visit the website, www.nzski.com *HSAC* hire ski equipment and *Hanmer Heli-ski and Heli-board*, T0800-888308, offer half-day trips from $395, full-day $650. For ski shuttles see 'Getting around', above.

There are plenty of good **walking** tracks around Hanmer, particularly in the Forest Park that offers both short/long and easy/moderate options. The one-hour **Conical Hill Lookout Walk**, with its views south across the town, is accessed from the top of Conical Hill Road and continues through the forest to link up with Jollies Pass Road and back into town. For more walks information contact the VIC.

Sleeping

There is plenty of choice in Hanmer to suit all budgets, with most of the options being modern, well appointed and within walking distance of the town centre. You are advised to book ahead in mid-summer and at weekends in the winter ski-season.

The new **LL-AL** ***Heritage Hotel and Resort***, 45 Conical Hill Rd, T3157021, F3157023, www.heritagehotels.co.nz is ideally located overlooking the town centre and has 64 rooms ranging from the honeymoon suite to the standard. It has all the usual facilities including a good restaurant, bar and a swimming pool. The hot pools are only 2 min away. The **LL** ***Braemar Lodge***, T3157049, F3157104, www.braemarlodge.co.nz is a fine modern luxury lodge located on a hillside 9 km from the town. It has beautifully appointed rooms, spa and excellent cuisine. Back in town the **AL** ***Cheltenham House B&B***, 13 Cheltenham St, T3157545, F3157645, www.cheltenham.co.nz is well located and offers good value en suites. The **AL** ***Alpen Rose***, T/F3157679, also on Cheltenham St (21), is similarly appointed. For a great view the **A** ***Hanmer View B&B***, 8 Oregon Heights (very end of Conical Hill Road), T3157947, F3157958, lawsurv@xtra.co.nz cannot be beaten, and the modern facilities and rooms are good value. For a cheaper option try the friendly **A** ***Glenalvon Lodge and B&B***, 29 Amuri Ave, T3157475, glenalvon@xtra.co.nz It has nice rooms with private bath and an en-suite. Self-contained modern units are also available.

The **motels** in Hanmer are generally excellent. The **A** ***Alpine Lodge***, 1 Harrogate St, T3157311, www.alpinelodgemotel.co.nz is modern lodge-style and well placed. The new **A** ***Scenic Views***, 10 Amuri Ave, T/F3157419, scenicviews@xtra.co.nz is located just at the entrance to the town and offers peace and quiet and, as it suggests, mountain views. The **A** ***Hanmer Inn Motel***, 16 Jack's Pass Rd, T3157516, motel@hanmer.com, is right in the heart of the town and a stone's throw from the thermal reserve. The **AL-A** ***Greenacres Chalets and Apartments***, 84 Conical Hill Rd, T3157125, www.greenacresmotel.co.nz is another modern option offering self-contained chalets and apartments overlooking the town, and has a spa. The **A-B** ***Willowbank Motel***, 121 Argelins Rd, T3157211, is the cheapest motel option in town. Backpackers need look no further than the friendly **C-D** ***Hanmer Backpackers***, 41 Conical Hill Rd, T3157196 which is close to the town centre, offering dorms and 2 good-value doubles. There are four motor parks to choose from, with the **B-D** ***Mountain View Top Ten***, T3157113, at the entrance to the town, and the **B-D** ***AA Tourist Park***, 200 Jacks Pass Rd, T3157112, south of the Thermal Resort, being recommended. Both have flats, cabins, powered/tent sites and clean modern facilities.

Eating

For fine dining the restaurant in the ***Heritage Hotel***, T3157021 (see above), is a good option (open for breakfast 0730, lunch 1200-1430 and dinner from 1800). Despite that, many folk still gravitate to the slightly cheaper and characterful ***Old Post Office Restaurant*** near the Thermal Resort at 2 Jack's Pass Rd, T3157461. It specialises in NZ cuisine and is open daily from 1800. The ***Alpine Village Inn***, Jack's Pass Rd, T3157005, is the local pub and does hearty, good-value pub food for lunch and dinner daily from 1200-1400 and 1730-2030, while ***PT's*** in the Mall, T3157685, offers good gourmet pizzas (open daily 1000-2200). There is a scattering of cafés along Amuri Ave, Conical Hill Road and in the Mall, all of which are quite similar in fare and value. ***Jollie Jacks Café and Bar***, 12A Conical Hill Rd, T3157388, does good coffee and value breakfasts, and is a good spot to watch the world go by. Open daily from 1100.

Directory

There is an **ATM** at the **Bank** of New Zealand beside the VIC, T3157220 (Open 0900-2100). **Internet** is available at the *Hanmer Business Centre*, 18 Conical Hill Rd (Open Mon-Fri 1200-1500). The **post office** is in the Four Square **Foodmarket**, which in turn is in the main shopping centre. **Traveller's cheques** are accepted and exchanged at the foodmarket. The **police** station is at 39 Amuri Av, T3157117, and the **Medical Centre** is located at 20 Amuri Av, T3157503.

Hanmer Springs to the West Coast

From Hanmer Springs SH7 crosses the northern ranges of the Great Divide (Southern Alps) to the West Coast via the **Lewis Pass**, **Maruia Springs**, **Springs Junction** and **Reefton**. Although not as dramatic as Arthur's Pass, further to the south, it offers some lovely scenery and a few good walking opportunities on the way. It also boasts a mountain with one of the most unusual names in the country. There are many with wonderful names, but frankly **Mons Sex Millia** has to take the honours.

At the top of the Hope River Valley from Hanmer the road skirts the borders of the **Lake Sumner Forest Park** and begins to follow the Lewis River to its headwaters and the saddle known as Lewis Pass (864 m). In pre-European times the Ngai Tahu Maori of Canterbury used this route to access the West Coast in search of greenstone (pounamu). Having negotiated the pass on their return, they are said to have dispensed with their slaves – alas not with a 'Thanks lads, see you next year', but a brutal death followed by a feast of their various bodily parts. A valley known as Cannibal Gorge remains testament to this rather grim form of the early 'transport café'.

The pass itself was named in 1860 after pioneer surveyor Henry Lewis. Ironically, Henry's daughter Eleanor married Arthur Dudley Dobson who surveyed 'Arthur's' Pass. But it doesn't end there. Arthur's sister then married the geologist and surveyor Julian Von Haast who is accredited with much of the exploration, survey work and many place names on the West Coast.

Lake Sumner Forest Park and the Lewis Pass offer some excellent **walks** from one hour to several days, and these are best outlined in various DOC leaflets, including the '*Lewis Pass Region*' broadsheet, which is available from the Hamner VIC. The lichen-covered beech forests are particularly superb in this region and well worth further investigation.

The five-day **St James Walkway** that begins near the Lewis Pass summit car park (and infamous Cannibal Gorge) is particularly good. There is a network of DOC huts, and the moderate track is best negotiated in summer or autumn. Just beyond the Lewis Pass, heading west, is the oasis of **Maruia Springs**, a small **thermal** resort with hot pools, comfortable accommodation, a restaurant and a bar (see below). It is it is a perfect stop for tired trampers. A further 21 km west is **Springs Junction**, the only significant settlement between Hanmer and Reefton, with accommodation, a café, and also a petrol station.

Sleeping **A-D** *Maruia Springs Thermal Resort*, T/F5238840, has lovely luxury/standard studio and family units and dorm accommodation for backpackers. The tariff includes unlimited access to the thermal pools. Two licensed restaurants one traditional/Kiwi, the other Japanese. Public access to the hot pools daily 0900-2100, from $7, child $4. Private pools available.

Around 12 km west of the hot pools is the **A** *Lewis Pass Motel*, SH7, T/F5238863, which offers 3 modern self-contained units in a pleasant country setting. In Springs Junction itself is the **B-D** *Alpine Inn*, T5238813, sj.alp.inn@xtra.co.nz offering studio units and separate backpackers accommodation. Attached is a café and shop selling light snacks. Internet. Open daily 0730-2030.

Transport Springs Junction is 95 km west of Hanmer Springs via SH7. **By bus** ***White Star*** T3236156 (Wesport to Christchurch Sun-Fri), and ***East-West***, T0800142622 (Westport to Christchurch daily via Lewis Pass). For more information contact the Hanmer VIC.

Kaikoura

Phone code: 03
Population: 4,000

So you have come to see Moby Dick and friends? Well, you have certainly come to the right spot. Kaikoura is a place that is not only aesthetically stunning but one that has one of the best sea creature 'who's who' in the world. They are all here: Moby, Flipper, Kaiko, Jaws, the lot – you might even bump into Marine Boy having a beer in the local boozer or a mermaid on the bus.

Okay, not quite. But for the wildlife enthusiast the Kaikoura coast is second only to the Otago Peninsula for richness and accessibility to some of New Zealand's biggest and most famous wildlife icons. The reason there is so much diversity matched with ease in accessibility is due to the topography and depth of the ocean floor. Just to the south of Kaikoura a trough comes unusually close to the coastline creating an upsurge of nutritious plankton soup, giving rise to the many creatures with which we are more familiar further up the food chain. At the very top of course, on the ocean throne, the majestic and much victimised king of them all – is the whale.

But even if you came to Kaikoura thinking that whales was a small and fine rugby playing nation somewhere in Britain, or indeed that seals clap and throw beach balls to each other, you cannot fail to be impressed. From the azure waters that surround the beautiful Kaikoura Peninsula, backed by the snow-capped peaks of the Kaikoura Ranges, you can get close up and personal with them all, from whales and dolphins, to seals, albatrosses and even sharks. So the place is very special and even before you arrive there is that sense of excitement.

Ins & outs

Getting there and around Kaikoura is 183 km north of Christchurch, 129 km south of Blenheim (154 km Picton) on SH1, and 136 km northwest of Hanmer Springs via SH70. By **bus** Kaikoura is served from Christchurch/Blenheim/Picton by ***Intercity***, 123 Worcester St, T3195641 (twice daily, book at the VIC); ***Atomic Shuttles***, T3195641 (daily); ***Southern Link***, T3588355, (daily); ***East Coast Express***, T050-8830900; ***South Island Connections***, T3666633; and ***Kiwilink***, T5778332. The fare to Christchurch or Blenheim costs from $15. ***Hanmer Connections***, T0800-377378, go to Hanmer Springs Tue/Thu/Sat at 1400 from $30; and ***South Island Connections*** go on Mon/Wed/Fri. Both drop-off in the centre of the village. By **train** Kaikoura is served by the TransCoastal, T0800-802802, daily (Christchurch 0700, from $19; Blenheim/Picton 1240, from $18). The train station is on Clarence St. For a **taxi** call T3196214.

Information & orientation

Kaikoura's human development is spread like a small rash either side of the neck and shoulders of the Kaikoura Peninsula, with the community being essentially split in two. SH1 connects both communities and essentially garrottes the peninsula. The main hub of activity is spread on the edge of its northern neck. Here you will find the commercial centre, VIC (West End) and **Train Station** (Clarence St). The Train Station houses *Whale Watch Kaikoura*. East of the 'West End', the **Esplanade**, that contains much of the accommodation, skirts the edge of the peninsula, terminating at **Point Kearn** and the peninsula walkway. This walkway crosses the scalp of the peninsula to link with **South Bay** on its southern edge. This is where the boats leave to encounter the whales and dolphins that inhabit the waters of deep ocean troughs off South Bay.

The Kaikoura **Visitor Information Centre** is located in the West End, T3195641, F3196819, www.kaikoura.co.nz Open daily 0800-1700 (Jun-Aug 0900-1700). It can provide information and arrange bookings for accommodation and onward transportation. There is also a 20-min precursory audio visual about the local environment and wildlife shown every hour or on demand, $3, child $1. All **DOC** information is also held at the VIC.

History

Although the peninsula was known to be heavily settled by Maori before the Europeans arrived, modern day Kaikoura was, ironically, first established as a whaling station in the early part of the 1800s. Its most noted pioneer was **George Fyffe**, who succeeded his uncle as the station manager. George built Kaikoura's oldest remaining house (**Fyffe House**) in 1860, located near the Old Wharf. The Fyffe name was also bestowed upon the mountain immediately

Kaikoura

To Blenheim, Picton, Mediterranean & Mussell Boys

To Old Convent & Donegal House

To Airport, Christchurch, Hanmer Springs, Limestone Cave, Kaikoura Wine Company, Fyffee Country Inn & campsites

Kaikoura Helicopters
Whale Watch Kaikoura
Kaikoura District Museum
Kodak Express
Dolphin Encounter
Pacific Ocean
Nga Niho Park
Scenic Reserve
Scenic Reserve
Lookout
Peninsula Walkway
Peninsula Walkway
Peninsula
South Bay

Beach Rd
Lyell Creek
Highway 1
Ludstone Rd
Grays
Kiwi St
Davidson
West End
Adelphi Terr
Chance Haven
Fyffe Av
Bayview St
Churchill St
Deal St
Hastings St
Takahanga
Killarney
Esplanade
Torquay St
Yarmouth
Brighton
Ramsgate
Scarborough St
Margate
Wakatu
Avoca St
Dover St
Austin St
Cromer
Ward St
Maui
Endeavour
Lookers-on
South Bay Parade
Kotare Pl
Takahe
Kotuku Rd
Kea
Tui
Weka
Moa Kaka Rd

Sleeping

1 Anchor Inn
2 Bayview B & B
3 Beach Road
4 Blue Seas
5 Central Backpackers
6 Cray Cottage
7 Dusky Lodge
8 Fifeshire B & B
9 Hilltop
10 Kaikoura (Maui) YHA
11 Kaikoura Top Ten Holiday Park
12 Nikau Guesthouse
13 Topspot Backpackers
14 White Morph

behind the township. After whaling it was mainly fishing, particularly for crayfish, that took over. Today of course Kaikoura is synonymous with its wildlife, thankfully now hunted only by the camera not the harpoon , and it is the resident and migratory whales that remain the focus.

Sights

Of course most of what you have probably come to see lies beneath the waves and has flippers, but Kaikoura offers a number of land-based features worthy of investigation. Paramount is the **Kaikoura Peninsula** that juts out into the ocean like a well-weathered head. The cliff-top and Shoreline **Peninsula Walkways** that link the northern and southern settlements of Kaikoura cross the head of the peninsula and offer superb coastal aesthetics (see below). A good spot to get an overall impression of the town, the peninsula and its mountain backdrop is from the **lookout** just off Scarborough Terrace (off SH1 between the northern and southern settlements).

There are three historical venues of note: The **Kaikoura District Museum**, 14 Ludstone Road, T3197440, was established in 1971 and offers an interesting insight into the early Maori and whaling activities. If the weather closes in and you cannot get out on to the water it can provide a good activity option and help pass the time. ■ *Mon-Fri 1230-1630, Sat/Sun 1400-1600, $2.* **Fyffe House** (see above) is located on Avoca Street, near the Old Wharf. ■ *Guided tours (30 minutes) are available daily between 1000-1600, $5, T3195835.* The 'Maori Leap Cave', located 2 km south of Kaikoura, was only discovered this century and is a sea-formed **limestone cave** featuring all the usual karst scenery. It can be visited on a 35-minute guided tour, T3195023, from $8.50, child $3.50. While in the area of the cave you might like to visit the **Kaikoura Winery** which is located just south of the

Lower Ward
Fyffe House
8
Walkway
Fyffe Quay
Point Kearn Car Park
Kaikoura Peninsula

● **Eating**
1 Act-one Bar & Café
2 Craypot Café & Bar
3 Finz Seafood & Wine Bar
4 Green Dolphin
5 Sonic Bar & Café
6 Why Not

Modern-day whaling in Kaikoura

The whale-watching experience is a wonderful mix of expectation, unpredictability and awe. Kaikoura is actually home to its own pod of ***Sperm Whales*** *– the species you are most likely to see. Although it is a complex social set- up and much is still not known, it is probably one or two of the young males from these resident bachelor pods that you will see. Of course this does not mean you are going to see a gang of prepubescent nippers – they are still enormous and are often joined by larger, visiting adults. A bull male can weigh as much as 50 tonnes and be up to 20 m in length. Other whale species that are seen regularly include* ***Humpbacks, Rights*** *and* ***Orcas****. If you are exceptionally lucky you may also see the endangered and truly industrial-size* ***Blue Whale****.*

Your boattrip to 'hunt down' and 'encounter' the whales is a fascinating and well-orchestrated performance of hydrophonics and simple 'eye-spy'. A combination of the two is used to locate the whales on or below the surface. It is tremendously exciting and timing is all important. They are known to dive for certain lengths of time and once surfaced remain there to catch their breath for around three minutes. This is your chance. When the great leviathan is spotted and the word is given, almost everybody jumps from their seat and clambers to get that illusive National Geographic shot from the decks. On rough days this can be quite riotous, with copious and unintentional bouts of head butting and hair pulling. Only a few poor souls are left strapped to their seat, their vision of a whale long lost at the bottom of a sick-bag. Believe it or not some folk even fall asleep. On calm days it is much more orderly and you will also get a better view of the whale's vast bulk. Whales are a bit like icebergs, for all you can see above the surface, there is an awful lot more beneath. However, regardless of conditions what you are guaranteed to see is the point when the whales dive, flipping their tail in the air and descending gracefully back to the depths. Of course there is no guarantee you will see a whale at all and you do receive a ***refund*** *if the trip is unsuccessful. But most often you can expect to see one to three on the two hours you are out in the bay. You will also be taken to encounter dolphins, which are equally as spectacular especially in huge pods of up to 100.*

town, T0800-4524568, www.kaikourawines.co.nz There are hourly tours daily (from $7.50), underground cellars and tastings.

Activities There are two things you need to bear in mind with the boat-based activities in Kaikoura. The first is simple – in mid-summer book the whale-watching and dolphin-swimming well in advance. Even the other less popular activities are worth **pre-booking** to avoid disappointment. The second is the notoriously fickle **weather**. Given its position on the Southern Ocean, Kaikoura is subject to the vagaries of wind and wave, and trips can be cancelled at a moment's notice. Again to avoid disappointment give yourself at least two days, just in case your trip is rescheduled. Also be sure to request your inclusion on another trip on cancellation, since this will not be done as a matter of course.

Whale watching The first commercial whale-watching operation in New Zealand was started in 1987 by the Maori-owned and-operated *Whale Watch Kaikoura*, T3196767, F3196545, www.kaikoura.co.nz/whalewatch The company now has four purpose-built vessels and can accommodate about 50,000 visitors annually. Their base is at the 'Whaleway Station' (next to the Railway Station), accessed off Beach Road (SH1) just beyond West End. They offer between three to four 2-3½-hour trips daily (seasonal departures) from

$95, child $60. Recommended. The boats all leave from South Bay, 10 minutes from the Whaleway Station. You can expect to see at least one whale on your trip but if the trip is unsuccessful there is an 80% refund. Expect to see not only whales, but dolphins, seals, albatrosses and other unusual seabirds. Trips are, of course, weather-dependent and can be cancelled at any time. Note: your inclusion on a later trip is not automatic and must be requested.

If you don't like the idea of a boat trip, then perhaps you might like to go whale-watching from the air. This can be particularly good in calmer sea conditions when you can see the whole whale from above (obviously not possible from the surface). *Wings Over Whales*, based at the Peketa Airfield 6 km south of Kaikoura, T3196580, www.kaikoura.co.nz/wow offer 30-45 minute-flights at 0900/1100/1300 and 1500, from $95, child $60; while *Kaikoura Helicopters*, based at the 'Whaleway Station', T3196609, www.kaikoura.co.nz/helicopters offer 30-40 minute-flights from $150-$230, child rates negotiable.

Dolphins The coastal waters around Kaikoura abound with dolphins, and not just one species. They range from the common and bottlenose dolphins to the smaller dusky and rare hectors dolphin. It is the dusky dolphin you are most likely to encounter (or swim with), and pods running into their hundreds, even thousands are not uncommon. Even from the deck of a boat the sight of an inquisitive playful pod is superb. The duskies are also well known for breaching, and will jump out of the water or even summersault in an almost choreographed display of 'being'. Depending on their mood they may show great interest in the boat or swimmers or, on other days, show complete indifference. The main operator is *Dolphin Encounter* who have an office at 58 West End, T3196777, F3196534, info@dolphin.co.nz In summer the 3-hr trips leave from West End at 0600,0900 and 1300, in winter 0900 and 1300, from $95, child $80 (viewing only $48, child $38). If you swim, and provided a pod is found (which is highly likely – refund if they are not!), you will have plenty of time in the water frolicking around with the dolphins. You will be given a safety briefing and will be encouraged to make high-pitched bagpipe-like noises to attract them. This in turn will keep the 'viewing-only' passengers highly entertained. Take a towel and warm clothing, and book well in advance. Recommended.

Seals With whales and dolphins being the main oceanic stars, the New Zealand fur seals are often overlooked. But encounters with these inquisitive 'fat-bodies' can be a memorable experience. On land they are undisputed 'beach-bum-couch-potatoes', but under water it is a completely different story, displaying an ease and grace in motion that would put any ballet dancer to shame. In Kaikoura there is the choice of observing them from land, boat, kayak, or to get up close and personal in the water.

NZ Sea Adventures, 85 West End, T3196622, www.kaikoura.co.nz/scuba offer boat-based swimming on a one-hour excursion, from $50, child $30 (viewing only $25, child $15); *Seal Swim Kaikoura*, T3196182, www.kaikoura.co.nz/sealswim offer two-hour land-based snorkelling tours, from $40, child $30 (November-April); *Topspot Seal Swim*, T3195540, offer the same, again from November-April from $40, child $30. Finally, a kayak can provide a great milieu from which to encounter seals, and *Seal Kayak Kaikoura*, T3195641, offer half-day guided tours taking in both the scenery and seals of the peninsula. Trips depart from the VIC daily at 0830, 1230 and (summer) 1630, from $55, child $35. *Kaikoura Seal Colony*

Tours, T0800273334, tanya.jenkins@paradise.net.nz, offer an excellent and very reasonable one-hour trip to the seal colony, crossing the tidal channel by inflatable raft, from $15 (October-March).

Sharks Your close (caged) encounter with Jaws and his toothy mates can be arranged through *Shark Dive Kaikoura*, T3196888, www.kaikoura.co.nz/shark three-hour (10 minutes in 'the cage') trips leave daily (November-April). All equipment supplied, from $110.

Seabirds New Zealand is considered the seabird capital of the world and a remarkable 70% of its bird list are pelagic species. Kaikoura offers the unique and world-class opportunity to see many that would otherwise involve long excursions far offshore. Of particular interest are the albatross, mollymawks, and numerous petrel species. Just two notable regulars include the giant petrel, which is as big as a goose, the Westland petrel, which is endemic to New Zealand, and the cape pigeon that could not be more aptly named. The birds are attracted to the boat using a block of 'chum' (fish guts) and almost the instant it hits the water the show begins. *Ocean Wings*, 58 West End, T3196777, www.kaikoura.co.nz/oceanwings run by the Dolphin Encounter outfit, offer 2-3-hour trips on demand, from $60, child $35. Recommended. *Acacia Downs Lake and Eco Tours*, T3196112, offer enjoyable and informative land-based birding trips to Lake Rotorua and elsewhere, from $50, child $30.

General Eco-tours *Down Under Water Adventures*, T0800-273334, go underwater offering snorkelling tours around the peninsula, from $40, child $30; seafood hunting from $65. (November-April); *Glass Bottom Boat Tours*, T3196777, can dispense with the snorkel, one-hour from $25, child $15.

Other activities

Fishing There are a number of fishing trips and charters, and the VIC has full listings. The *FV Bounty*, T3196682, brianb@xtra.co.nz *Impulse*, T3196477; and *The Sylver Ann*, T3195710 (two-hour fishing from $50) are three examples. *Flying Pilot A Plane*, based at the Peketa Airfield south of the town, T3196579, offer a unique opportunity to take the controls (momentarily) on a 30-minute scenic flight, from $79.

Four-wheel drive and Quad-bike Adventures *Four Wheeler Safaris*, T/F3196424, www.kaikoura.co.nz/safaris offer three-hour to half-day trips through hill country, riverbed and bush, from $90; while *Glenstrae Farm 4 Wheeler Adventures*, T3197021, T025355628, offer three-hour trips with great views. Depart 0900, 1330 and at dusk.

Horse Trekking *Fyffe Horse Treks*, T3195069 (two hours from $40); *Lake View Horse Treks*, T3195997 (inland and coast, 1-2 hours, from $25-$40); and *Ludley Horse Treks*, T3195925 (two hours-five days, from $40). *Scenic Tours TJ's Tours*, T/F3196803, offer a range of trips with the one-hour general sights and seal colony tour being the most popular, from $15; *Turf to Surf*, T3198621, combine a four-wheel drive farm tour with a jetboat trip and include a tasty lunch, from $118.

Walks around Kaikoura

The two hour-return Peninsula Walk that links the two settlements via the cliffs or shoreline is excellent and recommended. You can either walk along the cliff-top or the shoreline (depending on the tide) and start at the Point Kearn car park at the end of Avoca Street, or alternatively at the South Bay car park. You will encounter seals, lots of interesting rock pools, and some superb coastal scenery. A much longer jaunt is the celebrated three-day, 45 km,

Kaikoura Coast Track which combines sights inland and on the coast. This can be done as a package with *Sally and David Handyside*, T3192715, www.kaikoura.co.nz from $110. Mount Fyffe (1602), which is directly behind Kaikoura, offers spectacular views and can be accessed from the end of Postman's Road (junction Athelney Road/SH1 north of Beach Road) or Grange Road (SH1 north); eight-hour return, DOC huts en route. There is also a good lookout and short walk (Fyffe Palmer Track) at the end of Mount Fyffe Rd (8 km). To get there drive out of town on Ludstone Road (north) then turn right onto Mount Fyffe Road and follow it to its terminus. The VIC has DOC broadsheets on all these walks and others.

Sleeping

There is plenty of choice in Kaikoura, with motels the dominant force, but you are still advised to book in advance in mid-summer.

There is a scattering of good **B&Bs and inns** in and around Kaikoura, and the VIC has full listings. **A** *Fyffe Country Inn*, SH1 (south), T3196869, F3196865, fyffe@xtra.co.nz is a lovely homestead made of mud-block and wood, with pleasant gardens and great views. All rooms have private en suites and there is a characterful restaurant attached serving fine cuisine. At the northern end of town in a quiet setting is the unusual **L-AL** *Old Convent*, Mt Fyffe Rd, T3196603, www.theoldconvent.co.nz which again is full of character, friendly and has a good range of well-appointed en suites. A 3-course French dinner costs $50, crayfish $60. Nearby is the **A** *Donegal House*, Fyffe Rd, T/F3195083. It is run very much with an Irish influence and has good en suites, but what makes the place are the grounds and the Irish bar/restaurant that is attached. Out towards the peninsula and its walkway is **A** *Fifeshire B&B (The Point Farm)*, T/F3195059. It has a tidy double, twin and single and is very peaceful.

Elsewhere, cheaper options include the two-storey **A** *Nikau Guesthouse*, 53 Deal St, T/F3196973, with 2 en-suites and standard doubles. Good views across town (closed May-Sep). The **B** *Bayview B&B*, 296 Scarborough St, T/F3195480, and **B** *Hill-top*, 74 Churchill St, T3195624, are both comfortable, friendly, good value and have great views.

There are almost 20 **motels** to choose from, with most being located along the Esplanade or heading north out of town on Beach St (SH1). At the top end cost-wise is the **AL** White Morph, 92-94 Esplanade, T3195014, www.whitemorph.co.nz Also on the Esplanade the **AL-A** *Anchor Inn*, 208 Esplanade, T3195426, www.anchor-inn.co.nz and the **A** *Blue Seas*, 222 Esplanade, T3195441, blue.seas@xtra.co.nz are recommended. At the northern end of town the **A** *Mediterranean*, 239 Beach Rd, T3196776, medmotel@xtra.co.nz is a good choice. There is no shortage of **backpacker** beds. For the best sea and mountain views head for the **C-D** *Kaikoura (Maui) YHA*, 270 Esplanade, T/F3195931. It has dorms, twins and doubles and, a good atmosphere, and is worth the 10-min walk from the West End. The **C-D** *Cray Cottage* is also on the Esplanade (190), T3195152, and has good facilities, dorm and twins. Also worth the walk is the very tidy **C-D** *Topspot Backpackers*, 22 Deal St, T3195540, topspot@xtra.co.nz They have dorm and doubles and do their own value $40 seal swimming trips. At the northern end of town is the **C-D** *Dusky Lodge*, 67 Beach Rd, T3195959, which is modern, friendly with dorms, twins and doubles, and only 3 mins to the West End. Right in the heart of the West End is the aesthetically unremarkable **C-D** *Central Backpackers*, T3195141, stay@planetbackpackers.com but it is handy for all amenities and has a great deck overlooking the action.

The **B-D** *Kaikoura Top Ten Holiday Park*, 34 Beach Rd, T/F3195362, www.kaikouraholidaypark.co.nz is the best **motor park** and offers modern facilities, motel units, en suite units, powered/tent sites only 3 mins from the town centre and the beach. If it is full, or for a quieter option, try the very friendly **C-D** *69 Beach Road*

Holiday Park, across the road, T3196275. There are also a number of very pleasant beachside **D campsites** on the coastal roads south of Kaikoura, T3195348.

Eating For evening fine dining away from the town centre try the cosy restaurant at the ***Fyffe Country Inn*** (south on SH1), T3196869. Open daily for both lunch and dinner. For good seafood and a fine view (especially after a late whale-watch) the ***Finz Seafood Restaurant and Wine Bar***, 103 South Bay Par, T3196688, is recommended. Open daily from 1800 (closed Mon in winter). Also out of town, ***Donegal House***, Mt Fyffe Rd, T3195083, offers lunch (1100-1400) and dinner (1800-2100) in a lovely setting, and with that Irish edge. In town there are plenty of affordable options for both lunch and dinner, with most specialising in seafood. The ***Craypot Café and Bar***, West End, T3196027, is a good place to try crayfish at an affordable price while the ***Mussel Boys***, 80 Beach Rd, T3197160, serve up their standard plates of superb mussels and seafood dishes (open May-Sep from 1200, closed Mon).

At the far end of the Esplanade, ***The Green Dolphin***, 12 Avoca St, is another firm seafood favourite (open daily in summer lunch and dinner, Tue-Sun dinner only in winter). For pizza look no further than the ***Act-One Bar and Café***, 25 Beach Rd, T3196760 (open daily from 1700). For good coffee the ***Why Not Café***, 58 West End is recommended (open days in winter and also evenings in summer). ***Hislop's Café***, 33 Beach Rd, T3196971, is the place to find wholefoods and the best vegetarian dishes. Open daily for lunch and dinner, closed Tue evenings in winter. ***The Sonic Bar and Café***, 93 West End, T3196414, is the place for the best evening **entertainment**, with occasional live bands, and is the main backpackers hangout. It also serves a fine value meal. Open daily from 1000-late.

Directory **Internet** is available at *Kodak Express* on West End. The **post office** is at 41 West End (open Mon-Fri 0830-1700). There is a BNZ **bank** branch at 42 West End with an **ATM**. For the **police** T3195038.

West of Christchurch

There are basically two main reasons tourists 'head for the hills', west from Christchurch. The most obvious is to reach the West Coast via **SH73**, the **Craigieburn Forest Park** and **Arthur's Pass**, while the other is to ski the popular **Mountt Hutt ski fields** near **Methven**. SH73 is one of the most celebrated scenic drives in the country.

Methven and Mount Hutt

Phone code: 03
Population: 1000

The biggest attraction to the small, but congenial agricultural town of Methven is its location close to the **Mount Hutt Ski-field**. At an elevation of 2075 m and covering an area of 365 ha, 'The Hutt' is highly regarded by the ski fraternity. The reason for this lies not only due to its proximity to Christchurch, but also for its reputation for having some of the best snow in the country and the longest and most consistent season in the Southern Hemisphere (min May-October). It also has a new and modern base lodge with brasserie, bar, cafés, shops and snowboarding facilities.

Ins & outs **Getting there** Methven is 90 km southwest of Christchurch via SH73 and SH77. By **bus**, *Intercity*, T0800764444, operates daily from Christchurch. For other winter shuttles to Mount Hutt and Christchurch, contact Methven Travel, T3028106, methven.travel@clear.net.nz

Getting around *Mountain Transport*, 28 Spaxton St, T3028443, kdanna@paradise.net.nz and ***Mount Hutt Taxi and Shuttle***, T025-318604 offer a door to door service between Methven and the skifields, from $20 return. **Mountain bikes** can be hired from *Big Al's* in The Square, T3028003.

Information

The Methven **Visitor Information Centre** is located on the Main St, T0800-764444, www.nz-holiday.co.nz/metven/info Open daily 0900-1700 (winter 0730-1800). It has free town maps and detailed information about the skifields, **DOC** information covering regional walks, **internet**, and also administers transport and activity bookings. For specific **ski** information contact the Mt Hutt Ski-field, T3085074, www.nzski.com Snow reports, T3028605.

Sights & activities

Lift passes cost $58 but, as ever, check out the **NZ Superpass** policy (www.nzski.com). Ski equipment **hire** is available at the field itself or in various outlets in Methven, including *Big Al's*, The Square, T3028003, www.bigals.co.nz For transport to the field see getting around, above. **Heli-ski** trips are offered by *Methven Heliski*, Main Road, T3028108, www.heliskiing.co.nz

Even outside the ski season Methven offers a good range of activities year round. *Aoraki Hot Air Balloon Safaris*, T3028172, www.nzballooning.com offer relaxing flights with a champagne breakfast, from $245. Two **jetboat** operators, *Rakaia Gorge Scenic Jet*, T3186515, and *Rakaia Gorge Alpine Jet*, T3186574, www.rivertours.co.nz offer scenic trips and Heli-jet options on the Rakaia River from *Rangitata Rafts*, T/F6963534, www.rafts.co.nz offer day excursions down the scenic Rangitata River, south of Methven (Grade IV-V), from $130. To keep up the adrenaline, you might also consider a spot of **abseiling** or raft building with *Rock and Ice Adventures*, T3029227, www.rockice.co.nz or better still a tandem **skydive** with the **Parachute Centre**, T025-321135 (10,000ft from $245).

Mount Hutt Helicopters, Blackford Road, T3028401, offer **flightseeing** trips and a Heli-taxi service. For other scenic trips you can either go on 4 wheels with *Strathavon Quad Bike Tours*, T3028059, or on eight wheels with *Planet Argo*, T0800-2746386. Horse trekking is available with *Ranelagh Rides*, T3028626, from $30 per hour.

There are numerous **walks** or longer hikes on offer in the **Mount Hutt Forest** (14 km west), Mount Somers, **'The Foothills'** and the **Peel Forest** (south), with the climb to the summit of **Mount Somers** (1687) being particularly recommended. The VIC has details. There is an excellent **golf** course at Terrace Downs on the Lake Coleridge Road, T0800465373, info@terracedowns.co.nz Clubs can be hired from *Big Al's* in The Square, Methven.

Sleeping

Given its popularity, as a ski resort there is no shortage of beds in the town, with the majority being upper-to mid-range self-contained lodges with spas, open fires, drying rooms etc. There are also a good number of backpacker lodges and, again, these have that 'ski-lodge' feel with all the facilities. The VIC has full listings, and advanced bookings are advised in winter.

At the top-end is the **A** ***Sovereign Resort Hotel***, Main St, T3028724, info@sovresort.co.nz which has 2 suites and numerous tidy studios, a sauna, three outdoor hot pools and in-house restaurants and bar. Along the same lines and price range is the **AL** ***Brinkley Village Resort***, Barkers Rd, T3028885, brinkley@xtra.co.nz Both of the above offer attractive summer rates.

The **AL**Homestead on the Mount Hutt Station, T3028130, www.the-homestead.co.nz has all the same mod cons in a country setting, great cuisine, and the closest top-range accommodation to the ski-field. In Methven itself, and slightly cheaper, is the centrally located and friendly **A** ***Abisko Lodge***, 74 Main St, T3028875, abisko@clear.net.nz It has 12 en suites with great facilities including restaurant, bar, spa/sauna and a comfortable lounge with open fire. Another good mid-range self-catering option is the **B** ***Snow Denn Lodge***, corner of Bank and McMillan St, T3028999, huttski@voyager.co.nz The **AL-B** ***Methven Mt Hutt Holiday Homes***, 29 Patton St, T3029200, mmhhh@voyager.co.nz are a good bet for couples and groups, with a list of about 20 houses and units from deluxe to standard or budget. The **A-D** *Bed Post*, 177 Main St, T/F3028508, is the closest modern **motel** option to the centre of town and includes good budget rooms.

There are a good number of budget/**hostel** options including the **C-D** *Alpenhorn Chalet*, 44 Allen St, T3028779. It is a cosy bungalow with new facilities, dorms and doubles and a spa. The **C-D** *Skiwi Lodge*, 30 Chapman St, T3028772, skiwihouse@xtra.co.nz Well established, friendly and very comfortable with well-heated dorms and doubles. It is also good in summer given the enthusiasm offered in arranging other non-ski activities. The **C-D** *Redwood Lodges*, 5 Wayne Pl, T/F3028964, skired@voyager.co.nz provides two good-value purpose-built, self-catering lodges, one with shared facilities and one with great value en-suites. All the ski facilities are provided, and it has a cosy log fire and laundry. The **A-D** ***Kohuia Lodge of Pudding Hill***, on the Inland Scenic Highway (12 km west of Methven) T3028416, F3029255, www.kohuialodge.co.nz A tidy modern establishment close to Mt Hutt and the skifield. It has 1-2 bedroom studio units, budget lodge rooms, **powered/tent sites**, restaurant, bar and jacuzzi. In Methven itself is the more basic **D** *Methven Caravan Park*, Barkers Rd, T3028005.

Eating For fine dining, year round, the ***Sovereign*** and ***Brinkley Resort Restaurants*** (see above) are both reliable. Although some distance from Methven (30 km), the ***Stronechrubie Restaurant*** in Mt Somers, T3039814, is one of the best fine-dining restaurants in the region (outside Christchurch). For daytime dining the ***Café 131*** on Main St, T3029131, is quite classy and good value. Open 0900-1600 (winter 0700-1900). The ***Ski Time Restaurant***, Racecourse Av, T3028398, www.skitime.co.nz is another good-value option and has a cosy open fire. The ***Eagle Rock*** on Main St, T3028222, is also popular for a relaxed coffee, but is also good for lighter, traditional NZ meals. The Topnotch ***Foodmarket*** is located on McMillan St, T3028114.

Pubs The colourful pubs, ***The Blue*** on Barkers Rd, and ***The Brown*** just opposite, are both popular, with the former the most popular for après-ski. Other alternatives include the ***Eagle Rock*** on Main St and The American-style ***Last Post*** opposite the VIC. Most offer good pub lunches.

Directory The BNZ **bank** is on Main St, while the Westpac (**ATM**) is in the Mall. The **post office** is in Gifts Galore, Main St. The **Pharmacy** is on Main St, T3028103, and the **Medical** Centre is in The Square, T3028105.

The West Coast via Arthur's Pass

The route to the West Coast via SH73 from Christchurch, across The Great Divide and the northern ranges of the Southern Alps, is one of the most celebrated **scenic drives and rail journeys** in the country. It is most notable perhaps for its sheer range of dramatic South Island landscapes, from the flatlands of the Canterbury Plains to the east, through the rugged mountain peaks and river gorges in its centre, to the lush coastal valleys and lakes to the west. On the way, other than its aesthetics, are the **Craigieburn Forest** and

Arthur's Pass National Parks, which offer some excellent **walking, tramping, rock climbing** and **skiing** opportunities.

Ins & outs

Getting there By road it is 240 km from Christchurch to the West Coast. Arthur's Pass is 158 km. By **bus** *Coast to Coast*, T0800-800847, and *Alpine Coaches*, T0800-274888, operate daily from Christchurch, from $40 (Arthur's Pass from $25).

TransScenic's daily **rail** service **TranzAlpine** is touted as one of the most scenic rail journeys in the world and is a very popular way to get from Christchurch to Greymouth. The Alpine leaves Christchurch at 0900 arriving Arthur's Pass 1127 and than Greymouth at 1325. It then makes the return journey from Greymouth at 1425 to Arthur's Pass at 1630, arriving in Christchurch at 1835. A standard return is $119, child $62 (Arthur's Pass $78, child $46). T0800-802802, www.tranzscenic.co.nz

Sights & activities

From Christchurch, with the almost constant sight of the mountains looming ever larger, you pass through the small and aptly named rural settlements of Darfield and Springfield to reach the foot of the Torlesse Range. Just beyond Springfield the road climbs steeply through **Porters Pass** before falling once again into the valleys and unusual karst landscapes that border the **Craigieburn Forest Park** (100 km). The area offers a small flurry of **ski fields**, including Porter Heights, Mount Olympus, Mount Cheeseman, Broken Rivers and Craigieburn. All these are 'club fields', offering a wide range of slopes and conditions. For information contact the VIC in Christchurch or Methven, or consult the excellent website, www.nzski.com There are also plenty of walking opportunities. The DOC leaflet the '*Craigieburn Forest Park Day Walks*' is very useful and available from the VICs above. The rugged karst landscape of Kura Tawhiti or **Castle Hill Reserve** (30 km west of Springfield) provide more interesting walks and also some excellent **rock climbing**. *Rock and Ice Adventures*, T3029227, www.rockice.co.nz, based in Methven, offer abseiling trips in the area.

Six kilometres further west is the **Cave Stream Scenic Reserve** which is easily accessible from SH73. Here you will find the rather unique opportunity of a self-guided **black-water hike** in a limestone cave system that has been created over the millennia by the Waimakariri River and its tributaries. The cave system was used by for centuries, Maori on their transmigration west to the coast and still contains some examples of rock art and bones. The one-hour underground hike is of course more of a 'wade', but is well worth the soaking. Just be sure to take a good torch and dry clothing. The DOC Interpretative panels in the car park will keep you right, and leaflets are available from the VICs.

At the northern border of the Forest Park, and just beyond the tiny settlement of Cass, both road and rail penetrate the vast open-braided **Waimakariri River Valley** before entering the **Arthur's Pass National Park**. From there it is only a short drive to the enveloped outpost village of **Arthur's Pass.**

Sleeping

There are a number of good places to stay before you reach Arthur's Pass. In winter these are very popular with the ski fraternity, while in summer it is walking boots, not the skiing variety, that sit on the steps.

In Springfield the **C-D** *Smylie's YHA*, T3184740, in the centre of the village, is worth mentioning. It has cosy dorms and doubles and is an ideal base for both winter and summer activities. A further 40 km east of Arthur's Pass, ideally located close to the ski fields and the Craigieburn Forest Park walks, is the **A-D** *Flock Hill Lodge*, T3188196. It has tidy motel units, lodge backpackers and a **restaurant**.

Another 10 km further west sees the luxurious **LL** *Grassmere Lodge*, T3188407, which offers all mod cons, dinner and activities as part of the package. East of Arthur's

Pass (16 km) is the plush and slightly cheaper, **LL-L** ***Arthur's Pass Wilderness Lodge***, T3189246, a luxury B&B that is a similar set up offering activities inclusive of the price. The **A-D** ***Bealey Hotel***, T3189277, is only 4 km east of Arthur's pass and offers motel doubles and backpacker twins. Bealey is famous for its reputed moa sighting in recent years. Of course said sighting was an elaborate hoax, but it was successful enough to create a national hysteria deserving of a monument that stands looking decidedly giraffe-like beside the hotel. The Bealey Hotel has a bistro that is open daily.

Arthur's Pass

Phone code: 03
Population: 111

It was one Arthur Dudley Dobson, a pioneer surveyor, who first explored the route to the West Coast via the east Waimakariri and west Otira River Valleys in 1864. Although at the time Arthur was merely on a routine trip, his observations became an integral part of securing road access to the West Coast during the gold boom of the 1860s. Remarkably, or perhaps not, given the motivation, a basic road was built within a year, but the rail link that later served the coal and timber trade, took a further 60 years to complete. Now, long after all the gold has gone, the railway remains a monument to patience, while the road continues to need constant maintenance and improvement. These modern feats of road engineering and construction become obvious just beyond Arthur's Pass in the form of the impressive, and only recently opened, **Otira Viaduct.**

Even before the rail link to Arthur's Pass was complete, the area was proving popular for **tramping** and **skiing**, and by 1930 Arthur's Pass was gazetted as a National Park. The tiny settlement of Arthur's Pass is 924 m above sea level and is used as the base for activities in the park or as a welcome halfway stop en route to the West Coast.

Ins & outs

The **DOC** Arthur's Pass **Visitor Information Centre** is located in the heart of the village on the southern side of SH73, T3189211, F3189271, www.doc.govt.nz Open daily 0900-1600. There are various displays about the national park, a video ($1), walks information and all local accommodation and service details. Ask for the *'Village Information'* broadsheet and map. Before embarking on any long walks or tramps, check the weather forecast provided and ask the staff about up-to-date track conditions. Intentions sheets are provided. There is a **petrol** station and a **police** station in the village, T3189212. For emergencies call T111. For **Breakdown** T6189266. The **post office** (the smallest on the planet) is also on the Main St (limited hours).

Sleeping

Arthur's Pass village offers a small range of accommodation options, with one B&B lodge, a motel, two backpackers and a campsite. For eating there is only one bistro/à la carte restaurant and a café.

The **A** ***Chalet B&B***, T3182936, located at the western end of the village, is the most expensive, with comfortable doubles with 8 en suites and 3 with shared facilities. There is an in-house à la carte and a bistro/restaurant. The cheaper **A-B** ***Alpine Motel***, T3189233, has self-contained doubles and is just beyond the bridge on the right at the eastern end of the village. They also offer a 'car minding' service. In the centre of the village there is the choice of two equally congenial backpackers: the older **C-D** ***Sir Arthur Dudley Dobson Memorial YHA***, T3189230, next to the café, has dorm and doubles, while the newer and two-storied **C-D** ***Mountain View Backpackers***, T3189258, mountain.house@xtra.co.nz has dorms and tent sites.

Basic **camping** facilities are also available at the public shelter across the road from the VIC in the village ($4), or free at Klondyke Corner, 8 km east, and ***Kelly Shelter***, 17 km west. Other than the licensed *Chalet Restaurant* (above) eating options are limited to *Oscar's Haus Café*, T3189234, in the centre of town. It offers light snacks, home-made pies and questionable coffee. Open daily 0900-2100 (winter 1030-1600). There is also a tearoom offering basic fare, across the road. Open daily 0800-1900.

The Arthur's Pass National Park

The Arthur's Pass National Park was designated in 1929 and is 114,500 ha in area. It extends from the vicinity of Harper's Pass in the northern Southern Alps, to the mountains around the head of the Waimakariri and Otira Rivers. The park is essentially made up of high mountain ranges, gorges and expansive braided river valleys. One of the highest and most attractive mountains is **Mount Rolleston** (2270 m), which lies just to the southwest of the Arthur's Pass. Its impressive **'Bealey Face'** can be seen from the road just west of the village.

The mountain ranges are 'alpine' in nature, containing a broad range of vegetation which varies greatly from east to west in accordance with the varying climatic conditions and rainfall. To the east the forests are almost entirely made up of mountain beech, while to the west, on the other side of The Great Divide', it is more complex with a variety of podocarp species, beech, kamahi and kaiakawaka. The park is rich in alpine plant species, many of which thrive above the tree line and are endemic to New Zealand. Many native birds are also present, the most notable being the notoriously inquisitive and destructive native mountain parrot, the **kea**. Often, kea will come down to the village to see you before you go up into the mountains to see them, relieving you of your sandwiches in the process. If this is your first trip across to the West Coast you may also notice one other creature. One that will makes its presence known in no uncertain terms and, sadly for you I'm afraid, for the duration – the satanic sandfly.

The park offers a network of **tramping** tracks that are facilitated by over 30 DOC Backcountry Huts. Two of the best **day walks** are the 7-8 hour ascent of **Avalanche Peak**, directly behind the village on its southern side, or, further west still, the more difficult (mainly summer) climb to the summit of **Mount Rolleston**. The Avalanche Peak track begins from behind the DOC Information Centre, which can offer detailed information and advice on these tracks and others. Note that braided rivers and the small tributaries that feed them are notorious for **flash floods**, so extra care is required. History buffs might like to negotiate the 1 ½-hour **Arthur's Pass Village Historic Walk**. Leaflet from the VIC.

South on SH1

From Christchurch SH1 heads south through the flat heartland of the ***Canterbury Plains*** *to Timaru. With so much seemingly omnipresent and stunning scenery elsewhere in New Zealand, aesthetically it is often labelled as the least exciting drive in the country. Only the occasional glimpses of the distant Southern Alps far to the west, and the odd wide pebble-strewn river bed crossing, breaks the monotony of the endless roadside windbreaks and expansive fields. Even the cows look bored to death. Roughly half way between Christchurch and Timaru is the only major settlement, Ashburton.*

Ashburton

Population: 13,400
Phone code: 03

Due to its surrounding topography and perhaps its very location right on SH1, as well as its location so near Christchurch and so far from the principal tourist attractions to the south, Ashburton seldom lures tourists to stop for anything other than a hurried toilet stop, quick snack and cup of coffee. But having said that, it is not a bad little place and if you take a little time (especially on Sundays) it will reveal a few worthy attractions and tempting activities to complement the warm welcome offered by its friendly residents.

Ins & outs

Getting there Ashburton is 87 km south of Christchurch and 76 km north of Timaru on SH1. All the major **bus** companies heading south can stop in Ashburton including *Intercity*, T3088219, and *Atomic Shuttles*, T3228883. Buses stop outside the VIC.

Information The Ashburton **Visitor Information Centre** is located on the main road, East St, T/F3081064, infocentre@ashburton.co.nz Open Mon-Fri 0830-1700, Sat 1000-1500, Sun 1000-1300. It has a free town map and full accommodation and local activity listings.

Sights & activities

The main attractions are its small museums and craft outlets. The **Ashburton Art Gallery and Museum**, Baring Square East, T/F3083167, has the obvious focus on local history but is particularly noted for its displays of local and contemporary arts and crafts. ■ *Tue-Fri 1000-1600, Sat/Sun 1300-1600, donation.*

Also of note, though seldom open, is **The Plains Vintage Railway and Historical Museum**, which is located just over the Manoran Road level crossing (off SH1) in the **Tinwald Domain and Recreation Park** (south of the town centre), T3089621. Open on every second Sunday in the month (October-June) and most Sundays during the rest of the year, it offers short rides on some of its fine array of restored locos and traction engines. Sadly, the classic 'K88 Washington', built in the USA in 1877, is not one of them. After spending 47 years lying in a riverbed in Southland it was lovingly restored and returned to service in 1982. Looking 'the' classic archetype of an old steam engine and almost like something that would be drawn from a child's imagination, it is well worth seeing. You may like to follow this with a visit to the **Vintage Car Museum** which is also located in the Domain, T3087025. It has a collection that dates back to 1905 and is again only open on Sundays. For crafts, the **Ashford Craft Village**, 415 West Street, T3089085, is worth a look and can double as a good place for lunch.

For activities, Ashburton is home to *Adventure Skydives, tandem skydiving* (8,500 ft), T0800-666228, and *Rangitata Fishing Safaris*, T/F3081353, but pick-ups are provided for other activities to the west including **rafting** and **ballooning**. There are also some interesting day tours available to the **Foothills** and **Mount Somers**. Contact the VIC.

Sleeping

The **A** *Hotel Ashburton*, Racecourse Rd, T/F3083059, www.hotelash.co.nz has modern units in spacious grounds with in-house restaurant, bar and spas. There are a few motels, mainly on the main drag, including the **B** *Academy Lodge*, 782 East St, T3085503, and at the southern end the cheaper **B** *Riverside*, 1 Main Road South, T3088248. The **C-D** *Ashburton Holiday Park* in the Tinwald Domain (see above), T3086805, is ideally placed and has basic cabins, powered/tent sites and backpacker accommodation. For eating, *Jesters*, 9 Moana Sq, T3089983, and *Tuscany's* across the road from the VIC, T3083389, are both good and open daily for lunch and dinner. *Cactus Jacks*, 209 Wills St, T3080495, is also open daily and is good for a Tex-Mex. All the latter are licensed. For a good pub lunch try ***Kelly's Bar and Café***, 234 East St, T3088811. For coffee and light snacks the ***Ashford Café and Wine Bar***, T3089085, in the ***Ashford Craft Village***, 427 West St, is recommended. Open Mon-Fri 0900-1630, Sat/Sun 1000-1600.

South Canterbury

Timaru

Phone code: 03
Population: 27,300

The port city of Timaru, located roughly half way between Christchurch and Dunedin, provides a refreshing stop over on SH1, or a convenient starting point from which to head west, via SH8, to The 'MacKenzie Country', Mount Cook and Queenstown. The city is a pleasant one, boasting the popular Caroline Bay **beach** near the town centre, a few good parks, the region's main museum, a reputable art gallery and a few unique attractions, including some ancient seventh-century **Maori rock art** that adorn caves and rock overhangs near the city.

Ins & outs

Getting there Timaru is 163 km south of Christchurch and 199 km north of Dunedin on SH1; Lake Tekapo lies 104 km west via SH8. **By air** The airport in Timaru is located about 12 km north of town (SH1) and is served by ***Air New Zealand Link*** daily from Christchurch and Wellington, T0800-737000. By **bus** *Intercity*, T6886497; ***Atomic Shuttles***, T3228883, and ***Kiwilink***, T0800-802300, run daily services between Christchurch and Dunedin. *Intercity* stop outside the Railway Station, Station St. *AJ's Café* in the station are the booking agents, T6847195. ***GTS Country Link Tours***, 44 Omahau Cres, T4350052, take a return trip to Twizel every Fri. If the Southerner train service is still operative (service under threat at the time of going to print), it offers a daily service to Christchurch/Invercargill, T0800-802802.

Getting around From the airport contact ***Timaru Taxis*** T6888899, from $10. For **car hire** and **taxi** services see 'Directory' below. The VIC holds local suburban **bus** (CRC) timetables.

Information The Timaru **Visitor Information Centre** is located in the former Landing Service Building, 2 George St, T6886163, info@timaru.com/www.southisland.org Open Mon-Fri 0830-1700, Sat/Sun 1000-1500. **DOC** information is held at the VIC. For **Internet** and other essential services refer to 'Directory' below.

History

With the existence of over 500 sites featuring **Maori Rock art**, particularly in the caves and rock overhangs of the Opihi and Opuha Rivers, west of Timaru, historians have estimated that the Maori settled in the area as early as 1400 AD. During the 17th century the warring Ngati Tahu, from the north of the South Island, drove the descendants of these people, the Ngati Mamoe south into Fiordland. European settlement began with the establishment of a whaling station at Patiti Point, close to the present town, in 1837. This was followed by the purchase and creation of a sheep station known as 'The Levels' in 1852 by the influential Rhodes brothers from England. For over two decades disputes arose between the brothers and the government surrounding land ownership and development, but this was eventually settled and the two communities merged to form Timaru. With the reclamation of land in 1877, and the subsequent creation of the harbour at Caroline Bay, the town quickly developed as a major port. Today the port at Timaru is the second largest fishing port in New Zealand and is even visited by the odd cruise liner. The name Timaru is thought to be derived from the Maori 'te maru' meaning 'place of shelter', however, some authorities dispute this and suggest the literal translation of ti – meaning cabbage tree and maru – meaning shady is the correct one.

Sights At the VIC you are immediately confronted by the original 'bluestone' façade of the **Landing Service Building** which was built in 1870 to facilitate the export of wool and other goods from the surrounding district. This building now forms the starting point for the town's three main **heritage trails**.

The **South Canterbury Museum**, on Perth Street in the centre of town, is the main regional museum and contains some interesting exhibits on local maritime history, Maori rock art and the exploits of aviator **Richard Pearse** (1877-1953). In 1903 Pearse is said to have made the first manned flight, nine months before the Wright Brothers of America (see Temuka below). A full replica of the impressive contraption that allowed him to do so is on display. Other relics of Pearse's various flying inventions are held at the Pleasant Point Railway Museum in Pleasant Point (see 'Around Timaru' below). ■ *The South Canterbury Museum is free and open Tue-Fri 1000-1630, Sat/Sun 1330-1630.*

With the presence of **The Aigantighe** (pronounced 'egg and tie') **Art Gallery**, 49 Wai-iti Road, T6884424, Timaru can boast one of the best art galleries in the country. Founded in 1956, and set in a 1908 historic home surrounded by a sculpture garden, its hallowed walls feature exhibitions from a substantial permanent exhibition, which dates back to the 7th century, as well as contemporary works by **McCahon** and **C F Goldie**. The gallery also hosts an ongoing program of regional and national exhibitions. Aigantighe means 'at home' in Scots Gaelic. ■ *Tue-Fri 1000-1600, Mon/Sat/Sun 1200-1600 (gardens open dawn to dusk), free.*

The somewhat iconic **DB Mainland Brewery** on Sheffield Street (2 km north of town) offers free weekday tours and tastings at 1030, T6882059.

Timaru has some pleasant parks and beaches. The beach at **Caroline Bay**, to the north of the town centre, was formed as a result of land reclamation and original harbour development in 1877. Although in close proximity to the busy port, and therefore not aesthetically remarkable, the beach still remains a popular and safe haven for swimming.

The park alongside the beach has a number of attractions including a roller skating rink, a mini golf course, a maze and an open-air concert soundshell. Every summer, just after Christmas, this area is the focus for the **Summer Carnival**. Hugely popular amongst locals, this event attracts thousands who are entertained with organised concerts, fair ground rides, sideshows and the obligatory candyfloss stalls. The addition of the new **Piazza**, leading from the Bay Hill down to Caroline Bay in 1997, added a focus for a relaxed seaside café, restaurant and wine bar scene. Of more traditional and less convivial aesthetics are the **Timaru Botanical Gardens**, which were established in 1864. They are located just south of the town centre and best accessed on the corner of King and Queen Streets. ■ *Open daily 0800-dusk, T6886163.* **Centennial Park**, that follows the course of the Otipua Creek, also offers a peaceful escape and a lovely 3 ½ km one-hour one-way walk that begins from the old 'bluestone' Gleniti School on Clearmont Street, west of the town centre.

Activities Timaru is noted not only for its sand and surf but also for its inland rivers, which come complete with monster trout. *Aoraki Fly Fishing*, T6869266, www.flyfishing.co.nz are one of the best regional guides. *Timaru Marine Cruises*, T6886881, offer marine wildlife watching tours that often locate the rare and tiny hector's dolphin. The 'Caroline Cat' departs daily at 1015 from No1 Wharf in the harbour (corner of Port Loop and Ritchie Street), from $25. There are plenty of good short-walking opportunities in the town, with three Heritage Trails and the one-hour Dashing Rocks and 45-minute Caroline Bay Walks and the Centennial Park Walk (see above). The VIC has details.

Sleeping

The Piazza overlooking Caroline Bay is a fine place to be based and hosts a new and tidy motel, the **A-B** *Aorangi/Panorama Motor Lodge*, 50-52 The Bay Hill, T/F6880097, aorangi@timaru.co.nz It is handy for the restaurants on the Piazza and Caroline Bay. Further north the **AL-A** *Benvenue Hotel and Motor Inn*, 16-22 Evans St, T6884049,

Timaru

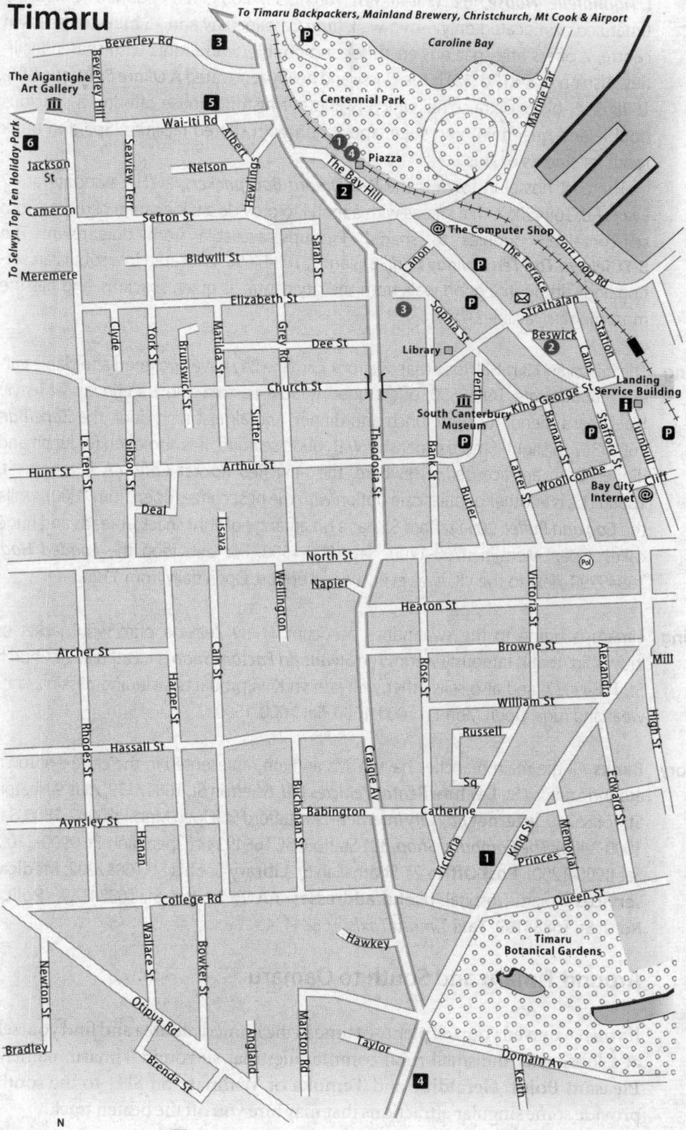

Sleeping
1 Ace-Hi Motel
2 Aorangi/Panorama Motor Lodge
3 Benvenue & Motor Inn
4 Cedar Motor Lodge
5 Okare Boutique B&B
6 Tighnafeile House

Eating
1 Boudicca's
2 Coq & Pullet
3 Red Rocket Café
4 Zanzibar

F6884048, which is also good, has an in-house restaurant. Close to the Botanical Gardens on King Street is the peaceful **B** *Ace-Hi Motel*, (51-53), T/F6883054, or the newer **A-B** *Cedar Motor Lodge*, (36), T6844084, cedarlodge@clear.net.nz

At the **B&B** top-end is the beautiful and historic, former run-holders station, **L** *Tighnafeile House*, 62 Wai-iti Rd, T6843333, F6843328, tighnafeile-house@timaru.co.nz Located only 5-min walk from Caroline Bay and 15 mins to the town centre, it offers fine spacious en-suites and double/twin rooms with shared facilities. Also on Wai-iti Rd (11) is the classy and newly renovated **A** ***Okare Boutique B&B***, T6880316, okare@xtra.co.nz which is another historic house offering a spacious double and queen with en suite, and a king with shared facilities. Spa and bunk room for singles or kids.

The best hostel in town is the **B-D** *Timaru Backpackers*, a YHA associate at 42 Evans Rd, T6845067, that shares with a motel to provide a wide range of rooms from self-contained doubles to shared. Pick-ups available from downtown. The **B-D** *Selwyn Top Ten Holiday Park*, 8 Glen St, T6847690, is located in a suburban setting and, although a good walk from the city centre, is quiet, spacious, and has the most modern facilities.

Eating

The Piazza and Bay Hill Road that overlook Caroline Bay have two good affordable eateries: ***Boudicca's***, T6888550, offers good Middle Eastern and traditional Kiwi-style blackboard menu, for both lunch and dinner; and almost next door, the ***Zanzibar***, T6884367, is slightly more expensive with good seafood. It is also open for lunch and dinner. Both are licensed. Elsewhere, the new ***Red Rocket Café***, 4A Elizabeth St, T6888313, is another popular café option with the best coffee (open from 1000), while the ***Coq and Pullet***, 209 Stafford St, has a great range of light snacks, breads and huge cakes. Open Mon-Fri 0700-1700, Sat 1000-1500. For pub food the ***Loaded Hog***, T6849999, next to the VIC is, as ever, a good option. Open daily from 1100.

Shopping

Timaru is home to the swanndri – an 'iconic' New Zealand pure wool jacket or 'bushshirt' that is famously warm. The *Swanndri Factory Shop* is located at 24 Church St, T6849037, and also sells other well-known Kiwi products including oilskins, knitwear and rugs. Open Mon-Fri 1000-1600, Sat 1000-1500.

Directory

Banks All the main branches have ATMs and are represented in the centre of town around Stafford St. **Car hire** *Rental Vehicles Ltd*, 6 Sefton St, T6847179; ***Avis*** 9 Heaton St, T6886240. **Internet** *Bay City Internet*, 47a Stafford St (Open Mon-Fri 0900-1800, Sat 1000-1400); *The Computer Shop*, 331 Stafford St, T6849333 (Open Mon-Fri 0900-1700, Sat 0900-1200). **Post Office** 21 Strathallan St. **Library** Sophia St, T6842202. **Medical services** Timaru Hospital. **Useful addresses AA** 26 Church St, T6884189. **Police** North St, T6884199. **Taxi** *Timaru Taxis*, T6884434.

Around Timaru and South to Oamaru

If you have given yourself plenty of time in the immediate area and find yourself at a loose end, the small rural communities that surround Timaru, namely, **Pleasant Point**, **Geraldine** and **Temuka** or **Waimate** off SH1 to the south, provide some singular attractions that may lure you off the beaten track.

Geraldine
Phone code: 03
Population: 2,323

The pleasant anglified country town of Geraldine, nestled amidst the Four Peaks and Peel Forest Mountain ranges, is home to a thriving arts and crafts community providing an attractive, if brief, diversion off SH1 (15 km).

Sir Edmund Hillary

Sir Edmund Hillary is one of New Zealand's most famous sons, and although most well known as the man that first conquered Mount Everest, he is also a noted Antarctic explorer and in more recent times is also well known for his welfare work in Nepal. Born in Auckland in 1919, he first worked as an apiarist, before serving with the air force in the Pacific during the Second World War.

It was after the war that Hillary was drawn, time and again, to the Mountains of the Southern Alps in New Zealand. Being both a committed mountaineer and having immense stamina and ability, it was not long before his obsession took him to the Himalayas. He almost immediately joined expeditions in 1951and 1952, but it was on the 29 May, 1953 as a member of John Hunt's British team, that Hillary and sherpa Tenzing Norgay made the first known, successful ascent of the summit. It was a feat that naturally brought instant fame.

After further expeditions to Nepal in 1954 and 55 Hillary turned his attentions to another of nature's last frontiers – the Antarctic. In 1956-58 he was a member of a team that completed the first tractor journey from Scott Base to the South Pole. After this successful expedition he returned once again to Everest where he lead several expeditions between 1961 and 1965, before embarking on another journey to Antarctica to lead the first successful ascent of Mount Herschel.

It is refreshing perhaps that Hillary has gone well beyond the mere desire of climbing, or ego of summit-bagging and has worked very hard to 'pay back' something to his much loved Nepal. There is no doubt he has developed a great respect for its people and worked tirelessly over the years to help raise funds for the creation of schools and hospitals in the region. The first hospital was built in 1966 and he went on to form the Himalayan Trust. His sterling work lead to his appointment as New Zealand's High Commissioner to India in 1985.

Still drawn to both Nepal and Antarctica and to satisfy the ever-present desire to explore, Hillary served as a tour guide on commercial flights over Antarctica in the 1970s and was still active in exploration of the great continent. With a love of nature added to his love of people, Hillary was also, for a time, the proud director of the World Wildlife Fund adding conservation to his list of interests and activities. He has published several books on his expeditions and two autobiographies. As a small nation New Zealand is proud of Hillary, perhaps because he stands for much of what New Zealand is all about a oneness with nature and the courage to venture where others have yet to. Perhaps Hillary reminds fellow New Zealanders of that everyday and in to the future, featuring on the nations $5 banknote.

The Geraldine **Visitor Information Centre** is located at 32 Talbot St, T6931006, information@geraldine.co.nz Open Mon-Fri 0830-1700, Sat/Sun 1000-1500. It has full listings for local accommodation. The free leaflet *'Geraldine'* has comprehensive listings including the varied arts and crafts outlets. **DOC** information is held at the VIC. **Internet** is available at the *Geraldine Berry Barn Complex* (see 'Essentials' below).

Other than the obvious attraction of a scattering of **arts and craft** galleries and shops (listing from the VIC), the town has two museums. The **Vintage Car Club and Machinery Museum**, 178 Talbot Street, T6938005, has a sizeable collection of cars and tractors dating back to 1900, as well as a few notable aircraft, including its star attraction, the unique 'Spartan'. ■ *Open daily 1000-1600, $4*. The small and fairly unremarkable town **museum** is house in the former 1885 Civic Centre on Cox Street. ■ *Open daily.*

The best way to negotiate the arts and crafts outlets is with the guidance and maps available at the VIC. Of particular note is **Barkers Berry Farm** on Talbot Street, T6939727, that offers tastings and sales from its fine range of fruity products. **The Giant Jersey**, 10 Wilson Street, is also worth a look, reputedly displaying the largest jersey in the world. There are a number of good walks in the vicinity, particularly in the **Talbot Forest Scenic Reserve** located next to the town, and the **Peel Forest** located 19 km northwest, via SH79 (The Peel Forest Road). The VIC has details. Geraldine is the base for some interesting activity operators including *4x4 New Zealand*, T6938847, www.southisland.org.nz/4x4 which are a reputable outfit offering 4WD Alpine and **scenic tours** locally and throughout the region; and *Rangitata Rafts*, T/F6963534, www.rafts.co.nz who offer day excursions down the scenic Rangitata River (Grade 4-5), from $130.

Sleeping The VIC has full accommodation listings. Of particular note is the luxurious boutique lodge **LL** *Kavanagh House*, SH1, Winchester, T6156150, F6159694, kavanaghhouse@kavanaghhouse.co.nz It has 2 sumptuous modern en-suites with spa or claw-bath and open fires. It is also well known for its fine cuisine. Also out of town but still in range (8 km), is the aptly named and affordable **B** *Struan Farm Retreat*, Thatcher Rd, Tripp, T6922852, www.struanretreat.com It is a self-contained 2 bedroom cottage in 20 acres with a lovely atmosphere and views. The guest-friendly animals make it especially good for kids. In Geraldine itself is the **AL** *Crossing*, Woodbury Rd, T6939689, which is an old 'gentleman's residence' with en-suites, pleasant gardens, open fire and in-house restaurant. The cheaper **B** *Crown Hotel*, 31 Talbot St, T6938458, Geraldine-crown@xtra.co.nz has character and some good-value en suites. There are a handful of motels including the pleasant and modern **B** *Four Peaks*, 28 MacKenzie St, T/F6938339. For budget accommodation try the friendly **D** *Olde Presbytery*, 13 Jollie St, T6939644. In town the **B-D** *Farmyard Holiday Park*, Coach Rd, T/F6939355, has self-contained units, cabins and powered/tent sites, while up in the Peel Forest you will find the basic but tidy **C-D** *Peel Forest Motor Camp*, T/F6963567. It offers cabins, powered/tent sites and nice walks nearby.

Eating For expensive fine dining the *Kavanagh House* is the obvious choice (see above), bookings essential. For more affordable evening dining in town itself, head for the *Totara Bar and Restaurant in the Crown Hotel*, open daily from 1100 (see above). During the day the *Plum's Café*, 44 Talbot St, T6939770, is a safe bet (open daily for lunch, Fri/Sat for dinner, great lunch specials on Sun); while the *Barkers Berry Farm* (see above) is definitely the place for smoothies and sundaes. Open daily 0900-1730.

Temuka
Phone code: 03
Population: 4,000

This small agricultural service town, 19 km north of Timaru, is the former home of farmer and eccentric inventor **Richard Pearse** (1877-1953). In April 1903, at the tender age of 26, Pearse created history by making the first ever powered flight in a 'heavier-than-air man-carrying aeroplane'. His flight, though neither long nor spectacular, was a world first and was completed nine months before the better-known and much-celebrated flight by the American pioneer aviator Orville Wright of the famous Wright brothers. A **memorial** to his muted achievement can be seen at Waitohi (signposted off SH1), which was the site of his brief and historic flight. It seems a sad testament really when you consider Pearse died an unrecognised recluse in a psychiatric hospital in Christchurch.

The Temuka **Visitor Information Centre** is located at 72-74 King St, T6159537, temlibrary@xtra.co.nz and has full accommodation listings.

The Legend of James 'Jock' McKenzie

The MacKenzie Country which lies west of the Burkes Pass from Fairlie is named after the legendary Scots sheep drover James 'Jock' McKenzie. Jock of course is a common label given to Scots folk, and the 'a' is optional in the 'Mac' – both Mac and Mc meaning, simply 'son of'. Anyway, the story goes that our James was caught in the Burke Pass, east of Lake Tekapo in 1855 with 1000 sheep. Nothing unusual in that (or is there?), except for the simple fact that they were not his. Said sheep actually belonged to the Rhodes brothers from the large Levels Station near Timaru (doubtless English!). The Rhodes boys had sent out a small party to look for the flock and found James happily droving them to pastures new. Being hopelessly outnumbered, but Scottish, James managed to escape and was later recaptured in Lyttelton near Christchurch. Re-captured and suitably arraigned he was found guilty of sheep rustling and sentenced to five years in jail. But that's where it all gets a bit hazy. Apparently, James then professed his innocence, claiming the sheep had in fact been bought and that he was taking his 'legally purchased' flock to a new claim in Otago. (another story goes that he was in fact coerced in to the theft) .Initially believing this to be a load of tartan codswallop he was jailed. But still determined, James escaped, not once, but two (some say three) times, by which time the powers that be were beginning to believe his story. Remarkably, after only nine months he was given a full pardon and released (but some say with the condition that he left New Zealand forever). Innocent or guilty, buried in the soils of New Zealand, or the glens back home in Scotland, we may never know. But still the stuff of legend he is immortalised by a monument and stone cairn on the roadside, just west of the Pass (which apparantly some say was not where he was captured at all). On the monument you can read the folowing immortal words...

'In this spot James MacKenzie (sic) freebooter, was captured by John Sidebottom (see, told you he was English!) and Maoris, Taiko and Seventeen and escaped the same night, 4th March 1855'...go Jimmy!

Besides the memory and memorial to its most famous son, Temuka is noted for its modern-day crafts outlets, particularly the **Temuka Pottery**, Thomas Street (tours every Wednesday at 1300). Its location is perhaps fitting given the fact that the town's name derived from the Maori Te-Umu-Kaha, meaning 'The Place of the Hot Ovens'!

Located 18 km northwest of Timaru (SH8), Pleasant Point offers a few brief diversions including the **Pleasant Point Museum and Railway**, T6862269, www.timaru.com/railway It is home to the world's only remaining 1925 Model T Ford Railcar. There are regular scheduled rides on a glistening restored loco, and kids will further delight at others that feature faces akin to 'Thomas the Tank Engine' and friends. Although rides are offered on most weekends (1030-1630) you are advised to phone for specific dates and details. After experiencing these working metal characters you may like to see another in the form of Gareth James at the **Artisan Forge**, 5 Maitland Street, T6147272. Gareth is one of New Zealand's few working blacksmiths. ■ *Open daily 1000-1700.*

Near Pleasant Point is one of the finest examples of **Maori rock art** in the country. The weathered 14-ft drawing known as the Opihi 'Taniwha' (Maori for 'monster') is considered to be the oldest, having been created sometime in the 16th century. It is located in a shallow limestone shelter on private farmland and is best viewed lying on your back. To visit the site you will need to be accompanied by a guide, which can be organised through the Timaru VIC.

Waimate
Population: 3,000

Although noted as being an atypical New Zealand rural township, Waimate, 47 km south of Timaru, is perhaps better known as a 'little bit of Aussie abroad', with its very furry resident population of cuddly marsupials. Known rather unfortunately perhaps as 'red necked' or bush **wallabies**, these appealing plump and bouncy little characters were originally introduced to the area in 1875 for fur and sport. But, like so many other intellectually wanting acts of 'wildlife familiarisation', it has resulted in a resident population of rapacious native plant-eaters that are now considered a major pest. Given this, the activities surrounding the wallabies are in complete contrast.

The Waimate Information Centre is located at 75 Queen St, T6897771, F6897791, info@waimatedc.govt.nz/www.waimate.org.nz It has detailed accommodation and local activity listings. **Internet** is available at the *Wildberry Café*, Queen St (open daily 0700-2100).

You can either take the indirect, sympathetic and close-range option, with copious amounts of petting and feeding, at the wallaby-friendly **EnkleDooVery Korna**, Bathgates Road, T6897197, or alternatively the more distant and direct approach, with a bullet (hunting details from the VIC). If you do take the former option you can cuddle the irresistible pouch babies. ■ *Open Oct-Apr, Fri 1300-1700, Sat/Sun 1000-1700, $2, child $1.* Wallabies can also be seen, petted and fed at the **Kelcey's Bush Holiday and Animal Park**, 7 km west of the town (signposted), T6898057, kelceysbush@xtra.co.nz

Of a more steadfast and historical nature is the less cuddly but very smart **Waimate Historical Museum**, housed in the former 1879 Waimate Courthouse, 28 Shearman Street, T6897832. It houses a small but significant array of memorabilia and forms part of the town's **Strawberry Heritage Trail**. ■ *Mon-Fri 1330-1630, Sun 1400-1600, $2.*

Also of historical interest, but of very different structural aesthetics, is the Te Waimate historic thatched **'cuddy'** which is almost as cute as the wallabies. Built in 1854 from a single totara tree, it was the home of Michael Studholme, the first European settler in the town. Waimate is often used as a short cut to the **Waimate River** and Benmore/Aviemore **Lakes**, which are famous for their water-sports activities and superb **fishing**. The huge and very uncuddly Quinnant salmon are the prime target. The VIC has details and listings of local guides. If you are in Waimate in February your visit may coincide with the annual **Busking Festival**, which attracts participants from far and wide.

Sleeping & eating

The **AL** *Te Kiteroa*, Point Bush Rd, T6898291, grakeen@xtra.co.nz is a fine old home in the Hunter Hills, with a formal garden. It offers well-appointed en suites and a self-contained former gardener's cottage. In-house massage and aromatherapy are a speciality. In town is the cheaper **B** *Locheil Motel and Guest House*, 100 Shearman St, T6897570, which offers self-contained studios and units. For budget accommodation try the spacious **D** *Hunter's Hill Lodge*, Hillary St, T6898726, hunters.hills@xtra.co.nz The **B-D** *Kelcey's Bush Farmyard*, Mill Rd (see above) is good for campervans and has tidy cabins and flats.

There is not a great deal of choice when it comes to eating, with only a handful of fairly unremarkable take-aways and tearooms in the town centre. *Zanders Restaurant*, 25 Queen St, T6896010, offers à la carte, while the *Wildberry Café*, also on Queen St, has light snacks (open daily 0500-2100). That aside you could do worse than fish and chips from the *Waimate Fish Supply*, 37 Queen St, T6898647.

The MacKenzie Country

The area known as the MacKenzie Country refers principally to the flat expanse of tussock grasslands that make up the watersheds of the Tekapo and Gray's Rivers. It is a strange barren landscape, devoid of trees and almost analogous to the plains of heartland USA. There is really nowhere else like it in New Zealand and it bears little semblance to the lofty peaks that rise from around its edge. The name MacKenzie was bestowed upon it through the almost legendary activities of Scots pioneer and sheep drover James 'Jock' Mckenzie (see page 517)

Fairlie

Phone code: 03
Population: 845

Lying relatively out on its own at the foot of the Hunter and Two Thumbs Ranges, the small rural settlement of Fairlie is often labelled as the rather dull gateway to the **MacKenzie Country** that lies just to the west through the portal of the **Burkes Pass**.

Ins & outs

All the daily west-east buses from Christchurch and Queenstown pass through Fairlie, including ***Intercity***, T0800-767080; ***Atomic Shuttles***, T3328883; and ***Southern Link Shuttles***, T3588355.

The closest you find to a **Visitor Information Centre** in Fairlie are the helpful folk in the *Sunflower Centre and Café*, 31 Main St, T6858258. Open daily 0900-1800. They stock leaflets and list local accommodation options. **Internet** is available at the *Old Library Café* (see below). ***The Ski Shack*** on the Main St, T/F6858088, sells and rents out **ski gear**.

While it is certain Fairlie will probably never set the world alight, it seems to have absolutely no intention of doing so and is, instead, perfectly happy with its pretty autumn colours and quiet existence. Quiet that is until winter when it is used as a base for the **Mount Dobson Ski-field**, T6858039, www.dobson.co.nz

If you look a little closer you will find considerable evidence that contradicts Fairlie's outward appearance and reputation of being just another dull rural town. It has in fact been home to some rather innovative folk. One such resident, **Rodolph Wigley**, for example, drove from Timaru to Mount Cook in 1906 in a De Dion Bouton single-cylinder car, taking three days and encountered atrocious conditions (and few roads) to do so. Not satisfied with this rather impressive mechanical feat, he then went on to develop a motor-coach service and later an air transport service to Mount Cook, thereby creating the **Mount Cook Company**. Still not satisfied with this thriving enterprise (and clearly still reeling with inherent tedium), he then added a threshing mill business to his list of achievements and a traction engine that could do the work of 16 bullocks at twice the speed. And it doesn't end there. Rodolph's son, Harry, went on to design a landing gear that allowed his aircraft to land on the snow and ice of the Tasman Glacier. Said gear was later to become the precursor to the landing gears in use today. So, you see it is in fact interesting after all.

Other little insights can be procured from the two small museums in town; the 1875 **Mabel Binney Cottage** and the **Vintage Machinery Museum**, both located on the main highway west of the town centre (open daily 1000-1700, seasonal). Further west still (5 km) is the historic 1879 limestone **Woolshed**, on the privately owned Three Springs Station, T6858174. ■ *Daily 1000-1600, seasonal.* At its peak this station accommodated nine 'blade' shearers, which to the layman is essentially a very hard working fella shearing with a very sharp pair of scissors – not the bionic electric clippers that are used today.

On a completely different 'footing' keep your eyes open for the utterly bizarre (and typically New Zealand) **'Shoe Monument'** that has formed along a fence beside the road through the Burkes Pass. It is in no particularly special place and exists, it seems, for no apparently sane reason. It just seems that somebody did that 'Forrest Gump' thing and tied a pair of shoes to the fence and started a craze. Now, after some months, they have reproduced into a 'booty' of styles and sizes that would make Imelda Marcos look modest.

Sleeping At the top end try the **L-AL** *Dobson Lodge*, Burkes Pass, T6858316, dobson_lodge@xtra.co.nz which although some distance west of Fairlie provides a lovely romantic self-contained stone cottage in a country setting. The self-contained farm-based **B** *Possum Cottage*, Bedeshurst, T6858075, possum.cottage@xtra.co.nz is a cheaper and very cosy alternative with an open fire.

There are a few basic but comfortable motels including the **B** *Aorangi*, 26 Denmark St, T/F6858340, and the newer **B** *Fairlie Lodge*, 16 School Rd, T6858452.

The riverside **B-D** *Fairlie Gateway Top Ten Holiday Park* is located on Allandale Rd, northwest of the town centre, T/F6858375, fairliegateway@xtra.co.nz It has backpacker accommodation.

Eating The *Old Library Café* in the centre of town, T6858999, is recommended, offering snacks to dinners including a great two-course 'skiers' menu for $12.50. Open daily from 1000.

Lake Tekapo

Phone code: 03
Population: 300

Between **Lake Tekapo** and Twizel is the heart of the **MacKenzie Country**. If you have come north from the heady highs of Mount Cook there could hardly be more contrast in scenery. Lake and mountain ranges quickly give way to a vast expanse of featureless tussock grasslands of the **Tekapo River** basin. Suddenly it seems you have been taken magically from the Swiss Alps to Mid-West USA, and on less than a litre of petrol. New Zealand is just like that. Switzerland one minute, the US the next, then round the corner the Highlands of Scotland – a landscape of incredible contrasts. From whichever direction you have come, SH8 delivers you to the southern shores of Lake Tekapo and the settlement of the same name. A pretty place, famous for its iconic lakeside **church** and an ever-watchful little **collie dog**.

Ins & outs **Getting there By road** Lake Tekapo is 226 km southwest of Christchurch and 58 km north of Twizel, SH8. All the daily west-east buses from Christchurch and Queenstown pass through Lake Tekapo, including *Intercity*, T0800-767080; *Atomic Shuttles*, T3328883; and *Southern Link Shuttles*, T3588355. Bookings can be made with *High Country Souvenirs and Crafts*, T6806895.

The independent Lake Tekapo **Visitor Information Centre** is located on the main street (along with just about everything else), at *'Kiwi Express'* (near the Godley Resort Hotel), T6806224. Open 0800-2000 (winter 1800). It is very small but has free town maps, all the information about accommodation in the village, and local activity listings. *'Kiwi Treasures'*, beside the **post shop**, also acts as a VIC, T6806686. There is only one **ATM** in Tekapo, next to the **petrol station**. The *Reflections Restaurant* at the top end of the village, the VIC and the Godley Resort Hotel, all on the Main Street, have **internet** terminals.

Sights

Just about everybody who visits Lake Tekapo pays homage to the town's stone church that sits alone, in almost picture postcard position, overlooking the lake.If it were a stage prop for some ecclesiastical Hollywood blockbuster it could not look more perfect. Even on closer inspection it is truly blessed, with an open door revealing a cross on the altar backed by a large stained glass window – minus the stain. With a view and a backdrop like that it is heavenly enough, thank you. The church is called '**The Church of the Good Shepherd**' and was built in 1935, primarily as a functional place of worship, but also as a memorial to the lives of the MacKenzie Country pioneers. Sadly though, its modern-day function is almost entirely aesthetic, and the poor minister – our good shepherd – who is in attendance almost daily, must tend a very superficial and transitory flock. The vast majority of people who fall out of the tour buses in droves and are guided to the church by yelping interpreters, come only to take pictures and worship the lord digital and Kodak, not to pray or worship the Lord God Almighty. And watching this mass and chaotic 'sheep-dip' you can't help but wonder whether his cheery smile and kind words hide more cynical thoughts about a world gone utterly mad. Whatever you do go early morning or late in the day to avoid the hordes.

A few pew's lengths from the church is a statue of a collie **sheepdog** which is a simple tribute to the shepherd's best friend. It's a lovely statue, with the dog facing the lake with an alert and loyal expression as if waiting for his master to appear from the mists of the lake. He has waited a long time, and may wait forever, his little nose covered in ice in winter, dripping with rain in spring and bleached by the sun in summer.

Activities

For full activity listings and contact numbers contact the VIC, T6806686

Although Lake Tekapo is a small place there is plenty to do beyond grabbing a coffee, taking pictures of a church and patting an attractive bust! Being the first major stop for the east-west tour buses and independent tourist traffic, there is the instant lure to leave the car parked and reach for the skies. There are a number of **flightseeing** options, and the airfield in Tekapo is the starting point for two main operators that also pick up passengers in Mount Cook, before embarking on world-class scenic flights across the Great Divide. On the main street is the office of *Air Safaris*, T0800-806880, www.airsafaris.co.nz and *Tekapo Helicopters*, T6806229, www.helicopterflights.co.nz Air Safari's popular *'Grand Traverse'* is a memorable 50-minute trip that takes in Mount Cook and the glaciers on both sides of the divide. It is a fairly unique combination that you would be hard pressed to find anywhere else in the world, so if you do not have time to visit Mount Cook Village or the West Coast, where similar options abound, it is well worth considering. There will also be plenty of other options in Wanaka and Queenstown, but this trip (beyond a flight to Milford Sound) is one of the best and, at $220, child $145, is good value for money. Helicopter trips are of course are a little more expensive, provide a different kind of experience and can land on the snow.

Still in the skies there is another unique opportunity to go **star-gazing** at the international observatory and US satellite tracking station, that sits discreetly atop Mount John at the western end of the village. Even a walk up here during the day provides some heavenly views. For details T6806565, 1 ½ hours $40 (minimum four). Also based in Tekapo is the highly experienced company *Alpine Recreation*, T6806736, www.alpinerecreation.co.nz which offers guided mountain climbing and trekking trips from the three-day Ball Pass Trek in the Tasman Glacier Valley to the full-monty six-day ascent of Cook, for the small mortgage of $3000. Of course Lake Tekapo provides both cruise and fishing opportunities. *Lake Tekapo Excursions and Adventures*,

T6806686, offer an attractive range of fishing, boating, hiking and sightseeing, from 1½ hours, $30.

Mountain bikes, **kayaks** ($15 for two hours) and **fishing rods** (half-day $12, license $20) can be hired from the *Lake Tekapo Alpine Inn*, T6806848. *Kiwi Express*, T6806224, nearby also hire out **mountain bikes** (full day $15) and kayaks.

Sleeping

In Maori the name Tekapo means 'sleeping mat', but thankfully the village can offer far more than a bivvy beside the lake. The main hotel in town is the **L-AL** *Godley Resort Hotel*, SH8, T6806848, F6806873, www.thegodley.com that is in prime position in the centre of the village overlooking the lake. It has comfortable suites with great views, and reputable Chinese and Japanese restaurants. It is of course very busy with tour groups in summer, which may not suit, but in winter, when rates are reduced or with the odd special deal, it can be great.

Slightly further up the road and right in the heart of the action is the new **AL-A** *Lake Tekapo Scenic Resort Motel*, T6806808, www.laketekapo.com which offers modern studio units with views and spas. Another fine motel option is the lodge-style **AL-A** *Chalet Boutique Motel*, T6806774, www.thechalet-laketekapo.co.nz that is lakeside (near the church) and offers a wide range of activities.

Tekapo has some fine B&Bs including the **LL-L** *Tekapo Lodge*, which sits above the main street in Aorangi Cres, T6806566, www.laketekapolodge.co.nz It offers 4 en suites, one with spa, and a nice guest lounge with open fire. The slightly cheaper but equally modern **A** *Tekapo House*, 8 O'Neill Place, T6806607, rayntek@xtra.co.nz is 10 min from the centre of the village and has 1 en-suite, 1 double and 1 twin with shared facilities. The **A** *Pioneer Cottage*, overlooking the lake (near the church) on Pioneer Drive, T6806755, is a good self-contained option and very cosy in winter with its log fire. For other good B&B options contact the VIC.

The **C-D** *Tekapo YHA*, 3 Simpson Lane, T6806857, yhatekapo@yha.org.nz is popular with backpackers due to its lakeside location at the western end of the village, offering great views. It has doubles, twins and dorms, and bike hire. Another alternative is the friendly and efficient **C-D** *Tailor-Made-Tekapo Backpackers*, 9-11 Aorangi Cres, T6806700, tailor-made-backpackers@xtra.co.nz Although not with the same views as the YHA, it has a good range of rooms with some good value en suites. The spacious, peaceful and lakeside **A-D** *Lake Tekapo Motels and Motor Camp*, at the western end of the village, Lakeside Drive, T6806825, F6806824, is a fine spot with self-contained motels, flats, cabins and powered/tent sites.

Lastly, should all the scenery and abounding nature lead to a sudden and dramatic desire to remove all your clothing, you would be welcome to do so with the naturist friendly *Aoraki Naturally*, T6806549, located 16 km south of Tekapo near Irishman Creek Bridge.

Eating

For fine dining your best bet is the *Kohan Japanese Restaurant* in the Godley Resort Hotel, T6806688 (open daily for lunch and dinner). But if Japanese cuisine is not to your liking then The *Reflections Restaurant*, T6806808, at the other end of the village is another safe bet (open daily from 1000). There are numerous café/bars and takeaways in the main street that offer light snacks and coffee, with most offering backdoor views across the lake.

Twizel

Phone code: 03
Population: 1,179

Right in the heart of the MacKenzie Basin, near the river after which it was named, is Twizel, a former hydroelectric scheme construction town built in the 1970s. The name Twizel was bestowed upon the town by pioneer surveyor John Thompson after the Twizel Bridge that crosses the River Tweed on the border between England and Scotland. Twizel's most famous residents are the critically endangered and endemic Kaki, or **black stilt**, which, along with the village's proximity to the **Mount Cook National Park** and **mountain biking**, is its biggest tourist draw.

Ins & outs

Getting there By road Twizel is 63 km from Mount Cook, 57 km west of Tekapo and 127 km north of Wanaka. By **bus** Twizel is served daily by most of the operators plying the Christchurch/Queenstown route, including ***Intercity***, T442800; ***Atomic Shuttles***, T4429708; ***Southern Link***, T3588355); ***Mount Cook Landline***, T0800-800904; and ***High Country Shuttles***, T0800-435050 (which connect daily with Christchurch-bound Intercity and Atomic Shuttles in Mount Cook). Buses stop outside DOC near the centre of town.***GTS Country Link Tours***, 44 Omahau Cres, T4350052, go to Timaru every Fri and also offer local tours.

Getting around Almost everything a body needs is located in or near Market Place, a small and modern shopping square in the heart of the village. Most accommodation is within walking distance from there.

Information The Twizel Visitor **Information Centre** is located beside the Mall (northern entrance to Market Place) in the centre of the village, T4353124, F4350537, www.twizel.com Open daily 0900-1900 (winter Mon-Fri 0900-1700, Sat 1000-1600). The free leaflet *'Twizel-Town of Trees'* has a detailed map and is very useful. **DOC** have an area office on Wairepo Rd, T3652766, KakiVisitorHide@doc.govt.nz and can provide local walks, tramping and mountain bike track information. Open Mon-Fri 0830-1730. **Internet** is available at the VIC.

Sights & activities

Twizel presents another excellent opportunity to see cutting-edge conservation at work, so typical of DOC and the country as a whole. Twizel is home to the internationally recognised efforts to maintain the wild populations of the **black stilt** – one of the rarest wading birds in the world. They are called 'Kaki' by the Maori and are considered by them to be a taonga species (living treasure). Once common in the heartlands and braided-river beds throughout New Zealand, thanks primarily to man's indirect introduction of non-native predatory species, like the weasel and stoat, numbers have been decimated and currently total less than 100 wild birds. A guided visit to the **viewing hide**, located 3 km south of the village, allows the public to view the stalwart survivors and captive population of 66, that are bred in enclosed aviaries and used to replenish (or hopefully increase) the wild population. Bookings are essential and visits are by prior arrangement only. ■ *Guided tours are available daily from late Oct-mid Apr (weekdays only in winter), from $12.50, child $5. Contact DOC or the VIC.*

The other big and relatively new attraction based in Twizel are the **mountain biking** opportunities. Of particular note are the **Heli-biking** trips to several locations including Benmore and Lake Ohau. Rides range from 1 ½ hours to 3 ½ hous and cost from $75. Contact *Heli-bike Twizel*, T/F4350626, www.helibike.com (bike hire available).

Independently, the numerous canals and their associated tracks that connect the waterways and hydroelectric schemes provide ideal biking opportunities. For more information contact the VIC or consult the DOC leaflet '*Ohau Conservation Area*'.

Other operators based in or around Twizel include *Twizel Horse Treks*, Ohau Canal Road, T4350530, from 1-3 days. *Tussock Country Horse Treks*, T4350484, located 9 km from Twizel, towards Mount Cook, provide similar trips. Shaun Norman of *High Country Expeditions*, T/F4350622, snorman@voyager.co.nz is a world-class mountain guide offering half-to multi-day climbing, **mountaineering** and abseiling trips. A number of Scenic **Heli-flightseeing** trips leave from beside the MacKenzie Country Inn on Wairepo Road, but you are advised to look at the numerous other choices available from elsewhere before parting with the cash (see Mount Cook National Park section). There are also some excellent fishing venues in the area; the VIC has details.

The VIC also lists over 60 other *'Things Twizel can offer'* in the way of activities, ranging from frisbee golf to ice-skating, although 'buying a house' and 'yoga' (unless done in unison perhaps) is slightly overdoing it. It also quite rightly suggests a visit to the 'fantastic information centre' – it and its staff are great.

Sleeping At the top end is the very plush **L-AL** *MacKenzie Country Inn*, corner of Ostler and Wairepo Rds, T4350869, F4350857, bookings@mackenzie.co.nz which has 'all the right knobs and switches' and is close to the town centre. There are a scattering of motels, including the modern A-frames of the **A** *Mountain Chalets Motel*, Wairepo Rd, T4350785, mt.chalets@xtra.co.nz A cheaper motel option with backpacker facilities is the vast **B-D** *High Country Holiday Lodge and Motel*, 23 MacKenzie Dr, T4350671, which has cheap en suites, doubles, singles and dorms. There is also a restaurant and bar on site and it is a stone's throw from Market Place. There are not many B&B's, but the VIC has a full list of those that are available. The **AL** *Heartland Lodge*, 19 North West Arm, T4350008, european@xtra.co.nz has some nice rooms and a self-contained loft that is good value for up to six. The **A** *Aoraki Lodge*, 32 MacKenzie Dr, T4350300, mtdb@mtcook.org.nz is a slightly cheaper and equally reliable option. There are two motor parks in the area, the **B-D** *Parklands Alpine Tourist Park*, 122 MacKenzie Dr, T4350507, which is in a sheltered spot and has self-contained and budget accommodation, and the **C-D** *Lake Ruataniwha Holiday Park*, T4350613, which is in a pleasant setting near the lake, 4 km south of the village.

Eating The options are few with almost all centred in Market Place. ***The Hunter's Bar and Café***, T4350303, is recommended and the local's choice for lunch, dinner and entertainment. The plush *MacKenzie Country Inn* also offers fine dining (see above). Open daily from 1100. For a quick coffee or light snack try the *Black Stilt Coffee Shop*, T4350627, which is also in Market Place.

Mount Cook National Park

This 70,696-ha park has, by its very name, got to be one of the most spectacular in New Zealand, and a natural 'cathedral' second only to Milford Sound. With the 3754 m peak of ***Mount Cook*** *as its altar, its robust ministers include* ***Tasman*** *(3498 m) and* ***Mount Sefton*** *(3158 m), surrounded by a supportive choir of 19 peaks over 3000 m. Rising up to this great chancel are the vast and impressive* ***Hooker*** *and* ***Tasman Glaciers****, which not only created the long nave but once blocked the very porch. All this natural architecture makes for world-class scenery and mountaineering. Indeed, it was here that Sir Edmund Hillary first started his career that was to reach its very 'peak' on the summit of Everest in 1953. The park is essentially connected to the Westland National Park by the Great (east-west)*

Divide and peaks of the Liebeg Range. Yet the two parks are significantly different. With such a dramatic upheaval of rock so close to the sea, the western side sees most rain and snow, creating slopes draped in dense rainforest and, higher up, huge snowfields, spawning the great Franz and Fox glaciers (to name but two). But in the Mount Cook National Park, there is almost no forest, with almost one-third of it being permanent snow and ice. In amongst the rock beds and valley floors rare ***alpine plants*** *flourish, some endemic and rare, and rummaging around in this heady garden are unique bird species, like the mountain parrot and resident vandal – the* ***kea****.*

The area is considered sacred by the Maori who see Aoraki (Mount Cook) as a powerful symbol of being, an ancestor from who the Tangata Whenua – the Ngai Tahu people – are descended, and a link between the supernatural and natural world.

The road to Mount Cook

About 8 km north of Twizel the famed **SH80** skirts the western banks and azure waters of **Lake Pukaki** to pay homage to **Aoraki-Mount Cook**. Before entering the chancel you are first advised to look at the cathedral from afar from the southern banks of Lake Pukaki. There is a car park, unmanned information centre and **lookout point** from which, on a clear day, the mountain beckons. Unless you are really pressed for time, or the weather is foul, it really is sacrilege not to make the scenic 55 km drive to Mount Cook Village. Located so close to the base of the Mountains and Hooker-Tasman Glacier Valleys, it is like a miniature Toy-Town that acts as the gateway to National Park. And once here, it seems a terrible waste to move on without exploring the park from even closer quarters.

Glentanner Park

For the first 32 km towards the mountain valleys your excitement grows in parallel with the vista before you, as the great snow-capped edifices get larger and larger and more poignantly – you – smaller and smaller. It really is a bit like entering the gaping mouth of Moby Dick. Once again we have nature at its wonderfully dominant best! Before reaching Mount Cook Village, and just beyond the water terminus of Lake Pukaki, you will encounter the motor park and scenic flightseeing base of **Glentanner Park**, T4351855, F4351854, www.glentanner.co.nz You are strongly advised to stop here and muse at the **scenic flights** and other **activities** on offer, perhaps over a coffee, in its **café** overlooking the mountain. Also, if you are in a camper van and intend to stay in the valley overnight, be aware that this will be home – there is no **motor park** in the National Park or Mount Cook Village.

On offer at **B-D** *Glentanner* are excellent facilities, self-contained and standard cabins, backpacker dorm and spacious powered/tent sites.

Activities

These and other activities are also available through the Hermitage and VIC in Mount Cook Village (see below)

The biggest draw at Glentanner are the **fixed-wing** and **helicopter flightseeing** trips. The choices are vast. *Helicopter Line*, T4351801, www.helicopter.co.nz whose Mount Cook (East) operations are based at the park, offer three trips from 20 minutes ($152) to 45 minutes ($325). If you can possibly afford it, their *'Mountains High'* (45 minutes) trip is truly memorable. First you are flown up and over the Tasman Valley Glacier, before making a snow landing at over 2000 m to sample the atmosphere and magnificent view of Mount Cook and its associate peaks. Then back in the air you cross the Great Divide. From here you encounter the views of the West Coast and the fractured bed of the upper Franz and Fox Glaciers, before skirting just below

Cook's awesome summit and dropping down the Hooker Valley, over Mount Cook Village and back to base. Not even the James Bond theme music or Holst's Planets Suite playing in the background could do that justice, believe me. *Cloud 9*, an adjunct operation to Helicopter Line, also offer some very appealing **Heli-hiking** trips of three to five hours, from $148, child $115. You might even have a full-on snowball fight or go tobogganing high above the snow line in mid summer. **Fixed-wing** trips are also offered by *Air Safaris*, T6806880, www.airsafaris.co.nz or *Mount Cook Ski Planes*, T4351026, www.skiplanes.co.nz These range from 25 minutes (from $160) to 55 minutes (from $315). The Ski Plane option also offers snow landings. The benefit of a fixed-wing adventure is that you are longer in the air for the money. Note that Mount Cook Ski Planes are based at the Mount Cook Airport, a few kilometres north, not at Glentanner itself.

Other activities available from *Glentanner* are the excellent *Glacier Explorer Trips*, T/F4351077, glacier 007@xtra.co.nz This involves a half-hour walk to the terminus of the Tasman Lake, followed by a fascinating two-hour boat trip to the very edges of the ice. Recommended, from $75, child $35; Glentanner has its own **horse trekking** operation, T4351855, from 30 minutes ($30) to three hours ($75); *Argo Adventure Tours* offer two hour trips on eight-wheel drive buggies, a good trip in wet weather, from $80, child $50; or 2 ½ hour four-wheel drive tours are on offer with *Alan's 4WD Tours*, T4351809, from $75, child $35. Book at the main desk, T4351855.

Guided **kayak** trips (T4351855, from $60) and **walking** adventures (T025-2577013, $90) are also on offer. The kayak trips offer the unique opportunity to explore independently the features of the glacier lakes. *Glentanner* offers mountain bike ($18 for half-day) and fishing tackle hire (fishing license $13).

Mount Cook Village

Phone code: 03
Population: 300 (summer)

From Glentanner you begin to enter the 'chancel' of the mountains and the National Park proper. In Mount Cook, about 23 km further towards the mountains, you will find yourself climbing out of your 'dinky-toy' car feeling like a termite. It's easy to get neck ache round here.

Ins & outs

Mount Cook village is 63 km from Twizel

Getting there By air Mount Cook **airport**, located 3 km to the south of Mount Cook Village, is served by ***Air New Zealand Link (Mount Cook Airlines)***, T0800-737000, from Christchurch and Queenstown. A shuttle bus meets most flights, from $5.

By bus *Intercity*, T0800-767080, offer a daily service from Christchurch (Queenstown-bound) departing at 1200. The tour buses ***Great Sights***, T0800-744487, www.greatsights, and ***Grey Line***, T0800-800904, also ply the Christchurch/Queenstown route daily, departing for Christchurch in the early afternoon. ***High Country Shuttles***, T4350506, offer a daily service to Mount Cook from Twizel (depart Twizel 0700/1035/1230). They connect with Atomic and Intercity services from Queenstown and Christchurch (in Twizel). ***The Cook Connection***, T0800-252666, www.cookconnect.co.nz offer a Mt Cook to Oamaru return ($80) and Mt Cook to Timaru return ($80), a minimum of 3 days a week.

Information The **DOC Visitor Information Centre** is located just below the Hermitage Hotel, on Bowen Drive, T4351818, F4351080, www.mtcook.org.nz Open daily 0830-1800 (winter 0830-1700). It has displays, an audio-visual (good in wet weather, $2.50) and information surrounding the park and its obvious attractions. There are walks leaflets, tramping information and they administer all hut bookings. An up-to-date weather forecast and intentions forms are also provided. Of immediate use is a map of the village contained in the handy leaflet '*Aoraki, Mount Cook Alpine Village*" which is available from DOC and the Hermitage Hotel.

Sights

After you have recovered from the incredible views that surround you, you will be immediately struck at how ordered and dull in colour Mount Cook, the village, is. This is not an accident, since the settlement comes within the boundary of the **Mount Cook National Park** and is therefore strictly controlled. The only real exception is the **Hermitage Hotel**, T4351809, F4351879, www.mount-cook.com which many claim to be the most famous in New Zealand, while others hail it merely as a blot on the landscape. Of course it is the setting that makes the hotel, with its boast of 'mountain views' taking on far more than mere honest credibility. But although the Hermitage has been well blessed by location it has also been cursed with misfortune. What you see today is not the original, in fact it is essentially the third. The original that was built in 1884 was located further down the valley and destroyed by flash floods in 1913. Relocated and rebuilt in its present position it was then gutted by fire 44 years later. Now at the beginning of the millennium it is undergoing renovation and tightly controlled (but still invasive?) expansion. No doubt you will find yourself continuously staring up at **Mount Cook** from the interior of *The Hermitage* or from its well-manicured lawns. Keep your eyes and ears open for **kea**, the cheeky green mountain parrots that hang about with – it seems – the sole intention of harrying anything with legs and dismantling all they possess.

As well as the gargantuan vista of Mount Cook and **Mount Sefton** (3158 m), the associate glacier valleys are well worthy of investigation. Directly north of the Hermitage is the **Hooker Valley**, and east, over the dwarfed **Wakefield Range**, the vast **Tasman Valley** with its own massive glacier – the longest in New Zealand. Both valleys act as the watersheds that feed Lake Pukaki and were once full of ice, hence the incredible expanse of **boulder-fields** that precede the lake's azure waters. It is incidentally the presence of fine glacial moraine ('rock flour') that gives the glacial lakes their exotic colour. There are a number of activities that focus on the glacier valleys and lakes which have already been mentioned (see Glentanner above), but they can of course also be explored by foot (see walks below).

Activities

Do not risk any climb without proper experience or equipment. Mount Cook National Park is serious business. If in doubt don't – and consult Alpine Guides

Note that all the activities already mentioned above (Glentanner Park) are also available from Mount Cook Village. **Bikes** can be hired from the *Hermitage Hotel*. *Alpine Guides*, located in the village, T4351834, F4351898, www.alpineguides.co.nz are the only resident guiding company in the national park and, given the terrain, the potential challenges and hazards at hand, their presence is welcome. They offer multi-day **mountaineering** and **trekking** trips as well as half- to full-day (8 km) **walks** from $90, child $60 (November-March). In winter full-day **skiing** and **Heli-skiing** trips are available on the upper Tasman Glacier and other equally remote locations, from $625. Although these trips are expensive, they provide the unique opportunity to ski on virgin snow in areas simply inaccessible to the masses.

Tramping

Mount Cook village is the gateway to the **Copeland Pass Track**, which is a 4-5 day tramp to the West Coast across the Great Divide. As attractive as this may seem, it is a tramp that requires considerable experience and proper mountaineering equipment. It is also ill advised at present due to rock falls at the higher altitudes. Conditions are expected to improve, however, especially with the planned relocation of the Hooker Hut. Although you are still currently permitted to attempt the crossing you are advised to seek advice and check with up-to-date conditions with DOC.

A far more realistic option is the overnight tramp to the **Muller Hut**, which sits in a superb position (1768 m) on the ridge of **Mount Oliver** (1933 m) behind Mount Cook Village. Although a strenuous climb, requiring a fair level of fitness, proper planning and equipment, it is a classic excursion. If you stay overnight in the Muller Hut the views at sunset and sunrise over the Hooker and Mount Cook especially are simply world class. In total it is a stiff four-hour climb each way. A further one-hour return will see you at the top of Mount Oliver which, rumour has it, was the first peak in the region that Sir Edmund Hillary climbed – and look what it did to him! For more information contact DOC and the '*Muller Hut Route*' leaflet, $1.

Walking

All times are standard return times. For all walks in the area get hold of the DOC 'Walks in Aoraki/Mount Cook National Park'

There are some very appealing walks in the vicinity that offer fine views and insights into the local hardy flora and fauna, with most beginning from the village. The shortest is the **Bowen Bush Walk**, which is only ten minutes but takes you through some classic **totara forest**. It starts from behind the Alpine Guides Centre. A similar 30-minute walk, the **Glencoe Walk**, starts from behind the *Hermitage Hotel* and another, the one-hour **Governors Bush Walk**, begins from the public shelter, just to the south of the Alpine Guides Centre. The latter also offers a good viewpoint of the mountains. Two longer options are the two-hour **Red Tarns Track** (which again begins from the public shelter) and the 2-3 hour **Sealy Tarns Track**, which is part of the Muller Hut ascent and begins from the Kea Point Track from the *Hermitage*. Both of these walks offer spectacular views from higher altitudes.

The **Kea Point Track** can be tackled from the *Hermitage* (two hours) or from the White Horse Hill campsite car park (one hour), which is accessed north via the Hooker Valley Road (which in turn is accessed from beside the Kitchener Stream Bridge just at the entrance to the village complex). At the terminus of the Kea Walk is a lookout deck that offers memorable views of Mount Sefton, Footstool, the Hooker Valley, Muller Glacier and of course Mount Cook. If you want to investigate the Hooker Valley you can do this from the village or, again, from the White Horse Hill car park. Other than the spectacular views of Mount Cook towering above, the four-hour **Hooker Valley Track** takes you all the way to the fascinating ice and melt water features of the Hooker Glacier **terminal lake.**

The **Tasman Valley** also offers some interesting walks that take in the snout of the vast, advancing glacier. From the village you will need to travel by car or mountain bike to the end of the Tasman Glacier Road (8 km) that is accessed off SH80 south of the village. There are two walks on offer: the 3-4 hour **Ball Shelter Walk** which skirts the side of the glacier, and the more remarkable one-hour **Glacier Walk** which investigates the terminal lake and head of the glacier. Both walks start from the car park.

Sleeping & eating

At the top end there is of course little alternative to The **LL-AL** *Hermitage Hotel*, T4351809, F4351879, www.mount-cook.com which owns most of the accommodation options on offer. Other than the rather tired and expensive traditional rooms in the hotel, there is a new luxury wing just opened (with remarkable views and modern decor), self-contained motel doubles, studios and chalets with basic facilities. Somewhere in there you may find what you are looking for (even economically for groups of four), but bear in mind that the price reflects the location, not necessarily the quality of accommodation. Bookings in the high season are advised. There is no faulting the hotel facilities, and the **restaurants** and bars are good, providing affordable and filling buffet meals. With all the tour buses lunch, however, can look a bit like a shark-feeding frenzy. Both the hotel and the motel complex have restaurants and bars and both offer buffet-style lunches and dinners. The **café** underneath the hotel serves a range of light snacks and bottomless cups of coffee. There is also a small store.

Backpackers should look no further than the busy **B-D** *Mount Cook YHA*, corner od Bowen and Kitchener Drs, T4351820, F4351821, yhamtck@yha.org.nz, which even if it had competition would compete very favourably. It has tidy double, twin and shared rooms, modern ski-lodge style facilities including a log fire and sauna. Internet. You are advised to book your bed at this hostel well in advance in summer.

Camper van owners are best to double back to The **B-D** *Glentanner Park* (see above) where they will find excellent facilities. If the YHA is full you may also get budget accommodation at Glentanner. With the many shuttles going back and forth to the village, transport is also possible. The basic **D** *White Horse Hill campsite* is located at the end of the Hooker Valley Road, 2 km from the village (see walks above).

For evening **entertainment** again you are looking at the bars in the *Hermitage Hotel* or its sister motel complex. The motel complex bar has a pool table and is the most popular with backpackers.

Directory

The *Hermitage Hotel* forms the hub of all activity and services in the village, housing two **restaurants, bars,** a small and expensive grocery **store,** and a café. The hotel also offers non-clients **internet**, **currency exchange**, a **post office**, **EFTPOS** and **activity** bookings. That's not a bad list to add to its comfy if over-priced beds with their world-class mountain views. The only thing it does not provide is **petrol**, which can be purchased (24 hr credit card and EFTPOS) near the *Alpine Guides Centre* just to the south (unmanned).

Omarama

Located at the head of the Waitaki Valley and north of the scenic Lindis Pass (from Wanaka and Queenstown), Omarama provides a convenient overnight stop and starting point from which to explore the **MacKenzie Country**. There are also a number of local activities that may hold you back, including **fishing** and **water sports** on Lakes Benmore and Aviemore, **gliding** from Omarama airfield and winter **skiing** at Lake Ohau.

Other than the obvious appeal of the local lakes, the **Clay Cliffs** situated between Omarama and Twizel are worthy of investigation, and echo the bizarre eroded rock and gravel formations of The Pinnacles in the Wairarapa, North Island. To reach them turn off SH8 west towards the mountains on Quailburn Road, 3 km north of the village (signposted), 15 km. There is a small charge ($5 in an honesty box) at the gate to the cliffs. *Omarama Four Seasons Tours*, T4389547, offer **scenic road tours** and interpretative visits to the Clay Cliffs, Waitaki Lakes and surrounding countryside. Omarama is world renowned for **gliding**, with the huge expanses of thermal-rich grasslands and mountain offering world-class conditions and scenic flights that are almost unparalleled. *Alpine Soaring*, T4389600, offer a range of options from the airfield in the village. For **fishing**, two good local guides can be found *in Doug Horton*, T4389808, and *Max Irons*, T4389468.

Sleeping and eating There is a good range of accommodation in the village. At the top end is the expansive **AL-A** *Heritage Gateway Hotel*, T4389805, F4389837, heritagegateway@xtra.co.nz with modern standard rooms and self-contained suites, a bar and restaurant. They can also arrange local tours and activities. Nearby is the very tidy **A** *Ahuriri Motel*, T/F4389451, which has 14 modern and comfortable self-contained units. The **B** *Briar's Country Homestay*, Ahuriri Heights, SH8, T4389615, is a good B&B option and the proprietors also offer garden tours.

For **backpackers** there is the popular **D** ***Buscot Station***, 8 km north of the village, T4389646 which provides dorms, en suite rooms and tent sites on a working cattle/sheep station. South (15 km), the **D** ***Killermont Station***, T4389864, provides a similar set up. Back in the village, camper vans are well catered for at the **B-D** ***Omarama Top Ten Holiday Park***, T/F4389875. It's nicely sheltered, well facilitated and has flats, cabins and powered/tent sites.

Other than the **restaurant** in the *Heritage Hotel* (above) the ***Clay Cliffs Vineyard*** and Café, T4389654, located 500 m south of the village on SH8, provides fine cuisine in a lovely setting. Tastings and sales. Open 1100-1800 (closed in Jun).

Lake Ohau Largely unbeaten by the nasty commercial stick, Lake Ohau provides a pleasant diversion off SH8 between Omarama and Twizel, and in winter a popular skiing venue. The **ski field** is best known for its scenic views, less frenzied atmosphere and the longest T bar in New Zealand (1033 m). For more information about skiing contact T/F4389885, or visit www.nzski.com Most of the activity centres around Lake Ohau **Alpine Village** which is located above the southern shores of Lake Ohau, just west of **Lake Middleton**, a small sub-lake separated from Lake Ohau by a narrow strip of land.

In summer the lake and its surroundings are popular for **walking**, **fishing** and **mountain biking**. It has six forests around its shores, with a number of tracks, access points and camp sites. The best information is contained in the DOC brochure *'Ohau Conservation Area'* available from the VIC in Twizel.

Sleeping Other than the **camping grounds** there is the very pleasant **L-AL**Lake Ohau Lodge, T4389885, F4389885, www.ohau.co.nz It is set lakeside and has standard self-contained studio and luxury units, a restaurant, bar and cosy open fire. Cheaper accommodation can be found at the **B**Weatherall Motel, T4389662, F4389839, which has self-contained units and shared units (30 mins from the ski-fields). The tidy **A**Lake Ohau Homestay, Ohau Dr, Ohau Alpine Village, T4389833, is the only B&B option, and is 5 mins from the ski fields.

Waitaki Valley From Oamaru you have the option of turning inland via SH83 through the picturesque Waitaki Valley to **Omarama**, The **MacKenzie Country** and **Mount Cook**. It is a pleasant drive, best negotiated in autumn when the poplar and lakeside weeping willows are draped in gold. Many of the orchards on the way also offer a palette of autumnal hues. The valley is best known for its lakes and the Waitaki River, which are regulated by an extensive system of hydroelectric dams that begin to dominate the waterways of the southwestern Canterbury Region. Fishing for both trout and salmon is just one of the more obvious leisure activities in the area.

Duntroon From east to west the first settlement of any significance is **Duntroon**. With the discovery of gold in 1868 the town enjoyed a very brief boom, before the diggings proved a failure, earning them the label of the 'poor man's field'. After a return to relative obscurity, there was more excitement with the discovery of a quartz reef between the Maerewhenua and Otekaike Rivers in 1870, but, like the gold, its extraction was short-lived.

Now merely a small farming settlement, it offers a number of amenities, activities and scenic attractions. There is a petrol station and the *Duntroon Tavern*, Main Street, T4312850, or the *Flying Pig Café*, Main St, T4312733 (which also acts as the **information** centre), for a snack, lunch or dinner. **Fishing** and **Jetboating** on the Waitaki and Maerewhenua Rivers is offered by *Trail Blazer Safaris*, T4348799. The **Elephant Rocks**, accessed from

Livingstone Rd, near the Maerewhenua River Bridge are an unusual set of limestone outcrops that are worthy of investigation and also provide good **rock climbing** possibilities, T4326855. There are also **Maori rock drawings** at Takiroa on the other side of the Maerewhenua River Valley dating back over 1,000 years (ask at the café for directions).

Sleeping The **L** *Tokarahi Homestead*, T4312500, F4312551, tokarahi@xtra.co.nz located 2 km down Dip Hill Rd, 11 km south of Duntroon on the Dansey's Pass Road, provides luxurious, beautifully appointed accommodation in 19th-century Victorian style. A perfect peaceful, historic retreat. The **D** ***Dansey's Pass Holiday Camp***, T4312564, at the end of Dansey's Pass Road, is cheaper and less salubrious but no less peaceful. They also offer an interesting range of local scenic tours.

Kurow to Omarama

From Kurow it is 52 km to Omarama and SH8

A further 23 km west of Duntroon is **Kurow**, which nestles at the confluence of the Hakataramea and Waitaki Rivers. Most of the residents work on the hydroelectric damns of the Lakes Benmore and Aviemore to the west, but for leisure they say there is one activity that stands head and shoulders above the rest – **fishing**. For insider information and guided trips contact *Waitaki Valley Fishing Guides*, 104 Gordon Street, T4360510. There is also **jetboating** on the Waitaki with *Waitaki Jets*, 15 Bledisloe Street, T4360778. South of Kurow is another potential distraction in the form of the former 1871 homestead of the Hon Robert Campbell now open to the public by arrangement, T4311111. West of Kurow you soon encounter **Lake Aviemore** and the higher, more extensive and truncated **Lake Benmore**. Both have **dams**. The Aviemore Dam has a 1-km long fish spawning race that is used by up to 3000 adult trout at a time. The dam at the head of Benmore is the largest in New Zealand and can also be investigated though the lakeside picnic grounds. Safe swimming and water sports in both lakes may prove more attractive. For more information contact the **Benmore Power Station and Visitor Centre**, T4389212 (open daily 1030-1630, tours 1100, 1300, 1500).

Sleeping The **C-D** *Kurow Holiday Park* is located at 76 Bledisloe St, T4360725.

15 The West Coast

The West Coast

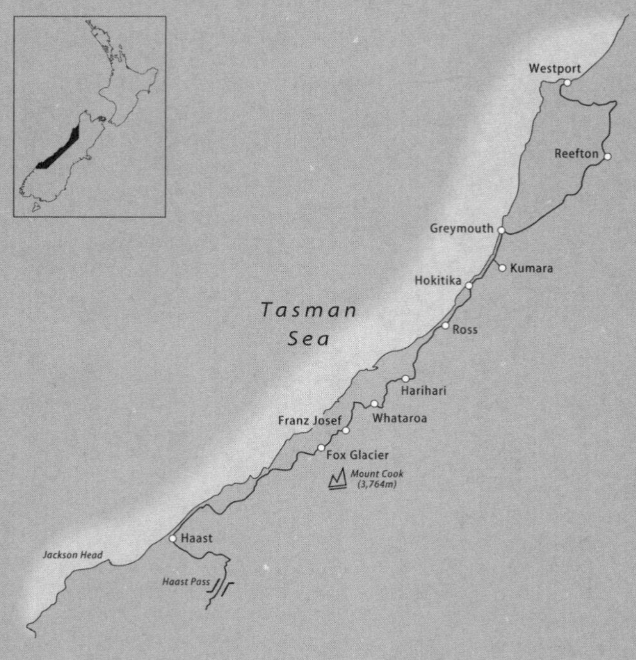

The West Coast of South Island, New Zealand is a land of extremes – extreme climate and extreme geography, extreme ecosystems and above all, extreme scenery. It is a place of majestic beauty. Bounded on one side by the Tasman Sea and on the other by the heady peaks of the ***Southern Alps****, it encompasses a narrow stretch of land that accounts for only 8% of the total landmass of New Zealand. Between these boundaries lies a quarter of all New Zealand's* ***native forest****, a lush and predominantly impenetrable landscape copiously watered by an average annual rainfall totalling over 5 m. The boundaries of five of the country's 14 national parks breach the West Coast region. Two of these,* ***Paparoa National Park*** *and the* ***Westland National Park****, it can call its very own. In one – the Westland – are the huge* ***Fox*** *and* ***Franz Josef*** *glaciers. The settlements of the region, strung along the 600 km length of SH6, from Karamea in the north to Jackson's Bay in the south, are not attractive places and stand in stark contrast to the beauty surrounding them. Nature, thankfully, has never made it easy for man to live here, nor plunder its resources. The modern-day West Coast is sparsely populated, with less than 1% of the country's total population. Indeed, there are less people living there now than in the late 19th century.*

Things to do in West Coast

- *Explore the ancient forests and awesome limestone features of the Oparara Basin.*
- *Feel the ground shake as the surf pounds Punakaiki's Pancake Rocks.*
- *Go 'on strike' in Blackball.*
- *Meet a possum and a giant sandfly at the Bushman's Centre near Lake Ianthe.*
- *Visit the colony of elegant Kotuku (White Herons), by jet boat, from Whataroa.*
- *Choose your favourite glacier – Franz Josef or Fox – and fly over them, land or climb on them.*
- *Explore the stunning coastal scenery of Munroe, Murphy's or Ship Creek beaches.*
- *Go jet boating from coast to mountain from Haast.*
- *Explore the pristine wilderness south of Haast. Follow the Jackson River Valley to the Cascade, then stop for the country's most remote fish and chip shop in Jackson's Bay.*

Ins and Outs

Getting there

Haast is 421 km from Dunedin, 261 km from Queenstown and 145 km from Wanaka. Greymouth is 258 km from Christchurch and 290 km from Nelson

By air The West Coast airports of Westport and Hokitika are serviced by ***Air New Zealand Link*** from Wellington and Christchurch respectfully, T0800-737000. **By bus** the West Coast is served by ***Intercity***, T3799020, www.intercitycoach.co.nz ***Atomic Shuttles***, T3228883; ***Coast Shuttles***, T7896837; ***West Coast Express***, T5465007 and ***White Star***, T5468687. **By car** There are 4 main routes to the West Coast. North to south they are: the Buller Gorge (SH6) from Blenheim and Nelson; Lewis Pass (SH7) from Kaikoura and Christchurch; Arthur's Pass (SH73) from Christchurch; and, the most recent, the Hasst Pass (SH6) from Wanaka. **By train** the West Coast is served by the world famous, scenic ***TranzAlpine*** from Christchurch to Greymouth, T0800-802802.

Getting around

The main highway SH6 down the length of the West Coast is generally well serviced by the bus companies above. Local bus companies are listed in the relevant text. Breaking down on the West Coast can be a frustrating experience and you would also be wise to join the **AA**. You should also be aware that **petrol** is hard to come by and there are long stretches between townships down the length of the West Coast: there are no petrol stations between Westport and Greymouth (101 km). So fill up. **Hitching** in the region is possible but at times difficult – and often very wet. **Motorcycling** and **cycling** are highly recommended

Information

The main website is www.west-coast.co.nz

There are main **VICs** in Westport, Greymouth and Hokitika, with a number of **DOC** Visitor Centres throughout the region including Franz Josef, Fox Glacier and Haast. Contact details are in the relevant sections.

The Buller Gorge

This will be your introduction to an unwelcome and almost constant companion on your West Coast journey – the ubiquitous sandfly

There are actually two gorges on the Buller River, the Upper Gorge and the Lower Gorge. They are separated by an area of relatively flat farmland around the small settlement of Inangahua, which lies roughly halfway between Murchison and Westport. Following the river is the northernmost arterial to the West Coast, SH6. This 100-km road journey from Murchison to the coast, is a scenic and at times dramatic experience, where you fall with the river through mountains and valleys draped in an ever-increasing veil of green. The drive to the coast is, in itself, pleasant enough but also holds a number of interesting attractions and stops along the way.

Sights & activities

Just beyond the junction of SH6 and SH65 the road crosses O'Sullivan's Bridge and the **Upper Gorge** begins proper. Almost immediately you come across the **Buller Gorge Swingbridge** which, at 110 m is New Zealand's longest. True to the New Zealand attitude, you can not only wet yourself crossing it by foot ($3), but also fly beside it, strapped to a small chair ($15). To create even more laundry for the week you can then descend to the river for a trip in a **jetboat** (from $50). All this can be done while the sensible watch with great amusement from afar, the fit go for a guided **walk** and the wishful thinking go **gold-panning**. The **Swingbridge Centre** is located right next to SH6 and there is a café on site, T5239809, www.bullergorge.co.nz

A little further on just before Newton Livery Hotel is the **(Eathquake White Creek Fault Slip) Lookout** where the violent (7.8 on the Richter scale) earthquake of 1929, was centred. A further 8 km will reveal the **Brunner Memorial**, which is a small metal plaque attached to the rock, commemorating the epic journeys of one Thomas Brunner. The intrepid Mr Brunner took three months to negotiate the gorge in 1846 with little except a group of Maori guides.

After a long bend in the river the road then passes through the old gold-mining town of **Lyell** – now very much a village. Former relics of the great but brief gold rush days including an old stamper battery can be seen on the **Lyell Walkway** (two hour return). A further 17 km will bring you to the rather unremarkable settlement of **Inangahua.** It has little more than a petrol pump and the rather dubious claim to fame of being nearly destroyed by another, more recent earthquake in 1968. If darkness is descending you can stay at the comfortable **D** *Inwoods Farm Backpackers*, T7890205.

From just beyond Inangahua the **Lower Gorge** begins its dramatic descent to the sea. At **Hawks Crag** the rock has been gouged out to form a dramatic overhang over the road. Its negotiation is really very interesting provided there is not a large petrol tanker coming the other way.

Westport

Phone code: 03
Population: 4,500

Westport, the West Coast's oldest town, is not a pretty place. On first acquaintance its long main street, fed by a flat expanse of unimaginative orderly blocks, and overly wide roads, is at the very least, uninspiring. Whether under clear blue skies, or more often a veil of rain, its drabness is all the more exposed by such beautiful surroundings. But although the place lacks heart its people do not. They retain the proud and stoic traditions of the old pioneers and coal miners: that down-to-earth working-class attitude, the warm welcome and the humour. Westport is most often used as an overnight base before heading north to Karamea and the Heaphy Track or south towards Greymouth. There are however a few attractions and activities on offer that may hold you back, including **rafting** on the Buller River and a large **seal colony** at Cape Foulwind.

Ins & outs

Getting there **By air** Wesport airport (8 km south) is served daily (except Sun) by *Air New Zealand Link*, T0800737000. For a **taxi** to the airport (from $12), T7896900. **By bus** Westport is served by *White Star* (Christchurch/Nelson), T7897177; *East-West*, (Christchurch) T7896251; *Atomic Shuttles* (Greymouth/Nelson), T3228883; *Coast Shuttles* (Nelson), T7896837; *Southern Link Shuttles* (Queenstown/ Christchurch/Nelson), T3588355; *Intercity* (Greymouth/Nelson), T7897819. Most buses stop just outside the VIC. *Intercity* stop at Craddock's Energy Centre, Caltex, 197 Palmerston St. For all services north to Karamea (and the Heaphy Track) call *Karamea Express*, T7826617, or *Cunningham's Coaches*, 179 Palmerston St, T7897177. **Bike hire** is available at *Becker's Sports*, 204 Palmerston St, T7898787.

The Westport **Visitor Information Centre** is located at 1 Brougham St, T7896658, F7896668, westport.info@xtra.co.nz Open daily 0900-1900 (winter 0900-1700). **DOC** information and enquiries are handled at the VIC.

Sights

If you wish to explore the coalmining heritage in more detail a 'Buller Coalfields Heritage Trail' leaflet is available free from the VIC

With such a tradition of gold and coal-mining in the area it is almost rude not to visit the excellent **Coaltown Museum**, at Queen Street South. It has an extensive and nicely presented range of displays, with an emphasis on coal-mining, but also gold, pioneer and maritime exhibitions. Of particular note is the interesting audio-visual presentation covering the history of coalmining in the region, the simulated walkthrough mine and the massive 20-ton brake drum (haulage rail-wagon) from the Denniston Incline. Pitched at a 47° angle (the steepest on the incline) the brake drum creates an almost fearful sight. Even if you have little interest in mining the sheer efforts made and feats of engineering cannot fail to impress. ■ *Open daily 0900-1630, Adult $6, child $4. T7898204.*

In contrast and yet, in a way, related is the **Miners Brewery** on Lyndhurst Street. Here various heady brews are created to quench the thirst of the modern-day miner. ■ *There are tours Mon-Sat at 1130 and 1330, $5. T7896201.*

Cape Foulwind, 11 km south of Westport, is a buttress of land, apparently named so by James Cook in 1770, after his ship was beset by gales and rain. It was formerly called Clyppygen Hoek – or Rocky Corner – by Abel Tasman in 1642 and before that, 'Tauranga' by the Maori, which meant 'a sheltered anchorage, or landing place'.

The main attraction on the Cape is the thriving fur **seal colony** at the very beautiful **Tauranga Bay**. You are guaranteed to see seals here at any time of year (be it from a lookout situated quite far above the rocks), but summer when the pups are born is the best time to see them, with over 500 in residence. The colony is best accessed from the Tauranga Bay car park. Before you set off, keep your eyes open for the rather comical and cheeky **weka** around the car park itself. Weka are a flightless, endemic, brown game-like bird about the size of a chicken. Although you are not supposed to feed them it is hard to resist.

From the seal colony the **Cape Foulwind Walkway** also takes in the lighthouse and offers great views (1½ hours, 4 km – one way). At the southern end of Tauranga Bay there is the fine Bay *House Café and Art Gallery*. It offers outdoor seating overlooking the bay and is a great place to sup a cup of coffee, or tuck into a cooked breakfast, while watching the surfers ride the waves beyond. Cape Foulwind and the seal colony are easily accessible and signposted from Westport. *Burning Mine Adventures*, T7897277 offer two hour tours that take in the seal colony, from $30.

Activities

There is an increasing range of interesting and quality activity operators based in Westport. *Norwest Adventures* (Underworld Rafting), T7896689, norwest@xtra.co.nz based in Charlestown (27 km south of Westport) offer adventure **caving** and **underground rafting** trips to the Te Tahi and Metro **limestone caves** in Paparoa National Park. With such underground feature names as the 'Lambada', 'The Iron Room' and 'The Witches Cauldron' it is hard to resist. Trips leave twice daily from Westport (four to five hours, from $105). *Buller Adventures* based east of Westport on SH6 (Buller Gorge Road), T7897286, www.adventuretours.co.nz offer rafting trips; half-day from $85; full-day from $120, heli-rafting from $245; jetboating (1½ hours, from $60) and horse trekking (2½ hours, from $45). *Burning Mine Adventures*, T7897277, offer mountain biking (four hours, from $45); kayaking (from $75); mining Tours (four hours, from $45) as well as land yachting and surfing. *Out West Tours*, T0800-688937, offer an interesting range of five-hour trips by four-wheel drive truck to the former Denniston Coalmines, down the coast or inland to explore the Buller Gorge. Trips depart daily from Brougham Street.

Sleeping

AL *River View Lodge*, Buller Gorge Rd, T/F7896037, is one of the best B&Bs in the area and is located 7 km from Westport. It is set in pleasant gardens overlooking the river it and has 4 en suites. Dinners by arrangement. In town the **AL** *Archer House*, 75 Queen St, T7898778, www.archerhouse.co.nz, is a new and classy B&B in the century-old former convent. Well appointed en-suites in a central location.

There are plenty of motels both new and old: The new **AL-A** *Chelsea Gateway Motor Lodge*, 330 Palmerston St, T7896835, is the most luxurious; the **A-B** *Westport Motor Hotel*, Palmerston St, T7897889, is popular, well-located and has a good in-house restaurant; and the **B** *Westport Motels*, 32 The Esplanade, T7897575 is one of the best budget options.

There are also plenty of backpacker beds in town: **C-D** *The TripInn*, 72 Queen St, T7897367, tripinn@clear.net.nz, is a grand, spacious villa, kept squeaky clean, with a wide range of rooms and good facilities including internet; **C-D** *Marg's Traveller's Rest*, 56 Russell St, T7898627, is a vast establishment close to the town centre, with a wide range of units, self-contained dorms, powered sites and good facilities and internet; **C-D** *Basils*, T7896410, next door, is a homely, well-kept villa with modern units, dorms and facilities and internet.

Out of town and south on SH6 (17 km), by the coast, is the popular **D** *Beaconstone Backpackers*, T025-310491. It is a slightly 'alternative' 12-bed lodge in a bush setting, with solar power and futon beds. There are two main motorcamps bot basic but functional. The **C-D** *Westport Holiday Park*, 37 Domett St, T7897043, is a short walk from the town centre and offers cabins, powered/tent sites and dorm beds. More popular is the **C-D** *Seal Colony Tourist Park*, Marine Parade, Carters Beach (6 km on Cape Foulwind /Carters Beach Road), T7898002. Note it is still a good 6 km from the seal colony!

Eating

Options are limited in the area. The best local restaurant is the *Bay House Café*, T7897133, which is located at the southern end of Tauranga Bay, Cape Foulwind (near the seal colony). It is a great restaurant, offering breakfast, lunch and an imaginative à la carte menu for dinner and is in a superb setting over looking the bay. In Westport the *Serengeti Restaurant* in the Westport Motor Hotel, Palmerston St, T7897889, is recommended. Open from 1800. For pub grub and good beer try the *Bailies Bar*, 187 Palmerston St, T7897289 (open from 1130) and for a daytime café *Freckles*, also on Palmerston St. Open 0900-1700.

Directory

Internet is available at the library across the road from the VIC. Open Mon-Thu 1000-1700, Fri 1000-1830 and Sat 1030-1300. The main **post office** and **bank** branches are on Palmerston St.

North to Karamea

From Westport, SH67 heads north to Karamea (100 km) and an eventual dead end at the trailhead of the Heaphy Track (111 km). If you have time there are a few places of interest and several good walks on offer along the way. Of particular note is the former coalmining township of **Denniston**. Perched high (900 m) on the Rochford Plateau and accessed via Waimangaroa, (15 km north of Westport), Denniston was once the largest producer of coal in the country and the surrounding area was a hive of industrial activity. The **Denniston Walkway** (two hours, 1 km, 520 m ascent), which follows the former supply route, is the best way to explore the area and eventually takes you to the former settlement. Little remains, except a few rusting pieces of machinery, but there are great views of the impressive **Denniston Incline**

(1878-1967) on which 20-ton brake drums brought millions of tonnes of coal down over 500 m to the railhead at terrific speeds. There is a small museum based in the old schoolhouse in Denniston (only open on Sundays).

Back on SH67 and 6 km north is the once bustling township of **Granity**. The *Drifters Café* on the main street is worth a stop and has some interesting artwork and mining remnants on display. Inland from Granity a road sweeps up the ranges to 'Porridge Hill' and two more former coal towns; **Millerton and Stockton**. Little remains of either, but again they are still worthy of some investigation. The short **Millerton Incline Walkway** (40 minutes) takes in a number of features and, as the name suggests, another incline, be it a far less impressive affair than the one at Dennniston. A further 1 km north of Granity is the very pleasant **Charming Creek Walkway** (two hours , 4 km one-way) which follows the old coal line through the Ngakawau River Gorge, taking in various old tunnels and other mining features along the way.

At the mouth of the Mokihinui River SH67 turns inland and climbs precariously around the bush-clad and scenic **Karamea Bluff**, before falling again to the coast towards Karamea.

Sleeping Located on the far side of the Mokihinui River Mouth (Gentle Annie's Beach) is the excellent **C-D** *Cowshed Café and Backpackers*, T7891826. It is a great spot for both food and accommodation with quiet, dorm or self-contained lodges and camping sites. The café is imaginatively housed in a former milking shed. It has detailed information about local walks and activities including kayaking on the river from $25.

Karamea

Phone code: 03
Population: 684

After the rather bleak nature of the former coal-mining towns encountered on its approach, you might expect Karamea to be similarly afflicted. But this former 'frontier' settlement, perched on its namesake river mouth, and overshadowed by the rising peaks of the **Kahurangi National Park**, offers a far more pleasing sight and a quiet (as opposed to dead) atmosphere. Although most often used as a base for the famed **Heaphy Track** (which begins at the road terminus 15 km north) Karamea also offers some lesser-known sights that are quite simply superb. Of particular note are the limestone caves and arches of the **Oparara Basin.**

Ins & outs **Getting there By air** The airstrip at Karamea is often used (from the north) for pick-up and drop-off for the Heaphy Track. The *Karamea Village Hotel*, T7826800, or the *Last Resort*, T7826617, act as agents or contact *Tasman Bay Aviation*, direct, T5472378. The *Last Resort* also has a helicopter at their disposal.

By bus For services to and from Karamea to the Heaphy Track trailhead contact *Karamea Motors*, T7826757 (Mon-Fri $5). For services to Westport contact *Karamea Express*, T7826617 or *Cunningham's Motors*, Westport T7897919 ($15). Karamea Motors also offer a general **taxi** service.

Information The Karamea **Visitor Information and Resource Centre** is located on Bridge St, just as you come into the village, T/F7826652, Karamea.info@xtra.co.nz Open daily 0900-1700 (seasonal hours). The staff are very helpful and there is plenty of information on local attractions and of course, all the latest on the Heaphy Track. They also issue DOC hut passes and have **internet**. There is no **bank** or ATM in the village but **postal** services are available in the Karamea Hardware Store across the road from the VIC. Most organized **activities** in the area can be arranged at the *Last Resort* (see Sleeping below).

Sights

The Oparara Basin, located 26 km north and east of Karamea, is a magical place that offers the most interesting concentration of 'karst' (limestone) topography in the Kahurangi National Park, and some of the most spectacular in the South Island. Although the karst features will keep you spellbound, the thick veil of ancient rainforest that covers it all creates a wonderful atmosphere all of its own – like some 'lost world'. There are (and certainly have been) some fantastical animals found here. Ancient moa bones have been discovered in the caves, along with others belonging to the now extinct New Zealand eagle, with a 3 m wingspan. Today, you may still stumble across the huge carnivorous snail (*Powelliphanta*). Also of note is the wonderfully named gradungula spider, the largest in New Zealand with a leg-span of 10 cm. But even if the prospect of such creatures leaves you cold, the Oparara Basin is still a 'must see'. From Karamea take the main road north for 10 km, then turn right at Break Creek Bridge (signposted) and head for the hills. Access to the basin is 16 km of narrow, winding and unsealed road. The basin is split into areas with both open and restricted public access.

At the very end of the track is the access point to the main feature of the basin – the **Honeycomb Caves**. They are a 15-km underground labyrinth that were only discovered 30-odd years ago, revealing all the usual limestone cave features, plus the bones of several moa and other extinct species. The Honeycomb Caves, can, due to their delicate nature and fragile eco-system, only be visited on a guided tour (*Oparara Tours* at the *Last Resort*, T7826617, two hours, $30). Nearby, is the **Honeycomb Arch** the first of three spectacular arches that have been formed by the age-old meanderings of the Oparara River. Although this arch is indeed impressive access is again restricted and is by kayak only (*Oparara Tours* at the *Last Resort*, $60). The **Oparara Arch**, which has free public access, is equally if not more impressive and is reached from a path (signposted) beside the road. A pleasant 20-minute (one-way) walk alongside the intriguing tannin coloured river, and through beautiful forest, will bring you to the awesome arch entrance. Once you have marvelled at the main entrance it is then well worth exploring the other end through the 140 m passage. This will involve getting your feet wet and crossing the river, so special care is required.

On a far lesser scale, but in a way more beautiful, is the **Moria (Little) Arch**, accessed from the other side of the road. Again it is reached by foot through attractive forest and a 40 minutes track that is both wet and difficult in places. What it lacks in grandeur,the Moria makes up for in serenity. Perhaps before or after the arches you can visit the **Crazy Paving** and **Box Canyon Caves** that are a short five minutes walk from the road. Beyond their unnerving darkness (take a torch), they are the least impressive of all the features. Note the river itself is beautiful and well worthy of investigation, particularly around the track to the small and self-explanatory **Mirror Tarn**. A small map of the Oparara basin is available free from the VIC.

Walks

Karamea is also a fine base for walking with the coastal stretch of the **Heaphy Track** being particularly good. From the **Kohaihai River** (trailhead), cross the swing bridge and walk through the forest to **Scotts Beach** (1½ hour return). From there you have the option of continuing along the coastline to **Kapito Shelter** (six hours return) or going the whole hog with an overnight stop at the **Heaphy Hut** (five-hours one-way) before retracing your steps. This stretch of coast is noted not only for its wild unspoilt beaches but also for its nikau palms, that gives it an almost tropical feel. Other tracks and expeditions include the **Fenian Track** (3-5 hours) which takes in a small cave system and a former gold-mining settlement and **Mount Stormy** (1084 m, 6-8 hours return) with its magnificent views. The VIC has detailed information on these walks and others. For details on the Heaphy Track see page 459.

Sleeping & eating The mainstay for accommodation in Karamea is the **AL-D** ***Last Resort***, 71 Waverley St, T7826617, F7826820, www.lastresort.co.nz It is a modern and imaginatively designed complex with lodge-style accommodation blocks all interconnected by walkways, with a large adjunct bar/café and restaurant. There are a wide variety of rooms on offer, from shared budget to self-contained en-suites. Note however there are no kitchen facilities. Internet is available at reception. The **A** ***Bridge Farm Motels***, Bridge St, T7826955, F7826748, www.karameamotels.co.nz by the river, is relatively new motel and offers 6 one and two bedroom self-contained suites.

Other comfortable backpacker accommodation is available at the **C-D** ***Punga Lodge Backpackers***, T7826667, or the **C-D** ***Karamea Village Hotel***, T7826800, both on Waverley St. The main motorcamp is the **C-D** ***Karamea Holiday Park***, Maori Point, T7826758, which is located just south of the village. It offers a range of cabins and powered/tent sites. **DOC** also has a basic **D** campsite at the Kohaihai River mouth (15 km north) at the trailhead of the Heaphy Track, T7826652.

Both the Karamea Village Hotel and the Last Resort have licensed **restaurants**. The ***LR Bar and café*** at the *Last Resort* also offers a cheaper pub-style menu and a great atmosphere (open daily). Other than that, the small ***Saracens Café*** across the road from the VIC is a good spot to watch the world go by over a coffee. Open 0830-1800 (seasonal).

Punakaiki and the Paparoa National Park

From Westport SH6 begins its relentless 600 km journey south, down the length of the West Coast. Once past the small and once booming gold-mining settlement of ***Charlestown****, the road hits the coast proper and then skirts the northern boundary of the* ***Paparoa National Park****. Designated in 1987, Paparoa covers a relatively small area (by New Zealand standards) of 30,000 ha and features a predominantly karst (limestone) topography. From mountaintop to coast, the park has everything from dramatic limestone bluffs to dramatic overhangs and caves. The most famous feature in the park are the much photographed and visited* ***pancake rocks*** *and* ***blowholes*** *of* ***Dolomite Point*** *at the small coastal settlement of* ***Punakaiki****. The park also offers some interesting features and notable walks inland, including the popular* ***Inland Pack Track****.*

nice accomodat Rocks & villas

Ins & outs **Getting there** Punakaiki is 60 km south of Westport and 50 km north of Greymouth. *Intercity*, T0800-767080, pass through the village daily and stop briefly for passengers to grab a snack and take quick look at the pancake rocks and blowholes. Note there is no **petrol** available in Punakaiki.

Information The **DOC** Paparoa National Park **Visitor Centre**, is located next to SH6 in the heart and commercial centre of Punakaiki, T7311895, F7311896. Open daily 0900-1800 (winter 0900-1630). There are some interesting displays about the park and detailed information available on local attractions, activities and walking conditions. **Internet** is available at the *Wild Coast Café* next door or the local backpackers. Although there is no real heart to the village, though most activities and amenities are found on the Main Street around the VIC. There are no **banks** but EFTPOS is available in the retail and food outlets.

The West Coast

A hard rain's gonna fall

The West Coast of the South Island, especially Fiordland, is one of the wettest places on earth. Moist prevailing westerly airstreams fan across the Tasman Sea and on encountering the mountain ranges of the Great Divide condense and dump rain or snow in huge quantities. At lower levels the annual rainfall is a rather aquatic 1 ½ m, but at higher levels this can rise to a staggering 5 m. Most of the rain falls on the seaward side of the mountains in what is called the 'rain shadow'. The contrast in rainfall is echoed in the types of vegetation.

On the western side of the Great Divide lush rainforests of podocarp and beech predominate, while only a few kilometres west this gives way to slopes of mainly scree and tussock. With such a high rainfall and gradient the rivers in Westland and Fiordland are regularly subject to flash flooding. For the uninitiated this may conjure up images of rivers merely in spate, but in reality it is an incredible thing to experience. There is such a bombardment of the senses you literally freeze with fear. The mere sight of a vast, all encompassing wall of water, like boiling brown soup, full of boulders tossed like croutons on the surface is bad enough – but the deafening roar and the shaking of the earth beneath your feet is almost more paralysing. Many unsuspecting trampers have been killed in such circumstances, so be advised to stay away from all riverbeds and tributaries following rain or even heavy showers.

On a more positive note – although it rains frequently on the West Coast, bear in mind it often clears quickly and the sun is never too far away. Besides, West Coast rain is real, industrial strength rain, so perhaps for once in your life get out there and enjoy it.

Sights and Activities

Immediately across the road from the visitor centre is **Dolomite Point** with its oddly shaped **pancake rocks** and crowd-pleasing **blowholes**. The fluted vertical columns are a lime/mudstone feature known as 'karren', which develop their layered appearance as a result of erosion by rain and sea spray. The track (20 minutes return) takes the form of a loop, offering various lookout points across the rocks, blowholes and down in to the surge pools. On a high tide and especially during a strong westerly, the 'show' can be amazing, with the ground physically shaking to the thunderous pounding of the waves and the sea-spray hissing from the cracks as if coming from the nostrils of some furious sea dragon. But note that when the tide is out or there is little swell the blowholes can be quiet and idle, leaving many visitors disappointed. Regardless of the activity the rocks are certainly intriguing and the views are stunning. Keep your eye open for **dolphins**. It is not unusual to see pods or individuals mingling with surfers, with the mutual intent to catch the best wave.

If you have time there is also some stunning coastal scenery, easily accessed via the **Truman Track**, which begins beside SH6, 3 km north of Punakaiki. A 15 minute walk through coastal rainforest and nikau palms delivers you on the sands and rocky outcrops of **Perpendicular Point**. The rock formations here are fascinating with fissures, holes and mosaics, and although it is quite hard going and should only be attempted at low tide, a thorough investigation of the Point, northwards, is well worthwhile.

Turning your attentions inland, the river valleys lead to some fine scenery and a number of other dramatic limestone features such as caves and overhangs. At Tiromoana, 13 km north of Punakaiki, the **Fox River** finds the sea, and a small car park north of the bridge acts as the northern trailhead for the **Inland Pack Track**. The entire track (which is usually walked from the

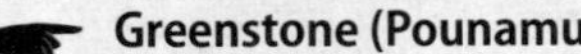

Greenstone (Pounamu)

*It would take a PhD in geology to describe the make-up, formation and various types of greenstone (nephrite). Greenstone – or jade as is better known – is precious (*taonga*) to the Maori and has been revered for centuries. The Maori called it* pounamu. *In New Zealand greenstone is found in the South Island, predominantly in Westland. The Maori called South Island* Te Wahi Pounamu *(the place of greenstone) and they went to great lengths to find and transport the precious stone, before carving it into a range of items, both practical and ornamental. Foremost among these was the* mere *(a flat hand-held weapon) which was a highly treasured and, in the hands of a warrior, lethal.* Heitiki, *or pendants, were also painstakingly carved, often in the form of mythical spirits and monsters. These* tiki *were passed on from generation to generation and in doing so, increased in* mana *(prestige or spiritual power). Nowadays, greenstone is mainly used to create ornaments and tiki for the commercial tourist market. Hokitika, on the West Coast of the South Island, is the best place to see it being made and buy it.*

southern trailhead in Punakaiki) is a 27 km, 2-3 day affair that takes in many limestone features, and inland valleys.

Its main highlights – the **Fox River Gorge, Caves** and **Ballroom Overhang** – can all be accessed from the Fox River mouth on an exciting 4-6 hour return walk. The track is well-formed for much of its length, but also involves crossing the river a number of times guided only by orange markers, so be prepared to get your feet wet. The Fox River Caves can be accessed with a short diversion before the first major river crossing. The main cave is over 100 m in length and decorated with the usual calcite formations. Once across the river, the track follows the base of the dramatic gorge before terminating temporarily at the confluence of the Fox and Dilemma Creek. Here you can leave the Inland Pack Track, cross the river, and then continue alongside the main Fox tributary to the Ballroom Overhang (1 km). Sitting like half an umbrella embedded the riverbed its 100 m by 30 m overhang is impressive, but spoilt somewhat by the graffiti on the walls.

Closer to Punakaiki are the **Bullock Creek** and **Pororari River** Valleys. The Pororari acts as the southern access of the Inland Pack Track which can be walked in part to join the Bullock Creek Valley and to access **Cave Creek**, a deeply incised limestone gorge and another karst feature worthy of investigation. It is also one that now serves more as a tragic memorial than a tourist attraction. In 1995 a viewing platform set high above the cavern collapsed sending 15 students to their deaths. As a result of the incident there was a complete review of all similar DOC structures countrywide and revised safety standards and protocols were subsequently put in place. Cave Creek can also be accessed via the Bullock Creek Valley, which is generally fun to explore by car, bike, or on foot. All walks in the area are subject to flooding to check with DOC at the VIC before setting off.

The area is also home to some rare wildlife. Of particular note is the **Westland black petrel (teiko)** – a gull-sized, black seabird which nests in burrows on the bush-clad slopes of Paparoa's mountains. They breed nowhere else in the world. Tours are available in season (March–December). Contact the VIC.

There is a wide range of other local activities available, above and beyond walking and tramping. For **kayaking** including independent hire, contact *Punakaiki Canoe Hire*, T7311870, from $15, plus $5 each hour after that. **Horse trekking** is available along the beaches or in to the Punakaiki River Valley, with *Paparoa Horse Treks*, T7311839 (one hour, from $30). For some excellent local **Eco-tours** contact *Green Kiwi Tours*, T0800-474733. To get out on the water **dolphin watching/swimming** contact *Kiwa Sea Adventures*, T7687765 (from $100, child $50). *Paparoa Guides*, T7311853, also offer half to full-day naturewalks (from $35) as well as **rock climbing** (from $90) and overnight wilderness trekking (from $135).

Essentials

Sleeping

Almost all the accommodation establishments are situated just off SH6, but vary in distance from the VIC. The most up-market accommodation is situated at the southern end of the village with the new **L** ***Punakaiki Rocks Hotel***, T7311167, punakaikihotel@xtra.co.nz Although the place has all the appeal of an airport departure lounge the individual units are very good and the views excellent. It also has a restaurant boasting great views across the beach.

Nearby is one of the best self-contained cottages on the coast, the very cute and reasonably priced **B** *Hydrangea Cottage*, T7311839, www.pancake-rocks.co.nz Another cottage is in the planning. A little further south (just off the main road) is the tidy and congenial **A** *Punakaiki Park Motel*, T7311883, www.paparoa.co.nz In the heart of the village is the older, but perfectly comfortable **A** ***Punakaiki Cottage Motels***, T7311008.

There are two hostels in the village: **C-D** ***Nikau Retreat***, T7311111, located in Te Miko, just north of the Truman Track, is simply superb. Run by an enthusiastic manager, who is no newcomer to the business, the establishment, with its range of stand-alone cottages set in the bush, creates a very special atmosphere. The facilities throughout are excellent and there are also self-contained options available. Internet. Closer to the village is the **C-D** ***Punakaiki Beach Hostel***, Webb St, T7311852. It's a well run, fairly compact establishment, with all the facilities and set across the road from the beach. Internet. For a good motorcamp look no further than the **C-D** ***Punakaiki Motor Camp***, T7311894, set next to the beach and only a short walk from the main village. It offers spacious grounds, cabins and powered/tent sites.

Eating

For fine dining the only real option in the village is in the ***Seascape Restaurant*** at the Punakaiki Rocks Hotel, T7311167. The food is perfectly acceptable and the views excellent. Open daily from 0700. The ***Punakaiki Tavern***, T7311188, next to the motorcamp (SH6) is the main hub of entertainment in the village offering palatable beer and the usual value pub-grub. Across the road from Dolomite Point and the pancake rocks is the ***Wild Coast Café***, Main Rd, T7311873. It has good coffee and an eclectic blackboard menu. There is also a small grocery **shop** attached, an internet terminal and yes, of course, it sells pancakes. Open daily 0800-2100 (winter 0800-1700)

Greymouth and around

Phone code: 03
Population: 10,000

From Punakaiki the coast road continues its relentless route south, treating you to some fine coastal scenery, before turning inland through Runanga to meet the Grey River and the West Coast's largest commercial centre – Greymouth. On initial acquaintance Greymouth seems to share the drab aesthetics of most northern West Coast towns and certainly lives up to its uninspiring name. That said, the people of Greymouth are welcoming, friendly and certainly not short of heart or colour. Today, the bustling town is mostly used by tourists as a short stop over point or supply base for further investigations of the coast. It does however have a few local attractions and some exciting activities on offer.

Ins and Outs

Getting there

Greymouth is 258 km west of Christchurch via SH73 and Arthur's Pass; 290 km south of Nelson via SH6 and 583 km north of Queenstown, also via SH6

By air Greymouth is served from Hokitika Airport (40 km) with *Air New Zealand Link*, T0800-737000. **By bus** The major companies serving the town include: *Intercity*, T0800-767080 (Nelson/Westport); *Coast to Coast Shuttles*, T0800-800847 (Christchurch to Hokitika); *Alpine Coaches*, T0800-274888 (Christchurch to Hokitika); *Atomic Shuttles*, T7685101 (Queenstown to Picton). Most buses stop at the **Travel Centre** in the railway station on Mackay St, T7687080. **By train** Greymouth is the western terminus of the famous *TranzAlpine* from Christchurch, which is considered a world class scenic journey, T0800-802802. The train arrives daily at Mackay St at 1325 and departs Greymouth again at 1425.

Getting around

The main **taxi** company is *Greymouth Taxis*, T76877078. **Car hire** companies include *Budget*, T7684343 and *Avis*, T7680902, both located at the train station. *Half-Price Rentals*, 170 Tainui St, T7680379 hire older, cheaper models. **Cycle hire** is available at *Coll's Sports/Avanti Pro Cycles* 53 Mackay St, T7684060.

Information

The Greymouth **Visitor Information Centre** is on the corner of Mackay and Herbert Sts, T7685101, F7680317, www.west-coast.co.nz Open daily 0900-1800. **DOC** information is also available in the VIC.

Greymouth enjoyed the former colonial names of Crescent City and Blaketown, before its present name (given in honour of the former New Zealand Governor, Sir George Grey) finally stuck. Not surprisingly its creation centred principally on gold prospecting and mining, but unlike so many of the other West Coast settlements that diminished with its exhaustion, Greymouth continued to thrive. This was due to the coal and timber industries, sound communication links and its status as the region's principal port. But its watery affairs have not all been smooth sailing. The Grey River Valley receives some of the heaviest rainfall in the country, and on more than one occasion, the town has been badly flooded.

Sights

One of Greymouth's most famous sights is the **Montieths Brewery**, on the corner of Turamaha and Herbert Street. Considered locally as a place of sanctity, its brands of 'Original', 'Black' and 'Celtic Red', are considered by most kiwis to be the country's greatest brews. Although not in the same league, nor enjoying the same reputation of Guinness or many other European beers, it is indeed a fine drop. In 2001 there was a major controversy when the powers that be decided to suddenly announce that operations were to be moved to Auckland of all places. This act of insanity resulted in an outcry of such proportions that the owners wisely decided to change their minds. ■ *Tours available for $5. T7684149, www.monteiths.co.nz*

If you are more culturally inclined you should head for the small but effective **History House Museum**, on Gresson Street. Its emphasis is naturally centred on the region's mining and nautical past, with a copious collection of old photographs. ■ *Mon-Fri 1000-1600. Adult $3, child $1. T7684028.* The creatively inclined will particularly enjoy the **Jade Boulder Gallery**, 1 Guinness Street. ■ *Daily 0830-2100, winter 1730. Free. T7680700.* Or the **Left Bank Art Gallery**, 1 Tainui Street. ■ *Daily 1000-1700. $2. T7680088.* Both are worthy of a look and display some fine crafted examples of the West Coasts ancient poanamu (greenstone) pieces.

For a short walk encompassing a memorable view of the town and the coast, visit the **Cobden Lookout** (also known as the Lions Walk). The track entrance is off Bright Street, Cobden, 200 m from the road bridge. The track zigzags steadily through the southern end of the **Rapahoe Range Scenic Reserve**. The **Point Elizabeth Track** (seven hours one-way) follows an old gold-miners trails along the Rapahoe Range and provides another good local jaunt. Access is north of Greymouth via Bright Street, then Domett Esplanade and North Beach Road (6 km) or via Rapahoe, Seven Mile Road.

For another longer tramp the 18 km, 6-7 hour **Croesus Track** from Barrytown (28 km north) to Blackball (25 km northeast) is recommended. It takes in the grand views of the coast from above the tree line of the Paparoa Ranges and includes some notable gold-mining relics. Also, most importantly perhaps, it has good pubs at both ends: *The Barrytown Tavern*, T7311812, and the former *Blackball Hilton*, T7324708. Both offer accommodation). The DOC broadsheet *'Central West Coast-Croesus Track'* is invaluable.

Activities

Most activities are water-based with a choice of **river-rafting, cave-rafting, dolphin watching** and **kayaking**. *Eco-Rafting Adventures* based at the *DP:One Café*, 108 Mawhera Quay, T7684005, www.ecorafting.co.nz offer half or multi-day trips on numerous West Coast rivers from $70. *Dragons Cave Rafting* (Wild West Adventures), Clifton Road, T0800-223456, offer an exhilarating half-day black-water rafting experience in the Taniwha Cave system from $95. *Dolphin Adventure Tours*, Mawhera Quay, T0800-929991, www.dolphintours.co.nz, offer both dolphin watching and swimming trips (two to four hour) from $67 and full-day kayaking trips from $87. Back on dry land but still good in wet conditions are the **quad bike** adventures with *On Yer Bike*, T7627438 (from $20-$100). *Kea West Coast Tours*, T0800-532868, offer a range of road trips to Punakaiki, Hokitika, The Glaciers, The Grey Valley and Shantytown, from $32-$165. To complete a threesome of water, land and air, contact *West Coast Scenic Flights*, T7680407.They fly locally or farther afield with a range of 1-5 hour trips.

Essentials

Sleeping

There are two main hotels in town the **AL-A** *Hotel Ashley*, 74 Tasman St, T0800-807787, ashley.grey@xtra.co.nz, and the **AL-A** *Quality Kings Hotel*, Mawhera Quay, T7685085, quality.kings@cdlhms.co.nz Both have comfortable rooms and good facilities with the Quality getting the vote for location and the Ashley the vote on the best restaurant.

Greymouth

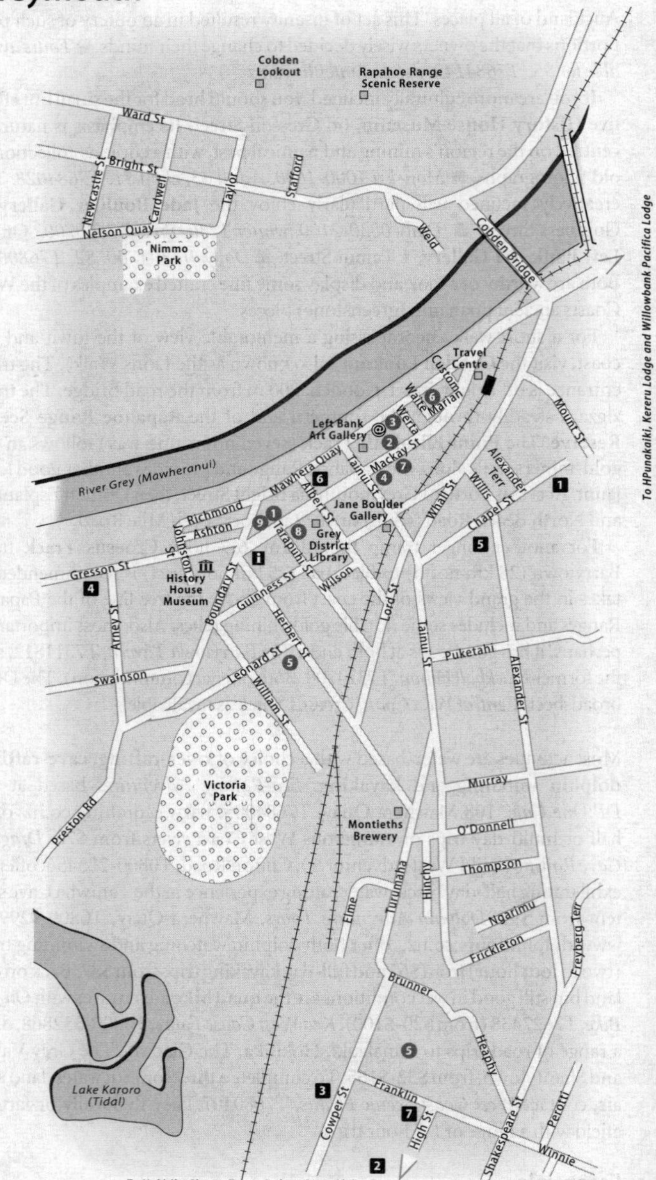

Cobden Lookout
Rapahoe Range Scenic Reserve
Ward St
Bright St
Newcastle St
Cardwell
Taylor
Stafford
Nelson Quay
Nimmo Park
Weld
Cobden Bridge
To HPunakaiki, Kereru Lodge and Willowbank Pacifica Lodge
Travel Centre
Custom
Marian
Werra
Mount St
Left Bank Art Gallery
Mackay St
Alexander Terr
Willis
River Grey (Mawheranui)
Mawhera Quay
Albert St
Tainui St
Richmond
Ashton
Chapel St
Jane Boulder Gallery
Whall St
Johnston St
Tarapuhi St
Grey District Library
Gresson St
History House Museum
Boundary St
Guinness St
Wilson
Lord St
Herbert St
Arney St
Leonard St
Puketahi
Alexander St
Swainson
William St
Victoria Park
Murray
Preston Rd
Montieths Brewery
O'Donnell
Thompson
Hinchy
Turumaha
Elme
Ngarimu
Frickleton
Freyberg Terr
Brunner
Heaphy
Lake Karoro (Tidal)
Franklin
Cowper St
High St
Shakespeare St
Perotti
Winnie
To Hokitika Shanty Town, Arthurs Pass, Alpine Rose, Ashleys and Top Ten Greymouth Holiday Park
Not to scale

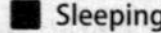

Sleeping
1 Ardwyn House
2 Gables Motor Lodge
3 Global Village Backpackers
4 Neptune's
5 Noah's Ark
6 Quality Kings
7 Rosewood

Eating
1 Bonzai Pizzeria
2 Café Cottage
3 DP:One Café
4 Jone's Café and Bar
5 Raceway Carvery
6 Railway
7 Smelting House Café
8 Steamers Café & Bar
9 West of the Border

For B&B and Homestays the value and centrally located **B** ***Ardwyn House***, 48 Chapel St, T7686107 and the slightly more expensive **A** ***Rosewood***, 20 High St, T7684674, rosewoodnz@xtra.co.nz are recommended. Out of town, 8 km north, the homely comforts of the **A** ***Kereru Lodge***, 58 Herd St, Dunollie, T/F7627077 are worth the journey, as are the great value delights of the **LL-AL** ***Kapitea Ridge Country Lodge and Cottage***, Chesterfield Rd (off SH6, 20 km south), T7556805, www.kapitea.co.nz

Most of the town's motels are located on the main drag (High St/SH6) heading south out of town. The **AL-A** ***Gables Motor Lodge***, (84), T7689991 and **AL-A** ***Alpine Rose*** (139), T7687586 are recommended. For a quieter option at a slightly cheaper price try the **A** ***Willowbank Pacifica Lodge***, just off SH6 3 km north of the town, T0800-668355.

Greymouth takes the prize for having the most imaginatively decorated hostels in the country with the Noah's Ark and Neptune backpackers both an excellent choice

The **C-D** ***Neptune's***, 43 Gresson St, T7684425, is run by the former owners of *Noah's Ark*. Already the former waterfront hotel/pub is showing signs of loving attention, mixed with an obvious deft touch. All things fishy is the emphasis this time, with the wide range of comfortable rooms and facilities (including baths) decorated accordingly. Neptune's is good value and particularly good for couples. Their former establishment the **C-D** ***Noah's Ark***, 16 Chapel St, T0800662472, noahsark@xtra.co.nz is a rambling old villa that has all the usual rooms and facilities but stands out a mile with its fauna-themed rooms. There is a positive zoo on site with everything from elephants and bears to the humble kiwi. Visitors often fall in love with both the place and their room and once departed continue to send themed articles to join the décor. Internet. Also noteworthy is the **C-D** ***Global Village Backpackers***, 42-54 Cowper St, T7687272, globalvillage@minidata.co.nz Managed by a partnership with an admiral wealth of travelling experience its only downfall is its location from the centre of town. Kayaking is available in the river that runs alongside it. Free pick-ups.

The best motorpark is the **B-D** ***Top Ten Greymouth Holiday Park***, Chesterfield St, T7686618. It is a spacious, well managed place, and located alongside the beach, offering self-contained units, cabins and powered/tent sites with excellent facilities.

Eating

Expensive *Café Collage*, 115 Mackay St (upstairs), T7685497, has a quality traditional-style menu and is open Tue-Sat from 1800. The à la carte restaurant and brasserie in Ashleys Hotel, 74 Tasman St, T0800-807787, also has a good reputation. Open daily for lunch and dinner.

Mid-range *The Smelting House Café*, 102 Mackay St, T7680012, is a local favourite located in a historic old bank building. It specialises in home-style food and serves good coffee. Open daily 0800-1700. ***Jone's Café and Bar***, 37 Tainui St, T7686468, is another good alternative that is open late, offers a traditional-style menu and has occasional live jazz and blues. Good breakfast.

Cheap For pizza the ***Bonzai Pizzeria***, 31 Mackay St, T7684170 (open 0700-late) will not let you down, for Tex-Mex try the hefty portions at ***West of the Border***, 25 Mackay St, T7685272 (dinner only) and for a good Sun Roast or pub grub try ***Steamers Café and Bar***, corner of Albert and Tarapuhi St, T7684193 (open daily 1200-1400/1700-2100). But for the real fill your face deal head for the ***Railway Hotel***, Mawhera Quay, T7687023 (open daily from 1830) or the ***Raceway Carvery*** (Union Hotel), 20 Herbert St, T7684013 (open for lunch and dinner). Both offer all-you-can-eat BBQs. The best (or certainly most interesting) café in town has to be ***DP:One*** on Mawhera Quay, T7687503 (open daily 0900-2230). It is a small place but full of character, resembling something like an extrovert artist's garage. It is also the best Internet venue in town.

Entertainment

Greymouth has 2 nightclubs that are something of a West Coast institution. The ***Opposition***, and the ***Pumphouse***, which are both on Boundary St. They are known locally and affectionately as the 'Proposition' and the 'Humphouse' – can't imagine why!

Directory **Banks** All bank branches can be found on or around Mackay St. **Communications Internet** is available at the *DPOne Café* on Mawhera Quay, the *Grey District Library*, Mackay St and the VIC. The **post office** is on Tainui St. Open Mon-Fri 0830-1700, Sat 1000-1230.

Around Greymouth

Shantytown

Should you pan a large nugget, don't try to sell it to a bank without a proper mining licence

Shantytown, situated just off SH6 (Rutherglen Rd), 11 km south of Greymouth, is a faithful recreation of an 1880s gold-mining settlement. It comes complete with shops, a bank, saloon, goal, livery stables, fire station, working sawmill and a working steam train. Although a little commercial, it provides an interesting insight into the lives of hopeful prospectors. The steam train operates daily from 0945-1600. You can also try your hand at gold- panning, or even tie the knot in the original church. More traditional facilities include a café and souvenir shop. ■ *Open daily 1830-1700. Adult $10.50, child $6.50. Gold panning is $3 extra. T7626634, www.shantytown.co.nz Kea West Coast Tours, T7689292, offer 3-hr guided trips from Greymouth for around $40.*

Lake Brunner

Moana is on the main TransAlpine train line between Greymouth and Christchurch, T0800-802802

Lake Brunner, 37 km east of Greymouth, is the West Coast's largest lake and certainly one of the prettiest. Other than fine scenery, Moana Kotuku (or Heron Sea as it is also known) offers some great fishing, walking, swimming and other water-based activities. The settlement of **Moana** on its northern bank is the main base for accommodation and activities. One of the best walks – the 20 minute **Arnold River Walkway** – is accessed via a swingbridge over the Arthur River at the western end of the village (Ahau Street). Keep your eye out for the beautiful **white heron** (Kotuku) which visit outside the summer breeding season. Guided fishing trips, tackle hire and the occasional kayak can be secured through the motorcamp, motel and hotel. The **Moana Conservation Park** near the motel on the Arnold Valley Road, displays a collection of native/non-native species including monkeys and otters, but no kiwi. ■ *Adult $10, child $4. T7380405.*

Sleeping The **C-D** *Lake Brunner Motor Camp*, Ahau St, T7380600, has a beautiful view across the lake and has basic facilities. **A-C** *Moana Hotel*, T7380083, also on Ahau St, has basic double rooms, cabins and motel units and an expert fishing guide. The **A** *Lake Brunner Country Motel*, T7380143, is on the Arnold Valley Road at the outskirts of the village towards Greymouth. It has modern self-contained chalets and can also arrange fishing and bush-walking excursions. At the southern end of the lake is the **LL-L** *Lake Brunner Lodge*, Mitchell's, Kumara-Inchbonnie Rd, T7380163, www.lakebrunner.com It is a historic, all-mod-cons fishing retreat with 11 luxury rooms and fine cuisine. For the more budget-conscious based in Moana your only eatery options are the Moana Hotel or the ***Station House Café and Gallery*** overlooking the lake and train station, T7380158 (seasonal hours)

The Grey Valley & Blackball

Between Greymouth and Reefton the Grey River heads coastward, hemmed in by the Paparoa Ranges and the northern flanks of the Southern Alps. Like much of the region, its small settlements were born during the heady days of the gold rush.

Although the small former gold-mining town of **Waiuta** (21 km south of Reefton) is of interest it is the coal-mining town of **Blackball** (accessed from Stillwater, 11 km north of Greymouth) that holds most interest. Founded on gold in 1866, but developed later on coal, it is most famous as the cradle of

Raise your glass (but not the price)

In 1931, Blackball became the venue for the longest strike in New Zealand history. During this 15-month uprising, extra police were even billeted in the local hotel. Now, you might think it was as a result of this action that the local miners gave up frequenting the hotel bar and set up their own working men's club., but you'd be wrong. The club was established as a result of protests over a one-penny-a-pint increase (to seven pence) in the price of beer in the hotel. And it doesn't finish there. One of the local hotels was christened the Blackball Hilton. The international Hilton Hotel chain did not like this idea and took legal action. Being a capitalist giant and having lots of money they won, but not surprisingly, it was Blackball that had the last word – literally. They just added the word 'Formerly' to the hotel's name.

working-class protest and unionism in the early 1900s. In 1908 an almost inevitable clash occurred when a 30-minute lunchbreak was sought (as opposed to 15). This debacle led to the formation of the Federation of Miners and subsequently the Red Federation of Labour – essentially the nation's Labour Movement. Such was the anti-capitalist feeling that, for a few years after the First World War, you could attend Marxism classes in the town.

Sleeping and eating **B-C** ***'Formerly the Blackball Hilton'*** on Hart St, T7324705, www.blackballhilton.co.nz, is now a comfortable and (believe it or not) very friendly backpackers and B&B. They can also arrange a number of local activities including gold-panning, horse trekking and walking. Check out the award-winning ***Blackball Salami Company***, T7324111, also on Hart St. Open Mon-Sat (Sun presumably being a day of protest or Marxism classes).

Reefton

Phone code: 03
Population: 1,200

Known as the inland capital of the West Coast, the former gold town of Reefton is a fairly unremarkable, but pleasant little place at the end (or beginning) of the Lewis Pass arterial to the coast. Famous for very little, except its claim as the first town in the southern hemisphere to receive a public electricity supply and street lighting in 1888, it is sustained by coal, forestry and farming. The nice thing about Reefton is its unpretentious atmosphere. It seems very real. Although underrated and rarely on the tourist agenda, Reefton offers some fine fishing in the local rivers as well as a wealth of walking, tramping and mountain biking opportunities, primarily in the vast and local 209,000 ha Victoria Forest Park – the largest forest park in the country.

Ins & outs

By road Reefton is 79 km Northeast of Greymouth and 80 km east of Wesport. Hanmer Springs is 130 km west via the Lewis Pass. Bus companies servicing the town are: ***White Star*** T3236156 (Wesport to Christchurch Sun-Fri); and ***East-West***, T7896251 (Westport to Chritchurch, via Lewis Pass/ Westport to Greymouth daily). For more information contact the VIC.

Information The main street of Broadway in Reefton provides most of the visitor's needs including the excellent **Visitor Information Centre**, T7328391, F7328616, refvin@nzhost.co.nz Open daily 0830-1730 (1630 in winter). It proudly boasts a small museum with a Cornish steam winding machine, once used in both the gold and coal mines and a simulated walkthrough mine shaft ($3). Next door in the **DOC** office there are various eco-based displays and lots of walking and tramping information.

Sights & activities The two most noted walks in town are the **Reefton Heritage Walk** and the **Powerhouse Walk**. The Heritage Walk takes in a number of interesting historical buildings including the newly renovated Courthouse, beautifully decorated Masonic Lodge and the former School of Mines. On The Strand you will find the lovingly restored, former workhorse R28 Fairlie Locomotive, the sole survivor of its type. The Powerhouse Walk is an easy 40-minute walk across the river to see the former powerhouse that once proudly lit up the town. Free leaflets outlining both walks are available from the VIC.

The **Blacks Point Museum**, just beside SH7 (Lewis Pass Road) in Black Point, has extensive displays surrounding the regions goldfields history. ■ *Open in summer Wed-Fri 0900-1600, Sat-Sun 1300-1600. $2. T7328808.* Spend some time in the VIC looking at the very attractive **walking, tramping** and **mountain biking** opportunities in the highly underrated and quiet **Victoria Forest Park**. There are numerous routes and half to multi-day walking /tramping options that take in a wealth of former gold-mining relics. An excellent 'helicopter in / mountain bike out' trip to Big River can be arranged by the VIC. Prices on application. The DOC leaflet *'Reefton-Victoria Conservation Park'* is useful.

The local **fishing** is also superb. Information, licenses and information about local guides are again available from the VIC. Tackle can be hired from *Sportsworld* in the centre of town. For a fine **view** of the town and the Inangahua Valley head south on SH7, turn left after 1 km into Soldier Flat Road and left again shortly afterwards. Follow this road to the lookout point in the pine forest.

Sleeping The perfectly comfortable **A** ***Quartz Lodge***, corner of Sheil and Sinnamon Sts, T7328383, and the cute and historic **A** ***Reef Cottage***, Broadway, T7328440, are the 2 principal B&Bs in town. The **B** ***Dawsons Hotel/Motel***, 74 Broadway, T7328406 has modern studio units. Spa and cafe/bar with lovely open fire. The **B** ***Bellbird Motel***, T7328444, also on Broadway. There are 2 backpackers on Sheil St: **D** ***Reefton Backpackers*** (at 64), T7328133 is a comfortable renovated villa with shared, single or double rooms with proper beds (not bunks); and the **C-D** ***Pog Mo Thon***, (at 104), T7328885 has 2 self-contained units, double, twin and singles and assures a warm Irish welcome. The basic **C-D** ***motorcamp*** in Reefton is located at the edge of town at the top of Broadway, T7328477. It has powered/tent sites and cabins and its coal fired water heater is typical of the town.

Eating The ***Dawsons Motel*** and ***Hotel Reefton***, T7328447 offer traditional pub-style meals. The ***Alfresco***, (summer only, Mon-Sat, lunch and dinner), across the road from the Domain Motorcamp on Broadway lives up to its name and does takeaway pizza, while the cosier ***Reef Cottage Café***, on Broadway in the centre of town, serves the best coffee and light snacks.

Directory **Internet** is available at the library/post office across the road from the VIC (open Mon-Fri 1030-1700)

Hokitika

Hokitika, or 'Hoki' as it is known on 'The Coast', shares the rather drab appearance and monotonous street grid system of its former gold-mining counterparts, but at least enjoys the same warm welcome and proud, healthy heartbeat felt the length and minimal breadth of the West Coast.

Phone code: 03
Population: 4,000

An important port until 1954, the town is also steeped in goldmining history. More of the precious metal passed through Hoki in the 1860s than any other town on the coast, with the port being one of the busiest in the country. Between 1865-67 over 37,000 hopefuls arrived from Australia, America and Britain, requiring a staggering 84 hotels to put them all up. In 1865 pioneer surveyor Julius von Haast described Hokitika as 'a scene of almost indescribable bustle and activity'. In those heady days it seemed only the river itself could hold the town back. At one point during the gold rush there was at least one grounding every ten weeks – and 21 in 1865 alone. Like everywhere else the gold ran out and old 'Hoki' slipped into decline. But today gold has been replaced by that other precious resource, tourism. Today, it is the craft capital of the West Coast and every summer sees cosmopolitan crowds of camera- toting visitors arrive by the bus load, to watch glass-blowing and greenstone carving and to browse in its numerous galleries.

Ins and outs

Getting there

By air Hoki boasts the West Coast' main airport, located 1 km east of the town centre, served daily by ***Air New Zealand Link***, T0800-737000. **By road** Hoki is 40 km south of Greymouth and 429 km north of Wanaka. Principal bus services are provided by ***Intercity***, T7558557 (points south to Greymouth/ Chrischurch); ***Atomic Shuttles***, T3228883 (Queenstown to Greymouth/Christchurch); ***Coast to Coast***, T0800-800847 (Greymouth/Christchurch) and ***Alpine Coaches***, T0800-274888 (Greymouth; Christchurch). All stop outside the **Travel Centre**, 65 Tancred St, T7558557. If you are heading south this is also your last chance to join the AA at the House of Travel, Weld St.

Getting around

For a **taxi** contact *Hokitika Taxis*, T7555075. **Bikes** can be hired at *Hokitika Cycles and Sports*, 33 Tancred St, T7558662.

Information

The Westland **Visitor Information Centre** is located in the rather grand Carnegie Building, corner of Hamilton and Tancred Sts, T7556166, F7555011, hkkvin@xtra.co.nz Open daily in summer 0830-1800 (winter Mon-Fri 0900-1700, Sat-Sun 1000-1400). **DOC** is located on Sewell St, T7558301 (open Mon-Fri 0800-1645) But the VIC will stock most of what you need.

Sights and activities

Hokitika is famous for its **arts** and **crafts**, particularly **greenstone** carving and **glass blowing**. Tancred Street is the hub of the many artisan outlets and factory shops. Not to be missed is the **Hokitika Glass Studio**, 28 Tancred Street, where you can see the glass been blown and crafted into rather lurid ornaments and *objets d'art*. ■ *Open daily 0900-1730 (longer in summer). T7557775. Shroders*, in the **Mountain Jade Complex**, 41 Weld St, T7558484, echoes the Glass Studio and also houses a jade factory shop. There are a number of other greenstone factory shops including **Westland Greenstone**, 34 Tancred Street. Here, once again you can see the beautiful and spiritual stone being cut and handcrafted in to a wide array of jewellery, ornaments and traditional Maori pendants (*tiki*). ■ *Open daily 0800-1700. T7558713.*

Also worthy of investigation is the **Gold Room** and **House of Wood**, both on Tancred Street. The huge natural nugget pendants in the Gold Room (at a hefty $8000) would delight the critical eye of Jimmy Saville or even Mr T.

If you fancy a go at jade carving yourself, then Gordon of the **Just Jade Experience**, 197 Revell Street, T7557612, will give you a full day of tuition from $80. Naturally you get to keep your masterpiece – or disaster!

Once crafted out and replete with souvenirs, you might like to absorb some local history at the **West Coast Historical Museum**, housed in the Carnegie Building (accessed through the VIC), 7 Tancred Street. As you might expect there is a heavy emphasis on gold and jade, but the troubled history of the port and its numerous shipwrecks provide some added excitement. ■ *Open daily 0930-1700 (seasonal). Adult $5, child $1. T7556898.*

The **Quay**, near the museum is worth a stroll with its centrepiece the 1897 Custom House now housing a small gallery. There is a free *'Hokitika Heritage Walk'* leaflet available from the VIC that outlines other places of historical interest.

Far removed from both craft and history is the small but effective **Westland's Water World**, Sewell Street. It is a small aquarium complex with a wide variety of native and non-native fish species, the stars of which are the New Zealand eels, the biggest eel species in the world. These unfeasible large, ugly and lethargic octogenarians are fed daily at 1000 and 1500. What perhaps lets the place down is the 'catch-yer-own' tank where death row salmon can be caught (hired rods $10) with little fuss or competition. Once caught

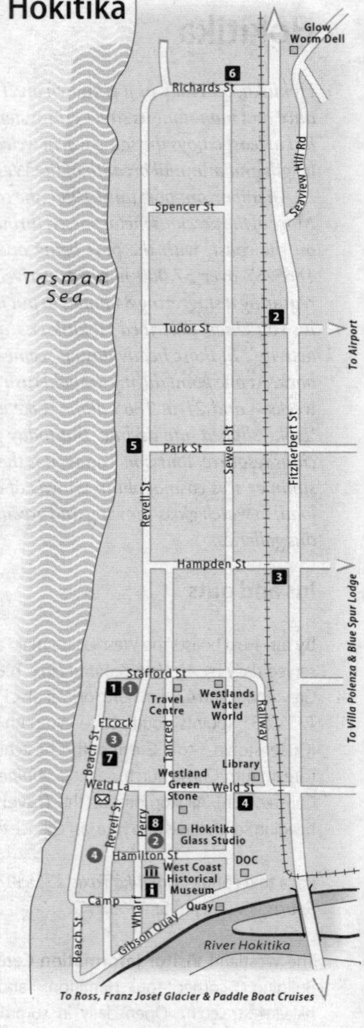

■ **Sleeping**
1 Beach House
2 Fitzherbert Court
3 Jade Court Motel
4 Mountain Jade Backbackers
5 Seaside Backpackers
6 Shining Star Log Chalets & Motorcamp
7 Southland
8 Teichelmann's B & B

● **Eating**
1 Beach House
2 Café de Paris
3 Tasman View
4 Trappers

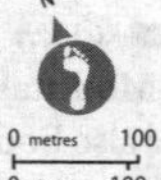

they are then quietly dispatched and vacuum packed for your total convenience. The young and enthusiastic staff at Water World are a credit to the place and will answer any fishy questions you may have. ■ *0900-1800 (winter 0930-1600), Adult $10, child $5, T7555251, www.waterworld.co.nz*

Still on the aquatic theme are the daily **Paddle Boat Cruises**, T7557239 which ply the creek to the picturesque **Mahinapua Lake** just south of the town. A 1½ hour trip will cost you from $20. Departs daily at 1400 (seasonal). **Flightseeing** to venues that include Mount Cook and The Glaciers is available from *Wilderness Wings*, T7558118, 20 minutes to 3 ½ hours, from $80. Last but not least is the town's very own **Glow-worm Dell** at the northern entrance to town. If you have never seen them before this is your chance.

Essentials

Sleeping

Hokitika is pretty well blessed with good accommodation but in summer, like everywhere else on the West Coast, you are advised to book well in advance

The sole remianing hotel is the **AL-A** ***Southland Hotel***, Revell St, T7558344, F7558250. It is comfortable enough, with its reputable restaurant/bar over-looking the beach being its best point. There are a few luxury **B&Bs** located near Hokitika with the **LL-L** ***Villa Polenza***, Brickfield Rd, T7557801, villapolenza@xtra.co.nz being the best. Built in a prime location in Italian style it offers luxuriously appointed king and queen rooms and 2 en suites. As you would expect, the cuisine is also excellent. In the town itself you cannot be better located than at the comfortable and friendly **A** ***Teichelmann's B&B***, 20 Hamilton St, T7558232, www.teichelmanns.co.nz For a motel-type option look no further than The **A-D** ***Shining Star Log Chalets and Motor Camp***, 11 Richards Dr, T7558921, shinning@xtra.co.nz It is a superb place with very tidy self-contained lodges designed and built by the owners. It is located close the beach in a quiet location and also takes campervans and tents. The facilities are excellent and include internet. If you find the lodges fully booked try the **A** ***Jade Court Motel***, 85 Fitzherbert St, T7558855 or the **A** ***Fitzherbert Court*** at 191, T7555342.

The **C-D** ***Mountain Jade Backpackers***, 41 Weld St, T0800-838301, is located in the centre of town. It is purpose built and a bit clinical, but certainly serves its purpose and has a restaurant downstairs. It takes the majority of the 'backpacker buses' so can get busy. The 2 other backpackers in town are both beachside, with the **C-D** ***Beach House***, 137 Revell St, T7556859, offering dorms, doubles, a restaurant and a popular 'bush-bath' and the **C-D** ***Seaside Backpackers***, 197 Revell St, T7557612, being smaller, more homely, and offering jade carving as its unique attraction. Located in the country 6 km east of town is the well-appointed and well-facilitated **C-D** ***Blue Spur Lodge Backpackers***, Hampden St, T7558445, bluespur@xtra.co.nz It has tidy doubles, twins and shared rooms as well as a fully self-contained cottage with 2 en suite rooms. It's a popular place noted for its peace and quiet and worth the effort to get there. Kayak hire, gold panning and bush walks on site.

Eating

For fine dining the award-winning *Café de Paris*, 19 Tancred St, T7558933 sets the benchmark. It has an imaginative French-style à la carte menu for dinner, a changing blackboard menu for breakfast and lunch and good coffee. It also has an interesting history (ask about the runaway pig). Open daily from 0730. The ***Tasman View Restaurant*** attached to the *Southland Hotel*, Revell St, T7558344, is popular not only for the views of the crashing waves but its seafood and value smorgasbords on Fri. Open for dinner Sat-Thu. The extremely wooden ***Trappers Restaurant***, 79 Revell St, T7555133, is also very good and touts itself as the original wild food restaurant, though it is definitely not one for the avid vegan. Open for lunch and dinner. For a good cheap meal the ***Beach House Café/Bar***, Stafford St, T7556859, is an old stalwart. Open from 1800.

Entertainment & events The main hub of entertainment is the ***O'Conners Bar***, Revell St. It's an Irish bar below the Southland Hotel with absolutely nothing Irish about it.

Hokitika goes mad each **Mar** and enjoys such a human influx that it can jog the memories of the gold rush days. The attraction – is not gold – but good food and lots and lots of beer and wine. The ***Hokitika Wildfoods Festival*** is a celebration of the West Coast's unique lifestyle, food and hospitality (not to mention drinking capacity). On offer is a vast array of culinary delights from BBQ possum to the famed whitebait fritter. A number of lesser events over 2-3 days (including such diverse activities as a basketball Exhibition match and a 0730 Monteiths Beer tasting) leads up the main festival and dance (monumental 'session') on the Sat. Tickets cost $12, T7558321, wildfoods@westlandddc.govt.nz

Directory **Banks** Most branches and ATMs are available in the town centre. Note if you are heading south there are no further banks, or ATMs until Wanaka. **Internet** is available at *the District Library*, 36 Weld St (Mon-Fri 1000-1700; Sat 0900-1200) and the **Travel Centre**, Tancred St.

Around Hokitika

Lake Kaniere Inland from Hokitika (14 km) is the picturesque Lake Kaniere, a popular haven in summer for swimming, water sports, picnicking and walking. The lake can be explored in a number of ways, by foot, car, boat or bicycle and there are many pleasant walks and features on offer. At the entrance to the **Lake Kaniere Scenic Reserve** there is an information kiosk outlining all the possibilities. The two best short walks, both of which include lovely beaches, are the Kahikatea Walk, at **Sunny Bight** (10 minute) and the **Canoe Cove** Walk (15 minute). If you are feeling more energetic the **Lake Kaniere Walkway** (four hours), which also starts at Sunny Bight, follows the western shore of the lake to Slip Bay at its southern edge. The road on the eastern edge will give you access to the hardest walk (seven hours) – the ascent of **Mount Tuhua** (1125 m). Further south are the **Dorothy Falls** (64 m) near Big Bay. There is a basic campsite at Hans Bay. The DOC leaflet *'Central West Coast-Hokitika'* outlines all these options and a few others ($1).

Hokitika Gorge Accessed directly from Hokitika (25 km) via the settlements of Kaniere and Kokatahi (end of Kowhitirangi and Whitcombe Road) or, alternatively, via Lake Kaniere (loop road to Kokatahi) is the picturesque and moody Hokitika Gorge. Other than the impressive scenery the highlight here is the **swingbridge** across the river. Although most of the time the river slides gracefully below, it can become a raging torrent after heavy rains, making the crossing an exciting prospect. Once across the bridge you can continue through the bush for another 100 m to emerge at a rock wall that offers an even better view of the gorge.

Lake Mahinapua Located just 10 km south of Hokitika, and shielded from SH6 by a narrow tract of bush, is Lake Mahinapua and the **Mahinapua Recreation Reserve**, another popular spot for swimming, fishing, kayaking and walking. At the road terminus there is a pleasant picnic spot, a campsite and the trailheads to a number of short walks. Perched in concrete near the car park is a former 15 m paddle steamer that used to ply the route to 'Hoki' carrying both freight and passengers. A modern working model runs daily (seasonal) **cruises** from the outlet creek to the lake, starting 6 km south of Hokitika (see page 555).

If you're hungry you could do a lot worse than a whitebait fritter and a pint of Monteiths in the Mahinapua Hotel, opposite the reserve

Hokitika to Franz Josef

Stocked up with cash, petrol and photographic film, you can now follow the human artery of SH6 in to the real wild West Coast. From here, the mountains rise higher and higher and become crowned with snow and impenetrable bush creeps steadily towards the road from all directions. Also, never far away, the pounding surf crashes onto lonely, driftwood-covered beaches. It all holds the promise of great things and, provided the weather is on your side, it will not disappoint. Even if you do nothing but simply gaze in wonder from the passenger seat, the 137 km journey to Franz Josef is a stunner, and will ease you gently in to West Coast time.

Ross

The first settlement of any consequence is the tiny and pretty **gold-mining** town of Ross, 30 km south of Hokitika. The most interesting thing about Ross is that mining still takes place here, in a very large hole at the edge of town, where the gentle chip, chip of the early pick-axe has long given way to the hum and roar of huge diggers and trucks. Even so, Ross retains the romance of its past with evidence of fond memories and many old remnants. During the great gold rush of the 1860s it was a bustling town of over 3000 hopefuls, who chipped away relentlessly at the alluvial gravels of the Totara Riverbeds in search of the 'big one'. Ironically, in 1909, towards the end of the great gold rush, one lucky miner fulfilled that dream. His find, named the '**Honourable Roddy**', after the erstwhile Minister of Mines, was a nugget weighing in at a healthy 3.1 kg. As you might expect, the nugget immediately took on a life of its own, at first being paraded from bar to bar then sold and sold again. Then after a short stint as a doorstop (apparently true) it was bought by the Government in 1911 as a coronation gift for King George V. Sadly, this act of generosity proved its demise. After a colourful life above ground, the good and the grateful Royals melted it down for use as a gold tea service at Buckingham Palace. Or that is what we are led to believe.

The Ross **Visitor Information Centre**, 4 Aylmer Street, T7554077, has some interesting displays and photographs of the gold rush days and information on a number of short local **walks**, including the **Water Race Walk** and the **Jones Flat Walk** (1-2 hours). Both take in some former mining relics. You can also go gold panning for $5. A short distance from the VIC is a renovated 1885 **Miners Cottage** with a replica of the great 'Honourable Roddy' nugget.

Sleeping and eating The basic but characterful and historic **B-D** *Empire Hotel*, Aylmer St, T7554005 has tent sites, backpacker cabins and en suite rooms. The **B** *Dahlia Cottage B&B*, 47 Aylmer St, T7554160 is a good B&B noted for its beautiful garden. For marginally god coffee and a snack your best bet is the *Roddy Nugget Café*, T7554245, on the Main Rd. Open daily from 0700 (summer).

Pukekura

About 18 km further south of Ross is the small settlement of Pukekura and the **Bushman's Centre**, T7554144. This place is instantly recognisable and notorious for the giant **sandfly** (*Renderus insanitus*) that hangs with menace from its walls (don't panic; despite local gossip, they could never grow that big). The Bushman's Centre is the ongoing project of local West Coaster and extrovert Peter Salter. As well as a fine **café** (with its superb 'road kill soup of the day') and **shop** it has a great little interactive **museum** ($4), where you can learn about bushcraft, meet a live possum, stroke a pig, baulk at ugly eels, then wantonly throw sharp knives and axes at the wall. It's brilliant. Other activities based at the centre include **horse trekking** and Canadian **canoe safaris**.

Sleeping and eating Across the road from the Bushman's Centre is a tidy **C-D** *Backpackers* (enquire at the Centre) offering dorms, 2 doubles and hot pools. The *Puke Pub* on the main road is without doubt one of the finest drinking establishments on the West Coast. It is full of character and offers pub-style grub. If you are a male only group ask to see the mock up view in to the ladies toilet – truly stunning.

Harihari

20 km south of Lake Ianthe and 80 km from Hokitika

From Pukekura the bush continues to envelope and you are blessed with your first occasional views of Mount Cook's snowy peak. At **Lake Ianthe**, there are opportunities to stop and take in the views or enjoy a picnic on its bush-clad bank. At the southern end of the lake a large **maitai tree** can be accessed with a short walk and is signposted. The maitai is the South Island's equivalent to the North Island's mighty kauri.

Harihari is a small farming settlement, nestled on the open alluvial plains of the Wanganui and Poerua Rivers. It is famous due to the unexpected visitation by a 21-year-old Australian aviator called Guy Menzies, in January 1931. Young Guy had set off unannounced and alone from Sydney, in his Avro-Avian plane called the Southern Cross, armed with little except a lot of courage and a good sense of direction. Just under 12 hours and an awful lot of sea later he crash-landed in a swamp near the town. The interesting thing is that the bold Guy had not officially told anybody of his attempt. But what was most interesting of all is that his crossing was actually completed in 2½ hours less than the much publicised success of Sir Charles Kingsford Smith, in a three-engine plane, with crew, three years earlier.

If you fancy some thorough exploration of the coastline, the **Harihari Coastal Walkway** (three hours) utilizes part of the old Wanganui River pack track and is a fine walk. It traverses kahikatea and rimu forest and essentially links the two river mouths. The car park and trailhead is accessed via La Fontaine Road at the southern end of Harihari (19 km). One of the many highlights of the walk is the lookout at the top of **Mount Doughboy** (or to give it its much more attractive name – Mount Oneone) Although not especially high it does afford a great view up and down the coast. The DOC leaflet '*Harihari Coastal Walk*' gives detailed information.

Sleeping and eating The **B-D** *Harihari Motor Inn*, Main Rd, T0800-833026 has tidy en suites, backpacker rooms, powered/tent sites and a licensed restaurant. The **B** *Tomsai Motel*, T7533116, across the road is another motel option with backpacker facilities. Other than the basic **restaurant** in the Harihari Motor Inn there is the *Glenalmond Tearooms*, which is again located on the main road through the town.

Whataroa

It is little wonder that the Maori have long revered the white heron (or kotuku). Although a non-native and essentially an Australian import, its presence here on the West Coast seems utterly befitting of the place. Somehow, with its colour echoing the snows of the mountaintops and its graceful unhurried flight in rhythm with West Coast time, there could be no better mascot. Whataroa, 35 km south of Harihari, provides your only opportunity to see these majestic birds congregated at their sole New Zealand breeding rookery. But you will have to time it right. The birds are only in residence from mid-October to mid-March. *White Heron Sanctuary Tours*, T0800-523456, www.whiteherontours.co.nz, have a small office in the centre of Whataroa and offer a three hour tour by jetboat, to access the hide that looks over the lagoon-based breeding area. ■ *All tours must be guided and the colony cannot be visited independently without a permit from DOC. Tours cost from $89, child $40 and leave daily at 0900, 1100, 1300 and 1500, in season.*

Outside the breeding season there is still an enjoyable 2 ½ hour *Rainforest Nature Tour* available, again by jetboat, to view the ancient Kahikatea forest and whatever birdlife that decides to show (40-minute jetboat tours on the Waitangitaona River are also available).

Sleeping and eating Accommodation is available at the **B-D** ***Sanctuary Tours Motel***, T0800-523456, in the form of units, cabins with cooking facilities. There are tent sites but no kitchen. The **C-D** ***Whataroa Hotel***, T7534076, has cabins and powered sites. More luxurious accommodation is available at **A** ***Sleepy Hollow***, T7534139, hollow@xtra.co.nz which is a very pleasant, modern and good value B&B with adjunct self-contained motel unit, located just off SH6, close to the village. The ***White Heron Store and Tearooms*** and the ***Whataroa Hotel,*** both on the main road, are the only eateries on offer.

Okarito
Population: 30 (formerly 3000)

Okarito, a small coastal settlement and former goldfields port is located 13 km off SH6 and 15 km south of Whataroa. This beautiful little paradise, set beachside next to the vast 3240-ha Okarito Lagoon backed by stunning views of the Southern Alps, is not surprisingly the favourite haunt of many a New Zealander. Thankfully most people shoot past the road junction from SH6 in their rush to see their first glacier – Franz Josef 29 km to the south. But for those who take the time and the diversion, they will be rewarded not only with Okarito's simple do-nothing appeal, but also some excellent walking, kayaking and birdwatching opportunities.

The best walk is the steady climb (1 ½ hours) via an old but well formed pack track, through native bush to the **Okarito Trig**. On a clear day, it affords a stunning view across the bush-clad hills to the Southern Alps and the peak of Mount Cook and its associates. As if that weren't enough, you can then turn to take in the expansive views back towards the Okarito Lagoon and north up the coast. The Trig Track starts from The Strand at the southern end of the village. Once you have negotiated the Trig you can then consider carrying on along the main pack track for about an hour to reach **Three Mile Lagoon**. It is a lovely spot with a quiet beach and more coastal views. If the tide is right, you can then walk back to Okarito via the beach where huge white-veined schist rocks that have been eroded from the Kohuamarua Bluff litter the beach. Also look out for dolphins playing just offshore.

The great expanse of **Okarito Lagoon** is a **birdwatcher's** paradise with almost every mainland bird species in New Zealand visiting at some point. Over 70 species have so far been recorded.The best way to view the birds and the lagoon is by **kayak** with *Okarito Nature Tours*, T7534014, www.okarito.co.nz, the only commercial operators in the village. They offer independent kayak rental (two hours, $30) and a range of guided trips from $65 and pick-up from SH6 for a small fee.

There are few remnants of Okarito's once bustling gold-mining past when the population remarkably ran into the thousands. Its hard to believe there were once 25 hotels, two banks, several stores, a busy school (now the *YHA*) and three theatres. Across the road from the obviously historic and incredibly cute YHA, is the almost unsightly obelisk commemorating Abel Tasman's first sighting of New Zealand, somewhere off Okarito in 1642.

Sleeping and eating **D** ***Okarito YHA Hostel***, The Strand, T7534124, is something of novelty with a limited number of bunks in what was the former 1870s schoolhouse. Bookings can be made via the Franz Josef VIC or payment made direct at the wardens house located close to the hostel. Facilities at the hostel are adequate, but showers are only available at the very pleasant, sheltered and basic **D** ***Campground***, T7534142 across the road. The **C-D** ***Royal Hostel and Motel***, also on the Strand, T7534080, offers comfortable dorms and doubles and can pick up from the junction with SH6 or even Franz Josef (for longer stay clients) There are no shops in Okarito so bring your own food.

The Glacier Region

As if New Zealand has not enough to offer in majestic scenery and ecological surprises, the two gigantic and dynamic monoliths of ice, Franz Josef and Fox Glaciers, provide a dramatic sight. They are the brightest jewels in the highly decorated crown of the Westland and Mount Cook National Parks, joined, yet separated on the map, by the jagged summits and peaks of the Southern Alps and the great Dividing Range. Descending from a height of 3000 m to 300 m at the remarkable speed of over 1 m a day, the glaciers create one of the best examples of glaciology in the world.

In summer there are only really two moods to the neighbouring villages of Franz and Fox. When the sun shines they are both a frenetic buzz of activity. From the moment the sun peeks from above the mountaintops, the skies fill with the sound of aircraft, the roads swarm with tour buses and the streets fill rapidly with expectant tourists. They seem excited, rushed, almost consumed with the desire to get there: to see them, walk on them, photograph them, perhaps even touch them. And yet, when the clouds gather (which is often) and the rain descends (correction; crashes down), the pace of everything slows, dramatically. Then, the streets fill with puddles and the tourists' glum faces stare at them from behind café windows. The air hangs heavy with silence. At Franz and Fox it's amazing just how much the weather and two, multi-million ton blocks of ice, dictates. Welcome to the Glaciers.

Franz Josef

Phone Code: 03
Population: 300

Franz Josef owes its very existence and, of course its name, to the great block of ice that sits 5 km to the south of the village. Of the two principally tourist-based settlements (Franz and Fox), Franz is the larger and better-serviced. As you might expect it is very much a seasonal destination, crowded in summer, quiet in winter. Although the glacier can of course be visited in the rain and the guided glacier-walks are rarely cancelled, the scenic flights, and essentially, an overall impression of the glaciers from above and below, are completely dependent on favourable conditions. As a rule, you should plan to give yourself at least two days in the area. If you have scenic flights booked, these can be forwarded and while you wait for the clouds to clear, there are still a few things to keep you occupied, even in the rain. The average annual rainfall in the area is about 5 m over 180 rain days. In summer always book your accommodation well in advance.

Ins & outs

There are no scheduled air services to Franz Josef

Getting there **By road** Franz Josef is 177 km south of Greymouth, 404 km north of Queenstown and 25 km north of Fox Glacier on SH6. ***Intercity*** and ***Atomic Shuttles***, T7520738, north and southbound bus services all stop in the centre of the village. The *Glacier Shop* in the Alpine Adventure Building act as the local ***Intercity*** agent, T7520131.

Getting around *Kamahi Tours*, T7520699 (book at the ***Alpine Adventure Centre***) provide transportation to the head of the glacier, from $5. Hitching to the glacier and back is rarely a problem. **Bike hire** is available from *Ice Flow* (opposite the VIC), T7520144.

Information Most of Franz Josef's services and amenities are on SH6 (Main Road) with everything (except the glacier itself) being in easy walking distance. The DOC Franz Josef Glacier **Visitor Information Centre** is situated at the southern end of town (seaward side), T7520796, F7520797. Open 0830-1800 (winter 0830-1700). There are plenty of displays, walks information and most importantly up to date weather forecasts.

Franz Josef Glacier

By far the best way to view the glacier is from the air

Franz Josef was first sighted and officially documented by both Abel Tasman in 1642 and Cook in 1770, but first properly explored and named by geologist and explorer Julius von Haast in 1865. When he first explored its lower reaches it was almost 3 km nearer the coast than it is today. His official title of 'Francis Joseph Glacier' was given in honour of the Emperor Franz Josef of Austria. The spelling was later changed to Franz Josef in accordance with the internationally accepted version – as in Franz Josef Land in the Arctic and Franz Josef Fjord in Greenland. Until 1985, and apart from a few sporadic advances last century, the glacier had actually been receding steadily since 1865. As it stands, it is unclear what it will do next. After advancing almost 1 km, at almost 1 m a day over the last 17 years, it is now slowing down. Many are worried that global warming will see the glaciers recede at an unnatural rate due to a lack of snow at the summits.

The glacier is about 5 km south of town and accessed by the Glacier Access Road which runs alongside the cold, grey **Waiho River** that dramatically appears from beneath its face. From the car park it is a one hour 40 minute return walk along the wide rocky river bed to the face of the glacier. Unless properly equipped you cannot walk on the glacier itself and to do that you are strongly advised to join one of the many and regular guided trips on offer. Perhaps the best view of the glacier is from the 280 m viewpoint on **Sentinel Rock** (a stubborn remnant of previous glacial erosion) which is easily accessed from near the main car park (20 minutes).

Activities

There are many operators based in Franz offering a wide range of methods and modes of transport with which to acquaint yourself with the great ice cube. Competition is pretty fierce so shop around. Most people do one, or preferably, all of three things: they **walk** to the glacier's terminal face independently, they take a **guided walk** on to the glacier (**glacier walking**) or they take to the **air**. What you do will of course depend on your budget and the weather. Although a glacier walk is both exciting and very informative, if you can possibly afford it, take an extended scenic flight around Mount Cook and down the face of the glacier, landing briefly on the snow at its crown. The atmosphere up there, and the silence on a calm, clear day, is simply unforgettable.

Flightseeing Fixed wing or helicopter? Twin engine or single? Snow landing or no landing? Weather permitting, these are the questions! Generally speaking fixed wing aircraft will allow longer in the air for the price and cover more 'air', but you miss out on that unique feel of a helicopter. Apparently, helicopters have twin or single engine with a twin being safer. Most helicopters offer ten minute snow-landings whereas most fixed-wing planes do not. All modes are intrinsically safe and all companies are accommodating regarding weather cancellations (payment takes place pre-flight and post-booking) even arranging another flight at sister locations.

Helicopter In Franz Josef there are three helicopter companies: *Helicopter Line*, Main Road T0800-807767, www.helicopter.co.nz, offer flights from

20-40 minutes all with snow landings and a 2 ½ hours Heli-hike option. They are a nationwide company and their helicopters are twin-engine; *Glacier Southern Lakes Helicopters*, Main Road, T7520755, www.heli-flights.co.nz, offer 10-40 minute flights with snow landings on flights over 30 minutes. They are a South Island based company (founded in 1970) and fly twin-engine helicopters; *Fox and Franz Josef Heli-services*, Alpine Adventure Centre, T7520793, www.newzealandnz.co.nz/helicopters/ offer flights from 20-40 minutes, again with snow landings on flights of 30 minute or more. These helicopters are smaller but still relatively comfortable. The company pride themselves in their flexibility and the fact they are locally owned and operated. Being perhaps the most competitive in price they better suit the budget traveller. Charters are also available. Prices range from around $120-$135 for 20 minutes to $270-$280 for 40 minutes.

Fixed-wing *Ski Plane Adventures* (Aoraki Aero Company), T7520714, aoraki@aorakiaero.co.nz offer flights with a snow landing (35 minutes from $170/ 55 minutes from $235) or without (40 minutes $210/ one hour $270); *Air Safaris*, Main Road, T7520716, www.airsafaris.co.nz offer a 50-minute 'Grand Traverse' flight over ten glaciers and the upper peaks of both National Parks with no snow landing, from $210. *Air Safaris* have been operating for 30 years.

Glacier walking, hiking and ice climbing Glacier walking is a unique experience and a magical way to experience a glacier properly. By climbing across the surface and descending into small crevasses you get a better feel of how they work and can witness the beautiful blue colour of the ice. The tours are also very informative. Fox is generally accepted as the better glacier for ice climbing, while Franz is steeper and more heavily crevassed which makes for better glacier walking.

Franz Josef Glacier Guides, Main Road, T7520763, www.franzjosefglacier.com have been operating since 1990 and are a highly experienced and professional outfit offering 4-8 hour excursions as well as Heli-hike and high level alpine-hut trips. The eight hour trip takes you to the impressive icefalls further up the glacier face. Their famous strap on 'Ice-Talonz' crampons make for comfortable walking. Trips leave throughout the day from 0900. Prices are from $39 (four hours) / $78 (eight hours); *The Guiding Company*, Main Road (Alpine Adventures Centre), T7520047, www.nzguides.com are a more recent outfit offering similar trips for about the same price. They also offer an ice climbing option. Ice climbing and Heli-hiking are also available with *Alpine Guides in Fox Glacier* (see Fox Glacier 'activities' below)

Other walking options are outlined in various DOC leaflets and broadsheets available at the VIC

Walking Other than the glacier terminal walk there are a number of other walking options in the glacier valley. The wonderfully christened **Lake Wombat** (after a gold miner's nickname) and another (don't ask) **Alex Knob** (1000 m), can be accessed about 350 m down the Glacier Access Road. The route, which traverses the valley wall, takes you through classic rata and kamahi forest, rich in birdlife. The 'kettle' lake, Lake Wombat can be reached in about 45 minutes, while the stunning view of the glacier from Alex Knob will take another fairly strenuous three hours.

A little further along the Glacier Access Road is the access point to the **Douglas Walk** and **Peter's Pool**. Named after a young camper who set up his tent there in 1894 it is an easy walk and the lake can be reached in about 10 minutes. The track continues to reunite with the road further up the valley (one hour). Located 1 km from the junction of the Glacier Access Road and SH6 is **Canavans Knob Walk** (40 minutes return), which like Sentinel Rock in the glacier valley, withstood the actions of the ice that completely covered it until about 10,000 years ago. Now covered only in rimu trees it offers views of the glacier and the mountains

Other activities *Skydive New Zealand*, T0800-7510080 offer 9,000 ft and 12,000 ft dives amidst what must be the most stunning scenery in the country, from $225; *Ferg's Kayaks*, Cron Street, T7520230 (T0800-423262), offer 2 ½ hour **kayaking** trips in the area from $45; *Wildtrax*, Alpine Adventure Centre, T7520793 offer 2 ½ hour **eight-wheel drive** amphibious buggy and truck trips from $50; *Kamahi Tours*, Heli-services Office, Main Road, T7520793 offer conventional road and walking tours of 1-3 hours, from $25. **Fishing** on pretty **Lake Mapourika**, 8 km north of Franz can be arranged through the *Alpine Adventure Centre* on Main Road.

Sleeping

Given the amount of tourist traffic in summer and the fickle weather, you are advised to book your accommodation in advance and add an additional night, just in case

LL *Waiho Stables Country Stay*, Docherty Creek, T7520747, F7520786, www.waiho.co.nz is a boutique B&B situated south of the village. It has 2 luxury en suite rooms. The food and the company are excellent. **L-AL** *Franz Josef Glacier Hotels*, Main Rd, T7520729, F7520709, is the largest (and only) hotel in the village with over 177 rooms, a restaurant, a café and 4 bars, plus a spa. It is mainly designed to cater for tour groups. **L-AL** *Westwood Lodge*, SH6, T/F7520111, www.westwood-lodge.co.nz is a well-appointed, modern, single-storey B&B, with six spacious, en-suite rooms, located 1 km north of the village.

There are about ten **motels** all quite similar including the modern **A** *Bella Vista*, T7520008, and the **AL-A** *Alpine Glacier Motor Lodge*, T7520224, in Cron St (village centre) and the quieter **AL-A** *The Glacier Gateway Motor Lodge*, T7520776, on the southern edge of town (nearest the glacier). The newest motel, the **AL-A** *Glenfern*, T7520054, is located near the Tatare River just north of the village. **A-D** *Forest Park*, Cron St, T7520220, www.forestpark.co.nz offer a fine selection of Eco-based log cabins and also have good campervan facilities and tent sites.

There are many backpacker beds available in the village, most being in **hostels** on Cron St, located just to the east of Main Rd. The 2 favourites are the **C-D** *Black Sheep*, T7520007, www.Franzjosef.co.nz which is located to the south of the village and the **C-D** *Chateau Franz* on Cron St, T/F7520766. The *Black Sheep* is bigger with a party type atmosphere (including the *Baah Bar*!) while the *Chateau* is more relaxing with a free spa. Both have internet. Other backpacker options include the **C-D** *YHA*, Cron St, T7520754, yhafzjo@yha.org.nz, and the **B-D** *Glow Worm Cottages*, also on Cron St, T0800151027, glowwormcottages@hotmail.com

Other than the Forest Park, the main **motorparks** are the **B-D** *Franz Josef Holiday Park*, SH6, T7520766 located 1 km south of the town and also the **A-D** *Mountain View Top Ten*, SH6, T0800467897, which, provided you are not a travel writer, will provide a warm welcome and a smile.

Eating & entertainment

The Landing, Main Rd, T7520229, is Franz Josef's newest eatery and seems to be 'going off' nicely with it's buffet dinners being especially popular ($34 all in). Open from 1800. A few doors down is the ***Beeches Café, Restaurant and Bar,*** T7520721, which offers stiff opposition to *The Landing*. Open from 0700. The restaurants in the ***Franz Josef Glacier Hotel***, T7520729, provide another à la carte option, but are often busy with bus tours. Bookings are recommended. ***The Cheeky Kea Café***, Main Rd, T7520139 is a slightly cheaper option for a snack and good breakfast (open 0700-21000) while the ***Café Franz*** in the Alpine Adventures Centre has good coffee and internet. Open 0700-1800 (seasonal). ***The Blue Ice Café/Pub***, T7520707, also serves up a good pizza and evening meals and is the main drinking and after hours entertainment establishment in the village. All out war on the free pool table a speciality. Open from 1100/ Bar 1700-0200 (seasonal). For grocery supplies you will find there is a well stocked, but expensive *Fern Grove Food Centre* on the Main Rd. Open 0745-2200 (seasonal).

Directory There are no **banks** or ATMs in the village but the *Mobil Service Station* (Glacier Motors Ltd) on Main Rd has **EFTPOS** and will cash TCs and give advance cash on credit cards, T7520725. They also act as the main **postal** agent. Open from 0800. **Foreign exchange** is available at *Fern Grove Souvenirs*, Main Rd, T7520731 (across the road from *Alpine Adventures*). **Internet** is available at *Café Franz* in the Alpine Adventure Centre, the *Franz Josef Glacier Guides/ Helicopter Line* office, Main Rd and in most backpackers. **Useful numbers Police** (Whataroa) T7534151; **Doctor** (Whataroa), T7534172; **Weatherline** T0900-99903.

Fox Glacier

Phone Code: 03
Population: 300

Many people visiting the Glacier Region only visit one of the great monoliths, with Franz Josef being the most favoured. However, if you have time, Fox Glacier (25 km south of Franz and a further 8 km southeast) is no less dramatic. The **Fox Glacier Valley** and the chilly **Fox River** which surges from the glacier terminus provide a significantly different atmosphere, with the more precipitous, ice-carved cliffs near the car park being particularly remarkable. The Fox Glacier was originally called the Victoria Glacier and was renamed in honour of former New Zealand Prime Minister, Sir William Fox, on a visit in 1872. The small village of Fox Glacier is the main service centre and sits on a site that was, as recently as 5,000 years ago, covered by the present glacier.

Although less commercial, Fox, like its neighbour Franz, can also be explored at its terminus independently, or with along with a guide, can be walked upon or climbed over. Once again however the recommendation is to admire it from the air. There are also a number of interesting walks within the valley, at the coast and around the reflective **Lake Matheson**, which lies 4 km west of the village.

Ins & outs

Note there is no petrol available between Fox Glacier and Haast (177 km)

Getting around By road Fox Glacier is 177 km north of Haast. *Intercity* (book at the Alpine Guides Centre, T7510825) and *Atomic Shuttles* (book at the Ivory Towers Backpackers, Sullivan's Rd, T7510838) provide daily, north/south **bus** services. They both stop in the centre of the village next to the Alpine Guides Centre. **Bikes** can be hired from the Fox Glacier Holiday Park, Fox Glacier Lodge and Ivory Towers Backpackers.

Information Fox village, like Franz Josef, is a small settlement based around SH6, Main Road. Everything you should need is within easy walking distance. The DOC Fox Glacier **Visitor Information Centre** is located on SH6, at the northern end (seaward side) of the village, T7510807, F7510858. Open daily 0830-1830 (winter 0900-1630). It provides detailed information about regional walks, the glacier itself and the Westland National Park. Maps and an up to date weather forecast are also provided.

Activities **Flightseeing** In Fox there are four helicopter companies (three of which also operate out of Franz); *The Helicopter Line*, Main Road T7510767, www.helicopter.co.nz offer flights from 20–40 minutes all with snow landings and a 2 ½ hours Heli-hike option; *Glacier Southern Lakes Helicopters*, Main Road, T7510803 (T0800-800732), www.heli-flights.co.nz offer flights from 10-40 minute with snow landings on flights over 30 minutes; *Fox and Franz Josef Heli-services*, Alpine Guides T7510866, www.newzealandnz.co.nz/

helicopters/ offer flights from 20-40 minute, again with snow landings on flights of 30 minutes or more; *Mountain Helicopters*, Fox Glacier Store, T7510045, www.mountainhelicopters.co.nz are another small, local company. Again as such they are perhaps the most competitive in price they better suit the budget traveller. Charters also available. Prices range from around $120-$135 for 20 minutes to $270-$280 for 40 minutes. *Ski Plane Adventures* (Aoraki Aero Company), T7520714, aoraki@aorakiaero.co.nz offer flights with a snow landing (35 minutes from $170/ 55 minutes from $235) or without (40 minutes $210/one hour $270); *Air Safaris*, Main Road, T7520716, www.airsafaris.co.nz offer a 50-minute 'Grand Traverse' flight over ten glaciers and the upper peaks of both National Parks with no snow landing, from $210. Air Safaris have been operating for 30 years.

Glacier walking, hiking and ice climbing Fox is generally accepted as the better glacier for ice climbing. *Alpine Guides*, Alpine Guides Building, Main Rd, T7510825 (T0800-111600), F7510857, www.foxguides.co.nz have been operating since 1975 and are a highly experienced and professional outfit offering 2-8 hour excursions as well as Heli-hike, ice climbing, multi-day mountaineering and high level (overnight) alpine-hut trips. Trips leave throughout the day from 0900 and include a basic guided excursion to the glacier terminus ($20). Prices are from $39 (four hours) to $385 (eight hours Heli-hike). Their ice climbing instruction days are a speciality ($150).

Walking The closest short walk is the (25 minute return) **Minnehaha Walk**, which starts beside the road just south of the village. It is a pretty rainforest walk that takes in a small **glow worm dell** ($2); best viewed with a torch at night. The glacier valley walks and the glacier itself is accessed via Glacier Road, which leaves SH6 about 1 km south of the village. The **Glacier terminus** can be accessed from the car park (one hour return) which is about 8 km from Fox village. About 3 km down Glacier Road is a small car park on the left which is the trailhead for the River (1 km, 30 minutes return) and **Chalet Lookout Walk** (4 km, two hours return). The very pleasant **River Walk** begins with a swingbridge crossing over the cold, grey, Fox River. Once across the river the track then climbs through the rainforest, offering the occasional view of the glacier, before reaching the car park and terminus of the Glacier View Road (which runs along the southern bank of the river). From here it is a steady climb through forest and across crystal clear streams to reach the lookout point. The walk itself is as good as the view. However, do not expect to get good photographs of the glacier from here since there is too much bush in the way. The walk around **Lake Matheson** (4 km west from Cook Flat, then Lake Matheson Road, 1 ½ hours return) and to the **seal colony** at **Gillespies Beach** (20 km west via Cook Flat Road) are another two excellent options. The marked route (six hours return) up **Mount Fox** (1021 m), 3 km south of the village provides great views across the higher peaks and surrounding forest.

Sleeping

AL *Glacier Country Hotel*, Main Rd, T7510847, F7510822, is an old hotel but has recently undergone refurbishment. It has a wide range of fairly unremarkable rooms from studio to single. Restaurant and bar with large open fire. Internet The slightly tired but cheaper **AL-C** *Fox Glacier Hotel*, Cook Flat Rd, T7510839, F7510868, fox.resort@xtra.co.nz is popular and spacious with standard en suites, economy twins and backpacker rooms with en suites. **AL-D** *Fox Glacier Lodge*, Main Rd, T/F7510888 has a tidy lodge with 5 en suites (two with spa) and powered sites with shared facilities. **A** *Homestead Farm B&B*, Cook Flat Rd, T7510835, is one of the few B&Bs in the village offering all the comforts of home in a century old farmhouse.

Most of the **motels** in Fox are located along Cooks Flat Rd and include the recommended; **A-B** *Rainforest Motel*, T7510140; The **B** *Lake Matheson Motel*, T7510830 and **A** *Mount Cook View Motel*, T/F7510814, listed in order of proximity to the village.

There are 2 main **hostels** in the village; The **C-D** *Fox Glacier Inn*, Sullivan's Rd, T7510022, foxglacierbackpackers@xtra.co.nz is the newest with tidy family, double or shared rooms, a café, restaurant and bar. Tents also welcome. **C-D** *Ivory Towers*, also on Sullivan's Rd, T7510838, ivorytowers@xtra.co.nz is an old favourite with a cosy atmosphere and great facilities, including a spa. Bike hire and internet. Their double rooms are especially good value. The main motorpark in the village is the very spacious **B-D** *Fox Glacier Holiday Park*, Cooks Flat Rd, T7510821. It has cabins, lodge rooms, flats, powered/tent sites and a backpacker dorm. Good facilities.

Eating & entertainment

The *Café Neve*, Main Rd, T7510110, is a pleasant place for breakfast, light snacks, home baking and coffee with outdoor seating that offers a good spot to watch the world go by. Open 0800-late (seasonal). A few doors up is the *Cook Saddle Café and Saloon*, T7510700. It offers a good meat lover's menu and has a bar. Open from 1000. The *Hobnail Café* in the Alpine Guides Centre, T7510005 offers a hearty, value breakfast and some fine home baking. Open daily 0700-1700 (seasonal). The café at Lake Matheson is a disappointment. For a beer try and a chat try the bar at the *Fox Glacier Inn*. The *General Store* on Main Rd, T7510829 is open daily from 0800-2100.

Once again there are **no banks** or ATMs but EFTPOS is accepted in most places. **Foreign currency exchange** and **postal services** are available at *Alpine Guides*, Main Rd, T7510825. Open daily 0800-2100 (winter 0830-1730). **Internet** is available upstairs in the *Glacier Country Hotel* and at the *Ivory Towers Backpackers*.

South to Haast

From Fox Glacier you leave the great glaciers and towering peaks of the National Parks behind and SH6 winds its scenic way ever southwards to Haast and to the most remote region of the West Coast – South Westland. For many years Fox was as far south as any tourist ventured, the road from there becoming rough and eventually non-existent at Paringa. With the opening of the great Haast Pass Highway in 1965 the two roads were eventually linked making the continuous journey possible. Given much of the terrain in South Westland, it is not difficult to understand why such a 'frontier' link was so late in coming. Luckily, despite the intrusion much of South Westland remains remote, unspoilt and remarkably beautiful.

Copeland Pass

The heavily forested **Copeland Valley**, 26 km south of Fox, heralds the trailhead of the **Copeland Track**. Although the complete 3-4 day tramp makes a spectacular high alpine crossing in to the Hooker Valley and, eventually, the haven of Mount Cook Village, recent rock falls have made the route very difficult and one only suited to the experienced mountaineer. Nevertheless, the 17 km overnight tramp up the Copeland Valley to the **Welcome Flat Hut** is recommended. This tramp acquaints you with some superb forest, river and mountain scenery and perhaps best of all, includes the **natural hot pools** at Welcome Flat. The one-way tramp to the hut takes about six hours. From Welcome Flat you then have the option of an overnight stay and a return, or the additional (three hours one-way) excursion higher up the valley to the Douglas Rock Hut. For detailed information get hold of the Copeland Track broadsheet from DOC. Hut fees are $8 per night and there is a resident warden at Welcome Flat between November-April.

Note that *Intercity* and *Atomic Shuttle* buses pass the Copeland Valley entrance and can drop-off or pick-up.

Bruce Bay

A further 20 km will see you rejoining the coast at Bruce Bay a quiet, scenic spot, once famous for a false **gold claim** made during the rush of 1865. Apparently in Hokitika, three miners initiated the story that they had secured a hundredweight of gold in Bruce Bay and, as a result, over 2000 hopeful souls made the long and difficult journey south. Frustrated and angry after finding nothing and realising it was a hoax, they then went on the rampage looting and destroying the makeshift stores and shanties. Although it is very pretty in itself, one of the most beautiful and scenic bays and beaches of the West Coast lies just over the headland, to the south. The much-photographed (from the air) **Heretaniwha Bay**'s golden curve of sand and rim of windshorn rimu epitomise the West Coast wilderness. With the **Bruce River** and trackless headland preventing easy access it is very difficult to reach, which is perhaps what makes it so special.

Paringa

Turning inland again the SH6 continues south to cross the **Paringa River** before arriving at **Lake Paringa**. The River is noted as the furthest point south that the intrepid early explorer **Thomas Brunner** reached in his epic 18-month journey from Nelson and the Buller Gorge in 1848. Considering it would be another 100 years before the road even reached this point, his 'feat' can only be admired. A plaque by the river honours his feat. At Lake Paringa you will find accommodation and a café. The lake is noted for its good trout **fishing** and the **Jamie Creek Walkway** (15 minutes) which negotiates a fine tract of beech and rimu, 1 km south of the café near the DOC campsite.

Sleeping and eating **B-D** *Lake Paringa Motels*, T7510894, have basic studios and units and an on-site cafe. It also rents out dinghies, canoes and issues fishing licenses. There is a DOC campsite located lakeside 1 km south of the motel. The licensed ***Salmon Farm Café***, located just north of the Paringa River, T7510837 is a popular 'quick-stop' eatery. You can either feed the salmon in the tanks below, or eat one in the café. If you are a complete heathen you can even do both! Open daily 0730-1700 (winter 0830-1600).

Lake Moeraki & Munroe Beach

The reflective waters of Lake Moeraki are a further 18 km south of Lake Paringa and 30 km north of Haast. Although popular for swimming, kayaking and birdwatching most people are in an understandable rush to share the intent of its outlet river and head straight for the beach. The car park and trailhead to Munroe Beach is located 200 m north of **Moeraki River** bridge. An easy, well-formed path through some beautiful coastal forest will deliver you to the pounding surf. It is a typical West Coast stunner and a place where wildlife abounds. In the breeding season (July-December), or during their moult in late summer, it is a great place to see the rare and beautiful **Fiordland Crested Penguin**. If you are lucky, and provided you are quiet and stay out of sight, you can watch them fighting their way through the crashing waves to waddle uneasily up the beach before disappearing quietly into the bush. It really is a wonderful spectator sport and there's not an iceberg in sight.

If the tide is well out try to investigate the beach and the Moeraki River mouth to the south of Munroe. It's even better. Note that there is one other species that is present in its thousands and a far less interesting or welcome – sandflys. Apply lots of repellent or you will re-emerge at the car park looking like a serious road accident.

Sleeping The **LL-L** *Moeraki Wilderness Lodge*, T7500881, F7500882, www.wildernesslodge.co.nz is an exclusive Eco-based DB&B establishment located beside SH6 at the Moeraki River outlet. The lodge has 22 rooms all with private facilities and an in-house restaurant. Guided nature/history walks and canoe trips are also available, with some being part of the package. The restaurant is open to non-guests.

Knight Point

South of Moeraki SH6 rejoins the coast and climbs to Knight Point with its spectacular views of sea stacks and near inaccessible beaches. Just south of the viewpoint you should be able to see **fur seals** dozing on the beach. It was just south of Knight Point that the Haast Highway was official opened in 1965 thereby connecting Otago with South Westland and the West Coast proper. At the base of the hill about 3 km south is a small car park allowing unadvertised access to **Murphy's beach**. This is a superb spot for a beach walk. If the tide is out you can explore this beautiful sweep of sand and the rugged coast north or south. Like Wharariki Beach near Farewell Spit, in the Nelson Region, you will do so feeling guilty at leaving a single set of footprints in the sand. The rock outcrops and pinnacles to the south of the beach provide some superb photo opportunities, especially at sunset.

Ship Creek

From Ship Creek SH6 hugs the coast and passes some spectacular examples of coastal rimu, rata and kahikatea forest on its approach to Haast and the Haast River crossing

A little further south is the more popular access to the beach at Ship Creek. Here you can choose from a number of excellent **short walks** that explore the beach, the coastal forest and a small lake held captive by the dunes. If the tide is out you can make the easy river crossing, negotiate the headland and explore the beaches heading north. In summer it is not unusual to see **Fiordland Crested Penguins** coming ashore to their breeding areas hidden in the coastal fringe. When it comes to an archetypal wild and remote coast it does not get much better than this. Ship Creek was named after a wreck that ironically occurred on the Australian Coast at Cape Otway in Victoria in 1854. On her maiden voyage, the 2600 tonne 'Schomberg' ran aground and several years later, pieces of the ill-fated vessel were washed up here over 1500 km away.

The Haast Region

The Haast Region of South Westland contains some of the most unspoiled eco-systems in New Zealand. The stunning scenery, from mountaintop to coastal plain, includes pristine streams that terminate in vast river mouths fringed with dense tracts of ancient coastal (Kahikatea) forests. Within the forest lie swamps and hidden lakes and all along their fringe endless swathes of beach covered in sculpted driftwood. Wildlife, too, abounds, from the playful keas of the summits to the sleepy fur seals on the coast. Few tourists stop long enough in the Haast region to truly appreciate or explore properly. But if you do Haast is an ideal base and gateway to a unique and timeless environment.

Haast

Phone Code: 03
Population: 300

From the north, a lush corridor of coastal forest and the 750 m Haast River Bridge brings you to the rather splintered settlement of Haast. The Haast River is a fitting introduction to the village and the stunning wilderness that surrounds. On the coastal plain of Haast the annual rainfall, at 5 m, is similar to that of much of the West Coast. But above 1500 m in altitude, the average can be over three times that and, after a deluge, the great river can turn into a menacing torrent. Haast is the epitome of a West Coast village – remote, unobtrusive and the home to characters full of pride and moulded by the wild, rugged and harsh environment that surrounds them.

Ins & outs

Getting there North and southbound *Intercity* and *Atomic Shuttle* services stop in Haast Township and/or the DOC VIC. *Haast Shuttles*, T7500827 provide local transportation and specialist cyclist shuttle services.

Information The DOC Haast **Visitor Information Centre** is located next to SH6 a few hundred metres past the Haast River Bridge, T7500809, F7500832. Open daily 0900-1800. As if the sculpted water features outside were not impressive enough the interior displays are memorable and all the usual information on local walks and natural attractions are provided. Ask to see the 20-min *'Edge of Wilderness'* Video which is a fine introduction to the local landscape ($3).

Haast is named after the geologist /explorer/surveyor Julius von Haast who first explored the then almost inaccessible coast in 1863. He did so via the pass to the east, which also bears his name and now provides the modern day road access. Locals, however, will pull your leg and tell you the name actually derived from a misquotation by Captain James Cook on his voyage of 1770. On sailing past he was, by all accounts, so appalled at the sight and inhospitable nature of the place, he ordered all the ships flags to be flown at half-mast. Perhaps tired and, for once, short of a name, he entered 'Half-mast' in his log. A century later, when the log was reopened, the fold in the page disguised the full name and it became known as Haast.

On initial acquaintance Haast (the 'settlement') is a bit confusing. Immediately on the southern side of the bridge is a huddle of buildings that form **Haast Junction**. This is home to the DOC Visitors Centre, a petrol station and the World Heritage Hotel. A further 4 km south of Haast Junction, on the Jackson Bay Road, is **Haast Beach** another small conglomerate, including another petrol station, a motel, foodstore and some private homes. From there the road continues for 50 km before reaching a dead-end and the remote village of **Jackson's Bay**. East of there an unsealed road accesses the **Arawata River** and the **Cascade Saddle**, a memorable day-trip. The main settlement of Haast – or **Haast Township** – is located 4 km inland and east of Haast Junction on SH6. Here you will find the major residential area, shops and most of the accommodation.

Jackson's Bay Road

Other than the obvious attractions of the coast to the north, the true wilderness of the **Arawata** and **Cascade River** Valleys south of Haast via the Jackson's Bay Road, is considered legendary. Though this stunning landscape is well worthy of some thorough investigation, the tiny pioneering settlement of **Jackson's Bay** is the main attraction.

From Haast Junction and Haast Beach, Jackson's Bay Road hosts the tiny, principally whitebaiting settlement of **Okuru** on the Okuru River before carving a straight 20 km path through native forest to the Arawata River. In the heart of this forest is the stubborn plug of bedrock known as **Mount McLean**, which like **Mosquito Hill** near Haast withstood the assaults of old glaciers. At the Arawata Bridge you are afforded a grand view up the valley before the road forks inland to the Cascade River Valley, or west along the coast to Jackson's Bay.

The unmetalled Cascade Road follows the beautiful Jackson River Valley (a tributary of the Awawata). The river itself provides a wonderful place to go fishing or simply kickback and admire the scenery but perhaps your first stop should be the walk to the hidden **Lake Ellery**. Beginning just beside the Ellery River Bridge a well-disguised track follows the river to the lake edge. It is neither well-signposted nor well-maintained, so expect to get both muddy and wet. But the beautiful reflections of the forest on the river and tranquil atmosphere of the lake itself, makes the one-hour return walk well worthwhile. Once at the lakehead you can go no further and must return the way you came.

From Lake Ellery River the Cascade Road rises steadily crossing the Martyr River and the evocatively named Monkey Puzzle Gorge, before reaching a highpoint in the valley and the road terminus. From here you are afforded an expansive view down to the **Cascade Valley** and the dramatic glacial sculpted sweep of the hills to the coast. Inland the Olivine Range and Red Hills herald the boundary of the Mount Aspiring National Park. The **Red Hills** are a particularly interesting and noted geological feature. The colouration is caused by high concentrations of magnesium and iron in the rock that has been forced up by the actions of the Austral and Pacific tectonic plates. What makes this mountain range of special interest is that their other half (Dun Mountain) now lies in the Nelson Region!

Jackson's Bay

Fighting hard to survive its wild remoteness is the interesting and historic little village of Jackson's Bay, at the end of Jackson's Bay Road. Jackson's Bay has an interesting and troubled history. Now a small fishing settlement of about 20 registered vessels moored in what is the nearest thing to a natural harbour the length of the West Coast, it was first settled by a hardy group of 400 settlers in 1875. A cosmopolitan bunch of Scandinavians, Germans, Poles, Italians, Irish, Scots and English, they set about trying to establish agriculture and the small port. However, due to the weather, poor soils and a general lack of interest from beyond, the project was a catastrophic failure. Within weeks whole families fell ill, or simply gave up and moved out. Only three years after landing the community shrank from 400 to a mere handful. Only a few of the most prosperous survivors managed to stay by founding large cattle runs.

The iron framed grave of pioneer settler Claude Morton Ollivier, who died of pneumonia only weeks after his arrival, is a fitting testament to the Europeans' failed attempts. It is the oldest known European grave on the West Coast and is located next to the main road above the beach.

Other than a wander around Jackson's Bay itself you might like to try the 1 ½ hour return **Smoothwater Track**. Beginning about 500 m north of the village it climbs the forested hill to take in the fine views north, before crossing a saddle and dropping down again to the Smoothwater River Valley and neighbouring Smoothwater Bay. One attraction not to miss in Jackson's Bay is the *Cray Pot Café*, on the waterfront (see next page).

Activities

River Safaris based in the 'Red Barn' between Haast Junction and Haast Township, T0800-865382, www.riversafaris.co.nz offer 'the world's only sea to mountain river safari' on the Waiatoto and Haast River. The two-hour trips on their purpose built (covered) jetboat depart daily at 0900,1200 and 1500 and cost from $99, child $55. Recommended. There is some superb local fishing on offer and Vern Harvey, is a local guide that will be delighted to lead the way. He also offers nature, canoe and photographic trips. Contact *Trout Fishing and Nature Tours*, South Westland, T7500820. Other personalised half-day fishing and crayfish diving trips are available with *Haast Fish and Dive*, T7500004, from $100. *Round About Haast Tours*, Jackson's Bay Road, T7500890, mauryne@xtra.co.nz operated by locals Mauryne and Bob Cannell, are an ideal way to acquaint yourself with the area, its history and folklore. The tours last from 3-4 hours and cost from $50.

Sleeping

The **AL-D** *Haast World Heritage Hotel*, Haast Junction, T0800-502444, F7500827, www.world-heritage-hotel.com has 54 en-suite units, and budget accommodation but is best known for its restaurant and bar. In Haast Beach is the modern and friendly **A-B** *Acacia and Erewhon Motel*, Jackson's Bay Rd, T7500803, F7500825. It has 3 elite (upper floor with coastal view), 4 studio and five standard units all self-contained. In Haast Township is the **A-B** *Heritage Park Lodge*, Marks Rd, T7500868, heritageparklodge@xtra.co.nz has a range of modern units and suites and a licensed restaurant on-site. Nearby, the **A-D** *Haast Highway Accommodation*, T7500703, also has a range of units, cabins, powered/tent sites and also acts as the local YHA associate. The favoured backpackers however, is the spacious, single-storey **C-D** *Wilderness Backpackers*, Pauareka Rd, T7500029. It has good value doubles, a pleasant atmosphere and Internet. Although there are powered/tent sites at the Haast Highway Accommodation, the **A-D** *Haast Beach Holiday Park* in Okuru (15 km), Jackson's Bay Rd, T/F7500860 is excellent. It offers a number of motel units, self-contained and standard cabins, but is mainly noted for its location, friendliness and good facilities.

Eating

In Haast Junction the best (and only) option is the hearty pub-grub in the *Haast World Heritage Hotel Café and Bar*, T0800502444. Open daily 0700-1000. On Marks Road in Haast Township, *Smithy's Tavern*, T7500034 is a good for pub-grub while the *Fantail Café and Restaurant*, T7500055 also offers basic meals all day from 0730-2200. The main supermarket is in **Haast Township**. Open 0730-1930 (seasonal). There is also a general store next to the motel in Haast Beach, T7500825. In **Jackson's Bay** is the *Cray Pot Café* , a quirky cross between a rail-carriage and a barge, it serves up the best fish and chips on the West Coast. You can eat in (recommended) or take away. Open 0830-1930 (winter 0900-1830).

Directory

Internet is available at the *Wilderness Backpackers*, Pauareka Rd, Haast Township. *Johnston Motors* (Caltex) in Haast Junction, beside the VIC, T7500846 has **EFTPOS** and provides AA recovery and an independent **breakdown recovery** service (a godsend!). Petrol is available 24 hrs with EFTPOS and credit cards. The Mobil Service Centre in Haast Beach, T7500802 also provides the same services and acts as **car hire** and **postal** agents.

The Haast Pass

From Haast Township SH6 turns inland and follows the bank of the **Haast River** before being enveloped by mountains and surmounting what was, until 1960, the insurmountable. The Haast Pass at 563 m is an ancient Maori greenstone trail known as Tiori-patea' which means 'the way ahead is clear'. Ironically, being the principal water catchment of the Haast River and plagued by frequent floods and landslips, the name is one of misplaced optimism as the modern day road can testify. However, although sometimes treacherous and difficult to negotiate, the crossing captures the mood of the place, with names such as the Valley of Darkness and Mount Awful. Even beside the road there is suggestion of this, with other evocative titles like 'Solitary Creek No 2' and the first of three waterfalls, **Roaring Billy**, which is located 28 km inland from Haast. Best viewed on a short (signposted) loop walk Roaring Billy plunges down mountain slopes on the opposite side of the river, and although it's only a steady flow most of the time, after heavy rains it most certainly lives up to its name.

A further 25 km, just before the 'Gates of Haast' another waterfall – the competitively named **Thunder Creek Falls** – drop a vertical 28 m into the Haast River. They too can be accessed and photographed on a short loop track from beside the road.

The gorge, known as the **'Gates of Haast',** is just a little further on and you can see the huge boulders and precipitous rock walls that proved such a barrier to road construction for so many years. Above the Gates the road and the river level off and the mountains take on a less menacing appearance, as do the waterfalls, with **Fantail Falls** (again signposted and accessed next to the road) proving far less threatening, with moderate plumes of white water tumbling over a series of rocky steps. From Fantail Falls it is only a short distance before the **Haast Pass** itself and the boundary of Westland and **Otago**. From here the scenery dramatically changes and you leave the West Coast behind (or indeed enter it).

Otago

Otago

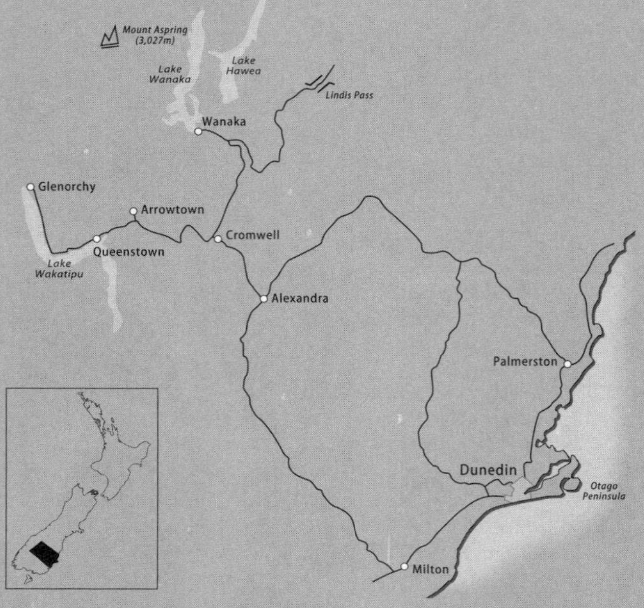

Mount Aspring (3,027m)
Lake Wanaka
Lake Hawea
Lindis Pass
Wanaka
Glenorchy
Arrowtown
Cromwell
Queenstown
Lake Wakatipu
Alexandra
Palmerston
Dunedin
Otago Peninsula
Milton

If the Otago Region were a girl she would be a very engaging sort, from a good Scots background, and good-looking. Her topography and scenery varies from the towering peaks of **Fiordland** *and* **Mount Aspiring National Parks** *in the west, to the gently rolling hills, harbours and golden beaches of the* **Otago Peninsula** *to the east. Her two large blue eyes would be* **Lakes Wakatipu** *and* **Wanaka**. *And down her entire length carves the vein of New Zealand's second longest river, the* **Clutha**. *In personality and mood too, there is also huge variety: from the student city buzz of* **Dunedin** *to the quiet whispers of* **Glenorchy** *or* **Clyde.** *Otago is also down-to-earth and wears her heart on her sleeve. She has distinct seasons: cold and snowy in winter; miserable with rain in spring; and boasting beautiful golden hues in autumn. Otago owes her considerable pedigree to her predominantly Scots heritage and the discovery of gold, a resource that was once her lifeblood. Now, though, the region pumps fast and furious with sheer adrenaline. Although Otago's head is in* **Dunedin**, *her heart is in* **Queenstown** *– the adventure sports capital of the world. Otago is not only pretty, she also knows how to have a good time.*

Things to do in Otago

- *Explore the Scots heritage and architecture of Dunedin. Try 'rolling your R's' with the locals.*
- *Go to a rugby game at Carrisbrook – the visitors' 'House of Pain'.*
- *Marvel at the grace of the albatross or the charms of the yellow-eyed penguins on the Otago Peninsula.*
- *Try gold panning in the historic Central Otago goldfields.*
- *Go canyoning, tandem skydiving or skiing in Wanaka. Take a scenic flight to Milford.*
- *Walk to the base of the Rob Roy Glacier – the best day-walk in the region.*
- *Take in the remarkable view from the Remarkables.*
- *Go on, make the jump in Queenstown!*
- *Visit the real Paradise north of Glenorchy.*

Ins and outs

Getting there By **road** Otago is reached from the north via the West Coast (SH6) or via the East Coast and Christchurch (SH1). Dunedin is the largest town and the capital, located 362 km south of Christchurch. Queenstown, the adrenaline capital, is 486 km south of Christchurch.

By **bus** the region is generally well served throughout. By **air** both Queenstown and Dunedin airports are served by ***Air New Zealand Link*** from Christchurch and Auckland. A the time of going to print the **train** service from Christchurch to Dunedin and south to Invercargill was threatened with extinction, or at the very least a period of dormancy, but this situation may change.

Getting around Queenstown is 283 km from Dunedin via SH8 and SH6, Wanaka 276 km via SH8. Wanaka is 117 km from Queenstown via SH6 and SH8 or 70 km via the newly sealed Cardrona Road. There are many and regular **bus** services from Dunedin to Queenstown and Wanaka. The principal operators are ***Intercity***, T4425628; ***Atomic Shuttles***, T4428178; and ***Southern Link***, T3588355. ***Wanaka Connections***, T0800-879926, run between Queenstown and Wanaka.

Information There are major VICs in Dunedin, Wanaka and Queenstown, with smaller local centres in Alexandra, Arrowtown, Cromwell and Oamaru. DOC has offices in Dunedin Queenstown, Wanaka and Alexandra. These are all listed in the relevant sections. The main websites are www.CityofDunedin.com/www.queenstown-nz.co.nz and www.lakewanaka.co.nz

Dunedin

Phone code: 03
Population: 120,000

There is perhaps nowhere else in the world – and certainly nowhere so far from its roots – that boasts a Scottish heritage like Dunedin, the South Island's second largest city. For those who have walked the centuries old streets of Edinburgh in Scotland, let alone lived there, a trip to Dunedin (which actually means 'Edin on the hill') is somewhat disconcerting. Immediately, one will notice the echo of Scottish architecture – grand buildings of stone, built to last, that go far beyond the merely functional and, in true Scots tradition, defy inclement weather. The streets are blatant in their similarity, even share the names of Edinburgh's most famous – Princes Street, George Street and Moray Place – and, presiding over the scene, in its very heart, a statue of one of Scotland's greatest sons, the poet Robert Burns. Now, as you ponder his gentle expression of intellect, with the seemingly omnipresent seagull perched on his head, you cannot help but wonder what he would say about this pseudo-Scots city, so very far from home.

Although a lively and attractive city, Dunedin has seen better days. In the 1860s, thanks to the great Otago gold boom, it enjoyed prosperity and considerable standing as the largest city in the land. Between 1861 and 65 its population grew by 500% to 10,000 and a decade later it was even the first place outside the USA to have a tram system. But as ever the gold ran out, decline set in and very quickly Dunedin, like so many other places in the South Island, had to learn how to survive where once it thrived. Having said that, modern day Dunedin has many assets, of which its university and rare wildlife are perhaps the best known. In term time the city boasts a population of 18,000 students who study at Otago University, New Zealand's oldest seat of learning, while the Otago Peninsula, Dunedin's beautiful backyard, is home to another form of wildlife – the only mainland-breeding colony of albatross, the rare yellow-eyed penguins and Hookers sealions. Other activities in the immediate area include sea kayaking, cruising and walking. There is one other undeniable asset to Dunedin, and one that can be attributed to its Scots heritage: without doubt it has the friendliest people and offers the warmest welcome in New Zealand.

Ins and outs

Getting there

Dunedin is 362 km south of Christchurch and 217 km north of Invercargill via SH1. Queenstown is 283 km south then west via SH8. **By bus** Dunedin is served by ***Intercity***, 205 St Andrew St, T4749600 (Christchurch/Invercargill/Queenstown/Wanaka); ***South Island Connections***, T3666633 (Christchurch); ***Atomic Shuttles***, T4774449 (Christchurch/Invercargill/Queenstown/Wanaka); ***Southern Link***, T3588355 (Queenstown/Wanaka). Both *Atomic Shuttles* and *Southern Link Shuttles* stop at the train station. The ***Catlins Coaster***, T4743300, and The ***Bottom Bus***, T4429708, serve the Catlins to Invercargill and provide pick-up/drop-off. Dunedin **airport** is located about 27 km south of the city; ***Air New Zealand Link***, T0800-737000; fly daily to Christchurch, Wellington, Auckland and Rotorua. ***Southern Air***, T2189129, fly to Stewart Island (Mon/Wed/Fri/Sun); ***Freedom Air***, T0800-600500, provide *Trans-Tasman* flights to Eastern Australia. Other domestic carriers and routes were under negotiation at the time of going to print. The daily 'Southerner' **train** service to Christchurch is under threat, but this situation may change, T4774499.

Getting around

Citibus, T4775577, are one of several suburban **bus** companies that serve Dunedin and its surrounds. The VIC has timetables. City buses stop in the **Octagon**, the distinctive heart of the city. For bus services to the Otago Peninsula see Otago Peninsula section below. For ***Airport Shuttles***, T4762519, or the major taxi firms (from $12-$15 one-way). For **taxis, car rental and bike** hire, see 'Directory' below. **Taxis** ***City Taxis***, T0800-771771, ***Dunedin Taxis***, T4777777..

Information & orientation

Although they could never be as ancient or as fine as their real namesakes in Edinburgh, **Princes St** and **George St** combine to form the main thoroughfare through the city centre, with the **Octagon** forming its heart. Generally the Central Business District is easily negotiated by foot, and even by car makes a pleasant change to the charmless, flat streets of Auckland or Christchurch. You will find most restaurants and cafés at the northern end of George St or around the Octagon.

The Dunedin **Visitor Information Centre** is located on the Octagon at Number 48, below the magnificent Municipal Chambers Building, T4743300, F4743311, www.CityofDunedin.com Open daily 0800-1800 (winter 0830-1700, Sat/Sun

Dunedin

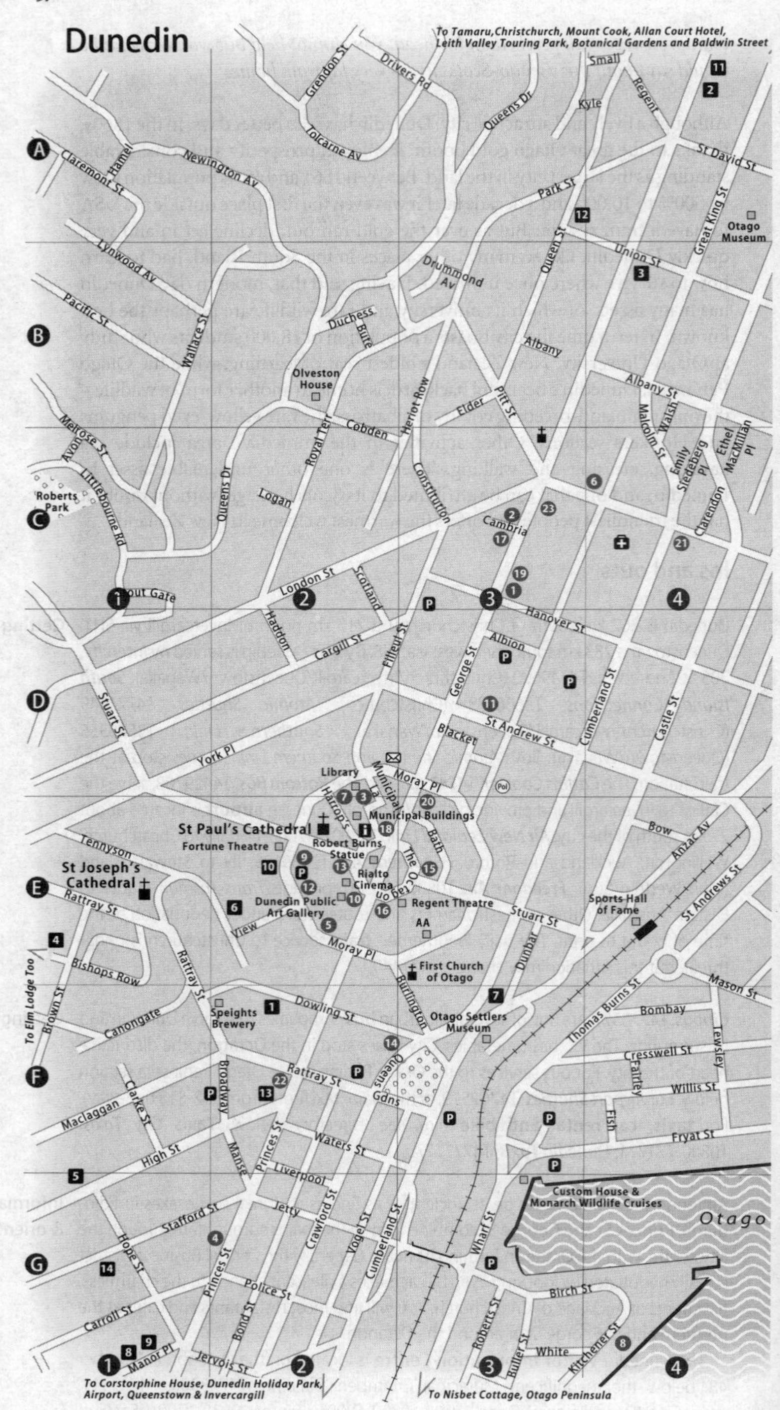
To Tamaru,Christchurch, Mount Cook, Allan Court Hotel, Leith Valley Touring Park, Botanical Gardens and Baldwin Street
Grendon St
Drivers Rd
Small
Kyle
Regent
Tolcarne Av
Queens Dr
St David St
Hamel
Claremont St
Newington Av
Park St
Great King St
Otago Museum
Queen St
Union St
Lynwood Av
Drummond Av
Pacific St
Wallace St
Duchess
Bute
Albany
Albany St
Olveston House
Heriot Row
Elder
Pitt St
Malcolm St
Walsh
Emily Siedeberg Pl
Ethel MacMillan Pl
Melrose St
Avonie
Cobden
Royal Terr
Littlebourne Rd
Queens Dr
Logan
Constitution
Roberts Park
Cambria
Clarendon
London St
Scotland
Out Gate
Hanover St
Haddon
Cargill St
Filleul St
Albion
George St
Stuart St
Blacket
St Andrew St
Cumberland St
Castle St
York Pl
Library
Municipal La
Harrop St
Moray Pl
Municipal Buildings
St Paul's Cathedral
Fortune Theatre
Robert Burns Statue
Bath
Tennyson
Rialto Cinema
The Octagon
Bow
Anzac Av
St Joseph's Cathedral
Dunedin Public Art Gallery
Regent Theatre
Stuart St
Sports Hall of Fame
St Andrews St
Rattray St
View
AA
Moray Pl
Bishops Row
First Church of Otago
Dunbar
To Elm Lodge Too
Brown St
Rattray St
Speights Brewery
Dowling St
Burlington
Otago Settlers Museum
Thomas Burns St
Mason St
Bombay
Canongate
Tewsley
Queens Gdns
Cresswell St
Fairley
Willis St
Rattray St
Broadway
Clarke St
Maclaggan
Manse
Princes St
Waters St
Fish
Fryat St
High St
Liverpool
Custom House & Monarch Wildlife Cruises
Otago
Stafford St
Jetty
Crawford St
Vogel St
Cumberland St
Wharf St
Hope St
Princes St
Police St
Birch St
Carroll St
Bond St
Roberts St
Butler St
White
Kitchener St
Manor Pl
Jervois St
To Corstorphine House, Dunedin Holiday Park, Airport, Queenstown & Invercargill
To Nisbet Cottage, Otago Peninsula

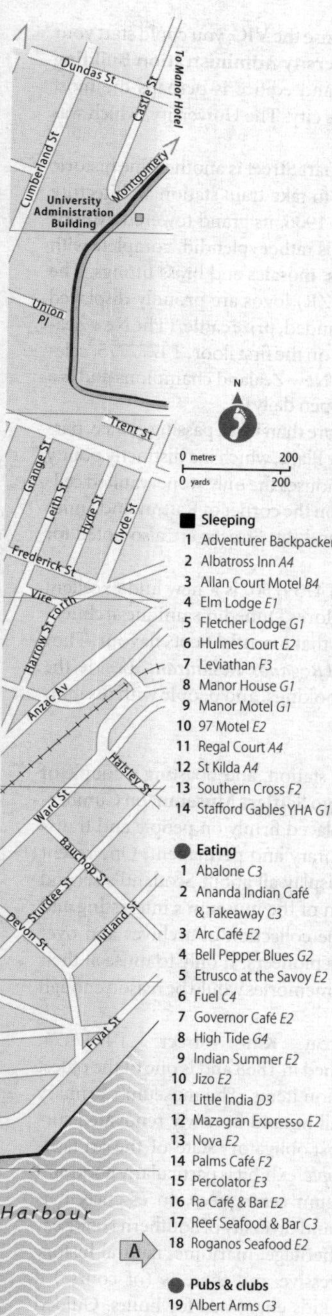

0900-1700). It is an efficient centre that can provide free city maps and advice on local tours and activities, particularly to the Otago Peninsula. **DOC** are located a short distance away, west, at 77 Lower Stuart St, T4770677. Open Mon-Fri 0800-1700.

Otago

History

The largest Maori *pa* in the area was located on the Otago Peninsula at Otakau, which saw its fair share of inter-tribal disputes before being ravaged by diseases brought by the early European whalers and sealers. Otakau is also the source of the name Otago that came about through a mispronunciation by the early pioneers. The first seeds of Dunedin's settlement and creation were sown in 1842 by Scots parliamentarian George Rennie, who, concerned at the levels of poverty and unemployment in Scotland, presented a plan for Presbyterian colonization in a 'New Edinburgh' of the south. Although this idea was initially declined, it was adapted and later accepted by a 300-strong Free Church colony that, arrived in 1848, under the leadership of Captain Cargill (of Invercargill fame) and the Reverend Dr Thomas Burns. With the discovery of gold just over a decade later the population exploded, and the town developed into a cosmopolitan, commercial centre, becoming the largest and most prosperous city in New Zealand by the late 1860's. Despite the loss of gold as a resource, Dunedin has been more successful than most in retaining a strong economic base, and is now a pleasant mix of old and new.

Sights

Architecture

A good way to get an immediate feel for Dunedin is with a quick tour of its finest architecture. Perhaps already acquainted with the Statue of **Robert Burns** presiding over the Octagon, and the grand **Municipal Buildings** that house the VIC, you could start your tour with a visit to the original **Otago University Administration Building and clock tower** on Leith Street. This grand edifice is perhaps the most famous and most photographed icon in the city. The University, which was New Zealand's first, was founded in 1869.

The **train station** at the end of Lower Stuart Street is another fine historic example, echoing that typical Scots desire to take train station architecture way beyond the purely functional. Built in 1906, its grand towered exterior cannot fail to impress, but the interior too is rather splendid, complete with stained glass windows, Royal Doulton tiles, mosaics and brass fittings. The almost omnipresent New Zealand Rail (NZR) logos are proudly displayed with more repetition than a large herd of branded, prize cattle. (The New Zealand **Sports Hall of Fame**, which is housed on the first floor, T4777775, celebrates the legacy of more than a century of New Zealand champions and is a worthy attraction for any avid sports fan (open daily).

The city's churches are also worthy of more than just a passing glance, particularly the **First Church of Otago**, Moray Place, which is a distinctly pointy affair, and **St Paul's** in the Octagon which houses the only stone-vaulted ceiling in the country. **St Joseph's Cathedral**, on the corner of Rattray and Smith Street and the **Knox Church**, on George and Pitt Streets, are also noted for their robust architectural aesthetics.

'Behind the Tartan', 19 Bond Street, T4739730, is a new and excellent guided 90-minute **heritage walk** that explores Dunedin's unique architectural and cultural heritage served up with that essential Scots flavour. They depart daily from the Highland Room (*Roganos Restaurant*, beside the VIC); $20, child $10. The VIC will take bookings, and people with disabilities are welcome.

Museums & galleries

Just a few hundred metres from the train station, and boasting a couple of monstrous historic steam trains, is the **Otago Settlers Museum**, on Cumberland Street, T4775052. The emphasis is placed firmly on people and transport, with many fine exhibits both temporary and permanent. One recent temporary exhibition was a fascinating display all about Scotland's second national drink – tea – which is a reflection of the museum's interesting and imaginative approach. There is also a fine collection of archives and over 20,000 photographic portraits of the early pioneers. If only to muse at their hardy, hopeful expressions and eyes full of memories would be reason enough to visit. ■ *Daily 1000-1700, $4, child, free.*

The **Otago Museum**, 419 Great King Street, T4747474, www.otagomuseum.govt.nz was established in 1868 and is one of the oldest in the country, with a staggering 1.7 million items. The museum's primary themes are culture, nature and science, all housed in newly renovated surroundings and displayed in the now almost obligatory state-of-the-art fashion. The new *'Southern Land-Southern People'* exhibit is particularly good and has been designed to become the museum centrepiece. In essence, it is intended to reflect the uniqueness, beauty and diversity of Southern New Zealand. The traditional Maori and Pacific heritage, maritime, natural history and archaeology displays are also impressive and there is (of course) a hands-on *'Discovery World'* to keep the kids engrossed for hours. Guided tours of the museum are available. ■ *Daily 1000-1700, donation ($5 encouraged). 'Discovery World' and some temporary exhibitions are extra.*

Aside from the safe, but unintentionally wobbly, grand-staircase in its foyer, the **Dunedin Public Art Gallery**, provides a grand and stable platform to display a fine collection of traditional and contemporary art. It is the oldest art gallery in the country and of special note is its collection of New Zealand works that date from 1860 to the present day. There are also some works by the more familiar iconic names like Turner, Gainsborough and Monet. ■ *Daily 1000-1700, free.*

The **Milford Galleries**, 18 Dowling Street, T4778275, are considered to be one of the countries leading dealer galleries and represent over 130 of New Zealand's foremost artists. ■ *Mon-Fri 0830-1700, Sat 1100-1500.*

At 42 Royal Terrace is the 1906 'Edwardian time capsule' of **Olveston House**. Bequeathed to the city in 1966 by the last surviving member of the wealthy and much travelled Theomin family, the 35-room mansion comes complete with an impressive 'collection of collections', containing many unique items from the Edwardian era. It gives an interesting insight into Dunedin of old, and the lives of the more prosperous pioneer! ■ *Guided tours are recommended and available daily at 0930/1045/1200/1330/1445 and 1600, $11, child $3.*

Otago

Breweries

Although Dunedin hosts many fine Scottish churches it also, not surprisingly, pays homage to that other great Scottish religion, the alcoholic beverage. South Island's iconic Speights Ale is the worship of many a 'Good Southern Man' and its communion is to be found in the hallowed walls of the surprisingly small **Speights Brewery**, 200 Rattray Street, T4777697, www.speights.co.nz Heritage **tours** and **tastings** are available daily but, unlike the churches these days, bookings are essential. From $12, child $4. If beer is not your tipple perhaps you might like to visit the **Weston Vintage Winery**, 25 Forresbank, Wakari, T4675544. Although not quite in the same league as its many New Zealand counterparts it can boast of being the world's most southerly winery.

The Taieri Gorge Railway & the Otago Central Rail Trail

The Taieri Gorge Railway is considered a world-class train trip, encompassing the scenic splendour and history of Otago's hinterland. The former goldfields supply line was completed in 1891, and as one negotiates the **Taieri Gorge**, with the aid of 12 viaducts and numerous tunnels, it very quickly becomes apparent why it took over 12 years to build. The four-hour trip gets off to a fine start amidst the splendour of Dunedin's grand train station, before heading inland to the gorge and Pukerangi. An informative commentary is provided along the way, and you are allowed to disembark at certain points of interest. Also, if you ask really nicely, you may also be able to ride alongside the locomotive engineer. Licensed snack bar on board. ■ *Trips depart daily Oct-Mar at 1430 and Apr-Sep at 1230, T4774449, $35.* If you wish you can extend the rail journey by coach across the rugged **Maniototo Plateau** to **Queenstown** (6 ½ hours), from $99. Another popular alternative is to take a mountain bike (no extra charge) and disembark at **Middlemarch** (only selected trains, but one-way fares available). From there you can negotiate the 150-km **Otago Central Rail Trail** (the former goldfields railway from Middlemarch to Clyde). It is a wonderful bike ride that includes over 60 bridges, viaducts and tunnels, and much of Central Otago's classic scenery. Horse trekking is also an option. For more details call in at the train station or T4774449, www.taieri.co.nz DOC in conjunction with the Otago Central Rail Trail Trust also provide an excellent leaflet *'Otago Central Rail Trail Middlemarch – Clyde'* that is available from DOC or the VIC.

Other attractions

There are many New Zealand 'firsts' in Dunedin, including the **Botanical Gardens** located on North Road. Nurtured since 1914, the 28-ha site is split into upper and lower gardens that straddle Signal Hill. Combined they form an interesting topography and all the usual suspects, with a particular bent on rhododendrons, plants from the Americas, Asia and Australia, native species, winter and wetland gardens. If you tire of the flora there is also a modern aviary complex, housing many exotic and native birds including the 'cheeky' kea and kaka parrots. Also on site are information points, a basic café and a small shop, all located in the Lower Garden. Access to the Lower Garden is from Cumberland Street, while the Upper Garden is reached via Lovelock Lane. The **Centennial Lookout** (6-km 1 ½ hours' walk) and **Lookout Point** offer grand views of the harbour and the city, and are accessed via Signal Hill Road (beyond Lovelock Avenue). ■ *Open from dawn to dusk.*

You might also like to visit the famed **Baldwin Street**, which at a gradient of nearly 1 in 3 (38° angle), is reputed to be the steepest street in the world. It's worth a look, if only to work out the building methodology and what happens when the residents are eating at a table, in the bath or shooting some pool.

The aptly named 'Gut-Busters' race is held annually during the Dunedin Festival to see who can reach the top and back again in around two minutes. Doubtless the street has been the scene of much fun over the years, but in 2001 the irresistible desire to defy or master gravity turned to tragedy when a young student took a 'wheelie-bin' (used for rubbish) to the top of the street, climbed in and launched herself down the hill toboggan-style. Sadly, the result was fatal and Baldwin Street claimed its first life. To reach Baldwin Street, head north via Great King Street then veer right at the Botanical Gardens on to North Road. Baldwin is about 1 km (10th street) on the right.

Tunnel Beach (1 km, one hour return), located south of the city centre near Blackhead (car park seaward end of Green Island Bush Rd off Blackhead Road), is a popular spot and a precursor to the splendid coastal scenery of the Otago Peninsula. A steep path through some bush delivers you to some impressive weathered sandstone cliffs and arches. For details see DOCs '*Tunnel Beach Walk*' broadsheet. If you do not have your own wheels take the Corstorphine bus from the city centre to Stenhope Crescent (start of Blackhead Road) and walk from there.

Activities & tours

For the highly popular attractions and tours beyond Dunedin to the Otago Peninsula see the Otago Peninsula, section below.

Flightseeing *Mainland Air*, Dunedin Airport, T4862200, www.mainlandair.com (from 30 minutes, $95), and *Dunedin Helicopters*, T4897322 offer flights locally or to Queenstown and Wanaka.

Golf Dunedin claims yet another first having created the first Golf Club in the Southern Hemisphere in 1871. From humble beginnings the *Otago Golf Club*, 125 Balmacewen Road, was officially formed in 1892 and is regarded as one of the best 18-hole courses in the country. The clubhouse also houses an interesting collection of early memorabilia, cups and medals, T4672099, green-fees from $50.

Horse trekking *Bums 'n' Saddles*, T4880097, are based in Blackhead, south of the city, and negotiate a network of coastal beach tracks, two hours from $25.

Mountain biking Other than the obvious attraction of the *Otago Central Rail Trail* (see 'Sights' above), there are a number of other shorter tracks available in the area. These are outlined in '*Mountain Bike Rides in Dunedin*', available free from the VIC.

Sightseeing tours

For Eco-Tours see page 20

Newton Tours, T4775577, provide a fun 1½-hour double-decker bus tour of the major city sights and depart from the VIC daily at 1000 and again at 1530. From $15, child $8. 'Under the Kilt' is run by the same outfit (excuse the pun), who do the popular 'Beyond the Tartan Tour' (see 'Sights' above). This one involves all the same features as the Tartan Tour with the added attraction of a lone piper and a modern-day Robbie Burns, who will provide exerts of poems in a suitable Scots brogue. There is also a *'Meal and Entertainment'* option (sadly salmon and venison as opposed to traditional haggis caught and exported from Scotland) and additional entertainment, or a 'Total Package' which combines the two. Tours depart Wednesdays from the 'Highland Room' of *Roganos Restaurant* beside the VIC. Bookings can be made at the VIC. Walk/Piper/Robbie Burns costs from $30, child $15; Meal and Entertainment $60, child $35; Total Package from $80, child $45. *Dunedin City Heritage Tours* offer a variety of scenic and informative road trips in classic jaguar limousines, and depart from the VIC daily at 1245, T0800-346370, from $54, child $40. *Country Tours*, T4675041, are a knowledgeable and friendly operator that offer individually designed trips from half- to multi-day, and specialize in garden and nature tours in Dunedin and beyond. Accommodation can also be arranged. *Arthur's Tours* are a similar operator, T0800-840729, www.arthurstours.co.nz *Otago Highland Safaris*, 19 Bond Street, T4739730, offer a wide array of day trips by road, bike or on foot to a number of attractions including the Taieri Gorge, working goldmines, historic homes, gardens and nature reserves.

Walking

Other than the **Centennial Lookout** (Signal Hill) and **Tunnel Beach** (see Sights above), another recommended local walk is to the summit of **Mount Cargill** with its wonderful views across the city and the Otago Peninsula. It can be accessed by foot (4 km, 3 ½ hours return) from Bethunes Gully (Norwood Street off North Road past the Botanical Gardens), or via Cowan Road (off Pine Hill Road which is off SH1 heading north). For details consult the DOC broadsheet *'Mt Cargill and Organ Pipes Walk'*, available from DOC or the VIC.

Essentials

Sleeping

Dunedin City has a good range of options, and you might also like to consider those available on the Otago Peninsula (see below). For both, pre-booking in summer is advised

L-A ***Southern Cross***, corner of Princes and High Sts, T4770752, F4775776, reservations@southerncross.co.nz is Dunedin's premier hotel, well located in the heart of the city centre, with 131 rooms and 8 suites. Its history dates back to 1883 when it was the original Grand Hotel, but it now boasts all the mod cons of the Scenic Circle Chain with an in-house bar/restaurant.The **LL** ***Corstorphine House***, 23A Milburn St, Corstorphine, T4876676, T4876672, www.corstorphine.co.nz is a popular 1863 Edwardian luxury lodge offering 6 en-suites with great views across the city. The house is beautifully appointed throughout and is surrounded by 12 acres of private gardens. **L** ***Fletcher Lodge***, 276 High St, T4775552, F4775551, lodge@es.co.nz This is another luxury establishment set in an elegant historic mansion. There are 5 en-suites all richly furnished with antiques.

The **AL-B** ***Leviathan Hotel***, located near the train station at 27 Queens Gdens, T4773160, F4772385, leviathan@xtra.co.nz is another historic, renovated place that is friendly, great value and well located. It has a range of rooms from self-contained suites (with spas) to budget rooms. Restaurant and internet. **AL-A** ***Hulmes Court***, 52 Tennyson St, T4775319, F4775310, www.hulmes.co.nz is a cheaper option set in an 1860s Victorian mansion close to the city centre, and comes complete with a friendly ex-stray cat called Solstice. It offers 1 en suite, 3 doubles and a single. **AL** ***Nisbet Cottage***, 6A Eliffe Pl, Sheil Hill, T4545169, F4545369, www.wingsokotuku.co.nz is conveniently located at the base of the Otago Peninsula and offers 3 very private rooms, one with a superb view across the city. The German couple also operate Otago Nature Tours (see Otago Peninsula activities) and can organize multi-day nature tours to the Catlins and Stewart Island. The **B** ***Albatross Inn***, 770 George St, T4772727, F4772108, albatross.inn@xtra.co.nz is a pleasant and spacious budget B&B with 13 rooms, well located close to the city centre.

There are plenty of **motels** to choose from in Dunedin, with most being located along the main drags in and out of town, particularly **George St**. The closest to the Octagon, and one of the best, is the friendly **AL-A** ***97 Motel*** hidden away at 97 Moray Pl, T4772050, F4771991, info@97 motel.co.nz It offers a wide variety of standard and executive units that are quiet, well appointed, and all within a stones throw of the Otagon. Along George St the award-winning **A** ***858 George St***, no prizes for guessing the number, T/F4740047, www.858georgestreetmotel.co.nz is recommended; other good options include the **A** ***Allan Court Motel***, at 590 T4777526, F4474937, allan.court@earthlight.co.nz, and the **A** ***Regal Court***, at 755, T/F4777729. Elsewhere the **A** ***Commodore Luxury***, 932 Cumberland St, T4777766, F4777750, commodore.motels@xtra.co.nz and cheaper **B** ***Manor Motel***, 22 Manor Place, T4776729, F4776729, manormotel@cartwright.co.nz and **B** ***St Kilda***, 105 Queens Drive, T/F4551151, are recommended.

Otago

The **C-D** ***Elm Lodge***, up the hill from the Octagon at 74 Elm Row, T4741872, is noted not so much for its accommodation (though there is no problem there) but for its superb adjunct operation the Elm Nature Tours, run by the friendly and nature-loving owners. (See Otago Peninsula activities.) The accommodation is comfortable with dorms and doubles, and fine views, and all comes amidst a very congenial atmosphere. Elm also run another over-flow establishment the ***Elm Lodge Too*** further up the hill. Pick-ups and internet. The **C-D** ***Stafford Gables YHA***, 71 Stafford St, T4741919, is a rambling old villa that has been recently renovated. Dorms, singles and doubles. Internet. The **C-D** ***Manor House***, 28 Manor Pl, T4770484, located near the YHA, is another historic colonial villa that has new kitchen and dining areas with dorms, twins and doubles. Bike hire. The **C-D** ***Adventurer Backpackers***, 37 Dowling St, T/F4777367, is yet another spacious, historic villa, and a popular choice with the highly active. Dorms, singles, twins and doubles. Open fire, No TV! Internet. Located close to the Octagon.

Motorcamps The **B-D** ***Leith Valley Touring Park***, 103 Malvern St, T4679936, is located towards the northern end of town in a sheltered setting next to the Leith Stream. It has modern self-contained cabins, powered and tent sites. Another option lying alongside St Kilda Beach at the other end of town is the **B-D** ***Dunedin Holiday Park***, 41 Victoria Rd, T/F4554690. It has modern facilities, en suite units, standard cabins, flats and powered and tent sites.

Eating

There is plenty of choice in Dunedin, with over 140 restaurants and cafés, with most being located along George St or around The Octagon. You will also find 2 ***Star 24 hr*** shops in George St.

Expensive ***Roganos Seafood Restaurant***, 38 The Octagon, T4775748, is an old seafood favourite and conveniently located next to the VIC. The seafood platter is monumental. Open daily 1730-late. ***Bell Pepper Blues***, 474 Princes St, T4740973, is a few mins' walk from the Octagon but worth it. The menu is highly imaginative and the service and presentation is excellent. Open lunch Wed-Fri, dinner Mon-Sat from 1830.

Mid-range Along with the cafés mentioned below, the following are recommended: The very grand ***Etrusco at the Savoy***, 8A Moray Pl (first floor), T4773737, is a fine Italian choice that is good value despite the plush surroundings. Open daily from 1730. ***High Tide***, 29 Kitchener St, T4779784, provides a convenient escape from the city centre and looks over the harbour. It has a mainly seafood and traditional NZ/Euro menu. Open Tue-Sat from 1800. The chic ***Abalone***, 1st Floor corner of

George and Hanover Sts, T4776877, is popular for traditional Euro/NZ fare. Open Mon-Fri 1200-late, Sat 1700-late. Other noted restaurants in the affordable range are ***Restaurant Ninety-Five***, 95 Filleul St, T4719265. Open Mon-Sat 0600-late; and ***The Two Chefs***, 428 George St, T4779117. Open Mon-Sat from 1800. Both of the latter have imaginative Euro/NZ menus. ***Little India***, 82 St Andrew St, T4776559, and ***Indian Summer***, Cnr Upper Stuart and Moray Pl, T4778880, are both affordable and recommended Indian restaurants

Cheap The ***London Lounge*** above the ***Albert Arms***, corner of George and Hanover Sts, T4778035, is recommended for traditional pub grub. Open Mon-Thu 1100-2230, Fri/Sat 1100-2300, Sun 1130-2130. For fish and chips look no further than the takeaway attached to the ***Reef Seafood Restaurant and Bar***, 329 George St, T4717185. On George St you will also find plenty of cheap **Asian** eateries and takeaways designed to keep poverty stricken students happy, with numerous Thai and Chinese options particularly between St Andrew and Fredrick Sts. The ***Ananda Indian Café and Takeaway***, 365 George St, T4771120, is noted for its vegetarian dishes. Open Mon-Sat 1130-1430 and 1700-2100.

Cafés

For the best coffee the specialist coffeehouse ***Mazagran Expresso***, 36 Moray Pl, T4779959, is recommended. There are plenty of cafés around the Octagon. ***The Nova*** (29), located next to the *Dunedin Art Gallery*, T4790808 (open Mon-Wed 0800-1800, Thu/Fri 0800-late, Sat 1000-late, Sun 1000-1700), is a good place for brunch, breakfast and even sells porridge. ***The Percolator***, 142 Lower Stuart St, T4775462 (open Sun-Thu 0900-2300, Fri/Sat 0900-late) is also recommended. The ***Governor Café***, 438 George St, T4776871, is no great shakes aesthetically but is very popular, with a cosmopolitan clientele, good-value meals (especially breakfasts) and an internet suite upstairs. Open daily 0800-late. The ***Arc Café***, 135 High St, T4741135, is a very popular place with local artists, 'musos' and laid-back students. It's great for a coffee and offers regular live gigs. Free email. Open Mon-Sat from 1200. ***Fuel***, 21 Frederick St, T4772575, provides plenty of the coffee variety and is a popular spot with students, subsequently having a lively atmosphere, pool and internet. Open Sun-Mon 0930-1800, Tue/Wed 0930-2100, Thu-Sat 0930-late. ***Palms Café***, 18 Queens Gardens, T4776534, is in a nice spot overlooking the war memorial, and is popular with locals. It offers a value four-course à la carte menu and does a 'Homeward Bound' special for $15 on Mon-Fri between 1700 and 1830. A la carte open daily from 1800. Lunches Wed-Sun. ***Jizo*** is a pleasant Japanese café at 56 Princes St, T4792692, offering very affordable sushi. Open Mon-Thu/Sat 1100-2100, Fri 1100-2200.

Entertainment

There is a healthy music, arts and cultural scene in Dunedin, and the best place to view current event and gig listings is in the *Otago Daily Times*. Dunedin hosts its own ***Fortune Theatre Company***, corner of Moray Pl and Stuart St, T4771292, www.fortunetheatre.co.nz with 2 venues: the Mainstage and Studio Theatres. They play from Feb to Dec, Tue-Sun. The ***Regent Theatre***, T4778597, on the Octagon, hosts the annual film festival and touring national and international shows. If gambling is your thing the small and smart ***Dunedin Casino*** is located in the Southern Cross Hotel, T4774545. Open Sun-Thu 1100-1500, Fri/Sat 1100-1600. The main cinema is the ***Multiplex*** on the Octagon, with the ***Rialto*** being another located on Moray Pl, T4742200 (Mon/Tue cheap night, $8). The ***Metro*** in the Town Hall is a venue that boasts 'No raincoats, no popcorn, no dinosaurs – just the finest films', hosting the best in Euro-Arthouse Film, T4743350, www.artfilms.co.nz

Pubs & clubs

The Scots pub ***Robert Burns*** on George St, and the ***Albert Arms*** across the road (corner of Hanover St), are both popular drinking establishments, especially with the younger set, and they often stage live gigs. The café/bars that surround the Octagon are also popular, especially at the weekends and with the mobile-phone brigade. Of these, ***The Ra Café and Bar*** at 21, T4776080, and the ***Bennu Café and Bar***, 12 Moray Pl, T4745055, are particularly well frequented. For a good all-round drinking, eating and music venue the ***Woolshed Bar and Grill***, 318 Moray Pl, T4773246, is good, while for the full 'shake of the pants' the ***Bath St***, 1 Bath St, T4776750 (open 2200-late), and the ***Bowler*** on Cumberland St (off Frederick St), are recommended.

Events The most noted annual events are ***The Dunedin Summer Festival***, which is held over 4 weeks kicking off in Feb, followed close on its heels by the ***Dunedin Food and Wine Festival*** and ***Scottish Week*** in Mar. The ***Dunedin Film Festival*** is focused on the Regent Theatre in Jul/Aug while ***Rhododendron Week*** blossoms in Oct. For more information on these or other annual events contact the VIC or www.CityofDunedin.com

Directory All the main **banks** are represented along Princes and George Sts, with many accommodating **currency exchange** services. *Thomas Cook* are on the corner of St Andrew and George St, T4777204 (open Mon-Fri 0830-1700, Sat 1000-1230). **Bike hire** ***Cycle Surgery***, 67 Stuart St, T4777473; ***Avanti Pro***, Lower Stuart St, T4777259 (from $25 per day). **Car hire** ***Pegasus***, 867 Cumberland St, T4776296; ***Jackie's Rent-a-Car***, 23 Cumberland St, T4777848; ***Reliable Rentals***, (deliver), T4883975. **Communications Internet** is available at the ***Dunedin Library***, Moray Place (open Mon-Fri 0930-2100, Sat 1000-1600, Sun 1400-1800); ***The Arc Café***, 135 High St, offers free email but in doing so gets very chaotic; ***The Governors Café***, 438 George St, is another good bet, with cheap email upstairs (open daily from 1100). ***Modak's*** is another café/internet option at 339 George St. The main **post office** is on the corner of Princes and Rattray Sts and they have post restante. **Medical services** Dunedin Hospital, 201 Great King St, T4740999; Urgent Doctor, 95 Hanover St, T4792900 (pharmacy next-door). **Useful addresses Police** 25 Great King St, T4776011. **AA** 450 Moray Pl, T4775945.

The Otago Peninsula

The beautiful Otago Peninsula, that stretches 33 km northeast from Dunedin out into the Pacific Ocean, is as synonymous with ***wildlife*** *as Dunedin is with Scotland. If there were any place that could honour the title of being the wildlife capital of the country, this would be it. It is home to an array of particularly rare species including the enchanting* ***yellow-eyed penguin*** *and the soporific* ***hookers sealion****, as well the more common* ***New Zealand fur seals****. But without doubt the peninsula's star attraction is the breeding colony of* ***royal albatross*** *on* ***Taiaroa Head****, located at the very tip of the peninsula. This colony is the only mainland breeding albatross colony in the world and offers a unique opportunity to observe these supremely beautiful masters of flight and long-haul travel. A day trip to see all these wildlife delights is highly recommended, and will leave a precious and lasting memory. Besides the wildlife the principal attractions on the Otago Peninsula are historic* ***Larnach Castle*** *and the stunning vista of* ***Sandfly Bay****, as well as the activities of* ***sea kayaking****,* ***cruising*** *and* ***walking****.*

Ins and outs

Getting there The best way to see the peninsula is by car, but if you have no wheels of your own or are not familiar with the wildlife, an organized **tour** is recommended. Some of the tours on offer can take you to several wildlife sites (and sights) that are out of bounds to the general public.

By road there are 2 main routes that penetrate the peninsula. On the western side, hugging the numerous small bays and inlets of the Otago Harbour, is the Portobello Road which serves the peninsula's main village, Portobello. From Portobello this road then continues past the small settlement of Harington Point to terminate at Taiaroa Head and the albatross colony. An alternative route to Portobello via Highcliff Road accesses two of the peninsula's major physical attractions, Larnach Castle and Sandfly Bay, and straddles the hilltops of the peninsula offering some memorable views. Note that both roads are sealed but very windy and dangerous. It is important to slow down and not maintain the pace and buzz of Dunedin city streets. Both Highcliff Rd and Portobello Rd are easily accessed via Cumberland St (city) across the railway line and then by skirting the Otago Harbour on Wharf St and Portsmouth Dr. The various tours are listed below. For a free map of the Otago Peninsula ask at the VIC.

Information

One of the principal raisons d'être of the **Dunedin VIC** is arranging half- to full-day trips out to the peninsula. The 3 principal attractions are the albatross and yellow-eyed penguin colonies and Larnach Castle. There are a number of options regarding the length of time of visit, the route and the sight itinerary, so it pays to study the options carefully before parting with your cash. The **DOC** office in Dunedin can provide further information on walks and wildlife. **Internet** is available at ***Stop Info Coffee***, 699 Highcliff Rd, T4781055 (open 0900-1700).

Sights

Albatrosses

Although **Taiaroa Head** is an interesting historic site in its own right, it is the colony of royal albatross that has really put the small rocky headland on the map. Ever since the first egg was laid in 1920 the site, which is the only mainland breeding colony in the world, has become an almost sacred preserve of these magnificent seabirds. The colony, now numbering almost 100, is fully protected and managed by the Department of Conservation and the Otago Peninsula Trust. With the opening of **The Royal Albatross Centre** in 1972, thousands of people have been given the unique opportunity to view the birds from an observatory and to learn about their fascinating lifestyle and the threats we place upon them. Even before you enter the centre, if the conditions are right, you can see the great birds wheeling in from the ocean on wings that span over 3 m (the largest of any bird) and with a grace that defies the effort. If there is such a thing as airborne ballet this is it.

The Albatross Centre has some superb exhibits that include static-displays, audio-visuals and even a live close-circuit TV feed from the occupied nests in the breeding season. It takes about eight months for the parent birds to 'rear' one of these avian B52s so your chances of seeing the 'industrial size' carpet-slipper-chicks are high. The activity of the adults does vary depending on courting, mating, incubating and feeding, with the best viewing times generally being between late-November and April. But having said that you would be fairly unlucky not to see at least one on any given visit at any time of year. ■ *The centre also has a café and a shop, and is open daily 0900-2000 (seasonal), T4780499, www.albatrosses.com*

Tours There are a number of tours available. The 90-minute '*Unique Taiaroa*' tour includes an introductory video, a viewing of the colony from the hilltop observatory, and a look at the remains of **Fort Taiaroa**. This is a series of underground tunnels, fortifications and a 'disappearing gun' that were originally built in 1885 in response to a perceived threat of invasion from Tsarist Russia. December-March; $30, child $15. April-September, $25, child

$12. The second tour on offer is the 60-minute '*Royal Albatross*' which includes all the above except the fort. December-March $24, child $12. April-September, $20, child $10. For those with no interest in seabirds and merely the forts, paranoia and guns you may like to join the 30-minute '*Fort Taiaroa Tour*' ($12, child $6). The 30-minute '*Albatross Insight Tour*' involves a guided tour of the centre and an introductory talk about the birds while viewing them on close-circuit TV, as opposed to first hand from the observatory ($8, child $4). Note that the observatory is closed between 17 September

Otago Peninsula

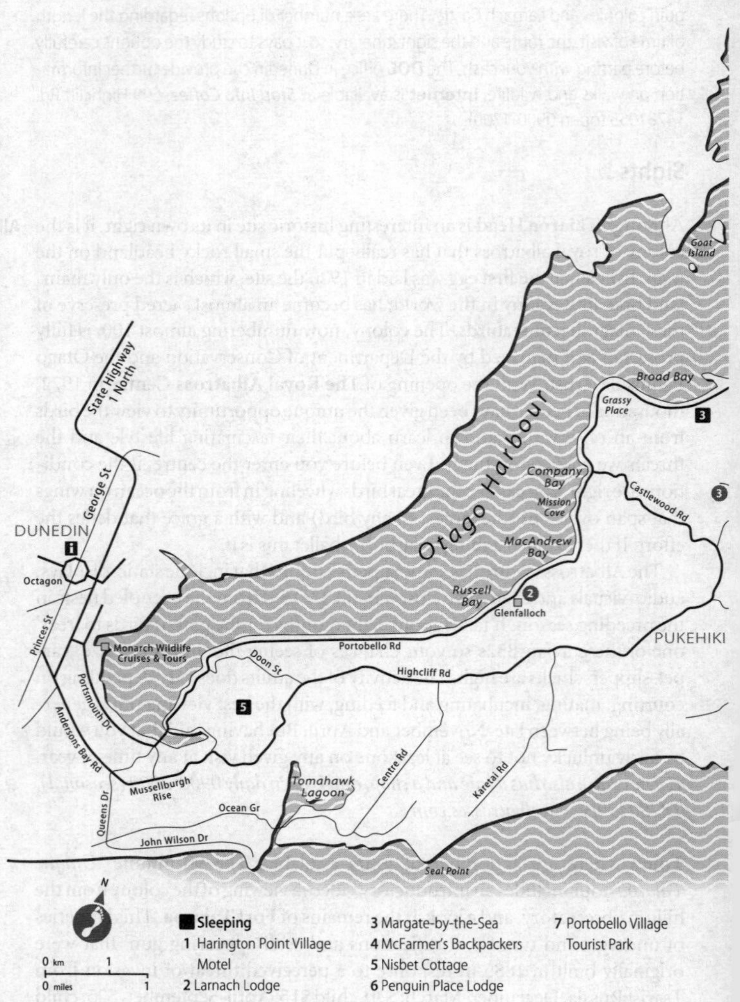

and 23 November each year, to allow the new season's birds to return and renew their pair bonds.

There is plenty of other wildlife to see on and around Taiaroa Head. Of particular note are the rare **Stewart Island shags** that also breed on the headland. They are beautiful birds, but when it comes to flight are the complete antithesis of the albatross. Also known as 'the flying brick', on a very windy day, it is not completely out of the ordinary for one to 'take out' you, your child and

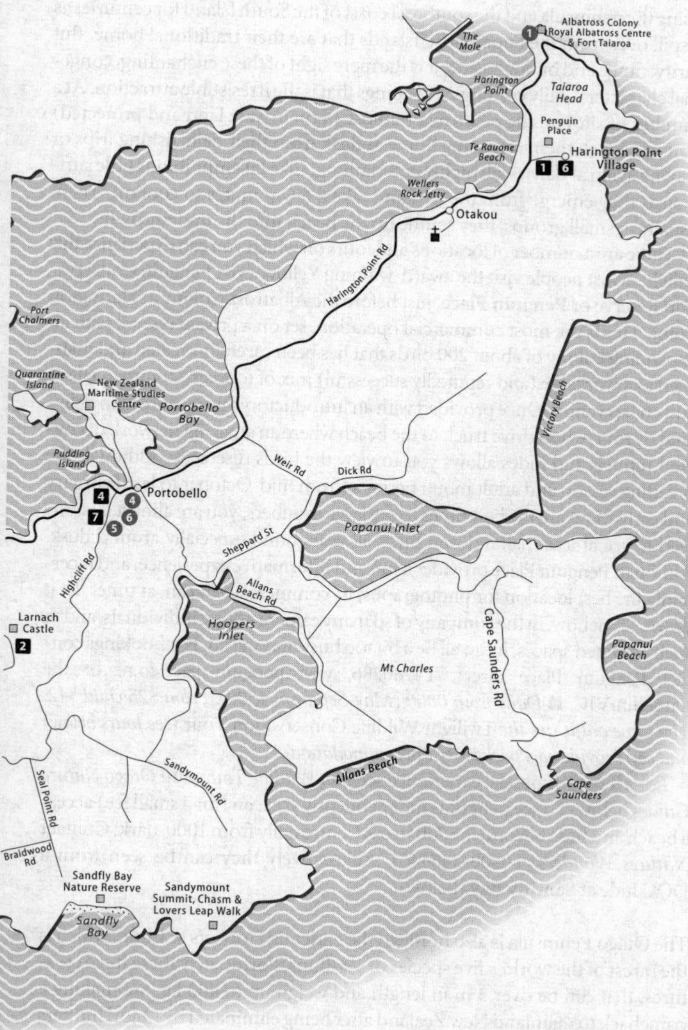

your ice cream from the viewing area near the centre. Around the base of the headland, **fur seals** and **little blue penguins** can regularly be seen and, if you have binoculars, the ocean will reveal a plethora of **petrels** and other seabirds.

Yellow-eyed penguins

The Otago Peninsula is a haven and breeding site for the yellow-eyed penguin, one of the rarest penguin species in the world. For many, the conditioning we have of the penguin/ice relationship and their near symbiosis is shattered amidst the golden sands and grasses of the peninsula's bays and inlets. The 'yellow eyes' or 'hoiho' (to give them their Maori name), have been using the peninsula and the southeast coast of the South Island for centuries as a spill over from the Subantartic Islands that are their traditional home. But rarity, range and biology aside, it is the mere sight of these enchanting, congenial characters' daily comings and goings that is the irresistible attraction. At a number of sites on the peninsula (almost all on private land and protected) you can watch them returning home at dusk from their daily fishing trips or leaving again at dawn – all highly entertaining. Like fat amphibious little surfboards they emerge from the surf and take a few minutes to cool off. Then, usually in small groups, they scuttle up the beach into the undergrowth.

There are a number of locations and tours on which you can experience this delight. Most people visit the award-winning Yellow-eyed Penguin Conservation Reserve or **Penguin Place**, just before the Albatross Colony at Harington Point. This is the most commercial operation, set on a private reserve with an expanding colony of about 200 birds that has been carefully created and managed as a workable (and reputedly successful) mix of tourism, commercialism and conservation. Once provided with an introductory talk you are then delivered by four-wheel drive truck to the beach where an amazing network of covered tunnels and hides allows you to view the birds discreetly. Although the breeding season and adult moult periods (from mid-October to late February and early May) are the best times to see large numbers, you are almost guaranteed to see at least half a dozen birds all year round especially around dusk. Although Penguin Place provides a fun and informative experience, and is certainly the best location for photographs, its commercialism can, at times, let it down. Somehow, in the company of so many camera-toting individuals, and in such confined spaces, it can all be a bit too busy and staged. For bookings contact Penguin Place direct, T4780286, www.penguin-place.co.nz or the Dunedin VIC. ■ *Daily from 0800 (May-Sep from 1500). From $25 child $12. The same outfit run the* Twilight Wildlife Conservation Tour *(see tours below) and can provide backpacker-style accommodation.*

For a less commercial experience see *Elm Wildlife Tours* and *Otago Nature Guides* below. To see penguins independently you can (for a small fee) access a beach and hide beyond the Albatross Centre daily from 1000-dark. Contact *Natures Wonders*, T0800-246446). Alternatively they can be seen from a DOC hide at **Sandfly Bay** (below).

Hookers sea-lions & New Zealand fur seals

The Otago Peninsula is also home to the endemic Hookers sea-lion, which is the rarest of the world's five species of sea-lions. Fortunately these huge creatures, that can be over 3 m in length and weigh up to 400 kg, are making a comeback to mainland New Zealand after being eliminated by Maori hunters centuries before the arrival of Europeans. In 1995 they bred again on the peninsula for the first time in 700 years. To encounter these ocean-going couch potatoes almost anywhere along the coast is an unforgettable experience. Seemingly devoid of any fear (and who wouldn't be, given those proportions and an impressive set of dentures housed in a mouth the size of a large bucket), they haul up on beaches and even the roads to rest. Having done so, they then display an overwhelming desire to do very little, except sleep, break wind (gas), scratch or eye you up occasionally with an expression of complete indifference. If you are lucky enough to see one do not go any nearer than 10 m. Despite their looks they can move like a slug from a slingshot and you would certainly lose the argument. Otago also has a number of fur seal colonies, the most accessible of which is around Taiaroa Head. Below the main car park you can usually find one or two hauled up in an almost enviable soporific state. Again, you can take a closer look but do not approach within 10 m.

Larnach Castle

Perched on the highest point of the peninsula, 16 km from Dunedin, is Larnach Castle, the former residence of Australian William Larnach (1833-98). As a minister of the Crown, banker, financier and merchant baron of the prosperous late 1880s, there is no doubt Larnach was a man of wealth and title, but he was far more renowned for his personal life and excesses. Excesses and events that finally lead to his tragic suicide surrounded by the very monument of his desires. Only the best would do for Larnach, who had both the will and the wherewithal to live up to the saying 'a man's home is his castle'. He employed 200 workmen for three years to build the exterior, and another 12 years was spent by master craftsmen embellishing the interior, with 32 different woods, marble from Italy, tiles from England, glass from Venice and France, and even slate from Wales. Both Larnach and his castle have a fascinating history. After his death the castle changed hands a number of times before falling into a state of disrepair. Then in 1967 the remains were purchased by the Barker family who have since lovingly renovated the castle to something very close to its former glory, and opened it to the public. Both the castle and its 14 acres of gracious grounds now remain open for self-guided tours and give a fascinating insight into the period and the man. There is a licensed café on site in the very Scottish ballroom, which comes complete with stags head and open fire. Larnach is signposted off Castlewood Road (from Portobello Rd). Most of the peninsula tour operators visit Larnach Castle as a matter of course. ■ *Daily 0930-1630. The castle also provides some of the best accommodation and views in the region. Daily 0900-1900 (1700 in winter), $12, child $4.50 (gardens only $6, child $2) T4761616, www.larnachcastle.co.nz*

Other sights

There are many scenic bays and walks on the peninsula, with perhaps the most dramatic and accessible being the idyllic, and at times wild **Sandfly Bay**, located on its eastern shore. From Highcliff Road take Seal Point Road to the reserve car park. From there the beach can then be accessed by foot (20 minutes). At the far end of the beach there is a small public hide overlooking the only free or publicly accessible Yellow-eyed penguin colony on the peninsula (40 minutes return). The best times for viewing are just before dawn and dusk. Beyond Sandfly Bay, and either accessible by foot (poled route) or via Sandymount Road (also off Highcliff Rd), is the **Sandymount Summit, Chasm and Lover's Leap Walk** (one hour). The Chasm and Lover's Leap are impressive coastal cliff features formed when the sea eroded the soft, lower layers of volcanic rock. For details about these walks and others on the peninsula get the *'Otago Peninsula Tracks'* leaflet from the Dunedin VIC and the peninsula walks broadsheets, available from DOC. **Glenfalloch** (Gaelic for 'hidden valley') is a pleasant wooded garden and historic estate located 9 km from Dunedin at 430 Portobello Road. The gardens are particularly noted for their rhododendrons, azaleas and camellias, which are at their bloomin' best between mid-September and mid-October. ■ *There is also a restaurant on site, T4761006. Daily, free.*

Located near Portobello on the shores of Otago Harbour is the **New Zealand Marine Studies Centre**, Hatchery Road, T4795826, www.otago.ac.nz/marinestudies On display there are a number of aquariums and 'touch tanks', with a range of native New Zealand sea creatures from sea horses to the octopus. There is even the opportunity to taste nutritious seaweed, and knowledgeable and friendly staff are on hand to answer any questions. ■ *Daily 1200-1630, $7, child $3.*

Tours There are a range of specialist **wildlife** tours available from Dunedin: *Elm Wildlife Tours*, T4741872, www.elmwildlifetours.co.nz operate out of the Elm Backpackers Lodge and provide an excellent award-winning Eco-tour of the peninsula. Their five- to six-hour trip takes in the Albatross Centre, a New Zealand fur seal colony and their own Yellow-eyed penguin-breeding beach at the remote Cape Saunders. The tour is fun, informative, yet nicely uncommercial, and gives you access to some of the most scenic private land on the peninsula. From $43 (albatross observatory tour extra). Pick-ups available. Recommended.

Otago Nature Guides, T4545169, www.nznatureguides.com specialize in highly personalized, small group tours at dawn to see the Yellow-eyed penguin colony at the beautiful Sandfly Bay. Tours in conjunction with their fine B&B accommodation in Nesbitt Cottage (see below) are recommended. Extended trips to the Catlins and Stewart Island are also available. German speaking.

Twilight Wildlife Conservation Tours, T4543116, wildsouth@clear.net.nz offer a relaxed and friendly tour of the albatross colony (entry optional), various wildlife sites, peninsula beaches and the Penguin Place reserve (see above). The Monarch Wildlife Cruise (see below) is also an optional extra. Tours depart from Dunedin March-October 1330 (November-February 1430). From $50, child $39.

The *Otago Peninsula Experience*, T4767261, offer a wildlife tour in a classic 1960s Jaguar and include Larnach Castle an optional extra on the itinerary, from $130, child $75.

Otago Explorer, T4743300, offer tours to Larnach Castle, departing from the city daily at 0900 and 1500, from $30.

For a personalized four-whell drive road tour of the peninsula contact *Sport 4x4 Adventures*, T4780878, four-hour day ($69) or 2½-hour evening tour ($35).

Etours, T4761960, allen.e-tours@xtra.co.nz offer interesting day ($89) or half-day ($40) tours of the peninsula by **bike** which really allows you the opportunity to get a feel for the place. Departs 0900.

Newton Tours (Citibus), T4775577, www.transportplace.co.nz offer a basic **sightseeing bus** trip to the peninsula, allowing the opportunity to get off at Larnach Castle, the Albatross Centre and the Penguin Place Yellow-eyed penguin colony. They can also drop off at the Monarch Wildlife Cruise jetty. Regular daily departures from the city are from $49-$89.

Other activities **Cruising** There are a number of opportunities to cruise the Otago Harbour with the most established operator being the award-winning *Monarch Wildlife Cruises and Tours*, corner of Wharf and Fryatt Streets, T4774276, www.wildlife.co.nz They offer a variety of trips from one hour to seven hours taking in all the harbour sights, with the main highlights being the Marine Studies Centre Aquarium at Portobello and the wildlife of Taiaroa Head. For a short trip you can join the boat at the Wellers Rock Jetty near Taiaroa Head.

Road trips are also available. Regular daily departures, one hour (Wellers Rock) $25, child $13, seven hours $150, child $90. Other charters include *Paranui Cruises*, T4778666, and Blue Wave, T4710804 (2 ½ hours from $40.

Horse trekking *Castle Discovery Horse Treks*, Camp Road, Broad Bay, T4780796, trek from harbour to hill top (Larnach Castle). Daily 0930-1230 and 1315-1615 from $45, child $35.

Sea kayaking Otago Harbour and Taiaroa Head provide some of the best sea kayaking in the country, with the added attraction of viewing and accessing wildlife in a manner simply not possible by land. Where else in the world can you kayak while viewing albatross at the same time? *Wild Earth Adventures*, T4736535, www.nzwildearth.com provide an excellent range of tours, the most popular of which is their three- to four-hour '*Taiaroa Ocean Tour*' around the heads. From $49. Recommended.

Essentials

Sleeping

The accommodation available at Larnach Castle is some of the best in the region, with views that are unsurpassed. The **L-AL** ***Larnach Lodge***, T4761616 offers a range of beautifully appointed 'themed' rooms – from 'The Scottish Room' with its tartan attire to the 'Goldrush Room' which comes complete with a king-size 'cart bed' made out of an original old cart found on the property. The views across the harbour and peninsula from every room are simply superb. Breakfast is served in the old stables, while dinner is optional in the salubrious interior of the castle. Book well in advance. Recommended.

The **A** ***Nisbet Cottage***, 6A Eliffe Pl, T4545169, www.wingsokotuku.co.nz is a comfortable and private B&B run by a friendly German couple who operate Otago Nature Tours. Ideal for that personalized peninsula experience. There are a number of other B&B and self-contained options on the peninsula, including **A** ***Margate-by-the-Sea***, 5 Margate Av, Broad Bay, T4780866, which is cosy and self-contained with spa, and the **A** ***Homestead***, 238 Harington Point Rd (2 km north of Portobello), T/F4780384, thehomestead@clear.net.nz which is set in a lovely position overlooking Portobello Bay. Further out on the peninsula, and conveniently placed for both the albatross and Penguin Place Yellow-eyed penguin colonies, is the small, modern and comfortable **A** ***Harington Point Village Motel***, Harrington Point, T4780287.

There are two backpacker options at **C-D** ***McFarmer's Backpackers***, 774 Portobello Rd, T4780389, which has dorms and doubles and is close to all village amenities, and **C-D** ***Penguin Place Lodge*** (Yellow-eyed penguin reserve), Harington Point, T4780286, which is basic but modern with single, twin and doubles with shared facilities. The only motorcamp is the **C-D** ***Portobello Village Tourist Park***, 27 Hereweka St, Portobello, T/F4780359, portobellotp@xtra.co.nz It has basic tourist flats, powered/tent sites and a bunk room. Bike hire is available.

Eating

There are only 2 restaurants and a scattering of cafés on the peninsula: ***Glenfalloch Restaurant***, 430 Portobello Rd, T4761006, is a licensed café-style establishment set in the pleasant Glenfalloch Gardens (open daily from 1100); Both *Larnach Castle* and The *Albatross Centre* have cafés (see above). The ***1908 Café/Restaurant***, 7 Harington Point Rd, Portobello, T4780801, is pleasant enough with a good Euro/NZ menu and a seafood edge. Open Mon-Sun for lunch and dinner. Nearby the ***Stop Info Coffee***, 699 Highcliff Rd, T4781055, has snacks, breakfast, acceptable coffee and internet. Open 0900-1700. There is a well-stocked **general store** located on the main street in Portobello, T4780555.

Central Otago

The barren, rugged and almost treeless landscapes of Central Otago have a unique atmosphere, that are almost dramatic in their sense of space and loneliness. Looking at these vistas now and passing through the quiet, unassuming towns of its back roads and river valleys, it is hard to imagine the immensity of the chaotic gold boom years that once made Otago the most populous region in the land. After gold was first discovered in 1861 by Gabriel Read, an Australian prospector, near Lawrence in the Clutha River Valley, Central Otago erupted into a gold fever that spread like wildfire across its barren landscape. It was a boom and a resource that would last until the turn of the 20th century, seeing the establishment of many towns including ***Alexandra****,* ***Clyde****,* ***Cromwell****,* ***Roxburgh****,* ***Ranfurly*** *and* ***St Bathans****, and the construction of the impressive* ***Taieri Gorge Railway*** *and what is now the* ***Otago Central Rail Trail****. Both once formed vital communication links with Dunedin. Many of the region's towns and goldfields heritage sites come within the boundaries of the* ***Otago Goldfields Park*** *administered by DOC.*

With the lure of Wanaka and Queenstown to the west, Central Otago sees little except transitory tourist traffic. But, if you have a couple of days to kill, a more thorough exploration of this historic gold-mining region can be rewarding and provide some respite from the crowds heading elsewhere.

Attractions of particular note include the Taieri Gorge Railway trips, a walk around historic St Bathans or Clyde, and the Otago Central Rail Trail. The latter is becoming increasingly popular, offering some of the best **mountain biking** in the region. Other less gold-orientated activities include **fishing**, **walking** and **horse trekking**.

For the serious historian the '*Otago Goldfields Heritage Trail*' booklet, available free from all of the region's VICs, provides a solid route-guide from which to explore the diverse historical sites scattered throughout the region.

Ins and outs

Getting there There are 3 main **roads** into Central Otago which essentially converge to form a loop. From Palmerston, 55 km north of Dunedin (via SH1 and the coast), SH85 turns inland to follow the 'Pig Root' to Ranfurly and Alexandra, with a small diversion to St Bathans. At Alexandra SH85 joins SH8 that follows the Clutha River Valley, south through Roxburgh, Raes Junction and Lawrence, before rejoining SH1 near Milton, 60 km south of Dunedin. At Mosgiel, 15 km south of Dunedin, SH87 follows close to the Taieri George Railway and Otago Central Rail Trail to merge with SH85 just east of Ranfurly. One of the best ways to get a taste of Central Otago is by **train** via the *Taieri Gorge Railway* and then by mountain **bike** from Middlemarch to Clyde on the now disused line that forms the *Otago Central Rail Trail*. Alternatively you can combine rail and **bus** to Queenstown (see Dunedin activities). Roxburgh, Alexandra, Clyde and Cromwell are all on the main highway to Queenstown (SH8) and are served by all the main bus companies that run between Dunedin and Queenstown/Wanaka (see Queenstown and Wanaka sections).

Information The principal **Visitor information centres** in Central Otago are located in Alexandra, Cromwell, with smaller centres in Ranfurly and Roxburgh. These are all listed in the text. **DOC** information is held at the Alexandra and Cromwell VICs. The Central Otago Regional Office is at 43 Dunstan Rd, T4488874. The **Otago Goldfields Heritage Trust**,

T4451516, has a useful website, www.nzsouth.co.nz/goldfields The website www.tco.org.nz may also prove useful, and the Otago Central Rail Trail has its own website, www.otagocentralrailtrail.co.nz

Alexandra

Phone code: 03
Population: 4,500

Situated at the junction of the Clutha and Manuherikia Rivers, Alexandra was one of the first goldmining towns to be established in Central Otago. Its creation was due to the first strikes made in 1862 by Horatio Hartley and Christopher Reilly in the once-rich Dunstan fields, in what is now the neighbouring town of Clyde. The river junction became known as Lower Dunstan and later, as the hopefuls descended, became the settlement of Alexandra. Once the gold ran out at the end of the 1800s the orchardists moved in, making fruitgrowing Alexandra's modern-day industry. The town is at its best in autumn when the riverside willows and poplars, ironically, bathe the valley in another hue of gold. Alexandra serves as the principal gateway to the **Otago Central Rail** and **Dunstan gold mining heritage trails**, which are a major attraction for mountain bikers and four-wheel drive enthusiasts.

Ins & outs

Getting there *Intercity* and *Atomic Shuttles* stop in Alexandra on the Queenstown and Wanaka to Dunedin route. *Catch-a-bus* and *Southern Link* both provide additional shuttle services to Queenstown and Wanaka. For information and bookings contact the VIC. For an on-demand shuttle service, T/F4492755.

Information The Central Otago **Visitor Information Centre** is located on the main drag, 22 Centennial Av, T4489515, F4402061, info@tco.org.nz Open Mon-Fri 0900-1700, Sat/Sun 1000-1500. It is an excellent centre almost as full of information as the staff are with enthusiasm for the region. There are free maps, leaflets and displays outlining the many historical aspects of the region and its most popular activities, including fishing and horse trekking. **DOC** is located at 43 Dunstan Rd, T4488874. **Internet** is available at the library and *Smith City*, Limerick St, in the centre of town (open Mon-Fri 0900-1700).

Sights

Almost instantly noticeable and visible from almost everywhere is the 11-m diameter **clock** on part of the Knobbies Range to the east of Alexandra. Completed in November 1968, its creation came about through no particular reason other than the pure and simple desire of one Alexander Jaycee. Somehow, after managing to get his idea endorsed by the town's residents, he then found the support and finances to build it – which was no mean feat in itself, requiring 1,264 man hours of work. Although hardly ugly, it does seem a little out of place, and certainly does not seem to reflect the general atmosphere or the pace of life in the town. One gets the feeling that if it ever stopped no one would be particularly bothered about going up there to give it a tap.

Besides the clock and its simple riverside aesthetics, the main attraction in town is the recently improved **Alexandra Historical Museum,** Skird Street, T4486230. It concentrates naturally on gold mining, but also includes some interesting displays on the role of the early Chinese settlers and sheep farmers. ■ *Mon-Fri 1000-1630, Sat 1000-1200, Entry by donation.*

A short walk from the centre of town will take you to the **Shaky Bridge** that crosses the Manuherikia River on Fox Street. Originally built in 1879, it was once used by wagons and horses. Now purely a footbridge, although aesthetically pleasing, it does not provide the impending adrenaline rush that its name suggests. As well as orchards the area has its fair share of **vineyards**. Ask at the VIC for the free *'Guide to Central Otago Wineries'*.

Activities Alexandra is the principal starting point for the **Otago Central Rail Trail** and **Dunstan Trails**. The VIC can provide information and free leaflets on the methods and negotiation of both, mainly by **mountain bike** or **four-wheel drive**. Accommodation listings are also available from the VIC. The Otago Central Rail Trail has its own website, www.otagocentralrailtrail.co.nz that may prove useful. Various transport operators provide luggage and bike pick-up or drop-offs and bike hire (and/or guided tours) for both trails. They include: *Central Outdoor Adventures*, T4488048, info@goldrush.co.nz *Henderson Cycles*, 14 Limerick Street, T4488917, and *Safari Excursions*, 41 Glencarron Street, T4487474, www.wildflowerwalks.co.nz *Dunstan Trail Rides*, Waikerikeri Valley Road, Clyde, T4492445, offer **horse trekking** on the Dunstan Trail from $20 per hour. **Fishing** permits and a list of local guides are available from the VIC.

Otago

Sleeping The VIC has full accommodation listings and can book on your behalf. There are a number of **motels**, with most being located on the main drag north, towards Clyde. These include the **A** ***Centennial Court***, 96 Centennial Av, T4486482, and the **A-B** ***Alexandra Heights***, 125 Centennial Av, T4486366. Elsewhere the **B** ***Alexandra Garden Court***, Manuherikia Rd, T4488295, is recommended.

For **B&Bs** try the very pleasant **L** ***Rocky Range***, Half Mile, T/F4486150, www.rockyrange.co.nz or the lovely orchard stay the **A** ***Iverson***, 47 Blackman Rd, T4492520. The main budget hostel in town is the YHA associate **C-D** ***Two Bob Backpackers***, 4 Dunorling St, T4488152, twobobs@xtra.co.nz which offers comfortable dorms, doubles and family rooms. They also provide guided mountain biking, tramping and walking trips.

There are 2 motorcamps in town: The **B-D** ***Alexandra Holiday Camp*** located on the Manuherikia Rod, T4488297 has cabins, backpackers, powered/tent sites and also hires kayaks and mountain bikes, while the smaller **B-D** ***Pine Lodge Holiday Camp***, Ngapara St, T4488861, has flats, units and powered/tent sites. Both of the parks are about a 10-15-min walk from the centre of town.

Eating Clyde, 10 km west of Alexandra, provides far better dining options than Alexandra, but if you wish to stay in town try the ***Briar and Tyme Café & Bar*** next door to the VIC at 26 Centennial Ave, T4489189. Open daily (Tue-Sat in winter). It is an historic single-storey villa and offers imaginative and affordable Euro/NZ lunches and dinners. In the centre of town there are a number of unremarkable cafés and takeaways, with the exception of the ***Red Brick Café***, Ennis St, T4489174, which is open daily for a good lunch or dinner.

Clyde

Phone code: 03
Population 1,000

Just 10 km west of Alexandra is the pretty and historic village of Clyde. Backed by the concrete edifice of the **Clyde Dam** that incarcerates **Lake Dunstan**, it offers a pleasant stop on the way to Queenstown or Wanaka. Originally called Dunstan and the hub of the rich Dunstan Goldfields, it assumed its present name in the late 1860s. Clyde in Scots Gaelic is 'Clutha' – which is the river that once flowed freely through the Cromwell Gorge and is the longest in the South Island. Amidst Clyde's very pleasant aesthetics are a number of historic old buildings including the Town Hall (1868), various pioneer cottages and a handful of its once 70 hotels. The **Old Courthouse** on Blyth Street is another fine example that was built in 1864. Many interesting artefacts are displayed inside, including the original courtroom dock, leg irons, handcuffs, and a set of scales. These scales, which no doubt were the focus of many an argument, are thought to have weighed over 70,000 ounces of gold. It is not surprising that during the gold boom, with so many hopefuls harbouring such a sense of greed, there were many disputes and disturbances in the town. Perhaps the worst of these was the $26,000 gold and banknotes robbery that set the town in uproar in 1879. ■ *The courthouse is open Tue-Sun 1400-1600, free.*

Nearby, on Fraser Street, is the **Clyde Historical Museum and Briar Herb Factory**, T4492092. The herb factory originally began operations in the 1930s processing local thyme, but has since grown into a museum housing not only the original herb-processing machinery, but a variety of exhibits illustrating the life of the early settlers. These include the workshops of blacksmith, farrier and wheelwrights, and stables with various horse-drawn vehicles. ■ *It is also open Tue-Sun 1400-1600, or at other times by arrangement.*

The trilogy of museums is completed by the **Clyde Station Museum** at the former railway station on Fraser Street, T4492400. It houses some lovingly restored locos and is open weekends 1400-1600, or by appointment. Although perhaps a bit morbid, the **cemetery** in Clyde (Springvale Road) can be an interesting place for reflection. Having been in use since the 1850's, the headstones provide some fascinating reading, particularly the ages, surnames and origins of the former settlers. Once you have enjoyed the atmosphere and historical aspects of the village, you might like to take the 30-minute walk to the **Clyde Lookout** hill (signposted) above the town and enjoy the views.

Sleeping & eating

L-AL ***Olivers Lodge***, 34 Sunderland St, T4492860, www.olivers.co.nz offers some charming individually styled rooms right in the heart of the village and next door to the restaurant. The old shower is simply superb. Across the road the historic former hotel **A** ***Dunstan House***, T4492295, www.dunstanhouse.co.nz offers elegant en suites decorated in turn-of-the-century style. The **A** ***Antique Lodge Motel***, 56 Sunderland St, T4492709, is a good motel option, while backpackers need look no further than the friendly **C-D** ***Hartley Arms Backpackers***, which is right in the thick of things on Sunderland St, T4492700. The **C-D** *Clyde Holiday Complex*, Whitby St, T4492713, has 1 cabin and powered/tent sites. For other accommodation options contact the VIC in Alexandra.

For eating try the award-winning ***Olivers Restaurant*** in the former 1863 general store, 34 Sunderland St, T4492860. The food is just as pleasant as the surroundings. Open daily for lunch and dinner (bookings advised). Across the road the equally historic ***Dunstan House*** offers a lunch and dinner menu that focuses mainly on local produce, T4492295. For lighter, imaginative meals and good coffee head for the ***Blues Bank Café and Bar***, a funky little place, also located on Sunderland St in the former bank, T4492147 (closed Mon-Wed). ***The Post Office Café and Bar*** also provides nice aesthetics and light meals and is located at 2 Blyth St, T/F4492488, open daily.

Cromwell

Phone code: 03
Population: 2,700

From Clyde, SH8 negotiates the Cromwell Gorge and plays tag with a section of Lake Dunstan, which on the map looks like the antenna of a large blue sea creature. At its head, 23 km to the north, is the tidy little town of Crowmwell. Cromwell is faced with five very large dilemmas – a pear, an apple, a peach, a lemon and its proximity to Queenstown. It is the latter of course with which it struggles the most. Just how do you stop any tourist so intent on reaching perhaps the busiest tourist town in the country? Well, it seems some bright spark (there is always one) thought a sculpture of four man-eating pieces of fruit might be a good idea. But you have to wonder if this has only added to the dilemma. Sure, people stop, they stare, make the suitable ohh and ahh noises, then take the inevitable photographs, but that is often the problem – they go no further. That's Cromwell. Forever and around the globe, Cromwell has

The highest bungy – so what does it feel like?

"Good morning, my name is Andy and I'll be your driver this morning. The journey to the 134-m Nevis Highwire Bungy – which, I'm sure, I don't need to remind you is the highest in New Zealand – will take about 40 minutes. But before I put on some 'sounds', do you have any questions?"

There's a pregnant pause, then Grant, a Yorkshireman from Leeds in England mutters... "Aye son... are we goin' t'die?"

A nervous giggle spreads through the bus.

Andy, a typical 'crew' member, replete with shaven hair and funky shades, smiles knowingly, then flips the tape player to 'deafen'. I look around to study my fellow 'pre-jumpers'. We are a cosmopolitan crowd; big, small, Asian, Euro, American, both male and female, young and not so young. But we all have one thing in common – a deep and suppressed sense of sheer and utter terror. And so, like a band of displaced refugees in the hands of a really nasty terrorist, we head south. Along the way, somehow oblivious to Queenstown's world-class scenery, we pass the original and now seemingly insignificant 43 m Kawarau Bridge Bungy – the world's first commercial site and where it all started in 1983. A little further on our bus turns onto an unsealed road and climbs a steep hill, then another. The thoughts are obvious. Over the crest of the hill we arrive at a barn-like building and all eyes turn to a gaping gorge. In its middle, suspended by wires, is a gleaming metal shed – the jump station – where it all happens. From a distance it seems to be dripping with bungy ropes and presumably various, as yet unseen, bodily fluids. The gorge seems to have no bottom and I mean no bottom. Yet elsewhere in almost audible unison all of ours suddenly clench. "Welcome to the Nevis Highwire", says Andy with obvious glee.

We get off and all walk like John Wayne (but with facial expressions like Stan Laurel) towards the reception centre. There we are signed in and weighed, then taken in small groups to a small open gondola that will take us out to the jump station. From terra firma we cross the abyss, the river looks like a stream, 180 m below.

"Bloody'ell", says Grant, going puce. We enter the jump station on to clear glass floor panels (nice touch folks) and are immediately welcomed by three Andy lookalikes. "Hi" they say in near unison as if we all had our pants down and they didn't.

Otago

become that place with the whooping fruit, ingrained forever in a million memories with a silly photo. However, that said, Cromwell is a pleasant place with a lot more to offer.

Ins & outs

Getting there *Intercity* and *Atomic Shuttles* stop in Cromwell on the Queenstown and Wanaka to Dunedin route. ***Catch-a-Bus*** and ***Southern Link*** provide additional shuttle services to Queenstown and Wanaka. For information and bookings contact the VIC.

Information The Cromwell and Districts **Visitor Information Centre and Museum** are located at 47 The Mall (along with just about everything else), T4450212, F4451319, crovin@nzhost.co.nz Open daily 1000-1600. The staff here are very enthusiastic and helpful and will do there best to make sure you see the financial and health benefits of staying in Cromwell as opposed to Queenstown. The website www.cromwell.org.nz is excellent. The museum, which is attached, focuses on the early history and building of the dam and is worth a look. Entry by donation. The Mall is located almost in the shadow of the giant fruit! For ski-field information contact Cardrona, T4437341, Coronet Peak, T4424620, The Remarkables, T4424615, Treble Cone, T4437443, and Waiorau, T4437542 (www.nzski.com). The *'Time for Real Adventure – Cromwell and Lake Dunstan'* is an excellent leaflet that is available from the VIC listing everything from climate statistics to local walks.

They seem almost annoyingly cool as they busy themselves with the routines of just another day and just another bunch of fools. Ropes are gathered, carabinas click and levers are pulled.

"Right, where's Darroch the travel writer?" 'Oh shit'... I mutter to myself, moving forward. "Hi" I answer sheepishly as if to say, 'come on guys it wasn't me'. "Right, your first man", says the Andy lookalike. "Over here please... just let me check your harness". While he tugs (hard) at my harness, I look at his name tag – 'Rod' it says... 'Satan' I'm thinking. "Right" says Rod. "Come over here and take a seat in the chair".

I walk (surprisingly unaided) towards 'said' chair which sits only inches from to the gaping exit and the inevitable abyss. Now this chair is not comfortable. It is metal, hard and imposing, with a black lining. Reluctantly, but trying very hard to look like I was about to sit down to steak and chips, I park my bum on the chair realising there was now, really no egotistically acceptable way of turning back. While dear Roderick straps the bungy to my ankles, I look out into the valley and down at oblivion. On the very edge of the platform is the well-worn launch pad. It is not even a foot square and yet it is a place of incredible significance. A place from where a million chaotic thoughts fight between fear and reason.

"OK", says Rod, "that's you.... now man, over to the launch pad". I stand up and now firmly attached to my lifesaving bungy, shuffle like a constipated penguin to the edge. My God I'm thinking, Neil Armstrong had it bloody lucky. I stand right on the edge, like you do a diving board. It was a moment I will never forget. I mean, how could you. You are about to do something that goes against every rule. While one billion brain cells unite in 'you must be joking!' there's one – just one – rebellious little sod saying: 'Hey its OK, it'll be great fun, it'll feel great, honest.'

"Smile at the camera", says Rod. I look down at what is effectively a free fall of 45 storeys – eight seconds by all accounts – and then the words and the thoughts fail me. Rod touches me lightly on the shoulders and says indifferently, "OK, mate... after three". Silence. I feel thirty expectant eyes boring into me from behind. Oh well, here goes...One... Two... Three...

Cromwell is of course another former gold town, and was originally called 'The Junction' due to its position at the confluence of the Clutha and Kawarau Rivers. These important bodies of water, which are now masked with the creation of Lake Dunstan, form an integral part of the South Island's Hydropower scheme. The decision to build the Clyde Dam in the 1980s, using Cromwell as the accommodation base, brought many changes to the town and gave rise to a mix of old-world charm and modern, tidy aesthetics. A wander through its very congenial Mall, followed by another in its historic precinct, provides a stark and interesting contrast. With the dam now established they say Cromwell's future lies in tourism, and of course its horticultural status as the 'Fruit Bowl of the South'. Cromwell is ideally situated between Wanaka, Queenstown, the Lindis Pass to Mount Cook and SH8 to Dunedin. The accommodation here is much cheaper than Queenstown and the place is far less stressful. Yet, still, the tourism capital of the South Island is only a scenic 60 km away. It is also in a great position to access five ski-fields (see information above). So it makes a lot of sense to base yourself here! Another thing – it is also one of the sunniest, warmest places in the South and has to be given considerable credit for being the only place in the world that has a reserve set aside especially for beetles.

Sights The main attraction in the town itself is the **Old Cromwell Town Precinct** located at the end of Melmore Place, at the point where the two rivers merge. Since the 1980s and encouraged by the disruption of the dam work, many of the former buildings have been restored or reconstructed and now house local **craftspeople**, **cafés** and shops. The precinct also serves as a base for **Lake Cruises**, and some of the restored buildings are open for view between 1000-1630, entry is free and the VIC has various free leaflets. *'In Search of the Main Street'* is particularly useful.

As you might expect, there are also numerous former goldmining sites and relics surrounding Cromwell. **Bannockburn**, **Bendigo** and the **Carrick Goldfields** are of particular interest. The VIC has details and maps, and *Gold Trail Tours*, T4450809, goldtrailtours@xtra.co.nz offer guided trips. The **Goldfields Mining Centre**, T4451037, in the **Kawarau Gorge** provides the opportunity to explore historic gold workings, a Chinese settlers village, gold stamper batteries and a sluice gun. You can also pan for gold, go horse trekking or jetboating ($65). ■ *Open daily 0900-1700, $14.* The Centre is located about 6 km towards Queenstown (but you must promise to come back!).

As well as its many orchards, the immediate area is also home to a number of **vineyards**. In Bannockburn, just to the south of Cromwell, you will find the *Felton Road Winery*, Felton Road, T4450885 (open 1000-1700, closed weekends May-October); the *Bannockburn Heights*, Cairnmuir Road, T4450887 (café/bar open daily 1000-1800); and the *Olssen's Garden Vineyard*, 306 Felton Road, T4451716 (tastings daily 1000-1600, closed weekends May-September). There are several orchard and vineyard **tour** operators including *Freeway Orchards*, T4451500, *Jackson Orchards Tours*, T/F4450596, and *Circuit Shuttles Sightseeing Tours*, T4450690.

Otago

Other activities Lake **cruises** are available on board the 1929 kauri launch 'MV Waitika' which departs from Old Cromwell Town Jetty daily in summer at 1200 and 1730, T4450203, two hours from $12. *Lake Dunstan Eco-experience*, T4450788, EcoExperience@xtra.co.nz offer an interesting three- to four-hour trip up Lake Dunstan to the Bendigo wetlands which are home to numerous waterbirds and waders. *Southern Lakes Pack Horse Trekking*, T/F4451444, are the local horse trekking operators. There are plenty of **walks** in the area and the *'Cromwell and Districts Guide to Walks and Outings'*, free from the VIC, will keep you literally on track. The area also provides excellent **fishing, mountain biking** and **four-wheel drive** opportunities, contact the VIC.

Sleeping There is a good range of accommodation in Cromwell and, given its popularity as a base close to (but cheaper) than Queenstown, the number of beds is increasing. The VIC has a full list of options and can book on your behalf. In summer it would still be wise to book ahead. The **AL** *Villa Amo*, Shine La, Pisa Moorings, T4450788, F4450711, VillaAmo@xtra.co.nz on Lake Dunstan is a modern spacious place and a good option in the upper B&B range. It is owned by the *Eco-experience* operators (see above). In town the peaceful **A** *Cottage Gardens B&B*, corner of Main Highway and Alpha St, T/F4450628, eco@xtra.co.nz is also a good choice.

There is a scattering of motels in town, from the new and upper range **A** *Colonial Manor*, corner of Barry and Mead Avs, T4450184, and **B** *Gateway Lakeside* on Alpha St, T4450385, to the cheaper and unremarkable **B** *Anderson Park Lodge*, Gair Av, T0800220550. The **B-D** *Cromwell Top Ten Holiday Park*, 1 Alpha St, T4450164, cromwell.holiday.park@xtra.co.nz has a wide range of modern motel, en suite/standard cabins and powered/tent sites in a quiet setting beside the golf course. For budget accommodation try the former revamped dam workers residences at the **C-D** *Chalets*

and Holiday Park, 102 Barry Av, T4451260, thechalets@xtra.co.nz It has bunk rooms and cheap but comfortable singles and doubles with shared facilities.

Eating

For fine dining the ***Bannockburn Heights Café and Wine Bar***, Cairnmuir Rd, Bannockburn,T4453211, is recommended. It is in a nice setting, boasts its own wines and beers and is open daily for lunch and dinner. In Cromwell itself the ***Ferryman Bistro and Bar*** on Melmore Terr (near the Old Cromwell Precinct), T4450607, is the best bet, while the Mall (61A) boasts the ***Junction Pizza Company***, T4450777. A good cheap feed can also be found at the ***Cromwell Golf and Country Club***, Neplusultra St, T4450566.

Directory

You will find a BNZ and National **Bank** in the Mall and the Westpac, which has an **ATM**. **Internet** is available at the *Library*, the *Resource Centre*, *Quick Photos* and ***Composite Computers*** all of which are again, in the Mall. The **post office** is in *Paper Plus* (Guess where?).

Queenstown

Phone code: 03
Population: 8,000

Oh dear, where do you start. Here goes. Ladies and Gentlemen, fasten your seat belts and welcome to Queenstown – Adrenaline Central, Thrillsville, New Zealand, the adventure capital of the world. You are perhaps studying this guide in your hotel room, or perched in your hostel bunk, with a pained expression trying to decide which of the 150-odd activities to try and, more especially, how your wallet can possibly cope? But first things first. Look out of the window. Now where else in the world do you have such accessible scenery like that? And all that is free!

Queenstown has come a long way since gold secured its destiny in the 1860s. It is now the biggest tourist drawcard in New Zealand and is now considered one of the top (and almost certainly the most scenic) adventure venues in the world. It simply has so much to offer. Amidst the stunning setting of mountain and lake, over 1,000,000 visitors a year partake in a staggering range of activities from a sedate steamboat cruise to the heart-stopping bungy jump. You can do almost anything here, from a gentle round of golf to paddling down a river in what looks like a blow-up carrot. Add to that a superb range of accommodation, services, restaurants and cafés, and you simply don't know where to turn. And it's all year round, day and night. In winter the hiking boots are simply replaced by skis, the T-shirt with a jumper and, after sunset, the activity guide with the wineglass, the knife and fork. It just goes on and on.

Ins and outs

Getting there

Queenstown **airport** is located 8 km east of the town in Frankton. ***Air New Zealand***, T4411900, have direct daily flights to Auckland, Christchurch, Wellington and Dunedin. Several airlines offer flights to Milford, including ***Air Fiordland***, T4423404, and ***Milford Sound Scenic Flights***, T4423065 (see activities section).

Queenstown is 486 km from Christchurch, 283 km from Dunedin, 117 km from Wanaka and 170 km from Te Anau (Milford Sound 291 km). **By bus** Queenstown is served daily by ***Intercity***, T442800 (Dunedin/Christchurch-via Mount Cook); ***Atomic Shuttles***, T4429708 (Dunedin/Christchurch); ***Southern Link***, T3588355 (Dunedin/Christchurch); ***Mount Cook Landline***, T0800-800904 (Christchurch via Mount Cook). Fares to Dunedin start from $30, Christchurch $40. ***Topline Tours***, T2498059, and ***Tracknet***, T2497777, go to Te Anau from $35. ***Catch-a-Bus***, T4428178, goes daily to Dunedin from $30. The ***Bottom Bus***, T4429708, serves Dunedin and the Southern Scenic Route to Invercargill and Te Anau. ***High Country Shuttles***,

T0800435050, connect daily with Christchurch-bound Intercity and Atomic Shuttles in Mount Cook, from $37. Intercity, Atomic Shuttles, Southern Link and the recommended ***Wanaka Connextions***, T4439122, go 3 times daily to Wanaka, from $20. For bus trips to Milford Sound see page 645.

Getting around The ***Shopper Bus***, T4426647 (stops outside *McDonalds*), and The ***Airport Bus***, T4426647 (door-to-door), serve the **airport** from $8. A taxi will cost about $18. The Shopper Bus stops at most major hotels and accommodation establishments and with a $10 day-pass

Queenstown

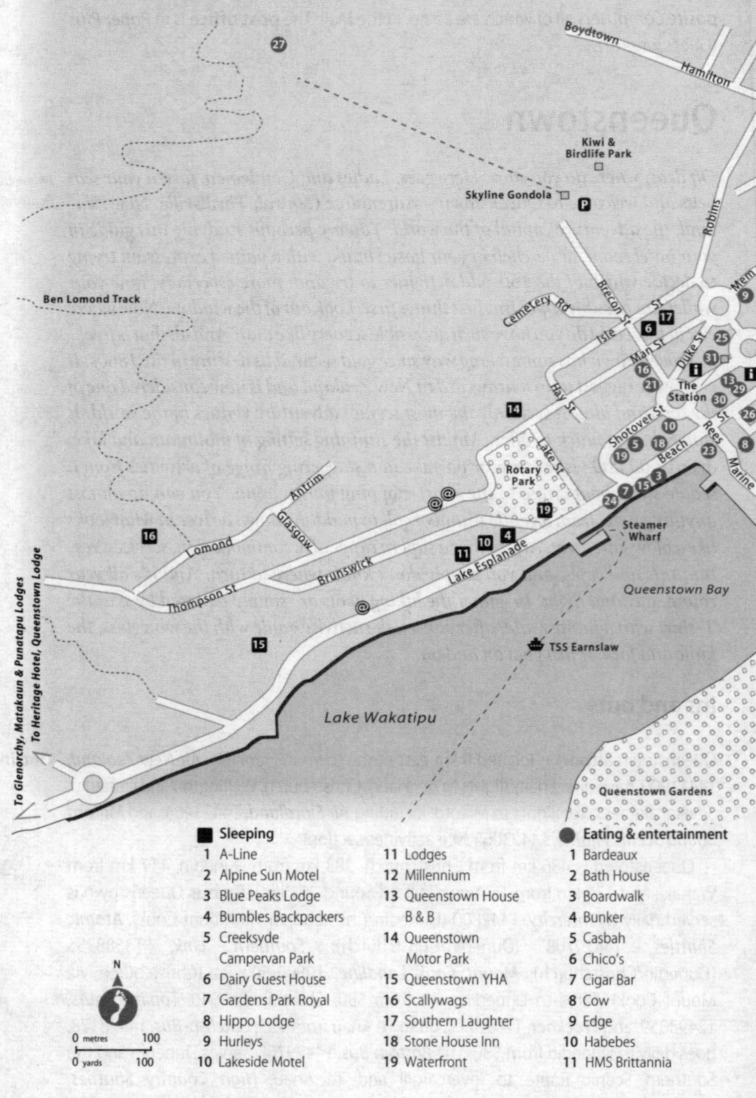

can be a good way to negotiate the **town** (timetable free from the VIC). ***Ski Shuttle*** T4426534, and ***AA Alpine Taxis***, T4426666 are the principal **ski field** shuttle operators serving Cardrona, Coronet Peak, The Remarkables and Treble Cone, from $25. The ***Arrow Express***, T4421900 (stops outside *McDonalds*) and ***Double-Decker Bus Tours*** (top of the Mall) go several times a day to **Arrowtown**, from $10 each way. ***Backpacker Express***, T4429939, runs daily to **Glenorchy**. For **taxi, car rental** and **bike hire** see 'Directory', below. You are advised to **book car rental** well in advance in summer. And remember, this is Queenstown – you can even hire your own modern bus complete with beds, the lot, contact ***InterNature***, T0800-005858, www.internature.co.nz

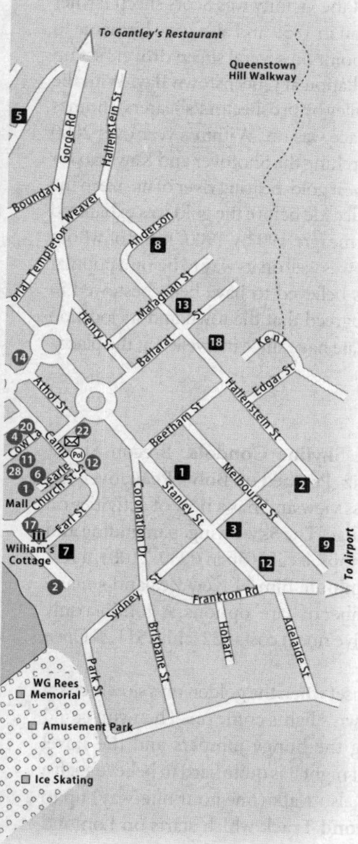

12 Joe's Garage
13 Leonardo's
14 Little India
15 Loaded Hog
16 Lone Star & Rattlesnake
17 McNeills Brewery
18 Minami Jujisei
19 Naff Caff
20 O'Connells Food Hall
21 Pasta Pasta Cucina
22 Pig & Whistle
23 Pog Mahone's
24 Queenstown Wharf Casino
25 Red Rock
26 Sky Alpine Casino
27 Skyline
28 Tardis
29 Tatler
30 Vudu Café
31 World

Tramping track transport For detailed information and trailhead bookings contact the **Information and Track Centre** (see information below). ***Tracknet***, T2497777, are the specialist tramping track operators to Te Anau (Kepler/Milford/Dusky). For Glenorchy and beyond (Routeburn/Greenstone-Caples/Rees-Dart) contact ***Backpacker Express***, T4429939, info@glenorchyinfocentre.co.nz For water-taxi transport via Lake Wakatipu and up the Rees/Dart, contact ***Glenorchy Cruising***, T4429951, WAKATIPU@xtra.co.nz or Backpacker Express (see above).

Otago

Information & orientation

Queenstown is compact and easily negotiable by foot. The main street for information and activity bookings is Shotover St while ***The Mall***, bordered by Camp St to the east and Marine Par on the waterfront, is the principal shopping and restaurant centre. The Esplanade (lakeside) and Steamer Wharf also have retail, information and activity outlets. Queenstown Gardens, located on the southern edge of Queenstown Bay, offer sanctuary from the chaotic town centre. There is total information overload in Queenstown. For non-biased advice head straight away to the very efficient and busy Queenstown **Travel and Visitor Centre** below the Clock Tower, corner of Shotover and Camp Sts, T4424100, F4428907, qvc@xtra.co.nz Open daily 0700-1900 (winter 1800). The website www.queenstownNZ.co.nz is excellent. **DOC**, T4427933, F4427932, are located across the road at 37 Shotover St, beside the **Information and Track Centre**, www.infotrack.co.nz/www.doc.govt.nz (Open daily 0830-1900, winter Mon-Fri

0900-1700, Sat/Sun 0930-1630.) They can provide all local walk and up-to-date major tramping information and deal with transportation and hut information and bookings. They also provide up-to-date weather forecasts. *Fiordland Travel Visitors Centre*, Steamer Wharf, T0800656503, T4424846, F4427504, www.fiordlandtravel.co.nz deals with a multitude of pleasures and trips to Milford and the Fiordland National Park. They also own and operate the TSS Earnslaw Steamship. For other **activity information** see 'Activities' below.

History

The first European known to have visited the vicinity was Scots sheep farmer Donald Hay, who explored Lake Wakatipu in 1859 and also gave his name to Lake Hayes near Arrowtown. From this point on several sheep drovers set up camp along the eastern shore of Lake Wakatipu at Queenstown Bay. With the discovery of gold in the Shotover River Valley by prospectors/shearers Thomas Arthur and Harry Redfern in 1862, the race was on. Within a year over 2000 hopefuls were camped in the area and searching the Shotover and Kawarau for gold. The Shotover is known to be the richest gold-bearing river of its size in the world. Despite that, it only took about a decade before the gold was exhausted and the population declined, reaching a meagre 190 by 1900, most of whom were farmers. By the mid-1900's the town was well on its way to being a popular tourist resort. The name Queenstown is believed to have been bestowed in 1863, when at a public gathering it was agreed that the town and its location were 'fit for a Queen'. Various heads of state have since marvelled at the place.

Sights

Perhaps the best place to start is the **Skyline Gondola**, Brecon Street, T4410101, F4426391, www.skyline.co.nz Perched on **Bob's Peak**, over 450 m above the town, it boasts a world-class view and has a host of activities on offer including The Ledge Bungy, The Luge, The Sky-Swing, paragliding and helicopter flightseeing. There are also shops, a café (open 0930-2100), a restaurant (see 'Eating' below) and a 27-minute film of New Zealand's many attractions, $8 child $4. There are a number of 'fare' options. A gondola only costs $14, child $5. Gondola and Luge (five rides) costs $22, child $11. ■ *Open from 0900-2100.*

A good time to go up is just before sunset when the golden rays slowly creep up the **Remarkables Range** and the town's lights come on. Then you could perhaps enjoy a meal before watching the bungy jumpers and the novel 'Sky-Swing' below the main building. At night it is quite hard to believe such a place and such activities exist. You can also **walk** (one hour one-way) up to the Skyline Complex via the **Ben Lomond Track** which starts on Lomond Crescent (via Brunswick St off the Lake Esplanade).

While at the base of the gondola you might like to see the obligatory **kiwi** and friends in the **Birdlife Park**, T4428059. Set in quiet(ish) pine forest it displays all the usual suspects, including kiwi, morepork (owl), parakeets, tui and of course the 'cheeky kea'. Of the 16 endangered species, the rarest is the delicate **black stilt**, sadly, one of only about 150 remaining. ■ *Open daily 0900-1900 (winter 0900-1700), $10.50, child $4.* Also in Brecon Street is **Caddy Shack City** Mini-Golf, T4426642. Here a plethora of weird and wonderful holes will keep small kids (and big kids) amused for hours on rainy days or evenings, $7 (open 0930-dusk). **Queenstown Gardens** offer some respite from the crowds and has oaks, sequoias and 1500 roses planted in 26 named rose beds. On the way you might like to pop into the historic 1865 **Williams Cottage**, on Marine Parade, which has been restored and now serves as a small museum.

There are also a number of **wineries** around Queenstown that boast surprisingly fine wines given their location, making them the most southerly vineyards in the world. *The Peregrine* and *Gibbston Valley vineyards*, T4426910, near the Kawarau Bungy Bridge are the two most noted. The VIC has details and tours are available (see tours below) For the **best view** around Queenstown, if not the region (see page 615). Finally if you have run out of money or simply want a good laugh, head for the **Kawarau Bridge Bungy** (23 km east on SH6) and watch the jumpers. It is a fascinating mix of fear and fun and watching the spectators is just as entertaining.

Activities

The choice is of course vast. There are over 150 activities to choose from, with everything from the tipples of a wine tour to the ripples of jetboating. And Queenstown is not just geared up for the young and the mad. There are activities to suit all ages, from infant to octogenarian and from the able to the disabled. If a 91-year-old can do a bungy jump, surely the possibilities are endless? Of course it is the bungy that Queenstown is most famous for, and no doubt if you are prepared to make 'the jump' and have been saving your pennies to do so, then it is here, in Queenstown, you must finally pluck up the courage. Heights vary from about 40 m to 134 m, and if there is any advice here (other than psychological and financial counselling), it is – if you are going to do it, do it in style and go high!

The **'big four'** activities in Queenstown are considered to be the **bungy**, **jetboating**, **rafting** and **flightseeing**. But you can use your imagination and manage your finances way beyond just those – and make sure you shop around. Do not be swayed by reputations or the Las Vegas-style advertising and marketing that confronts you the moment you arrive. Try to consider a variety of pursuits according to the budget at hand and the sheer variety available. For example consider something that costs nothing and is rather sedate, like a good walk taking in a stunning view, since this as just as much 'Queenstown' as anything else. Then by all means get the pulse racing with something high on the 'adrenalinometer', like a bungy, followed perhaps by something easy-going or an activity you can do nowhere else like a cruise on the TSS Earnslaw. Above all, don't only consider what you are 'supposed' to do, but also what most others do not. Queenstown is special and deserves far more of your attention and imagination.

Of course there are numerous **'combos'** on offer, and this is often a good way to go, saving you significant dollars. Some will take up about four hours, others are an exacting 12, it's all up to your stamina, your budget and of course your sheer 'guts'. A brief outline of the 'combos' available are listed below. One word of warning. If you are unsure of an activity and whether you can, or indeed will, actually do it, do not part with your cash. There will be no refunds.

In Queenstown you will be confronted with numerous sales and promotional outlets that can sniff your dollars in a dead calm, so be careful. The big players are *A J Hackett* (Lord of the bungy), *The Pipeline* (their major competitor) and *Shotover Jet*, with numerous others biting at their heels. A J Hackett and Shotover share an office in 'The Station', suitably situated right where the buses stop, at the corner of Shotover and Camp Street, T4425252, www.AJHackett.com Open 0700-2100, winter 0800-2000. Bookings can be made direct, but most accommodation establishments, especially backpackers, will book on your behalf. The Station is also the main pick-up and drop-off point for the relevant activities. Other offices in Shotover Street include *Pipeline*, 27 Shotover Street, T4425455, www.bungy.co.nz The best advice is first to take a wander into the unbiased VIC below the Clock Tower, have a chat and avail yourself of the leaflets and all the information.

Activity combos There are a huge number of combo packages available, from the main players like *A J Hackett*, *Pipeline* and *Shotover* to independents like *Adventure Marathon*. Most gravitate (no pun intended) between the big four – bungy, rafting, jetboating and flightseeing, with the odd 'luge' or movie thrown in. Bear in mind there are also others on offer like fish/trek, plus Heli-skiing or hiking. If you are short of time a combo is probably the best way to go, and with prices ranging from about $160 to $400 the savings can be quite attractive. One of the best, but most demanding combos is *Adventure Marathon's* full day (and at 12 hours it is exactly that) which includes the Nevis Bungy-jetboat-raft-gondola-luge, and ledge bungy for $395. They even throw in the Skyline movie. For details contact *Queenstown Combos*, T4427318.

A slightly less demanding value package is the *High Five* 3 ½-hour jetboat-helicopter-skyline-movie and luge offered by Shotover, T4427318, for $159. The half-day helicopter-raft and jetboat 'Triple Challenge' is also good value at $239. If you are still intent on a bungy this could perhaps be combined with one of the *Hackett* or *Pipeline* deals for multiple jumps. Again the best advice is to shop about and take your time.

Ballooning *Sunrise Balloons*, T4418248, balloons@queenstown.co.nz offer a three-hour flight with Champagne breakfast for $295, child $175. It is expensive, but given the scenery it is a great venue.

Bungy jumping The first commercial bungy jump in the world was created at **Kawarau Bridge**, about 12 km east of Queenstown, by *A J Hackett* and associates in 1988. Although perhaps the most famous spot and certainly the most accessible, at 43 m it is now dwarfed by most of the others. Since 1988 Hackett has created three other sites, the 71-m **Skippers Canyon** Bridge, the 47 m urban '**Ledge**' bungy beside the Skyline complex above Queenstown and, perhaps the mightiest and certainly the best, the awesome and the highest (ground based) 134-m **Nevis Highwire**. Not to be outdone Hackett's main competitors, *Pipeline*, are planning a **balloon bungy** option to add to their already established 102-m **Pipeline Bungy** over the Shotover River in Skippers Canyon. Jump prices range from $125 for the Ledge to $149 for the Nevis. This includes a 'T' shirt, but videos are usually extra. There are a number of **combos** on offer like *Hackett's* 'Bungy Thrillogy' or *Pipeline's* 'Grand Slam', from $199, which includes the 102-m bungy, jetboat, four-wheel drive and the 'Flying Fox' (see other activities below). A **second (24 hr) jump** at most sites is half price. For more information and bookings contact *A J Hackett* at 'The Station', corner of Shotover and Camp Streets, T4424007, www.AJHackett.com or *Pipeline* HQ, 27 Shotover Street, T4425455, www.bungy.co.nz

Canyoning Although Wanaka is famed for its canyoning activities, Queenstown's very own *12-Mile Delta*, T0800-222696, and *Vertigo Canyoning*, T4411261, offer similar exciting trips that involves abseiling, scrambling, rappelling and plunging your way down a mountain river. Note, this is not one for the acrophobic or the 'damn it darling, my shoes are wet'. Half or full day from $85.

Children's activities If you have kids and want to do the family thing, or conversely leave them in somebody else's capable hands, then the two companies to contact are *Family Adventures*, T4425112, and *Activekids*, T4421003, activekids@xtra.co.nz *Family Adventures* offer full- or half-day 'sedate' rafting trips for families from $125, child $90, while *Activekids* offer qualified care and day trips to Arrowtown and around Queenstown for those seven years and up.

Climbing, abseiling and mountaineering The possibilities are endless, and the **Mount Aspiring National Park** provides world-class venues. *Queenstown Mountain Guiding*, corner of Shotover and Rees Streets, T4413400, www.mountainguiding.co.nz offer a wide variety of trips from glacier walks and Heli-hikes to expeditions and instruction courses. They also guide on Mount Aspiring, Mount Cook and Mount Tasman. *Mountain Works*, 17 Shotover Street, T0508SUMMIT, www.mountainworks.co.nz are similar and offer abseiling and rock climbing trips and courses. Prices range from about $100 for a full-day trip to about $650 for a three-day mountain climb. If the weather closes in, or for practice, the Queenstown Events Centre, Joe O'Connell Drive, Frankton has a 12-m high **climbing wall**. T4423664, $10, child $5. Daily 0900-2100.

Cruising It won't take you long to spot the delightful *TSS Earnslaw* (TSS incidentally stands for Two Screw Steamer), plying the waters of Lake Wakatipu from the Steamer Wharf in Queenstown Bay. The TSS Earnslaw, named after the highest peak in the region Mount Earnslaw (2819 m), was launched at the most southerly end of **Lake Wakatipu**, Kingston, in 1912 and burns 1-ton of coal an hour. Despite her propensity to belch half of New Zealand's 'Kyoto nasty smoke quota' into the air she is a lovely sight indeed and there are a number of cruising options available. A standard one-hour 35-minute cruise heads west across the lake to its southern edge to the **Walter Peak Station**. They depart from the Steamer Wharf October-April every two hours from 1000-2000 (reduced winter schedule), from $33, child $10. A 3 ½ hour cruise, plus a farm tour of the Walter Peak Station which is designed to give an insight into typical Kiwi farming life (and to access lots of affectionate animals), costs $49, child $10. With a BBQ it is $14 extra. A four-hour evening dinner cruise costs $80, child $40. There are also 40-minute horse trekking and wagon-rides available at Walter Peak. *Fiordland Travel*, beside the Steamer Wharf, are the owner-operators and take bookings, T0800-656503, www.fiordlandtravel.co.nz

Note that there are also numerous **cruise/bus** and **cruise/fly options** on **Milford** and **Doubtful Sounds** that operate out of Queenstown (see Milford and Doubtful Sound sections). **Lion Cruises**, 78 Lower Shotover Road, T4423499, offer 1½-hour lake cruises aboard the lovingly restored 1908 Lion motor launch, from $48, child $24.

Fishing The region provides some excellent trout and salmon fishing, and there are numerous guides offering simple half-day to full-day Heli-fishing trips. Operators include *Fly Fishing NZ*, T4425363; *Queenstown Fishing Guides*, T4425363, www.wakatipu.co.nz; *Over the Top Helicopters*, T4422233, www.flynz.co.nz; and *Glenorchy Cruising* (see Glenorchy section) Prices vary from around $120 per hour to between $350 and $650 for the full-day. Heli trips range from half-day $565 to full-day $1220, both for two.

Flightseeing There are numerous options available and you are advised to shop around. If you do not have time to reach **Milford Sound** by road then a scenic flight is highly recommended. Note that there are numerous fly, fly/cruise/fly and bus/cruise/fly options on offer to Milford. **Fixed-wing** operators offering flights to Milford and Fiordland include *Air Fiordland*, T4423404, www.airfiordland.com *Queenstown Air*, T4422244, www.queenstownair.co.nz *Air Milford*, T4422351, www.airmilford.co.nz *Milford Sound Scenic Flights*, T4423065, milfordsound@queenstown.co.nz *Air Wakatipu*, T4423148, www.flying.co.nz Prices range from a one-hour local flight up to Glenorchy and around from $170, child $85, to the full four-hour Milford Sound and Mount Cook experience, from $345, child $205.

The principal **helicopter** companies are **Glacier Southern Lakes**, T4423061, www.heli-flights.co.nz *The Helicopter Line*, T4423034, www.helicopter.co.nz *Over The Top Helicopters*, T4423299, www.flynz.co.nz *Heliworks*, T4414011. Prices range from a 25-minute local flight across The Remarkables from $99, to a two-hour 'Peak Picnic' from $750. Over the Top provide a great range of Milford, Queenstown, **Heli-fishing and Heli-skiing** options. For more information on flightseeing trips to Milford Sound and Fiordland see Milford section page 643. If you fancy a flight with a difference try the three-hour aerobatics '*Pitts Special*'. Labelled as the 'Ferrari of the skies', it reaches speeds of up to 300 kmph with 3G turns. Fantastic. Contact *Actionflite*, T0800-360264, www.actionflite.co.nz

Otago

Flying-fox and Fly-by-Wire The Flying Fox is based in Skippers Canyon and run by Pipeline, T4425455. It basically involves being strapped into a harness and flying 250 m across the canyon suspended from a wire. Thankfully the brakes are hi-tech and actually provide the highlight, from $79. Combo-packages including bungy and jetboat are also available. The **Fly-by-Wire**, T4422116, is the sister operation to the original, created in Paekakariki, Wellington Region, from $145.

Golf One of the best courses in New Zealand is at the *Millbrook Resort*, Malaghan's Road, Arrowtown, T4417010, proshop@millbrook.co.nz It was designed by former Kiwi ace Bob Charles and opened in 1993. It is renowned for its long fairways, water hazards and of course its views. Green fees from $95.

Arrowtown itself also has a nice course at Centennial Avenue, T4421719, from $30. Of course Queenstown would have to have a **Frisbee Golf Course**, which is located in Queenstown Gardens, but don't be surprised if a dog disappears with your frisbee. Contact *Outside Sports*, Camp Street, T4428883, $2. They also sell frisbees, but no dog treats.

Horse trekking *Moonlight Stables*, T4421229, are located 15 minutes from Queenstown near Lake Hayes. A 1 ½-hour ride costs from $55, child $35. Full-day and fishing trips also available. *Shotover Stables*, T4429708, offer one-hour 45-minute or full-day treks from $48. For other operators see Glenorchy section, page 620. **Horse and carriage rides** are available in town from $20. Departs Steamer Wharf at 1200-1600 and from 1800 to late (seasonal).

Jetboating Such is the marketing, somehow you seem familiar with the *Shotover Jet* before you even arrive in Queenstown. That indelible blurred image of a red boat full of smiley faces and captain cool in shades at the wheel. Jetboating is one of the big four activities in Queenstown and, other than the thrills of the precipitous **Shotover Gorge**, there are also other independent operations on the **Kawarau** and the superb aesthetics of the **Dart River**. Shotover Jet are the originals, having been in existence for over 30 years, and offer the almost 'must-do' operation on the Shotover River – the only folks permitted to do so on the lower reaches. An efficient, safe and thrilling 30-minute, 70-kmph 'blat' down the river will see you too with a smiley face, interrupted only intermittently with one of shock as you are given the impression of coming perilously close to rock walls and jagged logs. The highlight of all the trips are the superb 360 degree turns that always soak some poor soul in the boat. Shotover Jet picks up from town several times a day for the 15-minute ride to the riverside. They can be booked at The Station, Shotover Street, T4428570, T0800SHOTOVER, www.shotoverjet.com From $75, child $35.

On Marine Parade (lakeside) you will find *Kawarau Jet*, T4426142, www.kjet.co.nz and *Twin River Jet*, T4423257, www.twinriversjet.co.nz both of whom zoom out across Queenstown Bay and down the Kawarau and up the lower reaches of the Shotover, one hour from $69, child $39. One of the best scenic jetboating trips in the world is also available with *Dart River Jetboats* or *Dart Wilderness Adventures* in Glenorchy (see Glenorchy section), 5-6 hours from $119, child $59. *Skippers Canyon Jet*, T4425455, www.grandcanyon.co.nz offer 16-km, 3 ½-hour trips (from Queenstown) to the upper reaches of the Shotover River in Skippers Canyon. This location gives an insight into the mining history and zips under the two historic suspension bridges (combo bungy/jetboat trips available), from $85, child $42.50.

Kayaking Some superb day to multi-day sea kayaking is offered on **Milford** and **Doubtful Sounds** (see relevant sections). Locally kayaks can usually be hired on the waterfront. For the very enjoyable ('blow-up carrot') **Funyak** trips on the Dart River see page 620; three hours from $179.

Mountain biking There are many options, from the manic Heli-bike to the low level mundane. *Adventure Biking*, T4429708, boxer@paradise.co.nz offer a three-hour easy-moderate trip from Queenstown that takes you from Moke Lake to Seffer Town – an area steeped in gold mining history, from $59. *Mountain Bike Adventures*, based at Outside Sports at the top of The Mall in town, T4428883, www.outsidesports.co.nz offer a three-hour trip from the top of Deer Park Heights, from $75. Again this is an easy to moderate ride. They also offer independent bike hire. *Skippers Canyon Mountain Biking*, T4429708, offer bike/raft, bike/bungy (but not on it!) and Heli-bike options in Skippers Canyon with almost all of the biking being downhill, from $105. *Gravity Action*, T4428178, offer half-day rides on the famous Skippers Pack Track, departing Queenstown at 0830 and 1230. Experience advised. For bike **rentals** see 'Directory' below.

Off-Road, trial-bike and snowmobile adventures *Nomad Safaris*, T4426699, www.outback.net.nz offer excellent two-hour to half-day 4x4 tours of the Skippers Canyon and Macetown goldfields. They also stop for a bit of gold panning. From $75, child $50. *Skippers Canyon 4WD*, run by Pipeline, T4425455; 6WD *Goldseekers*, T4425949, and *Outback Tours*, T4427386, offer a similar four-hour experience from $80, child $50. *Off Road Adventures*, 61A Shotover Street, T4427858, www.offroad.co.nz, have two-wheel and 4-wheel bike tour packages and rentals. Their two-hour guided trip costs from $100 and kids are welcome. In winter the self-drive or guided Heli/snowmobile adventures available through *Nevis Snowmobiles*, T4450843, www.snowmobilenz.co.nz are great fun. *Snowmobile Safaris* T4426699, run by Outback offer a similar package. Prices on application.

Parapenting, paraflying and hang-gliding When you arrive in Queenstown it won't be long before you see the colourful chutes of the tandem parapent descending gracefully down into the town from Bob's Peak and the Skyline Complex. It's a wonderful way to see the views, but a bit 'Queenstown' when your instructor answers his mobile phone mid-flight! Contact *Queenstown Parapenters*, T4425854, www.queenstown-tandem-paragliding.co.nz from $140. If you would rather be alone, then you might like to try paraflying across the lake with *Queenstown Parafly*, Main Pier, T4428507, 15 minutes from $69, child $55. For 15-25-minute tandem-hangliding trips contact *Antigravity*, T4418898, www.antigravity.co.nz from $160, or *Sky Trek*, T4426311, from $145.

Rafting There are three rafting operators in Queenstown: *Queenstown Rafting*, T4429792, www.rafting.co.nz a joint venture between Fiordland Travel and Kiwi Experience, who ply the rapids of the Shotover and Kawarau, with such enchanting highlights as 'The Toilet' and 'The Sharks Fin'. Depart Queenstown 0830 and 1315, from one to five hours, $109. Activity Combos also available. *Extreme Green Rafting*, T4428517, www.nzraft.com is the oldest company and also rafts the Shotover or Kawarau. Departures 0815 and 1245. One to five hours, from $99. *Challenge Rafting*, T4427318, www.raft.co.nz offer half-day or raft **combo** trips, again on the Shotover and Kawarau from $109. Minimum age for rafting is 13 years.

River sledging and surfing River surfing is basically the cunningly simple concept of replacing a raft with your own personal bodyboard. It is great fun and provides a far more intimate experience with the water! There are two companies; *Mad Dog*, T4427797, and *Serious Fun*, T4425262, www.riversurfing.com River sledging basically involves more drifting as opposed to surfing and provides more buoyancy. *Frogz Have More Fun*, T4439130, www.frogz.co.nz are based in Wanaka but pick up from Queenstown. All trips are about four hours (two hours on the water) and cost from $109.

Skiing Queenstown is as much a winter ski resort as it is a summer madhouse. From June to September the two local ski fields of **Coronet Peak** and **The Remarkables** spring into action. **Coronet Peak** (1649 m) is the larger of the two and the more accessible (25 minutes via SH6 west and Lower Shotover Rd). It also has a longer season, **night skiing** (Friday/Saturday 1600-2200), and a brasserie, bar, café and crèche. Slopes are suitable for the beginner to the advanced, with the intermediate being the best catered for. Day lift-pass costs $68, child $34, T4424620. **The Remarkables** ski field is higher (1935 m) and accessed from SH6, south of Frankton (45 minutes). The road is steep and often requires chains. Shuttle buses from Queenstown are recommended. Being the highest in the region, the snow conditions are often superior and then of course there are the stunning **views**. Slopes cater for all levels of ski and snowboard as well as cross-country. A day lift pass costs $65, child $32, T4424615. The **NZSuperpass**, two-day ($122, child $61) to 10-day ($530, child $265) give full access to both ski fields and also Mount Hutt in Canterbury. One-day ski/boots/poles rental $35, child $20. One-day snowboard and boots $50. Lessons from $70. Also within range of Queenstown are the **Cardrona** (45 km), T4437341, and **Treble Cone**, T4437443 (95 km). For ski **equipment hire** see 'Directory' below. For **transportation** see 'Getting around' above. For detailed information on both ski fields get your hands on the *'Queenstown Winter Resort*

Guide' from the VIC, or visit the website www.nzski.com Finally, for **snow reports**, T0900-99766 ($0.99 per minute).

Tandem skydiving Queenstown offers one of the most scenic skydiving venues on earth, the 'bungy without the bounce' – or the elastic rope for that matter. *Skydive Tandem*, T4425867, www.skydivetandem.co.nz, offer 3 ½-hours trips from Queenstown. Heights are from 9,000 to 15,000 ft, from $245.

Tours Vineyard, garden and general **sightseeing** tours offer a more sedate diversion from the mainstream adrenaline activities. There are many operators including *Awesome Wine Tours*, T4422905, five hours from $85. Includes lunch at the Gibbston Winery and free tastings. *Wine Time*, T0508946384, offer full- or half-day lunch and dinner tours. *Central Otago Wine Tours*, T4426622, www.winetoursnz.com take you to local vineyards and further afield to the Cromwell vineyards. Half- to full-day from $115. *Queenstown Wine Trail*, T4423799, visits all the main Kawarau Valley vineyards, four hours from $66. You can also visit the vineyards via jetboat with *Kawarau Jet*, T4426142, four hours from $135. For a good four hours local garden tour contact *Queenstown Garden Tours*, T4423799, from $69, and for a scenic 'Harley' motorcycle tour in a sidecar, contact *Scenic Motorcycle Tours*, T4427640, 30 minutes from $66.

Tramping Queenstown is a principal departure point for the Routeburn, Greenstone-Caples and Rees-Dart Tracks. For detailed information, hut and transportation bookings visit the Information and Track Centre (see information above). For guided walks on the Routeburn, Greenstone and Milford tracks from 1-6 days contact *Routeburn Walk Ltd*, T4428200, www.routeburn.co.nz Full day from $105, child $70. Lunch and morning tea provided. *Hollyford Track*, T4423760, www.hollyfordtrack.co.nz offer packages on the Hollyford with comfortable accommodation and jetboat options on part of the route. 3-4 days from $1300 all in. *Guided Nature Walks*, T4427126, www.nzwalks.com and *Arrowtown Lodge*, T4421101, offer a wide range of trips from half- and full- to multi-day from $75.

Walking For guided walks see above. The immediate Queenstown area offers many excellent walks from one hour to half a day. The DOC Visitor Centre on Shotover Street displays and can advise on the many local alternatives. If you have half a day, reliable wheels and walking boots, the walk to the lookout above the Remarkables ski field is highly recommended.

Other recommended walks: Queenstown Hill Accessed from York Street (look for DOC sign), this is a 2-3-hour moderate walk up to a scenic lookout above the town. The millennium gate on the way up is a nice and unusual piece of craftsmanship.

Ben Lomond (1747 m) dominates the scene above Bob's Peak and the Gondola and provides stunning views of the town and Lake Wakatipu. The full walk can be negotiated through forest from Lomond Street (from the Esplanade), but the best bet is to take the Gondola and join the track from there, 6-8 hours return. Details available from DOC.

Twelve-Mile Delta to Bob's Cove, an easy two-hour jaunt on the shores of Lake Wakatipu, accessed from the main Glenorchy Road (12 km). The **Mount Crichton Scenic Reserve** inland and just a bit further along the road also offers good options. Again DOC can provide details and leaflets.

Other activities Amongst the multitude of activities available at the Skyline (Gondola) Complex above the town is the **Luge**, the rather tame cousin of the famous course in Rotorua. The gondola trip and five rides will cost $26, child $19 (0930-dusk). The new invention with our activity junkie Hackett is the **Ledge Sky-Swing**, which is the delightful concept of being strapped into a harness and dropped from a great height and at mighty speeds, making the average park swing look like utter tedium, T4424007, from $79. One of the few opportunities to enjoy a **Maori Concert and Feast** is available in Queenstown, and if you missed out in Rotorua this is your chance. The hangi-style feast begins after a traditional 'powhiri' (Maori welcome) at 1900 with a concert at 2030-2130, T4428878, from $45. Train buffs will delight at the **Kingston Flyer**, T2488848, www.kingstonflyer.co.nz which puffs along for one hour 15 minutes on a 14-km track from Kingston, 47 km south of Queenstown. Daily 1015 and 1345, morning pick-ups available from Queenstown. Ride only $20, child $7. Also available is **Clay-bird Shooting**, T0800-273251, two hours from $115, **water-skiing, skating** and **gold panning**. The VIC has details.

Otago

Essentials

Sleeping Despite a healthy range of accommodation types and a total of 8,000 beds, it is essential to book 2 or 3 days in advance in mid summer or during the height of the ski season (especially during the Winter Festival in mid-Jul). This particularly applies to backpacker accommodation.

There is plenty of choice of **hotels**, with over a dozen major ones in town. The **LL-AL** *Heritage Hotel*, 91 Fernhill Rd, T4424988, F4424989, www.heritagehotels.co.nz offers a wide range of modern suites, has all the usual facilities and is particularly recommended for it's fine views. It even has a health club. The **LL-AL** *Millennium Hotel*, Cnr Frankton Rd and Stanley St, T4418888, F4418889, millennium.queenstown@cdlhms.co.nz is relatively new and very well positioned close to town. Again it has a wide range of suites and all the usual modern well-appointed facilities. The **LL-AL** *Gardens Park Royal*, corner of Earl St and Marine Par, T4427750, F4427469, reservations@queenstown.parkroyal.co.nz is in an ideal position at the edge of the town centre, right on the waterfront and a stone's throw from the peace and quiet of Queenstown Gardens. All that lets it down is its rather bizarre exterior architecture. The **AL-A** *A-Line Hotel*, 27 Stanley St, T4427700, aline@scenic-circle.co.nz offers well-appointed A-frame-style units with great views, within 2 mins of the town centre. For a very good budget hotel try the **B-D** *Hotel Esplanade*, 78 Park St, T4428611, which overlooks the lake in a quiet area of town. It is a no-nonsense place but perfectly comfortable, good value for money and has a magnificent outlook for the price. Out of town is the sumptuous **LL-AL** *Millbrook Resort*, T4417000, F4417025, www.millbrook.co.nz with its world-class golf course and luxury facilities. It has suites, villas and cottages, 2 restaurants, a bar, and a health and fitness complex.

Self-contained apartments Like the main cities, Queenstown has realized the preference for luxury fully self-contained and serviced apartments. Just 2 of the recommended examples are the new **LL-AL** *Point Luxury Apartments*, 239 Frankton Rd, T4411899, F4411898, www.thepoint.net.nz; and the **L-AL** *Lakefront Apartments*, 26 The Esplanade, T4418800, F4418806, lakefront@xtra.co.nz located close to the town centre with fine views.

With about 80 **B&Bs** the choice is huge with most being in the upper to luxury range. The VIC has full listings. Some of the finest include **LL** *Matakauri Lodge*, Farrycroft Row (off the Glenorchy Rd), T4411008, F4412180, www.matakauri.co.nz It is a magnificent place set in private bush 5 km west of Queenstown, with uninterrupted views across Lake Wakatipu. Accommodation is in modern villa-style, fully self-contained suites. The spacious lodge offers a library and four fireplaces, perfect for that après-ski. A further 7 km out on the Glenorchy Road is the **LL** ***Punatapu***, 1113 Rapid Gate, T4426624, F4426229, www.punatapu.co.nz an equally sumptuous place with an individually styled 'hamlet' of suites around a central courtyard. Again the views are stunning and there is a swimming pool, spa, sauna, and the works! At the other end of town is the enchanting **LL** ***Pear Tree Cottage***, 51 Mountain View Rd, T4429340, F4429349, www.peartree.co.nz Located at the base of the Coronet Peak ski field it is a quiet, lovingly restored 1870's cottage, tastefully appointed with two bedrooms. In summer flowers abound. A little further out, overlooking Lake Hayes near Arrowtown, is the new and elegant luxury retreat **LL** ***The Loose Box***, T4421802, F4421802, www.theloosebox.com It is very well appointed, has all mod cons and is full of beautiful antiques. South, along SH6, is the **LL** ***Remarkables Lodge***, T/F4422720, www.remarkables@xtra.co.nz a well-established luxury lodge with a fine reputation. It offers modern facilities and great cuisine and is expensive but worth it.

In Queenstown itself in the upper range is the **LL-L** ***Dairy Guesthouse***, 10 Isle St, T4425164, F4425166, www.thedairy@xtra.co.nz which has 10 cosy en-suites in period-style house restored and modelled on a 1920's dairy. Nicely appointed with antiques, Asian textiles and Persian rugs. On Hallenstein St (47) is the historic **L** ***Stone House Inn***, T4429812, F4418293, www.stonehouse.co.nz Built in 1874 from local stone it is full of character and offers nicely appointed en suites, an open fire, jacuzzi and a nice view across the town. Also on Hallenstein (69) is the cheaper **A** ***Queenstown House B&B***, T4429043, F4428755, queenstown.house@xtra.co.nz It offers comfortable en suites, good views and a memorable breakfast. The **A** ***Chalet Queenstown*** nearby on Dublin St, T4427117, F4427508, is a small Swiss chalet-style B&B-come-hotel which is well positioned and good value.

For a budget B&B try **C-D** ***Scallywags***, 27 Lomond St, T4427083. It is half way between a B&B and backpackers and is good-value, friendly and quiet, with a nice atmosphere.

Motels There are over 70 to choose from, so shop around. The VIC has full listings. Prices are generally more expensive than elsewhere, especially in mid-summer, so do not necessarily expect the value for money that you are used to. On the way into town is the **AL-A** ***Alpine Village Motor Inn***, 633 Frankton Rd, T4427795, F4427738, alpinevillage@xtra.co.nz a large place best noted for the views of The Remarkables from the rooms or chalets. In-house restaurant. As you come into town the **A-B** ***Goldfields***, 57 Frankton Rd, T4427211, goldfieldsmotel@xtra.co.nz is a pleasant, value option. Centrally located, at the upper range, try the hotel/motel **AL** ***Hurleys***, T4425999, F4425998, www.hurleys.co.nz which has tasteful fully self-contained studios supported with great facilities. Nearby the **AL** ***Blue Peaks Lodge***, Cnr Stanley and Sydney St, T4429224, F4426847, www.bluepeaks.co.nz is also recommended. At the mid-lower end is the **A** ***Alpine Sun Motel***, 18 Hallenstein St, T4428482, F4426432, alpine.sun@xtra.co.nz which is basic but comfortable and well positioned. Elsewhere on the waterfront, offering superb views (which you pay for), are the popular **AL** ***Waterfront***, 109 Beach Rd, T4425123, www.thewaterfront.co.nz, the **AL** ***Lodges***, 8 Lake Esplanade, T4427552, F4426493, www.thelodges.co.nz and the **AL** ***Lakeside Motel***, T4428976, F4428930, medward@es.co.nz

Hostels As you can imagine Queenstown is not short of backpacker hostels and with 20 establishments both old and new, staid or funky there is plenty to choose from. This is not the complete listing, just those that we recommend or that stand out. In summer you should book at least three days in advance. At the western end of town is the deservingly popular and new **C-D** *Queenstown YHA*, 80 Lake Esplanade, T4428413, F4426561, yhaqutn@yha.org.nz with its wide range of comfortable shared, twin and double rooms and modern facilities. Internet. A little further out is the friendly ski-lodge style **B-D** *Queenstown Lodge*, Sainsbury Rd, Fernhill, T4427107, F4426498, www.qlodge.co.nz It is quiet, has off-street parking, a pizza restaurant and excellent views. Back towards town is the well-established, spotlessly clean and efficient **C-D** *Bumbles Backpackers*, 2 Brunswick St, T4426298, which has a nice range of well-heated dorms, singles, twins and doubles, all with modern facilities and good views. Storage, drying rooms and internet.

Right in the heart of town is **B-D** *Thomas's Hotel* and Backpackers which is in an ideal position, with comfortable dorms and a wide range of doubles, some very good value with TV and phones and a grand view. The shared backpacker facilities are good, there is an in-house café and then of course there is Thomas the cat. Towards the Gondola, but still well positioned for town, is the **C-D** *Southern Laughter*, 4 Isle St, T4418828, which is small, but well established, has a nice atmosphere and facilities. The Larsson cartoon theme will keep you chuckling on rainy days. The **C-D** *Hippo Lodge*, 4 Anderson Heights, T/F4425785, hippolodge@xtra.co.nz is a superb place with the best backpackers view in town. It is modern, friendly, clean and well-facilitated, with dorms, twins and doubles, making it worth every step of the climb to get there. Parking can, however, be a problem.

Motor camps and campsites The popular **A-D** *Creeksyde Campervan Park*, 54 Robins Rd, T4429447, F4426621, creeksyde@camp.co.nz is the most centrally located and has modern motel units, flats, cabins, lodge rooms and good facilities including spa. It gets busy in summer, so pre-book. The huge and efficient **C-D** *Queenstown Motor Park*, on Man St, T4427252, info@motorpark.co.nz is spacious with cabins both old and new, powered/tent sites and a shop nearby. It is also good for information and activity bookings. Located about 6 km east and south on SH6 is the quieter and beautifully positioned **C-D** *Kawarau Falls Holiday Park*, T4423510, www.kaw.falls@xtra.co.nz set right next to the crystal clear river mouth from Lake Wakatipu. It is an ideal place to escape the stresses of town. It also has a Backpacker Lodge, with three grades of cabins, some self-contained. The shared facilities are fine.

Eating

There are 2 unique eating options in Queenstown, the Gondola restaurant and the TSS Earnslaw (see Sights above)

There are over 100 eateries in Queenstown, with a choice and quality to compete with any of the larger cities in New Zealand. There are Chinese, Mexican, Indian, Korean, Lebanese and Italian restaurants alongside the traditional New Zealand fare, with many doubling as bars and nightspots. Again, although prices can be slightly elevated, there are restaurants to suit all budgets.

Expensive Starting at the top, the ***Skyline Restaurant*** at the Skyline Gondola Complex, Brecon St, T4410101, offers a 6-course 'Taste of New Zealand' buffet which includes roast meats, seafood, local produce and salads followed by dessert and cheeseboard. The views obviously are exceptional, even at night. Open daily, lunch buffet 1200-1400, dinner from 1800. ***The Boardwalk***, 1st Floor, Steamer Wharf, T4425630, is well known for its superb seafood and great views. They are still dining out on the fact that it was Bill Clinton's choice when he visited in 1999. Open daily from 1200. Of equal reputation is the award-winning ***Gantley's***, Arthur's Point Rd, T4428999, www.gantleys.co.nz which is a very romantic affair set in an historic stone building 7 km out of town towards Arrowtown. Its wine list, like its cuisine, is superb. Open daily from 1830.

Mid-range The ***Bardeaux***, Eureka Arcade, The Mall, T4428284, is modern and classy, and especially popular with the après-ski crowd. Traditional NZ/Euro menu and a fine deck from which to watch the world go by. Open daily from 1700. For a nice mix of heritage and atmosphere try the ***McNeill's Cottage Brewery***, 14 Church St, T4429688. It's another award winner with a good selection of NZ meat, game, poultry

The Best View in Queenstown

*Although it takes a rugged drive and a fair scramble (in summer) to get there, the view of Lake Wakatipu and Queenstown from the **Remarkables Lookout** is worth every rut and step of the journey. Before considering this trip make sure the weather is clear and settled, since you will be at over 2000 m in altitude. Ensure that you are well prepared, with warm clothing and proper walking boots and that your car will survive the 1500 m climb up the unsealed road to the ski-fields (in winter you may need chains). The ski-field road is accessed off SH6 about 2 km south of Frankton. If the ski-field is open you might consider taking a shuttle from Queenstown, T4426534. From the Remarkables ski-field buildings, you are basically trying to reach the top of the Shadow Basin Chair Lift, the base of which is in the main car park. If the lift is open you have the option of using it, but in summer (or if you fancy the climb) then follow the path that zigzags up the slopes behind the main building to the 'Mid-Station'. From the Mid Station continue on the path in a rough line with the chairlift until you reach its terminus. The lookout is about 200 m directly behind and further up from this point. On a clear day surrounded by snow, you won't forget it!*

From the lookout (2 ½ hours) it is then possible to climb and scramble with care, further south along the ridge to the weather station. From here you will have even greater views including Lake Alta, the entire ski-field below and north, to Mount Aspiring. On an exceptional day you may even see Mount Cook almost 200km away.

Otago

and seafood. A little further along and perched on the edge of the beach, next to Queenstown Gardens, is the very romantic ***Bathhouse***, T4425626. It has an imaginative menu and is a lovely spot for both lunch and dinner, from 1000. If you have kids or simply enjoy good seafood try the ***HMS Britannia*** in The Mall, T4429600. It is a wee bit on the expensive side but the portions are huge and the walls are something of a museum exhibit. Also popular, though more for its exterior aesthetics and atmosphere is, ***The Cow***, Cow La, T4428588. Set in a former stone milking shed it is a little cramped but full of character. Pizza and pasta is the speciality. Another popular pizza place is ***Pasta Pasta Cucina***, 6 Brecon St, T4426762. Open daily from 1200. For a good Indian meal look no further than ***Little India***, 11 Shotover St, T4425335, either sit-in or takeaway; and for Japanese the ***Minami Jujisei***, 45 Beach St, T4429854. For pub food try ***Pog Mahone's***, 14 Rees St, T4425382; the ***Loaded Hog***, Steamer Wharf, T4412969; or the very pleasant al fresco spot at the ***Pig and Whistle***, 19 Camp St. All are great for food, atmosphere and beer, and are open daily from about 1100.

Cheap ***Habebes***, Wakatipu Arcade, Rees St, T4429861, is very popular day café for cheap vegetarian and Middle Eastern takeaways. Open daily 1100-1800 If you have a car ***Giuseppes*** on Fernhill Rd (west of town), is considered the best place in town for a good value pizza. The ***O'Connell's Food Hall***, Camp St, has all the usual cheap buffet lunch outlets and is open from 0700.

Cafés

The ***Naff Caff***, 1/66 Shotover St, T4428211, is one of Queenstown's best and offers great light snacks, coffee and a value breakfast. Open daily from 0730. Further up towards town next to the VIC is ***Leonardo's***, T4428542. It's small but in a perfect position for that essential caffeine hit after arriving back from all the activities based at the 'The Station'. ***Joe's Garage***, on Camp St is also noted for its great coffee. On Beach St, the ***Vudu Café***, T4425357, also has a loyal local following and again is good for breakfast.

Entertainment

Queenstown is very much a party town, and at New Year particularly goes off like a fire-cracker. It can all be a lot of fun, but at its busiest don't go out looking for refined culture and conversation. With so much adrenaline and testosterone flying around it doesn't go far beyond the standard yelps about the 'awesome' bungy jumping, or the double-flip-half-hernia on the snowboard, maaaan. The well-established favourites like the ***Loaded Hog***, Irish ***Pog Mahone's***, British-style ***Pig and Whistle*** and quaint ***McNeill's Brewery*** (all above), are all well known for a good beer and atmosphere. Slightly more upmarket and more popular with the upwardly mobiles (with mobiles) is the ***Cigar Bar*** in the Steamer Wharf, ***The Bardeaux*** (see above), ***The Tatler*** in The Mall, and the hard to find ***Bunker*** in Cow La. The ***Red Rock***, 48 Camp St, T4426850, ***The Lone Star***, Brecon St, and ***Rattlesnake*** (upstairs), provide regular live music or DJ's and are the favoured haunts of the younger set. As far as late-night drinking and dancing goes, try ***Chico's*** at the bottom of The Mall (open until 0230), or ***The Tardis*** and ***The Bunker*** in Cow La. The unfortunately named ***'Buff'*** at 26 Camp St, is very dark, very DJ, very late and, apparently, very popular. ***The Edge***, on the corner of Camp and Memorial Sts, is a new nightclub open from 2200 every night. The ***Casbah***, 54 Shotover St, and ***The World***, also on Shotover St, are the most commercial, chat-up or throw-up venues with regular happy hours. Again both stay open until about 0230.

Otago

Away from the pub scene and into the gambling, you have the ***Queenstown Wharf Casino***, Steamer Wharf, T4411495, which is open from 1100-0300, and The ***Sky Alpine Casino*** on Beach St, T4410400. The ***Embassy Cinema*** is located in The Mall, T4429990. For something different try the ***Maori Feast and Concert*** (see 'other activities' above).

Shopping For second-hand outdoor and ski equipment don't miss the ***Small Planet Recycling Co***, 17 Shotover St, T4426393. For new sports/outdoor/ski equipment ***Outside Sports***, top of the Mall (open 0700-2200), T4428883. Expensive souvenir shops abound. The ***Alpine Food Centre***, on Upper Shotover St, is handy for groceries and tramping food supplies. Open Mon-Sat 0800-2000, Sun 0900-2000.

Events & festivals Queenstown's most famous and popular event is the 9-day ***Queenstown Winter Festival*** (mid Jul) which of course has its focus on skiing, but also involves many other forms of entertainment, from live concerts, arts and fashion events, to mad-cap races. Later in the month is the internationally recognized ***K2 Snowboard Challenge***. Mid-Sep sees more extreme and zany ski competitions during the ***Spring Carnival*** at the Remarkables Ski Area. The ***Queenstown Jazz Festival***, which is now in its 13th successful year, is held over Labour weekend in Oct.

Christmas and particularly **New Year** see the town a-buzz with Kiwis and foreigners alike, while on the first Sat of the year are the ***Glenorchy Races***, a local affair generally regarded as reflecting Glenorchy's true colours as a wild west frontier town. Annually in Feb, gourmands gather in the town's gardens to sample the delicacies produced by 15 local vineyards at the ***Central Otago Wine Festival.*** Also in Feb is the annual ***Millbrook Outdoor Concert***, which last year featured the Beach Boys. Autumn and late Mar see the colourful and increasingly popular ***Arrowtown Autumn Festival*** and the ***Ben Lomond Assault*** in Queenstown, an exhausting race to the town's famous 1747 m lookout. There is more strain on 2 legs with the ***Queenstown Half Marathon*** in mid-Apr, which almost coincides with the 4-wheel races of the 3-day ***Silverstone Race to the Sky***, in the Cardrona Valley, the highlight of which is a car race to the summit to see who is 'king of the mountain'. Throughout the year there are many multisports events from triathlons, to mountain traverses, peak to peaks, jetboat races, marathons and even horse cavalcades. For more details visit www.queenstown-nz.co.nz

Directory **Airlines**: *Air NZ*, Queenstown Travel Centre, 41 Shotover St, T4411900. **Banks**: All the major banks are represented and ATMs are available in The Mall, Shotover St, Beach St, Rees St, Steamer Wharf and the O'Connell's Shopping Centre. **Currency exchange** ***BNZ*** on Rees St (open Mon-Fri 0900-2000, Sat/Sun 1000-2000); ***Thomas Cook***, corner of Camp St and The Mall; ***ANZ Postbank***, Beach St. There is a *Travelex* in the Clocktower Building and at the airport, open daily until 1900. **Car hire**: ***Avis***, 9 Duke St, T4427280; ***Budget***, Chester Bding, corner of Shotover and Camp Sts, T4429274; ***Hertz***, 2 Church St, T4424106; ***NZ Rent-A-Car***, corner of Shotover and Camp Sts, T4427465; ***Pegasus***, The Mall, T4427167; ***Queenstown Car Rentals***, 26 Shotover St, T4429220; ***Thrifty***, Queenstown Airport, T4428100. **Communications Internet**: The cheapest is usually ***Budget Communications***, 2nd Floor, O'Connell St Shopping Centre. Others include ***The E Café***, 50 Shotover St, which plays good music, and the biggest is ***Internet Outpost***, 27 Shotover St. Most outlets are open in summer from 0900-2300. Post Office: Cnr Camp and Ballarat Sts, T4427670 (open Mon-Fri 0830-2000, Sat 0930-2000, Sun 1000-1800). It has post restante. **Cycle hire** ***Queenstown Bike Hire*** (Lakefront Esplanade), T4426039; ***Outside Sports***, corner of The Mall and Camp St, T4428883, from $45 a day (open 0800-2100); ***Small Planet***, 17 Shotover St, T4426393, from $25 per day. **Library**: corner of Shotover St and George Rd. **Medical Services**: Hospital, Douglas St, Frankton, T4423053 (no Accident and Emergency Department); Doctor, Athol Street Surgery, T4427566; Queenstown Medical Centre, Shotover St, T4427301. **Ski and Snowboard hire** ***Outside Sports***, corner of The Mall and Camp St, T4428883, (open 0800-2100); ***Bad Jelly***, 26 Camp St, T4424064; ***Brown's Ski Shop***, 39 Shotover St, T4424003; ***Extreme Green Ski and Snowboard Rental***, 39 Camp St, T4428517; ***Quest***, 27 Shotover St, T/F4428330. **Taxis**: ***AA Taxis***, T4418222; ***Alpine Taxi***, T0800-4426666; (for a Mercedes complete with interpreter), ***Prestige Tourist Services***, T4429803. Ranks can be found at the top of The Mall and lower Shotover St. **Useful addresses Police**: Non-emergency, 11 Camp St,T4427900, Emergency T111.

Around Queenstown

Arrowtown

Phone code: 03
Population: 1,700

Providing some respite from the stress and adrenaline highs of Queenstown is Arrowtown, located 21 km to the northeast. Yet another former **gold mining** settlement, its pleasant tree-lined streets with their old historic buildings lie nestled below the foothills of the Crown Range – an apt name given their once rich reserves of gold. The origins of Arrowtown go back to 1862 when prospector William Fox made the first rich strike in the Arrow River Valley – a find that soon brought over 7,000 other hopefuls to the area. The first few weeks of mining produced 90 kg alone. Although first called Fox's, once the settlement was firmly established it was renamed Arrowtown after the river that revealed its riches. Once the gold was exhausted, the town's economy was centred first on agriculture and, in more recent years, the more lucrative resource of tourism. Looking down its quaint but almost Hollywood-style main street, one hopes this modern form of gold will not destroy its true aesthetic wealth and soul. Autumn sees the village at its most colourful both in scenery and spirit when the hugely popular **Arrowtown Autumn Festival** takes place (end of March), T4421570, www.autumnfestival.co.nz

Ins & outs

The Arrowtown ***Double Decker Bus Tour*** departs from the top of The Mall in Queenstown daily at 1000 and 1400, allowing 1 hr in Arrowtown and returning from outside the Museum. It visits Lake Hayes and the Kawarau Bungy Bridge on the way, T4426067, $27, child $10. The ***Arrow Express*** runs regularly between Queenstown and Arrowtown from outside *McDonalds* in Queenstown and the museum in Arrowtown, T4421900, $18, child $10 return. They are happy to take bikes and even gold pans!

Sights The Arrowtown **Visitors Information Centre** is located at 69 Buckingham Street in the Lakes District Museum building, T4421824, F4421149, apa@arrowtown.org.nz/www.arrowtown.org.nz ■ *Open daily 0900-1700.* The free brochures *'Welcome to Historic Arrowtown'* and *'Historic Arrowtown'* are both comprehensive guides to the history and historic sites of the village and the surrounding area. The **Lakes District Museum,** T4421806, museum@queenstown.co.nz offers plenty of insight into the 'calm before the storm', and then depicts the areas rather chaotic and feverish gold mining boom.■ *0900-1700, $5, child $0.50.*

Outside the museum the tree-lined avenue of **Buckingham Street** reveals several old historic cottages that add to the much-photographed aesthetics. At the far end of Buckingham Street the **Chinese Settlement** offers further insight with several mud-walled huts, and a reconstruction of a general store. The Chinese were subjected to much prejudice and derision by the European miners and, much of the time, instead of seeking claims of their own, would sift through the tailings looking for fine gold undetected or simply left by the other rapacious miners. In the hills up-river from Arrowtown, and accessed via a difficult 13-km track, is the former mining settlement of **Macetown**. Its remnants and lively negotiation is the focus for a number of interesting tours by foot, four-wheel drive or on horseback. (See 'Activities' below). In the centre of Arrowtown, along Buckingham Street, there is a rash of the inevitable souvenir shops, with the genuine nuggets in the **Gold Shop** being the most interesting.

Otago

Activities & tours *Nomad Safaris*, T4426699, www.outback.org.nz provide an exhilarating two-hour (4 ½ hours from Queenstown) four-wheel drive trip to Macetown. There are over 25 river crossings and a stop for a spot of gold panning in the Arrow River (summer only), from $75. For a more sedate 1 ½-hour local tour by foot with **gold panning** contact *Golden Fox Tours*, T025-416083, from $20, child $10. **Mountain bike** rentals are available from *Small Planet Adventures*, 25 Buckingham Street, T4420900, fun@smallplanetadventures.com For **walking** and **hiking** options see the *Arrowtown Lodge*, below.

Sleeping The VIC has full listings of the many charming B&Bs in the village and its surrounds. Located right in the heart of town, in the original church grounds, is the very smart **LL-L** ***Arrowtown House***, 10 Caernarvon St, T4420025, www.arrowtownhouse.co.nz It's a boutique luxury lodge with 5 well-appointed en suites. If you enjoy walking you might consider the walking or walking/accommodation packages of the **AL-A** ***Arrowtown Lodge and Hiking Company***, 7 Anglesea St, T4421101, www.arrowtownlodge.co.nz There are 4 cottage-style en suites all designed in keeping with the village's historic past. There is a scattering of motels including the value **A-B** ***Viking Lodge Motel***, 21 Inverness Cres, T/F4421765, viking@inq.co.nz It has self-contained A-frame units and a swimming pool. The more expensive **A** ***Settlers Cottage Motel***, 22 Hertford St, T4421734, settlersmotel@clear.net.nz has more characterful units. For budget accommodation, try the basic but friendly **B** ***New Orleans Hotel***, 27 Buckingham St, T/F4421745, which has a few cheap and comfortable doubles and twins; or the **C** ***Royal Oak Hotel***, 46 Buckingham St, T4421700, which has the cheapest beds in town. The **D** ***Arrowtown Holiday Park***, Suffolk St, T/F4421876, is centrally located and has powered/tent sites.

Eating The 3 main and most popular, affordable, à la carte restaurants in town are the modern ***Saffron***, 18 Buckingham St, T4420131, which has a good Pacific-rim menu and a fine wine list (open daily 1130-2130); the older and more historic ***Stables Café and Restaurant***, 28 Buckingham St, T4421818, which is especially popular for al fresco dining (open daily from 1100-late); and the new ***Vinefera Café and Bar***, corner of Buckingham and Wiltshire Sts, T4421860. Set in an historic stone cottage, it specializes in NZ cuisine and has a good local wine list. Open daily lunch and dinner. For cheaper pub-style food try the ***New Orleans*** or ***Royal Oak Hotels*** in Buckingham St, while coffee and light snacks are best served at the peaceful ***Wind in the Willows Bookshop Café***, Ramshaw Lane (turn right at the top of Buckingham St), overlooking the river, T4420055. Open daily.

Glenorchy

Population: 200

North of Queenstown (48 km) via the superb **Wakatipu Lake** scenic drive is the tiny former frontier village of Glenorchy. Backed and surrounded on both sides by the rugged peaks of the **Fiordland** and **Aspiring National Parks**, the glacier-fed **Rees** and **Dart Rivers** and ancient beech forests, it is little wonder it has been labelled the 'Gateway to Paradise'. Indeed, part of the attraction here, other than the pure scenic delights or activities is a visit to **Paradise** itself – an aptly named little farming settlement 20 km further north. If you have always been looking for it, now you can say you have actually been there.

Activities available in Glenorchy include **jetboating** and **horse trekking** and the village also serves as he main access point to the **Routeburn, Greenstone/Caples** and **Rees-Dart** tramping tracks. Glenorchy is named after Glen Orchy, through which the Orchy River runs on its way to Loch Awe in the highlands of Scotland. With such similar scenery to their native land it is obvious why Scots pioneers were especially drawn to the place.

Otago

Ins & outs

Backpacker Express, 2 Oban St, T4429939, info@glenorchyinfocentre.co.nz offer a comprehensive transport system between Queenstown, Glenorchy and the major tramping track trailheads by road ($10 one-way) and water-taxi. *Glenorchy Cruising*, T4429951, also provide water-taxi services to various points along the Dart-Rees Track.

The **DOC Visitor Information Centre** is located at the end of the Main Rd, T4429937. Open daily 0830-1630 (closed weekends in winter). Although providing all the relevant local walks and tramping information/bookings, if your intentions are merely to pass through Glenorchy on your way to one of the major tracks, you are advised to avail yourself of the information, and secure hut bookings at the Queenstown offices. Likewise for accommodation and activities, although the **Glenorchy Store** in the Holiday Park, 2 Oban St, can provide some information, the Queenstown VIC is your best bet. For more general pre-visit information on Glenorchy the website, www.Glenorchy.com is also useful. For information on the Routeburn and Greenstone and Caples Tracks see page 646. **Internet** is available at the *Glenorchy Café*, Mull St. The Mobil Station on Mull St acts as the local **postal** agent.

Sights & activities

Other than the stunning scenery and the services on offer to the tramping fraternity, the big attraction in Glenorchy is the **Jetboating** operations that ply the **Dart River**. Unlike the highly commercial rides of the Shotover and Kawarau in Queenstown, the remote Dart penetrates parts of the Aspiring National Park simply not accessible by road, and provides one of the most scenic jetboat trips in the world. *Dart Jet Boat River Safaris* are based in Mull Street, Glenorchy, T4429992, www.dartriverjet.co.nz but also provide transportation from Queenstown. There are two safaris on offer: the *'Original'* and the *'Backroad'*. The Original is a two-hour, 72-km trip with an optional short walk. The outward journey concentrates on the scenery while the return concentrates on sheer fun/madness; from $125, child $62.50. Departs Queenstown daily September-April 0800,1200, 1400, May-August

0800, 1130; Glenorchy September-April 0900,1300,1500, May-August 0900,1230. The Backroad is a two-hour four-wheel drive/jetboat trip. From Glenorchy the road trip takes you past the settlement of Paradise before a 20-minute bush-walk and then 1 ¼-hour 40-km of jetboating. From Queenstown it is a five- to six-hour trip, from $125, child $62.50. Departs Queenstown daily September-April 1000, May-August 1130; Glenorchy September-April 1100, May-August 1230. *Dart River Safaris* also offer a '**Funyak**' option which is a part jetboat (32-km 1 ¼-hour), part paddle on a blow-up carrot (Well, okay – a kayak), from $179, child $98. Lunch included and transport from Queenstown available (departs Queenstown September-April 0930, May-August 1100). *Dart Wilderness Adventures*, T4429939, www.glenorchyinfocentre.co.nz offer a 70-km three-hour trip on the Dart River for $119, child $59. Again pick-ups are available from Queenstown.

Dart Stables in Glenorchy, T4425688, offer two-hour ($65), five-hour ($130), 1 ½-day ($300) and three-day/two-night ($700) **horse trekking** trips through scenic forest trails near the Rees and Dart Rivers. *High Country Horses*, T4429915, www.high-country-horses.co.nz are another company based in the Rees Valley.

If you get sea sick or don't trust horses, but are not scared of heights then *Glenorchy Air*, T4422207, offer **flightseeing** trips around both national parks and to Milford Sound. There are also Milford flight/cruise and Dart jetboat **combinations** available. From $90. **Fishing** and **nature cruises** to the lake islands are available with *Glenorchy Cruising*, T4429951, or *Backpacker Express* (see Ins and outs above).

If you wish to explore the area under your own steam there are several **short walks** on offer immediately around Glenorchy, with the 2-km **wetlands boardwalk (Glenorchy Walkway)** just at the northern outskirts of the town (accessed from Islay Street) being particularly recommended. The reflections and views of **Mount Earnslaw** are superb and and there is an abundance of birdlife. By road you can head north of Glenorchy and explore the **Rees** or **Dart River (Routeburn) Valleys**, or better still visit **Paradise** and head to the western trailhead of the **Rees-Dart Tramping Track**. On the way you will pass some awesome scenery. From the trailhead, you can also take a short walk through the beech forest on the tramping track's first section. Again the views of Mount Earnslaw from the Paradise Road are excellent and you can also have some fun with silly photos at the Paradise **road sign**. For more information on walking in the area contact the DOC visitor centre in Glenorchy.

Sleeping

Given its size, there is not a huge amount of choice in Glenorchy, but that lends to its atmosphere. One of the most idyllic and peaceful places in the region is the **A-D** ***Kinloch Lodge*** that is on the opposite side of the Dart River, accessed via the Dart Valley Rd (Routeburn Track road), 862 Kinloch Rd, T4424900, www.kinlochlodge.co.nz An historic 1868 cottage, it has proved immensely popular with trampers for many years. It has both characterful self-contained and dorm accommodation and can also be reached by water-taxi. Evening meals are offered and it has a shop on-site.

In Glenorchy itself the **A** ***Glen-Roydon Lodge Hotel***, corner of Argyle and Mull Sts, T/F4429968, www.glenroydon.com offers ski-lodge-style en suites with a shared lounge and open fire. There is also an in-house restaurant/café and bar. Across the road, the older **A-D** ***Glenorchy Hotel***, T4429902, relax@glenorchy.org.nz offers traditional NZ-style hotel doubles, en-suites or a self-contained cottage. It also has backpacker dorms. The cheap in-house **restaurant** and bar is popular, with the outdoor upper-deck views proving a top spot! The **A** ***Mount Earnslaw Motel***, 87 Oban St, T4426993, Corrine@xtra.co.nz is Glenorchy's newest motel and offers tidy, modern en suite units. The **C-D** ***Glenorchy Holiday Park and Backpackers***, 2 Oban St, T4427171 has a self-contained villa, standard cabins, bunkrooms and powered/tent sites. There is also a small store and information centre. The ***Glenorchy Café*** on Mull St, T4429958 is a funky little place that offers light snacks and a good breakfast – all of which can be enjoyed to the dulcet tones of 80's hits, played on that wonderful old fossil, the LP (remember those?). Internet is also available.

Wanaka and around

Phone code: 03
Population: 3,700

Wanaka is almost unfeasibly pleasant, and has to rank as one of the most desirable places in New Zealand. With its lake of the same name, lapping rhythmically at its heels, and its picture-postcard mountain backdrops that border the Aspiring National Park, it is easy to understand why Wanaka is such a superb place to visit, or indeed live. In recent years Wanaka has seen a boom in both real estate sales and tourism, but it is reassuring that its manic neighbour, Queenstown, will always keep growth in check. As it is, Wanaka is just perfect; not to busy, not to quiet, developed, but not spoilt and a place for all to enjoy. It is also not just a place frequented by the rich and famous. If such a town in such a setting were in any other developed nation Wanaka would almost certainly be a very different place. Although now you would never guess it, Wanaka's history goes back to the 1860s when it played an important role as a service centre for the region's itinerant gold miners. Today, its resource are activities and its miners are tourists. Year round, there are a multitude of things to do, from water sports and tramping in summer, to skiing in winter. But it can also be the perfect to do little except relax and recharge your batteries beside the lake. Wanaka is that kind of town.

Otago

Ins and outs

Getting there

By air Wanaka is accessed via Queenstown airport which is served by***Air New Zealand Link***, T0800-737000. The airfield for the Wanaka Region is located 8 km east of the town via SH6. ***Aspiring Air*** fly between Queenstown and Wanaka, T4437943. **By bus** Wanaka is served daily by ***Intercity***, T4437885 (Christchurch/Dunedin); ***Atomic Shuttles***, T4437414 (Christchurch/Dunedin Queenstown) and ***Southern Link***, T4437414 (Christchurch/Dunedin/Queenstown). ***Wanaka Connections***, T0800-879926, www.wanakaconnexions.co.nz also run daily between Queenstown and Wanaka. Wanaka is 424 km southwest of Christchurch via SH1 and SH8; 276 km northwest of Dunedin via SH8; and 117 km north of Queenstown via SH8 and SH6. Or, alternatively, 70 km from Queenstown via the Cardrona Valley Road.

Getting around

Local shuttle services are available to Wanaka **airfield** ($12), the **ski fields** (from $20 return) and the Mount Aspiring **trailheads** with Alpine Shuttles (Good Sports), T4437966; ***Edgewater Adventures***, T4438422; ***The Bus Company***, T4438775; ***Mizzy Bee Bus Co***, T4431855 (Ski fields); and the ***Boarders Bus***, T4431230. ***Mount Aspiring Express***, T4438422, specialize in national park trailhead connections (Raspberry Creek, twice daily $45 return, Mount Roy $5, Diamond Lake $10). With ***Mount Aspiring Express*** you can also drive up/bike back ($5 extra – not hire). For **car rental** and **bike hire** see 'Directory' below.

Information

The Wanaka **Visitor Information Centre** is located in the Log Cabin on the lakefront, 100 Ardmore St, T4431233, F4431290, www.lakewanaka.co.nz Open daily 0900-1730 (winter 0930-1630). This office also administers most of the local activity and adventure bookings through ***Lakeland Adventures***, T4437495, www.lakelandadventures.co.nz The

DOC Visitor Information Centre is on Upper Ardmore St at the junction with McPherson St, T/F4437660, www.doc.govt.nz It deals with all national park/tramping hut bookings and local walks information. Up-to-date weather forecast also available. Open daily 0800-1645. **Internet** is available at ***Budget Communications***, 38 Helwick St, T4434440 (open daily 1000-2200), and ***WanakaWeb***, 3 Helwick St, T4437429 (open daily 0900-2100).

Sights

One of the most immediate ways to get acquainted with the area is to make the short 45-minute climb up **Mount Iron** (240 m), just 2 km before the township on the main road. A stubborn lump of rock left by the glaciers, its 360-degree views are very impressive and provide an ideal way to get your bearings. The track is well marked and there is a car park by the roadside. Wanaka town centre borders the very pretty **Roy's Bay** that opens out beyond **Ruby Island** into the southern and indented bays of **Lake Wanaka**. The lake, which is 274 m above sea level and over 45 km long, occupies an ancient glacier bed. The aesthetics speak for themselves, but the glistening waters are also

Otago

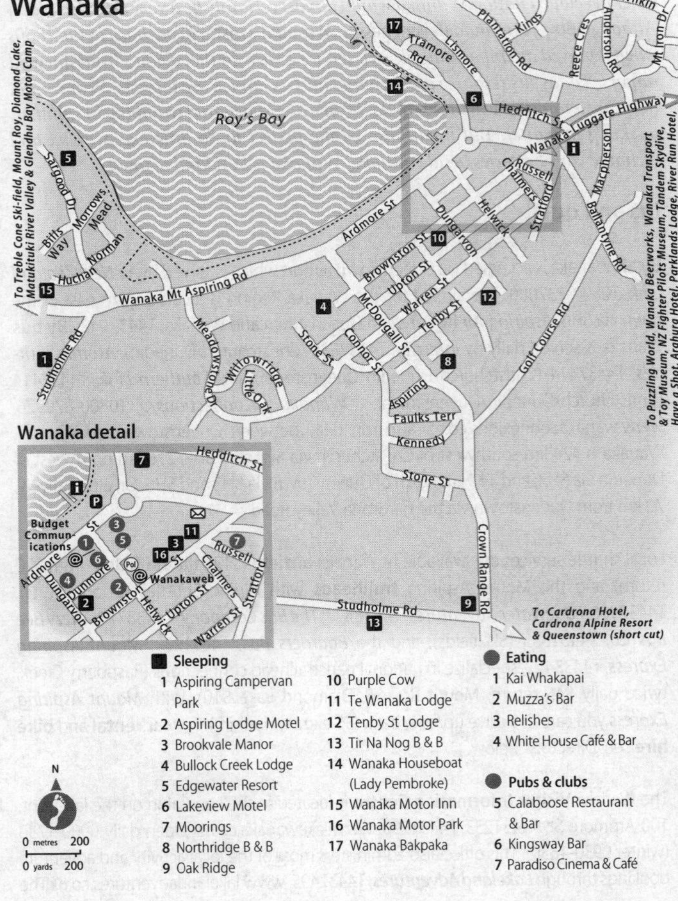

Sleeping
1 Aspiring Campervan Park
2 Aspiring Lodge Motel
3 Brookvale Manor
4 Bullock Creek Lodge
5 Edgewater Resort
6 Lakeview Motel
7 Moorings
8 Northridge B & B
9 Oak Ridge
10 Purple Cow
11 Te Wanaka Lodge
12 Tenby St Lodge
13 Tir Na Nog B & B
14 Wanaka Houseboat (Lady Pembroke)
15 Wanaka Motor Inn
16 Wanaka Motor Park
17 Wanaka Bakpaka

Eating
1 Kai Whakapai
2 Muzza's Bar
3 Relishes
4 White House Café & Bar

Pubs & clubs
5 Calaboose Restaurant & Bar
6 Kingsway Bar
7 Paradiso Cinema & Café

a prime attraction to boaties, water-skiers, kayakers and windsurfers. Even before you consider these activities you will find yourself simply admiring its beauty from Wanaka's attractive **Lakefront**.

On the way into town you cannot fail to miss New Zealand's 'Leaning Tower of Wanaka', the centrepiece of **Puzzling World**, T4437489. This is a madcap and indeed puzzling conglomerate of mazes, illusions and holograms. The toilets are particularly engaging. ■ *Open daily 0830-1730, from $4, child $3 (with maze $7/$4.50)*. A further 8 km east on SH6, surrounding Wanaka airfield, is the NZ Fighter Pilots Museum and The Wanaka Transport and Toy Museum, which also houses the Wanaka Beerworks. In these days when beer and transport make uncomfortable relations, it seems unusual to find a brewery at a transport museum, but so be it. **Wanaka Beerworks**, T4431865, is a craft brewery producing very palatable award winning beers for many Central Otago outlets. There are daily tours at 1400, tastings and of course sales. ■ *From $5, child, free. Daily 0930-1800.*

The **Wanaka Transport and Toy Museum**, T4438765, provides a good wet-weather option and is the largest privately owed vehicle and toy collection in New Zealand. There are over 15,000 items on display, including a staggering 9000 toys and 200 vehicles, comprising a tank, fire engines, trucks and the obligatory tractors. There is even a collection of spark plugs! ■ *Daily 0830-1700, from $5, child $2.*

Of more interest is the **NZ Fighter Pilots Museum**, T4437010, www.nzfpm.co.nz Although its main purpose is to honour the lives (and loss thereof) of New Zealand fighter pilots, this museum provides a fascinating insight into general aviation history. The museum's enviable and much-loved collection of flyable, classic Second World War fighters and trainers includes a Spitfire, Hurricane and a Mustang, all of which are the star attraction of Wanaka's main annual event, the 'Warbirds over Wanaka' which attracts thousands of spectators. Real enthusiasts will also delight in other unique aircraft on display; the 'Polikarpovs', housed in a separate hanger, are particularly unique. Also attached to the museum is the fun-filled **Compaq Computer Flightzone**. Here, you can have endless virtual dogfights with the bad guys. Though for the technophobe this sadly becomes a rather frustrating exercise, not so much in trying to spot the enemy (forget hitting any), as endlessly flying upside down into fields. It does make you wonder if you are even fit to drive a car, but the sound effects are great. ■ *The museum is open daily 0900-1600, from $7, child $4. While around the museum you might like to sit and watch terrified faces turn to ecstatic ones at the base of Wanaka Tandem Skydive*, T4437207.

Near the airfield is the '**Have a Shot**' complex, T4436656, with its range of 'smack it or shoot it' activities from clay-birds to archery or to the full golf range. **Alpine Shuttles** (see getting around) run regular shuttles to all the above attractions.

Activities

Most of the above can be booked at the **VIC/ Lakeland Adventures** office (see 'Information' above). **Good Sports**, T4437966, www.good-sports.co.nz on Dunmore Street hire out bikes, kayaks, 'funyaks', 'sit-on kayaks', fishing rods and tackle, plus the full range of ski and snow-sports equipment. The two main activity operators are *Edgewater Adventures*, T4438422, www.adventure.net.nz (trekking, cruising, fishing, four-wheel drive tours, jetboating), and *Lakeland Adventures*, T4437495, www.lakelandadventures.co.nz (fishing, jet boating, cruising).

Canyoning Most of the activities available in Wanaka you can also do elsewhere, but canyoning is a local speciality and recommended. It basically involves negotiating a mountain river with the assistance of gravity and in suitable attire. Methods of descent include scrambling, abseiling or just plain jumping – all great fun. *Deep Canyon*, T4437922, www.deepcanyon.co.nz 'do' the Emerald creek, Niger Stream and others (seven hours) from $165 (16 years of age minimum). Transport and lunch included.

Fishing The local fishing is excellent and there are many operators and guides including *Alpine Fishing Guides*, T4437655, www.cobwebs.co.nz/fishing ($385 per boat); *Southern Lakes Fishing Safaris*, T4439121, www.southernlakesfishing.co.nz (full day $395); *Wanaka Fishing Safaris*, T4437748, www.trout.net.nz (full day $395); *Edgewater Adventures*, T4438422, www.adventure.net.nz; *Lakeland Adventures*, T4437495, www.lakelandadventures.co.nz; *Gerald Telford*, T4439257, www.flyfishhunt.co.nz Most of the above can also organize more adventurous Heli-fishing trips throughout the region. Independent licences ($13) can be bought from *Good Sports* on Dunmore Street.

Flightseeing Wanaka is a superb base from which to reach **Milford Sound** by air, with the bonus of the stunning aesthetics of the **Aspiring National Park** on the way. Most flights from Queenstown and other centres (that cost about the same) do not follow quite the same spectacular flight path. *Aspiring Air*, T4437943, www.nz-flights.com, based out at the airfield, offer a range of flights from a 20-minute local flight for $70 to their highly recommended four-hour *'Majestic Milford Sound'* flight. Leaving at 1345 and arriving back at 1800 this epic involves a superb flight over Wanaka, up the Matukituki River Valley, past Mount Aspiring and then out across the national park and out to sea, before flying up the chancel of Milford Sound and Milford Sound village. Included in the trip is a 45-minute cruise on the Sound. It is a truly memorable experience and well worth the $280, child $160. If you want to buy someone an unusual present try their *'Mystery Flight'* from $140-$220. Also based at the airfield are *Wanaka Flightseeing*, T4438787, www.flightseeing.co.nz who offer similar trips including an interesting flight/jetboat experience with Dart River Jetboats in Glenorchy (see page 620), from $285.

Golf Wanaka's very scenic course is located on Ballantyne Road, just behind the town, and welcomes visitors, T4437888, green-fees are a very reasonable $20, club hire $15.

Horse trekking The Wanaka region offers some superb horse trekking possibilities. *Lake Wanaka Horse Trekking*, T4437777, offer two daily two-hour guided treks suitable for the beginner, from $45, child $40; while *NZ Backcountry Saddle Expeditions*, near Cardrona, T4438151, backcountry.saddle.expeditions@xtra.co.nz offer two-hour to 2-4 day treks, from $50, child $35 (full day $130).

Jetboating Lake Wanaka and its surrounding scenic rivers would almost have to incorporate a jetboat trip somewhere, and there are a number of operators: *Wanaka Jet*, T4438408, offer one-hour scenic trips on the Clutha and elsewhere, with an interesting commentary, from $65, child $35. A three-hour combined fishing trip is also available at $125 per hour. *Lakeland Adventures*, T4438422, based on the Lakefront, also offer one-hour trips

Mount Aspiring National Park

Of course like most of New Zealand's majestic national parks Mount Aspiring has an impressive list of vital statistics. First designated in 1964 the park has been extended to now cover 355,000 ha or 3,500 sq km, making it New Zealand's third largest. It extends for about 140 km from the Haast Pass to the Humbolt Range at the head of lake Wakatipu. It is 40 km at its widest. It contains five peaks over 2600 m, with the highest being Aspiring itself – at 3027 m, the highest outside the Mount Cook range. It contains over 100 glaciers, including the Bonar, Therma and Volta. It enjoys an annual rainfall of between 1000 mm-6000 mm a year. It is home to some unique wildlife like the New Zealand falcon, the kea and the giant weta. It is part of a World Heritage Area of international significance... the list just goes on. But, it is not figures that aptly describe this park. Without seeing it, it is without doubt names, words and phrases. How about Mount Awful, Mount Dreadful or Mount Dispute. Or Mount Chaos perhaps? Then there is The Valley of Darkness; Solitude Creek #2; Siberia River? How about Rob Roy, the Pope's Nose or the mind boggling 'Power Knob'. Are you getting the picture? This is without doubt a park and a wilderness worthy of investigation and well beyond mere imagination. The locals call the place 'Tiger Country'. A park of stunning wild and remote beauty. Enough said. Get in there and enjoy, but go prepared. For more information contact the DOC Information Centre in Wanaka or Makarora or visit the website www.doc.govt.nz.

Otago

down the Clutha for $60, child $30. Further afield in Makaroa, **Wilkin River Jets** ply the Makaroa and Wilkin Rivers (see page 630).

Kayaking *Alpine River Guides*, T4439023, www.alpinekayaks.co.nz run daily, guided whitewater day-trips on the Clutha, Matukituki and Hawea Rivers that are especially suitable for beginners. Transport and free pick-ups included, from $120, child $100. Independent kayak hire is available from *Lakeland Adventures* on the Lakefront, T4437495, from $20 per hour.

Mountaineering and rock climbing With Mount Aspiring and so many other attractive mountain climbs so close to Wanaka it is not surprising to find a number of quality mountaineering guiding companies offering a range of packages. *Alpinism and Ski Ltd*, 11 Rimu Lane, T4436593, www.alpinismski.co.nz offer guided trekking excursions throughout the region, and year-round to a number of peaks including Mount Aspiring and further afield to Mount Cook and the Westland National Park. Once you have flown over Aspiring you will appreciate that having a guide makes a lot of sense! Prices range from $100-$475. *Mount Aspiring Guides*, T4439422, www.mtaspiringguides.co.nz also offer a range of trips and packages all year round; while *Adventure Consultants*, T4438711, www.adventure.co.nz are very good for mountaineering and ice-climbing training courses. *Wanaka Rockclimbing*, T025762525, www.rockclimb.net.nz specialise in rock-climbing instruction, courses and ascents.

Mountain biking *Alpine & Heli Mountain Biking*, T4438943, www.mountainbiking.co.nz take the nasty, uphill part out of a trip and take you by helicopter to some of the country's highest and most scenic track trailheads including Mount Pisa, Mount Alpha and the Treble Cone ski field. From $195. Half-day road trips are also available from $95. Also of interest is the *Cardrona Alpine Resort*, T4437341, www.cardrona.com that stays open in summer to allow climbers, trampers and bikers to access the mountains. The chairlift operates daily from 1000-1600 and there are two purpose-built downhill bike tracks. Cardrona is 34 km southeast of Wanaka on the Crown Range Road.

Off-road and four-wheel drive adventures *Criffel Peak Safaris*, Mount Barker Road, T4431711, criffelpeak.safaris@xtra.co.nz are the local ATV four-wheel drive quad bike adventure specialists, offering guided one- to five-hour trips on farm and hill trails with great views, from $50-$160. *Edgewater Adventures*, T4438422, also offer four-wheel drive tours from $60.

Paragliding and paraflying *Wanaka Paragliding*, T4439193, www.wanakaparagliding.co.nz will gladly take you paragliding on nearby Mount Iron, from $135 for a tandem flight to $178 for an introductory course (September-April). The imaginatively named *Lucky Montana's Flying Circus*, T4431680, is another local company offering instruction from $140.

Rafting and river sledging Despite the stiff competition from Queenstown, Wanaka has its own rafting company in the form of *Pioneer Rafting*, T4431246, that offers fairly sedate eco-trips on the Clutha, full- or half-day from $95, child $55. Multi-day trips further afield are also available.

Whitewater sledging is growing in popularity and provides a far more intimate experience with the water on a modified boogie board. *Frogz Have More Fun*, T0800-338737, www.frogz.co.nz is not surprisingly a French-owned outfit offering one- to two-hour trips on the Clutha, Hawea and Kawarau Rivers, from $89 (minimum age 10-14 years depending on the river).

Skiing Wanaka has two great ski fields within 50 km of the town, Cardrona to the south and Treble Cone to the northwest. **Cardrona**, T4437341, www.cardrona.com is 34 km from Wanaka on the Crown Range (Cardrona) Road. It has a base area at 1670 m, and ski and board runs suitable for all levels, with the intermediates being especially well catered for. Facilities include bars and restaurants and, unusually, apartment accommodation. The ski season runs from 23 June-7 October but the resort (and some lifts) remain open in summer for trampers and mountain bikers. Lift passes from $60, child $30. Nearby, on the other side of the valley, is **Waiorau Snow Farm**, T4437542, www.snowfarm.co.nz a base for cross-country skiing with international standard tracks. It is open from mid June to the end of September and a pass costs from $20, child $10. The **Treble Cone Ski field** is located 20 km north west of Wanaka via Glendhu and is well known for its good snow and interesting terrain, not to mention its stunning views of Lake Wanaka and Mount Aspiring. It also offers more ski-able terrain than any other ski or board area in South Island and has the longest vertical rise in the Southern Lakes Region. Little wonder it is considered one of the best fields in the country. It is open from 0900-1600 late June-early October (no access in summer). Lift passes are from $61, child $31. Full clothing, ski and board hire are available on the mountain and there is a café, bar, childcare centre and ski/board schools. Daily **transport** from Wanaka is available with *Ski Shuttle* (transport and lift day-package from $90), T4424630. Other shuttle operators are listed in getting around above. *Harris Mountain Heli-skiing*, T4438589, www.heliski.co.nz are based in Wanaka and offer 3-7 run days from $595. Ski **equipment hire** is available from *Base* corner of Helwick and Dunmore Streets, T4436699, www.base.net.nz; *Good Sports*, Dunmore Street,

The Rob Roy Glacier Walk

If you haven't time or the energy for any of the major tramps, there is one-day walk in the Mount Aspiring National Park that is accessible from Wanaka and quite simply a 'must do'. From Wanaka drive (or arrange transportation) to the ***Raspberry Creek*** *Car Park in the West Matukituki Valley (one hour). From there follow the river, west to the footbridge over the river and up in to the* ***Rob Roy Valley****. From here the track gradually climbs, following the chaotic Rob Roy River, through beautiful rainforest, revealing the odd view of the* ***glacier*** *above. After about 1 ½ hours you will reach the treeline and enter a superb hidden valley rimmed with solid rock walls of* ***waterfall*** *and ice. It is simply stunning and well deserving of the label 'The Jewel of the Park'. Keep your eyes (and ears) open for kea and in the forest for the tiny rifleman. After some thorough investigation of the area, you can then retrace your steps back down the valley to the Matukituki River and the car park (five hours return). Mount Aspiring Express can shuttle you to Raspberry Creek for $45 return, T4438422.*

T4437966 (also arrange transport), and *Racer's Edge Planet Snow*, 99 Ardmore Street, T4437882, www.racersedge.co.nz Average prices – skis from $32, child $12/ Snowboard and boots from $38, child $20.

Skydiving The Wanaka Region is one of the most scenic in the country, which gives that added edge to any jump. *Tandem Skydive Wanaka*, T4437207, www.skydivenz.com operate out of the airfield from heights of 9,000 ($225) and 12,000 ($295), allowing 30-50 seconds of free-fall at around 200 kmph, followed by a gentle and peaceful 6-7-minute parachute ride to earth. Weight limit 100 kg/age limit seven years. Many people in the business recommend Wanaka, as we do! Pick-ups from Wanaka are free.

Walking Other than the **Mount Iron** Walk (see above) and the walk to **Rob Roy Glacier** (highly recommended), there are many other possibilities. Two popular alternatives are the ascent of Mount Roy or the easier, but still quite demanding, climb to the top of Rocky Mountain past Diamond Lake. From lakeside, the vision of **Mount Roy**, which dominates the western edge of Roy's Bay, can hardly be missed, but its ascent can reward you with some tremendous views. A well-formed path zigzags its way to the summit from a car park 6 km north of Wanaka towards Glendhu Bay. The walk takes about five hours return, and *Mount Aspiring Express*, T4438422, offer a shuttle service to the car park for $10 return.

Further up this road, past Glendhu and before the entrance to the Treble Cone Ski field, is the **Rocky Mountain** and **Diamond Lake Walk**. The appeal here is the view of Mount Aspiring and the Matukituki River Valley, as well as Lake Wanaka itself. The geology is also fascinating, with rocks that form unusual mounds and folds across the landscape. It is a stiff climb, but the path is marked and it is definitely worth the effort. At the end of Hospital Flat you will see the signposted car park. From there it is 20 minutes to the fairly unremarkable lake before the track skirts around the slopes to the top. On the descent be careful not to stray off the path far from the lower lookout. You need to double back here to rejoin the track. The walk takes about three hours return and again *Mount Aspiring Express* offer a shuttle from $20 return. For detailed walks information grab a copy of the '*Wanaka Walks*" broadsheet from *Edgewater Adventures* or the local walks leaflets from DOC. The Mount Aspiring National Park offers endless opportunities for walking and tramping.

Other activities *Mizzy Bee Bus Co*, T4431855, offer very pleasant 1-3 hour **sightseeing** tours of the region from $25. *Alpine Shuttles*, T4437966, also offer half- or full-day **wine** or **garden** tours. *Clean Green Images*, T4437951, www.cleangreen.co.nz offers **photo nature tours** from $60, while *Aspiring Images*, T4438358, grussell@xtra.co.nz also offer general Eco and four-wheel drive nature/photography tours from $50 per hour.

Essentials

Sleeping Although Wanaka has about 2800 beds you are advised to book at least 3 days in advance in summer (especially at New Year) and during the winter ski season. Although some distance from Wanaka (26 km), the **A** ***Cardrona Hotel***, Crown Range (Cardrona) Rd, T4438153, info@cardrona-hotel.co.nz is simply superb. The hotel is over 140 years old and still retains much of its former character. As it is, the comfortable rooms in the old stables are charming and front a beautiful enclosed garden and courtyard. There is a great rustic restaurant and bar attached. Further accommodation developments are planned. Bookings are essential.

Back in Wanaka, and in stark contrast, is the modern and classy (but hardly historic) **LL-AL** ***Edgewater Resort***, Sargood Dr, T4438311, F4438323, www.edgewater.co.nz Set overlooking Roy's Bay, its aesthetics cannot be faulted and it offers a wide range of en suites from the standard to luxurious. Lots of activities can be arranged in-house. Although called a Motor Inn, the cheaper **AL** ***Wanaka Motor Inn***, Mt Aspiring Rd, T4438216, F4439108, www.wanakanz.com is essentially a hotel complex and a popular choice, with comfortable, good-value studios and suites. Restaurant, bar and internet.

There are plenty of **motels** including the **A** ***Aspiring Lodge Motel***, corner of Dumore and Dungarvon Sts, T4437816, which offers good standard and executive suites and a spa. The **AL-A** ***Brookvale Manor***, 35 Brownston St, T4438333, www.brookvale.co.nz is slightly more expensive, with 1-bedroom and studio suites, pool, spa. The mid-range **A-B** ***Lakeview Motel***, 68 Lismore St, T4437029, BassGC@xtra.co.nz that has comfortable, good value singles, doubles and twins and good views. The **A** ***Tenby St Lodge***, 24 Tenby St, T4439294, tenbystlodge@amcom.co.nz backs on to the golf course and offers 10 quiet, well appointed en suites; and the classy **LL-AL** ***Moorings***, 17 Lakeside Rd, T4438479, has boutique motels and apartments overlooking the lake. Also of note are the ***Cardrona Alpine Resort*** units that are actually within the ski field complex, and sleep 1-8 from $320, T4437411, www.cardrona.com

There are many **B&Bs and homestays** available, from the luxury lodge or self-contained cottage to the basic B&B. The VIC has full listings. Out of Wanaka township and in the top range are the **LL** ***Arahura***, Faulks Rd, Mt Barker, T4437439, F4436503, www.arahura.com which is a top-quality country house lodge with 4 well-appointed double en-suites, singles and twins, tennis court, pleasant gardens and heated pool; The **L** ***Parklands Lodge***, Ballantyne Rd, T4437305, F4437345, www.parklandswanaka.co.nz is a new, spacious, single-storey place with 6 luxury en suites, pool, spa and 5-hole golf course, set in 10 acres of farmland. Again at the top end and out of town is the charming **LL** ***River Run***, Halliday Rd, T4439049, F4438454, www.riverrun.co.nz Set on an escarpment with sweeping views across the mountains, this huge 420-acre property provides a perfect retreat with imaginatively appointed rooms and furnishings, often using recycled materials in traditional NZ style. There are 5 en suites and the cuisine is superb.

Slightly closer to town is the new and sumptuous **LL-AL** ***Oak Ridge***, corner of Cardrona Valley and Studholme Rds, T4437707, F4437750, www.oakridge.co.

nz Puropse-built like a luxurious motel, it has well-appointed units that look out across spacious lawns and a swimming pool to the mountains. The Asian/Scots owners add an interesting flavour beyond the very reputable restaurant attached. Living areas are very spacious and comfortable with a large log fire. Nearby, at the cheaper end, is the **B** ***Tir Na Nog B&B***, Studholme Rd, T4437111, tirnanog@xtra.co.nz A pleasant self-contained cottage with spa. In town proper are the commanding views and very pleasant surroundings of the **AL** ***Northridge B&B***, 11 Botting Pl, T4438835, F4431835, s.atkinson@xtra.co.nz While in the town centre you can't go far past the excellent **AL** ***Te Wanaka Lodge***, 23 Brownston St, T4439224, F4439246, www.tewanaka.co.nz It is an alpine-style lodge complex with well-appointed en suites, self-contained cottage, spa, open fire, wine cellar and library. In Wanaka accommodation options even extend on to the water, with the ***Wanaka Houseboat (Lady Pembroke)***, T4437181, gratom@xtra.co.nz which is fully functional and sleeps up to 10 in 2 king-size bedrooms and 2 bunk rooms.

The **hostels** in Wanaka are all generally of a high standard. Three of the best are: the **C-D** ***Wanaka Bakpaka***, 117 Lakeside Rd, T4437837, wanakabakpaka@xtra.co.nz, 5 mins' walk from the centre of town but worth it. It has great views, a good range of dorm, twins and doubles (some new) and clean, modern facilities. It is very much a tramper's retreat with great walking advice and information. Kayaks for hire ($18 per hour) and internet; the **C-D** *Purple Cow*, 94 Brownston St, T4431880, www.purplecow.co.nz is a large place with stunning views across the lake. A wide range of comfortable dorms, twins and doubles all with en suites. Great facilities, internet, walks information and nice friendly atmosphere; the **C-D** ***Bullock Creek Lodge***, 46 Brownston St, T/F4431265, bullockcreeklodge@clear.net.nz has dorms, doubles and singles all with en suites, TV, decks, a great outlook and is close to the town centre.

Motor parks There are 3 choices here from the convenient, to the luxury and the aesthetic. Closest to town is the sprawling and rather unremarkable **C-D** ***Wanaka Motor Park***, 212 Brownston St, T/F4437883. It has adequate facilities, cabins and powered/tent sites. You will find an entirely different and new concept in motor camps at the **AL-C** ***Aspiring Campervan Park***, Studholme Rd, T4436603, www.campervanpark.co.nz It charges a hefty $30 for a powered site, but has all mod cons with new and modern facilities including a spa that looks out towards Mount Aspiring. Modern lodge, motel and tourist flats are also available. Internet; For the best aesthetics head for the basic but beautiful **C-D** ***Glendhu Bay Motor Camp***, Mount Aspiring Rd, T4437243, glendhucamp@xtra.co.nz It is 11 km from town, but offers lakeside sites with views up to Mount Aspiring. Facilities are basic but adequate. Friendly and busy in the ski season.

Eating

For daytime eating the best place is the ***Kai Whakapai***, Lakefront, T4437795. It has freshly baked breads, pies, foccacias, fresh pastas, pizzas and a good vegetarian selection. Breakfasts are also good value, the coffee is great and there is outside seating from which to watch the world go by on the waterfront. Open daily from 0700. For fine dining the ***White House Café and Bar***, corner of Dunmore and Dungarvon Sts, T4439595, is deservingly popular with an imaginative Mediterranean/Middle Eastern menu with vegetarian options. Fine wine list, outdoor eating and a big fat cat that jumps on your lap. Open daily from 1100. ***Relishes*** 1/99 Ardmore St, T4439018, is another good option offering a good value blackboard menu, outdoor dining in summer and fireside dining in winter. Good coffee and breakfasts. Open from 0900-1500 and 1800 til late. For good value pub food try the ***Muzza's Bar***, Cnr Brownston and Helwick Sts, T4437296. Out of town the historic and cosy *Cardrona Hotel* (see 'Sleeping' above) is well worth the 26-km journey for lunch or dinner, T4438153. Open daily from 1100.

Entertainment & events The *Kingsway Bar*, 21 Helwick St, T4437663, is popular among backpackers and famous for its pool competitions, while for a more sedate atmosphere try the new *Calaboose Restaurant and Bar*, 2 Dunmore St, T4436262. The *Paradiso Cinema and Café*, 3 Ardmore St, is famous for its one-of-a-kind movie offerings and comes complete with easy chairs and homemade ice cream. The café is just as laid back. The big annual event in the region is the increasingly popular *Warbirds Over Wanaka*, which is New Zealand's premier **airshow**, held at the end of Mar. The venue is of course the airfield, which hosts a wide variety of visiting 'birds', but also blows the dust off the NZ Fighter Pilots Museum's very own Spitfire. Entry is from $20, child $5 (3-day $70). For more information, T4438619, www.warbirdsoverwanaka.com

Directory **Banks** Currency exchange is available with the major bank branches in the town that include National, T4437521, and Westpac, T4437817. They also have ATMs. **Bike hire** is available at *Good Sports*, Dunmore St, T4437966, www.good-sports.co.nz from $25-$50 per day, and *Lakeland Adventures* on the Lakefront, T4437495. **Car hire** are available with *Aspiring*, T4437883, *Good Sports*, T4437966, *Lakeland Adventures*, T4437495, and *Wanaka Car Rentals*, T4438422. **Communications Post office** is at 39 Ardmore St, T/F4438211 (open Mon-Fri 0830-1730, Sat 0900-1200). **Medical Services** *Aspiring Medical Centre*, 28 Dungarvon St, T4431226; *Wanaka Medical Centre*, T4437811. **Police** 28 Helwick St, T4437272

Around Wanaka

Hawea North of Wanaka on SH6 towards the West Coast is **Lake Hawea** and the small holiday settlement of Hawea. Lake Hawea, like its neighbour Lake Wanaka, occupies an ancient glacier valley, and the two are only separated by a narrow strip of moraine known as The Neck. Lake Hawea is noted for its fishing and the beautiful scenery, with its mountain reflections that disappear towards its remote upper reaches, 35 km north of Hawea settlement. The lake level was risen by 18 m in 1958 as part of the Clutha River hydropower system. Hawea itself nestles on its southern shore and, although a fairly new settlement, was formerly the site of an important and strategic Maori *Pa*.

Sleeping The **A** *Lake Hawea Motor Inn*, 1 Capell Av, T4431224, and the slightly cheaper **A** *Lake Hawea Lodge Motel*, 60 Capell Av, T4431714, are 2 comfortable self-contained options. The Hawea Motor Inn also has budget accommodation. Eating is best done in Wanaka.

Makarora From Lake Hawea and the narrow Neck you revisit Lake Wanaka and head north through some beautiful 'Scottish' scenery to its northern edge and the small settlement of Makarora. At about 67 km from Wanaka, and almost on the **border** of the Otago and West Coast Regions, Makarora acts as the portal to the northern tramps and activities within the **Mount Aspiring National Park**. The village in itself offers little except a small conglomerate of tourist services reflecting the desires of most visitors who either pass through quickly or head for the hills.

Getting there All the major bus companies heading up or down the West Coast must pass through Makarora including *Intercity* and *Atomic* (for details ask at the Tourist Centre or phone the Wanaka VIC, see Wanaka above).

Information There is a small **DOC Visitors Information Centre** in the village, T4438365. Open daily 0800-1700 (closed weekends in winter). It has information on the northern sector of Aspiring National Park and the Haast Pass, and local short walks, and issues hut passes. Given the isolation and the potential for very wet weather conditions in the area you are advised to consult DOC before embarking on any of the major walks or tramps. Intentions sheets are provided.

Of special note in this area is the superb three-day **Gillespie Pass** Tramp and '**The Siberia Experience**' run by **Southern Alps Air** (in conjunction with Wilkin River Jet Boats). This evocatively named jaunt is a unique combination of scenic flight, tramp and jetboat, which gets consistently good reviews. You are first flown (25 minutes) into the beautiful and remote **Siberia Valley**, from where you tramp for about three hours to the **Wilkin River** to be picked up by Jetboat with a 30-minute scenic ride back to Makarora. At $160, child $100, it is good value. *Southern Alps Air* are housed in the café and shop, T4438666, F4438292, www.destination-nz.com and also offer **scenic flights** to Milford, Mount Cook or over the Aspiring National Park from 25 minutes ($100) to 2¼ hours ($450).

Makarora is also the base of the *Wilkin River Jet Boats*, T4438351, wilkinriverjets@xtra.co.nz that offer one hour trips on the scenic Wilkin from $55, child $22.50, as well as water-taxi services for trampers from $40.

Sleeping and eating The **B-D** ***Makarora Tourist Centre***, T4438372, F4431082, www.makaroa.co.nz offers motel, cabin, backpacker and camping facilities. The comfortable **A** ***Larrivee Homestay*** T4439177, andrea_larrivee@hotmail.com, near the visitor's centre, is another alternative and also offers a self-contained cottage and can do dinner. The licensed ***Country Café***, nearby, T4438207, serves light meals and refreshments and sells petrol.

Oamaru

Phone code: 03
Population: 12,000

Oamaru is a pleasant coastal town on the South Island's east coast, somehow befitting its position gracing the shores of 'Friendly' Bay. Primarily functioning as a port and an agricultural service town, its modern-day tourist attractions lie with the strange combination of stone, architecture and penguins. Given the prosperous times of the 1860s to 90s, and the discovery of a wealth of local limestone which could be easily carved and moulded, the early architects and stonemasons created a settlement rich in imposing, classic buildings, earning it the reputation of New Zealand's best-built town. Many old buildings remain, complete with Corinthian columns and gargantuan doorways, giving it a distinctly grand air. Add to that a small and congenial colony of rare Yellow-eyed penguins that waddle up to their burrows beside the port, like dignified gents in 'tux and tails', and the town's appeal becomes truly unique.

Ins & outs

Getting there By road Oamaru is 247 km south of Christchurch and 115 km north of Dunedin on SH1. Mount Cook is 216 km west via the Waitaki Valley. By **bus** all the major companies going north and south serve Oamaru, including ***Intercity***, T0800767080, and ***Atomic Shuttles***, T3328883. The ***Cook Connection***, T0800252666, www.cookconnect.co.nz go from Oamaru to Mt Cook and return a minimum of 3 days a week, from $80. All buses stop outside the ***Lagonda Coach Travel*** (tearooms) on the corner of Eden and Thames Street. Although the Southerner **train** service to Christchurch stops in Oamaru daily, at the time of going to print this service was under threat of extinction or at the very least a period of dormancy, but this situation may change, T0800-802802.

Getting around Most of the attractions in Oamaru can be easily negotiated by foot. *Coastline Tours*, T4395265, www.coastline-tours.co.nz and the *Penguin Express*, T4395265, offer shuttles to the penguin colony and other local attractions from $15.

Information The Oamaru **Visitor Information Centre** is on the corner of Itchen and Thames Sts, T4341656, F4341657, www.tourismwaitaki.co.nz Open Mon-Fri 0900-1700 (1800 summer), Sat/Sun 1000-1600 (1700 summer). The centre has town maps and a wealth of information surrounding the historical buildings, local tours and activities. The leaflet *'Historic Oamaru'* is very useful, and all local **DOC** walks leaflets are also available.

Internet is available at the Lagonda Coach Travel tearooms. You will find most of the major **bank** branches and ATMs on Thames St, with some housed in grand historic buildings. The **National Bank**, in the former 1871 Bank of Otago building, is the best example. The **post office** is on Severn St, near the intersection with Thames.

Sights Most of the historic buildings and associated attractions are located in the **Tyne-Harbour Street Historic Precinct** (begins at the southern end of Thames St), which boasts the largest and best-preserved collection of historic commercial buildings in the country. Although the *'Historic Oamaru'* leaflet will provide enough information for a self-guided tour, there are one-hour guided walks available on demand through the VIC, from $7.50, child $4. You will find that most of the buildings demonstrate a range of architectural styles from Venetian to Victorian and are now occupied with a variety of tourist lures, from antique and craft outlets to second-hand book stores, auto collections and cafés. The **Harbour and Tyne Market**, 2 Tyne Street, specialises in local crafts, food and produce. ■ *Open every Sat & Sun from 1000-1600.* It Another interesting attraction is the **Oamaru Steam Train**, T4345634, that is lovingly owned and operated by the local and very enthusiastic Steam and Rail Society. The shiny engine comes complete with a proud conductor in period uniform and hisses into action from beside the VIC to the Harbour on Sundays, from $5, child $2. As if there were not enough history on the streets, the town is also home to the **North Otago Museum**, 58-60 Thames St, T4348060, which has a modest collection, focusing on Maori history and the inevitable early settler collections. Of special interest are the information and displays about '**Oamaru Stone**', the white limestone for which the town is so famous. ■ *Mon-Fri 1300-1630, Sat 1000-1300, donations.*

Located in one of Oamaru's original banks is the **Forrester Art Gallery**, which is also on Thames Street, T4341653. It features local contemporary works as well as national and international touring exhibitions. ■ *Mon-Fri 1030-1630, Sat 1030-1300, Sun 1300-1630, donations.*

There are a number of historic **homesteads** that are open to the public, including the Victorian country mansion, *Burnside*, T4324194; the 1885 *Kuriheka*, T4395358; *the Tokarahi*, T4312500, and the Oamaru Stone farm; buildings of the *Totara Estate*, T4347169. Most of these offer regular guided tours from $3.50-$15. Ring for details and opening times.

If you get fed up with stone then head for the very pleasant **Oamaru Public Gardens**, accessed off Severn Street. Rated as one of the top 10 public gardens in the country, and first set aside in 1876, its 30 acres boast rose and Chinese gardens, fountains, statues and of course the ubiquitous duck pond. It's open from dawn to dusk and entry is free.

No visit to Oamaru would be complete without visiting its **penguin colonies**. The town has two species in residence – the enchanting **little blue penguin** (the smallest in the world) and the rare, larger, **yellow-eyed penguin**. There are two colonies and observation points, one at **Bushy Beach**, where you can watch the Yellow-eyed penguins from a hide for free, or the official harbour-side, **Oamaru Blue Penguin Colony** that you must pay to access. Obviously the free option is an attractive one, but if you know nothing about penguins and were always under the impression they lived on ice bergs and wore bow ties, then you are advised to join a tour, or visit the official Blue Penguin Colony, T4431195, before venturing out alone. The best (and only) time to view the penguins is from dusk (specific times are posted at the colony reception). There is a small covered stand from which you are given a brief talk before the penguins come ashore and waddle intently towards their burrows, from $8, child $6. The colony is accessed via Waterfront Road past the Historic Precinct (signposted).

The **Bushy Beach** yellow-eyed penguin colony and viewing hide is accessed on foot via the walkway at the end of Waterfront Road (30 minutes), or alternatively by car via Bushy Beach Road (end of Tyne Street from the Historic Precinct). One-hour guided tours leave from the car park at 1830 (check with the VIC), from $5 (November-March). The best time to view the birds is an hour or so before dawn and dusk when they come and go from their fishing expeditions. If you think one penguin species is just like another then think again, the two are very different in character and you are advised to see both. The *Penguin Express*, T4395265, combines transport with tours and entry fees, from $15.

As well as its historical aspects and penguin-watching, Oamaru has a number of other **activities** on offer including fresh and salt-water fishing, heritage tours, gold-mining tours and farm tours, jetboating, horse trekking and glider flights. The VIC has details.

Sleeping

The fairly unremarkable but comfortable **A** ***Quality Hotel Brydone***, 115 Thames St, T4349892, F4345719, qhbrydone@xtra.co.nz has standard doubles or suites. The popular Thomas's bar and brasserie housed in the hotel is the biggest attraction. Of more aesthetic appeal is the old **A** ***Criterion Hotel***, 3 Tyne St in the Historic Precinct, T4346247, F4349963. It offers two nicely restored Victorian-style bedrooms and a reputable bar and restaurant downstairs. Guests can dine in an attractive 'snug' complete with period furniture and fittings and open fire. Most of Oamaru's **motels** are located on the main drag (Thames Highway) heading out of town. These include the tidy and modern **AL-A** ***Heritage Court Motel***, 346 Thames Highway, T4372200, which has a nice range of suites and a spa; the **B** ***Alpine Motel***, 285 Thames St, T4345038, alpine.motel.oamaru@xtra.co.nz; and the new **B** ***Café 469 Motel***, 469 Thames Highway, T4371443, tskitto@ihug.co.nz

There are quite a few good **B&Bs and homestays** on offer with many being in historic surroundings. The VIC has full listings. At the top of the range is the **LL** ***Pen-Y-Bryn Lodge***, 41 Towey St, T4347939, F4349063, www.penybryn.co.nz It is a vast, lovely and historic Victorian villa which is actually the largest single-storeyed timber dwelling in the South Island. It offers luxury en suites and a sumptuous 5-course dinner included in the price. In the mid-range the **A** ***Clyde House***, 32 Clyde St, T/F4372774, www.clydehouse.co.nz is built of original Oamaru Stone and offers a peaceful setting and comfortable doubles. Dinner by arrangement.

Cheaper still is the very friendly **B** ***Glenhaven B&B***, 5 Forth St, T4370211, F4370201, which has a separate en suite and a triple room in the house. Anybody interested in cars or toys will be fascinated with the Matchbox car collection. Lastly there is the **B** ***Blue Penguin Lodge***, 2 Chelmer St, T/F4347072, bplodge@xtra.co.nz which is a spacious former 1910 gentlemen's residence. The rooms and the facilities are great value for the price.

There are 2 main hostels in town, both comfortable, clean and friendly: the **C-D** ***Red Kettle YHA*** is on the corner of Reed and Cross Sts, T4345008, offering dorm and twins, and the **C-D** ***Swaggers***, 25 Wansbeck St, T4349999, swaggers@es.co.nz is in a large suburban house offering 1 twin and 8 dorm beds. The basic **B-D** ***Oamaru Gardens Top Ten Holiday Park***, Chelmer St (signposted off Severn St, SH1), T4347666, backs on to the Oamaru Public Gardens and has flats, cabins, units, and powered/tent sites.

Eating & entertainment

Oamaru has a surprisingly good range of eateries, most of which are located on or around Thames St. For fine dining ***Thomas's Restaurant***, T4349892, in the Quality Hotel, 115 Thames St, is recommended, offering a nice ambience and good traditional NZ/Euro menu. Also of note, and again on Thames St (12), is the ***Last Post Bar and Restaurant*** in the former Oamaru Stone-built Post Office. It offers both casual and formal dining at reasonable prices (open Sun-Thu 1100-2200, Fri/Sat 1100-2400). For light snacks, a hearty breakfast and good coffee follow the locals to ***Emma's Café***, 30 Thames St, T4341165 (open Tue-Sun 0900-1800). Or for something different try the café at the ***Whitestone Cheese Factory***, Cnr Torridge and Humber Sts, T4348098. As well as the innovative blackboard menu you can of course sample and purchase their impressive range of 18 cheeses. Open Mon-Fri 0900-1700, Sat/Sun 1000-1600. For pub grub and good beer the ***Criterion Hotel*** (see Sleeping above) and the pseudo-Irish pub ***Annie Flannigan's***, 84 Thames St, T4348828, will not disappoint. Annie's offers live folk and rock mainly at weekends. The ***Penguin Entertainers Club***, Sea Side, Harbour St is another little-known spot for occasional visiting live acts. For dates and directions contact T025373922, F4345637. The annual ***Oamaru Victorian Heritage Celebrations*** take place in the Historic Precinct on the third weekend in Nov. It's all fun, top hats and penny-farthings.

Oamaru to Dunedin

If you are heading south and have time, take the quiet and **scenic coast road** from Oamaru, through **Kakanui** to rejoin SH1 at Waianakarua. About 10 km south of Waianakarua are the **Moeraki Boulders**, a strange and much-photographed collection of spherical boulders that litter the beach. Although Maori legend has it that these boulders are 'te kai hinaki', or food baskets and sweet potatoes, science has determined that they are in fact 'septarian concretions', a rather classy name for 'darn big rock gob-stoppers' left behind from the eroded coastal cliffs. To understand exactly how they are formed requires several PhDs in geology and physics, but you will find something near a layman's explanation at the **Moeraki Boulderpark Visitor Centre and Café**, T4394827, that is signposted just off SH1. Rather predictably shaped like the boulders themselves, it is open daily for lunch and dinner offering light meals and refreshments. The path to the boulders starts from the car park, where an interpretative panel will explain the formation of the boulders to the geologically wanting. You are requested to provide a donation of $2.

There are other, smaller boulders to be seen at **Katiki Beach** and **Shag Point** a few kilometres south, beyond the village of Moeraki. Sadly, there used to be many more, with most having been pilfered as souvenirs, prompting the protection of the larger boulders at Moeraki. The small fishing village of **Moeraki**, 3 km from the boulders, can be reached along the beach by foot (three hours return) or by car via SH1. Once a whaling settlement first settled as long ago as 1836, it now offers far more acceptable forms of fishing, as well as swimming, **wildlife watching** (including the rare Hector's dolphin) and some very pleasant **coastal walks**. The historic lighthouse is also worth a visit.

With the boulders still fresh in your mind your imagination can really run wild a further 20 km south on SH1 in **Palmerston**. There, dominating the scene above the town, is the rather spectacular phallus adorning **Puketapu Hill** (343 m). A monument to the late John McKenzie, a Scots runholder who rose to high office and pushed through the Land Settlement Act in the 1890s, the monument and its accompanying views can be reached from the northern end of town (signposted). From Palmerston it is a further 55 km through gently rolling hills to Dunedin.

Sleeping

Just south of Oamaru is the **D** ***Coastal Backpackers***, T034395411, seaside@coastalbackpackers.co.nz which is a popular and peaceful place within walking distance of the beach (All Day Bay). It has good-value doubles, twins and dorms, and canoes, body-boards and bikes can be hired. The nearest shop is 4 km away, so stock up. In Moeraki there is not much choice beyond the **B** ***Moeraki Motels***, T034394862, which has basic but comfortable self-contained units and cottages; or the **C-D** ***Moeraki Motor Camp***, T/F034394759. It has motel units, flats, cabins and powered/tent sites. Shop on site. Alternatively, there is the friendly **B-D** ***Joy's GuestHouse, B&B, Chalet and Backpackers***, T4394762. Also offers free English lessons! For eating your best bet is the ***Moeraki Boulderpark Café*** (see above).

Southland and the Fiords

Southland and the Fiords

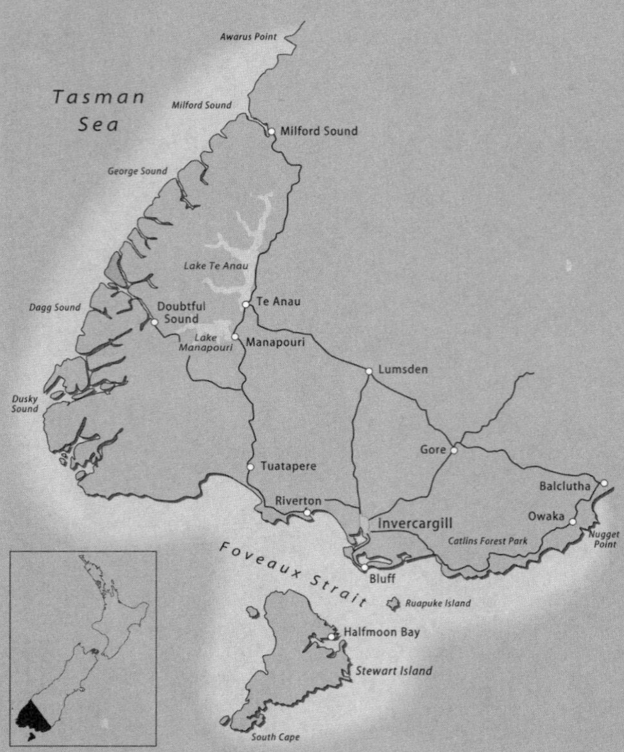

Southland is a region of stark contrasts. It is one of the most spectacular, yet inaccessible landscapes on earth. Even its boundaries are contrasting; stretching roughly in a straight line, from the fairly unremarkable and flat coastal town of **Balclutha***, in the east, to the towering peaks and fiord of* **Milford Sound***, to the west. Half of its coast is mountainous, remote and inhospitable – almost unchanged since* **Cook** *first landed (briefly) in 1770. The other half is home to Southland's largest town* **Invercargill***, the beautiful coastal holiday haunts of the* **Catlins** *and* **Riverton** *and an unsightly aluminium smelter. Amidst all that, knocking at its backdoor, is New Zealand's third island and newest national park,* **Stewart Island***.*

Most visitors head for the hills, and who can blame them. The **Fiordland National Park***, which is part of the internationally acclaimed* **Te Wahipounamu World Heritage Area***, is a staggering 12 ½ sq km of some of the world's most magnificent scenery. And, although the vast majority of it is wonderfully inaccessible, it still contains over 5000 km of walking tracks. But don't be fooled in to thinking the less spectacular parts are not worth a look. There, too, you will find a warm welcome and some pleasant surprises. Where else on earth, for example, can you meet a 150 year-old* **tuatara***, a reptile that has outlived the fiords themselves. Or see, unusuallyin daylight hours, the weird and and wonderful* **kiwi***, that flightless national icon.*

Things to do in Southland and the Fiords

- *Plan a major tramp in the Fiordland National Park: the 'moderate' Kepler; the 'challenging' Dusky; or the 'new' Hump Ridge Track.*
- *Drive to magnificent Milford Sound via the unforgettable Milford Road from Te Anau.*
- *Try kayaking under the waterfalls of Milford Sound.*
- *Stay overnight on Doubtful Sound where the silence is deafening.*
- *Cruise beautiful Lake Manapouri, and then go underground to the power station.*
- *Try to spot a wild kiwi on Stewart Island – New Zealand's newest National Park.*
- *Explore the quiet back roads and stunning scenery of the Catlins Coast.*
- *Watch the sunrise over Nugget Point.*

Ins and Outs

Getting there

By air The region's principal **airport** is in Invercargill, which is regularly serviced by ***Air New Zealand Link*** to Christchurch, T0800-737000. Te Anau and Milford Sound can be accessed by air from Queenstown with ***Mt Cook Airlines***, T2497516. ***Air New Zealand Link*** and ***Air Fiordland***, T2497505, www.airfiordland.co.nz Numerous helicopter companies (referred to in the text) provide charter flights or flightseeing trips to/from Queenstown or elsewhere.

By bus Southland is served by ***Intercity*** (From Christchurch/Dunedin/Queenstown to Invercargill/Te Anau), T0800-767080; ***Atomic Shuttles*** (Christchurch/Dunedin to Invercargill); ***Topline Tours***, (Queenstown to Te Anau), T050-8832628 and the backpacker oriented ***Bottom Bus*** (Dunedin/Queenstown to Invercargill/Te Anau), T4429708, www.bottombus.co.nz

By car Southland has a **good road network** and is accessed either from the East Coast via SH1, or from Queenstown via SH6. Those coming via Queenstown usually visit Te Anau, which lies 170 km southwest and from there, use it as the gateway to Milford Sound, a further 121 km north. Most then retrace their steps. Others, intent on exploring the region further, take the **Southern Scenic Route** (SH99) from Te Anau to Invercargill (168 km) and then north to Dunedin via the Catlins (272 km).

By train Invercargill also hosts the only **rail** link and is served by the daily Southerner service to Christchurch, T0800-802802.

Getting Around

Bus companies operating within Southland itself include; ***Spitfire Shuttles***, (Invercargill to Te Anau), T2497505; ***Caltlins Coaster*** (Dunedin to Invercargill via the Catlins coast), T0800304333, www.southern-nz.co.nz There are numerous **car hire** companies in Invercargill and Te Anau (refer to text)

Te Anau

Phone Code: 03
Population: 3000

*Located on the shores of New Zealand's second largest lake, **Lake Te Anau** and at the edge of the magnificent wilderness of the **Fiordland National Park** is the 'walking capital of the world', Te Anau. In summer it is like a busy gatehouse with crowds of eager trampers, intent and excited at the prospect of visiting its enormous garden. In winter it is like an unused holiday house, with only its resident caretaker, quietly waiting and wanting to turn the heating on again. As you drive in to Te Anau, often* *wedged between a convoy of tour buses, it can initially seem a rather dull little town, but once you acquaint yourself with its bustling centre, spacious open areas and beautiful lake views, your desire to move on quickly will fade. And although what lies beyond the town is what you have really come to see, it is worth giving Te Anau a little time. And, given the fickle weather in these parts, you my have little choice.*

Ins and outs

Getting there

Te Anau is 177 km southwest of Queenstown via SH6, 152 km from Invercargill via SH99 (Southern Scenic Route) and 290 km west of Dunedin via Gore and SH94

By air Te Anau is served from Queenstown by ***Air New Zealand Link*** (agents are the Te Anau Travel and Information Centre, Lakefront Dr, T2497516) and ***Air Fiordland***, T2497505. The airfield is located between Te Anau and Manapouri. For airfield transport contact ***Te Anau Taxis***, T2497777. **By bus** Te Anau is served by ***Intercity*** (Christchurch/Invercargill/Dunedin daily) T2497505; ***Topline Tours***, Caswell St (Queenstown daily), T0508832628; ***Catch-a-Bus*** (Dunedin daily), T2498900; ***Spitfire Shuttle*** (Invercargill), T2497505; and the backpacker oriented ***Bottom Bus*** (Queenstown/Dunedin/Invercargill), T034429708. All buses stop in the town centre. ***Back Track Transport***, T2497457, offer a rather unique way to get to Te Anau via Lake Wakapitu (Queenstown) and the Steamer TSS Earnslaw. Once ashore at the remote Walter Peak Station you can then travel by coach via the pretty Von Valley and Mavora Lakes to Te Anau (from $60)

Getting around

Forbus services to Milford see page 640

By air Both local fixed-wing and helicopter companies offer chartered transportation (or packages) to Milford and beyond (refer to activities) ***Te Anau Taxi and Tours*** provide local **taxi** services,T2497777. **Car hire** can be secured with ***Hertz***, T2497516, or ***Rent-a-Dent***, T2498363. Mini-vans can be hired with Te Anau Taxi and tours, T2497777 (from $65 per day). **Bike hire** is available with ***Fiordland Bike Hire***, 7 Mokonui St, T2497211, from $5 per hr.

Trampers Track Transport

By air ***Air Fiordland***, Town Centre, T2497505 (Hollyford/Milford); ***Waterwings Airways***, Lake Front (Milford/Dusky), T2497405; ***South-West Helicopters***, T2497133 offer helicopter charters throughout the region.

By shuttle bus ***Tracknet***, whose office is located behind the Moose Bar and Café, Lakefront Dr, offer shuttle services and packages to Queenstown ($66); Milford-Te Anau Downs ($12); Routeburn/Greenstone/Hollyford turn-off ($24); Kepler control gates ($5). All shuttle services run from Oct-May except the Milford Track service which is year round, T2497777, reservations@destinationnz.com On the water ***Sinbad Cruises*** based on the lakefront, T2497106, sinbad@teanau.co.nz offer an appealing way to reach the start of the Milford or Kepler Tracks on the 36 ft Gaff ketch 'Manuska'. From $60; ***Lakeland Boat Hire*** Te Anau, T2498364, stevsaunders@xtra.co.nz run a regular water-taxi service to Brod Bay and the Kepler Track from $15 one-way.

Information

Te Anau has a worryingly large number of information centres and booking offices. The most unbiased information is available from Fiordland **Visitor Information Centre**, Lakefront Dr, T2498900, F2497022, vin@fiordlandtravel.co.nz Open daily 0830-1800 (winter 0830-1700). It deals with all local information and serve as the agents for domestic air and bus bookings. Downstairs the ***Fiordland Travel*** arm deals with local sightseeing trips on Lake Te Anau (including the Te Anau Caves) and to Milford and Doubtful Sounds (open daily summer 0830-2100). The **DOC Fiordland National Park Visitor Centre** at the southern end of Lakefront Drive, T2497924, F2497613, fiordlandvc@doc.govt.nz is the principal source for track information, track bookings office and up to date weather forecasts. There is also a small museum and audio-visual theatre ($3). Open daily 0830-1800 (seasonal)

Other information and booking offices are: ***Te Anau Travel and Information Centre***, Lakefront Dr, T2497516, F2407518, teanau.travel@xtra.co.nz They are the handling agents for ***Air New Zealand***, including check in for Te Anau flights and take bookings for most local trips. ***Air Fiordland***, T2497505 have a local sightseeing booking office in their main office in the Town Centre, www.airfiordland.co.nz Open 0730-2000 (seasonal).

Sights

At 61 km long, 10 km at its widest point and a total of 344 sq.km in area, **Lake Te Anau** is the largest lake in the South Island and second largest in the land. Looking from the lakeside up its length to the Earl Mountains it certainly seems worthy of those dimensions and perhaps the label as one of the prettiest in the country. Directly opposite Te Anau, unseen in the bush, is the meanderings of the **Kepler Track** which begins at the southern end of the lake and skirts its southwestern edge, before climbing steadily towards the Kepler Mountains and the spectacular views from the **Luxmore Hut**. Also along the western edge between the Middle and South Fiords are the 200 m **Te Ana-au Caves**. Long revered by Maori, but only rediscovered by the Europeans in 1948, they provide the usual spectacular rock formations, fossils, whirlpools, waterfalls and glow-worms. The caves can only be accessed by boat and guided trips (2 ½ hours) leave from the wharf at Te Anau several times a day. After arriving by launch you are given a short video presentation before joining your guide on a short bush walk to the caves. The caves themselves are then explored by foot and on the water by punt. The 2015 (summer) or 1845 (winter) evening trips are recommended. Book with *Fiordland Travel*, Lakefront Drive, T2497416. From $43, child $10 ($49 for 2015).

On the southern shores of the lake on the road to Manapouri, is the DOC **Te Anau Wildlife Centre**, which is an important breeding centre for **takahe** and other rare native species. The story of the takahe is a fascinating one. Thought to be extinct for over fifty years, a small group were rediscovered in the Murchison Mountains above Lake Te Anau in 1948, by ornithologist and medical practitioner Dr Geoffrey Orbell. Although much of what goes on behind the scenes at the centre (in their efforts to maintain the new breeding colony in the Murchison Ranges) is off-limits, the open air aviaries and grounds are very appealing and well worth the visit. Once again it

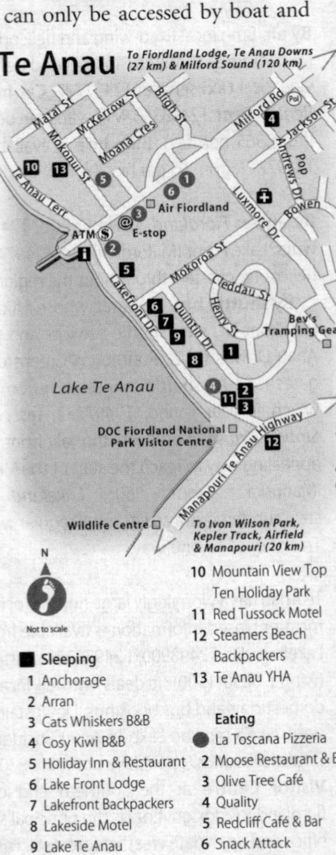

is very refreshing to see such efforts being made in wildlife conservation in New Zealand and witness these unique species in such a relaxed atmosphere. There are takahe, kea, morepork, and kaka to name but a few. Entry is very reasonably by donation (please give as much as you can). Across the road from the Wildlife Centre is the 35-ha **Ivor Wilson Park** (open dawn to dusk) which offers a number of pleasant tracks and picnic spots amongst native bush and surrounding Lake Henry.

Activities

The vast majority of visitors to Te Anau use it as a portal to Milford and Doubtful Sounds and the major tramping tracks. Note that there are other activity operators in Milford Sound, Manapouri and Queenstown offering a wide range of other trips in the region (refer to relevant texts)

Cruising *Sinbad Cruises* based on the lakefront, T2497106, sinbad@teanau.co.nz offer an appealing way to cruise the lake in the 36 ft Gaff ketch 'Manuska'. Trip options include five hour day cruise, cruise/walk, Heli/cruise and overnight cruises from $45.

Diving *Tawaki Dive*, T2499006, www.tawakidive.co.nz offer some unique full-day fiord diving trips for the experienced, from $220.

Flightseeing Without doubt the best way to see the Fiordland National Park is from the air. **Fixed-wing** operators based in Te Anau are *Air Fiordland*, Town Centre, T2497505, www.airfiordland.co.nz and *Waterwings Airways*, a **floatplane** that operates from the lakeshore, Lakefront Drive, T2497405, waterwings@teanau.co.nz Both offer a range of options principally to Milford and Doubtful Sound including flight only to flight/cruise and coach in/fly out, from one hour to 4 ½ hours and $220. The principal **helicopter** operator based in Te Anau are *Southern Lakes Helicopters*, Lakefront Drive, T2497167, slheli@teanau.co.nz who offer a range of flights and packages from 10 minutes ($100) to 1 ½ hours ($600). Again the principal locations are Milford and Doubtful Sounds though the remote Dusky Sound Trip (one hour, $495) is also very appealing as is the Heli-hike-cruise trip to the Mount Luxmore Hut on the Kepler Track, from $125.

Four-wheel drive *High Ride 4 Wheeler Adventures*, T2498591, www.highride.co.nz offer scenic (three hour) backcountry safaris on four-wheel drive ATVs from $98.

Golf Yes, you can even find a presentable golf course amidst all this splendour. For a reasonable fee *Golf Fiordland* can take care of all the arrangements, T2497247. *Te Anau Golf Club*, T2497474 ($25).

Horse Trekking The local operators are *Rainbow Downs*, located between Te Anau and Manapouri, T2498006 (one hour from $25).

Kayaking *Fiordland Wilderness Experiences* based in Te Anau, T2497700, www.fiordlandseakayak.co.nz also offer a day excursion on Milford and Doubtful Sounds from $95. The Milford trip is especially good taking in the scenery of the Milford Road. *Milford Sea Kayaks* are another company based in Milford Sound (see Milford 'activities'). *Kiwi Reel-Rifle Ltd*, 25 Cleddau Street, T2499071, www.kiwireelrifle.com offer an attractive 2-3 hour moonlight paddling experience on Lake Te Anau or Manapouri from $85. *Lakeland Boat Hire Te Anau*, T2498364 offer independent hire from $20 per hour; Other spectacular kayaking options are available in Milford and Doubtful Sound from Manapouri (See relevant section).

Sightseeing Tours *Trips and Tramps*, T2497081, offer day-trip to Milford Sound (including cruise ticket). It departs Te Anau at 0830 and returns at

1800 and costs $115, child $60. They also do a Milford Track day walk option from $110; *Fiordland Discoveries*, T2499205, www.fiordland-retreat.com, offer a wide range of personalised trips including tramping, fishing and horse riding. They also offer luxury accommodation and even massage, manicures and pedicures. Prices on application.

Walking The biggest local attraction here is of course the 67 km (2-3 day), **Kepler Track** which can be walked in whole or part. One of the most popular day or overnight walks is to capture the view from the **Luxmore Hut**, which is the first DOC hut on the track (in the traditional anticlockwise direction). To access the hut by foot, walk along the southern edge of the lake to the control gates. From there it is a fairly strenuous 11 km (six hours) one-way walk along the lake edge and up above the tree line to the hut. One very appealing way to cut out much of the strain is to get a water-taxi (T2498364, $30 return) or to join a walk/cruise trip (see Cruising) from Te Anau to **Brod Bay**. It is then a 16 km (eight hours) return trip. *Fiordland Travel*, T2497416 also offer **Milford Track day-walks** (five hours walking) on the Milford Track from $105, child $65. *Trips and Tramps*, T2497081 and *Fiordland Guides*, T2497832, www.fiordlandguides.co.nz offer a range of other guided walking options. *Bev's Tramping Gear*, 16 Homer St, T2497389, bevs.hire@max.net.co.nz hire a vast range of walking, tramping and camping equipment at competitive prices.

Essentials

Sleeping The most high profile **hotel** in town is the lakeside **AL-A** *Holiday Inn* (formerly the Centra), Lakefront Dr, T2499700, holidayinn.teanau@xtra.co.nz It has standard rooms, self-contained villas and 4 deluxe suites. A la carte restaurant, spa, pool and sauna.

There are a generous number of **B&Bs and homestays** with most being located out of town in a country setting. The **AL** *Fiordland Lodge*, 472 Te Anau-Milford Highway, (5 km north of Te Anau), T2497832 is a fine option with 2 self-contained log cabins. The owners also offer a wide range of guided excursions. The VIC has full listings of others. In town the German speaking **A** *Cosy Kiwi B&B*, 186 Milford Rd, T2497475, www.cosykiwi.com and **AL** *Cats Whiskers B&B*, 2 Lakefront Dr, T/F2498112, i.t.maher@paradise.net.nz are recommended.

There are plenty of **motels** scattered around town with the best and most expensive being located on Lakefront Dr and the older and cheaper tending to be elsewhere, particularly one street back on Quintin Dr. On Lakefront Drive, from the Town Centre heading south are the **AL-A** *Lake Front Lodge* (58), T2497728, www.LakefrontLodge.co.nz which is new and very well appointed and the **A** *Lakeside Motels* (36), T2497435, which is set amongst beautiful gardens. The **A** *Red Tussock Motel*, 10 Lakefront Dr, T2499110 at the southern end of Lakefront Dr, is also new and recommended. In Quintin Dr are the cheaper but comfortable **A** *Arran*, T2498826 and **A-B** *Anchorage*, T2497256.

There are plenty of backpacker **hostels** most of which are geared up to cater for trampers and muddy boots. The **C-D** *Te Anau YHA*, 29 Mokonui St, T2497847, yhatanau@yha.org.nz after years out of town has been relocated and purpose built right in the centre. It is the most popular backpacker option (deservingly so) with a wide range of rooms and a very comfortable lounge. Along the lakefront you will find the **C-D** *Lake Te Anau Backpackers*, 48 Lakefront Dr, T2497713, www.hostel.co.nz which is a large bustling place with all the usual facilities plus some excellent double or quad ex-motel units at reasonable prices. Spa and Internet. Right next-door is the smaller, quieter and more homely **C-D** *Lakefront Backpackers*, T2497974, lakefronthostel@xtra.co.nz

The newest backpackers in town is the **C-D** ***Steamers Beach Backpackers***, T2497737, steamers@destinationnz.com situated next to the Te Anau Holiday Park and across the road from the DOC Visitor Centre. Being purpose built to look like a ship it perhaps looks a little over the top but you'll find both fore and aft perfectly comfortable and fine facilities on deck.

The **motorpark A-D** ***Mountain View Top Ten Holiday Park***, 128 Te Anau Terr, T2497462, www.teanaumountainview.co.nz is a proud multi-award winner and is one of the best holiday parks in the country. The facilities are excellent and kept exceptionally clean and well maintained. You are even personally escorted to your site. It lives up to its name as having a 'bed for every budget'.

Eating

For fine dining the à la carte restaurants in the ***Holiday Inn*** (McKinnon Room), T2499700, and ***Quality Hotel*** (Bluestone), T2497421, are an option but the more congenial ***Redcliff Café and Bar***, 12 Mokonui St, T2497431 is recommended. Open daily 1600-late. There are plenty of affordable options in the Town Centre including the ***Moose Restaurant and Bar***, Lakeside Dr, T2497100. It has lost a little of its former atmosphere but can still serve up a good meal and has the town's most popular bar attached. Open daily from 1130 for lunch and dinner. On the main drag (Town Centre) ***La Toscana Pizzeria***, T2497756 is good value and recommended. Open Tue-Sun from 1730-late. For a good coffee try the ***Olive Tree Café*** which is also in theTown Centre, T2498496 (Open daily 0800-2200). For a traditional no-nonsense breakfast try the very entertaining ***Snack Attack***, 90 Town Centre, T2498895.

Directory

Banks There are 2 banks (***Westpac/BNZ***) in the town centre both have **ATMs** and offer **currency exchange** services. **Communications Internet** is available at ***E-stop,*** Jailhouse Mall, Town Centre (open 0900-2100, seasonal); ***Air Fiordland,*** Town Centre (open 0900-1900, seasonal), the Mountain View Holiday Park, Te Anau Terr and the ***Lake Te Anau Backpackers,*** 48 Lakefront Dr. The main **post office** is in 'Paper Plus', Town Centre. **Medical services** Doctor, Luxmore Dr, T2497007 (Mon-Fri 0800-1800/Thu 2000/Sat 0900-1200). **Shopping** ***Bev's Tramping Gear***, 16 Homer St, T2497389, bevs.hire@max.net.co.nz hire a vast range of walking, tramping and camping equipment at competitive prices. **Useful addresses Police**, Milford Rd, T2497600.

The Milford Road

If you are an independent traveller, you'll need to rely on tour buses. Almost 30 make the daily pilgrimage in summer, especially from about 1100 so go early or late in the day

The 119 km trip into the heart of the **Fiordland National Park** and **Milford Sound** is all part of the world class Milford Sound experience. In essence it is a bit like walking down the isle, past the interior walls of a great cathedral, to stand aghast at the chancel and the stunning stain-glassed windows above. This may sound like an exaggeration but if nature is your religion, then the trip to Milford is really nothing short of divine. Of course much depends on the weather. Ideally it should be of either extreme – cloudless, or absolutely thumping it down. Under clear blue skies it is of course magnificent, but many say that the trip through the mountains is actually better during very heavy rain. It is an incredibly moody place so don't necessarily be put off by foul weather.

From Te Anau you skirt the shores and enjoy the congenial scenery of Lake Te Anau before heading inland at **Te Anau Downs** (30 minutes). Te Anau Downs is principally a boat access point to the Milford Track (there is a motel, T0800-500805, and a hostel, T0800-478679). Another 30 minutes will see you through some low-lying alluvial flats and meadows as the Earl Mountains begin to loom large. After penetrating some beech forest you then suddenly emerge into the golden-grass expanse of the **Eglinton River Valley** with its viewpoints and stunning views towards the mountains. This is known as the 'Avenue of the Disappearing Mountain' and it speaks for itself.

At the northern end of the valley you then re-enter the shade of the beech forests and encounter **Mirror Lake**, which is a small body of water over looking the Earl Mountain Range. The lookout point is a short walk from the road. On a clear day you can, as the name suggests, capture the mood and the scene twice in the same shot.

Several kilometres further on is **Knobs Flat** where there is a DOC shelter and information/display centre and toilet facilities. For much of the next 25 minutes you negotiate the dappled shadows on a near constant tunnel of beautiful beech forest before reaching **Lake Gunn**, which offers some fine fishing and a very pleasant 45 minutes-nature walk through the forest. The copious growth of mosses and lichens here provide the rather unsubtle hint that the place can, very get very wet, very often!

From Lake Gunn you are really beginning to enter 'tiger country' as the road climbs to **The Divide** one of the lowest passes along the length of the Southern Alps. Here a shelter and an assortment of discarded boots marks the start of the **Routeburn** and **Greenstone/Caples Tracks**. The car park also serves as the starting point to a classic recommended (three hours return) walk to **Key Summit** which looks over the Humbolt and Darran Ranges. Round the corner there is the **Falls Creek (Pop's View) Lookout**, which looks down the **Hollyford Valley**. Depending on the weather this will be a scene of fairly quiet serenity or one of near epic proportions as the swollen **Hollyford River** rips its way down to the valley fed by a million fingers of white water.

Following the river is the **Lower Hollyford Road** and access to **Lake Marian** (1 km), a superb (three hours return) walk up through forest and past waterfalls into a glacial hanging valley that holds the lake captive. A further 7 km on is the Hollyford (Gun's) Camp, and the Hollyford Airfield, important access and accommodation points for the **Hollyford Track**, the trailhead for which is at the road terminus 6 km further on. The short 30 minutes return walk to the **Humboldt Falls**, which again are spectacular after heavy rain, starts just before the car park.

Back on the main Milford Road the mountains begin to close in on both sides as you make the ascent up to the **Homer Tunnel**, an incredible feat of engineering, and a bizarre and exciting experience, like being swallowed by a giant drain.

Once out of the tunnel you are now in the spectacular **Cleddau Canyon** and nearing Milford Sound. Instantly you will see the incredibly precipitous aspect of the mountains and bare valley walls. The rainfall is so high and rock and mudslides so frequent that the vegetation has little chance to establish itself. As a result the rainwater just cascades rapidly into the valleys. Note the creeks that cross under the road. There are so many they don't have names, but numbers! These all count up steadily to form the **Cleddau River** which, at **The Chasm** (20 minutes return), is really more waterfall than river, and has, over the millenia, sculpted round shapes and basins in the rock. From the Chasm it is five minutes before you see the tip of the altar of **Mitre Peak** (1692 m) and spire of **Mount Tutoko** (2746 m), Fiordland's highest peak. It's now only five minutes before your appointment with the Minister of Awe at the Chancel of **Milford Sound**.

Manapouri and Doubtful Sound

Phone Code: 03
Population: 400

As you drive in to Manapouri with its stunning vistas across the eponymous lake, you are immediately struck at how unobtrusive it is. If it were anywhere else in the developed world, it would be probably be an unsightly mass of exclusive real estate and tourist developments. Thankfully it is not, though perhaps the recent history of this pretty little village has something to do with that. Though you would never guess it, Manapouri has been the sight of some major altercations between the advocates of economics and conservation. Hidden away at the West Arm of the lake, and smack-bang in the heart of Fiordland National Park, is the country's largest hydroelectric power station, which has, over the years, created much controversy. Yet it is the very development of the power station that allows the tourist and conservationist access to some of the most remote parts of the park. Now it is home to an uneasy mix of power station workers and eco-friendly tourist operators and service providers. Manapouri is the main gateway and access point to activities on Lake Manapouri, Doubtful Sound and the incredible and challenging Dusky Track.

Ins & outs

There is no Information Centre in Manapouri per se, but **Fiordland Travel** have an office on the wharf (Pearl harbour) which is the base for all water activity on the lake and Doubtful Sound tour operations, T2496602, www.fiordlandtravel.co.nz For additional information contact the **VIC** (T2498900) or **DOC** (T2497924) in Te Anau.

Lake Manapouri

Lake Manapouri is stunning not only due to its backdrop of bush and mountain but also its moods. From the beach beside the village the whole scene echoes the constant change of Milford Sound. It is of course not so dramatic in its topography, but no less dynamic. Lake Manapouri has 35 islands which disguise its boundaries and, at a forbidding 420 m deep, is the second deepest lake in the country (the deepest is Lake Hauroko in southwestern Fiordland). To really appreciate the size and complex nature of Lake Manapouri it is necessary to get out on the water, which, thankfully, is a matter of course on the route to Doubtful Sound.

The Manapouri Underground Power Station

Located at the terminus of West Arm, and forming the main access point via Wilmot Pass to Doubtful Sound, is the Manapouri Underground Power Station. Although an unwelcome development to the conservationist, one cannot fail to admire the environmentally sympathetic way in which this incredible feat of engineering has been built or is indeed, maintained. Started in 1963 and completed eight years later, now only a few unsightly pylons, connected to a switchyard, control building and water intakes, belie the mammoth constructions underground – all supplied by a fairly unobtrusive barge that goes back and forth across the lake to Supply Bay near Manapouri. A 2040 m, 1 in 10 tunnel set in the hillside allows access to the main centre of operations– a large machine hall housing seven turbines and generators, fed by the water penstocks from 170 m above. What is most impressive is the 9.2 m diameter, tailrace tunnel that outputs the used water at the head of Doubtful Sound – an amazing 10 km from Lake Manapouri and 178 m below its surface. Started in 1964 the tailrace took four years to build.

Fiordland Travel, Pearl Harbour, Manapouri, T2496602, info@fiordlandtravel.co.nz offer three-hour trips to the power station alone (adult $50, child $10), but it is also a port of call on the Doubtful Sound day-excursion (see Doubtful Sound below). The bus drives down the dank and forbidding access tunnel and makes a very tight turn at the bottom where passengers are decanted to look at the interior of the machine hall. Even the most ardent luddite will be impressed.

Wilmot Pass

The road can be explored independently by mountain bike (provided you are fit enough) and acts as the northern trailhead to the Dusky Track

The 22 km road from West Arm to Doubtful Sound across the Wilmot Pass is a spectacular drive, encompassing remote mountain and beech and podocarp forest scenery, lookout points and waterfalls. The unsealed road, which took two years to complete, was built as part of the hydropower project. At a cost of nearly \$5 for every 2.5 cm, it is easily the most expensive road in the nation. With its numerous twists and turns and heady topography, together with a local annual rainfall of over 6 m, it is also a very hard road to maintain. Like the power station the road forms part of *Fiordland Travel*'s Doubtful Sound day trip (see below).

Doubtful Sound

Doubt nothing, this fiord like, Milford Sound, is all it is cracked up to be – and more. Many who have made the trip to Milford feel it may be very similar and therefore not worthy of the time or expense to get there. But Doubtful Sound has a very different atmosphere to Milford. With the mountain topography in Fiordland getting generally lower the further south you go, and the fiords becoming longer and more indented with coves, arms and islands, Doubtful Sound offers the sense of space and wilderness that Milford does not.

Getting there

Manapouri is 20 km south of Te Anau via SH95. Several **bus** companies pass through Manapouri on their way south via SH99 to Invercargill, including ***Spitfire Shuttles***, T2497505, ***Bottom Bus***, T4429708, and ***Topline Tours***, T2498059. Fiordland Travel is also regularly shuttling back and forth to Te Anau, T2496602.

Fiordland Explorer Charters, T2496616, offer **water-taxi** services on Lake Manapouri for trampers or mountain bikers who wish to explore the Wilmot Pass, or access the Dusky Track trailhead. ***Fiordland Travel***, Pearl Harbour, Manapouri, T2496602, info@fiordlandtravel.co.nz offer excellent day (8 hr) and overnight (24 hr) excursions to Doubtful Sound via Lake Manapouri and the Wilmot Pass (see next page).

Doubtful is, after Dusky, the second largest fiord and has ten times the surface area of Milford. At 40 km it is also over twice as long. Doubtful is deepest of the fiords at 421 m. There are three distinct arms and several outstanding waterfalls including the heady 619 m **Browne Falls** near Hall Arm. This is only marginally less than the near vertical Sutherland Falls on the famed Milford Track. At the entrance to Hall Arm is the impressive 900 m cliff of **Commander Peak** (1274 m), the only true echo of Milford's dramatic corridor.

Doubtful Sound hosts its own pod of about 60 bottlenose dolphins which are regularly seen by visitors as well as fur seals and fiordland crested penguins. But is also noted for its very lack of activity. On a calm night the silence is deafening.

Captain Cook originally named it Doubtful Harbour during his voyage of 1770. He decided not to explore past the entrance fearful that the prevailing winds would not allow him to get back out; hence the name. In doing so it seems, for once, Cook certainly missed out. It was not until 23 years later that Italian explorer Don Alessandro Malaspina, leading a Spanish expedition, dropped anchor and sent a small crew on a whaleboat in to the fiord to make observations. Although a brief excursion it was both brave and meticulous and left a number of present day names in its wake – Malaspina Reach being the most obvious.

Tours of the Sound

This trip is recommended not only because of the stunning natural scenery and the wildlife but because you are afforded such a stark contrast in the very bowels of the earth

After boarding a modern launch at Manapouri you cross the lake to West Arm (interesting commentary and free tea/coffee). From West Arm you then board a bus and negotiate the Wilmot Pass, stopping at a viewpoint over Doubtful Sound before descending past rivers, waterfalls and the hydropower tailrace outlet to the Doubtful Sound wharf. From there you board another launch for a superbly scenic and informative cruise through The Sound to the Tasman Sea. If time allows, you negotiate one or two of the fiords 'arms' and throughout the cruise can often encounter the resident dolphins. Once returned to the wharf, reunited with the bus and Lake Manapouri's West Arm, you then leave the dramatic scenery and daylight behind and negotiate the underground access tunnel to the machine hall of the hydropower station. There you stop for 30 mins to learn how it all works before re-emerging into daylight and catching the launch back to Manapouri. Trips depart daily at 0730 and 0930 and cost from $180 child $40.

The new **overnight trip** involves all of the above, plus an overnight stay on The Sound, aboard the new and comfortable 'Fiordland Navigator'. Designed along the lines of an of a traditional New Zealand trading scow, it comes complete with sails and offers private en-suite cabins or quad-share bunks. There are friendly nature guides on board and also kayaks with which you can do your own scheduled exploring. Trips depart daily November-April at 1230 from $245 child $170. Both these trips link in with Queenstown and Te Anau departures. *Fiordland Explorer Charters* also based in Pearl Harbour, T/F2496616, explorercharters@xtra.co.nz, offer a smaller scale more personalised operation and day-excursion (7 ½ hours) daily at 1000, from $120. For some excellent eco-tour options on Doubtful Sound (and others) see *Fiordland Ecology Holidays* below.

Eco-Tours Fiordland Ecology Holidays based on the main road in Manapouri, T2496600, www.foirdland.gen.nz, have developed an excellent range of holiday options from three days to two weeks on board their 12 passenger, 65 ft yacht 'Breaksea Girl'. The yacht is very comfortable and well-facilitated and the tours offer a very sensitive insight in to Fiordland's unique wildlife. Trips cost from $175 a day.

Kayaking Adventure Charters, Waiau St, T2496626, www.fiordlandadventure.co.nz offer day or overnight rental or fully equipped kayaks on Lake Manapouri (from $40 per day) as well as overnight kayak trips to Doubtful Sound, from $219. *Fiordland Wilderness Experiences* based in Te Anau (see page 643) offer 2-5 day trips to Doubtful, Breaksea and Dusky Sounds from $250. They also offer independent rental for the experienced only, from $45 a day.

Other activities

Mountain Biking The Wilmot Pass is a superb (but challenging 500 m ascent) road to explore by mountain bike. *Fiordland Explorer Charters*, T2496616 hire mountain bikes and offer water-taxi services across Lake Manapouri.

Walking and tramping The Wilmot Pass is the principal access point to the northern trailhead of the **Dusky Track** (see page 676). There are also a number of walks available around Manapouri most of which negotiate the **Garnock Burn** catchment and start on the southern bank of the Lake Manapouri outlet at Pearl Harbour. The most popular walk is the three hours Pearl Harbour **Circle Track** that follows the riverbank, up stream, before negotiating the forest ascent to a lookout point, then descending back to Pearl Harbour. The Circle Track also allows access to the longer **Back Valley** and **Hope Arm Hut** tracks that explore Hope Arm (Lake Manapouri) and the inland **Lake Rakatu**. For details pick up the *'Manapouri Walks'* leaflet ($1) from the DOC VIC in Te Anau. For dinghy hire across the river (call at the post centre next to the petrol station and café) or contact *Adventure Charters*, T2496626.

Essentials

Sleeping **LL** *Murrell's Grand View House*, 7 Murrell Av, T2496642, murrell@xtra.co.nz, is a historic rambling house near the mouth of the outlet and surrounded by spacious gardens. It offers double en-suites and fine cuisine. The **AL** *Beechwood Lodge*, 40 Cathedral Dr, T2496993, www.beechwoodlodge.com, is a new B&B that sits over looking the lake. It offers 2 well-appointed guest en suite bedrooms and has a glorious lounge from where you can watch the ever-changing moods of the lake. The older and more expensive.

The **B-D** *Lakeview Motor Inn*, Manapouri-Te Anau Highway, T2496652, manapouri@clear.net.nz overlooks the lake and has serviced units, plus two self-contained and 11 budget rooms, a café and internet. Almost next door is the wonderfully quirky **A-D** *Manapouri Lake View Motels and Motor Park*, Manapouri-Te Anau Highway, T2496624, whose elderly (and clearly) European owners tend a wonderful range of 'disney-esk' cottages, old Morris Minors and even a period costume collection. It has the cottages of course, which are a delight plus more conventional cabins, powered sites and good facilities. The lakeshore is just across the road.

The **B-D** *Manapouri Glade Motel and Motor Park*, T2496623, is located at the end of Murrell Av and right on the headland at the Waiau River mouth. It has 3 self-contained cottages, cabins and powered/tent sites. Lovely short walks nearby. For a backpackers you can't go far wrong with the small and cosy **C-D** *Possum Lodge* on the Lake Front and near the centre of the village, T2496660, possum.lodge@xtra.co.nz It has double/twin and 4 person share rooms some of which have a great view across the lake. Clean modern facilities, open fire and internet. Note this a popular hostel so book ahead-it may also be closed in mid winter. Provides pick-ups from Te Anau. The **D** *Deep Cove Hostel* at the head of Doubtful Sound is also a possibility outside school term-time but phone first for details, T2496602.

Eating There are few options in Manapouri and you would be better to head back to Te Anau for evening dining. During the day the ***Cathedral Café***, Cathedral Dr (next to the general store and petrol station) tries hard to serve up good coffee and snacks, while the ***Beehive*** in the Lakeview Motor Inn has a licensed café and bar, serving acceptable pub-style grub in to the evening T2496652. Open Mon-Sat 1100-0300, Sun 1200-1400 (seasonal).

The Southern Scenic Route

From Manapouri SH99 leaves the vast majority of tourist traffic behind, as most retrace their steps to Queenstown or cross-country east, to Dunedin. The Southern Scenic Route, which first heads south to the coast via ***Tuatapere*** *and* ***Invercargill****, then north, via the beautiful and underrated* ***Catlins*** *coast to* ***Dunedin****, provides an attractive alternative. The highlights of this trip, other than the sheer peace and quiet, are the potential stops in* ***Tuatapere*** *to walk the new and celebrated* ***Hump Ridge Track****,an overnight stay in the pleasant seaside resort of* ***Riverton****, a day or two in Invercargill, before a trip to* ***Stewart Island*** *and then, perhaps most recommended, the thorough exploration of the Catlins coast.*

Ins & Outs The Southern Scenic Route which is sometimes advertised as encompassing the entire journey from Dunedin to Milford Sound is a total of 440 km. **By bus** the route is served by *Spitfire Shuttle* (Invercargill), T2497505 and the backpacker oriente d *Bottom Bus* (Queenstown/Dunedin/Invercargill), T034429708. Local shuttle services are listed in the text.

Manapouri to Tuatapere

Still reeling from the highs of Fiordland's stunning scenery, your journey south could include the main drag of Vegas and still seem boring, so just accept that fact and sit back and enjoy the peace and quiet of the road. SH99 has to be one f the quietest main roads in the country and between Manapouri and Milford it's unusual to pass more than half a dozen cars even in summer. Generally speaking you will encounter very little with two legs. Instead what you will see is paddock upon paddock of sheep.

Although bird watchers can find considerable pleasure at the **Redcliffe Wetland Reserve** just north of Blackmount (38 km) there is little to justify a stop until **Clifden** (66 km). As well as its limestone caves, Clifden boasts one of the oldest and longest suspension bridges in the country (built in 1899). Though a little disappointing in global terms, it is still worth a look and makes a nice picnic spot by the river. Near Clifden (signposted off Clifden Gorge Road to Winton) are its very uncommercial and undeveloped limestone caves which can be explored carefully with a good torch and a little courage.

Just south of Clifden is the 30 km unsealed road to **Lake Hauroko**, the deepest body of water in New Zealand. Its remoteness is undoubtedly appealing and there is an interesting **walk** up a precipitous bluff to a lookout point. The area is also known for its many Maori (Ngai Tahu) burial sites. Lake Hauroko also provides jetboat access to the **Dusky Track**, one of the country's most challenging and remote treks. *Lake Hauroko Tours*, based in Tuatapere, T2266681, reinfo@es.co.nz, can provide access. On your way back from Lake Hauroko you may consider the short diversion north (off the Hauroko Road just before SH99) to sample the delights of **Dean Forest**. There, a pleasant short walk takes in its most famous native, a 1000-year-old totara tree. Once back on SH99 it is a further 13 km to Tuatapere, considered the gateway to the southeast corner of the Fiordland National Park (not that there are any roads!).

Tuatapere

Phone code: 03
Population: 800

Tuatapere is a quiet little town that wants to start making a big noise. The reason for this and the town's new and intended raison d'être, is the 53 km **Hump Ridge Track**, New Zealand's newest 'Great Walk' and one that is being advertised as being on a par with any of the others in Fiordland, or indeed the country (see page 678). The track starts at the western end of **Bluecliffs Beach**, which, in itself, is a nice spot to spend a couple of hours. Nearby, on the first section of the Hump Ridge Track is the 36 m high, 125 m **Percy Burn Viaduct** the largest wooden viaduct in the world. But even as it stood, this former saw-milling and farming town and (mysteriously) self proclaimed '**sausage capital**' of the nation, had a few other notable local attractions, including a fine jetboating operation down the **Wairaurahiri River**.

Ins & outs

The Tuatapere **Visitor Information Centre** is located at 31 Orawia Rd, T2266399, F2266074, reinfo@pop.es.co.nz The staff are very enthusiastic and helpful and there is infinite detail about the new Hump Ridge Track, www.humpridgetrack.co.nz Open daily 0900-1700 (winter Mon-Fri 0900-1700) **DOC** no longer has an office in Tuatapere with all the relevant administration being shifted to the VIC.

Activities *Wairaurahiri Jet*, T2084495 and worse still *Wairaurahiri Wilderness Jet*, T2258174, www.wildernessjet.co.nz offer exciting 6 ½ hour **jetboat** trips down a 10 km section of Lake Hauroko, before negotiating its 27 km 'outlet' river to the coast. It is a Grade III river, which to the layperson means very little, but what it does boast is the steepest lake-to-coast river fall in the country. From $130. Heli-jet, two-day trips and water taxi services to both Dusky and Hump Ridge Tracks are also available. *Lake Hauroko Tours*, T2266681, also offer transport and launch trips to and from the tracks.

Sleeping & eating Located right at the entrance to the Humpridge Track is the excellent **B-D** *Rarakau Farmstay and Lodge*, Papatotara Coast Rd, Bluecliffs Beach, T2258192, rarakau@southnet.co.nz They offer lodge bunkrooms, double B&B or private rooms. Cooking facilities or meals available and campervans are negotiable. Back in town the **C-D** *Five Mountains Holiday Park Backpackers and Camping*, corner of Half Mile and Clifden Rds, T2266418, is the principal backpackers while campervans are well catered for at the Tuatapere Motorpark, beside the river on Half Mile Rd, T2266502.

Elsewhere for a quick daytime snack the *Highway 99 Café/Bar and Takeaway* is another possibility. But, its biggest attraction is neither its coffee nor its sausages, but *'Brandy'* the cockatoo, with a level of conceit so great it would make the great Mohammed Ali seem modest. As you enter the shop you will be told in no uncertain terms that 'Brandy is a very (very) pretty boy'.

Southland and the Fiords

Tuatapere to Invercargill A further 10 km south and SH99 reaches the coast at the evocatively named **Te Waewae Bay**. Here you can stop at **McCraken's Rest** to admire the beach and the views west over southern Fiordland, or east, to **Monkey Island**. Monkey Island was the anchor site of the great Maori *waka* (canoe) Takitimu, which as legend tells, was wrecked on the bar of the Waiau River. Te Waewae Bay itself is quite a serene sight in fine weather and often the playground for hectors dolphin and the odd whale, but in winter the wind can come sweeping in from the Antarctic with a vengeance. This phenomenon is starkly highlighted in the next port of call – the intriguing village of **Orepuki** – where the macrocarpa trees have been sculpted in to amazing, tangled shapes, by the wind. Apparently, it is not in fact the wind that is directly responsible for this but the tree's aversion to sea salt swept in on the air. One has to wonder what the locals must look like.

The tiny former gold rush village of Orepuki is worth a little investigation, not only for its trees, but because it looks like the village that time forgot. The buildings seem to have changed little in decades. Also, 500 m north of the village is the **Orepuki Gemstone Beach**, which, for the geologist may reveal garnets, jasper, quartz, nephrite as well as the odd worm fossil or even sapphires. From Orepuki the road garrottes the Wakaputa Point before rejoining the coast again at the beachside settlement of **Colac Bay**. A place rich in Maori history it is now mainly frequented by surfers. Unless you have a board, you are best moving onto the far more ample amenities and sights of Riverton, a further 11 km east.

Riverton

Phone Code: 03
Population: 1900

Riverton – or Aparima, to use its former Maori name – is the oldest permanent European settlement in Southland and one of the oldest in the country. Located on the banks of the common estuary formed by the Aparima and Purakino Rivers, it was formerly a safe haven for whalers and sealers and was first established as early as the 1830s. Now having gradually developed into a popular coastal holiday resort Riverton is a fine place to stop for lunch, a short walk on the beach, or even to consider as a quieter alternative base to Invercargill, now only 42 km to the east.

Ins & outs

The Riverton **Visitor Information Centre** is located across the river (from the west) on Palmerston St, T2349991, therock@riverton.co.nz Open daily 0900-1700.

Sights

Given the rich history of the area the, **Wallace Early Settlers Museum**, 172 Palmerston Street, is worth a look. It houses displays and photographs focusing on the early Maori, whaling and gold mining days, with over 500 portraits of the early pioneers. It also provides genealogical research assistance. ■ *Open daily 1400-1600. Donation. T2348520.* Nearby the **South Coast Environment Centre**, proudly promotes the local environment and wildlife with displays and information. ■ *Open daily 1330-1630. T2348717.*

The **Riverton Rocks** and Howell's Point, located at the southern edge of Taramea Bay provides safe swimming, fishing, short walks and fine views across to Stewart Island. If you are looking for a good place for lunch then try the excellent *Beachhouse Café and Bar* (see below) . Other local **walks** are outlined in the free *'Riverton Scenic Walks'* leaflet; available free from the VIC. Southland is noted for its **paua** (abalone) industry, both for food and decorative jewellery. The *Southern Paua and Pacific Shell Factory and Shop*, 35 Bath Road, T2348825 and the *Riverton Paua Shoppe*, 134 Palmerston Street, T2349043 are the principal outlets.

Activities

Kiwi Wilderness Walks, T2348886, kiwiwalks@riverton.co.nz are a popular operator that provide guided eco-walks of 3-4 days Stewart Island and the Hump Ridge Track, from $795. The all expenses guided trips are best suited the older or less independent traveller but are no less exciting. The highlight of the Stewart Island trip is the good chance of observing kiwi in daylight, an unforgettable experience. Also based in Riverton are *Pourakino Jet Boat Tours*, T2246130, who offer trips on the local Pourakino or Fiordland's Wairaurahiri Rivers.

Sleeping & eating

The **A-D** ***Riverton Rock***, 136 Palmerston St, T2348886, www.riverton.co.nz is an excellent mid-budget establishment in a restored historic villa. It offers a range of very well appointed, 'themed' rooms including one with a superb original Victorian Bath. There is also an open fire in the 'paua' bunkroom. Modern facilities and good value. Campervan facilities available. The **AL** ***Harbour View B&B*** 12 Dallas St, T2348755, gail.w@ihug.co.nz , is a new and recommended B&B set in a historic villa and overlooking the harbour. For eating there is little competition with the ***Beachhouse Café and Bar***, 126 Rocks Highway, T2348274. Open Tue-Sun 1000-late. It overlooks the bay and is understandably popular. It also has Internet. There's also the award-winning and affordable ***Country Nostalgia Café***, 108 Palmerston St, T2349154. Open Wed-Mon for lunch and dinner.

Invercargill

Phone Code: 03
Population: 53,209

Invercargill suffers the same affliction of many towns in New Zealand and particularly those of South Island – it looks pretty awful. Stuck at the very rear end of New Zealand and sandblasted by the worst extremes of the southern weather, even its climate and geography are against it. On a brief visit, Mick Jagger described Invercargill as the 'rear-end of the universe', or words to that effect. And, to add insult to injury, it is even served by a transport carrier called 'Bottom Bus'. Despite all that, Invercargill has many good points, and although you will hear different, it is not quite the underdog it is reputed to be. For a start, it is the capital of the richest agricultural region in South Island and in 2000 had the strongest economic growth in the country.

Ins and outs

Getting there **By air** Invercargill airport is 2 ½ km south of the city and is served by *Air New Zealand Link*, T0800-737000. There are direct flights daily to Christchurch and Dunedin. ***Stewart Island Flights*** (Southern Air), T2189192, www.stewartislandflights.com, and ***Southeast Air***, T2145522, SOUTHEAST.AIR@xtra.co.nz, also serve Oban and Mason's Bay on Stewart Island.

Invercargill is 579 km from Christchurch and 217 km from Dunedin via SH1; 187 km from Queenstown via SH6 and 152 km from Te Anau via SH99 (Southern Scenic Route)

By bus Invercargill is served by ***Intercity*** (Christchurch/Dunedin), T2140598; ***Atomic Shuttles*** (Christchurch/Dunedin), T3228883; ***Spitfire Shuttles*** (Te Anau), T2187381;and the rather unfortunately named ***Bottom Bus***, which is a budget service (Southern Scenic Route/Catlins and Queenstown), T4429708, www.bottombus.co.nz Also plying the Southern Scenic Route is the ***Catlins Coaster***, (Catlins/Dunedin) T0800304333, www.southern-nz.co.nz Most buses leave from the **train** station on Leven St, T2140599, which provides the daily 'Southerner' service to Christchurch (leaves 0825). Note at the time of going to print this service was under threat.

For **ferry** services from Bluff to Stewart Island see page 658.

Getting around *Spitfire Shuttle*, T2187381, connect with Invercargill airport flights and will pick-up from your accommodation ($4). ***Invercargill Passenger Transport*** provide local suburban bus services, 100 Leven St, T2187108. Campbelltown Passenger Services, T2127404, provide shuttle services to Bluff and the Stewart Island ferry ($10) For taxis, car and bike rental see page 657.

Information The Invercargill **Visitor Information Centre** is located next to Queens Park and housed in the Southland Museum and Gallery Building, Victoria Av, T2146243, F2184415, ivcvin@nzhost.co.nz/www.southland.org.nz Open Mon-Fri 0900-1700 Sat/Sun 1000-1700. **DOC** information is held at the VIC or at the regional office, 7th Floor, State Insurance Building, 33 Don St, T2144589. Open Mon-Fri 0800-1700. The VIC has listings of local activities including flightseeing, sightseeing tours, golf, horse trekking and windsurfing. ***Southland Secrets***, T2369977 and ***Lynette Jack Tours***, T2157741 are two noted local and regional sightseeing tour operators.

History

Although the south coast was settled by European sealers and whalers as early as 1835, it was not until 1857, that the Chief Surveyor for Otago, one John Turnbull Thompson, was ordered by Governor Sir Thomas Gore Browne, to choose a site and take responsibility for the planning of what is now the country's most southerly city. When Southland seceded from Otago in 1861 to become a separate province, Invercargill became its capital. It is named in honour of Captain William Cargill (1784-1860), the first superintendent of Otago. 'Inver' is Scots Gaelic for 'at the mouth of' and refers, of course, to the city's proximity to the Waihopai River. Note also the many street names dedicated to Scottish rivers.

Sights

Ask to meet Lindsay Hadsley, the tuatara's proud custodian. There is nothing he does not know about tuataras and his enthusiasm is infectious

The main highlight in the town is the excellent **Southland Museum and Art Gallery** located on the edge of Queens Park, Victoria Avenue. Housed in a large pyramid in the southern hemisphere (27 m) it boasts all the usual fine Maori and early settler exhibits and national and international art exhibitions, but is particularly noted for its 'Roaring Forties Antarctic and Sub-Antarctic Island' display and audio-visual (25 minutes, $2) shown several times daily. Also excellent is the museum's **tuatara** display and breeding programme. The 'Tuatarium' is an utter delight and an opportunity to come face to face with a reptilian species older than the land on which you stand. Henry, the oldest resident at an estimated 120 years plus, usually sits only a foot or two away from the glass. You can try to stare the old fella out, but you will fail, because Henry has had plenty of practice. ■ *Mon-Fri 0900-1700 Sat/Sun 1000-1700. Donation. T2189753, www.southlandmuseum.co.nz*

Located beyond the museum is **Queens Park**, the city's saving grace. Its 80 ha of trees, flowerbeds and duck ponds provide a lovely setting for a walk, a picnic or a quiet doze. **Anderson Park**, McIvor Road, 27 km north of the city centre (signposted off SH6) is another 24 ha of beautiful parkland, with an interesting public art gallery. ■ *The gallery is open from Tue-Sun 1330-1700. The VIC has a very useful free* 'Parks and Gardens' *leaflet.*

If beaches and sand are your thing, then the huge 30 km expanse of **Oreti Beach**, 10 km west of the city (past the airport) will not disappoint. It has the added attraction of allowing vehicles (with sensible drivers) on the sand and safe swimming. Nearby **Sandy Point**, Sandy Point Road, offers a range of short walks and other recreation activities. There is an unmanned information point at the entrance to the park. For a fine view of the city (Sundays only) head for the very unusual 1889 **Water Tower**, corner of Gala Street and Queen Drive. ■ *Open 1330-1630.*

Sleeping

For farmstay options contact the very helpful Western Southland Farm Hosting Group, T2258608, www.nzcountry.co.nz/farmhost

The **LL-A** *Ascot Park Hotel*, corner of Tay St and Racecourse Rd, T2176195, ascot@ilt.co.nz is the city's top hotel. It is a large modern establishment offering a wide range of rooms and fine facilities in a quiet setting. Spa, pool and in-house restaurant and bar. For a **B&B** option 15 mins north of the city try the **A** *Tudor Park Country Stay*, 21 Lawrence Rd, Ryal Bush, T2217150, Tudorparksouth@hotmail.com Set in 4 ha of beautiful garden it is a neo-Tudor home with comfortable en-suite rooms. Meals available. In town the **A** *Gala Lodge*, 177 Gala St, T2188884, is another good option located across the road from Queens Park while the small and quiet **C-D** *Riverside*, 70 Filleul St, T2189207 is a budget guesthouse/backpackers next to the river off SH6 heading north.

There are plenty of **motels** in Invercargill some up-market and modern, others older and budget oriented. At the top range is the **A** *Homestead Villa*, Cnr Avenal and Dee Sts, T2140408, villa@southnet.co.nz ; The **A** *Balmoral Lodge*, Tay St, T2176109, accom@balmoral.ilt.co.nz and the **AL-A** *Birchwood Manor*, 189 Tay St, T2188881, www.birchwoodmanor.co.nz Mid-low range include the **B** *Garden Grove*, 161 North Rd, T2159555, ggrove@ihug.co.nz, and the **B** *Moana Court*, 554 Tay St, T2178443. The **A** *Queens Park Motel*, 85 Alice St, T2144504 is another good motel option within a short walk of Queens Park. The **B-D** *Tuatara Backpackers*, 30-32 Dee St, T08008828272, tuataralodge@xtra.co.nz is a new hostel ideally located in the centre of town. It offers very tidy shared standard double/twin and a few more luxurious doubles. Good kitchen facilities, Sky TV and an internet suite. The **C-D** *Southern Comfort Backpackers*, 30 Thomson St, T2183838, is an old, spacious villa near the museum and Queens Park. It is a traditional Southland favourite and offers dorms and doubles and free bike hire. For a motorpark look no further than the small, cosy and very friendly, **D** *Gum Tree Farm Motor Park*, 77 McIvor Rd (northern edge of town off SH6),

Invercargill

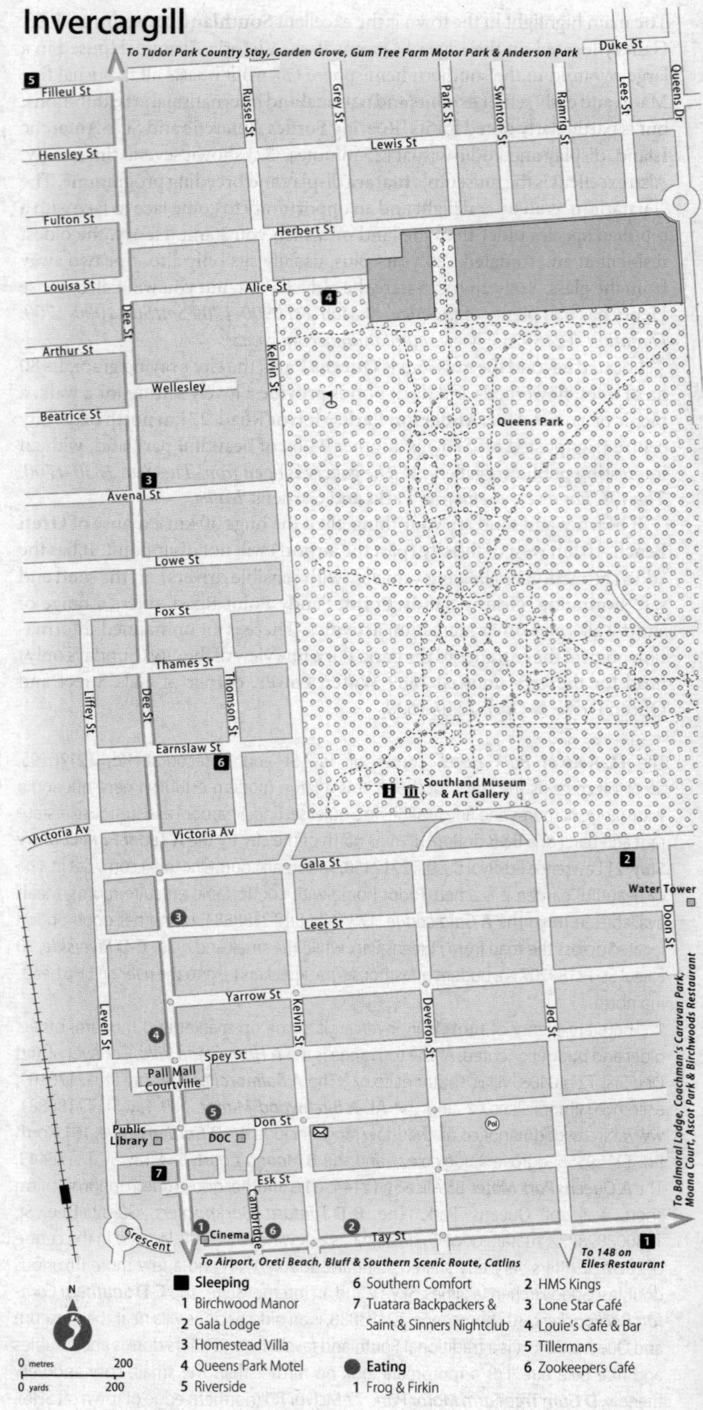

T2159032, gumtreefarmMP@xtra.co.nz If you must be in town try the **C-D** ***Coachman's Caravan Park***, 705 Tay St, T2176046.

Eating

There isn't a huge amount of choice in Invercargill

For fine dining the ***Birchwoods Restaurant*** in the Ascot Hotel, T2176195 (open for lunch Mon-Sat 1200-1400 dinner Mon-Sun from 1800), and the ***148 On Elles***, 148 Elles St, T2161000 (closed Sun) are recommended. For affordable evening dining try ***Louie's Café and Bar***, 142 Dee St, T2142913 (open Tue-Sun from 1800), or the very arty ***Tillermans***, 16 Don St, T2189240 (open Mon-Fri 1200-1400 and 1800, Sat from 1800). For seafood the ***HMS Kings*** 80 Tay St, T2183443, serves up a great seafood chowder amidst the nets and anchors (open daily lunch and dinner). For Tex-Mex the ***Lone Star Café***, corner of Leet and Dee St, T2146225 is recommended (open Mon-Sun from 1730). The best café in town is the licensed ***Zookeepers Café***, 50 Tay St, T2183373, which has a nice atmosphere, good coffee and good value evening meals (open daily from 1000-late). For pub-grub try the ***Frog and Firkin***, Dee St, next to the cinema, T2144001 (open for lunch 1200-1400, dinner Mon-Sat from 1700).

Entertainment

The Zookeepers, ***Lone Star*** and ***Frog and Firkin*** (see above) are all popular spots with the locals and usually have live gigs at the weekend. The dubious ***Saints and Sinners*** nightclub is below and beside the *Tuatara Backpackers* at 34 Dee St. The **Cinema** is located across the road at 29 Dee St, T2141110 and there is a **Ten Pin Bowling Centre**, corner of Kelvin and Leet Sts (licensed bar), T2144944. The *Southland Times* is the best source of local events and entertainment information.

Directory

Banks The main banks (most of whom offer **currency exchange**) are on or around Don St in the city centre. **Bike hire** *Wensley's Cycles*, corner of Tay and Nith Sts, T2186206. **Car hire** The airport has branches of most major players. Others include *Riverside Rentals*, corner of Bay and North Rds, T2159030; *Rent-a-Dent*, T2144820. **Communications Internet** is available at the VIC, *Public Library* (open Mon-Fri 0900-2000, Sat 1000-1300), *Tuatara Backpackers*, 30-32 Dee St, and *Gordon Data Services*, 124 Dee St. The main **post office** is on Don St in the city centre. **Medical services Doctor**, 103 Don St, T2188821. Open Mon-Fri from 1700, 24-hr Sat/Sun. **Taxi** *Blue Star*, T2186079; *Taxi Co*, T2144478. **Useful addresses Police**: Don St, T2144039.

Bluff

Phone Code: 03
Population: 2000

At 27 km south of Invercargill, the small port of Bluff heralds the end of the road in South Island. Most visitors to Bluff are either on their way or returning from Stewart Island, or come to stand and gawk at a windblasted signpost at the terminus of SH1, which tells them they several thousand miles from anywhere. Next stop Antarctica!

Ins & outs

Campbelltown Passenger Services offer a regular daily shuttle service to and from Invercargill to coincide with the Stewart Island ferries, T2127404 ($10 one-way). For **ferry** services see Stewart Island National Park text or contact *Foveaux Express*, T2127660.

The Bluff **Visitor Information Centre** is located in *Foveaux Souvenirs*, Gore St, T2128305. Open daily 1000-1600.

Sights

Visit the website www.bluff.co.nz

En route to the signpost is the quirky **Paua Shell House**, 258 marine Parade (open daily 0900-1700) which has over years become a bit of a New Zealand legend. For reasons best known to themselves, the elderly residents of this concrete crustacean took shell collecting to its extreme. Externally the house is nothing, compared to the interior. Enough said – you just have to see it! Sadly, Myrtle died last year, but Fred is still going strong.

Those with more time on their hands and a disturbing interest in aluminium smelting can take a free guided tour of the monstrous **Tiwai Smelter** sitting opposite Bluff harbour, T2185494. A far more aesthetically pleasing alternative is however **Bluff Hill** (270 m), which provides nice panoramic views past its chimney across Southland and back towards Stewart Island. If it is raining the **Maritime Museum**, Foreshore Road, is worth a look to soak up the towns long history. ■ *Open Mon-Fri 1000-1630 Sat/Sun 1300-1700, $2. T2127534.*

Bluff's biggest event of the year is the famous **Bluff Oyster Festival**, bluffoysterfest@icc.govt.nz usually held in May. It is a celebration of the world-class Bluff oysters and other local seafood delights. Of course there is lots of fine wine to wash it all down and plenty of entertainment, including live bands (noise annoys an oyster?) and oyster opening and eating competitions. The festival's raucous finale is the Southern Seas Ball.

Sleeping & eating

You can't go far wrong with the **A** ***Land's End Hotel***, a boutique hotel at the very end of SH1, T2127575, www.nzcountry.co.nz/landsend It has comfortable, well appointed en suite rooms and a wine bar/café. For a budget option try the **B-D** ***Flynn's Club Hotel***, 100 Gore St, T/F2128124 has a wide range of basic but comfortable rooms, plus a bar which sells meals. The basic ***Argyle Park Camping Ground*** is on Gregory St, T2128704. For eating there is the Land's End (above) which serves breakfast, lunch and dinner and will happily serve up the famous oysters when in season (Mar-Aug). The ***Harbour Lights Café***, 158 Gore St, T2128071, does good fish and chips.

Stewart Island (Rakiura National Park)

Phone Code: 03
Population: 390

Lying 20 km southwest off Bluff, across the antsy waters of Foveaux Strait, is the 'land of the glowing skies' (Racier) or Stewart Island. Often called New Zealand's third Island (making up 10% of its total area) and about the same size as Fiji, Stewart Island was described over a century ago, by pioneer botanist Leo Cockayne, as 'having a superabundance of superlatives'. There is much truth in that. It can be considered one of the country's most unspoilt and ecologically important areas. Such are its treasures that only the country's national parks can compare, which is why it was only a matter of time before it entered the fold, in May 2001, with 85% of the island now enjoying the limelight as the newest of New Zealand's 14 national parks.

Ins and outs

Getting there

Before booking anything independently it is advised to check with the Invercargill VIC for special rates and packages. These are most often targeted for 2 people, T2146243

By air Stewart Island can be reached by **air** (20 mins) from Invercargill to Half-moon Bay or the western Bays of Masons, Doughboy, West Ruggedy or Little Hellfire (trampers) with ***Stewart Island Flights***, T2189129, F2144681, www.stewartislandflights.com from $140 return. Scheduled flights Oct-Apr 0800/1300/1700 (May-Sep 0900/1300/1600) Only 15 kg of personal baggage can be flown over on a full flight (additional gear can be flown over on subsequent flights).

By sea ***Foveaux Express***, T2127660, F2128377, www.foveauxexpress.co.nz sail Sep-Apr; 0930/1700 and May-Aug; 0930/1630 from the port of Bluff. The crossing takes about 1 hr and costs $84 return, child $42. Secure parking is available in Bluff for $5 per day. ***Campbelltown Passenger Services*** offer a regular daily shuttle service to and from Invercargill to coincide with the Stewart Island ferries, T2127404 ($10 one-way).

Getting around

Once on the island you will find that most things are within walking distance, but many accommodation establishments will provide pick-ups. Both ***Oban Taxis and Tours***, T/F2191456 (0700-1930; later by special arrangement) and ***Sam and Billy the Bus*** (!), T2191269, F2191355 provide independent transportation. Oban Taxis and Tours also offer **car hire** (from $70 per-day) and **scooters** from $20 per-hr. Scooters can also be hired from ***Stewart Island Travel***, Main Rd, T2191269, who can also arrange tours, boat trips, water-taxis and car rentals. ***Innes Backpackers***, Argyle St hires **mountain bikes**, from $20, T2191080. ***Stewart Island Flights*** have a depot on the waterfront, T2189129. A **shuttle** to/from the airfield is included in the fare.

There are numerous **water-taxi** operators including ***Stewart Island Water Taxi***, T/F2191394, www.portofcall.co.nz ***Seaview Water Taxis***, T/F2191014; ***Seabuzzz***, T2191282, www.seabuzzz.co.nz and ***Rakiura Waterways/Blue water Taxis***, T2191414. Fares range between $20 and $50 one-way.

Information & orientation

Oban on Half-moon Bay is the principal settlement on the island. It is further connected to several smaller settlements including Golden Bay, Horseshoe Bay, Leask Bay and Butterfield Bay, by about 20 km of mainly sealed road.

Almost all of Oban's amenities and (non-B&B) accommodation establishments can be reached easily by foot from the wharf. The 2 principal streets are Elgin Terrace (the waterfront) and Main Road which hosts the **DOC Visitor Information and Field Centre**, T2191218, F2191555, www.stewartisland.co.nz/www.doc.govt.nz Open Mon-Fri 0800-1700, Sat/Sun 0900-1600. It is the principal source of accommodation and walk/tramping information and bookings on the island. There is a small interpretative display which is no doubt going to expand with the new national park status. They also provide toilets, a pay phone, storage lockers, sell maps and hire personal locator beacons. An excellent free location **map of the village** and its surrounds is available at the VIC and is an essential on your arrival.

Stewart Island Travel, Main Rd, T2191269, www.obantours.com and ***The Adventure Centre*** on the wharf (Foveaux Express), T2191134, F2191322, bookings@foveauxexpress.co.nz are the principal centres for land/water transportation and activity and non independent walking/tramping information and bookings.

Background

History

According to Maori legend Stewart Island is the anchor stone of the canoe of the mythological hero and explorer Maui and is therefore known as 'Te Puka-o-te-waka-a-Maui'. As early as the 13th century there is evidence that the island's rich natural resources were being utilized by the Maori, with the particular attraction being attributed to the vast numbers of muttonbirds (sooty shearwater) or 'Titi'. The first European visitor (no prizes for guessing), in 1770 sailed past and mistook the island to be the mainland, calling it Cape South. Thirty-nine years after Captain Cook, it took one William Stewart, the first officer aboard the whaling ship Pegasus, to get it right and bless the island with its modern name. In the first half of the 18th century whalers and sealers were beginning to establish themselves in the region and they were soon followed by fishermen and saw-millers who soon settled the island permanently.

In 1864 the island was officially bought from the Maori by the British, for the standard price of £6000. Besides a brief and sudden increase in population, thanks to a very unproductive gold rush in the late 1800s, the island has remained fairly uninhabited, with the current 390 residents mainly involved in fishing or tourism.

Flora & fauna Stewart Island has an indented coastline of river inlets, bays and offshore islands not dissimilar to parts of southern Fiordland. In many ways it is equally unspoiled and its heavily bush-clad landmass is host to a wealth of ecological habitats and a rich biodiversity. The most common species on the island are sadly, as ever, the non-natives and the introduced. The most unwelcome and destructive of these are the possums, the rats and feral cats. Also, for over a century, white-tailed deer have roamed the bush, put there to occupy the hunting interests we humans.

The island is home to 21 threatened plants, some of which are endemic or occur only on the island. With the absence of dominant and introduced trout, there are 15 native fish species and when it comes to birds the island is surrounded by a vast array of pelagic species, including mollymawks (a kind of albatross), petrels and shearwaters (muttonbirds), many of which breed on the offshore islets in vast numbers. Even on the main island (and fighting to survive the ravages of introduced vermin), its impressive bird breeding list includes two of the rarest and most unique in the world: a distinctly odd and enchanting, flightless parrot, called a kakapo (of which only about 60 remain) and perhaps most famous of all – *Apteryx australis lawryi* – better known as the Stewart Island Brown Kiwi, the largest and only diurnal kiwi in New Zealand. It is to see these whimsical birds on the beach by daylight that many visit the island. The thing is, though, you may have to watch them sidestep a yellowed-eyed penguin, which is one of the rarest penguins in the world. And, in turn, they may get their flippers in a twist to avoid the attentions of a dosing hookers sealion, which is one of the rarest sealions in the world. You've probably got the picture; Rakiura is a very special place indeed.

Stewart Island

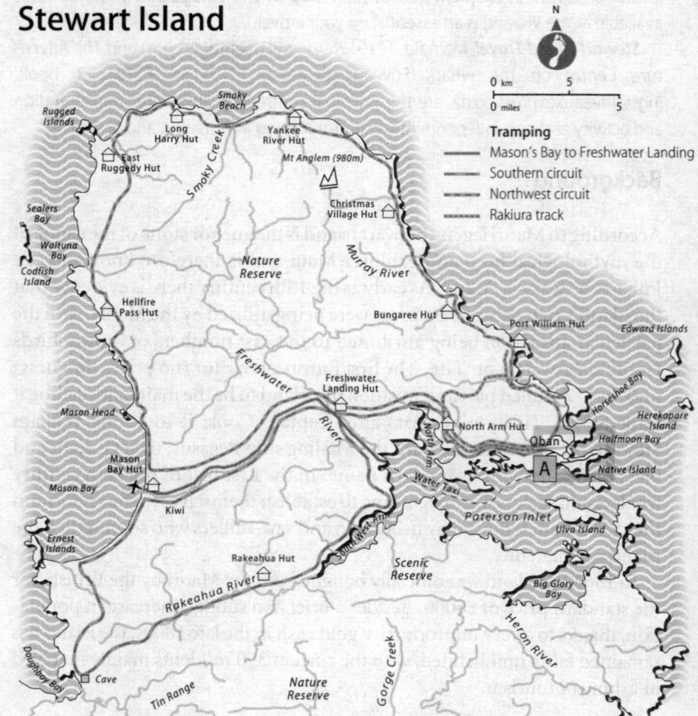

Related map
A Oban, page 662

Sights and activities

Other than to see kiwi, the boat trips and kayaking, people visit Stewart Island for two main reasons: either to bask in its tranquillity and do very little around the pleasant little village of Oban; or attempt one of its challenging, very long and very wet tramping tracks. Yes, it rains a lot here.

Around Oban

Perhaps the best place to start is by foot with a short, steady climb to **Observation Rock** (southern end of Oban village, up Ayr Street). From here you get a grand view of **Paterson Inlet** and the impenetrable forests that deck its southern shores and disappear beyond the horizon. This vista gives an idea of the rest of the island's wild and unspoilt make-up. In Oban itself the **Rakiura Museum** can entertain between rain showers, showcasing many aspects of the island's interesting history, including the very early Maori and their continued harvesting of muttonbirds (Titi) to whaling, saw-milling, gold mining and fishing. ■ *Mon-Sat 1000-1200, Sun 1200-1400. $2.*

The beach on the **waterfront** (Elgin Terrace) is a fine place to simply sit and watch the world go by, play industrial size chess, or decide on one of the many **water-based trips** that are available. As you can imagine there are a wide range of possibilities from **fishing** and **diving**, to simple daytime sightseeing, overnight or luxury multi-day adventures. The *VIC Adventure Centre* on the wharf or *Stewart Island Travel* list all the operators and charter possibilities, and *Oban Tours and Taxis*, T2191456, hire out diving gear. A one-hour **glass-bottom boat** trip will cost from $25 (*Seabuzz*, T2191282, 1100 daily) while a four- hour twilight bush-walking trip to attempt to see **kiwi** is available with *Bravo Adventure Cruises*, T/F2191144, from $60. Short of Mason's Bay this may be your best chance of seeing the kiwi in half-light (see page 663).

Those without sea legs might consider a 1½ hours **scenic bus trip** with *Sam and Billy the Bus*, T2191269. Sam, the naturalist/historian and Billy the wheels come petrol junkie have been providing entertaining and informative trips around Oban and its neighbouring settlements for 15 years. Tours leave from the Travel Centre on Main Road every hour from 1100-1430 (seasonal), from $18, child $9. Other similar tours are available with *Oban Tours and Taxis*, also from Main Road, T2191456. You may decide to do a self-guided trip by **scooter**, which can be hired from *Oban Tours and Taxis*, (two hours from $60).

You could head north of Oban towards Horseshoe Bay, which is a very pleasant walk in itself. On the way you can spend some time exploring or **swimming** at **Bathing Bay**, a lovely sheltered beach accessed via Kamahi Road off Horseshoe Bay Road. This walk can be extended to **Horseshoe Point** (3-4 hours), accessed from the southern end of **Horseshoe Bay**. On the southern entrance to Half-moon Bay the (three hours) **Harrold Bay to Ackers Point Lighthouse Walk**, accessed at the end of the southern bay road (Elgin Terrace), is another fine alternative. Harrold Bay is the site of **Ackers cottage** (1835), one of the oldest stone cottages in New Zealand. DOC has a very useful *'Day Walks'* leaflet available from the VIC ($1) which outlines other alternatives.

Ulva Island

Guarding the entrance of Paterson Inlet is Ulva Island, a nature reserve criss-crossed with trails and home to abundant and extremely tame and exuberant birdlife. The island provides the most popular **day or half-day trip** from Oban, with a number of water-taxi operators offering organized trips taking in the mussel and salmon farms in Big Glory Bay, as well as seal and shag colonies (four hours guided trips, $45, child $45, T2191066). Most companies also offer independent transportation. A trip to Ulva is recommended.

Ulva and Paterson Inlet also provide one of the many excellent **sea-kayaking** venues. The two main operators are *Stewart Island Sea Kayak Adventures*, T/F2191080 and *Completely Southern Kayaks*, T2191275, both of whom provide a range of guided single (from $60) to multi-day trips and independent hire. They also hire out camping equipment. You could also consider a **paddle/tramp** option with the trip up to the DOC Freshwater Hut and access from there to Mason's Bay.

Oban

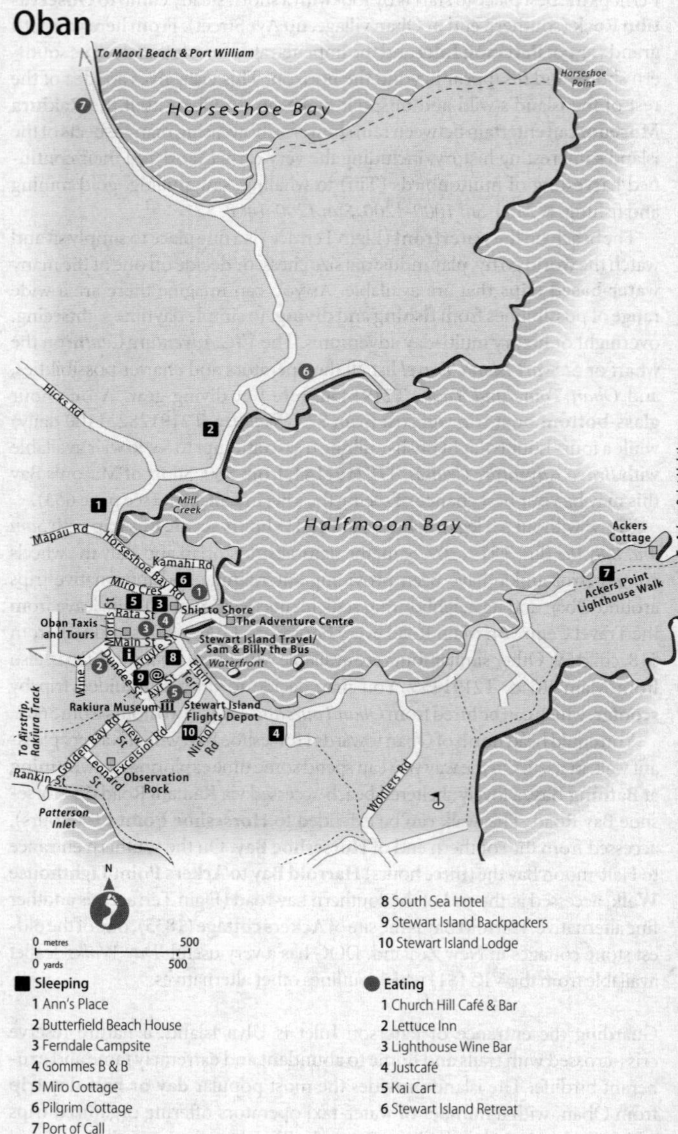

Sleeping
1 Ann's Place
2 Butterfield Beach House
3 Ferndale Campsite
4 Gommes B & B
5 Miro Cottage
6 Pilgrim Cottage
7 Port of Call
8 South Sea Hotel
9 Stewart Island Backpackers
10 Stewart Island Lodge

Eating
1 Church Hill Café & Bar
2 Lettuce Inn
3 Lighthouse Wine Bar
4 Justcafé
5 Kai Cart
6 Stewart Island Retreat

Kiwi-Spotting on Stewart Island

The tokoeka, or Stewart Island Brown Kiwi, is the reason many people come to Stewart Island. The Stewart Island sub-species, which number around 20,000, are the largest of the kiwis and the only one that is commonly active in daylight hours. Whatever the scientific reason fo9r this, it provides us with the unique opportunity to actually observe these fascinating birds in natural light, instead of having to peer at captive animals through the glass of some tacky kiwi house. You can encounter kiwi just about anywhere on Stewart Island, but the prime location is Mason's Bay on the west coast. It's best to go from an hour before sunrise to two hours after, or an hour or so before sunset, and walk quietly down the main tracks, looking particularly in the grassed areas. Look out for droppings (quite large and white) and/or probe holes in the ground. These indicate recent activity. If and when you spot a kiwi DO NOT approach more than 3 m, make sudden movements or any noise. If anything, let them come to you – which they often will. They are so blind (some say daft) and so busy they are even known to bump in to legs and rucksacks. They are just magical to watch and if they feel at all threatened will stop and listen intently, before sauntering off in to the scrub. If you do see one then just be very thankful. After all, there is nowhere else in the world you can see this bird in these circumstances, and maybe in 50 years time, sadly, the magical bird you're looking at will be found only in natural history books.

Southland and the Fiords

Tramping

With 245 km of walking tracks, Stewart Island is a popular venue for trampers. These tracks range from the many short 'warm-up' walks around Oban, to the Northwest Circuit, a mammoth 125 km, 10-12 day tramp around the island's northern coast. Some other, far more remote, routes are sometimes negotiated, including the fascinating **'Tin Range'** route on the island's south-western corner, but these require expert planning, logistics and a high level of fitness. Overall, tramping on Stewart Island presents its own challenges, not only because the island is so underdeveloped, remote and rugged, but mainly because it is particularly wet underfoot. There are numerous DOC huts that vary in size and standard, with the more remote obviously being the most basic. Hut details and bookings, maps and detailed track **information** is available with DOC and it is highly recommended you obtain all the details and if necessary fill in an intentions form for the longer or more remote tramps. In the south of the island you may need to apply for a permit to enter certain ecologically sensitive areas.

Two good companies offering **guided walks**, including the 'kiwi experience' are *Ruggedy Range Wilderness Experience*, based in Oban, T2191066, www.ruggedyrange.com or *Kiwi Wilderness Walks*, based in Riverton, T0800-248886, www.riverton.co.nz (See Riverton section).

Mason's Bay to Freshwater Landing

This is a 14 km four-hour walk with no road access that can be approached in various ways. You can either walk to Mason's Bay from Oban (37 km, three days one way), taking in part of the Rakiura Track, then reach Mason's Bay via Freshwater Landing. Once at Mason's Bay you can then walk or fly back to Oban. Or take a water-taxi or kayak to Freshwater Landing then make the return walk to Mason's Bay (28 km, two days return). The recommended alternative is to fly in to Mason's Bay, then make the leisurely return walk to Freshwater Landing (14 km, four hours) giving yourself an extra day to explore Mason's Bay (and give yourself the best chance of seeing **kiwi**). You can then get a water-taxi from Freshwater landing to Golden Bay and Oban. The track is low-level all the way, with a nice mix of open flax and tussock country and intriguing corridors of enclosed manuka tree. You will not manage to negotiate this trip without getting your feet wet and it is notoriously muddy, but there are boardwalks in the worst sections. The DOC Mason's Bay hut has 20 bunks but is popular and runs on a first come first served basis, so if you can take a tent.

Rakiura Track The Rakiura is one of New Zealand's 'Great Walks' immediately accessible by foot from Oban and is a 29-36 km track requiring 2-3 days. The appeal of the Rakiura, other than ease of access, is the mainly rimu and kamahi forest scenery, and views and secluded beaches of **Paterson Inlet**. There is also an abundance of **birdlife**. In the forest this includes kaka, tomtit, bellbirds, tui, and shining cuckoo, while wading birds including New Zealand dotterel or seabirds, including shags and little blue penguins, can be seen on the coast. The track can be negotiated clock or anticlockwise from Oban. In a clockwise direction the walking distances and times are as follows: Halfmoon Bay to Port William Hut, 12 km, 4-5 hours; Port William Hut to North Arm Hut, 12 km, six hours; North Arm to Halfmoon Bay 12 km, 4-5 hours. Port William and North arm huts are well facilitated and have 30 bunks each. You can purchase a Great Walks or campsite pass ($10/$6) from the VIC before departure or book over the net, greatwalksbooking@doc.govt.nz There are designated campsites with water and toilets at Maori Beach, Port William and Sawdust Bay.

The Northwest Circuit At 125 km and requiring at least 10 days this is one of the longest tramps in the country and done in total, is not for the faint-hearted. The appeal other than the sense of achievement and feeling of complete solitude, is the remote and rugged coastal scenery with its stunning bays and features, some with such evocative names as Hellfire Pass and Ruggedy Beach. The side trip to climb **Mount Anglem** (980 m), the island's highest peak, is also a recommended highlight. The track is also noted for its wildlife. Note that the track is notoriously muddy and wet at times but don't let that put you off. There are ten DOC huts on the route with 6-10 bunks. A Northwest Circuit Pass allowing ten nights in any hut on the route is available from the VIC for $40.

The track distances and minimum times are as follows: Halfmoon Bay to Port William, 12 km, four hours; Port William to Bungaree Hut, 6 km, three hours; Bungaree Hut to Christmas Village Hut, 11 km, five hours; Mount Anglem side trip, 11 km, six hours; Christmas Village Hut to Yankee River Hut 12 km, six hours; Yankee River Hut to Long Harry Hut, 11 km, five hours; Long Harry Hut to East Ruggedy Hut, 7 km, three hours; East Ruggedy Hut to Hellfire Pass, 14 km, seven hours; Hellfire Pass Hut to Mason's Bay Hut, 15 km, seven hours; Mason's Bay Hut to Freshwater Landing Hut 14 km, three hours; Freshwater Landing Hut to North Arm Hut 11 km, five hours; North Arm Hut to Halfmoon Bay, 12 km, five hours.

Southern Circuit The Southern Circuit is a 74 km 6-7 day tramp that takes in many similar (but more remote) aspects of the Rakiura Track and the delights of the rugged coastline from Doughboy Bay to Mason's Bay and Mason's Bay itself. Access to the recommended start and finish point of Freshwater Landing is by water-taxi. Four DOC huts and an interesting bivvy at Doughboy Bay provide accommodation. DOC can provide detailed information about the tramp.

Essentials

Sleeping

Most of the accommodation on the island takes the form of comfortable upper-mid range B&Bs and homestays and budget options but there is one hotel and a handful of motels. Note that none of the budget hostels take advance bookings in summer and beds must be secured on the day of departure from Bluff or Invercargill airport. Note also that there is much gossip surrounding certain bachelor-owned/operated hostels and the 'comfort' of single women travellers. The best advice is to check out a few hostels on your arrival (particularly those recommended below) and decide for yourself.

Set in an idyllic spot overlooking the entrance to Halfmoon Bay is the very cosy and friendly **L** ***Port of Call***, Jensen Bay, T/F2191394, www.portofcall.co.nz It offers a charming en-suite double, great breakfasts and views from the deck that are almost unsurpassed elsewhere. **L** ***Stewart Island Lodge***, 14 Nichol Rd, Halfmoon Bay, T/F2191085, www.StewartIslandLodge.co.nz is well established as one of the best upper-range B&Bs on the island. It provides five luxury en suites and notoriously good cuisine, amidst the perfect peaceful setting. **AL** *Gommes B&B*, Elgin Terr, T/F2191057 is another fine option with 2 well-appointed and cosy en suites and a lovely outlook over the bay. The owners also manage a number of other self-contained options from 2-4 bedrooms.

A ***South Sea Hotel***, corner of Elgin Terr and Main St, T2191059, F2191120, www.stewart-island.co.nz, is the main hotel on the waterfront. Although its in-house rooms are comfortable enough its new motel studio units out back are even better. In house restaurant and bar which is the local hub of evening entertainment. **A** ***Pilgrim Cottage*** and **A** ***Butterfield Beach House***, T219114, are 2 modern, tidy and affordable self-contained options, owned by the same couple. Kiwi trips a speciality, from $60. **A** ***Miro Cottage***, 113 Miro Cres, T/F2191180, janlance@xtra.co.nz is another fine self-contained option with two bedrooms and close to town.

C-D *Anne's Place*, Mill Creek, T2191065, is a no-nonsense, no TV, budget option run by a former VIC representative, so her knowledge knows no bounds. If Anne is full she can refer you on to another reputable hostel. In town the sprawling but highly functional **C-D** ***Stewart Island Backpackers***, Ayr St, T2191114, www.stewart-island.co.nz has a wide range of dorms and units. The basic **D** ***Ferndale Campsites***, Halfmoon Bay, T2191176 is close to all amenities.

Eating

Stewart Island has only a few eateries, with the famed muttonbird (Titi) being the speciality dish round these parts. By all accounts it is very tasty, being a bit like venison and certainly more 'oily' than chicken. But if you see these beautiful seabirds up close, never mind the chicks (which resemble fluffy brown slippers), you'll be picketing these establishments with a placard round your neck!

For fine dining the ***Church Hill Café Bar and Restaurant*** next (not in) the church on the headland above the wharf, T2191323, is the best bet. Open daily from 1000 (seasonal). In the village the ***South Sea Hotel*** provides a fine menu of no-nonsense lunch and dinner options including the unique muttonbird for $22 (Open 0800-0930/ 1200-1400/ 1800-2100, seasonal). The ***Lighthouse*** *Wine Bar* on Main St, T2191208, is good for a sit-in pizza (open from 1800, seasonal), while the ***Justcafe*** on the same street is the place for good coffee and a light meal, while absorbed with the internet, T2191208.

For some class fish and chips for lunch or dinner try the *Kai Cart* on Ayr St, T2191442. Outwith the village the café at the ***Stewart Island Retreat***, Horseshoe Bay, T2191071 is a great place for that refreshing cuppa! The ***Ship to Shore*** on the waterfront is the only general store while ***The Lettuce Inn***, 31 Main St is good for fresh meat, fruit and vegetables, T2191243.

Entertainment Without doubt the place to be for a beer and unpredictable entertainment is the ***South Sea Hotel***, Elgin Terr. But what kind of night you will have depends on who you bump in to and whether they are in good spirits or bad. They are great and welcoming bunch most of the time, so just place your cards on the table and give as good as you get!

Directory *Ship to Shore* on the waterfront, T2191069 (Open Mon-Fri 0800-1830, Sat/Sun 0900-1830, seasonal) is the only **general store** on the island and stock just about everything a body needs. They also have **EFTPOS** and accept NZ Travellers' Cheques. There are no **banks** or **ATMs** on the island. **Postal** services are administered by the Stewart Island Flights depot, also located on the waterfront (Elgin Terr), T2191090. **Internet** is available at the ***Justcafe***, Main St (open 0800-2200 seasonal) or the ***Stewart Island Backpackers***, Ayr St.

The Catlins

If you love remote and scenic coastlines you are going to love the Catlins. But the added bonus here is their location. Like the Wairarapa in the south-west of the North Island, the area is generally off the beaten track and certainly under-rated. You can negotiate the Catlins from the north or the south via the publicised **Southern Scenic Route**, encompassing a 187 km network of minor roads, about 30 km of which are **unsealed**. One word of warning here. Given the combination of 'difficult' road conditions, stunning scenery and often a time constraint, the Catlins have become a notorious black spot for **accidents** (take it from me!). 'Prangs' are so commonplace that most of the major car rental companies do not provide insurance coverage in the region. So if you are travelling in a rental, read the small print and check before setting off. Above all, **slow down**. The journey between Invercargill and Dunedin (or in reverse) is often attempted in one day, which is definitely a mistake. A more thorough, comfortable and less frustrating investigation will take at least **two days**, preferably three. But, if you can really only afford one day, the highlights not to be missed are – from the north – **Nugget Point** (for sunrise); the opportunity to see the seductively named **Hookers sealions** at **Cannibals Bay** (morning); the **Purakaunui Falls** and **Purakaunui Bay** (for lunch); then **Curio Bay** and **Slope Point** in the afternoon. The Catlins is also noted for its rich flora and fauna. Of particular note are the pinnipeds, or seals. The Catlins is the only mainland region of New Zealand where you can observe the New Zealand **fur seals**, **Hookers sealions** and **Southern Elephant seals** in the same location. The region is also within the very limited breeding range of the rarest penguin on the planet-the **Yellowed-Eyed Penguin (hoiho)** – and the rare and tiny **Hector's Dolphin**. Incredibly, with a little luck all these species can be observed quite easily, independently and at relatively close (safe!) range. The tracts of dense coastal forest that still remain are made up predominately of **podocarp** and **silver beech** and are home to native birds like **native pigeon** (kereru), **yellowhead** (mohua) and **fernbird**. The forests also hide a number of attractive **waterfalls**. Also, it is not only living trees that you can observe here. Curio Bay is home to a scattering of **petrified fossil trees** that are over 160 million years old.

Dong Won 529

Although you will almost certainly be blissfully unaware of it, Stewart Island holds the rather dubious honour of suffering New Zealand's worst and most recent major maritime oil spill. In October 1998 the Korean fishing vessel Dong Won 529 ran aground on the Breaksea Islands, on its most southeasterly point. Thankfully there was no loss of life, but the ship sunk and, most importantly, its 380 tonnes of diesel fuel.

Of course, its very remote location, the potential weather and most of all, the sheer variety and sheer scale of seabirds that might be affected, presented an instant and potentially disastrous situation. The only thing in everybody's favour (and most especially the wildlife), was the fact it was diesel oil and not crude. Had it been the thicker, more tenacious and potentially more damaging crude the consequences would have been catastrophic. Within hours after the ship's crew were rescued a full national oil spill response was initiated and experienced oiled wildlife responders brought in. The island became a frantic buzz of activity as helicopters hit the spill with dispersants and DOC crews and local residents were sent out to determine the impact on wildlife. Meanwhile in Invercargill the oil spill response HQ was set up and a temporary oiled wildlife treatment centre created in the city's old swimming pool complex. Thankfully the first few vital hours and days passed with no affected wildlife sighted. After a week the threat to wildlife was significantly decreased and miraculously not one oiled bird was received for rehabilitation. This was put down to the remote and inaccessible nature of the coastline and the wildlife itself. The fact that the birds in the area were predominantly 'tube-nosed' petrels may have also have been a factor, since they may have been able to smell the diesel and avoid it. However, even if any birds had been affected they would most likely come ashore and disappear down their breeding burrows never to be seen again. After the incident was over an impact assessment was initiated and, thankfully, the results seemed to be encouraging. It seemed on this occasion Stewart Island's precious wildlife and New Zealand as a whole, had been very lucky. Next time (and there will be a next time) things will almost certainly be different.

Ins and outs

Getting there

If you do not have your own transport the ***Bottom Bus***, T4429708, www.bottombus.co.nz, and the ***Catlins Coaster***, T0800304333, www.southern-nz.co.nz, provides transport and tour options from $79 (1-day). Refer also to activity operators below. **Petrol** is available at Owaka and Papatowai.

Information

Both the **VICs** in **Invercargill** and **Balclutha** can supply detailed information about the Catlins including accommodation. *'The Catlins'* is a useful free booklet. Within the region itself are the local seasonal VICs: **Owaka**, at the Catlins Diner, Main St, T/F4158371, info@catlins-nz.com Open Mon-Fri 0830-2030 Sat 0800-2030/Sun 0900-2130) T/F4158371; and **Waikawa**, Dolphin Magic Information Centre, T/F2468444, www.catlins.org.nz Open daily Oct-Apr. **DOC** also has leaflets ($1) on Catlin's walks and ecological highlights. **Internet** is available at the ***Hilltop Backpackers***, Papatowai and the VIC in Owaka. There is also an internet café a few doors down from the ***Lumberjack Café and Bar*** in Owaka. There are no banks in the Catlins but **EFTPOS** is available at the general stores and petrol stations the main centres.

History

The first human settlers in the region were the South Island Maori who utilized the abundant coastal resources and hunted the flightless moa as long ago as 1350AD. Within 200 years most of the moa had been plundered and the settlers turned their attentions to the fur seals, fish and other seafood. The thick almost impenetrable coastal forests of the region prevented easy access inland so the population waxed and waned and was never substantial. The forbidding forests were also thought by the Maori to be the home of a race of hairy giants known as Maeroero (probably a group of early Scots settlers looking for a pub). The Maori were joined, first by small groups of European whalers, then timber millers who began their relentless rape of the forest from the 1860s. Once depleted, as with most other parts of New Zealand, it was the farmers who then moved in. Thankfully a few tracts of the original coastal forest escaped the axe and can still be seen.

Organized activities & tours

The *Catlins Wildlife Trackers Eco-tours*, Papatowai, T4158613, www.catlins-ecotours.co.nz offer award winning two- (from $270) and four- (from $540) day eco-tours that explore the regions forest, coast, natural features and wildlife. They are very informative and accommodation is also provided. *Catlins Natural Wonders*, Balclutha, T0800353941, www.catlins-nz.com/canawn are another eco-based tour operator offering day trips (from $110) four times a week (depart from Balclutha) and two-day trips (from $350) from Invercargill to Dunedin on Thursdays which include accommodation. *Nugget Point Eco-Tours*, based in Kaka Point, T4128602, www.catlins.co.nz, offer water-based wildlife spotting and fishing trips around the Molyneux Bay and Nugget Point area, from $50. *Catlins Tours* based in Invercargill, T2304576, catlins@southnet.co.nz provide a more generalised tour Monday-Saturday. *Catlins Mini Tours*, Owaka, T0800-119370, sl_rlvalli@xtra.co.nz also offer Invercargill/Dunedin (or reverse) trips with a budget accommodation option from $60. *Dolphin Magic* based in Waikawa, T/F2468444, dolphinmagic@xtra.co.nz offer trips (1 ½ hours) to see the rare Hector's dolphin. Depart Waiwaka Dolphin Information Centre 1000/1300/1500 (from $50) and a (2 ½ hours) twilight trip at 1730 (from $75).

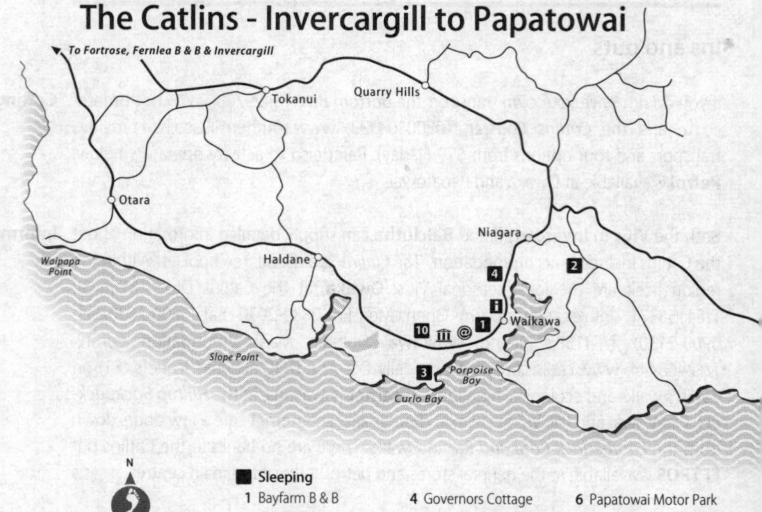

Invercargill to Papatowai

From Invercargill the Southern Scenic Route (SH92) crosses the **Southland Plains** to join the coast and the **Mataura River** mouth at the former coastal whaling station of **Fortrose** (42 km). At Fortrose you leave SH92 and begin to negotiate the coastal road networks of the Catlins towards **Otara** and Waikawa. The first potential diversion is to **Waipapa Point**. From just beyond Otara take the sign-posted road cross-country to a car park beside the lighthouse. The gently sloping beach is backed by dunes and decked with rock pools and offshore reefs. These reefs were the cause of New Zealand's second worst shipping disaster in 1881, when the *SS Tararua* ran aground with the loss of 131 lives. It was this tragedy that prompted the erection of the **lighthouse**. Completed in 1884 it was the last wooden lighthouse built in New Zealand. Keep your eyes open for hookers sealions which sometimes haul up on the beaches here for a doze. If there are none in evidence, don't worry, you will very probably see them further north.

Once back on the main route near Otara continue to Haldane and follow signs for **Slope Point**, which is actually the southernmost point in New Zealand, contrary to what most visitors believe. The real geographical point and obligatory signpost can be reached here via a short 10-minute walk from a roadside car park. From the car park you are also treated to the impressive views of the dramatic headlands that herald a distinct change from Waipapa's lowly dunescapes. Also note the macrocarpa trees which seem to get much photographic attention.

From Haldane the road skirts the Haldane Estuary before delivering you at the beautiful **Porpoise Bay**, a popular spot for swimming and surfing. From the junction it is a short drive (right) to the headland and **Curio Bay**.

The headland overlooking both bays is a superb spot to simply admire the coastal scenery, crashing waves and try to spot the tiny hector's dolphins. Some patience may be required for this but eventually you may see a pod (especially near the rocks that protect Porpoise Bay). They are a delight to observe breaching the surface in exuberant playfulness.

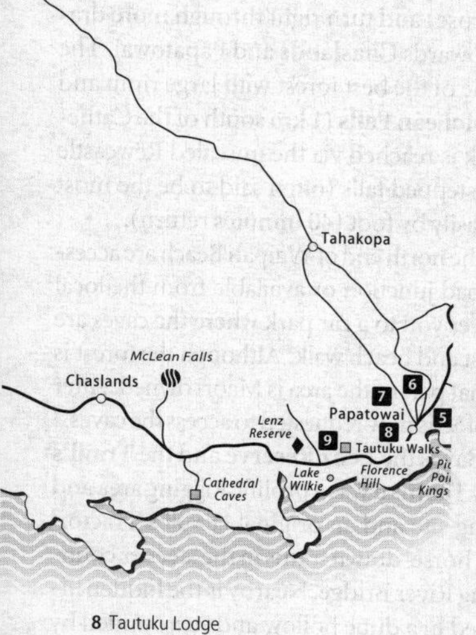

8 Tautuku Lodge
9 Waikawa Holiday Lodge

At Curio Bay, about 500 m west, is the **fossil forest**. At first glance it is difficult to make out the petrified stumps and logs that scatter the rock platform, but a more thorough investigation by foot will reveal the distinct features of these Jurassic ancestors. Although it is hard to drag yourself away from Curio Bay, the road now turns briefly inland to rejoin the Waikawa River Estuary at **Waikawa**. Here you will find a small **information centre** in the old church that also hosts *Dolphin Magic* (see activities above) and a small café, T2468444. ■ *Open daily Oct-Apr.* Across the road is the *Waikawa Holiday Lodge Backpackers* and the small **District Museum** which contains some relics from the whaling and saw-milling years. ■ *Open 1300-1600 daily (seasonal).*

Looking for a Hooker?

Gentlemen, Owaka, in South Island, New Zealand is perhaps the only place in the world where you can send a postcard home stating the following in complete innocence:

Dear Mum,
Went to the beach today in search of Hookers. Found ten huge, fat ones, asleep on the beach. Sat for a while watching and listening as they scratched, snored and broke wind, before moving in closer to take photographs. It was just great. Going back tomorrow to find more. Wish you were here. You're ever faithful and obedient son.

Hooker's sea lions are the most magical and amusing of pinnipeds (seals). Also called the New Zealand sea lion, they are the rarest of the world's five species of sea lions and are endemic to New Zealand. Today, they can be found lazing about a handful of beaches on the Otago or Southland coast, where they haul out to rest between fishing trips, particularly outwith the breeding season. But these soporific barrels of bad breath and wind (gas), often weighing in at over 400 kg and over 3 m in length, are not fussy about their choice of temporary couch. Coastal paths, boats and even roads come into their range of preferred 'hammock sites' and this can cause some troublesome, if not exactly entertaining, stand-offs. Polite words, a gentle prod or even a parking warden has little effect and usually the only solution is to wait until hunger drives them back to sea. But wherever they choose to take a nap, observing these great creatures from a safe distance is one of the highlights of any visit to the southern coast of New Zealand. And 'safe distance' is the important point. Despite the fact they may look about as agile as a sloth with a weight problem, looks are deceptive. Stray too close and their complacent bleary stare will explode into aggressive action. Be warned, these animals could play basketball with Arnie Schwarzenegger and in the water move faster than Michael Jordan.

From Waikawa the road then heads north past the former saw-milling village of **Niagara**. The name is said to be a somewhat facetious reference to the tiny falls at the bridge and their comparison to the Niagara Falls in North America. A few hundred metres past Niagara you then join the main SH92 Catlins road (from Tokanui and Fortrose) and turn right through more dramatic topography and coastal forest towards **Chaslands** and Papatowai. The **Chasland Scenic Reserve** boasts some of the best forest with large rimu and kamahi. Look out for the left turn to **McLean Falls** (1 km south of the Cathedral Caves turn-off). The falls car park is reached via the unsealed Rewcastle Road (3 km). The picturesque three-stepped falls (often said to be the most beautiful in the Catlins) are reached easily by foot (40 minutes return).

The 30-m high **Cathedral Caves** at the north end of Waipati Beach are accessible only at low tide (posted at the road junction or available from the local VICs). The 2 km access road will deliver you to a car park where the caves are accessed via a short (30 minutes) forest and beach walk. Although the forest is part of Waipati Scenic Reserve, note that part of the area is Maori owned. After several land claim disputes a small fee of $5 is now requested to access the caves.

Just before the beautiful Tautuku Bay is the **Lenz Reserve** and the **Traill's Tractor Historic Walk** (10 minutes). Tautuku was a prolific logging area and the walk takes you to a former milling site and an original 'Traill's Tractor' logging machine, that took over from horse-drawn trams in the steeper country. The walk starts from the Flemming River Bridge. Nearby is the hidden little scenic gem of **Lake Wilkie**. Formed in a dune hollow and surrounded by lush bush, it can be viewed from a lookout a mere five minutes' walk from the car park. You then have the option to complete a 30 minute circuit of the lake's coastal edge. The boardwalk provides another view across the lake and comes complete with interpretative signs that outline the botanical features of the unique habitat. Note there is no access to the beach from this point.

About 1 ½ km south of Lake Wilkie is the new **Tautuku Estuary Walk** (30 minutes return) which offers access to the estuary and coastal forest. The beach (which is a cracker) is best accessed via the **Tautuku Dune/Forest Walk** (15 minutes) which is just opposite the Tautuku Outdoor Education Centre on SH92. A stunning view of the whole bay and its thick fringe of coastal forest can be seen from the road as you climb **Florence Hill** at its eastern edge. Just offshore are the **Rainbow Isles** which owe their name to the effects of the sun on sea-spray, squirted skywards by a small blowhole on the main island. The Maori call it Rerekohu meaning 'flying mist'. From Florence Hill it is a short 2 km drive to **Papatowai** – the Catlins 'mid-point' and base for services and accommodation.

Sleeping

The **South Catlins Farmstay Group**, T/F2469876, Christine@xtra.co.nz are a co-operative group of 9 farmhouses and 5 self-contained cottages throughout the South Catlins region and are an excellent source of information. They can also arrange farm tours and garden visits.

The **A** *Fernlea B&B* in Motokua (20 mins from Invercargill) offers a lovely self-contained cottage (sleeps 4) with its own private garden on a large dairy farm. The very reasonable **A-B** *Catlins Farmstay*, located midway between Cathedral Caves and Curio Bay is on a 1000 acre working farm and offers 2 doubles and a twin, T2468843, catlinsfarmstay@xtra.co.nz The **B** *BayFarm B&B*, 595 Yorke Rd, Tokanui (and Waikawa Harbour), T/F2468833, bayfarm@xtra.co.nz is run by an American Alison Yorke and partner. They offer 2 good value options, the B&B near Tokanui or a self-contained cottage in Waikawa harbour. The **A** *Governors Cottage*, in Waikawa Harbour, T2468843, catlinsfarmstay@xtra.co.nz is another nice self-contained option.

The **A** *Southern Scenic Motel*, Papatowai, T/F4158600, catlinsbb@xtra.co.nz is a stylish modern place with four studio units, all with their own balcony. Close to amenities and coastal walks. The **B** *Papatowai Motels and Store*, T/F4158147 are a cheaper option nearby.

The basic **D** *Curio Bay Camp Ground*, T2468897, on the headland overlooking Porpoise Bay is a summer favourite and a superb location. It has powered/tent sites, showers and a small store. The **D** *Tautuku Lodge*, set in the Lenz Reserve at Tautuku, T4158024, dianan@clear.net.nz, is owned by the Forest and Bird Society. The lodge sleeps 10 but there is also a smaller cabin sleeping 4. Supply your own bedding. The **C-D** *Waikawa Holiday Lodge*, Waikawa, T2468552 provides comfortable budget doubles and dorms in a spacious house. In-house shop and café across the road at Dolphin Magic. The **C-D** *Hilltop Backpackers* in Papatowai, T4158028, hilltop@ihug.co.nz is an excellent place offering doubles (with a great view) and dorm beds. Log fire, modern facilities, hot tub, bikes, canoes, internet and much more. The **C-D** *Papatowai Motor Park*, T4158500, is located behind the **B** *Papatowai Motels and Store*, T/F4158147. It has budget dorms, cabins, powered/tent sites.

If you are not in a B&B or self-contained place then **eating** out in the South Catlins really takes the form of a stove or a BBQ with the sandflys. The store in Papatowai however does sell basic takeaways. Open daily 0830-2200, winter Sun-Thu 0900-1800, Fri/Sat 0900-1830.

Papatowai to Balclutha

There are a number of notable walks around Papatowai the most popular of which is the **Picnic Point Track** (40 minutes) which takes in both coast and forest and with a short diversion to the unusual **Kings Rock** formation.

From McLennan and the river of the same name you can access both the **Maitai** (north) and **Purakaunui Falls** (east). They are both easily accessed from the road (Maitai first via SH92), and significantly different and worthy of investigation. About 4 km east of the Purakaunui Falls is the access road to **Purakaunui Bay**. This is one of the most beautiful and supremely quiet spots on the Catlins Coast and is excellent for a short walk, surfing, a picnic or an overnight stay at the basic campsite. Be careful on this road, it is very narrow and winding.

Sleeping The **AL** *Greenstone Farmstay*, Purakaunui Falls Rd, T4158259, greenwoodfarm@xtra.co.nz has a en suite Queen, Twin and singles in a modern villa homestead situated on a 1900 acre farm. Dinners on request. Ideally located near the falls and Purakaunui Bay. Nearby is the small **C-D** *Falls Backpackers*, T4158724, sparx@es.co.nz which offers a double, single and shared twin rooms. Walking distance from the falls. The **DOC campsite** at **Purakaunui Bay** is basic but in a superb setting-its worth buying a tent for!

If you want a change from all the coastal scenery the **Catlins River Track** (five hours one-way) provides an excellent opportunity. Access is about 3 km south of Catlins Lake via Tawanui where there is a DOC campsite. Follow the road to **The Wisp** (farm lease) and the picnic site trailhead. The section between Wallis Stream and Franks Creek (1 ½ hours) is recommended.

Back on the coast many visitors are drawn along the western bank of the Catlins Lake and the Owaka Heads to see **Jacks Bay** and **Blowhole**. At 55 m deep, with an opening of 140 m by 70 m, it is quite an impressive sight, even without a storm to spur it into action.

Owaka & around
Population: 400

Returning back to Catlins Lake and SH92 it is then a short drive to the Catlins' largest settlement and supply centre, Owaka, which offers a host of basic facilities including a good restaurant, petrol, a grocery store, accommodation, visitors centre and even internet. But if the weather is fine, and you still have time on your hands before sunset, don't hang around. Instead, head back to the coast. **Pounawea** located 4 km south of Owaka offers a very pleasant (45 minutes) **nature walk** through podocarp forest and saltmarsh.

Just east of Pounawea is **Surat Bay**, which is reached across other side of the Owaka River (bridge 2 km south of Owaka). Although beach access is awkward (ask at the signposted Surat Bay Lodge) its golden swathes of sand and those of its neighbour, **Cannibals Bay** (access road from SH92, a few kilometres north of Owaka), provide the reasonable likelihood of encountering some dozing hooker sealions.

Cannibals Bay was mistakenly named in the late 1800s by geologist James Hector, who took the human remains from a Maori burial site to be something far more sinister. A very pleasant **walk** is to negotiate the length of Cannibals Bay (from the car park) to the **False Islet** headlands. Then, once you have taken in the views, from the west to Jacks Bay and then east, to the rocky outcrops of the Nugget Point, continue on to Surat Bay, before returning across the neck of the headland to Cannibals Bay (two hours).

Sleeping and eating **B** *Catlins Retreat B&B*, 27 Main Rd, T4158830, is a century old villa located right in the heart of Owaka. It has a spa and its BBQ's are a speciality. Across the road is the popular **C-D** *Blowhole Backpackers*, T4158830, which has doubles and dorms and is owned by the same people. Also has access to the spa. There are a small number of motels in the village, with the **A** *Catlins Area Motels*, 34 Ryley St,

Fiordland National Park

Fiordland National Park is 1.25 million ha and the largest of New Zealand's 14 national parks. In 1986 it was declared a World Heritage Area on account of its outstanding natural features, exceptional beauty and its important demonstration of the world's evolutionary history. Four years later, in 1990, Fiordland National Park was further linked with three others – Mount Aspiring, Westland and Mount Cook (Aoraki) to form the (United Nations) World Heritage Area of Southwest New Zealand. It was given the Maori name Te Waipounamu (literally: 'the waters greenstone'). Hopefully we can rest assured, that with such official labels and protection it will remain the stunning wilderness it is.

T/F4158821, and the slightly cheaper **B** ***Catlins Gateway Motel***, corner of Main Rd and Royal Terr, T/F4158592 being recommended.Tucked away near the coast and near Surat Bay (Owaka) is The delightful **A** ***Kepplestone B&B***, 9 Surat Bay Rd, T4158134, www.kepplestone@hostlinknz.com which has a range of en-suite rooms and offers fine cuisine. Nearby is the **C-D** ***Surat Bay Lodge***, T4158483 a small, peaceful backpackers which is a stone's throw from the beach. There is a basic motor park in Pounawea near Owaka, the **C-D** ***Pounawea Camp Ground***, Park Lane, T/F4191110.

The ***Lumber Jack Bar and Café*** on Owaka's main street, T4158747 is a new and fairly classy place, with a traditional NZ menu and good coffee. Open daily from 1200 (1600 in winter).

Nugget Point, Roaring Bay & Kaka Point

Back on SH92 the road turns inland again towards Balclutha. About 3 km east of Owaka is **Tunnel Hill**, which is a historic reserve featuring the 246-m long tunnel, once the most southerly railway tunnel in New Zealand. Completed in 1915 it was the most prominent feature on the Catlins branch railway line that ran between Balclutha and Tahakopa near McLennan. The line closed in 1971.

Just beyond the hill is the turn-off to Nugget Point, without doubt the highlight of the Catlins Coast. To get a proper feel for 'The Nuggets' they are best visited at sunrise, when the spectacular rock pillars and outcrops take on the orange glow of the sun. The track to the 1870 lighthouse starts at the terminus of a delightful road that skirts the beach and rock platforms of Molyneux Bay. It takes about 10 minutes to reach the lighthouse and its associated lookout point, but by far the best view is obtained from the hill, about 100 m short of it. Care must be taken here, but the views from the top are outstanding. The islets and rocky, inaccessible coastline, offers an important haven for **wildlife**, and is home to seals (all three species of fur, hookers and elephant), yellow-eyed and blue penguins, sooty shearwaters, gannets and occasionally royal spoonbills. Even below the waves life abounds, and the area boasts a wide diversity of underwater habitats. Keep your ears open for the plaintive wails of fur seal pups playing in and around the rock pools below the track and in the distance, look out for squadrons of shearwaters, skimming the waves in search of food. It really is a magical place.

Just inland from The Point is **Roaring Bay** that has a hide where **yellow-eyed penguins** can be seen coming ashore at dusk, or leaving again for their routine fishing trips at dawn. If you are lucky enough to see one, bear in mind you are looking at the rarest penguins in the world. Back along the edge of Molyneux Bay is **Kaka Point** (8 km), a charming little coastal settlement that, along with Owaka, provides the necessary visitor amenities and accommodation. From Kaka Point it is about 40 km to Balclutha and SH1 to Dunedin

Sleeping and eating The **A** ***Nugget View and Kaka Point Motels***, 11 Rata St. Kaka Point, T4128602, nugview@catlins.co.nz has what the name suggets from 10 comfortable studio units. They also run a small backpackers at 17Rata St and they offer boat based Eco-tours to The Nuggets. Only 2 km from Nugget Point right on the beach is the **A** ***Nugget Lodge Motels***, T4128783 which offer two new, modern units, one over-looking the bay. Back in Kaka Point you will find the small, homely and well-established **C-D** ***Fernlea Backpackers***, Moana St, T4128834. The view from the balcony is wonderful. The quiet **C-D** ***Kaka Point Motor Park*** is located on the edge of the town on Tarata St, T4128818. It offers two modern cabins.

In Kaka Point is the newest eatery/bar in the area is the ***Point Café and Bar*** on the Esplanade, T4128800. Both the food and the bar are very good and the place has been an instant hit. It also has a grocery store attached. Open daily 0800-2000.

Dunedin to Invercargill via SH1

The 217 km journey from Dunedin to Invercargill via SH1 takes in the two mainly agricultural service towns of **Balclutha** and **Gore**. Although the route via the Catlins coast (Southern Scenic Route) is by far the preferred and recommended option, both towns are often used as an overnight stop and have a few appealing attractions in themselves.

Balclutha
Phone Code: 03
Population: 4000

Balclutha (which is actually in South Otago) is 80 km southwest of Dunedin on the banks of the **Clutha River**, which, with its origins at Lake Wanaka, is the South Island's longest (322 km). Known as 'Big River Town' its name actually refers to the Scots Gaelic for 'town on the Clyde' after Glasgow's great river. The town's first known white resident was Scot Jim McNeill who used to run a ferry service across the river between 1853 and 1857. The modern day concrete bridge that provides the vital road link with Southland is not the original bridge. The first effort, which was constructed in 1866, was washed away in floods. Balclutha is most often used as a brief stop-over on the way to Invercargill via SH1 or as the gateway to the much-preferred route via the Catlins coast and **Southern Scenic Route**. Fishing is of course a popular local pursuit and the VIC has details of this and other local activities. The **South Otago Museum**, 1 Renfrew Street, T4182382 is particularly noted for its collection of bottles and displays surrounding the history of the local **Kaitangata** Coal Mine. ■ *Mon-Fri 1000-1600 Sun 1300-1600. Free.*

The Balclutha **Visitor Information Centre** is at 4 Clyde Street, T4180388, Balvin@nzhost.co.nz (open Monday-Friday 0830-1700 Saturday/Sunday 0930-1500). The centre can provide all the northbound information surrounding the Catlins and Southern Scenic Route.

Sleeping and eating The two principal motels are: **A** ***Rosebank Lodge Motor Hotel***, 265 Clyde St, T4181490, has comfortable units, spa, sauna and an in-house restaurant; and **A** ***Highway Lodge Motel***, 165 Clyde St, T4182363 is another modern option that sits at the start of the Southern Scenic Route and the Catlins coast. The basic **C-D** ***Balclutha Backpackers***, is at 20 Stewart St, T025-2917466. The only option for **campervans** in town is at the **C-D** ***Naish Park Motor Camp***, 56 Charlotte St, T4180088, which should adequately serve your needs. It also has a few cabins. For eating there really isn't a lot of choice, but restaurant at the ***Rosebank Lodge*** (see above) is recommended. Open daily for breakfast, lunch and dinner.

Transport Being on SH1 Balclutha is serviced by all the major north/south **bus** companies which stop at the VIC. Gore is also served by the daily 'Southerner' **train** service

Between a hot and a cold place

For those of you about to rejoice at reaching the Stirling Point Signpost at the terminus of SH1 in Bluff – take note – contrary to popular belief, it is not the most southerly tip of New Zealand's mainland. That honour goes to Slope Point in the Catlins, which is about 50 km east and 7 km further south! And one other interesting point to mull over. Did you know you are only 52% of the way between the Equator and the South Pole. Not that cold now then is it!

between Dunedin and Invercargill, T0800-802802. At the time of going to print this service was under threat.

Gore
Phone Code: 03
Population: 9000

Gore, located on the banks of the Mataura River, is Southland's second largest town and most famous for its unusual mix of trout **fishing**, **country music** and formerly (we can only presume), **illegal whiskey distilling**. So although on first acquaintance you might think the place to be a just another quiet back-water, beware. At times, particularly during the ten-day annual **New Zealand Gold Guitar Awards** held in May, sleepy Gore can go off like Dolly Parton in a lingerie shop. During the festival both amateurs and professionals artists compete and provide live entertainment, while the true fanatics get the chance to dust of their cowboy boots and line dance the night away (www.goldguitars.co.nz)

The Gore **Visitors Information Centre** is located on the corner of Hokonui Drive and Norfolk Street, T/F2089908, goreinfo@esi.co.nz Open Monday-Friday 0900-1700 Saturday/Sunday 1000-1600. The VIC has a list of local **walks** including the popular 1½ hour Whisky Falls Track **Internet** is available at the *Green Room Café*, 59 Irk Street, T2081005.

Other than the rod and reel, other local attractions include the **Hokonui Moonshine Museum**, which is housed in the **Gore Historical Museum**, next to the VIC, T2089908.There, the heady days of Gore district's insobriety and chaos, its times of prohibition and prudence, are all revealed, along with all the usual more mundane aspects of the region's history. Also planned is a **Fishing Museum** where the monster brown trout and the fishermen that come from around the globe to catch them are celebrated. ■ *Mon-Fri 0900-1700 Sat/Sun 1000-1600. $5 child, free.* Should you emerge from the museum intent on a bit of distillation or fishing yourself, you'll get a license for the latter only at the VIC ($25 per week). The VIC also has an extensive list of **local guides** and **tackle hire** outlets.

Also of note in the region is **Moth Restaurant and Bar** operated by the Croydon Aircraft Company, SH94, Mandeville, near Gore T2089662, www.themoth.co.nz Not only does it provide good food but also the unique opportunity to combine your visit with a flight in a Tiger Moth (from $35). Mandeville is located west of Gore on SH94. If you have animal-loving children, **The Reservation**, at the top of Coutts Road, T2081200, has a small menagerie of warm and fuzzies, from chinchillas to Clydesdale horses, all of whom are available for copious stroking and generous feeding. Open daily 1000-1730, $2, child $1.

Sleeping **A** *Croydon Lodge*, corner of SH94 and Waimea St, T2089029, is a large motel set in extensive grounds with a 9-hole golf course, à la carte restaurant and bar. The **A** *Oakleigh Motel*, 70 Hokonui Dr, T2084863, www.oakleighmotel.co.nz is another more upmarket motel in town. The small **C-D** *Old Fire Station Backpackers*,

19 Hokonui Dr (across the road from the VIC), T/F2081925 sleeps 11, with double/twin and dorms. The **C-D** ***Gore Motor Camp***, 35 Broughton St, T2084919 has basic cabins, powered/tent sites.

Out of town the ***Moth Restaurant and Bar*** (see above) is recommended (open Tue-Sun from 1100-2100). In town itself, the ***Table Talk Café***, 76 Main St, T2087110 has a modern NZ menu and serves a good all-day breakfast while ***Howl at the Moon***, at 2 Main St, T2083851, is a café/bar with a reasonable blackboard menu. Open daily from 1200.

Transport Being on SH1 Gore is serviced by all the major east/west and north/south **bus** companies which stop at the VIC. Gore is also served b the daily 'Southerner' **train** service between Dunedin and Invercargill, T0800-802802.

Tramping in Southland and the Fiords

The Dusky Track

Grade of Difficulty 9/10

Now this is a track for 'real trampers'; the sort with tree trunk legs, well-worn boots and copious facial hair. The Dusky offers the widest range of 'experiences' of any track in Fiordland, from stunning glacial valley and mountain scenery, to the possibility of complete immersion in icy water. It really is magnificent and thoroughly recommended. Perhaps the true attraction, other than the relative peace, is the sense of awe at the remote **Dusky Sound**, in the very heart of the Fiordland National Park. It is a true wilderness that has changed little since Captain Cook first set foot there over two centuries ago.

The Dusky attracts less than 1000 trampers a year, which is a reflection of its remote and difficult nature. Both its location and grade of difficulty make it a true challenge and one that should only be attempted in summer. Note the track is subject to bad flooding year round. Always consult with DOC before any attempt and fill in an intention sheet (Te Anau). Locator beacons are also recommended.

Walking times and distances: Hauroko (Hauroko Burn Hut) to Halfway Hut: 12 km, 4-6 hours. Halfway Hut to Lake Roe Hut: 7 km, 3-5 hours. Lake Roe Hut to Loch Maree Hut: 10 km, 4-6 hours. Loch Maree Hut to Supper Cove: 12 km, 6-8 hours. North Access (Wilmot Pass Road Access Point to Loch Maree): Wilmot Pass Road Access Point to Upper Spey Hut, 8 km, 4-5 hours (add 45 minutes to West Arm Wharf and Hut). Upper Spey Hut to Kintail Hut: 7 km, six hours. Kintail Hut to Loch Maree Hut: 11 km, 4-7 hours.

Ins & outs

Information For information (including DOC self-guided leaflet), the latest conditions on the Dusky and hut bookings contact the **DOC Visitor Information Centre** in Te Anau and the VIC in Tuatapere (see relevant sections). The DOC website www.doc.govt.nz is also useful.

Trailhead transport and access The Dusky Track can be accessed from the south via **Lake Hauroko** (64 km west of Tuatapere) or from the **Wilmot Pass** Road (40 mins from West Arm Wharf), accessed via boat and **Lake Manapouri**. By **road** Lake Manapouri is accessed from Manapouri (SH95), 21 km south of Te Anau. ***Spitfire Shuttles***, T2497505, can provide transport to Manapouri and Tuatapere (departs Te Anau 0830). ***Lake Hauroko Tours***, Tuatapere, T226668, reinfo@es.co.nz offer road and **jetboat** access to the southern trailhead via Lake Hauroko. Departs Mon and Thu from Tuatapere at 0900, from $50. ***Fiordland Travel***, T2496602 and ***Fiordland Explorer***

Charters, T/F2496616, explorercharters@xtra.co.nz both based in Pearl Harbour, Manapouri, provide daily boat transportation to and from West Arm and Wilmot Pass Road. It is also possible to fly in or out of Supper Cove or Lake Hauroko by **floatplane** (***Waterwings Airways***, Te Anau, T2497405) or **helicopter** (***Southern Lakes Helicopters***, T2497167, or ***South West Helicopters***, Te Anau/Tuatapere, T2497402). Prices on application. For more trailhead transport and trailhead access details see 'Tramping Track Transport' in the Te Anau section, page 641.

Essentials All 7 huts (Halfway, Lake Roe, Loch Maree, Supper Cove, Kintail, Upper Spey and West Arm Hut) are Category 3 ranging from 12-20 bunks with mattresses and toilet facilities. There are no gas cookers or wood fires. Huts must be booked through DOC and cost $5, child, $2.50 per night. For post walk accommodation see Manapouri/Te Anau and Tuatapere sections. For more booking information see the DOC website www.doc.govt.nz

The Hollyford Track

Grade of Difficulty 6/10

The Hollyford Track is essentially a low level (**bush**) 56 km four-day (one-way) tramp that negotiates the **Hollyford River Valley** and bank of **Lake McKerrow** to the remote **Martins Bay**. It is not a tramp for those expecting spectacular high level views, but does offer fine scenery and a superb sense of wilderness. The undeniable highlight is the **Martins Bay Hut** located at the mouth of the Hollyford River. Two days at Martins Bay taking in the coast and **seal colony** is a remote West Coast experience. The tramp is most often tackled in conjunction with **jetboat** returns/shortcuts via Lake McKerrow and a **flight** out from Martins Bay Lodge to Milford or Hollyford Valley airfield is highly recommended. Note that guided walks are available. Also note that the Hollyford can be extended or combined to include the long (9-10 day) and arduous **Pyke-Big Bay Track**. Martins Bay to Big Bay Hut offers a good day trip but the route is vague.

This is not a tramp to be tackled during or after **heavy rain**. The sections between The Trailhead car park and the Hidden Falls Hut (first hut) are especially tricky in wet weather. Some river crossings have **3-wire bridges** and the sandflys at the Martins Bay Hut are legendary!

Walking times and distances: Road End to Hidden Falls Hut: 9 km; 2-3 hours. Hidden Falls Hut to Alabaster Hut: 10 ½ km; 3-4 hours. Alabaster Hut to Demon Trail Hut: 14 ½ km; 4-5 hours. Demon Trail Hut to Hokuri Hut: 9 ½ km; 5-6 hours. Hokuri Hut to Martins Bay Hut: 13 ½ km; 4-5 hours.

Ins & outs

Trailhead transport and access For air transportation contact *Air Fiordland*, T2497080 (up to $375); for jetboat *Hollyford Track*, T0800832226 (T4423760); road to trailhead *Tracknet*, T2498685 ($35), *Trips 'n' Tramps*, T2497089. For more trailhead transport and trailhead access details see 'Tramping Track Transport' in the Te Anau section, page 641.

Information For information (including DoC self-guided leaflet), the latest conditions on the Rees-Dart Track and hut bookings contact the **DOC Information and Track Centre** in Queenstown or the **DOC Visitor Information Centre** in Te Anau (see relevant sections). Useful websites include www.doc.govt.nz/www.hollyfordtrack.co.nz

Essentials

All the DOC huts are **Category 3** ($5) from 12-20 bunks with wood fires but no gas cookers. **B** *Charlie's Place* on the northwestern bank of Lake McKerrow between the Hokuri and Martin's Bay Hut, T025-893570, www.webfactor.co.nz/charlies-place offers a comfortable, friendly and unique oasis mid tramp. Kayaks for hire. The Hollyford Guided Walk accommodation which includes The ***Martins Bay Lodge*** (located between the Hokuri and Martin's Bay Huts, accessible by jetboat and open to the public) are of a much higher standard than the DOC Huts. Guided trips Fully catered and guided fly in/walk out or walk in /walk out tramps are available with ***Hollyford Track***, T4423760, www.hollyfordtrack.co.nz From Te Anau a 3-day adventure costs from $1,290, child $970.

The Hump Ridge Track

Grade of Difficulty 5/10

The Hump Ridge Track opened in late 2000 and is New Zealand's newest tramping track. It is a 53 km three-day 'moderate' circuit track located at the southeastern end of the Fiordland National Park. Whether it can live up to all the promotional hype remains to be seen, but there is no doubt it offers an excellent tramping experience. Its combination of both coastal and podocarp/beech forest landscapes added to the unique historic appeal of its four viaducts are its main attractions. The 125 m Percy Burn Viaduct is reputed to be the largest wooden viaduct in the world. Wildlife to look out for include kea and bellbirds. Fur seals and the endangered hector's dolphins can be seen on the coast. The track is **boardwalk** through the areas most subject to any flooding, but you are still advised to check on track conditions before departure.

Walking times and distances: Bluecliffs Beach car park to Okaka Hut: 18 km; 8-9 hours. Okaka Hut to Port Craig Village Hut: 18 km; seven hours. Port Craig Village Hut to Bluecliffs Beach: 17 km; 6-7 hours.

Ins & outs

The Hump Ridge Track is administered by the Tuatapere Hump Ridge Track Trust

Trailhead transport and access The Hump Ridge Track starts and finishes at the western end of Blue Cliffs Beach on Te Wae Wae Bay (signposted from Tuatapere). An anticlockwise approach is generally recommended. **Road** transportation to the trailhead can be arranged through ***Lake Hauroko Tours***, Tuatapere, T226668, reinfo@es.co.nz or the VIC in Tuatapere. Independent vehicles can be left at the Tuatapere Hump Ridge Track office in Tuatapere, T2266739, or Rarakau Farm, Papatotara Coast Rd, Bluecliffs Beach, T2258192, rarakau@southnet.co.nz.

Information For information the latest conditions on the Humpridge Track and hut bookings contact the VIC in Tuatapere (see relevant section) or contact T2266739. www.humpridgetrack.co. nz is the official website. Bookings can be made on-line.

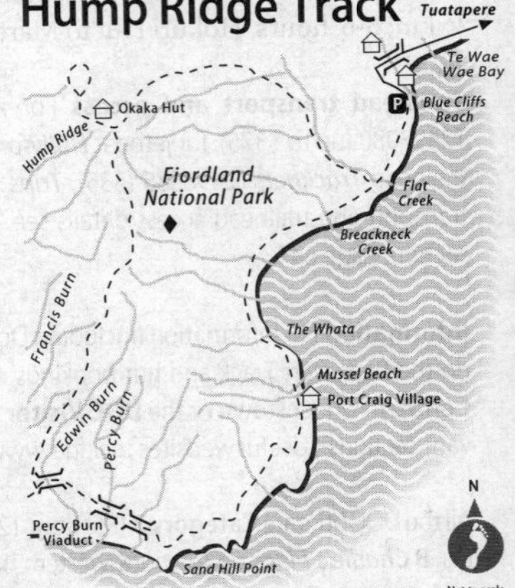

Essentials Both huts (Okaka and Port Craig Village) are maintained and managed by the Hump Ridge Track Trust. Wardens are seconded to each hut from Oct-Apr. The huts are very modern with 40 bunks, mattresses, lighting, cooking, heating and toilet facilities (limited hot water). Huts must be booked through the Track Trust direct, or through the VIC in Tuatapere. They cost $40, child, $20 per night. For post walk accommodation see Tuatapere sections. The **B-D *Rarakau Farmstay and Lodge***, Papatotara Coast Rd, Bluecliffs

Beach, T2258192, rarakau@southnet.co.nz is well placed and recommended (see Tuatapere 'Sleeping' section page 652.

The Kepler Track

Grade of Difficulty 6/10

The Kepler Track is a 67 km, 3-4 day **'Great Walk'**, that is easily accessible from Te Anau, providing a convenient and viable alternative to the Milford Track. It traverses the edge of the beautiful **Lake Te Anau** before ascending to the **Luxmore Hut** – reputed to offer one of the best 'hut views' in Fiordland. From the Luxmore Hut the track negotiates the scenic, open tops of the **Luxmore Range**, before falling through forest in to the **Iris Burn Valley** and back to civilisation via Shallow Bay on **Lake Manapouri**. The highlights are of course the views from the Luxmore Hut and the scenic combination of lake, mountain and river valley scenery. The forest is classic silver beech and podocarp, which at night often echoes to the cry of kiwi. New Zealand robin and blue duck are also seen occasionally. This track attracts over 10,000 trampers a year so book well in advance and expect company! The Kepler offers an excellent two-day (return) part-track walk to the Luxmore Hut and back.

Walking times and distances: Control Gates to Luxmore Hut: 14 km; six hours (Brod Bay campsite 1½ hours). Luxmore Hut to Iris Burn Hut: 18 ½ km; 5-6 hours. Irish Burn Hut to Moturau Hut: 17 km; 5-6 hours. Moturau Hut to Rainbow Reach: 6 km; 1 ½ hours.

Ins & outs

For more trailhead transport and trailhead access details see 'Tramping Track Transport' in the Te Anau section, page 641

Trailhead transport and access The Kepler Track starts at the Lake Te Anau outlet **control gates**, 5 km south of Te Anau and finishes at **Rainbow Reach** 11 km south of Te Anau near SH95. By **road** from Te Anau town to control gates ($5) or Rainbow Reach ($9) contact ***Tracknet***, T2498685 ($5). Tracknet also provide transportation from Queenstown. By **boat** the Kepler can be accessed opposite Te Anau at Brod Bay (missing out first 5 ½ km lakeside section of track), contact ***Sinbad Cruises***, T2497106, or ***Lakeland Boat Hire***, T2498364, from $15 (one-way). The Luxmore Hut can be reached by helicopter with ***Southern Lakes Helicopters***, T2497167, $100 per person (minimum 2 people).

Information

For information (including DOC self-guided leaflet), the latest conditions on Kepler and hut bookings contact the **DOC Information and Track Centre** in Queenstown or the **DOC Visitor Information Centre** in Te Anau (see relevant sections). The DOC website www.doc.govt.nz is also useful.

Essentials DOC Great Walk Tracks apply. All 3 huts (Luxmore, Iris Burn and Moturau) are of a good standard ranging from 40-60 bunks with mattresses and cooking facilities. Note huts do not have heating or cooking facilities in winter (May-mid Oct) They cost $10 per night or $25 for 3 nights, all year round. The campsite at Brod Bay costs $9, child $4.50. All bookings should be made with DOC well in advance, especially in mid summer. For trailhead accommodation see Te Anau sections. For more booking information see the DOC website www.doc.govt.nz (Great Walks).

Guided Walks ***Fiordland Guides***, Te Anau, T2497832, www.fiordlandguides.co.nz and ***Trips 'n' Tramps***, Te Anau, T2497081, trips@teanau.co.nz offer guided walks on the Kepler. Prices on application.

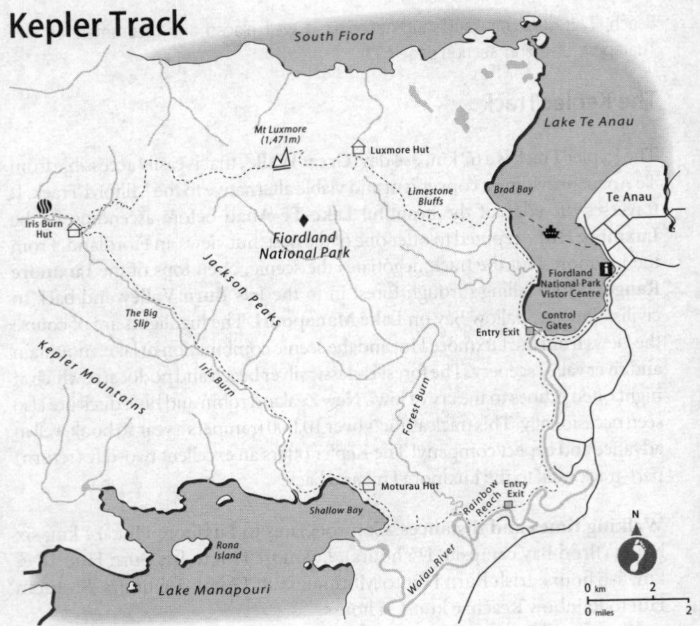

The Milford Track

Grade of Difficulty 6/10

Ever since the *National Geographic* Magazine hailed the mighty, 54 km, four-day, Milford Track as the **'World's Greatest Walk'** in the early 1980s, it has become a victim of its own reputation. It is now the hiking equivalent of the Old Course, St Andrews in Scotland – the home of golf and, as such, considered by golfers as the 'hallowed turf', worthy of near religious reverence and homage. So it is with the Milford. Of its utter scenic splendour there is no doubt, but there is also human traffic and commercialism .

That of course does not mean that it cannot be treated as a challenge. It is essentially a difficult tramp and should be tackled with enthusiasm, but more importantly, also, a sense of realism.

Highlights on the Milford are many, including the stunning vista of the **McKinnon Pass** (1073 m) and the 580 m **Sutherland Falls**. Then, of course, at track's end is the stunning and unforgettable **Milford Sound**. The Milford Track attracts up to 20,000 trampers a year so book well in advance (at least two months) and expect company! Bookings are on a first-come-first-served basis and start on 1 July for the following summer. Trampers should be of a suitable fitness level, allowing for four (six-hour, 20 km) days of walking with a heavy pack. The track is very well maintained but is still steep and rough in places. In winter the McKinnon Pass can be impassable due to snow and ice and there can be a severe avalanche danger. In winter always consult DOC before setting off, check weather forecasts, fill in an intentions sheet and consider taking locator beacons (can be hired from the DOC Visitor Centre).

Walking times and distances (Independent trampers): Glade House Wharf to Clinton Hut: 5 km; 1 ½ hours Clinton Hut to Mintaro Hut: 16 ½ km; 5 ½ hours. Mintaro Hut to Dumpling Hut: 14 km; six hours. Dumpling Hut to Sandfly Point: 18 km; six hours.

Ins & outs

Trailhead transport and access The Milford Track starts (by boat from Te Anau Downs) at **Glade House** (south) and finishes (by boat) at **Sandfly Point** near Milford Sound (north). The track can be tackled in either direction in winter (Apr-Oct) but if you are an independent tramper must be negotiated from south to north in summer (Oct-Apr). By **road** Te Anau Downs (and Milford Sound) is served by a number of Te Anau operators (see Te Anau 'Tramping Track transport' section, page 641. ***Tracknet***, T2498685 (Te Anau Downs $12; Milford Sound, departing Te Anau 0930/1500/1700, from $35) are recommended. Tracknet also provide transportation from Queenstown.

By **boat Glade House** can be accessed from Te Anau with Sinbad Cruises, T2497016 (1030; $60) or from Te Anau Downs with ***Fiordland Travel***, T2497416 (1030/1400; from $38). ***Waterwings Airways***, T2497405 can deliver you to Glade House by **floatplane**. Prices on application. From Milford Sound ***Red Boats***, T2497926 (1400/1500/1600; $22.50) and ***Rosco's Sea Kayaks*** (1400; $20) provide pick-ups and drop-offs to **Sandfly Point**. Sinbad Cruises and Tracknet (see above) both do complete transportation package deal for $110.

The DOC website www.doc.govt.nz/greatwalksbooking@doc.govt.nz and www.milfordtrack.co.nz are also useful

Information For information (including DOC self-guided leaflet), the latest conditions on the Milford Track contact the **DOC Information and Track Centre** in Queenstown or the **DOC Visitor Information Centre** in Te Anau (see relevant sections). The track is administered by DOC as a 'Great Walk' and Te Anau Visitors Centre serves as the principal booking office. Most mainstream bookshops stock specialist guides on the Milford or Fiordland Tracks. DOC also stock maps.

Southland and the Fiords

Essentials

The 3 DOC huts (Clinton, Mintaro and Dumpling)) are of a good standard with 40 bunks with mattresses, cooking, heating and toilet facilities. Wardens are seconded to all huts in summer. The cost of the three nights accommodation is $105, Child, $52.50). In winter Apr-Oct the huts revert to backcountry hut standard/category (no heating or cooking facilities) and cost $10, child $5. The Guided Walks companies have separate huts (Glade House, Quintin Hut and Milford Lodge). Given the popularity of the Milford, as an independent tramper you cannot stay consecutive nights in one hut and must move on. **There is no camping allowed.** All bookings should be made with DOCs Great Walks booking office (Te Anau), well in advance (preferably the year before), especially for a mid summer excursion.

Guided Walks *Milford Track Guided Walk*, T4411138, F4411124, www.milfordtrack.co.nz; *Ultimate Hikes*, T4351809, F4351879, www.ultimatehikes.co.nz offer full guided walk packages, from $1490. ***Trips 'n' Tramps***, Te Anau, T2497081, trips@teanau.co.nz and Koromiko Trek, Te Anau, T2498167 (winter T4810571) both offer guided day-walks and packages from $115 (from Te Anau).

Milford Sound

Population: 200
Phone Code: 03

There are simply not the words in a thesaurus to describe the sight of Milford Sound; let alone its moods. Come rain or shine, calm or storm, dawn or dusk, it is ever changing, always dramatic, and never dull. In every sense Milford Sound is quite simply New Zealand at its glorious and unparalleled best.

Given the enormity (quite literally) of the attraction you will probably be immediately struck with how underdeveloped Milford Sound is. With its conservative scatter of low-key buildings it seems only the boat terminal stands out like a sore thumb. This is quite deliberate. The fact that Milford is the jewel in the crown of the Fiordland National Park and administered by DoC means that further development is strictly controlled.

However, this is one of New Zealand's biggest tourist attractions. In mid-summer the place is a hum of propeller and diesel engines, as the masses are brought in to 'take the cruise'. Without proper investigation Milford can almost be too much for the senses, so it's best to arrive independently. By all means take a cruise, and more especially a scenic flight, but if you can linger a while, and wait until the buses have left, you can appreciate this incredible place even more.

Ins and outs

Getting there You can reach Milford Sound by air, by bus, independently by road, or in real style by foot, via the Milford Track. The best way to arrive, if you can afford it, is to take a scenic flight/cruise combination from Wanaka or Queenstown. Then, if you do not have your own wheels, hire a car from Queenstown or Te Anau and give yourself at least two days to explore the area properly.

Your arrival by **air** will almost certainly be in combination with a scenic flight or tour option from Wanaka, Queenstown or Te Anau (see Flightseeing below). The landing and take-off from the airfield in Milford, 1km from the Visitor Centre, is a memorable experience.

There is a vast array of **bus** and coach operators serving Milford Sound, with an equal number of tour options, from simple **bus-in/bus-out**, to **bus/cruise/bus** or **bus-in/cruise/fly-out** and even **bus/overnight cruise** options. Most operators are based in Queenstown, from where they make the 12 hr, 291km day-trip by road picking up passengers from Te Anau on the way. This is one of the most spectacular bus-trips in the world, provided the weather is favourable.

From **Queenstown** the principal upmarket operators can be booked through *Fiordland Travel*, 74 Shotover St, Queenstown, T4427509, www.fiordlandtravel.co.nz Expect to pay around $165 for a coach/cruise day-trip, from $250 for a coach/overnight cruise combo and $374 for the bus/cruise/fly option. Also from Queenstown the backpacker oriented *Kiwi Discovery*, Camp St, Queenstown, T4427340, and *Kiwi Experience*, 37 Shotover St, Queenstown, T4429708, offer similar coach/cruise options from $129. A fly/cruise/coach option with Kiwi Experience costs from $229.

Of course there are also many options available by bus from **Te Anau**, with many linking up with the Queenstown tours. Again *Fiordland Travel* (see the Te Anau section) are the principal operators. The VIC list others. From Te Anau for the coach/cruise option expect to pay around $95, and for a coach/overnight cruise around $208. Both *Kiwi Discovery* and *Kiwi Experience* pick up in Te Anau knocking around $30 off the Queenstown rate. Other smaller **independent tour operators** offer a range of day-trips to the Milford Sound area.

Information

If you have arrived independently and have not yet pre-booked any activities you can choose from the array of options at the Milford Sound *Visitors Centre* (Boat Terminal). Open 0900-1700. You are however advised to research the huge number of options prior to your visit. The VICs in Queenstown and Te Anau will assist.

Sights

Milford Sound is, in itself of course, just one huge sight but there are individual aspects worth noting. The centrepiece of the Sound is **Mitre Peak**. At 1,692 m it is not that high by New Zealand standards, but as with the entire corridor of Milford Sound, it is the sheer rate of ascent created by the actions of the glaciers that creates such an impact. Opposite Mitre Peak is **The Lion** (1,302 m) and further up the ridge behind it **Mount Pembroke** (2,045 m). **Milford Sound** itself is 15 km in length and about 290m at its deepest. The mouth of the fiord is only about 120 m due to melt action and the terminal moraines of the former glaciers. In heavy rains the fiord can seem like one great waterfall but by far the most impressive at any time are the 160 m **Bowen Falls** which can reached by a short 10-minute boardwalk from beside the boat terminal. About midway along the eastern well of the fiord are the **Stirling Falls** (154 m) whose mist and rainbows can only be visited by boat or kayak.

The fiords are home to some fairly unique and hardy wildlife. **Fur seals** are commonly seen lazing about on the rocks on almost every cruise, but it is below the water's surface that the real excitement lies. Milford Sound is home to an unusual **Underwater Observatory**, opened in 1995 and no mean engineering feat. Located in the sheltered waters of **Harrison Cove**, about a third of the way out of The Sound on its eastern edge, the observatory can be visited independently ($40), or in combination with a cruise from $59, T0800-326969, www.milforddeep.co.nz From the observatory's interesting interpretative centre you can descend 8 m in to a circular viewing chamber where a wide array of sea creatures can be observed at close quarters. Alternatively you have the option of descending in to the depths in a proper **submersible** (see activities below). There are many rare species to be seen in Milford including the very rare **black coral** (which is actually white), a species that can live for over 300 years. Another white resident you may encounter is '**Charlie**' the Kotuku (**white heron**). Charlie has been using Milford Sound as his winter residence for over 12 successive years. In summer Charlie reunites with his mate in Okarito on the West Coast, which is New Zealand's only breeding colony. The best place to spot Charlie is around the boat harbour or on the beach where he will probably be busy fishing or just watching the tourists go by.

Activities

Cruising

Day cruises *Fiordland Travel*, T2497416, www.fiordlandtravel.co.nz and *Milford Sound Red Boat Cruises*, T0800-657444, www.redboats.co.nz are the two principal cruise operators on the sound. The majority of cruises explore the entire 15 km length of The Sound to the Tasman Sea, taking in all the sights on the way, including the waterfalls (from very close range), precipitous rock overhangs, seal colonies and the underwater observatory (optional). There is an interesting commentary, with free tea or coffee, and you are encouraged to ask the crew questions. Free access is allowed all around the boat with the most hardy souls and budding National Geographic photographers braving the wind (and at times rain) on the upper decks. Additional luncheon options are also available. *Fiordland Travel* offer a

'Small Boat Daytime Cruise', a Standard (larger boat) 'Scenic Cruise' and a longer 'Nature Daytime Cruise'; prices range from $45 to $53. A cruise which includes a 30-minute stop at the underwater observatory is an additional $20. *Red Boat Cruises* offer very similar cruises and rates. *Mitre Peak Cruises* are another smaller independent operator offering a low-passenger number (smaller boat), nature-oriented day cruise. There are also numerous options that include air or bus transportation from Wanaka, Queenstown or Te Anau.

Overnight cruises On the overnight cruises you take in all the usual sights, but can enjoy an extended trip, meals, comfortable accommodation and other activities including boat-based kayaking. Given the fact you are not joined on the water by the fleets of day cruise ships you are also more likely to see the local wildlife, including dolphins. *Fiordland Travel* offer a small boat 'MV Friendship Overnight Cruise' (1700-0915; $145) and a larger boat 'MV Milford Mariner Overnight Cruise' (16 hours; $225); Another overnight alternative is on board the old trading scow the 'Milford Wanderer' which has less modern (but still comfortable) four-bunk cabin accommodation (departs 1700, 16 hours).

Diving *Tawaki Dive* based in Te Anau, T2499006, www.tawakidive.co.nz Offer full-day fiord diving trips for the experienced, from $220.

Flightseeing Flightseeing trips to Milford are readily and principally available from Wanaka, Queenstown and Te Anau. The most preferred option is the combination **fly/cruise** trips that combine an extended scenic flight with one of the regular daytime cruises. Expect to pay about $270-300 (Queenstown/Wanaka). Note however, that although exciting and well worth the money, this does not allow much time (two hours) in Milford itself. Another popular trip, missing out the long bus journey back, is the **bus-in/cruise/fly-back** option, which costs from $374 (Queenstown). Note also that the flight into and around Milford Sound has to rate right up there with the glacier and Mount Cook flights of the West Coast. *Milford Sound Fly & Cruise*, T034-422686, and *Milford Sound Helicopters*, T2498384, are two operators based in Milford.

Kayaking A far more serene and atmospheric way to see The Sound is by kayak, giving you an incredible sense of scale. *Milford Sound Kayaks* operated by Rosco Gaudin and based at Deep Water Basin (just east of the airfield), T2498500, www.kayakmilford.co.nz, offers a range of day-safaris, fly/kayak, paddle/walk (part of the Milford Track) twilight and even full moon trips from four hours ($49) to seven hours (with flight ex Queenstown) $275. *Fiordland Wilderness Experiences*, based in Te Anau, T2497700, www.fiordlandseakayak.co.nz offer a day excursion on The Sound from $95 which takes in the scenery of the Milford Road. *Kiwi Reel-Rifle* based in Te Anau, T2499071 also offer day trips ex Te Anau and independent kayak hire.

Submarine Adventures This is one of New Zealand's newest tourist activities. Based at the underwater observatory is a 5-person commercial submersible that can take you up to 200 m below the surface to view the fiord's underwater habitat. It is a dark, forbidding and fairly featureless place, with only a limited number of sea creatures on the tick list, but exciting nonetheless. What makes this two-hour experience so special is the unique nature of the wildlife. The main feature is the black (actually white) coral which you will see no where else in the world. It is very expensive, at $500, T4543782, www.submarines.co.nz

Essentials

For the independent traveller there really is only one place to stay in Milford Sound. The **C-D** ***Milford Sound Lodge***, T2498071, F2498075, milford.sound.lodge@xtra.co.nz, located just off the Milford Road about 1km east of the airfield. Being the only option it can be a very cosmopolitan place and in mid-summer forms the hub of Milford's leisure activity. Here you can mix it with all types, from the rich to locals and trampers. It has a comfortable range of double/twins, dorms and powered/tent sites. Bathroom facilities are shared. Although some of the facilities are a little tired improvements are planned. There is an in-house **restaurant** offering breakfast and pub-style evening meals, a large lounge, small grocery store and internet. The more salubrious ***Mitre Peak Lodge*** near the boat terminal caters only for clients of Milford Track guided walks, T4411138.

Other than the Milford Sound Lodge your eating options are the day-time **café** (next to the Mitre Peak Lodge and main car park) or the ***Shark Bar***, next door.

18 Background

Background

History

The Maori legends

According to Maori legend New Zealand was created by the great Polynesian Demigod **'Maui-Tikitiki-a Taranga'** who hailed from the original Polynesian homeland of **Hawaiki**. Maui was well known for his trickery and guile and through the magical powers of a magic jawbone given to him by his 'sorcerer' grandmother, he was blessed with many god-like powers, with which to confront the world around him. Once, while out fishing with his five brothers, Maui used a piece of his magic jawbone as a fishhook and his own blood as bait. Soon he caught an almighty fish and struggling to pull it to the surface placed a spell upon it to subdue it forever. This great fish became **Te-Ika-a-Maui** (The Fish of Maui) and in essence the North Island of New Zealand. The shape of the North Island is said to resemble the body of the fish with the mouth being Palliser Bay at its southernmost tip, the fins Taranaki and the East Cape and its tail Northland. The mountains and valleys were created when Maui's jealous brothers hacked hungrily at the fish with their greenstone *mere* (clubs). The South Island is **'Te-Waka-a-Maui'** (The Waka of Maui) and Stewart Island **'Te-Punga-o-te-Waka-a-Maui'** (The anchor)

Maori trace their ancestry to the homelands of 'Hawaiki' and the great Polynesian navigator **Kupe**. On a brave scouting mission, across the uncharted oceans to the southeast, Kupe made landfall on a new and as yet undiscovered land (Maui's fish) at a spot now called the Hokianga in Northland, around 800 AD. Finding the new land viable for settlement, Kupe named it **Aotearoa – The Land of the Long White Cloud**. Leaving his crew to colonise, Kupe then returned to Hawaiki to encourage further emigration. A century later the first fleet of *waka* left Hawaiki on the great migration to settle Aotearoa permanently. It was the crew of these great canoes that formed the first *iwi* (tribes) of a new race of people called the **Maori**.

Early beginnings

Due to its geographic isolation New Zealand was one of the last 'viable' lands to be settled by humans. Although it is a matter of debate, most modern historians speculate that the first peoples to discover and settle permanently in New Zealand were the ancestors of early Polynesians, who gradually spread southeast to the Pacific Islands from Indonesia around 1000 AD. The ancestral land called Hawaiki is thought to be Tahiti and The Society Islands. This late, ocean going migration is quite incredible if you consider that just across the Tasman, in Australia, the aborigines had already been happily ensconced for over 50,000 years. Again, exactly when and how these early Polynesians arrived and how they actually lived is in doubt. What is known is that they arrived sporadically in **double-hulled canoes** and initially struggled with the colder climate of New Zealand. Finding their traditional root crops like yam and **kumara** (sweet potato) hard to establish, they had to change their principal diet and methods of hunting. Fishing and seafood gathering took precedence over cultivation and seals and abundant flightless land birds (mainly moa) became principal food items. With such plentiful food, for many decades the early Maori thrived, but like the first aboriginal settlers of Australia they made the fatal mistake of plundering the environment without thought for the future or sustainability. They also brought with them **dogs** and **kiore** (rats) which, in the absence of predators, and along with hunting, reaped havoc on the flightless native birds.

Before long, especially in the South Island, much of the native bush had been burnt down and the hapless moa, along with a number of other species, were hunted to extinction. This period of colonisation was to become known as the **Archaic Period**. Facing starvation, many of the tribes that had ventured south returned to the warmer environment of the North Island where traditional crops could still be grown and seafood could easily be gathered. By the time the first European explorers arrived the Maori had developed their own culture based on the tight knit family unit and a tribal system not dissimilar to the Celts and Scots. In a desire to protect family, food resources and land the Maori, like the Scots, saw their fair share of brutal inter-tribal conflict. The Maori developed a highly effective community and defence system built within fortified villages or *pa* and cannibalism was also common. By the 16th century they had developed into a successful, fairly healthy, robust race, free from European diseases or intercontinental greed and were, by this time, like the aborigines millennia before them, beginning to develop a sustainable future in tune with the environment around them. This period is known as the **Classic Period**.

However despite the Maori successes of colonisation, in many ways, when the first human footprint was made on New Zealand shores, the subsequent environmental damage was inevitable and irreversible. A 'classic' dynamic of cause and effect was set in place that would compromise the land forever. The Maori had proved the nemesis of the unspoiled and isolated bio-diversity of the land. Now, with the sails of European ships appearing above the horizon and the first European shoe-print – it was, effectively, to become the turn of the Maori themselves to be facing threat.

European Exploration

Although there is a vicious rumour that the French or Spanish were actually the first Europeans to sight New Zealand, the first documented discovery was made by in 1642 by Dutch explorer **Abel Tasman**. Commissioned by the Dutch East India Company, Tasman was sent to confirm or otherwise the existence of the hotly rumoured Great Southern Continent (**Terra Australis Incognita**) and if discovered, to investigate its viability for trade. Doubtless with great satisfaction, he first set sight of the new continent (Aotearoa) off what is now Okarito in Westland, on 13 December 1642, before heading north and anchoring in **Golden Bay** at the northern tip of the South Island. However the excitement quickly turned to despair when the first encounter with the Maori proved hostile with a loss of life on both sides. Without setting foot on land Tasman turned tail and fled up the west coast of the North Island en route to Tonga and Fiji. He christened the new land 'Staten Landt' which was later renamed **'Nieuw Zeeland'**. It was Tasman's first and last encounter with the new land, but his visit led to New Zealand being put on the world map.

The next recorded European visit occurred with the arrival of the ubiquitous British explorer **Captain Cook** on board the **'Endeavour'** in **1769**. It would be the first of three voyages to New Zealand. Cook's first landing, on 7 October in **Poverty Bay** was 'eventful' to say the least, with what proved to be a classic culture clash with the resident Maori (see page 336). Ignorance and fear on both sides led to a mutual loss of life, but unlike Tasman, Cook persevered with his public relations efforts and after further encounters managed to establish a 'friendly' relationship with the new people he called tangata Maori (The 'ordinary people').

Cook spent a further six months in New Zealand coastal waters mapping and naming the geographical features as he went. From Poverty Bay he first sailed south

via The Bay of Plenty and Cape Kidnappers to Cape Turnagain (on the border of modern day Southern Hawkes Bay and the Wairarapa), before heading back north, around the North Island, then south again to the Cook Strait and **Ship Cove** in the Queen Charlotte Sound. Ship Cove was clearly a favourite of Cook's and would be revisited on every subsequent voyage. After refitting the Endeavour in Ship Cove, Cook returned to Cape Turnagain (via Cape Palliser), before sailing down the eastern coast of the South Island, passing Stewart Island (which he mapped as a headland), sighting the entrance to Dusky Sound in Fiordland, before returning via the West Coast back to Cook Strait. Perhaps reluctantly he then left for Australia, but not before naming Cape Farewell, just south of Farewell Spit.

Cook's second voyage in **1773** on board the **'Resolution'** saw him land briefly in Dusky Sound (to this day, virtually unchanged since that day) before returning to Ship Cove via the west coast of the South Island and from there on to South America. On his third and last voyage, three years later, he returned to Ship Cove and his beloved 'Sounds', before heading for Hawaii (**Sandwich Islands**), where he was killed by the natives. Modern-day New Zealand owes a great deal to Captain Cook, not least the long list of place names that he bestowed upon what was perhaps his favourite destination. There are at least six statutes around the country that now immortalise the great man.

European Settlement and the Clash of Cultures

After news spread of the Cook voyages and perhaps more so, due the observations of his colleague and ship's naturalist Joseph Banks, it did not take long for European **sealers** and **whalers** to reach New Zealand and rape the rich marine resources. Many set up stations around the south coast and Sub-Antarctic Islands and by the 1820s the New Zealand fur seal and numerous species of whale had been brought to the verge of extinction. As the industries subsequently declined they were quickly joined or replaced with a limited but still steady influx of timber and flax **traders**. Others including adventurers, ex-convicts from Australia and some very determined (and some would say, much needed) missionaries joined the steady influx. **Samuel Marsden** gave the first Anglican sermon in the Bay of Islands on Christmas Day on 1814.

Inevitably perhaps an uneasy and fractious integration occurred between the Maori and the new settlers and in the familiar stories of colonised peoples the world over, the consequences for the native people were disastrous. Western diseases quickly ravaged over 25% of the Maori population and the trade of food, land or even preserved heads, for the vastly more powerful and deadly European weapons resulted in the **Maori Musket Wars** of 1820-35, a swift and almost genocidal era of inter-tribal warfare. With such a melting pot of divergent cultures, greed and religion simmering on a fire of lawlessness and stateless disorganisation and, contrary to the glowing reports being given back in Europe, New Zealand was initially an awful place to be. Crime and corruption was rife. The Maori were colluded into ridiculously unfavourable land for weapons deals and, along with the spread of Christianity and disease, their culture and tribal way of life was gradually being undermined. Such were the realities of early settlement that Kororareka (now known as Russell) in the Bay of Islands, which was the largest European settlement in the 1830s, earned itself the name and reputation as the 'Hellhole of the Pacific'. Amidst all the chaos the settlers began to appeal to their governments for protection.

The Treaty of Waitangi

By 1838 there were about 2000 British subjects in New Zealand and by this time the country was under the nominal jurisdiction of New South Wales in Australia. In 1833 **James Busby** was sent to Waitangi in the Bay of Islands as the official 'British Resident'. He was given the responsibility of law and order, but without the means to enforce it. Matters were made worse with the arrival of boatloads of new British immigrants sent under the banner of the privately owned and non-government supported **New Zealand Company**. Four years after Busby's arrival British settlers petitioned William IV for protection, citing the fact that Frenchman Baron de Thierry was threatening to pre-empt any British attempt to claim sovereignty of New Zealand. Fearful of losing any possibility of control, Britain appointed **Captain William Hobson** as Lieutenant Governor to replace Busby in New Zealand. His remit was to effect the transfer of sovereignty over the land from the Maori Chiefs to the British Crown. In many ways the circumstances bore an uncanny resemblance to the situation in Britain before it became a United Kingdom. In essence the fact that the Maori were, like the Scots, a culture based on family (clan or tribe) and fought ferociously to protect *that* rather than a whole nation, would undoubtedly be in their favour. The lure for the Maori would of course be material gain in return for land and 'full protection' as British citizens. For many Maori iwi (tribes) whose power was inferior to that of others this would of course be an attractive proposition. With the help of Busby who was now familiar with the ways and desires of the Maori, Hobson created what was to become the most important and controversial document in New Zealand history, **The Treaty of Waitangi**.

In the hastily compiled document there were three main provisions. The first was the complete cession of sovereignty by the Maori to the Queen of England. The second was the promise of full rights and possession of Maori lands and resources (but with the right to sell, of course). The third, and perhaps the greatest, attraction, given the chaotic environment, was the full rights and protection of Maori as British citizens. After two days of discussions, a few amendments and amidst much pomp and ceremony, over 40 Maori Chiefs eventually signed the Treaty on 5 February, 1840. With these first few signatures from the predominantly Northland tribes, Hobson went on a tour of the country to secure others.

To this day the Treaty of Waitangi remains a very contentious document. From its very inception it was inevitably going to be a fragile bridge between two very different cultures. Given the many differences in communication, translation and meaning, at best it was spurious or vague, but worse still could, as a result, be easily manipulated in both actual meaning and subsequent enactment. Indeed, a modern day lawyer would look at the Treaty and rub his little hands with glee. In essence the best politician, public relations consultant or rabid optimist could only have sold it as a ' beginning' or a 'start' on the 'difficult road a stable bi-culturalism', while many a realist would have (and still) declare it an unworkable 'scam'.

By September of 1840 Hobson had gathered over 500 signatures, all in the North Island. Feeling this was enough to claim sovereignty over New Zealand he did so, and declaring the right of discovery over the South Island, made New Zealand a Crown Colony, independent of New South Wales and Australia. But the refusal and subsequent omittance of several key (and powerful) Maori chiefs paved the way for regional disharmony and eventually war.

The Maori (Land) Wars

In 1840 Hobson established Kororareka (The Hell-hole of the Pacific') as the first capital of New Zealand, but given its reputation and history, he moved the seat of government to Auckland within a year. With the increased influx of settlers, all greedy for land and resources, human nature very quickly superseded the legal niceties and undermined the fragile bridge of the new bi-cultural colony. In a frenzy of very dubious land deals between Maori and *Pakeha* (white settlers), as well as misunderstandings in methods of land use and ownership, resentment between the two was rife. This, plus the heavy taxes that were being demanded by the new and financially strapped government, strained the bridge to breaking point. The Maori were essentially beginning to feel disenfranchised and began to rebel against British authority.

One of the first disputes was initiated by a particularly fractious and persistent chief called **Hone Heke** who was one of the original chiefs to sign the Treaty in the Bay of Islands. In 1844 he protested in a way that he knew would hit hard on the British psyche by cutting down the flagpole that so proudly flew the Union Jack in Kororareka (later renamed Russell). He did this not once, but (almost admirably) four times. Hone Heke's actions lead to a bloody war with the British that was to last two years. Sadly, this clash was just the beginning. In 1852 the **Constitution Act** was created and in 1853 the country was divided in to six provinces each with a Provincial Council exercising the functions of local government which included land purchases and sales.

At the same time immigration was increasing and with the spread of disease, the Maori were becoming well outnumbered. Once again it seems, as with many native peoples around the world, the Maori were becoming a resented minority and a displaced people. Exacerbated by the provincial administration, the continued greed of the settlers and inter-tribal conflicts, the Maori continued to lose land at an alarming rate and often in return for only meagre material gains.

Some of the more savvy Maori chiefs became reluctant to sell land and, in 1858, several Waikato tribes went a step further by electing their own Maori king. This became known as the **King Movement**. Although initially designed to preserve cultural identity and serve as a land policy maker, supporters were encouraged to resist all land sales and *Pakeha* settlement. The British reacted with complete derision, seeing the movement only as a barrier to further colonisation. The Land Wars (or Maori Wars) inevitably ensued. Troops from both Britain and Australia were sent to aid the NZ militia in an attempt to quash the uprising, which spread outwith the Waikato to Northland and Taranaki. The East Coast later joined the fold with the formation of a Maori 'Hauhau' religious movement. One of the most noted Maori rebels was **Te Kooti** who for a time became the most wanted man in the land (see page 217).

It proved to be a bloody time in New Zealand's early history with the fierce and fearless Maori warriors putting up a determined and courageous fight. Their traditional methods of fighting from a fortified *pa*, with trenches, proved so effective (and later, so admired by the British) it became the chosen method of defence and attack in ground warfare until after the Second World War.

With far superior weaponry and organisation the British quickly subdued the rebels. In return for their disobedience, and despite the Treaty, they confiscated huge tracts of land. This land was then sold to new or already established settlers. By 1900 over 90% of the land was outwith Maori ownership or control. They were a defeated people and, with little or no power and continued integration, their culture was rapidly crumbling.

Natural Resources, Consolidation and Social Reform

Although development in the North Island suffered as a result of the conflicts, both timber, agriculture and gold came to the rescue. On an already solid base of productive agriculture, and with the lucrative rape of the upper North Island's **kauri forest** already in full swing, the discovery of **gold** in the Coromandel in 1852 sealed the economic boom. South Island too, which had been a relatively peaceful haven compared to the North, joined the party, with the discovery of gold from 1857 in the Nelson, Otago and West Coast Regions.

With much of the economic focus being on the South Island the seat of a new central (as opposed to provincial) government was moved to Wellington which became the capital in 1876. With gold fever the prime attraction the *Pakeha* population grew dramatically. With so much good fortune in the south, Dunedin's head count alone grew from 2000 in 1861 to 10,000 four years later, making it the largest town in the land. Although the gold boom lasted only a decade, the infrastructures that the boom set in place paved the way for agricultural, timer and coal industries to take over.

In the agriculture sector alone, especially through sheep and dairy cattle, New Zealand was becoming an internationally significant export nation and prosperity continued. Towards the end of the 19th century lead by the enigmatic Liberal Party leader **Richard 'King Dick' Seddon**, New Zealand's colonial settlers went through a dramatic and sweeping phase of **social reforms**. Well ahead of Britain, the USA and most other Western nations, women secured the vote and pioneering legislation was enacted introducing old-age pensions, minimum wage structures and arbitration courts.

But while the *Pakeha* prospered the Maori continued to suffer. The **Native Lands Act** of 1865 was established to investigate Maori land ownership and distribute land titles, but again, thanks mainly to Maori tribal structure and the split of land to individual as opposed to communal blocks, this only exacerbated the disintegration of the Maori culture and undermined its cohesion. Maori were given the vote in 1867 but only held four out of 95 seats in the parliamentary House of Representatives. By 1900 the Maori population had decreased to less than 50,000 and with the integration of Maori and *Pakeha* and many Maori/*Pakeha* marriages, the pure Maori were becoming even more of a minority.

Prosperity and The World Wars

By 1907 New Zealand progressed to the title of '**Dominion**' of Britain rather than merely a 'colony' and by the 1920s was in control of most of its own affairs. By virtue of its close links with Britain, New Zealand the newly formed (trans-Tasman) **Australia and New Zealand Army** Corps (ANZAC) became heavily embroiled in the Boer War of 1899-1902 and again in the First World War, at Gallipoli and the Western Front. Although noted for their steadfast loyalty, courage and bravery, the ANZACs suffered huge losses. Over 17,000 never returned with one in every three men aged between 20 and 40 being killed or wounded. Almost a century on there remains a palpable sense of pride in both Australia and New Zealand for those lives lost and quite rightly so; their First World War casualties remain the greatest of any combat nation.

New Zealand joined the Western world in the **Great Depression** of the 1920s but it recovered steadily and independently progressed in an increasing atmosphere of optimism. Again from a solid base of agricultural production it prospered and immigration, particularly from Britain, grew steadily. The population had now

passed one million. In 1935 New Zealand became the fist nation to enact a social welfare system, which included free health care and low-rental council properties. These most recent pioneering acts of social reform, along with the economy, resources and common attitude, secured one of the highest standards of living in the world and New Zealand was an envied, prime 'new-life' destination.

However, along with the rest of the world, water was temporarily thrown on the fires of progress and prosperity with the outbreak of the Second World War. Once again, New Zealand and the loyal ANZACs answered the call. This time, in both Europe and Asia, it was the turn of the **28th Maori Battalion** to earn a widespread admiration and respect for their tenacity and courage. It seemed their warrior spirit, if not their culture was still alive and well. Like most warring nations the war effort extended to the home shores where women replaced men in the vast majority of industrial and social practices. With the spread of the conflict across the Pacific, it proved a nervous time for the nation and although many would be correct in saying it was not for the first time, the people of New Zealand were under a renewed threat of invasion. However, with the dropping of the atomic bomb in Japan the threat ceased and the war was over.

Post 1945

Shortly after the war, in 1947, New Zealand was declared an independent nation but thanks to the war and its important agricultural exports, it maintained close defence and trade links with the Great Britain, the USA and Australia. In 1945 it became one of the original member states of the **United Nations** (UN) and later joined the **ANZUS Defence Pact** with the USA and Australia. Domestically, the country again prospered but the nagging problems of race relations, land and resource disputes between Maori and *Pakeha* still had to be addressed.

By the early 1970s the vast majority of Maori had moved to urban areas in search of work, but with many being unsuccessful social problems proved inevitable. In an attempt to spawn a new sense of spirit, the government passed the **Waitangi Day Act** in 1960 making 6 February a day of thanksgiving in celebration of the Treaty and the cohesive bi-cultural society it was supposed to have created. This was further emphasised with an official public holiday in 1973. But some Maori (and *Pakeha*) merely saw the day as an opportunity for protest and although the public holiday remains, the traditional pomp and ceremony annually enacted at Waitangi in the Bay of Islands, was scrapped for much more low key governmental diplomatic posturing. In 1975 more significant and realistic progress was made with the formation of the **Waitangi Tribunal** which was established to legally and officially hear Maori claims against the Crown. This method of addressing the problems continues to this day, but as ever, the misinterpretations of the Treaty and its translation have remains a major stumbling block.

New Zealand joined most of the developed world in the economic slump of the 70s and 80s. The traditionally strong agricultural exports to Europe declined, the price of oil and manufacturing imports rose and it was hit hard by the stock market crash of 1987. In response to the economic decline the government of the day, under **Robert Muldoon's** National Party deregulated the country's economy, paving the way for free trade. The most important and lasting trade agreement was the **Closer Economic Relations Trade Agreement** made with Australia in 1983, but New Zealand was beginning to see itself playing a far more significant role in the Asian markets as opposed to the traditional European ones.

In 1984 the Labour government, under its enigmatic leader **David Lange**, took control and made further sweeping and radical changes to the economy. These were dubbed **'Rogernomics'** after the then finance minister Roger Douglas. Although the policies of privatization, free enterprise and the deregulation of the labour market improved the situation, unemployment rose and the policies began to prove unpopular with the voting public. Fearful of losing re-election votes Lange sacked Douglas, but when the party reinstated him, this resulted in his own shock resignation in 1989, leaving the party in disarray. Subsequently, the National Party led by and the far less enigmatic **Jim Bolger** swept to power in 1990.

One of the most important landmark decisions made on foreign policy in the 1980s was New Zealand's staunch **anti-nuclear** stand. In 1984 Lange refused entry to any foreign nuclear powered ships in its coastal waters. This soured its relationship with the US who reacted by suspending defence obligations to NZ made under the ANZUS pack in the 1950s. This anti-nuclear stance is still maintained with considerable pride and is one that was only strengthened when the French Secret Service bombed the Greenpeace vessel **Rainbow Warrior** in 1985, causing national and international outrage. Relations with France were further soured in 1995 with the rather arrogant and insensitive testing of nuclear weapons in French Polynesia.

Throughout the 1990s the National Party continued successfully to nurture the free-market economic policies first initiated by Labour. In 1993 a national referendum voted unanimously in favour of a mixed-member proportional representation (**MMP**) system of government. This system, which has proved successful in Germany, gives electors two votes: one for a candidate in their own electorate and the second for their favoured political party. Maori can choose to vote in either a general or Maori electorate. There is a 120-seat parliament with 60 general electorate seats, five Maori and 55 allocated to parties according to the percentage of party votes received.

Whether this system of government has been good for the country as a whole is debatable, but what did result through some ugly internal politics and fragile power-sharing agreements, were two women prime ministers. The first in New Zealand History was **Jenny Shipley** of the National Party who engineered a 'coup' to seize party leadership from Jim Bolger in 1997and currently in power is **Helen Clark** of the 1999 elected Labour Party. The new system can also not exactly be accused of restricting a diverse representation. One Green Party MP, Nandor Tanczos, is a Rastafarian and a Labour Party MP, Georgina Beyer, is transgender.

A highly significant event outside politics in 1995 was New Zealand's win in the coveted **America's Cup** yachting race. It was the first time the cup had been won by any nation other than the US and, given the country's love of yachting, it was the cause of unprecedented national celebration and pride. Over 300,000 people lined Queen Street in Auckland to congratulate the heroic yachties return. With the successful defence of the cup again in 2000 it now seems yachting can join – or some would say replace – rugby as the nation's world-dominant sport.

Into the new millennium

Given its size and isolation New Zealand enjoyed its 15 minutes fo fame on 1 January 2000 when it was the first country to see the dawn of the new millennium. Returning to the shadows New Zealand remains a land blessed by an outstanding natural environment, healthy independence and the huge asset of a low and cosmopolitan population. Its current economic struggles lie in a poor exchange rate and its biggest social challenge is the continued and difficult journey down the road of bi-culturalism. But perhaps New Zealand's greatest challenge lies in the conservation

and protection of its environment, for which it is most famous and much loved. Dubbed the 'Clean Green Land' it remains to be seen whether its government and people can truly embrace the reality that its relatively healthy ecological condition is mainly due to its lack of population, as opposed to the common and traditional human attitudes that have proved to be so ruinous elsewhere. One can only hope that this wise, determined and attitude can blossom, even though it is very much against the international grain. Without doubt, New Zealand is a premier tourist destination with a great deal to offer. Like its much larger neighbour Australia, tourism is fast becoming the biggest and most important growth industry. Encompassed within that industry is the sensible, desirable and sustainable realm of eco-tourism, which it is hoped can assist in the country's efforts to conserve its many unique and vulnerable species. At the forefront of these conservation efforts is the on-going program to conserve the the iconic kiwi as well as the country's impressive position on International whaling and the creation of a South Pacific Whale Sanctuary. So, from the creation of the great fish by the Maori Demi-god Maui, to its current efforts to protect them, the land and the people remain on an inextricable and co-dependent voyage in to the new millennium.

Culture

People and population

The population of New Zealand currently stands at about 3.8 million. The population densities are unevenly spread between the two islands, with North Island home to about 2.8 million and the South island about 920,000. Greater Auckland alone is home to just over 1 million, almost a third of the total population. New Zealand is essentially a bi-cultural society made up of Maori and Europeans, but many Caucasian (*Pakeha*) nationalities are present. Maori make up about 15% of the total population, with the vast majority living in the North Island. Pacific islanders make up the second largest non-Caucasian group at around 6% with almost all living in Greater Auckland. Asians make up 3% of the total population and are the fastest growing minority group. Again the vast majority of Asians choose to live in Greater Auckland. New Zealanders are famous for being 'the world's greatest travellers' and at any one time a large proportion of citizens are absent or living abroad. Over 400,000 live and work in Australia alone. Through their close trans-Tasman ties Australian and New Zealand citizens are free to live and work in both countries.

Religion

The dominant religion is **Christianity**, with Anglican, Presbyterian and Roman Catholic denominations the most prominent. Other minority religions include Hinduism, Islam, Judaism and Buddhism. The Maori developed two of their own minority Christian based faiths; Ratana and Ringatu, both of which were formed in the late 19th to early 20th centuries. At least a quarter of the total population are atheists or have no religion.

Music

For such a small country New Zealand has a thriving **rock** scene with **Dunedin** considered the hotbed of talent. In the 70s and 80s **Split Enz** was New Zealand's best-known group, reaching international recognition. Other notable bands include

Crowded House and the **Exponents**. In the late 90s **OMC** (Otara Millionaires Club) shot to fame with their catchy hit 'How Bizarre', but despite their success have since broken up. Many alternative bands and singers like **Bic Runga** and **DJ Amanda**, who are fast developing a unique kiwi or rap sound, mixed with mainly Polynesian influences, thrive within the mainstream. **Neil Finn,** formerly of Crowded House, and **Dave Dobbyn** spearhead the most successful ageing-rocker solo careers. In the classical arena **Dame Kiri Te Kanawa** has for many years been New Zealand's most noted international opera star. Traditional domestic or world music outside of Maori performances and Irish pubs is quite hard to find, however the **Pacific Festival** held in Auckland in March, is one notable exception.

Film

New Zealand has produced a number of notable feature films and is (or was) home to a few internationally recognized actors and directors. Perhaps the most famous film (though many would describe it more as an alarming and uncomfortable experience) is *'Once Were Warriors'* (1994) – an adaptation of Kiwi writer Alan Duffs portrayal of a highly dysfunctional urban Maori family, directed by Lee Tamahori. For those looking for a reality check of the worst social aspects of the advertised, pleasant 'clean green land' it is a must-see, superbly demonstrating that New Zealand is not immune to the death of traditional cultures, poverty, alcoholism and domestic abuse.

On a lighter note, yet still depicting harsh times, is the romantic classic *'The Piano'* (1993) directed by New Zealand's most noted director **Jane Campion.** Starring Holly Hunter, Sam Neill and Hollywood tough guy, Harvey Keitel, it tells the haunting story of a Scottish immigrant (Hunter) and her daughter (Anna Paquin) who are brought to New Zealand in the early 19th century in an arranged marriage to troubled colonial landowner (Neill). Finding Neill to be as romantic and warm-hearted as the mud they seem to spend all their time trudging through, she turns to the brooding, yet caring employee (Keitel) for love and affection. Part of the attraction is also his willingness to transport her prized possession – a grand piano – inland from the beach where she and her daughter were so unceremoniously off-loaded. It is a deserving multi-award winner that is well acted and has a superb musical score. However, it may leave you thinking New Zealand is a very harsh, wet place of little more but tangled bush and mud – which essentially it once was. Although actor **Sam Neill** was not born in New Zealand, he grew up in the South Island and now lives in Queenstown, so is considered by many to be an adopted son. Another actor who was born in New Zealand, but grew up in Australia, is **Russell Crowe**, who recently shot to fame for his macho role in *Gladiator*. He now seems set to become one of Hollywood's golden boys and of course must always be envied for dating Meg Ryan.

Peter Jackson is a talented kiwi director who is already well known for the New Zealand classic *'Heavenly Creatures'* which is the tale of two troubled teenage girls. Further recognition will no doubt be accorded with the release of the first of *'The Lord of the Rings'* Trilogies in late 2001. And where would be the perfect filming location to meet the considerable and dramatic scenic requirements? – New Zealand, naturally!

Maori culture and traditions

The Maori are essentially a tribal race consisting of the **whanau** (family unit), extending to the **hapu** (sub-tribe) and then the **iwi** (full tribe). Together they are referred to as the **tangata whenua**, which directly translated means 'people of the land'. The Maori relationship with their ancestors (or **tipuna**) is considered to exist through their genetic

inheritors and an individual's own genealogy (or **whakapapa**) can be traced right back to the gods via one of the original migratory canoes (or **waka)**. There are over 40 iwi in New Zealand with the largest being the **Ngapuhi** (descendants of Puhi) in Northland who have over 100,000 members, to one of the smallest, the **Ngai Tahu** (descendants of Tahu) in South Island, who have only about 30,000 members. The Maori's very family-based social structure is in many ways remarkably similar to the early Scottish clan system that developed almost in parallel at the other end of the earth. Indeed, the Maori culture has some uncanny similarities to the Scots in their love of music, song (waiata), dance (haka), oration (particularly storytelling), socialising and unfortunately, to their equal detriment, fighting amongst themselves and against outside invaders with fearless courage and determination. The word **maori** does in itself not denote a common background but derives from a term of differentiation used between the ordinary people (natives) and the European explorers.

Traditional Maori life is bounded by the customs, concepts or conducts of **tapu** (meaning taboo, or sacred) and **noa** (meaning mundane, or the opposite of tapu). If something is tapu, whether an object, place, action or person, it must be given the accordant respect. To do otherwise can result in ostracism, bad luck or sickness. A good example would be a burial place that is forever tapu, or a food resource that is given seasonal tapu to encourage sustainability. One good example for the visiting tourist is the summit of **Moehau**, the Coromandel Peninsula's highest peak. It is currently 'tapu' which means, that despite the views, or absence of any guard (beyond the spiritual that is) it would be very culturally insensitive to go clambering all over it. Another is **Green Lake** (Rotokakahi) near Rotorua. The island on the lake is an ancient Maori burial ground and the lake is therefore tapu. As such you cannot use it for any recreational activity and you must not set foot on the island.

Noa is a term heard less often, but plays an important role in the balance or cancellation of tapu. For example, at some point the summit of Moehau may through ceremony have its 'tapu' rendered 'noa'. Once noa you can clamber away to your little heart's content! Of course in the modern day your average 'Maori Joe' cannot just place a tapu on anything he chooses – his beer for example, or the Visa bill! If this were the case there would be social mayhem! Placing a tapu is a matter that requires deliberation by the iwi and enactment by the **elders**, very often after a meeting or **hui**. All things whether living or otherwise possess **mauri** (see next page), **wairau** (spirit) and **mana**. The meaning of mana goes well beyond words, but in essence means prestige, standing, integrity or respectability. It is a term that is often used by both Maori, *Pakeha* and is even sometimes heard outside New Zealand. If a Maori warrior won a fight or a battle this would increase his mana, if he lost, it would undermine it, and so on. Objects too have mana. The pendants (or **tiki**) that you buy (for others, never yourself) can hold spiritual mana or can increase in mana as they are passed onto others. It is a lovely term and perhaps the one most tourists take away or remember once they leave.

Maori face showing typical facial tattoos

Maori values

To the Maori everything has a ***mauri****, an essence that gives everything its special character and everything is viewed as a living entity. Mauri pervades and infuses everything – things living and non-living, the earth and sky. Sometimes it is represented by a sacred stone, which is placed at a secret location in a forest or river, and sometimes it has no tangible presence at all. But always the mauri must be nurtured, cared for and respected. When kia moana (seafood) is taken from the sea, a tree is felled, or any other thing is harvested, a* ***karakia*** *should be said beforehand and thanks given afterwards.*

The concept of mauri leads to a sense of unity between man and nature. The unity extends to the opposing principles that make up the cosmos, as is expressed in the creation tradition. The tradition expounds how ***Rangi*** *the sky father and* ***Papa*** *the earth mother were once united and how* ***Tane Mahuta*** *the god of the forest tore them apart to let in the daylight. The separation brought great sorrow to Rangi and Papa. This sorrow continues in the clinging mists and falling rain, and rising of the dew.* ***Water*** *is therefore fundamental to the Maori world-view. Water is considered a basic essence, a part of every living thing, the linking medium between individuals and their environment. The water of a hapu or iwi is a fundamental source of their mana and plays a central role in many rituals.*

Maoritanga (The Way of the Maori) The Maori language, lifestyle, social structure, customs, spirituality, legends, arts and crafts, are all enjoying something of a revival in modern-day New Zealand. The unique Maori culture and history are all very well represented in museums throughout the country, with both **Auckland Museum** and the state-of-the-art **Museum of New Zealand (Te Papa)** in Wellington, in particular, offering a fascinating insight. Although there are thought to be no 'true' full-blooded Maori left in New Zealand, the majority of those of undisputed Maori descent remain staunch and rightly proud of their ancestry and cultural identity. It is a sad fact that their cultural journey in the face of what many would call a 'European invasion' has been, and continues to be, a difficult and troubled one. To that end it is important for the visitor to be aware of the basics and to realise that New Zealand culture, in total, goes a lot deeper than the practice or development of a cosmopolitan mix of cultures imported from elsewhere. In a country that essentially has a very short human history and one that some critics declare as 'historically wanting', Maoritanga is, in essence, as old as it gets.

The Marae The marae is essentially the sacred 'place of meeting' or of simply 'being', that exist around a **whare tupuna** (or ancestral meetinghouse). It is traditionally used as a communal centre, meeting place or sometimes a retreat. Strict customs and protocols (or **kawa**) surrounds the marae and for any tourist who wishes to visit or stay it is important to be aware of these customs and the protocols. It is akin to taking your shoes off in a Japanese house, offering the correct welcome, introduction and so on. Visitors are welcomed on to the marae with a **powhiri** (a welcome), which is multi-faceted. First, a warrior will greet you (or all visitors – **manuhiri**) with a **haka**, which is a traditional dance that can look decidedly threatening. In essence this is a challenge (or **wero)**. Do not return the gestures, unless you want to be considered uncouth, culturally ignorant, or have the desire to get your head removed. At the end of the wero there is a peace offering (or **teka**), which is placed on the ground between you and the warrior. Once accepted a female elder will then issue the **karanga** (a chant), that both welcomes and addresses the visitor and their ancestors.

On moving forward you must bow to acknowledge the ancestors. At the entrance to the whare the chief will then offer a **whaikorero** or mihi (a welcoming speech). If you can, you, or traditionally the leader (chief) elect of your group are supposed to respond accordingly. You, or your chief, then perform the **hongi** – the touching (not rubbing) of noses unique to Maori. The hongi is an action which is equivalent to a hug, or a kiss and is often accompanied with a handshake. The equivalent of English 'hello' is the Maori **'kiaora'**.

Once this protocol is enacted you are then a welcome guest on the marae and free to talk, stay, or feast. The feast (or **hangi**) is a superb experience of earth-oven, steamed meat and vegetables with a very distinctive, succulent taste. A **karakia** (or prayer) is traditionally said beforehand.

Pa

The Pa, or the traditional **fortified settlements** built by the Maori are worth special mention. Built predominantly on a headland or hill and from wood and often networked by trenches, they were used to protect against invasion by invading tribes and also the *Pakeha* during the Maori Land Wars. Within the *pa* boundary are the marae, whare and food storage facilities. So effective was this system defence and so impressed were the Colonial British forces, that the design was echoed in the First World War in the trenches of the Western Front. There are many subtle remains around the country with one of the best being the distinct earthworks and kumara (sweet potato storage) pits on **One Tree Hill** in Auckland. The volcanic plugs of the Auckland area made ideal *pa* sites.

Song & dance

Like the aborigine of Australia the Maori did not keep a written history, but rather passed down the essence of their culture and historical journey by song – **waiata** – and chants – **karakai**. The two most common song types are **waiata tangi** (songs of mourning) and waiata **aroha** (songs of love).

Maori dance is known as **haka.** The most famous form of this has been given somewhat false iconic status in the modern-day by the sporting rugby legends the **All Blacks** before the start of each game. This particular form of haka is a war chant made as a challenge to all opposition and is quite a sight to behold. Whether you were Captain Cook or a 120 kg lock forward in the English Rugby team, to be confronted with a Maori doing a haka is is to know you're in for quite a battle!

However, there are other far less threatening forms of dance called **taparahi**. These include the **poi** dance, very commonly seen in traditional Maori performances; the poi being balls of strings that are swung or twirled in harmony and synchronicity to the music. Traditional musical instruments are the flute or **putorino**. The beat is traditionally kept by the stamping of feet.

Arts & crafts

The artistic styles and media used by the Maori were already fairly well developed on their arrival in New Zealand and influenced heavily be Polynesian tradition. However, in the absence of clay for pottery and metals with which to fashion rock or wood, they developed their own unique style.

Wood or greenstone (pounamu) **carving** was the commonest form of craft both for functional purposes (like **waka**) or for decoration, on panels, **pou** (equivalent to Native American totem poles), or adorning **whare whakairo** (meeting houses). **Kauri** or **totara** were the commonest native wood types and it was fashioned in to highly distinctive patterns using **greenstone (pounamu)**, shells, or sharp stones. Sadly the early Christian missionaries often discouraged the Maori from producing their carvings, which they saw as containing obscene or inappropriate imagery. This is especially the case in Northland where elaborate carving is far less commonly

seem on the marae. Other forms of carving were the creation of pendants or **tiki**, which were made predominantly from whalebone or pounamu. These pendants often depict spiritual ancestors – or **hei tiki** – as well as legendary or sacred animals. Weapons like **taiaha pouwhenua** (long clubs) and **patu** (short clubs) were fashioned from wood, while **mere** (short, close combat club) were traditionally fashioned from greenstone.

One of the best places to see both traditional and contemporary Maori arts and crafts in creation is at the **Mario Arts and Crafts Institute**, at the Wakarewarewa Thermal Reserve in Rotorua. Aside from carving and other three-dimensional works, Maori rock art is in evidence, particularly around Timaru in the South Island. There are also some very interesting contemporary Maori artworks showpieced in the Rotorua Museum.

Moko The unique Maori facial tattoo (or **moko**) was traditionally fashioned, doubtless with considerable pain, using bone chisels, a mallet and blue pigment. The moko was predominantly the decoration of the higher classes with men covering their entire face (and sometimes their buttocks) while the women were decorated on the chin. Today Maori (especially those in the Maori gangs like the Mongrel Mob and Black Power) still procure moko, but this is done of course using modern tattooing techniques. To get the best idea of its design and permanence (let alone to imagine the pain), take a look at the superb realist paintings of the Maori elders done in the late 1800s by renowned New Zealand painters **Gottfried Lindauer** and **Charles F Goldie**. Examples can be seen in major art galleries throughout the country, with the Auckland Art Gallery being especially good.

Land and environment

Geography

New Zealand consists of three main islands – **North Island, South Island** and **Stewart Island** – with a handful of other small far-flung Subtropical and **Sub-Antarctic islands** (the largest being a group called the **Chathams**, which lie 853 km east of the South Island) completing the family. The total land area is 268,704 sq km (slightly larger than the UK).

New Zealand's geographical boundaries extend from 33° to 53° south latitude and from 162° east longitude, to 173° west longitude, which results in a broad climatic range from north to south. It is bounded north and east by the **South Pacific Ocean**, on the west by the **Tasman Sea** and on the south by the great **Southern Ocean**. The nearest mainland is Australia, which lies 1600 km west, roughly the same distance as New Zealand is in length.

Geographical features Although compact in size, New Zealand's landscape is rich and varied: glaciers, braided rivers, lakes, fiords (flooded glacial valleys), sounds (flooded riverbeds) – found predominantly in the South Island – lowlands, alluvial plains, wetlands, large natural coastal harbours and a rash of offshore islands. Given the fact New Zealand is located at the meeting point of the Pacific and Indo-Australian Plates, it is also a distinctly 'shaky' land of frequent earthquakes and constant **volcanic activity**. The **Taupo Volcanic Zone** in central North Island is one of the most active in the world. A string of volcanoes stretches from the currently active White Island in the Bay of Plenty, to the moody Mount Ruapehu in the heart of North Island. The area also has

numerous **thermal features,** including geysers, mineral springs, blowholes and mud pools, most of which can be found around Rotorua and Taupo. One of the largest **volcanic eruptions** in human history occurred in New Zealand in 186 AD, the remnants of which is the country's largest lake – Lake Taupo. The most recent eruption occurred in 1995 (and again in 1996), when Mount Ruapehu – North Island's highest peak – had a moderate stomach upset. The country's most dramatic **earthquake** in recent history occurred in Napier on North Island's East Coast in 1931.

Due to the 'uplift' created by the clash of the two tectonic plates, South Island has many more mountain ranges than the North and boasts the country's highest peak, **Mount Cook**. *Aoraki*, as the Maori call it, stands less than 40 km from the West Coast at a height of 3,753 m. The country's longest river is the **Waikato**, which stretches 425 km from Lake Taupo to the Tasman Sea.

Geology

New Zealand is an ancient land that has been so isolated from any other land mass for so long that its biodiversity is described by some scientists as the closest one can get to studying life on another planet. The oldest rocks, which make up part of the New Zealand we know today, were first rafted away from the great Gondwana land mass over 100 million years ago by a process called continental drift. The modern landscape is the dramatic result of geological uplift and volcanic activity created by New Zealand's location on the boundary of the Pacific and Indo-Australian Plates. Further 'sculpturing' occurred as a result of natural erosion, particularly the glacial erosion of numerous ice ages in the last two million years. Thanks to its long isolation, much of New Zealand's biodiversity is not only ancient, but also highly unique, with such incredible oddities like the kiwi, tuatara and weta still in evidence today. A useful comparison is with the endemic biodiversity of Great Britain: having been separated from continental Europe for a mere 10,000 years it has only one endemic plant and one endemic animal species. In contrast, as a result of over 80 million years of isolation, the vast majority of New Zealand species are endemic. Around 90% of its insects and marine molluscs, 80% of its trees, ferns and flowering plants and 25% of it bird species, all 60 reptiles, four remaining frogs, two species of bat and eel are found nowhere else on earth. So there is little doubt New Zealand could aptly be described as a 'paradise created'. But on the tragic day that man arrived, a mere 1000 years ago, it was not only 'paradise found', but was to become 'paradise lost'. Our arrival has caused more devastation to this 'clean green land' than anything else in 80 million years of evolution.

Wildlife

Urban

Birds To start with the humble, clever and ubiquitous **house sparrow**, some would claim it is a tribute to the little bird itself. As you emerge bleary-eyed from the airport terminal, the chances are you will see one before you do a taxi. Whether on high or at your feet, they are waiting and watching and have your every move and bag contents under close observation. After human beings and, in essence, thanks to them, these master scavengers are one of the most successful and omnipresent species on earth. In New Zealand, the humble sparrow was introduced in 1867 and like anywhere else the land provides a happy hunting ground.

New Zealand's urban landscape is home to many introduced plants and animals and Europeans especially will notice many familiar species. In the average garden these include birds like the **song thrush**, the **blackbird**, the **starling** and the **chaffinch**.

Almost all of these were, of course, introduced. One notable exception that is absent is the European **robin**. However, old habits die hard and they are still seen in two dimensions, annually, on the front of New Zealand Christmas cards.

Elsewhere, in the parks and open spaces, you will see (or more likely hear) the **Australasian magpie**, as well as the comical **pukeko** and on the urban waterways, the obligatory **mallard duck** and **black swan**. The Australasian magpie is the size of a crow. He's dressed in black and white – like a butler – and is melodious and very intelligent. They are, as the name suggests, an Australian import and very unpopular in New Zealand. While nesting they are fiercely territorial and every year newspapers are full of Hitckcockian tales of people being attacked. The **pukeko** is a much more amicable import from Australia, where it is known as the swamphen. They look like a cross between a chicken and a spider, with outrageously long feet, with which they walk on water. They are a gorgeous blue/purple colour and support a robust red beak. Get used to the 'pookie' as you will see them everywhere.

Often mistaken with the similar looking pukeko, the **takahe** is much larger (and certainly much rarer). The black swan takes the place of the mute swan in Europe and is common throughout. They are smaller than the mute variety, but just as daft and just as delighted to share your sandwiches. The most common urban 'seagull' is the antsy and stern-looking **red-billed gull**. They are also widely encountered on the coast and again will show up at your feet before your stomach even grumbles. The same applies of course to the **feral pigeon**. They too are commonplace, especially in sight of flat-whites and menus. Out and about almost anywhere in the North Island you will also see the street-wise **Indian myna**, a chestnut coloured, medium sized passerine that, like the sparrow, is an introduced, almost human-reliant 'opportunist'. Their speciality is dodging traffic, which they can do with admirable precision while catching dead insects on the road.

Mammals When it comes to mammals in suburbia you will find that Mrs Tiggywinkle (alias, the **hedgehog**) moved in long ago. By all accounts 'she' paid a visit, liked both the climate and the menu and decided to stay. While the hedgehog at least adds slugs and other such unwelcome garden pests to its menu of native bird's eggs, the notorious **cat** is just the wanton, careless and prolific killer of old. Literally millions of native and non-native birds are mauled by domestic and feral cats every year and next to man, the **stoat**, the **possum** and the **rat**, they are native wildlife's worst enemy.

Coastal

Seabirds Of course the coast is never far away in New Zealand and it is home to some of New Zealand's 'wildlife royalty', specifically the world's only mainland colony of **Royal Albatross**, found only on the Otago Peninsula near Dunedin. If you are from the northern hemisphere this is simply a must-see, since without an expensive trip to Antarctica, this is perhaps your only chance. To watch them in flight or see their fat, infant chicks awaiting their next inter-continental meal (looking like large, bemused, fluffy white slippers) is simply unforgettable. It is amazing to think that 'said slippers' must grow wings that will span over 3 m and that those wings will

Royal Albatross courtship display

then subsequently take them around the world more times than Michael Palin or Richard Branson.

New Zealand is actually known as the seabird capital of the world and a remarkable 70% of its total avian 'who's who' is pelagic (the world average is 3%). The list is long. Numerous types of **mollymawk**, which are similar to albatrosses, are common, especially off the southern tip of the South Island, where another family of seabirds, the **shearwaters**, also abound. If you go to **Stewart Island** you may get the opportunity to see many of them, but you are more likely to find one boiled, next to your ketchup and chips. The prolific **sooty shearwater (or Titi)** has been hunted by the Maori for centuries and is still harvested today for food. Other seabirds include numerous species of **petrel**, including the Westland, Pycroft's and Cook's, all of which are found nowhere else in the world. One, the **taiko**, which was collected during Captain Cook's voyages, was not encountered again for nearly two centuries, when it was finally tracked down to its sole breeding site on the Chatham Islands. Most petrels and shearwaters nest in burrows and in huge numbers on the many offshore islands. They come ashore mainly at night, so your best chance to see them is offshore from boats or promontories, especially in Otago and Southland. Sometimes you will see huge rafts of petrels or shearwaters surface feeding, looking from a distance like a huge brown oil spill. One member of the petrel family you may bump in to while out sea fishing is the **giant petrel**. He's big (about the size of a goose), uniform brown, and looks like an industrial-strength mole-grip on wings. So don't mess! Throw out your fish scraps and smile politely.

Background

Penguins Another huge treat for any visitor from the northern hemisphere are New Zealand's penguin species. Believe it or not, there are in fact three species perfectly at home in New Zealand and without an iceberg in sight! The **little blue** is the commonest, being found all round the coast. It is also the smallest of the penguin species and almost certainly has to be the cutest. They come ashore to their burrows at dusk, and there are many places where you can observe them doing this. Oamaru in Otago is one of the most noted sites.

Some reserves, like **Tiritiri Matangi** Island near Auckland provide nest boxes in which you can take a quick peek at little blues during the day. This can be highly entertaining as the enchanting little souls will merely look up at you with a pained expression as if to say 'Oh god, go away, you mustn't see me this fat'. Sometimes, if you encounter them on a path at night, by torchlight, they will look utterly bemused, stick their heads in the grass and point their bums in the air. Dead cute. Almost as enchanting are the endangered **Yellow-eyed penguins** of the Otago and Southland coasts. Enough is said about them in the subsequent chapters, but like the Albatross they are a must-see. Less easily encountered is the rarest penguin in the world, the **Fiordland crested penguin**. You best chance to see one of these is on the West Coast between Fox Glacier and Haast, again mainly as they come ashore at dusk or leave again at dawn.

Other notable seabird attractions include the colonies of greedy **gannets** at Murawai (near Auckland), Cape Kidnappers (near Napier, in the Hawkes Bay) and On Farewell Spit, off the northern tip of South Island. Several species of **shag** (cormorant) are also present in New Zealand. The most common are the large **black shag**, the black-and-white **pied shag** and again, as the name suggests, the petite (and again black-and-white), **little shag**. Some very rare, endemic and more colourful cousins include the **spotted shag**, the **Stewart Island shag** and **king shag**. Many other rare birds also inhabit the coastline including the **New Zealand dotterel** and one of the world's rarest birds, the **fairy tern**, of which tragically only 36 remain.

Marine mammals When it comes to **whales** the word common can only be used with extreme caution, with many species being more prevalent around the New Zealand coast than most countries worldwide. **Kaikoura** is, of course, synonymous with the whale and presents one of the best whale watching opportunities in the world. As well as its resident pods of **sperm whale**, it plays host to **humpback whales**, **southern right whales, orca** and occasionally, even the endangered and massive, **blue whale**. New Zealand is proud to host the great whales and is a world leader in promoting their conservation and the respect they so richly deserve. It certainly does not share the view that these awesome creatures that have been around for millions of years are – as one Japanese minister at the International Whaling Commission conference recently put it – 'cockroaches of the sea'. Now there's a man who needs a shark encounter without the cage! New Zealand is also a world leader in dealing with mass **whale strandings**, which are all too common, particularly in the natural trap of **Golden Bay**, at the northern tip of the South Island.

Still in the XXL department are the three Sub-Antarctic pinniped species (or seal). The **hooker's sea lion** (or New Zealand sea lion), the **leopard seal** and **southern elephant seals**. Although actual breeding is rare on the mainland, all three regularly visit the southern coast. The best place to see these soporific barrels of bad breath and wind (gas), are the Otago and Southland Coasts. Indeed, the Catlins coast in Southland often presents the opportunity to see all three species in one day – which is unheard of out of the Sub-Antarctic Islands.

Given plenty of mention throughout the text is the **New Zealand fur seal**, which is a character of infinite charm and one that you will almost certainly encounter at close range. Out of the water, their ability to look fat and lazy, break wind and scratch their privates (all at the same time), while looking at you through one eye as if you are a complete waste of space, is frankly legendary. Quite right too – having has their brains battered to near extinction around New Zealand's waters throughout the 19th century perhaps we deserve such derision. A little word of warning: do not go within 10 m of any seal that you encounter on the beach. In the water they are even more agile and can swim faster and with more grace than anything in Speedos. Underwater or on it is also the best place to encounter **seals**. Whether diving independently or on an organised seal swim, they will often check you out like a dog in the park.

Dolphins are also a major feature of New Zealand's coastal wildlife, with dolphin watching and swimming being one of the country's many world-class activities. Apart from New Zealand's 'speciality' species, the tiny and endemic **hector's dolphin** (one of the rarest in the world), and at least four others are regularly seen including, the **dusky dolphin**, the **common dolphin**, **striped dolphin** and **bottlenose dolphin.**

Offshore Islands The New Zealand coast features literally thousands of offshore islands that are proving crucial to the conservation of the country's native wildlife. Many combine to form an invaluable flotilla of '**arks**'; ultimately the only true hope for many species. Once the Department of Conservation has eradicated formerly introduced predators, for example cats, rats and possums, which involves an expensive and time-consuming poisoning and/or capture programme – the remaining small pockets of resident birds, plants and animals are encouraged to re-colonise, and captive endemic breeds can also be re-released. Some of the many species that are now reliant on the management of these 'arks' include birds like the kakapo, the kokako and takahe. Other non-avian species include the precious **tuatara**.

The most crucial of the island's re-introduction programmes concerns the ancient flightless parrot, the **kakapo**; the flagship of New Zealand conservation efforts. Only about 62 named individuals remain and each is closely monitored. The vast majority are kept on three island reserves, **Codfish Island** (off Stewart Island), **Maud Island** in the Marlborough Sounds and **Little Barrier Island**, near Auckland in the Hauraki Gulf. But the intense efforts being made to save the kakapo is, at best, merely plugging up the holes. Many species are in essence their own worst enemies, taking years and very specific habitat and environmental requirements to breed successfully. Tragically, many say it is only a matter of time.

However, to visit one of these vital reserves is to at least get a taste of the New Zealand of old and to experience the 'paradise lost'. On one of these islands you enter a world of unique and ancient wildlife that shows little fear of humans, creating a near bombardment of the senses. To encounter a kiwi at night or listen to the sublime dawn chorus of the near flightless **kokako** is one of the greatest wildlife experiences in the world. While most of the offshore islands are, understandably off limits to visitors, New Zealand is very refreshing in its attitudes towards the education and access of its endangered wildlife for the average person. The islands of **Tiritiri Matangi** (see page 125) and **Kapiti Island** off the Wellington coast (see page 406) are just two examples.

Rivers, lakes & wetlands

New Zealand is riddled with rivers, lakes and low lying wetlands all of which are home to both common, rare and unique species of animals and plants. From the rafts of mallard and black swan on **Lake Taupo**, to the endangered **brown teal** on the quiet backwaters of **Great Barrier Island**, there is much to hold your interest. Other than the brown teal, other waterfowl of particular note include the beautiful **New Zealand shoveler** and the unique **blue duck**. A resident of remote and fast flowing forest and mountain rivers, the blue duck uses highly specialised feeding methods to find algae and river insects and it is so unique it has no close relatives anywhere else in the world. Called the *whio* by Maori, which is an apt pronunciation of its call, they can sometimes be seen (or heard) from a kayak or raft, or even on the more remote tramps near mountain rivers. The rivers that feed **Lake Waikaremoana** in the **Te Urewera National Park** are just one good place to search.

Although not strictly confined to areas of wetland, another far more common duck you will almost certainly encounter in New Zealand is the **paradise shelduck**. Most often seen in pairs the male is relatively dark in colour, while the female is unmistakable with a predominantly chestnut plumage and a white head. In city parks and publicly utilised lakes they can often be approached with little protest, but in less urban areas they are shy and notoriously loud, often circling continuously overhead issuing a repetitive, high pitched call until you have left their territory.

On the lower reaches of glacial rivers, where they become vast braided beds of moraine, there are two '**waders**' that are very unique and special. The first is the **black stilt**, or kaki, of which only about 80 individuals remain, making it one of the rarest waders in the world. You can see these beautiful and fragile looking 'birds in black' on a guided tour of the DOC's captive breeding hides in **Twizel**, Canterbury. These form part of the excellent conservation and management programme put in place to protect them.

The black stilt's close cousin the **pied stilt** which is much more common and a regular sight in the shallows of lakes, estuaries and natural harbours. Again they are very delicate in stature and boast a smart, almost formal looking plumage of black and white. Also, like their pure black relative they have legs like busy knitting needles. Another unique wader with unusual appendages is the endemic **wrybill,**

The Tuatara

To describe the noble and endemic tuatara as the most ancient reptile on earth is impressive enough, but when you consider that these 'living fossils' are even older than the landscape itself, it seems truly remarkable they exist at all. They belong to a very singular order of reptiles known as 'beakheads' that once roamed the earth (be it very slowly) over 225 million years ago. Once common throughout the country, but subject to predation and a widespread loss of habitat, the tuatara, has sadly joined the long list of New Zealand creatures in decline and now exists on only 30 offshore islands. They grow to a maximum of 610 mm, live in burrows and feed mainly on ground-dwelling insects Given their status and natural habitat, your best chance of seeing a tuatara is in one of the country's zoos or museums. The ***Southland Museum*** *in Invercargill is without doubt the most famous venue, having the most successful breeding and research programme in the world. They also boast perhaps the most famous tuatara in the land –* ***'Henry'****. In appearance and mannerism tuatara generally (but Henry in particular), seem the very epitome of the word ancient and a true mascot of an older, far less manic world, before mobile phones and walkmans.Somehow, Henry, who is at least 120 years old, without expression or movement and in a time zone all of his own, makes a mockery of all this human nonsense. Yet he and his ilk are not like the human centenarian awaiting death in some old folks home, most probably devoid of dignity or normal function. Not the tuatara or Henry. He clearly looks like he has all the time in the world.*

which has a bill bent to one side. This remarkable adaptation assists this small bird in its specialist search for insects under small stones and driftwood. In winter they can be seen along with huge numbers of migratory waders at the **Miranda Naturalist's Trust Reserve** on the **Firth of Thames** south of Auckland, while in summer they join the stilts, breeding 'incognito' and well camouflaged among the moraines of the braided rivers of the South Island.

Very common in both the urban environment and especially around water is the non-native **Sacred Kingfisher**. Like its European counterpart it is a shy bird but does not share quite the same bright iridescent colours. Far less prevalent is the unmistakable **White Heron** or Kokutu. Although relatively common worldwide, there is only one colony in New Zealand, near Okarito in Westland, South Island. There around 200 birds gather between September and November to breed, before scattering throughout the country during the winter months. You can see these magnificent birds on one of the daily tours that visit the Okarito breeding colony from Whataroa, north of Franz Josef. In winter, if you find yourself in Milford Sound, look out for 'Charlie', a famous heron that has spent the last 12 winters in and around the boat terminal. Somehow, the sight of white heron in Westland seems like some eminently suitable signature to such a majestic scenic backdrop. Little wonder the Maori have always held the white heron in such high esteem. The other

far more common and smaller heron you will certainly see throughout New Zealand is the non-native **white-faced heron**.

Of course New Zealand's waterways are also home to many endemic fish and insects. Two native **eels**, the short-finned eel and the long-finned eel have been sacred to the Maori for generations and once provided an important food source. They are huge, reaching up to 2 m in length and are thought to live up to 100 years old. You can see them in many nature reserves and animal parks where they are often fed by hand. The DOC **Mount Bruce Wildlife Centre** in the Wairarapa and **Rainbow Springs** in Rotorua are just too good examples.

Lowlands & forest

Less than 25% of New Zealand is under 200 m so, despite appearances there is as much room as you think. When man arrived and set to with his short-sighted slash and burn policy, New Zealand's landscape was irrevocably altered and has now lost over 85% of its natural forest cover. The impact on the whole ecosystem has been immense; most of the native forest that remains is confined to inaccessible areas and mountain slopes, with almost a quarter of that being in South Islands' West Coast region alone.

One of the most evident yet hardly common species of the forests and low lying bush is the native **New Zealand pigeon** or **kereru**; a large, handsome colourful character, with a signature plumage of almost iridescent greens, browns, purples and white, with bright red eyes. Often heard crashing about in the leaf canopies before being spotted, they exhibit a congenial air of one who is over-fed and bring new meaning to the word plump. Little wonder the Maori prized the kereru as an important source of food. Today, despite being protected, their numbers are declining, mainly due to habitat loss and illegal hunting. The kereru can be also seen in gardens and parks, but if it remains illusive you can still see them at most animal parks and zoos. 'Pig' a rather daft Kereru residing in **Wellington Zoo** is amenable to visitors and nearly died once after swallowing a pencil!

The stitchbird, bellbird and tui are also found in the lowland and forest habitats and are New Zealand's three representatives of the **honeyeaters**. A New Zealand endemic, the **tui** is quite common throughout the country and you are bound to see, and certainly hear them. From a distance they look a dull-black colour with a distinctive white bib (that also earned it the name of the 'parson's bird'), but on closer inspection their plumage is a superb mix of iridescent blues and greens. Their song is almost legendary, a delight to listen to, but almost impossible to describe. In essence they boast a remarkable range of audible whistles, grunts and knocks – a bit like Björk on a good night. Much of the tui's repertoire is beyond our audible range which is why they often look as if someone kept the camera rolling but momentarily pressed the 'mute' button. One of the best places to see tui in large numbers is during spring in the blooming cherry trees behind the **Wairakei Golf Club**, near Taupo. There up to 30-odd birds can be seen in action, which is quite a sight and sound. The **stitchbird** and **bellbird** are not as common as the tui but are equally colourful and just marginally less melodic. They are best seen on the off-shore island reserves.

Of all the smaller birds encountered most folks' favourite is the enchanting little **fantail**. These charming little birds are a bit like butterflies on speed and your visit to New Zealand will more than once be enhanced by their inquisitive nature. While walking down any bush or forest park they will often appear from nowhere and with manic audible 'peeps' fly about your person as if deeply interested in making your acquaintance. They do this not once but for some time, flitting about and fanning their tails manically. In actuality, fantails are only interested in the insects you are disturbing within their individual territories, which is why, after a while, they

The kiwi

Of course the iconic kiwi is deserving of a special piece and no doubt you are dying to see one. Along with the platypus of Australia, or perhaps the peacock, it has to be one of the most curious and endearing creatures on earth. Almost half-bird half-mammal, it evolved over millions of years of isolation to fill a specific niche free from any predators. Although related to the ostrich of Africa, the emu of Australia and the extinct, native New Zealand moas, it is in many ways unusual and in some, absolutely unique. Flightless of course, they have no wings and their feathers are more like hairs. They are nocturnal and live in burrows. They have long whiskers almost like those of a cat, which, along with an acute sense of hearing and smell, are its ammunition in the hunt for food. It is the only bird with nostrils at the end of its beak and of course its egg-to-body weight ratio is legendary. The egg of a kiwi averages 15% of the female's body weight, compared to 2% for the ostrich. Females tend to be larger than males and when it comes to the brown kiwi, the male tends to do most of the incubating. They mate for life, sleep for almost 20 hours a day and live as long as thirty years. There are four identified species of kiwi. The ***brown kiwi****, is the most common species and the one you are most likely to see in captivity. Although relatively widespread in central and northern North Island there is only an isolated population of 160 birds occurring in the South Island at Okarito. The* ***little spotted kiwi*** *are extinct on the mainland and survive only as 1000 birds on Kapiti Island and 200 on four smaller islands. The* ***great spotted kiwi*** *is only found on the South Island and an estimated 20,000 remain. Lastly, the* ***tokoeka*** *are found on Stewart Island, Fiordland and around Haast. The tokoeka of* ***Stewart Island*** *are the only kiwi that can be seen during the day which creates something of a tourist pilgrimage to try to see them.*

The best and only chance the vast majority of visitors get to observe these quirky characters in one of the many darkened ***'kiwi houses'*** *scattered around the country. Some of the best are to be found at the Whangarei Museum, the DOC Wildlife Centre at Mount Bruce in the Wairarapa, Wellington Zoo, Orana Park in Christchurch and in Queenstown. Like so many New Zealand species, even the iconic kiwi is not immune from a tragic threat of extinction and it is feared that they too will no longer be found anywhere in the wild on mainland New Zealand within two decades. For more information on kiwi and the efforts being made to conserve them consult the website www.kiwirecovery.org.nz*

suddenly seem to lose interest. Another little charmer, that is less common and shares this behaviour, is the **tomtit**: a small, native black-and-white character that in many ways resembles the European robin. Trampers will become familiar with the tomtit, especially in South Island. New Zealand incidentally does have its own robin, the dull-coloured **New Zealand robin** which again can often be seen in the forests of both North, South and Stewart Islands.

The **morepork** is New Zealand's only native owl species. It is a small owl that feeds mainly on insects but is not impartial to the odd lesser-sized avian. Being very illusive and nocturnal, they are most often heard rather than seem and it is their distinctive butcher's shop request – 'more pork, more pork' – that earned them the name. The only other raptors (birds of prey) present in New Zealand are the native New Zealand falcon and the 'imported' **Australasian harrier**. Commonly seen soaring above hillsides and fields throughout the countryside, the harrier is often mistaken by the novice to be some sort of eagle. But eagles are much larger; the **Haast eagle**, that is now extinct but once ruled the skies in New Zealand, was over

26 times the harrier's weight and had a mammoth wing span of over 3 m, so large it would probably have been able to tackle a human.

Also with a curvaceous beak, the adorable **kaka** is one of New Zealand's three native parrot species. Once common throughout the country they are now confined mainly to old-growth beech and podocarp forests. Although unmistakable in both call and plumage the average visitor would be lucky to see one in the wild, making your best bet the zoos or DOC wildlife centres at **Mount Bruce** in the Wiararapa or Te Anau in Fiordland. At Mount Bruce, a small group has been successfully captive bred and were released locally. Now, although essentially wild, they remain in the vicinity, returning to the same spot at the same time each day to be fed. This daily spectacle provides the kind of quality entertainment of which parrots can always be relied upon and also offers a superb photo opportunity.

Even tamer than the kaka but sharing its love for a free lunch is the **weka**, a sort of flightless brown rail. Again, without any predators, the weka evolved to dispense with the need for flight and focused its hunting activity entirely to the forest floor. In modern times it is not just the forest, but the human car park and campground that offers rich pickings. If you are joined at any point by this appealing albeit uninvited guest, bear in mind they can be very persistent and notoriously quick with the steal.

Of course the lowlands and forests are also home to many non-avian species, but most of the true endemics are either reptiles or insects. Two notable exceptions are the much celebrated and impressively sounding **peripatus** and **powelliphanta**, both of which are as old as the land itself. Peripatus is like a cross between a worm and a centipede, while powelliphanta is a carnivorous land snail with a shell the size of a saucer. Both of course are remarkable creatures and were on the scene millions of years before man.

Mammals It is remarkable to think that New Zealand played host to only one mammal before he arrived, a small bat, of which two species evolved. The **log-tailed bat** and the **short-tailed bat** are rarely seen by the casual observer, living in small local populations and even then, mainly on only a few remote offshore islands. Of course in New Zealand today, besides the bat, there is now a thoroughly cosmopolitan and unsavoury list of mammalian guests. This extraordinary list of reprobates includes possums (an estimated 70 million – 20 to every person), stoats, weasels, rabbits, hares, wallabies, ferrets, rats, mice, pigs, cats, horses, deer, goats and the infamous Paul Holmes (watch NZ TV every weeknight at 1900).

Highlands

With over 75% of the country being above 200 m, this is a vast habitat that, due to its very inhospitable landscape, could never exactly be overrun with species. However, New Zealand's mountains and glacial valleys, like the rest of its ecosystem, boast a fair number of endemic animals and many unique plants that can often be spotted by the casual observer.

Most noted of the birds is of course, the notorious **kea** – the only alpine parrot in the world. This highly intelligent, entertaining, 'avian thug' lives high above the tree line, where it nests amongst rocks and feeds on just about anything edible. Although you may only ever hear them from a distance, if lucky you may encounter them at close range. If you do you are almost certainly in for a treat. Nicknamed the 'cheeky kea' – thanks to their inherently inquisitive nature and extrovert behaviour – they are particularly fascinated with cars, rucksacks and shoelaces, in fact anything that can be dismantled, demolished or preferably eaten. To have a flock descend in to the middle of your picnic is a bit like an encounter with a special class of infants, all unsupervised, out of control and with severe behavioural disorders. I say children

because that is truly how they behave and it certainly relates best to your subsequent reaction. They are so appalling, carefree and fun-loving that it is almost impossible not to just let then get on with it.

Another creature of the slopes and mountain valleys is the equally clever, but far less frivolous, **New Zealand falcon**. Quite elusive and capable of demolishing its prey like a surface-to-air-missile you would be lucky to see one, but once spotted they are unmistakable. Nothing else in New Zealand flies with such stealth or purpose, nor when it arrests momentarily (most probably still grasping its latest victim) is so stern in looks. Even keas don't mess with a falcon's lunch!

Another bird of the mountains and remote glacial valleys is the remarkable and flightless **takahe**. They are the most appealing of birds and look like some congenial, almost 'clueless', prehistoric, purple chicken. Another ancient species once thought to be extinct, they were dramatically rediscovered deep in the Murchison Mountains of Fiordland in 1948. There is now an intensive breeding programme to attempt to secure their conservation, with only about 100 birds remaining in the wild and about the same again kept in captivity or on predator-free islands. Without doubt the best place to see them is **Tiritiri Matangi** Island near Auckland, where several families (totalling about 20 birds) are allowed to roam free. Being incredibly tame and inquisitive it is both memorable and remarkable to sit amongst them and reflect on just how privileged you are in being able to do so. But, as with so many of the species on the brink, you do so perhaps with a deep sense of guilt and the overriding and worrying question – but for how much longer?

Insects New Zealand has an impressive range of creepy-crawlies, ranging from the noisy and the colourful to one that is the size of mouse. Although somewhat lacking in butterfly species and far more replete with moths, one large and perhaps familiar butterfly that you will see, especially in Auckland and the upper North Island, is the **monarch butterfly**. Famous the world over as a migratory species, these tawny-red and black-striped beauties, with a wingspan of 10 cm first arrived in New Zealand around 1840 (some say much earlier). It is very common in the urban and suburban habitats, but rarely seen in the bush or south of Christchurch. Although well known in the Americas for their swarming and long inter-state migrations, the butterflies found in New Zealand infrequently demonstrate either of these behaviours. However, like their American cousins and unlike most butterfly species, they often over-winter and live for several months.

One moth species that has a remarkable tendency to commit suicide by flying into any artificial light source at night is the large, native **puriri moth**. A beautiful lime-green colour with a wingspan of up to 15 cm, it is the country's largest moth species but is only found in the native forests of the North Island. Although the adults only live for a few days the caterpillars spend several years in tunnels bored in to trees.

By far the noisiest insect in the country is the **cicada**, which in summer and en masse can create an ear-splitting din in almost any area of bush or forest throughout the country. There are many species in New Zealand with the one of the most common being the clapping cicada which was one of the first insects noted by Joseph Banks, the naturalist accompanying Captain Cook on his first new Zealand voyage in 1769-70. They are fascinating creatures, about 30 mm in length with a wingspan up to 80 mm. The larvae of the very vocal adults can live in the ground for many years before aspiring to split eardrums. It is only the males that sing and the noise is created by the vibration of a unique ribbed structure called a 'tymbal' which resonates the sound in the almost hollow abdomen. Despite there being so many in

any given area of bush or even one tree take some time to focus on one song and try to locate the insect on the tree trunk branch or underside of leaves.

There are a number of spider species in New Zealand with the two most notable being the **katipo** and the **avondale**. The **katipo spider** is about 10 mm in length and, along with the average politician, are the only poisonous creatures in the land. Looking the part, with a shiny-black body, long legs and a red spot on its abdomen, it is a relative of the famous black widow and can deliver a nasty bite that can be incapacitating, but rarely fatal. You will doubtless be relieved to learn that they are a coastal species that frequent the undersides of logs rather than toilet seats!

The **Avondale spider** is a sub-species of the well known Australian huntsman. It is relatively harmless, but very large at over 10 cm in length. A unique, localised sub-species, found only in the suburb of Avondale in Auckland, it is an amenable easily handled species that was bred en masse in captivity and used in the film 'Arachnophobia'.

Perhaps the most remarkable native insect in New Zealand is the **glow-worm**. Although it is essentially a gnat, it is the worm-like larvae that frequent the damp limestone caves and sheltered cavities on both the North and South islands that are most famous. The sight of an ethereal 'galaxy' of glow-worms (often called 'grottoes') on the roof of a cave in the darkness, particularly at Waitomo in the Waikato is a truly memorable sight. What you are actually seeing, to put it bluntly, are the shiny bottoms of the larvae, which emit a bright blue/green light. It is a clever and remarkable mechanism and a chemical reaction known as bioluminescence used to attract insect prey; the prey flies towards the light and is caught in sticky threads that the worm hangs from like a row of fishing lines from the roof of the cave. To enter a grotto at night then emerge into a clear starlit sky is a very firm reminder of the incredible world in which we live.

Not to be outdone by a mere glowing bottom, the New Zealand **weta** is perhaps the king of all the New Zealand insects. They are an ancient creature that has been around for millions of years. A number of species are found in gardens, forests caves and rock crevices throughout the country ranging from the common tree wetas, to the cave weta and ground weta. But without doubt the most impressive is the **giant weta**. At up to 9 cm in length and weighing in at up to 80 gm they are about the size of a mouse and the largest insect in the world. With their huge abdomens, beady black eyes, long antenna and 'Alien' like legs you will either love or hate the weta. Your best bet to see one either live or dead is the country's zoos or museums. Once you see one it will incite one of two reactions: an instant and impressive 100 m dash or a deep desire to make their acquaintance. Weta are not dangerous despite a fine set of mandibles used to crunch up leaves, shoots and other small insects.

Of course, if you go anywhere near the West Coast of the South Island you will become very intimate with the infamous New Zealand **sandfly**.

Vegetation

Like the country's animal life, much of New Zealand's plant life is very beautiful, very ancient and very unique, making it a veritable paradise for any 'budding' botanist. Over 80% of the country's flowering plants are not endemic to any other land. But like the fauna, much of the country's plant life is in a worrying state of decline, not as a result of predation, but by the clear felling and burning that has taken place since the arrival of man. Tragically, only about 15% of the New Zealand's original forest cover remains. Even a brief description of New Zealand's plant species is beyond the scope of this guide, but the following are some of the most notable species that you are likely to see or hear about.

Fern species Alongside the iconic kiwi, the **ponga** or **silver fern** is New Zealand's other great national emblem and just one of a vast array of over 80 fern species. Depicted on everything from the national rugby jersey to the side of America's Cup yachts the silver fern is a common sight in both the natural and commercial world. It is found throughout the mainly subtropical bush landscape, forming stands of almost

National parks & forest parks

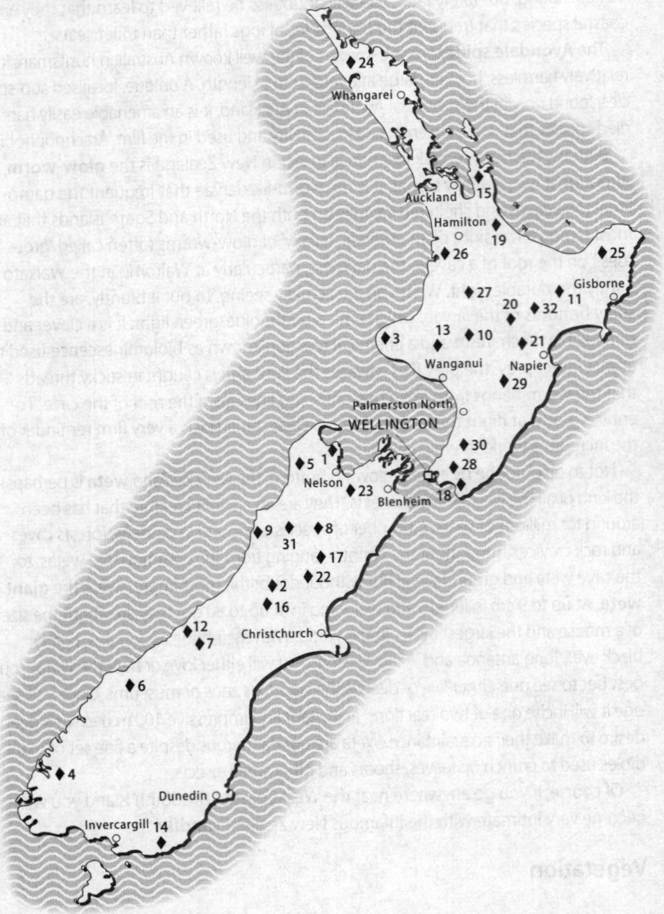

♦ **National park**
1 Abel Tasman
2 Arthur's Pass
3 Egmont
4 Fiordland
5 Kahurangi
6 Mt Aspiring
7 Mt Cook
8 Nelson Lakes
9 Paparoa
10 Tongariro
11 Urewera
12 Westland
13 Whanganui

♦ **Forest park**
14 Catlins
15 Coromandel
16 Craigieburn
17 Hanmer
18 Haurangi
19 Kaimai Mamaku
20 Kaimanawa
21 Kaweka
22 Lake Sumner
23 Mt Richmond
24 Northland
25 Raukumara
26 Pirongia
27 Pureora
28 Rimutaka
29 Ruahine
30 Tararua
31 Victoria
32 Whirinaki

N

Not to scale

prehistoric looking umbrellas. A lush green colour on top, it is the silver underside that has created their notoriety, and not just in pure aesthetics. One well known aspect of 'bush survival and rescue' is to lay out the fronds upside down in a clearing so as to capture the attention of a helicopter from above. Ferns generally have always been a very significant and sacred symbol of the Maori culture, especially in their tendency to 'unfurl' into 'being'. Often alongside the ubiquitous ponga, you will find the taller and more classic desert-island-type **nikau palm**, the **cabbage tree**, and numerous creepers, palm lilies, tree ferns and mosses.

Forest trees

The ancient New Zealand forest is traditionally one of **podocarp** and **beech trees**. Without doubt the most celebrated, yet overly utilised of the one hundred-odd forest tree species is the **kauri**. Occurring predominantly in the north of the North Island and a member of the podocarp family, it was once the dominant tree of the Auckland province and the Coromandel Peninsula. With vast trunks often over 15 m in diameter and 30 m tall, free from knots and blemishes, the kauri was prized by both the Maori for canoe building and by the early Europeans for masts and other ship-building materials. The tree's resin ('kauri gum') was also used as a derivative of varnishes and paint products and also made a medium suitable for carving into elaborate ornaments. Sadly, over 90% of the trees were harvested and only a few ancient individuals remain. Most noted of these is the impressive 1,200-year old '**Tane Mahuta**' ('Lord of the Forest') which still stands proud in the **Waipoua Forest** in Northland. Other notable podocarp species, utilised (and over-utilised) for canoes, boat building and timber generally, are the native **matai** (black pine), **rimu** (red pine), **totara, miro** and New Zealand's tallest tree – the **kahikatea** (white pine). The kahikatea can grow to over 60 m.

Another plant heavily utilised by the Maori is the tough stemmed **flax** plant, found predominantly in wetlands the length and breath of the country. It was used for everything from footwear to building.

Flowering trees

Two very colourful flowering trees, well known throughout the country, are the yellow flowering **kowhai** (New Zealand's national flower) and the red flowering **rata**, a climber that literally strangles its host tree to death. New Zealand's best known flowering tree is the beautiful **pohutukawa**; a gnarled looking coastal evergreen that bursts into bright crimson flower for three weeks in December, earning it the affectionate label as New Zealand's Christmas tree.

Endemic flowers

Of the many endemic flowers in New Zealand a large number are found in the high alpine areas, including the **Mount Cook lily**, the largest of all the buttercups. With flowers as big as its leaves it is an impressive sight, provided that is, you can find it amongst the 60 odd species of mountain daisies!

Conservation

Describing New Zealand's rich and unusual animal and plant species is an act of celebration, but it is also a sorry tale. Although the country is often dubbed '**clean and green**', many agree that it is a boast that is far more a result of low population rather than attitude. Since the arrival of man we have had a dramatic and tragic effect on the entire landscape and biodiversity of New Zealand. As a result of our presence 32% of indigenous land and freshwater birds and 18% of seabirds are now extinct. The most recent extinction occurred in 1907 with the last sighting of the beautiful huia, a relative of the kakako, which is now also endangered. Tragically, the loss of the huia occurred not only as a result of a decline in habitat, but man's ridiculous desire to adorn himself with its feathers. Many other unique and well known species have also disappeared, like the legendary **moa**, which was essentially hunted to extinction by the Maori. In the present day many others currently sit quietly on the brink and alas, the clean green land is gathering grey clouds and storms are brewing. As it stands, with endemic bird species alone, there are only 36 fairy terns remaining, 62 kakapo, about 70 Campbell Island teal, 70 taiko, 80 black stilt and 200 takahe, to name but a few. Even the kiwi, the very emblem of the nation and its people is severely under threat and without more financing, it too is expected to be completely absent on mainland New Zealand within the next two decades. To lose the kiwi itself – the very bird after which its native humans are named – seems unimaginable. One can only hope, that given its prestige, it may stir the people into action.

Government initiatives

Sterling efforts are being made in the war of conservation by governmental departments, for example the Department of Conservation, as well as independent organizations and individuals. Numerous captive breeding and predator eradication programmes have been initiated to stop, or at the very least slow down, the decline of so many species. Indeed, New Zealand is on the 'front-line' of the global conservation war and thankfully there has been some fine and victorious battles. The **black robin**, an endemic little bird found only on the Chatham Islands, is one such example and one of the most famous conservation successes in human history. From a population of only nine individuals in the mid 1970s, it has essentially been saved and now numbers around 250. But these battles all defy the short-sighted, financial and technologically driven society of the modern day. Since the very act of conservation is a drain of funds rather than a source, DOC are always under-funded and under-researched and it seems, tragically, a war that can perhaps never be won. Eco-tourism does offers a viable path in some areas but it is just part of a long and difficult climb towards salvation

Paradise Lost

In the New Zealand of today, the great clean, green land – the paradise, but really the paradise lost – it almost makes the heart cry to experience the deathly hush of forests once alive to the sound of birds. At times it really is like standing in an ancient church that has been sacked of all its contents and robbed of both congregation and choir. Instead of a heads held high in celebration, the whispers of prayer and beautiful arias of worship, the pose is one of despair, the atmosphere one of remorseful reflection and the sound, one of eternal silence. To lose the kakapo, the kokako or the kiwi itself, all species that have been around for millions of years is too tragic to contemplate.

19

Footnotes

Footnotes

Glossary of Maori Words

Aotearoa New Zealand
Ariki tribal leader
Atua spiritual being
Harakeke flax plant, leaves
Hawaiki ancestral Polynesian homeland
Hapu sub-tribe/to be pregnant
He Ao a land or a world
He tangata the people
Iwi tribe
Kaikaiawaro a dolphin (Pelorus Jack) who cruised the Sounds and became a guardian for iwi
Kaitiaki protector, caretaker
Kapa haka group of Maori performers
Kiaora welcome
Kaumatua elders
Kawa protocols
Kete basket
Kowhaiwhai rafter patterns
Mana integrity, prestige, control
Manawhenua people with tribal affiliations with the area
Maoritanga Maoriness
Marae sacred courtyard or plaza
Mauri life essence
Moana large body of water, sea
Moko tattoo
Muka flax fibre
Ngati people of
Pa a fortified residential area
Poi ball attached to flax string
Pounamu sacred greenstone
Rangatira tribal leader
Taiaha a fighting staff
Tangata people/person
Tangihanga death ritual
Taonga treasure, prized object (often passed down by ancestors)
Tapu sacred, out of bounds
Te Ika-a-Maui North Island
Tipuna ancestor
Tukutuku wall panels
Utu cost
Wahakatauki proverb or saying
Waiata song, flute music
Wairua soul
Waka canoe
Whakairo carving
Whakapapa origins of genealogy
Whanau extended family/to give birth
Whare house
Whenua land

Sales & distribution

Footprint Handbooks
6 Riverside Court
Lower Bristol Road
Bath BA2 3DZ England
T 01225 469141
F 01225 469461
discover
@footprintbooks.com

Australia
Peribo Pty
58 Beaumont Road
Mt Kuring-Gai
NSW 2080
T 02 9457 0011
F 02 9457 0022

Austria
Freytag-Berndt Artaria
Kohlmarkt 9
A-1010 Wien
T 01533 2094
F 01533 8685

Freytag-Berndt
Sporgasse 29
A-8010 Graz
T 0316 818230
F 3016 818230-30

Belgium
Craenen BVBA
Mechelsesteenweg 633
B-3020 Herent
T 016 23 90 90
F 016 23 97 11

Waterstones
The English Bookshop
Blvd Adolphe Max 71-75
B-1000 Brussels
T 02 219 5034

Canada
Ulysses Travel Publications
4176 rue Saint-Denis
Montréal
Québec H2W 2M5
T 514 843 9882
F 514 843 9448

Europe
Bill Bailey
16 Devon Square
Newton Abbott
Devon TQ12 2HR. UK
T 01626 331079
F 01626 331080

Denmark
Nordisk Korthandel
Studiestraede 26-30 B
DK-1455 Copenhagen K
T 3338 2638
F 3338 2648

Scanvik Books
Esplanaden 8B
DK-1263 Copenhagen K
T 3312 7766
F 3391 2882

Finland
Akateeminen Kirjakauppa
Keskuskatu 1
FIN-00100 Helsinki
T 09 121 4151
F 09 121 4441

Suomalainen Kirjakauppa
Koivuvaarankuja 2
01640 Vantaa 64
F 09 852751

France
FNAC – major branches

Guides Gallimard
Les Nouveaux Loisirs
5 rue Sébastien-Bottin
75007 Paris
T 00331 4954 1649
F 00331 4544 3945

L'Astrolabe
46 rue de Provence
F-75009 Paris 9e
T 01 42 85 42 95
F 01 45 75 92 51

Germany
GeoCenter ILH
Schockenriedstrasse 44
D-70565 Stuttgart
T 0711 781 94610
F 0711 781 94654

Brettschneider
Feldkirchnerstrasse 2
D-85551 Heimstetten
T 089 990 20330
F 089 990 20331

Geobuch
Rosental 6
D-80331 München
T 089 265030
F 089 263713

Gleumes
Hohenstaufenring 47-51
D-50674 Köln
T 0221 215650

Globetrotter Ausrustungen
Wiesendamm 1
D-22305 Hamburg
T040 679 66190
F 040 679 66183

Dr Götze
Bleichenbrücke 9
D-2000 Hamburg 1
T 040 3031 1009-0

Hugendubel Buchhandlung
Nymphenburgerstrasse 25
D-80335 München
T 089 238 9412
F 089 550 1853

Kiepert Buchhandlung
Hardenbergstrasse 4-5
D-10623 Berlin 12
T 030 311 880
F 030 311 88120

Greece
GC Eleftheroudakis
17 Panepistemiou
Athens 105 64
T 01 331 4180-83
F 01 323 9821

India
Roli Books
M-75 GK II Market
New Delhi 110048
T (011) 646 0886
F (011) 646 7185

Israel
Eco Trips
20a Ben Yehuda Street
Tel Aviv 63802
T 03 528 2811
F 03 528 8269

For a fuller list, see www.footprintbooks.com

Italy
Librimport
Via Biondelli 9
I-20141 Milano
T 02 8950 1422
F 02 8950 2811

Libreria del Viaggiatore
Via dell Pelegrino 78
I-00186 Roma
T/F 06 688 01048

Netherlands
Nilsson & Lamm bv
Postbus 195
Pampuslaan 212
N-1380 AD Weesp
T 0294 494949
F 0294 494455

Waterstones
Kalverstraat 152
1012 XE Amsterdam
T 020 638 3821

New Zealand
Auckland Map Centre
Dymocks

Norway
Schibsteds Forlag A/S
Akersgata 32 - 5th Floor
Postboks 1178 Sentrum
N-0107 Oslo
T 22 86 30 00
F 22 42 54 92

Tanum
Karl Johansgate 37-41
PO Box 1177 Sentrum
N-0107 Oslo 1
T 22 41 11 00
F 22 33 32 75

Olaf Norlis
Universitetsgt 24
N-1062 Oslo
T 22 00 43 00

Pakistan
Pak-American Commercial
Hamid Chambers
Zaib-un Nisa Street
Saddar, PO Box 7359
Karachi
T 21 566 0418
F 21 568 3611

South Africa
Faradawn CC
PO Box 1903
Saxonwold 2132
T 011 885 1787
F 011 885 1829

South America
Humphrys Roberts
Associates
Caixa Postal 801-0
Ag. Jardim da Gloria
06700-970 Cotia SP
Brazil
T 011 492 4496
F 011 492 6896

Southeast Asia
APA Publications
38 Joo Koon Road
Singapore 628990
T 865 1600
F 861 6438

In Hong Kong, Malaysia, Singapore and Thailand: MPH, Kinokuniya, Times

Spain
Altaïr
C/Balmes 69
08007 Barcelona
T 933 233062
F 934 512559

Altaïr
Gaztambide 31
28015 Madrid
T 0915 435300
F 0915 443498

Libros de Viaje
C/Serrano no 41
28001 Madrid
T 01 91 577 9899
F 01 91 577 5756

Il Corte Inglés – major branches

Sweden
Hedengrens Bokhandel
PO Box 5509
S-11485 Stockholm
T 08 611 5132

Kart Centrum
Vasagatan 16
S-11120 Stockholm
T 08 411 1697

Kartforlaget
Skolgangen 10
S-80183 Gavle
T 026 633000
F 026 124204

Lantmateriet Kartbutiken
Kungsgatan 74
S-11122 Stockholm
T 08 202 303
F 08 202 711

Switzerland
Office du Livre OLF
ZI3, Corminboeuf
CH-1701 Fribourg
T 026 467 5111
F 026 467 5666

Buchzentrum AG
Postfach
CH-4601 Olten
T 062 209 2525
F 062 209 2627

Travel Bookshop
Rindermarkt 20
Postfach 216
CH-8001 Zürich
T 01 252 3883
F 01 252 3832

Tanzania
A Novel Idea
The Slipway
PO Box 76513
Dar es Salaam
T/F 051 601088

USA
Publishers Group West
1700 Fourth Street
Berkeley
CA 94710
T 510 528 1444
F 510 528 9555

Barnes & Noble, Borders, specialist travel bookstores

Footprint travel list

Footprint publish travel guides to over 120 countries worldwide. Each guide is packed with practical, concise and colourful information for everybody from first-time travellers to travel aficionados. The list is growing fast and current titles are noted below. For further information check out the website **www.footprintbooks.com**

Andalucía Handbook
Argentina Handbook
Bali & the Eastern Isles Hbk
Bangkok & the Beaches Hbk
Barcelona Handbook
Bolivia Handbook
Brazil Handbook
Cambodia Handbook
Caribbean Islands Handbook
Central America & Mexico Hbk
Chile Handbook
Colombia Handbook
Costa Rica Handbook
Cuba Handbook
Cusco & the Sacred Valley Hbk
Dominican Republic Handbook
Dublin Handbook
East Africa Handbook
Ecuador & Galápagos Handbook
Edinburgh Handbook
Egypt Handbook
Goa Handbook
Guatemala Handbook
India Handbook
Indian Himalaya Handbook
Indonesia Handbook
Ireland Handbook
Israel Handbook
Jordan Handbook
Laos Handbook
Libya Handbook
London Handbook
Malaysia Handbook
Marrakech & the High Atlas Hbk
Myanmar Handbook
Mexico Handbook
Morocco Handbook
Namibia Handbook
Nepal Handbook
New Zealand Handbook
Nicaragua Handbook
Pakistan Handbook
Peru Handbook
Rajasthan & Gujarat Handbook
Rio de Janeiro Handbook
Scotland Handbook
Scotland Highlands & Islands Hbk
Singapore Handbook
South Africa Handbook
South American Handbook
South India Handbook
Sri Lanka Handbook
Sumatra Handbook
Syria & Lebanon Handbook
Thailand Handbook
Tibet Handbook
Tunisia Handbook
Turkey Handbook
Venezuela Handbook
Vietnam Handbook

Also available from Footprint
Traveller's Handbook
Traveller's Healthbook
Traveller's Internet Guide

Available at all good bookshops

Footprint Handbooks: a brief history

1924	First ***South American Handbook*** published for the business traveller by the *Royal Mail Steam Packet Company*.
1972	The printer of the *Handbook*, John Dawson buys the rights to the guidebook and forms *Trade & Travel* to continue publishing it.
1988	John and his sons, James and Patrick, begin publishing guides to destinations other than South America – *Caribbean Islands* is the first.
1997	Company name is changed to Footprint Handbooks, there are 15 titles in print.
1997-1998	As new editions are published, the livery of the books is changed from the cream of *Trade & Travel* to the multicolours of *Footprint*, though the books remain in hardback.
1998	The 1999 edition is the 75th annual edition of the *South American Handbook* – it has been updated every single year since 1924 (right through the Second World War) and is the longest running guidebook in the English language.
1999	In the second phase of the development of the series, titles are published in paperback for the first time, with totally redesigned text pages, colour highlights pages and colour maps.
2001	There are 60 travel guides in the series and many more in the pipeline.

What the papers say

"I carried the South American Handbook from Cape Horn to Cartagena and consulted it every night for two and a half months. I wouldn't do that for anything else except my hip flask."
Michael Palin, BBC Full Circle

"The titles in the Footprint Handbooks series are about as comprehensive as travel guides get."
Travel Reference Library

"If 'the essence of real travel' is what you have been secretly yearning for all these years, then Footprint are the guides for you."
Under 26 magazine

"Excellent, best buy whether travelling independently or with a tour operator."
Adventure Travel

"Footprint can be depended on for accurate travel information and for imparting a deep sense of respect for the lands and people they cover."
World News

"Footprint Handbooks, the best of the best."
Le Monde, Paris

Mail order

Available worldwide in bookshops and on-line. Footprint travel guides can also be ordered directly from us in Bath, via our website **www.footprintbooks.com** or from the address on the imprint page of this book.

Index

Footnotes

Footnotes

Footnotes

Footnotes

Footnotes

Map index

Shorts

Will you help us?

We try as hard as we can to make each Footprint Handbook as up-to-date and accurate as possible but, of course, things always change. Many people email or write to us – with corrections, new information, or simply comments. If you want to let us know about your experiences and adventures – be they good, bad or ugly – then don't delay; we're dying to hear from you. And please try to include all the relevant details and juicy bits. Your help will be greatly appreciated, especially by other travellers. In return we will send you details about our special guidebook offer.

email Footprint at:
new1_online@footprintbooks.com

or write to:

Elizabeth Taylor
Footprint Handbooks
6 Riverside Court
Lower Bristol Road
Bath
BA2 3DZ
UK

New Zealand

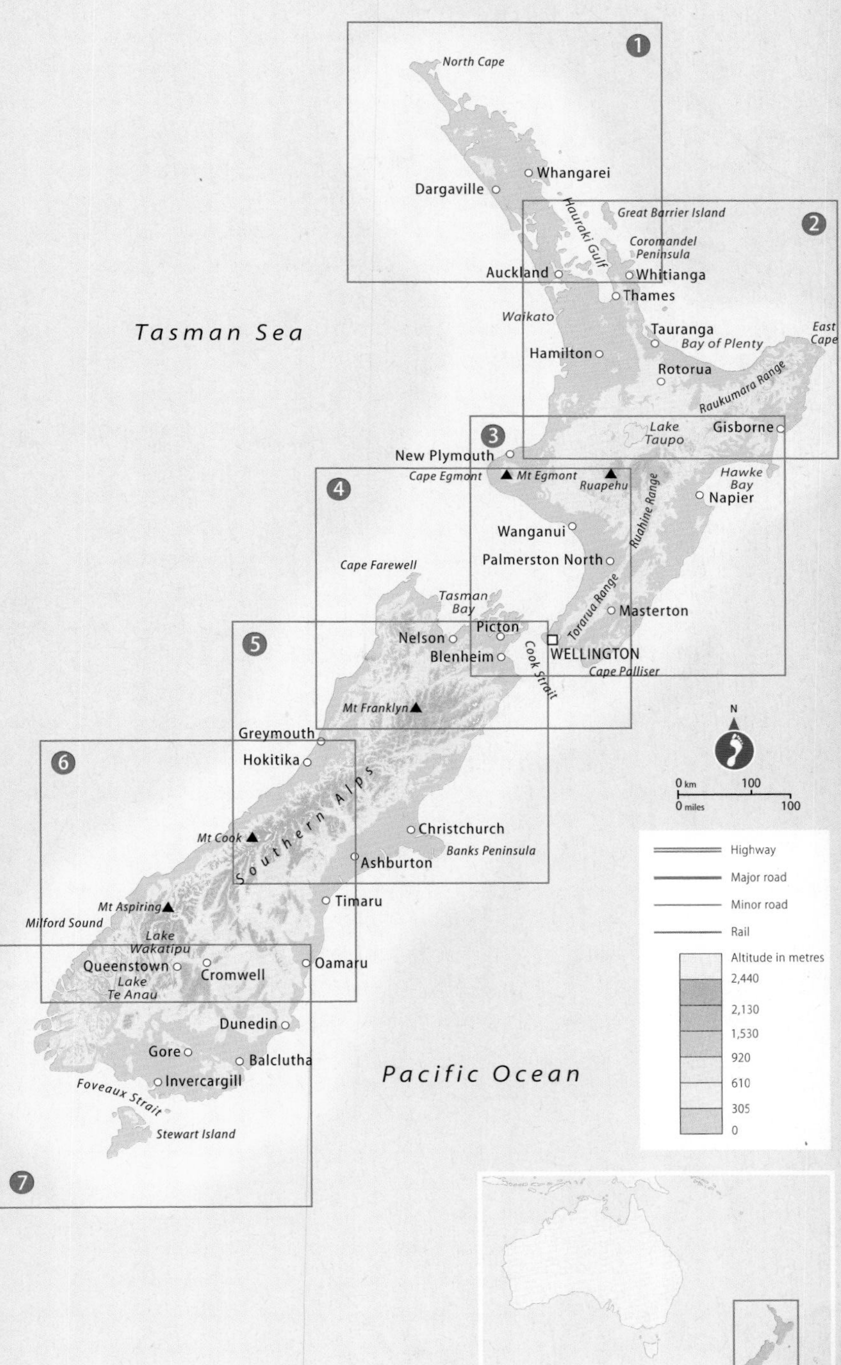

1
2
3
4
5
6
7
North Cape
Whangarei
Dargaville
Hauraki Gulf
Great Barrier Island
Coromandel Peninsula
Auckland
Whitianga
Thames
Waikato
Tasman Sea
Tauranga
Bay of Plenty
East Cape
Hamilton
Rotorua
Raukumara Range
Lake Taupo
Gisborne
New Plymouth
Cape Egmont
Mt Egmont
Ruapehu
Hawke Bay
Napier
Ruahine Range
Wanganui
Palmerston North
Cape Farewell
Tasman Bay
Tararua Range
Masterton
Picton
Nelson
Blenheim
WELLINGTON
Cook Strait
Cape Palliser
Mt Franklyn
Greymouth
Hokitika
Southern Alps
Mt Cook
Christchurch
Banks Peninsula
Ashburton
Timaru
Mt Aspiring
Milford Sound
Lake Wakatipu
Queenstown
Cromwell
Oamaru
Lake Te Anau
Dunedin
Gore
Balclutha
Invercargill
Foveaux Strait
Stewart Island
Pacific Ocean
N
0 km
100
0 miles
100
Highway
Major road
Minor road
Rail
Altitude in metres
2,440
2,130
1,530
920
610
305
0

Map 1 North Island

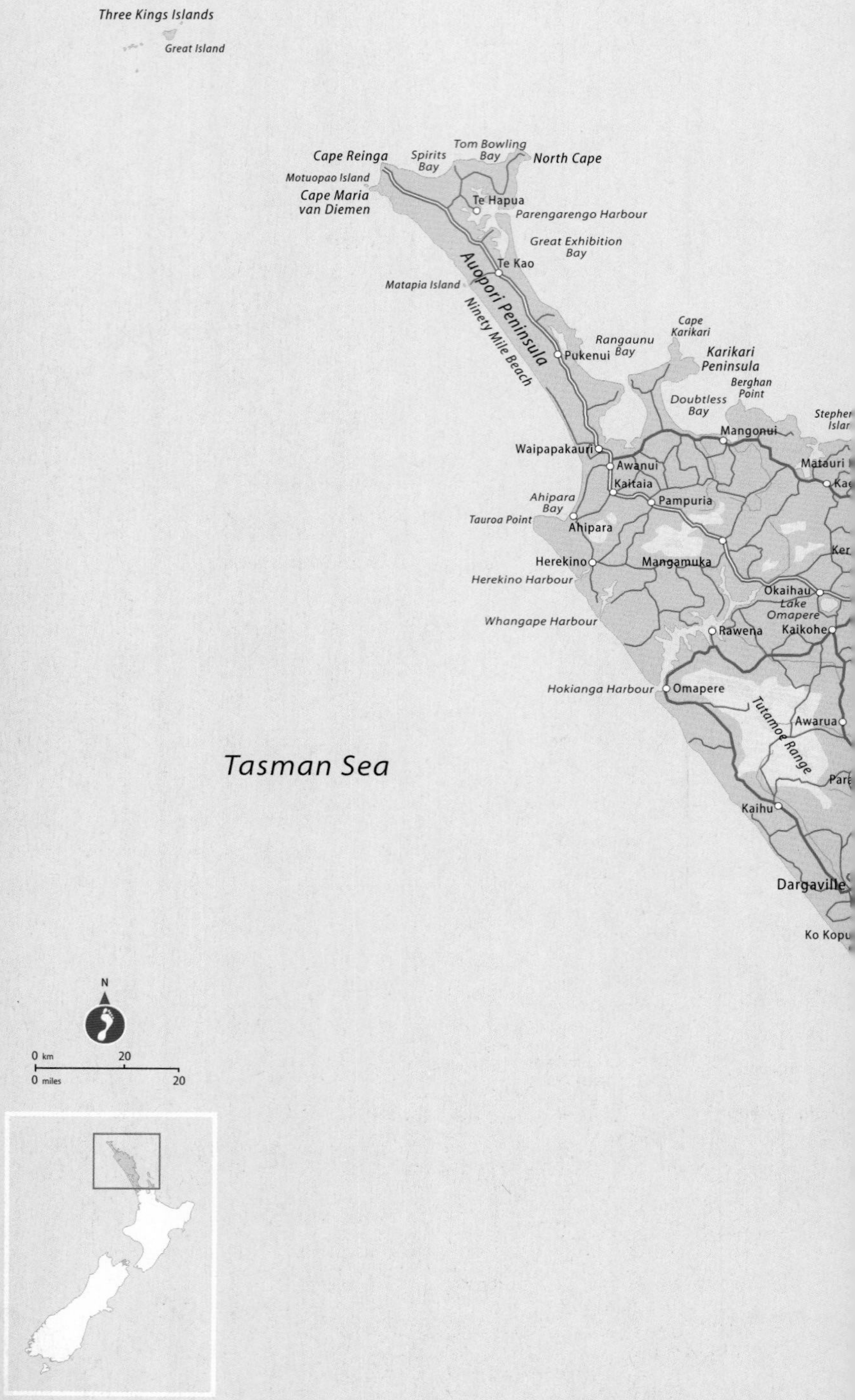

Three Kings Islands
Great Island
Cape Reinga
Spirits Bay
Tom Bowling Bay
North Cape
Motuopao Island
Cape Maria van Diemen
Te Hapua
Parengarengo Harbour
Great Exhibition Bay
Te Kao
Matapia Island
Auopori Peninsula
Ninety Mile Beach
Cape Karikari
Rangaunu Bay
Karikari Peninsula
Pukenui
Berghan Point
Doubtless Bay
Stephen Islar
Mangonui
Waipapakauri
Matauri
Awanui
Kaitaia
Kae
Ahipara Bay
Pampuria
Tauroa Point
Ahipara
Ker
Herekino
Mangamuka
Herekino Harbour
Okaihau
Lake Omapere
Whangape Harbour
Rawena
Kaikohe
Hokianga Harbour
Omapere
Tutamoe Range
Awarua
Tasman Sea
Pare
Kaihu
Dargaville
Ko Kopu

N

0 km 20
0 miles 20

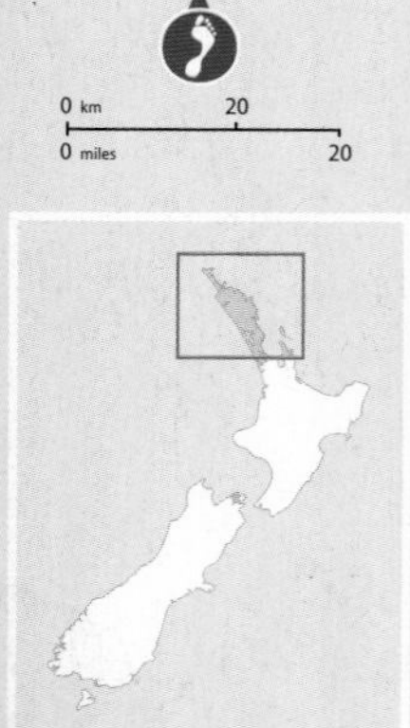

Pacific Ocean

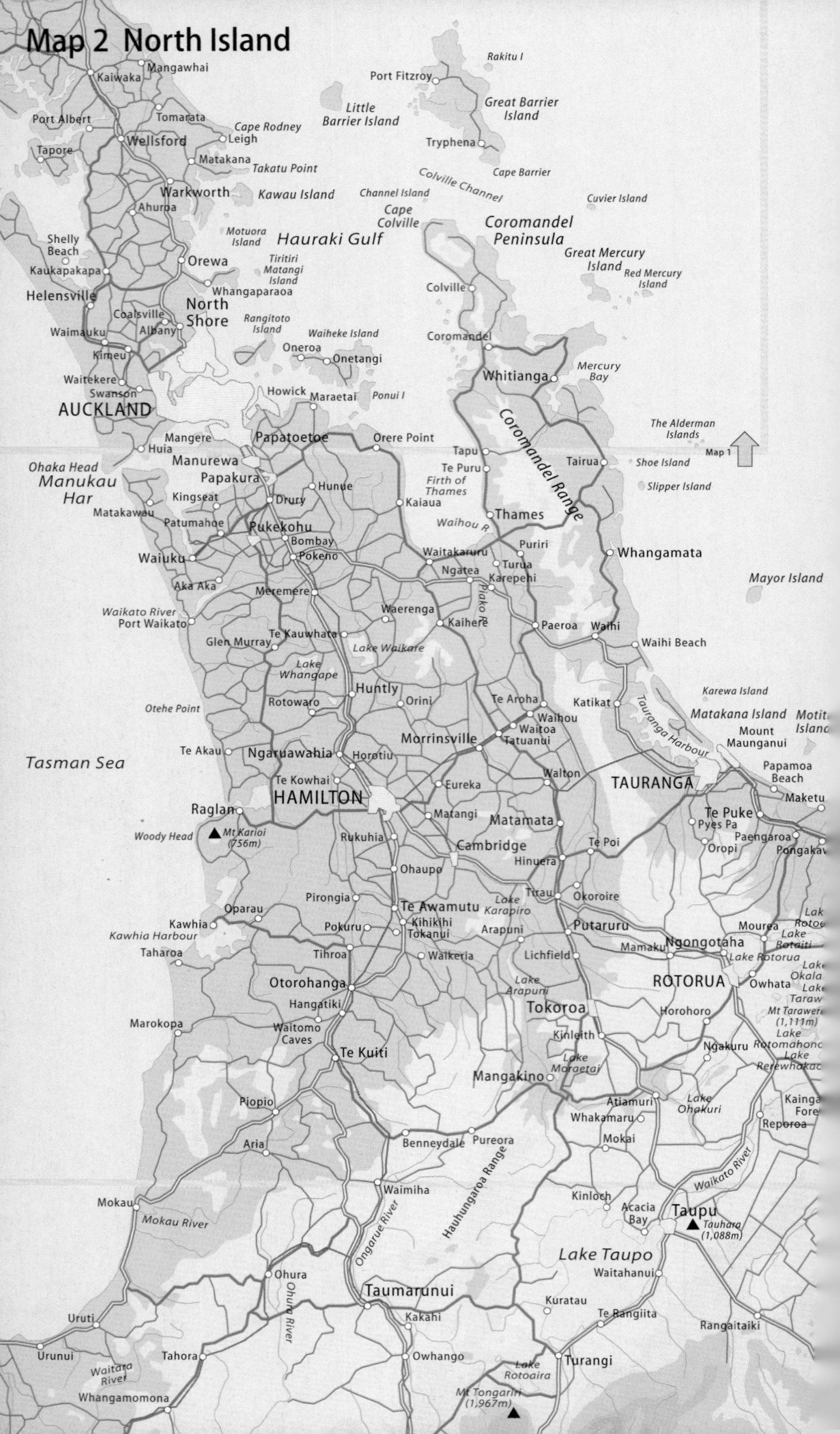

Map 2 North Island
Rakitu I
Mangawhai
Kaiwaka
Port Fitzroy
Little Barrier Island
Great Barrier Island
Port Albert
Tomarata
Cape Rodney
Leigh
Wellsford
Tryphena
Tapore
Matakana
Takatu Point
Cape Barrier
Colville Channel
Warkworth
Kawau Island
Channel Island
Cuvier Island
Ahuroa
Cape Colville
Coromandel Peninsula
Motuora Island
Hauraki Gulf
Shelly Beach
Great Mercury Island
Orewa
Tiritiri Matangi Island
Red Mercury Island
Kaukapakapa
Whangaparaoa
Colville
Helensville
North Shore
Coalsville
Rangitoto Island
Albany
Waimauku
Waiheke Island
Coromandel
Oneroa
Onetangi
Kimeu
Whitianga
Mercury Bay
Waitekere
Swanson
Howick
Maraetai
Ponui I
AUCKLAND
Coromandel Range
The Alderman Islands
Mangere
Papatoetoe
Orere Point
Huia
Tapu
Map 1
Manurewa
Tairua
Ohaka Head
Te Puru
Shoe Island
Manukau Har
Papakura
Firth of Thames
Hunue
Slipper Island
Kingseat
Drury
Kaiaua
Matakawau
Thames
Patumahoe
Waihou R
Pukekohu
Bombay
Puriri
Waiuku
Pokeno
Waitakaruru
Whangamata
Turua
Ngatea
Karepehi
Mayor Island
Aka Aka
Meremere
Piako R
Waerenga
Waikato River
Port Waikato
Kaihere
Paeroa
Waihi
Te Kauwhata
Waihi Beach
Glen Murray
Lake Waikare
Lake Whangape
Huntly
Karewa Island
Rotowaro
Orini
Te Aroha
Katikat
Otehe Point
Waihou
Tauranga Harbour
Matakana Island
Waitoa
Tatuanui
Mount Maunganui
Morrinsville
Te Akau
Ngaruawahia
Horotiu
Tasman Sea
Walton
Papamoa Beach
Te Kowhai
TAURANGA
Eureka
HAMILTON
Maketu
Raglan
Matangi
Matamata
Te Puke
Pyes Pa
Mt Karioi (756m)
Woody Head
Rukuhia
Paengaroa
Te Poi
Oropi
Cambridge
Hinuera
Ohaupo
Tirau
Okoroire
Pirongia
Lake Karapiro
Te Awamutu
Oparau
Kihikihi
Putaruru
Kawhia
Pokuru
Arapuni
Mourea
Kawhia Harbour
Tokanui
Ngongotaha
Mamaku
Lake Rotorua
Taharoa
Tihiroa
Waikeria
Lichfield
Otorohanga
ROTORUA
Owhata
Lake Arapuni
Hangatiki
Tokoroa
Marokopa
Horohoro
Mt Tarawera (1,111m)
Waitomo Caves
Kinleith
Te Kuiti
Ngakuru
Lake Maraetai
Mangakino
Piopio
Atiamuri
Lake Ohakuri
Whakamaru
Reporoa
Aria
Benneydale
Pureora
Mokai
Hauhungaroa Range
Waikato River
Waimiha
Mokau
Kinloch
Acacia Bay
Taupu
Ongarue River
Tauhara (1,088m)
Mokau River
Lake Taupo
Ohura
Waitahanui
Taumarunui
Ohura River
Kuratau
Uruti
Kakahi
Te Rangiita
Rangaitaiki
Urunui
Tahora
Owhango
Turangi
Waitara River
Lake Rotoaira
Whangamomona
Mt Tongariri (1,967m)

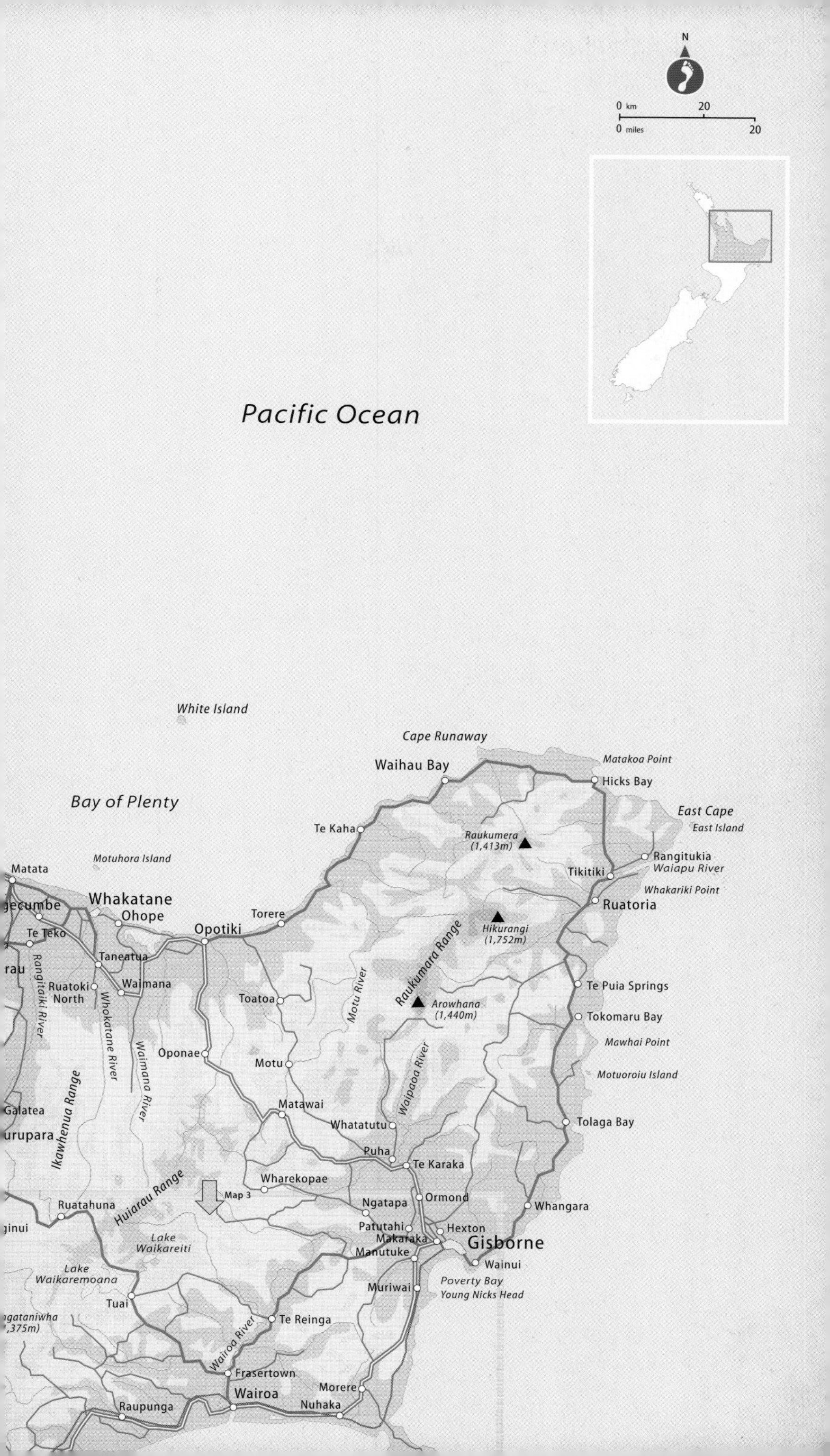

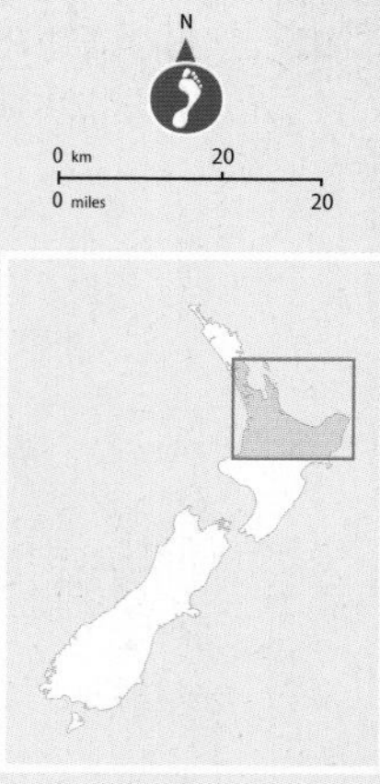

Pacific Ocean

White Island

Cape Runaway

Waihau Bay

Matakoa Point

Hicks Bay

Bay of Plenty

East Cape

East Island

Te Kaha

Raukumera (1,413m)

Motuhora Island

Rangitukia

Waiapu River

Matata

Tikitiki

Whakariki Point

Whakatane

Ruatoria

gecumbe

Ohope

Torere

Hikurangi (1,752m)

Te Teko

Opotiki

Raukumara Range

Taneatua

rau

Rangitaiki River

Ruatoki North

Waimana

Motu River

Te Puia Springs

Toatoa

Arowhana (1,440m)

Tokomaru Bay

Whokatane River

Waimana River

Mawhai Point

Oponae

Waipaoa River

Motu

Motuoroiu Island

Ikawhenua Range

Galatea

Matawai

Whatatutu

Tolaga Bay

urupara

Puha

Te Karaka

Wharekopae

Map 3

Ormond

Huiarau Range

Ruatahuna

Ngatapa

Whangara

ginui

Patutahi

Hexton

Lake Waikareiti

Makaraka

Gisborne

Manutuke

Wainui

Lake Waikaremoana

Poverty Bay

Muriwai

Young Nicks Head

Tuai

ngataniwha (1,375m)

Te Reinga

Wairoa River

Frasertown

Morere

Wairoa

Raupunga

Nuhaka

Map 3 North Island

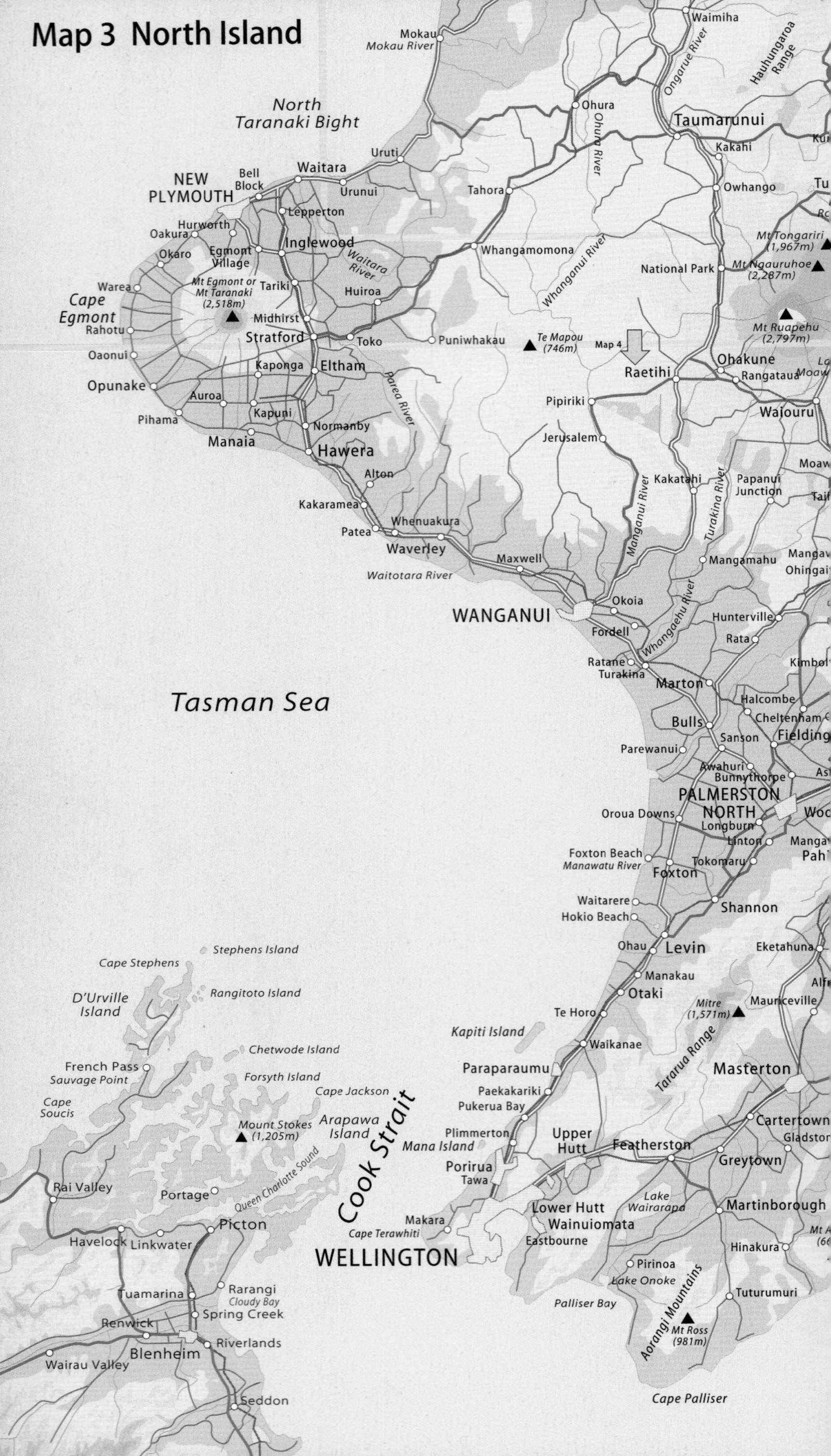

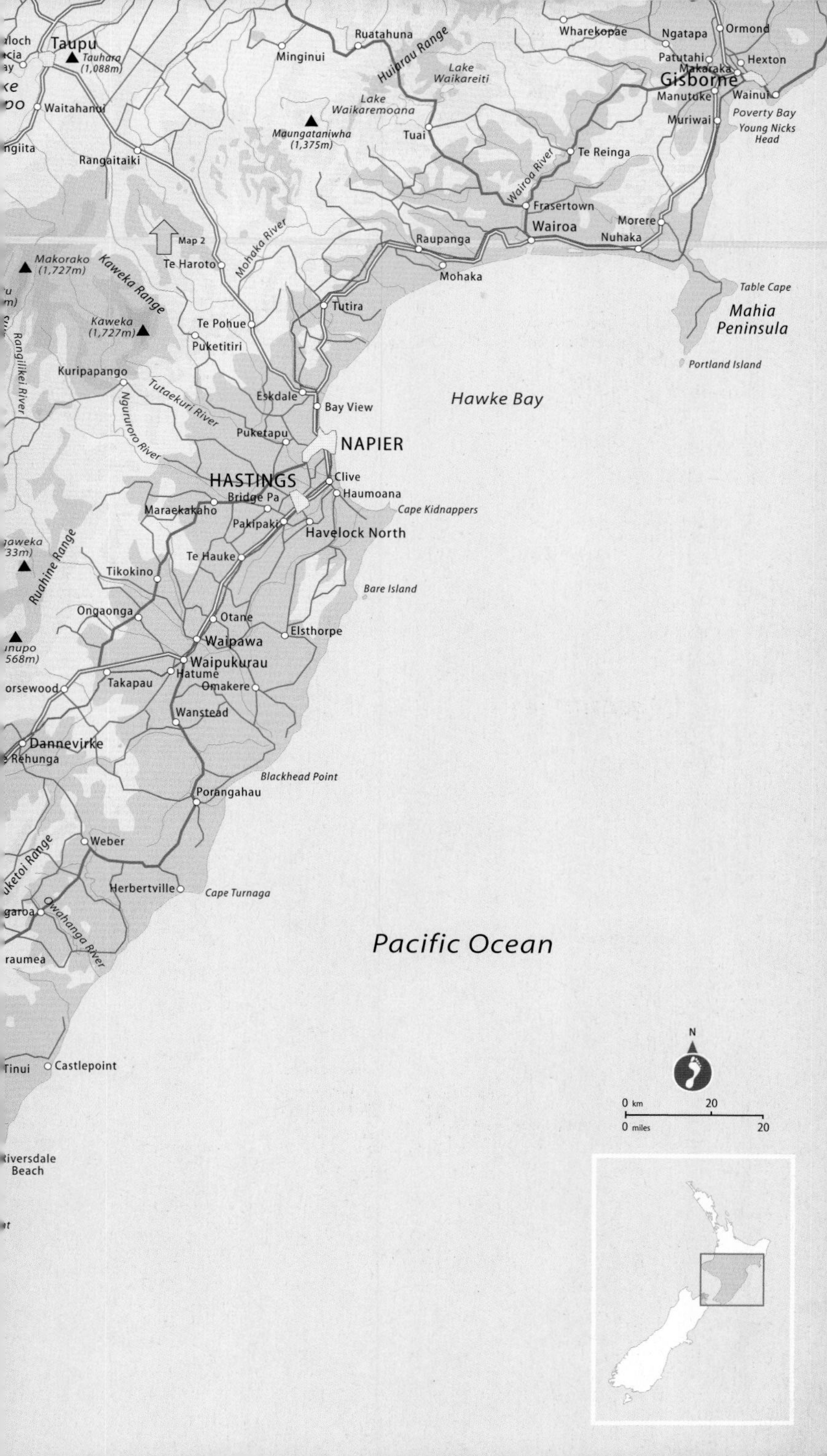

Taupu
Tauhara (1,088m)
Waitahanui
Rangaitaiki
Minginui
Ruatahuna
Huiarau Range
Lake Waikareiti
Lake Waikaremoana
Maungataniwha (1,375m)
Tuai
Wharekopae
Ngatapa
Ormond
Patutahi
Makaraka
Hexton
Gisborne
Manutuke
Wainui
Muriwai
Poverty Bay
Young Nicks Head
Te Reinga
Wairoa River
Frasertown
Wairoa
Morere
Nuhaka
Raupanga
Mohaka
Table Cape
Mahia Peninsula
Portland Island
Map 2
Te Haroto
Mohaka River
Makorako (1,727m)
Kaweka Range
Kaweka (1,727m)
Te Pohue
Puketitiri
Tutira
Rangitikei River
Kuripapango
Tutaekuri River
Ngururoro River
Eskdale
Bay View
Hawke Bay
Puketapu
NAPIER
HASTINGS
Clive
Haumoana
Bridge Pa
Maraekakaho
Cape Kidnappers
Pakipaki
Havelock North
Te Hauke
Ruahine Range
Tikokino
Bare Island
Ongaonga
Otane
Waipawa
Elsthorpe
Waipukurau
Hatume
Takapau
Omakere
Wanstead
Dannevirke
Rehunga
Blackhead Point
Porangahau
Weber
Herbertville
Cape Turnaga
Owahanga River
Pacific Ocean
Castlepoint
N
0 km
20
0 miles
20

Map 4 South Island

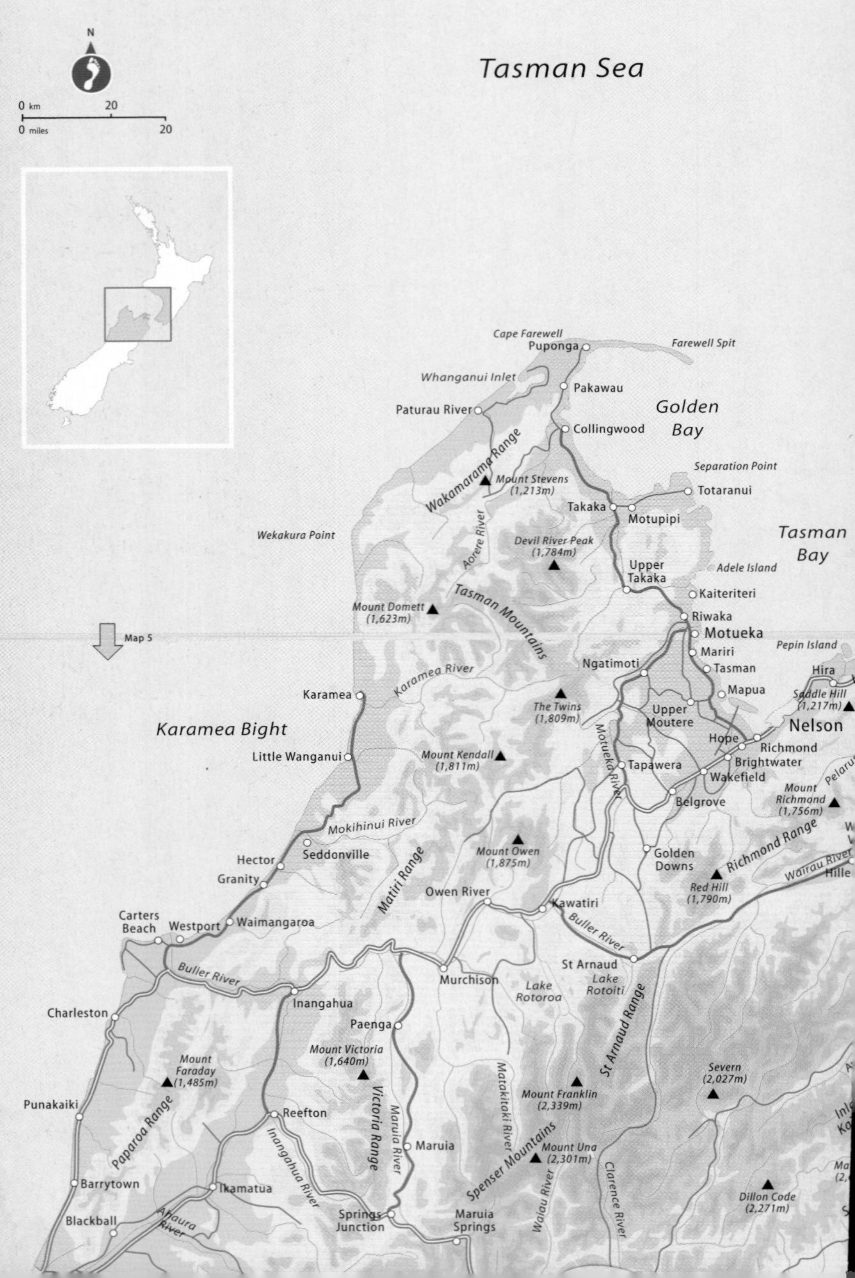

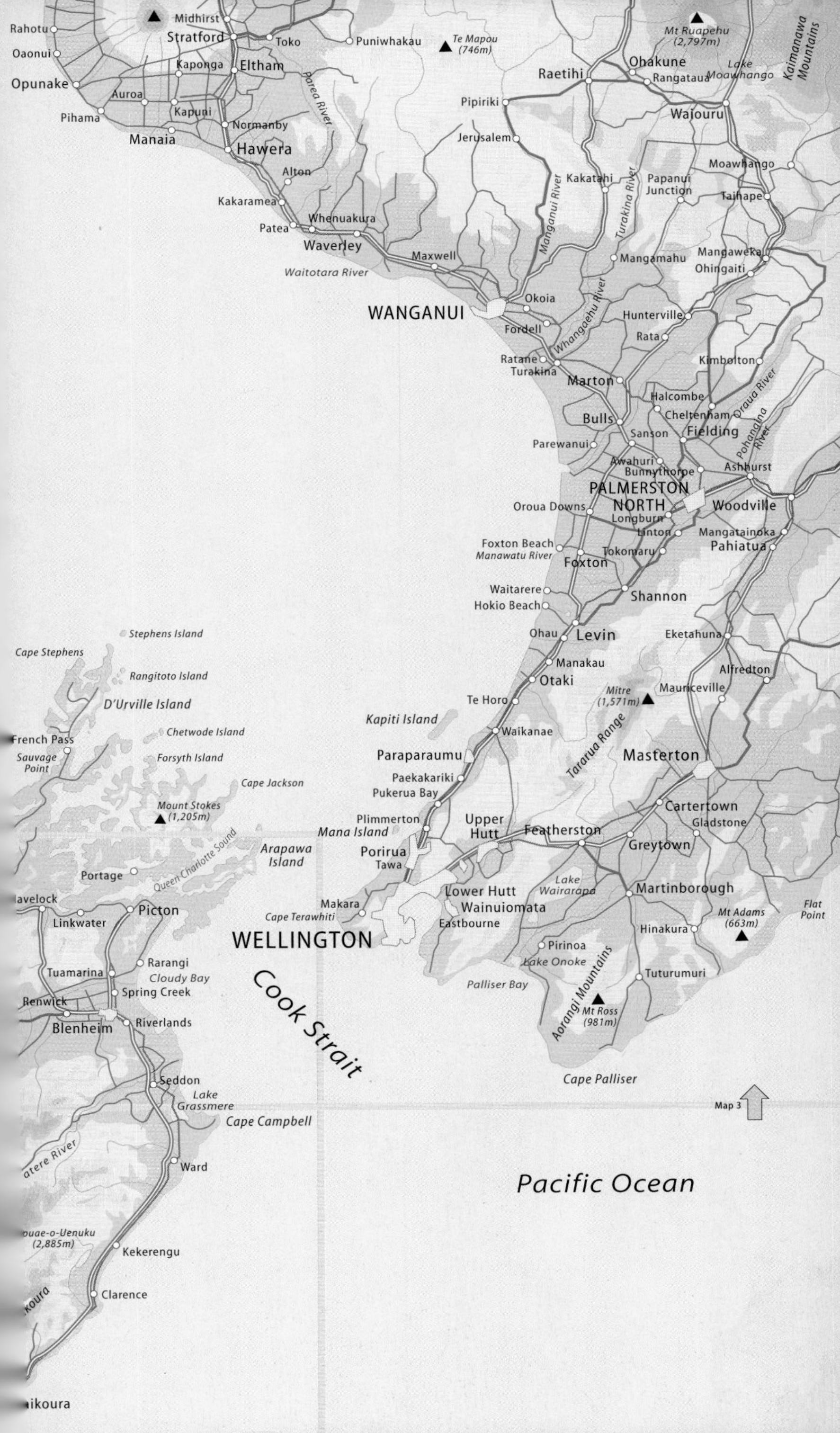

Rahotu
Midhirst
Stratford
Toko
Puniwhakau
Te Mapou
(746m)
Mt Ruapehu
(2,797m)
Kaimanawa Mountains
Oaonui
Kaponga
Eltham
Opunake
Auroa
Kapuni
Pihama
Normanby
Manaia
Hawera
Patea River
Raetihi
Ohakune
Rangataua
Lake Moawhango
Pipiriki
Waiouru
Jerusalem
Moawhango
Alton
Kakaramea
Patea
Whenuakura
Waverley
Maxwell
Waitotara River
Kakatahi
Manganui River
Turakina River
Papanui Junction
Taihape
Mangamahu
Mangaweka
Ohingaiti
WANGANUI
Okoia
Fordell
Whangaehu River
Hunterville
Rata
Ratane
Turakina
Kimbolton
Marton
Halcombe
Cheltenham
Oroua River
Bulls
Sanson
Fielding
Pohangina River
Parewanui
Awahuri
Bunnythorpe
Ashhurst
PALMERSTON NORTH
Oroua Downs
Longburn
Woodville
Linton
Mangatainoka
Foxton Beach
Manawatu River
Tokomaru
Pahiatua
Foxton
Waitarere
Shannon
Hokio Beach
Ohau
Levin
Eketahuna
Manakau
Alfredton
Otaki
Mitre
(1,571m)
Mauriceville
Te Horo
Waikanae
Tararua Range
Masterton
Stephens Island
Cape Stephens
Rangitoto Island
D'Urville Island
Kapiti Island
Chetwode Island
French Pass
Sauvage Point
Forsyth Island
Paraparaumu
Paekakariki
Pukerua Bay
Cape Jackson
Mount Stokes
(1,205m)
Plimmerton
Mana Island
Upper Hutt
Featherston
Cartertown
Gladstone
Greytown
Arapawa Island
Queen Charlotte Sound
Porirua
Tawa
Portage
Lake Wairarapa
Lower Hutt
Martinborough
Wainuiomata
Eastbourne
Makara
Cape Terawhiti
Linkwater
Picton
WELLINGTON
Mt Adams
(663m)
Flat Point
Hinakura
Pirinoa
Lake Onoke
Rarangi
Tuamarina
Cloudy Bay
Spring Creek
Cook Strait
Palliser Bay
Tuturumuri
Aorangi Mountains
Mt Ross
(981m)
Renwick
Blenheim
Riverlands
Seddon
Cape Palliser
Lake Grassmere
Cape Campbell
Map 3
Ward
Pacific Ocean
Kekerengu
Clarence

Map 5 South Island

Karamea
Karamea Bight
Map 4
Little Wanganui
Tasman Sea
Mokihinui River
Seddonville
Hector
Granity
Matiri Range
N
0 km 20
0 miles 20
Carters Beach
Westport
Waimangaroa
Buller River
Inangahua
Charleston
Paenga
Mount Victoria (1,640m)
Mount Faraday (1,485m)
Maruia River
Victoria Range
Punakaiki
Reefton
Paparoa Range
Maruia
Inangahua River
Barrytown
Ikamatua
Blackball
Springs Junction
Runanga
Ahaura River
Ngahere
Greymouth
Dobson
Mount Technico (1,867m)
Map 6
Paroa
Moana
Kopara
Mount Ajax (1,834m)
Lake Brunner
Kumara
Mount Longfello (1,901m)
Lake Sumn
Hokitika
Inchbonnie
Kaniere
Turiwhate
Lake Kaniere
Ruatapu
Otira
Ross
Kowhitirangi
Arthur's Pass
Arthur's Pass
Browning Pass
Esk River
Puketeraki Range
Cass
Chest Peak (1,935m)
Wanganui River
Wilberforce River
Lees Valley
Abut Head
Harihari
Whitcombe Pass
Rotokino
Mount Whitcombe (2,644m)
Okarito
Rakaia River
Lake Coleridge
Porters Pass
Oxford
Whatarea
Springfield
Mount Arrowsmith (2,795m)
Franz Josef Glacier
Lake Coleridge
Sheffield
Gillespies Beach
Mount D'Archiac (2,865m)
Mount Hutt (2,188m)
Coalgate
Fox Glacier
Lake Heron
Mount Hutt
Kirw
Mount Potts (2,194m)
Darfield
Hororata
The Thumbs (2,545m)
South Br
North Br
Greendale
Mount Cook (3,754m)
Godley River
Thumbs Range
Methven
Dunsande
Mount Somers
Rakaia River
Rangitata River
Lauriston
Landsborough River
Mount Cook
Rakaia
Chertsey
Two Thumbs Range
Mount Musgrave (2,246m)
Mayfield
Winchmore
Lake Tekapo
Mount Ward (2,644m)
Hinds River
Tinwald
Ashburton
Carew
Willowby
Dun Fiunary (2,499m)
Hinds
Lake Tekapo
Hakatere
Woodbury
Lake Pukaki
Geraldine
Lowcliffe
Fairlie
Orari
Canterbury Bigh
Winchester

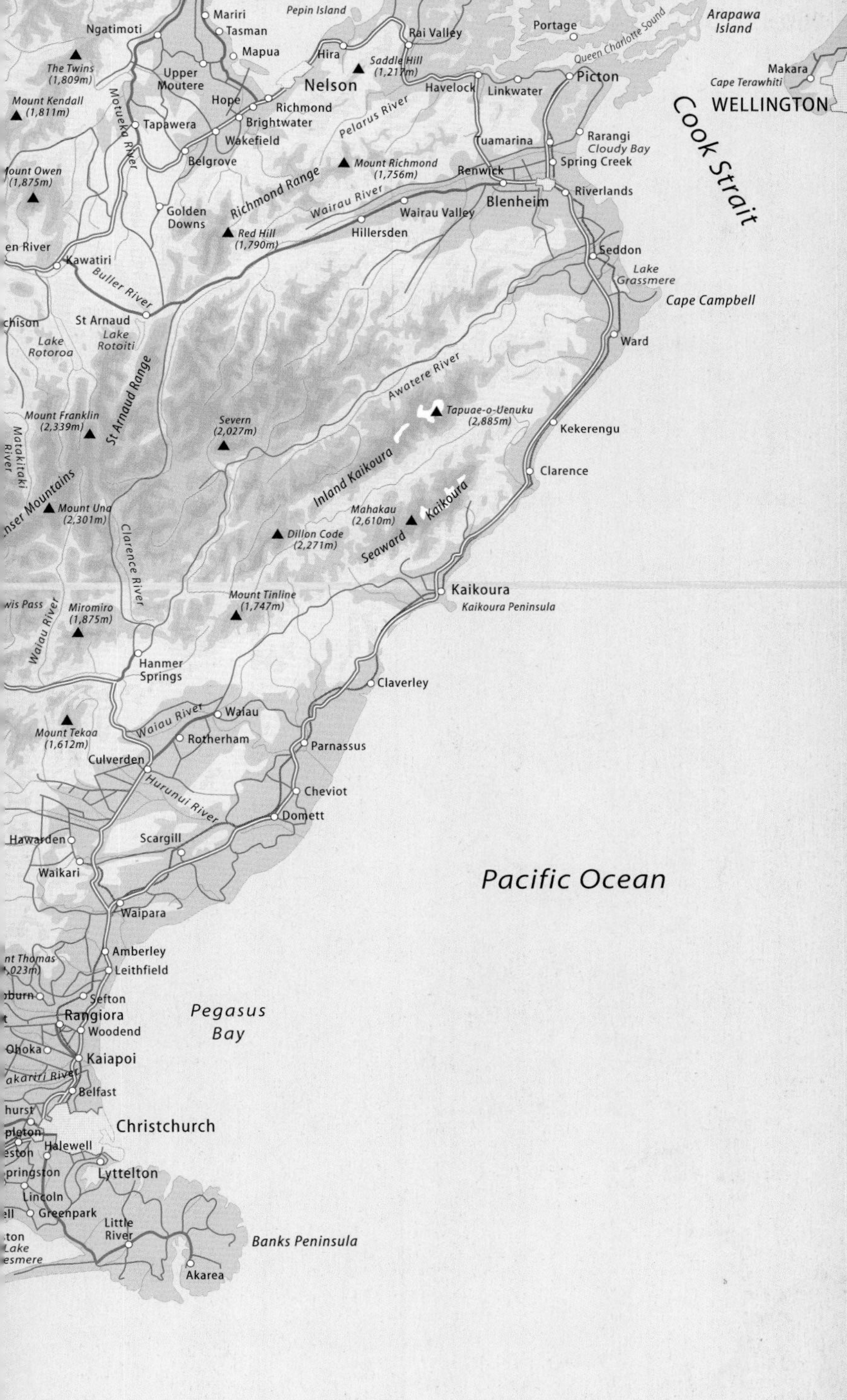
Mariri
Tasman
Pepin Island
Ngatimoti
Mapua
The Twins
(1,809m)
Upper
Moutere
Hira
Nelson
Saddle Hill
(1,217m)
Rai Valley
Portage
Queen Charlotte Sound
Arapawa
Island
Makara
Cape Terawhiti
WELLINGTON
Picton
Linkwater
Havelock
Mount Kendall
(1,811m)
Hope
Richmond
Brightwater
Tapawera
Wakefield
Motueka River
Pelarus River
Tuamarina
Rarangi
Cloudy Bay
Spring Creek
Cook Strait
Belgrove
Mount Richmond
(1,756m)
Renwick
Blenheim
Riverlands
Richmond Range
Wairau River
Wairau Valley
Hillersden
Golden
Downs
Red Hill
(1,790m)
Kawatiri
Buller River
Seddon
Lake
Grassmere
Cape Campbell
St Arnaud
Lake
Rotoiti
Lake
Rotoroa
Ward
St Arnaud Range
Awatere River
Tapuae-o-Uenuku
(2,885m)
Mount Franklin
(2,339m)
Severn
(2,027m)
Kekerengu
Matakitaki
River
Clarence
Inland Kaikoura
Mount Una
(2,301m)
Mahakau
(2,610m)
Seaward Kaikoura
Dillon Code
(2,271m)
Clarence River
Kaikoura
Kaikoura Peninsula
Mount Tinline
(1,747m)
Miromiro
(1,875m)
Waiau River
Hanmer
Springs
Claverley
Waiau River
Waiau
Mount Tekoa
(1,612m)
Rotherham
Culverden
Parnassus
Hurunui River
Cheviot
Domett
Hawarden
Scargill
Waikari
Pacific Ocean
Waipara
Amberley
Leithfield
Sefton
Rangiora
Pegasus
Bay
Woodend
Ohoka
Kaiapoi
Belfast
Christchurch
Halewell
Lyttelton
Lincoln
Greenpark
Little
River
Banks Peninsula
Akarea

Map 6 South Island

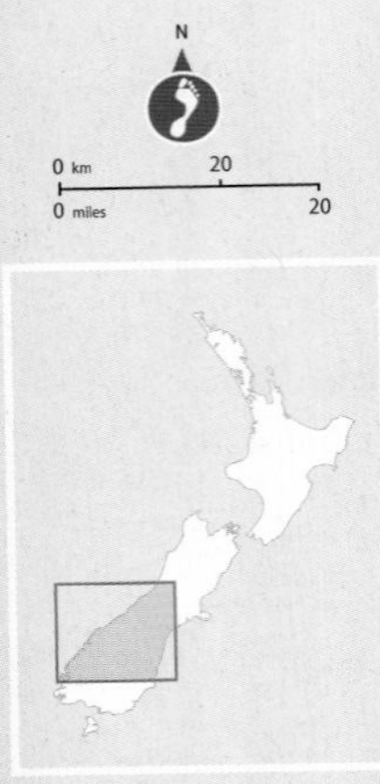

Tasman Sea

Haast
Hannahs Clearing
Jackson Head
Jackson Bay
Cascade Point
Olivine Range
Makaro
Makarora River
Lake Wana
Awarua Point
Big Bay
Martins Bay
Mount Aspiring (3,033m)
Mount Aha (2,347m)
Lake McKerrow
Yates Point
Milford Sound
Mount Tutoko (2,746m)
Humboldt Mountains
Mount Earnslaw (2,819m)
Richardson Mountains
Wanaka
Seabreeze Point
Milford Sound
Sutherland Sound
Bligh Sound
Mackinnon Pass
Homer Tunnel
Mount Bonpland (2,348m)
Glenorchy
Cardrona
Map 7
George Sound
Franklin Mountains
Cascade Creek
Arrowtown
Round Head
Queenstown
Frankton
Crom
Bannock
Coswell Sound
Mount Alexandra (1,323m)
Stuart Mountains
Charles Sound
Livingston Mountains
Lake Wakatipu
Cecil Peak (1,974m)
Nancy Sound
Thompson Sound
Secretary Island
Mount Irane (1,879m)
Lake Te Anau
Eyre Mountains
South West Point
Doubtful Sound
Jane Peak (2,035m)
Kingston
Garvie Mountains
Mararou River
Te Anau
Dagg Sound
Athol

Paroa
Moana
Kopara
Kumara
Lake Brunner
Hokitika
Kaniere
Turiwhate
Inchbonnie
Ruatapu
Lake Kaniere
Otira
Ross
Kowhitirangi
Arthur's Pass
Arthur's Pass
Browning Pass
Wilberforce River
Cass
Wanganui River
Abut Head
Harihari
Rotokino
Okarito
Mount Whitcombe (2,644m)
Whitcombe Pass
Rakaia River
Lake Coleridge
Porters Pass
Whatarea
Mount Arrowsmith (2,795m)
Lake Coleridge
Franz Josef Glacier
Gillespies Beach
Mount D'Archiac (2,865m)
Mount Hutt (2,188m)
Fox Glacier
Mount Potts (2,194m)
Lake Heron
Mount Hutt
South Br
North Br
Mount Cook (3,754m)
The Thumbs (2,545m)
Jacobs River
Methven
Godley River
Two Thumbs Range
Mount Somers
Rangitata River
Mount Cook
Lauriston
Landsborough River
Lake Tekapo
Mount Musgrave (2,246m)
Mayfield
Hinds River
Winchmore
Mount Ward (2,644m)
Ashburton
Tinwald
Dun Fiunary (2,499m)
Carew
Willowby
Mount Brewster (2,423m)
Lake Pukaki
Lake Tekapo
Woodbury
Rinds
Mount Huxley (2,499m)
Geraldine
Fairlie
Lowcliffe
Hunter River
Orari
Tekapo River
Winchester
Map 5
Lake Ohau
Albury
Pleasent Point
Temuka
Twizel
The Hunters Hills
Opihi River
Mount St Mary (2,332m)
Seadown
Cave
Levels
Clearburn
Timaru
Mount Melina (1,905m)
Lake Benmore
Fairview
Kirkliston Range
Omarama
Cattle Creek
Pareora
Lindis Pass
Blue Cliffs
St Andrews
Otematata
Lake Aviemore
Lake Waitaki
Hakataramea
Makikihi
Hawkdun Range
Lindis
Kurow
Waimato
Morven
Tarras
Otekaieke
Ikawai
Duntroon
Dunstan Mountains
St Bathans
Glenavy
Tokarahi
Ngapara
Becks
Naseby
Kakanui Mountains
Pukeuri Junction
Lauder
Weston
Omakau
Manuherikia River
Renfurly
Oamaru
Poolburn
Mahend
Waipiata
Kakanui
Herbert
Alexandra
Patearoa
Morrisons
Hampden
Macraes Flat
Summit Rock (1,450m)
Moeraki
Shag River
Dunback
Taieri River
Palmerston
Middlemarch

Map 7 South Island

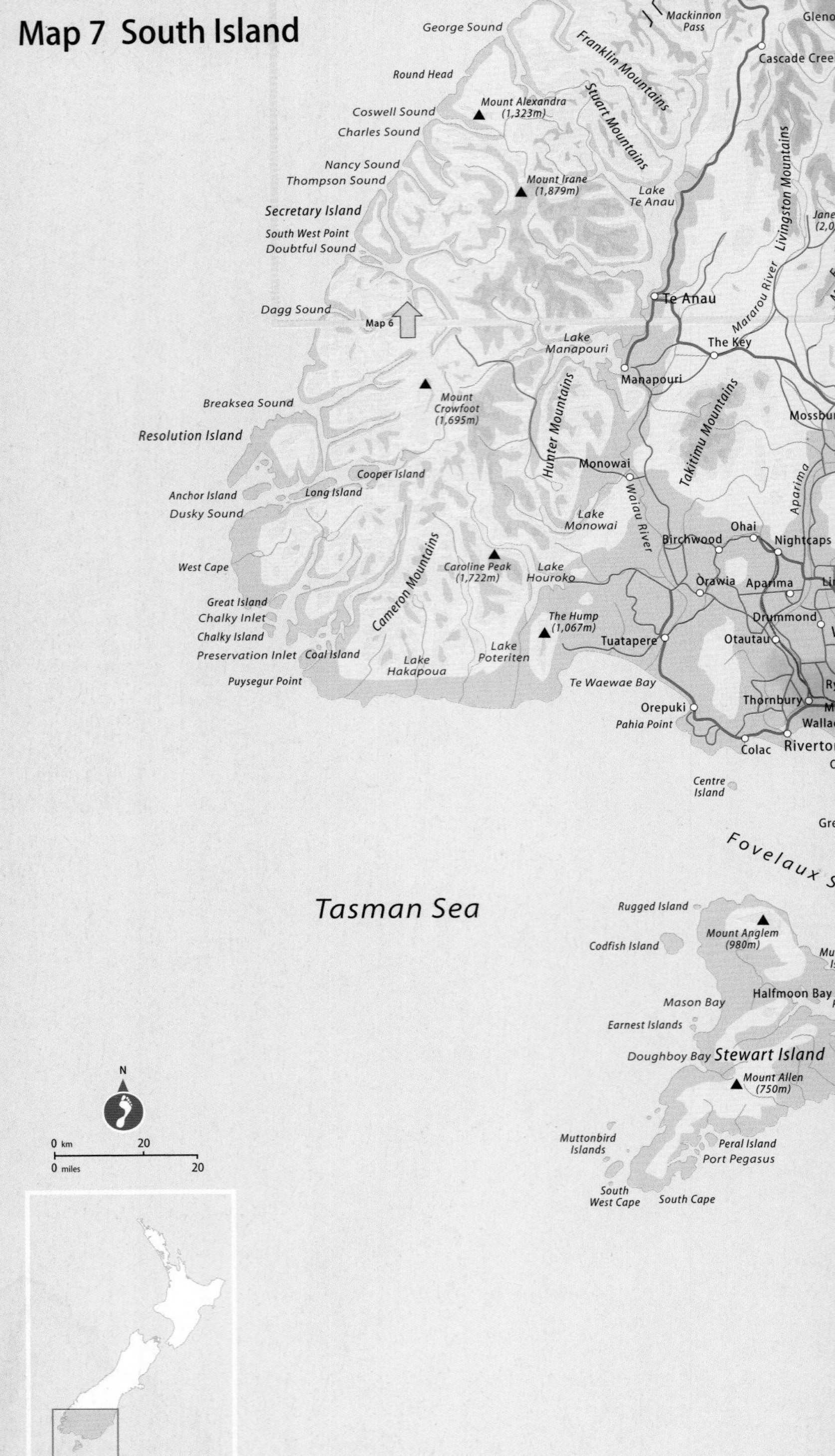

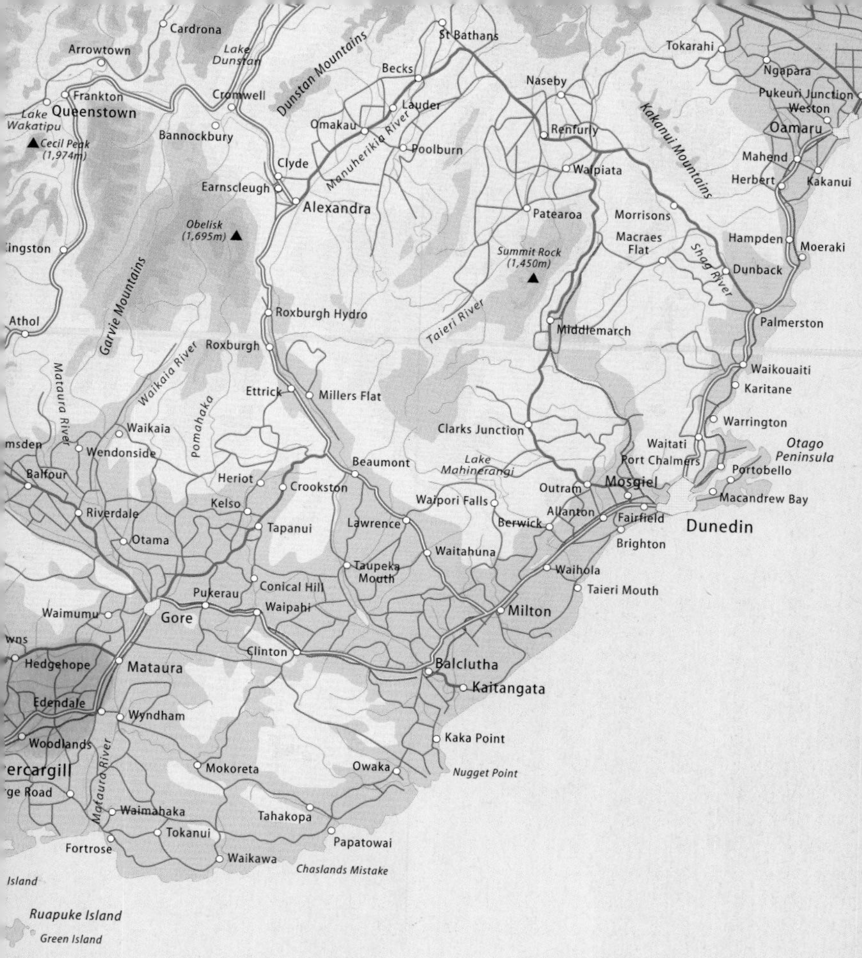

Cardrona
Arrowtown
Lake Dunstan
Dunstan Mountains
St Bathans
Becks
Tokarahi
Ngapara
Naseby
Pukeuri Junction
Weston
Oamaru
Frankton
Lake Wakatipu
Queenstown
Cromwell
Lauder
Omakau
Manuherikia River
Renfurly
Kakanui Mountains
Cecil Peak (1,974m)
Bannockbury
Poolburn
Mahend
Herbert
Kakanui
Clyde
Waipiata
Earnscleugh
Alexandra
Patearoa
Morrisons
Macraes Flat
Hampden
Moeraki
Obelisk (1,695m)
Kingston
Summit Rock (1,450m)
Shag River
Dunback
Garvie Mountains
Roxburgh Hydro
Taieri River
Palmerston
Athol
Middlemarch
Roxburgh
Waikaia River
Waikouaiti
Karitane
Mataura River
Ettrick
Millers Flat
Pomahaka
Waikaia
Warrington
Clarks Junction
Wendonside
Waitati
Otago Peninsula
Beaumont
Lake Mahinerangi
Port Chalmers
Balfour
Heriot
Crookston
Portobello
Outram
Mosgiel
Macandrew Bay
Waipori Falls
Kelso
Allanton
Riverdale
Lawrence
Berwick
Fairfield
Dunedin
Tapanui
Brighton
Otama
Waitahuna
Taupeka Mouth
Waihola
Conical Hill
Taieri Mouth
Pukerau
Waipahi
Waimumu
Milton
Gore
Clinton
Hedgehope
Mataura
Balclutha
Kaitangata
Edendale
Wyndham
Woodlands
Kaka Point
Mokoreta
Owaka
Nugget Point
Mataura River
Waimahaka
Tahakopa
Tokanui
Papatowai
Fortrose
Waikawa
Chaslands Mistake
Island
Ruapuke Island
Green Island
Pacific Ocean

Acknowledgements

Darroch Donald would like to thank all the staff and representatives of the many regional visitor information centres and regional tourism offices who provided invaluable advice and assistance, in particular New Zealand Tourism Board media representative Tracy Johnston, West Coast representative Lisa Stadler, Sharon Wesney in Queenstown, Shevaun Taberner in Fiordland and Karen Gear in Southland.

Also thanks to close friends Chris and Don Stuart in Auckland, John Andrew and Sharon Walker in Christchurch and Tony and Brigitte in Santa Barbara, for their valued friendship and for providing sanctuary from the rigours of the road.

Also thanks to all the team at Footprint, and Alan Murphy and Rachel Fielding in particular for their much appreciated patience, support and hard work.

Finally a special thanks, as ever, to my mother Grace for her steadfast encouragement and support, my brother Ghill for assisting with frequent cashflow problems and for the many 'tonic' email attachments, and my partner Rebecca, who knows that, although she is unable to join me on the road, she is always with me in my thoughts and in my heart.

About the author

Scot **Darroch Donald** has two major passions in life – wildlife and travel. After gaining a diploma in wildlife illustration and photography, in Wales in 1986, Darroch took up the position of assistant manager at a wildlife rehabilitation centre in Scotland. This unusual work took him to many far-flung places, including Saudi Arabia during the Gulf War eco-disaster in 1991 and eventually to New Zealand, where he emigrated in 1992. There he acted as an oiled wildlife consultant to the government and, in 1996 published his first book 'Creatures', an account of his wildlife encounters. Now Darroch has expanded his work to include both travel and nature. As well as being author of Footprint's New Zealand Handbook, he is also co-author of the Australia Handbook.